RELIGION AND THE STATE

Second Edition

STEVEN G. GEY
Stearns Weaver Miller Weissler
Alhadeff & Sitterson Professor
Florida State University
College of Law

LexisNexis

ISBN # 0-8205-7022-2

Library of Congress Cataloging-in-Publication Data

Gey, Steven G. (Steven Gene), 1956-
Religion and the state / by Steven G Gey. — 2nd ed.
  p. cm.
Includes bibliographical references and index.
ISBN 0-8205-7022-2 (hard cover)
1. Church and state — United States — Cases. I. Title.
KF4865.A7G49 2006
342.7308'52 — dc22   2006022689

Editorial Offices
744 Broad Street, Newark, NJ 07102 (973) 820-2000
201 Mission St., San Francisco, CA 94105-1831 (415) 908-3200
701 East Water Street, Charlottesville, VA 22902-7587 (434) 972-7600
www.lexis.com

(Pub.3138)

PREFACE

The First Amendment contains two Religion Clauses, comprised of just sixteen words: "Congress shall make no law respecting an establishment of religion, or prohibiting the free exercise thereof . . . ." Despite (or perhaps because of) their brevity, these two clauses are among the most frequently litigated in the United States Supreme Court, and generate more than their share of high-profile constitutional disputes in the lower courts.

On its face, the First Amendment seems to impose a constitutional mandate of strict separation between church and state. The Establishment Clause prohibits not only government favoritism of religion, but also government actions "respecting" an establishment of religion. The literal meaning of this clause would prohibit even indirect efforts by the state to aid or endorse religious beliefs or practices. Likewise, the language of the Free Exercise Clause also has separationist overtones, by suggesting that courts should uphold government action restricting religious exercise as long as that action does not "prohibit[] the free exercise thereof." If this were the approach taken by the modern courts, the United States would indeed have achieved Thomas Jefferson's stated goal of erecting a "wall of separation" between church and state. *See* Thomas Jefferson, Letter of January 1, 1802, to the Danbury Baptist Association, *reprinted in* Chapter One, *infra*.

Of course, if the Supreme Court had adopted and enforced the literal meaning of the First Amendment's terms, there would be little need for an entire casebook on the subject of church/state jurisprudence. As Justice Black argued frequently in the free speech context, the First Amendment's admonition that Congress may pass "no law" regarding religion would mean literally **NO** law. Under this literal interpretation of the Amendment, the courts would be obligated to strike down any law having the slightest tendency to favor religion, and would likewise be obligated to uphold any law restricting religious practice unless that law had the effect of outlawing the practice altogether.

Although the Supreme Court gave lip service to the strict separation approach in its early Establishment Clause decisions, the Court has never actually applied that approach. Instead, the Court has vacillated between a moderately separationist interpretation of the Religion Clauses and a more lenient approach that permits — and sometimes requires — government action accommodating religious belief and practice. Because the Court has gone beyond the First Amendment's text to define the proper limits of the relationship between church and state, interpretive issues have always been at the forefront of Religion Clause litigation. These interpretive issues are the main focus of the first four chapters of this text. Chapter One deals with the effect of history and original intent on the meaning of the modern Religion Clauses. Chapter Two considers the key theoretical questions underpinning the First Amendment. Specifically, what is the proper role for religion in a modern, religiously pluralist, secular democracy? This chapter also analyzes the difficulties of reconciling the two Religion Clauses if and when their principles conflict. Chapters Three and Four address two seemingly straightforward, but vexing questions of Religion Clause interpretation: First, what is "religion," and second, does the definition of "religion" that is applicable to the Establishment Clause necessarily apply also to the Free Exercise Clause?

These broad, theoretical issues permeate all Religion Clause litigation, but most of the judicial opinions in this area focus on the details of particular problems that arise in disputes over legislation that favors or disfavors religion. The remaining chapters address these specific areas of Establishment and Free Exercise Clause litigation. These chapters are divided according to the types of disputes: symbolic endorsement of religion by the government, government funding of religious activities, and government efforts to accommodate idiosyncratic religious practices. One of the difficulties in attempting to integrate these materials is that the Court has been inconsistent in its application of theory to the various different contexts in which church/state issues arise. In the Establishment Clause area, for example, the Court has recently been much more separationist in its approach to symbolic endorsement cases than in its approach to the financing cases. In the Free Exercise Clause area, a Court that is viewed as increasingly friendly to religious practitioners is nevertheless also responsible for virtually eviscerating Free Exercise Clause protections against generally applicable governmental restrictions that impinge on religious practices.

These issues will become even more contentious in the near future as a result of Justice O'Connor's departure from the Court. With the addition of Justice Alito, the Court may well be poised to inaugurate a major shift in its approach to issues of church and state. A majority of Justices may now be prepared to abandon altogether the Madisonian/Jeffersonian ideal of separation. Members of the new majority have yet to announce what constitutional guideposts they intend to offer as a substitute for the separation principle. The disputes over these issues will likely play out over many years — both on and off the Court — and students should return regularly to the questions posed in the first chapters of the casebook as they contemplate the pragmatic details of life in a country in which politics and religion are increasingly conjoined.

———————

Finally, the author would like to recognize the invaluable assistance of two people who contributed their time and abundant skill to produce this casebook. First, my research assistant Celeste Perrino devoted countless hours to editing and organizing the original manuscript, during which she managed to demonstrate a far more attentive eye for detail than the person whose name appears on the cover. Second, Megan Reynolds was equally helpful in reviewing the final drafts of the casebook, sacrificing a large portion of her summer break to review the entire book on a very short schedule. Many thanks to both Ms. Perrino and Ms. Reynolds for their helpful suggestions, editing skills, and unfailing good humor in the face of tedium and tight deadlines. They now have a formal acknowledgement that whatever they were paid for these tasks, it wasn't enough.

TABLE OF CONTENTS

Chapter 1

THE ROLE OF HISTORY IN INTERPRETING THE RELIGION CLAUSES

The role of history and the original intent of the framers in interpreting the Religion Clauses have been debated since the beginning of the modern constitutional era. But the historical interpretation of any constitutional provision is a dicey affair. It sometimes seems that there are as many different ways to read the original intent of the framers as there are different judges and constitutional theorists. Few constitutional terms are self-defining, so the modern interpreter must resort to ancillary evidence to define the meaning of ambiguous terms such as "establishment" and "free exercise." At the outset, therefore, the search for the original intent must confront three related issues: (1) What is the relevant time frame for establishing the meaning of constitutional terms? (2) Who are the "framers" whose interpretation of ambiguous terminology should govern modern meaning? (3) Which historical materials are helpful in documenting the relevant framers' views?

An originalist interpretation of the religion clauses must begin with a definition of the appropriate historical moment at which to pinpoint the framers' intent. The appropriate time frame is important because the religion clauses were ratified and applied to federal government activity long before the clauses were incorporated into the Fourteenth Amendment Due Process Clause and applied to the states. (James Madison introduced a separate amendment to protect freedom of conscience from interference by state governments. This Amendment passed the House, but was rejected by the Senate. *See* THOMAS CURRY, THE FIRST FREEDOMS: CHURCH AND STATE IN AMERICA TO THE PASSAGE OF THE FIRST AMENDMENT (1986)).

In light of the gap between the adoption of the First Amendment and its application to the states, several questions come to mind. First, what is the significance of the fact that in 1789, six of the original thirteen states had state constitutional provisions that permitted some form of state establishment of religion? *See* LEONARD LEVY, THE ESTABLISHMENT CLAUSE: RELIGION AND THE FIRST AMENDMENT 25-62 (1986). Second, how significant is it that all states prohibited establishment in any form as of 1833, when the last holdout (Massachusetts) eliminated its constitutional establishment provision? *Id.* at 38. This is arguably very significant; the final state establishment was eliminated thirty-five years before the Fourteenth Amendment was enacted, approximately sixty years before the Supreme Court began incorporating the Bill of Rights into the Fourteenth Amendment, and over one hundred years before the Court first stated that the Religion Clauses were incorporated into the Fourteenth Amendment. Finally, how significant is it that three of the six original states that allowed establishments in 1789 (Massachusetts, Connecticut, and Georgia) did not ratify the First Amendment until 1939, long after those states had eliminated their state establishments and only one year before the Court began incorporating the Religion Clauses into the Fourteenth Amendment? As Douglas Laycock has argued, "one does not need a full-blown theory to show that the understanding of religious liberty in states that ratified the religion clauses is more important than the understanding of religious liberty in states that did not." Douglas Laycock, *"Nonpreferential" Aid to Religion: A False Claim About Original Intent,* 27 WM. & MARY L. REV. 875 (1986).

One may argue that each of the above facts is relevant, and one may argue with equal logic that each of these facts is irrelevant. The answers to these questions will depend on the interpreter's choice of the relevant time frame for ascertaining constitutional meaning. Judges and constitutional theorists who depend on original intent must derive constitutional meaning from the context of constitutional development, yet the constitutional context constantly changes. Thus, the outcome of debates over constitutional meaning will depend largely on when one decides to take a snapshot of the constitutional ratification process.

The difficulties inherent in the originalist effort do not end with the choice of a constitutionally significant point in time. After defining the relevant time for determining original intent, the interpreter must then identify a relevant group of framers. Suppose an interpreter of the Religion Clauses selects as the relevant time for analysis the period during which the Religion Clauses were proposed, drafted, and ratified. The interpreter must then pick and choose among the relevant political actors during the chosen period. During any given period relevant to the adoption of the Bill of Rights, many candidates qualify for the role of "framer," and the selection of framers will depend on the point of view that the modern originalist wants to establish as legitimate. Consider, for example, then-Justice Rehnquist's opinion in the *Wallace v. Jaffree* excerpt reprinted below, in which Rehnquist attempts to discount Thomas Jefferson's views in the debate over the meaning of the Establishment Clause.

With regard to the Bill of Rights, the potential framers include the members of the state conventions that ratified the original Constitution (some of which did so on the condition that a Bill of Rights be adopted by the First Congress), the members of the First Congress (which proposed the amendments), particular members of the First Congress who had an especially significant role in drafting the amendments (such as James Madison), and the members of the state legislatures that finally ratified the amendments. Complications arise even within each group. For example, how much value should be accorded the opinions of Antifederalists, whose support for the adoption of what would become the Bill of Rights was part of a political effort to defeat ratification of the main document? *See* CURRY, *supra*, at 194-95. Conversely, how much weight should be given to the opinions of the Federalists, who did not believe the amendments were necessary at all, and who proposed them largely as a response to recommendations made by several state legislatures as conditions for ratifying the original document?

Finally, even if a relevant group of framers can be identified, practical problems of proof threaten to overwhelm the originalist effort. It is very difficult to establish the precise meaning the framers attached to the new amendments because documentation of the debate over the Bill of Rights is sparse. Neither the Senate nor the House of Representatives kept official records of the debates over the Bill of Rights. There are only sketchy (and perhaps unreliable) unofficial reports of the House debate, and no unofficial reports whatsoever of the Senate's secret sessions. Records of the state legislatures that ratified the amendments are also nonexistent. *See* LEVY, *supra*, at 187-89.

The dearth of official or quasi-official evidence of the framers' intent has forced historians into an endless debate regarding the proper inferences to be drawn from ambiguous and even metaphorical language used by framers in letters, speeches, and pamphlets distributed outside the official ratification proceedings. This evidence, although abundant, is equally unhelpful, because different aspects of the evidence lead the modern interpreter in different directions; some evidence supports the notion of strict separation between church and state, other evidence refutes it. Given the murky and conflicting state of historical evidence, it is possible to sympathize with Mark Tushnet's comment that "when all is said and done, the better the history we have, the less helpful that history is in resolving problems of constitutional interpretation." Mark Tushnet, *The Origins of the Establishment Clause,* 75 GEO. L.J. 1509, 1511 (1987). Despite these problems, heated debate over the historical meanings of the Religion Clauses continues. The readings that follow are intended primarily to illustrate the breadth of the modern debate, but it seems logical to start with James Madison's *Memorial and Remonstrance Against Religious Assessments*. The background of the *Memorial and Remonstrance* is discussed in the subsequent excerpt from *Everson v. Board of Education.*

A. PRELUDE TO THE FIRST AMENDMENT: THE VIRGINIA EXPERIENCE

James Madison
Memorial and Remonstrance
Against Religious Assessments (1785)

We, the subscribers, citizens of the said Commonwealth, having taken into serious consideration, a Bill printed by order of the last Session of General Assembly, entitled "A Bill establishing a provision for Teachers of the Christian Religion," and conceiving that the same, if finally armed with the sanctions of a law, will be a dangerous abuse of power, are bound as faithful members of a free State, to remonstrate against it, and to declare the reasons by which we are determined. We remonstrate against the said Bill,

1. Because we hold it for a fundamental and undeniable truth, "that Religion or the duty which we owe to our Creator and the Manner of discharging it, can be directed only by reason and conviction, not by force or violence." The Religion then of every man must be left to the conviction and conscience of every man; and it is the right of every man to exercise it as these may dictate. This right is in its nature an unalienable right. It is unalienable; because the opinions of men, depending only on the evidence contemplated by their own minds, cannot follow the dictates of other men: It is unalienable also; because what is here a right towards men, is a duty towards the Creator. It is the duty of every man to render to the Creator such homage, and such only, as he believes to be acceptable to him. This duty is precedent both in order of time and degree of obligation, to the claims of Civil Society. Before any man can be considered as a member of Civil Society, he must be considered as a subject of the Governor of the Universe: And if a member of Civil Society, who enters into any subordinate Association, must always do it with a reservation of his duty to the general authority; much more must every man who becomes a member of any particular Civil Society, do it with a saving of his allegiance to the Universal Sovereign. We maintain therefore that in matters of Religion, no man's right is abridged by the institution of Civil Society, and that Religion is wholly exempt from its cognizance. True it is, that no other rule exists, by which any question which may divide a Society, can be ultimately determined, but the will of the majority; but it is also true, that the majority may trespass on the rights of the minority.

2. Because if religion be exempt from the authority of the Society at large, still less can it be subject to that of the Legislative Body. The latter are but the creatures and vicegerents of the former. Their jurisdiction is both derivative and limited: it is limited with regard to the coordinate departments, more necessarily is it limited with regard to the constituents. The preservation of a free government requires not merely, that the metes and bounds which separate each department of power may be invariably maintained; but more especially, that neither of them be suffered to overleap the great Barrier which defends the rights of the people. The Rulers who are guilty of such an encroachment, exceed the commission from which they derive their authority, and are Tyrants. The People who submit to it are governed by laws made neither by themselves, nor by an authority derived from them, and are slaves.

3. Because, it is proper to take alarm at the first experiment on our liberties. We hold this prudent jealousy to be the first duty of citizens, and one of [the] noblest characteristics of the late Revolution. The freemen of America did not wait till usurped power had strengthened itself by exercise, and entangled the question in precedents. They saw all the consequences in the principle, and they avoided the consequences by denying the principle. We revere this lesson too much, soon to forget it. Who does not see that the same authority which can

establish Christianity, in exclusion of all other Religions, may establish with the same ease any particular sect of Christians, in exclusion of all other Sects? That the same authority which can force a citizen to contribute three pence only of his property for the support of any one establishment, may force him to conform to any other establishment in all cases whatsoever?

4. Because, the bill violates that equality which ought to be the basis of every law, and which is more indispensable, in proportion as the validity or expediency of any law is more liable to be impeached. If "all men are by nature equally free and independent," all men are to be considered as entering into Society on equal conditions; as relinquishing no more, and therefore retaining no less, one than another, of their natural rights. Above all are they to be considered as retaining an "equal title to the free exercise of Religion according to the dictates of conscience." Whilst we assert for ourselves a freedom to embrace, to profess and to observe the Religion which we believe to be of divine origin, we cannot deny an equal freedom to those whose minds have not yet yielded to the evidence which has convinced us. If this freedom be abused, it is an offence against God, not against man: To God, therefore, not to men, must an account of it be rendered. As the Bill violates equality by subjecting some to peculiar burdens; so it violates the same principle, by granting to others peculiar exemptions. Are the Quakers and Menonists the only sects who think a compulsive support of their religions unnecessary and unwarrantable? Can their piety alone be intrusted with the care of public worship? Ought their Religions to be endowed above all others, with extraordinary privileges, by which proselytes may be enticed from all others? We think too favorably of the justice and good sense of these denominations, to believe that they either covet preeminencies over their fellow citizens, or that they will be seduced by them, from the common opposition to the measure.

5. Because the bill implies either that the Civil Magistrate is a competent Judge of Religious truth; or that he may employ Religion as an engine of Civil policy. The first is an arrogant pretension falsified by the contradictory opinions of Rulers in all ages, and throughout the world: The second an unhallowed perversion of the means of salvation.

6. Because the establishment proposed by the Bill is not requisite for the support of the Christian Religion. To say that it is, is a contradiction to the Christian Religion itself; for every page of it disavows a dependence on the powers of this world: it is a contradiction to fact; for it is known that this Religion both existed and flourished, not only without the support of human laws, but in spite of every opposition from them; and not only during the period of miraculous aid, but long after it had been left to its own evidence, and the ordinary care of Providence: Nay, it is a contradiction in terms; for a Religion not invented by human policy, must have pre-existed and been supported, before it was established by human policy. It is moreover to weaken in those who profess this Religion a pious confidence in its innate excellence, and the patronage of its Author; and to foster in those who still reject it, a suspicion that its friends are too conscious of its fallacies, to trust it to its own merits.

7. Because experience witnesseth that ecclesiastical establishments, instead of maintaining the purity and efficacy of Religion, have had a contrary operation. During almost fifteen centuries, has the legal establishment of Christianity been on trial. What have been its fruits? More or less in all places, pride and indolence in the Clergy; ignorance and servility in the laity; in both, superstition, bigotry and persecution. Enquire of the Teachers of Christianity for the ages in which it appeared in its greatest lustre; those of every sect, point to the ages prior to its incorporation with Civil policy. Propose a restoration of this primitive state in which its Teachers depended on the voluntary rewards of their flocks; many of them predict its downfall. On which side ought their testimony to have greatest weight, when for or when against their interest?

8. Because the establishment in question is not necessary for the support of Civil Government. If it be urged as necessary for the support of Civil Government only as it is a means of supporting Religion, and it be not necessary for the latter purpose, it cannot be necessary for the former. If Religion be not within [the] cognizance of Civil Government, how can its legal establishment be said to be necessary to civil Government? What influence in fact have ecclesiastical establishments had on Civil Society? In some instances they have been seen to erect a spiritual tyranny on the ruins of Civil authority; in many instances they have been seen upholding the thrones of political tyranny; in no instance have they been seen the guardians of the liberties of the people. Rulers who wished to subvert the public liberty, may have found an established clergy convenient auxiliaries. A just government, instituted to secure & perpetuate it, needs them not. Such a government will be best supported by protecting every citizen in the enjoyment of his Religion with the same equal hand which protects his person and his property; by neither invading the equal rights of any Sect, nor suffering any Sect to invade those of another.

9. Because the proposed establishment is a departure from that generous policy, which, offering an asylum to the persecuted and oppressed of every Nation and Religion, promised a lustre to our country, and an accession to the number of its citizens. What a melancholy mark is the Bill of sudden degeneracy? Instead of holding forth an asylum to the persecuted, it is itself a signal of persecution. It degrades from the equal rank of Citizens all those whose opinions in Religion do not bend to those of the Legislative authority. Distant as it may be, in its present form, from the Inquisition it differs from it only in degree. The one is the first step, the other the last in the career of intolerance. The magnanimous sufferer under this cruel scourge in foreign Regions, must view the Bill as a Beacon on our Coast, warning him to seek some other haven, where liberty and philanthrophy in their due extent may offer a more certain repose from his troubles.

10. Because, it will have a like tendency to banish our Citizens. The allurements presented by other situations are every day thinning their number. To superadd a fresh motive to emigration, by revoking the liberty which they now enjoy, would be the same species of folly which has dishonoured and depopulated flourishing kingdoms.

11. Because, it will destroy that moderation and harmony which the forbearance of our laws to intermeddle with Religion, has produced amongst its several sects. Torrents of blood have been spilt in the old world, by vain attempts of the secular arm to extinguish Religious discord, by proscribing all difference in Religious opinions. Time has at length revealed the true remedy. Every relaxation of narrow and rigorous policy, wherever it has been tried, has been found to assuage the disease. The American Theatre has exhibited proofs, that equal and complete liberty, if it does not wholly eradicate it, sufficiently destroys its malignant influence on the health and prosperity of the State. If with the salutary effects of this system under our own eyes, we begin to contract the bonds of Religious freedom, we know no name that will too severely reproach our folly. At least let warning be taken at the first fruits of the threatened innovation. The very appearance of the Bill has transformed that "Christian forbearance, love and charity," which of late mutually prevailed, into animosities and jealousies, which may not soon be appeased. What mischiefs may not be dreaded should this enemy to the public quiet be armed with the force of a law?

Patrick Henry,
A Bill Establishing a Provision for Teachers of the Christian Religion (1784)

Whereas the general diffusion of Christian knowledge hath a natural tendency to correct the morals of men, restrain their vices, and preserve the peace of society, which cannot be effected without a competent provision for learned teachers, who may be thereby enabled to devote their time and attention to the duty of instructing such citizens, as from their circumstances and want of education, cannot otherwise attain such knowledge; and it is judged that such provision may be made by the Legislature, without counteracting the liberal principle heretofore adopted and intended to be preserved by abolishing all distinctions of preeminence amongst the different societies or communities of Christians;

Be it therefore enacted by the General Assembly, That for the support of Christian teachers, per centum on the amount, or in the pound on the sum payable for tax on the property within this Commonwealth, is hereby assessed, and shall be paid by every person chargeable with the said tax at the time the same shall become due; and the Sheriffs of the several Counties shall have power to levy and collect the same in the same manner and under the like restrictions and limitations, as are or may be prescribed by the laws for raising the revenues of this State.

And be it enacted, That for every sum so paid, the Sheriff or Collector shall give a receipt, expressing therein to what society of Christians the person from whom he may receive the same shall direct the money to be paid, keeping a distinct account thereof in his books. The Sheriff of every County, shall, on or before the __ day of __ in every year, return to the Court, upon oath, two alphabetical lists of the payments to him made, distinguishing in columns opposite to the names of the persons who shall have paid the same, the society to which the money so paid was by them appropriated; and one column for the names where no appropriation shall be made. One of which lists, after being recorded in a book to be kept for that purpose, shall be filed by the Clerk in his office; the other shall be the Sheriff be fixed up in the Court-house, there to remain for the inspection of all concerned. And the Sheriff, after deducting a five per centum for the collection, shall forthwith pay to such person or persons as shall be appointed to receive the same by the Vestry, Elders, or Directors, however, denominated of each such society, the sum so stated to be due to that society; or in default thereof, upon the motion of such person or persons to the next or any succeeding Court, execution shall be awarded for the same against the Sheriff and his security, his and their executors or administrators; provided that ten days previous notice be given of such motion. An upon every such execution, the Officer serving the same shall proceed to immediate sale of the estate taken, and shall not accept of security for payment at the end of three months, nor to have the goods forthcoming at the day of sale; for his better direction wherein, the Clerk shall endorse upon every such execution that no security of any kind shall be taken.

And be it further enacted, That the money to be raised by virtue of this Act, shall be by the Vestries, Elders, or Directors of each religious society, appropriated to a provision for a Minister or Teacher of the Gospel of their denomination, or the providing place of divine worship, and to none other use whatsoever; except in the denominations of Quakers and Menonists, who may receive what is collected from their members, and place it in their general fund, to be disposed of in a manner which they shall think best calculated to promote their particular mode of worship.

And be it enacted, That all sums which at the time of payment to the Sheriff or Collector may not be appropriated by the person paying the same, shall be accounted for with the Court in manner as by this Act is directed; and after deducting for his collection, the Sheriff shall pay the amount thereof (upon account certified by the Court to the Auditors of Public Accounts, and by them to the Treasurer) into the public Treasury, to be disposed of under the direction of the General Assembly, for the encouragement of seminaries of learning within the Counties whence such sums shall arise, and to no other use or purpose whatsoever.

Thomas Jefferson
A Bill for Establishing Religious Freedom (1777)

SECTION I. Well aware that the opinions and belief of men depend not on their own will, but follow involuntarily the evidence proposed to their minds; that Almighty God hath created the mind free, and manifested his supreme will that free it shall remain by making it altogether insusceptible of restraint; that all attempts to influence it by temporal punishments, or burthens, or by civil incapacitations, tend only to beget habits of hypocrisy and meanness, and are a departure from the plan of the holy author of our religion, who being lord both of body and mind, yet chose not to propagate it by coercions on either, as was in his Almighty power to do, but to extend it by its influence on reason alone; that the impious presumption of legislators and rulers, civil as well as ecclesiastical, who, being themselves but fallible and uninspired men, have assumed dominion over the faith of others, setting up their own opinions and modes of thinking as the only true and infallible, and as such endeavoring to impose them on others, hath established and maintained false religions over the greatest part of the world and through all time: That to compel a man to furnish contributions of money for the propagation of opinions which he disbelieves and abhors, is sinful and tyrannical; that even the forcing him to support this or that teacher of his own religious persuasion, is depriving him of the comfortable liberty of giving his contributions to the particular pastor whose morals he would make his pattern, and whose powers he feels most persuasive to righteousness; and is withdrawing from the ministry those temporary rewards, which proceeding from an approbation of their personal conduct, are an additional incitement to earnest and unremitting labours for the instruction of mankind; that our civil rights have no dependence on our religious opinions, any more than our opinions in physics or geometry; that therefore the proscribing any citizen as unworthy the public confidence by laying upon him any incapacity of being called to offices of trust and emolument, unless he profess or renounce this or that religious opinion, is depriving him injuriously of those privileges and advantages to which, in common with his fellow citizens, he has a natural right; that it tends also to corrupt the principles of that very religion it is meant to encourage, by bribing, with a monopoly of worldly honours and emoluments, those who will externally profess and conform to it; that though indeed these are criminals who do not withstand such temptation, yet neither are those innocent who lay the bait in their way; that the opinions of men are not the object of civil government, nor under its jurisdiction; that to suffer the civil magistrate to intrude his powers into the field of opinion and to restrain the profession or propagation of principles on supposition of their ill tendency is a dangerous fallacy, which at once destroys all religious liberty, because he being of course judge of that tendency will make his opinions the rule of judgment, and approve or condemn the sentiments of others only as they shall square with or differ from his own; that it is time enough for the rightful purposes of civil government for its officers to interfere when principles break out into overt acts against peace and good order; and finally, that truth is great and will prevail if left to herself; that she is the proper and sufficient antagonist to error, and has nothing to fear from the conflict unless by human interposition disarmed of her natural weapons, free argument and debate; errors ceasing to be dangerous when it is permitted freely to contradict them.

SECTION II. We the General Assembly of Virginia do enact that no man shall be compelled to frequent or support any religious worship, place, or ministry whatsoever, nor shall be enforced, restrained, molested, or burthened in his body or goods, nor shall otherwise suffer, on account of his religious opinions or belief; but that all men shall be free to profess, and by argument to maintain, their opinions in matters of religion, and that the same shall in no wise diminish, enlarge, or affect their civil capacities.

SECTION III. And though we well know that this Assembly, elected by the people for the ordinary purposes of legislation only, have no power to restrain the acts of succeeding Assemblies, constituted with powers equal to our own, and that therefore to declare this act irrevocable would be of no effect in law; yet we are free to declare, and do declare, that the rights hereby asserted are of the natural rights of mankind, and that if any act shall be hereafter passed to repeal the present or to narrow its operation, such act will be an infringement of natural right.

EVERSON v. BOARD OF EDUCATION
330 U.S. 1 (1947)

[In a suit by a taxpayer, the New Jersey appellate courts upheld a state statute authorizing reimbursement of bus fares paid for transporting children to private schools. The private schools involved were mostly Catholic, which operated under the superintendency of a Catholic priest and, in addition to secular education, gave religious instruction in the Catholic faith. By a 5-4 majority, the United States Supreme Court affirmed the holding of the New Jersey courts.]

MR. JUSTICE BLACK delivered the opinion of the Court. The New Jersey statute is challenged as a "law respecting an establishment of religion." The First Amendment, as made applicable to the states by the Fourteenth, *Murdock v. Pennsylvania,* 319 U.S. 105, commands that a state "shall make no law respecting an establishment of religion, or prohibiting the free exercise thereof. . . ." These words of the First Amendment reflected in the minds of early Americans a vivid mental picture of conditions and practices which they fervently wished to stamp out in order to preserve liberty for themselves and for their posterity. Doubtless their goal has not been entirely reached; but so far has the Nation moved toward it that the expression "law respecting an establishment of religion," probably does not so vividly remind present-day Americans of the evils, fears, and political problems that caused that expression to be written into our Bill of Rights. Whether this New Jersey law is one respecting an "establishment of religion" requires an understanding of the meaning of that language, particularly with respect to the imposition of taxes. Once again, therefore, it is not inappropriate briefly to review the background and environment of the period in which that constitutional language was fashioned and adopted.

A large proportion of the early settlers of this country came here from Europe to escape the bondage of laws which compelled them to support and attend government-favored churches. The centuries immediately before and contemporaneous with the colonization of America had been filled with turmoil, civil

strife, and persecutions, generated in large part by established sects determined to maintain their absolute political and religious supremacy. With the
power of government supporting them, at various times and places, Catholics
had persecuted Protestants, Protestants had persecuted Catholics, Protestant
sects had persecuted other Protestant sects, Catholics of one shade of belief had
persecuted Catholics of another shade of belief, and all of these had from time
to time persecuted Jews. In efforts to force loyalty to whatever religious group
happened to be on top and in league with the government of a particular time
and place, men and women had been fined, cast in jail, cruelly tortured, and
killed. Among the offenses for which these punishments had been inflicted were
such things as speaking disrespectfully of the views of ministers of government-
established churches, non-attendance at those churches, expressions of nonbelief in their doctrines, and failure to pay taxes and tithes to support them.
These practices of the old world were transplanted to and began to thrive in the
soil of the new America. The very charters granted by the English Crown to the
individuals and companies designated to make the laws which would control the
destinies of the colonials authorized these individuals and companies to erect
religious establishments which all, whether believers or non-believers, would be
required to support and attend. An exercise of this authority was accompanied
by a repetition of many of the old-world practices and persecutions. Catholics
found themselves hounded and proscribed because of their faith; Quakers who
followed their conscience went to jail; Baptists were peculiarly obnoxious to
certain dominant Protestant sects; men and women of varied faiths who happened to be in a minority in a particular locality were persecuted because they
steadfastly persisted in worshipping God only as their own consciences dictated. And all of these dissenters were compelled to pay tithes and taxes to support government-sponsored churches whose ministers preached inflammatory
sermons designed to strengthen and consolidate the established faith by generating a burning hatred against dissenters.

These practices became so commonplace as to shock the freedom-loving colonials into a feeling of abhorrence.[9] The imposition of taxes to pay ministers'
salaries and to build and maintain churches and church property aroused their
indignation. It was these feelings which found expression in the First Amendment. No one locality and no one group throughout the Colonies can rightly be
given entire credit for having aroused the sentiment that culminated in adoption of the Bill of Rights' provisions embracing religious liberty. But Virginia,
where the established church had achieved a dominant influence in political
affairs and where many excesses attracted wide public attention, provided a

---

[9] Madison wrote to a friend in 1774: "That diabolical, hell-conceived principle of persecution rages
among some . . . This vexes me the worst of anything whatever. There are at this time in the adjacent country not less than five or six well-meaning men in close jail for publishing their religious
sentiments, which in the main are very orthodox. I have neither patience to hear, talk, or think of
anything relative to this matter; for I have squabbled and scolded, abused and ridiculed, so long
about it to little purpose, that I am without common patience. So I must beg you to pity me, and pray
for liberty of conscience to all." I WRITINGS OF JAMES MADISON (1900) 18, 21.

great stimulus and able leadership for the movement. The people there, as elsewhere, reached the conviction that individual religious liberty could be achieved best under a government which was stripped of all power to tax, to support, or otherwise to assist any or all religions, or to interfere with the beliefs of any religious individual or group.

The movement toward this end reached its dramatic climax in Virginia in 1785-86 when the Virginia legislative body was about to renew Virginia's tax levy for the support of the established church. Thomas Jefferson and James Madison led the fight against this tax. Madison wrote his great Memorial and Remonstrance against the law. In it, he eloquently argued that a true religion did not need the support of law; that no person, either believer or non-believer, should be taxed to support a religious institution of any kind; that the best interest of a society required that the minds of men always be wholly free; and that cruel persecutions were the inevitable result of government-established religions. Madison's Remonstrance received strong support throughout Virginia, and the Assembly postponed consideration of the proposed tax measure until its next session. When the proposal came up for consideration at that session, it not only died in committee, but the Assembly enacted the famous "Virginia Bill for Religious Liberty" originally written by Thomas Jefferson. The preamble to that Bill stated among other things that "Almighty God hath created the mind free; that all attempts to influence it by temporal punishments or burthens, or by civil incapacitations, tend only to beget habits of hypocrisy and meanness, and are a departure from the plan of the Holy author of our religion, who being Lord both of body and mind, yet chose not to propagate it by coercions on either . . .; that to compel a man to furnish contributions of money for the propagation of opinions which he disbelieves, is sinful and tyrannical; that even the forcing him to support this or that teacher of his own religious persuasion, is depriving him of the comfortable liberty of giving his contributions to the particular pastor, whose morals he would make his pattern. . . ."

And the statute itself enacted "That no man shall be compelled to frequent or support any religious worship, place, or ministry whatsoever, nor shall be enforced, restrained, molested, or burthened in his body or goods, nor shall otherwise suffer on account of his religious opinions or belief. . . ."

This Court has previously recognized that the provisions of the First Amendment, in the drafting and adoption of which Madison and Jefferson played such leading roles, had the same objective and were intended to provide the same protection against governmental intrusion on religious liberty as the Virginia statute. *Reynolds v. United States, infra* Chapter 11; *Watson v. Jones,* 13 Wall. 679; *Davis v. Beason,* 133 U.S. 333, 342. Prior to the adoption of the Fourteenth Amendment, the First Amendment did not apply as a restraint against the states. Most of them did soon provide similar constitutional protections for religious liberty. But some states persisted for about half a century in imposing restraints upon the free exercise of religion and in discriminating against particular religious groups. In recent years, so far as the provision against the establishment of a religion is concerned, the question has most frequently arisen in connection with proposed state aid to church schools and efforts to carry on religious teachings in the public schools in accordance with the tenets of a particular sect. Some churches have either sought or accepted state financial support for their schools. Here again the efforts to obtain state aid or acceptance of it have not been limited to any one particular faith. The state courts, in the main, have remained faithful to the language of their own constitutional provisions designed to protect religious freedom and to separate religions and governments. Their decisions, however, show the difficulty in drawing the line between tax legislation which provides funds for the welfare of the general public and that which is designed to support institutions which teach religion.

The meaning and scope of the First Amendment, preventing establishment of religion or prohibiting the free exercise thereof, in the light of its history and the evils it was designed forever to suppress, have been several times elaborated by the decisions of this Court prior to the application of the First Amendment to the states by the Fourteenth. The broad meaning given the Amendment by these earlier cases has been accepted by this Court in its decisions concerning an individual's religious freedom rendered since the Fourteenth Amendment was interpreted to make the prohibitions of the First applicable to state action abridging religious freedom. There is every reason to give the same application and broad interpretation to the "establishment of religion" clause. The interrelation of these complementary clauses was well summarized in a statement of the Court of Appeals of South Carolina, quoted with approval by this Court in *Watson v. Jones*, 13 Wall. 679, 730: "The structure of our government has, for the preservation of civil liberty, rescued the temporal institutions from religious interference. On the other hand, it has secured religious liberty from the invasion of the civil authority."

The "establishment of religion" clause of the First Amendment means at least this: Neither a state nor the Federal Government can set up a church. Neither can pass laws which aid one religion, aid all religions, or prefer one religion over another. Neither can force nor influence a person to go to or to remain away from church against his will or force him to profess a belief or disbelief in any religion. No person can be punished for entertaining or professing religious beliefs or disbeliefs, for church attendance or non-attendance. No tax in any amount, large or small, can be levied to support any religious activities or institutions, whatever they may be called, or whatever form they may adopt to teach or practice religion. Neither a state nor the Federal Government can, openly or secretly, participate in the affairs of any religious organizations or groups and vice versa. In the words of Jefferson, the clause against establishment of religion by law was intended to erect "a wall of separation between church and State." *Reynolds v. United States*, 98 U.S. at 164.

MR. JUSTICE RUTLEDGE, with whom MR. JUSTICE FRANKFURTER, MR. JUSTICE JACKSON and MR. JUSTICE BURTON agree, dissenting.

No provision of the Constitution is more closely tied to or given content by its generating history than the religious clause of the First Amendment. It is at once the refined product and the terse summation of that history. The history includes not only Madison's authorship and the proceedings before the First Congress, but also the long and intensive struggle for religious freedom in America, more especially in Virginia, of which the Amendment was the direct culmination. In the documents of the times, particularly of Madison, who was leader in the Virginia struggle before he became the Amendment's sponsor, but also in the writings of Jefferson and others and in the issues which engendered them is to be found irrefutable confirmation of the Amendment's sweeping content.

For Madison, as also for Jefferson, religious freedom was the crux of the struggle for freedom in general. Madison was coauthor with George Mason of the religious clause in Virginia's great Declaration of Rights of 1776. He is credited with changing it from a mere statement of the principle of tolerance to the first official legislative pronouncement that freedom of conscience and religion are inherent rights of the individual. He sought also to have the Declaration expressly condemn the existing Virginia establishment. But the forces supporting it were then too strong.

Accordingly Madison yielded on this phase but not for long. At once he resumed the fight, continuing it before succeeding legislative sessions. As a member of the General Assembly in 1779 he threw his full weight behind Jefferson's historic Bill for Establishing Religious Freedom. That bill was a prime phase of Jefferson's broad program of democratic reform undertaken on his return from the Continental Congress in 1776 and submitted for the General Assembly's consideration in 1779 as his proposed revised Virginia code.[15] With Jefferson's departure for Europe in 1784, Madison became the Bill's prime sponsor. Enactment failed in successive legislatures from its introduction in June, 1779, until its adoption in January, 1786. But during all this time the fight for religious freedom moved forward in Virginia on various fronts with growing intensity. Madison led throughout, against Patrick Henry's powerful opposing leadership until Henry was elected governor in November, 1784.

---

15 Jefferson was chairman of the revising committee and chief draftsman. Corevisers were Wythe, Pendleton, Mason and Lee. The first enacted portion of the revision, which became known as Jefferson's Code, was the statute barring entailments. Primogeniture soon followed. Much longer the author was to wait for enactment of the Bill for Religious Freedom; and not until after his death was the corollary bill to be accepted in principle which he considered most important of all, namely, to provide for common education at public expense. See V [THE WORKS OF THOMAS JEFFERSON (Ford ed. 1904-05)] at 153. However, he linked this with disestablishment as corollary prime parts in a system of basic freedoms. I JEFFERSON, 78.

Jefferson, and Madison by his sponsorship, sought to give the Bill for Establishing Religious Freedom as nearly constitutional status as they could at the time. Acknowledging that one legislature could not "restrain the acts of succeeding Assemblies . . . and that thereof to declare this act irrevocable would be of no effect in law," the Bill's concluding provision as enacted nevertheless asserted: "Yet we are free to declare, and do declare, that the rights hereby asserted are of the natural rights of mankind, and that if any act shall be hereafter passed to repeal the present or to narrow its operation, such act will be an infringement of natural right." 1 RANDALL, [THE LIFE OF THOMAS JEFFERSON] 220 [(1858)].

The climax came in the legislative struggle of 1784-1785 over the Assessment Bill. This was nothing more nor less than a taxing measure for the support of religion, designed to revive the payment of tithes suspended since 1777. So long as it singled out a particular sect for preference it incurred the active and general hostility of dissentient groups. It was broadened to include them, with the result that some subsided temporarily in their opposition. As altered, the bill gave to each taxpayer the privilege of designating which church should receive his share of the tax. In default of designation the legislature applied it to pious uses. But what is of the utmost significance here, "in its final form the bill left the taxpayer the option of giving his tax to education."

Madison was unyielding at all times, opposing with all his vigor the general and nondiscriminatory as he had the earlier particular and discriminatory assessments proposed. The modified Assessment Bill passed second reading in December, 1784, and was all but enacted. Madison and his followers, however, maneuvered deferment of final consideration until November, 1785. And before the Assembly reconvened in the fall he issued his historic Memorial and Remonstrance.

This is Madison's complete, though not his only, interpretation of religious liberty. It is a broadside attack upon all forms of "establishment" of religion, both general and particular, nondiscriminatory or selective. Reflecting not only the many legislative conflicts over the Assessment Bill and the Bill for Establishing Religious Freedom but also, for example, the struggles for religious incorporations and the continued maintenance of the glebes, the Remonstrance is at once the most concise and the most accurate statement of the views of the First Amendment's author concerning what is "an establishment of religion." Because it behooves us in the dimming distance of time not to lose sight of what he and his coworkers had in mind when, by a single sweeping stroke of the pen, they forbade an establishment of religion and secured its free exercise, the text of the Remonstrance is appended at the end of this opinion for its wider current reference, together with a copy of the bill against which it was directed.

The *Remonstrance*, stirring up a storm of popular protest, killed the Assessment Bill. It collapsed in committee shortly before Christmas, 1785. With this, the way was cleared at last for enactment of Jefferson's Bill for Establishing Religious Freedom. Madison promptly drove it through in January of 1786, seven years from the time it was first introduced. This dual victory substantially ended the fight over establishments, settling the issue against them. The next year Madison became a member of the Constitutional Convention. Its work done, he fought valiantly to secure the ratification of its great product in Virginia as elsewhere, and nowhere else more effectively. Madison was certain in his own mind that under the Constitution "there is not a shadow of right in the general government to intermeddle with religion" and that "this subject is, for the honor of America, perfectly free and unshackled. The government has no jurisdiction over it. . . ." Nevertheless he pledged that he would work for a Bill of Rights, including a specific guaranty of religious freedom, and Virginia, with other states, ratified the Constitution on this assurance.

Ratification thus accomplished, Madison was sent to the first Congress. There he went at once about performing his pledge to establish freedom for the nation as he had done in Virginia. Within a little more than three years from his legislative victory at home he had proposed and secured the submission and ratification of the First Amendment as the first article of our Bill of Rights.

All the great instruments of the Virginia struggle for religious liberty thus became warp and woof of our constitutional tradition, not simply by the course of history, but by the common unifying force of Madison's life, thought and sponsorship. He epitomized the whole of that tradition in the Amendment's compact, but nonetheless comprehensive, phrasing.

As the Remonstrance discloses throughout, Madison opposed every form and degree of official relation between religion and civil authority. For him religion was a wholly private matter beyond the scope of civil power either to restrain or to support. Denial or abridgment of religious freedom was a violation of rights both of conscience and of natural equality. State aid was no less obnoxious or destructive to freedom and to religion itself than other forms of state interference. "Establishment" and "free exercise" were correlative and coextensive ideas, representing only different facets of the single great and fundamental freedom. The Remonstrance, following the Virginia statute's example, referred to the history of religious conflicts and the effects of all sorts of establishments, current and historical, to suppress religion's free exercise. With Jefferson, Madison believed that to tolerate any fragment of establishment would be by so much to perpetuate restraint upon that freedom. Hence he sought to tear out the institution not partially but root and branch, and to bar its return forever.

In no phase was he more unrelentingly absolute than in opposing state support or aid by taxation. Not even "three pence" contribution was thus to be exacted from any citizen for such a purpose. *Remonstrance*, Par. 3. Tithes had been the lifeblood of establishment before and after other compulsions disappeared. Madison and his coworkers made no exceptions or abridgments to the complete separation they created. Their objection was not to small tithes. It was to any tithes whatsoever. "If it were lawful to impose a small tax for religion, the admission would pave the way for oppressive levies." Not the amount but "the principle of assessment was wrong." And the principle was as much to prevent "the interference of law in religion" as to restrain religious intervention in political matters. In this field the authors of our freedom would not tolerate "the first experiment on our liberties" or "wait till usurped power had strengthened itself by exercise, and entangled the question in precedents." *Remonstrance*, Par. 3. Nor should we.

In view of this history no further proof is needed that the Amendment forbids any appropriation, large or small, from public funds to aid or support any and all religious exercises. But if more were called for, the debates in the First Congress and this Court's consistent expressions, whenever it has touched on the matter directly, supply it.

By contrast with the Virginia history, the congressional debates on consideration of the Amendment reveal only sparse discussion, reflecting the fact that the essential issues had been settled. Indeed the matter had become so well understood as to have been taken for granted in all but formal phrasing.

B. THE DEBATE OVER THE ORIGINAL INTENT OF THE RELIGION CLAUSES

Status of State Religious Establishments in 1789		
State	Status in 1789	Final Disestablishment
MA	multiple establishment	1833
NH	multiple establishment	1819
CT	multiple establishment	1818
MD	multiple establishment*	1810**
GA	multiple establishment*	1798
SC	multiple establishment*	1790
VA	none	1785
NY	none	1777
NC	none	1776
RI	none	never had establishment
PA	none	never had establishment
DE	none	never had establishment
NJ	none	never had establishment
VT***	multiple establishment	1807

Source: Information compiled from LEONARD LEVY, THE ESTABLISHMENT CLAUSE: RELIGION AND THE FIRST AMENDMENT (1986)

* In southern states the state constitutions merely permitted the establishment of religion by statute — these provisions did not establish religion explicitly.

** The MD legislature never implemented its constitutional authority.

*** Vermont was admitted to the union on March 7, 1791, prior to the ratification of the Bill of Rights on December 15, 1791.

WALLACE v. JAFFREE
472 U.S. 38 (1985)

[In this case, the Supreme Court struck down an Alabama silent prayer statute, on the ground that the legislature passed the statute with the impermissible intent to advance religion. Justice Rehnquist dissented, and used this opportunity to state his views on the role of original intent in the interpretation of the Establishment Clause.]

REHNQUIST, dissenting.

Thirty-eight years ago this Court, in *Everson v. Board of Education*, 330 U.S. 1, 16 (1947), summarized its exegesis of Establishment Clause doctrine thus:

> In the words of Jefferson, the clause against establishment of religion by law was intended to erect "a wall of separation between church and State." *Reynolds v. United States,* [98 U.S. 145, 164 (1879)].

This language from *Reynolds*, a case involving the Free Exercise Clause of the First Amendment rather than the Establishment Clause, quoted from Thomas Jefferson's letter to the Danbury Baptist Association the phrase "I contemplate with sovereign reverence that act of the whole American people which declared that their legislature should 'make no law respecting an establishment of religion, or prohibiting the free exercise thereof,' thus building a wall of separation between church and State." 8 WRITINGS OF THOMAS JEFFERSON 113 (H. Washington ed. 1861).[1]

It is impossible to build sound constitutional doctrine upon a mistaken understanding of constitutional history, but unfortunately the Establishment Clause has been expressly freighted with Jefferson's misleading metaphor for nearly 40 years. Thomas Jefferson was of course in France at the time the constitutional Amendments known as the Bill of Rights were passed by Congress and ratified by the States. His letter to the Danbury Baptist Association was a short note of courtesy, written 14 years after the Amendments were passed by Congress. He would seem to any detached observer as a less than ideal source of contemporary history as to the meaning of the Religion Clauses of the First Amendment.

Jefferson's fellow Virginian, James Madison, with whom he was joined in the battle for the enactment of the Virginia Statute of Religious Liberty of 1786, did play as large a part as anyone in the drafting of the Bill of Rights. He had two advantages over Jefferson in this regard: he was present in the United States, and he was a leading Member of the First Congress. But when we turn to the record of the proceedings in the First Congress leading up to the adoption

---

[1] *Reynolds* is the only authority cited as direct precedent for the "wall of separation theory." 330 U.S. at 16, 67 S. Ct., at 512. *Reynolds* is truly inapt; it dealt with a Mormon's Free Exercise Clause challenge to a federal polygamy law.

of the Establishment Clause of the Constitution, including Madison's significant contributions thereto, we see a far different picture of its purpose than the highly simplified "wall of separation between church and State."

During the debates in the Thirteen Colonies over ratification of the Constitution, one of the arguments frequently used by opponents of ratification was that without a Bill of Rights guaranteeing individual liberty the new general Government carried with it a potential for tyranny. The typical response to this argument on the part of those who favored ratification was that the general Government established by the Constitution had only delegated powers, and that these delegated powers were so limited that the Government would have no occasion to violate individual liberties. This response satisfied some, but not others, and of the 11 Colonies which ratified the Constitution by early 1789, 5 proposed one or another amendments guaranteeing individual liberty. Three — New Hampshire, New York, and Virginia — included in one form or another a declaration of religious freedom. See 3 J. ELLIOT, DEBATES ON THE FEDERAL CONSTITUTION 659 (1891); 1 *id.*, at 328. Rhode Island and North Carolina flatly refused to ratify the Constitution in the absence of amendments in the nature of a Bill of Rights. 1 *id.*, at 334; 4 *id.*, at 244. Virginia and North Carolina proposed identical guarantees of religious freedom:

> "[A]ll men have an equal, natural and unalienable right to the free exercise of religion, according to the dictates of conscience, and ... no particular religious sect or society ought to be favored or established, by law, in preference to others."

3 *id.*, at 659; 4 *id.*, at 244.[2]

On June 8, 1789, James Madison rose in the House of Representatives and "reminded the House that this was the day that he had heretofore named for bringing forward amendments to the Constitution." 1 ANNALS OF CONG. 424. Madison's subsequent remarks in urging the House to adopt his drafts of the proposed amendments were less those of a dedicated advocate of the wisdom of such measures than those of a prudent statesman seeking the enactment of measures sought by a number of his fellow citizens which could surely do no harm and might do a great deal of good. He said, inter alia:

> "It appears to me that this House is bound by every motive of prudence, not to let the first session pass over without proposing to the State Legislatures, some things to be incorporated into the Constitution, that will render it as acceptable to the whole people of the United States, as it has been found acceptable to a majority of them. I wish, among other reasons why something should be done, that those who had been friendly to the adoption of this Constitution may have the oppor-

---

[2] The New York and Rhode Island proposals were quite similar. They stated that no particular "religious sect or society ought to be favored or established by law in preference to others." 1 ELLIOT'S DEBATES, at 328; *id,* at 334.

tunity of proving to those who were opposed to it that they were as sincerely devoted to liberty and a Republican Government, as those who charged them with wishing the adoption of this Constitution in order to lay the foundation of an aristocracy or despotism. It will be a desirable thing to extinguish from the bosom of every member of the community, any apprehensions that there are those among his countrymen who wish to deprive them of the liberty for which they valiantly fought and honorably bled. And if there are amendments desired of such a nature as will not injure the Constitution, and they can be ingrafted so as to give satisfaction to the doubting part of our fellow-citizens, the friends of the Federal Government will evince that spirit of deference and concession for which they have hitherto been distinguished."

Id., at 431-432.

The language Madison proposed for what ultimately became the Religion Clauses of the First Amendment was this:

"The civil rights of none shall be abridged on account of religious belief or worship, nor shall any national religion be established, nor shall the full and equal rights of conscience be in any manner, or on any pretext, infringed."

Id., at 434.

On the same day that Madison proposed them, the amendments which formed the basis for the Bill of Rights were referred by the House to a Committee of the Whole, and after several weeks' delay were then referred to a Select Committee consisting of Madison and 10 others. The Committee revised Madison's proposal regarding the establishment of religion to read:

"[N]o religion shall be established by law, nor shall the equal rights of conscience be infringed."

Id., at 729.

The Committee's proposed revisions were debated in the House on August 15, 1789. The entire debate on the Religion Clauses is contained in two full columns of the "Annals," and does not seem particularly illuminating. *See id.,* at 729-731. Representative Peter Sylvester of New York expressed his dislike for the revised version, because it might have a tendency "to abolish religion altogether." Representative John Vining suggested that the two parts of the sentence be transposed; Representative Elbridge Gerry thought the language should be changed to read "that no religious doctrine shall be established by law." *Id.,* at 729. Roger Sherman of Connecticut had the traditional reason for opposing provisions of a Bill of Rights — that Congress had not delegated authority to "make religious establishments" — and therefore he opposed the adoption of the amendment. Representative Daniel Carroll of Maryland thought it desirable to adopt the words proposed, saying "[h]e would not contend with gentlemen about the phraseology, his object was to secure the substance in such a manner as to satisfy the wishes of the honest part of the community."

Madison then spoke, and said that "he apprehended the meaning of the words to be, that Congress should not establish a religion, and enforce the legal observation of it by law, nor compel men to worship God in any manner contrary to their conscience." *Id.,* at 730. He said that some of the state conventions had thought that Congress might rely on the Necessary and Proper Clause to infringe the rights of conscience or to establish a national religion, and "to prevent these effects he presumed the amendment was intended, and he thought it as well expressed as the nature of the language would admit." *Ibid.*

Representative Benjamin Huntington then expressed the view that the Committee's language might "be taken in such latitude as to be extremely hurtful to the cause of religion. He understood the amendment to mean what had been expressed by the gentleman from Virginia; but others might find it convenient to put another construction upon it." Huntington, from Connecticut, was concerned that in the New England States, where state-established religions were the rule rather than the exception, the federal courts might not be able to entertain claims based upon an obligation under the bylaws of a religious organization to contribute to the support of a minister or the building of a place of worship. He hoped that "the amendment would be made in such a way as to secure the rights of conscience, and a free exercise of the rights of religion, but not to patronise those who professed no religion at all." *Id.,* at 730-731.

Madison responded that the insertion of the word "national" before the word "religion" in the Committee version should satisfy the minds of those who had criticized the language. "He believed that the people feared one sect might obtain a pre-eminence, or two combine together, and establish a religion to which they would compel others to conform. He thought that if the word 'national' was introduced, it would point the amendment directly to the object it was intended to prevent." *Id.,* at 731. Representative Samuel Livermore expressed himself as dissatisfied with Madison's proposed amendment, and thought it would be better if the Committee language were altered to read that "Congress shall make no laws touching religion, or infringing the rights of conscience." *Ibid.*

Representative Gerry spoke in opposition to the use of the word "national" because of strong feelings expressed during the ratification debates that a federal government, not a national government, was created by the Constitution. Madison thereby withdrew his proposal but insisted that his reference to a "national religion" only referred to a national establishment and did not mean that the Government was a national one. The question was taken on Representative Livermore's motion, which passed by a vote of 31 for and 20 against. *Ibid.*

The following week, without any apparent debate, the House voted to alter the language of the Religion Clauses to read "Congress shall make no law establishing religion, or to prevent the free exercise thereof, or to infringe the rights of conscience." *Id.,* at 766. The floor debates in the Senate were secret, and therefore not reported in the Annals. The Senate on September 3, 1789, considered several different forms of the Religion Amendment, and reported this language back to the House:

> "Congress shall make no law establishing articles of faith or a mode of worship, or prohibiting the free exercise of religion."

C. ANTIEAU, A. DOWNEY, & E. ROBERTS, FREEDOM FROM FEDERAL ESTABLISHMENT 130 (1964).

The House refused to accept the Senate's changes in the Bill of Rights and asked for a conference; the version which emerged from the conference was that which ultimately found its way into the Constitution as a part of the First Amendment.

> "Congress shall make no law respecting an establishment of religion, or prohibiting the free exercise thereof."

The House and the Senate both accepted this language on successive days, and the Amendment was proposed in this form.

On the basis of the record of these proceedings in the House of Representatives, James Madison was undoubtedly the most important architect among the Members of the House of the Amendments which became the Bill of Rights, but it was James Madison speaking as an advocate of sensible legislative compromise, not as an advocate of incorporating the Virginia Statute of Religious Liberty into the United States Constitution. During the ratification debate in the Virginia Convention, Madison had actually opposed the idea of any Bill of Rights. His sponsorship of the Amendments in the House was obviously not that of a zealous believer in the necessity of the Religion Clauses, but of one who felt it might do some good, could do no harm, and would satisfy those who had ratified the Constitution on the condition that Congress propose a Bill of Rights. His original language "nor shall any national religion be established" obviously does not conform to the "wall of separation" between church and State idea which latter-day commentators have ascribed to him. His explanation on the floor of the meaning of his language — "that Congress should not establish a religion, and enforce the legal observation of it by law" is of the same ilk. When he replied to Huntington in the debate over the proposal which came from the Select Committee of the House, he urged that the language "no religion shall be established by law" should be amended by inserting the word "national" in front of the word "religion."

It seems indisputable from these glimpses of Madison's thinking, as reflected by actions on the floor of the House in 1789, that he saw the Amendment as designed to prohibit the establishment of a national religion, and perhaps to prevent discrimination among sects. He did not see it as requiring neutrality on the part of government between religion and irreligion. Thus the Court's opinion in

Everson — while correct in bracketing Madison and Jefferson together in their exertions in their home State leading to the enactment of the Virginia Statute of Religious Liberty — is totally incorrect in suggesting that Madison carried these views onto the floor of the United States House of Representatives when he proposed the language which would ultimately become the Bill of Rights.

The repetition of this error in the Court's opinion in *Illinois ex rel. McCollum v. Board of Education*, 333 U.S. 203 (1948), and, inter alia, *Engel v. Vitale*, 370 U.S. 421 (1962), does not make it any sounder historically. Finally, in *Abington School District v. Schempp*, 374 U.S. 203, 214 (1963), the Court made the truly remarkable statement that "the views of Madison and Jefferson, preceded by Roger Williams, came to be incorporated not only in the Federal Constitution but likewise in those of most of our States" (footnote omitted). On the basis of what evidence we have, this statement is demonstrably incorrect as a matter of history. And its repetition in varying forms in succeeding opinions of the Court can give it no more authority than it possesses as a matter of fact; stare decisis may bind courts as to matters of law, but it cannot bind them as to matters of history.

None of the other Members of Congress who spoke during the August 15th debate expressed the slightest indication that they thought the language before them from the Select Committee, or the evil to be aimed at, would require that the Government be absolutely neutral as between religion and irreligion. The evil to be aimed at, so far as those who spoke were concerned, appears to have been the establishment of a national church, and perhaps the preference of one religious sect over another; but it was definitely not concerned about whether the Government might aid all religions evenhandedly. If one were to follow the advice of Justice Brennan, concurring in *Abington School District v. Schempp, supra*, at 236, and construe the Amendment in the light of what particular " practices ... challenged threaten those consequences which the Framers deeply feared; whether, in short, they tend to promote that type of interdependence between religion and state which the First Amendment was designed to prevent," one would have to say that the First Amendment Establishment Clause should be read no more broadly than to prevent the establishment of a national religion or the governmental preference of one religious sect over another.

The actions of the First Congress, which reenacted the Northwest Ordinance for the governance of the Northwest Territory in 1789, confirm the view that Congress did not mean that the Government should be neutral between religion and irreligion. The House of Representatives took up the Northwest Ordinance on the same day as Madison introduced his proposed amendments which became the Bill of Rights; while at that time the Federal Government was of course not bound by draft amendments to the Constitution which had not yet been proposed by Congress, say nothing of ratified by the States, it seems highly unlikely that the House of Representatives would simultaneously consider proposed amendments to the Constitution and enact an important piece of territorial legislation which conflicted with the intent of those proposals. The Northwest Ordinance, 1 Stat. 50, reenacted the Northwest Ordinance of 1787 and provided that "[r]eligion, morality, and knowledge, being necessary to good government and the happiness of mankind, schools and the means of education shall forever be encouraged." *Id.*, at 52, n. (a). Land grants for schools in the Northwest Territory were not limited to public schools. It was not until 1845 that Congress limited land grants in the new States and Territories to non-sectarian schools. 5 Stat. 788; C. ANTIEAU, A. DOWNEY, & E. ROBERTS, FREEDOM FROM FEDERAL ESTABLISHMENT 163 (1964).

On the day after the House of Representatives voted to adopt the form of the First Amendment Religion Clauses which was ultimately proposed and ratified, Representative Elias Boudinot proposed a resolution asking President George Washington to issue a Thanksgiving Day Proclamation. Boudinot said he "could not think of letting the session pass over without offering an opportunity to all the citizens of the United States of joining with one voice, in returning to Almighty God their sincere thanks for the many blessings he had poured down upon them." 1 ANNALS OF CONG. 914 (1789). Representative Aedanas Burke objected to the resolution because he did not like "this mimicking of European customs"; Representative Thomas Tucker objected that whether or not the people had reason to be satisfied with the Constitution was something that the States knew better than the Congress, and in any event "it is a religious matter, and, as such, is proscribed to us." *Id.*, at 915. Representative Sherman supported the resolution "not only as a laudable one in itself, but as warranted by a number of precedents in Holy Writ: for instance, the solemn thanksgivings and rejoicings which took place in the time of Solomon, after the building of the temple, was a case in point. This example, he thought, worthy of Christian imitation on the present occasion. . . ." *Ibid.*

Boudinot's resolution was carried in the affirmative on September 25, 1789. Boudinot and Sherman, who favored the Thanksgiving Proclamation, voted in favor of the adoption of the proposed amendments to the Constitution, including the Religion Clauses; Tucker, who opposed the Thanksgiving Proclamation, voted against the adoption of the amendments which became the Bill of Rights.

Within two weeks of this action by the House, George Washington responded to the Joint Resolution which by now had been changed to include the language that the President "recommend to the people of the United States a day of public thanksgiving and prayer, to be observed by acknowledging with grateful hearts the many and signal favors of Almighty God, especially by affording them an opportunity peaceably to establish a form of government for their safety and happiness." 1 J. RICHARDSON, MESSAGES AND PAPERS OF THE PRESIDENTS, 1789-1897, p. 64 (1897). The Presidential Proclamation was couched in these words:

> "Now, therefore, I do recommend and assign Thursday, the 26th day of November next, to be devoted by the people of these States to the service of that great and glorious Being who is the beneficent author of

all the good that was, that is, or that will be; that we may then all unite in rendering unto Him our sincere and humble thanks for His kind care and protection of the people of this country previous to their becoming a nation; for the signal and manifold mercies and the favorable interpositions of His providence in the course and conclusion of the late war; for the great degree of tranquillity, union, and plenty which we have since enjoyed; for the peaceable and rational manner in which we have been enabled to establish constitutions of government for our safety and happiness, and particularly the national one now lately instituted; for the civil and religious liberty with which we are blessed, and the means we have of acquiring and diffusing useful knowledge; and, in general, for all the great and various favors which He has been pleased to confer upon us.

"And also that we may then unite in most humbly offering our prayers and supplications to the great Lord and Ruler of Nations, and beseech Him to pardon our national and other transgressions; to enable us all, whether in public or private stations, to perform our several and relative duties properly and punctually; to render our National Government a blessing to all the people by constantly being a Government of wise, just, and constitutional laws, discreetly and faithfully executed and obeyed; to protect and guide all sovereigns and nations (especially such as have shown kindness to us), and to bless them with good governments, peace, and concord; to promote the knowledge and practice of true religion and virtue, and the increase of science among them and us; and, generally, to grant unto all mankind such a degree of temporal prosperity as He alone knows to be best." *Ibid.*

George Washington, John Adams, and James Madison all issued Thanksgiving Proclamations; Thomas Jefferson did not, saying:

"Fasting and prayer are religious exercises; the enjoining them an act of discipline. Every religious society has a right to determine for itself the times for these exercises, and the objects proper for them, according to their own particular tenets; and this right can never be safer than in their own hands, where the Constitution has deposited it."

11 WRITINGS OF THOMAS JEFFERSON 429 (A. Lipscomb ed. 1904).

As the United States moved from the 18th into the 19th century, Congress appropriated time and again public moneys in support of sectarian Indian education carried on by religious organizations. Typical of these was Jefferson's treaty with the Kaskaskia Indians, which provided annual cash support for the Tribe's Roman Catholic priest and church. It was not until 1897, when aid to sectarian education for Indians had reached $500,000 annually, that Congress decided thereafter to cease appropriating money for education in sectarian schools. *See* Act of June 7, 1897, 30 Stat. 62, 79; cf. *Quick Bear v. Leupp*, 210 U.S. 50, 77-79 (1908); J. O'NEILL, RELIGION AND EDUCATION UNDER THE CONSTI-

TUTION 118-119 (1949). *See generally* R. CORD, SEPARATION OF CHURCH AND STATE 61-82 (1982). This history shows the fallacy of the notion found in Everson that "no tax in any amount" may be levied for religious activities in any form. 330 U.S., at 15-16.

Joseph Story, a Member of this Court from 1811 to 1845, and during much of that time a professor at the Harvard Law School, published by far the most comprehensive treatise on the United States Constitution that had then appeared. Volume 2 of STORY'S COMMENTARIES ON THE CONSTITUTION OF THE UNITED STATES 630-632 (5th ed. 1891) discussed the meaning of the Establishment Clause of the First Amendment this way:

> "Probably at the time of the adoption of the Constitution, and of the amendment to it now under consideration [First Amendment], the general if not the universal sentiment in America was, that Christianity ought to receive encouragement from the State so far as was not incompatible with the private rights of conscience and the freedom of religious worship. An attempt to level all religions, and to make it a matter of state policy to hold all in utter indifference, would have created universal disapprobation, if not universal indignation.
>
> . . .
>
> "The real object of the [First] [A]mendment was not to countenance, much less to advance, Mahometanism, or Judaism, or infidelity, by prostrating Christianity; but to exclude all rivalry among Christian sects, and to prevent any national ecclesiastical establishment which should give to a hierarchy the exclusive patronage of the national government. It thus cut off the means of religious persecution (the vice and pest of former ages), and of the subversion of the rights of conscience in matters of religion, which had been trampled upon almost from the days of the Apostles to the present age. . . ." (Footnotes omitted.)

Thomas Cooley's eminence as a legal authority rivaled that of Story. Cooley stated in his treatise entitled CONSTITUTIONAL LIMITATIONS that aid to a particular religious sect was prohibited by the United States Constitution, but he went on to say:

> "But while thus careful to establish, protect, and defend religious freedom and equality, the American constitutions contain no provisions which prohibit the authorities from such solemn recognition of a superintending Providence in public transactions and exercises as the general religious sentiment of mankind inspires, and as seems meet and proper in finite and dependent beings. Whatever may be the shades of religious belief, all must acknowledge the fitness of recognizing in important human affairs the superintending care and control of the Great Governor of the Universe, and of acknowledging with thanksgiving his boundless favors, or bowing in contrition when visited with the penalties of his broken laws. No principle of constitutional law is violated when thanks-

giving or fast days are appointed; when chaplains are designated for the army and navy; when legislative sessions are opened with prayer or the reading of the Scriptures, or when religious teaching is encouraged by a general exemption of the houses of religious worship from taxation for the support of State government. Undoubtedly the spirit of the Constitution will require, in all these cases, that care be taken to avoid discrimination in favor of or against any one religious denomination or sect; but the power to do any of these things does not become unconstitutional simply because of its susceptibility to abuse. . . ." *Id.,* at *470-*471.

Cooley added that

"[t]his public recognition of religious worship, however, is not based entirely, perhaps not even mainly, upon a sense of what is due to the Supreme Being himself as the author of all good and of all law; but the same reasons of state policy which induce the government to aid institutions of charity and seminaries of instruction will incline it also to foster religious worship and religious institutions, as conservators of the public morals and valuable, if not indispensable, assistants to the preservation of the public order." *Id.,* at *470.

It would seem from this evidence that the Establishment Clause of the First Amendment had acquired a well-accepted meaning: it forbade establishment of a national religion, and forbade preference among religious sects or denominations. Indeed, the first American dictionary defined the word "establishment" as "the act of establishing, founding, ratifying or ordaining," such as in "[t]he episcopal form of religion, so called, in England." 1 N. WEBSTER, AMERICAN DICTIONARY OF THE ENGLISH LANGUAGE (1st ed. 1828). The Establishment Clause did not require government neutrality between religion and irreligion nor did it prohibit the Federal Government from providing nondiscriminatory aid to religion. There is simply no historical foundation for the proposition that the Framers intended to build the "wall of separation" that was constitutionalized in *Everson.*

Notwithstanding the absence of a historical basis for this theory of rigid separation, the wall idea might well have served as a useful albeit misguided analytical concept, had it led this Court to unified and principled results in Establishment Clause cases. The opposite, unfortunately, has been true; in the 38 years since *Everson* our Establishment Clause cases have been neither principled nor unified. Our recent opinions, many of them hopelessly divided pluralities, have with embarrassing candor conceded that the "wall of separation" is merely a "blurred, indistinct, and variable barrier," which "is not wholly accurate" and can only be "dimly perceived." *Lemon v. Kurtzman*, 403 U.S. 602, 614 (1971); *Tilton v. Richardson*, 403 U.S. 672, 677-678 (1971); *Wolman v. Walter*, 433 U.S. 229, 236 (1977); *Lynch v. Donnelly*, 465 U.S. 668, 673 (1984).

Whether due to its lack of historical support or its practical unworkability, the *Everson* "wall" has proved all but useless as a guide to sound constitutional adjudication. It illustrates only too well the wisdom of Benjamin Cardozo's observation that "[m]etaphors in law are to be narrowly watched, for starting as devices to liberate thought, they end often by enslaving it." *Berkey v. Third Avenue R. Co.*, 244 N.Y. 84, 94, 155 N.E. 58, 61 (1926).

But the greatest injury of the "wall" notion is its mischievous diversion of judges from the actual intentions of the drafters of the Bill of Rights. The "crucible of litigation," ante, at 2488, is well adapted to adjudicating factual disputes on the basis of testimony presented in court, but no amount of repetition of historical errors in judicial opinions can make the errors true. The "wall of separation between church and State" is a metaphor based on bad history, a metaphor which has proved useless as a guide to judging. It should be frankly and explicitly abandoned.

NOTE ON THE "WALL OF SEPARATION" AND JEFFERSON'S LETTER TO THE DANBURY BAPTISTS

Jefferson's *Letter to the Danbury Baptists* and the phrase "wall of separation between Church & State," which appears in the letter, have been the source of numerous comments and critiques, some favorable (such as the references in the various *Everson* opinions) and some unfavorable (including Justice Rehnquist's *Wallace v. Jaffree* dissent). Jefferson's letter was written in 1802, in response to an address from the Danbury, Connecticut Baptist Association congratulating him on his election as president. In an article prepared for a Library of Congress exhibition on "Religion and the Founding of the American Republic," the chief of the Library's Manuscript Division provides a succinct explanation of the genesis and context of Jefferson's letter, including an examination of passages that were removed by Jefferson before the letter was sent. *See* James Hutson, *"A Wall of Separation": FBI Helps Restore Jefferson's Obliterated Draft*, LC Information Bulletin, available at http://www.loc.gov/loc/lcib/9806/danbury.html (June 1998). Mr. Hutson explains that Jefferson used his letter to the Danbury Baptists to express his ideas on the separation of church and state, explain his unwillingness to declare official days of religious thanksgiving, and respond to continuing Federalist attempts to paint him as an atheist and an infidel. "Federalist preachers had routinely used fast and thanksgiving days to revile Jefferson and his followers, going so far in 1799 as to suggest that a Philadelphia yellow fever epidemic was a divine punishment for Republican godlessness." *Id.* One way in which Jefferson counterattacked was to link the Federalists with the ecclesiastical tyranny associated with the British monarchy. "In indicting the Federalists for their 'Tory' taste for thanksgivings and fasts, Jefferson was playing rough. . . . [T]o sully them with Anglophobic mudslinging, generated by the partisan warfare of his own time, as Jefferson did, was a low blow. But who was being more unfair: Jefferson or his Federalist inquisitors, who continued to calumniate him as an atheist?" Ironically, Jefferson deleted much of the stronger language about official thanksgiving proclamations before the letter was sent. These edits were undertaken upon the advice of Attorney General Levi Lincoln of Massachusetts, who read an early draft and recognized that the original version might hurt Jefferson among the growing number of New England Republicans, whose political representatives were in the habit of issuing precisely the type of official proclamations decried by Jefferson. The final version of the letter appears in its entirety below. The original draft, with the deleted text restored by the FBI Laboratory, can be viewed on the Library of Congress website: http://www.loc.gov/loc/lcib/9806/danbury.html.

> To messers. Nehemiah Dodge, Ephraim Robbins, & Stephen S. Nelson, a committee of the Danbury Baptist association in the state of Connecticut.
>
> Gentlemen
>
> The affectionate sentiments of esteem and approbation which you are so good as to express towards me, on behalf of the Danbury Baptist association, give me the highest satisfaction. My duties dictate a faithful and zealous pursuit of the interests of my constituents, & in proportion as they are persuaded of my fidelity to those duties, the discharge of them becomes more and more pleasing.
>
> Believing with you that religion is a matter which lies solely between Man & his God, that he owes account to none other for his faith or his worship, that the legitimate powers of government reach actions only, & not opinions, I contemplate with sovereign reverence that act of the whole American people which declared that their legislature should "make no law respecting an establishment of religion, or prohibiting the free exercise thereof," thus building a wall of separation between Church & State. Adhering to this expression of the supreme will of the nation in behalf of the rights of conscience, I shall see with sincere satisfaction the progress of those sentiments which tend to restore to man all his natural rights, convinced he has no natural right in opposition to his social duties.
>
> I reciprocate your kind prayers for the protection & blessing of the common father and creator of man, and tender you for yourselves & your religious association, assurances of my high respect & esteem.
>
> Th Jefferson
> Jan. 1. 1802.

As one measure of the controversy that Jefferson's "wall of separation" is still capable of generating, note that James Hutson's account of Jefferson's letter to the Danbury Baptists itself became an object of dispute when it was issued in conjunction with a Library of Congress exhibition on the history of religion and the founding of the nation. *See* Laurie Goodstein, *Fresh Debate on 1802 Jefferson Letter*, N.Y. TIMES, Sept. 10, 1998, at A20. Christian conservatives seized on the references to the political context of Jefferson's letter in Hutson's account, arguing that this "was proof that Jefferson's 'wall' metaphor should never have been interpreted as an overarching principle." *Id.* Twenty-four scholars immediately responded to this assertion in a letter to the Library of Congress, arguing that the Hutson account presents an "unbalanced treatment of this important topic on the basis of questionable analysis that has not, as far as is known, been subjected to independent scholarly review." Robert S. Alley, et al, *The Library of Congress Misinterprets Thomas Jefferson: A Letter of Concern from Scholars* (1998). According to the NEW YORK TIMES, "Robert M. O'Neill, director of the Thomas Jefferson Center and a professor of law at the University of Virginia, who helped draft the scholars' letter, said, 'The fact that there may have been a political context for Jefferson's letter hardly disqualifies it as an assertion of principle, especially since it is so consistent with everything else he did or said on this issue.'" Goodstein, *supra.* For a full discussion of this controversy, including contributions from Hutson and O'Neill, *see Forum*, 56 WM. & MARY Q. 775 (1999).

Note that although Jefferson is usually credited (or blamed) for introducing the metaphor of a "wall of separation" into the lexicon of church/state discourse in this country, the concept can actually be traced to the seventeenth century Puritan minister Roger Williams, who wrote that "[W]hen they have opened a gap in the hedge or wall of Separation between the Garden of the Church and the Wilderness of the world, God hath ever broke down the wall itself, removed the Candlestick, and made his Garden a Wilderness, as at this day. And that ther[e]fore if he will ever please to restore his Garden and Paradise again, it must of necessity be walled in peculiarly unto himself from the world, and that all that shall be saved out of the world are to be transplanted out of the Wilderness of [the] world, and added unto his Church or Garden." Roger Williams, *Mr. Cotton's Letter Examined and Answered* (1644), *reprinted in* 1 THE COMPLETE WRITINGS OF ROGER WILLIAMS 313, 392 (Russel & Russel, Inc. 1963). For several nuanced views of the relationship between Jefferson's advocacy of a wall to prevent religion from undermining pluralist democracy and Williams' advocacy of a wall to protect the purity of religion from the corruption of the secular world, *see* MARK DEWOLFE HOWE, THE GARDEN AND THE WILDERNESS (1965); Timothy L. Hall, *Roger Williams and the Foundations of Religious Liberty*, 71 B.U. L. REV. 455 (1991); Arlin M. Adams & Charles J. Emmerich, *A Heritage of Religious Liberty*, 137 U. PA. L. REV. 1559 (1989).

Douglas Laycock
"Nonpreferential" Aid To Religion: A False Claim About Original Intent
27 WM. & MARY L. REV. 875 (1986)*

[In this article Prof. Laycock reviews the relevant history of the First Amendment and concludes that it "refutes one important claim about the establishment clause — that the Framers specifically intended to permit government aid to religion so long as that aid does not prefer one religion over others."]

The theory that the establishment clause forbids only preferential aid has long been a favorite of those who support government aid to religion. It does not go away despite repeated rejection by the United States Supreme Court. In the round of establishment clause debate triggered by the political coalition that elected Ronald Reagan to the Presidency, the "no preference" argument has been stated in one form or another by Attorney General Edwin Meese,[5] Chief Justice William Rehnquist,[6] political scientists Michael Malbin[7] and Robert Cord,[8] law professor Rodney Smith,[9] and my former student, Martin Nussbaum.[10] Malbin's pamphlet and Cord's book have become standard authorities for supporters of government aid to religion.

Professor Tushnet's prediction that Cord would be ignored was erroneous. Justice O'Connor's concurrence in *Wallace v. Jaffree* cites Cord, and Justice White's dissent was receptive. Justice Rehnquist's dissent drew heavily on Cord's history without citing it. Justice Stevens' opinion for the majority rejected Justice Rehnquist's conclusions on the basis of precedent, but it did not refute Justice Rehnquist's account of history.

The prominence and longevity of the nonpreferential aid theory is remarkable in light of the weak evidence supporting it and the quite strong evidence against it. I do not mean to overstate what we know about the establishment clause. Neither its history nor its text offers us a single unambiguous meaning. But they

---

* Copyright 1986 by Douglas Laycock. All Rights Reserved.

[5] Meese, *Toward a Jurisprudence of Original Intention*, 2 BENCHMARK 1, 5 (1986).

[6] *Wallace v. Jaffree*, 472 U.S. 38, 91-114 (1985) (Rehnquist, J., dissenting).

[7] M. MALBIN, RELIGION AND POLITICS: THE INTENTIONS OF THE AUTHORS OF THE FIRST AMENDMENT (1978).

[8] R. CORD, SEPARATION OF CHURCH AND STATE: HISTORICAL FACT AND CURRENT FICTION (1982); Cord, *Church-State Separation: Restoring the "No Preference" Doctrine of the First Amendment*, 9 HARV. J.L. & PUB. POL'Y 129 (1986).

[9] Smith, *Getting Off on the Wrong Foot and Back On Again: A Reexamination of the History of the Framing of the Religion Clauses of the First Amendment and a Critique of the Reynolds and Everson Decisions*, 20 WAKE FOREST L. REV. 569 (1984).

[10] Nussbaum, *A Garment for the Naked Public Square: Nurturing American Public Theology*, 16 CUM. L. REV. 53, 62, 68, 74 (1985); Comment, *Mueller v. Allen: Tuition Tax Relief and the Original Intent,* 7 HARV. J.L. & PUB. POL'Y 551, 566-77 (1984).

can eliminate some possible meanings, and to do that is real progress. So long as the debate is dominated by a false claim, it is hard to discuss the real issues.

I. THE NONPREFERENTIAL AID CLAIM

There are several versions of the nonpreferential aid argument, but all reach substantially the same conclusion. The claim is that the framers of the religion clauses intended a specific meaning with respect to the problems now treated under the establishment clause: government may not prefer one religion over others, but it may aid all religions evenhandedly. Under this view, the Supreme Court's more expansive interpretation is a usurpation that remains illegitimate no matter how long the Court adheres to it.

This claim is false. The framers of the religion clauses certainly did not consciously intend to permit nonpreferential aid, and those of them who thought about the question probably intended to forbid it. In fact, substantial evidence suggests that the Framers expressly considered the question and that they believed that nonpreferential aid would establish religion. To assert the opposite as historical fact, and to charge the Supreme Court with usurpation without acknowledging the substantial evidence that supports the Court's position, is to mislead the American people.

The fact is that the First Congress repeatedly rejected versions of the establishment clause that would have permitted nonpreferential aid, and nothing in the sparse legislative history gives much support to the view that the Framers intended to permit nonpreferential aid. Proposals for nonpreferential financial aid were squarely rejected in Maryland and Virginia in 1785 and 1786, amidst much public debate. No state offered nonpreferential aid to churches, and only Maryland and Virginia seriously proposed such aid. Some of the New England states provided financial aid to more than one church, but these systems were preferential in practice and were the source of bitter religious strife. There is no evidence that those schemes were the model for the establishment clause.

The Framers also had a second, less considered intention. Both the states and the federal government openly endorsed Protestantism and provided a variety of preferential, nonfinancial aid to Protestants. This aid was wholly noncontroversial, because the nation was so uniformly Protestant and hostile to other faiths. The early preference for Protestantism is not a precedent for nonpreferential aid, and it is not an attractive model for establishment clause interpretation. The Framers' generation thought about establishment clause issues in the context of financial aid; they did not think about those issues in connection with nonfinancial aid. We can make better sense of the establishment clause if we follow what the Framers did when they were thinking about establishment. Thus, to the extent that the Framers' intent is thought to matter, the relevant intent is their analysis of financial aid to churches.

II. THE BEST EVIDENCE OF THE FRAMERS' INTENT: THE TEXT OF THE ESTABLISHMENT CLAUSE

A. *The Rejected Drafts*

Professor Kurland mentions in passing the most important fact concealed by the proponents of nonpreferential aid: the First Congress considered and rejected at least four drafts of the establishment clause that explicitly stated the "no preference" view. So far as we can tell from the legislative journal, the issue was squarely posed in the Senate and again in the Conference Committee.

The House of Representatives sent to the Senate a draft of the establishment clause somewhat like the version ultimately ratified:

> Congress shall make no law establishing religion, or prohibiting the free exercise thereof, nor shall the rights of conscience be infringed.

The first motion in the Senate clearly presented the "no preference" position. The motion was to strike out "religion, or prohibiting the free exercise thereof," and to insert, "one religious sect or society in preference to others." The motion was first rejected, and then passed. The proposal on the floor then read:

> Congress shall make no law establishing one religious sect or society in preference to others, nor shall the rights of conscience be infringed.

Next, the Senate rejected two substantively similar substitutes. First, the Senate rejected language providing:

> Congress shall not make any law, infringing the rights of conscience, or establishing any Religious Sect or Society.

Second, it rejected an alternative that stated:

> Congress shall make no law establishing any particular denomination of religion in preference to another, or prohibiting the free exercise thereof, nor shall the rights of conscience be infringed.

The two motions to amend by substitution appear to have presented stylistic choices. But the first vote appears to have been substantive. At the very least, these three drafts show that if the First Congress intended to forbid only preferential establishments, its failure to do so explicitly was not for want of acceptable wording. The Senate had before it three very clear and felicitous ways of making the point.

Still later the same day, the Senate appears to have abandoned the "no preference" position. It adopted a draft that spoke of all religion generically:

> Congress shall make no law establishing religion, or prohibiting the free exercise thereof.

A week later, the Senate again changed its mind and adopted the narrowest version of the establishment clause considered by either House:

> Congress shall make no law establishing articles of faith or a mode of worship, or prohibiting the free exercise of religion. . . .

The House of Representatives rejected this version. James Madison and two others represented the House on the Conference Committee that produced the version of the establishment clause ultimately ratified:

> Congress shall make no law respecting an establishment of religion, or prohibiting the free exercise thereof. . . .

The establishment clause actually adopted is one of the broadest versions considered by either House. It forbids not only establishments, but also any law respecting or relating to an establishment. Most important, it forbids any law respecting an establishment of "religion." It does not say "a religion," "a national religion," "one sect or society," or "any particular denomination of religion." It is religion generically that may not be established.

Malbin is a major proponent of the "no preference" position. While parsing the legislative history for support of his position, he argues that there is a big difference between establishing "a religion" and establishing "religion." He notes that to forbid establishment of "a religion" would clearly state the nonpreferentialist position, but that to forbid establishment of "religion" would not. On that point, he is absolutely right. The rejected drafts pose the distinction even more clearly: establishing "religion" is not the same as establishing one sect or society, any particular denomination, or articles of faith and a mode of worship. If Congress paid any attention at all to the language it fought over, it rejected the "no preference" view.

The nonpreferentialists tend not to mention the rejected drafts, or to pass over the drafts as insignificant. Some nonpreferentialists rely heavily on similar resolutions from the state ratifying conventions. The Virginia, North Carolina and New York, conventions proposed establishment clauses similar to the rejected Senate drafts. James Madison's original bill in the First Congress provided: "nor shall any national religion be established." Like the Senate drafts, however, all of these proposals were rejected.

An approach to interpretation that disregards the ratified amendment and derives meaning exclusively from rejected proposals is strange indeed. The "no preference" position requires a premise that the Framers were extraordinarily bad drafters — that they believed one thing but adopted language that said something substantially different, and that they did so after repeatedly attending to the choice of language.

Perhaps the Framers did not understand what they were doing and viewed the textual choices as stylistic. All sorts of things become possible once one begins to speculate about what the Framers might have thought instead of giving primary weight to what they enacted. But responsible constitutional interpretation does not allow us to assume a mistake of this magnitude. When the record reflects a textual choice as clear as this one, only extraordinarily clear contrary evidence should persuade us not to follow the text.

III. THE DEBATE IN THE FIRST CONGRESS

A. *The Relevance of the Debate*

The nonpreferentialists rely heavily on the debate in the First Congress, but that debate adds little to current understanding. The only recorded debate occurred in the House. No verbatim record exists, the reporter's notes are incomplete and sometimes inaccurate, and the notes fill slightly less than two columns in the Annals of Congress. Because the Senate met in secret, only the Journal entries recording its votes are available. Thus, the attempt to override the evidence of the rejected drafts depends on those two columns of notes from the House. The nonpreferentialists rely on a puzzling statement by Madison that is probably wrong and in any event does not state the nonpreferentialist understanding of the clause. They also rely on attenuated inferences from the remarks of others. These remarks must be examined in light of the preliminary draft to which they referred.

The House debate occurred on August 15, 1789, before any of the events in the Senate. The debate concerned the draft submitted by a Select Committee, a draft somewhat narrower than the amendment ultimately adopted. Two things about this draft are important. First, it was ambiguous concerning nonpreferential aid. Second, and more important, the House promptly rejected this draft and substituted a version that was not ambiguous on this issue.

The Select Committee draft provided:

> [N]o religion shall be established by law, nor shall the equal rights of conscience be infringed.

The reference to "no religion" is consistent with the view that many religions exist, and that no one of them may be established by law. The possibility is best illustrated by comparing the following two formulations, which are identical except for the placement of the negative:

1. No religion shall be established by law.   No specific Religion Nationaly
2. Religion shall not be established by law.   Dont touch Religion AI ALL

The first formulation is the Select Committee draft. It might mean that no particular religion, or no specific religion, shall be established by law. It is not plausible to read the second formulation that way; it seems clearly to mean that religion generally shall not be established by law.

Again, I do not want to make too much of this textual inference. The first formulation is not unambiguous, especially if it is not compared to the second formulation. If the Select Committee meant to say "no particular religion," it could have said so. Nothing suggests that anyone thought of the second formulation and deliberately chose the first formulation instead. Finally, what the Select Committee draft meant ultimately makes no difference, because the House did not adopt it and the subsequent Senate and Conference Committee choices are much less ambiguous. The possible meaning of the Select Committee draft matters only because of the emphasis that has been placed on the August 15 debate. Anyone who thinks that the debate concerning this draft shows an intention to ban only preferential aid must keep in mind that the draft might have been so limited, or that some of the speakers might have so understood it.

Even more important, the House rejected the Select Committee draft at the end of the August 15 debate. Instead, it adopted the sweeping substitute offered by Mr. Livermore:

> Congress shall make no laws touching religion, or infringing the rights of conscience.

Any law aiding religion in any way would "touch" religion. Malbin concedes that the Livermore amendment would have forbidden nonpreferential aid and even incidental religious effects of secular programs. But the surviving notes of the debate do not mention that point, and nothing clearly indicates why a majority voted for the amendment. Livermore's language had been proposed by the ratifying convention in his home state of New Hampshire, and he may have been the draftsman. Probably no one will ever know whether he offered the amendment for a substantive reason, out of state pride, or out of personal pride of authorship.

Malbin speculates that the Antifederalists supported Livermore's amendment because it was more restrictive than the Select Committee's draft and, in their view, any restriction on federal power was good. I wish I thought he were right, because that theory devastates the claim that the Framers meant to permit nonpreferential aid. Indeed, a similar claim that the Framers intended the meaning that most severely limited federal power is a principal element of Leonard Levy's attack on the nonpreferentialists. Malbin's Antifederalist explanation of the Livermore amendment suggests that a substantial block of congressmen understood the restrictive implications of the Livermore amendment and supported it because of those implications. Malbin's claim that those who spoke on August 15 wanted to permit nonpreferential aid is inconsistent with his claim that the House adopted the Livermore amendment precisely because it forbade nonpreferential aid and even incidental aid.

Malbin offers his Antifederalist explanation of the Livermore amendment to show that the House was sparring on collateral issues. That is plainly true of some of the debate, and it further reduces the importance of the debate. To the extent that the members were really talking about collateral issues, it is that much more difficult to infer specific intentions about the establishment clause from their remarks.

The bottom line concerning the Livermore amendment is this: If the House had the distinction between preferential and nonpreferential aid in mind, its vote for the Livermore amendment was a vote to forbid nonpreferential aid, and the "no preference" interpretation of the debate must be wrong. If the House did not have the distinction in mind, the debate cannot speak to the issue. Either way, the debate is little help.

B. The Content of the Debate

Fifty-one representatives were present to vote on the Livermore amendment. Only eight of them said anything the reporter took down, and few of the eight addressed the meaning of the Select Committee draft. Mr. Vining suggested transposing the two clauses. Mr. Sherman said that the amendment was unnecessary because the Constitution conferred no power to establish religion. Mr. Carroll responded that the amendment would reassure those with honest doubts. Mr. Madison agreed with Mr. Carroll. Mr. Livermore offered his substitute without explanation. These remarks do not support any inference about the meaning of the amendment.

Elbridge Gerry spoke twice. His longer speech concerned a wholly collateral issue. Madison had suggested clarifying the amendment by inserting the word "national," and Gerry took the opportunity to denounce the Federalists. The opponents of the Constitution had argued all along that it created a national rather than a federal government, and Madison seemed to be confirming the charge. Madison withdrew his motion.

Gerry's other comment was a suggestion that the amendment "would read better if it was, that no religious doctrine shall be established by law." This substitute would have stated a narrow variant of the nonpreferentialist position, but it does not show the meaning of the draft under discussion. No one spoke in support of Gerry's substitute, it was not adopted, and it closely paralleled the final Senate draft that was rejected in the Conference Committee.

That leaves three speakers for the nonpreferentialists to rely on: Mr. Sylvester and Mr. Huntington, who appeared to resist the establishment clause, and Madison, who sponsored it. Sylvester feared that the Select Committee draft "might . . . have a tendency to abolish religion altogether." From this comment some have argued that Sylvester was friendly to religion and convinced that religion was dependent on state aid, so that he must have intended not to forbid such aid. Those inferences are not unreasonable, but it does not follow that Sylvester wanted to forbid preferential aid and permit nonpreferential aid. No one knows what kind of aid Sylvester would have permitted. A fair inference is that Sylvester opposed the establishment clause, that he wanted it narrowed in any way possible, and that he would have supported any kind of aid he could get. Whatever he thought, no evidence indicates that a majority shared his views. The Select Committee draft was not changed to accommodate his objection.

Mr. Huntington was the only speaker who endorsed Sylvester's remarks. Specifically, Huntington feared that the amendment would render federal courts unable to enforce pledges of money to the support of churches. On its face, Huntington's statement seems to say that the amendment would go too far if it rendered church contracts unenforceable. But context reveals that Huntington probably meant more than that. He offered the example of "congregations to the Eastward." These congregations were presumably in his home state of Connecticut, because Congress then met in New York. Pledges of money to churches in Connecticut were not voluntary contracts; every citizen was required to pay a church tax to the church of his choice. This scheme of taxation could be viewed as a form of multiple or nonpreferential establishment, although dissenters viewed it as preferential and oppressive. However the Connecticut scheme is characterized, Huntington seems to have said that these taxes should be enforceable in federal court. Count one vote for financial aid to religion. But like Sylvester, Huntington probably opposed the clause, and there is no evidence that the majority shared his views.

The reporter's notes of Huntington's speech continue:

> By the charter of Rhode Island, no religion could be established by law; he could give a history of the effects of such a regulation; indeed the people were now enjoying the blessed fruits of it. He hoped, therefore, the amendment would be made in such a way as to secure the rights of conscience, and a free exercise of the rights of religion, but not to patronize those who professed no religion at all.

This passage may contain more than meets the eye. Perhaps Huntington was serious about the "blessed fruits" of disestablishment so long as the concept was not taken too far, but more likely his reference to Rhode Island was sarcastic and his concluding remark was a request to omit the establishment clause altogether. Much of the country viewed Rhode Island as radical, libertine, and unsavory, and supporters of establishment thought that disestablishment was an important part of that state's problems.

The remark about patronizing those who professed no religion at all appears to be a second allusion to disputes in Connecticut about collection of the church tax from nonbelievers. Connecticut was willing to let each citizen pay the church of his choice, but it was not willing to exempt nonbelievers altogether. Huntington had just urged that the federal courts be available for suits to collect this tax; perhaps he thought that a refusal to collect the tax from those who did not pay voluntarily would "patronize those who professed no religion at all." References to the rights of conscience and to free exercise already had appeared in various drafts of the religion clauses. Huntington appears to have urged Congress to adopt the rights of conscience and free exercise clauses and to reject the establishment clause.

Nussbaum and Smith apparently conclude that Huntington authoritatively explained the establishment clause. But Huntington was probably an opponent of disestablishment, or at best a grudging supporter. His view that the clause should be construed narrowly is based on his preference for establishment. The clause was not changed to eliminate Huntington's fears. Further, as Professor Kurland mentions, the Constitution already patronized nonbelievers in an important way: the test oath clause made them eligible for federal office. Huntington probably thought the ban on test oaths was a bad idea too, but that is no reason to construe the test oath clause to require belief in God.

It is no more plausible to impute Huntington's views of the establishment clause to the majority.

The heart of the argument is Madison's puzzling comments about a national religion and compelled worship. Madison's tactic was not to argue with Sylvester and Huntington, but to reassure them and their sympathizers by portraying the establishment clause in the narrowest possible light.

Madison spoke twice. The first time, he obviously was responding to Sylvester's fear that the amendment might abolish religion altogether: "Mr. MADISON said, he apprehended the meaning of the words to be, that Congress should not establish a religion, and enforce the legal observation of it by law, nor compel men to worship God in any manner contrary to their conscience." Huntington responded that he understood the amendment to mean what Madison had said, but he feared "that the words might be taken in such latitude as to be extremely hurtful to the cause of religion." Huntington then made his speech about collecting Connecticut church taxes and the blessed fruits of disestablishment in Rhode Island.

Madison then spoke a second time. He proposed that the House insert the word "national" before the word "religion," so that the establishment clause would read: "No national religion shall be established by law." Madison explained that

> he believed that the people feared one sect might obtain a preeminence, or two combine together, and establish a religion to which they would compel others to conform. He thought that if the word "national" was introduced, it would point the amendment directly to the object it was intended to prevent.

Madison's two statements are obviously inconsistent with modern interpretations of the establishment clause, but they are equally inconsistent with the view that only preferential aid is forbidden. Almost everyone agrees that the establishment clause means more than Madison mentioned on August 15. If Congress appropriated one million dollars for the support of the United Methodist Church, it would not be enforcing the observation of Methodism by law. Nevertheless, the appropriation would be preferential aid, unconstitutional even under the "no preference" view of the clause. If Madison's second statement described the entire meaning of the clause, the later Senate draft forbidding uniform "articles of faith or a mode of worship" would have captured the meaning perfectly. But that draft also was rejected.

It is hard to know what Madison was thinking. The two statements are inconsistent with all his previous and subsequent statements concerning establishment. Nevertheless, he appears to have said the same thing clearly and twice, which reduces the risk that the reporter's notes are materially inaccurate. The statements also are consistent with Madison's June 8 draft of the clause, which provided only that no "national religion be established."

Perhaps Madison was willing to settle for such a narrow amendment if that were all he could get, but subsequent developments in the Senate and the Conference Committee opened the way to more. Perhaps he believed that pressure for a single establishment with compelled observance was the issue most likely to arise, so that he believed he was accurately describing the principal consequence of the amendment. Perhaps Professor McConnell is right that coercion rather than preference is the essence of the establishment clause, and Madison was describing the classic example of coercion. Perhaps he was dissembling. We will never know. But Madison plainly did not describe a ban on preferential aid.

Madison's proposal to insert "national" before "religion" would have strengthened the implication that only a single national establishment was forbidden. But he promptly withdrew that motion in the face of Gerry's attack on the word "national." He could have substituted a less offensive adjective; "particular," "specific," or "single" would have done nicely. Either he did not think of these words or he chose not to offer them. His failure to offer such alternatives is consistent with Professor Levy's suggestion that the word "national" was intended to emphasize that the clause bound only Congress. But even if Levy's suggestion explains Madison's attempt to insert "national" into the text of the clause, it does not account for Madison's narrow explanations of the meaning of the clause.

After Madison withdrew his amendment, someone called the question on Livermore's substitute, and the House adopted it. The only reported debate thus ended a lot further from the "no preference" position than it began. Gerry's substitute was ignored, Madison's amendment was withdrawn, and Livermore's sweeping substitute was adopted. No one explicitly argued that preferential establishments were bad while nonpreferential establishments were acceptable. Two of the remarks most relied on by nonpreferentialists came from apparent opponents of the clause, and neither they nor Madison stated the "no preference" position. Compared to the clear textual choices made in the Senate and in the Conference Committee, nothing in this brief debate casts any useful light on the problem.

VI. THE FRAMERS' OTHER INTENTION: NONFINANCIAL AID TO RELIGION

The state debates concerning establishment centered on financial aid. Nonfinancial government support for Protestantism was rampant and largely noncontroversial. Nonpreferentialists also invoke these practices in support of their theory. Supporters of government aid to religion also make the more general claim that the establishment clause does not forbid anything analogous to a practice that was common in 1791. The crèche case and especially the legislative prayer case are based on that claim.

The argument cannot be merely that anything the Framers did is constitutional. The unstated premise of that argument is that the Framers fully thought through everything they did and had every constitutional principle constantly in mind, so that all their acts fit together in a great mosaic that is absolutely consistent, even if modern observers cannot understand the organizing principle. That is not a plausible premise. Of course the state and federal establishment clauses did not abruptly end all customs in tension with their implications. No innovation ever does. Momentum is a powerful force in human affairs, and the Framers were busy building a nation and creating a government. Their failure to spend time examining every possible establishment clause issue is hardly surprising. The Framers did not think that everything they did was constitutional. Professor Kurland quotes Madison's 1787 observation that many of the state bills of rights were widely violated. Indeed, one of the arguments against the federal Bill of Rights was that the state bills of rights had been ineffectual.

Those who would rely on early government aid to religion must identify some principled distinction between the practices the Framers accepted and those they rejected. We can then consider whether we are bound by, or are willing to adopt for ourselves, the implicit principle on which they appear to have acted. The search for patterns requires a brief review of the kinds of aid to religion that the Framers supported or at least tolerated.

The Constitutional Convention did not appoint a chaplain, but the First Congress appointed chaplains, and even Madison apparently acquiesced. Presidents Washington, Adams, and Madison issued Thanksgiving proclamations, although Madison did so only in time of war and at the request of Congress, and his proclamations merely invited citizens so disposed to unite their prayers on a single day. President Jefferson refused to issue Thanksgiving proclamations, believing them to be an establishment. In retirement, Madison concluded that both the congressional chaplains and the Thanksgiving proclamations had violated the establishment clause. He said he had never approved of the decision to appoint a chaplain.

Congress also subsidized missionary work among the Indians, and even Jefferson signed a treaty agreeing to build a church and supply a Catholic priest in exchange for tribal lands of the Kaskaskias. Congress continued to support sectarian education on Indian reservations until 1898. Commentators have alleged that the First Congress reenacted the Northwest Ordinance, with its recital that "religion, morality, and knowledge" are necessary to good government. The claim is false, but I do not doubt that a large majority of the First Congress would have subscribed to the sentiment.

These examples undoubtedly evidence support for religion, but they are hard to explain as nonpreferential. Supplying a Catholic priest to a tribe of Catholic Indians may be a cheap way to buy land, but it is not a form of nonpreferential aid. A missionary or a church-run school inevitably represented a particular denomination, whatever that denomination might be. So did the congressional chaplain. Congress did not hire a chaplain from every faith, or even one from every faith represented by a Congressman. I assume that most of the Framers saw no constitutional problem with a chaplain, but I doubt that they rationalized the practice on the ground that it was nonpreferential.

Professor McConnell's theory that the establishment clause forbids only coercive aid to religion comes much closer to explaining the early activities of the federal government. But sectarian education of Indians required tax money, which McConnell agrees is coercive. So noncoercion cannot explain everything the government did either.

The substantial political resistance to establishment focused on tax support for churches. The Framers' generation must have seen tax support for missionaries to the Indians as different from tax support for churches. Probably they found missionaries a cheap and effective way to educate the Indians: they were hiring churches to provide government services. Even so, religious teaching was also an accepted part of the mission, and nobody talked of any accounting to separate the costs of education in secular and religious subjects.

Once again, the practice of the states helps to flesh out the pattern. The federal government had limited legislative powers; the states' general police power gave them more opportunities to act with respect to religion. Most state constitutions guaranteed religious liberty. The federal religious liberty clauses did not necessarily mean the same thing as the state religious liberty clauses, but again state practices may help show how the Framers' generation understood religious liberty.

State aid to religion was both preferential and coercive. The states continued practices that no one would defend today. All but two states had religious qualifications for holding public office, and at least five states denied full civil rights to Catholics. Blasphemy was commonly a crime; in Vermont blasphemy against the Trinity was a capital offense, although it presumably was not enforced as such. Observance of the Christian Sabbath was widely enforced, with little in the way of fictitious explanations about a neutrally selected day for families to be together. These laws aroused little controversy, and almost no one thought them inconsistent with constitutional guarantees of religious liberty. Yet tax support for churches was deeply controversial and widely thought inconsistent with religious liberty.

Several reasons probably contributed to the differing reactions to financial and nonfinancial aid. First, there is always opposition to taxes, whatever their purpose. In Virginia, the general assessment was debated at a time of high taxes and low tobacco prices in a tobacco economy. Second, the tax for churches was associated with earlier unitary establishments: Anglicans in the South, and Congregationalists in the North. Broadening the tax to include other denominations did not remove the taint or end the hostility. The Anglican clergy were far more dependent on tax support than denominations already accustomed to voluntary support. Third, and perhaps most important, the tax for churches split the Protestant denominations. Baptists and Quakers objected even to a nonpreferential system in which every taxpayer designated the church to receive his tax. When the Virginia Presbyterians reached the same conclusion in 1786, the assessment bill was doomed.

For all these reasons, there were widespread objections to tax support for churches. What is largely the same thing, there were Protestant objections. This opposition forced the Framers' generation to think about the tax issue. Once they thought about it, they concluded that any form of tax support for churches violated religious liberty. By the time of the first amendment, church taxes were repealed or moribund outside New England, and they were not working well in the four New England states that still tried to collect them.

The other government supports of Protestantism never aroused enough controversy to trigger similar examination. The nation was overwhelmingly Protestant and hostile to other faiths. Bare tolerance of other faiths was a major accomplishment, not yet safe from reaction; accepting other faiths as equals was far in the future. John Jay led an unsuccessful movement to banish Catholics from New York, and John Adams boasted that Catholics and Jacobites were as rare as comets and earthquakes in his hometown of Braintree. Professor Kurland quotes other examples of Protestant bigotry among political leaders. Non-Protestants could practice their religion, but they often could not vote, hold public office, or publicly criticize Protestantism. Non-Protestants certainly could not expect the government to refrain from preaching Protestantism. These conditions would not change easily. Half a century later, mob violence, church burnings, and deaths would result when Catholics objected to studying the "Protestant Bible" in public schools. The anti-Catholic, anti-immigrant Know Nothing Party would sweep elections in eight states.

In 1791, almost no one thought that government support of Protestantism was inconsistent with religious liberty, because almost no one could imagine a more broadly pluralist state. Protestantism ran so deep among such overwhelming numbers of people that almost no one could see that his principles on church taxes might have implications for other kinds of government support for religion. The exclusion of non-Protestants from pronouncements of religious liberty was not nearly so thorough or so cruel as the exclusion of slaves from pronouncements that all men were created equal, but both blind spots were species of the same genus.

In short, the appeal to the Framers' practice of nonfinancial aid to religion is an appeal to unreflective bigotry. It does not show what the Framers meant by disestablishment; it shows what they did without thinking about establishment at all. I believe that the relevant intention of the Framers is the one they thought about. But if that view is rejected — if both the considered and the unconsidered intentions of the Framers are binding — then the result would not be to approve nonpreferential aid. The Framers' implicit distinction was between financial aid and other aid. If both their intentions are followed, all financial aid will be forbidden, whether or not preferential. But unlimited nonfinancial aid will be permitted even if it is preferential and coercive. Few nonpreferentialists would defend that.

I am not even suggesting that we modify the principle the Framers considered. I would apply uniformly the very principle the Framers considered and accepted: that aid to religion is not saved by making it nonpreferential.

VIII. CONCLUSION

The principle that best makes sense of the establishment clause is the principle of the most nearly perfect neutrality toward religion and among religions. I do not mean neutrality in the formal sense of a ban on religious classifications,[241] but in the substantive sense of government conduct that insofar as possible neither encourages nor discourages religious belief or practice.[242] This is the principle that maximizes religious liberty in a pluralistic society, and this is the principle that the Framers identified in the context of tax support for churches. They did not substitute nonpreferential taxes for preferential taxes; they rejected all taxes. They did not substitute small taxes for large taxes; three pence was as bad as any larger sum. The principle was what mattered. With respect to money, religion was to be wholly voluntary. Churches either would support themselves or they would not, but the government would neither help nor interfere.

That is what disestablishment meant to the Framers in the context in which they thought about it. They applied the principle only in that context — only to tax support. Their society was so homogeneous that they had no occasion to think about other kinds of support. Now that we have thought about it, we are not unfaithful to the Framers' intent when we apply their principle to analogous problems. Congress cannot impose civil disabilities on non-Protestants or ban blasphemy against the Trinity just because the Framers did it. It is no more able to endorse the predominant religion just because the Framers did it. Our task is not to perpetuate the Framers' blind spots, but to implement their vision.

NOTE ON JAMES MADISON'S *DETACHED MEMORANDA*

Professor Laycock refers to the fact that in retirement James Madison expressed the view that the appointment of congressional chaplains and the issuance of presidential proclamations of thanksgiving should be considered unconstitutional actions. This is a reference to the views Madison expressed in a document entitled the *Detached Memoranda*, which was found in the papers

---

[241] This is the principle proposed in Kurland, *Of Church and State and the Supreme Court,* 29 U. CHI. L. REV. 1 (1961).

[242] *See* Laycock, *Equal Access and Moments of Silence: The Equal Status of Religious Speech by Private Speakers,* 81 NW. U. L. REV. 1, 3 (1986). This distinction is best illustrated by facially neutral laws that violate religious conscience. In Professor Kurland's view, a law prohibiting the consumption of alcohol could not contain an exception for sacramental wine. Such an exception would prefer religion. In my view, an exception would be required. A law banning wine at the Eucharist and the Seder would prohibit the free exercise of religion, however neutral its wording and however general its application. In this example, no compelling interest would justify the prohibition.

of Madison biographer William Cabell Rives in 1946. Historians believe the document was written sometime between 1817 and 1832. It is reprinted in full in *Madison's Detached Memoranda*, 3 WM. & MARY Q. 534 (Elizabeth Fleet ed., 1946). Consider Madison's perspective in the *Detached Memoranda* on the problems associated with presidential religious proclamations (Madison's abbreviations — such as "Xn" for "Christian" — are as they appear in the original document):

> The objections to them are 1. that Govts ought not to interpose in relation to those subject to their authority but in cases where they can do it with effect. An advisory Govt is a contradiction in terms. 2. The members of a Govt as such can in no sense, be regarded as possessing an advisory trust from their Constituents in their religious capacities. They cannot form an ecclesiastical Assembly, Convocation, Council, or Synod, and as such issue decrees or injunctions addressed to the faith or the Consciences of the people. In their individual capacities, as distinct from their official station, they might unite in recommendations of any sort whatever, in the same manner as any other individuals might do. But then their recommendations ought to express the true character from which they emanate. 3. They seem to imply and certainly nourish the erronious idea of a national religion. The idea just as it related to the Jewish nation under a theocracy, having been improperly adopted by so many nations which have embraced Xnity, is too apt to lurk in the bosoms even of Americans, who in general are aware of the distinction between religious & political societies. The idea also of a union of all to form one nation under one Govt in acts of devotion to the God of all is an imposing idea. But reason and the principles of the Xn religion require that all the individuals composing a nation even of the same precise creed & wished to unite in a universal act of religion at the same time, the union ought to be effected thro' the intervention of their religious not of their political representatives. In a nation composed of various sects, some alienated widely from others, and where no agreement could take place thro' the former, the interposition of the latter is doubly wrong: 4. The tendency of the practice, to narrow the recommendation to the standard of the predominant sect. The Ist proclamation of Genl Washington dated Jany 1. 1795 recommending a day of thanksgiving, embraced all who believed in a supreme ruler of the Universe. That of Mr. Adams called for a Xn worship. Many private letters reproached the Proclamations issued by J. M. for using general terms, used in that of Presit W — n; and some of them for not inserting particulars according with the faith of certain Xn sects. The practice if not strictly guarded naturally terminates in a conformity to the creed of the majority and a single sect, if amounting to a majority. 5. The last & not the least objection is the liability of the practice to a subserviency to political views; to the scandal of religion, as well as the increase of party animosities. Candid or incautious politicians will not always dis-

own such views. In truth it is difficult to frame such a religious Proclamation generally suggested by a political State of things, without referring to them in terms having some bearing on party questions. The Proclamation of Pres: W. which was issued just after the suppression of the Insurrection in Penna and at a time when the public mind was divided on several topics, was so construed by many. Of this the Secretary of State himself, E. Randolph seems to have had an anticipation.

ZELMAN v. SIMMONS-HARRIS
536 U.S. 639 (2002)

[In this case a five-Justice majority upheld a Cleveland, Ohio school voucher program under which students were given government tuition aid, which could be used to attend public or private schools, including religious schools. The majority opinion is excerpted in Chapter 9. Justice Thomas concurred with the majority's decision, but offered his own unique perspective on whether the Court's Establishment Clause jurisprudence should apply to state and local government programs to the same extent as to federal programs.]

JUSTICE THOMAS, concurring:

To determine whether a federal program survives scrutiny under the Establishment Clause, we have considered whether it has a secular purpose and whether it has the primary effect of advancing or inhibiting religion. *See Mitchell v. Helms* [*infra* Chapter 9]. I agree with the Court that Ohio's program easily passes muster under our stringent test, but, as a matter of first principles, I question whether this test should be applied to the States.

The Establishment Clause of the First Amendment states that "Congress shall make no law respecting an establishment of religion." On its face, this provision places no limit on the States with regard to religion. The Establishment Clause originally protected States, and by extension their citizens, from the imposition of an established religion by the Federal Government. Whether and how this Clause should constrain state action under the Fourteenth Amendment is a more difficult question.

The Fourteenth Amendment fundamentally restructured the relationship between individuals and the States and ensured that States would not deprive citizens of liberty without due process of law. It guarantees citizenship to all individuals born or naturalized in the United States and provides that "[n]o State shall make or enforce any law which shall abridge the privileges or immunities of citizens of the United States; nor shall any State deprive any person of life, liberty, or property, without due process of law; nor deny to any person within its jurisdiction the equal protection of the laws." As Justice Harlan noted, the Fourteenth Amendment "added greatly to the dignity and glory of American citizenship, and to the security of personal liberty." *Plessy v. Ferguson,* 163 U.S. 537, 555 (1896) (dissenting opinion). When rights are incorporated against the States through the Fourteenth Amendment they should advance, not constrain, individual liberty.

Consequently, in the context of the Establishment Clause, it may well be that state action should be evaluated on different terms than similar action by the Federal Government. "States, while bound to observe strict neutrality, should be freer to experiment with involvement [in religion] on a neutral basis than the Federal Government." *Walz* v. *Tax Comm'n of City of New York*, 397 U.S. 664, 699 (1970) (Harlan, J., concurring). Thus, while the Federal Government may "make no law respecting an establishment of religion," the States may pass laws that include or touch on religious matters so long as these laws do not impede free exercise rights or any other individual religious liberty interest. By considering the particular religious liberty right alleged to be invaded by a State, federal courts can strike a proper balance between the demands of the Fourteenth Amendment on the one hand and the federalism prerogatives of States on the other.

ELK GROVE UNITED SCHOOL DISTRICT v. NEWDOW
542 U.S. 1 (2004)

[In this case, which is discussed in Chapter 7, *infra*, a 5-3 majority of the Court rejected Michael Newdow's standing to challenge statutes exposing his daughter to daily recitations of the Pledge of Allegiance in her public school. Three Justices, including Justice Thomas, would have reached the merits and ruled that the Pledge is constitutional. In his concurring opinion, Justice Thomas elaborated on his theory regarding the incorporation of the Establishment Clause into the Fourteenth Amendment.]

JUSTICE THOMAS, concurring in the judgment.

II.

I accept that the Free Exercise Clause, which clearly protects an individual right, applies against the States through the Fourteenth Amendment. *See Zelman* (*Thomas*, J., concurring). But the Establishment Clause is another matter. The text and history of the Establishment Clause strongly suggest that it is a federalism provision intended to prevent Congress from interfering with state establishments. Thus, unlike the Free Exercise Clause, which does protect an individual right, it makes little sense to incorporate the Establishment Clause. In any case, I do not believe that the Pledge policy infringes any religious liberty right that would arise from incorporation of the Clause. Because the Pledge policy also does not infringe any free-exercise rights, I conclude that it is constitutional.

A.

The Establishment Clause provides that "Congress shall make no law respecting an establishment of religion." Amdt. 1. As a textual matter, this Clause probably prohibits Congress from establishing a national religion. *But see* P. HAMBURGER, SEPARATION OF CHURCH AND STATE 106, n. 40 (2002) (citing sources). Perhaps more importantly, the Clause made clear that Congress could not interfere with state establishments, notwithstanding any argument that could be made based on Congress' power under the Necessary and Proper Clause. *See* A. AMAR, THE BILL OF RIGHTS 36-39 (1998).

Nothing in the text of the Clause suggests that it reaches any further. The Establishment Clause does not purport to protect individual rights. By contrast, the Free Exercise Clause plainly protects individuals against congressional interference with the right to exercise their religion, and the remaining Clauses within the First Amendment expressly disable Congress from "abridging [particular] *freedom[s]*." (Emphasis added.) This textual analysis is consistent with the prevailing view that the Constitution left religion to the States. See, *e.g.,* 2 J. STORY, COMMENTARIES ON THE CONSTITUTION OF THE UNITED STATES § 1873 (5th ed. 1891); *see also* AMAR, THE BILL OF RIGHTS, at 32-42; *id.,* at 246-257. History also supports this understanding: At the founding, at least six States had established religions, *see* McConnell, *The Origins and Historical Understanding of Free Exercise of Religion*, 103 HARV. L. REV. 1409, 1437 (1990). Nor has this federalism point escaped the notice of Members of this Court. *See, e.g., Zelman, supra,* at 677-680 (THOMAS, J., concurring); *Lee, supra,* at 641 (SCALIA, J., dissenting).

Quite simply, the Establishment Clause is best understood as a federalism provision — it protects state establishments from federal interference but does not protect any individual right. These two features independently make incorporation of the Clause difficult to understand. The best argument in favor of incorporation would be that, by disabling Congress from establishing a national religion, the Clause protected an individual right, enforceable against the Federal Government, to be free from coercive federal establishments. Incorporation of this individual right, the argument goes, makes sense. I have alluded to this possibility before. *See Zelman, supra,* at 679 (THOMAS, J., concurring) ("States may pass laws that include or touch on religious matters so long as these laws do not impede free exercise rights *or any other individual liberty interest*" (emphasis added)).

But even assuming that the Establishment Clause precludes the Federal Government from establishing a national religion, it does not follow that the Clause created or protects any individual right. For the reasons discussed above, it is more likely that States and only States were the direct beneficiaries. *See also Lee, supra,* at 641 (SCALIA, J., dissenting). Moreover, incorporation of this putative individual right leads to a peculiar outcome: It would prohibit precisely what the Establishment Clause was intended to protect — *state* establishments of religion. *See Schempp,* 374 U.S. at 310 (Stewart, J., dissenting) (noting that "the Fourteenth Amendment has somehow absorbed the Establishment Clause, although it is not without irony that a constitutional provision evidently designed to leave the States free to go their own way should now have become a restriction upon their autonomy"). Nevertheless, the potential right against federal establishments is the only candidate for incorporation.

I would welcome the opportunity to consider more fully the difficult questions whether and how the Establishment Clause applies against the States. One observation suffices for now: As strange as it sounds, an incorporated Establishment Clause prohibits exactly what the Establishment Clause protected — state practices that pertain to "an establishment of religion." At the very least, the burden of persuasion rests with anyone who claims that the term took on a different meaning upon incorporation. We must therefore determine whether the Pledge policy pertains to an "establishment of religion."

Note on Justice Thomas's Federalism Interpretation of the Establishment Clause

Some of the language Justice Thomas uses in making his argument is quite broad. In his *Zelman* concurrence, there is language suggesting that Thomas may be attacking the incorporation doctrine in general, or that he may be making a somewhat narrower claim against the Court's adoption of the theory that the Bill of Rights is incorporated into the Fourteenth Amendment (in Justice Harlan's phrase) "jot-for-jot and case-by-case." *Duncan v. Louisiana*, 391 U.S. 146, 181 (1968) (Harlan, J., dissenting).

In his *Newdow* concurrence, on the other hand, he focuses more precisely on the incorporation of the Establishment Clause alone. In this opinion, Thomas proposes to distinguish the Establishment Clause from every other provision of the First Amendment (including the Free Exercise Clause). This argument is also made in the recent book *Separation of Church and State* by Philip Hamburger, which Thomas cites in his opinion. The essential claim is that, unlike the other provisions of the First Amendment (and the other parts of the Bill of Rights that have been incorporated into the Fourteenth Amendment), which were intended to protect individual liberty, the Establishment Clause is a structural limitation that was originally intended to protect the states from federal interference. For other versions of this argument, *see* Daniel O. Conkle, *Toward a General Theory of the Establishment Clause*, 82 Nw. U. L. Rev. 1113 (1988); Akhil Reed Amar, *Some Notes on the Establishment Clause*, 2 Roger Williams U. L. Rev. 1 (1996); Note, *Rethinking the Incorporation of the Establishment Clause: A Federalist View*, 105 Harv. L. Rev. 1700 (1992). Note that under his interpretation of the Establishment Clause, Justice Thomas specifically acknowledges the consequence that each state would be permitted to adopt a coercive religious establishment. This would include the legal establishment of a particular sect as the state's official church.

This is not an uncontroversial theory, to say the least. For a thorough rejoinder to this argument, with specific references to the changes in attitude toward the Establishment Clause during the period between the adoption of the Bill of Rights and the Fourteenth Amendment, *see* Kurt T. Lash, *The Second Adoption of the Establishment Clause: The Rise of the Nonestablishment Principle*, 27 ARIZ. ST. L.J. 1085 (1995). For criticism of some of Philip Hamburger's historical analysis, and in particular Hamburger's attempt to link radical anti-Catholic and anti-religious movements to the modern concepts of separation of church and state and disestablishment, *see* Kent Greenawalt, *History as Ideology: Philip Hamburger's Separation of Church and State*, 93 CAL. L. REV. 367 (2005) (reviewing Philip Hamburger, Separation of Church and State (2002)); Douglas Laycock, *The Many Meanings of Separation*, 70 U. CHI. L. REV. 1667 (2003) (same).

Some strange consequences logically flow from the argument that the Establishment Clause is structural rather than liberty-enhancing, and therefore does not apply to the states. Although the structural argument seems to be predicated on the assumption that the states are more capable than the federal government of defending religious liberty, implementation of this theory may produce a contrary result: A structural interpretation of the Establishment Clause would prevent the federal judiciary from interfering with state establishments of religion in general, or individual churches in particular. At the very least this may create an atmosphere of legally endorsed ostracism of those who do not belong to the established church, and may also involve coercion of non-adherents in contexts such as school prayer and other public endorsements of the state's established faith. If one assumes (in line with a majority of the current members of the Supreme Court) that ostracism and psychological coercion interfere with religious liberty, then the quantum of religious liberty in the nation would arguably go *down* if the courts adopted this view of the Establishment Clause. The structural argument also seems to lead to the conclusion that the federal government could not enact legislation (such as the Religious Freedom Restoration Act, 42 U.S.C. § 2000bb) intended to provide federal statutory protection of religious liberty in the states. For an example of this use of the structural argument, *see* Jeb Rubenfeld, *Antidisestablishmentarianism: Why RFRA Really Was Unconstitutional*, 95 MICH. L. REV. 2347 (1997), discussed in Chapter 14, *infra*.

Justice Thomas attempts to avoid this latter conclusion by arguing that "[t]he [Establishment] Clause prohibits Congress from enacting legislation 'respecting an *establishment* of religion' . . . ; it does not prohibit Congress from enacting legislation 'respecting religion' or 'taking cognizance of religion.'" *Cutter v. Wilkinson, infra* Chapter 14 (Thomas, J., concurring). In *Cutter*, the Supreme Court rejected an Establishment Clause challenge to the federal Religious Land Use and Institutionalized Persons Act. *See infra* Chapter 14. This statute prohibits state and local governments from substantially burdening religious exercise in the land use and institutionalized person contexts unless the burden is justified by a compelling interest. According to Justice Thomas:

> Even when enacting laws that bind the States pursuant to valid exercises of its enumerated powers, Congress need not observe strict separation between church and state, or steer clear of the subject of religion.

It need only refrain from making laws "respecting an establishment of religion"; it must not interfere with a state establishment of religion. For example, Congress presumably could not require a State to establish a religion any more than it could preclude a State from establishing a religion.

On its face — the relevant inquiry, as this is a facial challenge — RLUIPA is not a law "respecting an establishment of religion." . . . This provision does not prohibit or interfere with state establishments, since no State has established (or constitutionally could establish, given an incorporated Clause) a religion. Nor does the provision require a State to establish a religion: It does not force a State to coerce religious observance or payment of taxes supporting clergy, or require a State to prefer one religious sect over another. It is a law respecting religion, but not one respecting an establishment of religion.

In addition, RLUIPA's text applies to all laws passed by state and local governments, including "rule[s] of general applicability," *ibid.*, whether or not they concern an establishment of religion. State and local governments obviously have many laws that have nothing to do with religion, let alone establishments thereof. Numerous applications of RLUIPA therefore do not contravene the Establishment Clause, and a facial challenge based on the Clause must fail.

Cutter, 125 S. Ct. at 2128 (Thomas, J., concurring). Is it logical to argue that Congress may dictate how states apply their laws to religious individuals, but may not interfere with an outright state establishment of religion?

On the most basic level, putting aside the debate over the pre-incorporation views of the Establishment Clause, the structural reading of the Establishment Clause probably conflicts sharply with most citizens' popular understandings of the modern meaning of the Clause. It would probably come as something of a surprise to most modern citizens to be told that their states suddenly have the authority to establish a church and enforce that church's dictates against them through the force of state law. Even if these arguments about the original perspective on the Establishment Clause are correct, has history now moved beyond the point at which the Establishment Clause could be "disincorporated"?

Chapter 2

THE THEORY OF THE RELIGION CLAUSES: "WE ARE A RELIGIOUS NATION WHOSE INSTITUTIONS PRESUPPOSE A SUPREME BEING . . ."

One of the most vexing problems in Religion Clause jurisprudence is also the most important: What is the basic theory of the constitutional provisions on religion? This broad issue can be broken down into several smaller questions. Were the First Amendment religion provisions intended to protect religion from the state, or vice versa? Are these provisions designed to protect and facilitate each citizen's ability to practice his or her chosen religion, or are the provisions designed to protect citizens *from* religious beliefs and practices that they do not share? Is religion necessary for democratic government, or is it fundamentally incompatible with modern democracy? Must the state ignore religion, or must it act affirmatively to accommodate the religious beliefs and practices of citizens? The Supreme Court has seldom sought to provide a broad theory for its pronouncements on the subject of religion, but academic commentators have filled the breach with a wide range of responses to these problems. The following materials provide a representative sample of the differing approaches.

A. THE ARGUMENT FOR AN ACCOMMODATIONIST REPUBLIC

Michael W. McConnell
Accommodation of Religion
1985 SUP. CT. REV. 1*

It is sometimes forgotten that religious liberty is the central value and animating purpose of the Religion Clauses of the First Amendment. The separation of church and state — a phrase that does not appear in the First Amendment or in the debates surrounding its adoption — is a more problematical, a more contingent, ideal than is religious liberty. The main components of religious liberty are the autonomy of religious institutions, individual choice in matters of religion, and the freedom to put a chosen faith (if any) into practice. Both free exercise and nonestablishment directly protect religious liberty: the government may not interfere with a person's chosen religious belief and

---

practice by prohibiting it or by exerting power or influence in favor of any faith. The separation of church and state is a different matter; sometimes separation enhances religious liberty and sometimes separation diminishes it.

The much-discussed "tension" between the two Religion Clauses largely arises from the Court's substitution of a misleading formula (the three-part *Lemon* test, under which a law or government practice is deemed an establishment of religion if it lacks a "secular" purpose, if it has the "primary effect" of either "advancing" or "inhibiting" religion, or if it leads to an "excessive entanglement" between church and state) and subsidiary, instrumental, values (especially the separation of church and state) in place of the central value of religious liberty.

Accommodation is an increasingly important concept in the Court's thinking about the problem of religion, but one that does not fit comfortably within the current doctrines of free exercise and nonestablishment. It is here that the interests of religious liberty and the rigors of the *Lemon* test are most strikingly at cross-purposes. My thesis is that between the accommodations compelled by the Free Exercise Clause and the benefits to religion prohibited by the Establishment Clause there exists a class of permissible governmental actions toward religion, which have as their purpose and effect the facilitation of religious liberty. Neither strict neutrality nor separationism can account for the idea of accommodation or define its limits.

[I]t is not meaningful to ask whether a government accommodation to religion has a "secular" purpose or whether it "encourages" or "advances" religion; all protections of religious liberty, including the Free Exercise Clause itself, "advance" religion in a sense and are intended to do so. What is needed is an understanding of the role of religion under the Constitution, within a framework that acknowledges the legitimacy of encouraging and facilitating religious liberty.

Under this view, the emphasis is placed on freedom of choice and diversity among religious opinion. The nation is understood not as secular but as pluralistic. Religion is under no special disability in public life; indeed, it is at least as protected and encouraged as any other form of belief and association — in some ways more so. The idea of accommodation of religion, which is foreign to interpretations of the Religion Clauses based on strict neutrality or separation, follows naturally from the pluralist understanding. I believe that this view is more consistent than its competitors with the liberal political theory which underlies the Constitution.

Religion poses a special problem for a liberal republic. The experience of religious strife and persecution associated with the various establishments of religion in Europe has demonstrated the dangers of an overbearing church. If a single church obtained political supremacy, the result would be tyranny. The dominant church might be expected to use the power of the state to enforce conformity, even to the point of persecution, among adherents to other forms of belief. And if even the prospect of political supremacy existed, the various sects would contend with one another for preferment. "It was impossible," Justice Story stated in his famous commentaries on the Constitution, "that there should not arise perpetual strife and perpetual jealousy on the subject of ecclesiastical ascendancy, if the national government were left free to create a religious establishment."

But, while unable to establish a national religion, the liberal state also cannot reject in principle the possibility that a religion may be true; and if true, religious claims are of a higher order than anything in statecraft. The individual and the state may disagree on a point of secular ethics, but the claims of right arising from such a disagreement, even if assumed to be valid, do not give a priority to one or the other. The individual must do what he thinks right; the state (that is, the citizens collectively) must do what it thinks right. Though natural law may be viewed as higher authority than positive law, controversies arising from natural law claims will take the form of disputes over what the natural law is. Neither the individual's nor the government's interpretive power is presumptively superior. By contrast, religious claims — if true — are prior to and of greater dignity than the claims of the state. If there is a God, His authority necessarily transcends the authority of nations; that, in part, is what we mean by "God." For the state to maintain that its authority is in all matters supreme would be to deny the possibility that a transcendent authority could exist. Religious claims thus differ from secular moral claims both because the state is constitutionally disabled from disputing the truth of the religious claim and because it cannot categorically deny the authority on which such a claim rests.

These considerations lead to both pragmatic and principled reasons for government deference to religious scruple. The state might defer on issues of less than compelling importance in order to preserve harmony. Since some persons, otherwise good and law-abiding citizens, will view religious claims as higher authority than civil law, it may be preferable to accommodate them than to provoke confrontation and disobedience. The state might also defer — again on issues of less than compelling importance — simply because liberalism recognizes, in principle, the possibility of higher claims than those of government.

Finally, the liberal state itself cannot ultimately be the source (though it can be the reflection) of the people's values. Liberalism is foremost a regime of fair procedures. It leaves to the citizens the right and responsibility for determining their own interests and values. Other than by education — which at the time of the Founding was predominantly private and certainly not secular — and by the example of its laws, the liberal state has no direct means of shaping the nation's moral thinking. In a liberal regime, the recesses of mind and conscience are exempt from governmental regulation; the state "is not the examiner of consciences."

Nonetheless, any form of civil society must depend, in part, on the citizens' commitment to order and morality. Coercion is an insufficient basis for civil order, except perhaps in the more ruthless despotisms. And any democratic form of society must inevitably reflect the values of its people. The need for internalized constraints and natural sentiments of justice is thus particularly acute for citizens of a republic, in which rule by force is replaced by self-rule. As the Founders understood it, the republic was peculiarly dependent on public virtue to maintain the mutual respect and harmony on which republican liberty rests. If the people are corrupt, how can a republican government — in which sovereignty resides in the people — be just?

If the state is not itself responsible for morality and self-restraint, how is the deficiency to be supplied? A partial answer may be found in indirect democracy, whereby the views of the people are expected to be "refine[d] and enlarge[d] — not merely reflected — through the process of representation and deliberation. By the constitutional scheme, the Founders hoped to remedy the defects in human nature. But no less important an element in republican theory was its reliance on the "genius" of the American people and their social institutions for the formation of national character. Madison himself defended the proposed Constitution on the ground that "the people will have virtue and intelligence to select men of virtue and wisdom" and acknowledged that if there is "no virtue among us . . . we are in a wretched situation. No theoretical checks, no form of government, can render us secure."

A source of public virtue outside of government was therefore necessary to the ultimate success of the republican experiment. Private associations — families, civic groups, colleges and universities, above all, churches — supply the need. They are the principal means by which the citizens in a liberal polity learn to transcend their individual interests and opinions and to develop civic responsibility for articulating and inculcating values of morality and justice in the liberal republic. Frequently denominated "mediating" structures or institutions, these associations "have played a critical role in the culture and traditions of the Nation by cultivating and transmitting shared ideals and beliefs." It is in the context of these communal associations that individual citizens commonly derive their system of values, even their sense of personal identity and integrity. If the liberal community ultimately has worth in the classical sense of promoting the good for its citizens — that is, the virtuous life — that end is met not by the government but by the free associations of the people.

In differing degrees and largely without explicit textual foundation, the Court has recognized the protected status of key mediating institutions. This is especially true of the family, but can also be seen in other areas — witness the Court's recognition of the constitutional autonomy of political and civic associations and social clubs and of academic freedom. Historically and to the present day, however, no such institutions are as important to the process of developing, transmitting, communicating, and enforcing concepts of morality and justice as are the churches. It is in this sense that Tocqueville described religion as "the first of [America's] political institutions." The role of the churches has been especially notable in connection with public morality and justice, as recent public controversies over matters such as racial discrimination, nuclear disarmament, abortion, and immigration illustrate. The special status of religion under the Constitution — both the individual's choice of faith and the institution's autonomy — derives in large part from these considerations.

The "political" effects of religion must be distinguished, in this sense, from individual morality. Unlike individual moral thought, religion is communal and institutional. It is poised between the individual and the state; it is social but not universal. Religious thought is not the product solely of individual reason but is rooted in history and tradition. It commands veneration and not mere assent. It carries with it a system of internalized discipline (most pronounced in traditional theistic religions with their belief in divine punishments and rewards) far stronger than mere opinion of right and wrong. It was accordingly widely thought by the Founders that republican self-government could not succeed unless religion continued to foster a moral sense in the people.

Stanley Fish
Liberalism Doesn't Exist
1987 DUKE L.J. 997[*]

I find Stephen Carter's argument compelling and incisive, and my only quarrel is with its conclusion when he urges a "softened liberal politics" that would "acknowledge and genuinely cherish the religious beliefs that for many Americans provide their fundamental worldview."[1] He confesses that he has "not yet worked out the details" of such a politics, and it is my contention that he never could for reasons he himself enumerates. The chief reason is that liberalism is informed by a faith (a word deliberately chosen) in reason as a faculty that operates independently of any particular world view. It is therefore committed at once to allowing competing world views equal access to its deliberative arena, and to disallowing the claims of any one of them to be supreme, unless of course it is demonstrated to be at all points compatible with the principles of reason. It follows then that liberalism can only "cherish" religion as something under its protection; to take it seriously would be to regard it as it demands to be regarded, as a claimant to the adjudicative authority already deeded in liberal thought to reason. This liberalism cannot do because, as Carter points out, if you take away the "primacy of reason" liberal thought loses its integrity, has nothing at its center, becomes just one more competing ideology rather than a procedure (and it is in procedure or process that liberalism puts its faith) that outflanks or transcends ideology. The one thing liberalism cannot do is put reason *inside* the battle where it would have to contend with other adjudicative principles and where it could not succeed merely by invoking itself because its own status would be what was at issue.

Indeed, liberalism depends on not inquiring into the status of reason, depends, that is, on the assumption that reason's status is obvious: it is that

---

[1] Carter, *Evolutionism, Creationism, and Treating Religion as a Hobby*, 1987 DUKE L.J. 977, 995.

which enables us to assess the claims of competing perspectives and beliefs. Once this assumption is in place, it produces an opposition between reason and belief, and that opposition is already a hierarchy in which every belief is required to pass muster at the bar of reason. But what if reason or rationality itself rests on belief? Then it would be the case that the opposition between reason and belief was a false one, and that every situation of contest should be recharacterized as a quarrel between two sets of belief with no possibility of recourse to a mode of deliberation that was not itself an extension of belief. This is in fact my view of the matter and I would defend it by asking a question that the ideology of reason must repress: where do reasons come from? The liberal answer must be that reasons come from nowhere, that they reflect the structure of the universe or at least of the human brain; but in fact reasons always come from somewhere, and the somewhere they come from is precisely the realm to which they are (rhetorically) opposed, the realm of particular (angled, partisan, biased) assumptions and agendas. What this means is that not all reasons (or reasonable trains of thought) are reasons for everyone. If (to take a humble literary example) I am given as a reason for preferring one interpretation of a poem to another the fact that it accords with the poet's theological views, I will only hear it as a reason (as a piece of weighty evidence) if it is *already* my conviction that a poet's aesthetic performance could be influenced by his theology; if, on the other hand, I see poetry and theology as independent and even antagonistic forms of life (as did many of those new critics for whom the autonomy of the aesthetic was an article of faith) this fact will not be a reason at all, but something obviously beside the (literary) point. Similarly, a lawyer may give as a reason for acquitting his client the fact that his action was not intentional, but both the fact and the reason it becomes will be perspicuous only because the boundaries between the intentional and the unintentional have been drawn in ways that could themselves be contested, even if at the moment they are not being contested but assumed. It is not that reasons can never be given or that they are, when given, incapable of settling disputes, but that the force they exert and their status *as* reasons depends on the already-in-place institution of distinctions that themselves rest on a basis no firmer (no less subject to dispute) than the particulars they presently order. In short, what is and is not a reason will always be a matter of faith, that is, of the assumptions that are bedrock within a discursive system which because it rests upon them cannot (without self-destructing) call them into question. (Nor can one avoid this conclusion by invoking supposedly abstract — i.e. contentless — logical operations like the "law of contradiction"; for just what is and is not a contradiction will vary depending on the distinctions already in place; a contradiction must be a contradiction between something and something else and the shape of those somethings will always be the product of an interpretive rather than a formal determination.)

It follows then that persons embedded within *different* discursive systems will not be able to hear the other's reasons *as* reasons, but only as errors or even delusions. This, I think, is Carter's point when he observes that "to the devout fundamentalist . . . evolutionary theory is not simply contrary to religious teachings; . . . it is *demonstrably* false." I take the stress on the word *demonstrably* to mean that Carter understands fully that the clash between liberals and fundamentalists is a clash between two faiths, or if you prefer (and it is my thesis that these two formulations are interchangeable) between two ways of thinking undergirded by incompatible first principles, empirical verification and biblical inerrancy. Given this incompatibility it would not be possible for either party to "cherish" or "take" seriously the commitments and conclusions of the other, for to do so would be to abandon the foundation on which it rests. The fundamentalist cannot measure the statements in *Genesis* against a standard of scientific fact because for him the proper direction of measurement is the other way around; he knows (in the only sense that knowledge can possibly have) that whatever does not accord with the Word of God cannot be true; and he knows further that untruths are dangerous and should not be allowed to flourish. And in the eyes of the liberal, the pronouncements of fundamentalists are no less dangerous and for the same reason: they flow from ignorance and bigotry, and if they go unchecked they may succeed in turning the nation away from reason. Accordingly the liberal feels obliged to quarantine religious pronouncements, to confine them to contexts (the home, the Church) that present the least risk of general infection. He cannot allow them to enter into the general political conversation because he does not regard them, and *could* not regard them, as issuing from a respectable point of view on a par with the points of view, for example, of libertarians or utilitarians. And by his lights he is right: the debate between those who would maximize individual freedom and those who would achieve the greatest good for the greatest number is conducted according to principles (of argument and evidence) to which all parties subscribe; not only do fundamentalists not subscribe to these principles, they stigmatize them as the diabolical tools of godless humanism; obviously they cannot be given a place in the arena for they refuse to play by the rules. Of course, a humane society (another key notion in liberal thought) does not kill or imprison people just because they believe foolish and unprofitable things; indeed it is the disinclination to punish those with whom you disagree that distinguishes the liberal from his "fanatic" opposite; those who believe obviously false things must be protected. Nevertheless, this does not require that the fundamentalist be taken seriously, for according to liberal assumptions, he gave up his claim to serious consideration when he abandoned the rule of reason.

All of this is implicit (and sometimes explicit) in Carter's argument. Why then does he cling to the hope of "softening the tension inherent in the liberal principle of neutrality toward religion"? The answer, I think, is that he mistakes the essence of liberalism when he characterizes it as "steeped . . . in skepticism, rationalism and tolerance." "Tolerance" may be what liberalism claims for itself in contradistinction to other, supposedly more authoritarian, views; but liberalism is tolerant only *within* the space demarcated by the operations of reason; any one who steps outside that space will not be tolerated, will not be regarded as a fully enfranchised participant in the marketplace (of ideas) over which reason presides. In this liberalism does not differ from fundamentalism or from any other system of thought; for any ideology — and an ideology is what liberalism is — must be founded on some basic conception of what the world is like (it is the creation of God; it is a collection of atoms), and while the conception may admit of differences within its boundaries (and thus be, relatively, tolerant) it cannot legitimize differences that would blur its boundaries, for that would be to delegitimize itself. A liberalism that did not "insist on reason as the only legitimate path to knowledge about the world" would not be liberalism; the principle of a rationality that is above the partisan fray (and therefore can assure its "fairness") is not incidental to liberal thought; it *is* liberal thought, and if it is "softened" by denying reason its priority and rendering it just one among many legitimate paths, liberalism would have no content. Of course it is my contention (and Carter's too I think) that liberalism doesn't have the content it believes it has. That is, it does not have at its center an adjudicative mechanism that stands apart from any particular moral and political agenda. Rather it is a very particular moral agenda (privileging the individual over the community, the cognitive over the affective, the abstract over the particular) that has managed, by the very partisan means it claims to transcend, to grab the moral high ground, and to grab it from a discourse — the discourse of religion — that had held it for centuries. This victory certainly sets liberalism apart from the ideologies it has vanquished, but because the victory is political, liberalism cannot finally claim to be different from its competitors. Liberalism, however, defines itself by that difference — by its not being the program of any particular group or party — and therefore in the absence of that difference one can only conclude, and conclude nonparadoxically, that liberalism doesn't exist.

B. THE ARGUMENT FOR A SECULAR REPUBLIC

Steven G. Gey
Why is Religion Special?: Reconsidering the Accommodation of Religion Under the Religion Clauses of the First Amendment
52 U. PITT. L. REV. 75 (1990)*

IV. THE NATURE OF RELIGION AND ITS ROLE IN THE MODERN STATE

[There is a serious] inconsistency at the heart of the accommodation principle. The accommodation principle is premised on the notion that religion and religious ideas are "special" and, therefore, are deserving of heightened protection under the Constitution. The primary objective of the accommodation principle is to protect both behavior motivated by religion and the belief and

---

expression of religious ideas. These themes cannot be reconciled without introducing into religion clause jurisprudence a preference for traditional forms of religious belief and practice. Attempts to define the essence of religion broadly enough to encompass the full range of arguably religious beliefs render the protection of behavior motivated by religion impossible because, under such broad definitions, virtually all behavior would be constitutionally protected. Each attempt to define religion broadly within an accommodationist perspective arbitrarily narrows the definition of religion to protect only the more traditional or nonthreatening forms of religious belief and practice.

In this section I argue that these two themes of the accommodation principle conflict, and that each of the themes is fundamentally flawed. In the first subsection below I offer a much narrower definition of "religion" than those discussed in the previous section. In the second subsection I apply this narrow definition to specific problems raised by the religion clauses. In particular, I argue that the narrow definition illustrates the need to reinforce strong establishment clause prohibitions on the use of state agencies to advance religious goals. I also definitively rebut claims that the state may not pursue a secular agenda in education and social welfare when that agenda conflicts with the doctrines of particular religious sects. The second subsection also includes a rejoinder to Professor [Mark] Tushnet's and Professor McConnell's argument that religion serves a salutary political function in the modern state. In the third subsection, I argue that a broader definition is unnecessary to protect religious liberty because (a) religious ideas and expression are adequately protected under a broadly construed free speech doctrine, and (b) there is no constitutional justification for using the free exercise clause to prefer religiously motivated behavior over nonreligious behavior.

A. A Narrow Definition of Religion

In this section, I propose to adopt and expand upon a narrow definition of religion suggested recently by Professor Stanley Ingber. Professor Ingber argues that religion "consists of a 'unified system of beliefs and practices relative to sacred things.'" Although Ingber notes that the sacred aspects of religion are not necessarily bound within theistic concepts, "religious duties must be based in the 'otherworldly' or the transcendent . . . a transcendent *reality*." The extra-human nature of religious obligation "makes secular law which interferes with divinely ordained responsibilities suspect. Human beings may not undo an obligation not of human making." In sum, religion involves the subordination of the individual will to the unchallengeable dictates of an extra-human, transcendent force or reality. This definition is helpful because it focuses on the three key aspects of religion: (1) religious principles are derived from a source beyond human control; (2) religious principles are immutable and absolutely authoritative; and (3) religious principles are not based on logic or reason, and, therefore, may not be proved or disproved.

As a purely theoretical matter, the narrow definition is superior to the competing definitions discussed in the previous section because the narrow definition omits much of the sociological, psychological, and institutional epiphenomena of religion that characterize the broader definitions. The three elements of the narrow definition focus attention solely on the particular facets of religion that are significant for constitutional purposes.

The first element of the narrow definition is necessary because without some reference to an external authority, a claim of religious duty or obligation becomes indistinguishable from a purely solipsistic individual desire. Unless "religion" means "all strong human desire," the definition of religion must locate the source of an asserted religious obligation outside the individual. Claims of extra-human authority are commonly made by proponents of the accommodation principle, who often urge that the state refrain from placing adherents in a position to choose between competing authorities.

The second element of the definition is also required in order to formulate a sensible limitation on constitutional entitlements. Religious principles that are neither immutable nor absolutely authoritative would not lead to a conflict between secular and religious obligations because, by definition, mutable and non-absolute religious obligations can be modified or ignored by the adherent in order to comply with secular duties. Like the conflicting authority argument, the dilemma of conflicting obligations is a common justification for the accommodation principle.

The third element of the narrow definition is necessary because of the evolution in the philosophy of religion. At least since Immanuel Kant's publication of the *Critique of Pure Reason,* theistic forms of religion have been unable to rely upon the traditional logical proofs of God's existence.[440] This transformation in the nature of theistic religion rendered God unknowable and placed theistic religion on the same foundation with nontheistic religion — a manifestation of human faith alone. A.J. Ayer put a linguistic spin on this transformation by noting that the disappearance of demonstrable proof that God exists robs religious utterances of any cognitive value whatever. "[The theist's] assertions cannot possibly be valid, but they cannot be invalid either. As he says nothing at all about the world, he cannot justly be accused of saying anything false, or anything for which he has insufficient grounds." It is irrelevant for constitutional purposes whether the evolution of philosophy and theology have rendered religious utterances merely unprovable or utterly nonsensical. The significant fact is that a theology based on belief rather than on reason creates a far more precarious basis for political action, certainly far too unstable a

---

440 *See generally* J. COLLINS, GOD IN MODERN PHILOSOPHY (1959); F. ENGLAND, KANT'S CONCEPTION OF GOD (1968); F. MANUEL, THE EIGHTEENTH CENTURY CONFRONTS THE GODS (1959). Kant attempted to replace the intellectual proofs of God's existence with a moral proof of God's existence, which Kant believed could be derived from individual moral experiences. But Kant's moral postulate carried discourse over God's existence into another sphere, characterized to a substantial extent by faith rather than reason. This resort to faith led Bertrand Russell to comment that, like many people, "in intellectual matters [Kant] was skeptical, but in moral matters he believed implicitly in the maxims that he had imbided at his mother's knee." B. RUSSELL, WHY I AM NOT A CHRISTIAN 11 (1957).

foundation to serve as the basis for the coercive application of religious principles to everyone in society.

Although the narrow definition is initially compelling as a matter of abstract theory, the definition is problematic when considered within the context of present religion clause doctrine, which includes at least a weak form of the accommodation principle. When the narrow definition is incorporated into current jurisprudence and applied to nontraditional or new forms of religious doctrine, where most free exercise litigation occurs, it seems to present some of the same difficulties that the broader definitions present. In particular, the definition seems to be grossly underinclusive. For example, the narrow definition seems incapable of recognizing the religious significance of pantheistic beliefs, which view the temporal world as sacred. The narrow definition of religion seems as unlikely to protect MOVE as do the broader definitions discussed previously. [EDITOR'S NOTE: *See Africa v. Pennsylvania* in Chapter 3 *infra*.] The narrow definition also seems unlikely to protect many Eastern religions, such as Hinduism and Buddhism, which, unlike most Western religions, do not make a radical distinction between this world and the next.

Ingber himself directs a similar criticism at Jesse Choper's suggestion that religion be defined in terms of the extratemporal consequences of a set of beliefs. Dean Choper would protect religious beliefs or practices that a religious adherent believes entail consequences after death. Ingber notes that Choper's system "creates a strong bias favoring religious liberty for adherents of Western religions and disfavoring like liberties for those associated with Eastern religions lacking comparable afterlife conceptions." Although Ingber's definition would exclude fewer non-Western faiths (because it considers more than a single factor), to the extent that it fails to recognize any non-traditional faiths as religious, it is subject to the same criticism of exclusionary cultural bias.

Ingber suggests his only possible response in a footnote contesting Kent Greenawalt's argument that a "higher reality" standard is an unacceptable criterion for defining religion because it would deny free exercise protection to groups such as the Ethical Culture Society. "My position," Ingber writes, "is that . . . [cases protecting such groups] . . . were decided wrongly and such groups must seek constitutional protection from provisions other than the religion clauses." In other words, Ingber's definition of religion does not protect these beliefs because these beliefs are not truly religious. This response is tautological; it asserts that the narrow definition is correct and the contradictory evidence is wrong because the definition says so. To withstand analysis, however, any definition of religion must accord with our intuitive judgments about the religious nature of individual organizations and systems of belief. Therefore, the real issue concerns the validity of Professor Greenawalt's intuitive judgment that the Ethical Culture Society deserves the same protection afforded to the Scientologists, the Unification Church, and the agnosticism of Daniel Seeger. If Greenawalt's intuitive judgment correctly observes that groups such as these should be classified together, then the narrow definition must be modified to include the Ethical Culture Society or to rationalize the exclusion of groups such as the Scientologists.

My own view is that the Ethical Culture Society does belong with these other groups, but I also believe that the narrow definition of religion is a helpful analytical tool. The problem of reconciling these views does not lie with the narrow definition, but rather with the accommodation principle that the definition is forced to serve. Professor Ingber must defend what seems to me an unsatisfactory distinction between peripheral religious groups because he continues to accept at least a weak version of the accommodation principle. Under Ingber's proposal, "before an individual can demand an exemption or be granted an accommodation under the free exercise clause from a generally imposed legal obligation, the individual must claim that her inconsistent duty emanates from a sacred or divine source." Once the sacred source of the inconsistent duty is identified, Ingber would rely upon a balance-of-interest analysis to determine whether and to what degree an accommodation must be made. Professor Ingber, therefore, implicitly accepts Professor McConnell's frank acknowledgement that "to the extent that religious *actions* are protected under the Religion Clauses, there will be an asymmetry in the treatment of religion and unbelief." Thus, even under the narrow definition of religion, the accommodation principle would justify governmental dispensations to believers that are not available to nonbelievers and adherents with less rigorous religious views.

Professor Ingber's theory seems unsatisfactory because it might deny the substantial social benefits of the accommodation principle not only to truly out-of-the-mainstream groups such as the Ethical Cultural Society and MOVE, but also possibly to adherents of Buddhism and Hinduism. Once the accommodation principle is accepted, the lines drawn between different forms of faith become extremely important; the principle dictates that substantial benefits will turn on whether the adherent can shoehorn her beliefs into the governing definition of "religion."

I argue that Professor Ingber's narrow definition of religion is helpful for religion clause analysis not because it provides a mechanism for rationally distinguishing the entitlements of different groups under the accommodation principle, but because it undercuts the very premises of the accommodation principle by identifying the characteristics that make religion an inappropriate basis for political and constitutional favoritism.

A. *The Narrow Definition and the Application of the Accommodation Principle in Establishment Clause Cases*

As Professor McConnell acknowledged, the question "Why is Religion Different?" is the key to the establishment clause debate. The narrow definition of religion provides a conceptual framework within which that question may be answered. The narrow definition of religion helps to explain why a strongly separationist interpretation of the establishment clause remains compelling. Proponents of the accommodation principle necessarily contend just the opposite. Their basic attitude is expressed by Justice Powell:

> At this point in the 20th century we are quite far removed from the dangers that prompted the Framers to include the Establishment Clause in the Bill of Rights. The risk of significant religious or denominational control over our democratic processes — or even of deep political division along religious lines — is remote. . . .

The narrow definition of religion rebuts this Panglossian conclusion by focusing establishment clause analysis on the nature of religious principles and on their relationship to democratic self-governance. Recall the three key aspects of religion identified by the narrow definition: religion's guiding principles are derived from a source beyond human control; religious principles are immutable and absolutely authoritative; religious principles are not based on logic or reason, and therefore may not be proved or disproved. Each of these three characteristics is incompatible with any democratic theory of the modern state.

Indeed, one could summarize the basic attributes of modern democratic theory by stating the converse of the first and second elements of religion. First, popular control of government and law is the essence of democracy in any form. By definition, democratic theory views all government actions as reflections of temporal human authority. This authority may be channeled through representative agencies and mediated by constitutional processes, but a democratic government's ultimate claim to legitimacy must be that those subject to the dictates of the system acquiesce to the system's exercise of power. Conversely, when a government places its imprimatur on principles derived from an extra-human source, or uses its resources to cultivate allegiance to an extra-human authority, it implicitly places certain political questions beyond human control. Democracy depends on the perpetuation of a healthy anti-authoritarian mindset among the citizenry; religion cultivates deference to some authority or power that cannot be questioned or changed, or even fully comprehended by the human mind.

Likewise, whereas religion asserts that its principles are immutable and absolutely authoritative, democratic theory asserts just the opposite. The sine qua non of any democratic state is that everything political is open to question; not only specific policies and programs, but the very structure of the state itself must always be subject to challenge. Democracies are by nature inhospitable to political or intellectual stasis or certainty. Religion is fundamentally incompatible with this intellectual cornerstone of the modern democratic state. The irreconcilable distinction between democracy and religion is that, although there can be no sacrosanct principles or unquestioned truths in a democracy, no religion can exist without sacrosanct principles and unquestioned truths.

The third characteristic identified by the narrow definition of religion reinforces these tendencies. Because religious principles are essentially nonrational and unprovable, they are insulated from many ordinary forms of political critique. Because religion concedes at the outset that it reaches policy conclusions by other means, empirical and utilitarian challenges to these policies are foreclosed. For example, it is fruitless to dispute the veracity of creationism within the intellectual framework of the scientific method if adherents of creationism believe in the inviolability of the story of creation set forth in Genesis. It is also impossible to critique the inegalitarian implications of social or economic policies if the state may respond that it is obligated by God to enact into law the untestable commands and principles of theological doctrine.

Some commentators on the left have criticized the separationist interpretation of the religion clauses precisely because of its rationalistic premises about the nature of political action. For example, Mark Tushnet argues that "religion cannot comfortably fit into our constitutional scheme because it is a form of life whose essential characteristics cannot be reduced to the rationalist premises of our legal system." He suggests that in order to reintroduce religion into political discourse "the Constitution's rationalism ought to be questioned." Stanley Fish likewise objects to constitutional liberalism, which he contends "is informed by a faith (a word deliberately chosen) in reason as a faculty that operates independently of any particular world view." He goes on to argue that liberalism's faith in reason is part of "a very particular moral agenda (privileging the individual over the community, the cognitive over the affective, the abstract over the particular)." Stephen Carter also links current constitutional theory with liberal theory and asserts that, under the guise of neutrality, these theories are "really derogating religious belief in favor of other, more 'rational' methods of understanding the world." According to Professor Carter, the modern liberal "believes that reason is the most important human faculty, and that amenability to reason is the trait that distinguishes humans from the rest of creation."

These arguments are flawed because each relies upon an artificially narrow definition of reason and rationality. Each of these accommodationists of the left seem to view "reason" as limited to what Max Weber called "purposive reason" — that is, reason that is directed exclusively to finding the most efficient means of organizing society. Purposive reason elevates means over ends, and is incapable of defining the ends that its efficient society should pursue. The critics noted above seem to share Weber's pessimistic view that this form of rationalism forms an "iron cage" around society, and then populates the cage with ". . . [s]pecialists without spirit [and] sensualists without heart."

Reason, however, is not inevitably the sterile and bureaucratic creature that Weber and his modern cohorts fear. Other, more complex forms of reason also exist. The characteristics of reason differ depending on the cognitive interests reason serves. For example, borrowing Jurgen Habermas' examples, a narrow, technical cognitive interest will call for the use of a fairly constricted empirical rationality that is intended to do nothing more than find out why isolated objects behave as they do in a controlled context. Broader cognitive interests, however, require more complex forms of reason. Habermas' illustrative list of cognitive interests culminates with the "emancipatory" cognitive interest, which is the basis for critical self- reflection and social action. My theory of the religion clauses does not depend on the acceptance of Habermas' particular taxonomy of reason. My point is simply that some form of rational, critical analysis is the centerpiece of any democratic project to achieve political and social change. Such a project depends on its participants' ability to observe sociopolitical phenomena, to arrange the knowledge they obtain in a coherent way, to analyze the implications of a given set of social arrangements, to detect the unstated biases and hidden tendencies of a given system or policy, and to devise a manner of successfully challenging any undesirable aspects that have been noted during the critical process.

By virtue of their attack on constitutional rationalism, the critics concede that religion is an alternative system of nonrational and unprovable beliefs. As such, religion is fundamentally incompatible with the critical rationality on which democracy depends. In a proper democracy, political truth is developed, not discovered, and it may change over time as the individual components of political truth lose their usefulness or become counterproductive to the larger social undertaking. In a religious context, on the other hand, truth is discovered, not developed, and its essential verities cannot be challenged or disproved. The adherent's disapproval of received truth in a religious scheme is an indication of the adherent's inadequate faith or devotion, rather than an indication of flaws in the governing religious concepts. A democratic system should be structured in a way that encourages the development and application of critical reason. A government that places itself in the service of nonrational and unquestionable religious principles, therefore, loses its claim to democratic legitimacy.

This analysis is useful in rebutting another aspect of the special status claims raised by Professors Tushnet and McConnell. This aspect deals with what Professor McConnell calls the "political effect" of religion in the modern state. Recall that both Tushnet and McConnell assert that religion plays a special role in the modern state, by educating citizens in civic virtue. McConnell speaks of religion's ability to instill a commitment to order, morality, and internalized constraint among citizens. In the same vein, Tushnet argues that religion provides an important mechanism for inculcating communal, as opposed to individualistic values. Both Tushnet and McConnell emphasize that the institutional structure of religion is an important part of its appeal. Tushnet emphasizes the importance of "intermediate institutions" interposed between individuals and the state, which "provide a sound location for the inculcation of the appropriate balance of values" (i.e., civic responsibility and a concern for the public interest). McConnell uses slightly different terminology ("'mediating' structures or institutions") to describe the same phenomenon, noting that "no such institutions are as important to the process of developing, transmitting, communicating, and enforcing concepts of morality and justice as are the churches."

These views of religion are on the whole very benign; both Tushnet and McConnell are favorably inclined toward the intellectual and sociological matrix provided by religion. Both seem to desire an overall increase in the "political effect" of religion in American society. There is no question that some "political effect" is inherent in the very nature of religion, but it seems that the typical political effect would tend to support Professor McConnell's rightist political principles rather than Professor Tushnet's leftist political principles. Charles I once wrote that "[R]eligion is the only firm foundation of all power." The British historian Christopher Hill elaborated on this statement by noting that "[t]he function of a state church was not merely to guide men to heaven: it was also to keep them in subordination here on earth. Different societies, different churches: but to want no state church at all seemed to traditionalists a denial of all good order."

The proponents of the accommodation principle argue that the traditional function of the church in propping up the existing political order no longer prevails because of the increased diversity of religious thought and practice. Professor Tushnet goes even further, arguing that religion teaches ideals that are contrary to those of the existing order. But as I have argued above, the very structure of religious ideas and practice are contrary to the mode of thought necessary to foster democratic self-governance. Professor Tushnet argues that religious organizations are "communal organizations in which members are interdependent, giving life to the institution itself." I sympathize with Professor Tushnet's goal of finding ways to inculcate in citizens a desire to pursue public interest instead of private interest, but any definition of the "public interest" is unavoidably tendentious. The "public interest" will advance some elements of the public and harm others. Every ruler cloaks her goals in the blanket of the "public interest." Thus, in order to avoid the demagogic possibilities of the pursuit of "public interest," a democratic system must always allow for dissent and political opposition. The problem with using religious institutions as a model for inculcating civic virtues is that religious institutions are not terribly good at tolerating doubts about their own goals and aspirations. "Excommunication" is a religious response to radical dissent that should have no political corollary in a proper democracy.

I should emphasize that none of the above is a criticism of religion itself, the views of particular religious faiths, or the internal operation of religious orders. The arguments above relate only to extending the influence of religion and religious organizations into the political sphere. The very characteristics that define modern religion — its reliance on faith in what is unknowable, unprovable, but absolutely true — provide a recipe for oppression when transferred to the political sphere and enshrined into law. Faith ultimately may be rewarded, but it should not be rewarded with political power.

In sum, the narrow definition of religion is appealing in two respects regarding establishment clause issues. First, it places the establishment clause in its proper context, as an expression of the Enlightenment movement away from political theory's prior reliance on political certainty and immutable hierarchy, and toward a concept of the political structure that is fluid and (at least in theory) responsive to democratically determined decisions about the temporal needs of society. In other words, the establishment clause removed from political discourse the final resort to the Almighty that had previously characterized determinations of political truth, and simultaneously severed the state's tie with an unelected and very powerful clergy. The establishment clause is itself a value choice in favor of collective relativism and uncertainty about everlasting political truth. Religious values (and the expression of such values) that conflict with these themes of rationality and skepticism are protected, but because of their undemocratic nature, these values cannot be written into law, nor may the state use the adherence to these values as the basis for granting specific legal or political advantages.

The narrow definition of religion is also appealing because it leaves government free to pursue any social or regulatory goal that does not specifically endorse or deny the transcendental essence of religion. Thus, public schools may use reading materials that provide role models premised on gender equality because social theories advocating gender equality do not implicate the basic transcendental verities of religion. For the same reason, the state may teach the value of rationalism and critical thought in the humanities, and favor logically coherent theories in the sciences because those actions do not concern the fundamental questions that form the heart of the religious project.

Michael W. McConnell
Accommodation of Religion: An Update and a Response to the Critics
60 GEO. WASH. L. REV. 685 (1992)*

I consider the argument that accommodations of religion are by their very nature unconstitutional in purpose and effect extremely weak. By this I do not mean that all government benefits to religion called "accommodations" are constitutional, but that accommodations that comply with the standards set forth in the previous section are constitutional.

To begin with, there is no ambiguity with regard to the historical record: Accommodations of religion in the years up to the framing of the First Amendment were frequent and well known, and no one took the position that they constituted an establishment of religion. For the most part, the largely Protestant population of the states as of 1789 entertained few religious tenets in conflict with the civil law; but where there were conflicts, accommodations were a frequent solution. Although the existence of these exemptions does not necessarily establish that accommodations were mandatory, it at least demonstrates that they were permitted. The Continental Congress, for example, exempted members of the peace churches from military conscription, and Madison, at the urging of the ratifying conventions of North Carolina, Virginia, and Rhode

Island, proposed that this policy be enshrined in the Bill of Rights. Madison's proposal was narrowly defeated, but the principal opponents took the position that such exemptions should be left to the discretion of the legislature. Typical was the argument of Egbert Benson that "the Legislature will always possess humanity enough to indulge this class of citizens in a matter they are so desirous of; but they ought to be left to their discretion." The anti-accommodation position thus flies in the face of what we know about the purposes and understanding of the Religion Clauses.

It is significant, as well, that early nineteenth-century judicial decisions rejecting claims for mandatory accommodation under state constitutional free exercise provisions invariably assumed that accommodations were within the legislative discretion. Decisions granting such claims (as well as decisions containing dicta regarding the conditions under which such claims would be granted) are similarly inconsistent with the theory that accommodations are establishments. Indeed, the notion that exemptions violate the nonestablishment principle seems to have been absent from early nineteenth-century legal argument.

Much of the historical argument against accommodations is based on a straw man: that proponents of accommodation believe that in every conflict between religious conscience and the law, conscience must prevail, no matter what the consequence. Professor Ellis West, for example, writes that on historical grounds "it is simply not credible to say that the free exercise clause of the first amendment was intended to give persons or churches the right to disobey laws with impunity provided they had religious reasons for wishing to do so." Indeed, such an extreme assertion would not be credible. The actual question is of more limited scope: whether there are occasions in which the Free Exercise Clause requires that religious exercise be given precedence over civil law. To say that there are valid free exercise claims for exemption does not mean that all claims for free exercise exemption are valid.

Putting aside the historical question, it is exceedingly impractical to treat accommodations of religion as categorically unconstitutional. It stands to reason that when a particular law or government policy threatens to inflict serious injury to the legitimate interests of a particular segment of the population, whatever the reason, the government should consider making a special provision. That the injury happens to involve religious conscience — a matter of particular importance and concern in a liberal republic — makes the desirability of accommodations even more evident. If accommodations were deemed illegitimate in principle, the legislature frequently would be forced to choose between violating the religious conscience of a segment of the population or dispensing with legislation it considers beneficial to society as a whole. For example, must Congress choose between attacking the male Catholic priesthood and failing to forbid sex discrimination in employment? This seems both pointless and illiberal because it is possible both to protect religious conscience and to achieve the public purpose. To exempt churches from this aspect of the law seems manifestly more reasonable than either of the alternatives: no exemption or no law.

Opponents of accommodation simply do not face up to the practical consequences of their position — except by trotting out the occasional tired bogeymen of accommodation claims that would have terrible consequences. No one denies that some accommodations would be terrible. But is this an argument against making any accommodations at all? For the most part, arguments against accommodation proceed on a high level of abstraction, without descending to address the impact of this position on real people in real cases. For my part, it would require an extremely powerful argument to persuade me that it is *unconstitutional* to excuse a Muslim school child from class for a few moments at the appropriate hours of the day for prayer, to allow Jewish military personnel to wear a yarmulke, to permit a church to choose its minister without supervision by the Equal Employment Opportunity Commission (EEOC), or to excuse Jehovah's Witnesses from jury duty. How can such cruel consequences be read into a provision designed to protect the full and equal rights of religious conscience?

The argument that accommodations are unconstitutional turns out to be predicated, almost exclusively, on the claim that accommodations are a form of "subsidy" or "favoritism" toward religion — that accommodation "courts the possibility of aggressive state encouragement of religious activity." This can mean only one of two things. Either accommodations "favor religion" in the sense that they reward and encourage religious behavior, or they "favor religion" in the sense that they protect religion from interference even though nonreligious individuals and institutions would not receive the same degree of protection.

If the first meaning is adopted, the charge that accommodations "favor" religion is simply inaccurate. Under the Supreme Court's analysis of accommodation, set forth in the previous section, government action that rewards or encourages religion is unconstitutional. Accommodation is legitimate only to the point that it facilitates or removes obstacles to independent religious decisions; any supposed "accommodation" that induces or "aggressively encourages" a religious practice should be invalidated. There are many examples of accommodations that permit the religious observer to engage in a practice but create no incentive to do so: to wear a turban or a yarmulke, to say prayers at designated times, to limit one's diet, to attend religious services on particular occasions, to avoid personal photographs, to prevent an autopsy on the body of a loved one, to refuse to display an orange warning triangle on the back of one's buggy, to decline the benefits of ninth and tenth grade, to ingest a bitter and unpleasant drug, to decline medical care, or to refuse to participate in Social Security — just to mention a few examples from recent free exercise controversies. It is absurd to say that the government "promotes" these practices when it decides not to penalize them. As Justice Brennan once commented, exemptions from laws that burden the exercise of religion "reflect[ ] nothing more than the governmental obligation of neutrality in the face of religious differences."

It is particularly peculiar to say that accommodations "promote" religion in view of the fact that accommodations in the government sector arise, by definition, only when religious practices and government policy are in conflict. Far from "enacting into law the religious preferences of the political majority," or bringing about an "alliance between church and state," accommodations reflect a decision to tolerate dissent from the policies adopted by the political majority. Accommodations are forbearance, not alliance. They do not reflect *agreement* with the minority, but *respect* for the conflict between temporal and spiritual authority in which the minority finds itself.

The second possible interpretation of the charge that accommodations "favor religion" is that they protect religious freedom more than the freedom to conduct oneself in accordance with nonreligious norms. This kind of "favoritism toward religion," however, is inherent in the very text of the First Amendment. The government must refrain from actions that officially prefer one religion over another, or religion over nonreligion — even though it is free to embrace certain secular ideologies and organizations and to oppose others. The government must also refrain from actions that punish or penalize the practice of religion — though it is free to punish or penalize other forms of human conduct. How could the First Amendment forbid the establishment or protect the exercise of "religion," if religion cannot receive protection not accorded secular individuals or institutions?

Anti-accommodationists are not without response to this "simple fact," which one scholar has called "the textualist trap." One response is to attribute their conundrum to the First Amendment itself. If the Establishment Clause prohibits the advancement of religion, and if extending special constitutional protection to free exercise advances religion, then the Religion Clauses are contradictory; and we should be free to substitute non-textualist interpretations of the self-contradictory text. But it is surely more sensible to ask, instead, whether there is a reading of the two clauses that is not contradictory — especially since historians tell us that the free exercise and nonestablishment arguments were invoked interchangeably and "represented a double declaration of what Americans wanted to assert about Church and State" rather than being two separate, let alone inconsistent principles. In the context of their purposes and intellectual history, the Religion Clauses are complementary provisions guarding against two equal and opposite threats to the autonomy of religious life. The Establishment Clause guarantees that the federal (and after incorporation, state and local) government will not give official status or preference to any religion or religions, and the Free Exercise Clause guarantees that it will not interfere (without sufficient justification) with the beliefs and practices of any religion. In other words, decisions about whether and what religious practices to engage in will be left to individual citizens and their churches.

It is the anti-accommodationists who fail to appreciate the significance of the Establishment Clause for the accommodation question. Anti-accommodationists object to "singling out" religion for special protection under the Free

Exercise Clause, but they typically have no qualms about "singling" out religion for special prohibitions under the Establishment Clause. Government may advance secular causes such as feminism or capitalism, subsidize controversial private organizations such as Planned Parenthood or the Republican Party, and issue government propaganda about improper private habits such as smoking or teenage sex; but it may not identify itself officially with Christianity, subsidize churches as such, or propagandize for religious views. This half of the Religion Clauses suits the anti-accommodationists just fine. But when religion is singled out for protection, this strikes them as terribly unfair. My position is that the government must "single out" religion in *both* free exercise and establishment contexts, with the goal of approximating a substantive neutrality in a religiously pluralistic culture. The anti-accommodationists seemingly take the position that the government must never "advance" religion, but may inhibit, penalize, and punish it.

A second response by anti-accommodationists to the "textualist trap" is to argue that, properly read, the Free Exercise Clause does not "single out" religion. The purpose of the Clause, they say, is to make clear that religious expression is part of the First Amendment's "broad protection [of] all forms of expression without regard to their religious nature." The Free Exercise Clause has "a crucial role in First Amendment theory by expanding the concept of expression beyond the purely political context." But religion is protected as speech, and nothing more. Free exercise protection is strictly limited to "religious beliefs, verbal expression . . . and the symbolic representation of faith through religious iconography" — subject always to "traditional time, place, and manner regulation."

One need look no further than the Constitution's use of the term "exercise" to appreciate the implausibility of an interpretation that would confine the Clause to speech and belief. Even the modern Supreme Court, which has adopted an extraordinarily narrow view of free exercise, has unanimously rejected that reading. The Virginia Declaration of Rights, which was the principal precursor to the First Amendment, began: "That religion, or the duty which we owe to our CREATOR, and the manner of discharging it, can be directed only by reason and conviction, not by force or violence; and therefore all men are equally entitled to the free exercise of religion." Unless the duties we owe to our Creator are confined to speech and belief, this demonstrates that "free exercise of religion" was understood to extend beyond the rights of expression.

But if First Amendment protections for religion extend beyond speech and belief, to "exercise," then the anti-accommodationist construction of the Amendment collapses. It is not credible to argue that accommodation of religion violates the First Amendment on the ground that it protects religion and not other institutions and systems of belief, because the same argument could be made against the First Amendment itself.

The final point to be made against the claim that accommodations "favor religion" because they protect religious but not nonreligious objections is that this is not necessarily true. Accommodation of religion must not be viewed in isolation, as if no other personal interests of the citizens receive protection from otherwise applicable laws. To hold that accommodation of religion is unconstitutional is to hold that the government *must* refuse to accommodate, even if it would accommodate a secular concern of comparable strength.

Consider an example posited by Professor Steven Gey: the case of a female student whose religion does not permit her to bare her legs in public, but is compelled to attend gym class, where for "aesthetic" reasons the students are required to wear shorts. Gey does not identify the hypothetical student's religious belief, but it resembles that of many traditional Hindus and Moslems. Although recognizing that allowing the student to wear alternative dress "would not 'coerce, compromise, nor influence the religious beliefs of any school children,'" Gey maintains that this accommodation "would not be permissible." "By ceding authority over the objecting student to the higher religious authority," Gey states, "the school board subjugates democratic control over a particular policy area to a nondemocratic, extra-human force."

What are we to make of this argument? One can only presume that a reasonable school board would accommodate a student who had equally powerful secular claims for accommodation (though the Free Exercise Clause would not *require* it). To say that the board *may not* accommodate the objection if it is grounded in religious belief means that religion is given least-protected status. But what if the school board has refused to accommodate secular objections to the gym uniform? It does not necessarily follow that the board would refuse to accommodate *all* secular objections, no matter how strong they may be. The "governmental interest test" is the means by which we can evaluate these counterfactual cases. If the government has a "compelling" (perhaps even a "substantial") interest in enforcing the rule, then we can assume that secular interest would be overridden. (That is what we mean when we say that the government's interests are "compelling.") But if the government's interests are not particularly strong, as in this case, there is every reason to believe that some secular beliefs, if held with anything like the strength of the religious example, would be accommodated.

The example thus helps to explain why accommodation is permitted, and also why it is sometimes required. If there were a Hindu or Moslem majority in the community, the uniform would have a different design, and all the students would, in effect, conform to the Hindu and Moslem mores (unless they had other constitutionally cognizable objections). Indeed, a modest uniform would probably be viewed as "natural" or "traditional," and not religious at all. Because there is neither a Hindu nor a Moslem majority, and because the majority's view of aesthetics and convenience favors the wearing of shorts, those who have different mores (whether religious or secular) pose a problem for the officials with control over the program. The ordinary checks of the political process are fair guarantees that government officials will ordinarily exercise reasonable judgement and will not mindlessly subject their young citizens to oppressive rules. Accommodations will probably be made. But the peculiar circumstances of minority religions and the danger of religious majoritarianism make it necessary to buttress the political checks with constitutional protections when the objection is based on adherence to religion (which, given the majoritarian character of the rule, will virtually always be a minority religion). The only reason I can think of that school officials might deny the student's request for accommodation is that they are hostile to Hinduism or Islam, or (less likely, but still possible) to religion in general, or to any religion that deviates from the society's norm of conduct. That is what the Religion Clauses are designed to prevent. The claim that the Religion Clauses *require* accommodation seems perfectly consistent with the general constitutional commitment to the protection of minority rights; the claim that the Religion Clauses *outlaw* accommodation of this sort is both normatively and doctrinally wrong. What legitimate interest of the state is served by requiring a Moslem or Hindu girl to violate the tenets of her faith?

A final argument against accommodation of religion is that religious commitments — at least those most likely to give rise to claims of accommodation — are inconsistent with the democratic order. Although these commitments should not be suppressed, neither should they be encouraged. Professor Lupu calls this the principle of "secular advantage." He sees religious accommodation as a threat to "the project of constitutional democracy, which depends upon a citizenry capable of exercising independent and critical judgment concerning policies and leaders." "[R]eligious institutions . . . frequently claim divine inspiration of their principles and leaders as a basis of power and legitimacy." "Such claims," Lupu says, "discourage skepticism and make intense demands for obedience by adherents. The Constitution requires toleration of such institutions, but it would be constitutional folly to read the Establishment Clause to permit support and encouragement [for them]." Such institutions "undermine rather than mutually reinforce habits of mind necessary for democratic decisionmaking." In a similar vein, Professor Gey states that religion is "fundamentally incompatible" with the "intellectual cornerstone of the modern democratic state," which is the realization that "there can be no sacrosanct principles or unquestioned truths." Religions fail to inculcate the "anti- authoritarian mindset" on which democracy depends. The Establishment Clause, he says, "is itself a value choice in favor of collective relativism and uncertainty about everlasting political truth."

There is no way to know how much of the opposition to a vigorous Free Exercise Clause is attributable to sentiments of this sort. They are rarely expressed. Is it necessary to respond? Is it necessary to point out that the great attacks on the democratic ideal and the most intense demands for obedience in this century have come from those for whom no extraworldly source of decent limits exists? Or that their prison camps were filled with brave individuals who claimed divine inspiration for their adherence to principle? Is it not obvious that intolerance and ideological blindness come in secular as well as religious hues? That persons of varying faiths can be equal citizens in a pluralistic republic? Indeed, that the wellsprings of religious experience have made a certain contribution to the development of the democratic spirit?

The canard that the First Amendment was a deliberate "value choice in favor of collective relativism" is more often heard among religious demagogues than among those who count themselves as supporters of our pluralistic constitutional order. Let there be no doubt: The Establishment Clause was a deliberate choice to allow all sects and modes of belief, religious as well as secular, to compete for the allegiance of the people, without official preference. The attempt to press the Religion Clauses into service as an instrument for "collective relativism," or any other official orthodoxy, must be condemned in the strongest possible terms.

The view that religion "undermines" the democratic spirit certainly played no part in this country's adoption of the First Amendment. The Founders were far more likely to assume, as did Washington, that religion is the "indispensable support[ ]" for republican government. The reaction of the Founders to the subgroups among them whose religious convictions conflicted with the needs of the civil order was not to accuse them of undemocratic tendencies, but to protect their sincere claims of conscience. It was at the time of greatest national peril that the Continental Congress passed this resolution:

> As there are some people, who, from religious principles, cannot bear arms in any case, this Congress intend no violence to their consciences, but earnestly recommend it to them, to contribute liberally in this time of universal calamity, to the relief of their distressed brethren in the several colonies, and to do all other services to their oppressed Country, which they can consistently with their religious principles.

Tocqueville observed that the Americans of the early days of the Republic considered religion "necessary to the maintenance of republican institutions." He had come to agree with them. "Despotism may be able to do without faith, but freedom cannot. Religion is much more needed in the republic they advocate than in the monarchy they attack, and in democratic republics most of all." He said the French "pedants" find this "an obvious mistake" and believe that "freedom and human happiness" would be advanced by the spread of secular Enlightenment ideas. "To that," Tocqueville responded, "I have really no answer to give, except that those who talk like that have never been in America and have never seen either religious peoples or free ones."

Nor would the view that religion undermines democracy have received the support of more than a tiny segment of the population at any point since then. It is the narrow ideological position of the secular elite, and it can claim no democratic or constitutional warrant. It relegates the large majority of the American public, for whom religion is the most important source of normative understanding, to second-class citizenship. Some democracy.

I make no claim that religious positions should be privileged because they are religious, but only that secular positions should not be privileged because they are secular. In a regime of popular sovereignty, the people should be free to draw their normative insights from whatever sources they find convincing, without the government tipping the scales in one direction or another. The arguments for and against accommodation should not rest on dubious presuppositions about the degree to which religion is indispensable to democracy, as Washington and Tocqueville said, or undermines democracy, as Professors Lupu and Gey say. Ours is not a Christian republic, but it is not a secular republic, either. It is a free and pluralistic republic, in which religious voices from a variety of traditions, along with nonreligious voices from other traditions, have an equal right to speak and strive for their visions of justice.

NOTE ON THE CONSTITUTION AND THE "SECULAR REPUBLIC"

Compare Professor McConnell's argument that "[o]urs is not a Christian republic, but it is not a secular republic, either" with Kathleen Sullivan's counterargument that "[t]he bar against an establishment of religion entails the establishment of a civil order — the culture of liberal democracy — for resolving public moral disputes." Kathleen M. Sullivan, *Religion And Liberal Democracy*, 59 U. CHI. L. REV. 195, 198 (1992). Sullivan asserts that this civil public order is the product of a "social contract produced by religious truce. Religious teachings as expressed in public debate may influence the civil public order but public moral disputes may be resolved only on grounds articulable in secular terms." *Id.* at 197. "The correct baseline [for measuring Religion Clause violations] is not unfettered religious liberty, but rather religious liberty insofar as it is consistent with the establishment of the secular public moral order. On this view, the exclusion of religion from public programs is not, as McConnell would have it, an invidious 'preference for the secular in public affairs.' Secular governance of public affairs is simply an entailment of the settlement by the Establishment Clause of the war of all sects against all. From the perspective of the prepolitical war of all sects against all, the exclusion of any religion from public affairs looks like 'discrimination.' But from the perspective of the settlement worked by the Establishment Clause, it looks like proper treatment." *Id.* at 198-99 (quoting Michael W. McConnell, *Religious Freedom at a Crossroads*, 59 U. CHI. L. REV. 115, 169 (1992)).

Note that there is a subtle but important difference in the way Professors McConnell and Sullivan approach the Establishment Clause. McConnell treats the Establishment Clause as merely one aspect of the general protection of individual religious liberty provided by the First Amendment as a whole. Sullivan, on the other hand, approaches the Establishment Clause much more as a structural protection of government, rather than as an aspect of individual liberty. For a detailed discussion of the basis and implications of the structural view of the Establishment Clause (with conclusions somewhat different than those drawn by Professor Sullivan), *see* Carl H. Esbeck, *The Establishment Clause as a Structural Restraint on Governmental Power*, 84 IOWA L. REV. 1 (1998).

Michael J. Perry,
Religion, Politics, and the Constitution
7 J. CONTEMP. LEGAL ISSUES 407 (1996)*

VII. RELIGION IN POLITICS: CONSTITUTIONAL PERSPECTIVES

I have articulated, in this essay, the basic features of the freedom of religion, including the freedom of religious believers and nonbelievers alike from governmentally-imposed religion, protected by the constitutional law of the United States — the freedom of religion constituted by the free exercise and nonestablishment norms. The stage is now set for us to pursue the inquiry about the role it is constitutionally permissible for religious arguments to play, if any, in the politics of the United States. As I noted in the introduction to this essay, the controversy about the proper role of religious arguments in politics comprises two inquiries: an inquiry about the *constitutionally* proper role of religious arguments in politics and a related but distinct inquiry about their *morally* proper role. In the larger work from which this essay is drawn, I pursue the moral inquiry. In the remainder of this essay, I address this question: Given the freedom of religion protected by the constitutional law of the United States — given, in particular, the nonestablishment norm — what role, if any, is it constitutionally permissible for religious arguments to play, in the United States, either in public debate about what political choices to make or as a basis of political choice?

First, some clarifications are in order.

- The political choices with which I am principally concerned in this essay are those that ban or otherwise disfavor one or another sort of human conduct based on the view that it is immoral for human beings (whether all human beings or some human beings) to engage in the conduct. A law banning abortion is a paradigmatic instance of the kind of political choice I have in mind; a law banning homosexual sexual conduct is another.

- The religious arguments with which I am principally concerned are arguments that one or another sort of human conduct, like abortion or homosexual sexual conduct, is immoral.

- By a "religious" argument, I mean an argument that relies on (among other things) a religious belief: an argument that presupposes the truth of a religious belief and includes that belief as one of its essential premises. A "religious" belief is, for present purposes, either the belief that God exists — "God" in the sense of a transcendent reality that is the source, the ground, and the end of everything else — or a belief about the nature, the activity, or the will of God. A belief can be "nonreligious", then, in one of two senses. The belief that God

---

does not exist is nonreligious in the sense of "atheistic". A belief that is about something other than God's existence or nonexistence, nature, activity, or will is nonreligious in the sense of "secular". In addition to religious arguments, we can imagine both "atheistic" arguments and "secular" arguments. One who is "agnostic" about the existence of God — who neither believes nor disbelieves that God exists — will find only secular arguments persuasive.[82]

Let's begin with this question: Does a legislator or other public official, or even an ordinary citizen, violate the nonestablishment norm by presenting a religious argument in public political debate? For example, does a legislator violate the nonestablishment norm by presenting, in public debate about whether the law should recognize homosexual marriage, a religious argument that homosexual sexual conduct is immoral? An affirmative answer is wildly implausible. Every citizen, without regard to whether she is a legislator or other public official, is constitutionally free to present in public political debate whatever arguments about morality, including whatever religious arguments, she wants to present. Indeed, the freedom of speech protected by the constitutional law of the United States is so generous that it extends even to arguments, including secular arguments, that may not, as a constitutional matter, serve as a basis of political choice — for example, the argument that persons of nonwhite ancestry are not truly or fully human (which is an unconstitutional basis of political choice under the antidiscrimination part of the Fourteenth Amendment). Thus, whether or not religious arguments may, as a constitutional matter, serve as a basis of political choice, it is clear that citizens and even legislators and other public officials are constitutionally free to present such arguments in public political debate. The nonestablishment norm is not to the contrary.

Moreover, to disfavor religious arguments relative to secular ones would violate the core meaning — the antidiscrimination meaning — of the free exercise norm. After all, included among the religious practices protected by the free exercise norm are bearing public witness to one's religious beliefs and trying to influence political decisionmaking on the basis of those beliefs. As the Second Vatican Council of the Catholic Church observed in the document *Dignitatis Humanae*, true freedom of religion includes the freedom of persons and groups "to show the special value of their doctrine in what concerns the organization of society and the inspiration of the whole of human activity." Although the nonestablishment norm, as I have explained, forbids any branch or agency of gov-

---

[82] My position, in this essay, about the constitutionally permissible role of religion in politics is meant to apply to atheistic arguments as well as to religious ones: arguments that presuppose the truth of and include as one of their essential elements the belief that God does not exist. In a society that, like the United States, is overwhelmingly religious, it would not be acceptable to deprivilege religious arguments relative to atheistic ones. As Kent Greenawalt has cautioned, "[O]ne must present grounds for the [proposed principle of restraint] that have appeal to persons of religious and ethical views different from one's own." KENT GREENAWALT, PRIVATE CONSCIENCES AND PUBLIC REASONS 128 (1995). *Cf. id.* at 63 ("assum[ing] that a principle of restraint against reliance on religious grounds would also bar reliance on antireligious grounds").

ernment to do certain sorts of things, to engage in certain sorts of actions, it does not forbid any person — including any person who happens to be a legislator or other public official — to say whatever she wants to say, religious or not, in public political debate. The serious question, then, is not whether legislators or other public officials, much less citizens, violate the nonestablishment norm by presenting religious arguments in public political debate. The serious question, rather, is whether government would violate the nonestablishment norm by basing a political choice — for example, a law banning abortion — on a religious argument.

Recall that among the other things it forbids government to do, the nonestablishment norm forbids government to take any action based on the view that one or more religious tenets are closer to the truth or more authentically American or otherwise better than one or more competing religious or nonreligious tenets. For example, government may not base any action on the view that the Book of Genesis (read literally) is a truer account of human origins than one or more competing religious or nonreligious accounts. Thus, the nonestablishment norm *does* forbid government to base political choices on religious arguments in this sense: Government may not base any action — therefore, it may not base any choice, including one about the morality of human conduct — on the view that a religious belief is closer to the truth or otherwise better than one or more competing religious or nonreligious beliefs. (Again, a religious argument is an argument that presupposes the truth of a religious belief and includes that belief as one of its essential premises.) The nonestablishment norm forbids government to base political choices on religious arguments; at least as an ideal matter, the nonestablishment norm requires that if government wants to make a political choice, including one about the morality of human conduct, it do so only on the basis of a secular argument: an argument that relies neither on any religious belief nor on the belief that God does not exist.

As the foregoing discussion suggests, and as I explained earlier in this essay, the nonestablishment norm also forbids government to base political choices on secular arguments of a certain sort, namely, secular arguments to the effect that one or more religious tenets are more authentically American, or more representative of the sentiments of the community, or otherwise better, than one or more competing religious or nonreligious tenets. When I refer, in describing the requirements of the nonestablishment norm, to a "secular" argument or rationale, I do not mean to include arguments of the sort described in the preceding sentence, but only those that do not in any way valorize one or more religious tenets — that do not claim that one or more religious beliefs are better, along one or another dimension of value, than one or more competing religious or nonreligious beliefs. Again, the central point of the free exercise and nonestablishment norms, taken together, is that government may not make judgments about the value or disvalue — the truth value, the moral value, the social value — of religions or of religious practices or tenets (qua religious).

In making a political choice, especially a political choice about the morality of human conduct, legislators and other public officials sometimes rely *both* on a religious argument *and* on an independent secular argument: a secular argument that, if accepted, supports the choice without help from a religious argument. It is noteworthy, in that regard, that many of those who contend that abortion is immoral, like many of those who contend that homosexual sexual conduct is immoral, come armed with an independent secular argument as well as a religious argument; indeed, some of them come armed only with a secular moral argument. If government based a political choice about the morality of human conduct at least partly on a plausible secular argument that supports the choice, it would be extremely difficult for a court to discern whether government based the choice solely on the secular argument or, instead, only partly on the secular argument and partly on the religious argument. That government would have made the choice even in the absence of the religious argument, solely on the basis of the secular argument, is some evidence that the choice was based solely on the secular argument. Such evidence is not conclusive, however; that one would have made a choice in the absence of reason X does not mean that one did not base the choice on X; it does not even mean that, in making the choice, one did not rely solely on X. Moreover, counterfactual inquiry by a court into whether government "would have made" a political choice about the morality of human conduct in the absence of a religious argument on which some officials relied is so speculative as to be unusually vulnerable to distortion by a judge's own sympathies and hostilities. Indeed, an individual legislator or other public official, inquiring in good faith, might not be able to decide with confidence whether she herself would have made a political choice about the morality of human conduct in the absence of a religious argument on which she relied (or whether she would make it now).

As an ideal matter, the nonestablishment norm is probably best understood, as I have suggested, to forbid government to make any political choice, even one about the morality of human conduct, on the basis of a religious argument. But, given the difficulty emphasized in the preceding paragraph, we should probably conclude that *as a practical matter*, the nonestablishment norm requires only that government not make political choices of the kind in question here — political choices about the morality of human conduct — unless a plausible secular rationale supports the choice without help from a parallel religious argument. (Kathleen Sullivan has written that "the negative bar against establishment of religion implies the affirmative 'establishment' of a civil order for the resolution of public moral disputes. . . . [P]ublic moral disputes may be resolved only on grounds articulable in secular terms.") Under that approach — which, concededly, involves an "underenforcement" of the full ideal of nonestablishment — a court need not pretend that it can discern what it probably could rarely discern, namely, whether government based such a political choice solely on a secular moral argument or only partly on such an argument and partly on a religious moral argument. (How many legislators would have to base their votes at least partly on a religious moral argument before a court should conclude that "government" had based the political choice on such an argument? How could a court determine whether or not an individual legislator had based her vote on a religious moral argument?) Moreover, if it became known that political choices about the morality of human conduct would be struck down as unconstitutional if not based solely on a secular argument, public officials could, and many doubtless would, take steps to construct a legislative history that would make it even harder for a court to conclude that such a political choice was not based solely on a secular moral argument. The inevitability of such a strategy reinforces the conclusion that as a practical matter, the nonestablishment norm should be understood to require only that government not make a political choice about the morality of human conduct in the absence of a plausible secular rationale.[94] (An important qualification is necessary here. I explain in the larger work from which this essay is drawn why a religious argument in support of the claim that each and every human being is sacred presents a special case: Even if we assume that no secular argument supports the claim that every human being is sacred, government may, under the nonestablishment norm, rely on a religious argument in support of the claim.)

Douglas Laycock has dissented from the nonestablishment position I am defending here.[95] According to Laycock, although government may not require anyone to engage in an act of religious worship, government may make a coercive political choice about the morality of human conduct even if the only rationale that supports the choice is religious — that is, even if no plausible secular argument supports the choice. In Laycock's view, government would not violate the nonestablishment norm by outlawing homosexual sexual conduct, for example, or by denying legal recognition to homosexual marriage, even if *ex hypothesi* the only rationale that could support such government action were religious. The absence of a plausible secular rationale is not irrelevant, in Laycock's view, because it might tend to show that government is in fact compelling persons to engage in acts of religious worship. What finally matters for Laycock, however, what is finally determinative for him, is not the presence or absence of a plausible secular rationale but only whether government is compelling anyone to engage in an act of religious worship.

---

[94] Mark Tushnet has reached much the same conclusion by a different route. *See* Mark Tushnet, *The Limits of the Involvement of Religion in the Body Politic, in* THE ROLE OF RELIGION IN THE MAKING OF PUBLIC POLICY 191 (James E. Wood, Jr. & Derek Davis, eds., 1991).

Given the importance of the nonestablishment norm, and of the religious freedom it protects, once it has been established that a religious argument has played a nontrivial role in government making a political choice about the morality of human conduct, the party defending the choice in court properly bears the burden of final doubt about whether a plausible secular rationale supports the choice. Therefore, the defending party should be required to show that there is a plausible secular rationale, rather than the party challenging the choice required to show that no such rationale exists.

[95] *See* Douglas Laycock, *Freedom of Speech That is Both Religious and Political,* 29 U.C. DAVIS L. REV. 793 (1996) (commenting on a paper of mine).

Laycock's position is deeply problematic. True, government may not compel anyone to engage in an act of religious worship. But why may it not do so? Government may not compel anyone to engage in an act of religious worship *because the nonestablishment norm forbids government to impose one or another religion — including one or another understanding of God or of God's will — on anyone.* (Indeed, as I have emphasized in this essay, government may not make judgments about the value — the truth value, the moral value, the social value — of religions or of religious practices or tenets qua religious.) However, if government (a state legislature, say) makes a coercive political choice about the morality of human conduct, a choice requiring or forbidding persons to do something, and if the only reason or reasons that can support the political choice are religious — if no plausible secular rationale supports the choice — then government has undeniably imposed religion on those persons whom the choice coerces. This is so whether or not the political choice compels persons to engage in what is conventionally understood as an act of religious worship.

Moreover, it is to exalt form over substance to say that under the nonestablishment norm government may not compel anyone to engage in an act of religious worship but that government may make a coercive political choice about the morality of human conduct even if the only reason or reasons that can support the political choice are religious. If I am a gay man or a lesbian, forbidding me to fulfill my sexuality because it is believed that the will of God, as revealed in Leviticus, forbids me to do so is a much more profound and disabling imposition on me — a *religious* imposition — than requiring me, for example, to listen to my public school teacher begin class with a recitation of the Lord's Prayer. (Requiring me to listen to my teacher begin class with a recitation of the Lord's Prayer is a way of compelling me to attend a worship service.)

For reasons having to do both with the central prohibition and meaning of the nonestablishment norm and with the importance of not exalting form over substance, I think Laycock's ground for rejecting my position is quite weak. The nonestablishment rule that Laycock emphasizes, against government compelling anyone to engage in an act of religious worship, is only an instance — albeit, a very important instance — of a more general rule against government imposing one or another religion on anyone. For government to make a coercive political choice about the morality of human conduct that can be supported only be a religious reason or reasons is for government to impose religion.

Admittedly, that under the nonestablishment norm government may not make a political choice about the morality of human conduct unless a plausible secular rationale supports the choice has less practical significance than one might think, because there will be plausible secular rationales for most such political choices that government might want to make. (In adjudicating the constitutionality, under the nonestablishment norm, of a political choice about the morality of human conduct, the proper issue for a court is not whether a secular rationale is, in the court's own view, persuasive. After all, the judiciary does not have the principal policymaking authority or responsibility. The proper issue for a court is only whether a secular rationale is plausible — that is, whether a legislator or other public official could reasonably find the rationale persuasive.) However, that a political choice about the morality of human conduct does not violate the nonestablishment norm does not mean that the choice does not violate some other constitutional requirement. In my view, a state's denial of legal recognition to homosexual marriage probably violates the antidiscrimination part of the Fourteenth Amendment.

I said that under the nonestablishment norm, government may not make a political choice about the morality of human conduct unless a plausible secular rationale supports the choice. But what about an individual legislator or other public official: What should she do? Should she vote to support a political choice about the morality of human conduct if she is agnostic about whether, or even skeptical that, a plausible secular rationale supports the choice, leaving it up to others, and ultimately to the courts, to decide if such a rationale exists? Fidelity to the spirit of the nonestablishment norm seems to me to require more of her: She should vote to support a political choice about the morality of human conduct only if, in her view, a persuasive secular rationale exists. (I am not suggesting that such a constitutional duty could be, or even should be, judicially enforced. How could a court determine whether or not an individual legislator really believes that there is a persuasive secular rationale? The duty would have to be self-enforced.) That she cannot reach a judgment about the soundness of the relevant secular argument or arguments on her own is not disabling, because she can seek the help of those whose judgment she respects and trusts. In the larger work from which the essay is drawn I explain why as a matter of political morality, too, and not just as a matter of constitutionality, an individual legislator should vote to support a political choice about the morality of human conduct only if, in her view, a persuasive secular rationale exists.

Constitutional legality does not entail moral propriety; that an act would not violate any constitutional norm does not entail that the act would be, all things considered, morally appropriate. Similarly, constitutional illegality does not entail moral impropriety; that an act would violate a constitutional norm does not entail that the act would be, apart from its unconstitutionally, morally inappropriate. Indeed, if we conclude that an act that would violate a constitutional norm would not be, apart from its unconstitutionality, morally inappropriate — and especially if we conclude that the act would be morally appropriate — we can proceed to inquire whether the constitutional law of the United States shouldn't be revised by the Supreme Court, or even amended pursuant to Article V of the Constitution, to permit the act.

Beyond the constitutional inquiry, therefore, lies the moral inquiry.

- I have explained that citizens and even legislators and other public officials are constitutionally free to present religious arguments, including religious arguments about the morality of human conduct, in public political debate. The question remains, however, whether, all things considered, it isn't morally inappropriate for citizens and especially legislators and other public officials to present such arguments in public political debate.

- According to the construal of the nonestablishment norm I have defended in this chapter, government may rely on a religious argument in making a political choice about the morality of human conduct only if a plausible secular rationale supports the choice. The question remains, however, whether, all things considered, it isn't morally inappropriate for legislators and other public officials, and for citizens voting in a referendum or an initiative election, to rely on a religious argument in making a political choice about the morality of human conduct even if a plausible secular rationale — or even, in their view, a persuasive secular rationale — supports the choice. (I have suggested that those with the principal policymaking authority and responsibility — in particular, legislators — should ask themselves whether they find a secular rationale persuasive.) From the other side, the question remains whether, *apart from the nonestablishment norm*, it is not morally permissible for legislators and others to rely on a religious argument in making a political choice about the morality of human conduct even if, in their view, no persuasive or even plausible secular rationale supports the choice.

NOTE ON MICHAEL PERRY AND RELIGIOUS POLITICS

After arguing for many years that the Establishment Clause prohibits legislators from basing legislation on religious reasons, Michael Perry has recently abandoned his earlier resistance to religiously based legislation, and now argues that the Establishment Clause should permit the government to use the law to enforce explicitly religious moral mandates. *See* MICHAEL J. PERRY, UNDER GOD? RELIGIOUS FAITH AND LIBERAL DEMOCRACY 20-34 (2003). At one point, he even describes as "un-American" the argument that the government may not base its policies on religiously-based rationales. *Id.* at 124.

Perry cites several reasons to support his new position. First, he argues that there are serious problems with giving the courts the authority to enforce a constitutional rule prohibiting the government from adopting policies that are based on religious beliefs. According to Perry, requiring the judiciary to enforce the mandate that policies must have at least a plausible secular purpose would require the courts to second-guess the legislature's rationale for all legislation. This would come "perilously close to having judges act as supreme arbiters of controversial moral beliefs." *Id.* at 28. Second, Perry argues that a separationist Establishment Clause rule prohibiting the legal enforcement of religious morality would "deprivilege religious faith, relative to secular belief, as a ground of moral judgment — and unfairly deprivilege too, therefore, those moral judgments that . . . cannot stand independent of religious faith." *Id.* at 30. Perry therefore concludes that the government may explicitly base policies and legislation on purely religiously based moral judgments — even if those judgments cannot be validated by an alternative secular rationale.

Although Perry has abandoned his earlier position prohibiting religiously based laws, he continues to warn that religious practitioners should be wary of bringing a purely sectarian point of view to politics, emphasizing that the wiser approach would be to follow an "ecumenical politics," which emphasizes toleration and respect for different religious beliefs.

What is the likelihood that religious practitioners whose beliefs require the eradication of immorality and sin will voluntarily choose to tolerate views and behavior that they view as immoral or sinful? If as a constitutional matter the government may base moral legislation on the religious views of the political majority, what is the logical stopping point for such legislation? In his new work, Perry continues to assert that the Establishment Clause prevents the government from enacting legislation favoring one church over another. Is this limitation consistent with the notion that the government has the authority to enforce the majority's religiously based moral judgments? Is it any less an intrusion into the religious liberty of the religious minority for the religious majority to use its political clout to favor the material aspects of its church than it is to use the law to impose on dissenters the moral teachings of that church?

C. PHILOSOPHICAL APPROACHES TO THE ROLE OF RELIGION IN A MODERN CONSTITUTIONAL DEMOCRACY

The complicated issues surrounding the role of religion in modern democracies have increasingly garnered the attention of political philosophers as well as lawyers and legal academics. Three philosophers, in particular, have devoted significant time recently to the argument that religion and religious arguments are to some degree incompatible with modern democratic governance.

1. *Richard Rorty and Religious Foundationalism.* Richard Rorty is a philosopher who has attempted in recent years to update and advance the American pragmatist philosophical tradition in political philosophy. Among the features of his approach is the opposition to all forms of political and philosophical foundationalism (defined broadly to include any doctrine premised on the existence of a moral absolute or objective truth). In Rorty's approach to philosophical disputes, he rejects both religious claims about God-given eternal truth, as well as the secular Platonist goal of seeking to understand the essential reality of the world. He would replace these and other forms of foundationalism with a straightforward focus on the utility of knowledge and moral claims for present human needs. Ironically, this approach amounts to a form of relativism so extensive that it undermines the very characteristics of Enlightenment reason that made possible the philosophical attitude Rorty adopts. "The suggestion that everything we say and do is a matter of fulfilling human needs and inter-

ests might seem simply a way of formulating the secularism of the Enlightenment — a way of saying that human beings are on their own, and have no
supernatural light to guide them to the Truth. But of course the Enlightenment
replaced the idea of such supernatural guidance with the idea of a quasi-divine
faculty called 'reason.' It is this idea which American pragmatists and post-
Nietzschean European philosophers are attacking." Richard Rorty, *Relativism:
Finding and Meaning, in* PHILOSOPHY AND SOCIAL HOPE xxvii (1999).

With regard to the relationship between religion and politics, Rorty's antifoun-
dationalism leads him to adopt the project of his philosophical progenitors
William James and John Dewey to "redescribe" American politics in a thoroughly secular way. RICHARD RORTY, ACHIEVING OUR COUNTRY 15 (1997). Rorty
explains that "I use 'secularism' in the sense of 'anticlericalism' rather than
'atheism.' I have argued . . . that Dewey, like James, wanted pragmatism to be
compatible with religious belief — but only with a privatized religious belief, not
with the sort of religious belief that produces churches, especially churches
which take political positions." *Id.* at 142 n.8. Rorty offers two arguments in
favor of privatizing religion within a secularized state. The first is the need to
avoid the coercion inherent when general religious faith is translated into specific religious creeds. According to Rorty, "Both scientific realism and religious
fundamentalism are private projects which have got out of hand. They are
attempts to make one's own private way of giving meaning to one's own life —
a way which romanticizes one's relation to something starkly and magnificently
nonhuman, something Ultimately True and Real — obligatory to the general
public." Richard Rorty, *Religious Faith, Intellectual Responsibility and Romance,
in* PHILOSOPHY AND SOCIAL HOPE, *supra,* at 157. The second argument is that religion is a "conversation stopper," which makes sensible discussion of public
issues impossible. Such discussion is impossible because a religious person's
rationales for proposing a particular public policy are largely irrelevant to those
who do not share the proponent's religious perspective. "Surely the fact that one
of us gets his premises in church and the other in the library is, and should be,
of no interest to our audience in the public square. The arguments that take
place there, political arguments, are best thought of as neither religious nor nonreligious." Richard Rorty, *Religion as Conversation-Stopper, in* PHILOSOPHY AND
SOCIAL HOPE, *supra,* at 172.

2. John Rawls and the Idea of Public Reason. Richard Rorty's concern about
the "conversation-stopping" nature of religious justifications for public policy is
also a focal point of John Rawls' recent work on the role of religion in a pluralist political structure. Rawls is more sanguine than Rorty about the role of reason in public discourse, however. For many years Rawls has been developing a
theory of democracy under which people with radically different ultimate concerns can coexist peacefully. *See* JOHN RAWLS, A THEORY OF JUSTICE (1971). In his
more recent work, Rawls has focused on the role of "public reason" in preserving the conditions of pluralist democracy. *See* JOHN RAWLS, THE LAW OF PEOPLES
(1999); JOHN RAWLS, POLITICAL LIBERALISM (1993). The need for "public reason"
is a function of the diverse nature of democracy itself. In a democratic culture,

"[c]itizens realize that they cannot reach agreement or even approach mutual understanding on the basis of their irreconcilable comprehensive doctrines. In view of this, they need to consider what kinds of reasons they may reasonably give one another when fundamental political questions are at stake." John Rawls, *The Idea of Public Reason Revisited, in* THE LAW OF PEOPLES 131-32. A crucial element of public reason is the criterion of reciprocity. In other words, reasons offered for supporting a public policy must be reciprocal in the sense that they must be accessible to everyone in the society and perceived as reasonable even to citizens who do not share the same ultimate beliefs of the policy's proponent. The criterion of reciprocity is itself premised on the basic requirement that in a democracy all citizens must be regarded as free and equal, and must be treated by the political system as full participants in the making of policy. "As free persons, citizens claim the right to view their persons as independent from and not identified with any particular . . . conception [of the good] with its scheme of final ends." RAWLS, POLITICAL LIBERALISM, *supra*, at 30.

This theory necessarily entails constraints on the use of religion to justify or support public policies, although it is unclear exactly how severe those constraints may be. First, Rawls applies the requirements of public reason only in the context of discussions taking place in what Rawls calls the public political forum; i.e., "the discourse of judges in their decisions . . . ; the discourse of government officials . . . ; and finally, the discourse of candidates for public office and their campaign managers, especially in their public oratory, party platforms, and political statements." Rawls, *The Idea of Public Reason, in* THE LAW OF PEOPLES, *supra*, at 133-34. Second, it is unclear whether Rawls intends to entirely foreclose the use of religious arguments, as long as proponents of public policies are "*able* to explain their vote to one another in terms of a reasonable balance of public political values." RAWLS, POLITICAL LIBERALISM, *supra*, at 243. On the other hand, Rawls seems increasingly drawn to more rigorous limitations on the use of religious arguments in public debate. Rawls notes with favor Madison's argument in the *Memorial and Remonstrance* that religious establishments are not necessary to support civil society, and notes that "[w]ith some care, many if not all of [Madison's] arguments can be expressed in terms of the political values of public reason." Rawls, *The Idea of Public Reason, in* THE LAW OF PEOPLES, *supra*, at 165. In his more recent work, Rawls occasionally seems to embrace the sort of privatization argument espoused by Richard Rorty. *See id.* at 169-70 & n.82 (discussing the sorts of nonreligious arguments Roman Catholics may raise in public debate against abortion and noting that resistance to the contrary conclusions made by courts and the general public is unreasonable since "it would mean attempting to impose by force their own comprehensive doctrine that a majority of other citizens who follow public reason, not unreasonably, do not accept."). On the other hand, Rawls has recently weakened his public reason requirement by introducing a proviso that comprehensive doctrines (such as religious doctrines) may be introduced into public debate "provided that in due course public reasons, given by reasonable political conception, are presented sufficient to support whatever the comprehensive doctrines are introduced to support." RAWLS, POLITICAL LIBERALISM, *supra*, at li-lii.

3. Robert Audi and the Distinctiveness of Secular Reason. A third philosophical approach to the problem of reconciling religion and democracy is closely related to that of John Rawls. The philosopher Robert Audi has developed a full theory of church/state relations that incorporates a requirement that participants in debates over public policy use only secular rationales to support policies that would restrict the freedom of others in society. *See* ROBERT AUDI, RELIGIOUS COMMITMENT AND SECULAR REASON (2000); ROBERT AUDI & NICHOLAS WOLTERSTOFF, RELIGION IN THE PUBLIC SQUARE: THE PLACE OF RELIGIOUS CONVICTIONS IN POLITICAL DEBATE (1997); Robert Audi, *Religious Values, Political Action, And Civic Discourse*, 75 IND. L.J. 273 (2000); Robert Audi, *The Place Of Religious Argument In A Free And Democratic Society*, 30 SAN DIEGO L. REV. 677 (1993); Robert Audi, *The Separation of Church and State and the Obligations of Citizenship*, 18 PHIL. & PUB. AFF. 259 (1989).

Audi argues that three basic principles support the institutional separation of church and state in a liberal democracy: (1) the libertarian principle, which requires the state to tolerate all nonharmful religious practices; (2) the equalitarian principle, which prohibits the state from preferring one religion over another; and (3) the neutrality principle, which prohibits the state from favoring or disfavoring religion. *See* ROBERT AUDI, RELIGIOUS COMMITMENT AND SECULAR REASON 32-33. Audi argues that similar considerations require separation between secular and religious justifications for public policy. Thus, Audi proposes both a secular rationale and a secular motivation principle. The secular rationale principle is noted above; it states that "one has a prima facie obligation not to advocate or support any law or public policy that restricts human conduct, unless one has, and is willing to offer, adequate secular reason for this advocacy or support (say for one's vote)." *Id.* at 86. The secular motivation principle imposes the further restriction that "one has a (prima facie) obligation to abstain from advocacy or support of a law or public policy that restricts human conduct, unless in advocating or supporting it one is sufficiently *motivated* by (normatively) adequate secular reason." *Id.* at 96. Audi identifies several salient differences between religious and secular reasons for public policy, which justify restrictions on religious rationales. These include the fact that religious reasons are often attributed to an infallible supreme authority; the condemnatory tendencies of religious practitioners toward those who do not adopt the chosen faith; the threat of religious fanaticism and domination; and the tendencies of religious practitioners to be passionately concerned with the sinful behavior (including private behavior) of those outside the religious fold. *See id.* at 100-03. Professor Audi's secular rationale requirement serves much the same purpose as the concept of public reason in the system of John Rawls, but Audi's system closes some of the gaps left by Rawls' recent concession that religious rationales may be introduced into public debate as long as secular rationales are offered in "due course" for the same policy. *Compare* RAWLS, POLITICAL LIBERALISM, *supra*, at li-lii *with* AUDI, RELIGIOUS COMMITMENT AND SECULAR REASON, *supra*, at 159-61. Audi argues that secular reasons must be offered now, rather than in "due course," and also emphasizes that restrictions on religious motivation for

public policies as well as reasons articulated in public in support of those policies are equally important in preventing religious domination of the public
sphere.

4. Responses to Philosophical Separationism. The responses to these recent
separationist arguments from academic philosophers and theologians tend to
focus on the silencing effect of restrictions on the use of religious rationales in
public debate. The central assertion of those who oppose the various proposals
of Rorty, Rawls, and Audi is that separationist arguments — whether based on
constitutional history, text, theory, or philosophical notions of enlightenment liberalism — all have the invidious effect of excluding from public debate individuals who are motivated primarily by religious principles. As Philip Quinn has
argued, "if [Robert Audi's secular motivation principle] is to have any teeth at
all, it will have to exclude some people who are not sufficiently motivated by adequate secular reasons." Philip L. Quinn, *Political Liberalisms and Their Exclusion of the Religious, in* RELIGION AND CONTEMPORARY LIBERALISM 138, 142 (Paul
J. Weithman, ed. 1997). Quinn cites the example of a devout Catholic advocate
of restrictive abortion laws who "might also believe that, apart from religious
reasons, there simply are no true propositions that confer justification on more
restrictive abortion laws or their advocacy and so consider it unconscientious to
try to comply with the [secular motivation] principle by acquiring secular
motives, which by her lights either would fail to confer justification or would be
false beliefs. She might therefore be able to comply with the principle in good
conscience only by ceasing to engage in her advocacy of abortion laws, and I do
not think it reasonable to suppose that she is under an obligation to refrain from
advocacy in her circumstances." *Id.* at 142.

5. Stephen Carter and the Culture of Disbelief. Stephen Carter is a law professor who has written extensively on the subject of religion and the state,
including the philosophical arguments discussed above. *See* STEPHEN CARTER,
GOD'S NAME IN VAIN: THE WRONGS AND RIGHTS OF RELIGION IN POLITICS (2000);
STEPHEN CARTER, THE CULTURE OF DISBELIEF: HOW AMERICAN LAW AND POLITICS
TRIVIALIZE RELIGIOUS DEVOTION (1993). Carter's perspective is that philosophical arguments based on separationist or neutrality principles attempt to
describe a world that can never exist and, in any event, amount to the discriminatory exclusion of religious citizens from public debate. "The reason neutrality fails is that it imagines an impossible world. No true wall of separation
is possible. Religion and the state, the two great sources of control all through
human history, will never be fully separate from each other. Each will always
shade into the other's sphere. Schoolchildren learn this truth in their science
classes: All containers leak. The only interesting question is how fast. In the case
of religion and the state, the leakage is rapid, and constant. How could matters
be otherwise? Religion, by focusing the attention of the believer on the idea of
transcendent truth, necessarily changes the person the believer is, which in turn
changes the way the believer interacts with the world; which in turn changes
political outcomes. Although there have been some clever moves in political
philosophy to explain why the religious voice should not be a part of our public

debates, such theories wind up describing debates from which deeply religious people are simply absent." Stephen L. Carter, *Religious Freedom as if Religion Matters: A Tribute to Justice Brennan*, 87 CALIF. L. REV. 1059, 1063-64 (1999).

6. Richard John Neuhaus and the Naked Public Square. Another prominent variation on the anti-separationist theme from outside the professional philosophical literature is Richard John Neuhaus's book THE NAKED PUBLIC SQUARE: RELIGION AND DEMOCRACY IN AMERICA (1984). As the title indicates, Neuhaus argues that excluding religion from its central role in American political life creates a "naked public square," denuded of the core values shared by many (and perhaps most) American citizens. "[W]e have in recent decades systematically excluded from policy consideration the operative values of the American people, values that are overwhelmingly grounded in religious belief." *Id.* at 37. Neuhaus argues that proponents of strict separation of church and state empirically misjudge the basic values of an overwhelming number of Americans. In contrast to the assumption of collective secular pluralism that is sometimes offered as a justification for separationist theories, Neuhaus notes that "over ninety percent of the American people say they believe in God and think that the Judeo-Christian tradition is somehow morally normative for personal and public life." *Id.* at 145. The "naked public square" not only fails to reflect the central values of the people who populate the country, according to Neuhaus, but it has the further effect of replacing religion with something much more insidious: "because the naked square cannot remain naked, the direction is toward the state-as-church, toward totalitarianism." *Id.* at 89. In his more recent writings, Neuhaus has focused more specifically on the role of the courts in enforcing separationist conceptions of the Establishment Clause. "In its hostility to the robust, persistent, and apparently increasing religious vitality of American society, the Court has come very close to establishing in law its own functional religion of a relentless secularism." Richard John Neuhaus, *Rebuilding the Civil Public Square*, 44 LOY. L. REV. 119, 132 (1998).

7. The Role of Religion and the Secular Purpose Requirement. Many of the arguments regarding the proper role of religion in modern democratic governance are closely linked to arguments about the secular purpose requirement of the three-part *Lemon v. Kurtzman* Establishment Clause test and the general legitimacy of religious rationales for government action. These arguments will be considered in the context of the *Lemon* analysis in Chapter 5, *infra*.

NOTE ON THE RECENT ATTACKS ON THE PRINCIPLE OF SEPARATION OF CHURCH AND STATE

1. The Attacks on Separationism. For many years various members of the Supreme Court who would permit government to engage directly in "nonpreferential" religious activity have attacked the basic principle of separation of church and state. In his dissent in *Wallace v. Jaffree*, for example, then-Justice Rehnquist derided Thomas Jefferson's use of the term "wall of separation between church and state" and lamented that Establishment Clause doctrine has been "expressly freighted with Jefferson's misleading metaphor for 40 years." *Wallace v. Jaffree*, 472 U.S. 38, 92 (1985) (Rehnquist, J., dissenting). Likewise, Justice Thomas has argued that the First Amendment was not intended to interfere with state establishments of religion and asserted that although the First Amendment was written by James Madison, it did not reflect Madison's "extreme" views on separation of church and state, which are represented in the *Memorial and Remonstrance. See Elk Grove Unified Sch. Dist. v. Newdow*, 542 U.S. 1, 44, 54 (2004) (Thomas, J., concurring).

Until recently, those Justices have been on the fringe of the Court's Establishment Clause discussions. The vigor of these attacks has been heightened lately, however, by salvos from some prominent jurists and academics who argue that the entire separationist ideal is nothing but a cover for Protestant attempts to dominate Catholicism and/or secularist attempts to undermine organized religion generally. *See Mitchell v. Helms*, 530 U.S. 793, 829 (2000) (arguing that the separationist prohibition on government aid to pervasively sectarian institutions was targeted "almost exclusively at Catholic parochial schools" and was therefore "born of bigotry [and] should be buried now"); *County of Allegheny v. ACLU*, 492 U.S. 573, 657 (1989) (Kennedy, J., concurring in part and dissenting in part) (arguing that the Establishment Clause should be interpreted to permit "government some latitude in recognizing and accommodating the central role religion plays in our society" and that the rigorous enforcement of the separation of church and state would require government to recognize only the secular "to the exclusion and so the detriment of the religious"); PHILIP HAMBURGER, SEPARATION OF CHURCH AND STATE 193 (2002) (calling the separation of church and state a "Theologically Liberal, Anti-Catholic and American Principle").

These conservative Justices and academic critics of the separation ideal are joined by lawyers representing religious groups that seek to use the political process to advance their theological goals. Jay Sekulow, of Pat Robertson's American Center for Law and Justice (the ACLJ), has argued that the separation of church and state is "destructive" when viewed from the "political perspective of Jefferson" because it is "wrought with the anticlerical biases of the enlightenment." Jay Alan Sekulow, James Matthew Henderson, Sr., & Kevin E. Broyles, *Religious Freedom and the First Self-Evident Truth: Equality as a Guiding Principle in Interpreting the Religion Clauses*, 4 WM. & MARY BILL RTS. J. 351, 382-83 (1995).

It is not surprising that representatives of Pat Robertson and other political conservatives vigorously attack the concept of separation of church and state. On the other hand, it is surprising that some former advocates of separationism have also abandoned the Jeffersonian ideal. As noted earlier in this Chapter, Professor Michael Perry recently abandoned his earlier resistance to religiously based legislation, and now argues that the Establishment Clause should permit the legislature to enforce religious morality through law. Perry rejects the exclu-

example

sionist perspective of strong separationists because he believes that position "deprivilege[s] religious faith, relative to secular belief, as a ground of moral judgment." MICHAEL J. PERRY, UNDER GOD? RELIGIOUS FAITH AND LIBERAL DEMOCRACY 30 (2003).

Along similar lines, Professor Chip Lupu has argued that separationism is essentially already a dead ideal, and that part of the reason for this death is separationism's unfortunate favoritism toward "the ideology of secular rationality." Ira C. Lupu, *The Lingering Death of Separationism*, 62 GEO. WASH. L. REV. 230, 279 (1993). According to Lupu, the secular rationality favored by separationism is nonobjective (because it favors science and markets) and is not "particularly conducive to the life of the spirit, without which it may not be possible for a nation to thrive." *Id.* Professor Douglas Laycock has even forsaken the use of the term "separation of church and state" because "the phrase has no sufficiently agreed meaning to be of any use." Douglas Laycock, *The Many Meanings of Separation*, 70 U. CHI. L. REV. 1667, 1700 (2003). He notes that "to some people separation means protection of religious activity from government, and to other people it means suppression or subordination of religious activity by government." *Id.* Laycock himself would prefer to treat separation as essentially coextensive with a requirement that the government maintain a stance of substantive neutrality, under which the government would be required to "minimize government incentives to change religious behavior in either direction." Douglas Laycock, *The Underlying Unity of Separation and Neutrality*, 46 EMORY L.J. 43, 71 (1997).

In the end, the arguments of liberal opponents of separationism sound remarkably similar to the arguments used by conservative critics such as the ACLJ, Michael McConnell, and Richard Neuhaus. Both sets of anti-separationists would empower religious groups to influence the government and incorporate their views into law. Both groups base their conclusions on three assertions: first, that prohibiting government from adopting religiously based policies marginalizes and discriminates against religious practitioners; second, that the separation of church and state effectively enshrines secularism as the national faith; and third, that religion is necessary to provide the deeper values that a democracy needs to operate and thrive.

2. The Defense of Separationism. As other materials in this Chapter attest, these are debatable propositions. Consider the following response to the critics of separationism:

Professor Laycock and other critics of separationism identify two possible meanings of separation: "protection of religious activity from government, and . . . suppression or subordination of religious activity by government." Laycock, *The Many Meanings of Separation*, *supra*, at 1700. This characterization leaves out a third possible meaning, which probably comes closer to describing how a majority of the Court actually has used the term "separation" since the modern era of church/state jurisprudence began in *Everson v. Board of Education*. The third possible meaning of separation is "the insulation of government from religion." This third possible meaning of separation interprets the term as referring to the need to protect secular government from religious domination and the political distortions that such domination entails.

This third meaning probably comes much closer than Professor Laycock's to describing the attitude of James Madison and Thomas Jefferson. In his fight to convince the Virginia legislature to pass Jefferson's Bill for Religious Freedom, Madison repeatedly returned to the argument that the structure of government would be undermined by the intrusion of religion into politics. *See* MADISON, MEMORIAL AND REMONSTRANCE AGAINST RELIGIOUS ASSESSMENTS ¶8 ("What influence in fact have ecclesiastical establishments had on Civil Society? In some instances they have been seen to erect a spiritual tyranny on the ruins of Civil authority; in many instances they have been seen upholding the thrones of political tyranny; in no instance have they been seen the guardians of the liberties of the people.")

This interpretation of separation is consistent with the first meaning of separation identified by Professor Laycock, but it does not at all encompass the second of Laycock's possible meanings. When Laycock writes that a strong theory of separation leads to the "suppression or subordination of religious activity by government," the clear implication is that a secular government in a separationist regime would take as its central objective the "suppression or subordination" of religious activity in society at large. This is a common argument against separationism, even though it requires a significant logical leap that cannot be found in any separationist literature. Separationist limits on the religious influence over government in the public sphere have little or nothing to do with what that government may do to suppress or subordinate religious activity in the private sphere. Moreover, no prominent separationist on the Court or in academia has ever made the case that a separationist regime permits — much less requires — the suppression of religion in civil society.

From this perspective, opposition to separation does not turn on the purported fear of governmental suppression of religion in the private sector, but rather the more controversial fear that in a separationist regime, the religious majority in society will not be able to use the government to advance its deeply felt values. The third meaning of separation — i.e., viewing separation as primarily concerned with the protection of a secular government from religious domination — is resisted by those who argue that government should be more accommodating to religion because, like Professors Perry and Laycock, they resist putting limits on how the religious majority can exercise its political clout. Laycock is forthright about this point in his criticism of versions of separationism that link the theory to the requirement of a purely secular government:

> Professor Lupu accurately describes a certain faction in recent controversies, and that faction may call itself separationist; but its defining commitment seems to be to secular supremacy and religious subordination, or at least to religious marginalization. As I have argued else-

where, there is little basis for that version of separation in constitutional text, history, or structure. So-called separationism that would privilege secular beliefs and bar religious arguments from public debates mistakes freedom of speech and the working of democracy for establishment. It distorts constitutional provisions that protect the people from the government into provisions that protect the government from the people.

Laycock, *The Underlying Unity of Separation and Neutrality*, *supra*, at 47.

This quote indicates that even the liberal opponents of separation are much more concerned with the influence of religion over government policy than they are with the possibility that religion will be suppressed in civil society. But once again, this criticism caricatures the separationist argument; contrary to the assertions of Professor Laycock and others, no judicial opinion or mainstream academic treatment advocating the separation of church and state argues that a secular government should subordinate religion or enshrine atheism as the national anti-religion.

A government that is required to stand apart from controversies over the existence of God and the nature of His moral mandates seems much more likely to foster a vibrant and pluralistic private life than a government that is permitted to incorporate one particular set of ultimate beliefs into law. Nothing in a separationist political regime would bar religious arguments from public discussion, nor would such a regime privilege secular beliefs over religious beliefs. A separationist regime simply requires that some issues be taken off the government's table and left to the private sector, where individuals and private associations such as churches can join together and decide these issues among themselves free of majoritarian coercion through law.

Chapter 3

THE PROBLEM OF DEFINING RELIGION

The problems associated with defining religion for First Amendment purposes have multiplied in modern times due to the increasingly diverse ethnic and religious character of the population and the equally diverse nature of religious beliefs. To complicate matters further, the lines between ethical and religious doctrines have become very indistinct. At the same time, opportunities for conflict between religious practice and the state have become more numerous due to the growth of the bureaucratic welfare state since World War II. Government is now involved to some degree in virtually every aspect of human activity. The government's taxation, social, educational, and regulatory policies constantly impinge upon the religious views of some individuals and, therefore, are the source of much litigation under both the Establishment and Free Exercise Clauses.

If there were only one Religious Clause in the First Amendment, the problem of defining religion would be less pronounced. But even though the word "religion" is used only once in the First Amendment, it serves as the reference point for both the Establishment and Free Exercise Clauses. The phrasing of the Religion Clauses thus creates a definitional dilemma: If the Free Exercise Clause is intended to protect religious adherents from government action that impinges on their faith, then the term "religion" must be defined very broadly, to encompass all behavior that is motivated by religion. But if the same broad definition is used to limit government action under the Establishment Clause, then many activities of the modern regulatory state would suddenly be vulnerable to constitutional challenge as establishments of religion. This has led some commentators to suggest that the definition of "religion" should be bifurcated, using a broad definition for Free Exercise purposes and a narrow one for Establishment Clause purposes. *See* Laurence H. Tribe, American Constitutional Law § 14.6, at 826 (1st ed. 1978); Paul A. Freund, *Public Aid to Parochial Schools*, 82 Harv. L. Rev. 1680, 1686-87 n.14 (1969); Marc Galanter, *Religious Freedom in the United States: A Turning Point?*, 1966 Wis. L. Rev. 217, 266; Notes, *Toward a Constitutional Definition of Religion*, 91 Harv. L. Rev. 1056 (1978). The problems raised by this suggestion are discussed in *Malnak v. Yogi*, *infra*.

In considering the definitional dilemma, reflect on the different aspects of religion that affect the constitutional analysis. In particular, note the differences between the theological and the behavioral aspects of religion. The theological aspect of religion requires courts and commentators to analyze the structure of religious belief that forms the basis of a claim under either the Free Exercise or Establishment Clause. The following questions arise in the course of this analysis: What kinds of ideas are "religious"? For example, is any comprehensive moral doctrine "religious" or must the moral doctrine be derived from an extra-human metaphysical authority to satisfy the criteria for "religion"? May agnosticism or atheism ever qualify as a religion? Must religion exist within a structured set of beliefs and practices that establish a spiritual hierarchy? If so, will a pantheistic religion ever qualify? Is religion social? If the Free Exercise Clause is interpreted to require the government to accommodate religious behavior that conflicts with government policies, will the accommodation principle protect an undoubtedly devout individual whose idiosyncratic beliefs are not certified by recognized ecclesiastical authorities and do not include common religious indicia such as a catechism and liturgy?

In contrast to the theological aspect of religion, the behavioral aspect of religion concerns the relationship between government action and the religiously mandated behavior of adherents. Specifically, the courts must identify which religious obligations and duties are so significant to the religious life of the believer that they should be protected under the Free Exercise Clause. The most important question in confronting the problem of religious behavior is whether the Constitution protects only primary religious behavior and absolute religious duties and obligations, or whether it also protects the behavioral implications of religious belief that do not rise to the level of absolute theological obligations. Stated in practical terms, does the accommodation principle protect only the core aspects of religion such as the expression of religious ideas in prayer or worship, or does the principle also protect the manifold consequences that flow from the application of those ideas to a believer's daily life? Also, must the government accommodate religious practices that fall short of absolute religious mandates?

The behavioral aspect of religion poses the greatest problem for modern constitutional adjudication of religious freedom issues. Recognizing this, many proponents of broad religious accommodation argue that for purposes of applying the Free Exercise Clause, the constitutional term "religion" should be interpreted to include all elements of religious belief and practice, including behavior that is merely influenced by religion as well as behavior that is absolutely mandated by an adherent's faith. *See, e.g.*, Michael W. McConnell, *Accommodation of Religion*, 1985 SUP. CT. REV. 1, 10-11, 26-28. Indeed, proponents of the accommodation principle are logically compelled to insist upon the protection of a broad range of religious behavior, because protection of the core elements of religious faith would provide little more protection than is currently offered to religious speech under the Free Speech Clause.

The breadth of the accommodationist position on protecting religiously motivated behavior necessarily limits the extent to which accommodationists can extend the protections offered by the accommodation principle to religious minorities and nonbelievers. By insisting on protecting a broad range of religious behavior, proponents of religious accommodation must restrict the scope of the principle in other ways, such as by denying the theological legitimacy of nontraditional or unfamiliar faiths. These are the problems confronted in the materials that follow. Note how these courts deal with the problems of definition, and consider also the extent to which the nature of the claim before a court (i.e., whether it is an Establishment Clause or Free Exercise Clause claim) colors the court's treatment of the definitional dilemma.

A. RELIGIOUS OATHS AND PUBLIC OFFICE

TORCASO v. WATKINS
367 U.S. 488 (1961)

MR. JUSTICE BLACK delivered the opinion of the Court.

Article 37 of the Declaration of Rights of the Maryland Constitution provides:

> "[N]o religious test ought ever to be required as a qualification for any office of profit or trust in this State, other than a declaration of belief in the existence of God. . . ."

The appellant Torcaso was appointed to the office of Notary Public by the Governor of Maryland but was refused a commission to serve because he would not declare his belief in God. [The state courts rejected Torcaso's challenge to this constitutional provision], holding that the state constitutional provision is self-executing and requires declaration of belief in God as a qualification for office without need for implementing legislation.

There is, and can be, no dispute about the purpose or effect of the Maryland Declaration of Rights requirement before us — it sets up a religious test which was designed to and, if valid, does bar every person who refuses to declare a belief in God from holding a public "office of profit or trust" in Maryland. The power and authority of the State of Maryland thus is put on the side of one particular sort of believers — those who are willing to say they believe in "the existence of God." It is true that there is much historical precedent for such laws. Indeed, it was largely to escape religious test oaths and declarations that a great many of the early colonists left Europe and came here hoping to worship in their own way. It soon developed, however, that many of those who had fled to escape religious test oaths turned out to be perfectly willing, when they had the power to do so, to force dissenters from their faith to take test oaths in conformity with that faith. This brought on a host of laws in the new Colonies imposing burdens and disabilities of various kinds upon varied beliefs depending largely upon what group happened to be politically strong enough to legislate in favor of its own beliefs. The effect of all this was the formal or practical "establishment" of particular religious faiths in most of the Colonies, with consequent burdens imposed on the free exercise of the faiths of nonfavored believers.

There were, however, wise and far-seeing men in the Colonies — too many to mention — who spoke out against test oaths and all the philosophy of intolerance behind them. One of these, it so happens, was George Calvert (the first Lord Baltimore), who took a most important part in the original establishment of the Colony of Maryland. He was a Catholic and had, for this reason, felt compelled by his conscience to refuse to take the Oath of Supremacy in England at the cost of resigning from high governmental office. He again refused to take that oath when it was demanded by the Council of the Colony of Virginia, and as a result he was denied settlement in that Colony. A recent historian of the early period of Maryland's life has said that it was Calvert's hope and purpose to establish in Maryland a colonial government free from the religious persecutions he had known — one "securely beyond the reach of oaths. . . ."

When our Constitution was adopted, the desire to put the people "securely beyond the reach" of religious test oaths brought about the inclusion in Article VI of that document of a provision that "no religious Test shall ever be required as a Qualification to any Office or public Trust under the United States." Article VI supports the accuracy of our observation in *Girouard v. United States*, 328 U.S. 61, 69, that "[t]he test oath is abhorrent to our tradition." Not satisfied, however, with Article VI and other guarantees in the original Constitution, the First Congress proposed and the States very shortly thereafter adopted our Bill of Rights, including the First Amendment. That Amendment broke new constitutional ground in the protection it sought to afford to freedom of religion, speech, press, petition and assembly. Since prior cases in this Court have thoroughly explored and documented the history behind the First Amendment, the reasons for it, and the scope of the religious freedom it protects, we need not cover that ground again. What was said in our prior cases we think controls our decision here. [The Court then recounted statements made in *Cantwell v. Connecticut* and *Everson v. Board of Education*, regarding the scope of the Establishment Clause. The Court summed up these statements by quoting a portion of Justice Frankfurter's concurring opinion in *Illinois ex rel. McCollum v. Board of Education*, 333 U.S. 203 (1948):]

> "We are all agreed that the First and Fourteenth Amendments have a secular reach far more penetrating in the conduct of Government than merely to forbid an 'established church.' . . . We renew our conviction that 'we have staked the very existence of our country on the faith that complete separation between the state and religion is best for the state and best for religion.'"

The Maryland Court of Appeals thought, and it is argued here, that this Court's later holding and opinion in *Zorach v. Clauson*, 343 U.S. 306, had in part repudiated the statement in the *Everson* opinion quoted above and previously reaffirmed in *McCollum*. But the Court's opinion in *Zorach* specifically stated: "We follow the *McCollum* case." 343 U.S. at page 315. Nothing decided or written in *Zorach* lends support to the idea that the Court there intended to open up the way for government, state or federal, to restore the historically and constitutionally discredited policy of probing religious beliefs by test oaths or limiting public offices to persons who have, or perhaps more properly profess to have, a belief in some particular kind of religious concept.[1]

We repeat and again reaffirm that neither a State nor the Federal Government can constitutionally force a person "to profess a belief or disbelief in any religion." Neither can constitutionally pass laws or impose requirements which aid all religions as against non-believers,[2] and neither can aid those religions based on a belief in the existence of God as against those religions founded on different beliefs.[3]

In upholding the State's religious test for public office the highest court of Maryland said:

> "The petitioner is not compelled to believe or disbelieve, under threat of punishment or other compulsion. True, unless he makes the declaration of belief he cannot hold public office in Maryland, but he is not compelled to hold office."

The fact, however, that a person is not compelled to hold public office cannot possibly be an excuse for barring him from office by state-imposed criteria forbidden by the Constitution. This was settled by our holding in *Wieman v. Updegraff*, 344 U. S. 183. We there pointed out that whether or not "an abstract right to public employment exists," Congress could not pass a law providing ". . . that no federal employee shall attend Mass or take any active part in missionary work."

---

[1] In one of his famous letters of "a Landholder," published in December 1787, Oliver Ellsworth, a member of the Federal Constitutional Convention and later Chief Justice of this Court, included among his strong arguments against religious test oaths the following statement: "In short, test-laws are utterly ineffectual: they are no security at all; because men of loose principles will, by an external compliance, evade them. If they exclude any persons, it will be honest men, men of principle, who will rather suffer an injury, than act contrary to the dictates of their consciences. . . ." Quoted in FORD, ESSAYS ON THE CONSTITUTION OF THE UNITED STATES, 170.

[2] In discussing Article VI in the debate of the North Carolina Convention on the adoption of the Federal Constitution, James Iredell, later a Justice of this Court, said: ". . . [I]t is objected that the people of America may, perhaps, choose representatives who have no religion at all, and that pagans and Mahometans may be admitted into offices. But how is it possible to exclude any set of men, without taking away that principle of religious freedom which we ourselves so warmly contend for?" And another delegate pointed out that Article VI "leaves religion on the solid foundation of its own inherent validity, without any connection with temporal authority; and no kind of oppression can take place." 4 ELLIOT, *op. cit., supra*, at 194, 200.

[3] Among religions in this country which do not teach what would generally be considered a belief in the existence of God are Buddhism, Taoism, Ethical Culture, Secular Humanism and others. *See Washington Ethical Society v. District of Columbia*, 101 U.S. App. D.C. 371, 249 F.2d 127; *Fellowship of Humanity v. County of Alameda*, 153 Cal. App. 2d 673, 315 P.2d 394; II ENCYCLOPAEDIA OF THE SOCIAL SCIENCES 293; 4 ENCYCLOPAEDIA BRITANNICA (1957 ed.) 325-327; 21 *id.*, at 797; ARCHER, FAITHS MEN LIVE BY (2d ed. revised by Purinton), 120-138, 254-313; 1961 WORLD ALMANAC 695, 712; YEAR BOOK OF AMERICAN CHURCHES FOR 1961, at 29, 47.

This Maryland religious test for public office unconstitutionally invades the appellant's freedom of belief and religion and therefore cannot be enforced against him.

NOTE ON SECULAR HUMANISM AS A "RELIGION"

Despite the *Torcaso* Court's reference to Secular Humanism as a "religion" in footnote 11, subsequent opinions in the lower courts have been reluctant to extend the definition of religion to humanists in all contexts. The two cases cited in *Torcaso* involved especially formalized versions of nontheistic practices, which approximated very closely the form of traditional theistic practices. For example, the Washington Ethical Society held regular Sunday services with Bible reading, sermons, "singing and meditation familiar in services of many formal or traditional church organizations," and had "leaders" who preached and ministered to the group's members. *See Washington Ethical Soc' v. District of Columbia*, 249 F.2d 127, 128 (D.C. Cir. 1957). As one court of appeals has summarized the case law: "The [Supreme] Court's statement in *Torcaso* does not stand for the proposition that humanism, no matter in what form and no matter how practiced, amounts to a religion under the First Amendment. The Court offered no test for determining what system of beliefs qualified as a 'religion' under the First Amendment. The most one may read into the *Torcaso* footnote is the idea that a particular non-theistic group calling itself the 'Fellowship of Humanity' qualified as a religious organization under California law." *Kalka v. Hawk*, 215 F.3d 90 (D.C. Cir. 2000) (rejecting on qualified immunity grounds prisoner's claim that prison officials violated his Free Exercise Clause rights by refusing to allow him to form groups within prison chapels to promote humanism).

UNITED STATES v. SEEGER
380 U.S. 163 (1965)

MR. JUSTICE CLARK delivered the opinion of the Court.

These cases involve claims of conscientious objectors under § 6(j) of the Universal Military Training and Service Act, which exempts from combatant training and service in the armed forces of the United States those persons who by reason of their religious training and belief are conscientiously opposed to participation in war in any form. The cases were consolidated for argument and we consider them together although each involves different facts and circumstances. The parties raise the basic question of the constitutionality of the section which defines the term "religious training and belief," as used in the Act, as "an individual's belief in a relation to a Supreme Being involving duties superior to those arising from any human relation, but [not including] essentially political, sociological, or philosophical views or a merely personal moral code." The constitutional attack is launched under the First Amendment's

Establishment and Free Exercise Clauses and is twofold: (1) The section does not exempt nonreligious conscientious objectors; and (2) it discriminates between different forms of religious expression in violation of the Due Process Clause of the Fifth Amendment. Jakobson (No. 51) and Peter (No. 29) also claim that their beliefs come within the meaning of the section. Jakobson claims that he meets the standards of § 6(j) because his opposition to war is based on belief in a Supreme Reality and is therefore an obligation superior to one resulting from man's relationship to his fellow man. Peter contends that his opposition to war derives from his acceptance of the existence of a universal power beyond that of man and that this acceptance in fact constitutes belief in a Supreme Being, qualifying him for exemption.

We have concluded that Congress, in using the expression "Supreme Being" rather than the designation "God," was merely clarifying the meaning of religious training and belief so as to embrace all religions and to exclude essentially political, sociological, or philosophical views. We believe that under this construction, the test of belief "in a relation to a Supreme Being" is whether a given belief that is sincere and meaningful occupies a place in the life of its possessor parallel to that filled by the orthodox belief in God of one who clearly qualifies for the exemption. Where such beliefs have parallel positions in the lives of their respective holders we cannot say that one is "in a relation to a Supreme Being" and the other is not. We have concluded that the beliefs of the objectors in these cases meet these criteria.

THE FACTS IN THE CASES.

No. 50: Seeger was convicted in the District Court for the Southern District of New York of having refused to submit to induction in the armed forces. He was originally classified 1-A in 1953 by his local board, but this classification was changed in 1955 to 2-S (student) and he remained in this status until 1958 when he was reclassified 1-A. He first claimed exemption as a conscientious objector in 1957 after successive annual renewals of his student classification. Although he did not adopt verbatim the printed Selective Service System form, he declared that he was conscientiously opposed to participation in war in any form by reason of his "religious" belief; that he preferred to leave the question as to his belief in a Supreme Being open, "rather than answer 'yes' or 'no'"; that his "skepticism or disbelief in the existence of God" did "not necessarily mean lack of faith in anything whatsoever"; that his was a "belief in and devotion to goodness and virtue for their own sakes, and a religious faith in a purely ethical creed." He cited such personages as Plato, Aristotle and Spinoza for support of his ethical belief in intellectual and moral integrity "without belief in God, except in the remotest sense." His belief was found to be sincere, honest, and made in good faith; and his conscientious objection to be based upon individual training and belief, both of which included research in religious and cultural fields. Seeger's claim, however, was denied solely because it was not based upon a "belief in a relation to a Supreme Being" as required by § 6(j) of the Act. At trial Seeger's counsel admitted that Seeger's belief was not in relation to a

Supreme Being as commonly understood, but contended that he was entitled to the exemption because "under the present law Mr. Seeger's position would also include definitions of religion which have been stated more recently," and could be "accommodated" under the definition of religious training and belief in the Act. He was convicted and the Court of Appeals reversed, holding that the Supreme Being requirement of the section distinguished "between internally derived and externally compelled beliefs" and was, therefore, an "impermissible classification" under the Due Process Clause of the Fifth Amendment.

No. 51: Jakobson was also convicted in the Southern District of New York on a charge of refusing to submit to induction. On his appeal the Court of Appeals reversed on the ground that rejection of his claim may have rested on the factual finding, erroneously made, that he did not believe in a Supreme Being as required by § 6(j).

Jakobson was originally classified 1-A in 1953 and intermittently enjoyed a student classification until 1956. It was not until April 1958 that he made claim to noncombatant classification (1-A-O) as a conscientious objector. He stated on the Selective Service System form that he believed in a "Supreme Being" who was "Creator of Man" in the sense of being "ultimately responsible for the existence of" man and who was "the Supreme Reality" of which "the existence of man is the *result*." He explained that his religious and social thinking had developed after much meditation and thought. He had concluded that man must be "partly spiritual" and, therefore, "partly akin to the Supreme Reality"; and that his "most important religious law" was that "no man ought ever to wilfully sacrifice another man's life as a means to any other end. . . ." In December 1958 he requested a 1-O classification since he felt that participation in any form of military service would involve him in "too many situations and relationships that would be a strain on [his] conscience that [he felt he] must avoid." He submitted a long memorandum of "notes on religion" in which he defined religion as the "*sum and essence of one's basic attitudes to the fundamental problems of human existence*"; he said that he believed in "Godness" which was "the Ultimate Cause for the fact of the Being of the Universe"; that to deny its existence would but deny the existence of the universe because "anything that Is, has an Ultimate Cause for its Being." There was a relationship to Godness, he stated, in two directions, *i.e.,* "vertically, towards Godness directly," and "horizontally, towards Godness through Mankind and the World." He accepted the latter one. The Board classified him 1-A-O and Jakobson appealed. The hearing officer found that the claim was based upon a personal moral code and that he was not sincere in his claim. The Appeal Board classified him 1-A. It did not indicate upon what ground it based its decision, *i.e.,* insincerity or a conclusion that his belief was only a personal moral code. The Court of Appeals reversed, finding that his claim came within the requirements of § 6(j). Because it could not determine whether the Appeal Board had found that Jakobson's beliefs failed to come within the statutory definition, or whether it had concluded that he lacked sincerity, it directed dismissal of the indictment.

No. 29: Forest Britt Peter was convicted in the Northern District of California on a charge of refusing to submit to induction. In his Selective Service System form he stated that he was not a member of a religious sect or organization; he failed to execute section VII of the questionnaire but attached to it a quotation expressing opposition to war, in which he stated that he concurred. In a later form he hedged the question as to his belief in a Supreme Being by saying that it depended on the definition and he appended a statement that he felt it a violation of his moral code to take human life and that he considered this belief superior to his obligation to the state. As to whether his conviction was religious, he quoted with approval Reverend John Haynes Holmes' definition of religion as "the consciousness of some power manifest in nature which helps man in the ordering of his life in harmony with its demands. . .[; it] is the supreme expression of human nature; it is man thinking his highest, feeling his deepest, and living his best." The source of his conviction he attributed to reading and meditation "in our democratic American culture, with its values derived from the western religious and philosophical tradition." As to his belief in a Supreme Being, Peter stated that he supposed "you could call that a belief in the Supreme Being or God. These just do not happen to be the words I use." In 1959 he was classified 1-A, although there was no evidence in the record that he was not sincere in his beliefs. After his conviction for failure to report for induction the Court of Appeals, assuming *arguendo* that he was sincere, affirmed.

BACKGROUND OF § 6(J).

Chief Justice Hughes, in his opinion in *United States* v. *Macintosh*, 283 U. S. 605 (1931), enunciated the rationale behind the long recognition of conscientious objection to participation in war accorded by Congress in our various conscription laws when he declared that "in the forum of conscience, duty to a moral power higher than the state has always been maintained." In a similar vein Harlan Fiske Stone, later Chief Justice, drew from the Nation's past when he declared that:

> "both morals and sound policy require that the state should not violate the conscience of the individual. All our history gives confirmation to the view that liberty of conscience has a moral and social value which makes it worthy of preservation at the hands of the state. So deep in its significance and vital, indeed, is it to the integrity of man's moral and spiritual nature that nothing short of the self-preservation of the state should warrant its violation; and it may well be questioned whether the state which preserves its life by a settled policy of violation of the conscience of the individual will not in fact ultimately lose it by the process."
> Stone, *The Conscientious Objector*, 21 COL. UNIV. Q. 253, 269 (1919).

Governmental recognition of the moral dilemma posed for persons of certain religious faiths by the call to arms came early in the history of this country. Various methods of ameliorating their difficulty were adopted by the Colonies, and were later perpetuated in state statutes and constitutions. Thus by the time of the Civil War there existed a state pattern of exempting conscientious objectors on religious grounds. In the Federal Militia Act of 1862 control of conscription was left primarily in the States. However, General Order No. 99, issued by the Adjutant General pursuant to that Act, provided for striking from the conscription list those who were exempted by the States; it also established a commutation or substitution system fashioned from earlier state enactments. With the Federal Conscription Act of 1863, which enacted the commutation and substitution provisions of General Order No. 99, the Federal Government occupied the field entirely and in the 1864 Draft Act, it extended exemptions to those conscientious objectors who were members of religious denominations opposed to the bearing of arms and who were prohibited from doing so by the articles of faith of their denominations. Selective Service System Monograph No. 11, Conscientious Objection 40-41 (1950). In that same year the Confederacy exempted certain pacifist sects from military duty.

The need for conscription did not again arise until World War I. The Draft Act of 1917 afforded exemptions to conscientious objectors who were affiliated with a "well-recognized religious sect or organization [then] organized and existing and whose existing creed or principles [forbade] its members to participate in war in any form. . . ." The Act required that all persons be inducted into the armed services, but allowed the conscientious objectors to perform noncombatant service in capacities designated by the President of the United States. Although the 1917 Act excused religious objectors only, in December 1917, the Secretary of War instructed that "personal scruples against war" be considered as constituting "conscientious objection." Selective Service System Monograph No. 11, Conscientious Objection at 54-55 (1950). This Act, including its conscientious objector provisions, was upheld against constitutional attack in the *Selective Draft Law Cases*, [*Arver v. United States*] 245 U.S. 366, 389-390 (1918).

In adopting the 1940 Selective Training and Service Act Congress broadened the exemption afforded in the 1917 Act by making it unnecessary to belong to a pacifist religious sect if the claimant's own opposition to war was based on "religious training and belief." Those found to be within the exemption were not inducted into the armed services but were assigned to noncombatant service under the supervision of the Selective Service System. The Congress recognized that one might be religious without belonging to an organized church just as surely as minority members of a faith not opposed to war might through religious reading reach a conviction against participation in war. Indeed, the consensus of the witnesses appearing before the congressional committees was that individual belief — rather than membership in a church or sect — determined the duties that God imposed upon a person in his everyday conduct; and that "there is a higher loyalty than loyalty to this country, loyalty to God." See also the proposals which were made to the House Military Affairs Committee but rejected. Thus, while shifting the test from membership in such a church to one's individual belief the Congress nevertheless continued its historic practice of excusing from armed service those who believed that they owed an obligation, superior to that due the state, of not participating in war in any form.

Between 1940 and 1948 two courts of appeals held that the phrase "religious training and belief" did not include philosophical, social or political policy. Then in 1948 the Congress amended the language of the statute and declared that "religious training and belief" was to be defined as "an individual's belief in a relation to a Supreme Being involving duties superior to those arising from any human relation, but [not including] essentially political, sociological, or philosophical views or a merely personal moral code." The only significant mention of this change in the provision appears in the report of the Senate Armed Services Committee recommending adoption. It said simply this: "This section reenacts substantially the same provisions as were found in subsection 5(g) of the 1940 act. Exemption extends to anyone who, because of religious training and belief in his relation to a Supreme Being, is conscientiously opposed to combatant military service or to both combatant and non-combatant military service. (See United States v. Berman (sic), 156 F.(2d) 377, certiorari denied, 329 U.S. 795)" S. Rep. No. 1268, 80th Cong., 2d Sess., 14.

INTERPRETATION OF § 6(J).

1. The crux of the problem lies in the phrase "religious training and belief" which Congress has defined as "belief in a relation to a Supreme Being involving duties superior to those arising from any human relation." In assigning meaning to this statutory language we may narrow the inquiry by noting briefly those scruples expressly excepted from the definition. The section excludes those persons who, disavowing religious belief, decide on the basis of essentially political, sociological or economic considerations that war is wrong and that they will have no part of it. These judgments have historically been reserved for the Government, and in matters which can be said to fall within these areas the conviction of the individual has never been permitted to override that of the state. The statute further excludes those whose opposition to war stems from a "merely personal moral code," a phrase to which we shall have occasion to turn later in discussing the application of § 6(j) to these cases. We also pause to take note of what is not involved in this litigation. No party claims to be an atheist or attacks the statute on this ground. The question is not, therefore, one between theistic and atheistic beliefs. We do not deal with or intimate any decision on that situation in these cases. Nor do the parties claim the monotheistic belief that there is but one God; what they claim (with the possible exception of Seeger who bases his position here not on factual but on purely constitutional grounds) is that they adhere to theism, which is the "Belief in the existence of a god or gods; . . . Belief in superhuman powers or spiritual agencies in one or many gods," as opposed to atheism.

Our question, therefore, is the narrow one: Does the term "Supreme Being" as used in § 6(j) mean the orthodox God or the broader concept of a power or being, or a faith, "to which all else is subordinate or upon which all else is ultimately dependent"? WEBSTER'S NEW INTERNATIONAL DICTIONARY (Second Edition). In considering this question we resolve it solely in relation to the language of § 6(j) and not otherwise.

2. Few would quarrel, we think, with the proposition that in no field of human endeavor has the tool of language proved so inadequate in the communication of ideas as it has in dealing with the fundamental questions of man's predicament in life, in death or in final judgment and retribution. This fact makes the task of discerning the intent of Congress in using the phrase "Supreme Being" a complex one. Nor is it made the easier by the richness and variety of spiritual life in our country. Over 250 sects inhabit our land. Some believe in a purely personal God, some in a supernatural deity; others think of religion as a way of life envisioning as its ultimate goal the day when all men can live together in perfect understanding and peace. There are those who think of God as the depth of our being; others, such as the Buddhists, strive for a state of lasting rest through self-denial and inner purification; in Hindu philosophy, the Supreme Being is the transcendental reality which is truth, knowledge and bliss. Even those religious groups which have traditionally opposed war in every form have splintered into various denominations: from 1940 to 1947 there were four denominations using the name "Friends," Selective Service System Monograph No. 11, Conscientious Objection 13 (1950); the "Church of the Brethren" was the official name of the oldest and largest church body of four denominations composed of those commonly called Brethren, *id.*, at 11; and the "Mennonite Church" was the largest of 17 denominations, including the Amish and Hutterites, grouped as "Mennonite bodies" in the 1936 report on the Census of Religious Bodies, *id.*, at 9. This vast panoply of beliefs reveals the magnitude of the problem which faced the Congress when it set about providing an exemption from armed service. It also emphasizes the care that Congress realized was necessary in the fashioning of an exemption which would be in keeping with its long-established policy of not picking and choosing among religious beliefs.

In spite of the elusive nature of the inquiry, we are not without certain guidelines. In amending the 1940 Act, Congress adopted almost intact the language of Chief Justice Hughes in *United States v. Macintosh, supra*:

> "The essence of religion is belief in a relation to *God* involving duties superior to those arising from any human relation." At 633-634 of 283 U.S. (Emphasis supplied.)

By comparing the statutory definition with those words, however, it becomes readily apparent that the Congress deliberately broadened them by substituting the phrase "Supreme Being" for the appellation "God." And in so doing it is also significant that Congress did not elaborate on the form or nature of this higher authority which it chose to designate as "Supreme Being." By so refraining it must have had in mind the admonitions of the Chief Justice when he said in the same opinion that even the word "God" had myriad meanings for men of faith:

> "[P]utting aside dogmas with their particular conceptions of deity, freedom of conscience itself implies respect for an innate conviction of paramount duty. The battle for religious liberty has been fought and won with respect to religious beliefs and practices, which are not in conflict

with good order, upon the very ground of the supremacy of conscience within its proper field." At 634.

Moreover, the Senate Report on the bill specifically states that § 6(j) was intended to re-enact "substantially the same provisions as were found" in the 1940 Act. That statute, of course, refers to "religious training and belief" without more. Admittedly, all of the parties here purport to base their objection on religious belief. It appears, therefore, that we need only look to this clear statement of congressional intent as set out in the report. Under the 1940 Act it was necessary only to have a conviction based upon religious training and belief; we believe that is all that is required here. Within that phrase would come all sincere religious beliefs which are based upon a power or being, or upon a faith, to which all else is subordinate or upon which all else is ultimately dependent. The test might be stated in these words: A sincere and meaningful belief which occupies in the life of its possessor a place parallel to that filled by the God of those admittedly qualifying for the exemption comes within the statutory definition. This construction avoids imputing to Congress an intent to classify different religious beliefs, exempting some and excluding others, and is in accord with the well-established congressional policy of equal treatment for those whose opposition to service is grounded in their religious tenets.

3. The Government takes the position that since *Berman* v. *United States, supra*, was cited in the Senate Report on the 1948 Act, Congress must have desired to adopt the Berman interpretation of what constitutes "religious belief." Such a claim, however, will not bear scrutiny. First, we think it clear that an explicit statement of congressional intent deserves more weight than the parenthetical citation of a case which might stand for a number of things. Congress specifically stated that it intended to re-enact substantially the same provisions as were found in the 1940 Act. Moreover, the history of that Act reveals no evidence of a desire to restrict the concept of religious belief. On the contrary the Chairman of the House Military Affairs Committee which reported out the 1940 exemption provisions stated:

> "We heard the conscientious objectors and all of their representatives that we could possibly hear, and, summing it all up, their whole objection to the bill, aside from their objection to compulsory military training, was based upon the right of conscientious objection and in most instances to the right of the ministerial students to continue in their studies, and we have provided ample protection for those classes and those groups." 86 Cong. Rec. 11368 (1940).

During the House debate on the bill, Mr. Faddis of Pennsylvania made the following statement:

> "We have made provision to take care of conscientious objectors. I am sure the committee has had all the sympathy in the world with those who appeared claiming to have religious scruples against rendering military service in its various degrees. Some appeared who had consci-

entious scruples against handling lethal weapons, but who had no scruples against performing other duties which did not actually bring them into combat. Others appeared who claimed to have conscientious scruples against participating in any of the activities that would go along with the Army. The committee took all of these into consideration and has written a bill which, I believe, will take care of all the reasonable objections of this class of people." 86 Cong. Rec. 11418 (1940).

Thus the history of the Act belies the notion that it was to be restrictive in application and available only to those believing in a traditional God.

As for the citation to *Berman*, it might mean a number of things. But we think that Congress' action in citing it must be construed in such a way as to make it consistent with its express statement that it meant substantially to re-enact the 1940 provision. As far as we can find, there is not one word to indicate congressional concern over any conflict between *Kauten* and *Berman*. Surely, if it thought that two clashing interpretations as to what amounted to "religious belief" had to be resolved, it would have said so somewhere in its deliberations. Thus, we think that rather than citing *Berman* for what it said "religious belief" was, Congress cited it for what it said "religious belief" was not. For both *Kauten* and *Berman* hold in common the conclusion that exemption must be denied to those whose beliefs are political, social or philosophical in nature, rather than religious. Both, in fact, denied exemption on that very ground. It seems more likely, therefore, that it was this point which led Congress to cite *Berman*. The first part of the § 6(j) definition — belief in a relation to a Supreme Being — was indeed set out in *Berman*, with the exception that the court used the word "God" rather than "Supreme Being." However, as the Government recognizes, *Berman* took that language word for word from *Macintosh*. Far from requiring a conclusion contrary to the one we reach here, Chief Justice Hughes' opinion, as we have pointed out, supports our interpretation.

Admittedly, the second half of the statutory definition — the rejection of sociological and moral views — was taken directly from *Berman*. But, as we have noted, this same view was adhered to in *United States v. Kauten, supra*. Indeed the Selective Service System has stated its view of the cases' significance in these terms: "The *United States v. Kauten* and *Herman Berman v. United States* cases ruled that a valid conscientious objector claim to exemption must be based solely on 'religious training and belief' and not on philosophical, political, social, or other grounds. . . ." Selective Service System Monograph No. 11, Conscientious Objection 337 (1950). That the conclusions of the Selective Service System are not to be taken lightly is evidenced in this statement by Senator Gurney, Chairman of the Senate Armed Services Committee and sponsor of the Senate bill containing the present version of § 6(j):

> "The bill which is now pending follows the 1940 act, with very few technical amendments, worked out by those in Selective Service who had charge of the conscientious-objector problem during the war." 94 Cong. Rec. 7305 (1948).

Thus we conclude that in enacting § 6(j) Congress simply made explicit what the courts of appeals had correctly found implicit in the 1940 Act. Moreover, it is perfectly reasonable that Congress should have selected *Berman* for its citation, since this Court denied certiorari in that case, a circumstance not present in *Kauten*.

Section 6(j), then, is no more than a clarification of the 1940 provision involving only certain "technical amendments," to use the words of Senator Gurney. As such it continues the congressional policy of providing exemption from military service for those whose opposition is based on grounds that can fairly be said to be "religious." To hold otherwise would not only fly in the face of Congress' entire action in the past; it would ignore the historic position of our country on this issue since its founding.

4. Moreover, we believe this construction embraces the ever-broadening understanding of the modern religious community. The eminent Protestant theologian, Dr. Paul Tillich, whose views the Government concedes would come within the statute, identifies God not as a projection "out there" or beyond the skies but as the ground of our very being. The Court of Appeals stated in No. 51 that Jakobson's views "parallel [those of] this eminent theologian rather strikingly." In his book, SYSTEMATIC THEOLOGY, Dr. Tillich says:

> "I have written of the God above the God of theism. . . . In such a state [of self-affirmation] the God of both religious and theological language disappears. But something remains, namely, the seriousness of that doubt in which meaning within meaninglessness is affirmed. The source of this affirmation of meaning within meaninglessness, of certitude within doubt, is not the God of traditional theism but the 'God above God.' the power of being, which works through those who have no name for it, not even the name God." II SYSTEMATIC THEOLOGY 12 (1957).

Another eminent cleric, the Bishop of Woolwich, John A. T. Robinson, in his book, HONEST TO GOD (1963), states:

> "The Bible speaks of a God 'up there.' No doubt its picture of a three-decker universe, of 'the heaven above, the earth beneath and the waters under the earth,' was once taken quite literally. . . ." At 11. "[Later] *in place of a God who is literally or physically 'up there' we have accepted, as part of our mental furniture, a God who is spiritually or metaphysically 'out there'.* . . . But now it seems there is no room for him, not merely in the inn, but in the entire universe: for there are no vacant places left. In reality, of course, our new view of the universe had made not the slightest difference. . . ." At 13-14.

> "But the idea of a God spiritually or metaphysically 'out there' dies very much harder. Indeed, most people would be seriously disturbed by the thought that it should need to die at all. For it *is* their God, and they have nothing to put in its place. . . . Every one of us lives with some mental picture of a God 'out there,' a God who 'exists' above and beyond the

world he made, a God 'to' whom we pray and to whom we 'go' when we die." At 14.

"But the signs are that we are reaching the point at which the whole conception of a God 'out there,' which has served us so well since the collapse of the three-decker universe, is itself becoming more of a hindrance than a help." At 15-16 (Emphasis in original.)

The Schema of the recent Ecumenical Council included a most significant declaration on religion:

"The community of all peoples is one. One is their origin, for God made the entire human race live on all the face of the earth. One, too, is their ultimate end, God. Men expect from the various religions answers to the riddles of the human condition: What is man? What is the meaning and purpose of our lives? What is the moral good and what is sin? What are death, judgment, and retribution after death?

. . . .

"Ever since primordial days, numerous peoples have had a certain perception of that hidden power which hovers over the course of things and over the events that make up the lives of men; some have even come to know of a Supreme Being and Father. Religions in an advanced culture have been able to use more refined concepts and a more developed language in their struggle for an answer to man's religious questions.

. . . .

"Nothing that is true and holy in these religions is scorned by the Catholic Church. Ceaselessly the Church proclaims Christ, 'the Way, the Truth, and the Life,' in whom God reconciled all things to Himself. The Church regards with sincere reverence those ways of action and of life, precepts and teachings which, although they differ from the ones she sets forth, reflect nonetheless a ray of that Truth which enlightens all men."

Dr. David Saville Muzzey, a leader in the Ethical Culture Movement, states in his book, ETHICS AS A RELIGION (1951), that "[e]verybody except the avowed atheists (and they are comparatively few) believes in some kind of God," and that "The proper question to ask, therefore, is not the futile one, Do you believe in God? but rather, What *kind* of God do you believe in?" *Id.*, at 86-87. Dr. Muzzey attempts to answer that question:

"Instead of positing a personal God, whose existence man can neither prove nor disprove, the ethical concept is founded on human experience. It is anthropocentric, not theocentric. Religion, for all the various definitions that have been given of it, must surely mean the devotion of man to the highest ideal that he can conceive. And that ideal is a community of spirits in which the latent moral potentialities of men shall have been elicited by their reciprocal endeavors to cultivate the best in their fellow men. What ultimate reality is we do not know; but we have the faith that it expresses itself in the human world as the power which inspires in men moral purpose." At 95.

"Thus the 'God' that we love is not the figure on the great white throne, but the perfect pattern, envisioned by faith, of humanity as it should be, purged of the evil elements which retard its progress toward "the knowledge, love and practice of the right." At 98.

These are but a few of the views that comprise the broad spectrum of religious beliefs found among us. But they demonstrate very clearly the diverse manners in which beliefs, equally paramount in the lives of their possessors, may be articulated. They further reveal the difficulties inherent in placing too narrow a construction on the provisions of § 6(j) and thereby lend conclusive support to the construction which we today find that Congress intended.

5. We recognize the difficulties that have always faced the trier of fact in these cases. We hope that the test that we lay down proves less onerous. The examiner is furnished a standard that permits consideration of criteria with which he has had considerable experience. While the applicant's words may differ, the test is simple of application. It is essentially an objective one, namely, does the claimed belief occupy the same place in the life of the objector as an orthodox belief in God holds in the life of one clearly qualified for exemption?

Moreover, it must be remembered that in resolving these exemption problems one deals with the beliefs of different individuals who will articulate them in a multitude of ways. In such an intensely personal area, of course, the claim of the registrant that his belief is an essential part of a religious faith must be given great weight. Recognition of this was implicit in this language, cited by the *Berman* court from *State v. Amana Society*, 132 Iowa 304, 109 N.W. 894 (1906):

"Surely a scheme of life designed to obviate [man's inhumanity to man], and by removing temptations, and all the allurements of ambition and avarice, to nurture the virtues of unselfishness, patience, love, and service, ought not to be denounced as not pertaining to religion *when its devotees regard it as an essential tenet of their religious faith.*" 132 Iowa, at 315, 109 N.W., at 898, *cited in Berman v. United States*, 156 F.2d 377, 381. (Emphasis by the Court of Appeals.)

The validity of what he believes cannot be questioned. Some theologians, and indeed some examiners, might be tempted to question the existence of the registrant's "Supreme Being" or the truth of his concepts. But these are inquiries foreclosed to Government. As MR. JUSTICE DOUGLAS stated in *United States* v. *Ballard*, 322 U. S. 78, 86 (1944): "Men may believe what they cannot prove. They may not be put to the proof of their religious doctrines or beliefs. Religious experiences which are as real as life to some may be incomprehensible to others." Local boards and courts in this sense are not free to reject beliefs because they consider them "incomprehensible." Their task is to decide whether the beliefs professed by a registrant are sincerely held and whether they are, in his own scheme of things, religious.

But we hasten to emphasize that while the "truth" of a belief is not open to question, there remains the significant question whether it is "truly held." This is the threshold question of sincerity which must be resolved in every case. It is, of course, a question of fact — a prime consideration to the validity of every claim for exemption as a conscientious objector.

APPLICATION OF § 6(j) TO THE INSTANT CASES.

As we noted earlier, the statutory definition excepts those registrants whose beliefs are based on a "merely personal moral code." The records in these cases, however, show that at no time did any one of the applicants suggest that his objection was based on a "merely personal moral code." Indeed at the outset each of them claimed in his application that his objection was based on a religious belief. We have construed the statutory definition broadly and it follows that any exception to it must be interpreted narrowly. The use by Congress of the words "merely personal" seems to us to restrict the exception to a moral code which is not only personal but which is the sole basis for the registrant's belief and is in no way related to a Supreme Being. It follows, therefore, that if the claimed religious beliefs of the respective registrants in these cases meet the test that we lay down then their objections cannot be based on a "merely personal" moral code.

In *Seeger,* No. 50, the Court of Appeals failed to find sufficient "externally compelled beliefs." However, it did find that "it would seem impossible to say with assurance that [Seeger] is not bowing to 'external commands' in virtually the same sense as is the objector who defers to the will of a supernatural power." 326 F. 2d, at 853. It found little distinction between Jakobson's devotion to a mystical force of "Godness" and Seeger's compulsion to "goodness." Of course, as we have said, the statute does not distinguish between externally and internally derived beliefs. Such a determination would, as the Court of Appeals observed, prove impossible as a practical matter, and we have found that Congress intended no such distinction.

The Court of Appeals also found that there was no question of the applicant's sincerity. He was a product of a devout Roman Catholic home; he was a close student of Quaker beliefs from which he said "much of [his] thought is derived"; he approved of their opposition to war in any form; he devoted his spare hours to the American Friends Service Committee and was assigned to hospital duty.

In summary, Seeger professed "religious belief" and "religious faith." He did not disavow any belief "in a relation to a Supreme Being"; indeed he stated that "the cosmic order does, perhaps, suggest a creative intelligence." He decried the tremendous "spiritual" price man must pay for his willingness to destroy human life. In light of his beliefs and the unquestioned sincerity with which he held them, we think the Board, had it applied the test we propose today, would have granted him the exemption. We think it clear that the beliefs which prompted his objection occupy the same place in his life as the belief in a traditional deity holds in the lives of his friends, the Quakers. We are reminded once more of Dr. Tillich's thoughts:

> "And if that word [God] has not much meaning for you, translate it, and speak of the depths of your life, of the source of your being, or your ultimate concern, of *what you take seriously without any reservation.* Perhaps, in order to do so, you must forget everything traditional that you have learned about God. . . ." TILLICH, THE SHAKING OF THE FOUNDATIONS 57 (1948). (Emphasis supplied.)

It may be that Seeger did not clearly demonstrate what his beliefs were with regard to the usual understanding of the term "Supreme Being." But as we have said Congress did not intend that to be the test. We therefore affirm the judgment in No. 50.

In *Jakobson,* No. 51, the Court of Appeals found that the registrant demonstrated that his belief as to opposition to war was related to a Supreme Being. We agree and affirm that judgment.

We reach a like conclusion in No. 29. It will be remembered that Peter acknowledged "some power manifest in nature . . . the supreme expression" that helps man in ordering his life. As to whether he would call that belief in a Supreme Being, he replied, "you could call that a belief in the Supreme Being or God. These just do not happen to be the words I use." We think that under the test we establish here the Board would grant the exemption to Peter and we therefore reverse the judgment in No. 29.

It is so ordered.

MR. JUSTICE DOUGLAS, concurring.

If I read the statute differently from the Court, I would have difficulties. For then those who embraced one religious faith rather than another would be subject to penalties; and that kind of discrimination, as we held in *Sherbert v. Verner* [*infra* Chapter 12], would violate the Free Exercise Clause of the First Amendment. It would also result in a denial of equal protection by preferring some religions over others — an invidious discrimination that would run afoul of the Due Process Clause of the Fifth Amendment.

The legislative history of this Act leaves much in the dark. But it is, in my opinion, not a *tour de force* if we construe the words "Supreme Being" to include the cosmos, as well as an anthropomorphic entity. If it is a *tour de force* so to hold, it is no more so than other instances where we have gone to extremes to construe an Act of Congress to save it from demise on constitutional grounds. In a more extreme case than the present one we said that the words of a statute may be strained "in the candid service of avoiding a serious constitutional doubt." *United States v. Rumely,* 345 U.S. 41, 47.

The words "a Supreme Being" have no narrow technical meaning in the field of religion. Long before the birth of our Judeo-Christian civilization the idea of God had taken hold in many forms. Mention of only two — Hinduism and Buddhism — illustrates the fluidity and evanescent scope of the concept. In the Hindu *religion* the Supreme Being is conceived in the forms of several cult Deities. The chief of these, which stand for the Hindu Triad, are Brahma, Vishnu and Siva. Another Deity, and the one most widely worshipped, is Sakti, the Mother Goddess, conceived as power, both destructive and creative. Though Hindu religion encompasses the worship of many Deities, it believes in only one single God, the eternally existent One Being with his manifold attributes and manifestations. This idea is expressed in Rigveda, the earliest sacred text of the Hindus, in verse 46 of a hymn attributed to the mythical seer Dirghatamas (RIGVEDA, I, 164):

> "They call it Indra, Mitra, Varuna and Agni
> And also heavenly beautiful Garutman:
> The Real is One, though sages name it variously —
> They call it Agni, Yama, Matarisvan."

See SMART, REASONS AND FAITHS p. 35, n. 1 (1958); 32 HARVARD ORIENTAL SERIES pp. 434-435. (Lanman, ed. 1925). *See generally* 31 and 32 *id.*; EDITORS OF LIFE MAGAZINE, THE WORLD'S GREAT RELIGIONS Vol. 1, pp. 17-48 (1963).

Indian *philosophy*, which comprises several schools of thought, has advanced different theories of the nature of the Supreme Being. According to the UPANISADS, Hindu sacred texts, the Supreme Being is described as the power which creates and sustains everything, and to which the created things return upon dissolution. The word which is commonly used in the UPANISADS to indicate the Supreme Being is Brahman. Philosophically, the Supreme Being is the transcendental Reality which is Truth, Knowledge, and Bliss. It is the source of the entire universe. In this aspect Brahman is Isvara, a personal Lord and Creator of the universe, an object of worship. But, in the view of one school of thought, that of Sankara, even this is an imperfect and limited conception of Brahman which must be transcended: to think of Brahman as the Creator of the material world is necessarily to form a concept infected with illusion, or *maya* — which is what the world really is, in highest truth. Ultimately, mystically, Brahman must be understood as without attributes, as *neti neti* (not this, not that). *See* SMART, *op. cit., supra*, p. 133.

Buddhism — whose advent marked the reform of Hinduism — continued somewhat the same concept. As stated by Nancy Wilson Ross, "God — if I may borrow that word for a moment — the universe, and man are one indissoluble existence, one total whole. Only THIS — capital THIS — is. Anything and everything that appears to us as an individual entity or phenomenon, whether it be a planet or an atom, a mouse or a man, is but a temporary manifestation of THIS in form; every activity that takes place, whether it be birth or death, loving or eating breakfast, is but a temporary manifestation of THIS in activity. When we look at things this way, naturally we cannot believe that each individual person has been endowed with a special and individual soul or self. Each one of us is but a cell, as it were, in the body of the Great Self, a cell that comes into being, performs its functions, and passes away, transformed into another manifestation. Though we have temporary individuality, that temporary, limited individuality is not either a true self or our true self. Our true self is the Great Self; our true body is the Body of Reality, or the Dharmakaya, to give it its technical Buddhist name." THE WORLD OF ZEN, p. 18 (1960).

Does a Buddhist believe in "God" or a "Supreme Being"? That, of course, depends on how one defines "God," as one eminent student of Buddhism has explained:

> "It has often been suggested that Buddhism is an atheistic system of thought, and this assumption has given rise to quite a number of discussions. Some have claimed that since Buddhism knew no God, it could not be a religion; others that since Buddhism obviously was a religion which knew no God, the belief in God was not essential to religion. These discussions assume that *God* is an unambiguous term, which is by no means the case. CONZE, BUDDHISM, pp. 38-39 (1959).

Dr. Conze then says that if "God" is taken to mean a personal Creator of the universe, then the Buddhist has no interest in the concept. *Id.*, p. 39. But if "God" means something like the state of oneness with God as described by some Christian mystics, then the Buddhist surely believes in "God," since this state is almost indistinguishable from the Buddhist concept of Nirvana, "the supreme Reality;. . . the eternal, hidden and incomprehensible Peace." *Id.*, pp. 39-40. And finally, if "God" means one of the many Deities in an at least superficially polytheistic religion like Hinduism, then Buddhism tolerates a belief in many Gods: "the Buddhists believe that a Faith can be kept alive only if it can be adapted to the mental habits of the average person. In consequence, we find that, in the earlier Scriptures, the deities of Brahmanism are taken for granted and that, later on, the Buddhists adopted the local Gods of any district to which they came." *Id.*, p. 42.

When the present Act was adopted in 1948 we were a nation of Buddhists, Confucianists, and Taoists, as well as Christians. Hawaii, then a Territory, was indeed filled with Buddhists, Buddhism being "probably the major faith, if Protestantism and Roman Catholicism are deemed different faiths." STOKES AND PFEFFER, CHURCH AND STATE IN THE UNITED STATES, p. 560 (1964). Organized Buddhism first came to Hawaii in 1887 when Japanese laborers were brought to work on the plantations. There are now numerous Buddhist sects in Hawaii, and the temple of the Shin sect in Honolulu is said to have the largest congregation of any religious organization in the city. *See* MULHOLLAND, RELIGION IN HAWAII pp. 44-50 (1961).

In the continental United States Buddhism is found "in real strength" in Utah, Arizona, Washington, Oregon, and California. "Most of the Buddhists in the United States are Japanese or Japanese-Americans; however, there are

"English" departments in San Francisco, Los Angeles, and Tacoma." MEAD, HANDBOOK OF DENOMINATIONS, p. 61 (1961). The Buddhist Churches of North America, organized in 1914 as the Buddhist Mission of North America and incorporated under the present name in 1942, represent the Jodo Shinshu Sect of Buddhism in this country. This sect is the only Buddhist group reporting information to the annual YEARBOOK OF AMERICAN CHURCHES. In 1961, the latest year for which figures are available, this group alone had 55 churches and an inclusive membership of 60,000; it maintained 89 church schools with a total enrollment of 11,150. YEARBOOK OF AMERICAN CHURCHES, p. 30 (1965). According to one source, the total number of Buddhists of all sects in North America is 171,000. *See* WORLD ALMANAC, p. 636 (1965).

When the Congress spoke in the vague general terms of a Supreme Being I cannot, therefore, assume that it was so parochial as to use the words in the narrow sense urged on us. I would attribute tolerance and sophistication to the Congress, commensurate with the religious complexion of our communities. In sum, I agree with the Court that any person opposed to war on the basis of a sincere belief, which in his life fills the same place as a belief in God fills in the life of an orthodox religionist, is entitled to exemption under the statute. None comes to us an avowedly irreligious person or as an atheist;[2] one, as a sincere believer in "goodness and virtue for their own sakes." His questions and doubts on theological issues, and his wonder, are no more alien to the statutory standard than are the awe-inspired questions of a devout Buddhist.

WELSH v. UNITED STATES
398 U.S. 333 (1970)

MR. JUSTICE BLACK announced the judgment of the Court and delivered an opinion in which MR. JUSTICE DOUGLAS, MR. JUSTICE BRENNAN, and MR. JUSTICE MARSHALL join.

The controlling facts in this case are strikingly similar to those in *Seeger*. Both Seeger and Welsh were brought up in religious homes and attended church in their childhood, but in neither case was this church one which taught its members not to engage in war at any time for any reason. Neither Seeger nor Welsh continued his childhood religious ties into his young manhood, and neither belonged to any religious group or adhered to the teachings of any organized religion during the period of his involvement with the Selective Service System. At the time of registration for the draft, neither had yet come to accept pacifist principles. Their views on war developed only in subsequent years, but when their ideas did fully mature both made application to their local draft boards for conscientious objector exemptions from military service under § 6(j) of the Universal Military Training and Service Act.

---

[2] If he was an atheist, quite different problems would be presented. *Cf. Torcaso v. Watkins*, 367 U.S. 488.

In filling out their exemption applications both Seeger and Welsh were unable to sign the statement that, as printed in the Selective Service form, stated "I am, by reason of my religious training and belief, conscientiously opposed to participation in war in any form." Seeger could sign only after striking the words "training and" and putting quotation marks around the word "religious." Welsh could sign only after striking the words "my religious training and." On those same applications, neither could definitely affirm or deny that he believed in a "Supreme Being," both stating that they preferred to leave the question open. But both Seeger and Welsh affirmed on those applications that they held deep conscientious scruples against taking part in wars where people were killed. Both strongly believed that killing in war was wrong, unethical, and immoral, and their consciences forbade them to take part in such an evil practice. Their objection to participating in war in any form could not be said to come from a "still, small voice of conscience"; rather, for them that voice was so loud and insistent that both men preferred to go to jail rather than serve in the Armed Forces. There was never any question about the sincerity and depth of Seeger's convictions as a conscientious objector, and the same is true of Welsh. But in both cases the Selective Service System concluded that the beliefs of these men were in some sense insufficiently "religious" to qualify them for conscientious objector exemptions under the terms of § 6(j). Seeger's conscientious objector claim was denied "solely because it was not based upon a 'belief in a relation to a Supreme Being' as required by § 6 (j) of the Act," *United States v. Seeger*, 380 U.S. 163, 167 (1965), while Welsh was denied the exemption because his Appeal Board and the Department of Justice hearing officer "could find no religious basis for the registrant's beliefs, opinions and convictions." Both Seeger and Welsh subsequently refused to submit to induction into the military and both were convicted of that offense.

In resolving the question whether Seeger and the other registrants in that case qualified for the exemption, the Court stated that "[the] task is to decide whether the beliefs professed by a registrant are sincerely held and whether they are, *in his own scheme of things*, religious." The reference to the registrant's "own scheme of things" was intended to indicate that the central consideration in determining whether the registrant's beliefs are religious is whether these beliefs play the role of a religion and function as a religion in the registrant's life.

The Court made it clear that these sincere and meaningful beliefs that prompt the registrant's objection to all wars need not be confined in either source or content to traditional or parochial concepts of religion. It held that § 6(j) "does not distinguish between externally and internally derived beliefs," and also held that "intensely personal" convictions which some might find "incomprehensible" or "incorrect" come within the meaning of "religious belief" in the Act. What is necessary under *Seeger* for a registrant's conscientious objection to all war to be "religious" within the meaning of § 6(j) is that this opposition to war stem from the registrant's moral, ethical, or religious beliefs about what is right and wrong and that these beliefs be held with the strength of traditional religious convictions. Most of the great religions of today and of the past have embodied the idea of a Supreme Being or a Supreme Reality — a God — who communicates to man in some way a consciousness of what is right and should be done, of what is wrong and therefore should be shunned. If an individual deeply and sincerely holds beliefs that are purely ethical or moral in source and content but that nevertheless impose upon him a duty of conscience to refrain from participating in any war at any time, those beliefs certainly occupy in the life of that individual "a place parallel to that filled by. . . God" in traditionally religious persons. Because his beliefs function as a religion in his life, such an individual is as much entitled to a "religious" conscientious objector exemption under § 6(j) as is someone who derives his conscientious opposition to war from traditional religious convictions.

Applying this standard to Seeger himself, the Court noted the "compulsion to 'goodness'" that shaped his total opposition to war, the undisputed sincerity with which he held his views, and the fact that Seeger had "decried the tremendous 'spiritual' price man must pay for his willingness to destory human life." The Court concluded:

> "We think it clear that the beliefs which prompted his objection occupy the same place in his life as the belief in a traditional deity holds in the lives of his friends, the Quakers."

Accordingly, the Court found that Seeger should be granted conscientious objector status.

In the case before us the Government seeks to distinguish our holding in *Seeger* on basically two grounds, both of which were relied upon by the Court of Appeals in affirming Welsh's conviction. First, it is stressed that Welsh was far more insistent and explicit than Seeger in denying that his views were religious. For example, in filling out their conscientious objector applications, Seeger put quotation marks around the word "religious," but Welsh struck the word "religious" entirely and later characterized his beliefs as having been formed "by reading in the fields of history and sociology." The Court of Appeals found that Welsh had "denied that his objection to war was premised on religious belief" and concluded that "[t]he Appeal Board was entitled to take him at his word." We think this attempt to distinguish *Seeger* fails for the reason that it places undue emphasis on the registrant's interpretation of his own beliefs. The Court's statement in *Seeger* that a registrant's characterization of his own belief as "religious" should carry great weight, does not imply that his declaration that his views are nonreligious should be treated similarly. When a registrant states that his objections to war are "religious," that information is highly relevant to the question of the function his beliefs have in his life. But very few registrants are fully aware of the broad scope of the word "religious" as used in § 6(j), and accordingly a registrant's statement that his beliefs are nonreligious is a highly unreliable guide for those charged with administering the exemption. Welsh himself presents a case in point. Although he originally characterized his beliefs as nonreligious, he later upon reflection wrote a long and thoughtful letter to his

Appeal Board in which he declared that his beliefs were "certainly religious in the ethical sense of the word." He explained:

> "I believe I mentioned taking of life as not being, for me, a religious wrong. Again, I assumed Mr. [Bradey (the Department of Justice hearing officer)] was using the word "'religious" in the conventional sense, and, in order to be perfectly honest did not characterize my belief as 'religious.'"

The Government also seeks to distinguish *Seeger* on the ground that Welsh's views, unlike Seeger's, were "essentially political, sociological, or philosophical views or a merely personal moral code." As previously noted, the Government made the same argument about Seeger, and not without reason, for Seeger's views had a substantial political dimension. In this case, Welsh's conscientious objection to war was undeniably based in part on his perception of world politics. In a letter to his local board, he wrote:

> "I can only act according to what I am and what I see. And I see that the military complex wastes both human and material resources, that it fosters disregard for (what I consider a paramount concern) human needs and ends; I see that the means we employ to 'defend' our 'way of life' profoundly change that way of life. I see that in our failure to recognize the political, social, and economic realities of the world, we, *as a nation*, fail our responsibility *as a nation*."

We certainly do not think that § 6(j)'s exclusion of those persons with "essentially political, sociological, or philosophical views or a merely personal moral code" should be read to exclude those who hold strong beliefs about our domestic and foreign affairs or even those whose conscientious objection to participation in all wars is founded to a substantial extent upon considerations of public policy. The two groups of registrants that obviously do fall within these exclusions from the exemption are those whose beliefs are not deeply held and those whose objection to war does not rest at all upon moral, ethical, or religious principle but instead rests solely upon considerations of policy, pragmatism, or expediency. In applying § 6(j)'s exclusion of those whose views are "essentially political, sociological, or philosophical" or of those who have a "merely personal moral code," it should be remembered that these exclusions are definitional and do not therefore restrict the category of persons who are conscientious objectors by "religious training and belief." Once the Selective Service System has taken the first step and determined under the standards set out here and in *Seeger* that the registrant is a "religious" conscientious objector, it follows that his views cannot be "essentially political, sociological, or philosophical." Nor can they be a "merely personal moral code."

Welsh stated that he "believe[d] the taking of life — anyone's life — to be morally wrong." In his original conscientious objector application he wrote the following:

"I believe that human life is valuable in and of itself; in its living; there-fore I will not injure or kill another human being. This belief (and the corresponding "duty" to abstain from violence toward another person) is not "superior to those arising from any human relation." On the con-trary: *it is essential to every human relation.* I cannot, therefore, con-scientiously comply with the Government's insistence that I assume duties which I feel are immoral and totally repugnant." App. 10.

Welsh elaborated his beliefs in later communications with Selective Service officials. On the basis of these beliefs and the conclusion of the Court of Appeals that he held them "with the strength of more traditional religious convictions," 404 F.2d, at 1081, we think Welsh was clearly entitled to a conscientious objec-tor exemption. Section 6(j) requires no more. That section exempts from military service all those whose consciences, spurred by deeply held moral, ethical, or religious beliefs, would give them no rest or peace if they allowed themselves to become a part of an instrument of war.

The judgment is *Reversed.*

Mr. Justice White, with whom The Chief Justice and Mr. Justice Stewart join, dissenting.

I cannot hold that Congress violated the Clause in exempting from the draft all those who oppose war by reason of religious training and belief. In exempt-ing religious conscientious objectors, Congress was making one of two judg-ments, perhaps both. First, § 6(j) may represent a purely practical judgment that religious objectors, however admirable, would be of no more use in combat than many others unqualified for military service. Exemption was not extended to them to further religious belief or practice but to limit military service to those who were prepared to undertake the fighting that the armed services have to do. On this basis, the exemption has neither the primary purpose nor the effect of furthering religion. As Mr. Justice Frankfurter, joined by Mr. Justice Harlan, said in a separate opinion in the *Sunday Closing Law Cases,* 366 U.S. 420, 468 (1961), an establishment contention "can prevail only if the absence of any substantial legislative purpose other than a religious one is made to appear. *See Selective Draft Law Cases,* 245 U.S. 366."

Second, Congress may have granted the exemption because otherwise reli-gious objectors would be forced into conduct that their religions forbid and because in the view of Congress to deny the exemption would violate the Free Exercise Clause or at least raise grave problems in this respect. True, this Court has more than once stated its unwillingness to construe the First Amendment, standing alone, as requiring draft exemptions for religious believ-ers. *Hamilton v. Board of Regents,* 293 U.S. 245, 263–264 (1934); *United States v. Macintosh,* 283 U.S. 605, 623–624 (1931). But this Court is not alone in being obliged to construe the Constitution in the course of its work; nor does it even approach having a monopoly on the wisdom and insight appropriate to the task. Legislative exemptions for those with religious convictions against war date from colonial days. As Chief Justice Hughes explained in his dissent in *United States v. Macintosh, supra*, at 633, the importance of giving immunity to those having conscientious scruples against bearing arms has consistently been emphasized in debates in Congress and such draft exemptions are "indicative of the actual operation of the principles of the Constitution." However this Court might construe the First Amendment, Congress has regularly steered clear of free exercise problems by granting exemptions to those who conscientiously oppose war on religious grounds.

If there were no statutory exemption for religious objectors to war and failure to provide it was held by this Court to impair the free exercise of religion contrary to the First Amendment, an exemption reflecting this constitutional command would be no more an establishment of religion than the exemption required for Sabbatarians in *Sherbert v. Verner* [*infra* Chapter 12].

We have said that neither support nor hostility, but neutrality, is the goal of the religion clauses of the First Amendment. "Neutrality," however, is not self-defining. If it is "favoritism" and not "neutrality" to exempt religious believers from the draft, is it "neutrality" and not "inhibition" of religion to compel religious believers to fight when they have special reasons for not doing so, reasons to which the Constitution gives particular recognition? It cannot be ignored that the First Amendment itself contains a religious classification. The Amendment protects belief and speech, but as a general proposition, the free speech provisions stop short of immunizing conduct from official regulation. The Free Exercise Clause, however, has a deeper cut: it protects conduct as well as religious belief and speech. "[I]t safeguards the free exercise of the chosen form of religion. Thus the Amendment embraces two concepts — freedom to believe and freedom to act. The first is absolute but, in the nature of things, the second cannot be." *Cantwell v. Connecticut*, 310 U.S. 296, 303-304 (1940). Although socially harmful acts may as a rule be banned despite the Free Exercise Clause even where religiously motivated, there is an area of conduct that cannot be forbidden to religious practitioners but that may be forbidden to others. *See United States v. Ballard*, 322 U.S. 78 (1944); *Follett v. McCormick*, 321 U.S. 573 (1944). We should thus not labor to find a violation of the Establishment Clause when free exercise values prompt Congress to relieve religious believers from the burdens of the law at least in those instances where the law is not merely prohibitory but commands the performance of military duties that are forbidden by a man's religion.

MALNAK v. YOGI
592 F.2d 197 (3d Cir. 1979)

PER CURIAM.

This appeal requires us to decide whether the district court erred in determining that the teaching of a course called the Science of Creative Intelligence Transcendental Meditation (SCI/TM) in the New Jersey public high schools, under the circumstances presented in the record, constituted an establishment of religion in violation of the first amendment of the United States Constitution. Plaintiffs sought injunctive and declaratory relief and, after defendants had filed numerous depositions, answers to interrogatories, admissions, and other affidavits, the district court granted summary judgment in favor of plaintiffs. The court held that SCI/TM was religious activity for purposes of the establishment clause and that the teaching of SCI/TM in public schools is prohibited by the first amendment. The World Plan Executive Council United States and certain individual defendants have appealed. We affirm.

The course under examination here was offered as an elective at five high schools during the 1975-76 academic year and was taught four or five days a week by teachers specially trained by the World Plan Executive Council — United States, an organization whose objective is to disseminate the teachings of SCI/TM throughout the United States. The textbook used was developed by Maharishi Mahesh Yogi, the founder of the Science of Creative Intelligence. It teaches that "pure creative intelligence" is the basis of life, and that through the process of Transcendental Meditation students can perceive the full potential of their lives.

Essential to the practice of Transcendental Meditation is the "mantra"; a mantra is the sound aid used while meditating. Each meditator has his own personal mantra which is never to be revealed to any other person. It is by concentrating on the mantra that one receives the beneficial effects said to result from Transcendental Meditation.

To acquire his mantra, a meditator must attend a ceremony called a "puja." Every student who participated in the SCI/TM course was required to attend a puja as part of the course. A puja was performed by the teacher for each student individually; it was conducted off school premises on a Sunday; and the student was required to bring some fruit, flowers and a white handkerchief. During the puja the student stood or sat in front of a table while the teacher sang a chant and made offerings to a deified "Guru Dev." Each puja lasted between one and two hours.[2]

Puja

---

[2] For a comprehensive description of the puja, *see* 440 F. Supp. at 1305-08. The district court described the activities of a chanter at the puja ceremony:

> The chanter . . . makes fifteen offerings to Guru Dev and fourteen obeisances to Guru Dev. The chant then describes Guru Dev as a personification of "kindness" and of "the creative impulse of cosmic life," and the personification of "the essence of creation" . . . .

> The chanter then makes three more offerings to Guru Dev and three additional obeisances to Guru Dev. The chant then moves to a passage in which a string of divine epithets are applied to Guru Dev. Guru Dev is called "The Unbounded," "the omnipresent in all creation," "bliss of the Absolute," "transcendental joy," "the Self-Sufficient," "the embodiment of pure knowledge which is beyond and above the universe like the sky," "the One," "the Eternal," "the Pure," "the Immovable," "the Witness of all intellects, whose status

We agree with the district court's finding that the SCI/TM course was religious in nature. Careful examination of the textbook, the expert testimony elicited, and the uncontested facts concerning the puja convince us that religious activity was involved and that there was no reversible error in the district court's determination.

ADAMS, CIRCUIT JUDGE, concurring in the result.

I concur in the judgment of the Court that the teaching of a course in the Science of Creative Intelligence, which was offered as an elective in certain New Jersey public schools, and was funded, in part, by a grant from a federal agency, constitutes an establishment of religion proscribed by the first amendment. In contrast to the majority, however, I am convinced that this appeal presents a novel and important question that may not be disposed of simply on the basis of past precedent. Rather, as I see it, the result reached today is largely based upon a newer, more expansive reading of "religion" that has been developed in the last two decades in the context of free exercise and selective service cases but not, until today, applied by an appellate court to invalidate a government program under the establishment clause. Moreover, this is the first appellate court decision, to my knowledge, that has concluded that a set of ideas constitutes a religion over the objection and protestations of secularity by those espousing those ideas. Under these circumstances, and recalling Justice Frankfurter's admonition that an individual expression of opinion is useful when the way a result is reached may be important to results hereafter to be reached, I am impelled to state my views separately.

I. EXISTING PRECEDENT

The district court, while conceding that the decisions of the Supreme Court have avoided the creation of explicit criteria in determining what is a religion under the first amendment, nonetheless bases its result on those very decisions:

---

transcends thought," "the Transcendent along with the three gunas," and "the true preceptor." Manifestly, no one would apply all these epithets to a human being.

440 F. Supp. at 1308 (footnote omitted).

The district court concluded:

[T]he puja is sung at the direction of Maharishi Mahesh Yogi, a Hindu monk. The words and offerings of the chant invoke the deified teacher, who also was a Hindu monk, of Maharishi Mahesh Yogi. In the chant, this teacher is linked to names known as Hindu deities. Maharishi Mahesh Yogi places such great emphasis on the singing of this chant prior to the imparting of a mantra to each individual student that no mantras are given except at pujas and no one is allowed to teach the Science of Creative Intelligence/Transcendental Meditation unless he or she performed the puja to the personal satisfaction of Maharishi Mahesh Yogi or one of his aides. . . . Needless to say, neither Hinduism nor belief in "the Lord" constitute a dead religion. Both of these beliefs are held by hundreds of millions of people.

440 F. Supp. at 1311-12.

> The [district] court finds it unnecessary to improvise an unprecedented definition of religion under the first amendment because it appears that this case is governed by the teachings of prior Supreme Court decisions. Careful inspection of the facts in this suit reveal that the novel aspects of the case are more apparent than real.

It is my view that the teachings of those cases cited by the district court do indeed suggest the result reached by that court and affirmed today. But, as Judge Meanor's opinion amply illustrates, those opinions involve substantially different facts and problems than are presented here. And although the application of such cases to the factual situation here may be warranted, such an application is an extension of existing case law, and thus calls for both an explanation and a justification.

For purposes of the issues posed by this controversy, the arguably relevant decisional law may be divided into four principal groupings: cases announcing the traditional definition of religion, cases dealing with prayers recited in school, cases involving the conscientious objector exemption to the selective service laws, and cases touching on the newer constitutional definition of religion. Although the district court, and apparently the majority of this Court, consider these decisions to be controlling on the question raised here, careful reflection reveals as many differences as similarities.

A. *The Traditional Definition of Religion*

The original definition of religion prevalent in this country was closely tied to a belief in God. James Madison called religion "the duty which we owe to our creator, and the manner of discharging it." Basically, this was the position of the Supreme Court at the end of the nineteenth century. In *Davis v. Beason*, 133 U.S. 333 (1890), the Court declared:

> [T]he term "religion" has reference to one's views of his relations to his Creator, and to the obligations they impose of reverence for his being and character, and of obedience to his will.

This attitude remained unchallenged for many years. Chief Justice Hughes, writing a dissent in 1931, could conclude without concern that

> [t]he essence of religion is belief in a relation to God involving duties superior to those arising from any human relation.[6]

Thus, the traditional definition was grounded upon a Theistic perception of religion. It is not clear, however, given the absence of any concentration in SCI/TM on a "Supreme Being," that it may be considered a religion under this traditional formulation.

---

[6] *United States v. Macintosh*, 283 U.S. 605, 633-34 (1931) (Hughes, C.J., dissenting).

B. *The School Prayer Cases*

Facially, the Supreme Court decisions arguably most pertinent to this case are those involving school prayer. This is so, as I read the opinions of the district court and the majority of this Court, because an integral part of the preparation of the students for the practice of TM is the performance in Sanskrit of a chant called the Puja. Accordingly, we are urged to engage in a "textual analysis" of the Puja, and then to compare that analysis to the prayers outlawed in the school prayer cases. In that the English translation of the Puja sounds at least as "religious" as the New York Regents prayer invalidated in *Engel v. Vitale,* for instance, it is suggested that this case may be properly disposed of under that rubric.

I am not convinced, however, that the school prayer opinions provide particularly persuasive precedents for the resolution of the question presented here.[7] *Engel* concerned a prayer composed by the New York Board of Regents that had to be said aloud in every public school classroom by order of the local board of education, acting in its official capacity under state law. Students could be excused from attendance in a classroom where the prayer was said, but they needed the written request of a parent or guardian, and, of course, would have to take the initiative, and possible social consequences, if they chose to leave their classrooms during the recital of the prayer. That the prayer itself was religious in nature was not questioned. Indeed, it was specifically recommended by the Regents as an aid in "spiritual training" in the schools.

Similar to *Engel* is *Abington School District v. Schempp.* There, the Court invalidated a Pennsylvania statute that required the reading of at least ten verses of the Bible, without comment, at the opening of each school day. As in *Engel,* participation was voluntary in the sense that a child could be excused from the exercise, although Mr. Schempp had declined to have his children excused because he feared they would suffer social ostracism by their teachers and classmates. That the reading of the verses of the Bible was religious in nature does not seem to have been questioned by any of the parties or Justices who heard the appeal, although it was argued that a secular as well as a religious purpose was served by the readings.

The constitutional problems in *Engel* and *Schempp* are relatively straightforward. First, it is clear that the State, through the edict of a state agency or

---

[7] Nor am I persuaded that "textual analysis" — the comparison of wording of alleged prayers — is a meaningful way to scrutinize establishment clause cases. The actual wording of a school exercise, for example, may be far less important than its context and purpose. A textual analysis might well invalidate the pledge of allegiance, the singing of "America the Beautiful," or the performance of certain works from Handel or Bach by a school glee club. Yet, such activities have not been held to violate the establishment clause, even though they include references to God or a Supreme Being, because they are undertaken for patriotic, cultural or other secular reasons, and neither have, nor are intended to have, a religious effect on those participating in or witnessing them. These exercises, in other words, are not "prayers" within the meaning of *Engel* or *Schempp.*

by statute, may not seek to require that school districts engage in a particular form of obviously religious activity. Such religious partisanship, even though nonsectarian, is forbidden by the establishment clause. Second, the general nature of the activities raised serious free exercise questions because they were "voluntary" only in form, not in practice. In order to avoid the official exercises, individual students had to take specific steps that were almost certain to draw attention to them, attention that was unlikely to be desirable, given the majority orientation of the religious practices. In neither case was the "wording" of the exercises of particular importance in resolving the constitutional problem.

Lower court decisions deflecting efforts to introduce prayers into public schools have expanded the teachings of *Engel* and *Schempp* to reach almost any prayer recited as such on school grounds, but none has sought to label as "religious" that which was presented as "nonreligious."

In contrast, appellants here unwaveringly insist that the Puja chant has no religious meaning whatsoever and is, in fact, a "secular Puja," quite common in Eastern cultures. And, even if we reject this claim, we are still substantially removed from the facts of *Engel* and *Schempp*: (a) the Puja was never performed in a school classroom, or even on government property; (b) it was never performed during school hours, but only on a Sunday; (c) it was performed only once in the case of each student; (d) it was entirely in Sanskrit, with neither the student nor, apparently, the teacher who chanted it, knowing what the foreign words meant.

Moreover, the elements of involuntariness present in *Engel* and *Schempp* are wholly absent here. The SCI/TM course was an elective. No student in this case had to abandon his home classroom at the start of each school day or in any way risk notoriety for conscience sake. Only those students who sought a course in SCI/TM had any contact with the chant; they were specifically told that the chant had no religious meaning; and they stated in affidavits that they did not understand it to have such meaning.

Most important for our purposes, however a court might resolve a challenge to the Puja under the school prayer cases, those cases provide few insights regarding the constitutional definition of religion. Both the prayer in *Engel* and the Bible readings in *Schempp* are unquestionably and uncompromisingly Theist. Even under the most narrow and traditional definition of religion, prayers to a Supreme Being and readings from the Bible would be considered "religious." But the important question presented by the present litigation is how far the constitutional definition of religion extends beyond the Theistic formulation; that it comprehends all Theistic faiths has, to my knowledge, not been questioned. The school prayer cases, then, cannot be said to control, or, it would seem, even to address the question whether a particular belief-system should be considered a religion for first amendment purposes.

C. The Conscientious Objector Cases

In contradistinction to the school prayer cases, *United States v. Seeger* and *Welsh v. United States*, the leading selective service decisions bespeak a broader definition of religion. *Seeger* and *Welsh*, of course, are not constitutional cases but rather concern the proper interpretation of section 6(j) of the Universal Military Service and Training Act. This provision allowed for conscientious objector status for those who, "by reason of religious training and belief," were "opposed to participation in war in any form." The statute went on to define "religious training or belief" in Theistic terms.

The Supreme Court, in what has been characterized as "a remarkable feat of linguistic transmutation," recast the language of section 6(j) in order to give the exemption a much broader scope. Thus Seeger was granted C.O. status notwithstanding his refusal to affirm his faith in a Supreme Being because the Court concluded that "religious training and belief" encompass non- Theist faiths provided that they are "sincere religious beliefs which [are] based upon a power or being, or upon a faith, to which all else is subordinate or upon which all else is ultimately dependent." Welsh was similarly favored despite his assertion of only "moral" opposition to war, but in his case the Court was sharply divided.

Although *Seeger* and *Welsh* turned on statutory interpretation, and despite some indication that the Court has, to some degree, drawn back from the broadest possible reading of these cases, they remain constitutionally significant. As a matter of logic and language, if the Court is willing to read "religious belief" so as to comprehend beliefs based upon pantheistic and ethical views, it might be presumed to favor a similar inclusive definition of "religion" as that term appears in the first amendment. Such logical conclusion has considerably more force when one considers the varying contexts of the language in question. As the district judge perceptively observed: "the Court defined the phrase broadly in an exercise of statutory construction, an area in which the Court is far more circumscribed in defining terms than it is in the area of constitutional interpretation." It can hardly be denied that the Supreme Court's reading of the statutory language was strained at best. The Court's willingness to depart so drastically from the plain language of a statute in order to produce an expansive definition almost certainly unintended by Congress, implies, as Justice Harlan observed in *Welsh*, a "distortion to avert an inevitable constitutional collision."

Most importantly, the constitutional values prompting such a statutory construction can only be taken to suggest a broad definition of religion. Only four Justices explicitly discussed their constitutional concerns in *Welsh*. Justice Harlan was forthright in stating the problem:

> The constitutional question that must be faced in this case is whether a statute that defers to the individual's conscience only when his views emanate from adherence to theistic religious beliefs is within the power of Congress. Congress,. . . having chosen to exempt,. . . cannot draw the

line between theistic or non-theistic religious beliefs on the one hand and secular beliefs on the other. Any such distinctions are not, in my view, compatible with the Establishment Clause of the First Amendment.

Justice Harlan found § 6(j) constitutionally deficient for two reasons. First, the subsection appeared to prefer the religious over the secular. Second, despite what the Court had said in *Seeger*, Justice Harlan also argued that on its face the statute favored Theistic religions over non-Theistic beliefs and, therefore, "disadvantages adherents of religions that do not worship a Supreme Being." Thus Justice Harlan explicitly recognized as "religions" various non-Theistic belief systems.

The three dissenters, speaking through Justice White, were unprepared to extend § 6(j) to those professing no more than a philosophical or moral view. To Justice Harlan's assertion that such a result favors the religious over the secular, they replied that this was permissible as an accommodation of free exercise clause values. They dissented, then, because they were willing to read this accommodation as extending only to those with genuinely religious views, whether Theistic or non-Theistic and not to those with purely secular ideas to whom the free exercise clause offered "no protection whatsoever." Justice White's implicit definition of religion, therefore, included non-Theists but excluded economic, philosophical or merely personal opinions, however sincerely held.

In sum, then, all four Justices who addressed the constitutional issue concluded that "religion" should not be confined to a Theistic definition. Although four other Justices rested on statutory grounds and no exact definition was forthcoming in any event, *Seeger* and *Welsh* point to a definition at least somewhat broader than that advanced in the earlier decisions of the Supreme Court.

D. *Cases Suggesting a New Constitutional Definition*

Seeger and *Welsh*, however, are not the only cases presaging a broader reading of "religion" for first amendment purposes. The district court notes other cases more directly on point in that they concern constitutional, not statutory challenges.

The most important of these, and the only Supreme Court cases among them, is *Torcaso v. Watkins*. *Torcaso* involved a direct constitutional challenge to a Maryland provision that required an official to declare a belief in God in order to hold office in that state. A unanimous Court rejected this requirement, both as a matter of establishment clause values (the state may not favor Theism over pantheism or atheism) and free exercise clause values (an individual may not be barred from holding public office on the basis of his beliefs). In striking down the Maryland law, the Court specifically observed that neither the state nor the federal government "can aid those religions based on a belief in the existence of God as against those religions founded on different beliefs." The Court then added an instructive footnote:

Among religions in this country which do not teach what would generally be considered a belief in the existence of God are Buddhism, Taoism, Ethical Culture, Secular Humanism and others. *See Washington Ethical Society v. District of Columbia,* 101 U.S. App. D.C. 371, 249 F.2d 127; *Fellowship of Humanity v. County of Alameda*, 153 Cal. App. 2d 673, 315 P.2d 394; II ENCYCLOPAEDIA OF THE SOCIAL SCIENCES 293; 4 ENCYCLOPAEDIA BRITANNICA (1957 ed.) 325-327; 21 *id.*, at 797; ARCHER, FAITHS MEN LIVE BY (2d ed. revised by Purinton), 120-138, 254-313; 1961 WORLD ALMANAC 695, 712; YEAR BOOK OF AMERICAN CHURCHES FOR 1961, at 29, 47.

This note, although dictum, represents a rejection of the view that religion may, consonant with first amendment values, be defined solely in terms of a Supreme Being. Buddhism and Taoism are, of course, recognized Eastern religions. The other two examples given by the Court refer to explicitly non-Theist organized groups, discussed in cases cited in the footnote, that were found to be religious for tax exemption purposes primarily because of their organizational similarity to traditional American church groups. "Ethical Culture" is a reference to the organization in *Washington Ethical Society v. District of Columbia*, 101 U.S. App. D.C. 371, 249 F.2d 127 (1957), which held regular Sunday services and espoused a group of defined moral precepts. Similarly, "Secular Humanism," however broad the term may sound, appears to be no more than a reference to the group seeking an exemption in *Fellowship of Humanity v. County of Alameda*, 153 Cal. App. 2d 673, 315 P.2d 394 (1957), which, although non-Theist in belief, also met weekly on Sundays and functioned much like a church. In any event, the Court was willing to concede that these groups, "and others," were religious for constitutional purposes.

The broad reading of "religion" in *Torcaso* was drawn upon in *Founding Church of Scientology v. United States*, 133 U.S. App. D.C. 229, 409 F.2d 1146, *cert. denied*, 396 U.S. 963 (1969). There, Scientology, a belief system providing a "general account of man and his nature comparable in scope, if not in content, to those of some organized religions," was found to be a religion for purposes of the free exercise clause. Judge Wright was willing to accept, as religious, ideas that are sufficiently comprehensive to be comparable to traditional religions in terms of content and subject matter. But it must be added that he did so only after observing that the government did not contest Scientology's religious nature, or rebut the prima facie case for religious classification made by its supporters.

It would thus appear that the constitutional cases that have actually alluded to the definitional problem, like the selective service cases, strongly support a definition for religion broader than the Theistic formulation of the earlier Supreme Court cases. What this definition is, or should be, has not yet been made entirely clear.

II. THE MODERN DEFINITION OF RELIGION

It seems unavoidable, from *Seeger, Welsh*, and *Torcaso*, that the Theistic formulation presumed to be applicable in the late nineteenth century cases is no longer sustainable. Under the modern view, "religion" is not confined to the relationship of man with his Creator, either as a matter of law or as a matter of theology. Even theologians of traditionally recognized faiths have moved away from a strictly Theistic approach in explaining their own religions. Such movement, when coupled with the growth in the United States of many Eastern and non-traditional belief systems, suggests that the older, limited definition would deny "religious" identification to faiths now adhered to by millions of Americans. The Court's more recent cases reject such a result.

If the old definition has been repudiated, however, the new definition remains not yet fully formed. It would appear to be properly described as a definition by analogy. The *Seeger* court advertently declined to distinguish beliefs holding "parallel positions in the lives of their respective holders." Presumably beliefs holding the same important position for members of one of the new religions as the traditional faith holds for more orthodox believers are entitled to the same treatment as the traditional beliefs. The tax exemption cases referred to in *Torcaso* also rely primarily on the common elements present in the new challenged groups, the Ethical Society and the Fellowship of Humanity, as well as in the older unchallenged groups and churches. In like fashion, Judge Wright reasoned by analogy in crediting the prima facie claim made out for Scientology in *Founding Church of Scientology, supra*.[33] The modern approach thus looks to the familiar religions as models in order to ascertain, by comparison, whether the new set of ideas or beliefs is confronting the same concerns, or serving the same purposes, as unquestioned and accepted "religions."

But it is one thing to conclude "by analogy" that a particular group or cluster of ideas is religious; it is quite another to explain exactly what indicia are to be looked to in making such an analogy and justifying it. There appear to be three useful indicia that are basic to our traditional religions and that are themselves related to the values that undergird the first amendment.

---

[33] . . .[I]s Scientology a religion? On the record as a whole, we find that appellants have made out a *prima facie* case that the Founding Church of Scientology is a religion.

It is incorporated as such in the District of Columbia. It has ministers, who are licensed as such, with legal authority to marry and to bury. Its fundamental writings contain a general account of man and his nature comparable in scope, if not in content, to those of some recognized religions. The fact that it postulates no diety in the conventional sense does not preclude its status as a religion. The Government might have chosen to contest the claim that the Founding Church was in fact a religion. Not every enterprise cloaking itself in the name of religion can claim the constitutional protection conferred by that status. It might be possible to show that a self-proclaimed religion was merely a commercial enterprise, without the underlying theories of man's nature or his place in the Universe which characterize recognized religions.

409 F.2d at 1160. (citations omitted).

The first and most important of these indicia is the nature of the ideas in question. This means that a court must, at least to a degree, examine the content of the supposed religion, not to determine its truth or falsity, or whether it is schismatic or orthodox, but to determine whether the subject matter it comprehends is consistent with the assertion that it is, or is not, a religion. Thus the court was able to remark in *Founding Church of Scientology*:

> It might be possible to show that a self-proclaimed religion was merely a commercial enterprise, *without the underlying theories of man's nature or his place in the Universe which characterize recognized religions.*

Similarly, one of the conscientious objectors whose appeal was coupled with *Seeger*, submitted a long memorandum, noted by the Court, in which he defined religion as the *"Sum and essence of one's basic attitudes to the fundamental problems of human existence."*

Expectation that religious ideas should address fundamental questions is in some ways comparable to the reasoning of the Protestant theologian Dr. Paul Tillich, who expressed his view on the essence of religion in the phrase "ultimate concern." Tillich perceived religion as intimately connected to concepts that are of the greatest depth and utmost importance. His thoughts have been influential both with courts and commentators. Nor is it difficult to see why this philosophy would prove attractive in the American constitutional framework. One's views, be they orthodox or novel, on the deeper and more imponderable questions — the meaning of life and death, man's role in the Universe, the proper moral code of right and wrong — are those likely to be the most "intensely personal" and important to the believer. They are his ultimate concerns. As such, they are to be carefully guarded from governmental interference, and never converted into official government doctrine. The first amendment demonstrates a specific solicitude for religion because religious ideas are in many ways more important than other ideas. New and different ways of meeting those concerns are entitled to the same sort of treatment as the traditional forms.

Thus, the "ultimate" nature of the ideas presented is the most important and convincing evidence that they should be treated as religious. Certain isolated answers to "ultimate" questions, however, are not necessarily "religious" answers, because they lack the element of comprehensiveness, the second of the three indicia. A religion is not generally confined to one question or one moral teaching; it has a broader scope. It lays claim to an ultimate and comprehensive "truth." Thus the so-called "Big Bang" theory, an astronomical interpretation of the creation of the universe, may be said to answer an "ultimate" question, but it is not, by itself, a "religious" idea. Likewise, moral or patriotic views are not by themselves "religious," but if they are pressed as divine law or a part of a comprehensive belief-system that presents them as "truth," they might well rise to the religious level.

The component of comprehensiveness is particularly relevant in the context of state education. A science course may touch on many ultimate concerns,[41] but it is unlikely to proffer a systematic series of answers to them that might begin to resemble a religion. St. Thomas Aquinas once defined theology by asserting, ". . . this science commands all the other sciences as the ruling science. . . . This science uses for its service all the other sciences, as though its vassals. . . ." The teaching of isolated theories that might be thought to address "ultimate" questions is not the teaching of such a "ruling science." When these theories are combined into a comprehensive belief system, however, the result may well become such a "ruling science" that overflows into other academic disciplines as the guiding idea of the student's pursuits. It is just such a "ruling science" that the establishment clause guards against.

A third element to consider in ascertaining whether a set of ideas should be classified as a religion is any formal, external, or surface signs that may be analogized to accepted religions. Such signs might include formal services, ceremonial functions, the existence of clergy, structure and organization, efforts at propagation, observation of holidays and other similar manifestations associated with the traditional religions. Of course, a religion may exist without any of these signs, so they are not determinative, at least by their absence, in resolving a question of definition. But they can be helpful in supporting a conclusion of religious status given the important role such ceremonies play in religious life. These formal signs of religion were found to be persuasive proofs of religious character for tax exemption purposes in *Washington Ethical Society and Fellowship of Humanity,* discussed *supra.* They are noted as well in *Founding Church of Scientology supra.* Thus, even if it is true that a religion can exist without rituals and structure, they may nonetheless be useful signs that a group or belief system is religious.

Although these indicia will be helpful, they should not be thought of as a final "test" for religion. Defining religion is a sensitive and important legal duty. Flexibility and careful consideration of each belief system are needed. Still, it is important to have some objective guidelines in order to avoid *ad hoc* justice.

Before applying these guidelines to SCI/TM, however, a separate question must first be examined. Even conceding the propriety of the modern approach in certain contexts, the Court is urged to adopt the position that a less expansive definition is required in establishment clause cases. The broader definition has up until now been exclusively applied in response to free exercise clause values. Appellants contend that such broader definition is inappropriate in the context of the establishment clause.

---

[41]It is a widespread practice in high school biology courses, for instance, to include discussion of Darwin's theory of evolution. This theory is offensive to some religious groups, but it is not in itself religious. For a thoughtful discussion of this problem, *see* Note, *Freedom of Religion and Science Instruction in Public Schools,* 87 YALE L.J. 515 (1978).

III. A UNITARY DEFINITION FOR BOTH RELIGION CLAUSES

There has been considerable speculation whether the broader definition of religion developed in the free exercise cases should be applied under the establishment clause. Professor Tribe of Harvard has advanced the argument that the free exercise clause should be read broadly to include anything "arguably religious," but that the establishment clause should not be construed to encompass anything "arguably non-religious." In so doing, he has summarized the position of those favoring a dual definition:

Clearly, the notion of religion in the free exercise clause must be expanded beyond the closely bounded limits of theism to account for the multiplying forms of recognizably legitimate religious exercise. It is equally clear, however, that in the age of the affirmative and increasingly pervasive state, a less expansive notion of religion was required for establishment clause purposes lest all "humane" programs of government be deemed constitutionally suspect. Such a twofold definition of religion, expansive for the free exercise clause, less so for the establishment clause, may be necessary to avoid confronting the state with increasingly difficult choices that the theory of permissible accommodation. . . could not indefinitely resolve.[46]

Another commentator has come to the same conclusion, apparently for the same underlying reasons:

To borrow the ultimate concern test from the free exercise context and use it with present establishment clause doctrines would be to invite attack on all programs that further the ultimate concerns of individuals or entangle the government with such concerns. Doctrinal chaos might well result, and with it might come the wholesale invalidation of

---

[46]L. TRIBE, AMERICAN CONSTITUTIONAL LAW 827-28 (1978). Tribe's principal example is particularly relevant to the question presented here:

Consider, for example, the curious lawsuit in *Malnak v. Maharishi Mahesh Yogi*, where plaintiffs contend that the New Jersey school system is violating the establishment clause by allowing licensed teachers to use public school facilities to teach Transcendental Meditation (TM) as an elective course. The TM course trains students in a method or process of meditation. For some, it is a religion; but for thousands of people throughout the country it is a mental exercise, often engaged in by enthusiastic adherents of such formal religions as Christianity, Judaism, and Mohammedanism. Clearly, TM should be deemed a religion for purposes of the free exercise clause: if the government sought to forbid it as an activity, the free exercise clause would stand in the way. But if the same definition of religion were adopted for the establishment clause, offering the course proposed in *Malnak* would be unconstitutional even though many plausibly regard it as no more "religious" than courses in methods of concentration or body control. Are the teaching of psychology or of self-hypnosis forbidden by the establishment clause?

Id. Professor Tribe wrote before the facts of this case had been developed. He views the course as one in TM, not SCI/TM. Whether he would consider this particular SCI/TM course to be "arguably non-religious" is not entirely clear from the above. In any event, the teaching of this course is readily distinguishable from instruction in psychology or self- hypnosis.

programs which, if analyzed in light of the values underlying the establishment clause, would be found benign.

This view is not without other academic and some judicial support, and appellants here urge upon us a modified version of it.

Despite the distinguished scholars who advocate this approach, a stronger argument can be made for a unitary definition to prevail for both clauses. This would seem to be the preferable choice for several reasons. First, it is virtually required by the language of the first amendment. As Justice Rutledge put it over thirty years ago:

> "Religion" appears only once in the Amendment. But the word governs two prohibitions and governs them alike. It does not have two meanings, one narrow to forbid "an establishment" and another, much broader, for securing "the free exercise thereof." "Thereof" brings down "religion" with its entire and exact content, no more and no less, from the first into the second guaranty, so that Congress and now the states are as broadly restricted concerning the one as they are regarding the other.

Although the Constitution has often been subject to a broad construction, it remains a written document. It is difficult to justify a reading of the first amendment so as to support a dual definition of religion, nor has our attention been drawn to any support for such a view in the conventional sources that have been thought to reveal the intention of the framers. Moreover, the policy reasons put forward by the supporters of a dual definition, in my view at least, are unpersuasive.

The advocates of a dual definition appear to be motivated primarily by an anxiety that too extensive a definition under the establishment clause will lead to "wholesale invalidation" of government programs. Behind this fear lurks, I believe, too broad a reading of the teachings of *Seeger, Welsh*, and *Torcaso*. The selective service case did not hold that Seeger, Welsh and the other conscientious objectors were advancing views sufficient to qualify as a religion or religions, only that their views were based on religious belief. Were a school, or government agency, to advance the cause of peace, or opposition to war, such an official position would not qualify as a "religion" even though some citizens might come to adopt that very view because of their own religious beliefs. All programs or positions that entangle the government with issues and problems that might be classified as "ultimate concerns" do not, because of that, become "religious" programs or positions. Only if the government favors a comprehensive belief system and advances its teachings does it establish a religion. It does not do so by endorsing isolated moral precepts or by enacting humanitarian economic programs.

In this regard it should be noted that the modern definition of religion does not extend so far as to include those who hold beliefs however passionately regarding the utility of Keynesian economics, Social Democracy or, for that matter, Sociobiology. These ideas may in some instances touch on "ultimate concerns," but they are less analogous to religious views than they are to the political or sociological ideas that they are. Thus *Torcaso* does not stand for the proposition that "humanism" is a religion, although an organized group of "Secular Humanists" may be. An undefined belief in humanitarianism, or good intentions, is still far removed from a comprehensive belief system laying a claim to ultimate truth and supported by a formal group with religious trappings.[52]

Moreover, the establishment clause does not forbid government activity encouraged by the supporters of even the most orthodox of religions if that activity is itself not unconstitutional. The Biblical and clerical endorsement of laws against stealing and murder do not make such laws establishments of religion. Similarly, agitation for social welfare programs by progressive churchmen, even if motivated by the most orthodox of theological reasons, does not make those programs religious. The Constitution has not been interpreted to forbid those inspired by religious principle or conscience from participation in this nation's political, social and economic life.

Finally, in addition to these doubts whether "doctrinal chaos" would in fact result from resort to the new definition in the establishment clause context, the practical result of a dual definition is itself troubling. Such an approach would create a three-tiered system of ideas: those that are unquestionably religious and thus both free from government interference and barred from receiving government support; those that are unquestionably non-religious and thus subject to government regulation and eligible to receive government support; and those that are only religious under the newer approach and thus free from governmental regulation but open to receipt of government support. That belief systems classified in the third grouping are the most advantageously positioned is obvious. No reason has been advanced, however, for favoring the newer belief systems over the older ones. If a Roman Catholic is barred from receiving aid from the government, so too should be a Transcendental Meditator or a Scientologist if those two are to enjoy the preferred position guaranteed to them by the free exercise clause. It may be, of course, that they are not entitled to such a preferred position, but they are clearly not entitled to the advantages given by the first amendment while avoiding the apparent disadvantages. The rose cannot be had without the thorn.

For these reasons, then, I think it is correct to read religion broadly in both clauses and agree that the precedents developed in the free exercise context are properly relied upon here. Having reached this conclusion, two final questions remain: Does SCI/TM qualify as a religion under the criteria discussed above and, if it does, does the teaching and funding of this course constitute an establishment of that religion?

---

[52]The reference to "Secular Humanism" in the *Torcaso* footnote appears to be to just such a group. *See Fellowship of Humanity, supra.* A more difficult question would be presented by government propagation of doctrinaire Marxism, either in the schools or elsewhere. Under certain circumstances Marxism might be classifiable as a religion and an establishment thereof could result.

IV. SCI/TM AS A RELIGION

Although Transcendental Meditation by itself might be defended as appellants sought to do in this appeal as primarily a relaxation or concentration technique with no "ultimate" significance, the New Jersey course at issue here was not a course in TM alone, but a course in the Science of Creative Intelligence. Creative Intelligence, according to the textbook in the record, is "at the basis of all growth and progress" and is, indeed, "the basis of everything." Transcendental Meditation is presented as a means for contacting this "impelling life force" so as to achieve "inner contentment." Creative Intelligence can provide such "contentment" because it is "a field of unlimited happiness," which is at work everywhere and visible in such diverse places as in "the changing of the seasons" and "the wings of a butterfly." That the existence of such a pervasive and fundamental life force is a matter of "ultimate concern" can hardly be questioned. It is put forth as the foundation of life and the world itself.

The Science of Creative Intelligence provides answers to questions concerning the nature both of world and man, the underlying sustaining force of the universe, and the way to unlimited happiness. Although it is not as comprehensive as some religions — for example, it does not appear to include a complete or absolute moral code — it is nonetheless sufficiently comprehensive to avoid the suggestion of an isolated theory unconnected with any particular world view or basic belief system. SCI/TM provides a way — indeed in the eyes of its adherents *the way* — to full self realization and oneness with the underlying reality of the universe. Consequently, it can reasonably be understood as presenting a claim of ultimate "truth."

This conclusion is supported by the formal observances and structure of SCI/TM. Although there is no evidence in the record of organized clergy or traditional rites, such as marriage, burial or the like, there are trained teachers and an organization devoted to the propagation of the faith. And there is a ceremony, the Puja, that is intimately associated with the transmission of the mantra. The mantra is a word communicated privately to each newly-inducted practitioner, which is said to be vital to transcendental meditation and access to the field of unlimited happiness.

SCI/TM is not a Theistic religion, but it is nonetheless a constitutionally protected religion. It concerns itself with the same search for ultimate truth as other religions and seeks to offer a comprehensive and critically important answer to the questions and doubts that haunt modern man. That those who espouse these views and engage in the Puja, or meditate in the hope of reaching the transcendental reality of creative intelligence, would be entitled to the protection of the free exercise clause if threatened by governmental interference or regulation is clear. They are thus similarly subject, in my view, to the constraints of the establishment clause. When the government seeks to encourage this version of ultimate truth, and not others, an establishment clause problem arises.

V. THE NEW JERSEY SCI/TM COURSE AS AN ESTABLISHMENT OF RELIGION

Like the majority, I am convinced that the conclusion that SCI/TM is a religion is largely determinative of this appeal. There is nothing *per se* unconstitutional about offering a course in religion or religious writings. This was made clear by the Court in *Schempp* :

> It certainly may be said that the Bible is worthy of study for its literary and historic qualities. Nothing we have said here indicates that such study of the Bible or of religion, when presented objectively as part of a secular program of education, may not be affected consistently with the First Amendment.

A realistic appraisal of the course at issue here, however, demonstrates no such objective secular program.

In applying the three-prong *Nyquist* test for determining whether a particular program abridges the establishment clause, the district court credited the government with pursuing a secular purpose of sorts, but held that the means employed in pursuing this goal were forbidden by that clause:

> Owing to the religious nature of the concept of the field of pure creative intelligence. . ., it is apparent that the governmental agencies have sought to effect a secular goal by the propagation of a religious concept, a belief in an unmanifest field of life, which is perfect, pure, and infinite. . . . These means of effecting ostensibly secular ends are prohibited by the establishment clause.

I am in agreement with this conclusion, but entertain some doubt as to the secularity of purpose here. No federal or state agency has taken an appeal from the judgment of the district court, so we have not had the benefit of enlightenment as to what possible secular purpose was served by the decisions of the New Jersey educational authorities and the expenditure of federal tax dollars. Although a secular purpose, however unlikely, is usually conceded in establishment clause cases, there is some question whether one can be found in the record here. A careful review of the transcript, and the content of the course, reveals nothing other than an effort to propagate TM, SCI, and the views of Maharishi Mahesh Yogi. As the district court indicated, the government may have thought some "good" would come out of this instruction, but it is quite possible that some good would come out of instruction in the Protestant, Roman Catholic, Jewish or Islamic faiths. A conviction that religious education is "good" for students does not make out a secular purpose.

Religious observation and instruction in public schools may be sustainable if ideas are taught in an objective fashion, or if the overall impact of the religious observance is *de minimis*. Neither was true here. Once SCI/TM is found to be a religion, the establishment resulting from direct government support of that religion through the propagation of its religious ideas in the public school system is clear.

Although federal courts should be reluctant to interfere in the judgments of educational authorities on questions of what subject matter should be taught in the schools, our constitutional duty to guard against state efforts to promote religion may not be set aside out of deference to the policy choices of other officials. Whatever its merits, the program under consideration here, endorsed, as it is, by the State of New Jersey and the Department of Health, Education and Welfare, is forbidden by the first amendment. As such, it cannot stand.

AFRICA v. PENNSYLVANIA
662 F.2d 1025 (3d Cir. 1981)

ADAMS, CIRCUIT JUDGE.

Frank Africa, who claims to be a "Naturalist Minister" for the MOVE organization and who is a prisoner of the Commonwealth of Pennsylvania, appeals from a district court judgment holding that the state government is not required, under the religion clauses of the first amendment, to provide him with a special diet consisting entirely of raw foods. He maintains that to eat anything other than raw foods would be a violation of his "religion." After a careful consideration of the record in this case, we affirm.

I.

On July 15, 1981, Frank Africa was convicted of various state offenses by a Pennsylvania court and was sentenced to serve a term of up to seven years at the State Correctional Institution at Graterford, Pennsylvania. Prior to his sentence, Africa had been incarcerated in Holmesburg Prison, a facility under the jurisdiction of Philadelphia County. While at Holmesburg, Africa requested and received a special diet of uncooked vegetables and fruits.

Africa filed a motion for a temporary restraining order in federal district court on July 16, 1981, seeking an order either that he remain in Holmesburg for the duration of his sentence or that Graterford, upon his transfer there, be required to provide him with his dietary needs. In his pleading for relief, Africa averred that, as a Naturalist Minister for MOVE, "I eat an all raw food diet in accordance with my Religious principle. To eat anything else. . . would be a direct violation of my Religion and I will not violate my Religion for anyone." Africa's motion was assigned to Judge Hannum, who classified the matter as a civil rights action under 42 U.S.C. § 1983.

State authorities transferred Africa from Holmesburg to Graterford on July 17, 1981. Later that same day, at Judge Hannum's request, the Common Pleas Court of Philadelphia entered an order directing that Africa be returned to Holmesburg pending resolution of his request for injunctive relief. Pursuant to that order, Africa was sent back to Holmesburg on July 20 and his special diet was restored.

On July 27, 1981, the district court conducted a hearing on Africa's motion, which was treated as an application for a permanent injunction, and received testimony from Africa himself, Ramona Johnson, a "supporter" of MOVE, and Julius T. Cuyler, the superintendent of Graterford. At the hearing, Africa acted pro se and was questioned directly by the court. Judge Hannum sought to determine, among other things, whether Africa's diet was mandated by his "religion," and, if so, whether the Commonwealth could demonstrate a compelling interest sufficient to infringe upon Africa's dietary practices. Because our disposition of Africa's appeal depends so heavily upon the particular facts of this case, it will be necessary to set forth in some detail the evidence introduced in the proceeding below.

Based on Africa's testimony and on materials he provided the district court, MOVE is a "revolutionary" organization "absolutely opposed to all that is wrong." MOVE was founded, although the record does not reveal when, by John Africa, who serves as the group's revered "coordinator" and whose teachings Frank Africa and his fellow "family" members follow. MOVE has no governing body or official hierarchy; instead, because "everything is level" and "there are no ups or downs," all MOVE members, including John Africa, occupy an equivalent position within the organization. In fact, MOVE really has only "one member, one family, one body" since, according to Frank Africa, to talk to an individual MOVE "disciple" is to "talk to everybody."

Africa also summarized what he believed to be the tenets that defined the MOVE organization. MOVE's goals, he asserted, are "to bring about absolute peace,. . . to stop violence altogether, to put a stop to all that is corrupt." Toward this end, Africa and other MOVE adherents are committed to a "natural," "moving," "active," and "generating" way of life. By contrast, what they alternatively refer to as "this system" or "civilization" is "degenerating": its air and water are "perverted"; its food, education, and governments are "artificial"; its words are "gibberish." Members of MOVE shun matters "systematic" and "hazardous"; they believe in "using things (but) not misusing things." Thus, according to Africa:

> the air is first, but pollution is second. Water is first, but poison is second. The food is first, but the chemicals that hurt the food are second. . . . We believe in the first education, the first government, the first law. . . . This is the perception that *John Africa* has given us. The water's existence is to be drunk and *not* poisoned, the air's presence is to be breathed and not polluted, the food's purpose is to be eaten and *not* distorted. The abuse that life suffers MOVE suffers the *same*.

MOVE endorses no existing regime or lifestyle; it yields to none in its uncompromising condemnation of a society that it views as "impure," "unoriginal," and "blemished."

According to Africa, MOVE is a religion. In fact, he insists that "just as there is no comparison between the sun's perfection and the lightbulb's failure, there is no comparison between the absolute necessity of our belief and this system's interpretation of religion." Africa testified that MOVE members participate in no distinct "ceremonies" or "rituals"; instead, every act of life itself is invested with religious meaning and significance. In his words:

> We are practicing our religious beliefs all the time: when I run, when I put information out like I am doing now, when I eat, when I breathe. All of these things are in accordance to our religious belief. . . . We don't take a date out of the week to practice our religion and leave the other days and say that we are not going to practice our religion. . . It is not a one-day thing or a once-a-week thing or a monthly thing. It doesn't have anything to do with time. Our religion is constant. It is as constant as breathing. . . . Every time a MOVE person opens their mouth, according to the way we believe, according to the way we do things, we are holding church.

Similarly, Africa contends that, since no one day is any more special than another, for MOVE members every day of the year can be considered a religious "holiday."

Africa did not provide the district court with any purportedly official guidelines setting forth MOVE's religious credo. He did submit, however, a document, which he apparently authored, entitled *Brief to Define the Importance of MOVE's Religious Diet*. That document, which Africa asserts is wholly consonant with the teachings of John Africa, sets forth an elaborate explanation of the MOVE philosophical framework and consequently constitutes extremely pertinent evidence for purposes of assessing the nature of the organization. In the Brief, Africa contends that "while religion is seen as a way of life, our religion is simply the way of life, as our religion in fact is life." Individuals who subscribe to the MOVE ideology must live in harmony with what is natural, or untainted:

> Water is *raw*, which makes it *pure*, which means it is *innocent, trustworthy*, and *safe*, which is the same as *God*. . . . Our religion is raw, our belief is pure as original, reliable as chemical free water,. . . nourishing as the earth's soil that connects us to food, satisfying as the air that gives breath to all life.

By rejecting the "polluted" and the "fraudulent," and by concentrating instead on the "healthy" and the "original," men and women are put "in touch with life's vibration." Africa asserts that, "when flowing, moving along with the activity of life,. . . the less you resist the power that commands this flow the more you become forceful *as* the flow."

Central to this conception of an unadulterated existence is what Africa refers to as MOVE's "religious diet." That diet is comprised largely of raw vegetables and fruits; MOVE members who fully adhere to the diet decline to eat any foods that have been processed or cooked. "There is nothing unusual or special about our diet," Africa declares in his *Brief*; rather, "our religious diet is common and uncomplicated because our diet is provided by *God* and already *done*." Failure to follow the diet constitutes deviation from the "direct, straight, and true" and results in "confusion and disease." In part, Africa's total commitment to specific provisions appears prudently based, since he asserts that it is "impossible" for an individual's body to adjust to more traditional fare after it has become accustomed to natural foods. But Africa also insists that he is obligated to follow his diet:

> To take away our diet is to leave me to eat nothing, for I have *no* choice, because when given a choice between eating poison and eating nothing, I have no choice but to eat nothing, for I *can't* eat other than raw. This would be *suicidal* and suicide is against life's ministry.

Africa contends that the diet, in conjunction with "our founder's wisdom," transformed him from a weak, timid, and ailing being to a strong, confident, and healthy individual. "Our religious diet is work, hard work, simple consistent unmechanized unscientific self-dependent work," he concludes; "our religious diet is family, unity, consistency, (and) uncompromising togetherness."

Dietary considerations excepted, Africa shed little light upon what, if any, ethical commandments are part and parcel of the MOVE philosophy. In response to specific questioning by the district court, Africa testified that MOVE members would be unable to serve in the armed forces, since "it is impossible for us to defend this system." At the same time, though, he stressed that, from his point of view, there was nothing inconsistent in seeking judicial intervention to prevent his transfer to Graterford:

> We are taught to use anything, anything that is necessary to bring about our purpose. . . . I have to do whatever is necessary to get my point across, to teach people. . . . I am using this system as a bridge to get my purpose to people (and to get) the poor people on my side.

"When you are right, you are deserving of protection," Africa declared, "and everything that is in our interest is right."

Africa's discussion of the MOVE organization and its dietary precepts was corroborated by the testimony of Ramona Johnson, a self-labeled "MOVE supporter." Johnson testified that her "brother" was "ordained" as a naturalist minister of MOVE by John Africa, and that he is an ardent follower of his religion and its mandates. Johnson confirmed, but added little to Africa's description of the concerns that lie at the heart of the MOVE ideology. She contended that the MOVE "religion is total; it encompasses every aspect of MOVE members' lives; there is nothing that is left out." And she stressed that Africa's raw food diet is both a necessary "part of" and a sincere "reflection of" his religious commitment. In support of this last observation, Johnson testified that Africa in fact had gone without food for the four day period in July when he was imprisoned at Graterford.

The final witness at the hearing in the district court was Julius T. Cuyler, the superintendent of Graterford. Cuyler testified that his institution was unwilling to meet the dietary needs of Frank Africa. He expressed concern about the possibility of "a proliferation of other groups surfacing in our prison requesting special diets" and warned that, were a court to grant Africa's desired relief, MOVE would attract new "sympathizers." Cuyler contended that the prison's cafeteria already made available to inmates a number of raw foods, such as bananas, apples, and oranges. There were practical reasons, he explained, why Graterford could not be any more accommodating in this regard: it would be "quite a major problem to buy the items that are listed on this diet in the retail market"; the prison's accounting system would be unable to handle such a "major deviation" in the procurement process; some of the foods asked for by Africa, particularly the potatoes, rice, corn, and berries, if "not kept under strict security, . . . would probably be stolen and used for other purposes," such as to "make homemade booze"; accumulation of raw food might lead to a "rodent problem"; and furnishing special diets might delay the prison's feeding process, with the result that "our entire population will be deprived of just that much of recreation [time]." In short, according to Cuyler, providing Africa with a raw food diet "could be the straw that could break the camel's back."

On August 21, 1981, the district court denied Africa's application for injunctive relief. *Africa v. State of Pennsylvania*, 520 F.Supp. 967 (E.D.Pa.1981). In an opinion accompanying his order, Judge Hannum concluded that, because Africa's sentence was for a period of at least five years, it was not possible, under Pennsylvania law, to grant his request to serve the remainder of his term at Holmesburg. Moreover, Africa had failed to establish that MOVE is "a religion within the purview and definition of the first amendment." On the contrary, according to the district court, "MOVE is merely a quasi-back-to-nature social movement of limited proportion and with an admittedly revolutionary design." As an organization, it is concerned solely with "concepts of health and a return to simplistic living." This the district court found to be more akin to a "social philosophy" than to a religion:

> While MOVE members may respect and respond to religious concepts, these concepts are not subsumed by the MOVE ideology. Rather MOVE exists, as do virtually all other organizations in our society, independent of religion and with separate and distinct purposes while still respecting and abiding by external religious principles.

Consequently, the district court concluded that both Frank Africa and MOVE itself "are not entitled to the first amendment protections and rights respecting the exercise of religion."

Africa immediately appealed the district court's decision to this Court. On August 28, 1981, we ordered that Africa's transfer to Graterford be stayed pending determination of his appeal, which we expedited. In addition, we directed that Albert John Snite, Jr. of the Defender Association of Philadelphia be appointed counsel for Africa for this appeal.

II.

The relevant case law in the free exercise area suggests that two threshold requirements must be met before particular beliefs, alleged to be religious in nature, are accorded first amendment protection. A court's task is to decide whether the beliefs avowed are (1) sincerely held, and (2) religious in nature, in the claimant's scheme of things. *United States v. Seeger.* If either of these two requirements is not satisfied, the court need not reach the question, often quite difficult in the penological setting, whether a legitimate and reasonably exercised state interest outweighs the proffered first amendment claim.

A.

It is inappropriate for a reviewing court to attempt to assess the truth or falsity of an announced article of faith. Judges are not oracles of theological verity, and the Founders did not intend for them to be declarants of religious orthodoxy. *See United States v. Ballard,* 322 U.S. 78, 85-88 (1944). The Supreme Court has emphasized, however, that "while the 'truth' of a belief is not open to question, there remains the significant question whether it is 'truly held.'" *Seeger, supra,* 380 U.S. at 185. Without some sort of required showing of sincerity on the part of the individual or organization seeking judicial protection of its beliefs, the first amendment would become "a limitless excuse for avoiding all unwanted legal obligations."

The requirement of sincerity poses no obstacle to Africa in this case. Although the district court made no specific findings in this regard, the Commonwealth never intimated, either at the hearing below or on this appeal, that Africa's convictions, however they might be denominated, were other than deeply held and sincerely advanced. Moreover, we are persuaded from our review of the record that Africa's opinions, especially those having to do with his diet, are "truly held" within the meaning of *Ballard* and *Seeger.* We turn, therefore, to the second issue: whether Africa's beliefs, however sincerely possessed, are religious in nature.

B.

Few tasks that confront a court require more circumspection than that of determining whether a particular set of ideas constitutes a religion within the meaning of the first amendment. Judges are ill-equipped to examine the breadth and content of an avowed religion; we must avoid any predisposition toward conventional religions so that unfamiliar faiths are not branded mere secular beliefs. "Religions now accepted were persecuted, unpopular and condemned at their inception." *United States v. Kuch,* 288 F.Supp. 439, 443 (D.D.C.1968). Nonetheless, when an individual invokes the first amendment to shield himself or herself from otherwise legitimate state regulation, we are required to make such uneasy differentiations. In considering this appeal, then, we acknowledge that a determination whether MOVE's beliefs are religious and entitled to constitutional protection "present[s] a most delicate question"; at the same time, we recognize that "the very concept of ordered liberty precludes allowing" Africa, or any other person, a blanket privilege "to make his own standards on matters of conduct in which society as a whole has important interests." *Wisconsin v. Yoder* [*infra* Chapter 13].

The Supreme Court has never announced a comprehensive definition of religion for use in cases such as the present one. There can be no doubt, however, that the Court has moved considerably beyond the wholly theistic interpretation of that term expressed in cases such as *Davis v. Beason*, 133 U.S. 333, 342 (1890) ("'religion' has reference to one's views of his relations to his Creator"). In *United States v. Seeger*, the Court recognized as religious for purposes of the Universal Military Service and Training Act an individual's "sincere religious beliefs," even though not theistic in nature, if "based upon a power or being, or upon a faith, to which all else is subordinate or upon which all else is ultimately dependent." A similar "parallel"-belief approach was employed in *Welsh v. United States*, where conscientious objector status was extended to a military conscript even though he declined to profess belief in a Supreme Being. The four Justices in *Welsh* who considered the constitutional question, in addition to the statutory issue, either expressly or implicitly defined religion to include non-theistic ideologies. And in *Torcaso v. Watkins*, the Court struck down as a violation of the establishment clause a Maryland statute requiring public officials to declare their belief in God before taking office. Justice Black, writing for a unanimous Court, concluded that a state could not favor "those religions based on a belief in the existence of God as against those religions founded on different beliefs"; in a footnote, he observed that a number of religious groups within the United States do not hold to theistic doctrines.

Drawing upon these Supreme Court cases, a number of lower federal courts have adopted a broad, non-theistic approach to the definition-of-religion question. In considering a first amendment claim arising from a non-traditional "religious" belief or practice, the courts have "look[ed] to the familiar religions as models in order to ascertain, by comparison, whether the new set of ideas or beliefs is confronting the same concerns, or serving the same purposes, as unquestioned and accepted 'religions.'" *Malnak* (concurring opinion). In essence, the modern analysis consists of a "definition by analogy" approach. It is at once a refinement and an extension of the "parallel"-belief course first charged by the Supreme Court in *Seeger*.

In conducting its inquiry in the case at bar, the district court employed what it referred to as the "inherently vague definitional approach" enunciated in the concurring opinion in *Malnak, supra. Africa v. State of Pennsylvania,* 520 F.Supp. 967, 970 (E.D.Pa.1981). In the *Malnak* opinion, which explicitly adopted the "definition by analogy" process, three "useful indicia" to determine the existence of a religion were identified and discussed. First, a religion addresses fundamental and ultimate questions having to do with deep and imponderable matters. Second, a religion is comprehensive in nature; it consists of a belief-system as opposed to an isolated teaching. Third, a religion often can be recognized by the presence of certain formal and external signs. Applying these three factors, the concurring opinion in *Malnak* concluded that the Science of Creative Intelligence-Transcendental Meditation constituted a religion under the first amendment despite the contentions of its leaders to the contrary. After considering Africa's testimony in light of these guideposts, we reach the obverse result: in spite of his protestations, we conclude that MOVE, at least as described by Africa, is not a "religion," in the sense that that term is used in the first amendment.

Fundamental and ultimate questions. Traditional religions consider and attempt to come to terms with what could best be described as "ultimate" questions — questions having to do with, among other things, life and death, right and wrong, and good and evil. Not every tenet of an established theology need focus upon such elemental matters, of course; still, it is difficult to conceive of a religion that does not address these larger concerns. For, above all else, religions are characterized by their adherence to and promotion of certain "underlying theories of man's nature or his place in the Universe." *Founding Church of Scientology v. United States*, 409 F.2d 1146, 1160 (D.C.Cir.1969).

We conclude that the MOVE organization, as described by Africa at the hearing below, does not satisfy the "ultimate" ideas criterion. Save for its preoccupation with living in accord with the dictates of nature, MOVE makes no mention of, much less places any emphasis upon, what might be classified as a fundamental concern. MOVE does not claim to be theistic: indeed it recognizes no Supreme Being and refers to no transcendental or all-controlling force. Moreover, unlike other recognized religions, with which it is to be compared for first amendment purposes, MOVE does not appear to take a position with respect to matters of personal morality, human mortality, or the meaning and purpose of life. The organization, for example, has no functional equivalent of the Ten Commandments, the New Testament Gospels, the Muslim *Koran*, Hinduism's *Veda,* or Transcendental Meditation's Science of Creative Intelligence. Africa insists that he has discovered a desirable way to conduct his life; he does not contend, however, that his regimen is somehow morally necessary or required. Given this lack of commitment to overarching principles, the MOVE philosophy is not sufficiently analogous to more "traditional" theologies.

Despite having concluded that MOVE does not deal with "ultimate ideas," we concede that the matter is not wholly free from doubt. Appointed counsel for Africa argues that MOVE members do share a fundamental concern, namely, an all- consuming belief in a "natural" or "generating" way of life-a way of life that ultimately cannot be reconciled with "civilization" itself. According to counsel, Africa's insistence on keeping "in touch with life's vibration" amounts to a form of pantheism, wherein

> the entity of God is the world itself, and God is "swallowed up in that unity which may be designated 'nature'".... [MOVE's] return to nature is not simply a "preferred" state. It is the *only* state. It is the state of being in pure harmony with nature. This, MOVE calls godly. This is pantheism.

We decline to accept such a characterization of Africa's views, however. We recognize that, under certain circumstances, a pantheistic-based philosophy might qualify for protection under the free exercise clause. From the record in this case, though, we are not persuaded that Africa is an adherent of pantheism, as that word is commonly defined. His mindset seems to be far more the product of a secular philosophy than of a religious orientation. His concerns appear personal (*e.g.*, he contends that a raw food diet is "healthy" and that pollution and other such products are "hazardous") and social (*e.g.*, he claims that MOVE is a "revolutionary" organization, "absolutely opposed to all that is wrong" and unable to accept existing regimes), rather than spiritual or other-worldly. Indeed, if Africa's statements are deemed sufficient to describe a religion under the Constitution, it might well be necessary to extend first amendment protection to a host of individuals and organizations who espouse personal and secular ideologies, however much those ideologies appear dissimilar to traditional religious dogmas.

The Supreme Court would appear to have foreclosed such an expansive interpretation of the free exercise clause. In *Wisconsin v. Yoder*, the Court concluded that Wisconsin could not require members of the Amish sect to send their children to school beyond the eighth grade, where there was uncontested evidence that such a course was inconsistent with the Amish religion. The Court arrived at this result only after conducting a searching inquiry into the history and customs of the Amish people and into the nature of their religious teachings and practices. In the course of his opinion for the Court, Chief Justice Burger stressed that the objections of the Amish to compulsory secondary education derived from "deep religious conviction[s]" rather than from a "personal" or "secular" philosophy. According to the Chief Justice:

> [I]f the Amish asserted their claims because of their subjective evaluation and rejection of the contemporary secular values accepted by the majority, much as Thoreau rejected the social values of his time and isolated himself at Walden Pond, their claim would not rest on a religious basis. Thoreau's choice was philosophical and personal rather than religious, and such belief does not rise to the demands of the Religion Clauses.

Precisely the same distinction had been drawn by the Court in the *Seeger* and *Welsh* cases: while an individual could qualify for conscientious objector status on the basis of a genuine "religious belief," reliance upon a "merely personal moral code" was insufficient.

For purposes of the case at hand, then, it is crucial to realize that the free exercise clause does not protect all deeply held beliefs, however "ultimate" their ends or all-consuming their means. An individual or group may adhere to and profess certain political, economic, or social doctrines, perhaps quite passionately. The first amendment, though, has not been construed, at least as yet, to shelter strongly held ideologies of such a nature, however all-encompassing their scope. As the Supreme Court declared in *Yoder*, "[a] way of life, however virtuous and admirable, may not be interposed as a barrier to reasonable state regulation. . . if it is based on purely *secular* considerations; to have the protection of the Religion Clauses, the claims must be rooted in *religious* belief." While we do not necessarily agree with the district court's description of MOVE as "merely a quasi-back-to-nature social movement of limited proportion," we conclude that the concerns addressed by MOVE, even assuming they are "ultimate" in nature, are more akin to Thoreau's rejection of "the contemporary secular values accepted by the majority" than to the "deep religious conviction[s]" of the Amish.

Comprehensiveness. The concurring opinion in *Malnak* stressed that a religion must consist of something more than a number of isolated, unconnected ideas. "A religion is not generally confined to one question or one moral teaching; it has a broader scope. It lays claim to an ultimate and comprehensive 'truth.'" The Science of Creative Intelligence qualified as a religion, therefore, in part because of its comprehensive nature: its teachings consciously aimed at providing the answers to "questions concerning the nature both of world and man, the underlying sustaining force of the universe, and the way to unlimited happiness."

In contrast, we cannot conclude, at least on the basis of Africa's testimony, that MOVE members share a comparable "world view." MOVE appears to consist of a single governing idea, perhaps best described as philosophical naturalism. Apart from this desire to live in a "pure" and "natural" environment, however-a desire which we already have deemed insufficiently religious to qualify for first amendment protection-little more of substance can be identified about the MOVE ideology. It would not be possible, we believe, on the basis of the record in this case, to place Africa's dietary concerns within the framework of a "comprehensive belief system." Expressed somewhat differently, were we to conclude that Africa's views, taken as a whole, satisfied the comprehensiveness criterion, it would be difficult to explain why other single-faceted ideologies — such as economic determinism, Social Darwinism, or even vegetarianism — would not qualify as religions under the first amendment.

Again, we acknowledge that our conclusion in this regard is not unassailable. It could be argued that Africa's views are in a sense comprehensive, since, according to his testimony, his every effort and thought is attributable to and explained by his "religious" convictions. MOVE members, according to Africa, "are practicing our religious beliefs all the time," even when running, eating, and breathing. The notion that all of life's activities can be cloaked with religious significance is, of course, neither unique to MOVE nor foreign to more established religions. Such a notion by itself, however, cannot transform an otherwise secular, one-dimensional philosophy into a comprehensive theological system. It is one thing to believe that, because of one's religion, day-to-day living takes on added meaning and importance. It is altogether different, however, to contend that certain ideas should be declared religious and therefore accorded first amendment protection from state interference merely because an individual alleges that his life is wholly governed by those ideas. We decline to adopt such a self-defining approach to the definition-of-religion problem.

Structural characteristics. A third indicium of a religion is the presence of

any formal, external, or surface signs that may be analogized to accepted religions. Such signs might include formal services, ceremonial functions, the existence of clergy, structure and organization, efforts at propagation, observance of holidays and other similar manifestations associated with the traditional religions.

Malnak (concurring opinion). MOVE lacks almost all of the formal identifying characteristics common to most recognized religions. For example, Africa testified that his organization did not conduct any special services and did not recognize any official customs. Similarly, the group apparently exists without an organizational structure, since MOVE consists of only "one member" and since "everything is level." In this connection, although Africa claimed to be an ordained "Naturalist Minister," he did not make clear what responsibilities and benefits, if any, this title conferred on him in contradistinction to other MOVE members. Moreover, MOVE apparently celebrates no holidays, since it takes the position that every day of the year is equally important. Finally, although Africa referred to a series of guidelines that supposedly were written by John Africa and that allegedly set forth MOVE's principal tenets, no such documents were made available to the district court; thus, the record contains nothing that arguably might pass for a MOVE scripture book or catechism. Given what we know about the group from the record, we are of the view that MOVE is not structurally analogous to those "traditional" organizations that have been recognized as religions under the first amendment.

III.

We conclude first, that to the extent MOVE deals with "ultimate" ideas, a proposition in itself subject to serious doubt, it is concerned with secular matters and not with religious principles; second, that MOVE cannot lay claim to be a comprehensive, multi-faceted theology; and third, that MOVE lacks the defining structural characteristics of a traditional religion. The "new set of ideas or beliefs" presented by Africa does not appear to us to "confron[t] the same concerns, or serv[e] the same purposes, as unquestioned and accepted 'religions,'" *Malnak* (concurring opinion). We hold, therefore, that MOVE, at least as described by Africa, is not a religion for purposes of the religion clauses. We do not conclude that Africa's sincerely-held beliefs are false, misguided, or unacceptable, but only that those beliefs, as described in the record before us, are not "religious," as the law has defined that term.

As the result of our holding in this case, the Commonwealth of Pennsylvania is not required under the first amendment to supply Frank Africa with a special raw-food diet. Such a consequence, however troubling, follows directly from our declaration that MOVE is not a religion. We do not mean to suggest, however, that the requirements of the first amendment also define the proper scope of prudent state penological policy. Especially in light of the apparent willingness of Graterford officials to accede to the dietary requirements of other prisoners, both for religious and for medical reasons, it is not clear from the record why special accommodations cannot be made in this instance for a prisoner who obviously cares deeply about what food he eats. Nonetheless, as a matter of constitutional law, the Commonwealth prevails. Accordingly, the judgment of the district court will be affirmed.

BROWN v. PENA
441 F. Supp. 1382 (S.D. Fla. 1977)

JAMES LAWRENCE KING, DISTRICT JUDGE.

The plaintiff brought suit against the Director of the Equal Employment Opportunity Commission as a result of the dismissal of two employment discrimination charges filed with the Miami District Office. The charges claimed that the plaintiff had been discriminated against because of his religion. An E.E.O.C. affidavit executed by the plaintiff and filed with this court as an exhibit reveals that the charges were based upon the plaintiff's "personal religious creed" that "Kozy Kitten People/Cat Food. . . is contributing significantly to [his] state of well being. . . [and therefore] to [his] overall work performance" by increasing his energy. These charges were dismissed by the Miami District Office on July 14, 1976, as not falling under the jurisdiction of Title VII because plaintiff failed to establish a religious belief generally accepted as a religion.

The Supreme Court has characterized "a 'religious' belief or practice entitled to constitutional protection" as "not merely a matter of personal preference, but one of deep religious conviction, shared by an organized group, and intimately related to daily living." *Wisconsin v. Yoder* [*infra* Chapter 13] (exemption on religious grounds of the Amish from state compulsory education law). Similarly, that Court has construed the term "religious training and belief" as excluding a "merely personal moral code" which is "in no way related to a Supreme Being." *United States v. Seeger* (exemption on religious grounds of conscientious objectors under the Universal Military Training and Service Act [50 U.S.C.App. § 456(j) (1958)]). The Fifth Circuit has identified three major factors which enter into a determination of whether a belief is religious:

> the "religious" nature of a belief depends on (1) whether the belief is based on a theory of "man's nature or his place in the Universe," (2) which is not merely a personal preference but has an institutional quality about it, and (3) which is sincere.

Brown v. Dade Christian Schools, Inc., 556 F.2d 310, 324 (5th Cir. 1977) (dissent) (citations omitted) (alleged exemption on religious grounds from desegregation laws). It is significant that throughout these carefully reasoned opinions runs the exclusion of unique personal moral preferences from the characterization of religious beliefs. Plaintiff's "personal religious creed" concerning Kozy Kitten Cat Food can only be described as such a mere personal preference and, therefore, is beyond the parameters of the concept of religion as protected by the constitution or, by logical extension, by 42 U.S.C. § 2000e et seq.

Since plaintiff's belief in pet food does not qualify legally as a religion, the Equal Employment Opportunity Commission acted correctly in declining to pursue his charges of employment discrimination on religious grounds. Even if the appellate court were to grant plaintiff's appeal and find that this court did have subject matter jurisdiction, it would still be well within the E.E.O.C.'s discretion to determine that plaintiff's creed does not constitute a generally accepted religious belief within the ambit of Title VII. Therefore, plaintiff can make no rational argument on the law or facts which would enable him to prevail on appeal.

NOTE ON OTHER IDIOSYNCRATIC "RELIGIONS"

Some of the more idiosyncratic sets of beliefs that have been litigated involve so-called "New Age" practices, Wicca and Witchcraft, Satanism, and the Church of Marijuana. For the most part the courts have either rejected claims that these sets of beliefs and practices are "religious," or have held that the state has a compelling interest in regulating the practices even if they are "religious." *See Alvarado v. City of San Jose*, 94 F.3d 1223 (9th Cir. 1996) (holding that "New Age" beliefs do not constitute a religion for Establishment Clause purposes); *United States v. Meyers*, 95 F.3d 1475 (10th Cir. 1996) (holding that Church of Marijuana does not satisfy definition of "religion"). With regard to Wicca, Witchcraft, and Satanism, *see Kunselman v. Western Reserve Local Sch. Dist.*, 70 F.3d 931 (6th Cir. 1995) (assuming that Satanism and Church of Satan are religion, but holding that public school adoption of "Blue Devil" as school mascot did not violate the Establishment Clause); *Brown v. Woodland Joint Unified Sch. Dist.*, 27 F.3d 1373 (9th Cir. 1994) (assuming that witchcraft/Wicca is a religion, but holding that school activities that asked children to discuss witches and pretend they were witches and sorcerers did not establish religion); *Fleischfresser v. Directors of Sch. Dist. 200*, 15 F.3d 680 (7th Cir. 1994) (same); *Childs v. Duckworth*, 705 F.2d 915 (7th Cir. 1983) (upholding prison regulation of Satanism practices, and assuming that Satanism is a religion); *Dettmer v. Landon*, 799 F.2d 929 (4th Cir. 1986) (holding that witchcraft is a religion, but upholding prison regulations prohibiting possession of witchcraft-related materials); *Doty v. Lewis*, 995 F. Supp. 1081 (D. Ariz. 1998) (holding that prison regulations prohibiting possession of Satanic religious articles, including Satanic Bible, did not interfere with a tenet or belief that is central to the prisoner's religious doctrine); *Carpenter v. Wilkinson*, 946 F. Supp. 522 (N.D. Ohio 1996) (upholding prison regulation prohibiting possession of "The Satanic Bible" despite noting that Satanism "appears to have at least some of the indicia of a religion"); *McCorkle v. Johnson*, 881 F.2d 993 (11th Cir. 1989). *But see Howard v. United States*, 864 F. Supp. 1019 (D. Colo. 1994) (holding that prisoner had established likelihood of success on merits of claim that Satanism is a religion and that prison restrictions on Satanic practices violated prisoner's Free Exercise Clause rights).

As many of the Satanism and Witchcraft cases indicate, the constitutional protections of religious freedom in the prison context are much more limited than in civilian life. This is true even where restrictions on obvious religious exercises of more mainstream religions are at issue. In *O'Lone v. Estate of Shabazz*, 482 U.S. 342 (1987), the Supreme Court upheld a prison regulation that resulted in Muslim prisoners being unable to attend Jumu'ah, a weekly Muslim congregational service. The Court noted that "Jumu'ah is commanded by the Koran and must be held every Friday after the sun reaches its zenith and before the Asr, or afternoon prayer. *See* Koran 62:9-10." *Id.* at 345. Nevertheless, the Court upheld the regulation under a very lenient standard. The Court concluded that prison regulations impinging on religious and other fundamental rights are valid if they are "reasonably related to legitimate penological interests." *Id.* at 349 (quoting *Turner v. Safley*, 482 U.S. 78, 89 (1987)). According to the Court, "[t]his approach ensures the ability of corrections officials 'to anticipate security problems and to adopt innovative solutions to the intractable problems of prison administration,' and avoids unnecessary intrusion of the judiciary into problems particularly ill suited to 'resolution by decree.'" *Id.* (citations omitted).

The weak constitutional protections of religious liberty in prison have been substantially augmented by the Religious Land Use and Institutionalized Persons Act, which is discussed in Chapter 14, *infra*.

Chapter 4

RELIGION AND "RELIGION": THE LIMITATIONS OF THE CONCEPT

The previous chapter introduced the differences between the theological and behavioral aspects of religion. Many modern Religion Clause disputes are generated by the difficulties of reconciling the secular demands of the state and the conflicting mandates of many religious faiths — especially when secular state actions contradict or undermine religious faith. This chapter contains several specific examples of these disputes. Note that beneath the surface of these disputes — especially when they occur in the public schools — is an issue much larger than the simple question whether a single religious practitioner's actions violate a particular law. The real dispute in these cases is often over who controls the thought processes of the next generation. They are disputes, in other words, between the precepts of absolute intellectual freedom and the very different principles of faith-based adherence to spiritual commands. From the perspective of some religious practitioners, the materials in this chapter raise the following question: At what point does the comprehensive secular effort to acculturate and educate citizens in Enlightenment democratic values lapse into antireligious indoctrination? From another perspective, however, the question is quite different: Given the requirements of the Establishment Clause, how can the state endorse religious views that we "know" — based on empirical evidence, the techniques of modern science, and rational analysis — are invalid? Perhaps both concerns can be combined into a blunter question: When faith and reason conflict in the realm of state action, which should prevail?

A. CREATIONISM AS RELIGION

EPPERSON v. ARKANSAS
393 U.S. 97 (1968)

MR. JUSTICE FORTAS delivered the opinion of the Court.

I.

This appeal challenges the constitutionality of the "anti-evolution" statute which the State of Arkansas adopted in 1928 to prohibit the teaching in its public schools and universities of the theory that man evolved from other species of life. The statute was a product of the upsurge of "fundamentalist" religious fervor of the twenties. The Arkansas statute was an adaption of the famous Tennessee "monkey law" which that State adopted in 1925. The constitutionality of

155

the Tennessee law was upheld by the Tennessee Supreme Court in the celebrated *Scopes* case in 1927.[1]

The Arkansas law makes it unlawful for a teacher in any state-supported school or university "to teach the theory or doctrine that mankind ascended or descended from a lower order of animals," or "to adopt or use in any such institution a textbook that teaches" this theory. Violation is a misdemeanor and subjects the violator to dismissal from his position.[2]

The present case concerns the teaching of biology in a high school in Little Rock. According to the testimony, until the events here in litigation, the official textbook furnished for the high school biology course did not have a section on the Darwinian Theory. Then, for the academic year 1965 — 1966, the school administration, on recommendation of the teachers of biology in the school system, adopted and prescribed a textbook which contained a chapter setting forth "the theory about the origin. . . of man from a lower form of animal."

Susan Epperson, a young woman who graduated from Arkansas' school system and then obtained her master's degree in zoology at the University of Illinois, was employed by the Little Rock school system in the fall of 1964 to teach 10th grade biology at Central High School. At the start of the next academic year, 1965, she was confronted by the new textbook (which one surmises from the record was not unwelcome to her). She faced at least a literal dilemma because she was supposed to use the new textbook for classroom instruction and presumably to teach the statutorily condemned chapter; but to do so would be a criminal offense and subject her to dismissal.

---

[1] *Scopes v. State*, 154 Tenn. 105, 289 S.W. 363 (1927). The Tennessee court, however, reversed Scopes' conviction on the ground that the jury and not the judge should have assessed the fine of $100. Since Scopes was no longer in the State's employ, it saw "nothing to be gained by prolonging the life of this bizarre case." It directed that a *nolle prosequi* be entered, in the interests of "the peace and dignity of the state." 154 Tenn., at 121, 289 S.W., at 367.

[2] Initiated Act No. 1, Ark. Acts 1929; Ark. Stat. Ann. §§ 80-1627, 80-1628 (1960 Repl. Vol.). The text of the law is as follows:

"§ 80-1627. — Doctrine of ascent or descent of man from lower order of animals prohibited. — It shall be unlawful for any teacher or other instructor in any University, College, Normal, Public School, or other institution of the State, which is supported in whole or in part from public funds derived by State and local taxation to teach the theory or doctrine that mankind ascended or descended from a lower order of animals and also it shall be unlawful for any teacher, textbook commission, or other authority exercising the power to select textbooks for above mentioned educational institutions to adopt or use in any such institution a textbook that teaches the doctrine or theory that mankind descended or ascended from a lower order of animals.

"§ 80-1628. — Teaching doctrine or adopting textbook mentioning doctrine — Penalties — Positions to be vacated. — Any teacher or other instructor or textbook commissioner who is found guilty of violation of this act by teaching the theory or doctrine mentioned in section 1 hereof, or by using, or adopting any such textbooks in any such educational institution shall be guilty of a misdemeanor and upon conviction shall be fined not exceeding five hundred dollars; and upon conviction shall vacate the position thus held in any educational institutions of the character above mentioned or any commission of which he may be a member."

She instituted the present action in the Chancery Court of the State, seeking a declaration that the Arkansas statute is void and enjoining the State and the defendant officials of the Little Rock school system from dismissing her for violation of the statute's provisions. H.H. Blanchard, a parent of children attending the public schools, intervened in support of the action

Only Arkansas and Mississippi have such "anti-evolution" or "monkey" laws on their books.[8] There is no record of any prosecutions in Arkansas under its statute. It is possible that the statute is presently more of a curiosity than a vital fact of life in these States.[9]

II.

We do not rest our decision upon the asserted vagueness of the statute. On either interpretation of its language, Arkansas' statute cannot stand. It is of no moment whether the law is deemed to prohibit mention of Darwin's theory, or to forbid any or all of the infinite varieties of communication embraced within the term "teaching." Under either interpretation, the law must be stricken because of its conflict with the constitutional prohibition of state laws respecting an establishment of religion or prohibiting the free exercise thereof. The overriding fact is that Arkansas' law selects from the body of knowledge a particular segment which it proscribes for the sole reason that it is deemed to conflict with a particular religious doctrine; that is, with a particular interpretation of the Book of Genesis by a particular religious group.

III.

The antecedents of today's decision are many and unmistakable. They are rooted in the foundation soil of our Nation. They are fundamental to freedom.

Government in our democracy, state and national, must be neutral in matters of religious theory, doctrine, and practice. It may not be hostile to any religion or to the advocacy of no-religion; and it may not aid, foster, or promote one religion or religious theory against another or even against the militant opposite. The First Amendment mandates governmental neutrality between religion and religion, and between religion and nonreligion.

---

[8] Miss. Code Ann. §§ 6798, 6799 (1942). Ark. Stat. Ann. §§ 80-1627, 80-1628 (1960 Repl. Vol.). The Tennessee law was repealed in 1967. Oklahoma enacted an anti-evolution law, but it was repealed in 1926. The Florida and Texas Legislatures, in the period between 1921 and 1929, adopted resolutions against teaching the doctrine of evolution. In all, during that period, bills to this effect were introduced in 20 States. AMERICAN CIVIL LIBERTIES UNION (ACLU), THE GAG ON TEACHING 8 (2d ed., 1937).

[9] Clarence Darrow, who was counsel for the defense in the *Scopes* trial, in his biography published in 1932, somewhat sardonically pointed out that States with anti-evolution laws did not insist upon the fundamentalist theory in all respects. He said: "I understand that the States of Tennessee and Mississippi both continue to teach that the earth is round and that the revolution on its axis brings the day and night, in spite of all opposition." THE STORY OF MY LIFE 247 (1932).

As early as 1872, this Court said: "The law knows no heresy, and is committed to the support of no dogma, the establishment of no sect." *Watson v. Jones,* 13 Wall. 679, 728. This has been the interpretation of the great First Amendment which this Court has applied in the many and subtle problems which the ferment of our national life has presented for decision within the Amendment's broad command.

Judicial interposition in the operation of the public school system of the Nation raises problems requiring care and restraint. Our courts, however, have not failed to apply the First Amendment's mandate in our educational system where essential to safeguard the fundamental values of freedom of speech and inquiry and of belief. By and large, public education in our Nation is committed to the control of state and local authorities. Courts do not and cannot intervene in the resolution of conflicts which arise in the daily operation of school systems and which do not directly and sharply implicate basic constitutional values. On the other hand, "[t]he vigilant protection of constitutional freedoms is nowhere more vital than in the community of American schools," *Shelton v. Tucker,* 364 U.S. 479, 487 (1960). As this Court said in *Keyishian v. Board of Regents,* the First Amendment "does not tolerate laws that cast a pall of orthodoxy over the classroom." 385 U.S. 589, 603 (1967).

There is and can be no doubt that the First Amendment does not permit the State to require that teaching and learning must be tailored to the principles or prohibitions of any religious sect or dogma. In *Everson v. Board of Education,* this Court, in upholding a state law to provide free bus service to school children, including those attending parochial schools, said: "Neither [a State nor the Federal Government] can pass laws which aid one religion, aid all religions, or prefer one religion over another."

At the following Term of Court, in *McCollum v. Board of Education,* 333 U.S. 203 (1948), the Court held that Illinois could not release pupils from class to attend classes of instruction in the school buildings in the religion of their choice. This, it said, would involve the State in using tax-supported property for religious purposes, thereby breaching the "wall of separation" which, according to Jefferson, the First Amendment was intended to erect between church and state. While study of religions and of the Bible from a literary and historic viewpoint, presented objectively as part of a secular program of education, need not collide with the First Amendment's prohibition, the State may not adopt programs or practices in its public schools or colleges which "aid or oppose" any religion. This prohibition is absolute. It forbids alike the preference of a religious doctrine or the prohibition of theory which is deemed antagonistic to a particular dogma. As Mr. Justice Clark stated in *Joseph Burstyn, Inc. v. Wilson,* "the state has no legitimate interest in protecting any or all religions from views distasteful to them. . . ." 343 U.S. 495, 505 (1952). The test was stated as follows in *Abington School District v. Schempp*: "[W]hat are the purpose and the primary effect of the enactment? If either is the advancement or inhibition of religion then the enactment exceeds the scope of legislative power as circumscribed by the Constitution."

These precedents inevitably determine the result in the present case. The State's undoubted right to prescribe the curriculum for its public schools does not carry with it the right to prohibit, on pain of criminal penalty, the teaching of a scientific theory or doctrine where that prohibition is based upon reasons that violate the First Amendment. It is much too late to argue that the State may impose upon the teachers in its schools any conditions that it chooses, however restrictive they may be of constitutional guarantees. *Keyishian v. Board of Regents*, 385 U.S. 589, 605-606 (1967).

In the present case, there can be no doubt that Arkansas has sought to prevent its teachers from discussing the theory of evolution because it is contrary to the belief of some that the Book of Genesis must be the exclusive source of doctrine as to the origin of man. No suggestion has been made that Arkansas' law may be justified by considerations of state policy other than the religious views of some of its citizens.[15] It is clear that fundamentalist sectarian conviction was and is the law's reason for existence.[16] Its antecedent, Tennessee's "monkey law," candidly stated its purpose: to make it unlawful "to teach any theory that denies the story of the Divine Creation of man as taught in the Bible, and to teach instead that man has descended from a lower order of animals."[17]

---

[15] Former Dean Leflar of the University of Arkansas School of Law has stated that "the same ideological considerations underlie the anti-evolution enactment" as underlie the typical blasphemy statute. He says that the purpose of these statutes is an "ideological" one which "involves an effort to prevent (by censorship) or punish the presentation of intellectually significant matter which contradicts accepted social, moral or religious ideas." Leflar, *Legal Liability for the Exercise of Free Speech*, 10 ARK. L. REV. 155, 158 (1956). *See also* R. HOFSTADTER & W. METZGER, THE DEVELOPMENT OF ACADEMIC FREEDOM IN THE UNITED STATES 320-366 (1955) (*passim*); H. BEALE, A HISTORY OF FREEDOM OF TEACHING IN AMERICAN SCHOOLS 202-207 (1941); Emerson & Haber, *The* Scopes *Case in Modern Dress*, 27 U. CHI. L. REV. 522 (1960); Waller, *The Constitutionality of the Tennessee Anti-Evolution Act*, 35 YALE L.J. 191 (1925) (*passim*); ACLU, THE GAG ON TEACHING 7 (2d ed., 1937); J. SCOPES & J. PRESLEY, CENTER OF THE STORM 45 -53 (1967).

[16] The following advertisement is typical of the public appeal which was used in the campaign to secure adoption of the statute:

'THE BIBLE OR ATHEISM, WHICH?

"All atheists favor evolution. If you agree with atheism vote against Act No. 1. If you agree with the Bible vote for Act No. 1. . . . Shall conscientious church members be forced to pay taxes to support teachers to teach evolution which will undermine the faith of their children? The Gazette said Russian Bolshevists laughed at Tennessee. True, and that sort will laugh at Arkansas. Who cares? Vote FOR ACT NO. 1." THE ARKANSAS GAZETTE, Little Rock, Nov. 4, 1928, p. 12, cols. 4-5.

Letters from the public expressed the fear that teaching of evolution would be "subversive of Christianity," *id.*, Oct. 24, 1928, p. 7, col. 2; *see also id.*, Nov. 4, 1928, p. 19, col. 4; and that it would cause school children "to disrespect the Bible," *id.*, Oct. 27, 1928, p. 15, col. 5. One letter read: "The cosmogony taught by [evolution] runs contrary to that of Moses and Jesus, and as such is nothing, if anything at all, but atheism. . . . Now let the mothers and fathers of our state that are trying to raise their children in the Christian faith arise in their might and vote for this anti-evolution bill that will take it out of our tax supported schools. When they have saved the children, they have saved the state." *Id.*, at cols. 4-5.

[17] Arkansas' law was adopted by popular initiative in 1928, three years after Tennessee's law was enacted and one year after the Tennessee Supreme Court's decision in the *Scopes* case, *supra.*

Perhaps the sensational publicity attendant upon the *Scopes* trial induced Arkansas to adopt less explicit language.[18] It eliminated Tennessee's reference to "the story of the Divine Creation of man" as taught in the Bible, but there is no doubt that the motivation for the law was the same: to suppress the teaching of a theory which, it was thought, "denied" the divine creation of man.

Arkansas' law cannot be defended as an act of religious neutrality. Arkansas did not seek to excise from the curricula of its schools and universities all discussion of the origin of man. The law's effort was confined to an attempt to blot out a particular theory because of its supposed conflict with the Biblical account, literally read. Plainly, the law is contrary to the mandate of the First, and in violation of the Fourteenth, Amendment to the Constitution.

MR. JUSTICE BLACK, concurring.

It seems to me that in this situation the statute is too vague for us to strike it down on any ground but that: vagueness. Under this statute as construed by the Arkansas Supreme Court, a teacher cannot know whether he is forbidden to mention Darwin's theory, at all or only free to discuss it as long as he refrains from contending that it is true. It is an established rule that a statute which leaves an ordinary man so doubtful about its meaning that he cannot know when he has violated it denies him the first essential of due process. Holding the statute too vague to enforce would not only follow long-standing constitutional precedents but it would avoid having this Court take unto itself the duty of a State's highest court to interpret and mark the boundaries of the State's laws. And, more important, it would not place this Court in the unenviable position of violating the principle of leaving the States absolutely free to choose their own curriculums for their own schools so long as their action does not palpably conflict with a clear constitutional command.

The Court, not content to strike down this Arkansas Act on the unchallengeable ground of its plain vagueness, chooses rather to invalidate it as a violation of the Establishment of Religion Clause of the First Amendment. I would not decide this case on such a sweeping ground for the following reasons, among others.

1. In the first place I find it difficult to agree with the Court's statement that "there can be no doubt that Arkansas has sought to prevent its teachers from discussing the theory of evolution because it is contrary to the belief of some that the Book of Genesis must be the exclusive source of doctrine as to the origin of man." It may be instead that the people's motive was merely that it would be best to remove this controversial subject from its schools; there is no reason I can imagine why a State is without power to withdraw from its curriculum any subject deemed too emotional and controversial for its public

---

[18] In its brief, the State says that the Arkansas statute was passed with the holding of the *Scopes* case in mind. Brief for Appellee 1.

schools. And this Court has consistently held that it is not for us to invalidate a statute because of our views that the "motives" behind its passage were improper; it is simply too difficult to determine what those motives were. *See, e.g., United States v. O'Brien*, 391 U.S. 367, 382-383 (1968).

2. A second question that arises for me is whether this Court's decision forbidding a State to exclude the subject of evolution from its schools infringes the religious freedom of those who consider evolution an anti-religious doctrine. If the theory is considered anti-religious, as the Court indicates, how can the State be bound by the Federal Constitution to permit its teachers to advocate such an "anti-religious" doctrine to schoolchildren? The very cases cited by the Court as supporting its conclusion that the State must be neutral, not favoring one religious or anti-religious view over another. The Darwinian theory is said to challenge the Bible's story of creation; so too have some of those who believe in the Bible, along with many others, challenged the Darwinian theory. Since there is no indication that the literal Biblical doctrine of the origin of man is included in the curriculum of Arkansas schools, does not the removal of the subject of evolution leave the State in a neutral position toward these supposedly competing religious and anti-religious doctrines? Unless this Court is prepared simply to write off as pure nonsense the views of those who consider evolution an anti-religious doctrine, then this issue presents problems under the Establishment Clause far more troublesome than are discussed in the Court's opinion.

3. I am also not ready to hold that a person hired to teach school children takes with him into the classroom a constitutional right to teach sociological, economic, political, or religious subjects that the school's managers do not want discussed. This Court has said that the rights of free speech "while fundamental in our democratic society, still do not mean that everyone with opinions or beliefs to express may address a group at any public place and at any time." *Cox v. State of Louisiana*, 379 U.S. 536, 554; *Cox v. State of Louisiana*, 379 U.S. 559, 574. I question whether it is absolutely certain, as the Court's opinion indicates, that "academic freedom" permits a teacher to breach his contractual agreement to teach only the subjects designated by the school authorities who hired him.

Certainly the Darwinian theory, precisely like the Genesis story of the creation of man, is not above challenge. In fact the Darwinian theory has not merely been criticized by religionists but by scientists, and perhaps no scientist would be willing to take an oath and swear that everything announced in the Darwinian theory is unquestionably true. The Court, it seems to me, makes a serious mistake in bypassing the plain, unconstitutional vagueness of this statute in order to reach out and decide this troublesome, to me, First Amendment question. However wise this Court may be or may become hereafter, it is doubtful that, sitting in Washington, it can successfully supervise and censor the curriculum of every public school in every hamlet and city in the United States. I doubt that our wisdom is so nearly infallible.

I would either strike down the Arkansas Act as too vague to enforce, or remand to the State Supreme Court for clarification of its holding and opinion.

EDWARDS v. AGUILLARD
482 U.S. 578 (1987)

JUSTICE BRENNAN delivered the opinion of the Court

The question for decision is whether Louisiana's "Balanced Treatment for Creation-Science and Evolution-Science in Public School Instruction" Act (Creationism Act) is facially invalid as violative of the Establishment Clause of the First Amendment.

I

The Creationism Act forbids the teaching of the theory of evolution in public schools unless accompanied by instruction in "creation science." No school is required to teach evolution or creation science. If either is taught, however, the other must also be taught. The theories of evolution and creation science are statutorily defined as "the scientific evidences for [creation or evolution] and inferences from those scientific evidences."

Appellees, who include parents of children attending Louisiana public schools, Louisiana teachers, and religious leaders, challenged the constitutionality of the Act in District Court, seeking an injunction and declaratory relief. Appellants, Louisiana officials charged with implementing the Act, defended on the ground that the purpose of the Act is to protect a legitimate secular interest, namely, academic freedom. Appellees attacked the Act as facially invalid because it violated the Establishment Clause and made a motion for summary judgment. The District Court held that the Creationism Act violated the Establishment Clause either because it prohibited the teaching of evolution or because it required the teaching of creation science with the purpose of advancing a particular religious doctrine.

The Court of Appeals affirmed. The court observed that the statute's avowed purpose of protecting academic freedom was inconsistent with requiring, upon risk of sanction, the teaching of creation science whenever evolution is taught. The court found that the Louisiana Legislature's actual intent was "to discredit evolution by counterbalancing its teaching at every turn with the teaching of creationism, a religious belief."

II

The Establishment Clause forbids the enactment of any law "respecting an establishment of religion." The Court has applied a three-pronged test to determine whether legislation comports with the Establishment Clause. First, the legislature must have adopted the law with a secular purpose. Second, the statute's principal or primary effect must be one that neither advances nor inhibits religion. Third, the statute must not result in an excessive entanglement of government with religion. *Lemon v. Kurtzman*.**4** State action violates the Establishment Clause if it fails to satisfy any of these prongs.

The Court has been particularly vigilant in monitoring compliance with the Establishment Clause in elementary and secondary schools. Families entrust public schools with the education of their children, but condition their trust on the understanding that the classroom will not purposely be used to advance religious views that may conflict with the private beliefs of the student and his or her family. Students in such institutions are impressionable and their attendance is involuntary. The State exerts great authority and coercive power through mandatory attendance requirements, and because of the students' emulation of teachers as role models and the children's susceptibility to peer pressure.**5** Furthermore, "[t]he public school is at once the symbol of our democracy and the most pervasive means for promoting our common destiny. In no activity of the State is it more vital to keep out divisive forces than in its schools. . . ." *Illinois ex rel. McCollum v. Board of Education*, 333 U.S. 203, 231 (1948) (opinion of Frankfurter, J.).

Consequently, the Court has been required often to invalidate statutes which advance religion in public elementary and secondary schools. *See, e.g., Grand Rapids School Dist. v. Ball* [*infra* Chapter 8] (school district's use of religious school teachers in public schools); *Wallace v. Jaffree* [*infra* Chapter 6] (Alabama statute authorizing moment of silence for school prayer); *Stone v. Graham*, 449 U.S. 39 (1980) (posting copy of Ten Commandments on public classroom wall*); Epperson v. Arkansas* (statute forbidding teaching of evolution); *Abington School Dist. v. Schempp* [*infra* Chapter 6] (daily reading of Bible); *Engel v. Vitale* [*infra* Chapter 6] (recitation of "denominationally neutral" prayer).

III

Lemon's first prong focuses on the purpose that animated adoption of the Act. "The purpose prong of the *Lemon* test asks whether government's actual purpose is to endorse or disapprove of religion." *Lynch v. Donnelly* [*infra* Chapter 7] (O'CONNOR, J., concurring). A governmental intention to promote religion is

---

4 The *Lemon* test has been applied in all cases since its adoption in 1971, except in Marsh *v.* Chambers, 463 U.S. 783 (1983), where the Court held that the Nebraska Legislature's practice of opening a session with a prayer by a chaplain paid by the State did not violate the Establishment Clause. The Court based its conclusion in that case on the historical acceptance of the practice. Such a historical approach is not useful in determining the proper roles of church and state in public schools, since free public education was virtually nonexistent at the time the Constitution was adopted. *See Wallace v. Jaffree*, 472 U.S. 38, 80 (1985) (O'CONNOR, J., concurring in judgment) (citing *Abington School Dist. v. Schempp*, 374 U.S. 203, 238, and n. 7 (1963) (BRENNAN, J., concurring)).

5 The potential for undue influence is far less significant with regard to college students who voluntarily enroll in courses. "This distinction warrants a difference in constitutional results." *Abington School Dist. v. Schempp, supra*, at 253 (BRENNAN, J., concurring). Thus, for instance, the Court has not questioned the authority of state colleges and universities to offer courses on religion or theology. *See Widmar v. Vincent*, 454 U.S. 263, 271 (1981) (POWELL, J.); *id.,* at 281 (STEVENS, J., concurring in judgment).

clear when the State enacts a law to serve a religious purpose. This intention may be evidenced by promotion of religion in general, see *Wallace v. Jaffree* [*infra* Chapter 6] (Establishment Clause protects individual freedom of conscience "to select any religious faith or none at all"), or by advancement of a particular religious belief, *e.g., Stone v. Graham, supra,* 449 U.S., at 41 (invalidating requirement to post Ten Commandments, which are "undeniably a sacred text in the Jewish and Christian faiths") (footnote omitted); *Epperson v. Arkansas* (holding that banning the teaching of evolution in public schools violates the First Amendment since "teaching and learning" must not "be tailored to the principles or prohibitions of any religious sect or dogma"). If the law was enacted for the purpose of endorsing religion, "no consideration of the second or third criteria [of *Lemon*] is necessary." *Wallace v. Jaffree.* In this case, appellants have identified no clear secular purpose for the Louisiana Act.

True, the Act's stated purpose is to protect academic freedom. This phrase might, in common parlance, be understood as referring to enhancing the freedom of teachers to teach what they will. The Court of Appeals, however, correctly concluded that the Act was not designed to further that goal.[6] We find no merit in the State's argument that the "legislature may not [have] use[d] the terms "academic freedom" in the correct legal sense. They might have [had] in mind, instead, a basic concept of fairness; teaching all of the evidence." Even if "academic freedom" is read to mean "teaching all of the evidence" with respect to the origin of human beings, the Act does not further this purpose. The goal of providing a more comprehensive science curriculum is not furthered either by outlawing the teaching of evolution or by requiring the teaching of creation science.

A

While the Court is normally deferential to a State's articulation of a secular purpose, it is required that the statement of such purpose be sincere and not a sham.

It is clear from the legislative history that the purpose of the legislative sponsor, Senator Bill Keith, was to narrow the science curriculum. During the

---

[6] The Court of Appeals stated that "[a]cademic freedom embodies the principle that individual instructors are at liberty to teach that which they deem to be appropriate in the exercise of their professional judgment." 765 F.2d, at 1257. But, in the State of Louisiana, courses in public schools are prescribed by the State Board of Education and teachers are not free, absent permission, to teach courses different from what is required. Tr. of Oral Arg. 44-46. "Academic freedom," at least as it is commonly understood, is not a relevant concept in this context. Moreover, as the Court of Appeals explained, the Act "requires, presumably upon risk of *sanction* or *dismissal* for failure to comply, the teaching of creation-science whenever evolution is taught. Although states may prescribe public school curriculum concerning science instruction under ordinary circumstances, the compulsion inherent in the Balanced Treatment Act is, on its face, inconsistent with the idea of academic freedom as it is universally understood." 765 F.2d, at 1257 (emphasis in original). The Act actually serves to diminish academic freedom by removing the flexibility to teach evolution without also teaching creation science, even if teachers determine that such curriculum results in less effective and comprehensive science instruction.

legislative hearings, Senator Keith stated: "My preference would be that neither [creationism nor evolution] be taught." Such a ban on teaching does not promote — indeed, it undermines — the provision of a comprehensive scientific education.

It is equally clear that requiring schools to teach creation science with evolution does not advance academic freedom. The Act does not grant teachers a flexibility that they did not already possess to supplant the present science curriculum with the presentation of theories, besides evolution, about the origin of life. Indeed, the Court of Appeals found that no law prohibited Louisiana public school teachers from teaching any scientific theory. As the president of the Louisiana Science Teachers Association testified, "[a]ny scientific concept that's based on established fact can be included in our curriculum already, and no legislation allowing this is necessary." The Act provides Louisiana school teachers with no new authority. Thus the stated purpose is not furthered by it.

Furthermore, the goal of basic "fairness" is hardly furthered by the Act's discriminatory preference for the teaching of creation science and against the teaching of evolution.[7] While requiring that curriculum guides be developed for creation science, the Act says nothing of comparable guides for evolution. Similarly, resource services are supplied for creation science but not for evolution. Only "creation scientists" can serve on the panel that supplies the resource services. The Act forbids school boards to discriminate against anyone who "chooses to be a creation-scientist" or to teach "creationism," but fails to protect those who choose to teach evolution or any other non-creation science theory, or who refuse to teach creation science.

If the Louisiana Legislature's purpose was solely to maximize the comprehensiveness and effectiveness of science instruction, it would have encouraged the teaching of all scientific theories about the origins of humankind. But under the Act's requirements, teachers who were once free to teach any and all facets of this subject are now unable to do so. Moreover, the Act fails even to ensure that creation science will be taught, but instead requires the teaching of this theory only when the theory of evolution is taught. Thus we agree with the Court of Appeals' conclusion that the Act does not serve to protect academic freedom, but has the distinctly different purpose of discrediting "evolution by counterbalancing its teaching at every turn with the teaching of creationism. . . ."

B

Stone v. Graham invalidated the State's requirement that the Ten Commandments be posted in public classrooms. "The Ten Commandments are unde-

---

[7] The Creationism Act's provisions appear among other provisions prescribing the courses of study in Louisiana's public schools. These other provisions, similar to those in other States, prescribe courses of study in such topics as driver training, civics, the Constitution, and free enterprise. None of these other provisions, apart from those associated with the Creationism Act, nominally mandates "equal time" for opposing opinions within a specific area of learning. *See, e.g.*, La. Rev. Stat. Ann. §§ 17:261-17:281 (1982 and Supp. 1987).

niably a sacred text in the Jewish and Christian faiths, and no legislative recitation of a supposed secular purpose can blind us to that fact." As a result, the contention that the law was designed to provide instruction on a "fundamental legal code" was "not sufficient to avoid conflict with the First Amendment." Similarly *Abington School Dist. v. Schempp* held unconstitutional a statute "requiring the selection and reading at the opening of the school day of verses from the Holy Bible and the recitation of the Lord's Prayer by the students in unison," despite the proffer of such secular purposes as the "promotion of moral values, the contradiction to the materialistic trends of our times, the perpetuation of our institutions and the teaching of literature."

As in *Stone* and *Abington*, we need not be blind in this case to the legislature's preeminent religious purpose in enacting this statute. There is a historic and contemporaneous link between the teachings of certain religious denominations and the teaching of evolution.[9] It was this link that concerned the Court in *Epperson v. Arkansas*, which also involved a facial challenge to a statute regulating the teaching of evolution. In that case, the Court reviewed an Arkansas statute that made it unlawful for an instructor to teach evolution or to use a textbook that referred to this scientific theory. Although the Arkansas antievolution law did not explicitly state its predominant religious purpose, the Court could not ignore that "[t]he statute was a product of the upsurge of 'fundamentalist' religious fervor" that has long viewed this particular scientific theory as contradicting the literal interpretation of the Bible. After reviewing the history of antievolution statutes, the Court determined that "there can be no doubt that the motivation for the [Arkansas] law was the same [as other anti-evolution statutes]: to suppress the teaching of a theory which, it was thought, 'denied' the divine creation of man." The Court found that there can be no legitimate state interest in protecting particular religions from scientific views "distasteful to them," and concluded "that the First Amendment does not permit the State to require that teaching and learning must be tailored to the principles or prohibitions of any religious sect or dogma."

These same historic and contemporaneous antagonisms between the teachings of certain religious denominations and the teaching of evolution are present in this case. The preeminent purpose of the Louisiana Legislature was clearly to advance the religious viewpoint that a supernatural being created humankind. The term "creation science" was defined as embracing this particular religious doctrine by those responsible for the passage of the Creationism Act. Senator Keith's leading expert on creation science, Edward Boudreaux, testified at the legislative hearings that the theory of creation science included belief in the existence of a supernatural creator. *See* [Boudreaux legislative testimony] (noting that "creation scientists" point to high probability that life

---

9 *See McLean v. Arkansas Bd. of Ed.,* 529 F. Supp. 1255, 1258-1264 (ED Ark.1982) (reviewing historical and contemporary antagonisms between the theory of evolution and religious movements).

was "created by an intelligent mind").[12] Senator Keith also cited testimony from other experts to support the creation-science view that "a creator [was] responsible for the universe and everything in it."[13] The legislative history therefore reveals that the term "creation science," as contemplated by the legislature that adopted this Act, embodies the religious belief that a supernatural creator was responsible for the creation of humankind.

Furthermore, it is not happenstance that the legislature required the teaching of a theory that coincided with this religious view. The legislative history documents that the Act's primary purpose was to change the science curriculum of public schools in order to provide persuasive advantage to a particular religious doctrine that rejects the factual basis of evolution in its entirety. The sponsor of the Creationism Act, Senator Keith, explained during the legislative hearings that his disdain for the theory of evolution resulted from the support that evolution supplied to views contrary to his own religious beliefs. According to Senator Keith, the theory of evolution was consonant with the "cardinal principle[s] of religious humanism, secular humanism, theological liberalism, aetheistism [sic]." The state senator repeatedly stated that scientific evidence supporting his religious views should be included in the public school curriculum to redress the fact that the theory of evolution incidentally coincided with what he characterized as religious beliefs antithetical to his own.[14] The legislation therefore sought to alter the science curriculum to reflect endorsement of a religious view that is antagonistic to the theory of evolution.

In this case, the purpose of the Creationism Act was to restructure the science curriculum to conform with a particular religious viewpoint. Out of many possible science subjects taught in the public schools, the legislature chose to affect the teaching of the one scientific theory that historically has been opposed by

---

[12] Boudreaux repeatedly defined creation science in terms of a theory that supports the existence of a supernatural creator. *See, e.g.,* 2 App. E-501 - E-502 (equating creation science with a theory pointing "to conditions of a creator"); 1 App. E-153 - E-154 ("Creation . . . requires the direct involvement of a supernatural intelligence"). The lead witness at the hearings introducing the original bill, Luther Sunderland, described creation science as postulating "that everything was created by some intelligence or power external to the universe." *Id.,* at E-9 - E-10.

[13] Senator Keith believed that creation science embodied this view: "One concept is that a creator however you define a creator was responsible for everything that is in this world. The other concept is that it just evolved." *Id.,* at E-280. Besides Senator Keith, several of the most vocal legislators also revealed their religious motives for supporting the bill in the official legislative history. *See, e.g., id.,* at E-441, E-443 (Sen. Saunders noting that bill was amended so that teachers could refer to the Bible and other religious texts to support the creation-science theory); 2 App. E-561 - E-562, E-610 (Rep. Jenkins contending that the existence of God was a scientific fact).

[14] *See, e.g.,* 1 App. E-74 - E-75 (noting that evolution is contrary to his family's religious beliefs); *id.,* at E-313 (contending that evolution advances religions contrary to his own); *id.,* at E-357 (stating that evolution is "almost a religion" to science teachers); *id.,* at E-418 (arguing that evolution is cornerstone of some religions contrary to his own); 2 App. E-763 – E-764 (author of model bill, from which Act is derived, sent copy of the model bill to Senator Keith and advised that "I view this whole battle as one between God and anti-God forces. . . . if evolution is permitted to continue . . . it will continue to be made to appear that a Supreme Being is unnecessary . . .").

certain religious sects. As in *Epperson*, the legislature passed the Act to give preference to those religious groups which have as one of their tenets the creation of humankind by a divine creator. The "overriding fact" that confronted the Court in *Epperson* was "that Arkansas' law selects from the body of knowledge a particular segment which it proscribes for the sole reason that it is deemed to conflict with. . . a particular interpretation of the Book of Genesis by a particular religious group." Similarly, the Creationism Act is designed *either* to promote the theory of creation science which embodies a particular religious tenet by requiring that creation science be taught whenever evolution is taught or to prohibit the teaching of a scientific theory disfavored by certain religious sects by forbidding the teaching of evolution when creation science is not also taught. The Establishment Clause, however, "forbids *alike* the preference of a religious doctrine *or* the prohibition of theory which is deemed antagonistic to a particular dogma." *Epperson*. Because the primary purpose of the Creationism Act is to advance a particular religious belief, the Act endorses religion in violation of the First Amendment.

We do not imply that a legislature could never require that scientific critiques of prevailing scientific theories be taught. Indeed, the Court acknowledged in *Stone* that its decision forbidding the posting of the Ten Commandments did not mean that no use could ever be made of the Ten Commandments, or that the Ten Commandments played an exclusively religious role in the history of Western Civilization. In a similar way, teaching a variety of scientific theories about the origins of humankind to schoolchildren might be validly done with the clear secular intent of enhancing the effectiveness of science instruction. But because the primary purpose of the Creationism Act is to endorse a particular religious doctrine, the Act furthers religion in violation of the Establishment Clause.[15]

IV

Appellants contend that genuine issues of material fact remain in dispute, and therefore the District Court erred in granting summary judgment. Federal Rule of Civil Procedure 56(c) provides that summary judgment "shall be rendered forthwith if the pleadings, depositions, answers to interrogatories, and admissions on file, together with the affidavits, if any, show that there is no genuine issue as to any material fact and that the moving party is entitled to a judgment as a matter of law." A court's finding of improper purpose behind a statute is appropriately determined by the statute on its face, its legislative history, or its interpretation by a responsible administrative agency. The plain meaning of the statute's words, enlightened by their context and the contemporaneous leg-

---

[15] Neither the District Court nor the Court of Appeals found a clear secular purpose, while both agreed that the Creationism Act's primary purpose was to advance religion. "When both courts below are unable to discern an arguably valid secular purpose, this Court normally should hesitate to find one." *Wallace v. Jaffree*, 472 U.S., at 66 (POWELL, J., concurring).

islative history, can control the determination of legislative purpose. Moreover, in determining the legislative purpose of a statute, the Court has also considered the historical context of the statute, *e.g.*, *Epperson v. Arkansas*, and the specific sequence of events leading to passage of the statute, *e.g.*, *Arlington Heights v. Metropolitan Housing Dev. Corp.*, 429 U.S. 252 (1977).

In this case, appellees' motion for summary judgment rested on the plain language of the Creationism Act, the legislative history and historical context of the Act, the specific sequence of events leading to the passage of the Act, the State Board's report on a survey of school superintendents, and the correspondence between the Act's legislative sponsor and its key witnesses. Appellants contend that affidavits made by two scientists, two theologians, and an education administrator raise a genuine issue of material fact and that summary judgment was therefore barred. The affidavits define creation science as "origin through abrupt appearance in complex form" and allege that such a viewpoint constitutes a true scientific theory.

We agree with the lower courts that these affidavits do not raise a genuine issue of material fact. The existence of "uncontroverted affidavits" does not bar summary judgment. Moreover, the postenactment testimony of outside experts is of little use in determining the Louisiana Legislature's purpose in enacting this statute. The Louisiana Legislature did hear and rely on scientific experts in passing the bill, but none of the persons making the affidavits produced by the appellants participated in or contributed to the enactment of the law or its implementation.[18] The District Court, in its discretion, properly concluded that a Monday-morning "battle of the experts" over possible technical meanings of terms in the statute would not illuminate the contemporaneous purpose of the Louisiana Legislature when it made the law.[19] We therefore conclude that the District Court did not err in finding that appellants failed to raise a genuine issue of material fact, and in granting summary judgment.

---

[18] Appellants contend that the affidavits are relevant because the term "creation science" is a technical term similar to that found in statutes that regulate certain scientific or technological developments. Even assuming, *arguendo,* that "creation science" is a term of art as represented by appellants, the definition provided by the relevant agency provides a better insight than the affidavits submitted by appellants in this case. In a 1981 survey conducted by the Louisiana Department of Education, the school superintendents in charge of implementing the provisions of the Creationism Act were asked to interpret the meaning of "creation science" as used in the statute. About 75 percent of Louisiana's superintendents stated that they understood "creation science" to be a religious doctrine. 2 App. E-798 - E-799. Of this group, the largest proportion of superintendents interpreted creation science, as defined by the Act, to mean the literal interpretation of the Book of Genesis. The remaining superintendents believed that the Act required teaching the view that "the universe was made by a creator." *Id.*, at E-799.

[19] The Court has previously found the postenactment elucidation of the meaning of a statute to be of little relevance in determining the intent of the legislature contemporaneous to the passage of the statute. *See Wallace v. Jaffree,* 472 U.S., at 57, n. 45; *id.,* at 75 (O'CONNOR, J., concurring in judgment).

JUSTICE POWELL, with whom JUSTICE O'CONNOR joins, concurring.

I

This Court consistently has applied the three-pronged test of *Lemon v. Kurtzman* to determine whether a particular state action violates the Establishment Clause of the Constitution. The first requirement of the *Lemon* test is that the challenged statute have a "secular legislative purpose." If no valid secular purpose can be identified, then the statute violates the Establishment Clause.

A

"The starting point in every case involving construction of a statute is the language itself." *Blue Chip Stamps v. Manor Drug Stores*, 421 U.S. 723, 756 (1975) (POWELL, J., concurring). The Balanced Treatment for Creation-Science and Evolution-Science Act (Act or Balanced Treatment Act) provides in part:

> "[P]ublic schools within [the] state shall give balanced treatment to creation-science and to evolution-science. Balanced treatment of these two models shall be given in classroom lectures taken as a whole for each course, in textbook materials taken as a whole for each course, in library materials taken as a whole for the sciences and taken as a whole for the humanities, and in other educational programs in public schools, to the extent that such lectures, textbooks, library materials, or educational programs deal in any way with the subject of the origin of man, life, the earth, or the universe. When creation or evolution is taught, each shall be taught as a theory, rather than as proven scientific fact."

"Balanced treatment" means "providing whatever information and instruction in both creation and evolution models the classroom teacher determines is necessary and appropriate to provide insight into both theories in view of the textbooks and other instructional materials available for use in his classroom." "Creation-science" is defined as "the scientific evidences for creation and inferences from those scientific evidences." "Evolution-science" means "the scientific evidences for evolution and inferences from those scientific evidences."

Although the Act requires the teaching of the scientific evidences of both creation and evolution whenever either is taught, it does not define either term. "A fundamental canon of statutory construction is that, unless otherwise defined, words will be interpreted as taking their ordinary, contemporary, common meaning." *Perrin v. United States*, 444 U.S. 37, 42 (1979). The "doctrine or theory of creation" is commonly defined as "holding that matter, the various forms of life, and the world were created by a transcendent God out of nothing." WEBSTER'S THIRD NEW INTERNATIONAL DICTIONARY 532 (unabridged 1981). "Evolution" is defined as "the theory that the various types of animals and plants have their origin in other preexisting types, the distinguishable differences being due to modifications in successive generations." Thus, the Balanced Treatment Act mandates that public schools present the scientific evidence to support a theory of divine creation whenever they present the scientific evidence to support the theory of evolution. "[C]oncepts concerning God or a supreme being of some sort are manifestly religious. . . . These concepts do not shed that religiosity merely because they are presented as a philosophy or as a science." *Malnak v. Yogi.* From the face of the statute, a purpose to advance a religious belief is apparent.

A religious purpose alone is not enough to invalidate an act of a state legislature. The religious purpose must predominate. The Act contains a statement of purpose: to "protec[t] academic freedom." This statement is puzzling. Of course, the "academic freedom" of teachers to present information in public schools, and students to receive it, is broad. But it necessarily is circumscribed by the Establishment Clause. "Academic freedom" does not encompass the right of a legislature to structure the public school curriculum in order to advance a particular religious belief. *Epperson v. Arkansas.* Nevertheless, I read this statement in the Act as rendering the purpose of the statute at least ambiguous. Accordingly, I proceed to review the legislative history of the Act.

B

In June 1980, Senator Bill Keith introduced Senate Bill 956 in the Louisiana Legislature. The stated purpose of the bill was to "assure academic freedom by requiring the teaching of the theory of creation *ex nihilo* in all public schools where the theory of evolution is taught." 1 App E-1.[202] The bill defined the "theory of creation *ex nihilo*" as "the belief that the origin of the elements, the galaxy, the solar system, of life, of all the species of plants and animals, the origin of man, and the origin of all things and their processes and relationships were created *ex nihilo* and fixed by God." This theory was referred to by Senator Keith as "scientific creationism."

While a Senate committee was studying scientific creationism, Senator Keith introduced a second draft of the bill, requiring balanced treatment of "evolution-science" and "creation-science." Although the Keith bill prohibited "instruction in any religious doctrine or materials," it defined "creation-science" to include

"the scientific evidences and related inferences that indicate (a) sudden creation of the universe, energy, and life from nothing; (b) the insufficiency of mutation and natural selection in bringing about development of all living kinds from a single organism; (c) changes only within

---

202 Creation *"ex nihilo"* means creation "from nothing" and has been found to be an "inherently religious concept." *McLean v. Arkansas Board of Education*, 529 F. Supp. 1255, 1266 (ED Ark.1982). The District Court in *McLean* found:

"The argument that creation from nothing in [§] 4(a)(1) [of the substantially similar Arkansas Balanced Treatment Act] does not involve a supernatural deity has no evidentiary or rational support. To the contrary, 'creation out of nothing' is a concept unique to Western religions. In traditional Western religious thought, the conception of a creator of the world is a conception of God. Indeed, creation of the world 'out of nothing' is the ultimate religious statement because God is the only actor." *Id.*, at 1265.

fixed limits or originally created kinds of plants and animals; (d) separate ancestry for man and apes; (e) explanation of the earth's geology by catastrophism, including the occurrence of a worldwide flood; and (f) a relatively recent inception of the earth and living kinds."

Significantly, the model Act on which the Keith bill relied was also the basis for a similar statute in Arkansas. *See McLean v. Arkansas Board of Education*, 529 F. Supp. 1255 (ED Ark.1982). The District Court in *McLean* carefully examined this model Act, particularly the section defining creation science, and concluded that "[b]oth [its] concepts and wording. . . convey an inescapable religiosity." *Id.,* at 1265. The court found that "[t]he ideas of [this section] are not merely similar to the literal interpretation of Genesis; they are identical and parallel to no other story of creation." *Ibid.*

The complaint in *McLean* was filed on May 27, 1981. On May 28, the Louisiana Senate committee amended the Keith bill to delete the illustrative list of scientific evidences. According to the legislator who proposed the amendment, it was "not intended to try to gut [the bill] in any way, or defeat the purpose [for] which Senator Keith introduced [it]," and was not viewed as working "any violence to the bill." Instead, the concern was "whether this should be an all inclusive list."

The legislature then held hearings on the amended bill that became the Balanced Treatment Act under review. The principal creation scientist to testify in support of the Act was Dr. Edward Boudreaux. He did not elaborate on the nature of creation science except to indicate that the "scientific evidences" of the theory are "the objective information of science [that] point [s] to conditions of a creator." He further testified that the recognized creation scientists in the United States, who "numbe[r] something like a thousand [and] who hold doctorate and masters degrees in all areas of science," are affiliated with either or both the Institute for Creation Research and the Creation Research Society. Information on both of these organizations is part of the legislative history, and a review of their goals and activities sheds light on the nature of creation science as it was presented to, and understood by, the Louisiana Legislature.

The Institute for Creation Research is an affiliate of the Christian Heritage College in San Diego, California. The Institute was established to address the "urgent need for our nation to return to belief in a personal, omnipotent Creator, who has a purpose for His creation and to whom all people must eventually give account." A goal of the Institute is "a revival of belief in special creation as the true explanation of the origin of the world." Therefore, the Institute currently is working on the "development of new methods for teaching scientific creationism in public schools." The Creation Research Society (CRS) is located in Ann Arbor, Michigan. A member must subscribe to the following statement of belief: "The Bible is the written word of God, and because it is inspired throughout, all of its assertions are historically and scientifically true." To study creation science at the CRS, a member must accept "that the account of origins in Genesis is a factual presentation of simple historical truth."[3]

C

When, as here, "both courts below are unable to discern an arguably valid secular purpose, this Court normally should hesitate to find one." *Wallace v. Jaffree* (POWELL, J., concurring). My examination of the language and the legislative history of the Balanced Treatment Act confirms that the intent of the Louisiana Legislature was to promote a particular religious belief. The legislative history of the Arkansas statute prohibiting the teaching of evolution examined in *Epperson v. Arkansas*, was strikingly similar to the legislative history of the Balanced Treatment Act. In *Epperson*, the Court found:

> "It is clear that fundamentalist sectarian conviction was and is the law's reason for existence. Its antecedent, Tennessee's 'monkey law,' candidly stated its purpose: to make it unlawful 'to teach any theory that denies the story of the Divine Creation of man as taught in the Bible, and to teach instead that man has descended from a lower order of animals.' Perhaps the sensational publicity attendant upon the Scopes trial induced Arkansas to adopt less explicit language. It eliminated Tennessee's reference to 'the story of the Divine creation of man' as taught in the Bible, but there is no doubt that the motivation for the law was the same: to suppress the teaching of a theory which, it was thought, 'denied' the divine creation of man." *Id.*, at 107-109 (footnotes omitted).

Here, it is clear that religious belief is the Balanced Treatment Act's "reason for existence." The tenets of creation science parallel the Genesis story of creation,[4] and this is a religious belief. "[N]o legislative recitation of a supposed sec-

---

[3] The District Court in *McLean* noted three other elements of the CRS statement of belief to which members must subscribe:

> "'[i] All basic types of living things, including man, were made by direct creative acts of God during Creation Week as described in Genesis. Whatever biological changes have occurred since Creation have accomplished only changes within the original created kinds. [ii] The great Flood described in Genesis, commonly referred to as the Noachian Deluge, was an historical event, world-wide in its extent and effect. [iii] Finally, we are an organization of Christian men of science, who accept Jesus Christ as our Lord and Savior. The account of the special creation of Adam and Eve as one man and one woman, and their subsequent Fall into sin, is the basis for our belief in the necessity of a Savior for all mankind. Therefore, salvation can come only thru (sic) accepting Jesus Christ as our Savior.'" 529 F. Supp., at 1260, n. 7.

[4] After hearing testimony from numerous experts, the District Court in *McLean* concluded that "[t]he parallels between [the definition section of the model Act] and Genesis are quite specific." *Id.*, at 1265, n. 19. It found the concepts of "sudden creation from nothing," a worldwide flood of divine origin, and "kinds" to be derived from Genesis; "relatively recent inception" to mean "an age of the earth from 6,000 to 10,000 years" and to be based "on the genealogy of the Old Testament using the rather astronomical ages assigned to the patriarchs"; and the "separate ancestry of man and ape" to focus on "the portion of the theory of evolution which Fundamentalists find most offensive." *Ibid.* (citing *Epperson v. Arkansas*, 393 U.S. 97 (1968)).

ular purpose can blind us to that fact." *Stone v. Graham*, 449 U.S. 39, 41 (1980). Although the Act as finally enacted does not contain explicit reference to its religious purpose, there is no indication in the legislative history that the deletion of "creation ex nihilo" and the four primary tenets of the theory was intended to alter the purpose of teaching creation science. Instead, the statements of purpose of the sources of creation science in the United States make clear that their purpose is to promote a religious belief. I find no persuasive evidence in the legislative history that the legislature's purpose was any different. The fact that the Louisiana Legislature purported to add information to the school curriculum rather than detract from it as in *Epperson* does not affect my analysis. Both legislatures acted with the unconstitutional purpose of structuring the public school curriculum to make it compatible with a particular religious belief: the "divine creation of man."

That the statute is limited to the scientific evidences supporting the theory does not render its purpose secular. In reaching its conclusion that the Act is unconstitutional, the Court of Appeals "[did] not deny that the underpinnings of creationism may be supported by scientific evidence." And there is no need to do so. Whatever the academic merit of particular subjects or theories, the Establishment Clause limits the discretion of state officials to pick and choose among them for the purpose of promoting a particular religious belief. The language of the statute and its legislative history convince me that the Louisiana Legislature exercised its discretion for this purpose in this case.

JUSTICE SCALIA, with whom THE CHIEF JUSTICE joins, dissenting.

II

A

We have relatively little information upon which to judge the motives of those who supported the Act. About the only direct evidence is the statute itself and transcripts of the seven committee hearings at which it was considered. Unfortunately, several of those hearings were sparsely attended, and the legislators who were present revealed little about their motives. We have no committee reports, no floor debates, no remarks inserted into the legislative history, no statement from the Governor, and no postenactment statements or testimony from the bill's sponsor or any other legislators. *Cf. Wallace v. Jaffree.* Nevertheless, there is ample evidence that the majority is wrong in holding that the Balanced Treatment Act is without secular purpose.

At the outset, it is important to note that the Balanced Treatment Act did not fly through the Louisiana Legislature on wings of fundamentalist religious fervor — which would be unlikely, in any event, since only a small minority of the State's citizens belong to fundamentalist religious denominations. *See* B. QUINN, H. ANDERSON, M. BRADLEY, P. GOETTING, & P. SHRIVER, CHURCHES AND CHURCH MEMBERSHIP IN THE UNITED STATES 16 (1982). The Act had its genesis (so to speak) in legislation introduced by Senator Bill Keith in June 1980. After two hearings before the Senate Committee on Education, Senator Keith asked that his bill be referred to a study commission composed of members of both Houses of the Louisiana Legislature. He expressed hope that the joint committee would give the bill careful consideration and determine whether his arguments were "legitimate." The committee met twice during the interim, heard testimony (both for and against the bill) from several witnesses, and received staff reports. Senator Keith introduced his bill again when the legislature reconvened. The Senate Committee on Education held two more hearings and approved the bill after substantially amending it (in part over Senator Keith's objection). After approval by the full Senate, the bill was referred to the House Committee on Education. That committee conducted a lengthy hearing, adopted further amendments, and sent the bill on to the full House, where it received favorable consideration. The Senate concurred in the House amendments and on July 20, 1981, the Governor signed the bill into law.

Senator Keith's statements before the various committees that considered the bill hardly reflect the confidence of a man preaching to the converted. He asked his colleagues to "keep an open mind" and not to be "biased" by misleading characterizations of creation science. He also urged them to "look at this subject on its merits and not on some preconceived idea." Senator Keith's reception was not especially warm. Over his strenuous objection, the Senate Committee on Education voted 5-1 to amend his bill to deprive it of any force; as amended, the bill merely gave teachers *permission* to balance the teaching of creation science or evolution with the other. The House Committee restored the "mandatory" language to the bill by a vote of only 6-5, and both the full House (by vote of 52-35), and full Senate (23-15), had to repel further efforts to gut the bill.

The legislators understood that Senator Keith's bill involved a "unique" subject, and they were repeatedly made aware of its potential constitutional problems. Although the Establishment Clause, including its secular purpose requirement, was of substantial concern to the legislators, they eventually voted overwhelmingly in favor of the Balanced Treatment Act: The House approved it 71-19 (with 15 members absent), the Senate 26-12 (with all members present). The legislators specifically designated the protection of "academic freedom" as the purpose of the Act. We cannot accurately assess whether this purpose is a "sham," until we first examine the evidence presented to the legislature far more carefully than the Court has done.

Before summarizing the testimony of Senator Keith and his supporters, I wish to make clear that I by no means intend to endorse its accuracy. But my views (and the views of this Court) about creation science and evolution are (or should be) beside the point. Our task is not to judge the debate about teaching the origins of life, but to ascertain what the members of the Louisiana Legislature believed. The vast majority of them voted to approve a bill which explicitly stated a secular purpose; what is crucial is not their *wisdom* in believing that purpose would be achieved by the bill, but their *sincerity* in believing it would be.

Most of the testimony in support of Senator Keith's bill came from the Senator himself and from scientists and educators he presented, many of whom enjoyed academic credentials that may have been regarded as quite impressive by members of the Louisiana Legislature. To a substantial extent, their testimony was devoted to lengthy, and, to the layman, seemingly expert scientific expositions on the origin of life. These scientific lectures touched upon, *inter alia*, biology, paleontology, genetics, astronomy, astrophysics, probability analysis, and biochemistry. The witnesses repeatedly assured committee members that "hundreds and hundreds" of highly respected, internationally renowned scientists believed in creation science and would support their testimony.

Senator Keith and his witnesses testified essentially as set forth in the following numbered paragraphs:

(1) There are two and only two scientific explanations for the beginning of life — evolution and creation science. Both are bona fide "sciences." Both posit a theory of the origin of life and subject that theory to empirical testing. Evolution posits that life arose out of inanimate chemical compounds and has gradually evolved over millions of years. Creation science posits that all life forms now on earth appeared suddenly and relatively recently and have changed little. Since there are only two possible explanations of the origin of life, any evidence that tends to disprove the theory of evolution necessarily tends to prove the theory of creation science, and vice versa. For example, the abrupt appearance in the fossil record of complex life, and the extreme rarity of transitional life forms in that record, are evidence for creation science.

(2) The body of scientific evidence supporting creation science is as strong as that supporting evolution. In fact, it may be *stronger*. The evidence for evolution is far less compelling than we have been led to believe. Evolution is not a scientific "fact," since it cannot actually be observed in a laboratory. Rather, evolution is merely a scientific theory or "guess." It is a very bad guess at that. The scientific problems with evolution are so serious that it could accurately be termed a "myth."

(3) Creation science is educationally valuable. Students exposed to it better understand the current state of scientific evidence about the origin of life. Those students even have a better understanding of evolution. Creation science can and should be presented to children without any religious content.

(4) Although creation science is educationally valuable and strictly scientific, it is now being censored from or misrepresented in the public schools. Evolution, in turn, is misrepresented as an absolute truth. Teachers have been brainwashed by an entrenched scientific establishment composed almost exclusively of scientists to whom evolution is like a "religion." These scientists discriminate against creation scientists so as to prevent evolution's weaknesses from being exposed.

(5) The censorship of creation science has at least two harmful effects. First, it deprives students of knowledge of one of the two scientific explanations for the origin of life and leads them to believe that evolution is proven fact; thus, their education suffers and they are wrongly taught that science has proved

their religious beliefs false. Second, it violates the Establishment Clause. The United States Supreme Court has held that secular humanism is a religion. (Sen. Keith) (referring to *Torcaso v. Watkins* [*infra* Chapter 3]). Belief in evolution is a central tenet of that religion. Thus, by censoring creation science and instructing students that evolution is fact, public school teachers are *now* advancing religion in violation of the Establishment Clause.

Senator Keith repeatedly and vehemently denied that his purpose was to advance a particular religious doctrine. At the outset of the first hearing on the legislation, he testified: "We are not going to say today that you should have some kind of religious instructions in our schools. . . . We are not talking about religion today. . . . I am not proposing that we take the Bible in each science class and read the first chapter of Genesis." At a later hearing, Senator Keith stressed: "[T]o. . . teach religion and disguise it as creationism. . . is not my intent. My intent is to see to it that our textbooks are not censored." He made many similar statements throughout the hearings.

We have no way of knowing, of course, how many legislators believed the testimony of Senator Keith and his witnesses. But in the absence of evidence to the contrary, we have to assume that many of them did. Given that assumption, the Court today plainly errs in holding that the Louisiana Legislature passed the Balanced Treatment Act for exclusively religious purposes.

B.

Even with nothing more than this legislative history to go on, I think it would be extraordinary to invalidate the Balanced Treatment Act for lack of a valid secular purpose. Striking down a law approved by the democratically elected representatives of the people is no minor matter. "The cardinal principle of statutory construction is to save and not to destroy. We have repeatedly held that as between two possible interpretations of a statute, by one of which it would be unconstitutional and by the other valid, our plain duty is to adopt that which will save the act." *NLRB v. Jones & Laughlin Steel Corp.*, 301 U.S. 1, 30 (1937). So, too, it seems to me, with discerning statutory purpose. Even if the legislative history were silent or ambiguous about the existence of a secular purpose — and here it is not — the statute should survive *Lemon*'s purpose test. But even more validation than mere legislative history is present here. The Louisiana Legislature explicitly set forth its secular purpose ("protecting academic freedom") in the very text of the Act. We have in the past repeatedly relied upon or deferred to such expressions.

The Court seeks to evade the force of this expression of purpose by stubbornly misinterpreting it, and then finding that the provisions of the Act do not advance that misinterpreted purpose, thereby showing it to be a sham. The Court first surmises that "academic freedom" means "enhancing the freedom of teachers to teach what they will" — even though "academic freedom" in that sense has little scope in the structured elementary and secondary curriculums with which the Act is concerned. Alternatively, the Court suggests that it might mean "maximiz[ing] the comprehensiveness and effectiveness of science instruction" — though that is an exceedingly strange interpretation of the words, and one that is refuted on the very face of the statute. Had the Court devoted to this central question of the meaning of the legislatively expressed purpose a small fraction of the research into legislative history that produced its quotations of religiously motivated statements by individual legislators, it would have discerned quite readily what "academic freedom" meant: *students'* freedom from *indoctrination*. The legislature wanted to ensure that students would be free to decide for themselves how life began, based upon a fair and balanced presentation of the scientific evidence — that is, to protect "the right of each [student] voluntarily to determine what to believe (and what not to believe) free of any coercive pressures from the State." *Grand Rapids School District v. Ball, infra* Chapter 8. The legislature did not care whether the topic of origins was taught; it simply wished to ensure that *when* the topic was taught, students would receive "'all of the evidence.'"

As originally introduced, the "purpose" section of the Balanced Treatment Act read: "This Chapter is enacted for the purposes of protecting academic freedom. . . *of students*. . . and assisting *students* in their search for truth." Among the proposed findings of fact contained in the original version of the bill was the following: "Public school instruction in only evolution-science. . . *violates the principle of academic freedom because it denies students a choice between scientific models and instead indoctrinates them in evolution science alone.*" Senator Keith unquestionably understood "academic freedom" to mean "freedom from indoctrination."

If one adopts the obviously intended meaning of the statutory term "academic freedom," there is no basis whatever for concluding that the purpose they express is a "sham." To the contrary, the Act pursues that purpose plainly and consistently. It requires that, whenever the subject of origins is covered, evolution be "taught as a theory, rather than as proven scientific fact" and that scientific evidence inconsistent with the theory of evolution (viz., "creation science") be taught as well. Living up to its title of *"Balanced Treatment* for Creation-Science and Evolution-Science Act," it treats the teaching of creation the same way. It does *not* mandate instruction in creation science; *forbids* teachers to present creation science "as proven scientific fact"; and *bans* the teaching of creation science unless the theory is (to use the Court's terminology) "discredit[ed] '. . . at every turn'" with the teaching of evolution. It surpasses understanding how the Court can see in this a purpose "to restructure the science curriculum to conform with a particular religious viewpoint," "to provide a persuasive advantage to a particular religious doctrine," "to promote the theory of creation science which embodies a particular religious tenet," and "to endorse a particular religious doctrine."

The Act's reference to "creation" is not convincing evidence of religious purpose. The Act defines creation science as *"scientific evidenc[e],"* and Senator Keith and his witnesses repeatedly stressed that the subject can and should be presented without religious content. We have no basis on the record to conclude that creation science need be anything other than a collection of scientific data supporting the theory that life abruptly appeared on earth. Creation science, its proponents insist, no more must explain *whence* life came than evolution must explain whence came the inanimate materials from which it says life evolved. But even if that were not so, to posit a past creator is not to posit the eternal and personal God who is the object of religious veneration. Indeed, it is not even to posit the "*unmoved* mover" hypothesized by Aristotle and other notably nonfundamentalist philosophers. Senator Keith suggested this when he referred to "a creator *however you define a creator.*"

The Court cites three provisions of the Act which, it argues, demonstrate a "discriminatory preference for the teaching of creation science" and no interest in "academic freedom." First, the Act prohibits discrimination only against creation scientists and those who teach creation science. Second, the Act requires local school boards to develop and provide to science teachers "a curriculum guide on presentation of creation-science." Finally, the Act requires the Governor to designate seven creation scientists who shall, upon request, assist local school boards in developing the curriculum guides. But none of these provisions casts doubt upon the sincerity of the legislators' articulated purpose of "academic freedom" — unless, of course, one gives that term the obviously erroneous meanings preferred by the Court. The Louisiana legislators had been told repeatedly that creation scientists were scorned by most educators and scientists, who themselves had an almost religious faith in evolution. It is hardly surprising, then, that in seeking to achieve a balanced, "nonindoctrinating" curriculum, the legislators protected from discrimination only those teachers whom they thought were *suffering* from discrimination. (Also, the legislators were undoubtedly aware of *Epperson v. Arkansas*, and thus could quite reasonably have concluded that discrimination against evolutionists was already prohibited.) The two provisions respecting the development of curriculum guides are also consistent with "academic freedom" as the Louisiana Legislature understood the term. Witnesses had informed the legislators that, because of the hostility of most scientists and educators to creation science, the topic had been censored from or badly misrepresented in elementary and secondary school texts. In light of the unavailability of works on creation science suitable for classroom use (a fact appellees concede) and the existence of ample materials on evolution, it was entirely reasonable for the legislature to conclude that science teachers attempting to implement the Act would need a curriculum guide on creation science, but not on evolution, and that those charged with developing the guide would need an easily accessible group of creation scientists. Thus, the provisions of the Act of so much concern to the Court *support* the conclusion that the legislature acted to advance "academic freedom."

The legislative history gives ample evidence of the sincerity of the Balanced Treatment Act's articulated purpose. Witness after witness urged the legislators to support the Act so that students would not be "indoctrinated" but would instead be free to decide for themselves, based upon a fair presentation of the scientific evidence, about the origin of life.

Legislators other than Senator Keith made only a few statements providing insight into their motives, but those statements cast no doubt upon the sincerity of the Act's articulated purpose. The legislators were concerned primarily about the manner in which the subject of origins was presented in Louisiana schools — specifically, about whether scientifically valuable information was being censored and students misled about evolution. Representatives Cain, Jenkins, and F. Thompson seemed impressed by the scientific evidence presented in support of creation science. At the first study commission hearing, Senator Picard and Representative M. Thompson questioned Senator Keith about Louisiana teachers' treatment of evolution and creation science. At the close of the hearing, Representative M. Thompson told the audience:

> "We as members of the committee will also receive from the staff information of what is currently being taught in the Louisiana public schools. We really want to see [it]. I. . . have no idea in what manner [biology] is presented and in what manner the creationist theories [are] excluded in the public school[s]. We want to look at what the status of the situation is."

Legislators made other comments suggesting a concern about censorship and misrepresentation of scientific information.

It is undoubtedly true that what prompted the legislature to direct its attention to the misrepresentation of evolution in the schools (rather than the inaccurate presentation of other topics) was its awareness of the tension between evolution and the religious beliefs of many children. But even appellees concede that a valid secular purpose is not rendered impermissible simply because its pursuit is prompted by concern for religious sensitivities. If a history teacher falsely told her students that the bones of Jesus Christ had been discovered, or a physics teacher that the Shroud of Turin had been conclusively established to be inexplicable on the basis of natural causes, I cannot believe (despite the majority's implication to the contrary) that legislators or school board members would be constitutionally prohibited from taking corrective action, simply because that action was prompted by concern for the religious beliefs of the misinstructed students.

In sum, even if one concedes, for the sake of argument, that a majority of the Louisiana Legislature voted for the Balanced Treatment Act partly in order to foster (rather than merely eliminate discrimination against) Christian fundamentalist beliefs, our cases establish that that alone would not suffice to invalidate the Act, so long as there was a genuine secular purpose as well. We have, moreover, no adequate basis for disbelieving the secular purpose set forth in the Act itself, or for concluding that it is a sham enacted to conceal the legislators' violation of their oaths of office. I am astonished by the Court's unprecedented readiness to reach such a conclusion, which I can only attribute to an intellectual predisposition created by the facts and the legend of *Scopes v. State* — an instinctive reaction that any governmentally imposed requirements bearing upon the teaching of evolution must be a manifestation of Christian fundamentalist repression. In this case, however, it seems to me the Court's position is the repressive one. The people of Louisiana, including those who are Christian fundamentalists, are quite entitled, as a secular matter, to have whatever scientific evidence there may be against evolution presented in their schools, just as Mr. Scopes was entitled to present whatever scientific evidence there was for it. Perhaps what the Louisiana Legislature has done is unconstitutional because there is no such evidence, and the scheme they have established will amount to no more than a presentation of the Book of Genesis. But we cannot say that on the evidence before us in this summary judgment context, which includes ample uncontradicted testimony that "creation science" is a body of scientific knowledge rather than revealed belief. *Infinitely less* can we say (or should we say) that the scientific evidence for evolution is so conclusive that no one could be gullible enough to believe that there is any real scientific evidence to the contrary, so that the legislation's stated purpose must be a lie. Yet that illiberal judgment, that *Scopes*-in-reverse, is ultimately the basis on which the Court's facile rejection of the Louisiana Legislature's purpose must rest.

NOTES

1. *Inconvenient Facts and Religion.* Consider conservative columnist George Will's critique of Justice Scalia's *Edwards* dissent:

> "Creation science" is a theory for people who are only interested in facts that weigh against a rival theory. But as Gould has written, no scientist doubts the basic fact that life evolves. The uncertainties concern the mechanisms. When Scalia tries to make much of the fact that the original version of the Louisiana bill emphasized giving "students a choice between scientific models," he is only documenting the confusion of Louisiana's legislators. But that does not change the fact that they were legislating a religious assertion disguised as a scientific inquiry.
>
> There is poignancy in the plight of fundamentalists whose spiritual serenity is under siege from facts. It is for theologians to say what consequences the fact of evolution has for faith. But it is for every thoughtful citizen to say this: The bedrock of Western civilization is a willingness — no, an eagerness — to face and embrace facts. And if the facts inconvenience beliefs, too bad for the beliefs.

George F. Will, *Good Grief, Scalia!*, WASH. POST, June 25, 1987, at A17.

2. *The Scientific Community's Response to Scalia.* Scalia's *Edwards* dissent did not fare any better with the scientific community. "[T]hough it may form only part of his rationale, Scalia's argument relies crucially upon a false concept of science. . . . I regret to say that Justice Scalia does not understand the subject matter of evolutionary biology. He has simply adopted the creationists' definition and thereby repeated their willful mistake. . . . He equates creation and evolution because creationists can't explain life's beginning while evolutionists can't resolve the ultimate origin of the inorganic components that later aggregate to life. But this inability is the very heart of creationist logic and the central reason why their doctrine is not science, while science's inability to specify the ultimate origin of matter is irrelevant because we are not trying to do any such thing. We know that we can't, and we do not even consider such a question as part of science." Stephen Jay Gould, *Justice Scalia's Misunderstanding*, 5 CONST. COMMENT. 1, 8, 10 (1988).

3. *Individual Teachers, Free Speech, and Creationism in the Classroom.* The plaintiffs in *Epperson* and *Edwards* were both teachers and students who sought to avoid the teaching of creationism. For a case involving a plaintiff on the other side of this debate, *see Peloza v. Capistrano Unified Sch. Dist.*, 37 F.3d 517 (9th Cir. 1994) (holding that school did not violate teacher's free speech or free exercise rights by requiring teacher to teach theory of evolution in science class and prohibiting teacher from discussing his religious views with students).

4. *Creationism and the Clash Between Enlightenment Values and Religion.* The seemingly unending dispute over the teaching of creationism and evolution in the public schools is in many ways a perfect microcosm of the continuing cultural conflict between what is often perceived as the corrosive relativism of modern popular and political culture and the ancient certitudes and hierarchies of the mainstream Western religious culture. Stanley Fish's article in Chapter Two provides one perspective on this dichotomy, in which Fish perceives the conflict as essentially a battle to ultimate victory between two fundamentally irreconcilable worldviews. Stephen Carter has offered another variation on that theme. In an article published in the same law review symposium as Fish's article, Carter criticizes the Supreme Court for its *Edwards* decision and suggests that the larger problem is the inability of the secular liberal legal and political structure to come to terms with the basic attributes of religion. *See* Stephen L. Carter, *Evolution, Creationism, and Treating Religion as a Hobby*, 1987 DUKE L.J. 977. According to Carter, the liberal desire to impose on the government the requirement of neutrality toward religion does not foster religious liberty, but rather threatens to ultimately diminish religion so that "religious belief will ultimately become a kind of hobby: something so private that it is as irrelevant to public life as the building of model airplanes." *Id.* at 978.

Carter goes on to criticize the secular terms in which the evolution/creation battles tend to be fought in the courts. "The liberal critic may be right to say that creationism is bad science. But why should that issue be the crucial one? Creationists are not irrational merely because they are unscientific. Creationism was not created from thin air; creation theory developed as a consequence of the preferred hermeneutical method of many Christian fundamentalists for understanding the world." *Id.* at 980. The hermeneutical assumptions to which Carter refers are all derived from the common premise of biblical inerrancy. If one assumes that the Bible is factually true and is the true, received word of God, Carter argues, "what chance is there that the theory of evolution is correct? Virtually none." *Id.*

Like Fish, Carter believes that the root of the conflict is the "reliance of liberalism on dialogue and rationality as indispensable components of its political theory, and the often unstated premise of many liberal theorists that reasoning and religious belief are mutually exclusive means for understanding the world." *Id.* at 986. But it is unclear what Carter would do with these observations. At the end of his article he suggests the possibility of "transcend[ing] liberalism itself," which would find "ways to take seriously the deep religious feelings that motivate so many Americans in their daily lives." *Id.* at 995. It is unclear what this means. "A softened liberal politics would not insist on reason as the only legitimate path to knowledge about the world, and if, in the end, only one path were taught in school, at least it would not be taught as though no other path were possible." *Id.* Carter does not propose a definitive resolution of this issue, but it seems that he would interpret the Establishment Clause to at least permit statutes such as the Louisiana statute struck down in *Edwards*, and possibly to permit a broader scheme in which the religious perspective would be taught side-by-side with the worldview provided by the rational world of empirical science. Is there any way of doing this without undermining the most basic principles barring religious indoctrination in public schools? Is there any part of the "religious hermeneutic" that would fall outside even the narrowest definitions of religion in Establishment Clause doctrine?

For another discussion of the relationship between the liberal democratic reliance on rationality and the "supra-rational" phenomenon of religion, see Jane Rutherford, *Religion, Rationality, and Special Treatment*, 9 WM. & MARY BILL RTS. J. 303 (2001).

5. *The Third Generation of Creationism: Intelligent Design.* Creationism has gone through two major transformations in response to the legal decisions summarized above. The first generation of creationism statutes barred the teaching of evolution altogether. These statutes were the basis of the famous Scopes "Monkey Trial" in 1927, and were finally held unconstitutional by the Supreme Court in 1968 in *Epperson v. Arkansas*. The second generation of creationism statutes conceded that evolution could be taught, but required that creationist theory be given equal time. These so-called "balanced treatment" statutes were held unconstitutional in 1987 in *Edwards v. Aguillard*. The first two generations of creationism statutes often referred specifically to the precepts of young-earth creationist doctrine, which suggests that the earth is only approximately six thousand years old, all geological phenomena can be explained by catastrophism (a flood), and diverse new species do not evolve from common ancestors. In response to *Edwards*, a third generation of creationism has developed in the form of so-called "Intelligent Design" doctrine. Intelligent Design seeks to unite disparate branches of the creationist movement behind a streamlined

form of the doctrine, which avoids asserting the details of young-earth creationism, and does not specifically identify the identity of the "intelligent
designer" as God, although as with earlier advocates of creationism, Intelligent
Design proponents continue to deny common descent. Intelligent Design proposals come in various forms, including efforts by school boards to directly
advance the theory in science classes beside traditional scientific renditions of
evolution theory, incorporation of Intelligent Design precepts in state science
standards, and the placement of disclaimers in science textbooks. Although
the theory has had some political success in states such as Kansas and
Louisiana, it has thus far failed to survive judicial scrutiny under the Establishment Clause.

6. *Intelligent Design and State Science Standards.* In August 1999, the Kansas
state board of education decided by a 6-4 vote to eliminate all references to evolutionary biology from the statewide science achievement tests for students in
the seventh and tenth grades. The board also removed references to evolution
from the state's recommended science curriculum, although under Kansas law
local school boards retained control over the curricula in their own districts. In
making its decision, the state board took only a few hours to reject the contrary
recommendations of twenty-seven scientists and science teachers, who had
worked nearly two years to revise the state's recommended science curriculum
and standardized tests. Do the state board's actions violate the Establishment
Clause as interpreted in *Epperson* and *Edwards*? The decision led to conster-
nation among many within Kansas, including Republican Governor Bill Graves.
Outside Kansas, the state was subjected to ridicule from sources ranging from
the New York Times to late-night television comedians.

The state's electorate responded at the next election by defeating (in the
Republican primary) three conservative candidates who supported the board's
anti-evolution position. The new board's pro-evolution majority quickly moved
to reconsider the earlier board's decision on state science standards. On February 14, 2001, the new board voted 7-3 to adopt new state science testing
standards that incorporated evolution and effectively required all public schools
in the state to teach the subject. The 100-page document setting forth the new
standards also included the following statement under the heading "Teaching
With Tolerance and Respect":

> Teachers should not ridicule, belittle or embarrass a student for express-
> ing an alternative view or belief. If a student should raise a question in
> a natural science class that the teacher determines to be outside the
> domain of science, the teacher should treat the question with respect.
> The teacher should explain why the question is outside the domain of
> natural science and encourage the student to discuss the question fur-
> ther with his or her family and other appropriate sources."

In yet another twist, the control of the Kansas state board of education once
more shifted in favor of anti-evolution forces in the election of 2004. In November 2005, the new board voted to adopt science standards that criticize evolution,

once again rejecting the science standards proposed by the board's own twenty-seven-member science standards committee. The standards are presently due to be incorporated into the state's science assessment tests (which must be taken by all high school students in Kansas) in 2008.

7. *Intelligent Design and Disclaimers.* Although Kansas is still grappling with the dispute over creationism through the electoral process, officials in at least one section of Louisiana recently attempted to circumvent *Edwards* in a manner that required judicial attention. After a failed attempt to introduce creationism into the science curriculum in the Tangipahoa Parish (Louisiana) public schools, the school board enacted the following policy:

> Whenever, in classes of elementary or high school, the scientific theory of evolution is to be presented, whether from textbook, workbook, pamphlet, other written material, or oral presentation, the following statement shall be quoted immediately before the unit of study begins as a disclaimer from endorsement of such theory.

> It is hereby recognized by the Tangipahoa Board of Education, that the lesson to be presented, regarding the origin of life and matter, is known as the Scientific Theory of Evolution and should be presented to inform students of the scientific concept and not intended to influence or dissuade the Biblical version of Creation or any other concept.

> It is further recognized by the Board of Education that it is the basic right and privilege of each student to form his/her own opinion and maintain beliefs taught by parents on this very important matter of the origin of life and matter. Students are urged to exercise critical thinking and gather all information possible and closely examine each alternative toward forming an opinion.

Freiler v. Tangipahoa Parish Bd. of Educ., 185 F.3d 337, 341 (5th Cir. 1999), *cert. denied*, 530 U.S. 1251 (2000). The Fifth Circuit Court of Appeals held that the mandatory disclaimer violated the Establishment Clause:

> After careful consideration of the oral arguments, the briefs, the record on appeal, and the language of the disclaimer, we conclude that the primary effect of the disclaimer is to protect and maintain a particular religious viewpoint, namely belief in the Biblical version of creation. In reaching this conclusion, we rely on the interplay of three factors: (1) the juxtaposition of the disavowal of endorsement of evolution with an urging that students contemplate alternative theories of the origin of life; (2) the reminder that students have the right to maintain beliefs taught by their parents regarding the origin of life; and (3) the "Biblical version of Creation" as the only alternative theory explicitly referenced in the disclaimer. . . . The disclaimer, taken as a whole, encourages students to read and meditate upon religion in general and the "Biblical version of Creation" in particular.

Id. at 346. Is the Kansas board of education's statement on "Teaching with Tolerance and Respect" different in kind from the Tangipahoa Parish disclaimer? Would a Kansas-style statement survive the Fifth Circuit's Establishment Clause analysis if the board issuing the statement was in favor of teaching evolution and included only evolution in the curriculum?

For another recent decision striking down an anti-evolution disclaimer, see *Selman v. Cobb County Sch. Dist.*, 390 F. Supp. 2d 1286 (N.D.Ga. 2005).

8. *Intelligent Design as Science.* In the Supreme Court's two creationism decisions, the statutes in question were struck down because they lacked a secular purpose. By casting the decisions in this way, the Court did not have to grapple with the difficult question of ascertaining whether the nature of creationist doctrine was, as its proponents claimed, a legitimate body of scientific ideas or was instead merely a set of religious ideas regarding a supernatural creator's intervention in the natural universe. In a prominent recent case involving a Dover, Pennsylvania, school board's efforts to get Intelligent Design into its public school classrooms, a district judge considered and rejected the claims that Intelligent Design is science. The judge therefore ruled that the Dover policy was unconstitutional both on secular purpose and secular effect grounds as an impermissible endorsement of religion. *See Kitzmiller v. Dover Area Sch. Dist.*, below.

KITZMILLER v. DOVER AREA SCHOOL DISTRICT
400 F. Supp. 2d 707 (M.D. Pa. 2005)

JONES, CIRCUIT JUDGE:

INTRODUCTION:

On October 18, 2004, the Defendant Dover Area School Board of Directors passed by a 6-3 vote the following resolution:

> Students will be made aware of gaps/problems in Darwin's theory and of other theories of evolution including, but not limited to, intelligent design. Note: Origins of Life is not taught.

On November 19, 2004, the Defendant Dover Area School District announced by press release that, commencing in January 2005, teachers would be required to read the following statement to students in the ninth grade biology class at Dover High School:

> The Pennsylvania Academic Standards require students to learn about Darwin's Theory of Evolution and eventually to take a standardized test of which evolution is a part.

> Because Darwin's Theory is a theory, it continues to be tested as new evidence is discovered. The Theory is not a fact. Gaps in the Theory exist

for which there is no evidence. A theory is defined as a well-tested explanation that unifies a broad range of observations.

Intelligent Design is an explanation of the origin of life that differs from Darwin's view. The reference book, Of Pandas and People, is available for students who might be interested in gaining an understanding of what Intelligent Design actually involves.

With respect to any theory, students are encouraged to keep an open mind. The school leaves the discussion of the Origins of Life to individual students and their families. As a Standards-driven district, class instruction focuses upon preparing students to achieve proficiency on Standards-based assessments.

[A group of parents whose children attended the Dover schools challenged the resolution and the disclaimer. The court reviewed the relevant Establishment Clause doctrine, and concluded that it must analyze the Dover board's actions under *Lemon* and the endorsement analysis.

[With regard to the endorsement analysis, the court held that "an objective observer would know that ID and teaching about 'gaps' and 'problems' in evolutionary theory are creationist, religious strategies that evolved from earlier forms of creationism." The court also held that a reasonable student would view the disclaimer as an endorsement of religion. In discussing these conclusions, the court discussed the nature and history of the Intelligent Design movement.]

   1. *An Objective Observer Would Know that ID and Teaching About "Gaps" and "Problems" in Evoluntionary Theory are Creationist, Religious Strategies that Evolved from Earlier Forms of Creationism*

The concept of intelligent design (hereinafter "ID"), in its current form, came into existence after the *Edwards* case was decided in 1987. For the reasons that follow, we conclude that the religious nature of ID would be readily apparent to an objective observer, adult or child.

We initially note that John Haught, a theologian who testified as an expert witness for Plaintiffs and who has written extensively on the subject of evolution and religion, succinctly explained to the Court that the argument for ID is not a new scientific argument, but is rather an old religious argument for the existence of God. He traced this argument back to at least Thomas Aquinas in the 13th century, who framed the argument as a syllogism: Wherever complex design exists, there must have been a designer; nature is complex; therefore nature must have had an intelligent designer. Dr. Haught testified that Aquinas was explicit that this intelligent designer "everyone understands to be God." The syllogism described by Dr. Haught is essentially the same argument for ID as presented by defense expert witnesses Professors Behe and Minnich who employ the phrase "purposeful arrangement of parts."

Dr. Haught testified that this argument for the existence of God was advanced early in the 19th century by Reverend Paley and defense expert witnesses Behe and Minnich admitted that their argument for ID based on the "purposeful arrangement of parts" is the same one that Paley made for design. The only apparent difference between the argument made by Paley and the argument for ID, as expressed by defense expert witnesses Behe and Minnich, is that ID's "official position" does not acknowledge that the designer is God. However, as Dr. Haught testified, anyone familiar with Western religious thought would immediately make the association that the tactically unnamed designer is God, as the description of the designer in [Intelligent Design textbook] *Of Pandas and People* (hereinafter "*Pandas*") is a "master intellect," strongly suggesting a supernatural deity as opposed to any intelligent actor known to exist in the natural world. Moreover, it is notable that both Professors Behe and Minnich admitted their personal view is that the designer is God and Professor Minnich testified that he understands many leading advocates of ID to believe the designer to be God.

Although proponents of the IDM occasionally suggest that the designer could be a space alien or a time-traveling cell biologist, no serious alternative to God as the designer has been proposed by members of the IDM, including Defendants' expert witnesses. In fact, an explicit concession that the intelligent designer works outside the laws of nature and science and a direct reference to religion is *Pandas* ' rhetorical statement, "what kind of intelligent agent was it [the designer]" and answer: "On its own science cannot answer this question. It must leave it to religion and philosophy."

A significant aspect of the IDM is that despite Defendants' protestations to the contrary, it describes ID as a religious argument. In that vein, the writings of leading ID proponents reveal that the designer postulated by their argument is the God of Christianity. Dr. Barbara Forrest, one of Plaintiffs' expert witnesses, is the author of the book *Creationism's Trojan Horse*. She has thoroughly and exhaustively chronicled the history of ID in her book and other writings for her testimony in this case. Her testimony, and the exhibits which were admitted with it, provide a wealth of statements by ID leaders that reveal ID's religious, philosophical, and cultural content. The following is a representative grouping of such statements made by prominent ID proponents.

Phillip Johnson, considered to be the father of the IDM, developer of ID's "Wedge Strategy," and author of the 1991 book entitled *Darwin on Trial,* has written that "theistic realism" or "mere creation" are defining concepts of the IDM. This means "that God is objectively real as Creator and recorded in the biological evidence. . . " In addition, Phillip Johnson states that the "Darwinian theory of evolution contradicts not just the Book of Genesis, but every word in the Bible from beginning to end. It contradicts the idea that we are here because a creator brought about our existence for a purpose." ID proponents Johnson, William Dembski, and Charles Thaxton, one of the editors of *Pandas,* situate ID in the Book of John in the New Testament of the Bible, which begins, "In the

Beginning was the Word, and the Word was God." Dembski has written that ID is a "ground clearing operation" to allow Christianity to receive serious consideration, and "Christ is never an addendum to a scientific theory but always a completion." Moreover, in turning to Defendants' lead expert, Professor Behe, his testimony at trial indicated that ID is only a scientific, as opposed to a religious, project for him; however, considerable evidence was introduced to refute this claim. Consider, to illustrate, that Professor Behe remarkably and unmistakably claims that the *plausibility of the argument for ID depends upon the extent to which one believes in the existence of God.* As no evidence in the record indicates that any other scientific proposition's validity rests on belief in God, nor is the Court aware of any such scientific propositions, Professor Behe's assertion constitutes substantial evidence that in his view, as is commensurate with other prominent ID leaders, ID is a religious and not a scientific proposition.

Dramatic evidence of ID's religious nature and aspirations is found in what is referred to as the "Wedge Document." The Wedge Document, developed by the Discovery Institute's Center for Renewal of Science and Culture (hereinafter "CRSC"), represents from an institutional standpoint, the IDM's goals and objectives, much as writings from the Institute for Creation Research did for the earlier creation-science movement, as discussed in *McLean.* The Wedge Document states in its "Five Year Strategic Plan Summary" that the IDM's goal is to replace science as currently practiced with "theistic and Christian science." As posited in the Wedge Document, the IDM's "Governing Goals" are to "defeat scientific materialism and its destructive moral, cultural, and political legacies" and "to replace materialistic explanations with the theistic understanding that nature and human beings are created by God." The CSRC expressly announces, in the Wedge Document, a program of Christian apologetics to promote ID. A careful review of the Wedge Document's goals and language throughout the document reveals cultural and religious goals, as opposed to scientific ones. ID aspires to change the ground rules of science to make room for religion, specifically, beliefs consonant with a particular version of Christianity.

In addition to the IDM itself describing ID as a religious argument, ID's religious nature is evident because it involves a supernatural designer. The courts in *Edwards* and *McLean* expressly found that this characteristic removed creationism from the realm of science and made it a religious proposition. Prominent ID proponents have made abundantly clear that the designer is supernatural.

The weight of the evidence clearly demonstrates, as noted, that the systemic change from "creation" to "intelligent design" occurred sometime in 1987, *after* the Supreme Court's important *Edwards* decision. This compelling evidence strongly supports Plaintiffs' assertion that ID is creationism re-labeled. Importantly, the objective observer, whether adult or child, would conclude from the fact that *Pandas* posits a master intellect that the intelligent designer is God.

[The court also held that abundant evidence existed to support the conclusion that the board adopted the ID policy with the specific purpose of advancing religion in the classroom.

[Finally, the court specifically considered and rejected the scientific claims of ID proponents.]

4. *Whether ID is Science*

After a searching review of the record and applicable caselaw, we find that while ID arguments may be true, a proposition on which the Court takes no position, ID is not science. We find that ID fails on three different levels, any one of which is sufficient to preclude a determination that ID is science. They are: (1) ID violates the centuries-old ground rules of science by invoking and permitting supernatural causation; (2) the argument of irreducible complexity, central to ID, employs the same flawed and illogical contrived dualism that doomed creation science in the 1980's; and (3) ID's negative attacks on evolution have been refuted by the scientific community. As we will discuss in more detail below, it is additionally important to note that ID has failed to gain acceptance in the scientific community, it has not generated peer-reviewed publications, nor has it been the subject of testing and research.

As the National Academy of Sciences (hereinafter "NAS") was recognized by experts for both parties as the "most prestigious" scientific association in this country, we will accordingly cite to its opinion where appropriate. NAS is in agreement that science is limited to empirical, observable and ultimately testable data: "Science is a particular way of knowing about the world. In science, explanations are restricted to those that can be inferred from the confirmable data — the results obtained through observations and experiments that can be substantiated by other scientists. Anything that can be observed or measured is amenable to scientific investigation. Explanations that cannot be based upon empirical evidence are not part of science."

This rigorous attachment to "natural" explanations is an essential attribute to science by definition and by convention. We are in agreement with Plaintiffs' lead expert Dr. Miller, that from a practical perspective, attributing unsolved problems about nature to causes and forces that lie outside the natural world is a "science stopper." As Dr. Miller explained, once you attribute a cause to an untestable supernatural force, a proposition that cannot be disproven, there is no reason to continue seeking natural explanations as we have our answer.

ID is predicated on supernatural causation, as we previously explained and as various expert testimony revealed. ID takes a natural phenomenon and, instead of accepting or seeking a natural explanation, argues that the explanation is supernatural.

It is notable that defense experts' own mission, which mirrors that of the IDM itself, is to change the ground rules of science to allow supernatural causation of the natural world, which the Supreme Court in *Edwards* and the court in

McLean correctly recognized as an inherently religious concept. First, defense expert Professor Fuller agreed that ID aspires to "change the ground rules" of science and lead defense expert Professor Behe admitted that his broadened definition of science, which encompasses ID, would also embrace astrology. Moreover, defense expert Professor Minnich acknowledged that for ID to be considered science, the ground rules of science have to be broadened to allow consideration of supernatural forces.

Notably, every major scientific association that has taken a position on the issue of whether ID is science has concluded that ID is not, and cannot be considered as such. Initially, we note that NAS, the "most prestigious" scientific association in this country, views ID as follows:

> Creationism, intelligent design, and other claims of supernatural intervention in the origin of life or of species are not science because they are not testable by the methods of science. These claims subordinate observed data to statements based on authority, revelation, or religious belief. Documentation offered in support of these claims is typically limited to the special publications of their advocates. These publications do not offer hypotheses subject to change in light of new data, new interpretations, or demonstration of error. This contrasts with science, where any hypothesis or theory always remains subject to the possibility of rejection or modification in the light of new knowledge.

Additionally, the American Association for the Advancement of Science (hereinafter "AAAS"), the largest organization of scientists in this country, has taken a similar position on ID, namely, that it "has not proposed a scientific means of testing its claims" and that "the lack of scientific warrant for so-called 'intelligent design theory' makes it improper to include as part of science education. . . ." Not a single expert witness over the course of the six week trial identified one major scientific association, society or organization that endorsed ID as science. What is more, defense experts concede that ID is not a theory as that term is defined by the NAS and admit that ID is at best "fringe science" which has achieved no acceptance in the scientific community.

[The court then considered and rejected several empirical claims made by ID proponents, including the central ID claim that biological organisms are "irreducibly complex" and therefore could not have developed through evolution.]

H. Conclusion

The proper application of both the endorsement and *Lemon* tests to the facts of this case makes it abundantly clear that the Board's ID Policy violates the Establishment Clause. In making this determination, we have addressed the seminal question of whether ID is science. We have concluded that it is not, and moreover that ID cannot uncouple itself from its creationist, and thus religious, antecedents.

Both Defendants and many of the leading proponents of ID make a bedrock assumption which is utterly false. Their presupposition is that evolutionary theory is antithetical to a belief in the existence of a supreme being and to religion in general. Repeatedly in this trial, Plaintiffs' scientific experts testified that the theory of evolution represents good science, is overwhelmingly accepted by the scientific community, and that it in no way conflicts with, nor does it deny, the existence of a divine creator.

To be sure, Darwin's theory of evolution is imperfect. However, the fact that a scientific theory cannot yet render an explanation on every point should not be used as a pretext to thrust an untestable alternative hypothesis grounded in religion into the science classroom or to misrepresent well-established scientific propositions.

The citizens of the Dover area were poorly served by the members of the Board who voted for the ID Policy. It is ironic that several of these individuals, who so staunchly and proudly touted their religious convictions in public, would time and again lie to cover their tracks and disguise the real purpose behind the ID Policy.

With that said, we do not question that many of the leading advocates of ID have *bona fide* and deeply held beliefs which drive their scholarly endeavors. Nor do we controvert that ID should continue to be studied, debated, and discussed. As stated, our conclusion today is that it is unconstitutional to teach ID as an alternative to evolution in a public school science classroom.

Those who disagree with our holding will likely mark it as the product of an activist judge. If so, they will have erred as this is manifestly not an activist Court. Rather, this case came to us as the result of the activism of an ill-informed faction on a school board, aided by a national public interest law firm eager to find a constitutional test case on ID, who in combination drove the Board to adopt an imprudent and ultimately unconstitutional policy. The breathtaking inanity of the Board's decision is evident when considered against the factual backdrop which has now been fully revealed through this trial. The students, parents, and teachers of the Dover Area School District deserved better than to be dragged into this legal maelstrom, with its resulting utter waste of monetary and personal resources.

NOTE

In November 2005, the citizens of Dover voted to turn out of office all eight members of the Dover school board who had supported the anti-evolution policy. The new school board decided not to appeal the *Kitzmiller* decision. In return, the plaintiffs agreed to forego over half of their $2.067 million in attorneys' fees.

For a good journalistic account of the Dover trial, see Margaret Talbot, *Darwin in the Dock: Intelligent Design Has Its Day in Court*, THE NEW YORKER, Dec.

5, 2005, at 66. For a full history of the Intelligent Design (ID) movement, co-authored by one of the primary experts at the Dover trial, see BARBARA FORREST & PAUL R. GROSS, CREATIONISM'S TROJAN HORSE: THE WEDGE OF INTELLIGENT DESIGN (2004). For two of the central texts of the ID movement, see PHILIP JOHNSON, DARWIN ON TRIAL (1993), and MICHAEL J. BEHE, DARWIN'S BLACK BOX: THE BIOCHEMICAL CHALLENGE TO EVOLUTION (1998) (Behe was one of the school board's primary expert witnesses in the Dover trial.). For the best compendium of articles on ID (both pro and con), see INTELLIGENT DESIGN CREATIONISM AND ITS CRITICS: PHILOSOPHICAL, THEOLOGICAL, AND SCIENTIFIC PERSPECTIVES (Robert T. Pennock, ed. 2001). For law review discussions of legal issues raised by ID, see Matthew J. Brauer, Barbara Forrest & Steven G. Gey, *Is It Science Yet?: Intelligent Design Creationism and the Constitution*, 83 WASH. U. L.Q. 1 (2005) (arguing generally that ID cannot be taught in public schools); Jay D. Wexler, *Darwin, Design, and Disestablishment: Teaching the Evolution Controversy in Public Schools*, 56 VAND. L. REV. 749 (2003) (same); Jay D. Wexler, Note, *Of Pandas, People, and the First Amendment: The Constitutionality of Teaching Intelligent Design in the Public Schools*, 49 STAN. L. REV. 439 (1997) (same); David K. DeWolf, Stephen C. Meyer & Mark Edward DeForrest, *Teaching the Origins Controversy: Science, or Religion, or Speech?*, 2000 UTAH L. REV. 39, 93 (2000) (arguing that teaching ID in public schools is permissible).

B. SECULAR EDUCATION AS RELIGION

SMITH v. BOARD OF SCHOOL COMMISSIONERS OF MOBILE COUNTY
827 F.2d 684 (11th Cir. 1987)

JOHNSON, CIRCUIT JUDGE:

Appellants, Alabama State Board of Education and Wayne Teague ("Board") and Malcolm Howell, et al. ("Defendant-Intervenors") appeal the district court's order enjoining the use in Alabama public schools of forty-four textbooks approved by the Board for inclusion on the State-Adopted Textbook List, the use of which the district court found to be a violation of the establishment clause of the first amendment. We reverse.

I. BACKGROUND

A. Procedural History

This case is a continuation of the Alabama school prayer cases. In May 1982, Ishmael Jaffree brought an action on behalf of three of his minor children pursuant to 42 U.S.C.A. §1983 against the Mobile County School Board, various school officials, and three teachers seeking, *inter alia*, a declaratory judgment that certain classroom prayer activities conducted in the Mobile public school system violated the establishment clause of the first amendment and an injunction against classroom prayer. By his second amended complaint, Jaffree added as defendants the Governor of Alabama and other state officials, including Appellant Board, and challenged three Alabama statutes relevant to the school prayer issue as violative of the establishment clause. Douglas T. Smith and others ("Appellees") filed a motion to intervene in the Jaffree action alleging that an injunction against religious activity in the public schools would violate their right to free exercise of religion, and the district court allowed them to intervene as defendants. Subsequently, Appellees filed a motion entitled "Request for Alternate Relief" in which Appellees requested that, if an injunction were granted in favor of Jaffree, that injunction be enforced "against the religions of secularism, humanism, evolution, materialism, agnosticism, atheism and others" or, alternatively, that Appellees be allowed to produce additional evidence showing that these religions had been established in the Alabama public schools.

The district court granted Jaffree's motion for a preliminary injunction against enforcement of two of the challenged statutes, but determined after trial on the merits that Jaffree was not entitled to relief in either action because the Supreme Court of the United States had erred in holding that the establishment clause of the first amendment prohibits the states from establishing a religion. The district court therefore dismissed Jaffree's complaint for failure to state a claim upon which relief could be granted.

In its opinion denying relief in *Jaffree*, the district court had stated that "[i]f the appellate courts disagree with this Court in its examination of history and conclusion of constitutional interpretation thereof, then this Court will look again at the record in this case and reach conclusions which it is not now forced to reach." In a footnote, the district court indicated that the issues not reached dealt with (1) the free speech rights of teachers and students who wished to pray in school and (2) the teaching of the religion of secular humanism in the schools.[1] On remand, the district court issued an order in response to Jaffree's

---

[1] With regard to the secular humanism issue, the district court stated:

> It was pointed out in the testimony that the curriculum in the public schools of Mobile County is rife with efforts at teaching or encouraging secular humanism — all without opposition from any other ethic — to such an extent that it becomes a brainwashing effort. If this Court is compelled to purge "God is great, God is good, we thank Him for our daily food" from the classroom, then this Court must also purge from the classroom those things that serve to teach that salvation is through one's self rather than through a deity.

Jaffree, 554 F.Supp. at 1129 n. 41. The district court had expressed similar views on the merits of this issue in its earlier opinion granting a preliminary injunction, which was issued before Appellees had filed their "Request for Alternate Relief":

> The case law, in the opinion of the Court, has overlooked the totality of what is religion in its consideration when deciding issues under the establishment clause of the Constitution . . . . It is apparent from a reading of the decision law that the courts acknowledge that Christianity is the religion to be proscribed . . . . The religions of atheism, materialism, agnosticism, communism and socialism have escaped the scrutiny of the courts throughout the years, and make no mistake these are to the believers religions; they are ardently adhered to and quantitatively advanced in the teachings and literature that is

request for attorney's fees, finding that the relief requested by Appellees had not been fully addressed in the prior decisions in the case and, therefore, remained for consideration by the district court on remand. The district court interpreted the position of the Appellees as that "if Christianity is not a permissible subject of the curriculum of the public schools, then neither is any other religion, and under the evidence introduced it is incumbent upon this Court to strike down those portions of the curriculum demonstrated to contain other religious teachings." For the purpose of considering this issue, the district court *sua sponte* realigned the parties by making Appellees parties plaintiff, consolidated the cases, and invited the parties to submit briefs in support of their positions and to petition the Court to reopen the record for the presentation of additional evidence. The district court stated that the original plaintiffs could withdraw, if they felt their position had been "fully justified," in which case the district court would consider the attorney's fees question, or could remain in the litigation, in which event the motion for attorney's fees would be denied as premature. The original plaintiffs did withdraw, and Appellees filed a position statement in which they asserted, *inter alia*, that the curriculum in the Mobile County School System unconstitutionally advanced the religion of Humanism and unconstitutionally inhibited Christianity, and that the exclusion from the curriculum of "the existence, history, contributions and role of Christianity in the United States and the world" violated their constitutional rights of equal protection, teacher and student free speech, the student's right to receive information, and teacher and student free exercise of religion

The twelve Defendant-Intervenors, who are parents of children currently enrolled, or soon to be enrolled, in the Mobile County School System, filed a motion to intervene as defendants in the action, which was granted by the district court.

A bench trial was held October 6-22, 1986 with regard to Appellees' claims. Appellees' evidence focused on elementary and secondary school textbooks in the areas of history, social studies, and home economics, which were on the Alabama State Approved Textbook List, and which Appellees argued unconstitutionally established the religion of secular humanism. The district court found that use

---

presented to the fertile minds of the students in the various school systems. If the courts are to involve themselves in the proscription of religious activities in the schools, then it appears to this Court that we are going to have to involve ourselves in a whole host of areas, such as censoring, that we have heretofore ignored or overlooked. An example of what the Court heard reflecting on this point is in connection with the claimed use of foul language in literature read by a fourth grader and, though it might seem innocuous to some to condemn the use of the word "Goddamn" as it is used in the writings that are required reading, it can clearly be argued that as to Christianity it is blasphemy and is the establishment of an advancement of humanism, secularism or agnosticism. If the state cannot teach or advance Christianity, how can it teach or advance the Antichrist?

Jaffree, 544 F.Supp. at 732. In that opinion, the district court stated that "[i]t is common knowledge that miscellaneous doctrines such as evolution, socialism, communism, secularism, humanism, and other concepts are advanced in the public schools." *Id.* at n. 2.

of forty-four of these textbooks violated the establishment clause of the first amendment, and permanently enjoined the use of the textbooks in the Alabama public schools.

II. DISCUSSION

The first amendment provides in pertinent part that "Congress shall make no law respecting an establishment of religion. . . ." The district court found that secular humanism constitutes a religion within the meaning of the first amendment and that the forty-four textbooks at issue in this case both advanced that religion and inhibited theistic faiths in violation of the establishment clause. The Supreme Court has never established a comprehensive test for determining the "delicate question" of what constitutes a religious belief for purposes of the first amendment, and we need not attempt to do so in this case, for we find that, even assuming that secular humanism is a religion for purposes of the establishment clause, Appellees have failed to prove a violation of the establishment clause through the use in the Alabama public schools of the textbooks at issue in this case.

The Supreme Court has developed three criteria to serve as guidelines in determining whether this barrier has been breached by challenged government action:

> First, the statute must have a secular legislative purpose; second, its principal or primary effect must be one that neither advances nor inhibits religion; finally, the statute must not foster "an excessive government entanglement with religion." *Lemon v. Kurtzman*. Governmental action violates the establishment clause if it fails to meet any of these three criteria. *Stone v. Graham*, 449 U.S. 39, 40-41 (1980).

In applying the *Lemon* test to a situation involving the public schools, the Court "must do so mindful of the particular concerns that arise in the context of public elementary and secondary schools." *Edwards v. Aguillard*. This special context is one which requires a sensitivity on the part of the court to both the broad discretion given school boards in choosing the public school curriculum, which mandates that courts not intervene in the resolution of conflicts arising in the daily operation of school systems unless basic constitutional values are "directly and sharply implicate[d]," and the pervasive influence exercised by the public schools over the children who attend them, which makes scrupulous compliance with the establishment clause in the public schools particularly vital. *Epperson v. Arkansas*. For these reasons, the Court must be "particularly vigilant in monitoring compliance with the Establishment Clause in elementary and secondary schools."

The parties agree that there is no question of a religious purpose or excessive government entanglement in this case and our review of the record confirms that conclusion. Our inquiry, therefore, must center on the second *Lemon* criterion: whether use of the challenged textbooks had the primary effect of either advancing or inhibiting religion.

"The effect prong [of the *Lemon* test] asks whether, irrespective of government's actual purpose, the practice under review in fact conveys a message of endorsement or disapproval." *Jaffree* (O'Connor, J., concurring). If government identification with religion conveys such a message of government endorsement or disapproval of religion, then "a core purpose of the Establishment Clause is violated." *Ball* [*infra* Chapter 8]. In determining the message conveyed by use of the textbooks in this case, we recognize that we must use "particular care" as "many of the citizens perceiving the governmental message are children in their formative years."

The district court found that the home economics, history, and social studies textbooks both advanced secular humanism and inhibited theistic religion. Our review of the record in this case reveals that these conclusions were in error. As discussed below, use of the challenged textbooks has the primary effect of conveying information that is essentially neutral in its religious content to the school children who utilize the books; none of these books convey a message of governmental approval of secular humanism or governmental disapproval of theism.

A. Home Economics Textbooks

The district court found that the home economics textbooks required students to accept as true certain tenets of humanistic psychology, which the district court found to be "a manifestation of humanism." In particular, the district court found that the books "imply strongly that a person uses the same process in deciding a moral issue that he uses in choosing one pair of shoes over another,"[5] and teach that "the student must determine right and wrong based only on his own experience, feelings and [internal] values" and that "the validity of a moral choice is only to be decided by the student."[6] The district court stated that "[t]he emphasis and overall approach implies, and would cause any reasonable thinking student to infer, that the book is teaching that moral choices are just a matter of preferences, because, as the books say, 'you are the most important person in your life.'" The district court stated that "[t]his highly relativistic and individualistic approach constitutes the promotion of a funda-

---

[5] In support of this statement, the district court refers to a passage in one of the home economics textbooks in which the author lists the steps in the decision-making process and states that "[a]s you can see, the steps in decision-making can be applied to something as simple as buying a new pair of shoes" and "can also be applied to more complex decisions such as those which involve religious preferences; education and career choices; the use of alcohol, tobacco and drugs; and sexual habits." F. Parnell, *Homemaking Skills for Everyday Living* 26 (1984). The book lists the steps in decision-making as (1) Define the problem; (2) Establish your goals; (3) List your goals in order of importance; (4) Look for resources; (5) Study the alternatives; (6) Make a decision; (7) Carry out the decision; (8) Evaluate the results of your decision. *Id.*

[6] The district court acknowledged that the textbooks do not explicitly state that the validity of a moral choice is only to be decided by the student, but found that this conclusion was implicit in the books' repetition of statements to the effect that decisions are "yours alone," or "purely personal" or that "only you can decide." *Smith*, 655 F.Supp. at 986.

mental faith claim" that "assumes that self-actualization is the goal of every human being, that man has no supernatural attributes or component, that there are only temporal and physical consequences for man's actions, and that these results, alone, determine the morality of an action." According to the district court, "[t]his belief strikes at the heart of many theistic religions' beliefs that certain actions are in and of themselves immoral, *whatever the consequences*, and that, in addition, actions will have extra-temporal consequences." The district court stated that "some religious beliefs are so fundamental that the act of denying them will completely undermine that religion" and "[i]n addition, *denial* of that belief will result in the affirmance of a contrary belief and result in the establishment of an opposing religion." It concluded that, while the state may teach certain moral values, such as that lying is wrong, "if, in so doing it advances a reason for the rule, the possible different reasons must be explained evenhandedly" and "the state may not promote one particular reason over another in the public schools."

In order to violate the primary effect prong of the *Lemon* test through advancement of religion, it is not sufficient that the government action merely accommodates religion. The constitution "affirmatively mandates accommodation, not merely tolerance, of all religions, and forbids hostility towards any." *Lynch* [*infra* Chapter 7]. Nor is it sufficient that government conduct confers an indirect, remote or incidental benefit on a religion, or that its effect merely happens to coincide or harmonize with the tenets of a religion:

> [T]he Establishment Clause does not ban federal or state regulation of conduct whose reason or effect merely happens to coincide or harmonize with the tenets of some or all religions. In many instances, the Congress or state legislatures conclude that the general welfare of society, wholly apart from any religious considerations, demands such regulation. Thus, for temporal purposes, murder is illegal. And the fact that this agrees with the dictates of the Judaeo-Christian religions while it may disagree with others does not invalidate the regulation. So too with the questions of adultery and polygamy. The same could be said of theft, fraud, etc., because those offenses were also proscribed in the Decalogue.

McGowan v. Maryland, 366 U.S. 420, 442 (1961) (citations omitted). In order for government conduct to constitute an impermissible advancement of religion, the government action must amount to an endorsement of religion. Further, the primary effect of challenged government action must be determined in light of the overall context in which it occurs: "[f]ocus exclusively on the religious component of any activity would inevitably lead to its invalidation under the Establishment Clause."

Examination of the contents of these textbooks, including the passages pointed out by Appellees as particularly offensive, in the context of the books as a whole and the undisputedly nonreligious purpose sought to be achieved by their use, reveals that the message conveyed is not one of endorsement of secular humanism or any religion. Rather, the message conveyed is one of a governmental attempt to instill in Alabama public school children such values as independent thought, tolerance of diverse views, self-respect, maturity, self-reliance and logical decision-making. This is an entirely appropriate secular effect. Indeed, one of the major objectives of public education is the "inculcat[ion of] fundamental values necessary to the maintenance of a democratic political system." *Bethel School Dist. No. 403 v. Fraser*, 478 U.S. 675 (1986) (quoting *Ambach v. Norwick*, 441 U.S. 68, 77 (1979)) (brackets in original). It is true that the textbooks contain ideas that are consistent with secular humanism; the textbooks also contain ideas consistent with theistic religion. However, as discussed above, mere consistency with religious tenets is insufficient to constitute unconstitutional advancement of religion.

Nor do these textbooks evidence an attitude antagonistic to theistic belief. The message conveyed by these textbooks with regard to theistic religion is one of neutrality: the textbooks neither endorse theistic religion as a system of belief, nor discredit it. Indeed, many of the books specifically acknowledge that religion is one source of moral values and none preclude that possibility. While the Supreme Court has recognized that "the State may not establish a 'religion of secularism' in the sense of affirmatively opposing or showing hostility to religion, thus 'preferring those who believe in no religion over those who do believe,'" *Abington*, that Court also has made it clear that the neutrality mandated by the establishment clause does not itself equate with hostility towards religion. *See e.g., id.; McCollum v. Board of Ed.*, 333 U.S. 203, 211-12 (1948); *Engle v. Vitale*.[9] Rather, the separation of church and state mandated by the first amendment "rests upon the premise that both religion and government can best work to achieve their lofty aims if each is left free from the other within its respective sphere." *McCollum*, 333 U.S. at 212. Thus, it is a recognition that "[t]he place of religion in our society is an exalted one, achieved through a long tradition of reliance on the home, the church and the inviolable citadel of the individual heart and mind," and not hostility towards religion, which requires that the state remain "firmly committed to a position of neutrality." *Abington*; *accord, Engle* ("The Establishment Clause. . . stands as an expression of principle on the part of the Founders of our Constitution that religion is too personal, too sacred, too holy, to permit its 'unhallowed perversion' by a magistrate.")

It is obvious that Appellees find some of the material in these textbooks offensive. That fact, however, is not sufficient to render use of this material in the public schools a violation of the establishment clause. *See Epperson* (quoting *Joseph Burstyn, Inc. v. Wilson*, 343 U.S. 495, 505 (1952)) ("The state has no legitimate interest in protecting any or all religions from views distasteful to

---

[9] A contrary conclusion would totally eviscerate the establishment clause: "[i]f the establishment clause is to have any meaning, distinctions must be drawn to recognize not simply 'religious' and 'anti-religious' but 'non-religious' governmental activity as well." *Grove v. Mead School Dist. No. 354*, 753 F.2d 1528, 1536 (9th Cir.) (Canby, J., concurring), *cert. denied*, 474 U.S. 826 (1985).

them.").[10] The district court erred in concluding that the challenged home economics books advanced secular humanism and inhibited theistic religion.

B. History and Social Studies Textbooks

The district court's conclusion that the history and social studies textbooks violated the establishment clause was based on its finding that these books failed to include a sufficient discussion of the role of religion in history and culture. The district court found that the history books omit certain historical events with religious significance and "uniformly ignore the religious aspect of most American culture." The district court found that "[r]eligion, where treated at all, is generally represented as a private matter, only influencing American public life at some extraordinary moments," and that "[t]his view of religion is one humanists have been seeking to instill for fifty years." The district court concluded that the history books "assist that effort by perpetuating an inaccurate historical picture" and held that the books "lack so many facts as to equal ideological promotion." The district court also found that the history books "discriminate against the very concept of religion, and theistic religions in particular, by omissions so serious that a student learning history from them would not be apprised of relevant facts about America's history." Use of the social studies books was found unconstitutional because the books failed to integrate religion into the history of American society, ignored the importance of theistic religion as an influence in American society and contained "factual inaccuracies. . . so grave as to rise to a constitutional violation."

It is clear on the record of this case that, assuming one tenet of secular humanism is to downplay the importance of religion in history and in American society, any benefit to secular humanism from the failure of the challenged history and social studies books to contain references to the religious aspects of certain historical events or to adequately integrate the place of religion in modern American society is merely incidental. There is no doubt that these textbooks were chosen for the secular purpose of education in the areas of history and social studies, and we find that the primary effect of the use of these textbooks is consistent with that stated purpose. We do not believe that an objective observer could conclude from the mere omission of certain historical facts regarding religion or the absence of a more thorough discussion of its place in modern American society that the State of Alabama was conveying a message of approval of the religion of secular humanism. Indeed, the message that rea-

---

27 [10] Indeed, given the diversity of religious views in this country, if the standard were merely inconsistency with the beliefs of a particular religion there would be very little that could be taught in the public schools. As Justice Jackson has stated:

> Authorities list 256 separate and substantial religious bodies to exist in the . . . United States . . . . If we are to eliminate everything that is objectionable to any of these warring sects or inconsistent with any of their doctrines, we will leave public education in shreds. Nothing but educational confusion and a discrediting of the public school system can result . . . .

McCollum v. Board of Ed., 333 U.S. 203, 235 (1948) (Jackson, J., concurring).

sonably would be conveyed to students and others is that the education officials, in the exercise of their discretion over school curriculum, chose to use these particular textbooks because they deemed them more relevant to the curriculum, or better written, or for some other nonreligious reason found them to be best suited to their needs.

Nor can we agree with the district court's conclusion that the omission of these facts causes the books to "discriminate against the very concept of religion." Just as use of these books does not convey a message of governmental approval of secular humanism, neither does it convey a message of government disapproval of theistic religions merely by omitting certain historical facts concerning them.

The district court's reliance on *Epperson v. Arkansas* to support its conclusion that omission of certain material regarding religion in this case constituted a first amendment violation is misplaced. *Epperson* involved an Arkansas statute that made it a crime to teach the theory of evolution in the public schools. The Supreme Court found that the law violated the establishment clause under the purpose prong of the *Lemon* test: the state forbade the teaching of evolution because it conflicted with a particular religious doctrine. The Court stated that "the First Amendment does not permit the State to require that teaching and learning must be tailored to the principles or prohibitions of any religious sect or dogma." Thus, "[t]he State's undoubted right to prescribe the curriculum for its public schools does not carry with it the right to prohibit, on pain of criminal penalty, the teaching of a scientific theory or doctrine *where that prohibition is based upon reasons that violate the First Amendment.*"

There is no question in this case that the purpose behind using these particular history and social studies books was purely secular. Selecting a textbook that omits a particular topic for nonreligious reasons is significantly different from requiring the omission of material because it conflicts with a particular religious belief. Further, unlike the situation in *Epperson*, which involved total exclusion of information regarding evolution from the school curriculum, Appellees in this case merely complain that the historical treatment of religion in the challenged textbooks is inadequate. Finally, the record indicates that teachers in Alabama were free to supplement the discussion contained in the textbooks in areas they found inadequate. Thus, unlike the situation in *Epperson* where the State of Arkansas had made an attempt to teach the omitted material a criminal offense, there is no active policy on the part of Alabama that prohibits teaching historical facts about religion. There simply is nothing in this record to indicate that omission of certain facts regarding religion from these textbooks of itself constituted an advancement of secular humanism or an active hostility towards theistic religion prohibited by the establishment clause. While these textbooks may be inadequate from an educational standpoint, the wisdom of an educational policy or its efficiency from an educational point of view is not germane to the constitutional issue of whether that policy violates the establishment clause.

III. CONCLUSION

The home economics, social studies, and history textbooks at issue in this case do not violate the establishment clause of the first amendment. The district court's conclusions to the contrary reflect a misconception of the relationship between church and state mandated by the establishment clause. What is required of the states under the establishment clause is not "comprehensive identification of state with religion," but *separation* from religion. Yet implicit in the district court's opinion is the assumption that what the establishment clause actually requires is "equal time" for religion. Thus, the district court states that, while the state may teach certain moral values, it cannot advance any reason for those values unless "the possible different reasons [are] explained evenhandedly," and finds that history may not be taught constitutionally in the schools unless the textbooks contain more references to the place of religion in history.

"Separation is a requirement to abstain from fusing functions of Government and religious sects, not merely to treat them all equally." *McCollum*, 333 U.S. at 227 (Frankfurter, J., concurring), *quoted in Abington*. The public schools in this country are organized

> on the premise that secular education can be isolated from all religious teaching so that the school can inculcate all needed temporal knowledge and also maintain a strict and lofty neutrality as to religion. The assumption is that after the individual has been instructed in worldly wisdom he will be better fitted to choose his religion.

Abington (quoting *Everson* (Jackson, J., dissenting)). The district court's opinion in effect turns the establishment clause requirement of "lofty neutrality" on the part of the public schools into an affirmative obligation to speak about religion. Such a result clearly is inconsistent with the requirements of the establishment clause.

The judgment of the district court is REVERSED and the case is REMANDED for the sole purpose of entry by the district court of an order dissolving the injunction and terminating this litigation.

MOZERT v. HAWKINS COUNTY BOARD OF EDUCATION
827 F.2d 1058 (6th Cir. 1987)

LIVELY, CHIEF JUDGE.

This case arose under the Free Exercise Clause of the First Amendment, made applicable to the states by the Fourteenth Amendment. The district court held that a public school requirement that all students in grades one through eight use a prescribed set of reading textbooks violated the constitutional rights of objecting parents and students. The district court entered an injunction which required the schools to excuse objecting students from participating in reading classes where the textbooks are used and awarded the plaintiff parents more than $50,000 damages.

I.

A.

Early in 1983 the Hawkins County, Tennessee Board of Education adopted the Holt, Rinehart and Winston basic reading series (the Holt series) for use in grades 1-8 of the public schools of the county. In grades 1-4, reading is not taught as a separate subject at a designated time in the school day. Instead, the teachers in these grades use the reading texts throughout the day in conjunction with other subjects. In grades 5-8, reading is taught as a separate subject at a designated time in each class. However, the schools maintain an integrated curriculum which requires that ideas appearing in the reading programs reoccur in other courses. By statute public schools in Tennessee are required to include "character education" in their curricula. The purpose of this requirement is "to help each student develop positive values and to improve student conduct as students learn to act in harmony with their positive values and learn to become good citizens in their school, community, and society."

Like many school systems, Hawkins County schools teach "critical reading" as opposed to reading exercises that teach only word and sound recognition. "Critical reading" requires the development of higher order cognitive skills that enable students to evaluate the material they read, to contrast the ideas presented, and to understand complex characters that appear in reading material. Plaintiffs do not dispute that critical reading is an essential skill which their children must develop in order to succeed in other subjects and to function as effective participants in modern society. Nor do the defendants dispute the fact that any reading book will do more than teach a child how to read, since reading is instrumental in a child's total development as an educated person.

The plaintiff Vicki Frost is the mother of four children, three of whom were students in Hawkins County public schools in 1983. At the beginning of the 1983-84 school year Mrs. Frost read a story in a daughter's sixth grade reader that involved mental telepathy. Mrs. Frost, who describes herself as a "born again Christian," has a religious objection to any teaching about mental telepathy. Reading further, she found additional themes in the reader to which she had religious objections. After discussing her objections with other parents, Mrs. Frost talked with the principal of Church Hill Middle School and obtained an agreement for an alternative reading program for students whose parents objected to the assigned Holt reader. The students who elected the alternative program left their classrooms during the reading sessions and worked on assignments from an older textbook series in available office or library areas. Other students in two elementary schools were excused from reading the Holt books.

B.

In November 1983 the Hawkins County School Board voted unanimously to eliminate all alternative reading programs and require every student in the public schools to attend classes using the Holt series. Thereafter the plaintiff students refused to read the Holt series or attend reading classes where the series was being used. The children of several of the plaintiffs were suspended for brief periods for this refusal. Most of the plaintiff students were ultimately taught at home, or attended religious schools, or transferred to public schools outside Hawkins County. One student returned to school because his family was unable to afford alternate schooling. Even after the board's order, two students were allowed some accommodation, in that the teacher either excused them from reading the Holt stories, or specifically noted on worksheets that the student was not required to believe the stories.

On December 2, 1983, the plaintiffs, consisting of seven families — 14 parents and 17 children — filed this action pursuant to 42 U.S.C. §1983. In their complaint the plaintiffs asserted that they have sincere religious beliefs which are contrary to the values taught or inculcated by the reading textbooks and that it is a violation of the religious beliefs and convictions of the plaintiff students to be required to read the books and a violation of the religious beliefs of the plaintiff parents to permit their children to read the books. The plaintiffs sought to hold the defendants liable because "forcing the student-plaintiffs to read school books which teach or inculcate values in violation of their religious beliefs and convictions is a clear violation of their rights to the free exercise of religion protected by the First and Fourteenth Amendments to the United States Constitution."

II.

A.

Following remand the Commissioner of Education of the State of Tennessee was permitted to intervene as a defendant. At a pretrial hearing the parties made certain stipulations. Counsel for the defendants stipulated that the plaintiffs' religious beliefs are sincere and that certain passages in the reading texts offend those beliefs. However, counsel steadfastly refused to stipulate that the fact that the plaintiffs found the passages offensive made the reading requirement a burden on the plaintiffs' constitutional right to the free exercise of their religion. Similarly, counsel for the plaintiffs stipulated that there was a compelling state interest for the defendants to provide a public education to the children of Hawkins County. However, counsel stipulated only to a narrow definition of the compelling state interest — one that did not involve the exclusive use of a uniform series of textbooks. These stipulations left for trial the issues of whether the plaintiffs could show a burden on their free exercise right, in a constitutional sense, and whether the defendants could show a compelling interest in requiring all students in grades 1-8 of the Hawkins County public schools to use the Holt, Rinehart and Winston basal reading textbooks.

These were questions of law to be determined on the basis of evidence produced at trial.

B.

Vicki Frost was the first witness for the plaintiffs and she presented the most complete explanation of the plaintiffs' position. The plaintiffs do not belong to a single church or denomination, but all consider themselves born again Christians. Mrs. Frost testified that the word of God as found in the Christian Bible "is the totality of my beliefs." There was evidence that other members of their churches, and even their pastors, do not agree with their position in this case.

Mrs. Frost testified that she had spent more than 200 hours reviewing the Holt series and had found numerous passages that offended her religious beliefs. She stated that the offending materials fell into seventeen categories which she listed. These ranged from such familiar concerns of fundamentalist Christians as evolution and "secular humanism" to less familiar themes such as "futuristic supernaturalism," pacifism, magic and false views of death.

In her lengthy testimony Mrs. Frost identified passages from stories and poems used in the Holt series that fell into each category. Illustrative is her first category, futuristic supernaturalism, which she defined as teaching "Man As God." Passages that she found offensive described Leonardo da Vinci as the human with a creative mind that "came closest to the divine touch." Similarly, she felt that a passage entitled "Seeing Beneath the Surface" related to an occult theme, by describing the use of imagination as a vehicle for seeing things not discernible through our physical eyes. She interpreted a poem, "Look at Anything," as presenting the idea that by using imagination a child can become part of anything and thus understand it better. Mrs. Frost testified that it is an "occult practice" for children to use imagination beyond the limitation of scriptural authority. She testified that the story that alerted her to the problem with the reading series fell into the category of futuristic supernaturalism. Entitled "A Visit to Mars," the story portrays thought transfer and telepathy in such a way that "it could be considered a scientific concept," according to this witness. This theme appears in the testimony of several witnesses, *i.e.,* the materials objected to "could" be interpreted in a manner repugnant to their religious beliefs.

Mrs. Frost described objectionable passages from other categories in much the same way. Describing evolution as a teaching that there is no God, she identified 24 passages that she considered to have evolution as a theme. She admitted that the textbooks contained a disclaimer that evolution is a theory, not a proven scientific fact. Nevertheless, she felt that references to evolution were so pervasive and presented in such a factual manner as to render the disclaimer meaningless. After describing her objection to passages that encourage children to make moral judgments about whether it is right or wrong to kill animals, the witness stated, "I thought they would be learning to read, to have good

English and grammar, and to be able to do other subject work." Asked by plaintiffs' attorney to define her objection to the text books, Mrs. Frost replied:

> Very basically, I object to the Holt, Rhinehart [sic] Winston series as a whole, what the message is as a whole. There are some contents which are objectionable by themselves, but my most withstanding [sic] objection would be to the series as a whole.

Another witness for the plaintiffs was Bob Mozert, father of a middle school and an elementary school student in the Hawkins County system. His testimony echoed that of Vicki Frost in large part, though his answers to questions tended to be much less expansive. He also found objectionable passages in the readers that dealt with magic, role reversal or role elimination, particularly biographical material about women who have been recognized for achievements outside their homes, and emphasis on one world or a planetary society. Both witnesses testified under cross-examination that the plaintiff parents objected to passages that expose their children to other forms of religion and to the feelings, attitudes and values of other students that contradict the plaintiffs' religious views without a statement that the other views are incorrect and that the plaintiffs' views are the correct ones.

C.

The district court held that the plaintiffs' free exercise rights have been burdened because their "religious beliefs compel them to refrain from *exposure* to the Holt series," and the defendant school board "has effectively required that the student plaintiffs either read the offensive texts or give up their free public education."

The district court went on to find that the state had a compelling interest "in the education of its young," but that it had erred in choosing "to further its legitimate and overriding interest in public education by mandating the use of a single basic reading series," in the face of the plaintiffs' religious objections. The court concluded that the proof at trial demonstrated that the defendants could accommodate the plaintiffs without material and substantial disruption to the educational process by permitting the objecting students to "opt out of the school district's reading program," and meet the reading requirements by home schooling.

The court entered an injunction prohibiting the defendants "from requiring the student-plaintiffs to read from the Holt series," and ordering the defendants to excuse the student plaintiffs from their classrooms "[d]uring the normal reading period" and to provide them with suitable space in the library or elsewhere for a study hall.

III.

A.

The first question to be decided is whether a governmental requirement that a person be exposed to ideas he or she finds objectionable on religious grounds constitutes a burden on the free exercise of that person's religion as forbidden by the First Amendment. This is precisely the way the superintendent of the Hawkins County schools framed the issue in an affidavit filed early in this litigation. In his affidavit the superintendent set forth the school system's interest in a uniformity of reading texts. The affidavit also countered the claims of the plaintiffs that the schools were inculcating values and religious doctrines contrary to their religious beliefs, stating: "Without expressing an opinion as to the plaintiffs' religious beliefs, I am of the opinion that plaintiffs misunderstand the fact that exposure to something does not constitute teaching, indoctrination, opposition or promotion of the things exposed. While it is true that these textbooks expose the student to varying values and religious backgrounds, neither the textbooks nor the teachers teach, indoctrinate, oppose or promote any particular value or religion." That the district court accepted the issue as thus framed is clear from its reference to "exposure to the Holt series."

It is also clear that exposure to objectionable material is what the plaintiffs objected to albeit they emphasize the repeated nature of the exposure. The complaint mentioned only the textbooks that the students were required to read. It did not seek relief from any method of teaching the material and did not mention the teachers' editions. The plaintiffs did not produce a single student or teacher to testify that any student was ever required to affirm his or her belief or disbelief in any idea or practice mentioned in the various stories and passages contained in the Holt series. However, the plaintiffs appeared to assume that materials clearly presented as poetry, fiction and even "make-believe" in the Holt series were presented as facts which the students were required to believe. Nothing in the record supports this assumption.

At numerous places in her testimony Vicki Frost referred to various exercises and suggestions in the teachers' manuals as support for her view that objectionable ideas were being inculcated as truth rather than being offered as examples of the variety of approaches possible to a particular question. However, the students were not required to read the teachers' materials. While these materials suggested various ways of presenting the lessons, including "acting out" and round table discussions, there was no proof that any plaintiff student was ever called upon to say or do anything that required the student to affirm or deny a religious belief or to engage or refrain from engaging in any act either required or forbidden by the student's religious convictions. Mrs. Frost seemed to assume that each teacher used every suggested exercise or teaching tool in the teachers' editions. There was evidence that reading aloud and acting out the themes encountered in school lessons help young people learn. One of the teachers stated that students read some of the stories aloud. Proof that an objecting student was *required* to participate beyond reading and discussing assigned materials, or was disciplined for disputing assigned materials, might well implicate the Free Exercise Clause because the element of compulsion would then be present. But this was not the case either as pled or proved. The record leaves no doubt that the district court correctly viewed this case as one involving exposure to repugnant ideas and themes as presented by the Holt series.

Vicki Frost testified that an occasional reference to role reversal, pacifism, rebellion against parents, one-world government and other objectionable concepts would be acceptable, but she felt it was the repeated references to such subjects that created the burden. The district court suggested that it was a matter of balance, apparently believing that a reading series that presented ideas with which the plaintiffs agree in juxtaposition to those with which they disagree would pass constitutional muster. While balanced textbooks are certainly desirable, there would be serious difficulties with trying to cure the omissions in the Holt series, as plaintiffs and their expert witnesses view the texts.

However, the plaintiffs' own testimony casts serious doubt on their claim that a more balanced presentation would satisfy their religious views. Mrs. Frost testified that it would be acceptable for the schools to teach her children about other philosophies and religions, but if the practices of other religions were described in detail, or if the philosophy was "profound" in that it expressed a world view that deeply undermined her religious beliefs, then her children "would have to be instructed to [the] error [of the other philosophy]." It is clear that to the plaintiffs there is but one acceptable view — the Biblical view, as they interpret the Bible. Furthermore, the plaintiffs view every human situation and decision, whether related to personal belief and conduct or to public policy and programs, from a theological or religious perspective. Mrs. Frost testified that many political issues have theological roots and that there would be "no way" certain themes could be presented without violating her religious beliefs. She identified such themes as evolution, false supernaturalism, feminism, telepathy and magic as matters that could not be presented in any way without offending her beliefs. The only way to avoid conflict with the plaintiffs' beliefs in these sensitive areas would be to eliminate all references to the subjects so identified. However, the Supreme Court has clearly held that it violates the Establishment Clause to tailor a public school's curriculum to satisfy the principles or prohibitions of any religion. *Epperson v. Arkansas.*

The testimony of the plaintiffs' expert witness, Dr. Vitz, illustrates the pitfalls of trying to achieve a balance of materials concerning religion in a reading course. He found "markedly little reference to religion, particularly Christianity, and also remarkably little to Judaism" in the Holt series. His solution would be to "beef up" the references to these two dominant religions in the United States. However, an adherent to a less widely professed religion might then object to the slighting of his or her faith. Balance in the treatment of religion lies in the eye of the beholder. Efforts to achieve the particular "balance" desired by any individual or group by the addition or deletion of religious material would lead to a forbidden entanglement of the public schools in religious matters, if done with the purpose or primary effect of advancing or inhibiting religion. *Epperson; Schempp.*

B.

In this case the district court erroneously applied decisions based on governmental requirements that objecting parties make some affirmation or take some action that offends their religious beliefs. In each [of these decisions] the burden on the plaintiff's free exercise of religion consisted of being required to perform an act which violated the plaintiffs' religious convictions or forego benefits. In each case there was compulsion to do an act that violated the plaintiffs' religious convictions.

That element is missing in the present case. The requirement that students read the assigned materials and attend reading classes, in the absence of a showing that this participation entailed affirmation or denial of a religious belief, or performance or non-performance of a religious exercise or practice, does not place an unconstitutional burden on the students' free exercise of religion.

C.

The plaintiffs appear to contend that the element of compulsion was supplied by the requirement of class participation in the reading exercises. As we have pointed out earlier, there is no proof in the record that any plaintiff student was required to engage in role play, make up magic chants, read aloud or engage in the activity of haggling. In fact, the Director of Education for the State of Tennessee testified that most teachers do not adhere to the suggestions in the teachers' manuals and a teacher for 11 years in the Hawkins County system stated that she looks at the lesson plans in the teachers' editions, but "does her own thing." Being exposed to other students performing these acts might be offensive to the plaintiffs, but it does not constitute the compulsion described in the Supreme Court cases, where the objector was required to affirm or deny a religious belief or engage or refrain from engaging in a practice contrary to sincerely held religious beliefs.

IV.

A.

The Supreme Court has recently affirmed that public schools serve the purpose of teaching fundamental values "essential to a democratic society." These values "include tolerance of divergent political and religious views" while taking into account "consideration of the sensibilities of others." *Bethel School Dist. No. 403 v. Fraser*, 478 U.S. 675 (1986). The Court has noted with apparent approval the view of some educators who see public schools as an "assimilative force" that brings together "diverse and conflicting elements" in our society "on a broad but common ground." *Ambach v. Norwick*, 441 U.S. 68, 77 (1979), citing works of J. Dewey, N. Edwards and H. Richey. The critical reading approach furthers these goals. Mrs. Frost stated specifically that she objected to stories that develop "a religious tolerance that all religions are merely different roads to God." Stating that the plaintiffs reject this concept, presented as a recipe for an ideal world citizen, Mrs. Frost said, "We cannot be tolerant in that we accept other religious views on an equal basis with ours." While probably not an uncommon view of true believers in any religion, this statement graphically illustrates what is lacking in the plaintiffs' case.

The "tolerance of divergent. . . religious views" referred to by the Supreme Court is a civil tolerance, not a religious one. It does not require a person to accept any other religion as the equal of the one to which that person adheres. It merely requires a recognition that in a pluralistic society we must "live and let live." If the Hawkins County schools had required the plaintiff students either to believe or say they believe that "all religions are merely different roads to God," this would be a different case. No instrument of government can, consistent with the Free Exercise Clause, require such a belief or affirmation. However, there was absolutely no showing that the defendant school board sought to do this; indeed, the school board agreed at oral argument that it could not constitutionally do so. Instead, the record in this case discloses an effort by the school board to offer a reading curriculum designed to acquaint students with a multitude of ideas and concepts, though not in proportions the plaintiffs would like. While many of the passages deal with ethical issues, on the surface at least, they appear to us to contain no religious or anti-religious messages. Because the plaintiffs perceive every teaching that goes beyond the "three Rs" as inculcating religious ideas, they admit that any value-laden reading curriculum that did not affirm the truth of their beliefs would offend their religious convictions.

Although it is not clear that the plaintiffs object to all critical reading, Mrs. Frost did testify that she did not want her children to make critical judgments and exercise choices in areas where the Bible provides the answer. There is no evidence that any child in the Hawkins County schools was required to make such judgments. It was a goal of the school system to encourage this exercise, but nowhere was it shown that it was required. When asked to comment on a reading assignment, a student would be free to give the Biblical interpretation of the material or to interpret it from a different value base. The only conduct compelled by the defendants was reading and discussing the material in the Holt series, and hearing other students' interpretations of those materials. This is the exposure to which the plaintiffs objected. What is absent from this case is the critical element of compulsion to affirm or deny a religious belief or to engage or refrain from engaging in a practice forbidden or required in the exercise of a plaintiff's religion.

CORNELIA G. KENNEDY, CIRCUIT JUDGE, concurring.

I agree with Chief Judge Lively's analysis and concur in his opinion. However, even if I were to conclude that requiring the use of the Holt series or another similar series constituted a burden on appellees' free exercise rights, I would find the burden justified by a compelling state interest.

Appellants have stated that a principal educational objective is to teach the students how to think critically about complex and controversial subjects and to develop their own ideas and make judgments about these subjects. Several witnesses testified that the only way to achieve these objectives is to have the children read a basal reader, participate in class discussions, and formulate and express their own ideas and opinions about the materials presented in a basal reader. Thus, appellee students are required to read stories in the Holt series, make personal judgments about the validity of the stories, and to discuss why certain characters in the stories did what they did, or their values and whether those values were proper. Appellee parents testified that they object to their children reading the Holt readers, being exposed to controversial ideas in the classroom, and to their children making critical judgments and formulating their own ideas about anything for which they believe the Bible states a rule or position.

In *Bethel School Dist. No. 403 v. Fraser*, 478 U.S. 675 (1986), the Supreme Court stated: "The role and purpose of the American public school system was well described by two historians, saying 'public education must prepare pupils for citizenship in the Republic.'" Additionally, the *Bethel School* Court stated that the state through its public schools must "inculcate the habits and manners of civility as values in themselves conducive to happiness and as indispensable to the practice of self-government in the community and the nation." *Id.* (quoting C. Beard & M. Beard, New Basic History of the United States 228 (1968)). Teaching students about complex and controversial social and moral issues is just as essential for preparing public school students for citizenship and self-government as inculcating in the students the habits and manners of civility.

The evidence at trial demonstrated that mandatory participation in reading classes using the Holt series or some similar readers is essential to accomplish this compelling interest and that this interest could not be achieved any other way. Several witnesses for appellants testified that in order to develop critical reading skills, and therefore achieve appellants' objectives, the students must read and discuss complex, morally and socially difficult issues. Many of these necessarily will be subjects on which appellees believe the Bible states the rule or correct position. Consequently, accommodating appellees' beliefs would unduly interfere with the fulfillment of the appellants' objectives. Additionally, mandatory participation in the reading program is the least restrictive means of achieving appellants' objectives. Appellees' objections would arise even if the School Board selected another basal reading textbook series since the students would be required to engage in critical reading and form their own opinions and judgments on many of the same issues.

The state and the Hawkins County School Board also have a compelling interest in avoiding disruption in the classroom. Hawkins County Schools utilize an integrated curriculum, designed to prepare students for life in a complex, pluralistic society, that reinforces skills and values taught in one subject in other areas. The Director of Elementary Education testified that teachers use every opportunity within the school day to reinforce information taught in the different subject areas. For example, the students may discuss stories in the Holt readers dealing with evolution or conservation of natural resources in the science course. This approach to learning is well-recognized and enables the students to see learning "as part of their total life, not just [as] bits and pieces." This is particularly true in grades one through four where reading is taught throughout the school day, rather than in a particular period. Appellants would be unable to utilize effectively the critical reading teaching method and accommodate appellees' religious beliefs. If the opt-out remedy were implemented, teachers in all grades would have to either avoid the students discussing objectionable material contained in the Holt readers in non-reading classes or dismiss appellee students from class whenever such material is discussed. To do this the teachers would have to determine what is objectionable to appellees. This would either require that appellees review all teaching materials or that all teachers review appellees' extensive testimony. If the teachers concluded certain material fell in the objectionable classification but nonetheless considered it appropriate to have the students discuss this material, they would have to dismiss appellee students from these classes.[3] The dismissal of appellee students from the classes would result in substantial disruption to the public schools.

Additionally, Hawkins County Public Schools have a compelling interest in avoiding religious divisiveness. The Supreme Court has emphasized that the avoidance of religious divisiveness is nowhere more important than in public education, for "[t]he government's activities in this area can have a magnified impact on impressionable young minds. . . ." *Grand Rapids School Dist. v. Ball* [*infra* Chapter 8]. The opt-out remedy would permit appellee students to be released from a core subject every day *because* of their religion. Thus, although some students in the Hawkins County schools are presently released from class during the school day for special instruction, these students are not released because they have a religious objection to material being presented to the class. The present case is distinguishable from this Court's decision in *Spence v. Bailey*, 465 F.2d 797 (6th Cir.1972), inasmuch as the student in *Spence* was permitted to not participate in the school's R.O.T.C. program, a non-core subject. There is less divisiveness in excusing someone from military training then in excusing them from discussing a multitude of ideas. Accordingly, the opt-out remedy ordered by the court is inconsistent with the public schools' compelling interest in "promoting cohesion among a heterogenous democratic people." *Illinois ex rel. McCollum v. Board of Educ.*, 333 U.S. 203, 216 (1948) (Frankfurter, J., concurring).

The divisiveness and disruption caused by the opt-out remedy would be magnified if the schools had to grant other exemptions. Although the District Court found that no other objections to the Hawkins County public school curriculum have been raised and that Hawkins County is homogeneous from a religious perspective, this case would create a precedent for persons from other religions to request exemptions from core subjects because of religious objections. If the school district were required to accommodate exceptions and permit other students to opt-out of the reading program and other core courses with materials

---

[3] It is important to note that with respect to some of appellees' objections, any required discussion of objectionable materials would violate appellees' religious beliefs. It is not the mere "unbalanced treatment" of these materials that appellees find offensive.

others found objectionable, this would result in a public school system impossible to administer. As Justice Jackson stated in *McCollum*, every parent:

> has as good a right as this plaintiff to demand that the courts compel the schools to sift out of their teaching everything inconsistent with its doctrines. If we are to eliminate everything that is objectionable to any of these warring sects or inconsistent with any of their doctrines, we will leave public education in shreds. Nothing but educational confusion and a discrediting of the public school system can result from subjecting it to constant law suits.

Accordingly, I also would reverse the judgment of the District Court for these additional reasons, as well as the reasons so well stated by Chief Judge Lively.

BOGGS, CIRCUIT JUDGE, concurring.

II

I believe this is a more difficult case than outlined in the court's opinion. I disagree with the first proposition in the court's opinion, that plaintiffs object to any exposure to any contrary idea. I do not believe we can define for plaintiffs their belief as to what is religiously forbidden to be so comprehensive, where both they and the district court have spoken to the contrary. A reasonable reading of plaintiffs' testimony shows they object to the overall effect of the Holt series, not simply to any exposure to any idea opposing theirs. The district court specifically found that the objection was to exposure to the Holt series, not to any single story or idea.

Ultimately, I think we must address plaintiffs' claims as they actually impact their lives: it is their belief that they should not take a course of study which, on balance, to them, denigrates and opposes their religion, and which the state is compelling them to take on pain of forfeiting all other benefits of public education.

Their view may seem silly or wrong-headed to some, but it is a sincerely held religious belief. By focussing narrowly on references that make plaintiffs appear so extreme that they could never be accommodated, the court simply leaves resolution of the underlying issues here to another case, when we have plaintiffs with a more sophisticated understanding of our own and Supreme Court precedent, and a more careful and articulate presentation of their own beliefs.

Under the court's assessment of the facts, this is a most uninteresting case. It is not the test case sought, or feared, by either side. The court reviews the record and finds that the plaintiffs actually want a school system that affirmatively teaches the correctness of their religion, and prevents other students from mentioning contrary ideas. If that is indeed the case, then it can be very simply resolved. It would obviously violate the Establishment Clause for any school system to agree with such an extravagant view.

It should be noted and emphasized that if such is the holding, this decision is largely irrelevant to the national legal controversy over this case. The extent to which school systems may constitutionally require students to use educational materials that are objectionable, contrary to, or forbidden by their religious beliefs is a serious and important issue. The question of exactly how terms such as "contrary," "objectionable," and "forbidden," are to be assessed in the context of religious beliefs is a subtle and interesting one. But this decision, as I understand it, addresses none of those questions. When a case arises with more sophisticated or cagey plaintiffs, or less skillful cross-examination, that true issue must be faced anew, with little guidance from this decision. Since these plaintiffs' claims are rejected because they are read to be so extreme as obviously to violate the Establishment Clause, this case is no precedent for the more specific and narrowly drawn complaint that the district court and plaintiffs' counsel (and, to me, the plaintiffs) thought the plaintiffs were making.

I find the court's conclusion based on its reading of the record to be unsatisfactory on the factual basis of what was said at the trial. The trial strategies of the two sides were clear. The plaintiffs understood that the more thoroughgoing and extensive their objections, the less possible would it be to accommodate them within the bounds of the Constitution. Therefore, the plaintiffs repeatedly stated their objections in terms of the overall Holt series.

The defendants equally clearly sought to depict plaintiffs' objections in the most constitutionally offensive terms. By skillful cross-examination, they did elicit on some occasions the statements on which the court relies. I believe these two lines of apparently contradictory testimony can be reconciled by recognizing the different meanings or usage of the same words or phrases such as "objectionable," "want," or "opposed to." These words can cover a gamut from mild objection or desire to constitutional insistence. Something may be "objectionable," in the sense that one would rather it did not happen, but it is something that must be endured. Conversely, it may be "objectionable" in the sense that it should not be permitted or one should not be required to endure it. Thus, I may find Muzak on buses, or in-flight movies, "objectionable," but that's life. However, one might find the display of pornographic material in either location "objectionable" to the point that a relatively captive audience legally should not be subjected to it.

Similarly, plaintiffs may "want" a school system tailored exactly to their religious beliefs (that is why many people choose religious education), but they very well know that that is constitutionally impermissible. They "want" a particular type of accommodation that they have sought in this law suit, and they believe that they are constitutionally entitled to that. Judge Hull, who sat through eight days of trial testimony over these very issues, came to the same conclusion I do, expressed it in the form of a finding, and should not be overturned unless that finding is clearly erroneous. In my reading of the testimony, the judge's finding is not only not clearly erroneous, but it can only be reversed by a failure to recognize a distinction between the ideal education the parents want, and that level of accommodation and education which they believe is constitutionally required and which they "want" here. Thus, I believe we must take plaintiffs' claims as they have stated them — that they desire the accommodation of an opt-out, or alternative reading books, and no more. That is all they have ever asked for in their pleadings, in the arguments at trial and in appellate briefing and argument.

III

I also disagree with the court's view that there can be no burden here because there is no requirement of conduct contrary to religious belief. That view both slights plaintiffs' honest beliefs that studying the full Holt series would be conduct contrary to their religion, and overlooks other Supreme Court Free Exercise cases which view "conduct" that may offend religious exercise at least as broadly as do plaintiffs.

On the question of exposure to, or use of, books as conduct, we may recall the Roman Catholic Church's, *Index Librorum Prohibitorum.*" This was a list of those books the reading of which was a mortal sin, at least until the second Vatican Council in 1962. I would hardly think it can be contended that a school requirement that a student engage in an act (the reading of the book) which would specifically be a mortal sin under the teaching of a major organized religion would be other than "conduct prohibited by religion," even by the court's fairly restrictive standard. Yet, in what constitutionally important way can the situation here be said to differ from that? Certainly, a religion's size or formality of hierarchy cannot determine the religiosity of beliefs. Similarly, and analogous to our case, church doctrine before 1962 also indicated that portions of the banned books could be used or read in a context to show their error, and that references to, or small portions of, the books did not fall under the same ban. Again, it seems inconceivable that we would determine that a Catholic child had forfeited the right to object to committing a mortal sin by reading Hobbes because he was willing, in another context, to read small portions or excerpts of the same material.

While this argument would seem persuasive that studying objectionable material would be "conduct" contrary to religious belief, the court's opinion attempts to distinguish our case from *Thomas v. Review Board,* 450 U.S. 707 (1981), by emphasizing that the plaintiff there was asked to "engage in a practice" forbidden by his religion, and the plaintiffs here are not. I do not believe that distinction bears up under scrutiny. Thomas had to hook up chains to a conveyor in a factory. For Thomas, there was no commandment against hooking up chains. He asserted that this would be "aiding in the manufacture of items used in the advancement of war," because it was in a tank turret line, but he had also said that he would work in a steel factory that might ultimately sell to the military. (A fellow Witness was willing to work in the turret line.) This distinction appears as convoluted as plaintiffs' distinctions seem to some. Nevertheless, Thomas drew his line, and the Supreme Court respected it and dealt with it.

"[R]eligious beliefs need not be acceptable, logical, consistent, or comprehensible to others in order to merit First Amendment protection."

Here, plaintiffs have drawn their line as to what required school activities, what courses of study, do and do not offend their beliefs to the point of prohibition. I would hold that if they are forced over that line, they are "engaging in conduct" forbidden by their religion. The court's excellent summary of its holding on this point, *ante,* at 1070, appears to concede that what plaintiffs were doing in school was conduct, but that there "was no evidence that the conduct required of the students was forbidden by their religion." I cannot agree. The plaintiffs provided voluminous testimony of the conflict (in their view) between reading the Holt readers and their religious beliefs, including extensive Scriptural references. The district court found that "plaintiffs' religious beliefs *compel* them to refrain from exposure to the Holt series." I would think it could hardly be clearer that they believe their religion commands, not merely suggests, their course of action.

VI

However, constitutional adjudication, especially for a lower court, is not simply a matter of common sense use of words. We must determine whether the common sense burden on plaintiffs' religious belief is, in the context of a public school curriculum, a constitutional "burden" on their religious beliefs.

Running a public school system of today's magnitude is quite a different proposition [than that raised by other religious accommodation cases]. A constitutional challenge to the content of instruction (as opposed to participation in ritual such as magic chants, or prayers) is a challenge to the notion of a politically-controlled school system. Imposing on school boards the delicate task of satisfying the "compelling interest" test to justify failure to accommodate pupils is a significant step. It is a substantial imposition on the schools to *require* them to justify each instance of not dealing with students' individual, religiously compelled, objections (as opposed to *permitting* a local, rough and ready, adjustment), and I do not see that the Supreme Court has authorized us to make such a requirement.

Our interpretation of these key phrases of our Bill of Rights in the school context is certainly complicated by the fact that the drafters of the Bill of Rights never contemplated a school system that would be the most pervasive benefit of citizenship for many, yet which would be very difficult to avoid.

The average public expenditure for a pupil in Hawkins County is about 20% of the income of the average household there. Even the modest tuition in the religious schools which some plaintiffs attended here amounted to about a doubling of the state and local tax burden of the average resident. Had the Founders recognized the possibility of state intervention of this magnitude, they might have written differently. However, it is difficult for me to see that the words "free exercise of religion," at the adoption of the Bill of Rights, implied a freedom from state teaching, even of offensive material, when some alternative was legally permissible.

Therefore, I reluctantly conclude that under the Supreme Court's decisions as we have them, school boards may set curricula bounded only by the Establishment Clause, as the state contends. Thus, contrary to the analogy plaintiffs suggest, pupils may indeed be expelled if they will not read from the King James Bible, so long as it is only used as literature, and not taught as religious truth. *See Abington School Dist. v. Schempp; Donahoe v. Richards*, 38 Me. 379, 61 Am.Dec. 256 (1854). Contrary to the position of amicus American Jewish Committee, Jewish students may not assert a burden on their religion if their reading materials overwhelmingly provide a negative view of Jews or factual or historical issues important to Jews, so long as such materials do not assert any propositions as religious truth, or do not otherwise violate the Establishment Clause.

The court's opinion well illustrates the distinction between the goals and values that states may try to impose and those they cannot, by distinguishing between teaching *civil* toleration of other religions, and teaching *religious* toleration of other religions. It is an accepted part of public schools to teach the former, and plaintiffs do not quarrel with that. Thus, the state may teach that all religions have the same civil and political rights, and must be dealt with civilly in civil society. The state itself concedes it may not do the latter. It may not teach as truth that the religions of others are just as correct *as religions* as plaintiffs' own.

It is a more difficult question when, as here, the state presents materials that plaintiffs sincerely believe preach religious toleration of religions by consistent omission of plaintiffs' religion and favorable presentation of opposing views. Our holding requires plaintiffs to put up with what they perceive as an unbalanced public school curriculum, so long as the curriculum does not violate the Establishment Clause. Every other sect or type of religious belief is bound by the same requirement. The rule here is not a rule just for fundamentalist dissenters, for surely the rule cannot be that when the school authorities disagree with non-fundamentalist dissenters, the school loses. Rather, unless the Supreme Court chooses to extend the principle of *Thomas* to schools, the democratic principle must prevail.[14]

Schools are very important, and some public schools offend some people deeply. That is one major reason private schools of many denominations — fundamentalist, Lutheran, Jewish — are growing. But a response to that phenomenon is a political decision for the schools to make. I believe that such a significant change in school law and expansion in the religious liberties of pupils and parents should come only from Supreme Court itself, and not simply from

---

[14] Plaintiffs are, of course, free to work politically and by education to change the school curriculum, just as others worked and succeeded in making the changes to which plaintiffs object.

our interpretation. It may well be that we would have a better society if children and parents were not put to the hard choice posed by this case. But our mandate is limited to carrying out the commands of the Constitution and the Supreme Court.

Chapter 5

THE FRUSTRATING SEARCH FOR
AN ESTABLISHMENT CLAUSE STANDARD

In a logical world, this Chapter would begin with a summary of the Supreme Court's Establishment Clause standard, and then proceed to various critiques of that standard. Unfortunately, contemporary Establishment Clause jurisprudence is such that no one can say with certainty what standard the Supreme Court currently applies in Establishment Clause cases. The standard that has served as the focal point for Establishment Clause discussions in recent times is the three-part test described in the majority opinion in *Lemon v. Kurtzman*, 403 U.S. 602 (1971). Ever since the Supreme Court issued the so-called "*Lemon* test," debate has raged over what the test means, whether its terms are absolute, whether it is a good or a bad thing, and (in recent times) whether the test even has the support of a majority of the Justices currently on the Court. Lower courts are especially confused about the current state of Establishment Clause law and are often reduced to applying one or more other tests in addition to *Lemon*. They have a number of options from which to choose; there are nine Justices on the United States Supreme Court and some combination of these nine Justices have at one point or another have applied at least ten different Establishment Clause analyses. The situation is complicated even further by the fact that many of the Justices apply more than one standard, some of which contradict each other. See, for example, Justice Kennedy's application of a narrow coercion analysis in *County of Allegheny v. ACLU, infra* Chapter 6; a broad coercion analysis in his majority opinion in *Lee v. Weisman, infra* Chapter 6; and a neutrality analysis in *Rosenberger v. Rector and Visitors of the University of Virginia*, 515 U.S. 819 (1995).

This chapter provides a snapshot of all the standards currently supported by at least one Justice. Whether these formalistic standards have any significant relationship with the constitutional principles they are designed to enforce (or indeed, whether the standards do anything more than certify a decision reached on other grounds) is, as in every area of constitutional law, always open to debate. But at the very least the standards reflect the different concerns of different justices, and (perhaps more importantly) communicate to lower courts and litigants the terms they are supposed to use to characterize their church/state claims.

Like most lower courts, the materials below take *Lemon* as the starting point for developing a modern Establishment Clause analysis and then proceed to discuss the other possibilities. One should keep in mind, however, that the departure of Justice O'Connor from the Court may spell the demise of *Lemon*, at least for the near future.

A. THE *LEMON* TEST

LEMON v. KURTZMAN
403 U.S. 602 (1971)

[The Court stuck down two state statutes providing financial aid to religious schools, on the ground that the statutes fostered an unconstitutional entanglement between the states and the beneficiary religious institutions. Before discussing the particulars of the statutes, the Court defined the 3-part analysis that has dominated all subsequent Establishment Clause discussions.]

II.

In *Everson v. Board of Education*, this Court upheld a state statute that reimbursed the parents of parochial school children for bus transportation expenses. There Mr. Justice Black, writing for the majority, suggested that the decision carried to "the verge" of forbidden territory under the Religion Clauses. Candor compels acknowledgment, moreover, that we can only dimly perceive the lines of demarcation in this extraordinarily sensitive area of constitutional law.

The language of the Religion Clauses of the First Amendment is at best opaque, particularly when compared with other portions of the Amendment. Its authors did not simply prohibit the establishment of a state church or a state religion, an area history shows they regarded as very important and fraught with great dangers. Instead they commanded that there should be "no law *respecting* an establishment of religion." A law may be one "respecting" the forbidden objective while falling short of its total realization. A law "respecting" the proscribed result, that is, the establishment of religion, is not always easily identifiable as one violative of the Clause. A given law might not *establish* a state religion but nevertheless be one "respecting" that end in the sense of being a step that could lead to such establishment and hence offend the First Amendment.

In the absence of precisely stated constitutional prohibitions, we must draw lines with reference to the three main evils against which the Establishment Clause was intended to afford protection: "sponsorship, financial support, and active involvement of the sovereign in religious activity." *Walz v. Tax Commission* [*infra* Chapter 8].

Every analysis in this area must begin with consideration of the cumulative criteria developed by the Court over many years. Three such tests may be gleaned from our cases. First, the statute must have a secular legislative purpose; second, its principal or primary effect must be one that neither advances nor inhibits religion, *Board of Education v. Allen*, 392 U.S. 236, 243 (1968); finally, the statute must not foster "an excessive government entanglement with religion." *Walz*, at 674.

Michael Stokes Paulsen
Lemon is Dead
43 CASE W. RES. L. REV. 795 (1993)*

For many years, *Lemon* had been the subject of sharp criticism from legal commentators and even sharper criticism from members of the Court.[15] The criticism was well deserved. Each of Lemon's three "prongs" for evaluating the constitutionality of government action challenged under the Establishment Clause — (1) that the law or conduct have a "secular purpose"; (2) that it have a "primary effect" that "neither advances nor inhibits" religion; and (3) that it not foster "excessive entanglement" of the state with religion — had some major analytic flaw or ambiguity. In addition, packaging the test as one in which all three requirements must be satisfied compounded these problems by cumulating them. Finally, the ambiguity of the test left the Court leeway to interpret each prong in varying ways, producing a bewildering patchwork of decisions as the justices engaged in a tug-of-war over the interpretation of the test. Not all of the resulting decisions were wrong, of course, but they certainly lacked doctrinal coherence.

The difficulty begins with first premises. Much of the *Lemon* framework seemed to assume that the Establishment Clause imposes a constitutional disability on religion — that it is an "anti-religion" counterweight to the "pro-religion" Free Exercise Clause rather than a protection of religious liberty. The "secular purpose" prong was sometimes read to reflect this erroneous assumption. It misleadingly implied (and many courts thus held) that laws motivated by a desire to promote religious freedom or to accommodate religious practice automatically constitute an establishment of religion. The result was frequently a reading of the Establishment Clause that required functional hostility, or indifference to religion by treating the promotion of religious freedom as distinguished from the promotion of religion — as an improper government motivation. This produced a head-on confrontation with the Free Exercise Clause: The Establishment Clause was construed to forbid government from deliberately taking action that the Free Exercise Clause seemed to require gov-

---

[15] *See, e.g.*, County of Allegheny v. ACLU, 492 U.S. 573, 655-56 (1989) (Kennedy, J., concurring in part and dissenting in part) (collecting cases); Edwards v. Aguillard, 482 U.S. 578, 636-40 (1987) (Scalia, J., dissenting) (advocating elimination of the purpose prong of the Lemon test); Aguilar v. Felton, 473 U.S. 402, 426-30 (1985) (O'Connor, J., dissenting) (criticizing the entanglement prong); Wallace v. Jaffree, 472 U.S. 38, 108- 12 (1985) (Rehnquist, J., dissenting) (test lacking historical basis in the First Amendment); Roemer v. Maryland Bd. of Public Works, 426 U.S. 736, 768- 69 (1976) (White, J., concurring in the judgment) (entanglement prong unnecessary and superfluous); Lemon, 403 U.S. at 661 (White, J., dissenting).

For a sampling of academic criticism, see Philip B. Kurland, *The Irrelevance of the Constitution: The Religion Clauses of the First Amendment and the Supreme Court*, 24 VILL. L. REV. 3 (1978); Michael W. McConnell, *Religious Freedom at a Crossroads*, 59 U. CHI. L. REV. 115, 127-34 (1992); [Michael A.] Paulsen, [*Religion, Equality, and the Constitution: An Equal Protection Approach to Establishment Clause Adjudication*, 61 NOTRE DAME L. REV. 311 (1986),] *supra* note 3.

ernment to take, producing an untenable reading of the religion clauses as contradictory in principle.

Still worse, the "secular purpose" prong was often understood to render susceptible to Establishment Clause challenge laws *motivated* by religious convictions but not otherwise distinctively "religious" in character. Some of these challenges were unsuccessful, as in the challenge to the Hyde Amendment restricting government funding for abortion. But other challenges succeeded in invalidating laws simply because of the supposed religious motivations underlying their public support. Some of these laws might have failed other "prongs" of *Lemon* (and perhaps even a sensitive application of the coercion test) because they involved actual government inculcation of religion to a captive audience. But if a statute motivated by religion, or even intended to advance religion, is neutral in its effects on freedom of religious exercise and nonexercise, the Establishment Clause supplies no justification for outlawing it. The purpose prong of Lemon thus served no legitimate function, and several illegitimate ones. A law should not be considered unconstitutional because of the religious motives of the persons favoring it. Still less ought it be struck down because of the religious identity or affiliation of those favoring it. The purpose prong too readily became the doctrinal equivalent of the *ad hominem* fallacy — an attack on the person(s) making the argument (or statute), not on the argument (statute) itself.

It is not the motivation or identity of a law's supporters, but the *effects* of a law that properly determine its constitutionality. The "primary effect" prong of *Lemon* addressed this central inquiry, but floundered on two points: first, it was opaque and misleading as to what constituted the forbidden object of government "advancement"; second, it ignored the question of the proper baseline against which such effects would be measured. Put another way, the Court never clearly came to grips with either the "effects" yardstick or the "effects" baseline. It is not surprising that the Court's cases under *Lemon* were so incoherent, since the Court did not know what it was measuring or where it was starting from.

What is it that government may not "advance"? The Court at first spoke of the effects prong in terms of laws that advanced *religion* as opposed to the devilishly manipulable term "nonreligion." Near the end of *Lemon*'s life, the Court recognized that any law accommodating religion, by promoting religious freedom, in a sense "advanced" religion in a way that "nonreligion" was not similarly advanced. The Court adjusted its interpretation of the effects prong accordingly. As it stated in *Corporation of Presiding Bishop v. Amos*:

> A law is not unconstitutional simply because it allows churches to advance religion, which is their very purpose. For a law to have forbidden 'effects' under *Lemon*, it must be fair to say that the *government itself* has advanced religion through its own activities and influence.

As the concurring justices in *Amos* aptly observed, this comment confuses more than clarifies. It begs the question in all cases of government accommodation of religion (including *Amos* itself): does the "government itself" advance religion where it exempts religion from a burden it imposes on secular persons or entities? If the government really must be neutral as between religion and "nonreligion" — as the effects prong of *Lemon* asserted — the answer is no. Special treatment unconstitutionally advances religion. But that conclusion proved impossible to reconcile with the Court's cases holding that the Free Exercise Clause sometimes *requires* unique accommodation of religion. Such a conclusion also left no room for *permissive* accommodation of religion, a result the Court came to recognize as equally unacceptable. The Court never could resolve this tension.

The second serious problem with the effects test was the Court's repeated failure to confront the problem of selecting a realistic and consistent baseline from which to measure "advancement" (of whatever it is that may not be advanced). Does it advance religion to grant religion affirmative benefits where secular institutions are granted those same benefits (or similar but greater ones)? *Lemon v. Kurtzman* said yes. The program invalidated in the case that launched the "*Lemon* test" was one in which state governments made modest financial contributions to private, including religious, schools. Of course, government's financial support for *public* schools was infinitely greater. The programs in *Lemon* — and in a large number of subsequent cases testing its application to other forms of aid — merely made up this discrepancy in small part. Despite the implausibility of claiming that such treatment advances religion relative to nonreligion, the Court implicitly treated the baseline for the effects test as zero benefits, notwithstanding that secular entities received huge benefits.

The absurdity of this approach is highlighted by an example the Court frequently gave in opinions upholding the neutral inclusion of religion within some programs: "If the Establishment Clause barred the extension of general benefits to religious groups, 'a church could not be protected by the police and fire departments, or have its public sidewalk kept in repair.'" The irony (which the Court failed to note) is that this example contradicts *Lemon* in principle. What makes police and fire protection different from financial assistance to education? Neither benefit would be given to religion in a state of nature. If the baseline is what religion would get were there no government, then providing churches with fire protection in principle "advances" religion every bit as much as salary supplements for parochial schools, for it leaves religion better off than if there were no government. But if the baseline is the benefits the modern welfare state makes available to all similarly situated persons and groups, then it does not "advance" religion to make religious persons and groups eligible for benefits on the same terms as any other person or group. Still less does it advance religion to be granted a substitute, smaller benefit (as in *Lemon*).

Both of these problems are susceptible of a single answer, but it is an answer that guts the core of Lemon (at least as Lemon was often applied). The relevant comparison is not between a law's effects on the exercise of religion and the exercise of "non-religion" (which would seem to imply that laws must be neutral in their relative effects as between religious exercise and tennis-playing, or lawn-mowing, or photography). Rather, the proper comparison is between a law's effects on the exercise of religion and the non-exercise of religion — the freedom not to engage in the exercise of religion. A better "primary effect" prong would require that a law neither advance nor inhibit the exercise of any particular religion as against the exercise of any other religion, or as against the right not to exercise any religion.

Improvement

This standard addresses the relevant "effect": government action's impact on freedom of religious exercise and non-exercise. It also implicitly establishes the appropriate baseline from which neutrality should be measured — religious practice absent government action. This inquiry would focus on government effects on religious *conduct* — on actions — not effects on "religion" as an abstract concept. This has the salutary effect of being an easier and more appropriate task for judges to perform; courts can more readily judge effects on outward and visible signs than on inward and spiritual states. Moreover, this inquiry makes better textual sense as well as better practical sense. If non-establishment and free exercise are understood as correlative rather than contradictory principles, it is logical to read the clauses as mirror-image prohibitions on government prescription and proscription, respectively, of the same thing — religious *exercise*. As thus recast, the effects prong is properly a version of the "coercion" test: the Establishment Clause forbids government compulsion of religious exercise through means direct or indirect. But that is about all that usefully can be salvaged from *Lemon*.

The third prong of *Lemon* — "excessive entanglement" — was perhaps the most consistent object of criticism. It offered many problems from which to choose. First, the test belonged on the free exercise side of the coin: excessive entanglement of the state with religion is a form of burden on free religious exercise, abridging the liberty of the person or institution "entangled" with, not a means of coercing, promoting, or even endorsing religion. As such, it makes little sense to accord standing to raise an entanglement challenge to anyone but the burdened person or institution in an action under the Free Exercise Clause. Second, the test was hopelessly vague; it delegates essentially standardless discretion to judges to decide what is "excessive." Third, as employed by the Court in tandem with the primary effect prong, the entanglement prong created a damned-if-you-do-damned-if-you-don't dilemma. The very steps that government sometimes must take to assure that programs are neutral toward religion (so as to pass the effect prong) entail monitoring condemned under the entanglement prong. Finally, like the purpose prong, entanglement sometimes was construed to prohibit programs "divisive" along religious lines. The "divisiveness" variant implied that religious persons and groups could be excluded from public programs — discriminated against — if there was strong enough political opposition. The Court's more recent cases applying the entanglement prong had defanged it somewhat, but the problems with the test remained.

It is somewhat strange that the entanglement prong, with all its difficulties, lasted as long as the rest of *Lemon*. The explanation probably lies in the "separation of church and state" theme that has persistently dogged Establishment Clause interpretation since Jefferson's invocation of the metaphor of a "wall of separation" in a letter to the Danbury Baptists. A prohibition on "excessive entanglement" is simply a way of restating the imprecise idea that the Establishment Clause requires an appropriate degree of "separation" of church and state. It does not clarify what that degree is, nor does it justify Jefferson's characterization of the clause in such terms. The First Amendment does require "separation" or "non-entanglement," but it does so as a matter of the Free Exercise Clause's protection of religion from government intrusion on personal and institutional religious autonomy. That is, religion may be entitled to a private sphere separate and independent from government power and immune from its regulations. It never was legitimate to use the idea of separation to authorize *discrimination* against religion within the public sphere.

Steven G. Gey
Religious Coercion and the Establishment Clause
1994 U. ILL. L. REV. 463[*]

I. THE LONG AND WINDING WALL:
ENFORCING THE SEPARATION OF CHURCH AND STATE

The practical difficulties of enforcing the separation [of church and state] have produced a constant stream of litigation over the last forty years. These difficulties also have produced several failed efforts to precisely describe the standard by which courts judge government actions that benefit or endorse religion. The case law is littered with tests and guidelines that were intended to clarify the line separating church and state but which succeeded only in creating new disputes.

The governing standard for more than twenty years has been the three-part *Lemon* test. The longevity of this test does not mean that the Court has used it consistently, or even that a majority of Justices agree about what the test means. Instead, the *Lemon* test frequently has resembled a constitutional Rorschach test, reflecting the often contradictory constitutional views of different observers. These broad disagreements about the meaning and viability of *Lemon*, both inside and outside the Court, have rendered the *Lemon* test only an imperfect tool for enforcing the separation principle.

A. THE HONORABLE FAILURE OF *LEMON V. KURTZMAN*

In 1971, the Supreme Court used a case challenging state funding of religious education to articulate the modern standard for judging Establishment Clause violations. This standard includes three components: "First, the statute must

---

[*] Copyright © 1994. Reprinted by permission

have a secular legislative purpose; second, its principal or primary effect must be one that neither advances nor inhibits religion; finally, the statute must not foster 'an excessive government entanglement with religion.'" Except for three cases involving special circumstances,[13] the Court has applied the *Lemon* test to decide every Establishment Clause case since 1971. The almost uniform use of *Lemon* gives a misleading appearance of coherence and consistency in the application of this standard. In reality, the Court's application of *Lemon* has been erratic, contradictory, and arguably irrational. Although measuring such things scientifically is impossible, the three-part test for compliance with the Establishment Clause announced in *Lemon v. Kurtzman* is possibly the most maligned constitutional standard the Court has ever produced.

The *Lemon* test has been the subject of criticism almost from the day it was announced. Even *Lemon's* author eventually de-emphasized the precedent's importance and seemed happy to entertain suggestions that the test be abandoned.[15] Chief Justice Rehnquist was even less willing to permit *Lemon* to share the Establishment Clause stage with other tests. When he was not urging the Court to overrule *Lemon*, he was disparaging Lemon as "no more than [a] helpful signpos[t]."

After reading repeated comments of this nature from various Supreme Court Justices, many constitutional litigators and lower court judges inferred the imminent demise of the *Lemon* standard. In 1992, in *Lee v. Weisman*, the Bush administration joined conservative religious groups in urging the Court to explicitly abandon the *Lemon* test. For several years prior to *Weisman*, a number of lower court judges had also suggested that the separationist language of the *Lemon* test should be abandoned in favor of a more compliant standard based on the Court's recognition in *Marsh v. Chambers* that religion is "part of the fabric of our society." Other lower courts exhibited less enthusiasm for abandoning *Lemon*, but, in expectation that the Supreme Court might soon replace the *Lemon* test, carefully justified their Establishment Clause decisions on the basis of several different standards.

---

[13] Lee v. Weisman, 112 S. Ct. 2649, 2655 (1992) (striking down graduation prayer without applying *Lemon* because the "pervasive" nature of the religious activity conflicted with settled precedent regarding public school prayer); Marsh v. Chambers, 463 U.S. 783, 791 (1983) (upholding legislative prayer without applying *Lemon* because of the "unique history" of the practice); Larson v. Valente, 456 U.S. 228, 252-55 (1982) (applying one prong of *Lemon*, but noting that Lemon "is not necessary to the disposition of the case before us").

Justice Souter's majority opinion in Board of Education v. Grumet, 114 S. Ct. 2481 (1994), may be considered a fourth such decision, depending upon whether one accepts Justice Blackmun's or Justice O'Connor's interpretation of the majority rationale. Compare id. at 2495 (Blackmun, J., concurring) (majority relying on decisions "that explicitly rest[] on the criteria set forth in *Lemon*"), *with* id. at 2500 (O'Connor, J., concurring) (majority opinion demonstrating "the slide away from *Lemon's* unitary approach").

[15] Lynch v. Donnelly, 465 U.S. 668, 679 (1984) ("[W]e have repeatedly emphasized," Chief Justice Burger wrote in the Court's first Christmas creche case, "our unwillingness to be confined to any single test or criterion in this sensitive area.")

Doubt over *Lemon*'s continued viability, combined with confusion over the meaning of the *Lemon* test, has produced an area of law that is chaotic and almost entirely unpredictable. When the Fifth Circuit Court of Appeals recently rejected a challenge to the official use of a religious symbol by the city government of Austin, Texas, it nicely summarized the practical effect of most Establishment Clause precedents:

> In so holding, we obviously cannot fashion a bright line test to apply to future challenges to government use or depiction of religious symbols. Instead, as we must, we decide only the case before us. And in doing so, we have considered, and balanced, the totality of its unique facts and circumstances.[22]

In other words, the appellate court spent valuable time writing an opinion that has virtually no precedential value. Because of *Lemon*'s slippery nature, the slightest factual distinction makes each Establishment Clause case a whole new ball game.

The Supreme Court can blame only itself for the dissatisfaction and confusion that surrounds the *Lemon* standard. The Court produced the Lemon standard in 1971, during a period when the Court was evolving toward a more conservative position on church-state matters than it had taken during the Warren Court era. Chief Justice Burger's majority opinion made clear that the Court which produced *Lemon* would not support any constitutional standard that would ensure strict separation between church and state. Perhaps to emphasize that the strong terms of the new standard should not be read too literally, Chief Justice Burger commented that the Establishment Clause erects only a "blurred, indistinct, and variable barrier depending on all the circumstances of a particular relationship." Such a tepid statement of objectives is unlikely to produce a consistently applied constitutional standard, no matter how strongly that standard is phrased in the abstract.

One response to the muddle surrounding *Lemon* is simply to ignore the three-part test in analyzing Establishment Clause issues in favor of looking behind *Lemon* for other factors that explain the Court's Establishment Clause cases. Douglas Laycock suggests that courts can ignore the *Lemon* test when considering issues such as school prayer and religious school financing because "the three-part test does not help explain the Court's results and actually hampers understanding of the real issues." The notion that the Court's activity can be analyzed without reference to *Lemon* suggests that the Court has, at least subliminally, already abandoned the *Lemon* standard in practice, even though it continues to give lip service to the standard in theory. Other critics of *Lemon* advocate ignoring the standard because its terms are inherently meaningless and devoid of substance, even when judges conscientiously try to apply *Lemon* consistently.

---

[22] Murray [v. Austin, 947 F.2d 147, 158 (5th Cir. 1991)].

I believe that *Lemon* is neither useless nor meaningless. Applied rigorously, the operative terms of *Lemon* — secular purpose, secular effect, and entanglement — could be effective tools in separating government from religion. Contrary to the usual criticism of *Lemon*, the problem is not that the terms of *Lemon* mean too little; the problem is that the terms of *Lemon* mean too much. An honest application of the *Lemon* test would require a far more rigorous separation of church and state than a majority of the current Supreme Court is willing to enforce. This does not mean the test is flawed. Rather, the separation principle that gives the test meaning does not have the support necessary to provide courts applying Lemon with a consistent orientation. Criticism of *Lemon* is often conjoined with criticism of the separation principle. The criticism of the separation principle, however, involves a much more basic issue than does the debate over whether the *Lemon* test or some alternative will best fulfill a universally accepted goal of the Establishment Clause. The true target of the antagonism many critics direct toward the three-part *Lemon* test is the separation principle that is at the core of *Lemon*. Viewed from this perspective, the debate over the efficacy of *Lemon* is irrelevant.

One of the remarkable things about the Court's recent Establishment Clause decisions is that a majority of the Court has not been willing to abandon formally the *Lemon* test. If I am correct about the broader themes underlying the debate over the survival of the *Lemon* test, this unwillingness indicates that the majority is uncertain about its attitude toward the continued importance of the separation principle in Establishment Clause jurisprudence. In the Supreme Court's October 1992 Term, the majority turned down two opportunities to abandon *Lemon* in favor of some more lenient test. The majority's hesitancy to adopt a new Establishment Clause standard in these cases clearly drove some *Lemon* opponents on the Court to distraction.

The majority's hesitancy instigated the latest attack on *Lemon* by Justice Scalia, who has become the Court's most vocal opponent of the current Establishment Clause standard. The overheated language of Justice Scalia's attack indicates how caustic the debate over basic Establishment Clause principles has become. "Like some ghoul in a late-night horror movie that repeatedly sits up in its grave and shuffles abroad,. . ." he wrote, "*Lemon* stalks our Establishment Clause jurisprudence once again, frightening the little children and school attorneys of Center Moriches Union Free School District." After noting that five Justices (including himself) have "personally driven pencils through the creature's heart," he offers this opinion about *Lemon's* longevity:

> The secret of the *Lemon* test's survival, I think, is that it is so easy to kill. It is there to scare us (and our audience) when we wish it to do so, but we can command it to return to the tomb at will. . . . Such a docile and useful monster is worth keeping around, at least in a somnolent state; one never knows when one might need him.

Justice Scalia's flippancy aside, he is at least correct in noting that the present majority is ambivalent about *Lemon*. However, the majority's ambivalence about *Lemon* is not, as Justice Scalia suggests, simply a function of intellectual sloppiness and judicial inertia. Rather, it is founded on the majority's much deeper and quite serious ambivalence about the separation principle itself. Justice Scalia has no such ambivalence because, in his view, the Constitution accords religion preferential treatment. In his view, the Court should abandon the *Lemon* test because the separation principle that *Lemon* is intended to enforce violates the dominant religious values embedded in the First Amendment by "those who adopted our constitution, who believed that the public virtues inculcated by religion are a public good." The majority's hesitancy to abandon *Lemon* reflects its unwillingness to legitimize the sectarian political culture that Justice Scalia so readily embraces. The ambivalence about *Lemon* remains because the majority has not yet come to terms with what the separation principle entails and, in particular, with how much separation the principle requires.

NOTE ON *LEMON* AND THE SEPARATION PRINCIPLE

Does it seem plausible that the attacks on *Lemon* are really attacks on the separation principle? If so, is this a reflection of changes in the religious views of those belonging to the cultural elite, who populate the courts and legal academy? Consider Professor Lupu's analysis:

> Separationism thrived best when white Anglo-Saxon Protestants of low-level religious intensity constituted the bulk of our cultural elite. For members of this group, separationism reflected an attractive mix of privatized (hence unobtrusive) religion, opposition to a public subsidy of the educational mission of the Roman Catholic Church, and support for the mission of socializing Americans in what this elite perceived as the common American culture. Hence, separationism required reduction in public celebration of sectarian religion, stringent limits on public aid to parochial schools, and religiously "neutral" public schools.

> Many of the cultural and political conditions that sustained the concept of separationism have eroded considerably in the past twenty years. Our cultural elite has grown far more diverse. America has experienced a religious awakening, in which high-intensity, publicly oriented religion has expanded dramatically. The public schools have declined in their capacity to deliver a good education and are no longer considered the uncontroversial home of common culture. These phenomena have resulted in the rise of private parochial schools among many sects and denominations and have produced intensified combat about the propriety of religious thought and practice in both public schools and public life generally.

> Predictably, the Supreme Court has both led and followed these trends. As in the political culture itself, a set of themes compete within the Court for recognition as the successor to separationism. Chief among

these themes are neutrality and accommodation, although it is increasingly evident that some version of neutrality is winning out. As one would expect from an institution committed in some strong yet incomplete respect to stare decisis, however, the law of the Religion Clauses remains encrusted with significant aspects of the separationist motif. Like Captain Ahab at the climactic moment in Moby Dick, separationism beckons as it perishes.

Ira C. Lupu, *The Lingering Death of Separationism*, 62 GEO. WASH. L. REV. 230, 231-32 (1993). If Professor Lupu is correct about separationism perishing, is that a good thing? When considering the facts of the cases in the next chapters, consider whether any of the Establishment Clause approaches other than separationism will adequately protect religious dissenters — not just in elite institutions and diverse urban settings, but also in the small, rural, and religiously homogenous locales that often produce the most serious Establishment Clause conflicts.

NOTES ON THE "DEATH" OF *LEMON*

1. *The Court's Recent (Strong) Reaffirmation of Lemon.* The three-part *Lemon* analysis has been remarkably resistant to academic efforts to kill it off. In *Santa Fe Independent School District v. Doe*, 530 U.S. 313 (2000), the Supreme Court applied the *Lemon* test in striking down a Texas school board's policy of permitting student-led prayers before public-school football games. The school board argued that a facial challenge to the policy was premature in the absence of evidence that the policy would be used in a religious manner. The Court employed *Lemon* in rejecting this argument:

> This argument, however, assumes that we are concerned only with the serious constitutional injury that occurs when a student is forced to participate in an act of religious worship because she chooses to attend a school event. But the Constitution also requires that we keep in mind "the myriad, subtle ways in which Establishment Clause values can be eroded," *Lynch*, 465 U.S., at 694 (O'Connor, J., concurring), and that we guard against other different, yet equally important, constitutional injuries. One is the mere passage by the District of a policy that has the purpose and perception of government establishment of religion. Another is the implementation of a governmental electoral process that subjects the issue of prayer to a majoritarian vote.

> The District argues that the facial challenge must fail because "Santa Fe's Football Policy cannot be invalidated on the basis of some 'possibility or even likelihood' of an unconstitutional application." Brief for Petitioner 17 (quoting *Bowen v. Kendrick*, 487 U.S. 589, 613 (1988)). Our Establishment Clause cases involving facial challenges, however, have not focused solely on the possible applications of the statute, but rather have considered whether the statute has an unconstitutional purpose.

Writing for the Court in *Bowen*, the Chief Justice concluded that "[a]s in previous cases involving facial challenges on Establishment Clause grounds, *e.g.*, *Edwards v. Aguillard*, *Mueller v. Allen*, we assess the constitutionality of an enactment by reference to the three factors first articulated in *Lemon v. Kurtzman*, . . . which guides '[t]he general nature of our inquiry in this area,' *Mueller v. Allen*." 487 U.S., at 602. Under the *Lemon* standard, a court must invalidate a statute if it lacks "a secular legislative purpose." *Lemon v. Kurtzman*, 403 U.S. 602, 612 (1971). It is therefore proper, as part of this facial challenge, for us to examine the purpose of the October policy.

Santa Fe, 530 U.S. at 314. The Court went on to hold that the Santa Fe policy did not have a legitimate secular purpose. Chief Justice Rehnquist, in a dissenting opinion joined only by Justices Scalia and Thomas, objected that to reach its conclusion that the Santa Fe policy was unconstitutional, the majority "applies the most rigid version of the oft-criticized test of *Lemon v. Kurtzman*," and that "rather than look to *Lemon* as a guide, applies *Lemon*'s factors stringently and ignores *Bowen*'s admonition that mere anticipation of unconstitutional applications does not warrant striking a policy on its face." *Santa Fe*, 530 U.S. at 319 & n.1.

2. *The Court's More Recent (Weak) Reaffirmation of* Lemon. In the course of upholding the Cleveland school voucher plan (*see* Chapter 8), the Supreme Court reaffirmed the relevance of at least the first two parts of the three-part *Lemon* analysis:

The Establishment Clause of the First Amendment, applied to the States through the Fourteenth Amendment, prevents a State from enacting laws that have the purpose or effect of advancing or inhibiting religion. *Agostini* v. *Felton,* 521 U.S. 203, 222-223 (1997) ("[W]e continue to ask whether the government acted with the purpose of advancing or inhibiting religion [and] whether the aid has the effect of advancing or inhibiting religion" (citations omitted)). There is no dispute that the program challenged here was enacted for the valid secular purpose of providing educational assistance to poor children in a demonstrably failing public school system. Thus, the question presented is whether the Ohio program nonetheless has the forbidden effect of advancing or inhibiting religion.

Zelman v. Simmons-Harris, infra Chapter 9. Of course, the Court then went on to filter the secular effect component of the test through the lens of a "neutrality" analysis to uphold the voucher system. This, coupled with the fact that the majority opinion was joined by longstanding opponents of *Lemon* such as Justice Scalia, may lead to the conclusion that, at least in cases involving the government financing of religious institutions, the opponents of *Lemon* may have given up on burying *Lemon* in favor of killing it with kindness.

This is Justice O'Connor's perspective on the application of *Lemon* in the educational financing context:

> A central tool in our analysis of cases in this area has been the *Lemon* test. As originally formulated, a statute passed this test only if it "had a secular legislative purpose," if its "principal or primary effect" was one that "neither advance[d] nor inhibit[ed] religion," and if it "did not foster an excessive government entanglement with religion." *Lemon v. Kurtzman.* In *Agostini v. Felton*, we folded the entanglement inquiry into the primary effect inquiry. This made sense because both inquiries rely on the same evidence, see *ibid.*, and the degree of entanglement has implications for whether a statute advances or inhibits religion. The test today is basically the same as that set forth in *School Dist. of Abington Township v. Schempp* (citing *Everson v. Board of Ed. of Ewing*, 330 U.S. 1 (1947); *McGowan v. Maryland*, 366 U.S. 420, 442 (1961)), over 40 years ago.
>
> The Court's opinion in these cases focuses on a narrow question related to the *Lemon* test: how to apply the primary effects prong in indirect aid cases? Specifically, it clarifies the basic inquiry when trying to determine whether a program that distributes aid to beneficiaries, rather than directly to service providers, has the primary effect of advancing or inhibiting religion, *Lemon v. Kurtzman*, or, as I have put it, of endors[ing] or disapprov[ing] religion. Courts are instructed to consider two factors: first, whether the program administers aid in a neutral fashion, without differentiation based on the religious status of beneficiaries or providers of services; second, and more importantly, whether beneficiaries of indirect aid have a genuine choice among religious and nonreligious organizations when determining the organization to which they will direct that aid. If the answer to either query is no, the program should be struck down under the Establishment Clause. JUSTICE SOUTER portrays this inquiry as a departure from *Everson*. A fair reading of the holding in that case suggests quite the opposite. Justice Black's opinion for the Court held that the [First] Amendment requires the state to be a neutral in its relations with groups of religious believers and non-believers; it does not require the state to be their adversary. How else could the Court have upheld a state program to provide students transportation to public and religious schools alike? What the Court clarifies in these cases is that the Establishment Clause also requires that state aid flowing to religious organizations through the hands of beneficiaries must do so only at the direction of those beneficiaries. Such a refinement of the *Lemon* test surely does not betray *Everson*.

Three years after *Zelman*, the Court issued another series of opinions that, if anything, increased the confusion about the meaning and applicability of *Lemon*. First, in *Cutter v. Wilkinson*, *see infra* Chapter 14, the Court rejected an

Establishment Clause challenge to the Religious Land Use and Institutionalized Persons Act. In a cryptic footnote, the Court quoted the *Lemon* test and then stated "We resolve this case on other grounds." The Court gave no further explanation, nor did it clearly identify an alternative to the *Lemon* test. In contrast to the enigmatic reference to *Lemon* in the *Cutter* majority opinion, Justice Thomas's *Cutter* concurrence referred to *Lemon* as a "discredited test," and noted that under a proper application of *Lemon* "any accommodation of religion . . . might violate the Clause."

Justice Thomas' rush to inter *Lemon*, like so many other efforts before it, proved premature. Less than a month after *Cutter*, the Court issued an opinion regarding a constitutional challenge to the posting of the Ten Commandments in government buildings in two Kentucky counties. *McCreary Cty. v. American Civil Liberties Union of Kentucky, infra* Chapter 7. In that opinion, five members of the Court specifically relied on the secular purpose prong of *Lemon* to hold the displays unconstitutional. Meanwhile Justice Scalia filed a tart dissent, joined by two other Justices (a third — Justice Kennedy — also dissented, but did not endorse this part of Scalia's opinion), in which he attacked the basic notion that the government may not legally favor the majority's religion. He noted pointedly that "a majority of Justices on the current Court (including at least one Member of today's majority) have, in separate opinions, repudiated the brain-spun '*Lemon* test' that embodies the supposed principle of neutrality between religion and irreligion." He went on to chide the Court for its inconsistency in applying *Lemon*, and argued that "[a]s bad as the *Lemon* test is, it is worse for the fact that, since its inception, its seemingly simple mandates have been manipulated to fit whatever result the Court aimed to achieve."

To complicate matters even further, the same day it issued the *McCreary* opinion, the Court issued a second opinion involving another Ten Commandments display on the grounds outside the Texas state legislature. *Van Orden v. Perry, infra* Chapter 7. In that opinion, the Court upheld the religious display. The four-member plurality in *Van Orden* — whose members were also the dissenters in *McCreary* — asserted that *Lemon* is "not useful in dealing with the sort of passive monument that Texas has erected on its Capitol grounds. Instead, our analysis is driven both by the nature of the monument and by our Nation's history." Justice Breyer, who had been the fifth vote to strike down the Kentucky display, switched sides to vote in favor of the Texas display, but did not join the plurality's opinion. Instead, he relied on the context of the display and the fact that the display had not engendered serious divisiveness. With regard to the constitutional standard to be applied, Breyer essentially abandoned the effort to define one. Although he did not abandon *Lemon*, Breyer noted the "the Court has found no single mechanical formula that can accurately draw the constitutional line in every case."

Thus, before Justice O'Connor left the Court, the most that can be said of *Lemon* is that the test retained the support — at least in some cases — of five Justices, although two members of that majority (Justices Breyer and O'Connor) would be willing to ignore *Lemon* in what Justice Breyer referred to in *Van Orden* as "fact-intensive cases." Now that Justice O'Connor has been replaced by Justice Alito, it seems doubtful that *Lemon* can muster even a bare majority, even some of the time.

NOTE ON THE SECULAR PURPOSE REQUIREMENT

One of the more controversial aspects of both the *Lemon* and endorsement analyses is the requirement that government policies be motivated by a secular purpose. This requirement has been a central factor in several Supreme Court decisions over the years. *See, e.g., Edwards v. Aguillard*, 482 U.S. 578 (1987); *Wallace v. Jaffree*, 472 U.S. 38 (1985) (striking down silent prayer statute); *Stone v. Graham*, 449 U.S. 39 (1981) (striking down state statute requiring posting of copy of Ten Commandments on walls of each public school classroom); *Epperson v. Arkansas*, 393 U.S. 97 (1968) (striking down statute prohibiting the teaching of evolution); *Abington Sch. Dist. v. Schempp*, 374 U.S. 203 (1963) (striking down statute providing for opening exercises in public schools involving Bible reading and recitation of the Lord's Prayer). Despite the long lineage of this requirement, many constitutional analysts argue that the secular purpose requirement should not be part of the constitutional standard for judging Establishment Clause cases. There are at least three different criticisms of this requirement.

Argument 1: The Religious Hostility Argument. The broadest argument against the secular purpose requirement asserts that the requirement amounts to discrimination against those whose social and political views are based in religion. "Religion has long been placed in American private life. Religious belief in the Western tradition centers on a transcendent force or belief — that is, a force or belief beyond the material, phenomenal world. As such, religious belief is not subject to verification or falsification according to the objectivist conventions of public life. Secularism constitutes the test of residency in American public life, and religion by its nature cannot pass the test. Keeping religion and religious belief confined to private life enables the liberal state to marginalize religion without eliminating it." Frederick Mark Gedicks, *Public Life and Hostility to Religion*, 78 VA. L. REV. 671, 679-80 (1992). Similar criticisms of the secular purpose argument are made by Richard John Neuhaus and Stephen Carter in the materials discussed in Chapter 4 and Michael Stokes Paulsen, *supra. See also* David M. Smolin, *Regulating Religious and Cultural Conflict in a Postmodern America: A Response to Professor Perry*, 76 IOWA L. REV. 1067, 1078 (1992) (describing one version of the secular purpose requirement as designed to exclude "the religious groups most active in trying to displace the cultural hegemony of America's highly secularized elites"). Criticism of this type tends to be directed not just at the secular purpose requirement per se, but more broadly at the separation principle the secular purpose requirement is perceived to serve. There are two other critiques, however, which single out the secular purpose requirement for criticism even while accepting the need for some degree of constitutionally mandated separation between church and state.

Argument 2: The Theoretical Argument. Professor Douglas Laycock rejects the secular purpose requirement, and has even written that "[I]t is obvious that intelligent and important people think that these are important questions, but I must confess that I have never understood why that is. I wish that this enormous array of talent had spent less time on these questions and more time on other things." Douglas Laycock, *Freedom of Speech That Is Both Religious and Political*, 29 U.C. DAVIS L. REV. 793 (1996). As a matter of First Amendment Religion Clause and Free Speech Clause theory, Professor Laycock has three main arguments against the secular purpose requirement.

First, Laycock argues that religiously motivated political speech should be protected under the Free Speech Clause to the same high extent as other political speech. Prohibition of religious arguments in political debate, Laycock concludes, is "viewpoint discrimination, plain and simple." *Id.* at 798. The "essence of the Free Speech Clause," Laycock argues, is that "[a] speaker in an American political debate, in all but the most extraordinary cases, is entitled to make any substantive argument that she wants to make." *Id.*

Second, Laycock argues that attempts to prohibit legislation premised on religious grounds amount to discrimination on the basis of religion. He argues that proposals to exclude religious rationales from the list of available justifications for public policy are "futile attempt[s] at a coup d' etat, in which secularists would get to silence everybody on the religious side of the spectrum." *Id.* at 799. Those who would prohibit religious reasons for legislation are, therefore, doing so for partisan political reasons and are committed to "secular supremacy and religious subordination, or at least to religious marginalization." Douglas Laycock, *The Underlying Unity of Separation and Neutrality*, 46 EMORY L.J. 43, 47 (1997).

Third, Laycock argues that religion provides several major benefits to a democratic political culture, and therefore should not be frozen out of the process for developing and enacting political policies. He asserts that religion is a prime source of civic virtue and national unity, necessary even in a pluralist democracy. Laycock, *Freedom of Speech That Is Both Religious and Political*, *supra*, at 808. He argues that critics of religious involvement in politics often focus on "a small range of political positions they reject," *id.* at 800, and cites the abolitionist and civil rights movements as examples of the positive role religion can play in politics. Religion arguments "often speak to fundamental values. Democracy would be impoverished without them." *Id.* at 801.

Is it possible to respond to Laycock by distinguishing between private religious arguments for or against public policies (which the Establishment Clause does not prohibit) and religious arguments that are used by government actors to justify government policy (which the Establishment Clause *does* prohibit)? In this context, consider another passage from the work of Professor Laycock:

Under the religion clauses, as I understand them and as the Supreme Court has understood them, all religions are protected. But that commitment itself entails one choice about types of religion. There is one type of religion that cannot be fully protected. That is the religion of those people who believe that their religious exercise requires use of the instruments of government, either to directly impose their belief on others or to use government in their own worship services. This choice among types of religion is also a choice among types of liberty. I believe that it is not simply a raw choice. It is a principled choice, based on the view that the best you can do to maximize religious liberty for all citizens is to prevent anyone from using the government for religious purposes.

Douglas Laycock, *The Benefits of the Establishment Clause*, 42 DePaul L. Rev. 373, 374-75 (1992). One explanation of the seeming contradiction between this passage, which seems to defend the secular purpose requirement, and Laycock's criticisms of that requirement, is the distinction Laycock draws between religious matters that are "outside the jurisdiction of government" and religious matters that are "inside the jurisdiction of government." *Id.* at 374. This is how he explains this distinction:

> [I]t is occasionally suggested that the Establishment Clause helps keep religion out of politics. Simply put, that is nonsense. As history clearly demonstrates, religion is always a part of politics. . . . What the Establishment Clause separates from government is theology, worship, and ritual, the aspects of religion that relate only to things outside the jurisdiction of government. Questions of morality, of right conduct, of proper treatment of our fellow humans, are questions to which both church and state have historically spoken. They are questions within the jurisdiction of both. In a democratic society, the state will ultimately decide these questions at least to the extent of deciding what conduct will be subject to legal sanctions. But these are also questions on which churches are absolutely entitled to speak.

Id. at 381. Is Laycock's distinction perhaps too narrow to protect against many forms of religious coercion? If Laycock's "jurisdictional" distinction were used to dictate the application of the Establishment Clause, would it be possible to prevent a religious political majority from imposing rules and regulations on everyone in a community that, although clearly (and often exclusively) religious in nature, fall short of "theology, worship, and ritual"?

3. *The Pragmatic Argument.* There are two variations of pragmatic arguments against the secular purpose requirement. The broad variation of this argument is represented by Justice Scalia's dissent in *Edwards v. Aguillard*, Chapter 4, *supra*. Justice Scalia's broad pragmatic argument against the secular purpose requirement is part of his general skepticism about the power of courts to go beyond statutory texts to ascertain legal meaning. *See generally* Antonin Scalia, A Matter of Interpretation: Federal Courts and the Law

(1997). In Justice Scalia's words, "while it is possible to discern the objective 'purpose' of a statute, . . . or even the formal motivation for a statute where that is explicitly set forth . . . discerning the subjective motivation of those enacting the statute is, to be honest, almost always an impossible task." *Edwards*, 482 U.S. at 636 (Scalia, J., dissenting). Justice Scalia gives three reasons for this difficulty. First, there are many relevant actors involved in the adoption of any legislative policy whose reasons for supporting a particular policy are often vague and may vary widely; second, sources of information about the views of legislators and other government officials are "eminently manipulable" and untrustworthy as evidence of unconstitutional intent; *id.* at 638, and third, in some cases, only a few legislators may have an unconstitutional intention in voting to adopt a particular policy, and it is inappropriate to invalidate the legislation when "everyone else's intent was pure." *Id.*

The narrow version of this argument has been presented in several books and articles by Michael Perry. *See, e.g.*, MICHAEL J. PERRY, RELIGION IN POLITICS: CONSTITUTIONAL AND MORAL PERSPECTIVES (1997); MICHAEL J. PERRY, LOVE AND POWER: THE ROLE OF RELIGION AND MORALITY IN AMERICAN POLITICS (1991); Michael J. Perry, *Religion in Politics*, 29 U.C. DAVIS L. REV. 729 (1996). Professor Perry begins his argument regarding the constitutional limits on religion in politics by distinguishing between the expression of religious arguments about a public policy (which Perry believes is permissible) and reliance on those arguments in adopting that policy (which Perry would prohibit). With regard to the expression of religious arguments, Perry writes that "[e]very citizen, without regard to whether she is a legislator or other public official, is constitutionally free to present in public political debate whatever arguments about morality, including whatever religious arguments, she wants to present." Perry, *Religion in Politics, supra*, at 733. With regard to the government's actual reliance on those arguments, however, Perry's rule is quite different: "The nonestablishment norm forbids government to base political choices on religious arguments; thus, at least as an ideal matter, the nonestablishment norm requires that if government wants to make a political choice, including one about the morality of human conduct, it [must] do so only on the basis of a secular argument." *Id.* at 735.

Under Professor Perry's theory, therefore, a legislator may make religious arguments (apparently even on the floor of the Senate or House) but may not then rely on those arguments when it is time to vote. Although this distinction seems to impose an absolute prohibition against public officials relying on religious arguments to enact public policies, judicial enforcement of the reliance prohibition would be governed by a weak rule that would have the courts uphold any statute if "a plausible secular rationale supports the choice without help from a parallel religious argument." *Id.* at 737. Apparently, this "plausible secular rationale" would not have to be stated by the legislature (or government agency) at the time it adopts the policy; the rationale could be developed in litigation, or even by the courts themselves, without any proof that the "plausible secular rationale" was even considered (much less relied upon) by the relevant policymakers. Professor Perry concedes that this weak rule "involves an 'under-enforcement' of the full ideal of nonestablishment," *id.*, but argues that this is a necessary concession to the practical realities of ascertaining whether the government relied in part on impermissible religious reasons in adopting a particular policy.

Do both Scalia and Perry underestimate the ability of the courts to ferret out legislative intent from the various ancillary materials produced during the legislative process? Is the problem with Professor Perry's version of the pragmatic argument traceable to his unwillingness to permit courts to use a legislator's public statements of religious motivation (which Perry regards as unlimited by the Establishment Clause) as evidence of their *reliance* on those religious sentiments (which Perry regards as the primary prohibition of the Establishment Clause)?

In this regard, note that in *Wallace v. Jaffree, infra* Chapter 6, the Supreme Court struck down the Alabama moment-of-silence statute because it lacked a secular purpose. One of the key pieces of evidence supporting the Court's conclusion was a statement that the law's sponsor in the state senate placed in the legislative record. Part of this statement contains the following passage: "Since coming to the Alabama Senate I have worked hard on this legislation to accomplish the return of voluntary prayer in our public schools and return to the basic moral fiber [sic]." 472 U.S. at 57 n.43. The senator who made this statement later confirmed in testimony before the district court that returning prayer to the classroom was his only purpose in supporting the legislation. Based largely on this evidence, the Supreme Court struck down the statute. But suppose the same statute was litigated in a slightly different context. Suppose that instead of placing in the legislative record a statement about his intention to return prayer to school, the statute's sponsor embarked on a six-month crusade through the state, announcing at every opportunity his intention to return prayer to public schools as a means of returning to "the basic moral fiber." Then, when the legislation came up for a vote, the legislator and all his colleagues remained silent about their motives, and no one attached to the legislation a legislative record of any kind. Moreover, at a trial on the constitutionality of the statute, suppose that the legislator testified that his intention in supporting the statute was merely to provide a moment of quiet reflection at the beginning of the school day, and his colleagues all testified to the same effect. If, as Professor Perry asserts, the Establishment Clause "does not forbid any person — including any person who happens to be a legislator or other public official — to say whatever she wants to say, religious or not, in public policy debate," and if (as lower courts have held) the ostensible intent to provide a moment of quiet reflection constitutes what Perry calls a "plausible secular rationale," then under Perry's theory, the courts would be obligated to uphold the statute even though everyone in the process knows very well that the statute was devised and enacted for an unconstitutional purpose. Has Perry weakened the secular purpose argument to the point that it is ineffective as applied to all but the most inept politicians?

For a thoughtful and interesting treatment of the secular purpose requirement, *see* Andrew Koppelman, *Secular Purpose*, 88 VA. L. REV. 87 (2002). Professor Koppelman notes that several current Supreme Court Justices may be prepared to abandon the secular purpose requirement, and presents a detailed argument for why this is a bad idea. He also uses the secular purpose requirement as a vehicle for the exploration of other vexing problems of church/state jurisprudence, such as the accommodation principle and the possibility of conflict between the Establishment and Free Exercise Clauses. As Koppelman summarizes the argument in the introduction to his article:

> The [secular purpose] doctrine cannot be discarded . . . without effectively reading the Establishment Clause out of the Constitution altogether. The result would be heightened civil strife, corruption of religion, and oppression of religious minorities. Since a religious justification is available for nearly anything that the state wants to do to anyone, discarding this requirement would eventually devastate many constitutional protections that have nothing to do with religion. And this terrible price will have been paid for nothing. Present doctrine already allows for what the doctrine's critics most value: state recognition of the distinctive value of religion. The state is already free to recognize the uniqueness of religion as a human concern, and the law does so by treating religion as something special in a broad range of legislative and judicial actions. What the state may not do — what the doctrine properly forbids it to do — is declare any particular religious doctrine to be the true one, or enact laws that clearly imply such a declaration of religious truth.

Id. at 88.

In *McCreary County, Kentucky v. Am. Civil Liberties Union of Kentucky,* which is discussed in Chapter 7, five members of the Court reaffirmed their commitment to enforcing the secular purpose requirement of the *Lemon* test. Justice Souter, writing for the majority, noted the "intuitive importance of official purpose to the realization of Establishment Clause values" and rejected arguments by the government petitioners that the secular purpose mandate should be abandoned. In fact, the Court even seemed to strengthen the secular purpose analysis:

> After declining the invitation to abandon concern with purpose wholesale, we also have to avoid the Counties' alternative tack of trivializing the enquiry into it. The Counties would read the cases as if the purpose enquiry were so naive that any transparent claim to secularity would satisfy it, and they would cut context out of the enquiry, to the point of ignoring history, no matter what bearing it actually had on the significance of current circumstances. There is no precedent for the Counties' arguments, or reason supporting them.

> *Lemon* said that government action must have "a secular . . . purpose," and after a host of cases it is fair to add that although a legislature's stated reasons will generally get deference, the secular purpose

required has to be genuine, not a sham, and not merely secondary to a religious objective. Even the Counties' own cited authority confirms that we have not made the purpose test a pushover for any secular claim. True, *Wallace* [*v. Jaffree*] said government action is tainted by its object "if it is entirely motivated by a purpose to advance religion," a remark that suggests, in isolation, a fairly complaisant attitude. But in that very case the Court declined to credit Alabama's stated secular rationale of "accommodation" for legislation authorizing a period of silence in school for meditation or voluntary prayer, given the implausibility of that explanation in light of another statute already accommodating children wishing to pray. And it would be just as much a mistake to infer that a timid standard underlies the statement in *Lynch v. Donnelly* that the purpose enquiry looks to whether government "activity was motivated wholly by religious considerations," for two cases cited for that proposition had examined and rejected claims of secular purposes that turned out to be implausible or inadequate. As we said, the Court often does accept governmental statements of purpose, in keeping with the respect owed in the first instance to such official claims. But in those unusual cases where the claim was an apparent sham, or the secular purpose secondary, the unsurprising results have been findings of no adequate secular object, as against a predominantly religious one.

The Counties' second proffered limitation can be dispatched quickly. They argue that purpose in a case like this one should be inferred, if at all, only from the latest news about the last in a series of governmental actions, however close they may all be in time and subject. But the world is not made brand new every morning, and the Counties are simply asking us to ignore perfectly probative evidence; they want an absentminded objective observer, not one presumed to be familiar with the history of the government's actions and competent to learn what history has to show. The Counties' position just bucks common sense: reasonable observers have reasonable memories, and our precedents sensibly forbid an observer "to turn a blind eye to the context in which [the] policy arose."

B. THE ENDORSEMENT ANALYSIS

LYNCH v. DONNELLY
465 U.S. 668 (1984)

[The majority upheld the constitutionality of a city-owned display placed in a park owned by a nonprofit organization. The display included a Nativity scene, along with a Santa Claus house, reindeer pulling Santa's sleigh, candy-striped poles, a Christmas tree, carolers, cutout figures representing such characters as a clown, an elephant, and a teddy bear, hundreds of colored lights, a large banner that read "SEASONS GREETINGS."]

JUSTICE O'CONNOR, concurring.

I concur in the opinion of the Court. I write separately to suggest a clarification of our Establishment Clause doctrine. The suggested approach leads to the same result in this case as that taken by the Court, and the Court's opinion, as I read it, is consistent with my analysis.

I

The Establishment Clause prohibits government from making adherence to a religion relevant in any way to a person's standing in the political community. Government can run afoul of that prohibition in two principal ways. One is excessive entanglement with religious institutions, which may interfere with the independence of the institutions, give the institutions access to government or governmental powers not fully shared by nonadherents of the religion, and foster the creation of political constituencies defined along religious lines. *E.g., Larkin v. Grendel's Den*, 459 U.S. 116 (1982). The second and more direct infringement is government endorsement or disapproval of religion. Endorsement sends a message to nonadherents that they are outsiders, not full members of the political community, and an accompanying message to adherents that they are insiders, favored members of the political community. Disapproval sends the opposite message. *See generally Abington School District v. Schempp.*

Our prior cases have used the three-part test articulated in *Lemon v. Kurtzman* as a guide to detecting these two forms of unconstitutional government action. It has never been entirely clear, however, how the three parts of the test relate to the principles enshrined in the Establishment Clause. Focusing on institutional entanglement and on endorsement or disapproval of religion clarifies the *Lemon* test as an analytical device.

II

In this case, as even the District Court found, there is no institutional entanglement. Nevertheless, the appellees contend that the political divisiveness caused by Pawtucket's display of its creche violates the excessive-entanglement prong of the *Lemon* test. The Court's opinion follows the suggestion in *Mueller v. Allen*, 463 U.S. 388, 403 n. 11 (1983), and concludes that "no inquiry into potential political divisiveness is even called for" in this case. In my view, political divisiveness along religious lines should not be an independent test of constitutionality.

Although several of our cases have discussed political divisiveness under the entanglement prong of *Lemon, see, e.g., Committee for Public Education v. Nyquist*, 413 U.S. 756, 796 (1973); *Lemon v. Kurtzman, supra*, 403 U.S., at 623, we have never relied on divisiveness as an independent ground for holding a government practice unconstitutional. Guessing the potential for political divisiveness inherent in a government practice is simply too speculative an enterprise, in part because the existence of the litigation, as this case illustrates, itself may affect the political response to the government practice. Political divisiveness is admittedly an evil addressed by the Establishment Clause. Its existence may be evidence that institutional entanglement is excessive or that a government practice is perceived as an endorsement of religion. But the constitutional inquiry should focus ultimately on the character of the government activity that might cause such divisiveness, not on the divisiveness itself. The entanglement prong of the *Lemon* test is properly limited to institutional entanglement.

III

The central issue in this case is whether Pawtucket has endorsed Christianity by its display of the creche. To answer that question, we must examine both what Pawtucket intended to communicate in displaying the creche and what message the City's display actually conveyed. The purpose and effect prongs of the *Lemon* test represent these two aspects of the meaning of the City's action.

The meaning of a statement to its audience depends both on the intention of the speaker and on the "objective" meaning of the statement in the community. Some listeners need not rely solely on the words themselves in discerning the speaker's intent: they can judge the intent by, for example, examining the context of the statement or asking questions of the speaker. Other listeners do not have or will not seek access to such evidence of intent. They will rely instead on the words themselves; for them the message actually conveyed may be something not actually intended. If the audience is large, as it always is when government "speaks" by word or deed, some portion of the audience will inevitably receive a message determined by the "objective" content of the statement, and some portion will inevitably receive the intended message. Examination of both the subjective and the objective components of the message communicated by a government action is therefore necessary to determine whether the action carries a forbidden meaning.

The purpose prong of the *Lemon* test asks whether government's actual purpose is to endorse or disapprove of religion. The effect prong asks whether, irrespective of government's actual purpose, the practice under review in fact conveys a message of endorsement or disapproval. An affirmative answer to either question should render the challenged practice invalid.

A

The purpose prong of the *Lemon* test requires that a government activity have a secular purpose. That requirement is not satisfied, however, by the mere existence of some secular purpose, however dominated by religious purposes. In *Stone v. Graham*, 449 U.S. 39 (1980), for example, the Court held that posting copies of the Ten Commandments in schools violated the purpose prong of the Lemon test, yet the State plainly had some secular objectives, such as instilling most of the values of the Ten Commandments and illustrating their connection to our legal system, *but see id.*, at 41. *See also Abington School District v.*

Schempp, supra, 374 U.S., at 223-224. The proper inquiry under the purpose prong of *Lemon*, I submit, is whether the government intends to convey a message of endorsement or disapproval of religion.

Applying that formulation to this case, I would find that Pawtucket did not intend to convey any message of endorsement of Christianity or disapproval of non-Christian religions. The evident purpose of including the creche in the larger display was not promotion of the religious content of the creche but celebration of the public holiday through its traditional symbols. Celebration of public holidays, which have cultural significance even if they also have religious aspects, is a legitimate secular purpose.

The District Court's finding that the display of the creche had no secular purpose was based on erroneous reasoning. The District Court believed that it should ascertain the City's purpose in displaying the creche separate and apart from the general purpose in setting up the display. It also found that, because the tradition-celebrating purpose was suspect in the court's eyes, the City's use of an unarguably religious symbol "raises an inference" of intent to endorse. When viewed in light of correct legal principles, the District Court's finding of unlawful purpose was clearly erroneous.

B

Focusing on the evil of government endorsement or disapproval of religion makes clear that the effect prong of the Lemon test is properly interpreted not to require invalidation of a government practice merely because it in fact causes, even as a primary effect, advancement or inhibition of religion. The laws upheld in *Walz v. Tax Commission*, 397 U.S. 664 (1970) (tax exemption for religious, educational, and charitable organizations), in *McGowan v. Maryland*, 366 U.S. 420 (1960) (mandatory Sunday closing law), and in *Zorach v. Clauson*, 343 U.S. 306 (1952) (released time from school for off-campus religious instruction), had such effects, but they did not violate the Establishment Clause. What is crucial is that a government practice not have the effect of communicating a message of government endorsement or disapproval of religion. It is only practices having that effect, whether intentionally or unintentionally, that make religion relevant, in reality or public perception, to status in the political community.

Pawtucket's display of its creche, I believe, does not communicate a message that the government intends to endorse the Christian beliefs represented by the creche. Although the religious and indeed sectarian significance of the creche, as the district court found, is not neutralized by the setting, the overall holiday setting changes what viewers may fairly understand to be the purpose of the display — as a typical museum setting, though not neutralizing the religious content of a religious painting, negates any message of endorsement of that content. The display celebrates a public holiday, and no one contends that declaration of that holiday is understood to be an endorsement of religion. The holiday itself has very strong secular components and traditions. Government celebration of the holiday, which is extremely common, generally is not under-

stood to endorse the religious content of the holiday, just as government celebration of Thanksgiving is not so understood. The creche is a traditional symbol of the holiday that is very commonly displayed along with purely secular
symbols, as it was in Pawtucket.

These features combine to make the government's display of the creche in this
particular physical setting no more an endorsement of religion than such governmental "acknowledgments" of religion as legislative prayers of the type
approved in *Marsh v. Chambers*, 463 U.S. 783 (1983), government declaration
of Thanksgiving as a public holiday, printing of "In God We Trust" on coins, and
opening court sessions with "God save the United States and this honorable
court." Those government acknowledgments of religion serve, in the only ways
reasonably possible in our culture, the legitimate secular purposes of solemnizing public occasions, expressing confidence in the future, and encouraging the
recognition of what is worthy of appreciation in society. For that reason, and
because of their history and ubiquity, those practices are not understood as
conveying government approval of particular religious beliefs. The display of the
creche likewise serves a secular purpose — celebration of a public holiday with
traditional symbols. It cannot fairly be understood to convey a message of government endorsement of religion. It is significant in this regard that the creche
display apparently caused no political divisiveness prior to the filing of this lawsuit, although Pawtucket had incorporated the creche in its annual Christmas
display for some years. For these reasons, I conclude that Pawtucket's display
of the creche does not have the effect of communicating endorsement of Christianity.

The District Court's subsidiary findings on the effect test are consistent with
this conclusion. The court found as facts that the creche has a religious content,
that it would not be seen as an insignificant part of the display, that its religious
content is not neutralized by the setting, that the display is celebratory and not
instructional, and that the city did not seek to counteract any possible religious message. These findings do not imply that the creche communicates government approval of Christianity. The District Court also found, however, that
the government was understood to place its imprimatur on the religious content
of the creche. But whether a government activity communicates endorsement
of religion is not a question of simple historical fact. Although evidentiary submissions may help answer it, the question is, like the question whether racial
or sex-based classifications communicate an invidious message, in large part a
legal question to be answered on the basis of judicial interpretation of social
facts. The District Court's conclusion concerning the effect of Pawtucket's display of its creche was in error as a matter of law.

IV

Every government practice must be judged in its unique circumstances to
determine whether it constitutes an endorsement or disapproval of religion. In
making that determination, courts must keep in mind both the fundamental
place held by the Establishment Clause in our constitutional scheme and the

myriad, subtle ways in which Establishment Clause values can be eroded. Government practices that purport to celebrate or acknowledge events with religious significance must be subjected to careful judicial scrutiny.

The city of Pawtucket is alleged to have violated the Establishment Clause by endorsing the Christian beliefs represented by the creche included in its Christmas display. Giving the challenged practice the careful scrutiny it deserves, I cannot say that the particular creche display at issue in this case was intended to endorse or had the effect of endorsing Christianity. I agree with the Court that the judgment below must be reversed.

NOTE ON THE ROLE OF THE "REASONABLE OBSERVER" IN THE ENDORSEMENT ANALYSIS

In her concurring opinion in *County of Allegheny v. ACLU*, Justice O'Connor introduced the concept of the "reasonable observer" as the person who determines whether the government has improperly endorsed religion. According to *elitest*
O'Connor, "the 'history and ubiquity' of a practice is relevant because it provides part of the context in which a reasonable observer evaluates whether a challenged governmental practice conveys a message of endorsement of religion." 492 U.S. 573, 630 (1989) (O'Connor, J., concurring). In *Capital Square Review and Advisory Board v. Pinette*, 515 U.S. 753 (1995), Justice O'Connor and Justice Stevens disagreed about how much information the "reasonable observer" should be assumed to have before judging whether a particular government action conveyed an improper message of endorsement. In assessing whether a privately owned Latin cross placed in a public park could be attributed to the government in a way that conveyed improper endorsement, Justice Stevens argued:

> At least when religious symbols are involved, the question whether the State is "appearing to take a position" is best judged from the standpoint of a "reasonable observer." It is especially important to take account of the perspective of a reasonable observer who may not share the particular religious belief it expresses. A paramount purpose of the Establishment Clause is to protect such a person from being made to feel like an outsider in matters of faith, and a stranger in the political community. If a reasonable person could perceive a government endorsement of religion from a private display, then the State may not allow its property to be used as a forum for that display.

Justice O'Connor agrees that an "endorsement test" is appropriate and that we should judge endorsement from the standpoint of a reasonable observer. But her reasonable observer is a legal fiction, "'a personification of a community ideal of reasonable behavior, determined by the [collective] social judgment.'" The ideal human Justice O'Connor describes knows and understands much more than meets the eye. Her "reasonable person" comes off as a well-schooled jurist, a being finer than the tort-law model. With respect, I think this enhanced tort-law standard is singularly out of place in the Establishment Clause context. It strips of constitutional protection every reasonable person whose knowledge happens to fall below some "'ideal'" standard. Instead of protecting only the "'ideal'" observer, then, I would extend protection to the universe of reasonable persons and ask whether some viewers of the religious display would be likely to perceive a government endorsement.

Justice O'Connor's argument that "[t]here is always someone" who will feel excluded by any particular governmental action ignores the requirement that such an apprehension be objectively reasonable. A person who views an exotic cow at the zoo as a symbol of the government's approval of the Hindu religion cannot survive this test.

The existence of a "public forum" in itself cannot dispel the message of endorsement. A contrary argument would assume an "ultrareasonable observer" who understands the vagaries of this Court's First Amendment jurisprudence. I think it presumptuous to consider such knowledge a precondition of Establishment Clause protection. Many (probably most) reasonable people do not know the difference between a "public forum," a "limited public forum," and a "non-public forum." They do know the difference between a state capitol and a church. Reasonable people have differing degrees of knowledge; that does not make them "'obtuse,'" nor does it make them unworthy of constitutional protection. It merely makes them human. For a religious display to violate the Establishment Clause, I think it is enough that some reasonable observers would attribute a religious message to the State.

Id. at 799-800 & n.5, 807 (Stevens, J., dissenting). Justice O'Connor responded by proposing a more knowledgeable and sophisticated "reasonable observer":

[T]he reasonable observer in the endorsement inquiry must be deemed aware of the history and context of the community and forum in which the religious display appears. Nor can the knowledge attributed to the reasonable observer be limited to the information gleaned simply from viewing the challenged display. Today's proponents of the endorsement test all agree that we should attribute to the observer knowledge that the cross is a religious symbol, that Capitol Square is owned by the State, and that the large building nearby is the seat of state government. In my view, our hypothetical observer also should know the general history of the place in which the cross is displayed. Indeed, the fact that Capitol Square is a public park that has been used over time by private speakers of various types is as much a part of the display's context as its proximity to the Ohio Statehouse.

Id. at 780-81 (O'Connor, J., concurring).

If the "reasonable observer's" analysis of endorsement depends entirely on the amount of legal and historical knowledge fed into the observer before the analysis begins, how helpful is the analysis?

C. THE BROAD COERCION ANALYSIS

For many years, some prominent academic commentators on church/state issues have favored using coercion as a dominant motif in applying the Establishment Clause. *See, e.g.,* Michael W. McConnell, *Coercion: The Lost Element of Establishment*, 27 WM. & MARY L. REV. 933 (1986); Jesse H. Choper, *The Religion Clauses of the First Amendment: Resolving the Conflict*, 41 U. PITT. L. REV. 673 (1980). Some of the Court's current Justices, including Justices Kennedy and Scalia, have also periodically advocated this approach. Unfortunately, coercion theory suffers from many of the same problems that plague Justice O'Connor's endorsement theory. Specifically, coercion theory has been interpreted in broadly inconsistent ways, which means that one could logically construe some religious practices as either coercive or not, depending on how one interprets the term "coercion." The underlying problem with coercion theory is that an intellectually coherent version of the theory produces so few limits on government involvement with religion that it leaves the Establishment Clause virtually meaningless, and probably no more protective than the Free Exercise Clause. If the term "coercion" is used as commonly understood to mean the act of restraining or dominating by force, then few government actions can reasonably be described as "coercing" reluctant individuals to engage in religious activity against their will.

The only way of avoiding the unacceptable result of eviscerating the Establishment Clause is to ameliorate coercion theory by broadening the meaning of "coercion" to the point that even government inaction in the face of attenuated social pressure is considered unconstitutionally "coercive." Once coercion theory reaches this point, it becomes as unclear and unpredictable as other Establishment Clause standards, and therefore introduces into Establishment Clause theory the same level of uncertainty that coercion theory was intended to resolve. The choice seems to be between a narrow version of coercion theory, which produces coherent but unacceptable results, or a broad version of coercion theory, which is incoherent and unpredictable but can lead to consequences that are compatible with society's intuitive notion of what religious liberty entails. Proponents of both forms of coercion theory are presently represented on the Court, and (not surprisingly) the constitutional results stemming from the application of coercion theory have differed wildly depending on which version of coercion theory is used.

This subsection contains a brief excerpt from Justice Kennedy's *Lee v. Weisman* majority opinion, in which he explains his broad version of coercion theory. The next subsection contains an excerpt of Justice Scalia's dissenting opinion in *Lee*, in which he disputes the broad version of coercion theory and advocates a contrary and very narrow version. (In *Lee*, the Court held unconstitutional a prayer at a public school graduation ceremony. Fuller versions of both of these opinions are reprinted in Chapter 6.)

LEE v. WEISMAN
505 U.S. 577 (1992)

KENNEDY, J., delivered the opinion of the Court.

The principle that government may accommodate the free exercise of religion does not supersede the fundamental limitations imposed by the Establishment Clause. It is beyond dispute that, at a minimum, the Constitution guarantees that government may not coerce anyone to support or participate in religion or its exercise, or otherwise act in a way which "establishes a [state] religion or religious faith, or tends to do so." *Lynch* [*infra* Chapter 7]. The State's involvement in the school prayers challenged today violates these central principles.

That involvement is as troubling as it is undenied. A school official, the principal, decided that an invocation and a benediction should be given; this is a choice attributable to the State, and from a constitutional perspective it is as if a state statute decreed that the prayers must occur. The principal chose the religious participant, here a rabbi, and that choice is also attributable to the State. The reason for the choice of a rabbi is not disclosed by the record, but the potential for divisiveness over the choice of a particular member of the clergy to conduct the ceremony is apparent.

As we have observed before, there are heightened concerns with protecting freedom of conscience from subtle coercive pressure in the elementary and secondary public schools. Our decisions in *Engel* and *Schempp* recognize, among other things, that prayer exercises in public schools carry a particular risk of indirect coercion. The concern may not be limited to the context of schools, but it is most pronounced there. What to most believers may seem nothing more than a reasonable request that the nonbeliever respect their religious practices, in a school context may appear to the nonbeliever or dissenter to be an attempt to employ the machinery of the State to enforce a religious orthodoxy.

We need not look beyond the circumstances of this case to see the phenomenon at work. The undeniable fact is that the school district's supervision and control of a high school graduation ceremony places public pressure, as well as peer pressure, on attending students to stand as a group or, at least, maintain respectful silence during the invocation and benediction. This pressure, though subtle and indirect, can be as real as any overt compulsion. Of course, in our culture standing or remaining silent can signify adherence to a view or simple respect for the views of others. And no doubt some persons who have no desire to join a prayer have little objection to standing as a sign of respect for those who do. But for the dissenter of high school age, who has a reasonable perception that she is being forced by the State to pray in a manner her conscience will not allow, the injury is no less real. There can be no doubt that for many, if not most, of the students at the graduation, the act of standing or remaining silent was an expression of participation in the rabbi's prayer. That was the very point of the religious exercise. It is of little comfort to a dissenter, then, to be told that for her the act of standing or remaining in silence signifies mere respect, rather than participation. What matters is that, given our social conventions, a reasonable dissenter in this milieu could believe that the group exercise signified her own participation or approval of it.

Finding no violation under these circumstances would place objectors in the dilemma of participating, with all that implies, or protesting. We do not address whether that choice is acceptable if the affected citizens are mature adults, but we think the State may not, consistent with the Establishment Clause, place primary and secondary school children in this position. Research in psychology supports the common assumption that adolescents are often susceptible to pressure from their peers towards conformity, and that the influence is strongest in matters of social convention. Brittain, *Adolescent Choices and Parent-Peer Cross-Pressures*, 28 AM. SOCIOLOGICAL REV. 385 (June 1963); Clasen & Brown, *The Multidimensionality of Peer Pressure in Adolescence*, 14 J. OF YOUTH AND ADOLESCENCE 451 (Dec. 1985); Brown, Clasen & Eicher, *Perceptions of Peer Pressure, Peer Conformity Dispositions, and Self-Reported Behavior Among Adolescents*, 22 DEVELOPMENTAL PSYCHOLOGY 521 (July 1986). To recognize that the choice imposed by the State constitutes an unacceptable constraint only acknowledges that the government may no more use social pressure to enforce orthodoxy than it may use more direct means.

D. THE NARROW COERCION ANALYSIS

LEE v. WEISMAN
505 U.S. 577 (1992)

JUSTICE SCALIA, with whom THE CHIEF JUSTICE, JUSTICE WHITE, and JUSTICE THOMAS join, dissenting.

In holding that the Establishment Clause prohibits invocations and benedictions at public-school graduation ceremonies, the Court — with nary a mention that it is doing so — lays waste a tradition that is as old as public-school graduation ceremonies themselves, and that is a component of an even more longstanding American tradition of nonsectarian prayer to God at public celebrations generally. As its instrument of destruction, the bulldozer of its social engineering, the Court invents a boundless, and boundlessly manipulable, test of psychological coercion. Today's opinion shows more forcefully than volumes of argumentation why our Nation's protection, that fortress which is our Constitution, cannot possibly rest upon the changeable philosophical predilections of the Justices of this Court, but must have deep foundations in the historic practices of our people.

The Court presumably would separate graduation invocations and benedictions from other instances of public "preservation and transmission of religious beliefs" on the ground that they involve "psychological coercion." I find it a sufficient embarrassment that our Establishment Clause jurisprudence regarding holiday displays, see *County of Allegheny,*, has come to "requir[e] scrutiny more commonly associated with interior decorators than with the judiciary." *American Jewish Congress v. Chicago*, 827 F. 2d 120, 129 (7th Cir. 1987) (Easterbrook, J., dissenting). But interior decorating is a rock-hard science compared to psychology practiced by amateurs. A few citations of "[r]esearch in psychology" that have no particular bearing upon the precise issue here cannot disguise the fact that the Court has gone beyond the realm where judges know what they are doing. The Court's argument that state officials have "coerced" students to take part in the invocation and benediction at graduation ceremonies is, not to put too fine a point on it, incoherent.

The Court declares that students' "attendance and participation in the [invocation and benediction] are in a fair and real sense obligatory." But what exactly is this "fair and real sense"? According to the Court, students at graduation who want "to avoid the fact or appearance of participation" in the invocation and benediction are *psychologically* obligated by "public pressure, as well as peer pressure, . . . to stand as a group or, at least, maintain respectful silence" during those prayers. This assertion — *the very linchpin of the Court's opinion* — is almost as intriguing for what it does not say as for what it says. It does not say, for example, that students are psychologically coerced to bow their heads, place their hands in a Dürer-like prayer position, pay attention to the prayers, utter "Amen," or in fact pray. (Perhaps further intensive psychological research remains to be done on these matters.) It claims only that students are psychologically coerced "to stand. . . *or*, at least, maintain respectful silence." Both halves of this disjunctive (*both* of which must amount to the fact or appearance of participation in prayer if the Court's analysis is to survive on its own terms) merit particular attention.

To begin with the latter: The Court's notion that a student who simply *sits* in "respectful silence" during the invocation and benediction (when all others are standing) has somehow joined — or would somehow be perceived as having joined — in the prayers is nothing short of ludicrous. We indeed live in a vulgar age. But surely "our social conventions" have not coarsened to the point that anyone who does not stand on his chair and shout obscenities can reasonably be deemed to have assented to everything said in his presence. Since the Court does not dispute that students exposed to prayer at graduation ceremonies retain (despite "subtle coercive pressures") the free will to sit, there is absolutely no basis for the Court's decision. It is fanciful enough to say that "a reasonable dissenter," standing head erect in a class of bowed heads, "could believe that the group exercise signified her own participation or approval of it." It is beyond the absurd to say that she could entertain such a belief while pointedly declining to rise.

But let us assume the very worst, that the nonparticipating graduate is "subtly coerced". . . to stand! Even that half of the disjunctive does not remotely establish a "participation" (or an "appearance of participation") in a religious exercise. The Court acknowledges that "in our culture standing. . . can signify adherence to a view or simple respect for the views of others (Much more often the latter than the former, I think, except perhaps in the proverbial town meeting, where one votes by standing.) But if it is a permissible inference that one who is standing is doing so simply out of respect for the prayers of others that are in progress, then how can it possibly be said that a "reasonable dissenter. . . could believe that the group exercise signified her own participation or approval"? Quite obviously, it cannot. I may add, moreover, that maintaining respect for the religious observances of others is a fundamental civic virtue that government (including the public schools) can and should cultivate — so that even if it were the case that the displaying of such respect might be mistaken for taking part in the prayer, I would deny that the dissenter's interest in avoiding *even the false appearance of participation* constitutionally trumps the government's interest in fostering respect for religion generally.

I also find it odd that the Court concludes that high school graduates may not be subjected to this supposed psychological coercion, yet refrains from addressing whether "mature adults" may. I had thought that the reason graduation from high school is regarded as so significant an event is that it is generally associated with transition from adolescence to young adulthood. Many graduating seniors, of course, are old enough to vote. Why, then, does the Court treat them as though they were first-graders? Will we soon have a jurisprudence that distinguishes between mature and immature adults?

The deeper flaw in the Court's opinion does not lie in its wrong answer to the question whether there was state-induced "peer-pressure" coercion; it lies, rather, in the Court's making violation of the Establishment Clause hinge on such a precious question. The coercion that was a hallmark of historical establishments of religion was coercion of religious orthodoxy and of financial support *by force of law and threat of penalty*. Typically, attendance at the state church was required; only clergy of the official church could lawfully perform sacraments; and dissenters, if tolerated, faced an array of civil disabilities. L. LEVY, THE ESTABLISHMENT CLAUSE 4 (1986). Thus, for example, in the Colony of Virginia, where the Church of England had been established, ministers were required by law to conform to the doctrine and rites of the Church of England; and all persons were required to attend church and observe the Sabbath, were tithed for the public support of Anglican ministers, and were taxed for the costs of building and repairing churches. *Id.,* at 3-4.

The Establishment Clause was adopted to prohibit such an establishment of religion at the federal level (and to protect state establishments of religion from federal interference). I will further acknowledge for the sake of argument that, as some scholars have argued, by 1790 the term "establishment" had acquired an additional meaning — "financial support of religion generally, by public taxation" — that reflected the development of "general or multiple" establishments, not limited to a single church. But that would still be an establishment coerced *by force of law*. And I will further concede that our constitutional tradition, from the Declaration of Independence and the first inaugural address of Washington, quoted earlier, down to the present day, has, with a few aberrations, ruled out of order government-sponsored endorsement of religion — even when no legal coercion is present, and indeed even when no ersatz, "peer-pressure" psycho-coercion is present — where the endorsement is sectarian, in the sense of specifying details upon which men and women who believe in a benevolent, omnipotent Creator and Ruler of the world are known to differ (for example, the divinity of Christ). But there is simply no support for the proposition that the officially sponsored nondenominational invocation and benediction read by Rabbi Gutterman — with no one legally coerced to recite them — violated the Constitution of the United States. To the contrary, they are so characteristically American they could have come from the pen of George Washington or Abraham Lincoln himself.

Thus, while I have no quarrel with the Court's general proposition that the Establishment Clause "guarantees that government may not coerce anyone to support or participate in religion or its exercise," I see no warrant for expanding the concept of coercion beyond acts backed by threat of penalty — a brand of coercion that, happily, is readily discernible to those of us who have made a career of reading the disciples of Blackstone rather than of Freud. The Framers were indeed opposed to coercion of religious worship by the National Government; but, as their own sponsorship of nonsectarian prayer in public events demonstrates, they understood that "[s]peech is not coercive; the listener may do as he likes." *American Jewish Congress* v. *Chicago*, 827 F. 2d, at 132 (Easterbrook, J., dissenting).

This historical discussion places in revealing perspective the Court's extravagant claim that the State has "for all practical purposes," and "in every practical sense," compelled students to participate in prayers at graduation. Beyond the fact, stipulated to by the parties, that attendance at graduation is voluntary, there is nothing in the record to indicate that failure of attending students to take part in the invocation or benediction was subject to any penalty or discipline. Contrast this with, for example, the facts of *Barnette*: Schoolchildren were required by law to recite the Pledge of Allegiance; failure to do so resulted in expulsion, threatened the expelled child with the prospect of being sent to a reformatory for criminally inclined juveniles, and subjected his parents to prosecution (and incarceration) for causing delinquency. To characterize the "subtle coercive pressures," allegedly present here as the "practical" equivalent of the legal sanctions in *Barnette* is. . . well, let me just say it is not a "delicate and fact-sensitive" analysis.

Michael W. McConnell
Coercion: The Lost Element of Establishment
27 WM. & MARY L. REV. 933 (1986)*

Professor Kurland has warned against "law office" history — the history that "brief writers write," "picking and choosing statements and events favorable to the client's cause". His warning is well-taken. Few areas of the law have suffered so much from law office history as have the religion clauses of the first amendment. Perhaps I betray my recent past as a brief writer in this field, however, if I suggest that the damage wrought by the brief writers' law office histories pales into insignificance when compared to the law office history of the United States Supreme Court.

In these days of the Meese-Brennan debate about the significance of the original intention of the framers of the Constitution, it is like stepping into a time warp to read the establishment clause opinions of the 1940's, 1950's and 1960's. Was it really Justice Brennan in *Abington School District v. Schempp* who told us that, in deciphering the first amendment, "the line we must draw between the permissible and the impermissible is one which accords with history and faithfully reflects the understanding of the Founding Fathers"? Mr. Meese, I have a promising candidate for you for a judicial appointment.

Of course, a few changes have occurred since 1963. Not least among them has been the Court's realization — painful, as in cases like *Marsh v. Chambers* — that its rigorously separationist picture of the intentions and actions of the Founding Fathers was seriously misleading as a matter of history. One no longer can maintain, as Justice Rutledge did, that the Framers originally intended the religion clauses "to create a complete and permanent separation of the spheres of religious activity and civil authority by comprehensively forbidding every form of public aid or support for religion." Whatever directions our historical research ultimately may lead, it now seems beyond doubt that, as Justice Harlan observed, "the historical purposes of. . . the First Amendment are significantly more obscure and complex than [the Supreme] Court has heretofore acknowledged."

The Supreme Court's response to these developments has not been encouraging. Essentially, what once was declared necessary because of history now is declared necessary because of precedent. In his Article, Professor Kurland has refused "to dwell on whether the true meaning of the Constitution can be determined by seeking the intention of the Framers." For present purposes, I intend to follow his lead. In the jurisprudential shift from original intention to general principles, however, it seems only right to call time out to reexamine those holdings of the Court that were products of faulty history and that have yet to be justified on any other theoretical basis.

One such holding is the Court's statement in *Engel v. Vitale* that "[t]he Establishment Clause, unlike the Free Exercise Clause, does not depend upon any showing of direct governmental compulsion and is violated by the enactment of laws which establish an official religion whether those laws operate directly to coerce non-observing individuals or not." Before looking to the historical support, or lack of it, for this proposition, three brief observations about how this proposition came to enter the law are appropriate.

First, the Court's statement was without the support of precedent. In *Cantwell v. Connecticut*, the Court had paraphrased the establishment clause as "forestal[ling] compulsion by law of the acceptance of any creed or the practice of any form of worship," and the presence or lack of compulsion, respectively, had been central to the Court's decisions in *McCollum v. Board of Education* and *Zorach v. Clauson*, which concerned release time programs in the public schools. And just one year before *Engel*, Chief Justice Warren had explained the distinction between Sunday closing laws and the release time program in *McCollum* on the basis that Sunday closing laws did not compel religious participation. Finally, *Engel* itself conspicuously fails to supply supporting authority for the Court's position.

Second, the Court's statement was unnecessary to its decision. After informing us that compulsion — or at least "direct" compulsion — is not an element of an establishment clause claim, the Court pointed out, in its next breath: "This is not to say, of course, that [school prayers] do not involve coercion. . . . When the power, prestige, and financial support of government is placed behind a particular religious belief, the indirect coercive pressure upon religious minorities to conform to the prevailing officially approved religion is plain." I agree. If I did not agree, I would find it difficult to identify any substantial constitutional right violated by public school prayers.

My third observation is that the Court's decision to abjure coercion as an element of an establishment clause claim essentially was without explanation. In *Engel*, the Court stated that the purposes of the establishment clause "go much further" than preventing even indirect religious compulsion. The Court's reasons, however, were that a fully compulsory established church in the United States and in England historically had "incurred the hatred, disrespect and even contempt of those who held contrary beliefs," and that established churches "go hand in hand" with religious persecution. These facts seem merely to reinforce that compulsion — yes, even persecution — had been an element of the established church as our forefathers knew it.

The Court's statement in *Engel*, therefore, is mysterious in many ways. Nonetheless, without precedent, without explanation, and, as the Court admitted, without relevance to the case in which it was announced, the notion has been introduced into the law that the establishment clause does not involve an element of coercion. The proposition has been passed down, with an ever-lengthening string of citations, to be applied in cases in which so-called establishments can be found by courts even though nobody's religious liberty has been infringed in any way.

Lest it be thought that only the separationists have disregarded the coercion element of an establishment, then-Associate Justice Rehnquist seems to have done likewise in his dissenting opinion in *Wallace v. Jaffree*. According to Justice Rehnquist, the establishment clause "forbade establishment of a national religion, and forbade preference among religious sects or denominations" — nothing more. Despite having quoted Madison's words, Justice Rehnquist failed to mention that under the first amendment Congress cannot "compel men to worship God in any manner contrary to their conscience" or compel them to "conform" to any religion not of their own choosing. It is easy to imagine forms of nonpreferential aid, short of establishing a national church, that nonetheless would have the effect of coercing a religious observance. While the majority of the justices concern themselves with whether measures favor religion over non-religion, and their opponents focus instead on whether measures favor one religion over another, the central issue of religious choice is disregarded by both sides.

Let us turn then to the historical record. In the debates in the First Congress concerning the wording of the first amendment, James Madison, the principal draftsman and proponent, said of the committee draft that he "apprehended the meaning of the words to be, that Congress should not establish a religion, and enforce the legal observation of it by law, nor compel men to worship God in any manner contrary to their conscience." Upon further questioning by those who feared that the proposed amendment "might be taken in such latitude as to be extremely hurtful to the cause of religion," Madison clarified the point. He stated that he "believed that the people feared one sect might obtain a preeminence, or two combine together, and establish a religion to which they would compel others to conform." Is compulsion an element of an establishment clause violation? If Madison's explanations to the First Congress are any guide, compulsion is not just an element, it is the essence of an establishment.

Curiously, in all the pages of the United States Reports canvassing the history of the period for clues as to the meaning of the religion clauses, no majority or concurring opinion ever has relied on these words by Madison. Indeed, until Justice Rehnquist dissented in *Wallace v. Jaffree*, no justice ever had seriously analyzed the debates on the framing of the first amendment in any opinion on any side of any religion clause question. This is not because history was deemed irrelevant, because during much of that time the Court had purported to be judging in accordance with original intent. Nor is it because Madison's views were deemed unimportant. Madison's opinions concerning church-state questions propounded before the amendment, after the amendment, at every time except when he was explaining the meaning of the amendment to the First Congress, have been treated as key to an understanding of the amendment. Under ordinary principles of legislative history, Madison's statements on the floor of Congress are of the greatest weight.

But let us look as well at Madison's famous Memorial and Remonstrance Against Religious Assessments, what Justice Rutledge called Madison's "complete, though not his only, interpretation of religious liberty." The Court has relied on the Memorial and Remonstrance many times in its search for the original intent of the framers of the religion clauses. What does the Memorial and Remonstrance have to say about compulsion and establishment? It states: (1) that the proposed bill for the support of teachers of the Christian religion would be a "dangerous abuse" if "armed with the sanctions of a law"; (2) that religion "can be directed only by reason and conviction, not by force or violence"; (3) that government should not be able to "force a citizen to contribute" even so much as three pence to the support of a church; (4) that such a government would be able to "force him to conform to any other establishment in all cases whatsoever"; (5) that "compulsive support" of religion is "unnecessary and unwarrantable"; and (6) that "attempts to enforce by legal sanctions, acts obnoxious to so great a proportion of Citizens, tend to enervate the laws in general." Again, legal compulsion to support or participate in religious activities would seem to be the essence of an establishment.

The result of Madison's Memorial and Remonstrance, as Professor Kurland has recounted, was passage of Virginia's Act for Establishing Religious Freedom. Professor Kurland already has directed our attention to the key words: "[N]o man shall be compelled to frequent or support any religious worship, place, or ministry whatsoever, nor shall be enforced, restrained, molested, or burthened in his body or goods, nor shall otherwise suffer on account of his religious opinions or belief." It is difficult to see, on this evidence, how an establishment could exist in the absence of some form of coercion.

Professor Kurland also has noted that the religion clauses can be best understood "not merely by examining what its authors and contemporaries said about them, but also by examining the problems that the Founding Fathers encountered, remembered, and sought to solve." Here again, the problems that the Founders had encountered were that the government had sought to compel adherence to one religion or, in some colonies, one of several religions, and that the government had sought to restrain adherence to the others. The establishment and free exercise clauses arose out of these very problems.

Subsequent history confirms this thesis. Exponents of strict separation are embarrassed by the many breaches in the wall of separation countenanced by those who adopted the first amendment: the appointment of congressional chaplains, the provision in the Northwest Ordinance for religious education, the resolutions calling upon the President to proclaim days of prayer and thanksgiving, the Indian treaties under which Congress paid the salaries of priests and clergy, and so on. These actions, so difficult to reconcile with modern theories of the establishment clause, are much easier to understand if one sees religious coercion as the fundamental evil against which the clause is directed. Even if one would take a different view on the specific issues today, perhaps because of a broader sense of coercions stemming from the pervasive influence of the modern welfare-regulatory state, these examples demonstrate that noncoercive supports for religion were not within the contemporary understanding of an establishment of religion. Strong evidence suggests that discrimination among religious sects also was proscribed by the establishment clause, but I have run across no persuasive evidence that the Framers of the first amendment considered evenhanded support for all religions or religion in general, in the absence of a coercive impact, an establishment of religion.

Why does this matter? At the most obvious level, it suggests that the courts are wasting their time when they draw nice distinctions about various manifestations of religion in public life that entail no use of the taxing power and have no coercive effect. The simple answer to most such lawsuits is that the plaintiff has no standing to sue. More importantly, the analysis suggests that the courts should be more hospitable to liberty-enhancing accommodations of religion, like the Connecticut law struck down last year that prevented workers from being fired for refusing to work on their chosen Sabbath.

On the other hand, my analysis suggests that aid to religion must not be structured to influence or distort religious choice. Merely because aid may be neutral among religions does not mean that it is consistent with the noncoercion standard. For example, a program of tuition grants to attend private schools, limited to religious private schools, would be neutral among religions but obviously would interfere with religious choice. A noncoercion standard protects nonbelievers and those indifferent to religion no less than it protects believers.

Doctrinally, renewed attention to coercion suggests that the Court's three-part test for an establishment of religion should be modified. A rule that forbids government actions with the purpose or effect of advancing religion fails to distinguish between efforts to coerce and influence religious belief and action, on the one hand, and efforts to facilitate the exercise of one's chosen faith, on the other. It is meaningless to speak of "advancing" religion without specifying the reference point. To protect religious freedom against persecution "advances" religion, as does treating religion neutrally if the prior practice had been to discriminate against it.

Recognition of the centrality of coercion — or, more precisely, its opposite, religious choice — to establishment clause analysis would lead to a proscription of all government action that has the purpose and effect of coercing or altering religious belief or action. Under this standard, the Court would sustain many worthwhile, progressive social programs that it has struck down in the past — programs such as remedial education for economically and educationally deprived children on the premises of their own schools. The point here is not that the government may undertake to aid religion, but that it can pursue its legitimate purposes even if to do so incidentally assists the various religions.

A noncoercion standard, of course, would not answer all questions. For example, it obviously would not answer the question, "What is coercion?" Enormous variance exists between the persecutions of old and the many subtle ways in which government action can distort religious choice today. This is no less true under the establishment clause than it is under the free exercise clause, where the Court has recognized the problem. But while there will be room for continuing debate and disagreement concerning the definition of coercion, at least attention again would be directed to the right question. Not what flunks the three-part test, but what interferes with religious liberty, is an establishment of religion.

Steven G. Gey
Religious Coercion and the Establishment Clause
1994 U. Ill. L. Rev. 463*

For approximately fifty years, two principles have defined the Supreme Court's Establishment Clause jurisprudence. The first is the separation of church and state. The second is the protection of individual religious liberty. These principles interrelate in various ways, but they differ in three important respects. First, the separation principle is institutional rather than individual. In other words, issues involving the separation of church and state relate primarily to institutional political arrangements, rather than to the effects such arrangements have on individual citizens. Second, the separation principle addresses harms that are more diffuse than those the liberty principle addresses. The harms resulting from a direct denial of religious liberty are immediate and concrete and, therefore, easier to identify and redress than the harms arising from the close alliance of church and state. Third, the goal of separating church and state provides the courts with a far more comprehensive rationale for intervening in political affairs than does the religious liberty principle. Political favoritism of religion occurs in subtle ways, and the courts therefore must have a great deal of discretion to enforce the constitutional mandate of separation.

Despite the differences between these two Establishment Clause principles, the Court often has acted and spoken as if the principles were indistinguishable. Thus, when the Court began developing its modern Establishment Clause jurisprudence, it simultaneously emphasized the liberty principle and the separation principle. In more recent cases, the Court has denied that separation of church and state always coexists with the protection of religious liberty. These cases, however, seldom clearly define the circumstances that require the Court to enforce the separation principle or indeed, why separation is even necessary if religious liberty can be protected in other ways. Instead, the Court has left a constitutional muddle with a series of unsatisfactory and unclear standards and outcomes.

Recently, several Justices (along with their academic supporters) have argued that the Court should clean up its Establishment Clause jurisprudence by clarifying the principles the clause is intended to serve. These Justices would have the Court abandon the separation principle and exclusively focus Establishment Clause jurisprudence on protecting religious liberty. They would also abandon the three-part "*Lemon* test" that has governed this area since 1971 and analyze

---

all Establishment Clause cases under a coercion standard. Under this standard, courts would judge alleged Establishment Clause violations by assessing the coercive effect of the government's action. In other words, government actions advancing or endorsing a particular religious faith (or religion in general) would violate the Establishment Clause only if those actions were to coerce an individual to believe in or act in accordance with a religion against the individual's will.

A coercion analysis of Establishment Clause cases raises obvious practical questions. What is coercion? How is it measured? Is coercion systemic, such that certain governmental acts presumptively coerce all persons in society, or is coercion particularized, such that courts must judge each case according to the spiritual susceptibility of specific individuals?

Although these practical problems are significant, the new Establishment Clause coercion theories pose larger theoretical concerns. These concerns stem from a contradiction within coercion theory. Coercion theory seeks to abandon the traditional objective of separation in favor of a constitutional analysis more attuned to the specific religious views and actions of individuals affected by the government's action. This shift in emphasis is justified by the second traditional goal of the Establishment Clause — preserving the role of intellectual and spiritual autonomy in matters of religious faith. Under an Establishment Clause jurisprudence that is guided exclusively by the coercion standard, however, religion becomes a legitimate matter of collective governmental concern, limited only by the flexible condition that the political and religious majority may not use its control of government too heavy-handedly. Under this standard, theocratic government policies would no longer automatically violate the Constitution. Thus, coercion theory does not merely propose another series of modifications to an already flexible constitutional standard. Rather, coercion theory radically departs from existing attitudes about the role of government, the parameters of individual autonomy, and the nature of religion.

III. WHAT IS "COERCION?"

The coercion standard is not new. Professor Jesse Choper has been arguing since the early sixties that the Court should hold unconstitutional government-sponsored religious practices in public schools only if the government's primary purpose is religious and the practices are likely to coerce (i.e., compromise or influence) students' religious beliefs. In the late sixties, Alan Schwarz elaborated on the theme of coercion, arguing that the Establishment Clause should do "no more than prohibit government from compelling or influencing religious choice and from aiding others to influence religious choice." Although a majority of the Supreme Court has consistently rejected the coercion standard as the foundation of its Establishment Clause jurisprudence,[112] some Justices relied

---

[112] *See, e.g.*, Lee v. Weisman, 112 S. Ct. 2649, 2664 (1992) (Blackmun, J., concurring) ("The Court repeatedly has recognized that a violation of the Establishment Clause is not predicated on coercion."); Wallace v. Jaffree, 472 U.S. 38, 72 (1985) (O'Connor, J., concurring in the judgment) (cita-

upon the coercion standard in their dissents from the Court's early separationist holdings. Justice Stewart, for example, dissented from the prayer-in-school and bible reading cases, asserting that the outcome of the Establishment Clause issue "turns on the question of coercion."

Justice Kennedy and Professor McConnell have been the primary recent advocates of revamping Establishment Clause doctrine along the lines of the coercion standard. In 1985, Professor McConnell wrote that "the principal objects of the Religion Clauses. . . were to prevent coercion (and lesser forms of government pressure) in matters of religion and to encourage a multiplicity of religious sects." A year later he wrote that the proposed coercion standard would prohibit "all government action that has the purpose and effect of coercing or altering religious belief or action." In his more recent work, Professor McConnell criticized some applications of the coercion standard, but he continues to argue that Establishment Clause analysis should hinge on whether the government has the purpose or effect of "forcing or inducing a contrary religious practice. . . without sufficient justification."

These academic versions set out the broad outlines of the coercion standard, and Justice Kennedy's opinions have clarified the standard. Justice Kennedy initially set forth his version of the coercion standard in the Court's second creche case, *Allegheny v. ACLU*:

> Our cases disclose two principles: government may not coerce anyone to support or participate in any religion or its exercise; and it may not, in the guise of avoiding hostility or callous indifference, give direct benefits to religion in such a degree that it in fact "establishes a [state] religion or religious faith, or tends to do so."

He also provided examples of coercion, including "taxation to supply the substantial benefits that would sustain a state-established faith, direct compulsion to observance, or governmental exhortation to religiosity that amounts in fact to proselytizing." According to Justice Kennedy, government actions that are not analogous to these "more or less subtle [forms of] coercion" do not violate the Establishment Clause.

---

tion omitted) ("The decisions in [*Engel* and *Schempp*] acknowledged the coercion implicit under the statutory schemes, but they expressly turned only on the fact that the government was sponsoring a manifestly religious exercise."); Committee for Pub. Educ. v. Nyquist, 413 U.S. 756, 786 (1973) (citation omitted) ("[P]roof of coercion . . . [is] not a necessary element of any claim under the Establishment Clause."); Abington Sch. Dist. v. Schempp, 374 U.S. 203, 223 (1963) ("The distinction between the two [religion] clauses is apparent — a violation of the Free Exercise Clause is predicated on coercion while the Establishment Clause need not be so attended."); Engel v. Vitale, 370 U.S. 421, 430 (1962) ("The Establishment Clause, unlike the Free Exercise Clause, does not depend upon any showing of direct government compulsion and is violated by the enactment of laws which establish an official religion whether those laws operate directly to coerce nonobserving individuals or not."); *see also* Lee v. Weisman, 112 S. Ct. at 2671-76 (Souter, J., concurring) (arguing on basis of history, text, and theory of Constitution that coercion theory is inadequate to protect First Amendment values).

The coercion standard's proponents recognize that the standard is not an infallible litmus test for assessing compliance with the Establishment Clause. Professor McConnell notes that "[e]normous variance exists between the persecutions of old and the many subtle ways in which government action can distort religious choice today." The coercion standard's proponents, however, argue that coercion provides a much clearer guideline than the Court's other tests, and that the coercion standard more closely conforms to the Framers' intent than the Court's separationist approach. The proponents also argue that the coercion standard tends to further what Justice Kennedy calls "our Nation's historic traditions of diversity and pluralism." Religious pluralism, in turn, is viewed as the prime indicator of religious liberty, which the coercion theorists believe is the single objective of the Establishment Clause.[126]

In this section, I argue that none of these claims for the coercion standard can withstand scrutiny. I will leave aside the highly problematic issue of original intent, which is no more capable of sustaining the coercion standard than it is any other interpretation of the Establishment Clause. As to the other claims, it seems to me that the coercion standard is even more impractical than either the *Lemon* test or Justice O'Connor's endorsement standard, and is also less likely to protect religious liberty adequately.

The practical problems with the coercion standard arise because the standard's key term is very indefinite. As the divergent opinions in *Lee v. Weisman* indicate, the term coercion is open to a wide range of definitions, each leading to very different results. The range of possible results under the coercion standard is broader than under the *Lemon* test, and probably also broader than those produced by Justice O'Connor's endorsement standard. This means that the coercion standard is a very weak foundation for the preservation of religious liberty. The coercion standard's threat to religious liberty is underscored by the fact that the narrow, less protective definition of coercion proposed by Justice Scalia in *Weisman* is probably more defensible than the broader, more protective definition preferred by Justice Kennedy and Professor McConnell. This is disturbing because the narrow definition of coercion imposes almost no limit whatsoever on government-sponsored religious activity. Adopting this version of the coercion standard would rob the Establishment Clause of almost all its power. Even constitutional commentators such as Professor McConnell, who views the Establishment Clause primarily as a clarifying addendum to the Free Exercise Clause, should be uncomfortable at this prospect.

The logic and implications of the various versions of the coercion standard are best illustrated by discussing specific applications of the standard. Subsection

---

126 "[P]luralism, rather than assimilation, ecumenism, or secularism, [is] the organizing principle of church-state relations. . . . The Court should not ask, 'Will this advance religion?,' but rather, 'Will this advance religious pluralism?'" [Michael W.] McConnell, *Origins* [*The Origins and Historical Understanding of Free Exercise of Religion*, 103 HARV. L. REV. 1409, 1515 (1990)], *supra* note 94, at 1516.

A discusses the application of the coercion standard in the government endorsement context, which includes the school prayer and Christmas creche cases. Subsection B addresses the application of the coercion standard to the problem of public financing of religious education. In light of these specific examples, subsection C addresses the question of whether religious majoritarianism is an inherent and unavoidable characteristic of the coercion standard.

A. The Coercion Standard and Government Endorsement of Religion

The coercion standard is tailor-made for reversing the Court's separationist tendencies in government endorsement cases, which include two of the most frequently litigated Establishment Clause subjects: government-supported religious displays at holidays and prayer in public schools. The placement of passive religious symbols on government property almost always would be upheld under the coercion standard, in contrast to the separationist approach, because it is virtually inconceivable that any religious symbol would "coerce anyone to support or participate in any religion or its exercise." The same result would seem to apply in the public school prayer cases. As Justice Stewart argued in *Schempp*, so long as students who do not wish to participate are permitted to abstain from the state-endorsed prayer, their religious views have not been coerced in any noticeable manner. Yet Justice Kennedy takes the exact opposite stance (over Justice Scalia's strenuous objections) in his majority opinion in *Lee v. Weisman*. A comparison of Justice Kennedy's opinions in *Allegheny* and *Weisman* indicates that even the coercion standard's supporters recoil from the more oppressive implications inherent in a consistent application of the standard. The opinions also indicate that even those Justices who argue the loudest for abandoning the separation principle viscerally understand that the separation of church and state is indispensable to preserving religious liberty.

1. Coercion and Religious Displays

The *Allegheny* Court considered two holiday displays. The first, a creche placed on the grand staircase of the county courthouse, depicted the birth of Jesus, and was accompanied by an angel carrying a banner proclaiming "Gloria in Excelsis Deo!" [Glory to God in the Highest]. The second display stood outside the city-county building and included an eighteen-foot Menorah and a forty-five-foot Christmas tree, accompanied by a sign entitled "Salute to Liberty." A majority of the Court upheld the constitutionality of the second display, but held the first display unconstitutional.

Justice Kennedy was willing to find both displays constitutional, arguing that neither display violated the coercion standard, because

> [n]o one was compelled to observe or participate in any religious ceremony or activity. . . . Passersby who disagree with the message conveyed by these displays are free to ignore them, or even to turn their backs, just as they are free to do when they disagree with any other form of government speech.

The definition of coercion that Justice Kennedy employs in his *Allegheny* opinion is the very narrow, common understanding of the term. Under this definition, coercion occurs only when a person is compelled by force or threat to do something that he or she would not otherwise do.

According to Justice Kennedy, a religious dissenter's feelings of discomfort, exclusion, or offense do not, without more, amount to proof of coercion. The government action favoring one religion is constitutional, so long as it does not change the offended person's contrary religious behavior. After reviewing several examples of presidential religious proclamations, Justice Kennedy writes that "[i]t requires little imagination to conclude that these proclamations would cause nonadherents to feel excluded, yet they have been a part of our national heritage from the beginning." Justice Kennedy then approvingly notes the Court's opinion upholding legislative prayer in *Marsh v. Chambers*, and concludes that "[i]f the intent of the Establishment Clause is to protect individuals from mere feelings of exclusion, then legislative prayer cannot escape invalidation." Because Justice Kennedy believes that legislative prayer is constitutional, we must conclude from these comments that, in Justice Kennedy's view, a proper Establishment Clause standard (i.e., the coercion standard) would not take into account religious minorities' feelings of exclusion. This conclusion is reinforced when Justice Kennedy grumbles at the end of his *Allegheny* dissent that the majority's endorsement approach consigns the country's majority faiths to "least favored faiths so as to avoid any possible risk of offending members of minority religions."

Justice Kennedy's message in *Allegheny* to members of minority faiths (as well as agnostics and nonbelievers) is not encouraging. We will give you the freedom to worship as you please, Justice Kennedy tells them, but in return you must accept the fact that "the Establishment Clause permits government some latitude in recognizing and accommodating the central role religion plays in our society." In addition to permitting the government to adopt the symbols of a particular religion, the coercion standard also would permit the government to "recognize" the majority's faith in other ways. In particular, Justice Kennedy mentions legislative prayer, the national motto ("In God We Trust"), and a statute that is "a straightforward endorsement of the concept of 'turn[ing] to God in prayer.'"

From the separationist perspective, this is a radical proposal. Justice Kennedy's interpretation of the coercion standard in *Allegheny* would convert religious practices and symbols into political spoils, and the winner of an election in an overwhelmingly Christian (or, hypothetically, Jewish or Muslim) community would be able to use its political muscle to "recognize and accommodate" its own faith with government resources. This would convey subtly (or often not so subtly) to the religious minority their position in the political hierarchy. Justice Kennedy clearly intended the exclusionary implications of this proposal. His *Allegheny* opinion contains too many references to maligned religious majorities and hypersensitive religious minorities to believe otherwise.

Despite the majoritarian emphasis of Justice Kennedy's Allegheny opinion, the opinion also indicates that he might not be willing to tolerate the full exercise of the power the coercion standard would provide an aggressive religious majority. Immediately after he introduces the coercion standard in his *Allegheny* dissent, Justice Kennedy adds the caveat that a government's symbolic endorsement of religion may be deemed coercive "in an extreme case." He then adds an odd example of what may constitute an "extreme case": "I doubt not, for example, that the [Establishment] Clause forbids a city to permit the permanent erection of a large Latin cross on the roof of city hall." The problem with a permanent cross, Justice Kennedy says, is that "such an obtrusive year-round religious display would place the government's weight behind an obvious effort to proselytize on behalf of a particular religion." This seems true, but so what? Under the coercion standard, if no one is coerced into practicing the particular faith represented by the cross, where is the violation of the Establishment Clause?

Justice Kennedy does not explain why the permanent cross he describes should be considered ipso facto coercive. It is particularly puzzling that Justice Kennedy considers the cross more coercive than the creche he was willing to approve in *Allegheny*. First, everything he says about passersby being able to ignore the Christmas creche is equally true of a permanent cross on top of city hall. Also, he cannot object to the cross on the ground that (unlike the creche) it is unaccompanied by other secular symbols, because he specifically ridicules Justice O'Connor's endorsement standard for "trivializing constitutional adjudication" by requiring governments to place religious holiday displays in a secular context. Justice Kennedy says that the cross is problematic because it associates the government with a particular religion. The importance of this distinction is unclear because Justice Kennedy was willing to uphold a Christmas display that, as Justice Blackmun noted, "has the effect of endorsing a patently Christian message: Glory to God for the birth of Jesus Christ." It is very odd that Justice Kennedy would find a cross to be a more specifically religious symbol than the baby Jesus.

The only plausible factual distinction between the cross and the creche is that Justice Kennedy's hypothetical cross would be a permanent fixture, whereas the *Allegheny* creche was only temporary. But, why should this make a difference? Justice Kennedy relies heavily on the history and tradition of religious influence over the nation's political culture. Justice Kennedy's willingness to adopt a constitutional rule allowing the government to acknowledge the country's religious history and tradition only one month every year is inconsistent with this emphasis.[151] If, as Justice Kennedy argues, the government should be allowed to recognize the religious aspects of the culture it represents, it is not logical to

---

[151] Justice Kennedy's other caveat concerning the application of the coercion standard warrants similar criticism. At one point in *Allegheny*, he writes that "if a city chose to recognize . . . every significant Christian holiday while ignoring the holidays of all other faiths, the argument that the city

distinguish a cross on top of city hall from a large creche placed inside a government building and topped with a sign praising God.

I suspect that the minor factual distinctions between the cross and the creche are not the real point of Justice Kennedy's caveat in Allegheny. The real reason that Justice Kennedy's theory will not support his attempt to draw minute factual distinctions is that, at the most basic level, Justice Kennedy is not wholly committed to his theory. The city hall cross example is Justice Kennedy's way of leaving himself an escape hatch, which can be used whenever the religious majority pursues too aggressively the implications of everything Justice Kennedy has told them about the historical role of religion in our political process. When Justice Kennedy used this escape hatch in *Lee v. Weisman*, thereby igniting a debate within the Court over the meaning of coercion, he demonstrated the multiple flaws and inadequacies of coercion theory.

2. Coercion and Public School Prayer: The Kennedy Position

Lee v. Weisman is a distant successor to two of the Court's earliest and, at least at the time, most controversial Establishment Clause decisions. In *Engel v. Vitale*, the Court held unconstitutional government-sanctioned prayers in public school classrooms. In *Abington School District v. Schempp*, the Court used Engel as the basis for striking down government-sanctioned Bible reading in public school classrooms. In *Lee v. Weisman*, the Court considered a milder form of government-sanctioned prayer: prayer at a public school graduation ceremony.

In *Weisman*, the Court reviewed the policy of a Providence, Rhode Island, public school system permitting prayer at high school graduation ceremonies.

---

was simply recognizing certain holidays celebrated by its citizens without establishing an official faith or applying pressure to obtain adherents would be much more difficult to maintain." [*Allegheny*], at 664 n.3 (Kennedy, J., concurring in the judgment in part and dissenting in part). Why Justice Kennedy would be concerned by a government decision to recognize a single religious tradition is unclear. The notion that recognition of one religion must be ameliorated by recognition of one or more others seems analogous to Justice Blackmun's requirement that a specifically religious display must be ameliorated by a larger secular context. Yet Justice Kennedy derides this part of Justice Blackmun's *Allegheny* opinion. *See id.* at 674 (Kennedy, J., concurring in the judgment in part and dissenting in part).

Justice Kennedy's argument that constitutional problems would arise if the government were to favor the majority religion is also analogous to Justice Blackmun's argument that governmental use of religious symbols on behalf of a majority religion should be viewed more critically than governmental use of a minority religion's symbols. Justice Kennedy also derides this latter argument. *See id.* at 677 (Kennedy, J., concurring in the judgment in part and dissenting in part). Finally, the notion that in order to recognize one religion the government must recognize a number of others flies in the face of the pervasively Christian nature of government religious practices "acknowledging" religion, which Justice Kennedy relies upon to justify his position. *See id.* at 671-74 (Kennedy, J., concurring in the judgment in part and dissenting in part). The basic issue with regard to both selective government recognition of religious symbols and a permanent cross on top of city hall is this: if the government stops short of forcing everyone in society to change their religious behavior to comply with the majority faith embodied in the symbolic action, how can Justice Kennedy argue that such actions are coercive?

Members of the local clergy conducted the prayers at the Providence graduation ceremonies, guided by school policy guidelines suggesting that the clergy keep in mind "inclusiveness and sensitivity" when composing a graduation prayer. Using the prayer given at the plaintiff 's middle school graduation as an example of a typical graduation prayer in the Providence system, the Court found that the prayers were short (usually about one minute long) and nondenominational. Despite the efforts of the school district to make its prayer as non-confrontational as possible, a five-member majority of the Supreme Court held that the prayer violated the Establishment Clause. Surprisingly, Justice Kennedy wrote the majority opinion. Even more surprisingly, he used the coercion standard as the basis for his opinion.

The author of the *Weisman* majority opinion is in many respects a different Justice Kennedy than the Justice who wrote the angry dissent in *Allegheny*. Likewise, the coercion test that first appeared in Justice Kennedy's *Allegheny* dissent is a substantially different animal from the one that appears in *Weisman*. The version of the coercion standard that Justice Kennedy uses in *Weisman* to strike down a brief nondenominational graduation prayer is much stricter than the version he uses in *Allegheny* to approve a large display of the baby Jesus prominently placed in a public building. The root of the difference between the two versions is a very different conception of the term "coercion."

In *Allegheny*, the key indication of unconstitutional coercion is evidence that the government's action has interfered in fact with an individual's religious autonomy. In that case, Justice Kennedy argued that so long as a member of a religious minority retains the right to practice his or her own religion and to disassociate himself or herself from the public display of the religious majority's symbols, the placement of such symbols on public property is not coercive, and therefore is not a violation of the Establishment Clause. According to this version of the Establishment Clause issue, the government has the right to speak, even on the subject of religion, so long as individuals who disagree have the right "to ignore [the displays], or even to turn their backs, just as they are free to do when they disagree with any other form of government speech." Thus, in *Allegheny*, Justice Kennedy views coercion as a narrow, easily perceptible phenomenon. If government action endorsing another religion has not changed an individual religious practitioner's religious behavior, then there has been no coercion. Indications that members of the religious minority have felt excluded or offended by the government's religious speech are irrelevant.

The concept of coercion that forms the core of Justice Kennedy's *Weisman* opinion is much broader, looser, and more indefinite. Although Justice Kennedy quotes the key language from his *Allegheny* definition, he interprets and applies that language quite differently in *Weisman*. In *Weisman*, the Court held that the very fact that the government used its authority to endorse or further the cause of religion is itself evidence of coercion, without regard to the actual effect the government action has on the religious practices of anyone in the audience. Justice Kennedy writes that because school officials decided that the prayer should be given, "from a constitutional perspective it is as if a state statute decreed that the prayers must occur." He concludes that such a statute would be a per se violation of the Establishment Clause.

This conclusion is inconsistent with the broad outlines of Establishment Clause theory set forth in *Allegheny*. In *Allegheny*, Justice Kennedy argued that government speech about religion is not per se suspect, provided the speech does not "place the government's weight behind an obvious effort to proselytize on behalf of a particular religion." He takes exactly the opposite position in *Weisman*, asserting that the Establishment Clause specifically prohibits the government from participating in religious debate or expression. He also rejects the school district's claim (which seems to follow his own suggestion in *Allegheny*) that the government may make generalized references to civic religion, so long as it does not advance the creed of a particular faith. "The suggestion that government may establish an official or civic religion as a means of avoiding the establishment of a religion with more specific creeds strikes us as a contradiction that cannot be accepted." Justice Kennedy justifies his new position directly on the lesson "that was and is the inspiration for the Establishment Clause, the lesson that in the hands of government what might begin as a tolerant expression of religious views may end in a policy to indoctrinate and coerce." In this passage, he interprets the Establishment Clause to prohibit not only actual religious coercion, but also the cozy association of religion and government that "may end" in coercion. The notion that the coercion standard also covers government action that precedes coercion sounds suspiciously like the separation principle in disguise.

Justice Kennedy's *Weisman* opinion also contradicts his argument in *Allegheny* that the Establishment Clause standard should not turn on an individual's feelings of exclusion from the majority's religious culture. In *Weisman*, Justice Kennedy uses imagery highlighting the plaintiff's feelings of exclusion and religious isolation to demonstrate the existence of coercion, and thus to bolster his finding that graduation prayer violates the Establishment Clause. "[T]he school district's supervision and control. . . places public pressure, as well as peer pressure, on attending students to stand as a group, or, at least, maintain respectful silence during the Invocation and Benediction. This pressure, though subtle and indirect, can be as real as any overt coercion."

Three things are noteworthy about this passage. First, Justice Kennedy acknowledges that even a passive demonstration of respect by a member of the religious minority for the government's favored religious practice is tantamount to direct participation in the exercise. Second, he finds coercion even though the government itself does nothing whatsoever to pressure the dissenter to do anything. The existence of conformist religious pressures among the population is sufficient to provide the necessary coercion.[166] Third, Justice

---

[166] *Id.* at 2659 (holding that "the government may no more use social pressure to enforce orthodoxy than it may use more direct means").

Kennedy finds coercion even though there is no evidence that either governmental or nongovernmental actors did anything to pressure or threaten the religious minority to conform. He presumes coercion exists simply because conformist tendencies are likely to flow from the religious minority's feelings of social ostracism. I emphasize that I believe Justice Kennedy's perceptions about these tendencies are correct. It stretches the meaning of the word coercion, however, to apply that term to an individual's decision to modify beliefs that no other person has sought actively to change. Justice Kennedy's description of the constitutional problem in *Weisman* better fits Justice O'Connor's theory that the government should not make nonadherents feel like outsiders in society, a theory which Justice Kennedy criticized at great length in *Allegheny*.

Justice Kennedy's newfound sympathy for religious outsiders permeates his *Weisman* opinion. This kinder, gentler attitude toward the plight of religious minorities in a majoritarian culture provides the basis for some of the most striking differences in tone and emphasis between Justice Kennedy's *Weisman* and *Allegheny* opinions. In *Allegheny*, he asserts that "[g]overnment policies of accommodation, acknowledgement, and support for religion are an accepted part of our political and cultural heritage." The school district's attorneys in *Weisman* understandably incorporated a similar notion into their arguments defending the Providence graduation prayer, claiming that the prayer was a justifiable acknowledgement that "human achievements cannot be understood apart from their spiritual essence." In contrast to his statements in *Allegheny*, Justice Kennedy's *Weisman* opinion rejects the notion that official ceremonies can be used to demonstrate government's support for religion. "[The government] fails to acknowledge that what for many of Deborah's classmates and their parents was a spiritual imperative was for Daniel and Deborah Weisman religious conformance compelled by the State." Whereas in *Allegheny* Justice Kennedy emphasizes that members of religious minorities "are free to ignore" the government's use of religious symbols to which they object, in *Weisman* he writes that forcing the religious objector to "take unilateral and private action to avoid compromising religious scruples. . . turns conventional First Amendment analysis on its head."

In my view, Justice Kennedy cast his vote correctly in *Weisman*, but I do not believe that any defensible reading of the coercion standard can justify this result. The only way Justice Kennedy could reach the conclusion he reached in *Weisman* was to expand the coercion standard until it became virtually indistinguishable from the separationist views he rejected in *Allegheny*. If that is what the coercion standard now means, then Justice Kennedy's conclusions about the creche in *Allegheny* were wrong. Yet Justice Kennedy cited his *Allegheny* opinion in *Weisman*, and cited it again in a subsequent opinion criticizing both the *Lemon* test and Justice O'Connor's endorsement standard. Justice Kennedy thus has not become a sudden convert to the separation principle, but he clearly believes that coercion alone can explain the result in *Weisman*.

Professor McConnell agrees. In an article published when *Weisman* was pending before the Supreme Court, he wrote that "I would have thought that gathering a captive audience is a classic example of coercion." He cites two factors to support this conclusion, both of which are also emphasized by Justice Kennedy. First, he notes that the religious representatives chosen to give graduation prayers in the Providence school system were provided state-prepared guidelines on how the prayer should be composed. According to Professor McConnell, this amounted to "indirect governmental control [of the prayer's content], which is a species of coercion." But the Providence school district's guidelines represented the school district's effort to follow Professor McConnell's own mandate that government agencies should prevent public ceremonies from being used to "give official sponsorship to symbols or ceremonies that are inherently exclusionary." Religious representatives who could not in good faith follow the guidelines were not coerced to change their religious practices in any way; they were simply prevented from exercising their right to practice their religion during the government-organized ceremony. Thus, although the school district's guidelines definitively establish that the prayer was a state-sanctioned religious exercise subject to Establishment Clause limitations, the guidelines cannot be challenged legitimately (under Professor McConnell's own definition) as coercive.[179]

The second factor Professor McConnell cites to support the application of the coercion standard to strike down the Providence graduation prayer policy — the special nature of a high school graduation ceremony — is equally unconvincing. According to both Professor McConnell and Justice Kennedy, a high school graduation ceremony is, in effect, mandatory. "[A] student is not free to absent herself from the graduation exercise in any real sense of the term 'voluntary,' for absence would require forfeiture of those intangible benefits which have motivated the student through youth and all her high school years." Because the student, in effect, is required to attend the ceremony, "participation [in the prayer] is hardly voluntary if the cost of avoiding the prayer is to miss

---

[179] Justice Kennedy's version of Professor McConnell's first argument asserts that the coercive element of the guidelines was the likelihood that the religious representative would alter his or her views to fit the government mold. "Even if the only sanction for ignoring the instructions were that the rabbi would not be invited back, we think no religious representative who valued his or her continued reputation and effectiveness in the community would incur the State's displeasure in this regard." *Weisman*, 112 S. Ct. at 2656. It is true that the guidelines provide religious groups an incentive to draft an acceptable prayer in order to gain access to the public school graduation ceremony. Justice Kennedy, however, has written with regard to the Free Exercise Clause that it is not unconstitutional for a neutral government policy to burden private religious practices thereby creating an incentive for the religious practitioners to change their sacred practices. *See* Church of the Lukumi Babalu Aye, Inc. v. Hialeah, 113 S. Ct. 2217, 2226 (1993). If the burdens and incentives inherent in drug laws, *see, e.g.*, Employment Division v. Smith, 494 U.S. 872 (1990), social security laws, *see, e.g.*, United States v. Lee, 455 U.S. 252 (1982), and welfare laws, *see, e.g.*, Bowen v. Roy, 476 U.S 693 (1986), are not unconstitutionally coercive under the Establishment Clause, it is unclear why Justice Kennedy would find the Providence school district policy problematic. The Providence policy has the neutral purpose of encouraging religious tolerance and inclusiveness, and, unlike the criminal law and social welfare examples cited above, does not burden the private practice of religion at all.

one's graduation." Thus, graduation prayer is constitutionally indistinguishable from the Court's earlier classroom prayer cases.

The problem with this analysis is that it is inconsistent with both the common meaning of the term *coercion*, and with Justice Kennedy's use of the term in his *Allegheny* opinion. Justice Kennedy and Professor McConnell undoubtedly are correct in contending that graduating seniors are, in effect, compelled to attend their high school graduation ceremonies. But a citizen of Allegheny County may also be compelled to transact business in the county courthouse, which would inevitably require that person to pass by the prominent display of the birth of the Christian savior. If the Allegheny County citizen is not coerced by being required to respectfully pass by the religious display, why is the Providence student coerced by respectfully remaining silent during a one-minute prayer? Conversely, if "the act of standing or remaining silent" during a graduation prayer is "an expression of participation" in the prayer, why is walking by an overtly Christian display in respectful silence not also "an expression of participation" in the display?

The situations presented in *Allegheny* and *Weisman* offer the religious dissenter two choices. He or she may silently accept the government-sanctioned religious exercise, thereby suppressing deep disagreement with the exercise and misleading the rest of society about the dissenter's true views. Alternatively, the dissenter may make an overt gesture of dissent, which will be perceived by virtually everyone as inappropriate, rude, inflammatory, and probably sacrilegious, thereby increasing the dissenter's feelings of ostracism and the psychological pressure to conform. This is true without regard to the nature of the government's endorsement of religion. If psychological coercion is present in *Weisman*, it is also present in *Allegheny*.[184] Also, if psychological coercion is the main focus of the Establishment Clause, then Justice O'Connor correctly argues that the relevant standard should identify governmental practices that send nonadherents the message "that they are outsiders, not full members of the political community."

3. Coercion and Public School Prayer: The Scalia Position

If Justice Kennedy is sincere about distinguishing the coercion standard from Justice O'Connor's endorsement standard, then he must take seriously his own *Allegheny* definition of coercion. Under that definition, a person is coerced

---

[184] The problem cannot be solved by focusing on the fact that *Weisman* involved teenagers. First, Justice Kennedy himself notes that the concern over religious coercion is not limited to public schools, although he notes "it is most pronounced there." *Weisman*, 112 S. Ct. at 2658. Second, when Justice Kennedy explains why legislative prayer (which he approves) is different from graduation prayer, he does not even mention the age of the participants, choosing to focus instead on matters such as the formality of the proceedings and the extent of state control over the content of the prayer. *See id.* at 2660. Finally, as Justice Scalia points out, high school graduation "is generally associated with transition from adolescence to young adulthood." *Id.* at 2682 (Scalia, J., dissenting). With few exceptions, high school graduates are at least 18 years old. In Rhode Island, a person 18 years old is legally regarded as an adult. *See* R.I. Gen. Laws § 15-12-1 (1992) (lowering age of majority from 21 to 18 years of age).

if he or she is forced by some action of the government "to support or participate in any religion or its exercise." Psychological coercion, which is the focus of the *Weisman* opinion, does not fit this definition because the religious dissenter is not forced to participate in any religious act,[187] and because, in symbolic endorsement cases such as *Weisman*, the main source of the psychological pressure is society as a whole, not the particular government action. Therefore, if the coercion standard is to be a distinctive new reference point for Establishment Clause analysis, it must emphasize *legal*, rather than psychological, coercion.

Justice Scalia's dissenting opinion in *Weisman* drives this point home with sarcastic force. He labels Justice Kennedy's psychological coercion test "incoherent," and ridicules the idea that it can ever be applied consistently. In place of psychological coercion, Justice Scalia offers his concept of legal coercion, i.e., "coercion of religious orthodoxy and of financial support by force of law and threat of penalty." Justice Scalia's definition transforms *Weisman* into an easy case because "attendance at graduation is voluntary, [and] there is nothing in the record to indicate that failure of attending students to take part in the invocation or benediction was subject to any penalty or discipline." Ergo, state-sanctioned prayer at public school graduation ceremonies is constitutional. If Ms. Weisman does not like it, she can stay home.

If the coercion standard is interpreted consistently, taking into account the common understanding of the term coercion, and viewed against the background of a larger constitutional theory that distinguishes the coercion standard from the endorsement test and other separationist perspectives, then Justice Scalia's concept of the coercion standard is correct. The implications are harsh, because if the Supreme Court adopted this interpretation of the Establishment Clause, the next Ms. Weisman probably will take Justice Scalia's advice and stay home rather than attend her own graduation. I suppose Justice Scalia could respond that the Constitution does not guarantee that belonging to a religious minority will be easy.[192] Besides, he is simply following in the politi-

---

[187] In *Weisman*, Justices Kennedy and Scalia argue over whether a religious dissenter sitting quietly during a prayer would be construed by observers as participating in the prayer. *See Weisman*, 112 S. Ct. at 2658, 2681-82 (Scalia, J., dissenting). However, not even Justice Kennedy argues that the dissenter is forced by the graduation prayer to pray. The debate is over appearances, not actual participation, which is another reason why Justice Kennedy's *Weisman* opinion seems more in accord with Justice O'Connor's endorsement standard than with a coercion analysis.

[192] Justice Scalia has made this point in the free exercise context, where he noted that leaving religious accommodations to the political process "will place at a relative disadvantage those religious practices that are not widely engaged in; but that unavoidable consequence of democratic government must be preferred to a system in which each conscience is a law unto itself. . . ." Employment Division v. Smith, 494 U.S. 872, 890 (1990). In *Smith*, Justice Scalia argued that the Free Exercise Clause does not require the political branches of government to waive the application of religiously neutral laws when they conflict with the sacred practices of religious minorities. Justice Scalia's Establishment Clause position goes one step further. Under the coercion standard, the Establishment Clause permits the political branches to endorse partisan religious positions, even if these positions increase the existing social pressure on religious minorities to conform. Belonging to a religious minority will always be difficult, but it does not have to be as difficult as Justice Scalia seeks to make it.

cal tradition noted by Justice Kennedy in *Allegheny*: "It requires little imagination to conclude that. . . [religious] proclamations would cause nonadherents to feel excluded, yet they have been a part of our national heritage from the beginning." Putting the matter more crassly, this country has always made life difficult for religious minorities, so why stop now? To the historical certification of exclusionary prayers, Justice Scalia adds the practical point that government-certified public prayer serves as a "unifying mechanism" for a religiously diverse country. "To deprive our society of that important unifying mechanism, in order to spare the nonbeliever what seems to me the minimal inconvenience of standing or even sitting in respectful nonparticipation, is as senseless in policy as it is unsupported in law."

Justice Scalia's position is a radical departure from the traditional understanding of the First Amendment's countermajoritarian function. As Justice Jackson pointed out many years ago, the First Amendment specifically forbids the development of governmental mechanisms to unify citizens' opinions about matters such as religion. Justice Scalia's blunt opinion in *Weisman* indicates that he is anxious to abandon the traditional understanding of the First Amendment in favor of an interpretation favoring the interests of political and religious majorities. The opinion also indicates that Justice Scalia is much more willing than Justice Kennedy to face up to the exclusionary implications of the coercion standard. But even Justice Scalia stops short of embracing the full consequences of his argument. Whenever he refers to the general phenomenon of graduation prayer in his *Weisman* opinion, Justice Scalia emphasizes the benign, nondenominational content of the prayer given at Weisman's graduation. This is the type of prayer that Justice Scalia uses as his model in applying the coercion standard. As to other, not-so-benign prayers, Justice Scalia notes only that he is willing to concede that government-sponsored endorsement of religion may be unconstitutional "where the endorsement is sectarian, in the sense of specifying details upon which men and women who believe in a benevolent, omnipotent Creator and Ruler of the world, are known to differ (for example, the divinity of Christ)."

These overtures to nonsectarian tolerance offer some comfort, but if, as Justice Scalia argues, the Constitution permits "the expression of gratitude to God that a majority of the community wishes to make" so long as the community does not coerce others to participate in that expression, then there is no reason to limit the application of the coercion standard to friendly, nondenominational prayers. If dissenting audience members at a state-sponsored public event may walk away from the affair without subjecting themselves to legal penalties, it should not matter whether a prayer given at that function incorporates the tenets of a particular sect, or comments unfavorably on the tenets of another sect. It should not matter even if the government sponsors a prayer overtly hostile to one or more faiths, so long as the dissenters are allowed to ignore the government's advice and practice their own beliefs freely. As Justice Scalia repeatedly emphasizes, the amorphous fear or psychological pressure generated in the minds of religious minorities by such prayers is constitutionally irrelevant. According to Justice Scalia, the First Amendment is concerned only with "acts backed by threat of penalty — a brand of coercion that, happily, is readily discernible to those of us who have made a career of reading the disciples of Blackstone rather than of Freud."

In addition to dodging the unsavory implications of his theory for the actions of a government composed of a messianic religious majority, Justice Scalia also attempts to avoid the implications of his theory for the contentious issue of classroom prayer. After discussing his views on prayer at the high school graduation ceremony, Justice Scalia attempts to distinguish the Court's thirty-year-old rule against classroom prayer and Bible reading. He finds three differences between classroom and graduation prayer. First, he argues that classroom prayer does not fall within the permissive rule he asserts for graduation prayer because "school instruction is not a public ceremony." It is unclear why this fact should affect a constitutional analysis based on the coercion standard. If a student has the option of not participating in the government-sanctioned prayer (or leaving the room during a Bible reading), then the student's religious practice is not being coerced. It should not matter whether the context is a public graduation ceremony or a public school classroom. Both cases involve what Justice Scalia calls "the minimal inconvenience of standing or even sitting in respectful nonparticipation." The availability of simple expedients to avoid participating in the state-sanctioned prayer should lead the Court to uphold classroom prayer under the coercion standard.

Justice Scalia's second distinction is in part a response to this argument. According to Justice Scalia, the second distinction between classroom and graduation prayers is that attendance in a public school classroom is mandated by law, whereas participation in a graduation ceremony is purely voluntary. But this distinction is also unconvincing. It is certainly true that mandatory attendance laws compel students younger than a designated age to attend school. Mandatory attendance laws, however, do not — and under current constitutional doctrine cannot — require students to attend public school. Students who object to classroom prayers may always opt out of the public schools and attend purely secular private schools. More importantly, a law returning religion to the classroom easily could be written to avoid compelling any student in the classroom to recite the state-sanctioned prayer. Such a law should pass scrutiny under Justice Scalia's own "legal coercion" standard because, although attendance at school would be mandatory, participation in the religious exercise would not.

This is not a farfetched application of the coercion standard. Justice Stewart made precisely this argument in the original classroom prayer and Bible-reading cases, both of which involved "voluntary" religious exercises in the sense that students who objected could choose not to participate. Justice Stewart noted in *Engel* that no student was compelled by the state to recite the prayer sanctioned by the school board, and concluded that "I cannot see how an 'official religion' is established by letting those who want to say a prayer say it." Justice Stew-

274

THE SEARCH FOR AN ESTABLISHMENT CLAUSE STANDARD CH. 5

art's broader rationale resembles the underlying principles governing religion and society that Justice Scalia cites in *Weisman*. Like Justice Scalia, Justice Stewart argued that favoring the feelings of the children belonging to religious minorities over the wishes of the children belonging to the religious majority denies the majority children "the opportunity of sharing in the spiritual heritage of our Nation." Justice Stewart similarly argued in *Schempp* that the Establishment Clause requires the government to refrain "from so structuring the school environment as to put any kind of pressure on a child to participate in those exercises," but not to insulate children from religious practices with which they disagree.

The logic of Justice Scalia's graduation prayer opinion leads him in the direction of Justice Stewart's conclusions regarding state-sanctioned classroom prayer and Bible reading. At one point in his *Weisman* opinion, Justice Scalia even uses a version of Justice Stewart's very narrow coercion argument in discussing classroom recitation of the Pledge of Allegiance. Justice Scalia notes that the Pledge of Allegiance contains the words "under God," and argues that "[i]n *Barnette* we held that a public school student could not be compelled to *recite* the Pledge; we did not even hint that she could not be compelled to observe respectful silence — indeed, even to *stand* in respectful silence — when those who wished to recite it did so." It is a short step from this conclusion regarding the Pledge of Allegiance to the proposition that "voluntary" classroom prayer is constitutional.[211]

Justice Scalia's third attempt to distinguish classroom prayer from graduation prayer is even less persuasive than his first two distinctions. Classroom prayers are different than prayers at graduation ceremonies, Justice Scalia

---

[211] It is possible that Justice Scalia is giving away too much by acknowledging that a religiously devout public school system must permit a student to stand silently instead of participating in the school system's chosen prayer. Justice Frankfurter had in mind something akin to the coercion standard when he argued in West Virginia State Board of Education v. Barnette that Jehovah's Witness children could be forced to salute the flag despite their religious views to the contrary:

> Saluting the flag suppresses no belief nor curbs it. Children and their parents may believe what they please, avow their belief and practice it. It is not even remotely suggested that the requirement for saluting the flag involves the slightest restriction against the fullest opportunity on the part both of the children and of their parents to disavow as publicly as they choose to do so the meaning that others attach to the gesture of salute. All channels of affirmative free expression are open to both children and parents.

Barnette, 319 U.S. 624, 664 (1943) (Frankfurter, J., dissenting).

Taking a cue from Justice Frankfurter, it is possible to argue that saying a prayer "suppresses no belief nor curbs it." As with the flag salute, a local ordinance forcing all children to say a prayer does not in any way limit the ability of any child to disavow the prayer outside the classroom and practice a very different religious faith on his or her private time. All channels of affirmative free exercise of religion remain open to both parents and children. Ergo, no coercion. I note this possible interpretation of Justice Scalia's favored standard partly in jest and partly in order to underscore the point that the slope from the coercion principle to majoritarian religious tyranny is very slippery indeed.

argues, because parents are not present to counteract the pressures exerted by a student's teachers and peers. It seems unlikely, however, that devout religious students will fail to inform their parents when the students are confronted in the classroom with the prayers of another faith. The parents can then counteract the prayer in the same fashion as they would if they personally witnessed the prayer at the graduation ceremony. Indeed, the parental influence in the classroom situation may be even greater than in the graduation context because the parent probably will have advance warning that the classroom prayer will take place and therefore can make alternative arrangements for the child to avoid exposing the child to the state prayer in the first place. If the school observes the conditions on school prayer discussed above (i.e., dissenting students are given the opportunity to avoid participating), Justice Scalia logically cannot conclude that a classroom prayer interferes with "the liberty of parents to direct the religious upbringing of their children" to a significantly greater extent than a graduation prayer.

Justice Scalia cannot avoid this difficult issue by citing the imprecise social pressures imposed on dissenters, because he repeatedly emphasizes that social pressures are irrelevant to the constitutional analysis if they are unaccompanied by "acts backed by threat of penalty." If this is Justice Scalia's view of the Establishment Clause, then he must live with the consequences. One such consequence is clear: Justice Scalia and others who adopt the coercion standard must be willing to overrule *Engel* and *Schempp*, and uphold state-sanctioned, explicitly denominational classroom prayer, Bible reading, and any other form of governmental religious endorsement that is unaccompanied by civil or criminal sanctions for those who refuse to participate. At least on a symbolic level, government affairs could be infused with religion to a much greater extent than is possible today.

E. THE SUBSTANTIVE NEUTRALITY ANALYSIS

The theme of neutrality has been a mainstay of Establishment Clause analysis since the beginning of the modern era. The neutrality analysis is one of the more seasoned approaches to applying the Establishment Clause, but it is also one of the most inconsistent and least well developed by the Supreme Court. It is inconsistent in the sense that "neutrality" has been used over the years both to bolster and to attack claims advocating separation of church and state. The most prominent early proponent of the neutrality theory of the Establishment Clause was Philip Kurland, who argued that the Religion Clauses should be read together as the textual embodiment of the principle "that government cannot utilize religion as a standard for action or inaction because these clauses, read together as they should be, prohibit classification in terms of religion either to confer a benefit or to impose a burden." Philip B. Kurland, *Of Church and State and the Supreme Court*, 29 U. CHI. L. REV. 1, 96 (1961). This version of neutrality — sometimes referred to as "strict neutrality" — also can be found in the Justice Black's famous early description of the Establishment Clause standard in his majority opinion in *Everson*, *supra* Chapter 1. According to Justice Black: "The 'establishment of religion' clause of the First Amendment means at least this: Neither a state nor the Federal Government can set up a church. Neither can pass laws which aid one religion, aid all religions, or prefer one religion over another. Neither can force nor influence a person to go to or to remain away from church against his will or force him to profess a belief or disbelief in any religion. No person can be punished for entertaining or professing religious beliefs or disbeliefs, for church attendance or non-attendance. No tax in any amount, large or small, can be levied to support any religious activities or institutions, whatever they may be called, or whatever form they may adopt to teach or practice religion. Neither a state nor the Federal Government can, openly or secretly, participate in the affairs of any religious organizations or groups and vice versa. In the words of Jefferson, the clause against establishment of religion by law was intended to erect 'a wall of separation between church and State.' *Reynolds v. United States*, 98 U.S. at 164." *Everson*, 330 U.S. at 15.

This early version of neutrality is sometimes criticized as too rigidly separationist. "Professor Kurland's 'strict neutrality' approach, . . . while purporting to apply a neutral principle of equality of treatment to both clauses, in effect favors the anti-establishment prohibition 'at a cost of almost total emasculation of the free exercise provision.'" Michael A. Paulsen, *Religion, Equality, And The Constitution: An Equal Protection Approach To Establishment Clause Adjudication*, 61 NOTRE DAME L. REV. 311, 371 n.66 (1986)(quoting Gail Merel, *The Protection of Individual Choice: A Consistent Understanding of Religion Under the First Amendment*, 45 U. CHI. L. REV. 805, 808 (1978)).

The political philosopher Michael J. Sandel has presented a broad version of this same criticism, which links the neutrality theory with what he perceives to be the general tendency of secular liberal political regimes to exclude religion from the public sphere. Focusing on the early Kurland/*Everson* version of neutrality, Sandel argues that the mandate of religious neutrality is merely one example of how American society has abandoned the concern with developing and advancing the communitarian values of civic republicanism in favor of the individualistic values of what Sandel calls the "procedural republic": "The public philosophy of procedural liberalism, the one that emphasizes freedom of choice above all, holds out a liberating, even exhilarating, promise: what could freedom be if not the unfettered ability to choose my own way of life, my own conception of the good, without being imposed upon by government? But what we're finding now in our public life — and here is where philosophy comes down to earth — is that the arrival of the procedural republic has coincided with a loss of mastery, a growing sense of disempowerment. Despite the expansion of rights in recent decades, Americans find to their frustration that they are losing control of the forces that govern their lives." Michael J. Sandel, *The Constitution Of The Procedural Republic: Liberal Rights And Civic Virtues*, 66 FORDHAM L. REV. 1, 13-14 (1997). Sandel believes that religion serves an important function in providing a basis for the civic values that provide the organizing principles of society. Thus, Sandel — who situates himself on the political left — praises the fundamentalist Jerry Falwell. Sandel argues that Falwell is "right about the indispensable role of morality and religion in political discourse, right about the indispensability of the formative aspect of democratic life." *Id.* at 12. Sandel also joins religious conservatives in arguing that "the [Supreme Court's] emphasis on neutrality in the religion cases has led to an over-emphasis on the worry about establishment, even at a cost to accommodation of free exercise." *Id.* at 18.

Criticism of neutrality theory from conservative and civic republican quarters is ironic in light of the fact that a different version of neutrality theory has been used recently by Justices on the Supreme Court as the basis for rulings favoring increased government aid to religious individuals and organizations. Under this recent version of neutrality theory, government programs that provide benefits to religious individuals or organizations (such as government aid programs) would not violate the Establishment Clause as long as they offer the same aid under the same conditions to both religious and nonreligious recipients. This version of neutrality theory is very controversial and it is not clear that a majority of the Justices on the Supreme Court would apply it with full force. Compare the various opinions discussing this subject in *Mitchell v. Helms*, 530 U.S. 793 (2000). Justice Thomas, writing for himself and three other Justices, asserted a broad version of the new neutrality theory:

> In distinguishing between indoctrination that is attributable to the State and indoctrination that is not, we have consistently turned to the principle of neutrality, upholding aid that is offered to a broad range of groups or persons without regard to their religion. If the religious, irreligious, and areligious are all alike eligible for governmental aid, no one would conclude that any indoctrination that any particular recipient conducts has been done at the behest of the government. For attribution of indoctrination is a relative question. If the government is offering assistance to recipients who provide, so to speak, a broad range of indoctrination, the government itself is not thought responsible for any particular indoctrination. To put the point differently, if the government, seeking to further some legitimate secular purpose, offers aid on the same terms, without regard to religion, to all who adequately further that purpose. . . then it is fair to say that any aid going to a religious recipient only has the effect of furthering that secular purpose. . . . As a way of assuring neutrality, we have repeatedly considered whether any governmental aid that goes to a religious institution does so "only as a result of the genuinely independent and private choices of individuals." . . . We have viewed as significant whether the "private choices of individual parents," as opposed to the "unmediated" will of government, determine what schools ultimately benefit from the governmental aid, and how much. . . . Private choice . . . helps guarantee neutrality by mitigating the preference for pre-existing recipients that is arguably inherent in any governmental aid program, . . . and that could lead to

a program inadvertently favoring one religion or favoring religious private schools in general over nonreligious ones.

Mitchell, 530 U.S. at 809-10 (citations omitted).

Justice O'Connor, in a concurring opinion that was joined by Justice Breyer, asserted a much narrower view of neutrality and specifically rejected the notion that the "neutral" characteristics of a government aid program were alone sufficient to satisfy constitutional restrictions on government aid to religion:

> Reduced to its essentials, the plurality's rule states that government aid to religious schools does not have the effect of advancing religion so long as the aid is offered on a neutral basis and the aid is secular in content. . . . [T]he plurality's treatment of neutrality comes close to assigning that factor singular importance in the future adjudication of Establishment Clause challenges to government school-aid programs. . . . I do not quarrel with the plurality's recognition that neutrality is an important reason for upholding government-aid programs against Establishment Clause challenges. Our cases have described neutrality in precisely this manner, and we have emphasized a program's neutrality repeatedly in our decisions approving various forms of school aid. . . . Nevertheless, we have never held that a government-aid program passes constitutional muster solely because of the neutral criteria it employs as a basis for distributing aid. . . . As I have previously explained, neutrality is important, but it is by no means the only "axiom in the history and precedent of the Establishment Clause."

Mitchell, 530 U.S. at 839-40 (O'Connor, J., concurring in judgment)(citations omitted).

Justice Souter's *Mitchell* dissent (joined by two other Justices) rejected in even stronger terms the plurality's reliance on the new neutrality theory: "[T]he view revealed in the plurality opinion. . . espouses a new conception of neutrality as a practically sufficient test of constitutionality that would, if adopted by the Court, eliminate enquiry into a law's effects. The plurality position breaks fundamentally with Establishment Clause principle, and with the methodology painstakingly worked out in support of it." *Mitchell*, 530 U.S. at 869 (Souter, J., dissenting)(citations omitted). Justice Souter then provided a detailed description of the various ways in which the Court had used the term "neutrality" over the years:

> [W]e have used the term ["neutrality"] in at least three ways in our cases, and an understanding of the term's evolution will help to explain the concept as it is understood today, as well as the limits of its significance in Establishment Clause analysis. "Neutrality" has been employed as a term to describe the requisite state of government equipoise between the forbidden encouragement and discouragement of religion; to characterize a benefit or aid as secular; and to indicate even-handedness in distributing it. As already mentioned, the Court first

referred to neutrality in Everson, simply stating that government is required "to be a neutral" among religions and between religion and non-religion. Although "neutral" may have carried a hint of inaction when we indicated that the First Amendment "does not require the state to be [the] adversary" of religious believers, or to cut off general government services from religious organizations, Everson provided no explicit definition of the term or further indication of what the government was required to do or not do to be "neutral" toward religion. In practical terms, "neutral" in Everson was simply a term for government in its required median position between aiding and handicapping religion. The second major case on aid to religious schools, [Bd. of Educ. v.] Allen, used "neutrality" to describe an adequate state of balance between government as ally and as adversary to religion. . . . The term was not further defined, and a few subsequent school cases used "neutrality" simply to designate the required relationship to religion, without explaining how to attain it. . . . Allen similarly focused on the fact that the textbooks lent out were "secular" and approved by secular authorities, and assumed that the secular textbooks and the secular elements of education they supported were not so intertwined with religious instruction as "in fact [to be] instrumental in the teaching of religion." Such was the Court's premise in Lemon [v. Kurtzman] for shifting the use of the word "neutral" from labeling the required position of the government to describing a benefit that was nonreligious. We spoke of "[o]ur decisions from Everson to Allen [as] permitt[ing] the States to provide church-related schools with secular, neutral, or nonideological services, facilities, or materials," and thereafter, we regularly used "neutral" in this second sense of "secular" or "nonreligious.". . . The shift from equipoise to secular was not, however, our last redefinition, for the Court again transformed the sense of "neutrality" in the 1980's. Reexamining and reinterpreting Everson and Allen, we began to use the word "neutral" to mean "evenhanded," in the sense of allocating aid on some common basis to religious and secular recipients. Again, neither Everson nor Allen explicitly used "neutral" in this manner, but just as the label for equipoise had lent itself to referring to the secular characteristic of what a government might provide, it was readily adaptable to referring to the generality of government services, as in Everson's paradigms, to which permissible benefits were compared.

Mitchell, 530 U.S. at 878-81 (Souter, J., dissenting) (citations omitted). After describing the various ways in which the term "neutrality" had been used, he then noted the reasons why neutrality alone had not previously been considered sufficient to satisfy the Establishment Clause.

In the days when "neutral" was used in Everson's sense of equipoise, neutrality was tantamount to constitutionality; the term was conclusory, but when it applied it meant that the government's position was constitutional under the Establishment Clause. This is not so at all, however, under the most recent use of "neutrality" to refer to generality or evenhandedness of distribution. This kind of neutrality is relevant in judging whether a benefit scheme so characterized should be seen as aiding a sectarian school's religious mission, but this neutrality is not alone sufficient to qualify the aid as constitutional. It is to be considered only along with other characteristics of aid, its administration, its recipients, or its potential that have been emphasized over the years as indicators of just how religious the intent and effect of a given aid scheme really is. . . . The insufficiency of evenhandedness neutrality as a stand-alone criterion of constitutional intent or effect has been clear from the beginning of our interpretative efforts, for an obvious reason. Evenhandedness in distributing a benefit approaches the equivalence of constitutionality in this area only when the term refers to such universality of distribution that it makes no sense to think of the benefit as going to any discrete group. Conversely, when evenhandedness refers to distribution to limited groups within society, like groups of schools or schoolchildren, it does make sense to regard the benefit as aid to the recipients. . . . Hence, if we looked no further than evenhandedness, and failed to ask what activities the aid might support, or in fact did support, religious schools could be blessed with government funding as massive as expenditures made for the benefit of their public school counterparts, and religious missions would thrive on public money. This is why the consideration of less than universal neutrality has never been recognized as dispositive and has always been teamed with attention to other facts bearing on the substantive prohibition of support for a school's religious objective.

Mitchell, 530 U.S. at 883-85 (Souter, J., dissenting) (citations omitted). The various school-financing decisions discussed by the Justices in *Mitchell* will be considered at length in Chapters 8 and 9.

Professor Douglas Laycock has suggested that the differences between various types of neutrality are really distinctions between what he calls "formal neutrality" and "substantive neutrality." "Formal neutrality" is the theory that the Establishment Clause prohibits government classifications expressly conferring benefits or imposing burdens on the basis of religion. Douglas Laycock, *Formal, Substantive, and Disaggregated Neutrality Toward Religion*, 39 DEPAUL L. REV. 993, 999-1000 (1990). "Substantive neutrality" looks beyond the formal classifications in the law to assess whether a government policy actually encourages or discourages religious practice, observance, or belief. *Id.* at 1001-02. Despite its name, the theory of "substantive neutrality" is occasionally non-neutral in that it sometimes requires government to take affirmative steps to accommodate religion in order to ensure that secular government policies do not impinge on religious activity to the point that such activity is significantly discouraged. On the other hand, "formal neutrality" would permit substantial government funds to flow to religion as long as secular organizations have a formal opportunity to apply for the same funds. In general, substantive neutrality is a more complicated theory to apply than formal neutrality. Substantive neutrality requires courts to make sophisticated contextual judgments about the actual effects of government policy on religious activity, whereas formal neutrality requires merely an assessment of the formal terms of the government policy in question. In Laycock's nomenclature, the Court has been increasingly gravitating away from assessments of substantive neutrality and toward a stance of simple formal neutrality, as the excerpts from *Mitchell v. Helms* in the next subsection indicate.

Finally, there is a large and growing literature discussing the relationship between neutrality and separationist theories of the Establishment Clause. For examples, see Douglas Laycock, *The Underlying Unity Of Separation And Neutrality*, 46 EMORY L.J. 43 (1997) (arguing that neutrality and separationism are compatible); Carl H. Esbeck, *A Constitutional Case for Governmental Cooperation with Faith-Based Social Service Providers*, 46 EMORY L.J. 1, 3 (1997) (arguing that neutrality is separationism's "greatest competitor"); and Ira C. Lupu, *The Lingering Death of Separationism*, 62 GEO. WASH. L. REV. 230 (1994) (arguing that the theory of separationism is being superceded by the theory of neutrality). For other critical discussions of neutrality theory, see Daniel O. Conkle, *The Path of American Religious Liberty: From the Original Theology to Formal Neutrality and an Uncertain Future*, 75 IND. L.J. 1 (2000); Alan E. Brownstein, *Interpreting the Religion Clauses in Terms of Liberty, Equality, and Free Speech Values — A Critical Analysis of "Neutrality Theory" and Charitable Choice*, 13 NOTRE DAME J.L. ETHICS & PUB. POL'Y 243 (1999); Dhananjai Shivakumar, *Neutrality and the Religion Clauses*, 33 HARV. C.R.-C.L. L. REV. 505 (1998); Kathleen M. Sullivan, *Parades, Public Squares and Voucher Payments: Problems of Government Neutrality*, 28 CONN. L. REV. 243 (1996).

F. THE FORMAL NEUTRALITY ANALYSIS

MITCHELL v. HELMS
530 U.S. 793 (2000)

JUSTICE THOMAS announced the judgment of the Court and delivered an opinion, in which THE CHIEF JUSTICE, JUSTICE SCALIA, AND JUSTICE KENNEDY join.

[In this case the Court upheld a federal government program that distributes funds to state and local governmental agencies, which in turn lend educational materials and equipment to public and private schools, including many private schools that are religious. The decision is discussed in greater detail in Chapter 9.]

As we indicated in *Agostini*, and have indicated elsewhere, the question whether governmental aid to religious schools results in governmental indoctrination is ultimately a question whether any religious indoctrination that occurs in those schools could reasonably be attributed to governmental action.

We have also indicated that the answer to the question of indoctrination will resolve the question whether a program of educational aid "subsidizes" religion, as our religion cases use that term.

In distinguishing between indoctrination that is attributable to the State and indoctrination that is not, we have consistently turned to the principle of neutrality, upholding aid that is offered to a broad range of groups or persons without regard to their religion. If the religious, irreligious, and areligious are all alike eligible for governmental aid, no one would conclude that any indoctrination that any particular recipient conducts has been done at the behest of the government. For attribution of indoctrination is a relative question. If the government is offering assistance to recipients who provide, so to speak, a broad range of indoctrination, the government itself is not thought responsible for any particular indoctrination. To put the point differently, if the government, seeking to further some legitimate secular purpose, offers aid on the same terms, without regard to religion, to all who adequately further that purpose, then it is fair to say that any aid going to a religious recipient only has the effect of furthering that secular purpose. The government, in crafting such an aid program, has had to conclude that a given level of aid is necessary to further that purpose among secular recipients and has provided no more than that same level to religious recipients.

As a way of assuring neutrality, we have repeatedly considered whether any governmental aid that goes to a religious institution does so "only as a result of the genuinely independent and private choices of individuals." We have viewed as significant whether the "private choices of individual parents," as opposed to the "unmediated" will of government, determine what schools ultimately benefit from the governmental aid, and how much. For if numerous private choices, rather than the single choice of a government, determine the distribution of aid pursuant to neutral eligibility criteria, then a government cannot, or at least cannot easily, grant special favors that might lead to a religious establishment. Private choice also helps guarantee neutrality by mitigating the preference for pre-existing recipients that is arguably inherent in any governmental aid program, see, e.g., Gilder, *The Revitalization of Everything: The Law of the Microcosm*, HARV. BUS. REV. 49 (Mar./ Apr.1988), and that could lead to a program inadvertently favoring one religion or favoring religious private schools in general over nonreligious ones.

ZELMAN v. SIMMONS-HARRIS
536 U.S. 639 (2002)

CHIEF JUSTICE REHNQUIST delivered the opinion of the Court.

[In this case, the Court upheld a Cleveland, Ohio, program in which parents of school age children were given vouchers to send their children to private schools, 96 percent of which were religious in nature. The five-member majority held that the program was consistent with the Constitution because it was organized in a formally neutral manner — i.e., the government did not dictate that parents send their children to religious schools. This case is discussed in more detail in Chapter 9.]

[T]he Ohio program is neutral in all respects toward religion. It is part of a general and multifaceted undertaking by the State of Ohio to provide educational opportunities to the children of a failed school district. It confers educational assistance directly to a broad class of individuals defined without reference to religion, *i.e.*, any parent of a school-age child who resides in the Cleveland City School District. The program permits the participation of *all* schools within the district, religious or nonreligious. Adjacent public schools also may participate and have a financial incentive to do so. Program benefits are available to participating families on neutral terms, with no reference to religion. The only preference stated anywhere in the program is a preference for low-income families, who receive greater assistance and are given priority for admission at participating schools

There are no "financial incentive[s] that ske[w] the program toward religious schools." *Witters*. Such incentives "[are] not present where the aid is allocated on the basis of neutral, secular criteria that neither favor nor disfavor religion, and is made available to both religious and secular beneficiaries on a nondiscriminatory basis." *Agostini*. The program here in fact creates financial *dis*incentives for religious schools, with private schools receiving only half the government assistance given to community schools and one-third the assistance given to magnet schools. Adjacent public schools, should any choose to accept program students, are also eligible to receive two to three times the state funding of a private religious school. Families too have a financial disincentive to choose a private religious school over other schools. Parents that choose to participate in the scholarship program and then to enroll their children in a private school (religious or nonreligious) must copay a portion of the school's tuition. Families that choose a community school, magnet school, or traditional public school pay nothing. Although such features of the program are not necessary to its constitutionality, they clearly dispel the claim that the program creates "financial incentive[s] for parents to choose a sectarian school." *Zobrest*.

Respondents suggest that even without a financial incentive for parents to choose a religious school, the program creates a public perception that the State is endorsing religious practices and beliefs. But we have repeatedly recognized that no reasonable observer would think a neutral program of private choice, where state aid reaches religious schools solely as a result of the numerous independent decisions of private individuals, carries with it the *imprimatur* of government endorsement. The argument is particularly misplaced here since the reasonable observer in the endorsement inquiry must be deemed aware of the history and context underlying a challenged program. Any objective observer familiar with the full history and context of the Ohio program would reasonably view it as one aspect of a broader undertaking to assist poor children in failed schools, not as an endorsement of religious schooling in general.

There also is no evidence that the program fails to provide genuine opportunities for Cleveland parents to select secular educational options for their school-age children. Cleveland schoolchildren enjoy a range of educational choices: They may remain in public school as before, remain in public school with publicly funded tutoring aid, obtain a scholarship and choose a religious school, obtain a scholarship and choose a nonreligious private school, enroll in a community school, or enroll in a magnet school. That 46 of the 56 private schools now participating in the program are religious schools does not condemn it as a violation of the Establishment Clause. The Establishment Clause question is whether Ohio is coercing parents into sending their children to religious schools, and that question must be answered by evaluating *all* options Ohio provides Cleveland schoolchildren, only one of which is to obtain a program scholarship and then choose a religious school.

Respondents and Justice Souter claim that even if we do not focus on the number of participating schools that are religious schools, we should attach constitutional significance to the fact that 96% of scholarship recipients have enrolled in religious schools. They claim that this alone proves parents lack genuine choice, even if no parent has ever said so. We need not consider this argument in detail, since it was flatly rejected in *Mueller*, where we found it irrelevant that 96% of parents taking deductions for tuition expenses paid tuition at religious schools. Indeed, we have recently found it irrelevant even to the constitutionality of a direct aid program that a vast majority of program benefits went to religious schools. *See Agostini*; *see also Mitchell*. The constitutionality of a neutral educational aid program simply does not turn on whether and why, in a particular area, at a particular time, most private schools are run by religious organizations, or most recipients choose to use the aid at a religious school. As we said in *Mueller*, "[s]uch an approach would scarcely provide the certainty that this field stands in need of, nor can we perceive principled standards by which such statistical evidence might be evaluated."

In sum, the Ohio program is entirely neutral with respect to religion. It provides benefits directly to a wide spectrum of individuals, defined only by financial need and residence in a particular school district. It permits such individuals to exercise genuine choice among options public and private, secular and religious. The program is therefore a program of true private choice. In keeping with an unbroken line of decisions rejecting challenges to similar programs, we hold that the program does not offend the Establishment Clause.

G. THE NONPREFERENTIALIST ANALYSIS

Chief Justice Rehnquist was the Court's primary proponent of the nonpreferentialist analysis. In his dissent to the Alabama silent prayer decision — *Wallace v. Jaffree,* which is excerpted in Chapter 1 — Rehnquist set forth his view of the historical case for the nonpreferentialist approach. The radical implications of this analysis are clear from Rehnquist's summary:

It would seem from this evidence that the Establishment Clause of the First Amendment had acquired a well-accepted meaning: it forbade establishment of a national religion, and forbade preference among religious sects or denominations. Indeed, the first American dictionary defined the word "establishment" as "the act of establishing, founding, ratifying or ordaining," such as in "[t]he episcopal form of religion, so called, in England." 1 N. WEBSTER, AMERICAN DICTIONARY OF THE ENGLISH LANGUAGE (1st ed. 1828). The Establishment Clause did not require government neutrality between religion and irreligion nor did it prohibit the Federal Government from providing nondiscriminatory aid to religion. There is simply no historical foundation for the proposition that the Framers intended to build the "wall of separation" that was constitutionalized in *Everson.*

As indicated by Douglas Laycock's response to Rehnquist — which is also excerpted in Chapter 1 — Rehnquist's rendering of history is highly controversial. It is also unclear how much support remains for the nonpreferentialist approach after Chief Justice Rehnquist's departure from the Court. At least three of the current Justices seem to have embraced the approach. New Chief Justice Roberts, who replaced Rehnquist, wrote a memorandum discussing *Wallace v. Jaffree* while working for the Reagan Administration, in which he seems to have embraced Rehnquist's theory of the Establishment Clause. In describing Justice Rehnquist's dissent in that case, Roberts noted that Rehnquist "took a tenuous five-person majority and tried to revolutionize Establishment Clause jurisprudence, and ended up losing the majority." John G. Roberts, *Memorandum for Fred Fielding*, June 4, 1985, at 2, *available at* http://www.washingtonpost.com/wp-srv/nation/documents/roberts/Box48-JGR-SchoolPrayer1.pdf (last visited Feb. 13, 2006). Roberts then went on to praise Rehnquist's attempt to "revolutionize" the Establishment Clause jurisprudence by adopting the theory that the government may endorse religions, so long as it does not endorse a particular sect. "Which is not to say that the effort is misguided. In the larger scheme of things what is important is not whether this law is upheld or struck down, but what test is applied." *Id.*

The nonpreferentialist approach is also consistent with Justice Scalia's repeated statements that the Constitution allows the government to favor religion over nonreligion, *see McCreary Cty, Ky. v. American Civil Liberties Union of Ky.*, 125 S. Ct. 2722, 2748 (2005) (asserting that "the Court's oft repeated assertion that the government cannot favor religious practice is false"), and similar statements that the government may favor monotheism over polytheism, agnosticism, and atheism, *see id.* at 2753 (Scalia, J., dissenting) ("it is entirely clear from our Nation's historical practices that the Establishment Clause permits this disregard of polytheists and believers in unconcerned deities, just as it permits the disregard of devout atheists"). Justice Thomas joined the portions of Justice Scalia's opinion in which these statements appear.

H. THE NONINCORPORATION ANALYSIS

Justice Thomas's view that the Establishment Clause is not incorporated into the Fourteenth Amendment and therefore is not binding on the states is described fully in Chapter 1. He summarized his view in *Elk Grove United School District v. Newdow*, 542 U.S. 1, 50-51 (2004):

> Quite simply, the Establishment Clause is best understood as a federalism provision — it protects state establishments from federal interference but does not protect any individual right. These two features independently make incorporation of the Clause difficult to understand. The best argument in favor of incorporation would be that, by disabling Congress from establishing a national religion, the Clause protected an individual right, enforceable against the Federal Government, to be free from coercive federal establishments. Incorporation of this individual right, the argument goes, makes sense. I have alluded to this possibility before. *See Zelman, supra*, at 679 (Thomas, J., concurring) ("States may pass laws that include or touch on religious matters so long as these laws do not impede free exercise rights *or any other individual liberty interest*" (emphasis added)).

I. THE DIVISIVENESS ANALYSIS

In several recent cases, Justice Breyer has expressed concern about the potential for religious divisiveness in society as the barriers between church and state break down. In the following excerpts from *Zelman* and *Van Orden*, he discusses this concern in the context, respectively, of government financing of religion and government endorsement of religion. In some of the Court's earlier opinions, the concern with religious divisiveness was filtered through the entanglement prong of the three-part *Lemon* test. The excerpt from Justice O'Connor's *Lynch* opinion is an example of the recent resistance to this interpretation of *Lemon*.

ZELMAN v. SIMMONS-HARRIS
536 U.S. 639 (2002)

JUSTICE BREYER, with whom JUSTICE STEVENS AND JUSTICE SOUTER join, dissenting.

The principle underlying these cases — avoiding religiously based social conflict — remains of great concern. As religiously diverse as America had become when the Court decided its major 20th century Establishment Clause cases, we are exponentially more diverse today. America boasts more than 55 different religious groups and subgroups with a significant number of members. GRADUATE CENTER OF THE CITY OF NEW YORK, B. KOSMIN, E. MAYER, & A. KEYSAR, AMERICAN RELIGIOUS IDENTIFICATION SURVEY 12-13 (2001). Major religions include, among others, Protestants, Catholics, Jews, Muslims, Buddhists, Hindus, and Sikhs. *Ibid.* And several of these major religions contain different subsidiary sects with different religious beliefs. *See* Lester, *Oh, Gods!*, THE ATLANTIC MONTHLY 37 (Feb. 2002). Newer Christian immigrant groups are "expressing their Christianity in languages, customs, and independent churches that are barely recognizable, and often controversial, for European-ancestry Catholics and Protestants." H. EBAUGH & J. CHAFETZ, RELIGION AND THE NEW IMMIGRANTS: CONTINUITIES AND ADAPTATIONS IN IMMIGRANT CONGREGATIONS 4 (Abridged Student ed. 2002).

Under these modern-day circumstances, how is the "equal opportunity" principle to work — without risking the "struggle of sect against sect" against which Justice Rutledge warned? School voucher programs finance the religious education of the young. And, if widely adopted, they may well provide billions of dollars that will do so. Why will different religions not become concerned about, and seek to influence, the criteria used to channel this money to religious schools? Why will they not want to examine the implementation of the programs that provide this money — to determine, for example, whether implementation has biased a program toward or against particular sects, or whether recipient religious schools are adequately fulfilling a program's criteria? If so, just how is the State to resolve the resulting controversies without provoking legitimate fears of the kinds of religious favoritism that, in so religiously diverse a Nation, threaten social dissension?

In a society as religiously diverse as ours, the Court has recognized that we must rely on the Religion Clauses of the First Amendment to protect against religious strife, particularly when what is at issue is an area as central to religious belief as the shaping, through primary education, of the next generation's minds and spirits.

VAN ORDEN v. PERRY
125 S. Ct. 2854 (2005)

JUSTICE BREYER, concurring in the judgment.

[In this case the Court held that it was constitutional for the state of Texas to place a six-foot-high monolith containing one rendition of the Ten Commandments on the grounds of the Texas state capitol. Justice Breyer discussed several factors relating to the monolith, including the fact that there had been no major protests against it.]

As far as I can tell, 40 years passed in which the presence of this monument, legally speaking, went unchallenged (until the single legal objection raised by petitioner). And I am not aware of any evidence suggesting that this was due to a climate of intimidation. Hence, those 40 years suggest more strongly than can any set of formulaic tests that few individuals, whatever their system of beliefs, are likely to have understood the monument as amount-

[Margin note: Not strong Argument / Little objection]

ing, in any significantly detrimental way, to a government effort to favor a particular religious sect, primarily to promote religion over nonreligion, to "engage in" any "religious practic[e]," to "compel" any "religious practic[e]," or to "work deterrence" of any "religious belief." *Schempp* (Goldberg, J., concurring). Those 40 years suggest that the public visiting the capitol grounds has considered the religious aspect of the tablets' message as part of what is a broader moral and historical message reflective of a cultural heritage.

This case, moreover, is distinguishable from instances where the Court has found Ten Commandments displays impermissible. The display is not on the grounds of a public school, where, given the impressionability of the young, government must exercise particular care in separating church and state. This case also differs from *McCreary County*, where the short (and stormy) history of the courthouse Commandments' displays demonstrates the substantially religious objectives of those who mounted them, and the effect of this readily apparent objective upon those who view them. That history there indicates a governmental effort substantially to promote religion, not simply an effort primarily to reflect, historically, the secular impact of a religiously inspired document. And, in today's world, in a Nation of so many different religious and comparable nonreligious fundamental beliefs, a more contemporary state effort to focus attention upon a religious text is certainly likely to prove divisive in a way that this longstanding, pre-existing monument has not.

LYNCH v. DONNELLY
465 U.S. 668 (1984)

JUSTICE O'CONNOR, concurring.

In this case, as even the District Court found, there is no institutional entanglement. Nevertheless, the appellees contend that the political divisiveness caused by Pawtucket's display of its creche violates the excessive-entanglement prong of the *Lemon* test. The Court's opinion follows the suggestion in *Mueller v. Allen* [*infra* Chapter 8] and concludes that "no inquiry into potential political divisiveness is even called for" in this case. In my view, political divisiveness along religious lines should not be an independent test of constitutionality.

Although several of our cases have discussed political divisiveness under the entanglement prong of *Lemon, see, e.g., Committee for Public Education v. Nyquist* [*infra* Chapter 8]; *Lemon v. Kurtzman*, we have never relied on divisiveness as an independent ground for holding a government practice unconstitutional. Guessing the potential for political divisiveness inherent in a government practice is simply too speculative an enterprise, in part because the existence of the litigation, as this case illustrates, itself may affect the political response to the government practice. Political divisiveness is admittedly an evil addressed by the Establishment Clause. Its existence may be evidence that institutional entanglement is excessive or that a government practice is per-

[Margin note: Political Divisi Nothing to Do with entanglement]

ceived as an endorsement of religion. But the constitutional inquiry should focus ultimately on the character of the government activity that might cause such divisiveness, not on the divisiveness itself. The entanglement prong of the *Lemon* test is properly limited to institutional entanglement.

J. THE AD HOC ANALYSIS

Perhaps the best measure of how frustrating the search for a coherent Establishment Clause standard has become is the willingness of some Justices to give up the search altogether and resort to an unguided ad hoc approach to Establishment Clause jurisprudence. Justice O'Connor was the first modern Justice to suggest that no standard at all was preferable to any of the available alternatives, and with her departure from the Court, Justice Breyer has now picked up on this theme.

VAN ORDEN v. PERRY
125 S. Ct. 2854 (2005)

JUSTICE BREYER, concurring in the judgment.

[A]s Justices Goldberg and Harlan pointed out [in *Schempp*], the Court has found no single mechanical formula that can accurately draw the constitutional line in every case. Where the Establishment Clause is at issue, tests designed to measure "neutrality" alone are insufficient, both because it is sometimes difficult to determine when a legal rule is "neutral," and because "untutored devotion to the concept of neutrality can lead to invocation or approval of results which partake not simply of that noninterference and noninvolvement with the religious which the Constitution commands, but of a brooding and pervasive devotion to the secular and a passive, or even active, hostility to the religious."

Neither can this Court's other tests readily explain the Establishment Clause's tolerance, for example, of the prayers that open legislative meetings, see *Marsh, supra;* certain references to, and invocations of, the Deity in the public words of public officials; the public references to God on coins, decrees, and buildings; or the attention paid to the religious objectives of certain holidays, including Thanksgiving. *See, e.g., Lemon* (setting forth what has come to be known as the "*Lemon* test"); *Lynch* (O'Connor, J., concurring) (setting forth the "endorsement test"); *Capitol Square Review and Advisory Bd. v. Pinette* (Stevens, J., dissenting) (agreeing that an "endorsement test" should apply but criticizing its "reasonable observer" standard); *Santa Fe Independent School Dist. v. Doe,* (Rehnquist, C.J., dissenting) (noting *Lemon*'s "checkered career in the decisional law of this Court"); *County of Allegheny* (Kennedy, J., joined by Rehnquist, C.J., and White and Scalia, JJ., concurring in judgment in part and dissenting in part) (criticizing the *Lemon* test).

If the relation between government and religion is one of separation, but not of mutual hostility and suspicion, one will inevitably find difficult borderline cases. And in such cases, I see no test-related substitute for the exercise of legal judgment. That judgment is not a personal judgment. Rather, as in all constitutional cases, it must reflect and remain faithful to the underlying purposes of the Clauses, and it must take account of context and consequences measured in light of those purposes. While the Court's prior tests provide useful guideposts — and might well lead to the same result the Court reaches today; *Capitol Square* (O'Connor, J., concurring in part and concurring in judgment) — no exact formula can dictate a resolution to such fact-intensive cases.

BOARD OF EDUCATION OF KIRYAS JOEL v. GRUMET
512 U.S. 687 (1994)

[The state of New York created a special school district for religious enclave of Satmar Hasidim, practitioners of strict form of Judaism. The Court held that the state had violated the Establishment Clause by delegating the state's discretionary authority over public schools to a group defined by its common religion.]

JUSTICE O'CONNOR, concurring in part and concurring in the judgment.

III

I join Parts I, II-B, II-C, and III of the Court's opinion because I think this law, rather than being a general accommodation, singles out a particular religious group for favorable treatment. The Court's analysis of the history of this law and of the surrounding statutory scheme persuades me of this.

On its face, this statute benefits one group — the residents of Kiryas Joel. Because this benefit was given to this group based on its religion, it seems proper to treat it as a legislatively drawn religious classification. I realize this is a close question, because the Satmars may be the only group who currently need this particular accommodation. The legislature may well be acting without any favoritism, so that if another group came to ask for a similar district, the group might get it on the same terms as the Satmars. But the nature of the legislative process makes it impossible to be sure of this. A legislature, unlike the judiciary or many administrative decisionmakers, has no obligation to respond to any group's requests. A group petitioning for a law may never get a definite response, or may get a "no" based not on the merits but on the press of other business or the lack of an influential sponsor. Such a legislative refusal to act would not normally be reviewable by a court. Under these circumstances, it seems dangerous to validate what appears to me a clear religious preference.

Our invalidation of this statute in no way means that the Satmars' needs cannot be accommodated. There is nothing improper about a legislative intention to accommodate a religious group, so long as it is implemented through generally applicable legislation. New York may, for instance, allow all villages to operate their own school districts. If it does not want to act so broadly, it may set forth neutral criteria that a village must meet to have a school district of its own; these criteria can then be applied by a state agency, and the decision would then be reviewable by the judiciary. A district created under a generally applicable scheme would be acceptable even though it coincides with a village which was consciously created by its voters as an enclave for their religious group. I do not think the Court's opinion holds the contrary.

IV

One aspect of the Court's opinion in this case is worth noting: Like the opinions in two recent cases, *Lee v. Weisman* [*infra* Chapter 6]; *Zobrest v. Catalina Foothills School Dist.* [discussed in Chapter 9, *infra*], and the case I think is most relevant to this one, *Larson v. Valente*, 456 U.S. 228 (1982), the Court's opinion does not focus on the Establishment Clause test we set forth in *Lemon v. Kurtzman*.

It is always appealing to look for a single test, a Grand Unified Theory that would resolve all the cases that may arise under a particular clause. There is, after all, only one Establishment Clause, one Free Speech Clause, one Fourth Amendment, one Equal Protection Clause.

But the same constitutional principle may operate very differently in different contexts. We have, for instance, no one Free Speech Clause test. We have different tests for content-based speech restrictions, for content-neutral speech restrictions, for restrictions imposed by the government acting as employer, for restrictions in nonpublic fora, and so on. This simply reflects the necessary recognition that the interests relevant to the Free Speech Clause inquiry — personal liberty, an informed citizenry, government efficiency, public order, and so on — are present in different degrees in each context.

And setting forth a unitary test for a broad set of cases may sometimes do more harm than good. Any test that must deal with widely disparate situations risks being so vague as to be useless. I suppose one can say that the general test for all free speech cases is "a regulation is valid if the interests asserted by the government are stronger than the interests of the speaker and the listeners," but this would hardly be a serviceable formulation. Similarly, *Lemon* has, with some justification, been criticized on this score.

Moreover, shoehorning new problems into a test that does not reflect the special concerns raised by those problems tends to deform the language of the test. Relatively simple phrases like "primary effect. . . that neither advances nor inhibits religion" and "entanglement," *Lemon*, acquire more and more complicated definitions which stray ever further from their literal meaning. Distinctions are drawn between statutes whose effect is to advance religion and statutes whose effect is to allow religious organizations to advance religion. *See, e.g., Corporation of Presiding Bishop of Church of Jesus Christ of Latter-day Saints v. Amos* [*infra* Chapter 12]. Assertions are made that authorizing churches to veto liquor sales in surrounding areas "can be seen as having a 'primary' and 'principal' effect of advancing religion." *Larkin v. Grendel's Den, Inc.*, 459 U.S. 116, 125-126 (1982). "Entanglement" is discovered in public employers monitoring the performance of public employees — surely a proper enough function — on parochial school premises, and in the public employees cooperating with the school on class scheduling and other administrative details. Alternatives to *Lemon* suffer from a similar failing when they lead us to find "coercive pressure" to pray when a school asks listeners — with no threat of legal sanctions — to stand or remain silent during a graduation prayer. *Lee v. Weisman* [*infra* Chapter 6]. Some of the results and perhaps even some of the reasoning in these cases may have been right. I joined two of the cases cited above, *Larkin* and *Lee*, and continue to believe they were correctly decided. But I think it is more useful to recognize the relevant concerns in each case on their own terms, rather than trying to squeeze them into language that does not really apply to them.

Finally, another danger to keep in mind is that the bad test may drive out the good. Rather than taking the opportunity to derive narrower, more precise tests from the case law, courts tend to continually try to patch up the broad test, making it more and more amorphous and distorted. This, I am afraid, has happened with *Lemon*.   CRitic

Experience proves that the Establishment Clause, like the Free Speech Clause, cannot easily be reduced to a single test. There are different categories of Establishment Clause cases, which may call for different approaches. Some cases, like this one, involve government actions targeted at particular individuals or groups, imposing special duties or giving special benefits. Cases involving government speech on religious topics, *see, e.g., Lee v. Weisman* [*infra* Chapter 6]; *Allegheny County v. American Civil Liberties Union Greater Pittsburgh Chapter* [*infra* Chapter 7]; *Lynch v. Donnelly* [*infra* Chapter 7]; *Stone v. Graham*, 449 U.S. 39 (1980), seem to me to fall into a different category and to require an analysis focusing on whether the speech endorses or disapproves of religion, rather than on whether the government action is neutral with regard to religion.

Another category encompasses cases in which the government must make decisions about matters of religious doctrine and religious law. *See Serbian Eastern Orthodox Diocese v. Milivojevich* [*infra* Chapter 10] (which also did not apply *Lemon*). These cases, which often arise in the application of otherwise neutral property or contract principles to religious institutions, involve complicated questions not present in other situations. *See, e.g., id.* (looking at some aspects of religious law to determine the structure of the church, but refusing to look further into religious law to resolve the ultimate dispute). Government delegations of power to religious bodies may make up yet another category. As *Larkin* itself suggested, government impartiality towards religion may not be enough in such situations: A law that bars all alcohol sales within some distance of a church, school, or hospital may be valid, but an equally evenhanded law that gives each institution discretionary power over the sales may not be. *Larkin, supra,* 459 U.S., at 123-124. Of course, there may well be additional categories, or more opportune places to draw the lines between the categories.

As the Court's opinion today shows, the slide away from *Lemon's* unitary approach is well under way. A return to *Lemon*, even if possible, would likely be futile, regardless of where one stands on the substantive Establishment Clause questions. I think a less unitary approach provides a better structure for analysis. If each test covers a narrower and more homogeneous area, the tests may be more precise and therefore easier to apply. There may be more opportunity to pay attention to the specific nuances of each area. There might also be, I hope, more consensus on each of the narrow tests than there has been on a broad test. And abandoning the *Lemon* framework need not mean abandoning some of the insights that the test reflected, nor the insights of the cases that applied it.

Perhaps eventually under this structure we may indeed distill a unified, or at least a more unified, Establishment Clause test from the cases. But it seems to me that the case law will better be able to evolve towards this if it is freed from the *Lemon* test's rigid influence. The hard questions would, of course, still have to be asked; but they will be asked within a more carefully tailored and less distorted framework.

NOTE ON THE DIFFICULTIES OF MODERN ESTABLISHMENT CLAUSE ANALYSIS IN THE LOWER COURTS

However much an ad hoc approach might appeal to Justices overwhelmed by the task of making sense of the diversity of contexts in which Establishment Clause issues arise, such an approach is best described as a nightmare for lower court judges trying to ascertain what analysis the Supreme Court wants them to apply in a particular case. In the face of Supreme Court confusion and contradiction regarding the precise nature of Establishment Clause analysis, some lower courts have simply thrown up their hands and resorted to applying several different tests in each case. *See, e.g., Van Zandt v. Thompson,* 839 F.2d 1215 (7th Cir. 1988); *Albright v. Board of Educ. of Granite Sch. Dist.,* 765 F. Supp. 682, 689 (D. Utah 1991). The Fifth Circuit Court of Appeals has even formalized this approach. *See Freiler v. Tangipahoa Parish Bd. of Educ.,* 185 F.3d 337, 343 (5th Cir. 1999) (analyzing public school evolution disclaimer under *Lemon* and endorsement tests): "Our multi-test analysis in past cases has resulted from an Establishment Clause jurisprudence rife with confusion and from our own desire to be both complete and judicious in our decision-making." *See also Doe ex rel. Doe v. Beaumont Independent School District,* 173 F.3d 274, 295 (5th Cir. 1999) (analyzing school district's "Clergy in Schools" volunteer counseling program under *Lemon,* endorsement, and coercion tests); *Ingebretsen v. Jackson Public School District,* 88 F.3d 274, 280 (5th Cir. 1996) (examining state statute permitting prayer at public school school events under *Lemon,* endorsement, and coercion tests); *Jones v. Clear Creek Ind. Sch. Dist.,* 977 F.2d 963, 966-69, 972 (5th Cir. 1992) (analyzing graduation prayer at public school graduation ceremonies under *Lemon,* endorsement, and coercion tests); *Doe v. Santa Fe Independent School District,* 168 F.3d 806, 818 (5th Cir.

1999), *aff'd*, 530 U.S. 290 (2000) (analyzing policy regarding student prayer at public school football games under *Lemon* and endorsement tests).

By a happy coincidence, these various tests tend to all come out the same way in each case, which indicates either that the tests are not really different from each other after all, or that the courts are bending the tests to produce a false consistency. One Fifth Circuit panel has more or less acknowledged that the real consequence of this smorgasbord of legal standards is the very sort of ad hoc analysis that Justice O'Connor recommended in her *Kiryas Joel* concurrence. In rejecting an Establishment Clause challenge to the inclusion of a Christian cross in the Austin, Texas city insignia, the Fifth Circuit panel noted that "In so holding, we obviously cannot fashion a bright line test to apply in future challenges to government use or depiction of religious symbols. Instead, as we must, we decide only the case before us." *See Murray v. Austin*, 947 F.2d 147, 158 (5th Cir. 1991), *cert. denied*, 505 U.S. 1219 (1992). Is it fair to say that the Fifth Circuit's opinion in *Murray* has no precedential value, since according to the principles of that decision, every new case will turn on what the Fifth Circuit calls "the totality of its unique facts and circumstances"? *Id.* As a practical matter, does this mean that every case must be litigated to enforce the Establishment Clause? As a theoretical matter, if every case is decided entirely ad hoc, is there really any Establishment Clause standard at all?

Does all this really produce what William Marshall once called a "we know it when we see it" Establishment Clause jurisprudence? William P. Marshall, *"We Know It When We See It": The Supreme Court and Establishment,* 59 S. CAL. L. REV. 495 (1986). "[T]he [Court's] new term left establishment jurisprudence essentially in the same condition it had been in before; a patchwork of ad hoc decisions inside a legal framework that had long before lost its intellectual integrity." *Id.* at 498. Does this description of the Establishment Clause landscape in 1985 still apply over two decades later?

Chapter 6

EXPLICIT GOVERNMENT ENDORSEMENT OF RELIGION — THE SCHOOL PRAYER CASES

A. PRAYER IN THE CLASSROOM

In many respects, the Supreme Court's school prayer decisions in the early sixties are where modern Establishment Clause jurisprudence really begins. Certainly these are the cases that non-lawyers tend to focus on when discussing the constitutional relationship between church and state. From a bottom-line litigator's perspective, the outcomes of these cases have been remarkably uniform. The Supreme Court has issued five decisions on the subject of school prayer or school Bible-reading, and in every case a large majority of the Court has held the religious exercise unconstitutional. At the same time, popular opposition to these decisions remains strong in some quarters, and the more recent school prayer cases have generated some of the most vociferous dissents of any Religion Clause decisions in the Court's history.

The problems posed by prayer in public schools are illustrated in a series of decisions reproduced *infra* from the United States Court of Appeals for the Fifth Circuit. In the first of these decisions, the Fifth Circuit upheld a graduation prayer exercise at a public school, in an opinion that seems to reject many of the separationist principles of the Supreme Court's school prayer decisions. In subsequent cases, however, the Fifth Circuit has been forced to confront other, more pervasive religious exercises in public schools. In these cases, the Fifth Circuit has held the religious exercises unconstitutional, in opinions that return to the themes of separation and the protection of religious dissent.

Finally, in reading *Tanford v. Brand*, consider whether the Court's insistence on protecting religious dissenters from mandatory exposure to the religious exercises of the religious majority is limited to younger children. If so, then how can the courts explain the different constitutional rules? If not, then how can the courts explain the decisions in the next Chapter?

ENGEL v. VITALE
370 U.S. 421 (1962)

MR. JUSTICE BLACK delivered the opinion of the Court.

The respondent Board of Education of Union Free School District No. 9, New Hyde Park, New York, acting in its official capacity under state law, directed the School District's principal to cause the following prayer to be said aloud by each class in the presence of a teacher at the beginning of each school day:

"Almighty God, we acknowledge our dependence upon Thee, and we beg Thy blessings upon us, our parents, our teachers and our Country."

This daily procedure was adopted on the recommendation of the State Board of Regents, a governmental agency created by the State Constitution to which the New York Legislature has granted broad supervisory, executive, and legislative powers over the State's public school system. These state officials composed the prayer which they recommended and published as a part of their "Statement on Moral and Spiritual Training in the Schools," saying: "We believe that this Statement will be subscribed to by all men and women of good will, and we call upon all of them to aid in giving life to our program."

Shortly after the practice of reciting the Regents' prayer was adopted by the School District, the parents of ten pupils brought this action in a New York State Court insisting that use of this official prayer in the public schools was contrary to the beliefs, religions, or religious practices of both themselves and their children. The New York Court of Appeals, over the dissents of Judges Dye and Fuld, sustained an order of the lower state courts which had upheld the power of New York to use the Regents' prayer as a part of the daily procedures of its public schools so long as the schools did not compel any pupil to join in the prayer over his or his parents' objection.[2]

We think that by using its public school system to encourage recitation of the Regents' prayer, the State of New York has adopted a practice wholly inconsistent with the Establishment Clause. There can, of course, be no doubt that New York's program of daily classroom invocation of God's blessings as prescribed in the Regents' prayer is a religious activity. It is a solemn avowal of divine faith and supplication for the blessings of the Almighty. The nature of

---

[2] The trial court's opinion, which is reported at 18 Misc.2d 659, 191 N.Y.S.2d 453, had made it clear that the Board of Education must set up some sort of procedures to protect those who objected to reciting the prayer: "This is not to say that the rights accorded petitioners and their children under the 'free exercise' clause do not mandate safeguards against such embarrassments and pressures. It is enough on this score, however, that regulations, such as were adopted by New York City's Board of Education in connection with its released time program, be adopted, making clear that neither teachers nor any other school authority may comment on participation or non-participation in the exercise nor suggest or require that any posture or language be used or dress be worn or be not used or not worn. Non-participation may take the form either of remaining silent during the exercise, or if the parent or child so desires, of being excused entirely from the exercise. Such regulations must also make provision for those non-participants who are to be excused from the prayer exercise. The exact provision to be made is a matter for decision by the Board, rather than the Court, within the framework of constitutional requirements. Within that framework would fall a provision that prayer participants proceed to a common assembly while non-participants attend other rooms, or that non-participants be permitted to arrive at school a few minutes late or to attend separate opening exercises, or any other method which treats with equality both participants and non-participants." 18 Misc.2d, at 696, 191 N.Y.S.2d, at 492-493.

such a prayer has always been religious, none of the respondents has denied this and the trial court expressly so found.

The petitioners contend among other things that the state laws requiring or permitting use of the Regents' prayer must be struck down as a violation of the Establishment Clause because that prayer was composed by governmental officials as a part of a governmental program to further religious beliefs. For this reason, petitioners argue, the State's use of the Regents' prayer in its public school system breaches the constitutional wall of separation between Church and State. We agree with that contention since we think that the constitutional prohibition against laws respecting an establishment of religion must at least mean that in this country it is no part of the business of government to compose official prayers for any group of the American people to recite as a part of a religious program carried on by government.

It is a matter of history that this very practice of establishing governmentally composed prayers for religious services was one of the reasons which caused many of our early colonists to leave England and seek religious freedom in America. The Book of Common Prayer, which was created under governmental direction and which was approved by Acts of Parliament in 1548 and 1549, set out in minute detail the accepted form and content of prayer and other religious ceremonies to be used in the established, tax-supported Church of England. The controversies over the Book and what should be its content repeatedly threatened to disrupt the peace of that country as the accepted forms of prayer in the established church changed with the views of the particular ruler that happened to be in control at the time. Powerful groups representing some of the varying religious views of the people struggled among themselves to impress their particular views upon the Government and obtain amendments of the Book more suitable to their respective notions of how religious services should be conducted in order that the official religious establishment would advance their particular religious beliefs. Other groups, lacking the necessary political power to influence the Government on the matter, decided to leave England and its established church and seek freedom in America from England's governmentally ordained and supported religion.

By the time of the adoption of the Constitution, our history shows that there was a widespread awareness among many Americans of the dangers of a union of Church and State. These people knew, some of them from bitter personal experience, that one of the greatest dangers to the freedom of the individual to worship in his own way lay in the Government's placing its official stamp of approval upon one particular kind of prayer or one particular form of religious services. They knew the anguish, hardship and bitter strife that could come when zealous religious groups struggled with one another to obtain the Government's stamp of approval from each King, Queen, or Protector that came to temporary power. The Constitution was intended to avert a part of this danger by leaving the government of this country in the hands of the people rather than in the hands of any monarch. But this safeguard was not enough. Our Founders were no more willing to let the content of their prayers and their privilege of praying whenever they pleased be influenced by the ballot box than they were to let these vital matters of personal conscience depend upon the succession of monarchs. The First Amendment was added to the Constitution to stand as a guarantee that neither the power nor the prestige of the Federal Government would be used to control, support or influence the kinds of prayer the American people can say — that the people's religions must not be subjected to the pressures of government for change each time a new political administration is elected to office. Under that Amendment's prohibition against governmental establishment of religion, as reinforced by the provisions of the Fourteenth Amendment, government in this country, be it state or federal, is without power to prescribe by law any particular form of prayer which is to be used as an official prayer in carrying on any program of governmentally sponsored religious activity.

There can be no doubt that New York's state prayer program officially establishes the religious beliefs embodied in the Regents' prayer. The respondents' argument to the contrary, which is largely based upon the contention that the Regents' prayer is "nondenominational" and the fact that the program, as modified and approved by state courts, does not require all pupils to recite the prayer but permits those who wish to do so to remain silent or be excused from the room, ignores the essential nature of the program's constitutional defects. Neither the fact that the prayer may be denominationally neutral nor the fact that its observance on the part of the students is voluntary can serve to free it from the limitations of the Establishment Clause, as it might from the Free Exercise Clause, of the First Amendment, both of which are operative against the States by virtue of the Fourteenth Amendment. Although these two clauses may in certain instances overlap, they forbid two quite different kinds of governmental encroachment upon religious freedom. The Establishment Clause, unlike the Free Exercise Clause, does not depend upon any showing of direct governmental compulsion and is violated by the enactment of laws which establish an official religion whether those laws operate directly to coerce nonobserving individuals or not. This is not to say, of course, that laws officially prescribing a particular form of religious worship do not involve coercion of such individuals. When the power, prestige and financial support of government is placed behind a particular religious belief, the indirect coercive pressure upon religious minorities to conform to the prevailing officially approved religion is plain. But the purposes underlying the Establishment Clause go much further than that. Its first and most immediate purpose rested on the belief that a union of government and religion tends to destroy government and to degrade religion. The history of governmentally established religion, both in England and in this country, showed that whenever government had allied itself with one particular form of religion, the inevitable result had been that it had incurred the hatred, disrespect and even contempt of those who held contrary beliefs. That same history showed that many people had lost their respect for any religion that had relied upon the support for government to spread its faith. The

Establishment Clause thus stands as an expression of principle on the part of the Founders of our Constitution that religion is too personal, too sacred, too holy, to permit its "unhallowed perversion" by a civil magistrate. Another purpose of the Establishment Clause rested upon an awareness of the historical fact that governmentally established religions and religious persecutions go hand in hand. The Founders knew that only a few years after the Book of Common Prayer became the only accepted form of religious services in the established Church of England, an Act of Uniformity was passed to compel all Englishmen to attend those services and to make it a criminal offense to conduct or attend religious gatherings of any other kind — a law which was consistently flouted by dissenting religious groups in England and which contributed to widespread persecutions of people like John Bunyan who persisted in holding "unlawful [religious] meetings . . . to the great disturbance and distraction of the good subjects of this kingdom. . . ." And they knew that similar persecutions had received the sanction of law in several of the colonies in this country soon after the establishment of official religions in those colonies. It was in large part to get completely away from this sort of systematic religious persecution that the Founders brought into being our Nation, our Constitution, and our Bill of Rights with its prohibition against any governmental establishment of religion. The New York laws officially prescribing the Regents' prayer are inconsistent both with the purposes of the Establishment Clause and with the Establishment Clause itself.

It has been argued that to apply the Constitution in such a way as to prohibit state laws respecting an establishment of religious services in public schools is to indicate a hostility toward religion or toward prayer. Nothing, or course, could be more wrong. The history of man is inseparable from the history of religion. And perhaps it is not too much to say that since the beginning of that history many people have devoutly believed that "More things are wrought by prayer than this world dreams of." It was doubtless largely due to men who believed this that there grew up a sentiment that caused men to leave the cross-currents of officially established state religions and religious persecution in Europe and come to this country filled with the hope that they could find a place in which they could pray when they pleased to the God of their faith in the language they chose. And there were men of this same faith in the power of prayer who led the fight for adoption of our Constitution and also for our Bill of Rights with the very guarantees of religious freedom that forbid the sort of governmental activity which New York has attempted here. These men knew that the First Amendment, which tried to put an end to governmental control of religion and of prayer, was not written to destroy either. They knew rather that it was written to quiet well-justified fears which nearly all of them felt arising out of an awareness that governments of the past had shackled men's tongues to make them speak only the religious thoughts that government wanted them to speak and to pray only to the God that government wanted them to pray to. It is neither sacrilegious nor antireligious to say that each separate government in this country should stay out of the business of writing or sanctioning official prayers and leave that purely religious function to the people themselves and to those the people choose to look to for religious guidance.[21]

It is true that New York's establishment of its Regents' prayer as an officially approved religious doctrine of that State does not amount to a total establishment of one particular religious sect to the exclusion of all others — that, indeed, the governmental endorsement of that prayer seems relatively insignificant when compared to the governmental encroachments upon religion which were commonplace 200 years ago. To those who may subscribe to the view that because the Regents' official prayer is so brief and general there can be no danger to religious freedom in its governmental establishment, however, it may be appropriate to say in the words of James Madison, the author of the First Amendment:

> "[I]t is proper to take alarm at the first experiment on our liberties. . . . Who does not see that the same authority which can establish Christianity, in exclusion of all other Religions, may establish with the same ease any particular sect of Christians, in exclusion of all other Sects? That the same authority which can force a citizen to contribute three pence only of his property for the support of any one establishment, may force him to conform to any other establishment in all cases whatsoever?"

MR. JUSTICE STEWART, dissenting.

A local school board in New York has provided that those pupils who wish to do so may join in a brief prayer at the beginning of each school day, acknowledging their dependence upon God and asking His blessing upon them and upon their parents, their teachers, and their country. The Court today decides that in permitting this brief non-denominational prayer the school board has violated the Constitution of the United States. I think this decision is wrong.

The Court does not hold, nor could it, that New York has interfered with the free exercise of anybody's religion. For the state courts have made clear that those who object to reciting the prayer must be entirely free of any compulsion to do so, including any "embarrassments and pressures." Cf. *West Virginia State Board of Education v. Barnette*, 319 U.S. 624. But the Court says that in permitting school children to say this simple prayer, the New York authorities have established "an official religion."

---

[21] There is of course nothing in the decision reached here that is inconsistent with the fact that school children and others are officially encouraged to express love for our country by reciting historical documents such as the Declaration of Independence which contain references to the Deity or by singing officially espoused anthems which include the composer's professions of faith in a Supreme Being, or with the fact that there are many manifestations in our public life of belief in God. Such patriotic or ceremonial occasions bear no true resemblance to the unquestioned religious exercise that the State of New York has sponsored in this instance.

With all respect, I think the Court has misapplied a great constitutional principle. I cannot see how an "official religion" is established by letting those who want to say a prayer say it. On the contrary, I think that to deny the wish of these school children to join in reciting this prayer is to deny them the opportunity of sharing in the spiritual heritage of our Nation.

The Court's historical review of the quarrels over the Book of Common Prayer in England throws no light for me on the issue before us in this case. England had then and has now an established church. Equally unenlightening, I think, is the history of the early establishment and later rejection of an official church in our own States. For we deal here not with the establishment of a state church, which would, of course, be constitutionally impermissible, but with whether school children who want to begin their day by joining in prayer must be prohibited from doing so. Moreover, I think that the Court's task, in this as in all areas of constitutional adjudication, is not responsibly aided by the uncritical invocation of metaphors like the "wall of separation," a phrase nowhere to be found in the Constitution. What is relevant to the issue here is not the history of an established church in sixteenth century England or in eighteenth century America, but the history of the religious traditions of our people, reflected in countless practices of the institutions and officials of our government.

At the opening of each day's Session of this Court we stand, while one of our officials invokes the protection of God. Since the days of John Marshall our Crier has said, "God save the United States and this Honorable Court." Both the Senate and the House of Representatives open their daily Sessions with prayer. Each of our Presidents, from George Washington to John F. Kennedy, has upon assuming his Office asked the protection and help of God.

The Court today says that the state and federal governments are without constitutional power to prescribe any particular form of words to be recited by any group of the American people on any subject touching religion. One of the stanzas of "The Star-Spangled Banner," made our National Anthem by Act of Congress in 1931, contains these verses:

> Blest with victory and peace, may the heav'n rescued land
> Praise the Pow'r that hath made and preserved us a nation!
> Then conquer we must, when our cause it is just,
> And this be our motto "In God is our Trust."

In 1954 Congress added a phrase to the Pledge of Allegiance to the Flag so that it now contains the words "one Nation *under God,* indivisible, with liberty and justice for all." In 1952 Congress enacted legislation calling upon the President each year to proclaim a National Day of Prayer. Since 1865 the words "IN GOD WE TRUST" have been impressed on our coins.

Countless similar examples could be listed, but there is no need to belabor the obvious. It was all summed up by this Court just ten years ago in a single sentence: "We are a religious people whose institutions presuppose a Supreme Being." *Zorach v. Clauson,* 343 U.S. 306, 313.

I do not believe that this Court, or the Congress, or the President has by the actions and practices I have mentioned established an "official religion" in violation of the Constitution. And I do not believe the State of New York has done so in this case. What each has done has been to recognize and to follow the deeply entrenched and highly cherished spiritual traditions of our Nation — traditions which come down to us from those who almost two hundred years ago avowed their "firm Reliance on the Protection of divine Providence" when they proclaimed the freedom and independence of this brave new world.

SCHOOL DISTRICT OF ABINGTON TOWNSHIP v. SCHEMPP
374 U.S. 203 (1963)

MR. JUSTICE CLARK delivered the opinion of the Court.

Once again we are called upon to consider the scope of the provision of the First Amendment to the United States Constitution which declares that "Congress shall make no law respecting an establishment of religion, or prohibiting the free exercise thereof. . . ." These companion cases present the issues in the context of state action requiring that schools begin each day with readings from the Bible.

I.

[A Pennsylvania statute] requires that "At least ten verses from the Holy Bible shall be read, without comment, at the opening of each public school on each school day. Any child shall be excused from such Bible reading, or attending such Bible reading, upon the written request of his parent or guardian." The Schempp family, husband and wife and two of their three children, brought suit to enjoin enforcement of the statute, contending that their rights under the Fourteenth Amendment to the Constitution of the United States are, have been, and will continue to be violated unless this statute be declared unconstitutional as violative of these provisions of the First Amendment. The appellees Edward Lewis Schempp, his wife Sidney, and their children, Roger and Donna, are of the Unitarian faith and are members of the Unitarian Church in Germantown, Philadelphia, Pennsylvania, where they, as well as another son, Ellory, regularly attend religious services.

On each school day at the Abington Senior High School between 8:15 and 8:30 a.m., while the pupils are attending their home rooms or advisory sections, opening exercises are conducted pursuant to the statute. The exercises are broadcast into each room in the school building through an intercommunications system and are conducted under the supervision of a teacher by students attending the school's radio and television workshop. Selected students from this course gather each morning in the school's workshop studio for the exercises, which include readings by one of the students of 10 verses of the Holy Bible, broadcast to each room in the building. This is followed by the recitation of the

Lord's Prayer, likewise over the intercommunications system, but also by the students in the various classrooms, who are asked to stand and join in repeating the prayer in unison. The exercises are closed with the flag salute and such pertinent announcements as are of interest to the students. Participation in the opening exercises, as directed by the statute, is voluntary. The student reading the verses from the Bible may select the passages and read from any version he chooses, although the only copies furnished by the school are the King James version, copies of which were circulated to each teacher by the school district. During the period in which the exercises have been conducted the King James, the Douay and the Revised Standard versions of the Bible have been used, as well as the Jewish Holy Scriptures. There are no prefatory statements, no questions asked or solicited, no comments or explanations made and no interpretations given at or during the exercises. The students and parents are advised that the student may absent himself from the classroom or, should he elect to remain, not participate in the exercises.

At the first trial Edward Schempp and the children testified as to specific religious doctrines purveyed by a literal reading of the Bible "which were contrary to the religious beliefs which they held and to their familial teaching." The children testified that all of the doctrines to which they referred were read to them at various times as part of the exercises. Edward Schempp testified at the second trial that he had considered having Roger and Donna excused from attendance at the exercises but decided against it for several reasons, including his belief that the children's relationships with their teachers and classmates would be adversely affected.

V.

The wholesome "neutrality" of which this Court's cases speak thus stems from a recognition of the teachings of history that powerful sects or groups might bring about a fusion of governmental and religious functions or a concert or dependency of one upon the other to the end that official support of the State or Federal Government would be placed behind the tenets of one or of all orthodoxies. This the Establishment Clause prohibits. And a further reason for neutrality is found in the Free Exercise Clause, which recognizes the value of religious training, teaching and observance and, more particularly, the right of every person to freely choose his own course with reference thereto, free of any compulsion from the state. This the Free Exercise Clause guarantees. Thus, as we have seen, the two clauses may overlap. As we have indicated, the Establishment Clause has been directly considered by this Court eight times in the past score of years and, with only one Justice dissenting on the point, it has consistently held that the clause withdrew all legislative power respecting religious belief or the expression thereof. The test may be stated as follows: what are the purpose and the primary effect of the enactment? If either is the advancement or inhibition of religion then the enactment exceeds the scope of legislative power as circumscribed by the Constitution. That is to say that to withstand the strictures of the Establishment Clause there must be a secular legislative purpose and a primary effect that neither advances nor inhibits religion. *Everson v. Board of Education; McGowan v. Maryland, supra,* 366 U.S. at 442. The Free Exercise Clause, likewise considered many times here, withdraws from legislative power, state and federal, the exertion of any restraint on the free exercise of religion. Its purpose is to secure religious liberty in the individual by prohibiting any invasions thereof by civil authority. Hence it is necessary in a free exercise case for one to show the coercive effect of the enactment as it operates against him in the practice of his religion. The distinction between the two clauses is apparent — a violation of the Free Exercise Clause is predicated on coercion while the Establishment Clause violation need not be so attended.

Applying the Establishment Clause principles to the cases at bar we find that the States are requiring the selection and reading at the opening of the school day of verses from the Holy Bible and the recitation of the Lord's Prayer by the students in unison. These exercises are prescribed as part of the curricular activities of students who are required by law to attend school. They are held in the school buildings under the supervision and with the participation of teachers employed in those schools. The trial court has found that such an opening exercise is a religious ceremony and was intended by the State to be so. We agree with the trial court's finding as to the religious character of the exercises. Given that finding, the exercises and the law requiring them are in violation of the Establishment Clause.

[T]he State contends that the program is an effort to extend its benefits to all public school children without regard to their religious belief. Included within its secular purposes, it says, are the promotion of moral values, the contradiction to the materialistic trends of our times, the perpetuation of our institutions and the teaching of literature. The case came up on demurrer, of course, to a petition which alleged that the uniform practice under the rule had been to read from the King James version of the Bible and that the exercise was sectarian. The short answer, therefore, is that the religious character of the exercise was admitted by the State. But even if its purpose is not strictly religious, it is sought to be accomplished through readings, without comment, from the Bible. Surely the place of the Bible as an instrument of religion cannot be gainsaid, and the State's recognition of the pervading religious character of the ceremony is evident from the rule's specific permission of the alternative use of the Catholic Douay version as well as the recent amendment permitting nonattendance at the exercises. None of these factors is consistent with the contention that the Bible is here used either as an instrument for nonreligious moral inspiration or as a reference for the teaching of secular subjects.

The conclusion follows that in both cases the laws require religious exercises and such exercises are being conducted in direct violation of the rights of the appellees and petitioners. Nor are these required exercises mitigated by the fact that individual students may absent themselves upon parental request, for that fact furnishes no defense to a claim of unconstitutionality under the Establishment Clause. *See Engel v. Vitale.* Further, it is no defense to urge that the religious practices here may be relatively minor encroachments on the First Amendment. The breach of neutrality that is today a trickling stream may all too soon become a raging torrent and, in the words of Madison, "it is proper to take alarm at the first experiment on our liberties." *Memorial and Remonstrance Against Religious Assessments.*

It is insisted that unless these religious exercises are permitted a "religion of secularism" is established in the schools. We agree of course that the State may not establish a "religion of secularism" in the sense of affirmatively opposing or showing hostility to religion, thus "preferring those who believe in no religion over those who do believe." *Zorach v. Clauson, supra*, 343 U.S. at 314. We do not agree, however, that this decision in any sense has that effect. In addition, it might well be said that one's education is not complete without a study of comparative religion or the history of religion and its relationship to the advancement of civilization. It certainly may be said that the Bible is worthy of study for its literary and historic qualities. Nothing we have said here indicates that such study of the Bible or of religion, when presented objectively as part of a secular program of education, may not be effected consistently with the First Amendment. But the exercises here do not fall into those categories. They are religious exercises, required by the States in violation of the command of the First Amendment that the Government maintain strict neutrality, neither aiding nor opposing religion.

Finally, we cannot accept that the concept of neutrality, which does not permit a State to require a religious exercise even with the consent of the majority of those affected, collides with the majority's right to free exercise of religion.[10] While the Free Exercise Clause clearly prohibits the use of state action to deny the rights of free exercise to *anyone*, it has never meant that a majority could use the machinery of the State to practice its beliefs. Such a contention was effectively answered by Mr. Justice Jackson for the Court in *West Virginia Board of Education v. Barnette*:

> "The very purpose of a Bill of Rights was to withdraw certain subjects from the vicissitudes of political controversy, to place them beyond the reach of majorities and officials and to establish them as legal principles to be applied by the courts. One's right to . . . freedom of worship . . . and other fundamental rights may not be submitted to vote; they depend on the outcome of no elections."

The place of religion in our society is an exalted one, achieved through a long tradition of reliance on the home, the church and the inviolable citadel of

---

[10] We are not of course presented with and therefore do not pass upon a situation such as military service, where the Government regulates the temporal and geographic environment of individuals to a point that, unless it permits voluntary religious services to be conducted with the use of government facilities, military personnel would be unable to engage in the practice of their faiths.

the individual heart and mind. We have come to recognize through bitter experience that it is not within the power of government to invade that citadel, whether its purpose or effect be to aid or oppose, to advance or retard. In the relationship between man and religion, the State is firmly committed to a position of neutrality. Though the application of that rule requires interpretation of a delicate sort, the rule itself is clearly and concisely stated in the words of the First Amendment.

MR. JUSTICE BRENNAN, concurring.

[After reviewing the history and theory of the Religion Clauses, Justice Brennan addressed the arguments in favor of Bible-reading in public schools.]

A.

First, it is argued that however clearly religious may have been the origins and early nature of daily prayer and Bible reading, these practices today serve so clearly secular educational purposes that their religious attributes may be overlooked. I do not doubt, for example, that morning devotional exercises may foster better discipline in the classroom, and elevate the spiritual level on which the school day opens. The Pennsylvania Superintendent of Public Instruction, testifying by deposition in the *Schempp* case, offered his view that daily Bible reading "places upon the children or those hearing the reading of this, and the atmosphere which goes on in the reading . . . one of the last vestiges of moral value that we have left in our school system." The exercise thus affords, the Superintendent concluded, "a strong contradiction to the materialistic trends of our time." Baltimore's Superintendent of Schools expressed a similar view of the practices challenged in the *Murray* case, to the effect that "[t]he acknowledgment of the existence of God as symbolized in the opening exercises establishes a discipline tone which tends to cause each individual pupil to constrain his overt acts and to consequently conform to accepted standards of behavior during his attendance at school." These views are by no means novel, *see, e.g., Billard v. Board of Education*, 69 Kan. 53, 57-58, 76 P. 422, 423 (1904).[55]

It is not the business of this Court to gainsay the judgments of experts on matters of pedagogy. Such decisions must be left to the discretion of those administrators charged with the supervision of the Nation's public schools. The limited province of the courts is to determine whether the means which the educators have chosen to achieve legitimate pedagogical ends infringe the constitutional freedoms of the First Amendment. The secular purposes which devotional exercises are said to serve fall into two categories — those which depend upon an immediately religious experience shared by the participating children;

---

[55] In the *Billard* case, the teacher whose use of the Lord's Prayer and the Twenty-third Psalm was before the court testified that the exercise served disciplinary rather than spiritual purposes: "It is necessary to have some general exercise after the children come in from the playground to prepare them for their work. You need some general exercise to quiet them down." When asked again if the purpose were not at least partially religious, the teacher replied, "[I]t was religious to the children that are religious, and to the others it was not." 69 Kan., at 57-58, 76 P., at 423.

and those which appear sufficiently divorced from the religious content of the devotional material that they can be served equally by nonreligious materials. With respect to the first objective, much has been written about the moral and spiritual values of infusing some religious influence or instruction into the public school classroom. To the extent that only *religious* materials will serve this purpose, it seems to me that the purpose as well as the means is so plainly religious that the exercise is necessarily forbidden by the Establishment Clause. The fact that purely secular benefits may eventually result does not seem to me to justify the exercises, for similar indirect nonreligious benefits could no doubt have been claimed for the released time program invalidated in *McCollum*.

The second justification assumes that religious exercises at the start of the school day may directly serve solely secular ends — for example, by fostering harmony and tolerance among the pupils, enhancing the authority of the teacher, and inspiring better discipline. To the extent that such benefits result not from the content of the readings and recitation, but simply from the holding of such a solemn exercise at the opening assembly or the first class of the day, it would seem that less sensitive materials might equally well serve the same purpose. I have previously suggested that *Torcaso* and the *Sunday Law Cases* forbid the use of religious means to achieve secular ends where nonreligious means will suffice. That principle is readily applied to these cases. It has not been shown that readings from the speeches and messages of great Americans, for example, or from the documents of our heritage of liberty, daily recitation of the Pledge of Allegiance, or even the observance of a moment of reverent silence at the opening of class, may not adequately serve the solely secular purposes of the devotional activities without jeopardizing either the religious liberties of any members of the community or the proper degree of separation between the spheres of religion and government. Such substitutes would, I think, be unsatisfactory or inadequate only to the extent that the present activities do in fact serve religious goals. While I do not question the judgment of experienced educators that the challenged practices may well achieve valuable secular ends, it seems to me that the State acts unconstitutionally if it either sets about to attain even indirectly religious ends by religious means, or if it uses religious means to serve secular ends where secular means would suffice.

B.

Second, it is argued that the particular practices involved in the two cases before us are unobjectionable because they prefer no particular sect or sects at the expense of others. Both the Baltimore and Abington procedures permit, for example, the reading of any of several versions of the Bible, and this flexibility is said to ensure neutrality sufficiently to avoid the constitutional prohibition. One answer, which might be dispositive, is that any version of the Bible is inherently sectarian, else there would be no need to offer a system of rotation or alternation of versions in the first place, that is, to allow different sectarian versions to be used on different days. The sectarian character of the Holy Bible has been at the core of the whole controversy over religious practices in the public schools throughout its long and often bitter history. To vary the version as the Abington and Baltimore schools have done may well be less offensive than to read from the King James version every day, as once was the practice. But the result even of this relatively benign procedure is that majority sects are preferred in approximate proportion to their representation in the community and in the student body, while the smaller sects suffer commensurate discrimination. So long as the subject matter of the exercise is sectarian in character, these consequences cannot be avoided.

The argument contains, however, a more basic flaw. There are persons in every community — often deeply devout — to whom any version of the Judaeo-Christian Bible is offensive. There are others whose reverence for the Holy Scriptures demands private study or reflection and to whom public reading or recitation is sacrilegious, as one of the expert witnesses at the trial of the *Schempp* case explained. To such persons it is not the fact of using the Bible in the public schools, nor the content of any particular version, that is offensive, but only the *manner* in which it is used. For such persons, the anathema of public communion is even more pronounced when prayer is involved. Many deeply devout persons have always regarded prayer as a necessarily private experience. One Protestant group recently commented, for example: "When one thinks of prayer as sincere outreach of a human soul to the Creator, 'required prayer' becomes an absurdity." There is a similar problem with respect to comment upon the passages of Scripture which are to be read. Most present statutes forbid comment, and this practice accords with the views of many religious groups as to the manner in which the Bible should be read. However, as a recent survey discloses, scriptural passages read without comment frequently convey no message to the younger children in the school. Thus there has developed a practice in some schools of bridging the gap between faith and understanding by means of "definitions," even where "comment" is forbidden by statute. The present practice therefore poses a difficult dilemma: While Bible reading is almost universally required to be without comment, since only by such a prohibition can sectarian interpretation be excluded from the classroom, the rule breaks down at the point at which rudimentary definitions of Biblical terms are necessary for comprehension if the exercise is to be meaningful at all.

It has been suggested that a tentative solution to these problems may lie in the fashioning of a "common core" of theology tolerable to all creeds but preferential to none. But as one commentator has recently observed, "[h]istory is not encouraging to" those who hope to fashion a "common denominator of religion detached from its manifestation in any organized church." Sutherland, *Establishment According to* Engel, 76 HARV. L. REV. 25, 51 (1962). Thus, the notion of a "common core" litany or supplication offends many deeply devout worshipers who do not find clearly sectarian practices objectionable. Father Gustave Weigel has recently expressed a widely shared view: "The moral code held by each separate religious community can reductively be unified, but the consistent particular believer wants no such reduction." And, as the American Council on Education warned several years ago, "The notion of a common core suggests a watering down of the several faiths to the point where common essentials appear. This might easily lead to a new sect — a public school sect — which would take its place alongside the existing faiths and compete with them." *Engel* is surely authority that nonsectarian religious practices, equally with sectarian exercises, violate the Establishment Clause. Moreover, even if the Establishment Clause were oblivious to nonsectarian religious practices, I think it quite likely that the "common core" approach would be sufficiently objectionable to many groups to be foreclosed by the prohibitions of the Free Exercise Clause.

C.

A third element which is said to absolve the practices involved in these cases from the ban of the religious guarantees of the Constitution is the provision to excuse or exempt students who wish not to participate. Insofar as these practices are claimed to violate the Establishment Clause, I find the answer which the District Court gave after our remand of *Schempp* to be altogether dispositive:

> "The fact that some pupils, or theoretically all pupils, might be excused from attendance at the exercises does not mitigate the obligatory nature of the ceremony. . . . The exercises are held in the school buildings and perforce are conducted by and under the authority of the local school authorities and during school sessions. Since the statute requires the reading of the 'Holy Bible', a Christian document, the practice, as we said in our first opinion, prefers the Christian religion. The record demonstrates that it was the intention of the General Assembly of the Commonwealth of Pennsylvania to introduce a religious ceremony into the public schools of the Commonwealth." 201 F. Supp., at 819.

Thus the short, and to me sufficient, answer is that the availability of excusal or exemption simply has no relevance to the establishment question, if it is once found that these practices are essentially religious exercises designed at least in part to achieve religious aims through the use of public school facilities during the school day.

The more difficult question, however, is whether the availability of excusal for the dissenting child serves to refute challenges to these practices under the Free Exercise Clause. While it is enough to decide these cases to dispose of the establishment questions, questions of free exercise are so inextricably interwoven into the history and present status of these practices as to justify disposition of this second aspect of the excusal issue. The answer is that the excusal procedure itself necessarily operates in such a way as to infringe the rights of free exercise of those children who wish to be excused. We have held in *Barnette* and *Torcaso*, respectively, that a State may require neither public school students nor candidates for an office of public trust to profess beliefs offensive to religious principles. By the same token the State could not constitutionally require a student to profess publicly his disbelief as the prerequisite to the exercise of his constitutional right of abstention. And apart from *Torcaso* and *Barnette*, I think *Speiser v. Randall*, 357 U.S. 513, suggests a further answer. We held there that a State may not condition the grant of a tax exemption upon the willingness of those entitled to the exemption to affirm their loyalty to the Government, even though the exemption was itself a matter of grace rather than of constitutional right. We concluded that to impose upon the eligible taxpayers the affirmative burden of proving their loyalty impermissibly jeopardized the freedom to engage in constitutionally protected activities close to the area to which the loyalty oath related. *Speiser v. Randall* seems to me to dispose of two aspects of the excusal or exemption procedure now before us. First, by requiring what is tantamount in the eyes of teachers and schoolmates to a profession of disbelief, or at least of nonconformity, the procedure may well deter those children who do not wish to participate for any reason based upon the dictates of conscience from exercising an indisputably constitutional right to be excused.[68] Thus the excusal provision in its operation subjects them to a cruel dilemma. In consequence, even devout children may well avoid claiming their right and simply continue to participate in exercises distasteful to them because of an understandable reluctance to be stigmatized as atheists or nonconformists simply on the basis of their request.

Such reluctance to seek exemption seems all the more likely in view of the fact that children are disinclined at this age to step out of line or to flout "peer-group norms." Such is the widely held view of experts who have studied the behaviors and attitudes of children. This is also the basis of Mr. Justice Frankfurter's answer to a similar contention made in the *McCollum* case:

> "That a child is offered an alternative may reduce the constraint; it does not eliminate the operation of influence by the school in matters

---

[68] See the testimony of Edward L. Schempp, the father of the children in the Abington schools and plaintiff-appellee in No. 142, concerning his reasons for not asking that his children be excused from the morning exercises after excusal was made available through amendment of the statute:

> "We originally objected to our children being exposed to the reading of the King James version of the Bible . . . and under those conditions we would have theoretically liked to have had the children excused. But we felt that the penalty of having our children labeled as 'odd balls' before their teachers and classmates every day in the year was even less satisfactory than the other problem. . . .

> "The children, the classmates of Roger and Donna are very liable to label and lump all particular religious difference or religious objections as atheism, particularly, today the word 'atheism' is so often tied to atheistic communism, and atheism has very bad connotations in the minds of children and many adults today."

A recent opinion of the Attorney General of California gave as one reason for finding devotional exercises unconstitutional the likelihood that "[c]hildren forced by conscience to leave the room during such exercises would be placed in a position inferior to that of students adhering to the State-endorsed religion." 25 Cal.Op.Atty.Gen. 316, 319 (1955). Other views on this question, and possible effects of the excusal procedure, are summarized in Rosenfield, *Separation of Church and State in the Public Schools*, 22 U. of PITT. L. REV. 561, 581-585 (1961); Note, *Separation of Church and State: Religious Exercises in the Schools*, 31 U. OF CINC. L.REV. 408, 416 (1962); Note, 62 W. VA. L. REV. 353, 358 (1960).

sacred to conscience and outside the school's domain. The law of imitation operates, and non-conformity is not an outstanding characteristic of children. The result is an obvious pressure upon children to attend." 333 U.S., at 227.

Also apposite is the answer given more than 70 years ago by the Supreme Court of Wisconsin to the argument that an excusal provision saved a public school devotional exercise from constitutional invalidation:

> ". . . the excluded pupil loses caste with his fellows, and is liable to be regarded with aversion, and subjected to reproach and insult. But it is a sufficient refutation of the argument that the practice in question tends to destroy the equality of the pupils which the constitution seeks to establish and protect, and puts a portion of them to serious disadvantage in many ways with respect to the others." *State ex rel. Weiss v. District Board of School District No. 8*, 76 Wis. 177, 200, 44 N.W. 967, 975, 7 L.R.A. 330.

And 50 years ago a like answer was offered by the Louisiana Supreme Court:

> "Under such circumstances, the children would be excused from the opening exercises . . . because of their religious beliefs. And excusing such children on religious grounds, although the number excused might be very small, would be a distinct preference in favor of the religious beliefs to the majority, and would work a discrimination against those who were excused. The exclusion of a pupil under such circumstances puts him in a class by himself; it subjects him to a religious stigma; and all because of his religious belief. Equality in public education would be destroyed by such act, under a Constitution which seeks to establish equality and freedom in religious matters." *Herold v. Parish Board of School Directors*, 136 La. 1034, 1049-1050, 68 So. 116, 121, L.R.A.1915D, 941. *See also Tudor v. Board of Education*, 14 N.J. 31, 48-52, 100 A.2d 857, 867-868, 45 A.L.R.2d 729; *Brown v. Orange County Board of Public Instruction*, 128 So. 2d 181, 185 (Fla.App.).

Speiser v. Randall also suggests the answer to a further argument based on the excusal procedure. It has been suggested by the School Board, in *Schempp*, that we ought not pass upon the appellees' constitutional challenge at least until the children have availed themselves of the excusal procedure and found it inadequate to redress their grievances. Were the right to be excused not itself of constitutional stature, I might have some doubt about this issue. But we held in *Speiser* that the constitutional vice of the loyalty oath procedure discharged any obligation to seek the exemption before challenging the constitutionality of the conditions upon which it might have been denied. 357 U.S., at 529. Similarly, we have held that one need not apply for a permit to distribute constitutionally protected literature, *Lovell v. Griffin*, 303 U.S. 444, or to deliver a speech, *Thomas v. Collins*, 323 U.S. 516, before he may attack the constitutionality of a licensing system of which the defect is patent. Insofar as these cases implicate only questions of establishment, it seems to me that the availability of an excuse is constitutionally irrelevant. Moreover, the excusal procedure seems to me to operate in such a way as to discourage the free exercise of religion on the part of those who might wish to utilize it, thereby rendering it unconstitutional in an additional and quite distinct respect.

WALLACE v. JAFFREE
472 U.S. 38 (1985)

JUSTICE STEVENS delivered the opinion of the Court.

At an early stage of this litigation, the constitutionality of three Alabama statutes was questioned: (1) § 16-1-20, enacted in 1978, which authorized a 1-minute period of silence in all public schools "for meditation"; (2) § 16-1-20.1, enacted in 1981, which authorized a period of silence "for meditation or voluntary prayer"; and (3) § 16-1-20.2, enacted in 1982, which authorized teachers to lead "willing students" in a prescribed prayer to "Almighty God . . . the Creator and Supreme Judge of the world."

At the preliminary-injunction stage of this case, the District Court distinguished § 16-1-20 from the other two statutes. It then held that there was "nothing wrong" with § 16-1-20, but that §§16-1-20.1 and 16-1-20.2 were both invalid because the sole purpose of both was "an effort on the part of the State of Alabama to encourage a religious activity." After the trial on the merits, the District Court did not change its interpretation of these two statutes, but held that they were constitutional because, in its opinion, Alabama has the power to establish a state religion if it chooses to do so.

The Court of Appeals agreed with the District Court's initial interpretation of the purpose of both § 16-1-20.1 and § 16-1-20.2, and held them both unconstitutional. We have already affirmed the Court of Appeals' holding with respect to § 16-1-20.2. Moreover, appellees have not questioned the holding that § 16-1-20 is valid. Thus, the narrow question for decision is whether § 16-1-20.1, which authorizes a period of silence for "meditation or voluntary prayer," is a law respecting the establishment of religion within the meaning of the First Amendment.

Appellee Ishmael Jaffree is a resident of Mobile County, Alabama. On May 28, 1982, he filed a complaint on behalf of three of his minor children; two of them were second-grade students and the third was then in kindergarten. The complaint further alleged that two of the children had been subjected to various acts of religious indoctrination "from the beginning of the school year in September, 1981"; that the defendant teachers had "on a daily basis" led their classes in saying certain prayers in unison; that the minor children were exposed to ostracism from their peer group class members if they did not participate; and that Ishmael Jaffree had repeatedly but unsuccessfully requested that the devotional services be stopped.

On August 2, 1982, the District Court held an evidentiary hearing on appellees' motion for a preliminary injunction. At that hearing, State Senator Donald G. Holmes testified that he was the "prime sponsor" of the bill that was enacted in 1981 as § 16-1-20.1. He explained that the bill was an "effort to return voluntary prayer to our public schools . . . it is a beginning and a step in the right direction." Apart from the purpose to return voluntary prayer to public school, Senator Holmes unequivocally testified that he had "no other purpose in mind."

IV

The sponsor of the bill that became § 16-1-20.1, Senator Donald Holmes, inserted into the legislative record — apparently without dissent — a statement indicating that the legislation was an "effort to return voluntary prayer" to the public schools. Later Senator Holmes confirmed this purpose before the District Court. In response to the question whether he had any purpose for the legislation other than returning voluntary prayer to public schools, he stated: "No, I did not have no other purpose in mind." The State did not present evidence of *any* secular purpose.[45]

The unrebutted evidence of legislative intent contained in the legislative record and in the testimony of the sponsor of § 16-1-20.1 is confirmed by a consideration of the relationship between this statute and the two other measures that were considered in this case. The District Court found that the 1981 statute and its 1982 sequel had a common, nonsecular purpose. The wholly religious character of the later enactment is plainly evident from its text. When

---

[45] Appellant Governor George C. Wallace now argues that § 16-1-20.1 "is best understood as a permissible accommodation of religion" and that, viewed even in terms of the *Lemon* test, the "statute conforms to acceptable constitutional criteria." Brief for Appellant Wallace 5; *see also* Brief for Appellants Smith et al. 39 (§ 16-1-20.1 "accommodates the free exercise of the religious beliefs and free exercise of speech and belief of those affected"); *id.,* at 47. These arguments seem to be based on the theory that the free exercise of religion of some of the State's citizens was burdened before the statute was enacted. The United States, appearing as *amicus curiae* in support of the appellants, candidly acknowledges that "it is unlikely that in most contexts a strong Free Exercise claim could be made that time for personal prayer must be set aside during the school day." Brief for United States as *Amicus Curiae* 10. There is no basis for the suggestion that § 16-1-20.1 "is a means for accommodating the religious and meditative needs of students without in any way diminishing the school's own neutrality or secular atmosphere." *Id.,* at 11. In this case, it is undisputed that at the time of the enactment of § 16-1-20.1 there was no governmental practice impeding students from silently praying for one minute at the beginning of each schoolday; thus, there was no need to "accommodate" or to exempt individuals from any general governmental requirement because of the dictates of our cases interpreting the Free Exercise Clause. *See, e.g., Thomas v. Review Board, Indiana Employment Security Div.* [*infra* Chapter 10]; *Sherbert v. Verner* [*infra* Chapter 10]; *see also Abington School District v. Schempp* ("While the Free Exercise Clause clearly prohibits the use of state action to deny the rights of free exercise to *anyone,* it has never meant that a majority could use the machinery of the State to practice its beliefs"). What was missing in the appellants' eyes at the time of the enactment of § 16-1-20.1 — and therefore what is precisely the aspect that makes the statute unconstitutional—was the State's endorsement and promotion of religion and a particular religious practice.

the differences between §16-1-20.1 and its 1978 predecessor, § 16-1-20, are examined, it is equally clear that the 1981 statute has the same wholly religious character.

There are only three textual differences between § 16-1-20.1 and § 16-1- 20: (1) the earlier statute applies only to grades one through six, whereas § 16-1-20.1 applies to all grades; (2) the earlier statute uses the word "shall" whereas § 16-1-20.1 uses the word "may"; (3) the earlier statute refers only to "meditation" whereas § 16-1-20.1 refers to "meditation or voluntary prayer." The first difference is of no relevance in this litigation because the minor appellees were in kindergarten or second grade during the 1981-1982 academic year. The second difference would also have no impact on this litigation because the mandatory language of § 16-1-20 continued to apply to grades one through six. Thus, the only significant textual difference is the addition of the words "or voluntary prayer."

The legislative intent to return prayer to the public schools is, of course, quite different from merely protecting every student's right to engage in voluntary prayer during an appropriate moment of silence during the schoolday. The 1978 statute already protected that right, containing nothing that prevented any student from engaging in voluntary prayer during a silent minute of meditation. Appellants have not identified any secular purpose that was not fully served by § 16-1-20 before the enactment of § 16-1-20.1. Thus, only two conclusions are consistent with the text of § 16-1-20.1: (1) the statute was enacted to convey a message of state endorsement and promotion of prayer; or (2) the statute was enacted for no purpose. No one suggests that the statute was nothing but a meaningless or irrational act.

We must, therefore, conclude that the Alabama Legislature intended to change existing law and that it was motivated by the same purpose that the Governor's answer to the second amended complaint expressly admitted; that the statement inserted in the legislative history revealed; and that Senator Holmes' testimony frankly described. The legislature enacted § 16-1-20.1, despite the existence of § 16-1-20 for the sole purpose of expressing the State's endorsement of prayer activities for one minute at the beginning of each schoolday. The addition of "or voluntary prayer" indicates that the State intended to characterize prayer as a favored practice. Such an endorsement is not consistent with the established principle that the government must pursue a course of complete neutrality toward religion.

The importance of that principle does not permit us to treat this as an inconsequential case involving nothing more than a few words of symbolic speech on behalf of the political majority. For whenever the State itself speaks on a religious subject, one of the questions that we must ask is "whether the government intends to convey a message of endorsement or disapproval of religion." The well-supported concurrent findings of the District Court and the Court of Appeals — that §16-1-20.1 was intended to convey a message of state approval of prayer activities in the public schools — make it unnecessary, and indeed inappropriate, to evaluate the practical significance of the addition of the words "or voluntary prayer" to the statute. Keeping in mind, as we must, "both the fundamental place held by the Establishment Clause in our constitutional scheme and the myriad, subtle ways in which Establishment Clause values can be eroded," we conclude that § 16-1-20.1 violates the First Amendment.

JUSTICE O'CONNOR, concurring in the judgment.

I.

[Justice O'Connor first discussed her endorsement analysis of alleged Establishment Clause violations. This analysis is discussed in Chapter 5 *supra.*]

A

Twenty-five states permit or require public school teachers to have students observe a moment of silence in their classrooms. A few statutes provide that the moment of silence is for the purpose of meditation alone. The typical statute, however, calls for a moment of silence at the beginning of the schoolday during which students may meditate, pray, or reflect on the activities of the day. Federal trial courts have divided on the constitutionality of these moment of silence laws. Relying on this Court's decisions disapproving vocal prayer and Bible reading in the public schools, see *Abington School District v. Schempp; Engel v. Vitale,* the courts that have struck down the moment of silence statutes generally conclude that their purpose and effect are to encourage prayer in public schools.

The *Engel* and *Abington* decisions are not dispositive on the constitutionality of moment of silence laws. In those cases, public school teachers and students led their classes in devotional exercises. In *Engel,* a New York statute required teachers to lead their classes in a vocal prayer. The Court concluded that "it is no part of the business of government to compose official prayers for any group of the American people to recite as part of a religious program carried on by the government." In *Abington,* the Court addressed Pennsylvania and Maryland statutes that authorized morning Bible readings in public schools. The Court reviewed the purpose and effect of the statutes, concluded that they required religious exercises, and therefore found them to violate the Establishment Clause. Under all of these statutes, a student who did not share the religious beliefs expressed in the course of the exercise was left with the choice of participating, thereby compromising the nonadherent's beliefs, or withdrawing, thereby calling attention to his or her nonconformity. The decisions acknowledged the coercion implicit under the statutory schemes, but they expressly turned only on the fact that the government was sponsoring a manifestly religious exercise.

A state-sponsored moment of silence in the public schools is different from state-sponsored vocal prayer or Bible reading. First, a moment of silence is not inherently religious. Silence, unlike prayer or Bible reading, need not be associated with a religious exercise. Second, a pupil who participates in a moment of silence need not compromise his or her beliefs. During a moment of silence, a student who objects to prayer is left to his or her own thoughts, and is not compelled to listen to the prayers or thoughts of others. For these simple reasons, a moment of silence statute does not stand or fall under the Establishment Clause according to how the Court regards vocal prayer or Bible reading. Scholars and at least one Member of this Court have recognized the distinction and suggested that a moment of silence in public schools would be constitutional. *See Abington, supra*, 374 U.S., at 281 (BRENNAN, J., concurring) ("[T]he observance of a moment of reverent silence at the opening of class" may serve "the solely secular purposes of the devotional activities without jeopardizing either the religious liberties of any members of the community or the proper degree of separation between the spheres of religion and government"); L. TRIBE, AMERICAN CONSTITUTIONAL LAW § 14-6, p. 829 (1978); P. FREUND, THE LEGAL ISSUE, IN RELIGION AND THE PUBLIC SCHOOLS 23 (1965); Choper, 47 MINN. L. REV., at 371; Kauper, *Prayer, Public Schools, and the Supreme Court*, 61 MICH. L. REV. 1031, 1041 (1963). As a general matter, I agree. It is difficult to discern a serious threat to religious liberty from a room of silent, thoughtful schoolchildren.

By mandating a moment of silence, a State does not necessarily endorse any activity that might occur during the period. *Cf. Widmar v. Vincent*, 454 U.S. 263, 272, n. 11 (1981) ("[B]y creating a forum the [State] does not thereby endorse or promote any of the particular ideas aired there"). Even if a statute specifies that a student may choose to pray silently during a quiet moment, the State has not thereby encouraged prayer over other specified alternatives. Nonetheless, it is also possible that a moment of silence statute, either as drafted or as actually implemented, could effectively favor the child who prays over the child who does not. For example, the message of endorsement would seem inescapable if the teacher exhorts children to use the designated time to pray. Similarly, the face of the statute or its legislative history may clearly establish that it seeks to encourage or promote voluntary prayer over other alternatives, rather than merely provide a quiet moment that may be dedicated to prayer by those so inclined. The crucial question is whether the State has conveyed or attempted to convey the message that children should use the moment of silence for prayer.[2] This question cannot be answered in the abstract, but instead requires courts to examine the history, language, and administration of a particular statute to determine whether it operates as an endorsement of religion.

---

[2] Appellants argue that *Zorach v. Clauson*, 343 U.S. 306, 313-314 (1952), suggests there is no constitutional infirmity in a State's encouraging a child to pray during a moment of silence. The cited dicta from *Zorach*, however, is inapposite. There the Court stated that "[w]hen the state encourages religious instruction . . . *by adjusting the schedule of public events to sectarian needs*, it follows the best of our traditions." *Ibid.* (emphasis added). When the State provides a moment of silence during which prayer may occur at the election of the student, it can be said to be adjusting the schedule of public events to sectarian needs. But when the State also encourages the student to pray during a moment of silence, it converts an otherwise inoffensive moment of silence into an effort by the majority to use the machinery of the State to encourage the minority to participate in a religious exercise. *See Abington School District v. Schempp.*

Before reviewing Alabama's moment of silence law to determine whether it endorses prayer, some general observations on the proper scope of the inquiry are in order. First, the inquiry into the purpose of the legislature in enacting a moment of silence law should be deferential and limited. *See Everson v. Board of Education* (courts must exercise "the most extreme caution" in assessing whether a state statute has a proper public purpose). In determining whether the government intends a moment of silence statute to convey a message of endorsement or disapproval of religion, a court has no license to psychoanalyze the legislators. *See McGowan v. Maryland*, 366 U.S. 420, 466 (1961) (opinion of Frankfurter, J.). If a legislature expresses a plausible secular purpose for a moment of silence statute in either the text or the legislative history, or if the statute disclaims an intent to encourage prayer over alternatives during a moment of silence, then courts should generally defer to that stated intent. *See Committee for Public Education & Religious Liberty v. Nyquist* [*infra* Chapter 8]; *Tilton v. Richardson*, 403 U.S. 672, 678-679 (1971). It is particularly troublesome to denigrate an expressed secular purpose due to postenactment testimony by particular legislators or by interested persons who witnessed the drafting of the statute. Even if the text and official history of a statute express no secular purpose, the statute should be held to have an improper purpose only if it is beyond purview that endorsement of religion or a religious belief "was and is the law's reason for existence." *Epperson v. Arkansas* [*supra* Chapter 4]. Since there is arguably a secular pedagogical value to a moment of silence in public schools, courts should find an improper purpose behind such a statute only if the statute on its face, in its official legislative history, or in its interpretation by a responsible administrative agency suggests it has the primary purpose of endorsing prayer.

JUSTICE REHNQUIST suggests that this sort of deferential inquiry into legislative purpose "means little," because "it only requires the legislature to express any secular purpose and omit all sectarian references." It is not a trivial matter, however, to require that the legislature manifest a secular purpose and omit all sectarian endorsements from its laws. That requirement is precisely tailored to the Establishment Clause's purpose of assuring that government not intentionally endorse religion or a religious practice. It is of course possible that a legislature will enunciate a sham secular purpose for a statute. I have little doubt that our courts are capable of distinguishing a sham secular purpose from a sincere one, or that the *Lemon* inquiry into the effect of an enactment would help decide those close cases where the validity of an expressed secular purpose is in doubt. While the secular purpose requirement alone may rarely be determinative in striking down a statute, it nevertheless serves an important function. It reminds government that when it acts it should do so without endorsing a particular religious belief or practice that all citizens do not share. In this sense the secular purpose requirement is squarely based in the text of the Establishment Clause it helps to enforce.

Second, the *Lynch* concurrence suggested that the effect of a moment of silence law is not entirely a question of fact:

"[W]hether a government activity communicates endorsement of religion is not a question of simple historical fact. Although evidentiary submissions may help answer it, the question is, like the question whether racial or sex-based classifications communicate an invidious message, in large part a legal question to be answered on the basis of judicial interpretation of social facts." 465 U.S., at 693-694.

The relevant issue is whether an objective observer, acquainted with the text, legislative history, and implementation of the statute, would perceive it as a state endorsement of prayer in public schools. A moment of silence law that is clearly drafted and implemented so as to permit prayer, meditation, and reflection within the prescribed period, without endorsing one alternative over the others, should pass this test.

B

The analysis above suggests that moment of silence laws in many States should pass Establishment Clause scrutiny because they do not favor the child who chooses to pray during a moment of silence over the child who chooses to meditate or reflect. Alabama Code § 16-1-20.1 (Supp.1984) does not stand on the same footing. However deferentially one examines its text and legislative history, however objectively one views the message attempted to be conveyed to the public, the conclusion is unavoidable that the purpose of the statute is to endorse prayer in public schools. I accordingly agree with the Court of Appeals, 705 F.2d 1526, 1535 (1983), that the Alabama statute has a purpose which is in violation of the Establishment Clause, and cannot be upheld.

In finding that the purpose of § 16-1-20.1 is to endorse voluntary prayer during a moment of silence, the Court relies on testimony elicited from State Senator Donald G. Holmes during a preliminary injunction hearing. Senator Holmes testified that the sole purpose of the statute was to return voluntary prayer to the public schools. For the reasons expressed above, I would give little, if any, weight to this sort of evidence of legislative intent. Nevertheless, the text of the statute in light of its official legislative history leaves little doubt that the purpose of this statute corresponds to the purpose expressed by Senator Holmes at the preliminary injunction hearing.

First, it is notable that Alabama already had a moment of silence statute before it enacted §16-1-20.1. See Ala. Code § 16-1-20 (Supp.1984) Appellees do not challenge this statute — indeed, they concede its validity. The only significant addition made by § 16-1-20.1 is to specify expressly that voluntary prayer is one of the authorized activities during a moment of silence. Any doubt as to the legislative purpose of that addition is removed by the official legislative history. The sole purpose reflected in the official history is "to return voluntary prayer to our public schools." Nor does anything in the legislative history contradict an intent to encourage children to choose prayer over other alternatives during the moment of silence. Given this legislative history, it is not surprising that the State of Alabama conceded in the courts below that the purpose of the statute was to make prayer part of daily classroom activity, and that both the District Court and the Court of Appeals concluded that the law's purpose was to encourage religious activity. In light of the legislative history and the findings of the courts below, I agree with the Court that the State intended § 16-1-20.1 to convey a message that prayer was the endorsed activity during the state-prescribed moment of silence.[5] While it is therefore unnecessary also to determine the effect of the statute, *Lynch*, 465 U.S., at 690 (concurring opinion), it also seems likely that the message actually conveyed to objective observers by § 16-1-20.1 is approval of the child who selects prayer over other alternatives during a moment of silence.

Given this evidence in the record, candor requires us to admit that this Alabama statute was intended to convey a message of state encouragement and endorsement of religion. In *Walz v. Tax Comm'n*, 397 U.S., at 669, the Court stated that the Religion Clauses of the First Amendment are flexible enough to "permit religious exercise to exist without sponsorship and without interference." Alabama Code § 16-1-20.1 (Supp.1984) does more than permit prayer to occur during a moment of silence "without interference." It endorses the decision to pray during a moment of silence, and accordingly sponsors a religious exercise. For that reason, I concur in the judgment of the Court.

B. PRAYER AT GRADUATION

LEE v. WEISMAN
505 U.S. 577 (1992)

KENNEDY, J., delivered the opinion of the Court.

School principals in the public school system of the city of Providence, Rhode Island, are permitted to invite members of the clergy to offer invocation and benediction prayers as part of the formal graduation ceremonies for middle schools and for high schools. The question before us is whether including clerical members who offer prayers as part of the official school graduation ceremony is consistent with the Religion Clauses of the First Amendment, provisions the Fourteenth Amendment makes applicable with full force to the States and their school districts.

---

[5] THE CHIEF JUSTICE suggests that one consequence of the Court's emphasis on the difference between § 16-1-20.1 and its predecessor statute might be to render the Pledge of Allegiance unconstitutional because Congress amended it in 1954 to add the words "under God." I disagree. In my view, the words "under God" in the Pledge, as codified at 36 U.S.C. § 172, serve as an acknowledgment of religion with "the legitimate secular purposes of solemnizing public occasions, [and] expressing confidence in the future." *Lynch v. Donnelly* [*supra* Chapter 5].

I also disagree with The Chief Justice's suggestion that the Court's opinion invalidates any moment of silence statute that includes the word "prayer." As noted, "[e]ven if a statute specifies that a student may choose to pray silently during a quiet moment, the State has not thereby encouraged prayer over other specified alternatives."

I.

A.

Deborah Weisman graduated from Nathan Bishop Middle School, a public school in Providence, at a formal ceremony in June 1989. She was about 14 years old. For many years it has been the policy of the Providence School Committee and the Superintendent of Schools to permit principals to invite members of the clergy to give invocations and benedictions at middle school and high school graduations. Many, but not all, of the principals elected to include prayers as part of the graduation ceremonies. Acting for himself and his daughter, Deborah's father, Daniel Weisman, objected to any prayers at Deborah's middle school graduation, but to no avail. The school principal, petitioner Robert E. Lee, invited a rabbi to deliver prayers at the graduation exercises for Deborah's class. Rabbi Leslie Gutterman, of the Temple Beth El in Providence, accepted.

It has been the custom of Providence school officials to provide invited clergy with a pamphlet entitled "Guidelines for Civic Occasions," prepared by the National Conference of Christians and Jews. The Guidelines recommend that public prayers at nonsectarian civic ceremonies be composed with "inclusiveness and sensitivity," though they acknowledge that "[p]rayer of any kind may be inappropriate on some civic occasions." The principal gave Rabbi Gutterman the pamphlet before the graduation and advised him the invocation and benediction should be nonsectarian.

Rabbi Gutterman's prayers were as follows:

"INVOCATION

"God of the Free, Hope of the Brave:

"For the legacy of America where diversity is celebrated and the rights of minorities are protected, we thank You. May these young men and women grow up to enrich it.

"For the liberty of America, we thank You. May these new graduates grow up to guard it.

"For the political process of America in which all its citizens may participate, for its court system where all may seek justice we thank You. May those we honor this morning always turn to it in trust.

"For the destiny of America we thank You. May the graduates of Nathan Bishop Middle School so live that they might help to share it.

"May our aspirations for our country and for these young people, who are our hope for the future, be richly fulfilled.

AMEN"

"BENEDICTION

"O God, we are grateful to You for having endowed us with the capacity for learning which we have celebrated on this joyous commencement.

"Happy families give thanks for seeing their children achieve an important milestone. Send Your blessings upon the teachers and administrators who helped prepare them.

"The graduates now need strength and guidance for the future, help them to understand that we are not complete with academic knowledge alone. We must each strive to fulfill what You require of us all: To do justly, to love mercy, to walk humbly.

"We give thanks to You, Lord, for keeping us alive, sustaining us and allowing us to reach this special, happy occasion.

AMEN"

The school board (and the United States, which supports it as *amicus curiae*) argued that these short prayers and others like them at graduation exercises are of profound meaning to many students and parents throughout this country who consider that due respect and acknowledgment for divine guidance and for the deepest spiritual aspirations of our people ought to be expressed at an event as important in life as a graduation. We assume this to be so in addressing the difficult case now before us, for the significance of the prayers lies also at the heart of Daniel and Deborah Weisman's case.

II.

These dominant facts mark and control the confines of our decision: State officials direct the performance of a formal religious exercise at promotional and graduation ceremonies for secondary schools. Even for those students who object to the religious exercise, their attendance and participation in the state-sponsored religious activity are in a fair and real sense obligatory, though the school district does not require attendance as a condition for receipt of the diploma.

This case does not require us to revisit the difficult questions dividing us in recent cases, questions of the definition and full scope of the principles governing the extent of permitted accommodation by the State for the religious beliefs and practices of many of its citizens. *See County of Allegheny v. American Civil Liberties Union, Greater Pittsburgh Chapter* [*infra* Chapter 7]; *Wallace v. Jaffree* [*supra* this Chapter]; *Lynch v. Donnelly* [*supra* Chapter 7]. For without reference to those principles in other contexts, the controlling precedents as they relate to prayer and religious exercise in primary and secondary public schools compel the holding here that the policy of the city of Providence is an unconstitutional one. We can decide the case without reconsidering the general constitutional framework by which public schools' efforts to accommodate religion are measured. Thus we do not accept the invitation of petitioners and *amicus* the United States to reconsider our decision in *Lemon v. Kurtzman*. The government involvement with religious activity in this case is pervasive, to the point of creating a state-sponsored and state-directed religious exercise in a public school. Conducting this formal religious observance conflicts with settled rules pertaining to prayer exercises for students, and that suffices to determine the question before us.

The principle that government may accommodate the free exercise of religion does not supersede the fundamental limitations imposed by the Establishment Clause. It is beyond dispute that, at a minimum, the Constitution guarantees that government may not coerce anyone to support or participate in religion or its exercise, or otherwise act in a way which "establishes a [state] religion or religious faith, or tends to do so." *Lynch* [*infra* Chapter 7]. The State's involvement in the school prayers challenged today violates these central principles.

That involvement is as troubling as it is undenied. A school official, the principal, decided that an invocation and a benediction should be given; this is a choice attributable to the State, and from a constitutional perspective it is as if a state statute decreed that the prayers must occur. The principal chose the religious participant, here a rabbi, and that choice is also attributable to the State. The reason for the choice of a rabbi is not disclosed by the record, but the potential for divisiveness over the choice of a particular member of the clergy to conduct the ceremony is apparent.

Divisiveness, of course, can attend any state decision respecting religions, and neither its existence nor its potential necessarily invalidates the State's attempts to accommodate religion in all cases. The potential for divisiveness is of particular relevance here though, because it centers around an overt religious exercise in a secondary school environment where, as we discuss below, *see infra*, subtle coercive pressures exist and where the student had no real alternative which would have allowed her to avoid the fact or appearance of participation.

The State's role did not end with the decision to include a prayer and with the choice of a clergyman. Principal Lee provided Rabbi Gutterman with a copy of the "Guidelines for Civic Occasions," and advised him that his prayers should be nonsectarian. Through these means the principal directed and controlled the content of the prayers. Even if the only sanction for ignoring the instructions were that the rabbi would not be invited back, we think no religious representative who valued his or her continued reputation and effectiveness in the community would incur the State's displeasure in this regard. It is a cornerstone principle of our Establishment Clause jurisprudence that "it is no part of the business of government to compose official prayers for any group of the American people to recite as a part of a religious program carried on by government," *Engel v. Vitale*, and that is what the school officials attempted to do.

Petitioners argue, and we find nothing in the case to refute it, that the directions for the content of the prayers were a good-faith attempt by the school to ensure that the sectarianism which is so often the flashpoint for religious animosity be removed from the graduation ceremony. The concern is understandable, as a prayer which uses ideas or images identified with a particular religion may foster a different sort of sectarian rivalry than an invocation or benediction in terms more neutral. The school's explanation, however, does not resolve the dilemma caused by its participation. The question is not the good faith of the school in attempting to make the prayer acceptable to most persons, but the legitimacy of its undertaking that enterprise at all when the object is to produce a prayer to be used in a formal religious exercise which students, for all practical purposes, are obliged to attend.

We are asked to recognize the existence of a practice of nonsectarian prayer, prayer within the embrace of what is known as the Judeo-Christian tradition, prayer which is more acceptable than one which, for example, makes explicit references to the God of Israel, or to Jesus Christ, or to a patron saint. There may be some support, as an empirical observation, to the statement of the Court of Appeals for the Sixth Circuit, picked up by Judge Campbell's dissent in the Court of Appeals in this case, that there has emerged in this country a civic religion, one which is tolerated when sectarian exercises are not. If common ground can be defined which permits once conflicting faiths to express the shared conviction that there is an ethic and a morality which transcend human invention, the sense of community and purpose sought by all decent societies might be advanced. But though the First Amendment does not allow the government to stifle prayers which aspire to these ends, neither does it permit the government to undertake that task for itself.

The First Amendment's Religion Clauses mean that religious beliefs and religious expression are too precious to be either proscribed or prescribed by the State. The design of the Constitution is that preservation and transmission of religious beliefs and worship is a responsibility and a choice committed to the private sphere, which itself is promised freedom to pursue that mission. It must not be forgotten then, that while concern must be given to define the protection granted to an objector or a dissenting nonbeliever, these same Clauses exist to protect religion from government interference. James Madison, the principal author of the Bill of Rights, did not rest his opposition to a religious establishment on the sole ground of its effect on the minority. A principal ground for his view was: "[E]xperience witnesseth that ecclesiastical establishments, instead of maintaining the purity and efficacy of Religion, have had a contrary operation." *Memorial and Remonstrance Against Religious Assessments.*

These concerns have particular application in the case of school officials, whose effort to monitor prayer will be perceived by the students as inducing a participation they might otherwise reject. Though the efforts of the school officials in this case to find common ground appear to have been a good-faith attempt to recognize the common aspects of religions and not the divisive ones, our precedents do not permit school officials to assist in composing prayers as an incident to a formal exercise for their students. *Engel v. Vitale.* And these same precedents caution us to measure the idea of a civic religion against the central meaning of the Religion Clauses of the First Amendment, which is that all creeds must be tolerated and none favored. The suggestion that government may establish an official or civic religion as a means of avoiding the establishment of a religion with more specific creeds strikes us as a contradiction that cannot be accepted.

The degree of school involvement here made it clear that the graduation prayers bore the imprint of the State and thus put school-age children who objected in an untenable position. We turn our attention now to consider the position of the students, both those who desired the prayer and she who did not.

To endure the speech of false ideas or offensive content and then to counter it is part of learning how to live in a pluralistic society, a society which insists upon open discourse towards the end of a tolerant citizenry. And tolerance presupposes some mutuality of obligation. It is argued that our constitutional vision of a free society requires confidence in our own ability to accept or reject ideas of which we do not approve, and that prayer at a high school graduation does nothing more than offer a choice. By the time they are seniors, high school students no doubt have been required to attend classes and assemblies and to complete assignments exposing them to ideas they find distasteful or immoral or absurd or all of these. Against this background, students may consider it an odd measure of justice to be subjected during the course of their educations to ideas deemed offensive and irreligious, but to be denied a brief, formal prayer ceremony that the school offers in return. This argument cannot prevail, however. It overlooks a fundamental dynamic of the Constitution.

The First Amendment protects speech and religion by quite different mechanisms. Speech is protected by ensuring its full expression even when the government participates, for the very object of some of our most important speech is to persuade the government to adopt an idea as its own. The method for protecting freedom of worship and freedom of conscience in religious matters is quite the reverse. In religious debate or expression the government is not a prime participant, for the Framers deemed religious establishment antithetical to the freedom of all. The Free Exercise Clause embraces a freedom of conscience and worship that has close parallels in the speech provisions of the First Amendment, but the Establishment Clause is a specific prohibition on forms of state intervention in religious affairs with no precise counterpart in the speech provisions. The explanation lies in the lesson of history that was and is the inspiration for the Establishment Clause, the lesson that in the hands of government what might begin as a tolerant expression of religious views may end in a policy to indoctrinate and coerce. A state-created orthodoxy puts at grave risk that freedom of belief and conscience which are the sole assurance that religious faith is real, not imposed.

The lessons of the First Amendment are as urgent in the modern world as in the 18th century when it was written. One timeless lesson is that if citizens are subjected to state-sponsored religious exercises, the State disavows its own duty to guard and respect that sphere of inviolable conscience and belief which is the mark of a free people. To compromise that principle today would be to deny our own tradition and forfeit our standing to urge others to secure the protections of that tradition for themselves.

As we have observed before, there are heightened concerns with protecting freedom of conscience from subtle coercive pressure in the elementary and secondary public schools. Our decisions in *Engel* and *Schempp* recognize, among other things, that prayer exercises in public schools carry a particular risk of indirect coercion. The concern may not be limited to the context of schools, but it is most pronounced there. What to most believers may seem nothing more than a reasonable request that the nonbeliever respect their religious practices, in a school context may appear to the nonbeliever or dissenter to be an attempt to employ the machinery of the State to enforce a religious orthodoxy.

We need not look beyond the circumstances of this case to see the phenomenon at work. The undeniable fact is that the school district's supervision and control of a high school graduation ceremony places public pressure, as well as peer pressure, on attending students to stand as a group or, at least, maintain respectful silence during the invocation and benediction. This pressure, though subtle and indirect, can be as real as any overt compulsion. Of course, in our culture standing or remaining silent can signify adherence to a view or simple respect for the views of others. And no doubt some persons who have no desire to join a prayer have little objection to standing as a sign of respect for those who do. But for the dissenter of high school age, who has a reasonable perception that she is being forced by the State to pray in a manner her conscience will not allow, the injury is no less real. There can be no doubt that for many, if not most, of the students at the graduation, the act of standing or remaining silent was an expression of participation in the rabbi's prayer. That was the very point of the religious exercise. It is of little comfort to a dissenter, then, to be told that for her the act of standing or remaining in silence signifies mere respect, rather than participation. What matters is that, given our social conventions, a reasonable dissenter in this milieu could believe that the group exercise signified her own participation or approval of it.

Finding no violation under these circumstances would place objectors in the dilemma of participating, with all that implies, or protesting. We do not address whether that choice is acceptable if the affected citizens are mature adults, but we think the State may not, consistent with the Establishment Clause, place primary and secondary school children in this position. Research in psychology supports the common assumption that adolescents are often susceptible to pressure from their peers towards conformity, and that the influence is strongest in matters of social convention. Brittain, *Adolescent Choices and Parent-Peer Cross-Pressures*, 28 AM. SOCIOLOGICAL REV. 385 (June 1963); Clasen &

Brown, *The Multidimensionality of Peer Pressure in Adolescence*, 14 J. OF YOUTH AND ADOLESCENCE 451 (Dec. 1985); Brown, Clasen & Eicher, *Perceptions of Peer Pressure, Peer Conformity Dispositions, and Self-Reported Behavior Among Adolescents*, 22 DEVELOPMENTAL PSYCHOLOGY 521 (July 1986). To recognize that the choice imposed by the State constitutes an unacceptable constraint only acknowledges that the government may no more use social pressure to enforce orthodoxy than it may use more direct means.

The injury caused by the government's action, and the reason why Daniel and Deborah Weisman object to it, is that the State, in a school setting, in effect required participation in a religious exercise. It is, we concede, a brief exercise during which the individual can concentrate on joining its message, meditate on her own religion, or let her mind wander. But the embarrassment and the intrusion of the religious exercise cannot be refuted by arguing that these prayers, and similar ones to be said in the future, are of a *de minimis* character. To do so would be an affront to the rabbi who offered them and to all those for whom the prayers were an essential and profound recognition of divine authority. And for the same reason, we think that the intrusion is greater than the two minutes or so of time consumed for prayers like these. Assuming, as we must, that the prayers were offensive to the student and the parent who now object, the intrusion was both real and, in the context of a secondary school, a violation of the objectors' rights. That the intrusion was in the course of promulgating religion that sought to be civic or nonsectarian rather than pertaining to one sect does not lessen the offense or isolation to the objectors. At best it narrows their number, at worst increases their sense of isolation and affront.

There was a stipulation in the District Court that attendance at graduation and promotional ceremonies is voluntary. Petitioners and the United States, *as amicus,* made this a center point of the case, arguing that the option of not attending the graduation excuses any inducement or coercion in the ceremony itself. The argument lacks all persuasion. Law reaches past formalism. And to say a teenage student has a real choice not to attend her high school graduation is formalistic in the extreme. True, Deborah could elect not to attend commencement without renouncing her diploma; but we shall not allow the case to turn on this point. Everyone knows that in our society and in our culture high school graduation is one of life's most significant occasions. A school rule which excuses attendance is beside the point. Attendance may not be required by official decree, yet it is apparent that a student is not free to absent herself from the graduation exercise in any real sense of the term "voluntary," for absence would require forfeiture of those intangible benefits which have motivated the student through youth and all her high school years. Graduation is a time for family and those closest to the student to celebrate success and express mutual wishes of gratitude and respect, all to the end of impressing upon the young person the role that it is his or her right and duty to assume in the community and all of its diverse parts.

The importance of the event is the point the school district and the United States rely upon to argue that a formal prayer ought to be permitted, but it becomes one of the principal reasons why their argument must fail. Their contention, one of considerable force were it not for the constitutional constraints applied to state action, is that the prayers are an essential part of these ceremonies because for many persons an occasion of this significance lacks meaning if there is no recognition, however brief, that human achievements cannot be understood apart from their spiritual essence. We think the Government's position that this interest suffices to force students to choose between compliance or forfeiture demonstrates fundamental inconsistency in its argumentation. It fails to acknowledge that what for many of Deborah's classmates and their parents was a spiritual imperative was for Daniel and Deborah Weisman religious conformance compelled by the State. While in some societies the wishes of the majority might prevail, the Establishment Clause of the First Amendment is addressed to this contingency and rejects the balance urged upon us. The Constitution forbids the State to exact religious conformity from a student as the price of attending her own high school graduation. This is the calculus the Constitution commands.

The Government's argument gives insufficient recognition to the real conflict of conscience faced by the young student. The essence of the Government's position is that with regard to a civic, social occasion of this importance it is the objector, not the majority, who must take unilateral and private action to avoid compromising religious scruples, hereby electing to miss the graduation exercise. This turns conventional First Amendment analysis on its head. It is a tenet of the First Amendment that the State cannot require one of its citizens to forfeit his or her rights and benefits as the price of resisting conformance to state-sponsored religious practice. To say that a student must remain apart from the ceremony at the opening invocation and closing benediction is to risk compelling conformity in an environment analogous to the classroom setting, where we have said the risk of compulsion is especially high. Just as in *Engel* and *Schempp*, where we found that provisions within the challenged legislation permitting a student to be voluntarily excused from attendance or participation in the daily prayers did not shield those practices from invalidation, the fact that attendance at the graduation ceremonies is voluntary in a legal sense does not save the religious exercise.

Inherent differences between the public school system and a session of a state legislature distinguish this case from *Marsh v. Chambers*. The considerations we have raised in objection to the invocation and benediction are in many respects similar to the arguments we considered in *Marsh*. But there are also obvious differences. The atmosphere at the opening of a session of a state legislature where adults are free to enter and leave with little comment and for any number of reasons cannot compare with the constraining potential of the one school event most important for the student to attend. The influence and force of a formal exercise in a school graduation are far greater than the prayer exercise we condoned in *Marsh*. The *Marsh* majority in fact gave specific recognition to this distinction and placed particular reliance on it in upholding the prayers at issue there. Today's case is different. At a high school graduation, teachers and principals must and do retain a high degree of control over the precise contents of the program, the speeches, the timing, the movements, the dress, and the decorum of the students. In this atmosphere the state-imposed character of an invocation and benediction by clergy selected by the school combine to make the prayer a state-sanctioned religious exercise in which the student was left with no alternative but to submit. This is different from *Marsh* and suffices to make the religious exercise a First Amendment violation. Our Establishment Clause jurisprudence remains a delicate and fact-sensitive one, and we cannot accept the parallel relied upon by petitioners and the United States between the facts of *Marsh* and the case now before us. Our decisions in *Engel* and *Schempp* require us to distinguish the public school context.

We do not hold that every state action implicating religion is invalid if one or a few citizens find it offensive. People may take offense at all manner of religious as well as nonreligious messages, but offense alone does not in every case show a violation. We know too that sometimes to endure social isolation or even anger may be the price of conscience or nonconformity. But, by any reading of our cases, the conformity required of the student in this case was too high an exaction to withstand the test of the Establishment Clause. The prayer exercises in this case are especially improper because the State has in every practical sense compelled attendance and participation in an explicit religious exercise at an event of singular importance to every student, one the objecting student had no real alternative to avoid.

Our society would be less than true to its heritage if it lacked abiding concern for the values of its young people, and we acknowledge the profound belief of adherents to many faiths that there must be a place in the student's life for precepts of a morality higher even than the law we today enforce. We express no hostility to those aspirations, nor would our oath permit us to do so. A relentless and all-pervasive attempt to exclude religion from every aspect of public life could itself become inconsistent with the Constitution. We recognize that, at graduation time and throughout the course of the educational process, there will be instances when religious values, religious practices, and religious persons will have some interaction with the public schools and their students. But these matters, often questions of accommodation of religion, are not before us. The sole question presented is whether a religious exercise may be conducted at a graduation ceremony in circumstances where, as we have found, young graduates who object are induced to conform. No holding by this Court suggests that a school can persuade or compel a student to participate in a religious exercise. That is being done here, and it is forbidden by the Establishment Clause of the First Amendment.

JUSTICE SCALIA, with whom THE CHIEF JUSTICE, JUSTICE WHITE, and JUSTICE THOMAS join, dissenting.

Three Terms ago, I joined an opinion recognizing that the Establishment Clause must be construed in light of the "[g]overnment policies of accommodation, acknowledgment, and support for religion [that] are an accepted part of our political and cultural heritage." That opinion affirmed that "the meaning of the Clause is to be determined by reference to historical practices and understandings." It said that "[a] test for implementing the protections of the Establishment Clause that, if applied with consistency, would invalidate longstanding traditions cannot be a proper reading of the Clause." *County of Allegheny v. American Civil Liberties Union, Greater Pittsburgh Chapter* (KENNEDY, J., concurring in judgment in part and dissenting in part).

These views of course prevent me from joining today's opinion, which is conspicuously bereft of any reference to history. In holding that the Establishment Clause prohibits invocations and benedictions at public-school graduation ceremonies, the Court — with nary a mention that it is doing so — lays waste a tradition that is as old as public-school graduation ceremonies themselves, and that is a component of an even more longstanding American tradition of nonsectarian prayer to God at public celebrations generally. As its instrument of destruction, the bulldozer of its social engineering, the Court invents a boundless, and boundlessly manipulable, test of psychological coercion. Today's opinion shows more forcefully than volumes of argumentation why our Nation's protection, that fortress which is our Constitution, cannot possibly rest upon the changeable philosophical predilections of the Justices of this Court, but must have deep foundations in the historic practices of our people.

I

The history and tradition of our Nation are replete with public ceremonies featuring prayers of thanksgiving and petition. Since the Court is so oblivious to our history as to suggest that the Constitution restricts "preservation and transmission of religious beliefs . . . to the private sphere," it appears necessary to provide another brief account. [Justice Scalia then reviews religious references in the Declaration of Independence, presidential inaugural addresses, presidential Thanksgiving Proclamations, congressional prayers, and the opening invocation of the Supreme Court, "God save the United States and this Honorable Court."]

In addition to this general tradition of prayer at public ceremonies, there exists a more specific tradition of invocations and benedictions at public school graduation exercises. By one account, the first public high school graduation ceremony took place in Connecticut in July 1868 — the very month, as it happens, that the Fourteenth Amendment (the vehicle by which the Establishment Clause has been applied against the States) was ratified — when "15 seniors from the Norwich Free Academy marched in their best Sunday suits and dresses into a church hall and waited through majestic music and long prayers." Brodin-

sky, *Commencement Rites Obsolete? Not At All, A 10-Week Study Shows*, 10
UPDATING SCHOOL BOARD POLICIES, No. 4, p. 3 (Apr. 1979). As the Court obliquely
acknowledges in describing the "customary features" of high school graduations, and as respondents do not contest, the invocation and benediction have
long been recognized to be "as traditional as any other parts of the [school]
graduation program and are widely established." H. MCKOWN, COMMENCEMENT
ACTIVITIES 56 (1931); *see also* Brodinsky, *supra*, at 5.

II

The Court presumably would separate graduation invocations and benedictions from other instances of public "preservation and transmission of religious beliefs" on the ground that they involve "psychological coercion." I find it
a sufficient embarrassment that our Establishment Clause jurisprudence
regarding holiday displays, *see County of Allegheny*, has come to "requir[e]
scrutiny more commonly associated with interior decorators than with the judiciary." *American Jewish Congress v. Chicago*, 827 F.2d 120, 129 (7th Cir. 1987)
(Easterbrook, J., dissenting). But interior decorating is a rock-hard science
compared to psychology practiced by amateurs. A few citations of "[r]esearch in
psychology" that have no particular bearing upon the precise issue here cannot
disguise the fact that the Court has gone beyond the realm where judges know
what they are doing. The Court's argument that state officials have "coerced"
students to take part in the invocation and benediction at graduation ceremonies is, not to put too fine a point on it, incoherent.

The Court identifies two "dominant facts" that it says dictate its ruling that
invocations and benedictions at public school graduation ceremonies violate
the Establishment Clause. Neither of them is in any relevant sense true.

A

The Court declares that students' "attendance and participation in the [invo-
cation and benediction] are in a fair and real sense obligatory." But what exactly
is this "fair and real sense"? According to the Court, students at graduation who
want "to avoid the fact or appearance of participation" in the invocation and
benediction are *psychologically* obligated by "public pressure, as well as peer
pressure, . . . to stand as a group or, at least, maintain respectful silence" during those prayers. This assertion — *the very linchpin of the Court's opinion* —
is almost as intriguing for what it does not say as for what it says. It does not
say, for example, that students are psychologically coerced to bow their heads,
place their hands in a Dürer-like prayer position, pay attention to the prayers,
utter "Amen," or in fact pray. (Perhaps further intensive psychological research
remains to be done on these matters.) It claims only that students are psychologically coerced "to stand . . . *or*, at least, maintain respectful silence." Both
halves of this disjunctive (*both* of which must amount to the fact or appearance
of participation in prayer if the Court's analysis is to survive on its own terms)
merit particular attention.

To begin with the latter: The Court's notion that a student who simply *sits* in "respectful silence" during the invocation and benediction (when all others are standing) has somehow joined — or would somehow be perceived as having joined — in the prayers is nothing short of ludicrous. We indeed live in a vulgar age. But surely "our social conventions" have not coarsened to the point that anyone who does not stand on his chair and shout obscenities can reasonably be deemed to have assented to everything said in his presence. Since the Court does not dispute that students exposed to prayer at graduation ceremonies retain (despite "subtle coercive pressures") the free will to sit, there is absolutely no basis for the Court's decision. It is fanciful enough to say that "a reasonable dissenter," standing head erect in a class of bowed heads, "could believe that the group exercise signified her own participation or approval of it." It is beyond the absurd to say that she could entertain such a belief while pointedly declining to rise.

But let us assume the very worst, that the nonparticipating graduate is "subtly coerced" . . . to stand! Even that half of the disjunctive does not remotely establish a "participation" (or an "appearance of participation") in a religious exercise. The Court acknowledges that "in our culture standing . . . can signify adherence to a view or simple respect for the views of others. (Much more often the latter than the former, I think, except perhaps in the proverbial town meeting, where one votes by standing.) But if it is a permissible inference that one who is standing is doing so simply out of respect for the prayers of others that are in progress, then how can it possibly be said that a "reasonable dissenter . . . could believe that the group exercise signified her own participation or approval"? Quite obviously, it cannot. I may add, moreover, that maintaining respect for the religious observances of others is a fundamental civic virtue that government (including the public schools) can and should cultivate — so that even if it were the case that the displaying of such respect might be mistaken for taking part in the prayer, I would deny that the dissenter's interest in avoiding *even the false appearance of participation* constitutionally trumps the government's interest in fostering respect for religion generally.

The opinion manifests that the Court itself has not given careful consideration to its test of psychological coercion. For if it had, how could it observe, with no hint of concern or disapproval, that students stood for the Pledge of Allegiance, which immediately preceded Rabbi Gutterman's invocation? The government can, of course, no more coerce political orthodoxy than religious orthodoxy. *West Virginia Bd. of Ed. v. Barnette* [*infra* Chapter 11]. Moreover, since the Pledge of Allegiance has been revised since *Barnette* to include the phrase "under God," recital of the Pledge would appear to raise the same Establishment Clause issue as the invocation and benediction. If students were psychologically coerced to remain standing during the invocation, they must also have been psychologically coerced, moments before, to stand for (and thereby, in the Court's view, take part in or appear to take part in) the Pledge. Must the Pledge therefore be barred from the public schools (both from graduation ceremonies and from the classroom)? In *Barnette* we held that a public school student could not be compelled to *recite* the Pledge; we did not even hint that she could not be compelled to observe respectful silence — indeed, even to *stand* in respectful silence — when those who wished to recite it did so. Logically, that ought to be the next project for the Court's bulldozer.

I also find it odd that the Court concludes that high school graduates may not be subjected to this supposed psychological coercion, yet refrains from addressing whether "mature adults" may. I had thought that the reason graduation from high school is regarded as so significant an event is that it is generally associated with transition from adolescence to young adulthood. Many graduating seniors, of course, are old enough to vote. Why, then, does the Court treat them as though they were first-graders? Will we soon have a jurisprudence that distinguishes between mature and immature adults?

B

The other "dominant fac[t]" identified by the Court is that "[s]tate officials direct the performance of a formal religious exercise" at school graduation ceremonies. "Direct[ing] the performance of a formal religious exercise" has a sound of liturgy to it, summoning up images of the principal directing acolytes where to carry the cross, or showing the rabbi where to unroll the Torah. A Court professing to be engaged in a "delicate and fact-sensitive" line-drawing would better describe what it means as "prescribing the content of an invocation and benediction." But even that would be false. All the record shows is that principals of the Providence public schools, acting within their delegated authority, have invited clergy to deliver invocations and benedictions at graduations; and that Principal Lee invited Rabbi Gutterman, provided him a two-page pamphlet, prepared by the National Conference of Christians and Jews, giving general advice on inclusive prayer for civic occasions, and advised him that his prayers at graduation should be nonsectarian. How these facts can fairly be transformed into the charges that Principal Lee "directed and controlled the content of [Rabbi Gutterman's] prayer," that school officials "monitor prayer," and attempted to "'compose official prayers,'" and that the "government involvement with religious activity in this case is pervasive," is difficult to fathom. The Court identifies nothing in the record remotely suggesting that school officials have ever drafted, edited, screened, or censored graduation prayers, or that Rabbi Gutterman was a mouthpiece of the school officials.

These distortions of the record are, of course, not harmless error: without them the Court's solemn assertion that the school officials could reasonably be perceived to be "enforc[ing] a religious orthodoxy," would ring as hollow as it ought.

III

The deeper flaw in the Court's opinion does not lie in its wrong answer to the question whether there was state-induced "peer-pressure" coercion; it lies, rather, in the Court's making violation of the Establishment Clause hinge on such a precious question. The coercion that was a hallmark of historical establishments of religion was coercion of religious orthodoxy and of financial support *by force of law and threat of penalty*. Typically, attendance at the state church was required; only clergy of the official church could lawfully perform sacraments; and dissenters, if tolerated, faced an array of civil disabilities. L. Levy, The Establishment Clause 4 (1986). Thus, for example, in the Colony of Virginia, where the Church of England had been established, ministers were required by law to conform to the doctrine and rites of the Church of England; and all persons were required to attend church and observe the Sabbath, were tithed for the public support of Anglican ministers, and were taxed for the costs of building and repairing churches. *Id.,* at 3-4.

The Establishment Clause was adopted to prohibit such an establishment of religion at the federal level (and to protect state establishments of religion from federal interference). I will further acknowledge for the sake of argument that, as some scholars have argued, by 1790 the term "establishment" had acquired an additional meaning — "financial support of religion generally, by public taxation" — that reflected the development of "general or multiple" establishments, not limited to a single church. But that would still be an establishment coerced *by force of law*. And I will further concede that our constitutional tradition, from the Declaration of Independence and the first inaugural address of Washington, quoted earlier, down to the present day, has, with a few aberrations, ruled out of order government-sponsored endorsement of religion — even when no legal coercion is present, and indeed even when no ersatz, "peer-pressure" psycho-coercion is present — where the endorsement is sectarian, in the sense of specifying details upon which men and women who believe in a benevolent, omnipotent Creator and Ruler of the world are known to differ (for example, the divinity of Christ). But there is simply no support for the proposition that the officially sponsored nondenominational invocation and benediction read by Rabbi Gutterman — with no one legally coerced to recite them — violated the Constitution of the United States. To the contrary, they are so characteristically American they could have come from the pen of George Washington or Abraham Lincoln himself.

Thus, while I have no quarrel with the Court's general proposition that the Establishment Clause "guarantees that government may not coerce anyone to support or participate in religion or its exercise," I see no warrant for expanding the concept of coercion beyond acts backed by threat of penalty — a brand of coercion that, happily, is readily discernible to those of us who have made a career of reading the disciples of Blackstone rather than of Freud. The Framers were indeed opposed to coercion of religious worship by the National Government; but, as their own sponsorship of nonsectarian prayer in public events demonstrates, they understood that "[s]peech is not coercive; the listener may do as he likes." *American Jewish Congress v. Chicago*, 827 F.2d, at 132 (Easterbrook, J., dissenting).

This historical discussion places in revealing perspective the Court's extravagant claim that the State has "for all practical purposes," and "in every practical sense," compelled students to participate in prayers at graduation. Beyond the fact, stipulated to by the parties, that attendance at graduation is voluntary, there is nothing in the record to indicate that failure of attending students to take part in the invocation or benediction was subject to any penalty or discipline. Contrast this with, for example, the facts of *Barnette*: Schoolchildren were required by law to recite the Pledge of Allegiance; failure to do so resulted in expulsion, threatened the expelled child with the prospect of being sent to a reformatory for criminally inclined juveniles, and subjected his parents to prosecution (and incarceration) for causing delinquency. To characterize the "subtle coercive pressures," allegedly present here as the "practical" equivalent of the legal sanctions in *Barnette* is . . . well, let me just say it is not a "delicate and fact-sensitive" analysis.

The Court relies on our "school prayer" cases, *Engel* and *School Dist. of Abington v. Schempp*. But whatever the merit of those cases, they do not support, much less compel, the Court's psycho-journey. In the first place, *Engel* and *Schempp* do not constitute an exception to the rule, distilled from historical practice, that public ceremonies may include prayer; rather, they simply do not fall within the scope of the rule (for the obvious reason that school instruction is not a public ceremony). Second, we have made clear our understanding that school prayer occurs within a framework in which legal coercion to attend school (i.e., coercion under threat of penalty) provides the ultimate backdrop. In *Schempp*, for example, we emphasized that the prayers were "prescribed as part of the curricular activities of students who are *required by law* to attend school." *Engel*'s suggestion that the school prayer program at issue there — which permitted students "to remain silent or be excused from the room," — involved "indirect coercive pressure," should be understood against this backdrop of legal coercion. The question whether the opt-out procedure in *Engel* sufficed to dispel the coercion resulting from the mandatory attendance requirement is quite different from the question whether forbidden coercion exists in an environment *utterly devoid of legal compulsion*. And finally, our school prayer cases turn in part on the fact that the classroom is inherently an instructional setting, and daily prayer there — where parents are not present to counter "the students' emulation of teachers as role models and the children's susceptibility to peer pressure," *Edwards v. Aguillard*, might be thought to raise special concerns regarding state interference with the liberty of parents to direct the religious upbringing of their children: "Families entrust public schools with the education of their children, but condition their trust on the understanding that the classroom will not purposely be used to advance religious views that may conflict with the private beliefs of the student and his or her family." *Ibid*. Voluntary prayer at graduation — a one-time ceremony at which parents, friends, and relatives are present — can hardly be thought to raise the same concerns.

IV

Our Religion Clause jurisprudence has become bedeviled (so to speak) by reliance on formulaic abstractions that are not derived from, but positively conflict with, our long-accepted constitutional traditions. Foremost among these has been the so-called *Lemon* test, which has received well-earned criticism from many Members of this Court. The Court today demonstrates the irrelevance of *Lemon* by essentially ignoring it, and the interment of that case may be the one happy byproduct of the Court's otherwise lamentable decision. Unfortunately, however, the Court has replaced *Lemon* with its psycho-coercion test, which suffers the double disability of having no roots whatever in our people's historic practice, and being as infinitely expandable as the reasons for psychotherapy itself.

Another happy aspect of the case is that it is only a jurisprudential disaster and not a practical one. Given the odd basis for the Court's decision, invocations and benedictions will be able to be given at public school graduations next June, as they have for the past century and a half, so long as school authorities make clear that anyone who abstains from screaming in protest does not necessarily participate in the prayers. All that is seemingly needed is an announcement, or perhaps a written insertion at the beginning of the graduation program, to the effect that, while all are asked to rise for the invocation and benediction, none is compelled to join in them, nor will be assumed, by rising, to have done so. That obvious fact recited, the graduates and their parents may proceed to thank God, as Americans have always done, for the blessings He has generously bestowed on them and on their country.

* * *

The reader has been told much in this case about the personal interest of Mr. Weisman and his daughter, and very little about the personal interests on the other side. They are not inconsequential. Church and state would not be such a difficult subject if religion were, as the Court apparently thinks it to be, some purely personal avocation that can be indulged entirely in secret, like pornography, in the privacy of one's room. For most believers it is *not* that, and has never been. Religious men and women of almost all denominations have felt it necessary to acknowledge and beseech the blessing of God as a people, and not just as individuals, because they believe in the "protection of divine Providence," as the Declaration of Independence put it, not just for individuals but for societies; because they believe God to be, as Washington's first Thanksgiving Proclamation put it, the "Great Lord and Ruler of Nations." One can believe in the effectiveness of such public worship, or one can deprecate and deride it. But the longstanding American tradition of prayer at official ceremonies displays with unmistakable clarity that the Establishment Clause does not forbid the government to accommodate it.

The narrow context of the present case involves a community's celebration of one of the milestones in its young citizens' lives, and it is a bold step for this

Court to seek to banish from that occasion, and from thousands of similar celebrations throughout this land, the expression of gratitude to God that a majority of the community wishes to make. The issue before us today is not the abstract philosophical question whether the alternative of frustrating this desire of a religious majority is to be preferred over the alternative of imposing "psychological coercion," or a feeling of exclusion, upon nonbelievers. Rather, the question is *whether a mandatory choice in favor of the former has been imposed by the United States Constitution.* As the age-old practices of our people show, the answer to that question is not at all in doubt.

I must add one final observation: The Founders of our Republic knew the fearsome potential of sectarian religious belief to generate civil dissension and civil strife. And they also knew that nothing, absolutely nothing, is so inclined to foster among religious believers of various faiths a toleration — no, an affection — for one another than voluntarily joining in prayer together, to the God whom they all worship and seek. Needless to say, no one should be compelled to do that, but it is a shame to deprive our public culture of the opportunity, and indeed the encouragement, for people to do it voluntarily. The Baptist or Catholic who heard and joined in the simple and inspiring prayers of Rabbi Gutterman on this official and patriotic occasion was inoculated from religious bigotry and prejudice in a manner that cannot be replicated. To deprive our society of that important unifying mechanism, in order to spare the nonbeliever what seems to me the minimal inconvenience of standing or even sitting in respectful nonparticipation, is as senseless in policy as it is unsupported in law.

C. "VOLUNTARY" PRAYER AT PUBLIC SCHOOL GRADUATION CEREMONIES AND EXTRACURRICULAR EVENTS

JONES v. CLEAR CREEK INDEPENDENT SCHOOL DISTRICT
977 F.2d 963 (5th Cir. 1992)

REAVLEY, CIRCUIT JUDGE:

In *Jones v. Clear Creek Independent School Dist.*, 930 F.2d 416 (5th Cir.1991) (*Jones I*), *vacated,* 505 U.S. 1215 (1992), we held that Clear Creek Independent School District's Resolution[1] permitting public high school seniors to choose

---

[1] The Resolution provides:

1. The use of an invocation and/or benediction at high school graduation exercise shall rest within the discretion of the graduating senior class, with the advice and counsel of the senior class principal;

2. The invocation and benediction, if used, shall be given by a student volunteer; and

3. Consistent with the principle of equal liberty of conscience, the invocation and benediction shall be nonsectarian and nonproselytizing in nature.

student volunteers to deliver nonsectarian, nonproselytizing invocations at their graduation ceremonies does not violate the Constitution's Establishment Clause. In applying the tripartite test of *Lemon v. Kurtzman*, we reasoned that the Resolution has a secular purpose of solemnization, that the Resolution's primary effect is to impress upon graduation attendees the profound social significance of the occasion rather than advance or endorse religion, and that Clear Creek does not excessively entangle itself with religion by proscribing sectarianism and proselytization without prescribing any form of invocation.

Then, in *Lee v. Weisman*, the Supreme Court held that Robert E. Lee, a public-school principal acting in accord with the policy of his Providence, Rhode Island school district, violated the Establishment Clause by inviting a local clergy member, Rabbi Leslie Gutterman, to deliver a nonsectarian, nonproselytizing invocation at his school's graduation ceremony. The Court reasoned that Lee's actions represent governmental coercion to participate in religious activities, a paradigmatic establishment of religion. The Court then granted certiorari in this case, vacated our judgment, and remanded it to us for further consideration in light of *Lee*. Upon reconsideration, we hold that *Lee* does not render Clear Creek's invocation policy unconstitutional, and again affirm the district court's summary judgment in Clear Creek's favor.

I. THE SUPREME COURT TELLS THIS COURT WHAT THE ESTABLISHMENT CLAUSE MEANS

Although the Supreme Court's doctrinally-centered manner of resolving Establishment Clause disputes may be credited with accommodating a society of remarkable religious diversity, it requires considerable micromanagement of government's relationship to religion as the Court decides each case by distilling fact-sensitive rules from its precedents.

The Court has repeatedly held that the Establishment Clause forbids the imposition of religion through public education. That leads to difficulty because of public schools' responsibility to develop pupils' character and decisionmaking skills, a responsibility more important in a society suffering from parental failure. If religion be the foundation, or at least relevant to these functions and to the education of the young, as is widely believed, it follows that religious thought should not be excluded as irrelevant to public education. There is a deep public concern that radical efforts to avoid pressuring children to be religious actually teach and enforce notions that pressure the young to avoid all that is religious.

Nevertheless, it is neither our object nor our place to opine whether the Court's Establishment Clause jurisprudence is good, fair, or useful. What the Establishment Clause finally means in a specific case is what the Court says it means. We sit only to apply the analytical methods sanctioned by the Court in accord with its precedent.

II. FROM *LEMON* TO *LEE*

In *Jones I*, we applied *Lemon's* tripartite test. The *Lee* Court considered *Lemon* analysis unnecessary to decide whether Lee violated the Establishment Clause. The Court instead held Lee's actions unconstitutional under a coercion analysis. At least four Justices would also hold that Lee's actions had the effect of unconstitutionally endorsing religion. We address any statements in *Lee* that bear on our analysis in *Jones I* and apply *Lee's* coercion test for the first time.

A. SECULAR PURPOSE

Nothing in *Lee* abrogates our conclusion that the Resolution has a secular purpose of solemnization, and thus satisfies *Lemon's* first requirement. The Resolution represents Clear Creek's judgment that society benefits if people attach importance to graduation. A meaningful graduation ceremony can provide encouragement to finish school and the inspiration and self-assurance necessary to achieve after graduation, which are secular objectives.

The *Lee* Court stated that the Providence school district's solemnization argument would have "considerable force were it not for the constitutional constraints applied to state action. . . ." The Court did not question its members' previous acknowledgements that solemnization is a legitimate secular purpose of ceremonial prayer. Thus, we take the *Lee* Court to agree with our holding in *Jones I* that a law may pass *Lemon's* secular-purpose test by solemnizing public occasions, yet still be stricken as an unconstitutional establishment under another test mandated by the Court.

B. PRIMARY EFFECT

In *Jones I*, we held that the Resolution's *primary* effect was to solemnize graduation ceremonies, not to "advance religion" in contravention of *Lemon's* second requirement. *Lee* calls into question three statements that we made in support of our advancement holding. We stated that graduating high school seniors would be less easily influenced by prayer than would be their junior schoolmates, but the Court held that all students under school supervision would be unduly influenced by Rabbi Gutterman's prayers. We distinguished the graduation setting from the classroom setting because parents and guests are present only at graduation and school officials can pay much greater attention to individual students in the classroom than at graduation, but the Court stated that the two settings are "analogous." We stated that the brevity and infrequency of the permissible prayers under the Resolution tempered any advancement of religion, *Jones I*, but the Court rejected a *de minimis* characterization of the brief prayers at issue in *Lee*.

Lee commands that we not rely on these three points in deciding whether the Resolution's primary effect is to advance religion. Yet even without them, we remain convinced that the Resolution's primary effect is to solemnize graduation ceremonies.

The Resolution can only advance religion by increasing religious conviction among graduation attendees, which means attracting new believers or increasing the faith of the faithful. Its requirement that any invocation be nonsectarian and nonproselytizing minimizes any such advancement of religion. The *Lee* Court held that the nonsectarian nature of the prayers there at issue did not change the fact that Lee directed graduation attendees to participate in a religious exercise. Nevertheless, the nonsectarian nature of a prayer remains relevant to the extent to which a prayer advances religion.

The fact that *Lemon* only condemns government action that has the *primary* effect of advancing religion, requires us to compare the Resolution's secular and religious effect. The Resolution may or may not have any religious effect. The students may or may not employ the name of any deity; heads may or may not be bowed; indeed, an invocation may or may not appear on the program. If the students choose a nonproselytizing, nonsectarian prayer, the effect may well marshall attendees' extant religiosity for the secular purpose of solemnization; but no one would likely expect the advancement of religion by the initiation or increase of religious faith through these prayers. The Resolution's primary effect is secular.

C. ENTANGLEMENT

We held in *Jones I* that the Resolution's proscription of sectarianism does not, of itself, excessively entangle government with religion. We know of no authority that holds yearly review of unsolicited material for sectarianism and proselytization to constitute excessive entanglement. Moreover, nothing in *Lee* abrogates our reading of the Court's entanglement precedent to limit violative entanglement to *institutional* entanglement. That a rabbi wrote and delivered the prayer at issue in *Lee* makes entanglement analysis relevant to that case, but the Resolution keeps Clear Creek free of all involvement with religious institutions.

D. ENDORSEMENT

Like *Lemon*'s advancement test, the Court's endorsement analysis focuses on the *effect* of a challenged governmental action. This is why, perhaps mistakenly, we conflated advancement and endorsement analysis in *Jones I*. Because the Court has never tolerated a government endorsement of religion that is incidental to a primary secular effect, as it has with incidental religious advancements, we will not now compare endorsement to legitimate effects of the Resolution.

From the Court's various pronouncements, we understand government to unconstitutionally endorse religion when a reasonable person would view the challenged government action as a disapproval of her contrary religious choices.

We may compare the Resolution to the facts in two somewhat similar cases where members of the Court discussed endorsement of religion. Both *Lee* concurrences consider invocations directed by Lee to be unconstitutional endorsements of religion. On the other hand, a plurality of the Court recently held that a public school does not unconstitutionally endorse religion by permitting a Christian club to meet on school grounds after class and recruit members through the school's newspaper, bulletin boards, public address system, and annual Club Fair, as long as the school accords equal privileges to other non-curriculum-oriented student organizations. *See Board of Educ. of Westside Community Sch. v. Mergens*

To compare the Resolution with *Lee* and *Mergens*, we consider exactly what it does. Unlike the policy at issue in *Lee,* it does not mandate a prayer. The Resolution does not even mandate an invocation; it merely permits one if the seniors so choose. Moreover, the students present Clear Creek with *their* proposed invocation under the Resolution, while in *Lee* the school explained its idea for an invocation to a member of an organized religion and directed him to deliver it. The Resolution is passive compared to the governmental overture toward religion at issue in *Lee.*

Concerning endorsement, the instant case more closely parallels *Mergens* because a graduating high school senior *who participates in the decision as to whether her graduation will include an invocation by a fellow student volunteer* will understand that any religious references are the result of student, not government, choice. The *Mergens* plurality states the point directly:

> there is a crucial difference between *government* speech endorsing religion, which the Establishment Clause forbids, and *private* speech endorsing religion, which the Free Speech and Free Exercise Clauses protect. We think that secondary school students are mature enough and are likely to understand that a school does not endorse or support student speech that it merely permits on a nondiscriminatory basis.

In *Jones I*, we recognized that invocations permitted by the Resolution "may" include supplication to a deity. But the Resolution permits invocations free of all religious content, and the 1987 student proposal was acceptable to the plaintiff-appellants. The record does not disclose how each senior class chooses whether to include an invocation nor how the student volunteer who delivers the speech is chosen. We can imagine discriminatory methods of implementing the Resolution that would make it a tool for governmental endorsement of religion, but the Resolution itself is constitutional unless there is no way to implement it on a nondiscriminatory basis.

We think that Clear Creek does not unconstitutionally endorse religion if it submits the decision of graduation invocation content, if any, to the majority vote of the senior class. Clear Creek is legitimately concerned with solemnizing its graduation ceremonies, and the Resolution simply permits each senior class to decide how this can best be done. School districts commonly provide similarly secular criteria for the selection of other student graduation speakers, and no court has held that their religious speech at graduation represents government endorsement of religion.[11] After participating in a student determination of what kind of invocation their graduation will contain, we do not believe that students will perceive any more government endorsement of religion from the Resolution than do students in Westside Community schools who are regularly recruited during school hours to join a Christian club. Clear Creek students certainly perceive a less-direct relationship between state and religion under the Resolution than Providence students did before *Lee*. We find no unconstitutional endorsement.

E. COERCION

Instead of directly considering any of the tests that we have previously discussed, the *Lee* Court invalidated the Providence school district's policy on its evaluation of the coercive effect of Lee's actions. The Court held that Lee *coerced* graduation attendees to join in a formal religious exercise. The Court summarized its entire analysis of the constitutionality of the school policy at issue in *Lee* as follows:

> These dominant facts mark and control the confines of our decision: State officials direct the performance of a formal religious exercise at promotional and graduation ceremonies for secondary schools. Even for those students who object to the religious exercise, their attendance and participation in the state-sponsored religious activity are in a fair and real sense obligatory. . . .

Id. Thus, *Lee* identifies unconstitutional coercion when (1) the government directs (2) a formal religious exercise (3) in such a way as to oblige the participation of objectors. Before *Lee*, no one contended that the Resolution coerced participation in prayer at Clear Creek's graduation ceremonies, and we failed to appreciate the need to address this issue from the Court's precedent that we discussed in *Jones I*. Upon considering this case in light of *Lee*'s coercion analysis, we find that the Resolution does not succumb to one, let alone all three, of the elements of unconstitutional coercion, and thus survives the analysis that felled graduation prayer in *Lee*.

1. Direction

Throughout *Lee*'s entire coercion analysis, the Court repeatedly stresses the government's direct and complete control over the graduation prayers there at issue as determinative of the establishment question. The Court deplored three instances of government involvement in graduation prayer in *Lee*, none of which is tolerated, let alone prescribed, by the Resolution. First, the Court found that Lee "decided that an invocation and benediction should be given; this is a choice attributable to the State, and from a constitutional perspective it is as if a state statute decreed that the prayers must occur." The Resolution

---

[11] That some attendees choose to stand and remain silent during an invocation is indistinguishable from their decision to accord a standing ovation to a moving valedictory address with religious inferences.

requires that the state *not* decide whether an invocation will occur; it respects the graduating class's choice on the matter. The Resolution acknowledges that a school official may offer "advice and counsel" to the senior class in deciding whether to include invocations at graduation, and officials could exploit this clause to impose their will on the students. But, again, in evaluating the Resolution's facial constitutionality, we are only concerned with whether the Resolution necessarily charges government with the decision of whether to include invocations. Unlike the policy at issue in *Lee*, the Resolution does not.

Second, the Court was critical of the fact that "[t]he principal chose the religious participant, here a rabbi, and that choice is also attributable to the State." *Id.* In contrast, the Resolution explicitly precludes anyone but a student volunteer from delivering Clear Creek's invocations. Moreover, the Resolution says nothing of government involvement in the selection of the person who delivers any invocation. That the government can remain detached from this selection consistent with the Resolution maintains the Resolution's facial constitutionality.

The Court recognized that Lee completed his control over the invocation at his school's graduation ceremonies when he "provided Rabbi Gutterman with a copy of the 'Guidelines for Civic Occasions,' and advised him that his prayers should be nonsectarian." In three respects, Clear Creek exercises significantly less control over the content of invocations at its schools. Clear Creek does not solicit invocations; the Resolution only forbids Clear Creek schools from *accepting* sectarian or proselytizing invocations. Moreover, because a graduating senior drafts proposed invocations each year under the Resolution, the same person will never repeatedly propose an invocation. *Compare id.* (noting that Lee could refine an official prayer by repeatedly inviting the same clergy member to deliver invocations). Finally, the Resolution imposes two one-word restrictions "nonsectarian and nonproselytizing" which enhance solemnization and minimize advancement of religion, instead of a pamphlet full of invocation suggestions.

We conclude that Clear Creek does not direct prayer presentations at its graduation ceremonies.

2. Religiosity

Lee directed Rabbi Gutterman to pray, and the Court characterized this as a "formal religious observance." By contrast, the Resolution tolerates nonsectarian, nonproselytizing prayer, but does not require or favor it.

3. Participation

The *Lee* Court held that government-mandated prayer at graduation places a constitutionally impermissible amount of psychological pressure upon students to participate in religious exercises. We think that the graduation prayers permitted by the Resolution place less psychological pressure on students than the prayers at issue in *Lee* because all students, *after having participated in the decision of whether prayers will be given*, are aware that any prayers represent the will of their peers, who are less able to coerce participation than an authority figure from the state or clergy.

We also consider the age of the graduating seniors relevant to the determination of whether prayers under the Resolution can coerce these young people into participating in a religious exercise. *Lee* explains that the *state-initiated clergy prayers there at issue* have a coercive effect on public-school students regardless of age, but it nowhere compromises the Court's previous recognition that graduating seniors "are less impressionable than younger students."

Accordingly, we think that the coercive effect of any prayer permitted by the Resolution is more analogous to the innocuous "God save the United States and this Honorable Court" stated *by and to* adults than the government-mandated message delivered to young people from religious authority that the Court considered in *Lee*. *Cf. Lee* (refusing to "address whether [the choice between participation and protest] is acceptable if the affected citizens are mature adults").[13]

None of *Lee's* three elements of coercive effect exist here. Prayers allowed under the Resolution do not unconstitutionally coerce objectors into participation.

III. FROM SEA TO SHINING SEA, GREAT GOD OUR KING[14]

The practical result of our decision, viewed in light of *Lee*, is that a majority of students can do what the State acting on its own cannot do to incorporate prayer in public high school graduation ceremonies. In *Lee*, the Court forbade schools from exacting participation in a religious exercise as the price for attending what many consider to be one of life's most important events. This case requires us to consider *why* so many people attach importance to graduation ceremonies. If they only seek government's recognition of student achievement, diplomas suffice. If they only seek God's recognition, a privately-sponsored baccalaureate will do. But to experience the *community's* recognition of student achievement, they must attend the public ceremony that other interested community members also hold so dear. By attending graduation to experience and participate in the community's display of support for the graduates, people

---

[13] Nor did the Court criticize the fact that, before Rabbi Gutterman delivered the prayers ordered by Lee, the assembly stood for the Pledge of Allegiance, which of course recounts our subjugation to a deity.

[14] America! America!
God shed His grace on thee,
And crown thy good with brotherhood
From sea to shining sea.
America the Beautiful
Long may our land be bright.
With freedom's holy light;
Protect us by Thy might,
Great God, our King.
   America

should not be surprised to find the event affected by community standards. The Constitution requires nothing different.

DOE v. DUNCANVILLE INDEPENDENT SCHOOL DISTRICT
70 F.3d 402 (5th Cir. 1995)

W. EUGENE DAVIS, Circuit Judge:

I. FACTS

Plaintiffs in this case are Jane Doe, a student in the Duncanville Independent School District [DISD], and John Doe, her father. Jane Doe first enrolled in the DISD in 1988, when she entered the seventh grade at the age of twelve. Doe qualified to play on the girls' basketball team and was placed in an athletic class specially designated for team members. This class was held during the last class period of the day and extended into after school practice. Students received academic credit for this class and for their participation in the sport. During her first class, Doe learned that the girls' basketball coach, Coach Smith, included the Lord's Prayer in each basketball practice. The basketball team also said prayers in the locker rooms before games began, after games in the center of the basketball court in front of spectators, and on the school bus traveling to and from basketball games. Coach Smith initiated or participated in these prayers. These prayers had been a tradition for almost twenty years.

When she first became a team member, Doe participated in these prayers because she did not wish to single herself out. After Doe's father attended a game and saw his daughter joining in the center court prayer, he asked her how she felt about participating. When told that she preferred not to participate, John Doe told his daughter that she did not have to take part in the prayers. Thereafter, Jane Doe no longer participated. At games away from home and at least one home game, Doe was required to stand by while the team prayed. Her non-participation drew attention from her fellow students, who asked her "Aren't you a Christian?" and from one spectator, who called out "Well, why isn't she praying? Isn't she a Christian?" At one point during her history class, Doe's history teacher referred to her as a "little atheist."

John Doe complained about the prayers to the assistant superintendent of schools, Ed Parker, and his successor, Marvin Utecht. Utecht halted the prayers at pep rallies, although he insisted there was nothing he could do about the post-game prayers. [Parker's response to Doe's complaint was blunt: "Parker stated that 'unless [Doe] had grandparents buried in the Duncanville Cemetery he had no right to tell [Parker] how to run his schools.'" *See Doe I*, 994 F.2d at 162 n.1.]

Jane Doe also joined the choir program at DISD. Students in this program also receive academic credit for their participation. In the seventh and eighth grade choruses, Doe was required to sing the choir theme song *Go Ye Now in Peace*, which is based on Christian text. Upon progressing to the high school choirs, Doe was required to sing another Christian theme song, *The Lord Bless You and Keep You*. David McCullar, the director for the ninth through twelfth grade choirs, testified that *The Lord Bless You and Keep You* had been the choirs' theme song for at least 20 years; he did not know how it had originally been chosen. The choirs learn this song as part of their overall repertoire, sing it at the end of class on Fridays, at the end of some performances and during choral competitions. They also sing this song on the bus on the way home from performances. The parties stipulated that the choir's theme song is a "Christian religious song."

DISD also engaged in a number of other religious practices or customs, such as holding prayers and distributing pamphlets containing religious songs at awards ceremonies, allowing student-initiated prayers before football games, allowing Gideon Bibles to be distributed to fifth grade classes, and until 1990, including prayers during school pep rallies.

On August 15, 1991, the Does filed an application for a temporary restraining order and preliminary injunction. Following a two-day trial, the district court entered a preliminary injunction forbidding DISD from permitting its employees to lead, encourage, promote or participate in prayer with or among students during curricular or extra-curricular activities, including sporting events. DISD appealed the preliminary injunction, which was affirmed by this Court.

At the permanent injunction hearing, the parties stipulated that since May 1991, DISD stopped all prayers during class-time.[3] Students are still allowed to initiate prayers during athletic events, but the coaches no longer do so. After the hearing, the district court found that DISD violated the Establishment Clause by (1) permitting its employees to lead, encourage, promote or participate in prayers with students during curricular or extracurricular events; (2) permitting its employees to initiate, lead, authorize, encourage or condone the recitation or singing of religious songs as the theme songs of the schools' choirs; and (3) authorizing, permitting or condoning the distribution at Duncanville schools of Gideon Bibles to fifth grade students by representatives of the Gideon Society, except to the extent permitted by the Equal Access Act. Based on these conclusions, the court enjoined DISD from continuing these practices. We discuss each of Appellants' arguments below.

II. ANALYSIS

A. Prayer at Curricular and Extra-Curricular Activities

The district court enjoined DISD, its employees and its agents from:

> 1. leading, encouraging, promoting, or participating in prayers with or among students during curricular or extracurricular activities, including before, during, or after school-related sporting events. Students, however, are not enjoined from praying, either individually or in groups.

---

[3] However, it appears that prayers did not stop during basketball practice.

Students may voluntarily pray together, provided such prayer is not done with school participation or supervision.

DISD argues that the district court erred by forbidding DISD employees from participating in or supervising student-initiated prayers. We will address each asserted error separately.

1. Participation

DISD contends that it cannot prevent its employees from participating in student prayers without violating their employees' rights to the free exercise of religion, to association, and to free speech and academic freedom. We do not agree. As we noted in *Doe I*, " 'the principle that government may accommodate the free exercise of religion does not supersede the fundamental limitations imposed by the Establishment Clause.' " 994 F.2d at 165 (quoting *Lee*, 505 U.S. at 586-87). *See also Berger v. Rensselaer Central School Corp.*, 982 F.2d 1160, 1168 (7th Cir.1993) (free expression rights must bow to the Establishment Clause prohibition on school-endorsed religious activities). This is particularly true in the instant context of basketball practices and games. The challenged prayers take place during school-controlled, curriculum-related activities that members of the basketball team are required to attend. During these activities DISD coaches and other school employees are present as representatives of the school and their actions are representative of DISD policies. *See Bishop v. Aronov*, 926 F.2d 1066, 1073 (11th Cir.1991) ("a teacher's [religious] speech can be taken as directly and deliberately representative of the school"). DISD representatives' participation in these prayers improperly entangles it in religion and signals an unconstitutional endorsement of religion. *See also Board of Education of Westside Community Schools v. Mergens*, 496 U.S. 226, 251 (1990) (quoting *Edwards v. Aguillard*, 482 U.S. 578, 584 (1987)) (EAA valid because it expressly forbids teacher participation and "avoids the problems of 'the students' emulation of teachers as role models' ").[4]

For these reasons, we find that the district court did not err in enjoining DISD employees and agents from participating in student-initiated prayers.

2. Supervision

DISD contends that the district court's statement that "[s]tudents may voluntarily pray together, provided such prayer is not done with school participation or supervision" contradicts the Supreme Court's holding in *Mergens*.

---

[4] However, we note that neither the Establishment Clause nor the district court's order prevent DISD employees from treating students' religious beliefs and practices with deference and respect; indeed, the constitution requires this. Nothing compels DISD employees to make their non-participation vehemently obvious or to leave the room when students pray in, for example, a *Mergens* style setting. However, if while acting in their official capacities, DISD employees join hands in a prayer circle or otherwise manifest approval and solidarity with student religious exercises, they cross the line between respect for religion and endorsement of religion.

In *Mergens*, the Supreme Court upheld the Equal Access Act (EAA) require-ment that a non-curricular student prayer group be given the same access to school facilities as other student groups. Under the EAA, school employees can be present at these religious meetings for custodial purposes.

However, as we explained in *Doe I*, *Mergens* does not apply to the type of activities at issue here. The facts before us do not even vaguely resemble a *Mergens* situation. Membership on the basketball team is at least extra-cur-ricular: it is directly related to the school's physical education classes and stu-dents receive academic credit for their participation. The games are school-sponsored and -controlled events that do not provide any sort of open forum for student expression and DISD makes no claim that it has created such a forum for its basketball team or any other athletic group. Because nei-ther the injunction nor the facts of this case purport to address a genuine *Mer-gens* situation, we decline to do so here.

We also note that *Jones II* does not require a different result. *Jones II* upheld a school resolution which permitted high school students to choose whether to have a student volunteer deliver a non-sectarian and non-proselytizing invo-cation and benediction during high school graduation. In concluding that this resolution did not violate the Establishment Clause, we emphasized that high school graduation is a significant, once-in-a-lifetime event that could be appro-priately marked with a prayer, that the students involved were mature high school seniors, and that the challenged prayer was to be non-sectarian and non-proselytizing. Here, we are dealing with a setting that is far less solemn and extraordinary, a quintessentially Christian prayer, and students of twelve years of age (the age at which Jane Doe first encountered basketball team prayers). These facts place the prayer at issue here in a materially different position than the one we permitted in *Jones II*.

B. DISD Choirs' Theme Song

DISD contends that the district court erred by enjoining DISD from permit-ting DISD choirs to sing songs with religious content as their theme songs. The district court enjoined DISD, its employees and agents from:

> 2. initiating, leading, authorizing, encouraging, or condoning the recita-tion or singing of religious songs as a theme song of the Duncanville school choirs. Religious songs may be sung, however, for their artis-tic and historic qualities if presented objectively as part of a secular program of education.

The district court made only two findings specific to this issue: (1) that "Jane Doe is a member of the DISD choir and receives academic credit for her par-ticipation in the choir"; and (2) that "[a]s a DISD choir member, Jane Doe was required to sing a religious Christian song entitled, *The Lord Bless You and Keep You*. This song is sung at each DISD choir performance and has been adopted by school personnel and students as the choir's theme song."

All parties recognize that the Establishment Clause does not prohibit DISD choirs from singing religious songs as part of a secular music program, in accord with *School District of Abington Township v. Schempp*. Thus, the Does essentially contend that the act of treating *The Lord Bless You and Keep You* as the theme song, rather than as simply one song in the repertoire, transforms the permissible practice of singing this song into an endorsement of religion. The record reveals that two practical effects flow from designating this as the theme song: it is sung often and it is carried over from year to year.

Legitimate secular reasons exist for maintaining *The Lord Bless You and Keep You* as the theme song. As the choir director, David McCullar, testified, this song is particularly useful to teach students to sight read and to sing *a capella*. In Mr. McCullar's words, it is also "a good piece of music . . . by a reputable composer."

Neither does utilizing *The Lord Bless You and Keep You* as a theme song advance or endorse religion. The Does do not argue that the choir sings the theme song as a religious exercise per se so we do not accept the notion that repeated singing of a particular religious song amounts to an endorsement of religion. At trial, Mr. McCullar estimated that 60-75 percent of serious choral music is based on sacred themes or text. Given the dominance of religious music in this field, DISD can hardly be presumed to be advancing or endorsing religion by allowing its choirs to sing a religious theme song. As a matter of statistical probability, the song best suited to be the theme is more likely to be religious than not. Indeed, to forbid DISD from having a theme song that is religious would force DISD to disqualify the majority of appropriate choral music simply because it is religious. Within the world of choral music, such a restriction would require hostility, not neutrality, toward religion.[8]

A position of neutrality towards religion must allow choir directors to recognize the fact that most choral music is religious. Limiting the number of times a religious piece of music can be sung is tantamount to censorship and does not send students a message of neutrality. Where, as here, singing the theme song is not a religious exercise, we will not find an endorsement of religion exists merely because a religious song with widely recognized musical value is sung more often than other songs. Such animosity towards religion is not required or condoned by the Constitution.

We conclude that the district court erred by enjoining DISD from using songs with religious content as theme songs for its choirs.

---

[8] The argument that students likely identify their choir by its theme song is well taken but misses the crucial point that particularly in the world of choral music, singing about religion is not the same as endorsing or exercising religion. Students who identify DISD's choir with *The Lord Bless and Keep You* will certainly feel unity with past choirs from the same school but we are hard pressed to find that this unity necessarily stems from a common belief in Christianity or Judaism rather than the fact that the earlier students also attended the same high school.

C. Distribution of Gideon Bibles

[The court held that the plaintiff did not have standing to challenge the distribution of Gideon Bibles.]

EDITH H. JONES, CIRCUIT JUDGE, concurring and dissenting:

I concur in Judge Davis's opinion insofar as it rejects an Establishment Clause challenge to the DISD choir's choice of songs or "theme song" and holds the Gideon Bible controversy moot. I dissent with qualifications in the majority's upholding an injunction against active teacher "participation" and "supervision" of the voluntary student-initiated prayers. "Participation," in one sense, cannot constitutionally be prevented by this court, while "supervision," rightly understood, cannot be broader than the concept of the school's encouraging, promoting or leading the prayers.

This decision, like that in *Doe I*, does not prevent students from exercising their constitutional rights of free speech, association and free exercise by praying at appropriate times and in an appropriate manner during athletic practices or games. Further, we must abide by the Supreme Court's decisions, reflected in the injunction, that prevent active school leadership, encouragement or promotion of the prayers. The only questions here are how teachers may respond to student-initiated prayers and to what extent the school may "supervise" the prayers. My differences with the majority are those of emphasis.

There is practically no doubt that the trend in Supreme Court establishment clause cases supports the majority's decision insofar as it prevents teachers from actively joining in the student-led prayers, e.g., by joining hands in the prayer circle. Such actions would, according to at least five members of the Supreme Court, too easily connote official endorsement and would imply coercion of non-participants. As the majority properly observed, however, teachers are not prohibited from exercising deference and respect toward student-initiated prayers. I would add to this that the line between deference and sympathetic reverence is a fine one that cannot and should not be policed, if teachers' individual freedom of conscience is to retain any meaning in this context. The federal courts may currently prevent school-sponsored or -promoted religious devotional exercises, but surely they may not reach into the minds of individual teachers to prescribe their responses to student-initiated prayers. Neither Jane Doe nor any federal court in the United States of America may insist upon a purge of the teachers' spiritual response to student prayers.

As for the term "supervision," I agree that this is not technically a *Mergens* case involving the Equal Access Act. What "supervision" means in the context of basketball practices and games is, however, ambiguous. At a broad level, everything that goes on during practice or competition, including student-initiated locker-room or basketball court prayer, is subject to the coaches' "supervision." To outlaw supervision on this level would be to outlaw the otherwise constitutional student-led prayers. Neither the majority nor the district court intends this untenable result. It must be, then, that the injunction pertains only to *active* supervision and is thus redundant of the cautions that the school may not promote, encourage or lead prayers.

MAHON, DISTRICT JUDGE, dissenting in part:

Although I join in the majority opinion with respect to DISD's involvement in prayer and the distribution of Gideon Bibles, I respectfully disagree with my colleagues that DISD's choice of religious theme songs for its choirs is consistent with the First Amendment. Viewed as a whole, the facts in this case fully support the district court's prohibition of DISD's participation, in any form, in the use by its choirs of religious theme songs. Accordingly, I dissent from the majority's decision to reverse the district court's ruling on this issue.

Although the majority opinion sets forth many of the facts in the case, it will help to recount here those facts which demonstrate the similarity between the DISD's choice of a religious theme song and its other religious practices, which the majority agree are unconstitutional.

It is undisputed that for some twenty years, DISD, through the actions of its teachers and other employees, permitted, encouraged and even sponsored the recitation of prayers during curricular and extracurricular activities. Prayers were recited during classes. Many events were begun and closed with a prayer. Sports teams recited prayers before games in the locker rooms, after games on the field and in the buses returning to school. At award ceremonies, prayers were recited and DISD teachers distributed pamphlets of religious songs for participants to sing. The prayers and songs were always Christian.

During the same twenty year period, DISD choir teachers treated as the theme song for the ninth grade and high school choirs what the parties have stipulated is a Christian religious song entitled *The Lord Bless You and Keep You*. The song is in the form of a prayer seeking God's blessings on behalf of a third party.[1] The theme song was sung at the end of each performance except when circumstances made it inappropriate, such as when members of the choir performed as a barbershop quartet. In addition, the choir sang the song on the bus on the way home from performances and at the end of class each Friday. The students were not given an opportunity to choose a new theme song each year or to determine whether to have a theme song at all. Rather, the song was passed on as an established tradition to incoming choir teachers, who in turn taught it to each new group of students. Although there apparently was no for-

---

[1] The words of the song are:

"The Lord bless you and keep you, the Lord lift His countenance upon you; and give you peace, and give you peace, the Lord make his face to shine upon you, and be gracious unto you, be gracious, the Lord be gracious, gracious unto you. Amen, Amen, Amen, Amen, Amen."

This text, taken from the Old Testament, Numbers VI, 24-26, would be better characterized as Judeo-Christian.

mal, written designation of the theme song, choir teachers and students were aware that the specified song was the theme song and treated it accordingly.

DISD's intermediate school choir had a different theme song, which was also a Christian religious song. Although the record is less developed as to this song, *Go Ye Now in Peace*, the evidence shows that it also was sung at the end of each performance.

The district court did not err in viewing DISD's choice of religious theme songs as an inseparable part of its historical pattern of encouraging and endorsing Christian religious beliefs through the activities of its teachers. This is not a case where the choice of theme songs was the only arguably religious practice involved, but one where expression of religious belief was permitted and approved at almost every level of school life. In virtually the same way that prayers were recited during classes, sports and other events, the choirs' theme songs were used to mark the close of performances and the week, and to unify participants in a common outlook. Viewed in this context, the theme songs served as yet another vehicle for inculcating a Christian attitude, and their singing constituted a religious exercise.

The majority does not disagree with the legal principles applied by the district court. Instead, by ignoring the role and effect of theme songs in general, and the connection between DISD's theme songs and its other religious practices in particular, the majority reaches the conclusion that DISD's religious theme songs had a secular purpose and did not have the effect of advancing or endorsing religion. An analysis of the majority's reasoning shows it to be faulty in several respects.

Before addressing the majority's conclusions, it is important to review DISD's own justification for the choice of religious theme songs for each of its choirs. DISD has offered two purportedly secular reasons for this practice. It asserts, first, that the theme songs solemnize events as did the prayer found to be constitutional in *Jones v. Clear Creek Indep. Sch. Dist.* The holding in *Jones*, however, was limited to very specific circumstances which are not present here. *Jones* upheld a school district resolution that permitted the delivery of a non-sectarian, non- proselytizing prayer in only one context, a high school graduation ceremony, where solemnization was found appropriate to mark a once-in-a-lifetime occasion. By contrast, DISD's choirs' theme songs were sung repeatedly, not only at performances throughout the year, but also on the buses returning from performances and at the end of class each Friday, occasions not generally thought of as requiring a solemnizing ceremony. In asserting that a religious theme song is needed to achieve solemnity in such circumstances, some of the same ones in which DISD traditionally initiated or permitted the recitation of prayers, DISD inadvertently supports the conclusion that it chose religious theme songs not for any secular reason, but for the very purpose of encouraging religious reverence through yet another avenue.

DISD next contends its theme songs provide unity and comraderie for choir members. To the extent DISD means simply that having a theme song serves to unify choir members, this explanation adds nothing to the analysis, because the challenged injunction does not forbid the use of theme songs, *per se*. Nor does the reference to unity and comraderie, by itself, answer the question of the purpose of having *religious* theme songs. DISD does not specify which elements of its theme songs are critical to creating unity and comraderie. We already know, however, that DISD believes the songs have a solemnizing function, that is, a function most often played by prayer. See *Jones v. Clear Creek Indep. Sch. Dist.* (indicating there is no secular equivalent of a prayer for solemnization purposes). The theme songs were sung in circumstances likely to emphasize their religious message. Further, we cannot ignore the long history of this school district authorizing and encouraging the recitation of Christian prayers, especially as a means to unify the school and its teams before and after competitions and other special events. In light of this history, DISD's choice of theme songs that essentially are prayers can hardly be viewed as a coincidence. Rather, the religious nature of the songs clearly was expected to be an inextricable part of their role in fostering unity and group identification.

Apparently not satisfied with DISD's explanation, the majority finds its own secular reasons for maintaining *God Bless You and Keep You* as the high school choirs' theme song: the song's usefulness for teaching students to sing *a capella* and its worth as a good piece of music by a reputable composer. These characteristics of the song, however, do not answer the question of DISD's purpose in designating it, or any religious song, as a *theme* song. DISD is free to teach religious songs and obtain their secular benefits as part of the music curriculum without giving them the special treatment it has accorded its theme songs. Moreover, the evidence shows that *God Bless You and Keep You* is not unique in the characteristics singled out by the majority. DISD's high school choir director testified that there are from 25 to 50 secular songs that are sung *a capella* and would make suitable theme songs for the choir. In fact, DISD itself has not argued that it chose religious theme songs for their educational or musical qualities, as the majority suggests. Under the circumstances, the majority's attempt to propose secular reasons not even offered by DISD carries no weight. Once it was clear DISD's purported secular purposes for using religious theme songs were actually religious in nature, the district court was justified in concluding that the choice of religious theme songs had no secular purpose.

As with the question of purpose, the majority's narrow findings regarding the effects of designating a religious theme song — that the song was sung often and was carried over from year to year — disregard the characteristic role and resulting effects of a theme song. In common understanding, a theme song is a song used by a group to represent or identify itself. *See* WEBSTER'S NEW WORLD DICTIONARY OF THE AMERICAN LANGUAGE 1474 (2d College ed. 1972). By choosing a particular song, the group expresses a shared emotion, experience or outlook. The theme song is played at each of the group's meetings or performances and has special significance for the group and for others who identify the group by its song.

DISD intended its choirs' religious theme songs to play this role. Though the theme songs were singled out from the overall music program by their continual singing throughout the year, thereby achieving a prominence not enjoyed by other songs, this was not the sole effect of their designation. More importantly, the theme songs were given special emphasis by their placement at the close of performances and, in the case of the high school choirs' song, its use to end class on Fridays, treatment that served to highlight the songs' sacred character.[4] Choir members were informed that the song was their theme song and a tradition at the school, thereby being directed, in effect, to at least superficially identify themselves with it. Indeed, the choir teacher testified that the theme song was supposed to give the students a sense of unity, camaraderie, belonging, and something to identify with. Since any student, upon learning that a particular song is his or her group's theme song, would look to the words of the song as an important part of its special meaning, the school's designation of a theme song that consists entirely of calls for God's blessing could not help but reinforce existing religious belief and convey the impression to believers and nonbelievers alike that the school favored religion. In fact, Jane Doe indicated she felt the choirs' theme songs reflected and embodied DISD's favor for Christian beliefs. The district court did not err in determining that DISD's choice of religious theme songs had the primary effect of advancing and endorsing religion. *See Jones II* (practice advances religion if it increases religious conviction); *County of Allegheny v. American Civil Liberties Union* (endorsement occurs where government gives message that religion or a particular religious belief is favored or preferred).

Adopting DISD's reasoning, the majority attempts to minimize the significance of the choice of a religious theme song by pointing to the choir teacher's estimate that 60-75 percent of serious choral music is based on sacred themes or text. Considering these figures, it suggests, statistical probability would predict that a religious song would be best suited to serve as the theme song. This apparent logic obscures the real questions at issue — the purpose and effects of DISD choosing religious theme songs. This is not a case where the students, or even the teachers, have picked a theme song each year and statistics would predict the choice of a religious song some percentage of the time. Nor has DISD directly claimed that it chose its particular theme songs because they were better suited to that purpose than any secular songs. Thus, there is no basis to conclude that the relative percentages of religious and secular music have had any bearing on DISD's purpose in choosing a religious theme song. Similarly,

---

4 The evidence suggests that DISD choir performances were carefully arranged to give religious songs, including the theme songs, the role that prayers played in other DISD events. For example, during the time that Jane Doe was in the intermediate school choir, one performance began with the song *Before Our Lord and King* and ended with the theme song. The rest of the songs in the performance were secular in nature.

that religious songs may constitute the majority of serious choral music does not minimize the religious effects, discussed above, of DISD designating a religious theme song.

Not only does the majority stretch to circumvent the district court's reasonable conclusions, but it grants greater relief than DISD has argued for in its appellate briefs. The district court's injunction enjoins DISD from "initiating, leading, authorizing, encouraging or condoning" the recitation or singing of religious songs as theme songs. DISD does not argue that this entire part of the injunction should be overturned, as the majority has done, but only that, under *Jones II*, if *students* choose a religious theme song, the school should be able to lead, authorize and condone its singing. In other words, DISD essentially concedes that the school district itself may not properly initiate or encourage the choice of a religious song as a theme song. Therefore, at a minimum, we should affirm the injunction to the extent it prohibits the school from initiating or encouraging the choice of religious theme songs.

In addition, however, we should also affirm as to the prohibition on DISD authorizing, leading or condoning a student-chosen religious theme song. First, the evidence shows that a large number of DISD students are well aware, through the chain of siblings and teachers, that the district schools have a tradition of prayer and using specific religious theme songs. Most DISD students have supported these traditions. As a result, any choice of a theme song by students from a pool of songs that includes DISD's "traditional" theme songs is unlikely to be truly free.

Moreover, even if made without pressure of any sort, a majority student vote would not validate the choice of a religious theme song. Since DISD has not indicated otherwise, we can assume that if students chose a religious theme song, DISD would treat it in the same fashion as in the past. In other words, the sacred qualities of the song would be emphasized such that its singing would be a form of religious exercise. This would be true in any event because, as discussed earlier, designation of a theme song, whether by faculty or students, is certain to endow the words of the song with special meaning and demand facial allegiance from the group. School supervision, leadership and control of the choir, including the teaching, practicing and performance of the theme song, would place pressure on all choir members to participate in and identify with that song. Thus, the school district's authorizing, leading and condoning of a student-chosen religious theme song would still have the effect of advancing and endorsing religion and would act as a coercive force on dissenters. *See Lee* (school district's supervision and control of graduation ceremony pressures attending students, at a minimum, to show respect for invocation and benediction). As the majority notes with respect to student-initiated prayer, neither *Jones* nor *Mergens* permit this kind of school involvement in student-initiated religious activities during the regular curriculum-related program.

Because the record supports the injunction against any school involvement in the choice or use of a religious theme song, I would affirm the district court on this issue.

INGEBRETSEN v. JACKSON PUBLIC SCHOOL DISTRICT
88 F.3d 274 (5th Cir. 1996)

W. EUGENE DAVIS, Circuit Judge:

I.

On a wave of public sentiment and indignation over the treatment of a Principal, Dr. Bishop Knox, who allowed students to begin each school day with a prayer over the intercom, the Mississippi legislature passed the School Prayer Statute at issue here. The language at the center of this controversy is of the statute which reads:

> [o]n public school property, or other public property, invocations, benedictions or nonsectarian, nonproselytizing student-initiated voluntary prayer shall be permitted during compulsory or noncompulsory school-related student assemblies, student sporting events, graduation or commencement ceremonies and other school-related student events.

The statute includes a lengthy preamble stating that it shall not be construed to violate the constitution and that its purpose is to accommodate religion and the right to free speech. The School Prayer Statute also contains a severability clause which permits any provision of the statute found to be invalid or unconstitutional to be severed without affecting the remainder of the statute.

A group of parents, students, and taxpayers in the Jackson Public School District, including Ingebretsen, filed suit along with the American Civil Liberties Union of Mississippi in July of 1994 to enjoin enforcement of the School Prayer Statute on the ground that it violates the establishment clause. A motion for a preliminary injunction to preserve the status quo was filed simultaneously with the complaint.

The district court enjoined enforcement of the statute in its entirety with the exception of the portion which permits prayers to take place at graduation ceremonies in accordance with *Jones v. Clear Creek Indep. School Dist.*

III.

Mississippi argues next that the district court erred in issuing the preliminary injunction. To obtain a preliminary injunction, Ingebretsen was required to show: 1) a substantial likelihood of success on the merits; 2) a substantial threat that he will suffer irreparable injury if the injunction is not issued; 3) that the threatened injury to him outweighs any damage the injunction might cause to the state and its citizens; and 4) that the injunction will not disserve the public interest. The district court made findings under all of these factors and con-cluded that the injunction was appropriate. This court will reverse the district court only upon a showing of abuse of discretion. *Id.*

A. Substantial likelihood of success

The Fifth Circuit has identified three tests that the Supreme Court has used to determine whether a government action or policy constitutes an establish-ment of religion. First, the Establishment Clause test of longest lineage: the *Lemon* test. Under *Lemon*, a government practice is constitutional if (1) it has a secular purpose, (2) its primary effect neither advances nor inhibits religion, and (3) it does not excessively entangle government with religion. Second, the Court has analyzed school-sponsored religious activity in terms of the coercive effect that the activity has on students. *Lee v. Weisman.* Third, the Court has dis-approved of governmental practices that appear to endorse religion. *County of Allegheny v. ACLU.* The district court did not make an exhaustive analysis under each of the tests because it found that the statute was defective under any of the tests. We agree.

The School Prayer Statute fails all three prongs of the *Lemon* test because its purpose is to advance prayer in public schools, its effect is to advance religion in the schools and it excessively entangles the government with religion. The leg-islature declared that its purpose in enacting the School Prayer Statute was "to accommodate the free exercise of religious rights of its student citizens in the public schools." This statement of purpose cannot be characterized as "secular" because its clear intent is to inform students, teachers and school administra-tors that they can pray at any school event so long as a student "initiates" the prayer (ostensibly by suggesting that a prayer be given). Further, when we view this statute along with this same legislature's resolution commending Dr. Knox for his "unswerving dedication to prayer in public schools," and in the con-text of the uproar over Dr. Knox's treatment after allowing prayer in his school, the conclusion that the School Prayer Statute was intended to advance religion becomes unavoidable. Returning prayer to public schools is not a secular pur-pose.

The statute's effect is to advance religion over irreligion because it gives a preferential, exceptional benefit to religion that it does not extend to anything else. *See Herdahl v. Pontotoc County School District*, 887 F. Supp. 902, 908-09 (N.D. Miss.1995) (school policy of turning public address system over to religious club for morning invocation and scripture reading has primary effect of advanc-ing religion). Students are required by law to attend school and a state policy of prayer at school tells students that the state wants them to pray.

The final prong of *Lemon* is also violated by the School Prayer Statute because representatives of the government are allowed to lead students in prayer and punish students who leave class or assemblies in order to avoid lis-tening to a prayer. The statute will inevitably involve school officials in deter-mining which prayers are "nonsectarian and nonproselytizing" and in determining who gets to say the prayer at each event. To the extent that school administrators participate in prayers in their official capacity or review the content of prayers to ensure that they meet these requirements, the School Prayer Statute excessively entangles government with religion.

The School Prayer Statute is also unconstitutional under the "coercion test" of *Lee*. The statute would allow prayers to be given by any person, including teachers, school administrators and clergy at school functions where attendance is compulsory. The coercion here is even greater than that in *Lee* where students had the option of not attending the graduation ceremony where the challenged prayer was offered. Here, students will be a captive audience that cannot leave without being punished by the state or School Board for truancy or excessive absences.

This brings us to the final test: the endorsement test. Government unconstitutionally endorses religion whenever it appears to "'take a position on questions of religious belief,'" or makes "'adherence to a religion relevant in any way to a person's standing in the political community,'" *Allegheny*. The government creates this appearance when it conveys a message that religion is "favored," "preferred," or "promoted" over other beliefs. The School Prayer Statute is an unconstitutional endorsement of religion because it allows school officials in their capacity as representatives of the state to lead students in prayer and sets aside special time for prayer that it does not set aside for anything else. It also places the coercive power of the state in the position of forcing students to attend school and then forcing them to listen to prayers offered there.

Under any of these tests, the District Court's determination that Ingebretsen had shown a substantial likelihood of prevailing on the merits was not an abuse of discretion.

B. A substantial threat of irreparable injury

Ingebretsen has shown that the School Prayer Statute represents a substantial threat to his First Amendment rights. Loss of First Amendment freedoms, even for minimal periods of time, constitute irreparable injury.

C. The threatened injury outweighs any damage the injunction might cause to Mississippi and its citizens

The only harm asserted by the Attorney General is that the injunction would have a chilling effect on students who would like to pray at school. However, the court correctly held that the injunction affected only the School Prayer Statute and would not affect students' existing rights to the free exercise of religion and free speech. Therefore, students continue to have exactly the same constitutional right to pray as they had before the statute was enjoined. They can pray silently or in a non-disruptive manner whenever and wherever they want, *Wallace v. Jaffree* (O'Connor, J., concurring), in groups before or after school or in any limited open forum created by the school. *See Mergens*.

D. The injunction will not disserve the public interest.

The School Prayer Statute is unconstitutional so the public interest was not disserved by an injunction preventing its implementation.

All four requirements of a preliminary injunction were properly met. The district court did not abuse its discretion in determining that a preliminary injunction was warranted.

IV.

We decline Ingebretsen's invitation to reconsider our holding in *Jones II* which allows students to choose to solemnize their graduation ceremonies with a student-initiated, non-proselytizing and nonsectarian prayer given by a student. To the extent the School Prayer Statute allows students to choose to pray at high school graduation to solemnize that once-in-a-lifetime event, we find it constitutionally sound under *Jones II*.

DISSENT FROM DENIAL OF REHEARING EN BANC

EDITH H. JONES, CIRCUIT JUDGE, with whom E. GRADY JOLLY, JERRY E. SMITH, RHESA HAWKINS BARKSDALE, EMILIO M. GARZA and DEMOSS, CIRCUIT JUDGES, join, dissenting:

The First Amendment says Congress shall make no law respecting an establishment of religion, and under Supreme Court rulings, the Amendment has come to mean that states shall make no such laws. The First Amendment, in other words, limits government action that creates an establishment of religion. But the Supreme Court has never held that *students* may not express their *private* religious convictions by means of appropriate voluntary prayer in school. In overturning the Mississippi school prayer statute, leaving a sliver of liberty for student-initiated graduation ceremony prayers, the Fifth Circuit has transformed the Establishment Clause from a shield against government religious indoctrination to a sword attacking personal religious behavior.

Just as unfortunate as the court's invasion of civil liberty is its misapplication of traditional doctrines of judicial restraint to achieve that result. The court had no warrant either to adjudicate a case in which plaintiffs have not been injured and cannot assert a justiciable controversy, or to decide the facial constitutionality of this statute. Sadly, this exercise of judicial boldness may be explained, though it cannot be justified, by the lack of guidance from the Supreme Court's Establishment Clause jurisprudence. The Court's decisions in this area more closely resemble *ad hoc* Delphic pronouncements than models of guiding legal principle. It is no wonder lower courts and the public are led adrift and astray. Religious liberty has invariably been the victim of the uncertainty. From the Fifth Circuit's refusal to rehear this case *en banc*, I respectfully dissent.

I. *The Statute and its Treatment by the Panel*

The Mississippi School Prayer Statute aimed at enabling the conduct of voluntary, student-initiated prayer in connection with public schooling. The statute states as its purpose:

> . . . to protect the freedom of speech guaranteed by the First Amendment
> to the United States Constitution, to define for the citizens of Mississippi the rights and privileges that are accorded them on public school
> property, other public property or other property at school-related
> events; and to provide guidance to public school officials on the rights
> and requirements of law that they must apply. The intent and purpose
> of the Legislature is to accommodate the free exercise of religious rights
> of its student citizens in the public schools and at public school events
> as provided to them by the First Amendment to the United States Constitution and the judicial interpretations thereof as given by the United
> States Supreme Court.

Without otherwise limiting the free exercise of religion and speech, the statute permits:

> [o]n public school property, other public property or other property,
> invocations, benedictions or nonsectarian, nonproselytizing student-initiated voluntary prayer . . . during compulsory or noncompulsory
> school-related student assemblies, student sporting events, graduation
> or commencement ceremonies and other school-related student events.

The statute disclaims state support, approval or sanction of any prayer or similar activity that occurs on public property, and it disavows the promotion or establishment of any religion or religious belief. A severability clause seeks to protect the bulk of the statute to the extent any of its provisions is held invalid or unconstitutional.

There is no doubt of the breadth of this statute, and notwithstanding its disclaimer, the vulnerability of some of its aspects to constitutional challenge. Whether, for instance, participation in student-initiated prayer could be imposed on unwilling students in a "compulsory" setting may be dubious. *Compare Lee v. Weisman.* But to admit a potential for unconstitutional application is not to condemn the entire statute.

Any simplistic description of the statute's operation is belied by the daunting variety of activities daily undertaken on school property. Students gather before, during and after school, at lunch, in activity rooms or on the field, for all sorts of curricular, extracurricular and quasi-curricular events. Testimony in this case listed a few of the types of assemblies alone: scholastic achievement assemblies, beauty pageants, guest speakers, programs, athletics, matters initiated by students, PTA, civic clubs, Boy Scouts, pep rallies. Precisely because the initiation of voluntary student prayer rests with students rather than school administrators, and because federal courts never permitted the law to take effect, there was no evidence in the district court as to how or when the statute might be invoked.

Rather than admit that construing this statute depends upon private, not state action, the Fifth Circuit found guilt by mischaracterization. Relying on conclusional statements of school officials and the "enormous interest in prayer" related to the Bishop Knox suspension, the court declares, "[i]mplementation of the statute would inevitably lead to improper state involvement in school prayer" and would require school officials "to decide who prays" and to monitor prayers' content. *Ingebretsen v. Jackson Public School District*, 88 F.3d 274, 278 (5th Cir.1996). The court assumes that prayers may even be given by teachers, administrators or clergy, that attendance will be compulsory and non-attendants punished. These conclusions are not based on any facts but solely on predictions and hypotheticals spawned by a broadly drafted statute.

Once the panel accepted this mistaken impression of state control over the prayers, its result was predictable. The panel deployed three "tests" that the Supreme Court has used to determine the parameters of the Establishment Clause. Although one of these tests has been repeatedly discredited but not overruled, and the other two have never been fully adopted or explained, they were deemed sufficient to the panel's task of holding the school prayer statute *qua* "state prayer statute" unconstitutional. Unfortunately, its blow struck not just the mythical ogre of state-sponsored prayer but the sincere, praiseworthy desire of students to join in prayers of their own making.

IV. *Why This Case Matters*

This case matters because it breaches the limits of judicial authority to achieve results that are offensive to religious liberty and the sound upbringing of our children. The panel's departures from standard rules of judicial restraint have been explained above. It has long been thought prudent, indeed obligatory, for a court to avoid discussing difficult but unnecessary constitutional issues. Here, neither plaintiffs' lack of standing nor trepidation over a premature declaration of facial invalidity persuaded the panel to forebear.

But beyond the errors of judicial craft lies a deeper significance. The panel's decision is the latest in a long line of cases whose inevitable consequence has been to remake society in a secular image. Two examples suffice: courts have held that the mere existence of a Good Friday holiday "establishes" the Christian religion,[12] and the venerable inscription on a courthouse "The World Needs God" likewise constitutionally offends . . . someone.[13] Only by recognizing the absurdity of holding otherwise have courts allowed us still to pledge that we are "one nation under God, indivisible" and to maintain "In God We Trust" on the currency. When our cultural heritage and tradition, indeed the three-millennial history of the Western world threatens to be erased by three decades of federal

---

[12] *Metzl v. Leininger*, 57 F.3d 618 (7th Cir. 1995).

[13] *Doe v. County of Montgomery, Il.*, 41 F.3d 1156 (7th Cir. 1994).

court pronouncements, something is amiss. As Prof. Stephen Carter arrestingly concluded, our elite cultural institutions, including federal courts, have imposed on us an historically unprecedented "culture of disbelief."

The elites' tin ear for religious belief and practice has been particularly evident in cases regarding the public schools. Federal courts often seem unable to draw fundamental distinctions between school-sponsored religious "establishment" and benign teaching about religion or, as in this case, students' constitutionally protected free exercise of speech and religion. School officials, averse to the emotional and financial costs of litigation, have systematically excised religious references from school curricula and activities in response to the caselaw. This widespread Establishment Clause misconstruction occurs notwithstanding that Supreme Court justices have repeatedly acknowledged the importance of teaching about religion in public schools and that no Supreme Court authority limits students' nondisruptive religious self-expression. Not to belabor the point, I note that Congress passed and the Supreme Court upheld the Equal Access Act, a law guaranteeing students' rights to meet in religious clubs on public school property, in order to overturn lower federal court decisions to the contrary. Only last summer, President Clinton spoke of the problem of hostility to religion in public schools and instructed the Departments of Justice and Education to formulate guidelines for the protection of public school students' religious speech and conduct. Every time a federal court writes an unduly broad Establishment Clause decision concerning public schools, we encourage further misunderstandings, to the detriment of students' constitutional rights and the goal of teaching about religion in public schools.

The courts' broad decisions in this area are not only in my view, uncompelled by precedent, they are also extraordinarily shortsighted. Decisions fostering rigidly secular public education strip school officials of moral tools that lie at the heart of the educational process. Character education, whose roots lie deepest and firmest in precepts of religious morality, has been the ultimate casualty of the courts' careless Establishment Clause jurisprudence.

Eager judicial intrusions into the educational process have also spawned decrees that inhibit school leaders' flexibility to accommodate varying social conditions. Intuitively, it appears that different approaches are required to encourage educational success, including character building success, in a Chicago ghetto, a Dallas suburb or a small Tennessee town. Yet local control of schools, a cornerstone of American public education, has had to give way to a growing body of federalized, nationally binding Establishment Clause jurisprudence.

Paraphrasing George Orwell, we have sunk to the point at which it becomes one's duty to restate the obvious. What seems obvious to me is that disputes like these, deeply enmeshed in social and political policy, are not well handled by the adjudication process. Court decrees, focused on the single goal of pure "non-establishment," supplant decisions based on compromise and consensus which reflect the multifaceted wisdom of the people acting through democratically accountable elected officials and educators. Moreover, the accumulated precedential effect of the courts' secularizing decisions has stretched beyond each particular dispute to discourage and thwart moral and religious elements in public education.[20] It is precisely because of the tension between adjudicative decisionmaking and well-rounded social policy-making that courts fashioned self-constraints on declarations of facial unconstitutionality. It is because the Founders recognized the distinction between mere adjudication and lawmaking that Article III requires a real case or controversy, implicating standing to sue, ripeness and justiciability. A forthright sense of judicial modesty also compels such limitations on the judicial process. Neither judicial modesty nor principles of judicial restraint have been notably evident in decisions involving religion and the public schools.

This case, striking down Mississippi's attempt to accommodate students' desire — and constitutional right — voluntarily to pray aloud at school, is a paradigm of the errors that bedevil Establishment Clause jurisprudence. The court reached out to condemn the entire statute on its face even though no plaintiff had been injured or could realistically assert standing, and even though certain constitutional applications of it are mandated by our caselaw. The court's decision was premised not on actual facts but upon a hypothetical, worst-case application of the statute. The court dealt unsympathetically, to say the least, with the motivation for the statute, a motivation shared by the vast majority of the American people that life is more meaningful, education more dignified, morality fortified when voluntary, student-initiated prayer is permitted. It was not the court's prerogative under traditional principles of judicial restraint to strike down this statute. I DISSENT from the denial of rehearing *en banc*.

NOTES ON THE CONTINUING BATTLES OVER RELIGION IN THE PUBLIC SCHOOLS

1. Mississippi has had more than its representative share of school prayer cases. Another case litigated approximately the same time as *Ingebretsen* involved a public school in Ecru, Mississippi. In this case, Lisa Herdahl — a mother of five children in the school (which included a kindergarten and all twelve grades) — complained about the school's practice of permitting the broadcast of Bible readings and prayers over the intercom each morning, and vocal group prayers in classrooms before lunch. The school refused to stop the religious practices, and the school superintendent told Mrs. Herdahl that "We've done this for 50 years here and we're going to continue." Diane Eicher, *Prayer-Fight Film Seeks to Keep Balance*, DENVER POST, July 24, 1999, at G5. Mrs. Herdahl's children were ostracized, called "devil-worshippers," and in one widely reported response to the mother's protests, her "7-year-old son was called 'foot-

---

20 *Jones v. Clear Creek ISD, supra,* authorizing voluntary, student-initiated graduation prayer; *Doe v. Duncanville ISD, II, supra* authorizing voluntary student sports prayers.

ball head' after a teacher made him wear headphones to drown out the prayers broadcast over the school's intercom." *Mother Files Suit to Halt Prayer in a Public School in Mississippi*, N.Y. TIMES, Dec. 23, 1994, at A22. In another response to the mother's actions, U.S. House of Representatives Speaker Newt Gingrich commented publicly that it is "nonsense to say that one person can dictate to 3,000," and suggested that Ms. Herdahl "[g]o find a school you like. But don't dictate to everyone else in your community based on your particular prejudices." *Gingrich Voucher Remark is Called 'Nuts'; Mississippi Mother Rejects Criticism of Her Fight Against School Prayer*, WASH. POST, June 18, 1995, at A11. Ms. Herdahl's "particular prejudices" were Lutheran. *Id.* A federal district court ultimately ruled that the school district had violated the rules set forth by the Supreme Court over thirty years earlier in *Schempp* and *Engel*. *Herdahl v. Pontotoc County School District*, 887 F. Supp. 902 (N.D. Miss. 1995). What do the facts of this case suggest about Judge Jones' argument in *Ingebretsen* that in school prayer cases, the courts should avoid using the adjudicatory process to "supplant decisions based on compromise and consensus which reflect the multifaceted wisdom of the people acting through democratically accountable elected officials and educators"?

   2. Alabama has had almost as many difficulties in regulating religious ostracism in its public schools as Mississippi. Two years after Mrs. Herdahl won her lawsuit against the Pontotoc, Mississippi, school district, another family encountered its own problems with the governmentally condoned religious practices in Alabama's public schools. In this case Paul, David, and Sarah Herring were the only Jewish students in the Pike County, Alabama, school system. During their six years in the Pike County schools, Christian students taunted the Herring boys; called them "Jew boys" and "Jewish jokers"; drew swastikas on their lockers, book bags, and jackets; and ripped Yarmulkes from their heads. Sue Anne Pressley, *Tough Lessons in Alabama Town; Jewish Children Persecuted at School, Parents Charge in Lawsuit*, WASH. POST, Sept. 2, 1997, at A3. School officials contributed their own abuse. In addition to distributing Bibles in classes, producing a "Birth of Jesus" play, and having a "Happy Birthday Jesus" party in Paul's class, the teachers and administrators also targeted the children individually. "When Paul Herring, 14, was sent to the school office to be disciplined for disrupting class, he was ordered by the vice principal to write an essay on 'Why Jesus Loves Me.' When David Herring, 13, failed to bow his head during a school assembly prayer, a teacher allegedly reached over and lowered it for him. After Sarah Herring, 11, heard a minister deliver a fire-and-brimstone sermon at her elementary school, she said, she had nightmares for weeks about burning in hell." *Id.* Paul Herring's teacher also once ordered him to remove a Star of David lapel pin "because she said it was a prohibited gang symbol." *Id.* In response to the litany of problems the children faced, the Pike County school superintendent defended the abusive students and teachers and placed at least part of the blame on the Herring children themselves. He told the Washington Post: "Sometimes children, and I'm not going to say these, bring these things on themselves. The teachers try to prevent it, but if you have kids who brag and talk, other kids are going to do things to them." *Id.* The parents' case against Pike County was settled when the county signed a consent decree repeating most of the major features of a federal district court's ruling against another Alabama school district. *See Chandler v. James*, 958 F. Supp. 1550, *reaff'd*, 998 F. Supp. 1255 (M.D. Ala. 1997), *aff'd in part and rev'd in part*, 180 F.3d 1254 (11th Cir. 1999), *cert. granted, judgment vacated*, 530 U.S. 1256, *opinion reinstated*, 230 F.3d 1313 (2000); Gita M. Smith, *Alabama County Vows Tolerance: Jewish Family's Suit Charging Discrimination by School Teachers and Staff Members is Settled*, ATLANTA CONST., Apr. 22, 1998, at 8A.

3. Even conscientious school administrators in the South often have a difficult time deciphering the confusing directions on public school religious activity issued by the federal appellate courts in the region. In the Fifth Circuit, the spirit (if not the actual holding) of *Jones* is difficult to reconcile with *Doe* and *Ingebretsen*. The Eleventh Circuit's opinions on the subject are equally incoherent. In its most recent effort in the area, the Eleventh Circuit upheld most of the district court order in *Chandler v. James* (mentioned in the previous note), but invalidated the portion of the district court's injunction that required school officials to prohibit student "prayer or other devotional speech in situations which are not purely private, such as aloud in the classroom, over the public address system, or as part of the program at school-related assemblies and sporting events, or at a graduation ceremony." *Chandler*, 180 F.3d at 1257. After a lengthy discussion of the students' rights to engage in certain private religious activity on public school property, the court concluded with this cryptic caveat:

> A student's right to speak religiously is not, however, without limit. The school may impose the same reasonable restrictions on the time, place, and manner of religious speech as it does on secular student speech. Furthermore, a student's right to express his personal religious beliefs does not extend to using the machinery of the state as a vehicle for converting his audience. *See Abington*, 374 U.S. at 228. The Constitution requires that schools permit religious expression, not religious proselytizing. "The principle that government may accommodate the free exercise of religion does not supersede the fundamental limitations imposed by the Establishment Clause." *Lee*, 505 U.S. at 587. Proselytizing speech is inherently coercive and, the Constitution prohibits it from the government's pulpit. *Id.*

180 F.3d at 1265.

What does the Eleventh Circuit mean? If a student prays aloud in a public school classroom or at a public school assembly or graduation ceremony, isn't the student by definition "using the machinery of the state as a vehicle for converting his audience"? How can a prayer by a speaker at a formal graduation ceremony not be viewed as "religious proselytizing"? Does the phrasing of the prayer matter? Compare the following two statements made by a student speaker at a public school graduation ceremony: (1) "Oh Lord, thank you for the blessings you have bestowed upon me." (2) "Let us pray together for the blessings the Lord has bestowed upon us." Is the first statement "religious speech" or "religious proselytizing"? Is the second statement more likely to be deemed "proselytizing" because it invites the audience to participate? Can this semantic exercise be enforced consistently?

SANTA FE INDEPENDENT SCHOOL DISTRICT v. DOE
530 U.S. 290 (2000)

JUSTICE STEVENS delivered the opinion of the Court.

Prior to 1995, the Santa Fe High School student who occupied the school's elective office of student council chaplain delivered a prayer over the public address system before each varsity football game for the entire season. This practice, along with others, was challenged in District Court as a violation of the Establishment Clause of the First Amendment. While these proceedings were pending in the District Court, the school district adopted a different policy that permits, but does not require, prayer initiated and led by a student at all home games. The District Court entered an order modifying that policy to permit only nonsectarian, nonproselytizing prayer. The Court of Appeals held that, even as modified by the District Court, the football prayer policy was invalid. We granted the school district's petition for certiorari to review that holding.

I

Respondents commenced this action in April 1995 and moved for a temporary restraining order to prevent the District from violating the Establishment Clause at the imminent graduation exercises. In their complaint the Does alleged that the District had engaged in several proselytizing practices, such as promoting attendance at a Baptist revival meeting, encouraging membership in religious clubs, chastising children who held minority religious beliefs, and distributing Gideon Bibles on school premises. They also alleged that the District allowed students to read Christian invocations and benedictions from the stage at graduation ceremonies, and to deliver overtly Christian prayers over the public address system at home football games.

On May 10, 1995, the District Court entered an interim order addressing a number of different issues. With respect to the impending graduation, the order provided that "non-denominational prayer" consisting of "an invocation and/or benediction" could be presented by a senior student or students selected by members of the graduating class. The text of the prayer was to be determined by the students, without scrutiny or preapproval by school officials. References to particular religious figures "such as Mohammed, Jesus, Buddha, or the like" would be permitted "as long as the general thrust of the prayer is non-proselytizing."

In response to that portion of the order, the District adopted a series of policies over several months dealing with prayer at school functions. The policies enacted in May and July for graduation ceremonies provided the format for the August and October policies for football games. The May policy provided:

> "The board has chosen to permit the graduating senior class, with the advice and counsel of the senior class principal or designee, to elect by secret ballot to choose whether an invocation and benediction shall be part of the graduation exercise. If so chosen the class shall elect by secret ballot, from a list of student volunteers, students to deliver non-sectarian, nonproselytizing invocations and benedictions for the purpose of solemnizing their graduation ceremonies."

The parties stipulated that after this policy was adopted, "the senior class held an election to determine whether to have an invocation and benediction at the commencement [and that the] class voted, by secret ballot, to include prayer at the high school graduation." In a second vote the class elected two seniors to deliver the invocation and benediction.[4]

In July, the District enacted another policy eliminating the requirement that invocations and benedictions be "nonsectarian and nonproselytising," but also providing that if the District were to be enjoined from enforcing that policy, the May policy would automatically become effective.

The August policy, which was titled "Prayer at Football Games," was similar to the July policy for graduations. It also authorized two student elections, the first to determine whether "invocations" should be delivered, and the second to select the spokesperson to deliver them. Like the July policy, it contained two parts, an initial statement that omitted any requirement that the content of the invocation be "nonsectarian and nonproselytising," and a fallback provision that automatically added that limitation if the preferred policy should be enjoined. On August 31, 1995, according to the parties' stipulation, "[t]he district's high school students voted to determine whether a student would deliver prayer at varsity football games. . . . The students chose to allow a student to say a prayer at football games." A week later, in a separate election, they selected a student "to deliver the prayer at varsity football games."

The final policy (October policy) is essentially the same as the August policy, though it omits the word "prayer" from its title, and refers to "messages" and "statements" as well as "invocations." It is the validity of that policy that is before us.

---

[4] The student giving the invocation thanked the Lord for keeping the class safe through 12 years of school and for gracing their lives with two special people and closed: "Lord, we ask that You keep Your hand upon us during this ceremony and to help us keep You in our hearts through the rest of our lives. In God's name we pray. Amen." The student benediction was similar in content and closed: "Lord, we ask for Your protection as we depart to our next destination and watch over us as we go our separate ways. Grant each of us a safe trip and keep us secure throughout the night. In Your name we pray. Amen."

The District Court did enter an order precluding enforcement of the first, open-ended policy. Relying on our decision in *Lee v. Weisman*, it held that the school's "action must not 'coerce anyone to support or participate in' a religious exercise." Applying that test, it concluded that the graduation prayers appealed "to distinctively Christian beliefs," and that delivering a prayer "over the school's public address system prior to each football and baseball game coerces student participation in religious events." Both parties appealed, the District contending that the enjoined portion of the October policy was permissible and the Does contending that both alternatives violated the Establishment Clause. The Court of Appeals majority agreed with the Does.

The decision of the Court of Appeals followed Fifth Circuit precedent that had announced two rules. In *Jones v. Clear Creek Independent School Dist.*, that court held that student-led prayer that was approved by a vote of the students and was nonsectarian and nonproselytizing was permissible at high school graduation ceremonies. On the other hand, in later cases the Fifth Circuit made it clear that the *Clear Creek* rule applied only to high school graduations and that school-encouraged prayer was constitutionally impermissible at school-related sporting events. Thus, in *Doe v. Duncanville Independent School Dist.*, it had described a high school graduation as "a significant, once in-a-lifetime event" to be contrasted with athletic events in "a setting that is far less solemn and extraordinary."

In its opinion in this case, the Court of Appeals explained:

> "The controlling feature here is the same as in *Duncanville*: The prayers are to be delivered *at football games* — hardly the sober type of annual event that can be appropriately solemnized with prayer. The distinction to which [the District] points is simply one without difference. Regardless of whether the prayers are selected by vote or spontaneously initiated at these frequently-recurring, informal, school-sponsored events, school officials are present and have the authority to stop the prayers. Thus, as we indicated in *Duncanville*, our decision in *Clear Creek II* hinged on the singular context and singularly serious nature of a graduation ceremony. Outside that nurturing context, a Clear Creek Prayer Policy cannot survive. We therefore reverse the district court's holding that [the District's] alternative Clear Creek Prayer Policy can be extended to football games, irrespective of the presence of the nonsectarian, nonproselytizing restrictions."

The dissenting judge rejected the majority's distinction between graduation ceremonies and football games. In his opinion the District's October policy created a limited public forum that had a secular purpose and provided neutral accommodation of noncoerced, private, religious speech.

We granted the District's petition for certiorari, limited to the following question: "Whether petitioner's policy permitting student-led, student-initiated prayer at football games violates the Establishment Clause." We conclude, as did the Court of Appeals, that it does.

II

In *Lee v. Weisman*, we held that a prayer delivered by a rabbi at a middle school graduation ceremony violated that Clause. Although this case involves student prayer at a different type of school function, our analysis is properly guided by the principles that we endorsed in *Lee*.

As we held in that case:

> "The principle that government may accommodate the free exercise of religion does not supersede the fundamental limitations imposed by the Establishment Clause. It is beyond dispute that, at a minimum, the Constitution guarantees that government may not coerce anyone to support or participate in religion or its exercise, or otherwise act in a way which 'establishes a [state] religion or religious faith, or tends to do so.' "

In this case the District first argues that this principle is inapplicable to its October policy because the messages are private student speech, not public speech. It reminds us that "there is a crucial difference between *government* speech endorsing religion, which the Establishment Clause forbids, and *private* speech endorsing religion, which the Free Speech and Free Exercise Clauses protect. *Mergens* (opinion of O'Connor, J.). We certainly agree with that distinction, but we are not persuaded that the pregame invocations should be regarded as "private speech."

These invocations are authorized by a government policy and take place on government property at government-sponsored school-related events. Of course, not every message delivered under such circumstances is the government's own. We have held, for example, that an individual's contribution to a government-created forum was not government speech. *See Rosenberger v. Rector and Visitors of Univ. of Va.*. Although the District relies heavily on *Rosenberger* and similar cases involving such forums, it is clear that the pregame ceremony is not the type of forum discussed in those cases. The Santa Fe school officials simply do not "evince either 'by policy or by practice,' any intent to open the [pregame ceremony] to 'indiscriminate use,' . . . by the student body generally." *Hazelwood School Dist. v. Kuhlmeier*, 484 U.S. 260, 270 (1988) (quoting *Perry Ed. Assn. v. Perry Local Educators' Assn.*, 460 U.S. 37, 47 (1983)). Rather, the school allows only one student, the same student for the entire season, to give the invocation. The statement or invocation, moreover, is subject to particular regulations that confine the content and topic of the student's message. By comparison, in *Perry* we rejected a claim that the school had created a limited public forum in its school mail system despite the fact that it had allowed far more speakers to address a much broader range of topics than the policy at issue here. As we concluded in *Perry*, "selective access does not transform government property into a public forum."

Granting only one student access to the stage at a time does not, of course, necessarily preclude a finding that a school has created a limited public forum. Here, however, Santa Fe's student election system ensures that only those messages deemed "appropriate" under the District's policy may be delivered. That is, the majoritarian process implemented by the District guarantees, by definition, that minority candidates will never prevail and that their views will be effectively silenced. [T]his student election does nothing to protect minority views but rather places the students who hold such views at the mercy of the majority. Because "fundamental rights may not be submitted to vote; they depend on the outcome of no elections," *West Virginia Bd. of Ed. v. Barnette* [*infra* Chapter 11], the District's elections are insufficient safeguards of diverse student speech.

In *Lee*, the school district made the related argument that its policy of endorsing only "civic or nonsectarian" prayer was acceptable because it minimized the intrusion on the audience as a whole. We rejected that claim by explaining that such a majoritarian policy "does not lessen the offense or isolation to the objectors. At best it narrows their number, at worst increases their sense of isolation and affront." Similarly, while Santa Fe's majoritarian election might ensure that *most* of the students are represented, it does nothing to protect the minority; indeed, it likely serves to intensify their offense.

Moreover, the District has failed to divorce itself from the religious content in the invocations. It has not succeeded in doing so, either by claiming that its policy is "'one of neutrality rather than endorsement'" or by characterizing the individual student as the "circuit-breaker" in the process. Contrary to the District's repeated assertions that it has adopted a "hands-off" approach to the pregame invocation, the realities of the situation plainly reveal that its policy involves both perceived and actual endorsement of religion. In this case, as we found in *Lee*, the "degree of school involvement" makes it clear that the pregame prayers bear "the imprint of the State and thus put school-age children who objected in an untenable position."

The District has attempted to disentangle itself from the religious messages by developing the two-step student election process. The text of the October policy, however, exposes the extent of the school's entanglement. The elections take place at all only because the school "board *has chosen to permit* students to deliver a brief invocation and/or message." The elections thus "shall" be conducted "by the high school student council" and "[u]pon advice and direction of the high school principal." The decision whether to deliver a message is first made by majority vote of the entire student body, followed by a choice of the speaker in a separate, similar majority election. Even though the particular words used by the speaker are not determined by those votes, the policy mandates that the "statement or invocation" be "consistent with the goals and purposes of this policy," which are "to solemnize the event, to promote good sportsmanship and student safety, and to establish the appropriate environment for the competition."

In addition to involving the school in the selection of the speaker, the policy, by its terms, invites and encourages religious messages. The policy itself states that the purpose of the message is "to solemnize the event." A religious message is the most obvious method of solemnizing an event. Moreover, the requirements that the message "promote good citizenship" and "establish the appropriate environment for competition" further narrow the types of message deemed appropriate, suggesting that a solemn, yet nonreligious, message, such as commentary on United States foreign policy, would be prohibited.[18] Indeed, the only type of message that is expressly endorsed in the text is an "invocation" — a term that primarily describes an appeal for divine assistance. In fact, as used in the past at Santa Fe High School, an "invocation" has always entailed a focused religious message. Thus, the expressed purposes of the policy encourage the selection of a religious message, and that is precisely how the students understand the policy. The results of the elections described in the parties' stipulation make it clear that the students understood that the central question before them was whether prayer should be a part of the pregame ceremony. We recognize the important role that public worship plays in many communities, as well as the sincere desire to include public prayer as a part of various occasions so as to mark those occasions' significance. But such religious activity in public schools, as elsewhere, must comport with the First Amendment.

The actual or perceived endorsement of the message, moreover, is established by factors beyond just the text of the policy. Once the student speaker is selected and the message composed, the invocation is then delivered to a large audience assembled as part of a regularly scheduled, school-sponsored function conducted on school property. The message is broadcast over the school's public address system, which remains subject to the control of school officials. It is fair to assume that the pregame ceremony is clothed in the traditional indicia of school sporting events, which generally include not just the team, but also cheerleaders and band members dressed in uniforms sporting the school name and mascot. The school's name is likely written in large print across the field and on banners and flags. The crowd will certainly include many who display the school colors and insignia on their school T-shirts, jackets, or hats and who may also be waving signs displaying the school name. It is in a setting such as this that "[t]he board has chosen to permit" the elected student to rise and give the "statement or invocation."

In this context the members of the listening audience must perceive the pregame message as a public expression of the views of the majority of the student body delivered with the approval of the school administration. In cases involving state participation in a religious activity, one of the relevant questions is "whether an objective observer, acquainted with the text, legislative history,

---

[18] THE CHIEF JUSTICE'S hypothetical of the student body president asked by the school to introduce a guest speaker with a biography of her accomplishments obviously would pose no problems under the Establishment Clause.

and implementation of the statute, would perceive it as a state endorsement of prayer in public schools." Regardless of the listener's support for, or objection to, the message, an objective Santa Fe High School student will unquestionably perceive the inevitable pregame prayer as stamped with her school's seal of approval.

The text and history of this policy, moreover, reinforce our objective student's perception that the prayer is, in actuality, encouraged by the school. When a governmental entity professes a secular purpose for an arguably religious policy, the government's characterization is, of course, entitled to some deference. But it is nonetheless the duty of the courts to "distinguis[h] a sham secular purpose from a sincere one."

According to the District, the secular purposes of the policy are to "foste[r] free expression of private persons . . . as well [as to] solemniz[e] sporting events, promot[e] good sportsmanship and student safety, and establis[h] an appropriate environment for competition." We note, however, that the District's approval of only one specific kind of message, an "invocation," is not necessary to further any of these purposes. Additionally, the fact that only one student is permitted to give a content-limited message suggests that this policy does little to "foste[r] free expression." Furthermore, regardless of whether one considers a sporting event an appropriate occasion for solemnity, the use of an invocation to foster such solemnity is impermissible when, in actuality, it constitutes prayer sponsored by the school. And it is unclear what type of message would be both appropriately "solemnizing" under the District's policy and yet nonreligious.

Most striking to us is the evolution of the current policy from the long-sanctioned office of "Student Chaplain" to the candidly titled "Prayer at Football Games" regulation. This history indicates that the District intended to preserve the practice of prayer before football games. The conclusion that the District viewed the October policy simply as a continuation of the previous policies is dramatically illustrated by the fact that the school did not conduct a new election, pursuant to the current policy, to replace the results of the previous election, which occurred under the former policy. Given these observations, and in light of the school's history of regular delivery of a student-led prayer at athletic events, it is reasonable to infer that the specific purpose of the policy was to preserve a popular "state-sponsored religious practice."

School sponsorship of a religious message is impermissible because it sends the ancillary message to members of the audience who are nonadherents "that they are outsiders, not full members of the political community, and an accompanying message to adherents that they are insiders, favored members of the political community." The delivery of such a message — over the school's public address system, by a speaker representing the student body, under the supervision of school faculty, and pursuant to a school policy that explicitly and implicitly encourages public prayer — is not properly characterized as "private" speech.

III

The District next argues that its football policy is distinguishable from the graduation prayer in *Lee* because it does not coerce students to participate in religious observances. Its argument has two parts: first, that there is no impermissible government coercion because the pregame messages are the product of student choices; and second, that there is really no coercion at all because attendance at an extracurricular event, unlike a graduation ceremony, is voluntary.

The reasons just discussed explaining why the alleged "circuit-breaker" mechanism of the dual elections and student speaker do not turn public speech into private speech also demonstrate why these mechanisms do not insulate the school from the coercive element of the final message. In fact, this aspect of the District's argument exposes anew the concerns that are created by the majoritarian election system. The parties' stipulation clearly states that the issue resolved in the first election was "whether a student would deliver prayer at varsity football games," and the controversy in this case demonstrates that the views of the students are not unanimous on that issue.

One of the purposes served by the Establishment Clause is to remove debate over this kind of issue from governmental supervision or control. We explained in *Lee* that the "preservation and transmission of religious beliefs and worship is a responsibility and a choice committed to the private sphere." The two student elections authorized by the policy, coupled with the debates that presumably must precede each, impermissibly invade that private sphere. The election mechanism, when considered in light of the history in which the policy in question evolved, reflects a device the District put in place that determines whether religious messages will be delivered at home football games. The mechanism encourages divisiveness along religious lines in a public school setting, a result at odds with the Establishment Clause. Although it is true that the ultimate choice of student speaker is "attributable to the students," the District's decision to hold the constitutionally problematic election is clearly "a choice attributable to the State."

The District further argues that attendance at the commencement ceremonies at issue in *Lee* "differs dramatically" from attendance at high school football games, which it contends "are of no more than passing interest to many students" and are "decidedly extracurricular," thus dissipating any coercion. Attendance at a high school football game, unlike showing up for class, is certainly not required in order to receive a diploma. Moreover, we may assume that the District is correct in arguing that the informal pressure to attend an athletic event is not as strong as a senior's desire to attend her own graduation ceremony.

There are some students, however, such as cheerleaders, members of the band, and, of course, the team members themselves, for whom seasonal commitments mandate their attendance, sometimes for class credit. The District also minimizes the importance to many students of attending and participating in extracurricular activities as part of a complete educational experience. As we noted in *Lee,* "[l]aw reaches past formalism." To assert that high school students do not feel immense social pressure, or have a truly genuine desire, to be involved in the extracurricular event that is American high school football is "formalistic in the extreme." We stressed in *Lee* the obvious observation that "adolescents are often susceptible to pressure from their peers towards conformity, and that the influence is strongest in matters of social convention." High school home football games are traditional gatherings of a school community; they bring together students and faculty as well as friends and family from years present and past to root for a common cause. Undoubtedly, the games are not important to some students, and they voluntarily choose not to attend. For many others, however, the choice between whether to attend these games or to risk facing a personally offensive religious ritual is in no practical sense an easy one. The Constitution, moreover, demands that the school may not force this difficult choice upon these students for "[i]t is a tenet of the First Amendment that the State cannot require one of its citizens to forfeit his or her rights and benefits as the price of resisting conformance to state-sponsored religious practice."

Even if we regard every high school student's decision to attend a home football game as purely voluntary, we are nevertheless persuaded that the delivery of a pregame prayer has the improper effect of coercing those present to participate in an act of religious worship. For "the government may no more use social pressure to enforce orthodoxy than it may use more direct means." As in *Lee,* "[w]hat to most believers may seem nothing more than a reasonable request that the nonbeliever respect their religious practices, in a school context may appear to the nonbeliever or dissenter to be an attempt to employ the machinery of the State to enforce a religious orthodoxy." The constitutional command will not permit the District "to exact religious conformity from a student as the price" of joining her classmates at a varsity football game.

[N]othing in the Constitution as interpreted by this Court prohibits any public school student from voluntarily praying at any time before, during, or after the schoolday. But the religious liberty protected by the Constitution is abridged when the State affirmatively sponsors the particular religious practice of prayer.

IV

[In Section IV of its opinion, the Court ruled that a facial challenge to the voluntary prayer policy was appropriate in applying the secular purpose component of the three-part *Lemon* analysis.] Under the *Lemon* standard, a court must invalidate a statute if it lacks "a secular legislative purpose." It is therefore proper, as part of this facial challenge, for us to examine the purpose of the October policy. [The Court then analyzed the text of the policy and the history of its adoption and concluded that the policy was motivated by an impermissible nonsecular purpose.]

The District, nevertheless, asks us to pretend that we do not recognize what every Santa Fe High School student understands clearly — that this policy is about prayer. The District further asks us to accept what is obviously untrue: that these messages are necessary to "solemnize" a football game and that this single-student, year-long position is essential to the protection of student speech. We refuse to turn a blind eye to the context in which this policy arose, and that context quells any doubt that this policy was implemented with the purpose of endorsing school prayer.

Therefore, the simple enactment of this policy, with the purpose and perception of school endorsement of student prayer, was a constitutional violation. We need not wait for the inevitable to confirm and magnify the constitutional injury.

[E]ven if no Santa Fe High School student were ever to offer a religious message, the October policy fails a facial challenge because the attempt by the District to encourage prayer is also at issue. Government efforts to endorse religion cannot evade constitutional reproach based solely on the remote possibility that those attempts may fail.

CHIEF JUSTICE REHNQUIST, with whom JUSTICE SCALIA and JUSTICE THOMAS join, dissenting.

The Court distorts existing precedent to conclude that the school district's student-message program is invalid on its face under the Establishment Clause. But even more disturbing than its holding is the tone of the Court's opinion; it bristles with hostility to all things religious in public life. Neither the holding nor the tone of the opinion is faithful to the meaning of the Establishment Clause, when it is recalled that George Washington himself, at the request of the very Congress which passed the Bill of Rights, proclaimed a day of "public thanksgiving and prayer, to be observed by acknowledging with grateful hearts the many and signal favors of Almighty God." [The Chief Justice then devoted much of his dissent to the argument that the majority should not have permitted a facial challenge to the policy, but rather should have waited until the policy was put into practice.] Had the policy been put into practice, the students may have chosen a speaker according to wholly secular criteria — like good public speaking skills or social popularity — and the student speaker may have chosen, on her own accord, to deliver a religious message. Such an application of the policy would likely pass constitutional muster.

NOTES ON SANTA FE AND THE CONTINUING RELEVANCE OF RELIGIOUS DIVISIVENESS

1. The Court of Appeals opinion in *Santa Fe* continued the Fifth Circuit trend of narrowing the scope of the *Jones* decision without renouncing the precise holding of the case. In *Doe v. Santa Fe Independent School District*, 168 F.3d 806 (5th Cir. 1999), the Fifth Circuit held that football games are "hardly the sober type of annual event that can be appropriately solemnized with prayer." 168 F.3d at 823. Thus, the court held that the *Jones* decision "hinged on the singular context and singularly serious nature of a graduation ceremony. Outside that nurturing context, a [*Jones*] Prayer Policy cannot survive." *Id.* After *Doe v. Santa Fe*, the school prayer permitted by the *Jones* decision is apparently limited by the Fifth Circuit to the narrow range of cases involving identical policies and factual circumstances — i.e., "nonsectarian, nonproselytizing prayers" at formal graduation ceremonies. But given the Fifth Circuit's rulings in *Doe*, *Ingebretsen*, and *Santa Fe*, and the Supreme Court's even stronger opinion in *Santa Fe*, can even a narrow interpretation of *Jones* be justified under current Establishment Clause doctrine?

Apparently the Eleventh Circuit Court of Appeals thinks so. In response to a remand order from the Supreme Court, the Eleventh Circuit produced an opinion containing a strained reading of *Santa Fe*, which the Eleventh Circuit employed to reaffirm a previous decision upholding one Florida county's policy to permit students to vote on graduation speakers, most of whom used the occasion to pray. *See Adler v. Duval County Sch. Bd.*, 250 F.3d 1330 (11th Cir. 2001). According to the Eleventh Circuit majority, the Supreme Court's *Santa Fe* holding was limited by two facts: first, that the Santa Fe school board had reviewed the content of the student messages and second, that the Santa Fe school board invited and encouraged student religious messages. The Eleventh Circuit held that neither factor was evident in the Florida case, arguing that "the text setting forth the Duval County, [Florida] policy contains no language approving an 'invocation' and no other provision that could fairly be read to require or approve a 'religious' theme." The students selected under the Florida procedure had presented graduation messages with some sort of religious content, *id.* 1339, and despite the fact that the school board's Policy Memo introducing the policy was entitled "Graduation Prayers." *See id.* at 1345 (Kravitch, J., dissenting). One judge who had originally voted to uphold the policy dissented from the court's post-*Santa Fe* reaffirmation of its earlier opinion.

> [T]he majority opinion says the policy is not about prayer, but instead is about student messages in general and permitting student participation in graduation ceremonies. . . . I disagree. The policy is not entitled "Student Messages" or "Student Participation in Graduation," but "Graduation Prayers." . . . And the board's mandate that the student "message" be no longer than two minutes comports nicely with the length of a good, short prayer. The memorandum that became the board's policy refers repeatedly not to free speech or democratic participation cases but to a school prayer decision.

Id. at 1350 (Carnes, J. dissenting).

Do lower-court decisions like *Adler* illustrate the problem with flexible Establishment Clause standards? Given the ease with which the Eleventh Circuit circumvented the strong language of Justice Stevens' *Santa Fe* majority opinion, will it ever be possible for the Supreme Court to articulate an Establishment

Clause standard that will effectively prevent a lower court from failing to enforce constitutional decisions with which the lower court disagrees?

2. Justice Powell once wrote that "At this point in the 20th century we are quite far removed from the dangers that prompted the Framers to include the Establishment Clause in the Bill of Rights. The risk of significant religious or denominational control over our democratic processes or even of deep political division along religious lines is remote." *Wolman v. Walter*, 433 U.S. 229, 263 (1977) (Powell, J., concurring in part, concurring in judgment in part, and dissenting in part) (citations omitted). Do the facts of cases like *Doe*, *Santa Fe*, and the cases cited in the previous Note suggest this assessment is premature, at least in the context of rural, religiously homogeneous locales? In this context, consider the following exchange in the United States Supreme Court between Justice Scalia and Anthony Giffin, the attorney for "Susan Doe":

> MR. GRIFFIN: Mr. Chief Justice, may it please the Court: In July of 1996 there was a hearing held in the district court in Galveston, Texas. In that hearing, the court, the district court, took testimony and part of the testimony came from the Does, as they're affectionately known, in this case.

> QUESTION: Could I ask you about that? That's just a curiosity I have in this case. I don't even know who the plaintiffs are. Is there — how come it's Jane Doe? I mean, are these minors? Is — or what?

> MR. GRIFFIN: One parent is — one parent, one group of plaintiffs were Catholic, a Catholic family. Another group of families were a Mormon family.

> QUESTION: Do people have rights to sue anonymously in Federal court? Is anybody who just doesn't want it known that he's bring a lawsuit, he's ashamed of it for one reason or another, can sue anonymously? I didn't know we could do that.

> MR. GRIFFIN: I think the jurisprudence is, if there is a threat of intimidation, if there's a threat of violence, if there's a threat — and I think there was testimony that — within the temporary injunction when the case first started that there was this threat, and the district court had entered an order instructing not to ferret out the names, and when there was an attempt to ferret out the names —

> QUESTION: Well, how does the district court have authority to do that?

> MR. GRIFFIN: Well, he had an attempt — he had the authority to protect the plaintiffs, in other words, from any threat. The names of the plaintiffs were known to the defendant.

> QUESTION: What was the threat?

> MR. GRIFFIN: The threat was, we had information that certain children were intimidated, certain children were pushed, certain plaintiffs,

certain people who were not plaintiffs had to pull their children out of the school because of protesting the prayer policies that existed in Santa Fe, and that there was a intimate threat that the district court saw it necessary to protect.

QUESTION: Well, do you think the district court just has complete discretion to grant anonymity that way?

MR. GRIFFIN: I don't think the district court has the complete discretion, and I think that one of the issues that we briefed at the trial court below was that issue, and when we got to the — into the hearing of July of 19 and 96, the district court said, now that we're going into a hearing, these names must be revealed, but we will do it under protection. He did not seal that courtroom. He asked the press not to publish their names, but their names ultimately became —

QUESTION: Their names ultimately were —

MR. GRIFFIN: Yes. Their names ultimately became known to the public and — but they were not published in the newspaper, and in this hearing one of the most fundamental things that happened in the hearing after the district court had gone through the problem of the injunction, after the district court had instructed not to ferret out the names, after the court had heard testimony in terms of intimidation, the district court looked at the plaintiff, known as Susan Doe in the record, and he asked her, what is the big deal? And she looked at the court and she said, I teach my children at home religion, and I don't want to go down, and I don't think it's necessary for me to go down to the school and interview every one of the teachers and find out their religious faith. That's the backdrop of this case.

In Justice Stevens' majority opinion in *Santa Fe* he notes that the District Court entered the anonymity order to protect the Does from intimidation and harassment. Stevens also quoted the Fifth Circuit's conclusion that this was a decision that the school officials "apparently neither agreed with nor particularly respected." Stevens then quoted the order the district court entered a month after the complaint was filed:

[A]ny further attempt on the part of District or school administration, officials, counsellors, teachers, employees or servants of the School District, parents, students or anyone else, overtly or covertly to ferret out the identities of the Plaintiffs in this cause, by means of bogus petitions, questionnaires, individual interrogation, or downright "snooping", will cease immediately. ANYONE TAKING ANY ACTION ON SCHOOL PROPERTY, DURING SCHOOL HOURS, OR WITH SCHOOL RESOURCES OR APPROVAL FOR PURPOSES OF ATTEMPTING TO ELICIT THE NAMES OR IDENTITIES OF THE PLAINTIFFS IN THIS CAUSE OF ACTION, BY OR ON BEHALF OF ANY OF THESE INDIVIDUALS, WILL FACE THE HARSHEST POSSIBLE CON-

TEMPT SANCTIONS FROM THIS COURT, AND MAY ADDITION-
ALLY FACE CRIMINAL LIABILITY. The Court wants these proceedings addressed on their merits, and not on the basis of intimidation or
harassment of the participants on either side.

Santa Fe, 530 U.S. at 294 n.1 (emphasis in original). For other cases discussing
the need to sue pseudonymously in religious rights cases, *see Doe v. Harlan Cty
Sch. Dist.*, 96 F. Supp. 2d 667 (E.D. Ky. 2000); *Doe v. Stegall*, 653 F.2d 180 (5th
Cir. 1981).

D. SCHOOL PRAYER IN THE PUBLIC UNIVERSITY CONTEXT

TANFORD v. BRAND
104 F.3d 982 (7th Cir. 1997)

CUMMINGS, Circuit Judge.

On May 5, 1995, the Bloomington commencement activities began at the
University President's home. The following day a university-wide Commence-
ment Ceremony took place in the University's football stadium at 10:00 a.m.
Special events followed for graduates of the various schools and their families.
A committee consisting of faculty, staff and students was responsible for plan-
ning the commencement activities.

Thirty thousand to 35,000 people attended the Saturday morning stadium
Commencement Ceremony. All graduating students were invited to attend, but
attendance is voluntary and no penalty is imposed for non-attendance. Of the
7,400 graduating students in the undergraduate and graduate schools, approximately 5,000 attended.

Five thousand students and 150 University officials and faculty members
formed the academic procession to the Commencement Ceremony. These persons proceeded to chairs placed in the football field whereas the 25,000 to
30,000 visitors and guests were seated in the stadium's permanent seats. The
ceremony consisted of the national anthem, a nonsectarian invocation, an
address by the commencement speaker, the conferral of honorary degrees, the
presentation of the graduating classes, student remarks, the charge to the
graduating classes, the conferral of degrees, the induction ceremony, the singing
of the University's song, and a nonsectarian benediction. Fifteen to fifty-five percent of the students graduating from the law school attend the university-wide
Commencement Ceremony.

In 1840, the University commenced having a nonsectarian invocation and
benediction to open and close the morning Commencement Ceremony. A religious leader from the Bloomington area is invited to give the invocation and

benediction. The prayers usually refer to a deity.[1] A different person is chosen each year and in addition to the invocation that person is invited to give an uplifting and unifying benediction. In 1995, Father Ralph W. Sims of the St. Paul Catholic Center delivered the invocation and benediction. His parish serves the University's Catholic students. In the previous year, the invocation and benediction were given by Reverend Barbara Carlson of the Unitarian Universalist Church. Over the previous five years the invocation and benediction were delivered by clergymen from the First Presbyterian Church, the First United Methodist Church, and the B'Nai B'Rith Hillel Foundation. Most of those seated in the stadium do not stand for the invocation and benediction.

University President Brand has explained that this ceremony is not to sponsor any particular religious faith or even to endorse religion but is meant to serve secular objectives by emphasizing the solemnity and dignity of the ceremony.

The four plaintiffs may be described as follows:

1. Professor Tanford is 45 years old and has tenure at the University. His undergraduate degree was obtained from Princeton University and he received his J.D. and L.L.M. degrees from Duke University. He has taught at the law school since 1979. He attended only one Commencement Ceremony since 1979 when he commenced teaching law. He attended the 1987 Commencement Ceremony because he was asked to "hood" students there. However, he absented himself when the invocation began, returned for the hooding and left before the benediction. He said that he did not think all 7,000 people who stood during the invocation and benediction believed in the religious message conveyed and that the Commencement Ceremony would not affect the religious beliefs of those in attendance. In 1988 or 1989, he wrote the student newspaper urging the faculty and University community generally to boycott graduations because of the "inappropriateness of having prayer."

2. Third-year law student MacDonald was expected to graduate in May 1995. She had received her Bachelor of Arts degree from Indiana University in May 1992. She stated that she attended the May 1992 Commencement Ceremony when she received her undergraduate degree although she was uncomfortable in participating in a service led by someone of a different faith. She stated that her conscience would be offended if there were an invocation and benediction in

---

[1] The May 1995 benediction read as follows:

"Let us pray. Gracious God we have gathered as dreamers. People who believe deep inside that things can be better. We have been called into being by you to make a difference. We like giving. Be with us as we endeavor to reach out to those who feel distance from the joy and the challenge of truth. We pray that we might touch with our learning those who feel that there is no hope, no reason to believe in life and love, and the possibility itself. Strengthen us for the journeys of mind, of heart, of spirit, of body, so that we might be right in truth for one another, and for our world. We ask this in the name of our common god. Amen."

1995. She also attended the Commencement Ceremony in May 1994, being curious about the invocation and benediction. She planned to attend the 1995 Saturday afternoon law school Recognition Ceremony, knowing it would not have an invocation or benediction. She knew that she was not required to attend the stadium Commencement Ceremony and was uncertain whether she would attend if there were an invocation and benediction, even though her parents, family and friends were interested in attending. She stated that she would be bothered if her daughter saw a religious figure on the stage with the University president or giving a prayer. She did not disclose whether she attended the 1995 Commencement Ceremony after the preliminary injunction was denied.

3. Plaintiff Suess was a first-year law student, expected to graduate from the law school in May 1997. He is of the Jewish faith and stated that he was offended by the giving of a nonsectarian invocation and benediction because it is a form of proselytizing although he said it would not have any effect on his personal religious beliefs. He had attended an invocation and benediction at his undergraduate commencement ceremony at the University of Chicago, although he did not participate in it. Suess said he had been advised of the 1995 law school activities by law school friends and quite possibly would attend the morning Commencement Ceremony at the stadium. He did not say whether he attended the ceremony after the preliminary injunction was denied. He was planning to attend the 1995 graduating Recognition Ceremony at the law school although he did not know whether there would be an invocation or benediction. As customary there was none.

4. Urbanski was an undergraduate plaintiff and was added after the preliminary injunction was denied. He opposes graduation prayer because he believes there should be a separation between church and state in a public institution. Prayer makes him uncomfortable. However, he agreed with his public high school policy which permitted students to have a moment of silence or a short prayer during commencement speeches. He expected to attend the 1999 Commencement Ceremony and would stay during the invocation and benediction because it is inconvenient to leave during parts of the ceremony. He would sit quietly until the prayer was over but would not participate in it. His beliefs would not be impacted by the ceremony.

Thomas Bolyard, Director of University Field Services, said one of his responsibilities is to accommodate persons who have special problems or requests related to the Commencement Ceremony. He said it would be an easy matter to accommodate plaintiff Tanford and others who wished to be seated where they could enter or exit the Ceremony at will. He said that it was common for seated students or faculty members to get up and move around during the ceremony. He stated that some students and faculty members arrive late and leave early and often leave their seats to get a drink or use the restrooms.

In May 1995 the district court denied a preliminary injunction. After filing an amended complaint and answer, plaintiffs filed a motion for summary judgment which was denied. We affirm.

Discussion

All parties discuss *Lee v. Weisman* Unlike *Lee*, here there was no coercion — real or otherwise — to participate. Many students chose not to attend the stadium exercises. Others left during the invocation, then returned and exited before the benediction. Still others sat during both events, as did most stadium attendees. At the afternoon ceremonies, no prayer was involved. Finally, the mature stadium attendees were voluntarily present and free to ignore the cleric's remarks. Most remained seated. Under these facts, in which the special concerns underlying the Supreme Court's decision in *Lee* are absent, the district court correctly determined that *Lee* does not require the challenged practices to be struck down. *Cf. Widmar v. Vincent* ("University students . . . are less impressionable than younger students and should be able to appreciate that the University's policy is one of neutrality of religion.").

Lemon v. Kurtzman is plaintiffs' other principal reliance. There Pennsylvania and Rhode Island each gave financial aid to church-related educational institutions, a far cry from the non-denominational invocation and benediction at the Bloomington commencement.

Here the University's practice of having an invocation and benediction at its commencements has prevailed for 155 years and is widespread throughout the nation. Rather than being a violation of the Establishment Clause, it is "simply a tolerable acknowledgment of beliefs widely held among the people of this country." *Marsh v. Chambers*. As we held in *Sherman v. Community Consolidated School District 21*, 980 F.2d 437 (7th Cir. 1992), Illinois public schools may lead the Pledge of Allegiance, including its reference to God, without violating the Establishment Clause of the First Amendment. Similarly here, the invocation and benediction serve legitimate secular purposes of solemnizing public occasions rather than approving particular religious beliefs. As the concurring opinion in *Sherman* summarized, "the First Amendment was not intended to prohibit states [here a university] from sanctioning ceremonial invocations of God. Such . . . action simply does not amount to an establishment of religion" Finally, as the district court correctly determined, the University's inclusion of a brief non-sectarian invocation and benediction does not have a primary effect of endorsing or disapproving religion, and there is no excessive entanglement of church and state by virtue of the University's selection of a cleric or its instruction to the cleric that his or her remarks should be unifying and uplifting. Insofar as there is any advancement of religion or governmental entanglement, it is *de minimis* at best. *See Metzl v. Leininger*, 57 F.3d 618, 620 (7th Cir. 1995) (observing that "a law that promotes religion may nevertheless be upheld . . . because the effect in promoting religion is too attenuated to worry about").

NOTES ON GRADUATION PRAYER IN THE UNIVERSITY CONTEXT

1. *University Graduation Prayer and the Unruly Audience.* Dr. Dilip Chaudhuri is a professor of mechanical engineering at Tennessee State University who practices the Hindu religion. Since joining the university, Dr. Chaudhuri had complained for many years about the university's custom of having prayers offered at university functions such as graduation exercises, faculty meetings, dedication ceremonies, and guest lectures. In response to his complaints, the university's General Counsel issued an opinion letter in May 1988 stating that prayers could still be offered at these functions, but that they should not endorse or favor any particular religious point of view. At several graduation ceremonies following the issuance of this letter, the university invited various clergymen to give prayers, with the stipulation that the prayers be nonsectarian and that references to Jesus Christ be omitted. At the May 1991 ceremony, a clergyman offered a prayer that did not refer to Jesus Christ, but contained several references to God and the Heavenly Father. Dr. Chaudhuri sued the university for violating the Establishment Clause.

In April 1993, Dr. Chaudhuri's lawyers filed a preliminary injunction motion to prevent the university from permitting similar prayers at the upcoming May graduation. At approximately the same time, the university announced that a moment of silence would be included in the May graduation ceremony in lieu of a spoken prayer. This is how the court of appeals described the scene that ensued: "The program for the May graduation exercises included a moment of silence. On reaching that point in the program, the speaker asked everyone to rise and remain silent. The moment that followed proved less than silent. Someone, or a group of people, began to recite the Lord's Prayer aloud. Many audience members joined in — spontaneously, by all accounts — and loud applause followed. TSU officials say they had no advance knowledge of what was going to happen." At the summer graduation ceremony three months later, the university invited as a speaker a local educator. According to the court of appeals: "As noted in the commencement program, Dr. Jones was also the pastor at a local church. When Dr. Jones asked the audience to stand for a moment of silence, a portion of the audience again recited the Lord's Prayer. TSU officials denied complicity in this incident as well."

The federal district court subsequently granted the university's motion for summary judgment against Dr. Chaudhuri and the Sixth Circuit Court of Appeals affirmed. With regard to the spoken prayers, the Sixth Circuit held that since the prayers lacked any direct reference to Jesus Christ, they "do not strike us as overtly Christian. The prayers did, to be sure, evoke a monotheistic tradition not shared by Hindus such as Dr. Chaudhuri. But '[t]he content of the prayer is not of concern to judges where, as here, there is no indication that the prayer opportunity has been exploited to proselytize or advance any one, or to disparage any other, faith or belief. That being so, it is not for us to embark on a sensitive evaluation or to parse the content of a particular prayer.'" *Chaudhuri v. Tennessee*, 130 F.3d 232, 236-37 (6th Cir. 1997), *cert. denied*, 523 U.S.

1024 (1988) (quoting *Marsh v. Chambers*, 463 U.S. 783, 794-95 (1983)). With regard to the audience recitation of the Lord's Prayer during the ceremonies' moments of silence, the court held that the university could not be held accountable for the religious expression of audience members. Are the Sixth Circuit's conclusions consistent with the Establishment Clause principles discussed elsewhere in this Chapter?

2. *Prayer in Military Academies and Colleges.* In *Mellen v. Bunting*, 327 F.3d 355 (4th Cir. 2003), *cert. denied*, 541 U.S. 1019 (2004), the Fourth Circuit Court of Appeals held unconstitutional the practice of reading a supper prayer before dinner every night at the Virginia Military Institute, a state-operated military college located in Lexington, Virginia. The court distinguished cases such as *Tanford v. Brand* and *Chaudhuri v. Tennessee*, on the grounds that the conformity demanded of cadets attending a military college rendered the practice of group prayer more coercive than a prayer recited in a more informal educational setting:

> Although VMI's cadets are not children, in VMI's educational system they are uniquely susceptible to coercion. . . . At VMI, even upperclassmen must submit to mandatory and ritualized activities, as obedience and conformity remain central tenets of the school's educational philosophy. In this atmosphere, General Bunting reinstituted the supper prayer in 1995 to build solidarity and bring the Corps together as a family. In this context, VMI's cadets are plainly coerced into participating in a religious exercise. Because of VMI's coercive atmosphere, the Establishment Clause precludes school officials from sponsoring an official prayer, even for mature adults.

Id. at 371-72. This decision is in line with the District of Columbia Circuit's decision in *Anderson v. Laird*, 466 F.2d 283 (D.C. Cir.), *cert. denied*, 409 U.S. 1076 (1972), which held unconstitutional a federal regulation requiring all cadets and midshipmen at the military academies to attend "Protestant, Catholic or Jewish chapel services on Sundays."

3. *Religious Texts in University Settings.* Consider the following episode that occurred recently at the University of North Carolina.

> The University of North Carolina at Chapel Hill ("UNC") has an orientation program prior to the beginning of classes for all incoming freshman. The stated goals of the orientation program are to: (1) stimulate discussion and critical thinking around a current topic, (2) introduce the student to academic life at UNC, (3) enhance a sense of community between students, faculty and staff, and (4) provide a common experience for incoming students.

> UNC seeks to accomplish these goals by assigning a selected book, requesting that the students consider study questions and prepare a written response to the book, and holding a two-hour small-group discussion meeting led by volunteers. . . . For the 2002 orientation program,

UNC selected portions of Michael Sells' *Approaching the Qur'án: The Early Revelations* (White Cloud Press 1999). Sells is "a ranking Islamicist" and professor of religion at Haverford College. UNC stated in the assignment that it chose the book because Westerners have long been puzzled about the traditions of Islam and because it thought that a book exploring Islam was highly relevant in light of the terrorist attacks of September 11, 2001. UNC eventually changed the writing assignment for the 2002 orientation in order to allow those with religious objections to the book to write a short paper explaining their objections to reading the book instead of analyzing the book itself.

Yacovelli v. Moeser, 2004 U.S. Dist. LEXIS 9152 (M.D.N.C. May 20, 2004). Several students objected that the favorable portrayal of Islam amounted to an endorsement of the faith. They also objected to the study questions, which queried their religious views and responses to the Islamic literature. The study questions included the following: "What did you really know about the Qur'an before reading this book?" "What ideas or impressions did you have about Muslim cultures more generally? Has reading these parts of the Qur'an affected or changed those ideas or impressions about Islam? How?" "What are the main human and personal virtues and vices or flaws that these readings emphasize?" "From your perspective, how comprehensive are these lists of virtues and vices? Is there anything you would add? Or de-emphasize? Why?" *Id.*

The students sued the University, claiming that the assignment violated both the Establishment and Free Exercise clauses. The federal district court disagreed, and granted the University's motion to dismiss the complaint. According to the court:

> The book simply explains certain religious tenets of Islam and discusses the ambiguities involved in some situations as well as the long-standing cultural issues involved in Islam. Although the book does not include any passages addressing an obligation to kill non-believers, a fact which Plaintiffs point to in finding the book to be pro-Islam, the aim of the book does not pretend to be an exhaustive review of Islam. The book instead acts as an anthropological, literary and historical review of one of the world's most widespread and controversial religions. Reading and discussing the book is not properly deemed a religious practice.

> *Approaching the Qur'án* simply cannot be compared to religious practices which have been deemed violative of the Establishment Clause, such as posting the Ten Commandments, reading the Lord's Prayer or reciting prayers in school. The book does include Suras, which are similar to Christian Psalms. However, by his own words, the author endeavors only to explain Islam and not to endorse it. Furthermore, listening to Islamic prayers in an effort to understand the artistic nature of the readings and its connection to a historical religious text does not have the primary effect of advancing religion. The fact that few students are likely to have understood the Arabic readings lends support to the posi-

tion that the purpose of the CD was to aid academic discussion and not to promote the religion of Islam. A reasonable observer would not believe that the orientation program was an attempt to promote the Islamic faith.

Is it significant that Islam is very much a minority faith among students and faculty members at the University of North Carolina? Does this make the study of a sacred text less likely to be construed as endorsement by the University? Would the same assumption of nonendorsement prevail if a public university in an overwhelmingly Christian community required all its incoming freshmen to study the Bible and then asked the students (including the Jewish and Muslim students) to answer a study question such as "Has reading these parts of the Bible affected or changed those ideas or impressions about Christianity? How?"

Chapter 7

EXPLICIT GOVERNMENT ENDORSEMENT OF RELIGION IN OTHER CONTEXTS

The previous chapter illustrates the Supreme Court's tendency to impose fairly rigid rules restricting religious involvement in public schools. In other contexts, however, the rules regarding symbolic church/state relationships are noticeably less strict (and, not coincidentally, noticeably less clear). Outside the school prayer context, the courts have permitted religion to permeate public life in many subtle ways. As proponents like to point out, the courts do not seriously question the constitutionality of the phrase "In God We Trust" on the currency. Likewise, federal, state, and local legislatures routinely permit prayers in official meetings, and the Supreme Court itself opens its proceedings with the phrase "God save the United States and this Honorable Court."

This chapter focuses on several related symbolic endorsement problems other than school prayer. The cases in the first half of this chapter involve some of the most contentious issues to reach the courts during the last few decades: prayer in official proceedings, religious holiday displays, and official monuments or plaques containing renditions of the Ten Commandments or other religious symbols and phrases.

The last of the non-school cases in this chapter — *Capital Square v. Pinette* — raises the question whether private religious speech can ever be attributed to the government. This question returns us to the public school arena, which is the focal point of the cases in the last portion of this chapter. These cases deal with the permissibility of private religious speech on public school property. These cases are distinguished from the school prayer cases in that they depend on the determination of very sensitive questions of attribution. This is the crucial issue in these cases: In a society where most communities will be dominated by one or a very limited number of faiths, should the courts tend to attribute private religious speech to the government? Putting the same issue another way, does the Establishment Clause of the First Amendment limit the protection of religious speech under the Free Speech Clause in situations where religious dissenters are likely to attribute private religious speech on public property to the government?

A. LEGISLATIVE PRAYER

MARSH v. CHAMBERS
463 U.S. 783 (1983)

CHIEF JUSTICE BURGER delivered the opinion of the Court.

The question presented is whether the Nebraska Legislature's practice of opening each legislative day with a prayer by a chaplain paid by the State violates the Establishment Clause of the First Amendment.

I

The Nebraska Legislature begins each of its sessions with a prayer offered by a chaplain who is chosen biennially by the Executive Board of the Legislative Council and paid out of public funds. Robert E. Palmer, a Presbyterian minister, has served as chaplain since 1965 at a salary of $319.75 per month for each month the legislature is in session.

Ernest Chambers is a member of the Nebraska Legislature and a taxpayer of Nebraska. Claiming that the Nebraska Legislature's chaplaincy practice violates the Establishment Clause of the First Amendment, he brought this action under 42 U.S.C. § 1983, seeking to enjoin enforcement of the practice.

The Court of Appeals for the Eighth Circuit [applied] the three-part test of *Lemon v. Kurtzman*, [and] held that the chaplaincy practice violated all three elements of the test: the purpose and primary effect of selecting the same minister for 16 years and publishing his prayers was to promote a particular religious expression; use of state money for compensation and publication led to entanglement.

II

The opening of sessions of legislative and other deliberative public bodies with prayer is deeply embedded in the history and tradition of this country. From colonial times through the founding of the Republic and ever since, the practice of legislative prayer has coexisted with the principles of disestablishment and religious freedom. In the very courtrooms in which the United States District Judge and later three Circuit Judges heard and decided this case, the proceedings opened with an announcement that concluded, "God save the United States and this Honorable Court." The same invocation occurs at all sessions of this Court.

The tradition in many of the colonies was, of course, linked to an established church, but the Continental Congress, beginning in 1774, adopted the traditional procedure of opening its sessions with a prayer offered by a paid chaplain. Although prayers were not offered during the Constitutional Convention, the First Congress, as one of its early items of business, adopted the policy of selecting a chaplain to open each session with prayer. Thus, on April 7, 1789, the

Senate appointed a committee "to take under consideration the manner of electing Chaplains." On April 9, 1789, a similar committee was appointed by the House of Representatives. On April 25, 1789, the Senate elected its first chaplain; the House followed suit on May 1, 1789. A statute providing for the payment of these chaplains was enacted into law on September 22, 1789.

On Sept. 25, 1789, three days after Congress authorized the appointment of paid chaplains, final agreement was reached on the language of the Bill of Rights. Clearly the men who wrote the First Amendment Religion Clause did not view paid legislative chaplains and opening prayers as a violation of that Amendment, for the practice of opening sessions with prayer has continued without interruption ever since that early session of Congress. It has also been followed consistently in most of the states, including Nebraska, where the institution of opening legislative sessions with prayer was adopted even before the State attained statehood. Neb. Jour. of Council, General Assembly, 1st Sess., 16 (Jan. 22, 1855).

Standing alone, historical patterns cannot justify contemporary violations of constitutional guarantees, but there is far more here than simply historical patterns. In this context, historical evidence sheds light not only on what the draftsmen intended the Establishment Clause to mean, but also on how they thought that Clause applied to the practice authorized by the First Congress — their actions reveal their intent.

No more is Nebraska's practice of over a century, consistent with two centuries of national practice, to be cast aside. It can hardly be thought that in the same week Members of the First Congress voted to appoint and to pay a chaplain for each House and also voted to approve the draft of the First Amendment for submission to the States, they intended the Establishment Clause of the Amendment to forbid what they had just declared acceptable. In applying the First Amendment to the states through the Fourteenth Amendment, *Cantwell v. Connecticut*, 310 U.S. 296 (1940), it would be incongruous to interpret that Clause as imposing more stringent First Amendment limits on the States than the draftsmen imposed on the Federal Government.

In light of the unambiguous and unbroken history of more than 200 years, there can be no doubt that the practice of opening legislative sessions with prayer has become part of the fabric of our society. To invoke Divine guidance on a public body entrusted with making the laws is not, in these circumstances, an "establishment" of religion or a step toward establishment; it is simply a tolerable acknowledgment of beliefs widely held among the people of this country. As Justice Douglas observed, "[w]e are a religious people whose institutions presuppose a Supreme Being." *Zorach v. Clauson,* 343 U.S. 306, 313 (1952).

III

We turn then to the question of whether any features of the Nebraska practice violate the Establishment Clause. Beyond the bare fact that a prayer is offered, three points have been made: first, that a clergyman of only one denomination — Presbyterian — has been selected for 16 years; second, that the chaplain is paid at public expense; and third, that the prayers are in the Judeo-Christian tradition.[1] Weighed against the historical background, these factors do not serve to invalidate Nebraska's practice.

The Court of Appeals was concerned that Palmer's long tenure has the effect of giving preference to his religious views. We cannot, any more than Members of the Congresses of this century, perceive any suggestion that choosing a clergyman of one denomination advances the beliefs of a particular church. To the contrary, the evidence indicates that Palmer was reappointed because his performance and personal qualities were acceptable to the body appointing him. Palmer was not the only clergyman heard by the Legislature; guest chaplains have officiated at the request of various legislators and as substitutes during Palmer's absences. Absent proof that the chaplain's reappointment stemmed from an impermissible motive, we conclude that his long tenure does not in itself conflict with the Establishment Clause.

Nor is the compensation of the chaplain from public funds a reason to invalidate the Nebraska Legislature's chaplaincy; remuneration is grounded in historic practice initiated, as we noted earlier, by the same Congress that adopted the Establishment Clause of the First Amendment. The Continental Congress paid its chaplain, as did some of the states. Currently, many state legislatures and the United States Congress provide compensation for their chaplains. Nebraska has paid its chaplain for well over a century. The content of the prayer is not of concern to judges where, as here, there is no indication that the prayer opportunity has been exploited to proselytize or advance any one, or to disparage any other, faith or belief. That being so, it is not for us to embark on a sensitive evaluation or to parse the content of a particular prayer.

JUSTICE BRENNAN, with whom JUSTICE MARSHALL joins, dissenting.

III

A

The Court's main argument for carving out an exception sustaining legislative prayer is historical. The Court cannot — and does not — purport to find a pattern of "undeviating acceptance" of legislative prayer. It also disclaims exclusive reliance on the mere longevity of legislative prayer. The Court does, however, point out that, only three days before the First Congress reached agreement on the final wording of the Bill of Rights, it authorized the appointment of paid chaplains for its own proceedings, and the Court argues that in light of this "unique history," the actions of Congress reveal its intent as to the meaning of the Establishment Clause. I agree that historical practice is "of

---

[1] Palmer characterizes his prayers as "nonsectarian," "Judeo Christian," and with "elements of the American civil religion." App. 75 and 87. (deposition of Robert E. Palmer). Although some of his earlier prayers were often explicitly Christian, Palmer removed all references to Christ after a 1980 complaint from a Jewish legislator. *Id.,* at 49.

considerable import in the interpretation of abstract constitutional language," *Walz*, 397 U.S., at 681 (BRENNAN, J., concurring). This is a case, however, in which — absent the Court's invocation of history — there would be no question that the practice at issue was unconstitutional. And despite the surface appeal of the Court's argument, there are at least three reasons why specific historical practice should not in this case override that clear constitutional imperative.[30]

First, it is significant that the Court's historical argument does not rely on the legislative history of the Establishment Clause itself. Indeed, that formal history is profoundly unilluminating on this and most other subjects. Rather, the Court assumes that the Framers of the Establishment Clause would not have themselves authorized a practice that they thought violated the guarantees contained in the clause. This assumption, however, is questionable. Legislators, influenced by the passions and exigencies of the moment, the pressure of constituents and colleagues, and the press of business, do not always pass sober constitutional judgment on every piece of legislation they enact, and this must be assumed to be as true of the Members of the First Congress as any other. Indeed, the fact that James Madison, who voted for the bill authorizing the payment of the first congressional chaplains, later expressed the view that the practice was unconstitutional, is instructive on precisely this point. Madison's later views may not have represented so much a change of *mind* as a change of *role*, from a Member of Congress engaged in the hurly-burly of legislative activity to a detached observer engaged in unpressured reflection. Since the latter role is precisely the one with which this Court is charged, I am not at all sure that Madison's later writings should be any less influential in our deliberations than his earlier vote.

Second, the Court's analysis treats the First Amendment simply as an Act of Congress, as to whose meaning the intent of Congress is the single touchstone. Both the Constitution and its Amendments, however, became supreme law only by virtue of their ratification by the States, and the understanding of the States should be as relevant to our analysis as the understanding of Congress. This observation is especially compelling in considering the meaning of the Bill of Rights. The first 10 Amendments were not enacted because the Members of the First Congress came up with a bright idea one morning; rather, their enactment was forced upon Congress by a number of the States as a condition for their ratification of the original Constitution. To treat any practice authorized by the First Congress as presumptively consistent with the Bill of Rights is therefore somewhat akin to treating any action of a party to a contract as presumptively

---

[30] Indeed, the sort of historical argument made by the Court should be advanced with some hesitation in light of certain other skeletons in the congressional closet. *See, e.g.,* An Act for the Punishment of certain Crimes against the United States, § 16, 1 Stat. 116 (1790) (enacted by the First Congress and requiring that persons convicted of certain theft offenses "be publicly whipped, not exceeding thirty-nine stripes"); Act of July 23, 1866, 14 Stat. 216 (reaffirming the racial segregation of the public schools in the District of Columbia; enacted exactly one week after Congress proposed Fourteenth Amendment to the States).

consistent with the terms of the contract. The latter proposition, if it were accepted, would of course resolve many of the heretofore perplexing issues in contract law.

Finally, and most importantly, the argument tendered by the Court is misguided because the Constitution is not a static document whose meaning on every detail is fixed for all time by the life experience of the Framers. We have recognized in a wide variety of constitutional contexts that the practices that were in place at the time any particular guarantee was enacted into the Constitution do not necessarily fix forever the meaning of that guarantee. To be truly faithful to the Framers, "our use of the history of their time must limit itself to broad purposes, not specific practices." *Abington School Dist. v. Schempp*, 374 U.S., at 241 (BRENNAN, J., concurring). Our primary task must be to translate "the majestic generalities of the Bill of Rights, conceived as part of the pattern of liberal government in the eighteenth century, into concrete restraints on officials dealing with the problems of the twentieth century. . . ." *West Virginia State Bd. of Education v. Barnette*, 319 U.S. 624, 639 (1943).

The inherent adaptability of the Constitution and its amendments is particularly important with respect to the Establishment Clause. "[O]ur religious composition makes us a vastly more diverse people than were our forefathers. . . . In the face of such profound changes, practices which may have been objectionable to no one in the time of Jefferson and Madison may today be highly offensive to many persons, the deeply devout and the nonbelievers alike." *Schempp*, 374 U.S., at 240-241 (BRENNAN, J., concurring). *Cf. McDaniel v. Paty*, 435 U.S. 618, 628 (plurality opinion). President John Adams issued during his Presidency a number of official proclamations calling on all Americans to engage in Christian prayer. Justice Story, in his treatise on the Constitution, contended that the "real object" of the First Amendment "was, not to countenance, much less to advance Mahometanism, or Judaism, or infidelity, by prostrating Christianity; but to exclude all rivalry among Christian sects. . . ." Whatever deference Adams' actions and Story's views might once have deserved in this Court, the Establishment Clause must now be read in a very different light. Similarly, the members of the First Congress should be treated, not as sacred figures whose every action must be emulated, but as the authors of a document meant to last for the ages. Indeed, a proper respect for the Framers themselves forbids us to give so static and lifeless a meaning to their work. To my mind, the Court's focus here on a narrow piece of history is, in a fundamental sense, a betrayal of the lessons of history.

B

Of course, the Court does not rely entirely on the practice of the First Congress in order to validate legislative prayer. There is another theme which, although implicit, also pervades the Court's opinion. It is exemplified by the Court's comparison of legislative prayer with the formulaic recitation of "God save the United States and this Honorable Court." It is also exemplified by the Court's apparent conclusion that legislative prayer is, at worst, a "mere shadow" on the Establishment Clause rather than a "real threat" to it. Simply put, the Court seems to regard legislative prayer as at most a *de minimis* violation, somehow unworthy of our attention. I frankly do not know what should be the proper disposition of features of our public life such as "God save the United States and this Honorable Court," "In God We Trust," "One Nation Under God," and the like. I might well adhere to the view expressed in *Schempp* that such mottos are consistent with the Establishment Clause, not because their import is *de minimis*, but because they have lost any true religious significance. Legislative invocations, however, are very different.

First of all, as JUSTICE STEVENS' dissent so effectively highlights, legislative prayer, unlike mottos with fixed wordings, can easily turn narrowly and obviously sectarian. I agree with the Court that the federal judiciary should not sit as a board of censors on individual prayers, but to my mind the better way of avoiding that task is by striking down all official legislative invocations.

More fundamentally, however, *any* practice of legislative prayer, even if it might look "nonsectarian" to nine Justices of the Supreme Court, will inevitably and continuously involve the state in one or another religious debate. Prayer is serious business — serious theological business — and it is not a mere "acknowledgment of beliefs widely held among the people of this country" for the State to immerse itself in that business. Some religious individuals or groups find it theologically problematic to engage in joint religious exercises predominantly influenced by faiths not their own. Some might object even to the attempt to fashion a "non-sectarian" prayer. Some would find it impossible to participate in any "prayer opportunity," marked by Trinitarian references. Some would find a prayer *not* invoking the name of Christ to represent a flawed view of the relationship between human beings and God. Some might find any petitionary prayer to be improper. Some might find any prayer that lacked a petitionary element to be deficient. Some might be troubled by what they consider shallow public prayer, or non- spontaneous prayer, or prayer without adequate spiritual preparation or concentration. Some might, of course, have *theological* objections to any prayer sponsored by an organ of government. Some might object on theological grounds to the level of political neutrality generally expected of government-sponsored invocational prayer. And some might object on theological grounds to the Court's requirement, that prayer, even though religious, not be proselytizing. If these problems arose in the context of a religious objection to some otherwise decidedly secular activity, then whatever remedy there is would have to be found in the Free Exercise Clause. But, in this case, we are faced with potential religious objections to an activity at the very center of religious life, and it is simply beyond the competence of government, and inconsistent with our conceptions of liberty, for the state to take upon itself the role of ecclesiastical arbiter.

NOTES ON THE SCOPE OF THE *MARSH* PRINCIPLE

1. *Regulating the Legislature's Religious Choices.* Does *Marsh* inevitably place the government in the role of religious arbiter over the content of prayers given at government meetings? Consider the following scenario. Since 1982, Murray City, Utah, has opened its city council meetings with an invocation or devotional. The city asserts that the devotional is intended to "encourage lofty thoughts, promote civility, and cause the participants to set aside other matters in order to focus on the topics to be addressed at the meeting." The city has permitted various religious adherents to present devotionals, including Christians, Navajos, Quakers, and Zen Buddhists. Problems arose, however, when an agnostic individual submitted a request to present the following prayer during the devotional period:

> OUR MOTHER, who art in heaven (if, indeed there is a heaven and if there is a God that takes a woman's form) hallowed be thy name, we ask for thy blessing for and guidance of those that will participate in this meeting and for those mortals that govern the state of Utah;

> We fervently ask that you guide the leaders of this city, Salt Lake County and the State of Utah so that they may see the wisdom of separating church and state and so that they will never again perform demeaning religious ceremonies as part of official government functions;

> We pray that you prevent self-righteous politicians from mis-using the name of God in conducting government meetings; and, that you lead them away from the hypocritical and blasphemous deception of the public, attempting to make the people believe that bureaucrats' decisions and actions have thy stamp of approval if prayers are offered at the beginning of government meetings;

> We ask that you grant Utah's leaders and politicians enough courage and discernment to understand that religion is a private matter between every individual and his or her deity; we beseech thee to educate government leaders that religious beliefs should not be broadcast and revealed for the purpose of impressing others; we pray that you strike down those that mis-use your name and those that cheapen the institution of prayer by using it for their own selfish political gains;

> We ask that the people of the State of Utah will some day learn the wisdom of the separation of church and state; we ask that you will teach the people of Utah that government should not participate in religion; we pray that you smite those government officials that would attempt to censor or control prayers made by anyone to you or to any other of our Gods;

> We ask that you deliver us from the evil of forced religious worship now sought to be imposed upon the people of the State of Utah by the

actions of mis-guided, weak and stupid politicians, who abuse power in their own self- righteousness;

All of this we ask in thy name and in the name of thy son (if in fact you had a son that visited earth) for the eternal betterment of all of us who populate the Great State of Utah.

Amen.

The city council denied the request to present this prayer on the ground that it did not meet the objectives set by the city. According to the city, the devotional period "is not a time to express political views, attack city policies or practices, or mock city practices or policies." The Tenth Circuit Court of Appeals upheld the city's action against Free Exercise and Establishment Clause challenges. *See Snyder v. Murray City Corp.*, 124 F.3d 1349 (10th Cir. 1997).

Is the exclusion of this prayer consistent with the presumption in *Marsh* that legislative prayers are nonexclusionary? Is the nonexclusionary presumption even a part of *Marsh*? The *Marsh* majority hints that prayers might be problematic if they "disparage any other, faith or belief." Can an atheist or agnostic ever express his or her views as part of a public devotional without implicitly disparaging the beliefs of theists?

Mr. Snyder did not give up after losing in federal court. He persisted in bringing his claim to the state courts, which eventually ruled in his favor. The Utah Supreme Court ruled that Murray City had violated Snyder's rights under article 1, section 4 of the Utah Constitution. *See Snyder v. Murray City Corp.*, 73 P.3d 325 (Utah 2003). Among other things, this Section provides that "No public money or property shall be appropriated for or applied to any religious worship exercise or instruction, or for the support of any ecclesiastical establishment." The Utah courts have read into this provision a neutrality principle, which requires that any use of public money or property for a religious exercise must be on a nondiscriminatory basis and be equally accessible to all. The Utah Supreme Court ruled that Murray City violated this requirement when it rejected Mr. Snyder's prayer:

Murray City's rejection of Snyder's prayer was discriminatory in that the rejection was made after a review of the prayer's content and was based upon Murray City's disagreement with the beliefs expressed therein. Because Murray City's means of selecting those entitled to offer the prayer at the opening of its city council meetings was not nondiscriminatory, and therefore not neutral, the city's practice of opening its meetings with prayer constitutes a direct benefit to the exercise of religion and violates article I, section 4. . . .

Two other recent decisions regarding legislative prayer take somewhat different approaches to the subject. In *Simpson v. Chesterfield County Bd. of Supervisors*, 404 F.3d 276 (4th Cir. 2005), the Court denied a constitutional challenge brought against the county board of supervisors' legislative prayer by a person practicing the Wiccan religion. The plaintiff had requested the right to participate in the county's prayer program. The county submitted an invitation to local religious leaders every year. The bulk of the participants were from mainstream Christian denominations, although there were some Muslim and Jewish participants as well. When the plaintiff sought to be added to the list, she was told by the county attorney that " 'Chesterfield's non-sectarian invocations are traditionally made to a divinity that is consistent with the Judeo-Christian tradition,' a divinity that would not be invoked by practitioners of witchcraft." The Fourth Circuit held that the exclusion of the plaintiff from the list of participants did not violate the principles of *Marsh v. Chambers.*

In contrast to *Simpson*, the Fourth Circuit held in *Wynne v. Town of Great Falls, South Carolina*, 376 F.3d 292 (4th Cir. 2004), that the town's prayer practices were unconstitutional. The court found that the town's prayers "frequently refer[ ] to Jesus, Jesus Christ, Christ or Savior in the opening or closing portion." The court held that the frequent and specific references to Christianity were impermissible under *Marsh*:

> *Marsh* does not permit legislators to do what the district court, after a full trial, found the Town Council of Great Falls did here — that is, to engage, as part of public business and for the citizenry as a whole, in prayers that contain explicit references to a deity in whose divinity only those of one faith believe. The invocations at issue here, which specifically call upon Jesus Christ, are simply not constitutionally acceptable legislative prayer like that approved in *Marsh*. Rather, they embody the precise kind of "advance[ment]" of one particular religion that *Marsh* cautioned against.

Id. at 301-02.

2. *Marsh and School Boards.* Does *Marsh* apply to school boards? In *Coles v. Cleveland Board of Education*, 171 F.3d. 369 (6th Cir. 1999), the Sixth Circuit Court of Appeals refused to apply the *Marsh* holding to a public board of education that opened its public meetings with a prayer led by a local clergyman. The court noted that the school board usually met in public school buildings and was often asked to rule on student disciplinary matters and student grievances, and also regularly invited students to receive awards at the public sessions. The court also noted that teachers regularly attended the board meetings to address the board about school matters, and were therefore also required to participate in the prayer. The court held that "[a]lthough meetings of the school board might be of a 'different variety' than other school-related activities, the fact remains that they are part of the same 'class' as those other activities in that they take place on school property and are inextricably intertwined with the public school system." Thus, the court found that *Lee v. Weisman* was the applicable precedent rather than *Marsh*:

> Although the school board, like many other legislative bodies, is composed of publicly elected officials drawn from the local community, that

is where the similarity ends. What actually occurs at the school board's meetings is what sets it apart from the deliberative processes of other legislative bodies. Simply stated, the fact that the function of the school board is uniquely directed toward school-related matters gives it a different type of "constituency" than those of other legislative bodies — namely, students. Unlike ordinary constituencies, students cannot vote. They are thus unable to express their discomfort with state-sponsored religious practices through the democratic process. Lacking a voice in the electoral process, students have a heightened interest in expressing their views about the school system through their participation in school board meetings.

Coles, 171 F.3d. at 381. Are students who attend the state legislative sessions in which school financing legislation is considered any less interested in the legislature's business than the students in *Coles*? If so, then why should *Marsh* apply to the legislative session and not to the school board? Is the student disciplinary function of the school board sufficient to distinguish it from the legislature? Are legislative staff members any less coerced by forced participation in legislative prayers than teachers attending a school board meeting?

3. *Marsh and State Courts.* Does *Marsh* also apply to state courts as well as legislative bodies? *See North Carolina Civil Liberties Union Foundation v. Constangy*, 947 F.2d 1145 (4th Cir. 1991), *cert. denied*, 505 U.S. 1219 (1992) (holding unconstitutional a state judge's practice of saying a long prayer from the bench at the beginning of every day).

4. *Madison's Views on Legislative Chaplains.* Justice Brennan's *Marsh* dissent refers to James Madison's later views on the subject of congressional chaplains. This is a reference to the following passage from Madison's "Detached Memoranda" (abbreviations and punctuation are as in the original):

Is the appointment of Chaplains to the two Houses of Congress consistent with the Constitution, and with the pure principle of religious freedom?

In strictness the answer on both points must be in the negative. The Constitution of the U.S. forbids everything like an establishment of a national religion. The law appointing Chaplains establishes a religious worship for the national representatives, to be performed by Ministers of religion, elected by a majority of them; and these are to be paid out of the national taxes. Does not this involve the principle of a national establishment, applicable to a provision for a religious worship for the Constituent as well as of the representative Body, approved by the majority, and conducted by Ministers of religion paid by the entire nation.

The establishment of the chaplainship to Congs is a palpable violation of equal rights, as well as of Constitutional principles: The tenets of the chaplains elected [by the majority] shut the door of worship agst the members whose creeds & consciences forbid a participation in that of the majority. To say nothing of other sects, this is the case with that of Roman Catholics & Quakers who have always had members in one or both of the Legislative branches. Could a Catholic clergyman ever hope to be appointed a Chaplain? To say that his religious principles are obnoxious or that his sect is small, is to lift the evil at once and exhibit in its naked deformity the doctrine that religious truth is to be tested by numbers. [O]r that the major sects have a right to govern the minor.

If Religion consist in voluntary acts of individuals, singly, or voluntarily associated, and it be proper that public functionaries, as well as their Constituents shd discharge their religious duties, let them like their Constituents, do so at their own expence. How small a contribution from each member of Congs wd suffice for the purpose? How just wd it be in its principle? How noble in its exemplary sacrifice to the genius of the Constitution; and the divine right of conscience? Why should the expence of a religious worship be allowed for the Legislature, be paid by the public, more than that for the Ex. or Judiciary branch of the Govt?

B. NATIVITY SCENES AND OTHER RELIGIOUS HOLIDAY DISPLAYS

LYNCH v. DONNELLY
465 U.S. 668 (1984)

CHIEF JUSTICE BURGER delivered the opinion of the Court.

We granted certiorari to decide whether the Establishment Clause of the First Amendment prohibits a municipality from including a crèche, or Nativity scene, in its annual Christmas display.

I

Each year, in cooperation with the downtown retail merchants' association, the city of Pawtucket, R.I., erects a Christmas display as part of its observance of the Christmas holiday season. The display is situated in a park owned by a nonprofit organization and located in the heart of the shopping district. The display is essentially like those to be found in hundreds of towns or cities across the Nation — often on public grounds — during the Christmas season. The Pawtucket display comprises many of the figures and decorations traditionally associated with Christmas, including, among other things, a Santa Claus house, reindeer pulling Santa's sleigh, candy-striped poles, a Christmas tree, carolers, cutout figures representing such characters as a clown, an elephant, and a teddy bear, hundreds of colored lights, a large banner that reads "SEASONS GREETINGS," and the crèche at issue here. All components of this display are owned by the City.

The crèche, which has been included in the display for 40 or more years, consists of the traditional figures, including the Infant Jesus, Mary and Joseph, angels, shepherds, kings, and animals, all ranging in height from 5' to 5?. In 1973, when the present crèche was acquired, it cost the City $1,365; it now is valued at $200. The erection and dismantling of the crèche costs the City about $20 per year; nominal expenses are incurred in lighting the crèche. No money has been expended on its maintenance for the past 10 years.

III

In this case, the focus of our inquiry must be on the crèche in the context of the Christmas season. *See, e.g., Stone v. Graham*, 449 U.S. 39 (1980) (per curiam); *Abington School District v. Schempp* [*supra* Chapter 6]. In *Stone*, for example, we invalidated a state statute requiring the posting of a copy of the Ten Commandments on public classroom walls. But the Court carefully pointed out that the Commandments were posted purely as a religious admonition, not "integrated into the school curriculum, where the Bible may constitutionally be used in an appropriate study of history, civilization, ethics, comparative religion, or the like." Similarly, in *Abington*, although the Court struck down the practices in two States requiring daily Bible readings in public schools, it specifically noted that nothing in the Court's holding was intended to "indicat[e] that such study of the Bible or of religion, when presented objectively as part of a secular program of education, may not be effected consistently with the First Amendment." Focus exclusively on the religious component of any activity would inevitably lead to its invalidation under the Establishment Clause.

The Court has invalidated legislation or governmental action on the ground that a secular purpose was lacking, but only when it has concluded there was no question that the statute or activity was motivated wholly by religious considerations.

The District Court inferred from the religious nature of the crèche that the City has no secular purpose for the display. In so doing, it rejected the city's claim that its reasons for including the crèche are essentially the same as its reasons for sponsoring the display as a whole. The District Court plainly erred by focusing almost exclusively on the crèche. When viewed in the proper context of the Christmas Holiday season, it is apparent that, on this record, there is insufficient evidence to establish that the inclusion of the crèche is a purposeful or surreptitious effort to express some kind of subtle governmental advocacy of a particular religious message. In a pluralistic society a variety of motives and purposes are implicated. The city, like the Congresses and Presidents, however, has principally taken note of a significant historical religious event long celebrated in the Western World. The crèche in the display depicts the historical origins of this traditional event long recognized as a National Holiday.

The narrow question is whether there is a secular purpose for Pawtucket's display of the crèche. The display is sponsored by the City to celebrate the Holiday and to depict the origins of that Holiday. These are legitimate secular purposes. The District Court's inference, drawn from the religious nature of the crèche, that the City has no secular purpose was, on this record, clearly erroneous.

The District Court found that the primary effect of including the crèche is to confer a substantial and impermissible benefit on religion in general and on the Christian faith in particular. Comparisons of the relative benefits to religion of different forms of governmental support are elusive and difficult to make. But to conclude that the primary effect of including the crèche is to advance religion in violation of the Establishment Clause would require that we view it as more beneficial to and more an endorsement of religion, for example, than expenditure of large sums of public money for textbooks supplied throughout the country to students attending church-sponsored schools, *Board of Education v. Allen, supra*; expenditure of public funds for transportation of students to church-sponsored schools, *Everson v. Board of Education, supra*; federal grants for college buildings of church-sponsored institutions of higher education combining secular and religious education, *Tilton,* supra; noncategorical grants to church-sponsored colleges and universities, *Roemer v. Board of Public Works,* 426 U.S. 736 (1976); and the tax exemptions for church properties sanctioned in *Walz*. It would also require that we view it as more of an endorsement of religion than the Sunday Closing Laws upheld in *McGowan v. Maryland,* 366 U.S. 420 (1961); the release time program for religious training in *Zorach*; and the legislative prayers upheld in *Marsh, supra*.

We are unable to discern a greater aid to religion deriving from inclusion of the crèche than from these benefits and endorsements previously held not violative of the Establishment Clause. What was said about the legislative prayers in *Marsh*, and implied about the Sunday Closing Laws in *McGowan* is true of the City's inclusion of the creche: its "reason or effect merely happens to coincide or harmonize with the tenets of some . . . religions."

The dissent asserts some observers may perceive that the City has aligned itself with the Christian faith by including a Christian symbol in its display and that this serves to advance religion. We can assume, *arguendo*, that the display advances religion in a sense; but our precedents plainly contemplate that on occasion some advancement of religion will result from governmental action. The Court has made it abundantly clear, however, that "not every law that confers an 'indirect,' 'remote,' or 'incidental' benefit upon [religion] is, for that reason alone, constitutionally invalid." Here, whatever benefit to one faith or religion or to all religions, is indirect, remote and incidental; display of the crèche is no more an advancement or endorsement of religion than the Congressional and Executive recognition of the origins of the Holiday itself as "Christ's Mass," or the exhibition of literally hundreds of religious paintings in governmentally supported museums.

The District Court found that there had been no administrative entanglement between religion and state resulting from the City's ownership and use of the crèche. But it went on to hold that some political divisiveness was engendered by this litigation. Coupled with its finding of an impermissible sectarian purpose and effect, this persuaded the court that there was "excessive entanglement."

Entanglement is a question of kind and degree. In this case, however, there is no reason to disturb the District Court's finding on the absence of administrative entanglement. There is no evidence of contact with church authorities concerning the content or design of the exhibit prior to or since Pawtucket's purchase of the crèche. No expenditures for maintenance of the crèche have been necessary; and since the City owns the crèche, now valued at $200, the tangible material it contributes is *de minimis*. In many respects the display requires far less ongoing, day-to-day interaction between church and state than religious paintings in public galleries. There is nothing here, of course, like the "comprehensive, discriminating, and continuing state surveillance" or the "enduring entanglement" present in *Lemon*.

The Court of Appeals correctly observed that this Court has not held that political divisiveness alone can serve to invalidate otherwise permissible conduct. And we decline to so hold today. This case does not involve a direct subsidy to church-sponsored schools or colleges, or other religious institutions, and hence no inquiry into potential political divisiveness is even called for. In any event, apart from this litigation there is no evidence of political friction or divisiveness over the crèche in the 40-year history of Pawtucket's Christmas celebration. The District Court stated that the inclusion of the crèche for the 40 years has been "marked by no apparent dissension" and that the display has had a "calm history." Curiously, it went on to hold that the political divisiveness engendered by this lawsuit was evidence of excessive entanglement. A litigant cannot, by the very act of commencing a lawsuit, however, create the appearance of divisiveness and then exploit it as evidence of entanglement.

IV

JUSTICE BRENNAN describes the crèche as a "re-creation of an event that lies at the heart of Christian faith." The crèche, like a painting, is passive; admittedly it is a reminder of the origins of Christmas. Even the traditional, purely secular displays extant at Christmas, with or without a crèche, would inevitably recall the religious nature of the Holiday. The display engenders a friendly community spirit of good will in keeping with the season. The crèche may well have special meaning to those whose faith includes the celebration of religious Masses, but none who sense the origins of the Christmas celebration would fail to be aware of its religious implications. That the display brings people into the central city, and serves commercial interests and benefits merchants and their employees, does not, as the dissent points out, determine the character of the display. That a prayer invoking Divine guidance in Congress is preceded and followed by debate and partisan conflict over taxes, budgets, national defense, and myriad mundane subjects, for example, has never been thought to demean or taint the sacredness of the invocation.

Of course the crèche is identified with one religious faith but no more so than the examples we have set out from prior cases in which we found no conflict with the Establishment Clause. *See, e.g., McGowan, supra; Marsh, supra.* It would be ironic, however, if the inclusion of a single symbol of a particular historic religious event, as part of a celebration acknowledged in the Western World for 20 centuries, and in this country by the people, by the Executive Branch, by the Congress, and the courts for two centuries, would so "taint" the City's exhibit as to render it violative of the Establishment Clause. To forbid the use of this one passive symbol — the crèche — at the very time people are taking note of the season with Christmas hymns and carols in public schools and other public places, and while the Congress and Legislatures open sessions with prayers by paid chaplains, would be a stilted overreaction contrary to our history and to our holdings. If the presence of the crèche in this display violates the Establishment Clause, a host of other forms of taking official note of Christmas, and of our religious heritage, are equally offensive to the Constitution.

The Court has acknowledged that the "fears and political problems" that gave rise to the Religion Clauses in the 18th century are of far less concern today. We are unable to perceive the Archbishop of Canterbury, the Bishop of Rome, or other powerful religious leaders behind every public acknowledgment of the religious heritage long officially recognized by the three constitutional branches of government. Any notion that these symbols pose a real danger of establishment of a state church is far-fetched indeed.

Justice O'Connor, concurring.

[Justice O'Connor's concurring opinion is reproduced in Chapter 5, *supra.*]

Justice Brennan, with whom Justice Marshall, Justice Blackmun and Justice Stevens join, dissenting.

I.

B.

The Court advances two principal arguments to support its conclusion that the Pawtucket crèche satisfies the *Lemon* test. Neither is persuasive.

First. The Court, by focusing on the holiday "context" in which the nativity scene appeared, seeks to explain away the clear religious import of the creche and the findings of the District Court that most observers understood the crèche as both a symbol of Christian beliefs and a symbol of the city's support for those beliefs. Thus, although the Court concedes that the city's inclusion of the nativity scene plainly serves "to depict the origins" of Christmas as a "significant historical religious event," and that the crèche "is identified with one religious faith," we are nevertheless expected to believe that Pawtucket's use of the crèche does not signal the city's support for the sectarian symbolism that the nativity scene evokes. The effect of the crèche, of course, must be gauged not only by its inherent religious significance but also by the overall setting in which it appears. But it blinks reality to claim, as the Court does, that by including such a distinctively religious object as the crèche in its Christmas display, Pawtucket has done no more than make use of a "traditional" symbol of the holiday, and has thereby purged the crèche of its religious content and conferred only an "incidental and indirect" benefit on religion.

The Court's struggle to ignore the clear religious effect of the crèche seems to me misguided for several reasons. In the first place, the City has positioned the crèche in a central and highly visible location within the Hodgson Park display. The District Court's findings in this regard are unambiguous:

> "[D]espite the small amount of ground covered by the creche, viewers would not regard the creche as an insignificant part of the display. It is an almost life sized tableau marked off by a white picket fence. Furthermore, its location lends the creche significance. The creche faces the Roosevelt Avenue bus stops and access stairs where the bulk of the display is placed. Moreover, the creche is near two of the most enticing parts of the display for children — Santa's house and the talking wishing well. Although the Court recognizes that one cannot see the creche from all possible vantage points, it is clear from the City's own photos that people standing at the two bus shelters and looking down at the display will see the creche centrally and prominently positioned." 525 F. Supp., at 1176-1177 (citations omitted).

Moreover, the City has done nothing to disclaim government approval of the religious significance of the crèche, to suggest that the crèche represents only one religious symbol among many others that might be included in a seasonal display truly aimed at providing a wide catalogue of ethnic and religious celebrations, or to disassociate itself from the religious content of the crèche. In *Abington School Dist. v. Schempp*, we noted that reading aloud from the Bible would be a permissible schoolroom exercise only if it was "presented objectively as part of a secular program of education" that would remove any message of governmental endorsement of religion. Similarly, when the Court of Appeals for the District of Columbia approved the inclusion of a crèche as part of a national "Pageant of Peace" on federal parkland adjacent to the White House, it did so on the express condition that the government would erect "explanatory plaques" disclaiming any sponsorship of religious beliefs associated with the crèche. In this case, by contrast, Pawtucket has made no effort whatever to provide a similar cautionary message.

Third, we have consistently acknowledged that an otherwise secular setting alone does not suffice to justify a governmental practice that has the effect of aiding religion. In *Hunt v. McNair*, 413 U.S. 734, 743 (1973), for instance, we observed that "[a]id normally may be thought to have a primary effect of advancing religion . . . when it [supports] a specifically religious activity in an otherwise substantially secular setting." The demonstrably secular context of public education, therefore, did not save the challenged practice of school prayer in *Engel* or in *Schempp*. Similarly, in *Tilton v. Richardson*, 403 U.S. 672, 683 (1971), despite the generally secular thrust of the financing legislation under review, the Court unanimously struck down that aspect of the program which permitted church-related institutions eventually to assume total control over the use of buildings constructed with federal aid.

Finally, and most importantly, even in the context of Pawtucket's seasonal celebration, the crèche retains a specifically Christian religious meaning. I refuse to accept the notion implicit in today's decision that non-Christians would find that the religious content of the crèche is eliminated by the fact that it appears as part of the City's otherwise secular celebration of the Christmas holiday. The nativity scene is clearly distinct in its purpose and effect from the rest of the Hodgson Park display for the simple reason that it is the only one rooted in a biblical account of Christ's birth. It is the chief symbol of the characteristically Christian belief that a divine Savior was brought into the world and that the purpose of this miraculous birth was to illuminate a path toward salvation and redemption. For Christians, that path is exclusive, precious and holy. But for those who do not share these beliefs, the symbolic re-enactment of the birth of a divine being who has been miraculously incarnated as a man stands as a dramatic reminder of their differences with Christian faith.[14] When government appears to sponsor such religiously inspired views, we cannot say that the practice is "'so separate and so indisputably marked off from the religious function,'. . . that [it] may fairly be viewed as reflect[ing] a neutral posture toward religious institutions." *Nyquist*, 413 U.S., at 782 (quoting *Everson*, 330 U.S., at 18). To be so excluded on religious grounds by one's elected government is an insult and an injury that, until today, could not be countenanced by the Establishment Clause.

Second. The Court also attempts to justify the crèche by entertaining a beguilingly simple, yet faulty syllogism. The Court begins by noting that government may recognize Christmas day as a public holiday; the Court then asserts that the crèche is nothing more than a traditional element of Christmas celebrations; and it concludes that the inclusion of a crèche as part of a government's annual Christmas celebration is constitutionally permissible. The Court apparently believes that once it finds that the designation of Christmas as a public holiday is constitutionally acceptable, it is then free to conclude that virtually every form of governmental association with the celebration of the holiday is also constitutional. The vice of this dangerously superficial argument is that it overlooks

---

[14] For Christians, of course, the essential message of the nativity is that God became incarnate in the person of Christ. But just as fundamental to Jewish thought is the belief in the "non-incarnation of God, . . . [t]he God in whom [Jews] believe, to whom [Jews] are pledged, does not unite with human substance on earth." M. BUBER, ISRAEL AND THE WORLD (1948) (reprinted in F. TALMAGE, DISPUTATION AND DIALOGUE: READINGS IN THE JEWISH-CHRISTIAN ENCOUNTER 281-282 (1975)) (emphasis deleted). This distinction, according to Buber, "constitute[s] the ultimate division between Judaism and Christianity." *Id.*, at 281. *See also* R. REUTHER, FAITH AND FRATRICIDE 246 (1974).

Similarly, those who follow the tenets of Unitarianism might well find Pawtucket's support for the symbolism of the creche, which highlights the trinitarian tradition in Christian faith, to be an affront to their belief in a single divine being. *See* J. WILLIAMS, WHAT AMERICANS BELIEVE AND HOW THEY WORSHIP 316-317 (3d ed. 1969). *See also* C. OLMSTEAD, HISTORY OF RELIGION IN THE UNITED STATES 296-299 (1960).

the fact that the Christmas holiday in our national culture contains both secular and sectarian elements. To say that government may recognize the holiday's traditional, secular elements of gift-giving, public festivities and community spirit, does not mean that government may indiscriminately embrace the distinctively sectarian aspects of the holiday. Indeed, in its eagerness to approve the crèche, the Court has advanced a rationale so simplistic that it would appear to allow the Mayor of Pawtucket to participate in the celebration of a Christmas Mass, since this would be just another unobjectionable way for the City to "celebrate the holiday." As is demonstrated below, the Court's logic is fundamentally flawed both because it obscures the reason why public designation of Christmas Day as a holiday is constitutionally acceptable, and blurs the distinction between the secular aspects of Christmas and its distinctively religious character, as exemplified by the crèche.

When government decides to recognize Christmas Day as a public holiday, it does no more than accommodate the calendar of public activities to the plain fact that many Americans will expect on that day to spend time visiting with their families, attending religious services, and perhaps enjoying some respite from preholiday activities. The Free Exercise Clause, of course, does not necessarily compel the government to provide this accommodation, but neither is the Establishment Clause offended by such a step. *Cf. Zorach v. Clauson*, 343 U.S. 306 (1952). Because it is clear that the celebration of Christmas has both secular and sectarian elements, it may well be that by taking note of the holiday, the government is simply seeking to serve the same kinds of wholly secular goals — for instance, promoting goodwill and a common day of rest — that were found to justify Sunday Closing Laws in *McGowan*. If public officials go further and participate in the *secular* celebration of Christmas — by, for example, decorating public places with such secular images as wreaths, garlands or Santa Claus figures — they move closer to the limits of their constitutional power but nevertheless remain within the boundaries set by the Establishment Clause. But when those officials participate in or appear to endorse the distinctively religious elements of this otherwise secular event, they encroach upon First Amendment freedoms. For it is at that point that the government brings to the forefront the theological content of the holiday, and places the prestige, power, and financial support of a civil authority in the service of a particular faith.

The inclusion of a crèche in Pawtucket's otherwise secular celebration of Christmas clearly violates these principles. Unlike such secular figures as Santa Claus, reindeer and carolers, a nativity scene represents far more than a mere "traditional" symbol of Christmas. The essence of the crèche's symbolic purpose and effect is to prompt the observer to experience a sense of simple awe and wonder appropriate to the contemplation of one of the central elements of Christian dogma — that God sent His son into the world to be a Messiah. Contrary to the Court's suggestion, the crèche is far from a mere representation of a "particular historic religious event." It is, instead, best understood as a mystical re-creation of an event that lies at the heart of Christian faith. To suggest, as the Court does, that such a symbol is merely "traditional" and therefore no different from Santa's house or reindeer is not only offensive to those for whom the crèche has profound significance, but insulting to those who insist for religious or personal reasons that the story of Christ is in no sense a part of "history" nor an unavoidable element of our national "heritage."

For these reasons, the crèche in this context simply cannot be viewed as playing the same role that an ordinary museum display does. The Court seems to assume that prohibiting Pawtucket from displaying a crèche would be tantamount to forbidding a state college from including the Bible or Milton's *Paradise Lost* in a course on English literature. But in those cases the religiously-inspired materials are being considered solely as literature. The purpose is plainly not to single out the particular religious beliefs that may have inspired the authors, but to see in these writings the outlines of a larger imaginative universe shared with other forms of literary expression. The same may be said of a course devoted to the study of art; when the course turns to Gothic architecture, the emphasis is not on the religious beliefs which the cathedrals exalt, but rather upon the "aesthetic consequences of [such religious] thought."

In this case, by contrast, the crèche plays no comparable secular role. Unlike the poetry of *Paradise Lost* which students in a literature course will seek to appreciate primarily for esthetic or historical reasons, the angels, shepherds, Magi and infant of Pawtucket's nativity scene can only be viewed as symbols of a particular set of religious beliefs. It would be another matter if the crèche were displayed in a museum setting, in the company of other religiously-inspired artifacts, as an example, among many, of the symbolic representation of religious myths. In that setting, we would have objective guarantees that the crèche could not suggest that a particular faith had been singled out for public favor and recognition. The effect of Pawtucket's crèche, however, is not confined by any of these limiting attributes. In the absence of any other religious symbols or of any neutral disclaimer, the inescapable effect of the crèche will be to remind the average observer of the religious roots of the celebration he is witnessing and to call to mind the scriptural message that the nativity symbolizes. The fact that Pawtucket has gone to the trouble of making such an elaborate public celebration and of including a crèche in that otherwise secular setting inevitably serves to reinforce the sense that the city means to express solidarity with the Christian message of the crèche and to dismiss other faiths as unworthy of similar attention and support.

COUNTY OF ALLEGHENY v. ACLU
492 U.S. 573 (1989)

[EDITOR'S NOTE: Given the fractured nature of many of the Supreme Court's modern opinions, some measure of nose-counting is required in all constitutional litigation these days. In the Establishment Clause area, the task of discerning from new opinions the precise rules that command majority support on the Court often must proceed on a paragraph-by-paragraph basis. A good summary illustration of this phenomenon can be seen in the official rendering of Justices' votes in *County of Allegheny*:]

BLACKMUN, J., announced the judgment of the Court and delivered the opinion of the Court with respect to Parts III-A, IV, and V, in which BRENNAN, MARSHALL, STEVENS, and O'CONNOR, JJ., joined, an opinion with respect to Parts I and II, in which STEVENS, and O'CONNOR, JJ., joined, an opinion with respect to Part III-B, in which STEVENS,, J., joined, an opinion with respect to Part VII, in which O'CONNOR, J., joined, and an opinion with respect to Part VI. O'CONNOR, J., filed an opinion concurring in part and concurring in the judgment, in Part II of which BRENNAN and STEVENS,, JJ., joined. BRENNAN, J., filed an opinion concurring in part and dissenting in part, in which MARSHALL and STEVENS,, JJ., joined. STEVENS, J., filed an opinion concurring in part and dissenting in part, in which BRENNAN and MARSHAL JJ., joined. KENNEDY, J., filed an opinion concurring in the judgment in part and dissenting in part, in which REHNQUIST, C.J., and WHITE and SCALIA, JJ., joined.

I

A

The county courthouse is owned by Allegheny County and is its seat of government. It houses the offices of the county commissioners, controller, treasurer, sheriff, and clerk of court. Civil and criminal trials are held there. The "main," "most beautiful," and "most public" part of the courthouse is its Grand Staircase, set into one arch and surrounded by others, with arched windows serving as a backdrop.

Since 1981, the county has permitted the Holy Name Society, a Roman Catholic group, to display a crèche in the county courthouse during the Christmas holiday season. Christmas, we note perhaps needlessly, is the holiday when Christians celebrate the birth of Jesus of Nazareth, whom they believe to be the Messiah. Western churches have celebrated Christmas Day on December 25 since the fourth century. As observed in this Nation, Christmas has a secular, as well as a religious, dimension.

The crèche in the county courthouse, like other crèches, is a visual representation of the scene in the manger in Bethlehem shortly after the birth of Jesus, as described in the Gospels of Luke and Matthew. The crèche includes figures of the infant Jesus, Mary, Joseph, farm animals, shepherds, and wise men, all placed in or before a wooden representation of a manger, which has at its crest an angel bearing a banner that proclaims "Gloria in Excelsis Deo!"[5]

---

[5] This phrase comes from Luke, who tells of an angel appearing to the shepherds to announce the birth of the Messiah. After the angel told the shepherds that they would find the baby lying in a manger, "suddenly there was with the angel a multitude of the heavenly host praising God, and saying, Glory to God in the highest, and on earth peace, good will towards men." Luke 2:13-14 (King James Version). It is unlikely that an observer standing at the bottom of the Grand Staircase would be able to read the text of the angel's banner from that distance, but might be able to do so from a closer vantage point.

During the 1986-1987 holiday season, the crèche was on display on the Grand Staircase from November 26 to January 9. It had a wooden fence on three sides and bore a plaque stating: "This Display Donated by the Holy Name Society." Sometime during the week of December 2, the county placed red and white poinsettia plants around the fence. The county also placed a small evergreen tree, decorated with a red bow, behind each of the two endposts of the fence. These trees stood alongside the manger backdrop and were slightly shorter than it was. The angel thus was at the apex of the crèche display. Altogether, the crèche, the fence, the poinsettias, and the trees occupied a substantial amount of space on the Grand Staircase. No figures of Santa Claus or other decorations appeared on the Grand Staircase.

B

The City-County Building is separate and a block removed from the county courthouse and, as the name implies, is jointly owned by the city of Pittsburgh and Allegheny County. The city's portion of the building houses the city's principal offices, including the mayor's. The city is responsible for the building's Grant Street entrance which has three rounded arches supported by columns.

For a number of years, the city has had a large Christmas tree under the middle arch outside the Grant Street entrance. Following this practice, city employees on November 17, 1986, erected a 45-foot tree under the middle arch and decorated it with lights and ornaments. A few days later, the city placed at the foot of the tree a sign bearing the mayor's name and entitled "Salute to Liberty." Beneath the title, the sign stated:

"During this holiday season, the city of Pittsburgh salutes liberty. Let these festive lights remind us that we are the keepers of the flame of liberty and our legacy of freedom."

At least since 1982, the city has expanded its Grant Street holiday display to include a symbolic representation of Chanukah, an 8-day Jewish holiday that begins on the 25th day of the Jewish lunar month of Kislev. The 25th of Kislev usually occurs in December, and thus Chanukah is the annual Jewish holiday that falls closest to Christmas Day each year. In 1986, Chanukah began at sundown on December 26.

According to Jewish tradition, on the 25th of Kislev in 164 B.C.E. (before the common era (165 B.C.)), the Maccabees rededicated the Temple of Jerusalem after recapturing it from the Greeks, or, more accurately, from the Greek-influenced Seleucid Empire, in the course of a political rebellion. Chanukah is the holiday which celebrates that event. The early history of the celebration of Chanukah is unclear; it appears that the holiday's central ritual — the lighting of lamps — was well established long before a single explanation of that ritual took hold.

Chanukah, like Christmas, is a cultural event as well as a religious holiday. Indeed, the Chanukah story always has had a political or national, as well as a religious, dimension: it tells of national heroism in addition to divine intervention. Also, Chanukah, like Christmas, is a winter holiday; according to some historians, it was associated in ancient times with the winter solstice. Just as some Americans celebrate Christmas without regard to its religious significance, some nonreligious American Jews celebrate Chanukah as an expression of ethnic identity, and "as a cultural or national event, rather than as a specifically religious event."

The cultural significance of Chanukah varies with the setting in which the holiday is celebrated. In contemporary Israel, the nationalist and military aspects of the Chanukah story receive special emphasis. In this country, the tradition of giving Chanukah gelt has taken on greater importance because of the temporal proximity of Chanukah to Christmas. Indeed, some have suggested that the proximity of Christmas accounts for the social prominence of Chanukah in this country. Whatever the reason, Chanukah is observed by American Jews to an extent greater than its religious importance would indicate: in the hierarchy of Jewish holidays, Chanukah ranks fairly low in religious significance. This socially heightened status of Chanukah reflects its cultural or secular dimension.

On December 22 of the 1986 holiday season, the city placed at the Grant Street entrance to the City-County Building an 18-foot Chanukah menorah of an abstract tree-and-branch design. The menorah was placed next to the city's 45-foot Christmas tree, against one of the columns that supports the arch into which the tree was set. The menorah is owned by Chabad, a Jewish group, but is stored, erected, and removed each year by the city. The tree, the sign, and the menorah were all removed on January 13.

III

B

The rationale of the majority opinion in *Lynch* [v. *Donnelly*] is none too clear: the opinion contains two strands, neither of which provides guidance for decision in subsequent cases. First, the opinion states that the inclusion of the crèche in the display was "no more an advancement or endorsement of religion" than other "endorsements" this Court has approved in the past, but the opinion offers no discernible measure for distinguishing between permissible and impermissible endorsements. Second, the opinion observes that any benefit the government's display of the crèche gave to religion was no more than "indirect, remote, and incidental," *ibid.* — without saying how or why.

Although JUSTICE O'CONNOR joined the majority opinion in *Lynch*, she wrote a concurrence that differs in significant respects from the majority opinion. The main difference is that the concurrence provides a sound analytical framework for evaluating governmental use of religious symbols.

First and foremost, the concurrence squarely rejects any notion that this Court will tolerate some government endorsement of religion. Rather, the concurrence recognizes any endorsement of religion as "invalid," because it "sends a message to nonadherents that they are outsiders, not full members of the political community, and an accompanying message to adherents that they are insiders, favored members of the political community."

Second, the concurrence articulates a method for determining whether the government's use of an object with religious meaning has the effect of endorsing religion. The effect of the display depends upon the message that the government's practice communicates: the question is "what viewers may fairly understand to be the purpose of the display." That inquiry, of necessity, turns upon the context in which the contested object appears: "[A] typical museum setting, though not neutralizing the religious content of a religious painting, negates any message of endorsement of that content." *Ibid.* The concurrence thus emphasizes that the constitutionality of the crèche in that case depended upon its "particular physical setting," *ibid.*, and further observes: "Every government practice must be judged in its unique circumstances to determine whether it [endorses] religion."

The concurrence applied this mode of analysis to the Pawtucket crèche, seen in the context of that city's holiday celebration as a whole. In addition to the crèche, the city's display contained: a Santa Claus house with a live Santa distributing candy; reindeer pulling Santa's sleigh; a live 40- foot Christmas tree strung with lights; statues of carolers in old-fashioned dress; candy-striped poles; a "talking" wishing well; a large banner proclaiming "SEASONS GREETINGS"; a miniature "village" with several houses and a church; and various "cut-out" figures, including those of a clown, a dancing elephant, a robot, and a teddy bear. The concurrence concluded that both because the crèche is "a traditional symbol" of Christmas, a holiday with strong secular elements, and because the crèche was "displayed along with purely secular symbols," the crèche's setting "changes what viewers may fairly understand to be the purpose of the display" and "negates any message of endorsement" of "the Christian beliefs represented by the crèche."

The four *Lynch* dissenters agreed with the concurrence that the controlling question was "whether Pawtucket ha[d] run afoul of the Establishment Clause by endorsing religion through its display of the crèche." The dissenters also agreed with the general proposition that the context in which the government uses a religious symbol is relevant for determining the answer to that question. They simply reached a different answer: the dissenters concluded that the other elements of the Pawtucket display did not negate the endorsement of Christian faith caused by the presence of the crèche. They viewed the inclusion of the crèche in the city's overall display as placing "the government's imprimatur of approval on the particular religious beliefs exemplified by the crèche." Thus, they stated: "The effect on minority religious groups, as well as on those who may reject all religion, is to convey the message that their views are not similarly worthy of public recognition nor entitled to public support."

Thus, despite divergence at the bottom line, the five Justices in concurrence and dissent in *Lynch* agreed upon the relevant constitutional principles: the government's use of religious symbolism is unconstitutional if it has the effect of endorsing religious beliefs, and the effect of the government's use of religious symbolism depends upon its context. These general principles are sound, and have been adopted by the Court in subsequent cases. Since *Lynch*, the Court has made clear that, when evaluating the effect of government conduct under the Establishment Clause, we must ascertain whether "the challenged governmental action is sufficiently likely to be perceived by adherents of the controlling denominations as an endorsement, and by the nonadherents as a disapproval, of their individual religious choices." *Grand Rapids,* 473 U.S., at 390. Accordingly, our present task is to determine whether the display of the crèche and the menorah, in their respective "particular physical settings," has the effect of endorsing or disapproving religious beliefs.[47]

IV

We turn first to the county's crèche display. There is no doubt, of course, that the crèche itself is capable of communicating a religious message. Indeed, the crèche in this lawsuit uses words, as well as the picture of the Nativity scene, to make its religious meaning unmistakably clear. "Glory to God in the Highest!" says the angel in the crèche — Glory to God because of the birth of Jesus. This praise to God in Christian terms is indisputably religious — indeed sectarian — just as it is when said in the Gospel or in a church service.

Under the Court's holding in *Lynch,* the effect of a crèche display turns on its setting. Here, unlike in Lynch, nothing in the context of the display detracts from the crèche's religious message. The *Lynch* display composed a series of figures and objects, each group of which had its own focal point. Santa's house and his reindeer were objects of attention separate from the crèche, and had their specific visual story to tell. Similarly, whatever a "talking" wishing well may be, it obviously was a center of attention separate from the crèche. Here, in contrast, the crèche stands alone: it is the single element of the display on the Grand Staircase.[48]

---

[47] The county and the city argue that their use of religious symbols does not violate the Establishment Clause unless they are shown to be "coercive." Reply Brief for Petitioners County of Allegheny et al. 1-6; Tr. of Oral Arg. 9, 11. They recognize that this Court repeatedly has stated that "proof of coercion" is "not a necessary element of any claim under the Establishment Clause." *Committee for Public Education and Religious Liberty v. Nyquist,* 413 U.S., at 786; *see also Abington School District v. Schempp,* 374 U.S., at 222-223; *Engel v. Vitale,* 370 U.S., at 430. But they suggest that the Court reconsider this principle. Reply Brief for Petitioner Allegheny County et al. 3; *cf. American Jewish Congress v. Chicago,* 827 F. 2d 120, 137 (7th Cir. 1987) (dissenting opinion); McConnell, *Coercion: The Lost Element of Establishment,* 27 WM. & MARY L. REV. 933 (1986). The Court declines to do so, and proceeds to apply the controlling endorsement inquiry, which does not require an independent showing of coercion.

[48] The presence of Santas or other Christmas decorations elsewhere in the county courthouse, and of the nearby gallery forum, fail to negate the endorsement effect of the crèche. The record demonstrates clearly that the crèche, with its floral frame, was its own display distinct from any other decorations or exhibitions in the building. Tr. of Oral Arg. 7.

The floral decoration surrounding the crèche cannot be viewed as somehow equivalent to the secular symbols in the overall *Lynch* display. The floral frame, like all good frames, serves only to draw one's attention to the message inside the frame. The floral decoration surrounding the crèche contributes to, rather than detracts from, the endorsement of religion conveyed by the crèche. It is as if the county had allowed the Holy Name Society to display a cross on the Grand Staircase at Easter, and the county had surrounded the cross with Easter lilies. The county could not say that surrounding the cross with traditional flowers of the season would negate the endorsement of Christianity conveyed by the cross on the Grand Staircase. Its contention that the traditional Christmas greens negate the endorsement effect of the crèche fares no better.

Nor does the fact that the crèche was the setting for the county's annual Christmas-carol program diminish its religious meaning. First, the carol program in 1986 lasted only from December 3 to December 23 and occupied at most one hour a day. The effect of the crèche on those who viewed it when the choirs were not singing — the vast majority of the time — cannot be negated by the presence of the choir program. Second, because some of the carols performed at the site of the crèche were religious in nature, those carols were more likely to augment the religious quality of the scene than to secularize it.

Furthermore, the crèche sits on the Grand Staircase, the "main" and "most beautiful part" of the building that is the seat of county government. No viewer could reasonably think that it occupies this location without the support and approval of the government.[50] Thus, by permitting the "display of the crèche in this particular physical setting," *Lynch*, 465 U.S., at 692 (O'CONNOR, J., concurring), the county sends an unmistakable message that it supports and promotes the Christian praise to God that is the crèche's religious message.

The fact that the crèche bears a sign disclosing its ownership by a Roman Catholic organization does not alter this conclusion. On the contrary, the sign simply demonstrates that the government is endorsing the religious message of that organization, rather than communicating a message of its own. But the Establishment Clause does not limit only the religious content of the govern-

---

[50] The Grand Staircase does not appear to be the kind of location in which all were free to place their displays for weeks at a time, so that the presence of the crèche in that location for over six weeks would then not serve to associate the government with the crèche. Even if the Grand Staircase occasionally was used for displays other than the crèche (for example, a display of flags commemorating the 25th anniversary of Israel's independence, *id.*, at 176), it remains true that any display located there fairly may be understood to express views that receive the support and endorsement of the government. In any event, the county's own press releases made clear to the public that the county associated itself with the crèche. JEV 28 (flier identifying the choral program as county sponsored); *id.*, at 30; App. 174 (linking the crèche to the choral program). Moreover, the county created a visual link between itself and the crèche: it placed next to official county signs two small evergreens identical to those in the crèche display. In this respect, the crèche here does not raise the kind of "public forum" issue, *cf. Widmar v. Vincent*, 454 U.S. 263 (1981), presented by the crèche in *McCreary v. Stone*, 739 F. 2d 716 (2d Cir. 1984), *aff'd by an equally divided Court sub nom. Board of Trustees of Scarsdale v. McCreary*, 471 U.S. 83 (1985) (private crèche in public park).

ment's own communications. It also prohibits the government's support and promotion of religious communications by religious organizations. *See, e.g., Texas Monthly, Inc. v. Bullock*, 489 U.S. 1 (1989) (government support of the distribution of religious messages by religious organizations violates the Establishment Clause). Indeed, the very concept of "endorsement" conveys the sense of promoting someone else's message. Thus, by prohibiting government endorsement of religion, the Establishment Clause prohibits precisely what occurred here: the government's lending its support to the communication of a religious organization's religious message.

Finally, the county argues that it is sufficient to validate the display of the crèche on the Grand Staircase that the display celebrates Christmas, and Christmas is a national holiday. This argument obviously proves too much. It would allow the celebration of the Eucharist inside a courthouse on Christmas Eve. While the county may have doubts about the constitutional status of celebrating the Eucharist inside the courthouse under the government's auspices, this Court does not. The government may acknowledge Christmas as a cultural phenomenon, but under the First Amendment it may not observe it as a Christian holy day by suggesting that people praise God for the birth of Jesus.

In sum, *Lynch* teaches that government may celebrate Christmas in some manner and form, but not in a way that endorses Christian doctrine. Here, Allegheny County has transgressed this line. It has chosen to celebrate Christmas in a way that has the effect of endorsing a patently Christian message: Glory to God for the birth of Jesus Christ. Under *Lynch*, and the rest of our cases, nothing more is required to demonstrate a violation of the Establishment Clause. The display of the crèche in this context, therefore, must be permanently enjoined.

VI

The display of the Chanukah menorah in front of the City-County Building may well present a closer constitutional question. The menorah, one must recognize, is a religious symbol: it serves to commemorate the miracle of the oil as described in the Talmud. But the menorah's message is not exclusively religious. The menorah is the primary visual symbol for a holiday that, like Christmas, has both religious and secular dimensions.

Moreover, the menorah here stands next to a Christmas tree and a sign saluting liberty. While no challenge has been made here to the display of the tree and the sign, their presence is obviously relevant in determining the effect of the menorah's display. The necessary result of placing a menorah next to a Christmas tree is to create an "overall holiday setting" that represents both Christmas and Chanukah — two holidays, not one.

The mere fact that Pittsburgh displays symbols of both Christmas and Chanukah does not end the constitutional inquiry. If the city celebrates both Christmas and Chanukah as religious holidays, then it violates the Establishment Clause. The simultaneous endorsement of Judaism and Christianity is no less constitutionally infirm than the endorsement of Christianity alone.[61]

Conversely, if the city celebrates both Christmas and Chanukah as secular holidays, then its conduct is beyond the reach of the Establishment Clause. Because government may celebrate Christmas as a secular holiday, it follows that government may also acknowledge Chanukah as a secular holiday. Simply put, it would be a form of discrimination against Jews to allow Pittsburgh to celebrate Christmas as a cultural tradition while simultaneously disallowing the city's acknowledgment of Chanukah as a contemporaneous cultural tradition.

Accordingly, the relevant question for Establishment Clause purposes is whether the combined display of the tree, the sign, and the menorah has the effect of endorsing both Christian and Jewish faiths, or rather simply recognizes that both Christmas and Chanukah are part of the same winter-holiday season, which has attained a secular status in our society. Of the two interpretations of this particular display, the latter seems far more plausible and is also in line with *Lynch*.

The Christmas tree, unlike the menorah, is not itself a religious symbol. Although Christmas trees once carried religious connotations, today they typify the secular celebration of Christmas. Numerous Americans place Christmas trees in their homes without subscribing to Christian religious beliefs, and when the city's tree stands alone in front of the City-County Building, it is not considered an endorsement of Christian faith. Indeed, a 40-foot Christmas tree was one of the objects that validated the crèche in *Lynch*. The widely accepted view of the Christmas tree as the preeminent secular symbol of the Christmas holiday season serves to emphasize the secular component of the message communicated by other elements of an accompanying holiday display, including the Chanukah menorah.

The tree, moreover, is clearly the predominant element in the city's display. The 45-foot tree occupies the central position beneath the middle archway in front of the Grant Street entrance to the City-County Building; the 18-foot menorah is positioned to one side. Given this configuration, it is much more sensible to interpret the meaning of the menorah in light of the tree, rather than vice versa. In the shadow of the tree, the menorah is readily understood as simply a recognition that Christmas is not the only traditional way of observing the winter-holiday season. In these circumstances, then, the combination of the tree and the menorah communicates, not a simultaneous endorsement of both the Christian and Jewish faiths, but instead, a secular celebration of

---

[61] The display of a menorah next to a crèche on government property might prove to be invalid. *Cf. Greater Houston Chapter of American Civil Liberties Union v. Eckels*, 589 F. Supp. 222 (SD Tex. 1984), *appeal dism'd*, 755 F.2d 426 (5th Cir.), *cert. denied*, 474 U.S. 980 (1985) (war memorial containing crosses and a Star of David unconstitutionally favored Christianity and Judaism, discriminating against the beliefs of patriotic soldiers who were neither Christian nor Jewish).

Christmas coupled with an acknowledgment of Chanukah as a contemporaneous alternative tradition.

Although the city has used a symbol with religious meaning as its representation of Chanukah, this is not a case in which the city has reasonable alternatives that are less religious in nature. It is difficult to imagine a predominantly secular symbol of Chanukah that the city could place next to its Christmas tree. An 18-foot dreidel would look out of place and might be interpreted by some as mocking the celebration of Chanukah. The absence of a more secular alternative symbol is itself part of the context in which the city's actions must be judged in determining the likely effect of its use of the menorah. Where the government's secular message can be conveyed by two symbols, only one of which carries religious meaning, an observer reasonably might infer from the fact that the government has chosen to use the religious symbol that the government means to promote religious faith. *See Abington School District v. Schempp*, 374 U.S., at 295 (BRENNAN, J., concurring) (Establishment Clause forbids use of religious means to serve secular ends when secular means suffice). But where, as here, no such choice has been made, this inference of endorsement is not present.

The mayor's sign further diminishes the possibility that the tree and the menorah will be interpreted as a dual endorsement of Christianity and Judaism. The sign states that during the holiday season the city salutes liberty. Moreover, the sign draws upon the theme of light, common to both Chanukah and Christmas as winter festivals, and links that theme with this Nation's legacy of freedom, which allows an American to celebrate the holiday season in whatever way he wishes, religiously or otherwise. While no sign can disclaim an overwhelming message of endorsement, an "explanatory plaque" may confirm that in particular contexts the government's association with a religious symbol does not represent the government's sponsorship of religious beliefs. Here, the mayor's sign serves to confirm what the context already reveals: that the display of the menorah is not an endorsement of religious faith but simply a recognition of cultural diversity.

Given all these considerations, it is not "sufficiently likely" that residents of Pittsburgh will perceive the combined display of the tree, the sign, and the menorah as an "endorsement" or "disapproval . . . of their individual religious choices." While an adjudication of the display's effect must take into account the perspective of one who is neither Christian nor Jewish, as well as of those who adhere to either of these religions, *ibid.*, the constitutionality of its effect must also be judged according to the standard of a "reasonable observer." When measured against this standard, the menorah need not be excluded from this particular display. The Christmas tree alone in the Pittsburgh location does not endorse Christian belief; and, on the facts before us, the addition of the menorah "cannot fairly be understood to" result in the simultaneous endorsement of Christian and Jewish faiths. On the contrary, for purposes of the Establishment Clause, the city's overall display must be understood as conveying the city's secular recognition of different traditions for celebrating the winter-holiday season.[69]

JUSTICE O'CONNOR, concurring in part and concurring in the judgment.

III

For reasons which differ somewhat from those set forth in Part VI of JUSTICE BLACKMUN'S opinion, I also conclude that the city of Pittsburgh's combined holiday display of a Chanukah menorah, a Christmas tree, and a sign saluting liberty does not have the effect of conveying an endorsement of religion. I agree with JUSTICE BLACKMUN that the Christmas tree, whatever its origins, is not regarded today as a religious symbol. Although Christmas is a public holiday that has both religious and secular aspects, the Christmas tree is widely viewed as a secular symbol of the holiday, in contrast to the crèche which depicts the holiday's religious dimensions. A Christmas tree displayed in front of city hall, in my view, cannot fairly be understood as conveying government endorsement of Christianity. Although JUSTICE BLACKMUN'S opinion acknowledges that a Christmas tree alone conveys no endorsement of Christian beliefs, it formulates the question posed by Pittsburgh's combined display of the tree and the menorah as whether the display "has the effect of endorsing *both* Christian and Jewish faiths, or rather simply recognizes that both Christmas and Chanukah are part of the same winter-holiday season, which has attained a secular status in our society."

That formulation of the question disregards the fact that the Christmas tree is a predominantly secular symbol and, more significantly, obscures the religious nature of the menorah and the holiday of Chanukah. The opinion is correct to recognize that the religious holiday of Chanukah has historical and cultural as well as religious dimensions, and that there may be certain "secular aspects" to the holiday. But that is not to conclude, however, as JUSTICE BLACKMUN seems to do, that Chanukah has become a "secular holiday" in our society. The Easter holiday celebrated by Christians may be accompanied by certain "secular aspects" such as Easter bunnies and Easter egg hunts; but it is nevertheless a religious holiday. Similarly, Chanukah is a religious holiday with strong historical components particularly important to the Jewish people. Moreover, the menorah is the central religious symbol and ritual object of that religious holiday. Under JUSTICE BLACKMUN'S view, however, the menorah "has been relegated to the role of a neutral harbinger of the holiday season," almost devoid of any religious significance. In my view, the relevant question for Establishment Clause purposes is whether the city of Pittsburgh's display of the menorah, the religious symbol of a religious holiday, next to a Christmas tree and a sign

---

[69] This is not to say that the combined display of a Christmas tree and a menorah is constitutional wherever it may be located on government property. For example, when located in a public school, such a display might raise additional constitutional considerations. *Cf. Edwards v. Aguillard* [*supra* Chapter 4] (Establishment Clause must be applied with special sensitivity in the public-school context).

saluting liberty sends a message of government endorsement of Judaism or whether it sends a message of pluralism and freedom to choose one's own beliefs.

In characterizing the message conveyed by this display as either a "double endorsement" or a secular acknowledgment of the winter holiday season, the opinion states that "[i]t is distinctly implausible to view the combined display of the tree, the sign, and the menorah as endorsing Jewish faith alone." That statement, however, seems to suggest that it would be implausible for the city to endorse a faith adhered to by a minority of the citizenry. Regardless of the plausibility of a putative governmental purpose, the more important inquiry here is whether the governmental display of a minority faith's religious symbol could ever reasonably be understood to convey a message of endorsement of that faith. A menorah standing alone at city hall may well send such a message to nonadherents, just as in this case the crèche standing alone at the Allegheny County Courthouse sends a message of governmental endorsement of Christianity, whatever the county's purpose in authorizing the display may have been. Thus, the question here is whether Pittsburgh's holiday display conveys a message of endorsement of Judaism, when the menorah is the only religious symbol in the combined display and when the opinion acknowledges that the tree cannot reasonably be understood to convey an endorsement of Christianity. One need not characterize Chanukah as a "secular" holiday or strain to argue that the menorah has a "secular" dimension in order to conclude that the city of Pittsburgh's combined display does not convey a message of endorsement of Judaism or of religion in general.

In setting up its holiday display, which included the lighted tree and the menorah, the city of Pittsburgh stressed the theme of liberty and pluralism by accompanying the exhibit with a sign bearing the following message: "'During this holiday season, the city of Pittsburgh salutes liberty. Let these festive lights remind us that we are the keepers of the flame of liberty and our legacy of freedom.'" This sign indicates that the city intended to convey its own distinctive message of pluralism and freedom. By accompanying its display of a Christmas tree — a secular symbol of the Christmas holiday season — with a salute to liberty, and by adding a religious symbol from a Jewish holiday also celebrated at roughly the same time of year, I conclude that the city did not endorse Judaism or religion in general, but rather conveyed a message of pluralism and freedom of belief during the holiday season. "Although the religious and indeed sectarian significance" of the menorah "is not neutralized by the setting," this particular physical setting "changes what viewers may fairly understand to be the purpose of the display — as a typical museum setting, though not neutralizing the religious content of a religious painting, negates any message of endorsement of that content."

The message of pluralism conveyed by the city's combined holiday display is not a message that endorses religion over nonreligion. Just as government may not favor particular religious beliefs over others, "government may not favor religious belief over disbelief." Here, by displaying a secular symbol of the Christmas holiday season rather than a religious one, the city acknowledged a public holiday celebrated by both religious and nonreligious citizens alike, and it did so without endorsing Christian beliefs. A reasonable observer would, in my view, appreciate that the combined display is an effort to acknowledge the cultural diversity of our country and to convey tolerance of different choices in matters of religious belief or nonbelief by recognizing that the winter holiday season is celebrated in diverse ways by our citizens. In short, in the holiday context, this combined display in its particular physical setting conveys neither an endorsement of Judaism or Christianity nor disapproval of alternative beliefs, and thus does not have the impermissible effect of "mak[ing] religion relevant, in reality or public perception, to status in the political community."

My conclusion does not depend on whether or not the city had "a more secular alternative symbol" of Chanukah, just as the Court's decision in Lynch clearly did not turn on whether the city of Pawtucket could have conveyed its tribute to the Christmas holiday season by using a "less religious" alternative to the crèche symbol in its display of traditional holiday symbols. *See Lynch, supra*, 465 U.S., at 681, n. 7 ("JUSTICE BRENNAN argues that the city's objectives could have been achieved without including the crèche in the display, [465 U.S.,] at 699. True or not, that is irrelevant. The question is whether the display of the crèche violates the Establishment Clause"). In my view, JUSTICE BLACKMUN'S new rule that an inference of endorsement arises every time government uses a symbol with religious meaning if a "more secular alternative" is available is too blunt an instrument for Establishment Clause analysis, which depends on sensitivity to the context and circumstances presented by each case. Indeed, the opinion appears to recognize the importance of this contextual sensitivity by creating an exception to its new rule in the very case announcing it: the opinion acknowledges that "a purely secular symbol" of Chanukah is available, namely, a dreidel or four-sided top, but rejects the use of such a symbol because it "might be interpreted by some as mocking the celebration of Chanukah." This recognition that the more *religious* alternative may, depending on the circumstances, convey a message that is least likely to implicate Establishment Clause concerns is an excellent example of the need to focus on the specific practice in question in its particular physical setting and context in determining whether government has conveyed or attempted to convey a message that religion or a particular religious belief is favored or preferred.

JUSTICE STEVENS, with whom JUSTICE BRENNAN and JUSTICE MARSHALL join, concurring in part and dissenting in part.

Governmental recognition of not one but two religions distinguishes these cases from our prior Establishment Clause cases. It is, therefore, appropriate to reexamine the text and context of the Clause to determine its impact on this novel situation.

Relations between church and state at the end of the 1780s fell into two quite different categories. In several European countries, one national religion, such as the Church of England in Great Britain, was established. The established church typically was supported by tax revenues, by laws conferring privileges only upon members, and sometimes by violent persecution of nonadherents. In contrast, although several American Colonies had assessed taxes to support one chosen faith, none of the newly United States subsidized a single religion. Some States had repealed establishment laws altogether, while others had replaced single establishments with laws providing for nondiscriminatory support of more than one religion.

[Stevens then discussed the various drafts of the First Amendment Religion Clauses, culminating with the expansive language ultimately adopted by Congress.]

Similarly expanded was the relationship between government and religion that was to be disallowed. Whereas earlier drafts had barred only laws "establishing" or "touching" religion, the final text interdicts all laws "respecting an establishment of religion." This phrase forbids even a partial establishment, not only of a particular sect in favor of others, but also of religion in preference to nonreligion. It is also significant that the final draft contains the word "respecting." Like "touching," "respecting" means concerning, or with reference to. But it also means with respect — that is, "reverence," "good will," "regard" — to. Taking into account this richer meaning, the Establishment Clause, in banning laws that concern religion, especially prohibits those that pay homage to religion.

Treatment of a symbol of a particular tradition demonstrates one's attitude toward that tradition. Thus the prominent display of religious symbols on government property falls within the compass of the First Amendment, even though interference with personal choices about supporting a church, by means of governmental tithing, was the primary concern in 1791. Whether the vice in such a display is characterized as "coercion," or "endorsement," or merely as state action with the purpose and effect of providing support for specific faiths, *cf. Lemon*, it is common ground that this symbolic governmental speech "respecting an establishment of religion" may violate the Constitution.

In my opinion the Establishment Clause should be construed to create a strong presumption against the display of religious symbols on public property. There is always a risk that such symbols will offend nonmembers of the faith being advertised as well as adherents who consider the particular advertisement disrespectful. Some devout Christians believe that the crèche should be placed only in reverential settings, such as a church or perhaps a private home; they do not countenance its use as an aid to commercialization of Christ's birthday. In this very suit, members of the Jewish faith firmly opposed the use to which the menorah was put by the particular sect that sponsored the display at Pittsburgh's City-County Building. Even though "[p]assersby who disagree with the message conveyed by these displays are free to ignore them, or even to turn their backs," *see* [Justice Kennedy's opinion *infra*], displays of this kind inevitably have a greater tendency to emphasize sincere and deeply felt differences among individuals than to achieve an ecumenical goal. The Establishment Clause does not allow public bodies to foment such disagreement.

Application of a strong presumption against the public use of religious symbols scarcely will "require a relentless extirpation of all contact between government and religion," *see* [Justice Kennedy's opinion *infra*] for it will prohibit a display only when its message, evaluated in the context in which it is presented, is nonsecular. For example, a carving of Moses holding the Ten Commandments, if that is the only adornment on a courtroom wall, conveys an equivocal message, perhaps of respect for Judaism, for religion in general, or for law. The addition of carvings depicting Confucius and Mohammed may honor religion, or particular religions, to an extent that the First Amendment does not tolerate any more than it does "the permanent erection of a large Latin cross on the roof of city hall." *See* [Justice Kennedy's opinion *infra*]. Placement of secular figures such as Caesar Augustus, William Blackstone, Napoleon Bonaparte, and John Marshall alongside these three religious leaders, however, signals respect not for great proselytizers but for great lawgivers. It would be absurd to exclude such a fitting message from a courtroom, as it would to exclude religious paintings by Italian Renaissance masters from a public museum. Far from "border[ing] on latent hostility toward religion," *see post*, at 3135 (KENNEDY, J., concurring in judgment in part and dissenting in part), this careful consideration of context gives due regard to religious and nonreligious members of our society.

Thus I find wholly unpersuasive JUSTICE KENNEDY's attempts to belittle the importance of the obvious differences between the display of the crèche in this case and that in *Lynch v. Donnelly*. Even if I had not dissented from the Court's conclusion that the crèche in *Lynch* was constitutional, I would conclude that Allegheny County's unambiguous exposition of a sacred symbol inside its courthouse promoted Christianity to a degree that violated the Establishment Clause. Accordingly, I concur in the Court's judgment regarding the crèche for substantially the same reasons discussed in JUSTICE BRENNAN's opinion, which I join, as well as Part IV of JUSTICE BLACKMUN's opinion and Part I of JUSTICE O'CONNOR's opinion.

I cannot agree with the Court's conclusion that the display at Pittsburgh's City-County Building was constitutional. Standing alone in front of a governmental headquarters, a lighted, 45-foot evergreen tree might convey holiday greetings linked too tenuously to Christianity to have constitutional moment. Juxtaposition of this tree with an 18-foot menorah does not make the latter secular, as JUSTICE BLACKMUN contends. Rather, the presence of the Chanukah menorah, unquestionably a religious symbol, gives religious significance to the Christmas tree. The overall display thus manifests governmental approval of the Jewish and Christian religions. Although it conceivably might be interpreted as sending "a message of pluralism and freedom to choose one's own beliefs," the message is not sufficiently clear to overcome the strong presumption that the display, respecting two religions to the exclusion of all others, is the very kind of double establishment that the First Amendment was designed to outlaw. I would, therefore, affirm the judgment of the Court of Appeals in its entirety.

JUSTICE KENNEDY, with whom THE CHIEF JUSTICE, JUSTICE WHITE, and JUSTICE SCALIA join, concurring in the judgment in part and dissenting in part.

[In Part I of his opinion, Justice Kennedy states his conclusion that "[r]ather than requiring government to avoid any action that acknowledges or aids religion, the Establishment Clause permits government some latitude in recognizing and accommodating the central role religion plays in our society. Any approach less sensitive to our heritage would border on latent hostility toward religion, as it would require government in all its multifaceted roles to acknowledge only the secular, to the exclusion and so to the detriment of the religious. A categorical approach would install federal courts as jealous guardians of an absolute 'wall of separation,' sending a clear message of disapproval. In this century, as the modern administrative state expands to touch the lives of its citizens in such diverse ways and redirects their financial choices through programs of its own, it is difficult to maintain the fiction that requiring government to avoid all assistance to religion can in fairness be viewed as serving the goal of neutrality." Justice Kennedy therefore argues in favor of a coercion test, under which "[n]oncoercive government action within the realm of flexible accommodation or passive acknowledgment of existing symbols does not violate the Establishment Clause unless it benefits religion in a way more direct and more substantial than practices that are accepted in our national heritage."]

II

These principles are not difficult to apply to the facts of the cases before us. In permitting the displays on government property of the menorah and the crèche, the city and county sought to do no more than "celebrate the season," and to acknowledge, along with many of their citizens, the historical background and the religious, as well as secular, nature of the Chanukah and Christmas holidays. This interest falls well within the tradition of government accommodation and acknowledgment of religion that has marked our history from the beginning. It cannot be disputed that government, if it chooses, may participate in sharing with its citizens the joy of the holiday season, by declaring public holidays, installing or permitting festive displays, sponsoring celebrations and parades, and providing holiday vacations for its employees. All levels of our government do precisely that. As we said in *Lynch*, "Government has long recognized — indeed it has subsidized — holidays with religious significance."

If government is to participate in its citizens' celebration of a holiday that contains both a secular and a religious component, enforced recognition of only the secular aspect would signify the callous indifference toward religious faith that our cases and traditions do not require; for by commemorating the holiday only as it is celebrated by nonadherents, the government would be refusing to acknowledge the plain fact, and the historical reality, that many of its citizens celebrate its religious aspects as well. Judicial invalidation of government's attempts to recognize the religious underpinnings of the holiday would signal not neutrality but a pervasive intent to insulate government from all things religious. The Religion Clauses do not require government to acknowledge these holidays or their religious component; but our strong tradition of government accommodation and acknowledgment permits government to do so.

There is no suggestion here that the government's power to coerce has been used to further the interests of Christianity or Judaism in any way. No one was compelled to observe or participate in any religious ceremony or activity. Neither the city nor the county contributed significant amounts of tax money to serve the cause of one religious faith. The crèche and the menorah are purely passive symbols of religious holidays. Passersby who disagree with the message conveyed by these displays are free to ignore them, or even to turn their backs, just as they are free to do when they disagree with any other form of government speech.

There is no realistic risk that the crèche and the menorah represent an effort to proselytize or are otherwise the first step down the road to an establishment of religion.[3] *Lynch* is dispositive of this claim with respect to the crèche, and I find no reason for reaching a different result with respect to the menorah. Both are the traditional symbols of religious holidays that over time have acquired a secular component. Without ambiguity, *Lynch* instructs that "the focus of our inquiry must be on the [religious symbol] in the context of the [holiday] season." In that context, religious displays that serve "to celebrate the Holiday and to depict the origins of that Holiday" give rise to no Establishment Clause concern. If Congress and the state legislatures do not run afoul of the Establishment Clause when they begin each day with a state-sponsored prayer for divine guidance offered by a chaplain whose salary is paid at government expense, I cannot comprehend how a menorah or a crèche, displayed in the limited context of the holiday season, can be invalid.

Respondents say that the religious displays involved here are distinguishable from the crèche in *Lynch* because they are located on government property and are not surrounded by the candy canes, reindeer, and other holiday paraphernalia that were a part of the display in *Lynch*. Nothing in Chief Justice Burger's opinion for the Court in *Lynch* provides support for these purported distinctions. After describing the facts, the *Lynch* opinion makes no mention of either of these factors. It concentrates instead on the significance of the creche as part of the entire holiday season. Indeed, it is clear that the Court did not view the

---

[3] One can imagine a case in which the use of passive symbols to acknowledge religious holidays could present this danger. For example, if a city chose to recognize, through religious displays, every significant Christian holiday while ignoring the holidays of all other faiths, the argument that the city was simply recognizing certain holidays celebrated by its citizens without establishing an official faith or applying pressure to obtain adherents would be much more difficult to maintain. On the facts of these cases, no such unmistakable and continual preference for one faith has been demonstrated or alleged.

secular aspects of the display as somehow subduing the religious message conveyed by the crèche, for the majority expressly rejected the dissenters' suggestion that it sought "'to explain away the clear religious import of the crèche'" or had "equated the crèche with a Santa's house or reindeer." Crucial to the Court's conclusion was not the number, prominence, or type of secular items contained in the holiday display but the simple fact that, when displayed by government during the Christmas season, a crèche presents no realistic danger of moving government down the forbidden road toward an establishment of religion. Whether the crèche be surrounded by poinsettias, talking wishing wells, or carolers, the conclusion remains the same, for the relevant context is not the items in the display itself but the season as a whole.

The fact that the crèche and menorah are both located on government property, even at the very seat of government, is likewise inconsequential. In the first place, the *Lynch* Court did not rely on the fact that the setting for Pawtucket's display was a privately owned park, and it is difficult to suggest that anyone could have failed to receive a message of government sponsorship after observing Santa Claus ride the city fire engine to the park to join with the mayor of Pawtucket in inaugurating the holiday season by turning on the lights of the city-owned display. Indeed, the District Court in *Lynch* found that "people might reasonably mistake the Park for public property," and rejected as "frivolous" the suggestion that the display was not directly associated with the city.

Our cases do not suggest, moreover, that the use of public property necessarily converts otherwise permissible government conduct into an Establishment Clause violation. To the contrary, in some circumstances the First Amendment may *require* that government property be available for use by religious groups, *see Widmar v. Vincent* [*infra* Chapter 7.D]. and even where not required, such use has long been permitted. The prayer approved in *Marsh v. Chambers*, for example, was conducted in the legislative chamber of the State of Nebraska, surely the single place most likely to be thought the center of state authority.

Nor can I comprehend why it should be that placement of a government-owned crèche on private land is lawful while placement of a privately owned crèche on public land is not. If anything, I should have thought government ownership of a religious symbol presented the more difficult question under the Establishment Clause, but as *Lynch* resolved that question to sustain the government action, the sponsorship here ought to be all the easier to sustain. In short, nothing about the religious displays here distinguishes them in any meaningful way from the crèche we permitted in *Lynch*.

III

A

I take it as settled law that, whatever standard the Court applies to Establishment Clause claims, it must at least suggest results consistent with our precedents and the historical practices that, by tradition, have informed our

First Amendment jurisprudence. It is true that, for reasons quite unrelated to the First Amendment, displays commemorating religious holidays were not commonplace in 1791. *See generally* J. BARNETT, THE AMERICAN CHRISTMAS: A STUDY IN NATIONAL CULTURE 2-11 (1954). But the relevance of history is not confined to the inquiry into whether the challenged practice itself is a part of our accepted traditions dating back to the Founding.

Whatever test we choose to apply must permit not only legitimate practices two centuries old but also any other practices with no greater potential for an establishment of religion. The First Amendment is a rule, not a digest or compendium. A test for implementing the protections of the Establishment Clause that, if applied with consistency, would invalidate longstanding traditions cannot be a proper reading of the Clause.

If the endorsement test, applied without artificial exceptions for historical practice, reached results consistent with history, my objections to it would have less force. But, as I understand that test, the touchstone of an Establishment Clause violation is whether nonadherents would be made to feel like "outsiders" by government recognition or accommodation of religion. Few of our traditional practices recognizing the part religion plays in our society can withstand scrutiny under a faithful application of this formula.

Some examples suffice to make plain my concerns. Since the Founding of our Republic, American Presidents have issued Thanksgiving Proclamations establishing a national day of celebration and prayer. The first such proclamation was issued by President Washington at the request of the First Congress, and "recommend[ed] and assign[ed]" a day "to be devoted by the people of these States to the service of that great and glorious Being who is the beneficient author of all the good that was, that is, or that will be," so that "we may then unite in most humbly offering our prayers and supplications to the great Lord and Ruler of Nations, and beseech Him to . . . promote the knowledge and practice of true religion and virtue. . . ." 1 J. RICHARDSON, A COMPILATION OF MESSAGES AND PAPERS OF THE PRESIDENTS, 1789-1897, p. 64 (1899). Most of President Washington's successors have followed suit, and the forthrightly religious nature of these proclamations has not waned with the years. President Franklin D. Roosevelt went so far as to "suggest a nationwide reading of the Holy Scriptures during the period from Thanksgiving Day to Christmas" so that "we may bear more earnest witness to our gratitude to Almighty God." Presidential Proclamation No. 2629, 58 Stat. 1160. It requires little imagination to conclude that these proclamations would cause nonadherents to feel excluded, yet they have been a part of our national heritage from the beginning.

The Executive has not been the only Branch of our Government to recognize the central role of religion in our society. The fact that this Court opens its sessions with the request that "God save the United States and this honorable Court" has been noted elsewhere. The Legislature has gone much further, not only employing legislative chaplains, but also setting aside a special prayer room in the Capitol for use by Members of the House and Senate. The room is decorated with a large stained glass panel that depicts President Washington kneeling in prayer; around him is etched the first verse of the 16th Psalm: "Preserve me, O God, for in Thee do I put my trust." Beneath the panel is a rostrum on which a Bible is placed; next to the rostrum is an American Flag. *See* L. AIKMAN, WE THE PEOPLE: THE STORY OF THE UNITED STATES CAPITOL 122 (1978). Some endorsement is inherent in these reasonable accommodations, yet the Establishment Clause does not forbid them.

The United States Code itself contains religious references that would be suspect under the endorsement test. Congress has directed the President to "set aside and proclaim a suitable day each year . . . as a National Day of Prayer, on which the people of the United States may turn to God in prayer and meditation at churches, in groups, and as individuals." 36 U.S.C. § 169h. This statute does not require anyone to pray, of course, but it is a straightforward endorsement of the concept of "turn[ing] to God in prayer." Also by statute, the Pledge of Allegiance to the Flag describes the United States as "one Nation under God." 36 U.S.C. § 172. To be sure, no one is obligated to recite this phrase, *see West Virginia State Board of Education v. Barnette*, 319 U.S. 624 (1943), but it borders on sophistry to suggest that the "'reasonable'" atheist would not feel less than a "'full membe[r] of the political community'" every time his fellow Americans recited, as part of their expression of patriotism and love for country, a phrase he believed to be false. Likewise, our national motto, "In God we trust," which is prominently engraved in the wall above the Speaker's dias in the Chamber of the House of Representatives and is reproduced on every coin minted and every dollar printed by the Federal Government, must have the same effect.

If the intent of the Establishment Clause is to protect individuals from mere feelings of exclusion, then legislative prayer cannot escape invalidation. It has been argued that "[these] government acknowledgments of religion serve, in the only ways reasonably possible in our culture, the legitimate secular purposes of solemnizing public occasions, expressing confidence in the future, and encouraging the recognition of what is worthy of appreciation in society." *Lynch, supra,* at 693 (O'CONNOR, J., concurring). I fail to see why prayer is the only way to convey these messages; appeals to patriotism, moments of silence, and any number of other approaches would be as effective, were the only purposes at issue the ones described by the *Lynch* concurrence. Nor is it clear to me why "encouraging the recognition of what is worthy of appreciation in society" can be characterized as a purely secular purpose, if it can be achieved only through religious prayer. No doubt prayer is "worthy of appreciation," but that is most assuredly not because it is secular. Even accepting the secular-solemnization explanation at face value, moreover, it seems incredible to suggest that the average observer of legislative prayer who either believes in no religion or whose faith rejects the concept of God would not receive the clear message that his faith is out of step with the political norm. Either the endorsement test must invalidate scores of traditional practices recognizing the place religion holds in our culture, or it must be twisted and stretched to avoid inconsistency with practices we know to have been permitted in the past, while condemning similar practices with no greater endorsement effect simply by reason of their lack of historical antecedent. Neither result is acceptable.

C. "IN GOD WE TRUST," THE TEN COMMANDMENTS, AND OTHER RELIGIOUS INSCRIPTIONS

One of the most contentious (and frequently litigated) Establishment Clause issues in recent years has involved efforts by various state officials to post or otherwise enshrine copies of the Ten Commandments on state property. The Supreme Court's initial foray into the Ten Commandments controversy occurred over twenty years ago in the public school context. In *Stone v. Graham*, 449 U.S. 39 (1981), the Supreme Court struck down a Kentucky statute mandating the display of the Ten Commandments in public school classrooms. As in most other situations involving the governmental posting of the Ten Commandments, the state of Kentucky argued that the posting of the Commandments served the secular purpose of acknowledging the Ten Commandments as the inspiration for the "fundamental legal code of Western Civilization and the Common Law of the United States." The Supreme Court rejected this argument:

> The pre-eminent purpose for posting the Ten Commandments on schoolroom walls is plainly religious in nature. The Ten Commandments are undeniably a sacred text in the Jewish and Christian faiths, and no legislative recitation of a supposed secular purpose can blind us to that fact. The Commandments do not confine themselves to arguably secular matters, such as honoring one's parents, killing or murder, adultery, stealing, false witness, and covetousness. Rather, the first part of the Commandments concerns the religious duties of believers: worshipping the Lord God alone, avoiding idolatry, not using the Lord's name in vain, and observing the Sabbath Day. . . . Posting of religious texts on the wall serves no . . . [secular] educational function. If the posted copies of the Ten Commandments are to have any effect at all, it will be to induce the schoolchildren to read, meditate upon, perhaps to venerate and obey, the Commandments. However desirable this might be as a matter of private devotion, it is not a permissible state objective under the Establishment Clause.

Id. at 41-42 (citations omitted).

The Supreme Court's assertion in *Stone* that the Ten Commandments are predominantly religious in nature has colored most of the lower courts' treatment of other uses of the Commandments outside the public school context. Prior to 2005, plaintiffs challenging the use of the Ten Commandments in non-school contexts won most, but not all of the lower-court cases. *See, e.g., Books v. City of Elkhart, Ind.*, 235 F.3d 292 (7th Cir. 2000), *cert. denied*, 532 U.S. 1058 (2001) (holding unconstitutional a city's display of a monument inscribed with the Ten Commandments on the lawn of the city's municipal building); *Adland v.*

Russ, 307 F.3d 471 (6th Cir. 2002), *cert. denied*, 538 U.S. 999 (2003) (holding unconstitutional the proposed relocation to a permanent site on state capitol grounds of a monument inscribed with the Ten Commandments). *But see Suhre v. Haywood County*, 55 F. Supp. 2d 384 (W.D.N.C. 1999) (holding that a county courtroom display of plaques containing an abridged version of Ten Commandments did not violate the Establishment Clause). The cases in which plaintiffs have lost such challenges arise mostly where the Ten Commandments are incorporated into a display that is historical or artistic in nature. *See, e.g., Freethought Soc. of Greater Philadelphia v. Chester County*, 334 F.3d 247 (3d Cir. 2003) (upholding the display of a eighty-two-year-old plaque inscribed with the text of the Ten Commandments).

The phenomenon of Ten Commandments monuments has a rather strange history. Here is one rendition of the story from a Seventh Circuit Court of Appeals opinion in 2000, holding unconstitutional a Ten Commandments monument in Elkhart, Indiana:

> In the 1940s, a juvenile court judge in Minnesota, E.J. Ruegemer, inaugurated the Youth Guidance Program. Disheartened by the growing number of youths in trouble, he sought to provide them with a common code of conduct. He believed that the Ten Commandments might provide the necessary guidance. Judge Ruegemer originally planned to post paper copies of the Ten Commandments in juvenile courts, first in Minnesota and then across the country. To help fund his idea, he contacted the Fraternal Order of Eagles ("FOE"), a service organization dedicated to promoting liberty, truth, and justice. At first, FOE rejected Judge Ruegemer's idea because it feared that the program might seem coercive or sectarian. In response to these concerns, representatives of Judaism, Protestantism, and Catholicism developed what the individuals involved believed to be a nonsectarian version of the Ten Commandments because it could not be identified with any one religious group. After reviewing this version, FOE agreed to support Judge Ruegemer's program.

> Around this same time, motion picture producer Cecil B. DeMille contacted Judge Ruegemer about the program. DeMille, who was working to produce the movie "The Ten Commandments," suggested that, rather than posting mere paper copies of the Ten Commandments, the program distribute bronze plaques. Judge Ruegemer replied that granite might be a more suitable material because the original Ten Commandments were written on granite. DeMille agreed with Judge Ruegemer's suggestion, and the judge thereafter worked with two Minnesota granite companies to produce granite monuments inscribed with the Ten Commandments. Local chapters of FOE financed these granite monuments and then, throughout the 1950s, donated them to their local communities.

Books v. City of Elkhart, Indiana, 235 F.3d at 294-95. What was once in part a movie promotion has continued to have constitutional implications a half-century later. The FOE/DeMille granite Ten Commandments monuments are still being litigated. *See, e.g., ACLU Nebraska Foundation v. City of Plattsmouth, Nebraska*, 419 F.3d 772 (8th Cir. 2005) (holding that an FOE-donated granite Ten Commandments display in a city park did not violate the Establishment Clause).

Nothing in previous Ten Commandments litigation, however, can rival the events of the summer of 2003. In *Glassroth v. Moore*, 335 F.3d 1282 (11th Cir. 2003), *cert. denied*, 540 U.S. 1000 (2003), the Eleventh Circuit Court of Appeals ruled that Alabama Supreme Court Chief Justice Roy Moore violated the Establishment Clause when he erected in the rotunda of the Alabama State Judicial Building a 5280-pound granite monument on which was chiseled tablets quoting the Ten Commandments. The defendant in this case became prominent when he was serving as an Alabama Circuit Court judge. During that time, Judge Moore hung a hand-carved wooden plaque depicting the Ten Commandments in his courtroom and "routinely invited clergy to lead prayer at jury organizing sessions." *Glassroth*, 335 F.3d at 1284. He later ran for Chief Justice of the Alabama Supreme Court. According to the Eleventh Circuit:

> During his campaign for the Chief Justice position in the November 2000 election, then-Judge Moore's campaign committee, capitalizing on name recognition from the lawsuits, decided to refer to him as the "Ten Commandments Judge." Although the Chief Justice says he never described himself that way, he did not disagree with his campaign committee's decision. As a result, most of his campaign materials, including billboards, television and radio commercials, telephone scripts, and mailings, described him as the "Ten Commandments Judge" or otherwise referred to the Ten Commandments. The central platform of his campaign was a promise "to restore the moral foundation of law."
>
> After he was elected, Chief Justice Moore fulfilled his campaign promise by installing the Ten Commandments monument in the rotunda of the Alabama State Judicial Building. That building houses the Alabama Supreme Court, the Court of Criminal Appeals, the Court of Civil Appeals, the state law library, and the state's Administrative Office of the Courts.

Id. at 1285.

The monument was privately financed and was placed in a position that made it a primary feature of the rotunda. The monument was installed during the evening, and the installation was filmed by an evangelical Christian organization that, according to the court, "used the exclusive footage of the installation to raise funds for its own purpose and for Chief Justice Moore's legal defense, which [the group] has underwritten." *Id.* at 1286. The day after the installation, the Chief Justice gave a speech commemorating the event, in which "[h]e explained that the location of the monument was 'fitting and proper' because: 'this monument will serve to remind the appellate courts and judges of the circuit and district courts of this state, the members of the bar who appear before them, as well as the people who visit the Alabama Judicial Building, of the truth stated in the preamble of the Alabama Constitution, that in order to establish justice, we must invoke "the favor and guidance of Almighty God."'" *Id.* The Chief Justice also told the audience that they would "find no documents surrounding the Ten Commandments because they stand alone as an acknowledgment of that God that's contained in our pledge, contained in our motto, and contained in our oath." *Id.* at 1287.

The Eleventh Circuit applied the three-part *Lemon* test and found that the Chief Justice's placement of the monument in the rotunda violated both the secular purpose and the secular effect prongs of that test. With regard to Moore's purpose, the court held that it was "self-evident" that Moore's purpose was not secular. "Chief Justice Moore testified candidly that his purpose in placing the monument in the Judicial Building was to acknowledge the law and sovereignty of the God of the Holy Scriptures, and that it was intended to acknowledge 'God's overruling power over the affairs of men.'" *Id.* at 1296. With regard to the effect of the monument, the court of appeals agreed with the district court's finding that "a reasonable observer would view the monument's primary effect as an endorsement of religion," based on "the appearance of the monument itself; its location and setting in the rotunda; the selection and location of the quotations on its sides; and the inclusion on its face of the text of the Ten Commandments, which is an 'undeniably . . . sacred text,' . . . all of which contributed to 'the ineffable but still overwhelming holy aura of the monument.' . . . The court also considered: the fact that the Chief Justice campaigned as the 'Ten Commandments Judge'; his statements at the monument's unveiling; and the fact that the rotunda is not a public forum for speech." *Id.* at 1297.

The Roy Moore episode did not end with the Eleventh Circuit's opinion. After the Eleventh Circuit rendered its decision, the District Court ordered Moore to comply by removing the monument. Moore refused, and a motion to hold Moore in contempt was filed. The contempt motion was rendered moot when the other Justices of the Alabama Supreme Court ordered the monument removed from the Supreme Court rotunda. Moore was later removed from office by a unanimous vote of the state Judicial Inquiry Commission. The Commission held:

> Chief Justice Moore not only willfully and publicly defied the orders of a United States district court, but upon direct questioning by the court he also gave the court no assurances that he would follow that order or any similar order in the future. In fact, he affirmed his earlier statements in which he said he would do the same. Under these circumstances, there is no penalty short of removal from office that would resolve this issue. Anything short of removal would only serve to set up another confrontation that would ultimately bring us back to where we are today.

In re Roy S. Moore, Ct. of the Judiciary, Case No. 33, at 12 (Nov. 13, 2003).

The last gasp of the Alabama Ten Commandments litigation took the form of a suit brought by supporters of Moore. In *McGinley v. Houston*, 361 F.3d 1328 (11th Cir. 2004), the Eleventh Circuit Court of Appeals rejected the supporters' argument that "(1) the appellees' removal of the Ten Commandments monument constituted an impermissible endorsement of the 'religion of nontheistic belief by the state,' and (2) the removal 'creates hostility against religion by the government pitting and favoring the religion of nontheistic beliefs over the Judeo-Christian faith.'" The court rejected these arguments, holding that complying with the Establishment Clause did not constitute an establishment of the "religion" of secularism.

As the litigation over Judge Moore's monument was winding down, the Supreme Court agreed to review two cases involving Ten Commandments displays. The Court ultimately split 5-4 in both of these cases, with four Justices (Ginsburg, O'Connor, Souter, and Stevens) voting to hold both displays unconstitutional, four Justices (the Chief Justice, Kennedy, Scalia, and Thomas) voting to hold both displays constitutional, and one Justice (Breyer) voting to hold one display constitutional and the other unconstitutional. The split nature of the opinions makes it unlikely that these decisions will quell the furor over Ten Commandments monuments and plaques in public buildings. The fact that there were a total of nine different opinions in the two cases, coupled with the diffuse nature of Justice Breyer's crucial opinion, accentuates this perception.

There was a great deal of discussion in these opinions about issues ranging far beyond the narrow context of Ten Commandment displays. These portions of the opinions are excerpted elsewhere in other chapters. Justice Scalia's opinion arguing that the government's endorsement of monotheism is consistent with the country's constitutional tradition (along with Justice Stevens' rejoinder) is excerpted in Chapter 2. Justice Souter's opinion on behalf of the majority reaffirming the secular purpose requirement of *Lemon v. Kurtzman* is excerpted in Chapter 5, as is a discussion of the continuing applicability of *Lemon* generally. The excerpts below deal more specifically with the analysis pertaining to Ten Commandments displays.

McCREARY COUNTY, KENTUCKY v. AMERICAN CIVIL LIBERTIES UNION OF KENTUCKY
125 S. Ct. 2722 (2005)

[After petitioners, two Kentucky Counties, each posted large copies of the Ten Commandments in their courthouses, the ACLU sued to enjoin the displays on the ground that they violated the First Amendment's Establishment Clause. The Counties then adopted nearly identical resolutions calling for a more extensive exhibit meant to show that the Commandments are Kentucky's "precedent legal code." The resolutions noted several grounds for taking that position, including the state legislature's acknowledgment of Christ as the "Prince of

Ethics." The displays around the Commandments were modified to include eight smaller, historical documents containing religious references as their sole common element, *e.g.,* the Declaration of Independence's "endowed by their Creator" passage. The District Court held that the new display lacked a secular purpose under *Lemon*. After changing counsel, the Counties revised the exhibits again. No new resolution authorized the new exhibits, nor did the Counties repeal the resolutions that preceded the second one. The new posting, entitled "The Foundations of American Law and Government Display," consists of nine framed documents of equal size. One sets out the Commandments explicitly identified as the "King James Version," quotes them at greater length, and explains that they have profoundly influenced the formation of Western legal thought and this Nation. With the Commandments are framed copies of, *e.g.,* the Star Spangled Banner's lyrics and the Declaration of Independence, accompanied by statements about their historical and legal significance. Both the District Court and the Court of Appeals held the third display unconstitutional under the *Lemon* secular purpose analysis.]

JUSTICE SOUTER delivered the opinion of the Court.

II

A

Ever since *Lemon v. Kurtzman* summarized the three familiar considerations for evaluating Establishment Clause claims, looking to whether government action has "a secular legislative purpose" has been a common, albeit seldom dispositive, element of our cases. Though we have found government action motivated by an illegitimate purpose only four times since *Lemon*, and "the secular purpose requirement alone may rarely be determinative . . . , it nevertheless serves an important function."

The touchstone for our analysis is the principle that the "First Amendment mandates governmental neutrality between religion and religion, and between religion and nonreligion." When the government acts with the ostensible and predominant purpose of advancing religion, it violates that central Establishment Clause value of official religious neutrality, there being no neutrality when the government's ostensible object is to take sides. "*Lemon*'s 'purpose' requirement aims at preventing [government] from abandoning neutrality and acting with the intent of promoting a particular point of view in religious matters"). Manifesting a purpose to favor one faith over another, or adherence to religion generally, clashes with the "understanding, reached . . . after decades of religious war, that liberty and social stability demand a religious tolerance that respects the religious views of all citizens. . . ." By showing a purpose to favor religion, the government "sends the . . . message to . . . nonadherents 'that they are outsiders, not full members of the political community, and an accompanying message to adherents that they are insiders, favored members. . . .'"

[margin note: Great Def]

[margin note: O'CONN]

[The Court then discussed its reasons for reaffirming the secular purpose analysis under *Lemon*. This part of the Court's opinion is reprinted in Chapter 5.]

III

We take *Stone* as the initial legal benchmark, our only case dealing with the constitutionality of displaying the Commandments. *Stone* recognized that the Commandments are an "instrument of religion" and that, at least on the facts before it, the display of their text could presumptively be understood as meant to advance religion: although state law specifically required their posting in public school classrooms, their isolated exhibition did not leave room even for an argument that secular education explained their being there. But *Stone* did not purport to decide the constitutionality of every possible way the Commandments might be set out by the government, and under the Establishment Clause detail is key. Hence, we look to the record of evidence showing the progression leading up to the third display of the Commandments.

A

The display rejected in *Stone* had two obvious similarities to the first one in the sequence here: both set out a text of the Commandments as distinct from any traditionally symbolic representation, and each stood alone, not part of an arguably secular display. *Stone* stressed the significance of integrating the Commandments into a secular scheme to forestall the broadcast of an otherwise clearly religious message, and for good reason, the Commandments being a central point of reference in the religious and moral history of Jews and Christians. They proclaim the existence of a monotheistic god (no other gods). They regulate details of religious obligation (no graven images, no sabbath breaking, no vain oath swearing). And they unmistakably rest even the universally accepted prohibitions (as against murder, theft, and the like) on the sanction of the divinity proclaimed at the beginning of the text. Displaying that text is thus different from a symbolic depiction, like tablets with 10 roman numerals, which could be seen as alluding to a general notion of law, not a sectarian conception of faith. Where the text is set out, the insistence of the religious message is hard to avoid in the absence of a context plausibly suggesting a message going beyond an excuse to promote the religious point of view. The display in *Stone* had no context that might have indicated an object beyond the religious character of the text, and the Counties' solo exhibit here did nothing more to counter the sectarian implication than the postings at issue in *Stone*. Actually, the posting by the Counties lacked even the *Stone* display's implausible disclaimer that the Commandments were set out to show their effect on the civil law. What is more, at the ceremony for posting the framed Commandments in Pulaski County, the county executive was accompanied by his pastor, who testified to the certainty of the existence of God. The reasonable observer could only think that the Counties meant to emphasize and celebrate the Commandments' religious message.

This is not to deny that the Commandments have had influence on civil or secular law; a major text of a majority religion is bound to be felt. The point is simply that the original text viewed in its entirety is an unmistakably religious statement dealing with religious obligations and with morality subject to religious sanction. When the government initiates an effort to place this statement alone in public view, a religious object is unmistakable.

C

1

[The Court then discussed the history of the three displays.] These new statements of purpose [passed in conjunction with the third display] were presented only as a litigating position, there being no further authorizing action by the Counties' governing boards. And although repeal of the earlier county authorizations would not have erased them from the record of evidence bearing on current purpose, the extraordinary resolutions for the second display passed just months earlier were not repealed or otherwise repudiated. Indeed, the sectarian spirit of the common resolution found enhanced expression in the third display, which quoted more of the purely religious language of the Commandments than the first two displays had done; ("I the LORD thy God am a jealous God") (text of Second Commandment in third display); ("the LORD will not hold him guiltless that taketh his name in vain") (from text of Third Commandment); and ("that thy days may be long upon the land which the LORD thy God giveth thee") (text of Fifth Commandment). No reasonable observer could swallow the claim that the Counties had cast off the objective so unmistakable in the earlier displays.

Nor did the selection of posted material suggest a clear theme that might prevail over evidence of the continuing religious object. In a collection of documents said to be "foundational" to American government, it is at least odd to include a patriotic anthem, but to omit the Fourteenth Amendment, the most significant structural provision adopted since the original Framing. And it is no less baffling to leave out the original Constitution of 1787 while quoting the 1215 Magna Carta even to the point of its declaration that "fish-weirs shall be removed from the Thames." If an observer found these choices and omissions perplexing in isolation, he would be puzzled for a different reason when he read the Declaration of Independence seeking confirmation for the Counties' posted explanation that the "Ten Commandments . . . influence is clearly seen in the Declaration," in fact the observer would find that the Commandments are sanctioned as divine imperatives, while the Declaration of Independence holds that the authority of government to enforce the law derives "from the consent of the governed." If the observer had not thrown up his hands, he would probably suspect that the Counties were simply reaching for any way to keep a religious document on the walls of courthouses constitutionally required to embody religious neutrality.

2

In holding the preliminary injunction adequately supported by evidence that the Counties' purpose had not changed at the third stage, we do not decide that the Counties' past actions forever taint any effort on their part to deal with the subject matter. We hold only that purpose needs to be taken seriously under the Establishment Clause and needs to be understood in light of context; an implausible claim that governmental purpose has changed should not carry the day in a court of law any more than in a head with common sense. It is enough to say here that district courts are fully capable of adjusting preliminary relief to take account of genuine changes in constitutionally significant conditions.

Nor do we have occasion here to hold that a sacred text can never be integrated constitutionally into a governmental display on the subject of law, or American history. We do not forget, and in this litigation have frequently been reminded, that our own courtroom frieze was deliberately designed in the exercise of governmental authority so as to include the figure of Moses holding tablets exhibiting a portion of the Hebrew text of the later, secularly phrased Commandments; in the company of 17 other lawgivers, most of them secular figures, there is no risk that Moses would strike an observer as evidence that the National Government was violating neutrality in religion.

[Justice O'Connor's concurring opinion is omitted.]

JUSTICE SCALIA, with whom THE CHIEF JUSTICE and JUSTICE THOMAS oin and with whom JUSTICE KENNEDY joins, dissenting.

[Justice Scalia's argument in favor of governmental endorsement of monotheism is reprinted in Chapter 2.]

III

Even accepting the Court's *Lemon*-based premises, the displays at issue here were constitutional.

A

To any person who happened to walk down the hallway of the McCreary or Pulaski County Courthouse during the roughly nine months when the Foundations Displays were exhibited, the displays must have seemed unremarkable — if indeed they were noticed at all. The walls of both courthouses were already lined with historical documents and other assorted portraits; each Foundations Display was exhibited in the same format as these other displays and nothing in the record suggests that either County took steps to give it greater prominence.

B

On its face, the Foundations Displays manifested the purely secular purpose that the Counties asserted before the District Court: "to display documents that played a significant role in the foundation of our system of law and government." That the Displays included the Ten Commandments did not transform their apparent secular purpose into one of impermissible advocacy for Judeo-Christian beliefs. Even an isolated display of the Decalogue conveys, at worst, "an equivocal message, perhaps of respect for Judaism, for religion in general, or for law."

Perhaps in recognition of the centrality of the Ten Commandments as a widely recognized symbol of religion in public life, the Court is at pains to dispel the impression that its decision will require governments across the country to sandblast the Ten Commandments from the public square. The constitutional problem, the Court says, is with the Counties' *purpose* in erecting the Foundations Displays, not the displays themselves. The Court adds in a footnote: "One consequence of taking account of the purpose underlying past actions is that the same government action may be constitutional if taken in the first instance and unconstitutional if it has a sectarian heritage."

This inconsistency may be explicable in theory, but I suspect that the "objective observer" with whom the Court is so concerned will recognize its absurdity in practice. By virtue of details familiar only to the parties to litigation and their lawyers, McCreary and Pulaski Counties, Kentucky, and Rutherford County, Tennessee, have been ordered to remove the same display that appears in courthouses from Mercer County, Kentucky to Elkhart County, Indiana. Displays erected in silence (and under the direction of good legal advice) are permissible, while those hung after discussion and debate are deemed unconstitutional. Reduction of the Establishment Clause to such minutiae trivializes the Clause's protection against religious establishment; indeed, it may inflame religious passions by making the passing comments of every government official the subject of endless litigation.

VAN ORDEN v. PERRY
125 S. Ct. 2854 (2005)

[Among the 21 historical markers and 17 monuments surrounding the Texas State Capitol is a 6-foot-high monolith inscribed with the Ten Commandments. The monolith challenged here stands 6-feet high and 3 1/2 -feet wide. It is located to the north of the Capitol building, between the Capitol and the Supreme Court building. Its primary content is the text of the Ten Commandments. An eagle grasping the American flag, an eye inside of a pyramid, and two small tablets with what appears to be an ancient script are carved above the text of the Ten Commandments. Below the text are two Stars of David and the superimposed Greek letters Chi and Rho, which represent Christ. The bottom of the monument bears the inscription "PRESENTED TO THE PEOPLE AND YOUTH OF TEXAS BY THE FRATERNAL ORDER OF EAGLES OF TEXAS 1961." The legislative record surrounding the State's acceptance of the monument from the Eagles — a national social, civic, and patriotic organization — is limited to legislative journal entries. After the monument was accepted, the

State selected a site for the monument based on the recommendation of the state organization responsible for maintaining the Capitol grounds. The Eagles paid the cost of erecting the monument, the dedication of which was presided over by two state legislators.]

CHIEF JUSTICE REHNQUIST announced the judgment of the Court and delivered an opinion, in which JUSTICE SCALIA, JUSTICE KENNEDY, and JUSTICE THOMAS join.

Our cases, Januslike, point in two directions in applying the Establishment Clause. One face looks toward the strong role played by religion and religious traditions throughout our Nation's history. The other face looks toward the principle that governmental intervention in religious matters can itself endanger religious freedom.

This case, like all Establishment Clause challenges, presents us with the difficulty of respecting both faces. Our institutions presuppose a Supreme Being, yet these institutions must not press religious observances upon their citizens. One face looks to the past in acknowledgment of our Nation's heritage, while the other looks to the present in demanding a separation between church and state. Reconciling these two faces requires that we neither abdicate our responsibility to maintain a division between church and state nor evince a hostility to religion by disabling the government from in some ways recognizing our religious heritage.

Whatever may be the fate of the *Lemon* test in the larger scheme of Establishment Clause jurisprudence, we think it not useful in dealing with the sort of passive monument that Texas has erected on its Capitol grounds. Instead, our analysis is driven both by the nature of the monument and by our Nation's history.

In this case we are faced with a display of the Ten Commandments on government property outside the Texas State Capitol. Such acknowledgments of the role played by the Ten Commandments in our Nation's heritage are common throughout America. We need only look within our own Courtroom. Since 1935, Moses has stood, holding two tablets that reveal portions of the Ten Commandments written in Hebrew, among other lawgivers in the south frieze. Representations of the Ten Commandments adorn the metal gates lining the north and south sides of the Courtroom as well as the doors leading into the Courtroom. Moses also sits on the exterior east facade of the building holding the Ten Commandments tablets.

Of course, the Ten Commandments are religious — they were so viewed at their inception and so remain. The monument, therefore, has religious significance. According to Judeo-Christian belief, the Ten Commandments were given to Moses by God on Mt. Sinai. But Moses was a lawgiver as well as a religious leader. And the Ten Commandments have an undeniable historical meaning, as the foregoing examples demonstrate. Simply having religious content or promoting a message consistent with a religious doctrine does not run afoul of the Establishment Clause.

There are, of course, limits to the display of religious messages or symbols. For example, we held unconstitutional a Kentucky statute requiring the posting of the Ten Commandments in every public schoolroom. *Stone v. Graham.* In the classroom context, we found that the Kentucky statute had an improper and plainly religious purpose. As evidenced by *Stone's* almost exclusive reliance upon two of our school prayer cases, it stands as an example of the fact that we have "been particularly vigilant in monitoring compliance with the Establishment Clause in elementary and secondary schools." Neither *Stone* itself nor subsequent opinions have indicated that *Stone's* holding would extend to a legislative chamber, or to capitol grounds.[11]

[Justice Scalia's and Thomas' concurring opinions are omitted.]

JUSTICE BREYER, concurring in the judgment.

In *School Dist. of Abington Township v. Schempp,* Justice Goldberg, joined by Justice Harlan, wrote, in respect to the First Amendment's Religion Clauses, that there is "no simple and clear measure which by precise application can readily and invariably demark the permissible from the impermissible." One must refer instead to the basic purposes of those Clauses. They seek to "assure the fullest possible scope of religious liberty and tolerance for all." They seek to avoid that divisiveness based upon religion that promotes social conflict, sapping the strength of government and religion alike. *Zelman v. Simmons-Harris* (BREYER, J., dissenting). They seek to maintain that "separation of church and state" that has long been critical to the "peaceful dominion that religion exercises in [this] country," where the "spirit of religion" and the "spirit of freedom" are productively "united," "reign[ing] together" but in separate spheres "on the same soil." A. DE TOCQUEVILLE, DEMOCRACY IN AMERICA 282-283 (1835) (H. Mansfield & D. Winthrop transls. and eds.2000). They seek to further the basic principles set forth today by JUSTICE O'CONNOR in her concurring opinion in *McCreary County.*

The Court has made clear, as Justices Goldberg and Harlan noted, that the realization of these goals means that government must "neither engage in nor compel religious practices," that it must "effect no favoritism among sects or between religion and nonreligion," and that it must "work deterrence of no religious belief." The government must avoid excessive interference with, or promotion of, religion. But the Establishment Clause does not compel the government to purge from the public sphere all that in any way partakes of the reli-

---

11 Nor does anything suggest that *Stone* would extend to displays of the Ten Commandments that lack a "plainly religious," "pre-eminent purpose," *see Edwards v. Aguillard,* ("[*Stone*] did not mean that no use could ever be made of the Ten Commandments, or that the Ten Commandments played an exclusively religious role in the history of Western Civilization"). Indeed, we need not decide in this case the extent to which a primarily religious purpose would affect our analysis because it is clear from the record that there is no evidence of such a purpose in this case.

gious. Such absolutism is not only inconsistent with our national traditions, but would also tend to promote the kind of social conflict the Establishment Clause seeks to avoid.

Thus, as Justices Goldberg and Harlan pointed out, the Court has found no single mechanical formula that can accurately draw the constitutional line in every case. Where the Establishment Clause is at issue, tests designed to measure "neutrality" alone are insufficient, both because it is sometimes difficult to determine when a legal rule is "neutral," and because "untutored devotion to the concept of neutrality can lead to invocation or approval of results which partake not simply of that noninterference and noninvolvement with the religious which the Constitution commands, but of a brooding and pervasive devotion to the secular and a passive, or even active, hostility to the religious."

Neither can this Court's other tests readily explain the Establishment Clause's tolerance, for example, of the prayers that open legislative meetings, certain references to, and invocations of, the Deity in the public words of public officials; the public references to God on coins, decrees, and buildings; or the attention paid to the religious objectives of certain holidays, including Thanksgiving.

If the relation between government and religion is one of separation, but not of mutual hostility and suspicion, one will inevitably find difficult borderline cases. And in such cases, I see no test-related substitute for the exercise of legal judgment. That judgment is not a personal judgment. Rather, as in all constitutional cases, it must reflect and remain faithful to the underlying purposes of the Clauses, and it must take account of context and consequences measured in light of those purposes. While the Court's prior tests provide useful guideposts — and might well lead to the same result the Court reaches today, no exact formula can dictate a resolution to such fact-intensive cases.

The case before us is a borderline case. It concerns a large granite monument bearing the text of the Ten Commandments located on the grounds of the Texas State Capitol. On the one hand, the Commandments' text undeniably has a religious message, invoking, indeed emphasizing, the Deity. On the other hand, focusing on the text of the Commandments alone cannot conclusively resolve this case. Rather, to determine the message that the text here conveys, we must examine how the text is *used*. And that inquiry requires us to consider the context of the display.

In certain contexts, a display of the tablets of the Ten Commandments can convey not simply a religious message but also a secular moral message (about proper standards of social conduct). And in certain contexts, a display of the tablets can also convey a historical message (about a historic relation between those standards and the law) — a fact that helps to explain the display of those tablets in dozens of courthouses throughout the Nation, including the Supreme Court of the United States.

Here the tablets have been used as part of a display that communicates not simply a religious message, but a secular message as well. The circumstances surrounding the display's placement on the capitol grounds and its physical setting suggest that the State itself intended the latter, nonreligious aspects of the tablets' message to predominate. And the monument's 40-year history on the Texas state grounds indicates that that has been its effect.

The group that donated the monument, the Fraternal Order of Eagles, a private civic (and primarily secular) organization, while interested in the religious aspect of the Ten Commandments, sought to highlight the Commandments' role in shaping civic morality as part of that organization's efforts to combat juvenile delinquency. The Eagles' consultation with a committee composed of members of several faiths in order to find a nonsectarian text underscores the group's ethics-based motives. *See* Brief for Respondents 5-6, and n. 9. The tablets, as displayed on the monument, prominently acknowledge that the Eagles donated the display, a factor which, though not sufficient, thereby further distances the State itself from the religious aspect of the Commandments' message.

The physical setting of the monument, moreover, suggests little or nothing of the sacred. The monument sits in a large park containing 17 monuments and 21 historical markers, all designed to illustrate the "ideals" of those who settled in Texas and of those who have lived there since that time. The setting does not readily lend itself to meditation or any other religious activity. But it does provide a context of history and moral ideals. It (together with the display's inscription about its origin) communicates to visitors that the State sought to reflect moral principles, illustrating a relation between ethics and law that the State's citizens, historically speaking, have endorsed. That is to say, the context suggests that the State intended the display's moral message — an illustrative message reflecting the historical "ideals" of Texans — to predominate.

If these factors provide a strong, but not conclusive, indication that the Commandments' text on this monument conveys a predominantly secular message, a further factor is determinative here. As far as I can tell, 40 years passed in which the presence of this monument, legally speaking, went unchallenged (until the single legal objection raised by petitioner). And I am not aware of any evidence suggesting that this was due to a climate of intimidation. Hence, those 40 years suggest more strongly than can any set of formulaic tests that few individuals, whatever their system of beliefs, are likely to have understood the monument as amounting, in any significantly detrimental way, to a government effort to favor a particular religious sect, primarily to promote religion over nonreligion, to "engage in" any "religious practice," to "compel" any "religious practice," or to "work deterrence" of any "religious belief." Those 40 years suggest that the public visiting the capitol grounds has considered the religious aspect of the tablets' message as part of what is a broader moral and historical message reflective of a cultural heritage.

This case, moreover, is distinguishable from instances where the Court has found Ten Commandments displays impermissible. The display is not on the grounds of a public school, where, given the impressionability of the young, government must exercise particular care in separating church and state. *See, e.g., Lee v. Weisman; Stone v. Graham.* This case also differs from *McCreary County,* where the short (and stormy) history of the courthouse Commandments' displays demonstrates the substantially religious objectives of those who mounted them, and the effect of this readily apparent objective upon those who view them. That history there indicates a governmental effort substantially to promote religion, not simply an effort primarily to reflect, historically, the secular impact of a religiously inspired document. And, in today's world, in a Nation of so many different religious and comparable nonreligious fundamental beliefs, a more contemporary state effort to focus attention upon a religious text is certainly likely to prove divisive in a way that this longstanding, pre-existing monument has not.

For these reasons, I believe that the Texas display might satisfy this Court's more formal Establishment Clause tests. But, as I have said, in reaching the conclusion that the Texas display falls on the permissible side of the constitutional line, I rely less upon a literal application of any particular test than upon consideration of the basic purposes of the First Amendment's Religion Clauses themselves. This display has stood apparently uncontested for nearly two generations. That experience helps us understand that as a practical matter of *degree* this display is unlikely to prove divisive. And this matter of degree is, I believe, critical in a borderline case such as this one.

At the same time, to reach a contrary conclusion here, based primarily upon on the religious nature of the tablets' text would, I fear, lead the law to exhibit a hostility toward religion that has no place in our Establishment Clause traditions. Such a holding might well encourage disputes concerning the removal of longstanding depictions of the Ten Commandments from public buildings across the Nation. And it could thereby create the very kind of religiously based divisiveness that the Establishment Clause seeks to avoid.

Justices Goldberg and Harlan concluded in *Schempp* that

> "[t]he First Amendment does not prohibit practices which by any realistic measure create none of the dangers which it is designed to prevent and which do not so directly or substantially involve the state in religious exercise or in the favoring of religion as to have meaningful and practical impact."

That kind of practice is what we have here. I recognize the danger of the slippery slope. Still, where the Establishment Clause is at issue, we must "distinguish between real threat and mere shadow." Here, we have only the shadow.

In light of these considerations, I cannot agree with today's plurality's analysis. Nor can I agree with JUSTICE SCALIA's dissent in *McCreary County.* I do agree with JUSTICE O'CONNOR's statement of principles in *McCreary County,* though

I disagree with her evaluation of the evidence as it bears on the application of those principles to this case.

JUSTICE STEVENS, with whom JUSTICE GINSBURG joins, dissenting

The sole function of the monument on the grounds of Texas' State Capitol is to display the full text of one version of the Ten Commandments. The monument is not a work of art and does not refer to any event in the history of the State. It is significant because, and only because, it communicates the following message:

"I AM the LORD thy God.
"Thou shalt have no other gods before me.
"Thou shalt not make to thyself any graven images.
"Thou shalt not take the Name of the Lord thy God in vain.
"Remember the Sabbath day, to keep it holy.
"Honor thy father and thy mother, that thy days may be long upon the land which the Lord thy God giveth thee.
"Thou shalt not kill.
"Thou shalt not commit adultery.
"Thou shalt not steal.
"Thou shalt not bear false witness against thy neighbor.
"Thou shalt not covet thy neighbor's house.
"Thou shalt not covet thy neighbor's wife, nor his manservant, nor his maidservant, nor his cattle, nor anything that is thy neighbor's."

Viewed on its face, Texas' display has no purported connection to God's role in the formation of Texas or the founding of our Nation; nor does it provide the reasonable observer with any basis to guess that it was erected to honor any individual or organization. The message transmitted by Texas' chosen display is quite plain: This State endorses the divine code of the "Judeo-Christian" God.

For those of us who learned to recite the King James version of the text long before we understood the meaning of some of its words, God's Commandments may seem like wise counsel. The question before this Court, however, is whether it is counsel that the State of Texas may proclaim without violating the Establishment Clause of the Constitution. If any fragment of Jefferson's metaphorical "wall of separation between church and State" is to be preserved — if there remains any meaning to the "wholesome "neutrality' of which this Court's [Establishment Clause] cases speak" — a negative answer to that question is mandatory.

I

This case, however, is not about historic preservation or the mere recognition of religion. The issue is obfuscated rather than clarified by simplistic commentary on the various ways in which religion has played a role in American life, and by the recitation of the many extant governmental "acknowledgments" of the role the Ten Commandments played in our Nation's heritage. Surely, the mere compilation of religious symbols, none of which includes the full text of the Commandments and all of which are exhibited in different settings, has only marginal relevance to the question presented in this case.

II

When the Ten Commandments monument was donated to the State of Texas in 1961, it was not for the purpose of commemorating a noteworthy event in Texas history, signifying the Commandments' influence on the development of secular law, or even denoting the religious beliefs of Texans at that time. To the contrary, the donation was only one of over a hundred largely identical monoliths, and of over a thousand paper replicas, distributed to state and local governments throughout the Nation over the course of several decades. This ambitious project was the work of the Fraternal Order of Eagles, a well-respected benevolent organization whose good works have earned the praise of several Presidents. [Justice Stevens then recounts the history of the placement of the monuments, including the involvement of Cecil B. DeMille.]

> " 'The erection of these monoliths is to inspire all who pause to view them, with a renewed respect for the law of God, which is our greatest strength against the forces that threaten our way of life.' "

The desire to combat juvenile delinquency by providing guidance to youths is both admirable and unquestionably secular. But achieving that goal through biblical teachings injects a religious purpose into an otherwise secular endeavor. By spreading the word of God and converting heathens to Christianity, missionaries expect to enlighten their converts, enhance their satisfaction with life, and improve their behavior. Similarly, by disseminating the "law of God" — directing fidelity to God and proscribing murder, theft, and adultery — the Eagles hope that this divine guidance will help wayward youths conform their behavior and improve their lives. In my judgment, the significant secular by-products that are intended consequences of religious instruction — indeed, of the establishment of most religions — are not the type of "secular" purposes that justify government promulgation of sacred religious messages.

Though the State of Texas may genuinely wish to combat juvenile delinquency, and may rightly want to honor the Eagles for their efforts, it cannot effectuate these admirable purposes through an explicitly religious medium.

The reason this message stands apart is that the Decalogue is a venerable religious text. As we held 25 years ago, it is beyond dispute that "[t]he Ten Commandments are undeniably a sacred text in the Jewish and Christian faiths." *Stone v. Graham.* For many followers, the Commandments represent the literal word of God as spoken to Moses and repeated to his followers after descending from Mount Sinai. The message conveyed by the Ten Commandments thus cannot be analogized to an appendage to a common article of commerce ("In God we Trust") or an incidental part of a familiar recital ("God save the United States and this honorable Court"). Thankfully, the plurality does not attempt to minimize the religious significance of the Ten Commandments. Attempts to secularize what is unquestionably a sacred text defy credibility and disserve people of faith.

[D]espite the Eagles' best efforts to choose a benign nondenominational text,[15] the Ten Commandments display projects not just a religious, but an inherently sectarian message. There are many distinctive versions of the Decalogue, ascribed to by different religions and even different denominations within a particular faith; to a pious and learned observer, these differences may be of enormous religious significance.[16] *See* Lubet, *The Ten Commandments in Alabama*, 15 CONSTITUTIONAL COMMENTARY 471, 474-476 (Fall 1998). In choosing to display this version of the Commandments, Texas tells the observer that the State supports this side of the doctrinal religious debate. The reasonable observer, after all, has no way of knowing that this text was the product of a compromise, or that there is a rationale of any kind for the text's selection.[17]

The Establishment Clause, if nothing else, forbids government from "specifying details upon which men and women who believe in a benevolent, omnipotent Creator and Ruler of the world are known to differ." Given that the chosen text inscribed on the Ten Commandments monument invariably places the State at the center of a serious sectarian dispute, the display is unquestionably unconstitutional under our case law.

---

15 Despite the Eagles' efforts, not all of the monuments they donated in fact conform to a "universally-accepted" text. *Compare, e.g.,* Appendix, *infra* (including the command that "Thou shalt not make to thyself any graven images"), , with *Freedom From Religion Foundation*, 898 P.2d at 1016 (omitting that command altogether). The distinction represents a critical divide between the Protestant and Catholic faiths. During the Reformation, Protestants destroyed images of the Virgin Mary and of Jesus Christ that were venerated in Catholic churches. Even today there is a notable difference between the imagery in different churches, a difference that may in part be attributable to differing understandings of the meaning of what is the Second Commandment in the King James Bible translation and a portion of the First Commandment in the Catholic translation. *See* Finkelman, *The Ten Commandments on the Courthouse Lawn and Elsewhere*, 73 FORD. L.REV. 1477, 1493-1494 (2005).

16 For example, in the Jewish version of the Sixth Commandment God commands: "You shall not murder"; whereas, the King James interpretation of the same command is: "Thou shalt not kill." *Compare* W. PLAUT, THE TORAH: A MODERN COMMENTARY 534 (1981), *with* Appendix, *infra*. The difference between the two versions is not merely semantic; rather, it is but one example of a deep theological dispute. *See* Finkelman, *supra,* at 1481-1500; P. Maier, *Enumerating the Decalogue; Do We Number the Ten Commandments Correctly?* 16 CONCORDIA J. 18, 18-26 (1990). Varying interpretations of this Commandment explain the actions of vegetarians who refuse to eat meat, pacifists who refuse to work for munitions makers, prison officials who refuse to administer lethal injections to death row inmates, and pharmacists who refuse to sell morning-after pills to women. *See* Finkelman, *supra,* at 1494-1496; Brief for American Jewish Congress et al. as *Amici Curiae* 22-23. Although the command is ambiguous, its power to motivate likeminded interpreters of its message cannot be denied.

17 JUSTICE SCALIA's willingness to dismiss the distinct textual versions adhered to by different faiths in the name of generic "monotheism" based on mere speculation regarding their significance is not only somewhat ironic, *see* A. SCALIA, A MATTER OF INTERPRETATION 23-25 (1997), but also serves to reinforce the concern that interjecting government into the religious sphere will offend "adherents who consider the particular advertisement disrespectful."

Even if, however, the message of the monument, despite the inscribed text, fairly could be said to represent the belief system of all Judeo-Christians, it would still run afoul of the Establishment Clause by prescribing a compelled code of conduct from one God, namely a Judeo-Christian God, that is rejected by prominent polytheistic sects, such as Hinduism, as well as nontheistic religions, such as Buddhism. And, at the very least, the text of the Ten Commandments impermissibly commands a preference for religion over irreligion. Any of those bases, in my judgment, would be sufficient to conclude that the message should not be proclaimed by the State of Texas on a permanent monument at the seat of its government.

[The dissenting opinions of Justices Souter and O'Connor are omitted.]

NOTES

1. *The Relevant Factors in Assessing Ten Commandments Displays.* The Eleventh Circuit decision in *Glassroth* seems generally consistent with *McCreary County* and *Van Orden*, but do any of these decisions really provide much assistance in assessing other Ten Commandments displays in somewhat different contexts? In light of the highly contextualized nature of all these decisions, how would an attorney advise a city or county regarding a plaque or monument depicting the Ten Commandments? Is the key factor the explicit (and plausible) disavowal by the government officials of any intent to endorse the religious message of the Commandments? Or is the key the size and placement of the plaque or monument? Is the simple age of the monument the deciding factor? Is the divisiveness surrounding the placement of a particular display crucial? If so, are groups and individuals opposed to these displays obligated to oppose the displays as early and loudly as possible?

2. *Government Mottoes.* Government use of traditional religious symbols in winter holiday displays produce the most litigation over government use of religious symbols, but other symbols are litigated year-round. Government mottoes containing references to religion are frequent targets. Although the Supreme Court has never actually ruled on the constitutionality of the government's adoption of the national motto "In God We Trust," in *Lynch v. Donnelly* several Justices stated their views that the government's adoption of the motto does not violate the Constitution. *See Lynch*, 465 U.S. at 676 (motto is merely a "reference to our religious heritage"); *id.* at 693 (O'Connor, J., concurring) (motto serves "the legitimate secular purposes of solemnizing public occasions, expressing confidence in the future, and encouraging the recognition of what is worthy of appreciation in society"); *id.* at 716-17 (Brennan, J., dissenting) (motto "In God We Trust" is merely "ceremonial deism," which has "lost through rote repetition any significant religious content." Also, "these references are uniquely suited to serve such wholly secular purposes as solemnizing public occasions, or inspiring commitment to meet some national challenge in a manner that simply could not be fully served in our culture if government were limited to purely non-religious phrases. . . . The practices by which the government has long acknowledged religion are therefore probably necessary to serve certain secular functions, and that necessity, coupled with their long history, gives those practices an essentially secular meaning."). The lower courts have expressly upheld a federal statute requiring the motto "In God We Trust" to be inscribed on coins and currency, *see O'Hair v. Murray*, 588 F.2d 1144 (5th Cir. 1979); *Aronow v. United States*, 432 F.2d 242 (9th Cir. 1970), and have also upheld the constitutionality of the Pledge of Allegiance's reference to God. *See Sherman v. Cmty. Consol. Sch. Dist. 21 of Wheeling Twp.*, 980 F.2d 437 (7th Cir. 1992). *See also ACLU v. Capitol Square Review and Advisory Bd.*, 243 F.3d 289 (6th Cir. 2001) (upholding the constitutionality of Ohio's state motto "With God All Things Are Possible" on the grounds that (1) no reasonable observer would perceive motto to be an endorsement of Christianity, (2) the motto serves a secular legislative purpose by boosting morale and serving as a symbol of a common identity, and (3) the motto has a secular effect because it "merely pays lip service to the puissance of God"). Consider one of the points made in Judge Boyce's dissenting opinion in *Capitol Square*: "When Jesus' key to eternal salvation is lumped in the Ohio statutes with the Buckeye tree and tomato juice, the signal sent is that religion is no more important than those two nice but ultimately inconsequential things. To many, religion is much more important, perhaps the most important force in their lives. I fear that Ohio has given Christianity a crutch it is better left without." *Id.* at 312.

3. *Religious Symbols in Government Insignias.* A final source of litigation involving government use of religious symbols involves the inclusion of religious symbols in government insignias. *See Murray v. Austin*, 947 F.2d 147 (5th Cir. 1991) (holding that the use of Christian cross in city insignia does not violate the Establishment Clause); *Harris v. Zion*, 927 F.2d 1401 (7th Cir. 1991), *cert. denied*, 505 U.S. 1229 (1992) (holding unconstitutional the use of a Latin cross in city insignias); *Friedman v. Bd. of County Comm'rs of Bernalillo*, 781 F.2d 777 (10th Cir. 1985) (en banc), *cert. denied*, 476 U.S. 1169 (1986) (holding unconstitutional county seal that contained the Spanish motto "CON ESTA VENCEMOS" ("With This We Conquer" or "With This We Overcome") over a Latin cross, highlighted by edging and rays of light); *ACLU v. Stow*, 29 F. Supp. 2d 845 (N.D. Ohio 1998) (holding unconstitutional a city seal containing a Christian cross).

4. *The Concept of Ceremonial Deism.* For a comprehensive review of the cases involving what Dean Rostow called "ceremonial deism" — including legislative prayers, public oaths, and religious invocations and mottoes — see Steven B. Epstein, *Rethinking The Constitutionality Of Ceremonial Deism*, 96 COLUM. L. REV. 2083 (1996). Epstein argues that ceremonial deism cannot be reconciled with existing Establishment Clause doctrine, and that the Court "can and should hold most forms of ceremonial deism unconstitutional." *Id.* at 2091.

D. THE PLEDGE OF ALLEGIANCE

Few of the cases cited in this Chapter have generated anything like the visceral reaction to the Ninth Circuit Court of Appeals' ruling regarding the insertion of the words "under God" into the Pledge of Allegiance. In a lawsuit brought by the noncustodial father of a child attending a public elementary school in California, the Ninth Circuit Court of Appeals held unconstitutional a policy mandating the daily recitation of the official Pledge in classrooms throughout the school district. The Ninth Circuit's original opinion in the case also held unconstitutional the 1954 federal statute adding the words "under God" to the original, nonreligious version of the Pledge that had been adopted by Congress in 1942, a holding that was omitted from the final, amended opinion.

The Ninth Circuit's opinion in *Newdow* ignited a virtual firestorm of criticism. Within hours of the opinion's release, President Bush dismissed the decision as "ridiculous." The Democratic Senate majority leader Tom Daschle called the decision "just nuts." The Senate then proceeded to vote 99-0 (Senator Helms was ill) denouncing the court and instructing Senate lawyers to file a brief seeking reversal of the decision. The House of Representatives voted in favor of a similar resolution by a vote of 416-3.

The Supreme Court quickly granted certiorari. Even that decision generated controversy when Justice Scalia was forced to recuse himself after making comments critical of the Ninth Circuit in a public speech. The comments were made during a speech at a Knights of Columbus meeting in Fredericksberg, Virginia. (Coincidentally, the Knights of Columbus were instrumental in getting Congress to add the words "under God" to the Pledge in 1954.) At the meeting, Scalia told his audience that the Ninth Circuit's decision was an example of how courts were misinterpreting the Constitution to "exclude God from the public forums and from public life." *See* Linda Greenhouse, *Supreme Court to Consider Case on "Under God" in Pledge to Flag*, N.Y. TIMES, Oct. 15, 2003, at A1.

In the end, Justice Scalia's recusal may not have mattered. Five Justices on the Supreme Court reversed the Ninth Circuit on standing grounds, holding that although Mr. Newdow satisfied the Article III requirements of standing, he failed to satisfy the prudential standing requirements imposed by the Court to limit its own jurisdiction. Three Justices (who presumably would have been joined by Scalia) would have overturned the Ninth Circuit opinion on the merits of the Establishment Clause issue. Given the procedural nature of the Court's decision, it is highly likely that the Court will see this issue again in the near future. Therefore, although it has now been overturned, the Ninth Circuit opinion is reproduced below to provide some flavor of the debate over the merits of the Establishment Clause claim against the "under God" language in the Pledge. The Supreme Court opinion is reproduced after the Ninth Circuit excerpt.

NEWDOW v. U.S. CONGRESS
292 F.3d 597 (9th Cir. 2002)

GOODWIN, CIRCUIT JUDGE:

Michael Newdow appeals a judgment dismissing his challenge to the constitutionality of the words "under God" in the Pledge of Allegiance to the Flag.
Newdow argues that the addition of these words by a 1954 federal statute to the
previous version of the Pledge of Allegiance (which made no reference to God)
and the daily recitation in the classroom of the Pledge of Allegiance, with the
added words included, by his daughter's public school teacher are violations of
the Establishment Clause of the First Amendment to the United States Constitution.

FACTUAL AND PROCEDURAL BACKGROUND

Newdow is an atheist whose daughter attends public elementary school in the
Elk Grove Unified School District ("EGUSD") in California. In accordance with
state law and a school district rule, EGUSD teachers begin each school day by
leading their students in a recitation of the Pledge of Allegiance ("the Pledge").

The classmates of Newdow's daughter in the EGUSD are led by their teacher
in reciting the Pledge codified in federal law. On June 22, 1942, Congress first
codified the Pledge as "I pledge allegiance to the flag of the United States of
America and to the Republic for which it stands, one Nation indivisible, with liberty and justice for all." On June 14, 1954, Congress amended Section 1972 to
add the words "under God" after the word "Nation." ("1954 Act"). The Pledge is
currently codified as "I pledge allegiance to the Flag of the United States of
America, and to the Republic for which it stands, one nation under God, indivisible, with liberty and justice for all." 4 U.S.C. § 4 (1998).

Newdow does not allege that his daughter's teacher or school district requires
his daughter to participate in reciting the Pledge.[3] Rather, he claims that his
daughter is injured when she is compelled to "watch and listen as her state-
employed teacher in her state-run school leads her classmates in a ritual proclaiming that there is a God, and that our's [sic] is 'one nation under God.'"

DISCUSSION

D. Establishment Clause

Over the last three decades, the Supreme Court has used three interrelated
tests to analyze alleged violations of the Establishment Clause in the realm of
public education: the three-prong test set forth in *Lemon v. Kurtzman*; the
"endorsement" test, first articulated by Justice O'Connor in her concurring
opinion in *Lynch* [*v. Donnelly*], and later adopted by a majority of the Court in

---

[3] Compelling students to recite the Pledge was held to be a First Amendment violation in *West
Virginia State Board of Education v. Barnette* [see Text Chapter 9]. *Barnette* was decided before the
1954 Act added the words "under God" to the Pledge.

County of Allegheny v. ACLU; and the "coercion" test first used by the Court in *Lee* [*v. Weisman*].

We are free to apply any or all of the three tests, and to invalidate any measure that fails any one of them. The Supreme Court has not repudiated *Lemon*; in *Santa Fe* [*Independent School District v. Doe*], it found that the application of each of the three tests provided an independent ground for invalidating the statute at issue in that case; and in *Lee*, the Court invalidated the policy solely on the basis of the coercion test. Although this court has typically applied the *Lemon* test to alleged Establishment Clause violations, we are not required to apply it if a practice fails one of the other tests. Nevertheless, for purposes of completeness, we will analyze the school district policy and the 1954 Act under all three tests.

We first consider whether the 1954 Act and the EGUSD's policy of teacher-led Pledge recitation survive the endorsement test. The magistrate judge found that "the ceremonial reference to God in the pledge does not convey endorsement of particular religious beliefs." Supreme Court precedent does not support that conclusion.

In the context of the Pledge, the statement that the United States is a nation "under God" is an endorsement of religion. It is a profession of a religious belief, namely, a belief in monotheism. The recitation that ours is a nation "under God" is not a mere acknowledgment that many Americans believe in a deity. Nor is it merely descriptive of the undeniable historical significance of religion in the founding of the Republic. Rather, the phrase "one nation under God" in the context of the Pledge is normative. To recite the Pledge is not to describe the United States; instead, it is to swear allegiance to the values for which the flag stands: unity, indivisibility, liberty, justice, and — since 1954 — monotheism. The text of the official Pledge, codified in federal law, impermissibly takes a position with respect to the surely religious question of the existence and identity of God. A profession that we are a nation "under God" is identical, for Establishment Clause purposes, to a profession that we are a nation "under Jesus," a nation "under Vishnu," a nation "under Zeus," or a nation "under no god," because none of these professions can be neutral with respect to religion. "[T]he government must pursue a course of complete neutrality toward religion." *Wallace*, 472 U.S. at 60. Furthermore, the school district's practice of teacher-led recitation of the Pledge aims to inculcate in students a respect for the ideals set forth in the Pledge, and thus amounts to state endorsement of these ideals. Although students cannot be forced to participate in recitation of the Pledge, the school district is nonetheless conveying a message of state endorsement of a religious belief when it requires public school teachers to recite, and lead the recitation of, the current form of the Pledge.

The Supreme Court recognized the normative and ideological nature of the Pledge in *Barnette*. There, the Court held unconstitutional a school district's wartime policy of punishing students who refused to recite the Pledge and salute the flag. The Court noted that the school district was compelling the students "to declare a belief," and "requir[ing] the individual to communicate by word and sign his acceptance of the political ideas [the flag] . . . bespeaks." "[T]he compulsory flag salute and pledge requires affirmation of a belief and an attitude of mind." The Court emphasized that the political concepts articulated in the Pledge were idealistic, not descriptive: " '[L]iberty and justice for all,' if it must be accepted as descriptive of the present order rather than an ideal, might to some seem an overstatement." The Court concluded that: "If there is any fixed star in our constitutional constellation, it is that no official, high or petty, can prescribe what shall be orthodox in politics, nationalism, religion, or other matters of opinion or force citizens to confess by word or act their faith therein."

The Pledge, as currently codified, is an impermissible government endorsement of religion because it sends a message to unbelievers "that they are outsiders, not full members of the political community, and an accompanying message to adherents that they are insiders, favored members of the political community." *Lynch* (O'Connor, J., concurring). Justice Kennedy, in his dissent in *Allegheny*, agreed:

> [B]y statute, the Pledge of Allegiance to the Flag describes the United States as "one nation under God." To be sure, no one is obligated to recite this phrase, . . . but it borders on sophistry to suggest that the reasonable atheist would not feel less than a full member of the political community every time his fellow Americans recited, as part of their expression of patriotism and love for country, a phrase he believed to be false.

Allegheny (Kennedy, J., dissenting). Consequently, the policy and the Act fail the endorsement test.

Similarly, the policy and the Act fail the coercion test. Just as in *Lee*, the policy and the Act place students in the untenable position of choosing between participating in an exercise with religious content or protesting. As the Court observed with respect to the graduation prayer in that case: "What to most believers may seem nothing more than a reasonable request that the nonbeliever respect their religious practices, in a school context may appear to the nonbeliever or dissenter to be an attempt to employ the machinery of the State to enforce a religious orthodoxy." *Lee*. Although the defendants argue that the religious content of "one nation under God" is minimal, to an atheist or a believer in certain non-Judeo-Christian religions or philosophies, it may reasonably appear to be an attempt to enforce a "religious orthodoxy" of monotheism, and is therefore impermissible. The coercive effect of this policy is particularly pronounced in the school setting given the age and impressionability of schoolchildren, and their understanding that they are required to adhere to the norms set by their school, their teacher and their fellow students.[8] Furthermore, under *Lee*, the fact that students are not required to par-

---

[8] The "subtle and indirect" social pressure which permeates the classroom also renders more acute the message sent to non-believing schoolchildren that they are outsiders. *See Lee*, 505 U.S. at

ticipate is no basis for distinguishing *Barnette* from the case at bar because, even without a recitation requirement for each child, the mere fact that a pupil is required to listen every day to the statement "one nation under God" has a coercive effect. The coercive effect of the Act is apparent from its context and legislative history, which indicate that the Act was designed to result in the daily recitation of the words "under God" in school classrooms. President Eisenhower, during the Act's signing ceremony, stated: "From this day forward, the millions of our school children will daily proclaim in every city and town, every village and rural schoolhouse, the dedication of our Nation and our people to the Almighty." 100 Cong. Rec. 8618 (1954) (statement of Sen. Ferguson incorporating signing statement of President Eisenhower). Therefore, the policy and the Act fail the coercion test.[10]

Finally we turn to the *Lemon* test, the first prong of which asks if the challenged policy has a secular purpose. Historically, the primary purpose of the 1954 Act was to advance religion, in conflict with the first prong of the *Lemon* test. The federal defendants "do not dispute that the words 'under God' were intended" "to recognize a Supreme Being," at a time when the government was publicly inveighing against atheistic communism. Nonetheless, the federal defendants argue that the Pledge must be considered as a whole when assessing whether it has a secular purpose. They claim that the Pledge has the secular purpose of "solemnizing public occasions, expressing confidence in the future, and encouraging the recognition of what is worthy of appreciation in society." *Lynch*.

The flaw in defendants' argument is that it looks at the text of the Pledge "as a whole," and glosses over the 1954 Act. The problem with this approach is apparent when one considers the Court's analysis in *Wallace*. There, the Court struck down Alabama's statute mandating a moment of silence for "meditation or voluntary prayer" not because the final version "as a whole" lacked a primary secular purpose, but because the state legislature had amended the statute specifically and solely to add the words "or voluntary prayer."

By analogy to *Wallace*, we apply the purpose prong of the *Lemon* test to the amendment that added the words "under God" to the Pledge, not to the Pledge in its final version. As was the case with the amendment to the Alabama statute in *Wallace*, the legislative history of the 1954 Act reveals that the Act's *sole* pur-

---

592-93 (stating that "the risk of indirect coercion" from prayer exercises is particularly "pronounced" in elementary and secondary public school because students are subjected to peer pressure and public pressure which is "as real as any overt compulsion").

[10] In *Aronow v. United States*, 432 F.2d 242 (9th Cir. 1970), this court, without reaching the question of standing, upheld the inscription of the phrase "In God We Trust" on our coins and currency. *But cf. Wooley v. Maynard*, 430 U.S. 705, 722 (1977) (Rehnquist, J., dissenting) (stating that the majority's holding leads logically to the conclusion that "In God We Trust" is an unconstitutional affirmation of belief). In any event, *Aronow* is distinguishable in many ways from the present case. The most important distinction is that school children are not coerced into reciting or otherwise actively led to participating in an endorsement of the markings on the money in circulation.

pose was to advance religion, in order to differentiate the United States from nations under communist rule. "[T]he First Amendment requires that a statute must be invalidated if it is entirely motivated by a purpose to advance religion." As the legislative history of the 1954 Act sets forth:

> At this moment of our history the principles underlying our American Government and the American way of life are under attack by a system whose philosophy is at direct odds with our own. Our American Government is founded on the concept of the individuality and the dignity of the human being. Underlying this concept is the belief that the human person is important because he was created by God and endowed by Him with certain inalienable rights which no civil authority may usurp. The inclusion of God in our pledge therefore would further acknowledge the dependence of our people and our Government upon the moral directions of the Creator. At the same time it would serve to deny the atheistic and materialistic concepts of communism with its attendant subservience of the individual.

H.R. Rep. No. 83-1693, at 1-2 (1954), *reprinted in* 1954 U.S.C.C.A.N. 2339, 2340. This language reveals that the purpose of the 1954 Act was to take a position on the question of theism, namely, to support the existence and moral authority of God, while "deny[ing] . . . atheistic and materialistic concepts." Such a purpose runs counter to the Establishment Clause, which prohibits the government's endorsement or advancement not only of one particular religion at the expense of other religions, but also of religion at the expense of atheism.

In language that attempts to prevent future constitutional challenges, the sponsors of the 1954 Act expressly disclaimed a religious purpose. "This is not an act establishing a religion. . . . A distinction must be made between the existence of a religion as an institution and a belief in the sovereignty of God. The phrase 'under God' recognizes only the guidance of God in our national affairs." H.R.Rep. No. 83-1693, at 3 (1954), *reprinted in* 1954 U.S.C.C.A.N. 2339, 2341-42. This alleged distinction is irrelevant for constitutional purposes. The Act's affirmation of "a belief in the sovereignty of God" and its recognition of "the guidance of God" are endorsements by the government of religious beliefs. The Establishment Clause is not limited to "religion as an institution"; this is clear from cases such as *Santa Fe*, where the Court struck down student-initiated and student-led prayer at high school football games. The Establishment Clause guards not only against the establishment of "religion as an institution," but also against the endorsement of religious ideology by the government. Because the Act fails the purpose prong of *Lemon*, we need not examine the other prongs.

Similarly, the school district policy also fails the *Lemon* test. Although it survives the first prong of *Lemon* because, as even Newdow concedes, the school district had the secular purpose of fostering patriotism in enacting the policy, the policy fails the second prong. [T]he second *Lemon* prong asks "whether the challenged government action is sufficiently likely to be perceived by adherents of the controlling denominations as an endorsement, and by the nonadherents as a disapproval, of their individual religious choices." Given the age and impressionability of schoolchildren, as discussed above, particularly within the confined environment of the classroom, the policy is highly likely to convey an impermissible message of endorsement to some and disapproval to others of their beliefs regarding the existence of a monotheistic God. Therefore the policy fails the effects prong of *Lemon*, and fails the *Lemon* test. In sum, both the policy and the Act fail the *Lemon* test as well as the endorsement and coercion tests.[12]

In conclusion, we hold that (1) the 1954 Act adding the words "under God" to the Pledge, and (2) EGUSD's policy and practice of teacher-led recitation of the Pledge, with the added words included, violate the Establishment Clause.

FERNANDEZ, CIRCUIT JUDGE, concurring and dissenting:

[Judge Fernandez concurred in the majority's various jurisdictional rulings, then dissented on the Establishment Clause issue.]

We are asked to hold that inclusion of the phrase "under God" in this nation's Pledge of Allegiance violates the religion clauses of the Constitution of the United States. We should do no such thing. We should, instead, recognize that those clauses were not designed to drive religious expression out of public thought; they were written to avoid discrimination.

We can run through the litany of tests and concepts which have floated to the surface from time to time. Were we to do so, the one that appeals most to me, the one I think to be correct, is the concept that what the religion clauses of the First Amendment require is neutrality; that those clauses are, in effect, an early kind of equal protection provision and assure that government will neither discriminate for nor discriminate against a religion or religions. But, legal world abstractions and ruminations aside, when all is said and done, the danger that "under God" in our Pledge of Allegiance will tend to bring about a theocracy or suppress somebody's beliefs is so minuscule as to be de minimis. The danger that phrase presents to our First Amendment freedoms is picayune at most.

Some, who rather choke on the notion of de minimis, have resorted to the euphemism "ceremonial deism." *See, e.g., Lynch* (Brennan, J., dissenting). But whatever it is called (I care not), it comes to this: such phrases as "In God We Trust," or "under God" have no tendency to establish a religion in this country or to suppress anyone's exercise, or non-exercise, of religion, except in the fevered eye of persons who most fervently would like to drive all tincture of reli-

---

[12] We recognize that the Supreme Court has occasionally commented in dicta that the presence of "one nation under God" in the Pledge of Allegiance is constitutional. *See Allegheny*, 492 U.S. at 602-03; *Lynch*, 465 U.S. at 676; *id.* at 693 (O'Connor, J., concurring); *Abington Sch. Dist. v. Schempp*, 374 U.S. 203, 303-04 (1963) (Brennan, J., concurring); *id.* at 306-08 (Goldberg, J., joined by Harlan, J., concurring); *Engel*, 370 U.S. at 435 n. 21. However, the Court has never been presented with the question directly, and has always clearly refrained from deciding it. Accordingly, it has never applied any of the three tests to the Act or to any school policy regarding the recitation of the Pledge. That task falls to us, although the final word, as always, remains with the Supreme Court.

gion out of the public life of our polity. Those expressions have not caused any real harm of that sort over the years since 1791, and are not likely to do so in the future. As I see it, that is not because they are drained of meaning. Rather, as I have already indicated, it is because their tendency to establish religion (or affect its exercise) is exiguous.

My reading of the stelliscript suggests that upon Newdow's theory of our Constitution, accepted by my colleagues today, we will soon find ourselves prohibited from using our album of patriotic songs in many public settings. "God Bless America" and "America the Beautiful" will be gone for sure, and while use of the first three stanzas of the Star Spangled Banner will still be permissible, we will be precluded from straying into the fourth. And currency beware! Judges can accept those results if they limit themselves to elements and tests, while failing to look at the good sense and principles that animated those tests in the first place. But they do so at the price of removing a vestige of the awe we all must feel at the immenseness of the universe and our own small place within it, as well as the wonder we must feel at the good fortune of our country. That will cool the febrile nerves of a few at the cost of removing the healthy glow conferred upon many citizens when the forbidden verses, or phrases, are uttered, read, or seen.

In short, I cannot accept the eliding of the simple phrase "under God" from our Pledge of Allegiance, when it is obvious that its tendency to establish religion in this country or to interfere with the free exercise (or non-exercise) of religion is de minimis.[9]

NOTE

The Revised Newdow Opinion. On February 28, 2003, the full Ninth Circuit Court of Appeals denied the defendants' motion for a rehearing en banc of the three-judge panel's June 26, 2002, decision. *Newdow v. U.S. Congress*, 328 F.3d 466 (9th Cir. 2003) [*Newdow II*]. At the same time, the original *Newdow* panel issued an amended opinion. In his lawsuit, Mr. Newdow alleged that two government actions violate the Establishment Clause: (1) the federal statute adding the words "under God" to the official Pledge, and (2) the policy mandating the daily recitation of the official Pledge in classrooms throughout the public school district in which Mr. Newdow's daughter attends elementary school. *See Newdow I*, 292 F.3d at 600. In its original opinion, the Ninth Circuit panel held unconstitutional both the federal statute and local school district policy. *Id.* at 612. In its amended opinion, the panel held the school district policy unconstitutional but declined to reach the question regarding the constitutionality of the

---

[9] Lest I be misunderstood, I must emphasize that to decide this case it is not necessary to say, and I do not say, that there is such a thing as a de minimis constitutional violation. What I do say is that the de minimis tendency of the Pledge to establish a religion or to interfere with its free exercise is no constitutional violation at all.

federal statute. *Newdow II*, 328 F.3d at 490. In addition to narrowing its actual holding, the panel also omitted from its amended opinion some of the earlier opinion's discussion of the constitutionality of the federal statute adding the words "under God" to the official Pledge. *Compare Newdow II*, 328 F.3d at 489-90 (discussing the court's holding regarding the school district policy) with *Newdow I*, 292 F.3d at 609-12 (discussing the court's holding regarding the federal Pledge statute).

The amended opinion does not, however, ignore the effects of the federal statute. Although the court omits from its amended opinion some of the original opinion's discussion of the unconstitutionality of the 1954 statute adding the words "under God" in the official Pledge, the court's pointed description of the unconstitutional religious effect of that statute remains in the amended opinion. *See Newdow II*, 328 F.3d at 487 ("A profession that we are a nation 'under God' is identical, for Establishment Clause purposes, to a profession that we are a nation 'under Zeus,' or a nation 'under no God,' because none of these professions can be neutral with respect to religion."). For this reason, the Ninth Circuit judges who dissented from the denial of the rehearing en banc describe the amended *Newdow* opinion as "differ[ing] little from *Newdow I* in its central holding." *Newdow II*, at 473 (O'Scannlain, J., dissenting from the denial of rehearing en banc). As one of the en banc dissenters noted, although the amended opinion avoided the "technical question of the constitutionality of the 1954 Act," the amended opinion "necessarily *implies* that both an Act of Congress and a California law are unconstitutional." *Id.*

ELK GROVE UNIFIED SCHOOL DISTRICT v. NEWDOW
542 U.S. 1 (2004)

JUSTICE STEVENS delivered the opinion of the Court.

Each day elementary school teachers in the Elk Grove Unified School District (School District) lead their classes in a group recitation of the Pledge of Allegiance. Respondent, Michael A. Newdow, is an atheist whose daughter participates in that daily exercise. Because the Pledge contains the words "under God," he views the School District's policy as a religious indoctrination of his child that violates the First Amendment. A divided panel of the Court of Appeals for the Ninth Circuit agreed with Newdow. In light of the obvious importance of that decision, we granted certiorari to review the First Amendment issue and, preliminarily, the question whether Newdow has standing to invoke the jurisdiction of the federal courts. We conclude that Newdow lacks standing and therefore reverse the Court of Appeals' decision.

II

In March 2000, Newdow filed suit in the United States District Court for the Eastern District of California against the United States Congress, the President of the United States, the State of California, and the Elk Grove Unified School

District and its superintendent. At the time of filing, Newdow's daughter was enrolled in kindergarten in the Elk Grove Unified School District and participated in the daily recitation of the Pledge. Styled as a mandamus action, the complaint explains that Newdow is an atheist who was ordained more than 20 years ago in a ministry that "espouses the religious philosophy that the true and eternal bonds of righteousness and virtue stem from reason rather than mythology." The complaint seeks a declaration that the 1954 Act's addition of the words "under God" violated the Establishment and Free Exercise Clauses of the United States Constitution, as well as an injunction against the School District's policy requiring daily recitation of the Pledge. It alleges that Newdow has standing to sue on his own behalf and on behalf of his daughter as "next friend."

III

In every federal case, the party bringing the suit must establish standing to prosecute the action. "In essence the question of standing is whether the litigant is entitled to have the court decide the merits of the dispute or of particular issues." The standing requirement is born partly of "'an idea, which is more than an intuition but less than a rigorous and explicit theory, about the constitutional and prudential limits to the powers of an unelected, unrepresentative judiciary in our kind of government.'" *Allen v. Wright*, 468 U.S. 737, 750 (1984).

The command to guard jealously and exercise rarely our power to make constitutional pronouncements requires strictest adherence when matters of great national significance are at stake. Even in cases concededly within our jurisdiction under Article III, we abide by "a series of rules under which [we have] avoided passing upon a large part of all the constitutional questions pressed upon [us] for decision." *Ashwander v. TVA,* 297 U.S. 288, 346 (1936) (Brandeis, J., concurring). Always we must balance "the heavy obligation to exercise jurisdiction," *Colorado River Water Conservation Dist. v. United States*, 424 U.S. 800, 820 (1976), against the "deeply rooted" commitment "not to pass on questions of constitutionality" unless adjudication of the constitutional issue is necessary, *Spector Motor Service, Inc. v. McLaughlin*, 323 U.S. 101, 105 (1944).

Consistent with these principles, our standing jurisprudence contains two strands: Article III standing, which enforces the Constitution's case or controversy requirement, and prudential standing, which embodies "judicially self-imposed limits on the exercise of federal jurisdiction." The Article III limitations are familiar: The plaintiff must show that the conduct of which he complains has caused him to suffer an "injury in fact" that a favorable judgment will redress. Although we have not exhaustively defined the prudential dimensions of the standing doctrine, we have explained that prudential standing encompasses "the general prohibition on a litigant's raising another person's legal rights, the rule barring adjudication of generalized grievances more appropriately addressed in the representative branches, and the requirement that a plaintiff's complaint fall within the zone of interests protected by the law invoked." *Allen*, 468 U.S., at 751. "Without such limitations — closely related to Art. III concerns but essentially matters of judicial self-governance — the courts would be called upon to decide abstract questions of wide public significance even though other governmental institutions may be more competent to address the questions and even though judicial intervention may be unnecessary to protect individual rights." *Warth [v. Seldin]*, 422 U.S., at 500.

One of the principal areas in which this Court has customarily declined to intervene is the realm of domestic relations. Long ago we observed that "[t]he whole subject of the domestic relations of husband and wife, parent and child, belongs to the laws of the States and not to the laws of the United States." *In re Burrus,* 136 U.S. 586, 593-594 (1890). So strong is our deference to state law in this area that we have recognized a "domestic relations exception" that "divests the federal courts of power to issue divorce, alimony, and child custody decrees." *Ankenbrandt v. Richards,* 504 U.S. 689, 703 (1992). We have also acknowledged that it might be appropriate for the federal courts to decline to hear a case involving "elements of the domestic relationship," *id.*, at 705, even when divorce, alimony, or child custody is not strictly at issue.

Thus, while rare instances arise in which it is necessary to answer a substantial federal question that transcends or exists apart from the family law issue, *see, e.g., Palmore v. Sidoti,* 466 U.S. 429, 432-434 (1984), in general it is appropriate for the federal courts to leave delicate issues of domestic relations to the state courts.

As explained briefly above, the extent of the standing problem raised by the domestic relations issues in this case was not apparent until August 5, 2002, when Banning filed her motion for leave to intervene or dismiss the complaint following the Court of Appeals' initial decision. At that time, the child's custody was governed by a February 6, 2002, order of the California Superior Court. That order provided that Banning had "'*sole* legal custody as to the rights and responsibilities to make decisions relating to the health, education and welfare of'" her daughter. *Newdow II,* 313 F.3d, at 502. The order stated that the two parents should "'consult with one another on substantial decisions relating to'" the child's "'psychological and educational needs,'" but it authorized Banning to "'exercise legal control'" if the parents could not reach "'mutual agreement.'" *Ibid.*

That family court order was the controlling document at the time of the Court of Appeals' standing decision. After the Court of Appeals ruled, however, the Superior Court held another conference regarding the child's custody. At a hearing on September 11, 2003, the Superior Court announced that the parents have "joint legal custody," but that Banning "makes the final decisions if the two . . . disagree." App. 127-128.

Newdow contends that despite Banning's final authority, he retains "an unrestricted right to inculcate in his daughter — free from governmental interference — the atheistic beliefs he finds persuasive." The difficulty with that argument is that Newdow's rights, as in many cases touching upon family relations, cannot be viewed in isolation. This case concerns not merely Newdow's interest in inculcating his child with his views on religion, but also the rights of the child's mother as a parent generally and under the Superior Court orders specifically. And most important, it implicates the interests of a young child who finds herself at the center of a highly public debate over her custody, the propriety of a widespread national ritual, and the meaning of our Constitution.

The interests of the affected persons in this case are in many respects antagonistic. Of course, legal disharmony in family relations is not uncommon, and in many instances that disharmony poses no bar to federal-court adjudication of proper federal questions. What makes this case different is that Newdow's standing derives entirely from his relationship with his daughter, but he lacks the right to litigate as her next friend. In marked contrast to our case law on *jus tertii*, *see, e.g., Singleton v. Wulff,* 428 U.S. 106, 113-118 (1976) (plurality opinion), the interests of this parent and this child are not parallel and, indeed, are potentially in conflict.[7]

Nothing that either Banning or the School Board has done, however, impairs Newdow's right to instruct his daughter in his religious views. Instead, Newdow . . . wishes to forestall his daughter's exposure to religious ideas that her mother, who wields a form of veto power, endorses, and to use his parental status to challenge the influences to which his daughter may be exposed in school when he and Banning disagree. The California cases simply do not stand for the proposition that Newdow has a right to dictate to others what they may and may not say to his child respecting religion. The cases speak not at all to the problem of a parent seeking to reach outside the private parent-child sphere to restrain the acts of a third party. A next friend surely could exercise such a right, but the Superior Court's order has deprived Newdow of that status.

In our view, it is improper for the federal courts to entertain a claim by a plaintiff whose standing to sue is founded on family law rights that are in dispute when prosecution of the lawsuit may have an adverse effect on the person who is the source of the plaintiff's claimed standing. When hard questions of domestic relations are sure to affect the outcome, the prudent course is for the federal court to stay its hand rather than reach out to resolve a weighty question of federal constitutional law. There is a vast difference between Newdow's right to communicate with his child — which both California law and the First Amendment recognize — and his claimed right to shield his daughter from influences to which she is exposed in school despite the terms of the custody order. We conclude that, having been deprived under California law of the right

---

[7] "There are good and sufficient reasons for th[e] prudential limitation on standing when rights of third parties are implicated — the avoidance of the adjudication of rights which those not before the Court may not wish to assert, and the assurance that the most effective advocate of the rights at issue is present to champion them." *Duke Power Co. v. Carolina Environmental Study Group, Inc.,* 438 U.S. 59, 80 (1978). Banning tells us that her daughter has no objection to the Pledge, and we are mindful in cases such as this that "children themselves have constitutionally protectible interests." *Wisconsin v. Yoder* [*infra* Chapter 11] (Douglas, J., dissenting). In a fundamental respect, "[i]t is the future of the student, not the future of the parents," that is at stake.

to sue as next friend, Newdow lacks prudential standing to bring this suit in federal court.

The judgment of the Court of Appeals is reversed.

CHIEF JUSTICE REHNQUIST, with whom JUSTICE O'CONNOR joins, and with whom JUSTICE THOMAS joins as to Part I, concurring in the judgment.

I

[The Chief Justice argued that Mr. Newdow had standing to raise his constitutional challenge.]

We have, in the past, judicially self-imposed clear limits on the exercise of federal jurisdiction. In contrast, here is the Court's new prudential standing principle: "[I]t is improper for the federal courts to entertain a claim by a plaintiff whose standing to sue is founded on family law rights that are in dispute when prosecution of the lawsuit may have an adverse effect on the person who is the source of the plaintiff's claimed standing." The Court loosely bases this novel prudential standing limitation on the domestic relations exception to diversity-of-citizenship jurisdiction pursuant to 28 U.S.C. § 1332, the abstention doctrine, and criticisms of the Court of Appeals' construction of California state law, coupled with the prudential standing prohibition on a litigant's raising another person's legal rights.

The domestic relations exception is not a prudential limitation on our federal jurisdiction. It is a limiting construction of the statute defining federal diversity jurisdiction, which "divests the federal courts of power to issue divorce, alimony, and child custody decrees." This case does not involve diversity jurisdiction, and respondent does not ask this Court to issue a divorce, alimony, or child custody decree. Instead it involves a substantial federal question about the constitutionality of the School District's conducting the Pledge ceremony, which is the source of our jurisdiction. Therefore, the domestic relations exception to diversity jurisdiction forms no basis for denying standing to respondent.

II

As pointed out by the Court, California law requires public elementary schools to "conduc[t] . . . appropriate patriotic exercises" at the beginning of the schoolday, and notes that the "giving of the Pledge of Allegiance to the Flag of the United States of America shall satisfy the requirements of this section." The School District complies with this requirement by instructing that "[e]ach elementary school class recite the [P]ledge of [A]llegiance to the [F]lag once each day." Students who object on religious (or other) grounds may abstain from the recitation. *West Virginia Bd. of Ed. v. Barnette,* 319 U.S. 624, 642 (1943) (holding that the government may not compel school students to recite the Pledge).

Notwithstanding the voluntary nature of the School District policy, the Court of Appeals, by a divided vote, held that the policy violates the Establishment Clause of the First Amendment because it "impermissibly coerces a religious act." To reach this result, the court relied primarily on our decision in *Lee v. Weisman*.

I do not believe that the phrase "under God" in the Pledge converts its recital into a "religious exercise" of the sort described in *Lee*. Instead, it is a declaration of belief in allegiance and loyalty to the United States flag and the Republic that it represents. The phrase "under God" is in no sense a prayer, nor an endorsement of any religion, but a simple recognition of the fact noted in H.R. Rep. No. 1693, at 2: "From the time of our earliest history our peoples and our institutions have reflected the traditional concept that our Nation was founded on a fundamental belief in God." Reciting the Pledge, or listening to others recite it, is a patriotic exercise, not a religious one; participants promise fidelity to our flag and our Nation, not to any particular God, faith, or church.

[handwritten margin note: History Argument]

There is no doubt that respondent is sincere in his atheism and rejection of a belief in God. But the mere fact that he disagrees with this part of the Pledge does not give him a veto power over the decision of the public schools that willing participants should pledge allegiance to the flag in the manner prescribed by Congress. There may be others who disagree, not with the phrase "under God," but with the phrase "with liberty and justice for all." But surely that would not give such objectors the right to veto the holding of such a ceremony by those willing to participate. Only if it can be said that the phrase "under God" somehow tends to the establishment of a religion in violation of the First Amendment can respondent's claim succeed, where one based on objections to "with liberty and justice for all" fails. Our cases have broadly interpreted this phrase, but none have gone anywhere near as far as the decision of the Court of Appeals in this case. The recital, in a patriotic ceremony pledging allegiance to the flag and to the Nation, of the descriptive phrase "under God" cannot possibly lead to the establishment of a religion, or anything like it.

[handwritten margin note: Slippery Slope]

When courts extend constitutional prohibitions beyond their previously recognized limit, they may restrict democratic choices made by public bodies. Here, Congress prescribed a Pledge of Allegiance, the State of California required patriotic observances in its schools, and the School District chose to comply by requiring teacher-led recital of the Pledge of Allegiance by willing students. Thus, we have three levels of popular government — the national, the state, and the local — collaborating to produce the Elk Grove ceremony. The Constitution only requires that schoolchildren be entitled to abstain from the ceremony if they chose to do so. To give the parent of such a child a sort of "heckler's veto" over a patriotic ceremony willingly participated in by other students, simply because the Pledge of Allegiance contains the descriptive phrase "under God," is an unwarranted extension of the Establishment Clause, an extension which would have the unfortunate effect of prohibiting a commendable patriotic observance.

JUSTICE O'CONNOR, concurring in the judgment.

The Court has permitted government, in some instances, to refer to or commemorate religion in public life. *See, e.g., Pinette; Allegheny; Lynch; Marsh v.*

Chambers. While the Court's explicit rationales have varied, my own has been consistent; I believe that although these references speak in the language of religious belief, they are more properly understood as employing the idiom for essentially secular purposes. One such purpose is to commemorate the role of religion in our history. In my view, some references to religion in public life and government are the inevitable consequence of our Nation's origins. Just as the Court has refused to ignore changes in the religious composition of our Nation in explaining the modern scope of the Religion Clauses, *see, e.g., Wallace* [*v. Jaffree*] at 52-54 (even if the Religion Clauses were originally meant only to forestall intolerance between Christian sects, they now encompass all forms of religious conscience), it should not deny that our history has left its mark on our national traditions. It is unsurprising that a Nation founded by religious refugees and dedicated to religious freedom should find references to divinity in its symbols, songs, mottoes, and oaths. Eradicating such references would sever ties to a history that sustains this Nation even today.

Facially religious references can serve other valuable purposes in public life as well. Twenty years ago, I wrote that such references "serve, in the only ways reasonably possible in our culture, the legitimate secular purposes of solemnizing public occasions, expressing confidence in the future, and encouraging the recognition of what is worthy of appreciation in society." *Lynch* ([O'CONNOR, J.,] concurring opinion). For centuries, we have marked important occasions or pronouncements with references to God and invocations of divine assistance. Such references can serve to solemnize an occasion instead of to invoke divine provenance. The reasonable observer discussed above, fully aware of our national history and the origins of such practices, would not perceive these acknowledgments as signifying a government endorsement of any specific religion, or even of religion over nonreligion.

There are no *de minimis* violations of the Constitution — no constitutional harms so slight that the courts are obliged to ignore them. Given the values that the Establishment Clause was meant to serve, however, I believe that government can, in a discrete category of cases, acknowledge or refer to the divine without offending the Constitution. This category of "ceremonial deism" most clearly encompasses such things as the national motto ("In God We Trust"), religious references in traditional patriotic songs such as the Star-Spangled Banner, and the words with which the Marshal of this Court opens each of its sessions ("God save the United States and this honorable Court"). These references are not minor trespasses upon the Establishment Clause to which I turn a blind eye. Instead, their history, character, and context prevent them from being constitutional violations at all.

This case requires us to determine whether the appearance of the phrase "under God" in the Pledge of Allegiance constitutes an instance of such ceremonial deism. Although it is a close question, I conclude that it does, based on my evaluation of the following four factors.

History and Ubiquity

The constitutional value of ceremonial deism turns on a shared understanding of its legitimate nonreligious purposes. That sort of understanding can exist only when a given practice has been in place for a significant portion of the Nation's history, and when it is observed by enough persons that it can fairly be called ubiquitous. By contrast, novel or uncommon references to religion can more easily be perceived as government endorsements because the reasonable observer cannot be presumed to be fully familiar with their origins. As a result, in examining whether a given practice constitutes an instance of ceremonial deism, its "history and ubiquity" will be of great importance. As I explained in *Allegheny*:

> "Under the endorsement test, the 'history and ubiquity' of a practice is relevant not because it creates an 'artificial exception' from that test. On the contrary, the 'history and ubiquity' of a practice is relevant because it provides part of the context in which a reasonable observer evaluates whether a challenged governmental practice conveys a message of endorsement of religion."

Fifty years have passed since the words "under God" were added, a span of time that is not inconsiderable given the relative youth of our Nation. In that time, the Pledge has become, alongside the singing of the Star-Spangled Banner, our most routine ceremonial act of patriotism; countless schoolchildren recite it daily, and their religious heterogeneity reflects that of the Nation as a whole. As a result, the Pledge and the context in which it is employed are familiar and nearly inseparable in the public mind. No reasonable observer could have been surprised to learn the words of the Pledge, or that petitioner school district has a policy of leading its students in daily recitation of the Pledge.

It cannot be doubted that "no one acquires a vested or protected right in violation of the Constitution by long use, even when that span of time covers our entire national existence and indeed predates it. Yet an unbroken practice . . . is not something to be lightly cast aside." *Walz*. And the history of a given practice is all the more relevant when the practice has been employed pervasively without engendering significant controversy. In *Lynch*, where we evaluated the constitutionality of a town Christmas display that included a creche, we found relevant to the endorsement question the fact that the display had "apparently caused no political divisiveness prior to the filing of this lawsuit" despite its use for over 40 years. Similarly, in the 50 years that the Pledge has been recited as it is now, by millions of children, this was, at the time of its filing, only the third reported case of which I am aware to challenge it as an impermissible establishment of religion. The citizens of this Nation have been neither timid nor unimaginative in challenging government practices as forbidden "establishments" of religion. Given the vigor and creativity of such challenges, I find it telling that so little ire has been directed at the Pledge.

Absence of worship or prayer

"[O]ne of the greatest dangers to the freedom of the individual to worship in his own way [lies] in the Government's placing its official stamp of approval upon one particular kind of prayer or one particular form of religious services." *Engel v. Vitale.* Because of this principle, only in the most extraordinary circumstances could actual worship or prayer be defended as ceremonial deism. We have upheld only one such prayer against Establishment Clause challenge, and it was supported by an extremely long and unambiguous history. *See Marsh v. Chambers.* Any statement that has as its purpose placing the speaker or listener in a penitent state of mind, or that is intended to create a spiritual communion or invoke divine aid, strays from the legitimate secular purposes of solemnizing an event and recognizing a shared religious history. *Santa Fe Independent School Dist. v. Doe.*

Of course, any statement *can* be imbued by a speaker or listener with the qualities of prayer. But, as I have explained, the relevant viewpoint is that of a reasonable observer, fully cognizant of the history, ubiquity, and context of the practice in question. Such an observer could not conclude that reciting the Pledge, including the phrase "under God," constitutes an instance of worship. I know of no religion that incorporates the Pledge into its canon, nor one that would count the Pledge as a meaningful expression of religious faith. Even if taken literally, the phrase is merely descriptive; it purports only to identify the United States as a Nation subject to divine authority. That cannot be seen as a serious invocation of God or as an expression of individual submission to divine authority. *Cf. Engel* (describing prayer as "a solemn avowal of faith and supplication for the blessing of the Almighty"). A reasonable observer would note that petitioner school district's policy of Pledge recitation appears under the heading of "Patriotic Exercises," and the California law which it implements refers to "appropriate patriotic exercises." Cal. Educ. Code § 52720. Petitioner school district also employs teachers, not chaplains or religious instructors, to lead its students' exercise; this serves as a further indication that it does not treat the Pledge as a prayer. *Cf. Lee v. Weisman* (reasoning that a graduation benediction could not be construed as a *de minimis* religious exercise without offending the rabbi who offered it).

It is true that some of the legislators who voted to add the phrase "under God" to the Pledge may have done so in an attempt to attach to it an overtly religious message. *See* H.R. Rep. No. 1693, 83d Cong., 2d Sess., pp. 2-3 (1954). But their intentions cannot, on their own, decide our inquiry. First of all, those legislators also had permissible secular objectives in mind — they meant, for example, to acknowledge the religious origins of our Nation's belief in the "individuality and the dignity of the human being." *Id.*, at 1. Second — and more critically — the *subsequent* social and cultural history of the Pledge shows that its original secular character was not transformed by its amendment. In *School Dist. of Abington Township v. Schempp*, we explained that a government may initiate a practice "for the impermissible purpose of supporting religion" but nevertheless "retai[n] the la[w] for the permissible purpose of furthering overwhelmingly secular ends." Whatever the sectarian ends its authors may have had in mind, our continued repetition of the reference to "one Nation under God" in an exclusively patriotic context has shaped the cultural significance of that phrase to conform to that context. Any religious freight the words may have been meant to carry originally has long since been lost. See *Lynch* (Brennan, J., dissenting) (suggesting that the reference to God in the Pledge might be permissible because it has "lost through rote repetition any significant religious content").

Absence of reference to particular religion

"The clearest command of the Establishment Clause is that one religious denomination cannot be officially preferred over another." *Larson v. Valente*, 456 U.S. 228, 244 (1982). While general acknowledgments of religion need not be viewed by reasonable observers as denigrating the nonreligious, the same cannot be said of instances "where the endorsement is sectarian, in the sense of specifying details upon which men and women who believe in a benevolent, omnipotent Creator and Ruler of the world are known to differ." *Weisman* (SCALIA, J., dissenting). As a result, no religious acknowledgment could claim to be an instance of ceremonial deism if it explicitly favored one particular religious belief system over another.

The Pledge complies with this requirement. It does not refer to a nation "under Jesus" or "under Vishnu," but instead acknowledges religion in a general way: a simple reference to a generic "God." Of course, some religions — Buddhism, for instance — are not based upon a belief in a separate Supreme Being. But one would be hard pressed to imagine a brief solemnizing reference to religion that would adequately encompass every religious belief expressed by any citizen of this Nation. The phrase "under God," conceived and added at a time when our national religious diversity was neither as robust nor as well recognized as it is now, represents a tolerable attempt to acknowledge religion and to invoke its solemnizing power without favoring any individual religious sect or belief system.

Minimal religious content

A final factor that makes the Pledge an instance of ceremonial deism, in my view, is its highly circumscribed reference to God. In most of the cases in which we have struck down government speech or displays under the Establishment Clause, the offending religious content has been much more pervasive. *See, e.g., Weisman* (prayers involving repeated thanks to God and requests for blessings). Of course, a ceremony cannot avoid Establishment Clause scrutiny simply by avoiding an explicit mention of God. *See Wallace v. Jaffree* (invalidating Alabama statute providing moment of silence for meditation or voluntary prayer). But the brevity of a reference to religion or to God in a ceremonial exercise can be important for several reasons. First, it tends to confirm that the reference is being used to acknowledge religion or to solemnize an event rather than to endorse religion in any way. Second, it makes it easier for those participants who wish to "opt out" of language they find offensive to do so without having to reject the ceremony entirely. And third, it tends to limit the ability of government to express a preference for one religious sect over another.

The reference to "God" in the Pledge of Allegiance qualifies as a minimal reference to religion; respondent's challenge focuses on only two of the Pledge's 31 words. Moreover, the presence of those words is not absolutely essential to the Pledge, as demonstrated by the fact that it existed without them for over 50 years. As a result, students who wish to avoid saying the words "under God" still can consider themselves meaningful participants in the exercise if they join in reciting the remainder of the Pledge.

I have framed my inquiry as a specific application of the endorsement test by examining whether the ceremony or representation would convey a message to a reasonable observer, familiar with its history, origins, and context, that those who do not adhere to its literal message are political outsiders. But consideration of these factors would lead me to the same result even if I were to apply the "coercion" test that has featured in several opinions of this Court.

The coercion test provides that, "at a minimum . . . government may not coerce anyone to support or participate in religion or its exercise, or otherwise act in a way which 'establishes a [state] religion or religious faith, or tends to do so.'" Any coercion that persuades an onlooker to participate in an act of ceremonial deism is inconsequential, as an Establishment Clause matter, because such acts are simply not religious in character. As a result, symbolic references to religion that qualify as instances of ceremonial deism will pass the coercion test as well as the endorsement test. This is not to say, however, that government could *overtly* coerce a person to participate in an act of ceremonial deism. Our cardinal freedom is one of belief; leaders in this Nation cannot force us to proclaim our allegiance to *any* creed, whether it be religious, philosophic, or political. That principle found eloquent expression in a case involving the Pledge itself, even before it contained the words to which respondent now objects. *See West Virginia Bd. of Ed. v. Barnette.* The compulsion of which Justice Jackson was concerned, however, was of the direct sort — the Constitution does not guarantee citizens a right entirely to avoid ideas with which they disagree. It would betray its own principles if it did; no robust democracy insulates its citizens from views that they might find novel or even inflammatory.

Justice Thomas, concurring in the judgment.

[Justice Thomas expressed the opinion that the "under God" language in the Pledge indeed violates the Supreme Court's current Establishment Clause jurisprudence, but argued that the Court should abandon its current jurisprudence and hold instead that the Establishment Clause does not apply to the states. This part of his opinion is reproduced in Chapter 1, *supra*.]

NOTES

1. *The Standing Issue and Parental Rights.* The majority draws a distinction between Mr. Newdow's right to present his religious views to his daughter, and his right to limit what third parties — including the government — say to his daughter. According to the Court, Newdow simply has no legally cognizable interest in the latter. But suppose the facts of the case were somewhat different. Suppose the school were engaged in what everyone would concede were substantial constitutional violations. Suppose, for example, that the school presented daily Bible readings in class from the perspective of Protestant Christianity and pointedly noted that those who did not believe in the Bible were going to Hell. Suppose further that teachers singled out Mr. Newdow as a prime example of someone who was not going to make it to heaven. Suppose finally that the teachers directly suggested to Newdow's daughter that if she continued to associate with her father, her own eternal salvation would be put at risk. Would the *Newdow* majority still conclude that Mr. Newdow has no right to sue "to shield his daughter from influences to which she is exposed in school despite the terms of the custody order"?

In a related vein, the *Newdow* majority emphasizes several times that Mr. Newdow's daughter and her mother do not object to the school mandating the daily recitation of the religious language in the Pledge. In footnote 7, the Court describes the daughter's interest as "constitutionally protectible." The Court uses the daughter's "constitutionally protectible" interest as a justification for denying Mr. Newdow standing and avoiding a ruling on the constitutionality of the government's actions. But assume that Mr. Newdow is correct in claiming that the government is acting unconstitutionally. Does anyone have a "constitutionally protectible" interest in insulating from judicial review the government's unconstitutional behavior?

2. *The Standing Issue and Institutional Deference.* At one point, the majority cites *Warth v. Seldin* for the proposition that without strong limitations on standing, "the courts would be called upon to decide abstract questions of wide public significance even though other governmental institutions may be more competent to address the questions and even though judicial intervention may be unnecessary to protect individual rights." Which governmental institutions are more competent that the courts to address the issues relating to the Pledge? By suggesting that the elected bodies of government are "more competent" to decide these matters, hasn't the *Newdow* majority effectively conceded to the dissent on the merits of the constitutional issue? As Chief Justice Rehnquist points out, the elected bodies of government have made their position on this matter very clear: "Here, Congress prescribed a Pledge of Allegiance, the State of California required patriotic observances in its schools, and the School District chose to comply by requiring teacher-led recital of the Pledge of Allegiance by willing students. Thus, we have three levels of popular government — the national, the state, and the local — collaborating to produce the Elk Grove ceremony." Is the *Newdow* majority conceding that on matters of this sort it should defer institutionally to the political branches of government? If so, then what are "matters of this sort"? If the Court defers on the Pledge, then why not school prayer? Conversely, if the Court is not conceding that it should defer to the political branches, then what explanation (other than a reluctance to issue an unpopular decision) can the majority provide for exercising its discretion to avoid adjudicating the claim of someone with an injury that is constitutionally cognizable under Article III?

3. *The Pledge and Precedent.* The response of politicians to the Ninth Circuit decision in *Newdow* is not surprising, and may have as much to do with politics as piety. Many undoubtedly recall the political price paid during the 1988 presidential campaign by Massachusetts Governor Michael Dukakis for vetoing a bill requiring the pledge be recited in all Massachusetts schools. But some legal scholars were also quick to deride the Ninth Circuit panel's decision. University of Chicago law professor Cass Sunstein told the Chicago Daily Herald that "[i]t is a very surprising decision and it's not compelled by any precedent." Cass Cliatt, *Pledge Won't Affect Illinois; Expert Predicts Rededication to Pledge After Court's Ban*, CHI. DAILY HERALD, June 27, 2002, at 1. Sunstein went on to note, "This is not a religious ritual, it's a patriotic ritual, so the decision is almost certain to be overruled."

What does the Ninth Circuit's *Newdow* opinion and its aftermath tell us about the constitutionality of "ceremonial deism" in light of the Supreme Court's other Establishment Clause precedents? Are examples of this phenomenon so inconsequential that they should be ignored as unworthy of constitutional adjudication, or are they actually significant evidence of a persistent effort by the religious majority to subtly underscore its continuing dominance?

Is Professor Sunstein correct that the Ninth Circuit's decision is "not compelled by any precedent"? Are there any flaws in Judge Goodwin's analysis of the relevant precedent? Note that Judge Fernandez's dissent does not dispute the majority's application of the relevant *Lemon*, endorsement, and coercion precedents. Instead, Fernandez focuses on (1) statements in dicta by several individual Justices that the various references to God in official documents, public building inscriptions, and ceremonies may serve the legitimate secular purpose of solemnizing certain functions; (2) the possibility that overturning the "under God" portion of the pledge would lead to bans on other examples of ceremonial deism; and (3) the argument that the "under God" portion of the pledge poses only a "de minimis" threat of establishing a religion.

Consider the following possible responses to Judge Fernandez's three main points: (1) Previous statements approving references to God are not dispositive in *Newdow* because (a) these references did not focus specifically on the pledge in a public school classroom — with all the attendant coercive elements identified by the Court in the school prayer cases; (b) it is implausible that the addition of the words "under God" added any solemnity to a pledge that had seen the country through two world wars without those words; (c) the Court has consistently rejected the solemnization argument proffered by school boards trying to justify public school prayer; and (d) the solemnization rationale is inconsistent with the evidence in the record as to the actual religious purpose motivating the 1954 statute. (2) Barring the use of "under God" in a public school classroom — which the Court has singled out for special protection from coercive state-mandated religious exercises — would not necessarily bar the use of similar phrases in any other less-coercive context. (3) The argument that the use of "under God" in the pledge is trivial or "de minimis" is refuted by the furor generated by *Newdow*, which included not only routine denunciations of the court and its decision from virtually the entire political community, but also multiple hostile responses, including death threats, directed at the plaintiff and his daughter. These reactions were almost all specifically oriented toward perpetuating the government's direct endorsement of a religious belief in God — and, more ominously, contained implicit — and sometimes explicit — attacks on someone who had chosen in a very public way not to conform to the government's preferred form of religious belief.

Judge Fernandez's argument that the "under God" phrase poses only a de minimis threat to constitutional values is related to the widespread perception that Newdow's case is at most a trivial matter litigated by someone who, in one commentator's words, must have a lot of time on his hands. But is Newdow's constitutional principle really more trivial than some others that have led to decisions that have become an accepted part of our First Amendment jurisprudence? Is the claim here more trivial than that of the Jehovah's Witness children and parents in *West Virginia v. Barnette*? What about *Wooley v. Maynard*, 430 U.S. 705 (1977) (holding on free speech grounds that a Jehovah's Witness had a constitutional right to cover up the state motto "Live Free or Die" on his automobile tag because the motto offended his religious, moral, and political beliefs)? Or for that matter, *Engel*, *Lee v. Weisman*, and *Santa Fe*? Also, note that the triviality argument cuts both ways. If it is silly for Mr. Newdow to litigate all the way up to the Ninth Circuit Court of Appeals over two trivial little words, then it is presumably just as silly for the government to respond by expending precious resources to take the case on appeal to an en banc panel — much less on certiorari to the Supreme Court — just to reinstate those same two trivial words. Justice O'Connor may have inadvertently highlighted this point in her concurrence when she notes that "respondent's challenge focuses on only two of the Pledge's 31 words. [T]he presence of those words is not absolutely essential to the Pledge, as demonstrated by the fact that it existed without them for over 50 years."

Finally, are Professor Sunstein and Justice O'Connor correct in asserting that the pledge is "not a religious ritual, it's a patriotic ritual"? Is this consistent with the quotations from legislative history in *Newdow*? Is Justice O'Connor correct as a legal matter to suggest that "history and ubiquity" can sanitize a government action that may have originally been motivated by an impermissible religious motive? Is her factual assumption correct — i.e., that the original religious motive for the "under God" language has been replaced through historical usage with a permissible secular meaning? Consider in this light another of President Bush's comments on the case: "America is a nation that values our relationship with the Almighty," President Bush told reporters. "We need commonsense judges who understand that our rights were derived from God."

4. *Religion and the State in Times of National Crisis.* Should the attacks on the World Trade Center on September 11, 2001 (or some similarly traumatic national event) change the Establishment Clause analysis of public religious displays by the government and its officials? In a recent article, William Marshall notes the heavy infusion of religion in many post-September 11 ceremonies, and notes also that these religious elements could be viewed as violations of the secularism mandate of the Establishment Clause. Professor Marshall tentatively suggests "that the tension between the constitutional commitment to anti-establishment and the societal need to engage in collective religious exercise can be accommodated by a doctrine that allows for government support for religions in limited and exceptional circumstances." William P. Marshall, *The Limits of Secularism: Public Religious Expression in Moments of National Crisis and Tragedy*, 78 NOTRE DAME L. REV. 11, 33 (2002). He suggests three basic rationales for permitting the government to enlist the services of religion in times of crisis. First, "[a]n attack upon the Nation's religious identity literally cries out for religious response: the assertion that we are a godless, materialistic culture requires an answer." *Id.* at 29. Second, "basic human needs may require a relaxation of the prohibition against state support of religious exercise in times of crisis. Humanity most looks toward religion for comfort and meaning in times of upheaval and stress." *Id.* The third rationale "pertains to public grief. Religion and death are inextricably bound together. Indeed, fear of death may be the singularly most powerful reason that humanity seeks religion, and providing comfort in times of loss may be one of religion's most essential functions." *Id.* at 30. Taking into consideration these three rationales, Professor Marshall suggests that "One possible compromise is to employ something like an exceptional circumstances test that would require a number of factors — such as a national crisis and public mourning combined with a limited temporal nexus between the precipitating event and the state response — in order to sustain a state-supported religious exercise." *Id.* at 31-32.

Does Professor Marshall's proposed compromise sufficiently take into account the exclusionary possibilities of religious responses to national crises? In the context of the September 11 attacks, for example, could this compromise proposal be implemented in a way that would satisfactorily incorporate the views of American Muslims in the national religious response to the attack? What about atheists and agnostics? If a religious response is necessary to prove that the United States is not a "godless, materialist culture," then are non-religious citizens simply sent to the sidelines of the political culture until the national crisis subsides?

WIDMAR v. VINCENT
454 U.S. 263 (1981)

JUSTICE POWELL delivered the opinion of the court.

This case presents the question whether a state university, which makes its facilities generally available for the activities of registered student groups, may close its facilities to a registered student group desiring to use the facilities for religious worship and religious discussion.

I

It is the stated policy of the University of Missouri at Kansas City to encourage the activities of student organizations. The University officially recognizes over 100 student groups. It routinely provides University facilities for the meetings of registered organizations. Students pay an activity fee of $41 per semester (1978-1979) to help defray the costs to the University.

From 1973 until 1977 a registered religious group named Cornerstone regularly sought and received permission to conduct its meetings in University facilities.[2] In 1977, however, the University informed the group that it could no longer meet in University buildings. The exclusion was based on a regulation, adopted by the Board of Curators in 1972, that prohibits the use of University buildings or grounds "for purposes of religious worship or religious teaching."

Eleven University students, all members of Cornerstone, brought suit to challenge the regulation in the Federal District Court for the Western District of Missouri. They alleged that the University's discrimination against religious activity and discussion violated their rights to free exercise of religion, equal protection, and freedom of speech under the First and Fourteenth Amendments to the Constitution of the United States.

III

A

The University first argues that it cannot offer its facilities to religious groups and speakers on the terms available to other groups without violating the Establishment Clause of the Constitution of the United States. We agree that the interest of the University in complying with its constitutional obligations may be characterized as compelling. It does not follow, however, that an "equal access" policy would be incompatible with this Court's Establishment Clause

---

[2] Cornerstone is an organization of evangelical Christian students from various denominational backgrounds. According to an affidavit filed in 1977, "perhaps twenty students . . . participate actively in Cornerstone and form the backbone of the campus organization." Affidavit of Florian Chess (Sept. 29, 1977), *quoted in Chess v. Widmar*, 480 F. Supp. 907, 911 (WD Mo.1979). Cornerstone held its on-campus meetings in classrooms and in the student center. These meetings were open to the public and attracted up to 125 students. A typical Cornerstone meeting included prayer, hymns, Bible commentary, and discussion of religious views and experiences.

cases. Those cases hold that a policy will not offend the Establishment Clause if it can pass a three-pronged test: "First, the [governmental policy] must have a secular legislative purpose; second, its principal or primary effect must be one that neither advances nor inhibits religion . . . ; finally, the [policy] must not foster 'an excessive government entanglement with religion.'" *Lemon v. Kurtzman.*

In this case two prongs of the test are clearly met. Both the District Court and the Court of Appeals held that an open-forum policy, including nondiscrimination against religious speech,[9] would have a secular purpose and would avoid entanglement with religion. But the District Court concluded, and the University argues here, that allowing religious groups to share the limited public forum would have the "primary effect" of advancing religion.

The University's argument misconceives the nature of this case. The question is not whether the creation of a religious forum would violate the Establishment Clause. The University has opened its facilities for use by student groups, and the question is whether it can now exclude groups because of the content of their speech.[13] In this context we are unpersuaded that the primary effect of the public forum, open to all forms of discourse, would be to advance religion.

We are not oblivious to the range of an open forum's likely effects. It is possible — perhaps even foreseeable — that religious groups will benefit from access to University facilities. But this Court has explained that a religious organization's enjoyment of merely "incidental" benefits does not violate the prohibition against the "primary advancement" of religion.

We are satisfied that any religious benefits of an open forum at UMKC would be "incidental" within the meaning of our cases. Two factors are especially relevant.

First, an open forum in a public university does not confer any imprimatur of state approval on religious sects or practices. As the Court of Appeals quite

---

[9] As the dissent emphasizes, the Establishment Clause requires the State to distinguish between "religious" speech — speech, undertaken or approved by the State, the primary effect of which is to support an establishment of religion — and "nonreligious" speech — speech, undertaken or approved by the State, the primary effect of which is not to support an establishment of religion. This distinction is required by the plain text of the Constitution. It is followed in our cases. *E.g., Stone v. Graham,* 449 U.S. 39 (1980). The dissent attempts to equate this distinction with its view of an alleged constitutional difference between religious "speech" and religious "worship." *See post,* at 282, and n. 3. We think that the distinction advanced by the dissent lacks a foundation in either the Constitution or in our cases, and that it is judicially unmanageable.

[13] This case is different from the cases in which religious groups claim that the denial of facilities *not* available to other groups deprives them of their rights under the Free Exercise Clause. Here, the University's forum is already available to other groups, and respondents' claim to use that forum does not rest solely on rights claimed under the Free Exercise Clause. Respondents' claim also implicates First Amendment rights of speech and association, and it is on the bases of speech and association rights that we decide the case. Accordingly, we need not inquire into the extent, if any, to which free exercise interests are infringed by the challenged University regulation. Neither do we reach the questions that would arise if state accommodation of free exercise and free speech rights should, in a particular case, conflict with the prohibitions of the Establishment Clause.

aptly stated, such a policy "would no more commit the University . . . to religious goals" than it is "now committed to the goals of the Students for a Democratic Society, the Young Socialist Alliance," or any other group eligible to use its facilities.[14]

Second, the forum is available to a broad class of nonreligious as well as religious speakers; there are over 100 recognized student groups at UMKC. The provision of benefits to so broad a spectrum of groups is an important index of secular effect. *See, e.g., Committee for Public Education v. Nyquist,* [*infra* Chapter 8]. If the Establishment Clause barred the extension of general benefits to religious groups, "a church could not be protected by the police and fire departments, or have its public sidewalk kept in repair." *Roemer v. Maryland Public Works Bd.* [*infra* Chapter 8] (plurality opinion). At least in the absence of empirical evidence that religious groups will dominate UMKC's open forum, we agree with the Court of Appeals that the advancement of religion would not be the forum's "primary effect."

LAMB'S CHAPEL v. CENTER MORICHES UNION FREE SCHOOL DISTRICT
508 U.S. 384 (1993)

JUSTICE WHITE delivered the opinion of the Court.

New York [Education Law] authorizes local school boards to adopt reasonable regulations for the use of school property for 10 specified purposes when the property is not in use for school purposes. Among the permitted uses is the holding of "social, civic and recreational meetings and entertainments, and other uses pertaining to the welfare of the community; but such meetings, entertainment and uses shall be non-exclusive and shall be open to the general public." The list of permitted uses does not include meetings for religious purposes, and a New York appellate court in *Trietley v. Board of Ed. of Buffalo*, 409 N.Y.S.2d 912, 915 (App. Div. 1978), ruled that local boards could not allow student bible clubs to meet on school property because "[r]eligious purposes are not included in the enumerated purposes for which a school may be used under section 414." In [later cases] the Court of Appeals for the Second Circuit accepted *Trietley* as an authoritative interpretation of state law. Furthermore, the Attor-

---

[14] University students are, of course, young adults. They are less impressionable than younger students and should be able to appreciate that the University's policy is one of neutrality toward religion. *See Tilton v. Richardson, supra*, at 685-686. The University argues that the Cornerstone students themselves admitted in affidavits that "[s]tudents know that if something is on campus, then it is a student organization, and they are more likely to feel comfortable attending a meeting." Affidavit of Florian Frederick Chess, App. 18, 19. In light of the large number of groups meeting on campus, however, we doubt students could draw any reasonable inference of University support from the mere fact of a campus meeting place. The University's student handbook already notes that the University's name will not "be identified in any way with the aims, policies, programs, products, or opinions of any organization or its members." 1980-1981 UMKC Student Handbook 25.

ney General of New York supports *Trietley* as an appropriate approach to deciding this case.

Pursuant to [the state law], the Board of Center Moriches Union Free School District (District) has issued rules and regulations with respect to the use of school property when not in use for school purposes. The rules allow only 2 of the 10 purposes authorized by [state law]: social, civic, or recreational uses (Rule 10) and use by political organizations if [properly authorized] (Rule 8). Rule 7, however, consistent with the judicial interpretation of state law, provides that "[t]he school premises shall not be used by any group for religious purposes."

The issue in this case is whether, against this background of state law, it violates the Free Speech Clause of the First Amendment, made applicable to the States by the Fourteenth Amendment, to deny a church access to school premises to exhibit for public viewing and for assertedly religious purposes, a film series dealing with family and child-rearing issues faced by parents today.

I

Petitioners (Church) are Lamb's Chapel, an evangelical church in the community of Center Moriches, and its pastor John Steigerwald. Twice the Church applied to the District for permission to use school facilities to show a six-part film series containing lectures by Doctor James Dobson.[2] A brochure provided on request of the District identified Dr. Dobson as a licensed psychologist, former associate clinical professor of pediatrics at the University of Southern California, best-selling author, and radio commentator. The brochure stated that the film series would discuss Dr. Dobson's views on the undermining influences of the media that could only be counterbalanced by returning to traditional, Christian family values instilled at an early stage. The brochure went on to describe the contents of each of the six parts of the series. The District denied the first application, saying that "[t]his film does appear to be church related and therefore your request must be refused." The second application for permission to use school premises for showing the film series, which described it as a "Family oriented movie — from a Christian perspective," was denied using identical language.

II

The District, as a respondent, would save its judgment below on the ground that to permit its property to be used for religious purposes would be an estab-

---

[2] Shortly before the first of these requests, the Church had applied for permission to use school rooms for its Sunday morning services and for Sunday School. The hours specified were 9 a.m. to 1 p.m. and the time period one year beginning in the next month. 959 F.2d 381, 383 (2d Cir. 1992). Within a few days the District wrote petitioner that the application "requesting use of the high school for your Sunday services" was denied, citing both N.Y. Educ. Law § 414 and the District's Rule 7 barring uses for religious purposes. The Church did not challenge this denial in the courts and the validity of this denial is not before us.

lishment of religion forbidden by the First Amendment. This Court suggested in *Widmar v. Vincent*, that the interest of the State in avoiding an Establishment Clause violation "may be [a] compelling" one justifying an abridgment of free speech otherwise protected by the First Amendment; but the Court went on to hold that permitting use of university property for religious purposes under the open access policy involved there would not be incompatible with the Court's Establishment Clause cases.

We have no more trouble than did the *Widmar* Court in disposing of the claimed defense on the ground that the posited fears of an Establishment Clause violation are unfounded. The showing of this film series would not have been during school hours, would not have been sponsored by the school, and would have been open to the public, not just to church members. The District property had repeatedly been used by a wide variety of private organizations. Under these circumstances, as in *Widmar,* there would have been no realistic danger that the community would think that the District was endorsing religion or any particular creed, and any benefit to religion or to the Church would have been no more than incidental.

NOTES ON THE CONCEPT OF OPEN ACCESS

1. In *Board of Education v. Mergens*, 496 U.S. 226 (1990), the Supreme Court upheld the federal Equal Access Act, 20 U.S.C. §§ 4071-4074 (1994). The Act provides that "It shall be unlawful for any public secondary school which receives Federal financial assistance and which has a limited open forum to deny equal access or a fair opportunity to, or discriminate against, any students who wish to conduct a meeting within that limited open forum on the basis of the religious, political, philosophical, or other content of the speech at such meetings." A "limited open forum" is deemed to exist "whenever such school grants an offering to or opportunity for one or more noncurriculum related student groups to meet on school premises during noninstructional time." In upholding the application of the Act in a public secondary school against an Establishment Clause challenge, the Court emphasized that the meetings were held in noninstructional time, did not interfere with the educational program of the school, were not endorsed by the school, involved no participation by school officials, were held in an atmosphere in which the religious club was merely one of many different student-initiated voluntary clubs, and were undertaken in a way that avoided coercing unwilling students to attend.

2. Suppose a religious group requests permission to use a public school facility every Sunday on a regular basis "for the purpose of conducting worship services." Can a public school board deny this request without violating *Lamb's Chapel? See Bronx Household of Faith v. Cmty. Sch. Bd.*, 127 F.3d 207 (2d Cir. 1997) (upholding the District Court's denial of church request). Recall that in footnote 2 of the *Lamb's Chapel* majority opinion, the Court noted that the plaintiffs in that case had dropped their claim for permission to hold regular religious services in the public school.

The Second Circuit Court of Appeals recently revisited its decision in *The Bronx Household of Faith. See The Bronx Household of Faith v. Bd. of Educ. of the City of N.Y.*, 331 F.3d 342 (2d Cir. 2003). In its new decision, the Court of Appeals upheld a preliminary injunction issued by a district court on behalf of a religious group seeking to use a public middle school auditorium for Sunday morning worship services. The court held that the facts of *Bronx Household of Faith* were largely indistinguishable from the facts before the Supreme Court in *Good News Club v. Milford Central School.*

> Central to our conclusion is a candid acknowledgment of the factual parallels between the activities described in *Good News Club* and the activities at issue in the present litigation. Although the majority in *Good News Club* characterized the Club's activity as "the teaching of morals and character development from a particular viewpoint," this characterization cannot be divorced from Justice Souter's detailed description of the Club's activities that the majority adopted as accurate. In Justice Souter's view, the Club's meetings did not consist solely of teaching, but also included elements consistent with "an evangelical service of worship." The majority did not say that the meetings were somehow distinct from worship services, but simply observed that they were not "mere religious worship, divorced from any teaching of moral values."

> We find no principled basis upon which to distinguish the activities set out by the Supreme Court in *Good News Club* from the activities that the Bronx Household of Faith has proposed for its Sunday meetings at Middle School 206B.

331 F.3d at 354 (citations omitted). The court did not abandon its previous holding that religious worship could be treated differently than other religious expression, but it noted that the Supreme Court's efforts in this area had left many important issues unresolved.

> We decline to review the trial court's further determinations that, after *Good News Club*, religious worship cannot be treated as an inherently distinct type of activity, and that the distinction between worship and other types of religious speech cannot meaningfully be drawn by the courts. We recognize that these conclusions are in obvious tension with our previous holding that a permissible distinction may be drawn between religious worship and other forms of speech from a religious viewpoint, a proposition that was seriously undermined but not explicitly rejected in *Good News Club*. It is unnecessary for us to reach these issues in order to affirm the trial court's grant of a preliminary injunction in this case.

> We pause, however, to note some unresolved issues that arise from the recent Supreme Court precedent that, as an appellate court, we are bound to follow. Would we be able to identify a form of religious worship

that is divorced from the teaching of moral values? Should we continue to evaluate activities that include religious worship on a case-by-case basis, or should worship no longer be treated as a distinct category of speech? How does the distinction drawn in our earlier precedent between worship and other forms of speech from a religious viewpoint relate to the dichotomy suggested in *Good News Club* between "mere" worship on the one hand and worship that is not divorced from the teaching of moral values on the other?

Further, how would the state, without imposing its own views on religion, define which values are morally acceptable and which are not? And, if such a choice is impossible to make, would the state be required to permit the use of public school property by religious sects that preach ideas commonly viewed as hateful? When several religious groups seek to use the same property at the same time, would not the state have to choose between them? What criteria would govern that choice? In all of this process, is there not a danger of excessive entanglement by the state in religion?

How the Supreme Court answers these difficult questions will no doubt have profound implications for relations between church and state. The American experiment has flourished largely free of the religious strife that has stricken other societies because church and state have respected each other's autonomy. Religion and government thrive because each, conscious of the corrosive perils of intrusive entanglements, exercises restraint in making claims on the other. The beneficiaries are a diverse populace that enjoys religious liberty in a nation that honors the sanctity of that freedom.

331 F.3d at 355.

For another variation on the *Good News Club* theme, *see Child Evangelism Fellowship of Maryland v. Montgomery County Public Schools,* 373 F.3d 589 (4th Cir. 2004), in which the Fourth Circuit Court of Appeals ordered the district court to issue a preliminary injunction on behalf of a Christian evangelical group seeking access to a "take-home flyer program" at a public elementary school. Under this program, the school district "permits certain governmental and non-profit organizations to use the 'take-home flyer forum' in those schools to distribute flyers and permission slips for students to take home to their parents." *Id.* at 592. Groups participating in this program receive permission to distribute their literature, deliver the literature to the school, and the teachers pass out the literature to the students at the end of the school day. Students are expected to bring all of these flyers home to their parents. According to the Fourth Circuit, this program is covered by the principles articulated in *Good News Club.* The court held that the exclusion of proselytizing literature constituted viewpoint discrimination, which could not be justified by the fear that the distribution would violate the Establishment Clause. The school district emphasized that this program was different from *Good News Club* in two important respects: first, the literature was distributed during the school day, instead of after school hours, and second, teachers were directly involved in the activity. The Fourth Circuit found these differences insufficient to distinguish *Good News Club*. According to the court, "simply issuing a communication involving a religious organization during school hours does not render the communication state speech, nor does it invariably create a perception of endorsement or coercion by government officials." *Id.* at 596. Likewise, "teachers only act in an administrative capacity — picking up flyers from their mailboxes and distributing them to students' cubbies." *Id.* at 601-02. The court also concluded (over the vociferous objections of the dissenting judge) that requiring students to take the literature home to their parents did not coerce the students to participate in a religious exercise.

3. The New York City Board of Education policy regarding the private use of public school facilities contains the following provision:

> No outside organization or group may be allowed to conduct religious services or religious instruction on school premises after school. However, the use of school premises by outside organizations or groups after school for the purposes of discussing religious material or material which contains a religious viewpoint or for distributing such material is permissible.

Is the distinction between "religious services or religious instruction" and "discussing religious material" consistent with *Lamb's Chapel*? *See Bronx Household of Faith v. Cmty. Sch. Bd., supra* (upholding policy).

CAPITAL SQUARE REVIEW AND ADVISORY BOARD v. PINETTE
515 U.S. 753 (1995)

JUSTICE SCALIA announced the judgment of the Court and delivered the opinion of the Court with respect to Parts I, II, and III, and an opinion with respect to Part IV, in which THE CHIEF JUSTICE, JUSTICE KENNEDY and JUSTICE THOMAS join.

The Establishment Clause of the First Amendment, made binding upon the States through the Fourteenth Amendment, provides that government "shall make no law respecting an establishment of religion." The question in this case is whether a State violates the Establishment Clause when, pursuant to a religiously neutral state policy, it permits a private party to display an unattended religious symbol in a traditional public forum located next to its seat of government.

I

Capitol Square is a 10-acre, state-owned plaza surrounding the Statehouse in Columbus, Ohio. For over a century the square has been used for public speeches, gatherings, and festivals advocating and celebrating a variety of causes, both secular and religious. Ohio Admin. Code Ann. § 128-4-02(A) (1994) makes the square available "for use by the public . . . for free discussion of public questions, or for activities of a broad public purpose," and Ohio Rev. Code Ann. § 105.41 (1994), gives the Capitol Square Review and Advisory Board responsibility for regulating public access. To use the square, a group must simply fill out an official application form and meet several criteria, which concern primarily safety, sanitation, and non-interference with other uses of the square, and which are neutral as to the speech content of the proposed event.

It has been the Board's policy "to allow a broad range of speakers and other gatherings of people to conduct events on the Capitol Square." Such diverse groups as homosexual rights organizations, the Ku Klux Klan and the United Way have held rallies. The Board has also permitted a variety of unattended displays on Capitol Square: a state-sponsored lighted tree during the Christmas season, a privately-sponsored menorah during Chanukah, a display showing the progress of a United Way fundraising campaign, and booths and exhibits during an arts festival. Although there was some dispute in this litigation regarding the frequency of unattended displays, the District Court found, with ample justification, that there was no policy against them.

In November 1993, after reversing an initial decision to ban unattended holiday displays from the square during December 1993, the Board authorized the State to put up its annual Christmas tree. On November 29, 1993, the Board granted a rabbi's application to erect a menorah. That same day, the Board received an application from respondent Donnie Carr, an officer of the Ohio Ku Klux Klan, to place a cross on the square from December 8, 1993, to December 24, 1993. The Board denied that application on December 3, informing the Klan by letter that the decision to deny "was made upon the advice of counsel, in a good faith attempt to comply with the Ohio and United States Constitutions, as they have been interpreted in relevant decisions by the Federal and State Courts."

Two weeks later, having been unsuccessful in its effort to obtain administrative relief from the Board's decision, the Ohio Klan, through its leader Vincent Pinette, filed the present suit in the United States District Court for the Southern District of Ohio, seeking an injunction requiring the Board to issue the requested permit. The Board defended on the ground that the permit would violate the Establishment Clause. The District Court determined that Capitol Square was a traditional public forum open to all without any policy against freestanding displays; that the Klan's cross was entirely private expression entitled to full First Amendment protection; and that the Board had failed to show that the display of the cross could reasonably be construed as endorsement of Christianity by the State. The District Court issued the injunction and, after the Board's application for an emergency stay was denied, the Board permitted the Klan to erect its cross. The Board then received, and granted, several additional applications to erect crosses on Capitol Square during December 1993 and January 1994.

II

First, a preliminary matter: Respondents contend that we should treat this as a case in which freedom of speech (the Klan's right to present the message of the cross display) was denied because of the State's disagreement with that message's political content, rather than because of the State's desire to distance itself from sectarian religion. They suggest in their merits brief and in their oral argument that Ohio's genuine reason for disallowing the display was disapproval of the political views of the Ku Klux Klan. Whatever the fact may be, the case was not presented and decided that way. The record facts before us and the opinions below address only the Establishment Clause issue; that is the question upon which we granted certiorari; and that is the sole question before us to decide.

Respondents' religious display in Capitol Square was private expression. Our precedent establishes that private religious speech, far from being a First Amendment orphan, is as fully protected under the Free Speech Clause as secular private expression. *Lamb's Chapel v. Center Moriches Union Free School Dist.; Board of Ed. of Westside Community Schools (Dist. 66) v. Mergens; Widmar v. Vincent; Heffron v. International Soc. for Krishna Consciousness, Inc.,* 452 U.S. 640 (1981). Indeed, in Anglo-American history, at least, government suppression of speech has so commonly been directed *precisely* at religious speech that a free-speech clause without religion would be Hamlet without the prince. Accordingly, we have not excluded from free-speech protections religious proselytizing, *Heffron,* or even acts of worship, *Widmar.* Petitioners do not dispute that respondents, in displaying their cross, were engaging in constitutionally protected expression. They do contend that the constitutional protection does not extend to the length of permitting that expression to be made on Capitol Square.

It is undeniable, of course, that speech which is constitutionally protected against state suppression is not thereby accorded a guaranteed forum on all property owned by the State. The right to use government property for one's private expression depends upon whether the property has by law or tradition been given the status of a public forum, or rather has been reserved for specific official uses. If the former, a State's right to limit protected expressive activity is sharply circumscribed: it may impose reasonable, content-neutral time, place and manner restrictions (a ban on all unattended displays, which did not exist here, might be one such), but it may regulate expressive *content* only if such a restriction is necessary, and narrowly drawn, to serve a compelling state interest. These strict standards apply here, since the District Court and the Court of Appeals found that Capitol Square was a traditional public forum.

Petitioners do not claim that their denial of respondents' application was based upon a content-neutral time, place, or manner restriction. To the contrary, they concede — indeed it is the essence of their case — that the Board rejected the display precisely because its content was religious. Petitioners advance a single justification for closing Capitol Square to respondents' cross: the State's interest in avoiding official endorsement of Christianity, as required by the Establishment Clause.

IV

Petitioners argue that one feature of the present case distinguishes it from *Lamb's Chapel* and *Widmar*: the forum's proximity to the seat of government, which, they contend, may produce the perception that the cross bears the State's approval. They urge us to apply the so-called "endorsement test," and to find that, because an observer might mistake private expression for officially endorsed religious expression, the State's content-based restriction is constitutional.

We must note, to begin with, that it is not really an "endorsement test" of any sort, much less the "endorsement test" which appears in our more recent Establishment Clause jurisprudence, that petitioners urge upon us. "Endorsement" connotes an expression or demonstration of approval or support. THE NEW SHORTER OXFORD ENGLISH DICTIONARY 818 (1993); WEBSTER'S NEW DICTIONARY 845 (2d ed. 1950). Our cases have accordingly equated "endorsement" with "promotion" or "favoritism." We find it peculiar to say that government "promotes" or "favors" a religious display by giving it the same access to a public forum that all other displays enjoy. And as a matter of Establishment Clause jurisprudence, we have consistently held that it is no violation for government to enact neutral policies that happen to benefit religion. *See, e.g., Bowen v. Kendrick*, [Chapter 9, *infra*]; *Witters v. Washington Dept. of Services for Blind*, [Chapter 8, *infra*]; *Mueller v. Allen*, [Chapter 8, *infra*]; *McGowan v. Maryland*, 366 U.S. 420 (1961). Where we have tested for endorsement of religion, the subject of the test was either expression *by the government itself, Lynch, supra,* or else government action alleged *to discriminate in favor* of private religious expression or activity, *Board of Ed. of Kiryas Joel Village School Dist. v. Grumet*, 512 U.S. 687, 708-710 (1994), *Allegheny, supra*. The test petitioners propose, which would attribute to a neutrally behaving government *private* religious expression, has no antecedent in our jurisprudence, and would better be called a "transferred endorsement" test.

Petitioners rely heavily on *Allegheny* and *Lynch*, but each is easily distinguished. In *Allegheny* we held that the display of a privately-sponsored crèche on the "Grand Staircase" of the Allegheny County Courthouse violated the Establishment Clause. That staircase was not, however, open to all on an equal basis, so the County was *favoring* sectarian religious expression. We expressly distinguished that site from the kind of public forum at issue here, and made clear that if the staircase were available to all on the same terms, "the presence of the crèche in that location for over six weeks would then *not* serve to associate the government with the crèche." In *Lynch* we held that a city's display of a crèche did not violate the Establishment Clause because, in context, the display did not endorse religion. The opinion does assume, as petitioners contend, that the *government's* use of religious symbols is unconstitutional if it effectively endorses sectarian religious belief. But the case neither holds nor even remotely assumes that the government's neutral treatment of *private* religious expression can be unconstitutional.

Petitioners argue that absence of perceived endorsement was material in *Lamb's Chapel* and *Widmar*. We did state in *Lamb's Chapel* that there was "no realistic danger that the community would think that the District was endorsing religion or any particular creed." But that conclusion was not the result of empirical investigation; it followed directly, we thought, from the fact that the forum was open and the religious activity privately sponsored. See *ibid.* It is significant that we referred only to what would be thought by "the community" — not by outsiders or individual members of the community uninformed about the school's practice. Surely some of the latter, hearing of religious ceremonies on school premises, and not knowing of the premises' availability and use for all sorts of other private activities, *might* leap to the erroneous conclusion of state endorsement. But, we in effect said, given an open forum and private sponsorship, erroneous conclusions do not count. So also in *Widmar*. Once we determined that the benefit to religious groups from the public forum was incidental and shared by other groups, we categorically rejected the State's Establishment Clause defense.

What distinguishes *Allegheny* and the dictum in *Lynch* from *Widmar* and *Lamb's Chapel* is the difference between government speech and private speech. "[T]here is a crucial difference between *government* speech endorsing religion, which the Establishment Clause forbids, and *private* speech endorsing religion, which the Free Speech and Free Exercise Clauses protect." Petitioners assert, in effect, that that distinction disappears when the private speech is conducted too close to the symbols of government. But that, of course, must be merely a subpart of a more general principle: that the distinction disappears whenever private speech can be mistaken for government speech. That proposition cannot be accepted, at least where, as here, the government has not fostered or encouraged the mistake.

Of course, giving sectarian religious speech preferential access to a forum close to the seat of government (or anywhere else for that matter) would violate the Establishment Clause (as well as the Free Speech Clause, since it would involve content discrimination). And one can conceive of a case in which a governmental entity manipulates its administration of a public forum close to the seat of government (or within a government building) in such a manner that only certain religious groups take advantage of it, creating an impression of endorsement *that is in fact accurate*. But those situations, which involve governmental *favoritism*, do not exist here. Capitol Square is a genuinely public forum, is known to be a public forum, and has been widely used as a public forum for many, many years. Private religious speech cannot be subject to veto by those who see favoritism where there is none.

The contrary view, most strongly espoused by JUSTICE STEVENS, but endorsed by JUSTICE SOUTER and JUSTICE O'CONNOR as well, exiles private religious speech to a realm of less-protected expression heretofore inhabited only by sexually explicit displays and commercial speech. It will be a sad day when this Court casts piety in with pornography, and finds the First Amendment more hospitable to private expletives, than to private prayers. This would be merely bizarre were religious speech simply *as* protected by the Constitution as other forms of private speech; but it is outright perverse when one considers that private religious expression receives *preferential* treatment under the Free Exercise Clause. It is no answer to say that the Establishment Clause tempers religious speech. By its terms that Clause applies only to the words and acts of *government*. It was never meant, and has never been read by this Court, to serve as an impediment to purely *private* religious speech connected to the State only through its occurrence in a public forum.

Since petitioners' "transferred endorsement" principle cannot possibly be restricted to squares in front of state capitols, the Establishment Clause regime that it would usher in is most unappealing. Petitioners' rule would require school districts adopting similar policies in the future to guess whether some undetermined critical mass of the community might nonetheless perceive the district to be advocating a religious viewpoint. Policymakers would find themselves in a vise between the Establishment Clause on one side and the Free Speech and Free Exercise Clauses on the other. Every proposed act of private, religious expression in a public forum would force officials to weigh a host of imponderables. How close to government is too close? What kind of building, and in what context, symbolizes state authority? If the State guessed wrong in one direction, it would be guilty of an Establishment Clause violation; if in the other, it would be liable for suppressing free exercise or free speech (a risk not run when the State restrains only its *own* expression).

The "transferred endorsement" test would also disrupt the settled principle that policies providing incidental benefits to religion do not contravene the Establishment Clause. That principle is the basis for the constitutionality of a broad range of laws, not merely those that implicate free-speech issues. It has radical implications for our public policy to suggest that neutral laws are invalid whenever hypothetical observers may — *even reasonably* — confuse an incidental benefit to religion with state endorsement.

Religious expression cannot violate the Establishment Clause where it (1) is purely private and (2) occurs in a traditional or designated public forum, publicly announced and open to all on equal terms. Those conditions are satisfied here, and therefore the State may not bar respondents' cross from Capitol Square.

JUSTICE O'CONNOR, with whom JUSTICE SOUTER and JUSTICE BREYER join, concurring in part and concurring in the judgment.

I

There is, as the plurality notes, "a crucial difference between *government* speech endorsing religion, which the Establishment Clause forbids, and *private* speech endorsing religion, which the Free Speech and Free Exercise Clauses protect." *Board of Ed. of Westside Community Schools (Dist. 66) v. Mergens*. But the quoted statement was made while applying the endorsement test itself; indeed, the sentence upon which the plurality relies was followed immediately by the conclusion that "secondary school students are mature enough and are likely to understand that a school does not endorse or support student speech that it merely permits on a nondiscriminatory basis." *Ibid.* Thus, as I read the decisions JUSTICE SOUTER carefully surveys, our prior cases do not imply that the endorsement test has no place where private religious speech in a public forum is at issue. Moreover, numerous lower courts (including the Court of Appeals in this case) have applied the endorsement test in precisely the context before us today. Given this background, I see no necessity to draw new lines where "[r]eligious expression . . . (1) is purely private and (2) occurs in a traditional or designated public forum."

None of this is to suggest that I would be likely to come to a different result from the plurality where truly private speech is allowed on equal terms in a vigorous public forum that the government has administered properly. That the religious display at issue here was erected by a private group in a public square available "for use by the public . . . for free discussion of public questions, or for activities of a broad public purpose," Ohio Admin.Code Ann. § 128-4-02(A) (1994), certainly informs the Establishment Clause inquiry under the endorsement test. Indeed, many of the factors the plurality identifies are some of those I would consider important in deciding cases like this one where religious speakers seek access to public spaces: "The State did not sponsor respondents' expression, the expression was made on government property that had been opened to the public for speech, and permission was requested through the same application process and on the same terms required of other groups." And, as I read the plurality opinion, a case is not governed by its proposed *per se* rule where such circumstances are otherwise — that is, where preferential placement of a religious symbol in a public space or government manipulation of the forum is involved.

To the plurality's consideration of the open nature of the forum and the private ownership of the display, however, I would add the presence of a sign disclaiming government sponsorship or endorsement on the Klan cross, which would make the State's role clear to the community. This factor is important because, as JUSTICE SOUTER makes clear, certain aspects of the cross display in this case arguably intimate government approval of respondents' private religious message — particularly that the cross is an especially potent sectarian symbol which stood unattended in close proximity to official government buildings. In context, a disclaimer helps remove doubt about State approval of respondents' religious message. On these facts, then, "the message [of inclusion] is one of neutrality rather than endorsement." *Mergens*.

Our agreement as to the outcome of this case, however, cannot mask the fact that I part company with the plurality on a fundamental point: I disagree that "[i]t has radical implications for our public policy to suggest that neutral laws are invalid whenever hypothetical observers may — *even reasonably* — confuse an incidental benefit to religion with State endorsement." On the contrary, when the reasonable observer would view a government practice as endorsing religion, I believe that it is our *duty* to hold the practice invalid. The plurality today takes an exceedingly narrow view of the Establishment Clause that is out of step both with the Court's prior cases and with well-established notions of what the Constitution requires. The Clause is more than a negative prohibition against certain narrowly defined forms of government favoritism; it also imposes affirmative obligations that may require a State, in some situations, to take steps to avoid being perceived as supporting or endorsing a private religious message. That is, the Establishment Clause forbids a State from hiding behind the application of formally neutral criteria and remaining studiously oblivious to the effects of its actions. Governmental intent cannot control, and not all state policies are permissible under the Religion Clauses simply because they are neutral in form.

Where the government's operation of a public forum has the effect of endorsing religion, even if the governmental actor neither intends nor actively encourages that result, the Establishment Clause is violated. This is so not because of "'transferred endorsement,'" or mistaken attribution of private speech to the State, but because the State's own actions (operating the forum in a particular manner and permitting the religious expression to take place therein), and their relationship to the private speech at issue, *actually convey* a message of endorsement. At some point, for example, a private religious group may so dominate a public forum that a formal policy of equal access is transformed into a demonstration of approval. Other circumstances may produce the same effect — whether because of the fortuity of geography, the nature of the particular public space, or the character of the religious speech at issue, among others. Our Establishment Clause jurisprudence should remain flexible enough to handle such situations when they arise.

II

Conducting the review of government action required by the Establishment Clause is always a sensitive matter. Unfortunately, as I noted in *Allegheny*, "even the development of articulable standards and guidelines has not always resulted in agreement among the Members of this Court on the results in individual cases." Today, JUSTICE STEVENS reaches a different conclusion regarding whether the Board's decision to allow respondents' display on Capitol Square constituted an impermissible endorsement of the cross' religious message. Yet I believe it is important to note that we have not simply arrived at divergent results after conducting the same analysis. Our fundamental point of departure, it appears, concerns the knowledge that is properly attributed to the test's "reasonable observer [who] evaluates whether a challenged governmental practice conveys a message of endorsement of religion." In my view, proper application of the endorsement test requires that the reasonable observer be deemed more informed than the casual passerby postulated by [the dissent].

Because an Establishment Clause violation must be moored in government action of some sort, and because our concern is with the political community writ large, the endorsement inquiry is not about the perceptions of particular individuals or saving isolated non-adherents from the discomfort of viewing symbols of a faith to which they do not subscribe. Indeed, to avoid "entirely sweep[ing] away all government recognition and acknowledgment of the role of religion in the lives of our citizens," *Allegheny* (O'CONNOR, J., concurring in part and concurring in judgment), our Establishment Clause jurisprudence must seek to identify the point at which the government becomes responsible, whether due to favoritism toward or disregard for the evident effect of religious speech, for the injection of religion into the political life of the citizenry.

I therefore disagree that the endorsement test should focus on the actual perception of individual observers, who naturally have differing degrees of knowledge. Under such an approach, a religious display is necessarily precluded so long as some passersby would perceive a governmental endorsement thereof. In my view, however, the endorsement test creates a more collective standard to gauge "the 'objective' meaning of the [government's] statement in the community." In this respect, the applicable observer is similar to the "reasonable person" in tort law, who "is not to be identified with any ordinary individual, who might occasionally do unreasonable things" but is "rather a personification of a community ideal of reasonable behavior, determined by the [collective] social judgment." W. KEETON ET AL., PROSSER AND KEETON ON THE LAW OF TORTS 175 (5th ed. 1984). Thus, "we do not ask whether there is *any* person who could find an endorsement of religion, whether *some* people may be offended by the display, or whether *some* reasonable person *might* think [the State] endorses religion." Saying that the endorsement inquiry should be conducted from the perspective of a hypothetical observer who is presumed to possess a certain level of information that all citizens might not share neither chooses the perceptions of the majority over those of a "reasonable non-adherent," nor invites disregard for the values the Establishment Clause was intended to protect. It simply recognizes the fundamental difficulty inherent in focusing on actual people: there is always *someone* who, with a particular quantum of knowledge, reasonably might perceive a particular action as an endorsement of religion. A State has not made religion relevant to standing in the political community simply because a particular viewer of a display might feel uncomfortable.

It is for this reason that the reasonable observer in the endorsement inquiry must be deemed aware of the history and context of the community and forum in which the religious display appears. As I explained in *Allegheny*, "the 'history and ubiquity' of a practice is relevant because it provides part of the context in which a reasonable observer evaluates whether a challenged governmental practice conveys a message of endorsement of religion." Nor can the knowledge attributed to the reasonable observer be limited to the information gleaned simply from viewing the challenged display. Today's proponents of the endorsement test all agree that we should attribute to the observer knowledge that the cross is a religious symbol, that Capitol Square is owned by the State, and that the large building nearby is the seat of state government. In my view, our hypothetical observer also should know the general history of the place in which the cross is displayed. Indeed, the fact that Capitol Square is a public park that has been used over time by private speakers of various types is as much a part of the display's context as its proximity to the Ohio Statehouse. This approach does not require us to assume an "'ultra-reasonable observer' who understands the vagaries of this Court's First Amendment jurisprudence" (STEVENS, J., dissenting). An informed member of the community will know how the public space in question has been used in the past — and it is that fact, not that the space may meet the legal definition of a public forum, which is relevant to the endorsement inquiry.

[The dissent's] property-based argument fails to give sufficient weight to the fact that the cross at issue here was displayed in a forum traditionally open to the public. "The very fact that a sign is installed on public property," the dissent suggests, "implies official approval of its message." While this may be the case where a government building and its immediate curtilage are involved, it is not necessarily so with respect to those "places which by long tradition or by government fiat have been devoted to assembly and debate, . . . [particularly] streets and parks which 'have immemorially been held in trust for the use of the public and, time out of mind, have been used for purposes of assembly, communicating thoughts between citizens, and discussing public questions.'" To the extent there is a presumption that "structures on government property — and, in particular, in front of buildings plainly identified with the State — imply state approval of their message," *post* (STEVENS, J., dissenting), that presumption can be rebutted where the property at issue is a forum historically available for private expression. The reasonable observer would recognize the distinction between speech the government supports and speech that it merely allows in a place that traditionally has been open to a range of private speakers accompanied, if necessary, by an appropriate disclaimer.

On the facts of this case, therefore, I conclude that the reasonable observer would not interpret the State's tolerance of the Klan's private religious display in Capitol Square as an endorsement of religion.

JUSTICE SOUTER, with whom JUSTICE O'CONNOR and JUSTICE BREYER join, concurring in part and concurring in the judgment.

Although I agree in the end that, in the circumstances of this case, petitioners erred in denying the Klan's application for a permit to erect a cross on Capitol Square, my analysis of the Establishment Clause issue differs from JUSTICE SCALIA's, and I vote to affirm in large part because of the possibility of affixing a sign to the cross adequately disclaiming any government sponsorship or endorsement of it.

The plurality's opinion declines to apply the endorsement test to the Board's action, in favor of a *per se* rule: religious expression cannot violate the Establishment Clause where it (1) is private and (2) occurs in a public forum, even if a reasonable observer would see the expression as indicating state endorsement. This *per se* rule would be an exception to the endorsement test, not previously recognized and out of square with our precedents.

I

My disagreement with the plurality on the law may receive some focus from attention to a matter of straight fact that we see alike: in some circumstances an intelligent observer may mistake private, unattended religious displays in a public forum for government speech endorsing religion. The Klan concedes this possibility as well, saying that, in its view, "on a different set of facts, the government might be found guilty of violating the endorsement test by permitting a private religious display in a public forum."

An observer need not be "obtuse" to presume that an unattended display on government land in a place of prominence in front of a government building either belongs to the government, represents government speech, or enjoys its location because of government endorsement of its message. Capitol Square, for example, is the site of a number of unattended displays owned or sponsored by the government, some permanent (statues), some temporary (such as the Christmas tree and a "Seasons Greetings" banner), and some in between (flags, which are, presumably, taken down and put up from time to time). Given the domination of the square by the government's own displays, one would not be a dimwit as a matter of law to think that an unattended religious display there was endorsed by the government, even though the square has also been the site of three privately sponsored, unattended displays over the years (a menorah, a United Way "thermometer," and some artisans' booths left overnight during an arts festival), *cf. Allegheny County* ("Even if the Grand Staircase occasionally was used for displays other than the crèche . . . it remains true that any display located there fairly may be understood to express views that receive the support and endorsement of the government"), and even though the square meets the legal definition of a public forum and has been used "[f]or over a century" as the site of "speeches, gatherings, and festivals." When an individual speaks in a public forum, it is reasonable for an observer to attribute the speech, first and foremost, to the speaker, while an unattended display (and any message it conveys) can naturally be viewed as belonging to the owner of the land on which it stands.

In sum, I do not understand that I am at odds with the plurality when I assume that in some circumstances an intelligent observer would reasonably perceive private religious expression in a public forum to imply the government's endorsement of religion. My disagreement with the plurality is simply that I would attribute these perceptions of the intelligent observer to the reasonable observer of Establishment Clause analysis under our precedents, where I believe that such reasonable perceptions matter.

II

Even if precedent and practice were otherwise, however, and there were an open question about applying the endorsement test to private speech in public forums, I would apply it in preference to the plurality's view, which creates a serious loophole in the protection provided by the endorsement test. In JUSTICE SCALIA's view, as I understand it, the Establishment Clause is violated in a public forum only when the government itself intentionally endorses religion or willfully "foster[s]" a misperception of endorsement in the forum, or when it "manipulates" the public forum "in such a manner that only certain religious groups take advantage of it." If the list of forbidden acts is truly this short, then governmental bodies and officials are left with generous scope to encourage a multiplicity of religious speakers to erect displays in public forums. As long as the governmental entity does not "manipulat[e]" the forum in such a way as to exclude all other speech, the plurality's opinion would seem to invite such government encouragement, even when the result will be the domination of the forum by religious displays and religious speakers. By allowing government to encourage what it can not do on its own, the proposed *per se* rule would tempt a public body to contract out its establishment of religion, by encouraging the private enterprise of the religious to exhibit what the government could not display itself.

Something of the sort, in fact, may have happened here. Immediately after the District Court issued the injunction ordering petitioners to grant the Klan's permit, a local church council applied for a permit, apparently for the purpose of overwhelming the Klan's cross with other crosses. The council proposed to invite all local churches to erect crosses, and the Board granted "blanket permission" for "all churches friendly to or affiliated with" the council to do so. The end result was that a part of the square was strewn with crosses, see Appendices A & B to this opinion, and while the effect in this case may have provided more embarrassment than suspicion of endorsement, the opportunity for the latter is clear.

JUSTICE STEVENS, dissenting.

The Establishment Clause should be construed to create a strong presumption against the installation of unattended religious symbols on public property. Although the State of Ohio has allowed Capitol Square, the area around the seat of its government, to be used as a public forum, and although it has occasionally allowed private groups to erect other sectarian displays there, neither fact provides a sufficient basis for rebutting that presumption. On the contrary, the sequence of sectarian displays disclosed by the record in this case illustrates the importance of rebuilding the "wall of separation between church and State" that Jefferson envisioned.

I

At issue in this case is an unadorned Latin cross, which the Ku Klux Klan placed, and left unattended, on the lawn in front of the Ohio State Capitol.

The Court decides this case on the assumption that the cross was a religious symbol. I agree with that assumption notwithstanding the hybrid character of this particular object. The record indicates that the "Grand Titan of the Knights of the Ku Klux Klan for the Realm of Ohio" applied for a permit to place a cross in front of the State Capitol because "the Jews" were placing a "symbol for the Jewish belief" in the Square. Some observers, unaware of who had sponsored the cross, or unfamiliar with the history of the Klan and its reaction to the menorah, might interpret the Klan's cross as an inspirational symbol of the crucifixion and resurrection of Jesus Christ. More knowledgeable observers might regard it, given the context, as an antisemitic symbol of bigotry and disrespect for a particular religious sect. Under the first interpretation, the cross is plainly a religious symbol.[3] Under the second, an icon of intolerance expressing an anti-clerical message should also be treated as a religious symbol because the Establishment Clause must prohibit official sponsorship of irreligious as well as religious messages. This principle is no less binding if the anti-religious message is also a bigoted message. *See United States v. Ballard*, 322 U.S. 78, 86-89 (1944) (government lacks power to judge truth of religious beliefs); *Watson v. Jones*, 13 Wall. 679, 728 (1872) ("The law knows no heresy, and is committed to the support of no dogma, the establishment of no sect").

Thus, while this unattended, freestanding wooden cross was unquestionably a religious symbol, observers may well have received completely different messages from that symbol. Some might have perceived it as a message of love, others as a message of hate, still others as a message of exclusion — a Statehouse sign calling powerfully to mind their outsider status. In any event, it was a message that the State of Ohio may not communicate to its citizens without violating the Establishment Clause.

II

The plurality does not disagree with the proposition that the State may not espouse a religious message. It concludes, however, that the State has not sent such a message; it has merely allowed others to do so on its property. Thus, the State has provided an "incidental benefit" to religion by allowing private parties access to a traditional public forum. In my judgment, neither precedent nor respect for the values protected by the Establishment Clause justifies that conclusion.

The Establishment Clause, "at the very least, prohibits government from appearing to take a position on questions of religious belief or from 'making

---

[3] Indeed, the Latin cross is identifiable as a symbol of a particular religion, that of Christianity; and, further, as a symbol of particular denominations within Christianity. *See American Civil Liberties Union v. St. Charles*, 794 F. 2d 265, 271 (7th Cir. 1986) ("Such a display is not only religious but also sectarian. This is not just because some religious Americans are not Christians. Some Protestant sects still do not display the cross. . . . The Greek Orthodox church uses as its symbol the Greek (equilateral) cross, not the Latin cross.... [T]he more sectarian the display, the closer it is to the original targets of the [establishment] clause, so the more strictly is the clause applied").

adherence to a religion relevant in any way to a person's standing in the political community.'" *County of Allegheny,* quoting *Lynch v. Donnelly*, (O'CONNOR, J., concurring). At least when religious symbols are involved, the question of whether the state is "appearing to take a position" is best judged from the standpoint of a "reasonable observer." It is especially important to take account of the perspective of a reasonable observer who may not share the particular religious belief it expresses. A paramount purpose of the Establishment Clause is to protect such a person from being made to feel like an outsider in matters of faith, and a stranger in the political community. If a reasonable person could perceive a government endorsement of religion from a private display, then the State may not allow its property to be used as a forum for that display. No less stringent rule can adequately protect non-adherents from a well-grounded perception that their sovereign supports a faith to which they do not subscribe.[5]

In determining whether the State's maintenance of the Klan's cross in front of the Statehouse conveyed a forbidden message of endorsement, we should be mindful of the power of a symbol standing alone and unexplained. Even on private property, signs and symbols are generally understood to express the owner's views. The location of the sign is a significant component of the message it conveys.

> "Displaying a sign from one's own residence often carries a message quite distinct from placing the same sign someplace else, or conveying the same text or picture by other means. Precisely because of their location, such signs provide information about the identity of the 'speaker.' As an early and eminent student of rhetoric observed, the identity of the speaker is an important component of many attempts to persuade. A sign advocating 'Peace in the Gulf' in the front lawn of a retired general or decorated war veteran may provoke a different reaction than the same sign in a 10-year-old child's bedroom window or the same message on a bumper sticker of a passing automobile. An espousal of socialism may carry different implications when displayed on the grounds of a stately mansion than when pasted on a factory wall or an

---

[5] JUSTICE O'CONNOR agrees that an "endorsement test" is appropriate and that we should judge endorsement from the standpoint of a reasonable observer. But her reasonable observer is a legal fiction, "'a personification of a community ideal of reasonable behavior, determined by the [collective] social judgment.'" The ideal human JUSTICE O'CONNOR describes knows and understands much more than meets the eye. Her "reasonable person" comes off as a well-schooled jurist, a being finer than the tort-law model. With respect, I think this enhanced tort-law standard is singularly out of place in the Establishment Clause context. It strips of constitutional protection every reasonable person whose knowledge happens to fall below some "'ideal'" standard. Instead of protecting only the "'ideal'" observer, then, I would extend protection to the universe of reasonable persons and ask whether some viewers of the religious display would be likely to perceive a government endorsement.

JUSTICE O'CONNOR's argument that "there is always *someone*" who will feel excluded by any particular governmental action, ignores the requirement that such an apprehension be objectively reasonable. A person who views an exotic cow at the zoo as a symbol of the Government's approval of the Hindu religion cannot survive this test.

ambulatory sandwich board." *City of Ladue v. Gilleo*, 512 U.S. 43, 56-57 (1994) (footnote omitted).

Like other speakers, a person who places a sign on her own property has the autonomy to choose the content of her own message. Thus, the location of a stationary, unattended sign generally is both a component of its message and an implicit endorsement of that message by the party with the power to decide whether it may be conveyed from that location.

So it is with signs and symbols left to speak for themselves on public property. The very fact that a sign is installed on public property implies official recognition and reinforcement of its message. That implication is especially strong when the sign stands in front of the seat of the government itself. The "reasonable observer" of any symbol placed unattended in front of any capitol in the world will normally assume that the sovereign — which is not only the owner of that parcel of real estate but also the lawgiver for the surrounding territory — has sponsored and facilitated its message.

That the State may have granted a variety of groups permission to engage in uncensored expressive activities in front of the capitol building does not, in my opinion, qualify or contradict the normal inference of endorsement that the reasonable observer would draw from the unattended, freestanding sign or symbol. Indeed, parades and demonstrations at or near the seat of government are often exercises of the right of the people to petition their government for a redress of grievances — exercises in which the government is the recipient of the message rather than the messenger. Even when a demonstration or parade is not directed against government policy, but merely has made use of a particularly visible forum in order to reach as wide an audience as possible, there usually can be no mistake about the identity of the messengers as persons other than the State. But when a statue or some other freestanding, silent, unattended, immoveable structure — regardless of its particular message — appears on the lawn of the Capitol building, the reasonable observer must identify the State either as the messenger, or, at the very least, as one who has endorsed the message. Contrast, in this light, the image of the cross standing alone and unattended, and the image the observer would take away were a hooded Klansman holding, or standing next to, the very same cross.

This Court has never held that a private party has a right to place an unattended object in a public forum.[7] Today the Court correctly recognizes that a State may impose a ban on all private unattended displays in such a forum. This is true despite the fact that our cases have condemned a number of laws that foreclose an entire medium of expression, even in places where free speech is

---

[7] Despite the absence of any holding on this point, JUSTICE O'CONNOR assumes that a reasonable observer would not impute the content of an unattended display to the Government because that observer would know that the State is required to allow all such displays on Capitol Square. JUSTICE O'CONNOR thus presumes a reasonable observer so prescient as to understand legal doctrines that this Court has not yet adopted.

otherwise allowed. The First Amendment affords protection to a basic liberty: "the freedom of speech" that an individual may exercise when using the public streets and parks. The Amendment, however, does not destroy all property rights. In particular, it does not empower individuals to erect structures of any kind on public property. Thus our cases protecting the individual's freedom to engage in communicative conduct on public property (whether by speaking, parading, handbilling, waving a flag, or carrying a banner), or to send messages from her own property by placing a sign in the window of her home, do not establish the right to implant a physical structure (whether a campaign poster, a burning cross, or a statue of Elvis Presley) on public property. I think the latter "right," which creates a far greater intrusion on government property and interferes with the Government's ability to differentiate its own message from those of public individuals, does not exist.

Because structures on government property — and, in particular, in front of buildings plainly identified with the state — imply state approval of their message, the Government must have considerable leeway, outside of the religious arena, to choose what kinds of displays it will allow and what kinds it will not. Although the First Amendment requires the Government to allow leafletting or demonstrating outside its buildings, the state has greater power to exclude unattended symbols when they convey a type of message with which the state does not wish to be identified. I think it obvious, for example, that Ohio could prohibit certain categories of signs or symbols in Capitol Square — erotic exhibits, commercial advertising, and perhaps campaign posters as well — without violating the Free Speech Clause. Moreover, our "public forum" cases do not foreclose public entities from enforcing prohibitions against all unattended displays in public parks, or possibly even limiting the use of such displays to the communication of non-controversial messages. Such a limitation would not inhibit any of the traditional forms of expression that have been given full constitutional protection in public fora.

The State's general power to restrict the types of unattended displays does not alone suffice to decide this case, because Ohio did not profess to be exercising any such authority. Instead, the Capitol Square Review Board denied a permit for the cross because it believed the Establishment Clause required as much, and we cannot know whether the Board would have denied the permit on other grounds. Accordingly, we must evaluate the State's rationale on its own terms. But in this case, the endorsement inquiry under the Establishment Clause follows from the State's power to exclude unattended private displays from public property. Just as the Constitution recognizes the State's interest in preventing its property from being used as a conduit for ideas it does not wish to give the appearance of ratifying, the Establishment Clause prohibits government from allowing, and thus endorsing, unattended displays that take a position on a religious issue. If the State allows such stationary displays in front of its seat of government, viewers will reasonably assume that it approves of them. As the picture appended to this opinion demonstrates, a reasonable observer would likely infer endorsement from the location of the cross erected by the Klan in this case. Even if the disclaimer at the foot of the cross (which stated that the cross was placed there by a private organization) were legible, that inference would remain, because a property owner's decision to allow a third party to place a sign on her property conveys the same message of endorsement as if she had erected it herself.[13]

E. THE ESTABLISHMENT CLAUSE AND RELIGIOUS FREE SPEECH

NOTES ON THE ESTABLISHMENT CLAUSE AND RELIGIOUS FREE SPEECH

1. An analog of *Pinette* in the educational context is *Rosenberger v. Rector & Visitors of the University of Virginia*, 515 U.S. 819, 829 (1995). In *Rosenberger*, the Court struck down the University of Virginia's denial of student activity funds to a Christian magazine. The Court held that First Amendment free speech public forum principles applied to the allocation of funds intended to facilitate a broad range of private student speech. "The [Student Activites Fund] is a forum more in a metaphysical than in a spatial or geographic sense, but the same principles are applicable." *Id.* at 830. The Court held that by denying funds to religious speakers, the University had engaged in unconstitutional viewpoint discrimination. The Court rejected the theory that the Establishment Clause prohibited the government from providing funds collected by the government to advance a religious perspective. The Court responded to this argument by noting that the program did not single out religious viewpoints for favorable treatment, but rather was neutral with regard to the perspective of speakers receiving funds. "The neutrality of the program distinguishes the student fees from a tax levied for the direct support of a church or group of churches." *Id.* at 840. Four Justices based their dissent on the Establishment Clause issue, arguing that the direct provision of government funds to facilitate religious proselytizing violated several of the Court's precedents regarding government financing of religious activity. Writing for the four dissenters, Justice Souter asked rhetorically:

> Why does the Court not apply this clear law to these clear facts and conclude, as I do, that the funding scheme here is a clear constitutional violation? The answer must be in part that the Court fails to confront the

---

[13] Indeed, I do not think *any* disclaimer could dispel the message of endorsement in this case. Capitol Square's location in downtown Columbus, Ohio, makes it inevitable that countless motorists and pedestrians would immediately perceive the proximity of the cross to the Capitol without necessarily noticing any disclaimer of public sponsorship. The plurality thus correctly abjures inquiry into the possible adequacy or significance of a legend identifying the owner of the cross. JUSTICE SOUTER is of the view that an adequate disclaimer is constitutionally required, but he does not suggest that the attachment to the Klan's cross in this case was adequate.

evidence [regarding the religious nature of the activity in question]. Throughout its opinion, the Court refers uninformatively to Wide Awake's "Christian viewpoint," or its "religious perspective," and in distinguishing funding of Wide Awake from the funding of a church, the Court maintains that "[Wide Awake] is not a religious institution, at least in the usual sense." The Court does not quote the magazine's adoption of Saint Paul's exhortation to awaken to the nearness of salvation, or any of its articles enjoining readers to accept Jesus Christ, or the religious verses, or the religious textual analyses, or the suggested prayers. And so it is easy for the Court to lose sight of what the University students and the Court of Appeals found so obvious, and to blanch the patently and frankly evangelistic character of the magazine by unrevealing allusions to religious points of view.

Id. at 876-77 (Souter, J., dissenting).

2. *Rosenberger* holds that the Free Speech Clause of the First Amendment protects religious speech, even to the extent of mandating that the government give religious groups access to government funds. Are the outcomes of *Widmar*, *Mergens*, *Lamb's Chapel*, and *Pinette* also dictated by the Free Speech Clause as well as the Religion Clauses? If so, does Justice O'Connor (and the other four Justices who join her on this point in *Pinette*) deny religious practitioners their full First Amendment free speech rights when she rejects the majority's proposed rule that "[r]eligious expression cannot violate the Establishment Clause where it (1) is purely private and (2) occurs in a traditional or designated public forum, publicly announced and open to all on equal terms"? How does one determine when private religious speech in a public forum becomes problematic under the Establishment Clause? One key factor seems to be the extent to which the religious speech dominates the forum. "At some point . . . a private religious group may so dominate a public forum that a formal policy of equal access is transformed into a demonstration of approval." *Pinette*, 515 U.S. at 777 (O'Connor, J., concurring in part and concurring in the judgment). According to Justice O'Connor, private religious domination of a government forum, like direct governmental approval of religious ideas, potentially sends "a message to nonadherents that they are outsiders, not full members of the political community, and an accompanying message to adherents that they are insiders, favored members of the political community." *Id.* at 773 (quoting *Lynch v. Donnelly*, 465 U.S. at 688 (O'Connor, J., concurring)). This is consistent with caveats the Court has expressed elsewhere with regard to its holdings in the open access cases. In those cases, the Court has suggested that domination of a public school's "limited open forum" by religious groups would alone probably be sufficient to violate the Establishment Clause. *See Mergens*, 496 U.S. at 252 (noting the wide variety of nonreligious student groups at school). "At least in the absence of empirical evidence that religious groups will dominate [the university's] open forum, . . . the advancement of religion would not be the forum's 'primary effect.'" *Id.* (citing *Widmar*); *Widmar*, 454 U.S. at 274 (noting that over 100 student groups existed at the school and emphasizing that "[t]he provision of benefits to so broad a spectrum of groups is an important index of secular effect").

Justice O'Connor's *Pinette* opinion also identifies several factors other than outright domination of a public forum that may also contribute to a finding that private religious speech ostracizes nonadherents and, therefore, violates the Establishment Clause. These factors include "the fortuity of geography, the nature of the particular public space, or the character of the religious speech at issue." *Pinette*, 515 U.S. at 778 (O'Connor, J., concurring in part and concurring in the judgment). What do these factors mean exactly? O'Connor does not define these factors precisely, so consider the following suggestion:

> With regard to "the fortuity of geography" and "the nature of the par-
> ticular public space," several additional elements may indicate that a
> particular example of private religious speech on government property
> violates the Establishment Clause: (1) the scale of the religious exercise
> is such that it essentially monopolizes a significant portion of a partic-
> ular forum; (2) the religious speech is repetitive and frequent, thus con-
> stantly reinforcing the perceived link between the government forum
> and the religious perspective; (3) the religious speech takes a form that
> is especially intrusive on unwilling observers; and (4) the religious
> speech alters the forum in a way that draws attention to the relation-
> ship between religion and government. If any of these elements are
> found in a case involving private religious speech on government prop-
> erty, then this should constitute strong evidence that religious dis-
> senters are being forced to opt out of that forum in violation of the
> Establishment Clause.

Steven G. Gey, *When is Religious Speech Not "Free Speech"?*, 2000 U. ILL. L. REV. 379, 445.

3. How should these factors apply in particular cases? Consider the following examples:

In *Doe v. Village of Crestwood*, 917 F.2d 1476 (7th Cir. 1990), *cert. denied*, 505 U.S. 1218 (1992), the village of Crestwood, Illinois, sponsored a municipal festival called "A Touch of Italy." A "Beer Garden tent" in the Park housed several of the Festival's activities. An employee of the Village invited a Roman Catholic priest, to celebrate mass in the tent on Saturday afternoon. The mass would have included the customary prayers and Eucharist of the Roman Catholic church. An altar would have been installed in the Beer Garden tent for the occasion, along with a cross and lighted candles. None of the costs of these displays would have been borne by the village. The court held that although the park was a public forum, "everything turns on who is putting on this mass. Is it the Village, or is the church or a private club sponsoring a mass in the Village's public forum? The district court found that the Village is the sponsor, and we do not believe this to be clearly erroneous. Doe's verified complaint states that the Village is the sponsor. The Village concedes that one of its employees selected and recruited the priest. An article in a newspaper published by the Village bears the headline: 'Italian Mass to be celebrated at our Italian Fest.' As the district judge emphasized, 'our' implies that the mass and Festival alike are under the Village's sponsorship." Based on this assumption of village sponsorship, the court of appeals upheld a preliminary injunction issued against the mass.

In *O'Hair v. Andrus*, 613 F.2d 931 (D.C. Cir. 1979), the court rejected an Establishment Clause challenge to a large outdoor Mass conducted by Pope John Paul II on public land including the National Mall, the Washington Monument grounds, the Ellipse, and the Lincoln Memorial green. The court held that this land had regularly been made available to demonstrators speaking on a variety of topics. The estimated cost of the Park Police service of the Mass was between $100,000 and $150,000 and an estimated additional $28,450 would be required for the other services. The court held that these expenditures did not violate the constitutional prohibition on financing religious activity. The government estimated that approximately 500,000 people would attend the Mass.

In contrast to *O'Hair*, see *Gilfillan v. Philadelphia*, 637 F.2d 924 (3d Cir. 1980), *cert. denied*, 451 U.S. 987 (1981), in which the court held unconstitutional several actions undertaken by the city of Philadelphia to prepare for the Pope's outdoor mass at a public park in downtown Philadelphia. The unconstitutional actions included the city's expenditure of more than $200,000 to construct a special platform used to celebrate the Mass, the rental of 20,000 chairs for seating guests who obtained tickets from Archdiocese, the rental of a sound system, the planting of shrubbery and flowers, and the building of a smaller choir platform.

Does the fact that a public forum is essentially taken over by a religious group for a period of time constitute "domination" of the forum under O'Connor's theory in *Pinette*?

4. How do the rules regarding free speech and religion apply in the context of public schools? *Widmar* and the other open access cases deal with aspects of after-school allocation of space on public forum principles, but what about teacher and student speech during the school day? Consider the following examples:

In *C.H. ex rel Z.H. v. Oliva*, 195 F.3d 167 (3d Cir. 1999), *aff'd by an equally divided vote*, 226 F.3d 198 (3d Cir. 2000), *cert. denied*, 533 U.S. 915 (2001), the Third Circuit Court of Appeals rejected free speech and Religion Clause claims against a school for two incidents allegedly infringing on the rights of an elementary school student. In the first incident, the student had produced a Thanksgiving poster indicating that he was thankful for Jesus. This poster was initially hung in the hallway outside the student's kindergarten class, but later was moved to a less prominent location because of its religious content. In a second incident a year later, the same student was invited to read one of his favorite stories to his first-grade class. The student chose to read a story from a book entitled "The Beginner's Bible: Timeless Children's Stories," which was a cartoon-illustrated collection of ninety-five children's stories based on the Bible. The story was entitled "A Big Family," and was based on *Genesis* 29:1-33:20. The teacher informed the student that he could not read the story to the class because of its religious content (although he was permitted to read the story to the teacher).

The court held that the teacher had acted appropriately in light of legitimate pedagogical concerns in refusing to allow the student to read the Bible story in class. "For children at this level, the teacher is a primary source of authority in their lives. They look to their teacher for signals of appropriate behavior. As a result, lessons that a first-grade teacher imparts to a class, or allows to be imparted in a classroom under her supervision, are likely to be understood as carrying her imprimatur. While older students may be able to distinguish messages a teacher specifically advocates from those she merely allows to be expressed in the classroom, most first graders cannot be counted on to make this nuanced distinction." *Oliva*, 195 F.3d at 174-75. The court also noted that in this context, the other students in the class were in effect a captive audience, and it "is not unreasonable to expect that parents of non-Christian children would resent exposure of their six-year-old children to a reading from the Bible." *Id.* at 175. The court also upheld the school's decision to temporarily remove the religious poster, on the ground that "[g]iven the sensitivity of the issues raised by student religious expression, coupled with the notable immaturity of the students involved and the relatively public display of the posters in the school hallway," the action related to legitimate pedagogical concerns and thus did not violate the student's First Amendment rights.

Judge Samuel Alito dissented to the Third Circuit's en banc ruling in *Oliva*. He called the majority's ground for dismissing the plaintiffs' claims "spurious," and went on to argue that the school district and teacher had violated Z.H.'s First Amendment rights. Judge Alito stated a very broad principle to defend this result: "I would hold that discriminatory treatment of the poster because of its 'religious theme' would violate the First Amendment. Specifically, I would hold that public school students have the right to express religious views in class discussion or in assigned work, provided that their expression falls within the scope of the discussion or the assignment and provided that the school's restriction on expression does not satisfy strict scrutiny." *Oliva*, 226 F.3d at 210 (Alito, J., dissenting).

In *Settle v. Dickson County School Board*, 53 F.3d 152 (6th Cir. 1995), the court denied a free speech claim against a junior high school teacher who rejected a student's proposal to write a ninth-grade research paper on "The Life of Jesus Christ." The court held that the teacher had wide discretion to regulate classroom speech in performing her teaching function. "It is not for us to overrule the teacher's view that the student should learn to write research papers by beginning with a topic other than her own theology. Papers on the transfiguration of Jesus and similar topics may display more faith than rational analysis in the hands of a young student with a strong religious heritage — at least the teacher is entitled to make such a judgment in the classroom." *Id.* at 156.

In *DeNooyer v. Livonia Public Schools.*, 799 F. Supp. 744 (E.D. Mich. 1992), *aff'd in unpublished disposition*, 12 F.3d 211 (6th Cir. 1993), *cert. denied*, 511 U.S. 1031 (1994), the court upheld a school district's order prohibiting a student from showing a videotape of herself singing a proselytizing religious song to a second-grade class during show and tell. The teacher in this case had created a program under which students would make verbal presentations to the class about items that were interesting or important to them. One student brought a videotape to class and asked that it be shown. The videotape recorded her performance of a religious song at a worship service at the Baptist Church of which she and her parents were members. The song described the benefits of a child's early relationship with Jesus Christ and the importance of turning over one's "childish heart of sin" in order to be saved. In her deposition, the student testified that she wanted to share the message of the song with her classmates "[b]ecause I might have a chance to help people get saved." Among other things, the teacher testified that she was concerned about the videotape's religious message, which she believed was inappropriate for second graders in a public school classroom, and could potentially be viewed as communicating the school's endorsement of the message of the song. She was also concerned that the video might embarrass or offend other students in the classroom who were not Christians. In an unpublished affirmance of the district court's summary judgment ruling in favor of the school, the court of appeals held that the proposed presentation was part of the class curriculum and was therefore school-sponsored expression that could be regulated based on any legitimate pedagogical concern.

In *Duran v. Nitsche*, 780 F. Supp. 1048 (E.D. Pa. 1991), *order vacated and appeal dismissed*, 972 F.2d 1331 (3d Cir. 1992), the court denied an injunction against school officials who prohibited a student from distributing a survey on God and giving an oral presentation on "The Power of God" to a fifth-grade class. The court held that the classroom was not a designated public forum and that the teacher had exercised reasonable judgment in refusing the student's proposed project.

In considering cases involving religious speech in the school context, note that the Supreme Court has permitted far more restrictions on speech than would be permitted outside the confines of the school. *See, e.g., Hazelwood Sch. Dist. v. Kuhlmeier*, 484 U.S. 260 (1988) (giving school authorities broad authority to edit a student's speech in a school-sponsored newspaper); *Bethel Sch. Dist. No. 403 v. Fraser*, 478 U.S. 675 (1986) (broadly construing a school's authority to punish "disruptive" student speech, even as applied to mildly salacious speech by a student council candidate).

5. Most of the cases in note 4, *supra*, address the problems raised by the religious expression of students in public schools. In addition to these cases, there also are a significant number of cases involving the religious expression of public school teachers. As the cases in note 4 indicate, the courts generally defer to public school administrators in regulating student religious speech; if anything, the courts are even more willing to defer to public school administrators in limiting religious speech by teachers. In part, this greater deference is attributable to the fact that public school teachers (at least below the university level) probably have fewer free speech rights in the classroom than the students they teach. This is due to the fact that the Supreme Court has given public employers wide leeway in limiting public employee speech at work whenever that speech threatens to become disruptive. *See Connick v. Myers*, 461 U.S. 138 (1983); *Waters v. Churchill*, 511 U.S. 661 (1994).

> [W]e have consistently given greater deference to government predictions of harm used to justify restriction of employee speech than to predictions of harm used to justify restrictions on the speech of the public at large. . . . [W]e have given substantial weight to government employers' reasonable predictions of disruption, even when the speech involved is on a matter of public concern. . . . Similarly, we have refrained from intervening in government employer decisions that are based on speech that is of entirely private concern. Doubtless some such speech is sometimes nondisruptive; doubtless it is sometimes of value to the speakers and the listeners. But we have declined to question government employers' decisions on such matters.

Waters, 511 U.S. at 673-74.

The deference afforded to limitations on speech when the government acts as an employer probably is constrained somewhat in the educational environment by academic freedom concerns, especially at the university level, although the Supreme Court has not delineated clearly the extent to which academic freedom provides an independent basis for First Amendment protection of speech by individual public school teachers and professors. *Compare Keyishian v. Bd. of Regents*, 385 U.S. 589, 603 (1967) (the First Amendment "does not tolerate laws that cast a pall of orthodoxy over the classroom"), *with Urofsky v. Gilmore*, 216 F.3d 401, 412, 414 (4th Cir. 2000) (asserting that the concept of academic freedom is merely a recognition of "an institutional right of self-governance in academic affairs," which means that individual professors at a public university have no First Amendment right "to determine for themselves the content of their courses and scholarship").

In applying these principles to the religious expression of individual public school teachers, the clearest examples in which courts have deferred to public school limitations on expression have been cases in which the teacher overtly injects his or her own religious ideas or perspective into classroom discussions — especially when the context of the expression may be interpreted by students as implicitly coercive. *See Marchi v. Bd. of Coop. Educ. Servs. of Albany*, 173 F.3d 469 (2d Cir.), *cert. denied*, 528 U.S. 869 (1999) (upholding school board's cease and desist order against a teacher who converted to Christianity and then modified his instructional program to discuss topics such as forgiveness, reconciliation, and God). Although the government interests in limiting in-class religious discussion are presumably strongest below the university level, at least one court has upheld government limitations on a public university professor's religious speech in a university classroom. *See Bishop v. Aronov*, 926 F.2d 1066 (11th Cir. 1991) (upholding university action requiring professor to refrain from injecting his religious views into an exercise psychology class, and also to refrain from holding "optional" classes to discuss the Christian perspective on academic matters). The Second Circuit's broad conclusion in *Marchi* seems to be the standard response to public educational authorities' efforts to limit teachers' in-class religious discussions:

> [W]hen government endeavors to police itself and its employees in an effort to avoid transgressing Establishment Clause limits, it must be accorded some leeway, even though the conduct it forbids might not inevitably be determined to violate the Establishment Clause and the limitations it imposes might restrict an individual's conduct that might well be protected by the Free Exercise Clause if the individual were not acting as an agent of government.

Marchi, 173 F.3d at 476.

Harder questions of free speech are presented where the teacher does not purposely inject his or her religious views into classroom discussions, but rather passively expresses religious views through the wearing of religious articles or clothing. One federal district court rejected a free speech challenge to a public school's action prohibiting a teacher from wearing in class during instructional time a t-shirt with the inscription "JESUS 2000-J2K." *Downing v. West Haven Bd. of Educ.*, 162 F. Supp. 2d 19 (D.Conn. 2001). Upon learning that the teacher was wearing the shirt, and after consulting with school district lawyers, the vice principal ordered the teacher to cover the shirt or change into other clothes. She covered the shirt with a lab coat for the rest of the day. In rejecting the teacher's lawsuit for violations of her free exercise and free speech rights, the court relied heavily on the Second Circuit's opinion in *Marchi*, without discussing the possible differences between the protection of active and passive religious expression by teachers. The district court concluded that since the teacher wore the offending shirt during the school day there was a substantial likelihood that the students would attribute the teacher's expression to the school itself. If viewed as a statement endorsed by the school, the t-shirt inscription would clearly violate the Establishment Clause. The court went on to note that even if the shirt did not constitute a clear-cut violation of the Establishment Clause, the school was still entitled to prohibit the teacher from wearing it in class. "[W]hatever First Amendment rights were implicated by Downing wearing her tee shirt must give way to the defendants' legitimate concerns about a potential Establishment Clause violation in the public school." *Id.* at 28.

Is the result in *Downing* limited by the fact that the religious expression in that case was relatively obtrusive and explicit? What if the school district broadened its prohibition on individual teacher religious expression to include a ban on even unobtrusive religious symbols, such as crucifixes and yarmulkes? The Court has already upheld religious expression regulations that are this restrictive in the military context. *See Goldman v. Weinberger, infra* Chapter 11.

Is the real problem in *Downing* that the students might misattribute the teachers' speech as speech endorsed by the government? Would a simple memorandum from the vice principal to the students disavowing the teacher's religious views extinguish any Establishment Clause concern? If so, what would be the result if a public school allowed all or virtually all its teachers to exercise their rights to religious speech in class and in exactly the same way? In Orlando, Florida, for example, public school officials permitted teachers to celebrate "Friday Spirit Day" by wearing to class t-shirts inscribed with the phrase "Champions in Christ" on the front and a New Testament verse on the back. See Mark I. Pinsky, *Christian Groups Seek Converts at Schools; A Friendlier Legal Environment Finds at Least Five Outreach Groups Active in Area Public Schools*, ORLANDO SENTINEL, Sept. 14, 1997, at A1. The school officials bowed to the obvious Establishment Clause problems inherent in this activity simply by circulating a memo "explaining that the shirts 'are purely the private expression of that teacher or staff member and do not reflect the policy of or endorsement from the high school.'" *Id.* Does this satisfy Establishment Clause concerns, or on the contrary does it illustrate how permitting private religious expression by public school teachers can effectively undermine Establishment Clause restrictions on symbolic endorsement of religion?

To deal with the problems addressed in cases such as *Downing*, some states have adopted explicit "religious garb" statutes prohibiting public school teachers from wearing any religious articles or clothing to class. The Pennsylvania statute (which was originally enacted in 1895) contains the following provisions:

> (a) That no teacher in any public school shall wear in said school or while engaged in the performance of his duty as such teacher any dress, mark, emblem or insignia indicating the fact that such teacher is a member or adherent of any religious order, sect or denomination.

> (b) Any teacher employed in any of the public schools of this Commonwealth, who violates the provisions of this section, shall be suspended from employment in such school for the term of one year, and in case of a second offense by the same teacher he shall be permanently disqualified from teaching in said school. Any public school director who after notice of any such violation fails to comply with the provisions of this section shall be guilty of a misdemeanor, and upon conviction of the first offense, shall be sentenced to pay a fine not exceeding one hundred dollars ($100), and on conviction of a second offense, the offending school director shall be sentenced to pay a fine not exceeding one hundred dollars ($100) and shall be deprived of his office as a public school director. A person thus twice convicted shall not be eligible to appointment or election as a director of any public school in this Commonwealth within a period of five (5) years from the date of his second conviction.

24 Pa. Cons. Stat. Ann. § 11-1112 (2002).

There have been several cases involving the Pennsylvania statute. In *United States v. Board of Education of School District of Philadelphia*, 911 F.2d 882 (3d Cir. 1990), the Third Circuit denied a Title VII religious discrimination claim brought against the Philadelphia board of education by a devout Muslim teacher who was fired as a substitute teacher. The board's rationale for firing the teacher was the teacher's refusal to conform to the requirements of the Pennsylvania religious garb statute. The plaintiff sought to wear a "head scarf which covered her head, neck, and bosom leaving her face visible and a long loose dress which covered her arms to her wrists." *Id.*, 911 F.2d at 884. The Third Circuit found that the teacher's actions could not be accommodated without undue hardship by the board of education because the board itself would be subject to criminal penalties if they did not enforce the Pennsylvania statute. In another case, a district court ruled in favor of another Muslim applicant who was denied a third grade counseling position because of her religious dress, on the ground that a simple head covering (such as a scarf) would not necessarily be perceived as religious garb by students and therefore does not come within the ambit of the Pennsylvania statute. *E.E.O.C. v. Reads, Inc.*, 759 F. Supp. 1150 (E.D. Pa. 1991).

In the most recent decision involving the Pennsylvania statute, a federal district court held that the statute violates both the Free Speech and Free Exercise Clauses of the First Amendment. *See Nichol v. Arin Intermediate Unit 28*, 268 F. Supp. 2d 536 (W.D. Pa. 2003). The case involved a woman who was suspended for one year for refusing to remove or tuck in a small cross necklace while working as an instructional assistant at a public elementary school. The school argued that the Pennsylvania statute did not permit instructional personnel to wear religious items such as the cross. The court held that school's implementation of the state religious garb statute violates the free exercise protection because it "is openly and overtly averse to religion because it singles out and punishes *only* symbolic speech by its employees having religious content or viewpoint, while permitting its employees to wear jewelry containing secular messages or no messages at all." The court concluded that the policy also violates the free speech provision of the First Amendment because it is "a content driven regulation which violates plaintiff's right to free (symbolic or expressive) speech on a matter of public concern." The court rejected the school district's Establishment Clause concerns. Despite the fact that the speech took place during the school day in a public elementary school — where Establishment Clause concerns are at their highest — the court held that "[g]iven the inconspicuous nature of plaintiff's expression of her religious beliefs by wearing a small cross on a necklace, and the fact that other jewelry with secular messages or no messages is permitted to be worn at school, it is extremely unlikely that even elementary students would perceive [the school] to be *endorsing* her otherwise unvoiced Christian viewpoint." The court also rejected the school's reliance on the Third Circuit's decision in *United States v. Board of Education of School District of Philadelphia*. The district court gave three reasons for distinguishing the appellate decision: First, the district court noted that *School District* involved

Title VII and not the Establishment Clause; second, the district court implied that the cross necklace in *Nichol* was significantly more subtle and ambiguous than the head scarf in *School District*; and third, the district court asserted that "significant doctrinal developments" undermined the precedential value of *School District*.

Nichol is unlikely to be the final word on the Pennsylvania religious garb statute. The district court in that case interpreted several First Amendment doctrines very expansively. In rejecting the school's Establishment Clause concerns, for example, the court relied heavily on cases such as *Widmar v. Vincent* and *Good News Club* (*see supra* Chapter 7). These cases all involved private groups seeking to use public school facilities after hours, and it is by no means clear that the holdings of those cases can be expanded to cover religious speech by public school employees during the school day. Also, although the district court noted "significant doctrinal developments" in refusing to follow Third Circuit precedent set forth in *School District*, the only case cited as evidence of this doctrinal development was *Employment Division v. Smith* (*see infra* Chapter 14), a case that actually reduced Free Exercise Clause protections compared to the governing precedents when the Third Circuit decided *School District*. On the other hand, the Supreme Court's growing emphasis on governmental neutrality toward religion, which is most evident in school funding decisions such as *Zelman v. Simmons-Harris* (*see infra* Chapter 9), may lend support to the district court's decision in *Nichol*.

One of the most significant religious garb decisions outside Pennsylvania involved the Oregon religious garb statute. In *Cooper v. Eugene School District No. 4J*, 723 P.2d 298 (Or. 1986), the Oregon Supreme Court upheld the statute. The Oregon court's decision includes a long discussion of the genesis of religious garb statutes across the country and notes that many of the statutes (including Oregon's) were motivated originally by anti-Catholic animus. *See id.* at 308. The court noted, however, that the statute was reenacted in 1965, and "[t]here is no reason to believe that . . . the Legislature . . . [then] had any aim other than to maintain the religious neutrality of the public schools, to avoid giving children or their parents the impression that the school, through its teacher, approves and shares the religious commitment of one group and perhaps finds that of others less worthy." *Id.* The court thus upheld the statute as a mechanism for reinforcing Establishment Clause protections in the classroom and "contribut[ing] to the child's right to the free exercise and enjoyment of its religious opinions or heritage, untroubled by being out of step with those of the teacher." *Id.* at 310.

5. How do the free speech concerns expressed in some of these cases relate to the secular purpose requirement of *Lemon* and its variants? Consider the following scenario. A "motivational assembly" is held for students at a public high school during a school day. The students (who assumed the assembly was mandatory) are joined by hundreds of members of a local Baptist church and the assembled group sings religious songs, hears religious testimonials, and listens to a local minister leading the students in "confessions of faith in Jesus." They also hear a speech by a prominent government official who is the highest-ranking law-enforcement official in the county. The official tells the assembled students how "he once told his nine-year-old daughter that the Supreme Court says people can't use the name of Jesus Christ in school, 'yet here we are, in defiance of the U.S. Supreme Court, calling the name of Jesus Christ.'" *See* Doug Cumming, *Assembly of God*, NEW REPUBLIC, Mar. 30, 1998, at 11 (describing episode in Atlanta public school). Has the public official violated the Establishment Clause? If so, is it because he made the remarks in a public school? If he made the same remarks in a prayer breakfast attended only by adults, would the constitutional result be different? Assume that these comments were made by the public school superintendent at a prayer breakfast that was open to the public and attended only by adults. Could the comments at least be used as evidence of the superintendent's impermissible nonsecular purpose if the school system was later charged with authorizing impermissible religious activity in the public schools? If so, does this restrict the school superintendent's religious free speech rights? If not, can the secular purpose analysis be enforced effectively?

Chapter 8
GOVERNMENT FINANCIAL SUPPORT OF RELIGION: THE TRADITIONAL MODEL

Government financing of religious activity is in many ways the central issue in Establishment Clause jurisprudence. Even before the nation was formed, disputes over state financing of religion — usually in the form of mandatory contribution statutes — dominated discussions about the proper relationship of church and state. One of the new nation's first major political battles over church and state was fought in Virginia over the financing issue, with forces led by Patrick Henry supporting a statute renewing a tax levy for the established church. Not only did this effort to renew the tax fail in the face of opposition by several Protestant denominations, but at the instigation of James Madison, the Virginia legislature instead enacted Thomas Jefferson's Virginia Bill for Religious Liberty. It was in the course of this battle over the Virginia tax that Madison wrote his famous *Memorial and Remonstrance Against Religious Assessments*, which is excerpted in Chapter 1, *supra*. Madison's separationist views on the subject of state financing are reflected in his famous statement in the *Memorial* that even a mandatory contribution of "three pence" for the support of religion would constitute an impermissible establishment of religion. Until very recently, this statement was viewed by the Supreme Court as the basic principle regarding the government financing of religious activity, although the Court has always been inconsistent in applying this principle.

Many of the Supreme Court's earliest Establishment Clause decisions involved the financing issue. The Court chose a financing case to announce that the Establishment Clause is incorporated into the Fourteenth Amendment and therefore applicable to the states. *See Everson v. Bd. of Educ., infra.* The holding in *Everson* illustrates the difficulties the Court has had in defining the proper limits of state financial relationships with religion. Although the Court was essentially unanimous in endorsing a strict separationist interpretation of the Establishment Clause, the Court split 5-4 on applying these principles to the facts before the Court. Since *Everson*, the situation has gotten even more complicated as the essential consensus on the Court about abstract principles fractured into many different variations on the themes of separation, neutrality, coercion, and accommodation. In the last decade, for the first time since *Everson*, a majority of the Court has essentially abandoned the earlier reluctance to permit government to finance religious activities, and coalesced around a standard that permits the government to aid religion so long as the government packages its aid in a form that formally is available to nonreligious institutions on the same terms as religious institutions. This new perspective has the potential to radically alter the church/state landscape, in ways that will hearken back to the country's earliest battles over religious liberty and government coercion.

The cases in this chapter illustrate the basic principles of the Establishment Clause model the Court has traditionally applied to financial relationships between church and state. The next chapter is devoted to cases decided during the last decade, in which a new majority of the Court has largely abandoned the traditional model, in favor of a new vision of the Establishment Clause, under which government financing of religious activities and institutions is permitted to a far greater degree than it was under the traditional model.

A. TAX DEDUCTIONS FOR RELIGIOUS INSTITUTIONS

WALZ v. TAX COMMISSION OF THE CITY OF NEW YORK
397 U.S. 664 (1970)

MR. CHIEF JUSTICE BURGER delivered the opinion of the Court.

Appellant, owner of real estate in Richmond County, New York, sought an injunction in the New York courts to prevent the New York City Tax Commission from granting property tax exemptions to religious organizations for religious properties used solely for religious worship. The exemption from state taxes provides in relevant part:

> "Exemptions from taxation may be granted only by general laws. Exemptions may be altered or repealed except those exempting real or personal property used exclusively for religious, educational or charitable purposes as defined by law and owned by any corporation or association organized or conducted exclusively for one or more of such purposes and not operating for profit."

The essence of appellant's contention was that the New York City Tax Commission's grant of an exemption to church property indirectly requires the appellant to make a contribution to religious bodies and thereby violates provisions prohibiting establishment of religion under the First Amendment which under the Fourteenth Amendment is binding on the States.

I

The course of constitutional neutrality in this area cannot be an absolutely straight line; rigidity could well defeat the basic purpose of these provisions, which is to insure that no religion be sponsored or favored, none commanded, and none inhibited. The general principle deducible from the First Amendment and all that has been said by the Court is this: that we will not tolerate either governmentally established religion or governmental interference with religion. Short of those expressly proscribed governmental acts there is room for play in the joints productive of a benevolent neutrality which will permit religious exercise to exist without sponsorship and without interference.

Each value judgment under the Religion Clauses must therefore turn on whether particular acts in question are intended to establish or interfere with religious beliefs and practices or have the effect of doing so. Adherence to the policy of neutrality that derives from an accommodation of the Establishment and Free Exercise Clauses has prevented the kind of involvement that would tip the balance toward government control of churches or governmental restraint on religious practice.

Adherents of particular faiths and individual churches frequently take strong positions on public issues including, as this case reveals in the several briefs *amici*, vigorous advocacy of legal or constitutional positions. Of course, churches as much as secular bodies and private citizens have that right. No perfect or absolute separation is really possible; the very existence of the Religion Clauses is an involvement of sorts — one that seeks to mark boundaries to avoid excessive entanglement.

II

The legislative purpose of a property tax exemption is neither the advancement nor the inhibition of religion; it is neither sponsorship nor hostility. New York, in common with the other States, has determined that certain entities that exist in a harmonious relationship to the community at large, and that foster its "moral or mental improvement," should not be inhibited in their activities by property taxation or the hazard of loss of those properties for nonpayment of taxes. It has not singled out one particular church or religious group or even churches as such; rather, it has granted exemption to all houses of religious worship within a broad class of property owned by nonprofit, quasi-public corporations which include hospitals, libraries, playgrounds, scientific, professional, historical, and patriotic groups. The State has an affirmative policy that considers these groups as beneficial and stabilizing influences in community life and finds this classification useful, desirable, and in the public interest. Qualification for tax exemption is not perpetual or immutable; some tax-exempt groups lose that status when their activities take them outside the classification and new entities can come into being and qualify for exemption.

Governments have not always been tolerant of religious activity, and hostility toward religion has taken many shapes and forms — economic, political, and sometimes harshly oppressive. Grants of exemption historically reflect the concern of authors of constitutions and statutes as to the latent dangers inherent in the imposition of property taxes; exemption constitutes a reasonable and balanced attempt to guard against those dangers. The limits of permissible state accommodation to religion are by no means co-extensive with the noninterference mandated by the Free Exercise Clause. To equate the two would be to deny a national heritage with roots in the Revolution itself. We cannot read New York's statute as attempting to establish religion; it is simply sparing the exercise of religion from the burden of property taxation levied on private profit institutions.

We find it unnecessary to justify the tax exemption on the social welfare services or "good works" that some churches perform for parishioners and others — family counseling, aid to the elderly and the infirm, and to children. Churches vary substantially in the scope of such services; programs expand or contract according to resources and need. As public-sponsored programs enlarge, private aid from the church sector may diminish. The extent of social services may vary, depending on whether the church serves an urban or rural, a rich or poor constituency. To give emphasis to so variable an aspect of the work of religious bodies would introduce an element of governmental evaluation and standards as to the worth of particular social welfare programs, thus producing a kind of continuing day-to-day relationship which the policy of neutrality seeks to minimize. Hence, the use of a social welfare yardstick as a significant element to qualify for tax exemption could conceivably give rise to confrontations that could escalate to constitutional dimensions.

Determining that the legislative purpose of tax exemption is not aimed at establishing, sponsoring, or supporting religion does not end the inquiry, however. We must also be sure that the end result — the effect — is not an excessive government entanglement with religion. The test is inescapably one of degree. Either course, taxation of churches or exemption, occasions some degree of involvement with religion. Elimination of exemption would tend to expand the involvement of government by giving rise to tax valuation of church property, tax liens, tax foreclosures, and the direct confrontations and conflicts that follow in the train of those legal processes.

Granting tax exemptions to churches necessarily operates to afford an indirect economic benefit and also gives rise to some, but yet a lesser, involvement than taxing them. In analyzing either alternative the questions are whether the involvement is excessive, and whether it is a continuing one calling for official and continuing surveillance leading to an impermissible degree of entanglement. Obviously a direct money subsidy would be a relationship pregnant with involvement and, as with most governmental grant programs, could encompass sustained and detailed administrative relationships for enforcement of statutory or administrative standards, but that is not this case. The hazards of churches supporting government are hardly less in their potential than the hazards of government supporting churches; each relationship carries some involvement rather than the desired insulation and separation. We cannot ignore the instances in history when church support of government led to the kind of involvement we seek to avoid.

The grant of a tax exemption is not sponsorship since the government does not transfer part of its revenue to churches but simply abstains from demanding that the church support the state. No one has ever suggested that tax exemption has converted libraries, art galleries, or hospitals into arms of the state or put employees "on the public payroll." There is no genuine nexus between tax exemption and establishment of religion. As Mr. Justice Holmes commented in a related context "a page of history is worth of volume of logic." *New York Trust Co. v. Eisner*, 256 U.S. 345, 349 (1921). The exemption creates only a minimal and remote involvement between church and state and far less than taxation of churches. It restricts the fiscal relationship between church and state, and tends to complement and reinforce the desired separation insulating each from the other.

Nothing in this national attitude toward religious tolerance and two centuries of uninterrupted freedom from taxation has given the remotest sign of leading to an established church or religion and on the contrary it has operated affirmatively to help guarantee the free exercise of all forms of religious belief. Thus, it is hardly useful to suggest that tax exemption is but the "foot in the door" or the "nose of the camel in the tent" leading to an established church. If tax exemption can be seen as this first step toward "establishment" of religion, as MR. JUSTICE DOUGLAS fears, the second step has been long in coming. Any move that realistically "establishes" a church or tends to do so can be dealt with "while this Court sits."

Mr. Justice Cardozo commented in THE NATURE OF THE JUDICIAL PROCESS 51 (1921) on the "tendency of a principle to expand itself to the limit of its logic"; such expansion must always be contained by the historical frame of reference of the principle's purpose and there is no lack of vigilance on this score by those who fear religious entanglement in government.

MR. JUSTICE BRENNAN, concurring.

II

Government has two basic secular purposes for granting real property tax exemptions to religious organizations. First, these organizations are exempted because they, among a range of other private, nonprofit organizations contribute to the well-being of the community in a variety of nonreligious ways, and thereby bear burdens that would otherwise either have to be met by general taxation, or be left undone, to the detriment of the community. Thus, New York exempts "[r]eal property owned by a corporation or association organized exclusively for the moral or mental improvement of men and women, or for religious, bible, tract, charitable, benevolent, missionary, hospital, infirmary, educational, public playground, scientific, literary, bar association, medical society, library, patriotic, historical or cemetery purposes, for the enforcement of laws relating to children or animals, or for two or more such purposes. . . ." N.Y. Real Prop. Tax Law § 420, subd. 1 (Supp. 1969-1970).

Appellant seeks to avoid the force of this secular purpose of the exemptions by limiting his challenge to "exemptions from real property taxation to religious organizations on real property used exclusively for religious purposes." Appellant assumes, apparently, that church-owned property is used for exclusively religious purposes if it does not house a hospital, orphanage, weekday school, or the like. Any assumption that a church building itself is used for exclusively religious activities, however, rests on a simplistic view of ordinary church operations. As the appellee's brief cogently observes, "the public welfare activities and the sectarian activities of religious institutions are . . . intertwined . . .. Often a particular church will use the same personnel, facilities and source of funds to carry out both its secular and religious activities." Thus, the same people who gather in church facilities for religious worship and study may return to these facilities to participate in Boy Scout activities, to promote antipoverty causes, to discuss public issues, or to listen to chamber music. Accordingly, the funds used to maintain the facilities as a place for religious worship and study also maintain them as a place for secular activities beneficial to the community as a whole. Even during formal worship services, churches frequently collect the funds used to finance their secular operations and make decisions regarding their nature.

Second, government grants exemptions to religious organizations because they uniquely contribute to the pluralism of American society by their religious activities. Government may properly include religious institutions among the variety of private, nonprofit groups that receive tax exemptions, for each group contributes to the diversity of association, viewpoint, and enterprise essential to a vigorous, pluralistic society. To this end, New York extends its exemptions not only to religious and social service organizations but also to scientific, literary, bar, library, patriotic, and historical groups, and generally to institutions "organized exclusively for the moral or mental improvement of men and women." The very breadth of this scheme of exemptions negates any suggestion that the State intends to single out religious organizations for special preference. The scheme is not designed to inject any religious activity into a nonreligious context, as was the case with school prayers. No particular activity of a religious organization — for example, the propagation of its beliefs — is specially promoted by the exemptions. They merely facilitate the existence of a broad range of private, non-profit organizations, among them religious groups, by leaving each free to come into existence, then to flourish or wither, without being burdened by real property taxes.

MR. JUSTICE DOUGLAS, dissenting.

Petitioner is the owner of real property in New York and is a Christian. But he is not a member of any of the religious organizations, "rejecting them as hostile." The New York statute exempts from taxation real property "owned by a corporation or association organized exclusively for . . . religious . . . purposes" and used "exclusively for carrying out" such purposes. Yet nonbelievers who own realty are taxed at the usual rate. The question in the case therefore is whether believers — organized in church groups — can be made exempt from real estate taxes, merely because they are believers, while non-believers, whether organized or not, must pay the real estate taxes.

My Brother HARLAN says he "would suppose" that the tax exemption extends to "groups whose avowed tenets may be antitheological, atheistic, or agnostic." If it does, then the line between believers and nonbelievers has not been drawn.

But, with all respect, there is not even a suggestion in the present record that the statute covers property used exclusively by organizations for "antitheological purposes," "atheistic purposes," or "agnostic purposes."

In *Torcaso v. Watkins,* 367 U.S. 488, we held that a State could not bar an atheist from public office in light of the freedom of belief and religion guaranteed by the First and Fourteenth Amendments. Neither the State nor the Federal Government, we said, "can constitutionally pass laws or impose requirements which aid all religions as against non-believers, and neither can aid those religions based on a belief in the existence of God as against those religions founded on different beliefs." *Id.,* at 495.

That principle should govern this case.

There is a line between what a State may do in encouraging "religious" activities, and what a State may not do by using its resources to promote "religious" activities, or bestowing benefits because of them. Yet that line may not always be clear. Closing public schools on Sunday is in the former category; subsidizing churches, in my view, is in the latter. Indeed I would suppose that in common understanding one of the best ways to "establish" one or more religions is to subsidize them, which a tax exemption does. The State may not do that any more than it may prefer "those who believe in no religion over those who do believe." *Zorach v. Clauson, supra,* 343 U.S. at 314.

In affirming this judgment the Court largely overlooks the revolution initiated by the adoption of the Fourteenth Amendment. That revolution involved the imposition of new and far-reaching constitutional restraints on the States. Nationalization of many civil liberties has been the consequence of the Fourteenth Amendment, reversing the historic position that the foundations of those liberties rested largely in state law.

The process of the "selective incorporation" of various provisions of the Bill of Rights into the Fourteenth Amendment, although often provoking lively disagreement at large as well as among the members of this Court, has been a steady one. It started in 1897 with *Chicago, B. & Q.R. Co. v. Chicago,* 166 U.S. 226, in which the Court held that the Fourteenth Amendment precluded a State from taking private property for public use without payment of just compensation, as provided in the Fifth Amendment. The first direct holding as to the incorporation of the First Amendment into the Fourteenth occurred in 1931 in *Stromberg v. California,* 283 U.S. 359, a case involving the right of free speech, although that holding in *Stromberg* had been foreshadowed in 1925 by the Court's opinion in *Gitlow v. New York,* 268 U.S. 652. As regards the religious guarantees of the First Amendment, the Free Exercise Clause was expressly deemed incorporated into the Fourteenth Amendment in 1940 in *Cantwell v. Connecticut,* 310 U.S. 296, although that holding had been foreshadowed in 1923 and 1934 by the Court's dicta in *Meyer v. Nebraska,* 262 U.S. 390, 399 and *Hamilton v. Regents,* 293 U.S. 245, 262. The Establishment Clause was not incorporated in the Fourteenth Amendment until *Everson v. Board of Education* was decided in 1947.

Those developments in the last 30 years have had unsettling effects. It was, for example, not until 1962 that state-sponsored, sectarian prayers were held to violate the Establishment Clause. *Engel v. Vitale.* That decision brought many protests, for the habit of putting one sect's prayer in public schools had long been practiced. Yet if the Catholics, controlling one school board, could put their prayer into one group of public schools, the Mormons, Baptists, Moslems, Presbyterians, and others could do the same, once they got control. And so the seeds of Establishment would grow and a secular institution would be used to serve a sectarian end.

Hence the question in the present case makes irrelevant the "two centuries of uninterrupted freedom from taxation," referred to by the Court. If history be our guide, then tax exemption of church property in this country is indeed highly suspect, as it arose in the early days when the church was an agency of the state. *See* W. TORPEY, JUDICIAL DOCTRINES OF RELIGIOUS RIGHTS IN AMERICA 171 (1948). The question here, though, concerns the meaning of the Establishment Clause and the Free Exercise Clause made applicable to the States for only a few decades at best.

With all due respect the governing principle is not controlled by *Everson v. Board of Education, supra. Everson* involved the use of public funds to bus children to parochial as well as to public schools. Parochial schools teach religion; yet they are also educational institutions offering courses competitive with public schools. They prepare students for the professions and for activities in all walks of life. Education in the secular sense was combined with religious indoctrination at the parochial schools involved in *Everson.* Even so, the *Everson* decision was five to four and, though one of the five, I have since had grave doubts about it, because I have become convinced that grants to institutions teaching a sectarian creed violate the Establishment Clause. *See Engel v. Vitale* (DOUGLAS, J., concurring).

This case, however, is quite different. Education is not involved. The financial support rendered here is to the church, the place of worship. A tax exemption is a subsidy. Is my Brother BRENNAN correct in saying that we would hold that state or federal grants to churches, say, to construct the edifice itself would be unconstitutional? What is the difference between that kind of subsidy and the present subsidy?

Certainly government may not lay a tax on either worshiping or preaching. In *Murdock v. Pennsylvania*, 319 U.S. 105, we ruled on a state license tax levied on religious colporteurs as a condition to pursuit of their activities. In holding the tax unconstitutional we said:

> "The power to tax the exercise of a privilege is the power to control or suppress its enjoyment. *Magnano Co. v. Hamilton*, 292 U.S. 40, 44-45, and cases cited. Those who can tax the exercise of this religious practice can make its exercise so costly as to deprive it of the resources necessary for its maintenance. Those who can tax the privilege of engaging in

this form of missionary evangelism can close its doors to all those who do not have a full purse. Spreading religious beliefs in this ancient and honorable manner would thus be denied the needy. Those who can deprive religious groups of their colporteurs can take from them a part of the vital power of the press which has survived from the Reformation." *Id.*, at 112.

Churches, like newspapers also enjoying First Amendment rights, have no constitutional immunity from all taxes. As we said in *Murdock*:

"We do not mean to say that religious groups and the press are free from all financial burdens of government. *See Grosjean v. American Press Co.*, 297 U.S. 233, 250. We have here something quite different, for example, from a tax on the income of one who engages in religious activities or a tax on property used or employed in connection with those activities. It is one thing to impose a tax on the income or property of a preacher. It is quite another thing to exact a tax from him for the privilege of delivering a sermon." *Ibid.*

State aid to places of worship, whether in the form of direct grants or tax exemption, takes us back to the Assessment Bill and the Remonstrance. The church *qua* church would not be entitled to that support from believers and from nonbelievers alike. Yet the church *qua* nonprofit, charitable institution is one of many that receive a form of subsidy through tax exemption. To be sure, the New York statute does not single out the church for grant or favor. It includes churches in a long list of nonprofit organizations: for the moral or mental improvement of men and women; for charitable, hospital, or educational purposes; for playgrounds; for scientific or literary objects; for bar associations, medical societies, or libraries; for patriotic and historical purposes; for cemeteries; for the enforcement of laws relating to children or animals; for opera houses; for fraternal organizations; for academies of music; for veterans' organizations; for pharmaceutical societies; and for dental societies. While the beneficiaries cover a wide range, "atheistic," "agnostic," or "antitheological" groups do not seem to be included.

Churches perform some functions that a State would constitutionally be empowered to perform. I refer to nonsectarian social welfare operations such as the care of orphaned children and the destitute and people who are sick. A tax exemption to agencies performing those functions would therefore be as constitutionally proper as the grant of direct subsidies to them. Under the First Amendment a State may not, however, provide worship if private groups fail to do so.

That is a major difference between churches on the one hand and the rest of the nonprofit organizations on the other. Government could provide or finance operas, hospitals, historical societies, and all the rest because they represent social welfare programs within the reach of the police power. In contrast, government may not provide or finance worship because of the Establishment

Clause any more than it may single out "atheistic" or "agnostic" centers or groups and create or finance them.

The Brookings Institution, writing in 1933, before the application of the Establishment Clause of the First Amendment to the States, said about tax exemptions of religious groups:

> "Tax exemption, no matter what its form, is essentially a government grant or subsidy. Such grants would seem to be justified only if the purpose for which they are made is one for which the legislative body *would be equally willing to make* a direct appropriation from public funds equal to the amount of the exemption. This test would not be met except in the case where the exemption is granted to encourage certain activities of private interests, which, if not thus performed, would have to be assumed by the government at an expenditure at least as great as the value of the exemption." (Emphasis added.)

Since 1947, when the Establishment Clause was made applicable to the States, that report would have to state that the exemption would be justified only where "the legislative body *could make*" an appropriation for the cause.

On the record of this case, the church *qua* nonprofit, charitable organization is intertwined with the church *qua* church. A church may use the same facilities, resources, and personnel in carrying out both its secular and its sectarian activities. The two are unitary and on the present record have not been separated one from the other. The state has a public policy of encouraging private public welfare organizations, which it desires to encourage through tax exemption. Why may it not do so and include churches *qua* welfare organizations on a nondiscriminatory basis? That avoids, it is argued, a discrimination against churches and in a real sense maintains neutrality toward religion which the First Amendment was designed to foster. Welfare services, whether performed by churches or by nonreligious groups, may well serve the public welfare.

Whether a particular church seeking an exemption for its welfare work could constitutionally pass muster would depend on the special facts. The assumption is that the church is a purely private institution, promoting a sectarian cause. The creed, teaching, and beliefs of one may be undesirable or even repulsive to others. Its sectarian faith sets it apart from all others and makes it difficult to equate its constituency with the general public. The extent that its facilities are open to all may only indicate the nature of its proselytism. Yet though a church covers up its religious symbols in welfare work its welfare activities may merely be a phase of sectarian activity. I have said enough to indicate the nature of this tax exemption problem.

Direct financial aid to churches or tax exemptions to the church *qua* church is not, in my view, even arguably permitted. Sectarian causes are certainly not antipublic and many would rate their own church or perhaps all churches as the highest form of welfare. The difficulty is that sectarian causes must remain in the private domain not subject to public control or subsidy. That seems to me to be the requirement of the Establishment Clause. As Edmond Cahn said:

> "In America, Madison submitted most astutely, the rights of conscience must be kept not only free but *equal* as well. And in view of the endless variations — not only among the numerous sects, but also among the organized activities they pursued and the relative emotional values they attached to their activities — how could any species of government assistance be considered genuinely equal from sect to sect? If, for example, a state should attempt to subsidize all sectarian schools without discrimination, it would necessarily violate the principle of equality because certain sects felt impelled to conduct a large number of such schools, others few, others none. How could the officers of government begin to measure the intangible factors that a true equality of treatment would involve, i.e., the relative intensity of religious attachment to parochial education that the respective groups required of their lay and clerical members? It would be presumptuous even to inquire. Thus, just as in matters of race our belated recognition of intangible factors has finally led us to the maxim 'separate therefore unequal,' so in matters of religion Madison's immediate recognition of intangible factors led us promptly to the maxim 'equal therefore separate.' Equality was out of the question without total separation." CONFRONTING INJUSTICE 186-187 (1967).

The exemptions provided here insofar as welfare projects are concerned may have the ring of neutrality. But subsidies either through direct grant or tax exemption for sectarian causes, whether carried on by church *qua* church or by church *qua* welfare agency, must be treated differently, lest we in time allow the church *qua* church to be on the public payroll, which, I fear, is imminent.

As stated by my Brother BRENNAN in *Abington School Dist. v. Schempp*, "It is not only the nonbeliever who fears the injection of sectarian doctrines and controversies into the civil polity, but in as high degree it is the devout believer who fears the secularization of a creed which becomes too deeply involved with and dependent upon the government."

Madison as President vetoed a bill incorporating the Protestant Episcopal Church in Alexandria, Virginia, as being a violation of the Establishment Clause. He said, *inter alia*:

> "[T]he bill vests in the said incorporated church an authority to provide for the support of the poor and the education of poor children of the same, an authority which, being altogether superfluous if the provision is to be the result of pious charity, would be a precedent for giving to religious societies as such a legal agency in carrying into effect a public and civil duty."

He also vetoed a bill that reserved a parcel of federal land "for the use" of the Baptist Church, as violating the Establishment Clause.

What Madison would have thought of the present state subsidy to churches — a tax exemption as distinguished from an outright grant — no one can say with certainty. The fact that Virginia early granted church tax exemptions cannot be credited to Madison. Certainly he seems to have been opposed. In his paper Monopolies, Perpetuities, Corporations, Ecclesiastical Endowments he wrote: "Strongly guarded as is the separation between Religion & Govt in the Constitution of the United States the danger of encroachment by Ecclesiastical Bodies, may be illustrated by precedents already furnished in their short history." And he referred, inter alia, to the "attempt in Kentucky for example, where it was proposed to exempt Houses of Worship from taxes." From these three statements, Madison, it seems, opposed all state subsidies to churches. *Cf.* D. ROBERTSON, SHOULD CHURCHES BE TAXED? 60-61 (1968).

The religiously used real estate of the churches today constitutes a vast domain. *See* M. LARSON & C. LOWELL, THE CHURCHES: THEIR RICHES, REVENUES, AND IMMUNITIES (1969). Their assets total over $141 billion and their annual income at least $22 billion. *Id.*, at 232. And the extent to which they are feeding from the public trough in a variety of forms is alarming. *Id.*, c. 10.

We are advised that since 1968 at least five States have undertaken to give subsidies to parochial and other private schools — Pennsylvania, Ohio, New York, Connecticut, and Rhode Island. And it is reported that under two federal Acts, the Elementary and Secondary Education Act of 1965, 79 Stat. 27, and the Higher Education Act of 1965, 79 Stat. 1219, *billions of dollars* have been granted to parochial and other private schools.

[F]ederal grants to private institutions of higher education are revealed in Department of Health, Education, and Welfare (HEW), Digest of Educational Statistics 16 (1969). These show in billions of dollars the following:

```
1965-66  . . . . . . . . . .$1.4
1966-67  . . . . . . . . . .$1.6
1967-68  . . . . . . . . . . $1.7
1968-69  . . . . . . . . . .$1.9
1969-70  . . . . . . . . . .$2.1
```

It is an old, old problem. Madison adverted to it:

"Are there not already examples in the U.S. of ecclesiastical wealth equally beyond its object and the foresight of those who laid the foundation of it? In the U.S. there is a double motive for fixing limits in this case, because wealth may increase not only from additional gifts, but from exorbitant advances in the value of the primitive one. In grants of vacant lands, and of lands in the vicinity of growing towns & Cities the increase of value is often such as if foreseen, would essentially control the liberality confirming them. The people of the U.S. owe their Independence & their liberty, to the wisdom of descrying in the minute tax of 3 pence on tea, the magnitude of the evil comprised in the precedent. Let them exert the same wisdom, in watching agst every evil lurking under plausible disguises, and growing up from small beginnings."[17]

If believers are entitled to public financial support, so are nonbelievers. A believer and nonbeliever under the present law are treated differently because of the articles of their faith. Believers are doubtless comforted that the cause of religion is being fostered by this legislation. Yet one of the mandates of the First Amendment is to promote a viable, pluralistic society and to keep government neutral, not only between sects, but also between believers and nonbelievers. The present involvement of government in religion may seem *de minimis*. But it is, I fear, a long step down the Establishment path. Perhaps I have been misinformed. But as I have read the Constitution and its philosophy, I gathered that independence was the price of liberty.

I conclude that the tax exemption is unconstitutional.

TEXAS MONTHLY, INC. v. BULLOCK
489 U.S. 1 (1989)

JUSTICE BRENNAN announced the judgment of the Court and delivered an opinion, in which JUSTICE MARSHALL and JUSTICE STEVENS join.

I

Prior to October 2, 1984, Texas exempted from its sales and use tax magazine subscriptions running half a year or longer and entered as second class mail. This exemption was repealed as of October 2, 1984, before being reinstated effective October 1, 1987. Throughout this 3-year period, Texas continued to exempt from its sales and use tax periodicals published or distributed by a reli-

---

[17]In 1875 President Grant in his State of the Union Message referred to the vast amounts of untaxed church property:

"In 1850, I believe, the church property of the United States which paid no tax, municipal or State, amounted to about $83,000,000. In 1860 the amount had doubled; in 1875 it is about $1,000,000,000. By 1900, without check, it is safe to say this property will reach a sum exceeding $3,000,000,000. So vast a sum, receiving all the protection and benefits of Government without bearing its proportion of the burdens and expenses of the same, will not be looked upon acquiescently by those who have to pay the taxes. In a growing country, where real estate enhances so rapidly with time, as in the United States, there is scarcely a limit to the wealth that may be acquired by corporations, religious or otherwise, if allowed to retain real estate without taxation. The contemplation of so vast a property as here alluded to, without taxation, may lead to sequestration, without constitutional authority and through blood.

"I would suggest the taxation of all property equally, whether church or corporation, exempting only the last resting place of the dead and possibly, with proper restrictions, church edifices." 9 MESSAGES AND PAPERS OF THE PRESIDENTS 4288-4289 (1897).

gious faith consisting entirely of writings promulgating the teaching of the faith, along with books consisting solely of writings sacred to a religious faith.

Appellant Texas Monthly, Inc., publishes a general interest magazine of the same name. Appellant is not a religious faith, and its magazine does not contain only articles promulgating the teaching of a religious faith. Thus, it was required during this 3-year period to collect and remit to the State the applicable sales tax on the price of qualifying subscription sales. In 1985, appellant paid sales taxes of $149,107.74 under protest and sued to recover those payments in state court.

III

In proscribing all laws "respecting an establishment of religion," the Constitution prohibits, at the very least, legislation that constitutes an endorsement of one or another set of religious beliefs or of religion generally. It is part of our settled jurisprudence that "the Establishment Clause prohibits government from abandoning secular purposes in order to put an imprimatur on one religion, or on religion as such, or to favor the adherents of any sect or religious organization." *Gillette v. United States*, 401 U.S. 437, 450 (1971). The core notion animating the requirement that a statute possess "a secular legislative purpose" and that "its principal or primary effect . . . be one that neither advances nor inhibits religion," *Lemon v. Kurtzman*, is not only that government may not be overtly hostile to religion but also that it may not place its prestige, coercive authority, or resources behind a single religious faith or behind religious belief in general, compelling nonadherents to support the practices or proselytizing of favored religious organizations and conveying the message that those who do not contribute gladly are less than full members of the community.

It does not follow, of course, that government policies with secular objectives may not incidentally benefit religion. The nonsectarian aims of government and the interests of religious groups often overlap, and this Court has never required that public authorities refrain from implementing reasonable measures to advance legitimate secular goals merely because they would thereby relieve religious groups of costs they would otherwise incur. *See Mueller v. Allen.* Nor have we required that legislative categories make no explicit reference to religion. *See Wallace v. Jaffree* (O'CONNOR, J., concurring in judgment) ("The endorsement test does not preclude government from acknowledging religion or from taking religion into account in making law and policy"). Government need not resign itself to ineffectual diffidence because of exaggerated fears of contagion of or by religion, so long as neither intrudes unduly into the affairs of the other.

Thus, in *Widmar v. Vincent*, we held that a state university that makes its facilities available to registered student groups may not deny equal access to a registered student group desiring to use those facilities for religious worship or discussion. Although religious groups benefit from access to university facilities, a state university may not discriminate against them based on the content of their speech, and the university need not ban all student group meetings on campus in order to avoid providing any assistance to religion. Similarly, in *Mueller v. Allen, supra*, we upheld a state income tax deduction for the cost of tuition, transportation, and nonreligious textbooks paid by a taxpayer for the benefit of a dependent. To be sure, the deduction aided parochial schools and parents whose children attended them, as well as nonsectarian private schools and their pupils' parents. We did not conclude, however, that this subsidy deprived the law of an overriding secular purpose or effect. And in the case most nearly on point, *Walz v. Tax Comm'n of New York City*, we sustained a property tax exemption that applied to religious properties no less than to real estate owned by a wide array of nonprofit organizations, despite the sizable tax savings it accorded religious groups.

In all of these cases, however, we emphasized that the benefits derived by religious organizations flowed to a large number of nonreligious groups as well. Indeed, were those benefits confined to religious organizations, they could not have appeared other than as state sponsorship of religion; if that were so, we would not have hesitated to strike them down for lacking a secular purpose and effect.

In *Widmar v. Vincent*, we noted that an open forum in a public university would not betray state approval of religion so long as the forum was available "to a broad class of nonreligious as well as religious speakers. . . . The provision of benefits to so broad a spectrum of groups," we said, "is an important index of secular effect." We concluded that the primary effect of an open forum would not be to advance religion, "[a]t least in the absence of empirical evidence that religious groups will dominate" it. Likewise, in *Mueller v. Allen*, we deemed it "particularly significant" that "the deduction is available for educational expenses incurred by *all* parents, including those whose children attend public schools and those whose children attend nonsectarian private schools or sectarian private schools."

Finally, we emphasized in *Walz* that in granting a property tax deduction, the State "has not singled out one particular church or religious group or even churches as such; rather, it has granted exemption to all houses of religious worship within a broad class of property owned by nonprofit, quasi-public corporations which include hospitals, libraries, playgrounds, scientific, professional, historical, and patriotic groups." The breadth of New York's property tax exemption was essential to our holding that it was "not aimed at establishing, sponsoring, or supporting religion," but rather possessed the legitimate secular purpose and effect of contributing to the community's moral and intellectual diversity and encouraging private groups to undertake projects that advanced the community's well-being and that would otherwise have to be funded by tax revenues or left undone. Moreover, "[t]he scheme [was] not designed to inject any religious activity into a nonreligious context, as was the case with school prayers. No particular activity of a religious organization — for example, the propagation of its beliefs — [was] specially promoted by the exemptions." As Justice Harlan observed:

> "To the extent that religious institutions sponsor the secular activities that this legislation is designed to promote, it is consistent with neutrality to grant them an exemption just as other organizations devoting resources to these projects receive exemptions. . . . As long as the breadth of exemption includes groups that pursue cultural, moral, or spiritual improvement in multifarious secular ways, including, I would suppose, groups whose avowed tenets may be antitheological, atheistic, or agnostic, I can see no lack of neutrality in extending the benefit of the exemption to organized religious groups." *Id.*, at 697 (separate opinion) (footnote omitted).

Texas' sales tax exemption for periodicals published or distributed by a religious faith and consisting wholly of writings promulgating the teaching of the faith lacks sufficient breadth to pass scrutiny under the Establishment Clause. Every tax exemption constitutes a subsidy that affects nonqualifying taxpayers, forcing them to become "indirect and vicarious 'donors.'" *Bob Jones University v. United States*, 461 U.S. 574, 591 (1983). Insofar as that subsidy is conferred upon a wide array of nonsectarian groups as well as religious organizations in pursuit of some legitimate secular end, the fact that religious groups benefit incidentally does not deprive the subsidy of the secular purpose and primary effect mandated by the Establishment Clause. However, when government directs a subsidy exclusively to religious organizations that is not required by the Free Exercise Clause and that either burdens nonbeneficiaries markedly or cannot reasonably be seen as removing a significant state-imposed deterrent to the free exercise of religion, as Texas has done, it "provide[s] unjustifiable awards of assistance to religious organizations" and cannot but "conve[y] a message of endorsement" to slighted members of the community. *Corporation of Presiding Bishop of Church of Jesus Christ of Latter-day Saints v. Amos, infra* Chapter 12 (O'CONNOR, J., concurring in judgment). This is particularly true where, as here, the subsidy is targeted at writings that *promulgate* the teachings of religious faiths. It is difficult to view Texas' narrow exemption as anything but state sponsorship of religious belief, regardless of whether one adopts the perspective of beneficiaries or of uncompensated contributors.

How expansive the class of exempt organizations or activities must be to withstand constitutional assault depends upon the State's secular aim in granting a tax exemption. If the State chose to subsidize, by means of a tax exemption, all groups that contributed to the community's cultural, intellectual, and moral betterment, then the exemption for religious publications could be retained, provided that the exemption swept as widely as the property tax exemption we upheld in *Walz*. By contrast, if Texas sought to promote reflection and discussion about questions of ultimate value and the contours of a good or meaningful life, then a tax exemption would have to be available to an extended range of associations whose publications were substantially devoted to such matters; the exemption could not be reserved for publications dealing solely with religious issues, let alone restricted to publications advocating rather than criticizing religious belief or activity, without signaling an endorsement of religion that is offensive to the principles informing the Establishment Clause.

It is not our responsibility to specify which permissible secular objectives, if any, the State should pursue to justify a tax exemption for religious periodicals. That charge rests with the Texas Legislature. Our task, and that of the Texas courts, is rather to ensure that any scheme of exemptions adopted by the legislature does not have the purpose or effect of sponsoring certain religious tenets or religious belief in general. As Justice Harlan remarked: "The Court must survey meticulously the circumstances of governmental categories to eliminate, as it were, religious gerrymanders. In any particular case the critical question is whether the circumference of legislation encircles a class so broad that it can be fairly concluded that religious institutions could be thought to fall within the natural perimeter." Because Texas' sales tax exemption for periodicals promulgating the teaching of any religious sect lacks a secular objective that would justify this preference along with similar benefits for nonreligious publications or groups, and because it effectively endorses religious belief, the exemption manifestly fails this test.

IV

A

In defense of its sales tax exemption for religious publications, Texas claims that it has a compelling interest in avoiding violations of the Free Exercise and Establishment Clauses, and that the exemption serves that end. Without such an exemption, Texas contends, its sales tax might trammel free exercise rights, as did the flat license tax this Court struck down as applied to proselytizing by Jehovah's Witnesses in *Murdock v. Pennsylvania*, 319 U.S. 105 (1943). In addition, Texas argues that an exemption for religious publications neither advances nor inhibits religion, as required by the Establishment Clause, and that its elimination would entangle church and state to a greater degree than the exemption itself.

We reject both parts of this argument. Although Texas may widen its exemption consonant with some legitimate secular purpose, nothing in our decisions under the Free Exercise Clause prevents the State from eliminating altogether its exemption for religious publications. "It is virtually self-evident that the Free Exercise Clause does not require an exemption from a governmental program unless, at a minimum, inclusion in the program actually burdens the claimant's freedom to exercise religious rights." *Tony and Susan Alamo Foundation v. Secretary of Labor*, 471 U.S. 290, 303 (1985) (citations omitted). In this case, the State has adduced no evidence that the payment of a sales tax by subscribers to religious periodicals or purchasers of religious books would offend their religious beliefs or inhibit religious activity. The State therefore cannot claim persuasively that its tax exemption is compelled by the Free Exercise

Clause in even a single instance, let alone in every case. No concrete need to accommodate religious activity has been shown.

Moreover, even if members of some religious group succeeded in demonstrating that payment of a sales tax — or, less plausibly, of a sales tax when applied to printed matter — would violate their religious tenets, it is by no means obvious that the State would be required by the Free Exercise Clause to make individualized exceptions for them. In *United States v. Lee* [*infra* Chapter 13], we ruled unanimously that the Federal Government need not exempt an Amish employer from the payment of Social Security taxes, notwithstanding our recognition that compliance would offend his religious beliefs. We noted that "[n]ot all burdens on religion are unconstitutional," and held that "[t]he state may justify a limitation on religious liberty by showing that it is essential to accomplish an overriding governmental interest." Although the balancing test we set forth in *Lee* must be performed on a case-by-case basis, a State's interest in the uniform collection of a sales tax appears comparable to the Federal Government's interest in the uniform collection of Social Security taxes, and mandatory exemptions under the Free Exercise Clause are arguably as difficult to prove. No one has suggested that members of any of the major religious denominations in the United States — the principal beneficiaries of Texas' tax exemption — could demonstrate an infringement of their free exercise rights sufficiently serious to overcome the State's countervailing interest in collecting its sales tax.

B

Texas' further claim that the Establishment Clause mandates, or at least favors, its sales tax exemption for religious periodicals is equally unconvincing. Not only does the exemption seem a blatant endorsement of religion, but it appears, on its face, to produce greater state entanglement with religion than the denial of an exemption. As JUSTICE STEVENS has noted: "[There exists an] overriding interest in keeping the government — whether it be the legislature or the courts — out of the business of evaluating the relative merits of differing religious claims. The risk that governmental approval of some and disapproval of others will be perceived as favoring one religion over another is an important risk the Establishment Clause was designed to preclude." The prospect of inconsistent treatment and government embroilment in controversies over religious doctrine seems especially baleful where, as in the case of Texas' sales tax exemption, a statute requires that public officials determine whether some message or activity is consistent with "the teaching of the faith." *See, e.g., Jones v. Wolf* [*infra* Chapter 10].

While Texas is correct in pointing out that compliance with government regulations by religious organizations and the monitoring of their compliance by government agencies would itself enmesh the operations of church and state to some degree, we have found that such compliance would generally not impede the evangelical activities of religious groups and that the "routine and factual inquiries" commonly associated with the enforcement of tax laws "bear no resemblance to the kind of government surveillance the Court has previously held to pose an intolerable risk of government entanglement with religion." *Tony and Susan Alamo Foundation v. Secretary of Labor*, 471 U.S., at 305.

JUSTICE BLACKMUN, with whom JUSTICE O'CONNOR joins, concurring in the judgment.

The Texas statute at issue touches upon values that underlie three different Clauses of the First Amendment: the Free Exercise Clause, the Establishment Clause, and the Press Clause. As indicated by the number of opinions issued in this case today, harmonizing these several values is not an easy task.

The Free Exercise Clause value suggests that a State may not impose a tax on spreading the gospel. *See Follett v. McCormick*, 321 U.S. 573 (1944), and *Murdock v. Pennsylvania*, 319 U.S. 105 (1943). The Establishment Clause value suggests that a State may not give a tax break to those who spread the gospel that it does not also give to others who actively might advocate disbelief in religion. *See Torcaso v. Watkins* [*supra* Chapter 3]; *Everson v. Board of Education of Ewing* [*infra* Chapter 6]. The Press Clause value suggests that a State may not tax the sale of some publications, but not others, based on their content, absent a compelling reason for doing so. *See Arkansas Writers' Project, Inc. v. Ragland*, 481 U.S. 221, 231 (1987).

It perhaps is fairly easy to reconcile the Free Exercise and Press Clause values. If the Free Exercise Clause suggests that a State may not tax the sale of religious literature by a religious organization, this fact alone would give a State a compelling reason to exclude this category of sales from an otherwise general sales tax. In this respect, I agree generally with what JUSTICE SCALIA says in Part II of his dissenting opinion.

I find it more difficult to reconcile in this case the Free Exercise and Establishment Clause values. The Free Exercise Clause suggests that a special exemption for religious books is required. The Establishment Clause suggests that a special exemption for religious books is forbidden. This tension between mandated and prohibited religious exemptions is well recognized. *See, e.g., Walz v. Tax Comm'n of New York City*. Of course, identifying the problem does not resolve it.

JUSTICE BRENNAN's opinion, in its Part IV, would resolve the tension between the Free Exercise and Establishment Clause values simply by subordinating the Free Exercise value, even, it seems to me, at the expense of longstanding precedents. JUSTICE SCALIA's opinion, conversely, would subordinate the Establishment Clause value. This position, it seems to me, runs afoul of the previously settled notion that government may not favor religious belief over disbelief.

Perhaps it is a vain desire, but I would like to decide the present case without necessarily sacrificing either the Free Exercise Clause value or the Establishment Clause value. It is possible for a State to write a tax-exemption statute consistent with both values: for example, a state statute might exempt the sale not only of religious literature distributed by a religious organization but also of philosophical literature distributed by nonreligious organizations devoted to such matters of conscience as life and death, good and evil, being and nonbeing, right and wrong. Such a statute, moreover, should survive Press Clause scrutiny because its exemption would be narrowly tailored to meet the compelling interests that underlie both the Free Exercise and Establishment Clauses.

To recognize this possible reconciliation of the competing First Amendment considerations is one thing; to impose it upon a State as its only legislative choice is something else. JUSTICE SCALIA rightly points out that the Free Exercise and Establishment Clauses often appear like Scylla and Charybdis, leaving a State little room to maneuver between them. The Press Clause adds yet a third hazard to a State's safe passage through the legislative waters concerning the taxation of books and journals. We in the Judiciary must be wary of interpreting these three constitutional Clauses in a manner that negates the legislative role altogether.

I believe we can avoid most of these difficulties with a narrow resolution of the case before us. We need not decide today the extent to which the Free Exercise Clause requires a tax exemption for the sale of religious literature by a religious organization; in other words, defining the ultimate scope of *Follett* and *Murdock* may be left for another day. We need decide here only whether a tax exemption *limited* to the sale of religious literature by religious organizations violates the Establishment Clause. I conclude that it does.

In this case, by confining the tax exemption exclusively to the sale of religious publications, Texas engaged in preferential support for the communication of religious messages. Although some forms of accommodating religion are constitutionally permissible, this one surely is not. A statutory preference for the dissemination of religious ideas offends our most basic understanding of what the Establishment Clause is all about and hence is constitutionally intolerable.

At oral argument, appellees suggested that the statute at issue here exempted from taxation the sale of atheistic literature distributed by an atheistic organization. If true, this statute might survive Establishment Clause scrutiny, as well as Free Exercise and Press Clause scrutiny. But, as appellees were quick to concede at argument, the record contains nothing to support this facially implausible interpretation of the statute. Thus, constrained to construe this Texas statute as exempting religious literature alone, I concur in the holding that it contravenes the Establishment Clause, and in remanding the case for further proceedings not inconsistent with this holding.

JUSTICE SCALIA, with whom THE CHIEF JUSTICE and JUSTICE KENNEDY join, dissenting.

As a judicial demolition project, today's decision is impressive. The machinery employed by the opinions of JUSTICE BRENNAN and JUSTICE BLACKMUN is no more substantial than the antinomy that accommodation of religion may be required but not permitted, and the bold but unsupportable assertion (given such realities as the text of the Declaration of Independence, the national Thanksgiving Day proclaimed by every President since Lincoln, the inscriptions on our coins, the words of our Pledge of Allegiance, the invocation with which sessions of our Court are opened and, come to think of it, the discriminatory protection of freedom of religion in the Constitution) that government may not "convey a message of endorsement of religion." With this frail equipment, the Court topples an exemption for religious publications of a sort that expressly appears in the laws of at least 15 of the 45 States that have sales and use taxes — States from Maine to Texas, from Idaho to New Jersey. In practice, a similar exemption may well exist in even more States than that, since until today our case law has suggested that it is not only permissible but perhaps required. *See Follett v. McCormick*, 321 U.S. 573 (1944); *Murdock v. Pennsylvania*, 319 U.S. 105 (1943). I expect, for example, that even in States without express exemptions many churches, and many tax assessors, have thought sales taxes inapplicable to the religious literature typically offered for sale in church foyers.

When one expands the inquiry to sales taxes on items other than publications and to other types of taxes such as property, income, amusement, and motor vehicle taxes — all of which are likewise affected by today's holding — the Court's accomplishment is even more impressive. At least 45 States provide exemptions for religious groups without analogous exemptions for other types of nonprofit institutions. For over half a century the federal Internal Revenue Code has allowed "minister[s] of the gospel" (a term interpreted broadly enough to include cantors and rabbis) to exclude from gross income the rental value of their parsonages. In short, religious tax exemptions of the type the Court invalidates today permeate the state and federal codes, and have done so for many years.

I dissent because I find no basis in the text of the Constitution, the decisions of this Court, or the traditions of our people for disapproving this longstanding and widespread practice.

I

The opinions of Justice BRENNAN and Justice BLACKMUN proceed as though this were a matter of first impression. It is not. Nineteen years ago, in *Walz v. Tax Comm'n of New York*, we considered and rejected an Establishment Clause challenge that was in all relevant respects identical. Since today's opinions barely acknowledge the Court's decision in that case (as opposed to the separate concurrences of Justices BRENNAN and Harlan), it requires some discussion here. *Walz* involved New York City's grant of tax exemptions, pursuant to a state statute and a provision of the State Constitution, to "religious organizations for religious properties used solely for religious worship." In upholding the exemption, we conducted an analysis that contains the substance of the three-pronged "test" adopted the following Term in *Lemon v. Kurtzman*. First, we concluded that "[t]he legislative purpose of the property tax exemption is neither the advancement nor the inhibition of religion." We reached that conclusion because past cases and the historical record established that property tax exemption "constitutes a reasonable and balanced attempt to guard against" the "latent dangers" of government hostility to religion. We drew a distinction between an unlawful intent to favor religion and a lawful intent to "'accommodat[e] the public service to [the people's] spiritual needs,'" (quoting *Zorach v. Clauson*, 343 U.S. 306 (1952)), and found only the latter to be involved in "sparing the exercise of religion from the burden of property taxation levied on private profit institutions."

We further concluded that the exemption did not have the primary effect of sponsoring religious activity. We noted that, although tax exemptions may have the same economic effect as state subsidies, for Establishment Clause purposes such "indirect economic benefit" is significantly different.

> "The grant of a tax exemption is not sponsorship since the government does not transfer part of its revenue to churches but simply abstains from demanding that the church support the state. . . . There is no genuine nexus between tax exemption and establishment of religion."

JUSTICE BRENNAN also recognized this distinction in his concurring opinion:

> "Tax exemptions and general subsidies, however, are qualitatively different. Though both provide economic assistance, they do so in fundamentally different ways. A subsidy involves the direct transfer of public monies to the subsidized enterprise and uses resources exacted from taxpayers as a whole. An exemption, on the other hand, involves no such transfer." *Id.*, at 690 (footnote omitted).

Third, we held that the New York exemption did not produce unacceptable government entanglement with religion. In fact, quite to the contrary. Since the exemptions avoided the "tax liens, tax foreclosures, and the direct confrontations and conflicts that follow in the train of those legal processes," we found that their elimination would increase government's involvement with religious institutions.

We recognized in *Walz* that the exemption of religion from various taxes had existed without challenge in the law of all 50 States and the National Government before, during, and after the framing of the First Amendment's Religion Clauses, and had achieved "undeviating acceptance" throughout the 200-year history of our Nation. "Few concepts," we said, "are more deeply embedded in the fabric of our national life, beginning with pre-Revolutionary colonial times, than for the government to exercise at the very least this kind of benevolent neutrality toward churches and religious exercise generally so long as none was favored over others and none suffered interference."

It should be apparent from this discussion that *Walz*, which we have reaffirmed on numerous occasions in the last two decades, is utterly dispositive of the Establishment Clause claim before us here. The Court invalidates § 151.312 of the Texas Tax Code only by distorting the holding of that case and radically altering the well-settled Establishment Clause jurisprudence which that case represents.

JUSTICE BRENNAN explains away *Walz* by asserting that "[t]he breadth of New York's property tax exemption was essential to our holding that it was 'not aimed at establishing, sponsoring, or supporting religion.'" This is not a plausible reading of the opinion. At the outset of its discussion concerning the permissibility of the legislative purpose, the *Walz* Court did discuss the fact that the New York tax exemption applied not just to religions but to certain other "nonprofit" groups, including "hospitals, libraries, playgrounds, scientific, professional, historical, and patriotic groups." The finding of valid legislative purpose was not rested upon that, however, but upon the more direct proposition that "exemption constitutes a reasonable and balanced attempt to guard against" the "latent dangers" of governmental hostility towards religion "inherent in the imposition of property taxes." The venerable federal legislation that the Court cited to support its holding was not legislation that exempted religion along with other things, but legislation that exempted *religion alone. See, e.g.,* ch. 17, 6 Stat. 116 (1813) (remitting duties paid on the importation of plates for printing Bibles); ch. 91, 6 Stat. 346 (1826) (remitting duties paid on the importation of church vestments, furniture, and paintings); ch. 259, 6 Stat. 600 (1834) (remitting duties paid on the importation of church bells). Moreover, if the Court had intended to rely upon a "breadth of coverage" rationale, it would have had to identify some characteristic that rationally placed religion within the same policy category as the other institutions. JUSTICE BRENNAN's concurring opinion in *Walz* conducted such an analysis, finding the New York exemption permissible only because religions, like the other types of nonprofit organizations exempted, "contribute to the well-being of the community in a variety of nonreligious ways," and (incomprehensibly) because they "uniquely contribute to the pluralism of American society by their religious activities." (I say incomprehensibly because to favor religion for its "unique contribution" is to favor religion as religion.) Justice Harlan's opinion conducted a similar analysis, finding that the New York statute "defined a class of nontaxable entities whose common denominator is their nonprofit pursuit of activities devoted to cultural and moral improvement and the doing of 'good works' by performing certain social services in the community that might otherwise have to be assumed by government." The Court's opinion in *Walz*, however, not only failed to conduct such an analysis, but — seemingly in reply to the concurrences — *explicitly and categorically disavowed reliance upon it*, concluding its discussion of legislative purpose with a paragraph that begins as follows: "We find it unnecessary to justify the tax exemption on the social welfare services or 'good works' that some churches perform for parishioners and others." This should be compared with today's rewriting of *Walz*: "[W]e concluded that the State might reasonably have determined that religious groups generally contribute to the cultural and moral improvement of the community, perform useful social services, and enhance a desirable pluralism of viewpoint and enterprise, just as do the host of other nonprofit organizations that qualified for the exemption." This is a marvelously accurate description of what Justices BRENNAN and Harlan believed, and what the Court specifically rejected. The Court did not approve an exemption for charities that happened to benefit religion; it approved an exemption for religion as an exemption for religion.

Today's opinions go beyond misdescribing *Walz*, however. In repudiating what *Walz* in fact approved, they achieve a revolution in our Establishment Clause jurisprudence, effectively overruling other cases that were based, as *Walz* was, on the "accommodation of religion" rationale. According to JUSTICE BRENNAN's opinion, no law is constitutional whose "benefits [are] confined to religious organizations" — except, of course, those laws that are unconstitutional *unless* they contain benefits confined to religious organizations. Our jurisprudence affords no support for this unlikely proposition. *Walz* is just one of a long line of cases in which we have recognized that "the government may (and sometimes must) accommodate religious practices and that it may do so without violating the Establishment Clause." *Hobbie v. Unemployment Appeals Comm'n of Fla.*, 480 U.S. 136, 144-145 (1987). In such cases as *Sherbert v. Verner* [*infra* Chapter 11], *Wisconsin v. Yoder* [*infra* Chapter 13], *Thomas v. Review Bd. of Ind. Employment Security Div.* [*infra* Chapter 12], and *Hobbie v. Unemployment Appeals Comm'n of Fla.*, we held that the Free Exercise Clause of the First Amendment *required* religious beliefs to be accommodated by granting religion-specific exemptions from otherwise applicable laws. We have often made clear, however, that "[t]he limits of permissible state accommodation to religion are by no means co-extensive with the noninterference mandated by the Free Exercise Clause."

The novelty of today's holding is obscured by JUSTICE BRENNAN's citation and description of many cases in which "breadth of coverage" *was* relevant to the First Amendment determination. Breadth of coverage is essential to constitutionality whenever a law's benefiting of religious activity is sought to be defended not specifically (or not exclusively) as an intentional and reasonable accommodation of religion, but as merely the incidental consequence of seeking to benefit *all* activity that achieves a particular secular goal. But that is a different rationale — more commonly invoked than accommodation of religion but, as our cases show, not preclusive of it. Where accommodation of religion is the justification, by definition religion is being singled out. The same confusion of rationales explains the facility with which JUSTICE BRENNAN's opinion can portray the present statute as violating the first prong of the *Lemon* test, which is usually described as requiring a "secular legislative purpose." *Lemon.* That is an entirely accurate description of the governing rule when, as in *Lemon* and most other cases, government aid to religious institutions is sought to be justified on the ground that it is not religion *per se* that is the object of assistance, but rather the secular functions that the religious institutions, along with other institutions, provide. But as I noted earlier, the substance of the *Lemon* test (purpose, effect, entanglement) was first roughly set forth in *Walz* — and in that context, the "accommodation of religion" context, the purpose was said to be valid so long as it was "neither the advancement nor the inhibition of religion;

. . . neither sponsorship nor hostility." Of course rather than reformulating the *Lemon* test in "accommodation" cases (the text of *Lemon* is not, after all, a statutory enactment), one might instead simply describe the protection of free exercise concerns, and the maintenance of the necessary neutrality, as "secular purpose and effect," since they are a purpose and effect approved, and indeed to some degree mandated, by the Constitution. However the reconciliation with the *Lemon* terminology is achieved, our cases make plain that it is permissible for a State to act with the purpose and effect of "limiting governmental interference with the exercise of religion." *Corporation of Presiding Bishop.*

It is not always easy to determine when accommodation slides over into promotion, and neutrality into favoritism, but the withholding of a tax upon the dissemination of religious materials is not even a close case. The subjects of the exemption before us consist exclusively of "writings promulgating the teaching of the faith" and "writings sacred to a religious faith." If there is any close question, it is not whether the exemption is permitted, but whether it is constitutionally compelled in order to avoid "interference with the dissemination of religious ideas." *Gillette.*

Although JUSTICE BRENNAN's opinion places almost its entire reliance upon the "purpose" prong of *Lemon*, it alludes briefly to the second prong as well, finding that § 151.312 has the impermissible "effect of sponsoring certain religious tenets or religious belief in general." Once again, *Walz* stands in stark opposition to this assertion, but it may be useful to explain why. Quite obviously, a sales tax exemption aids religion, since it makes it less costly for religions to disseminate their beliefs. But that has never been enough to strike down an enactment under the Establishment Clause. "A law is not unconstitutional simply because it *allows* churches to advance religion, which is their very purpose." *Corporation of Presiding Bishop.* The Court has consistently rejected "the argument that any program which in some manner aids an institution with a religious affiliation" violates the Establishment Clause. To be sure, we have set our face against the subsidizing of religion — and in other contexts we have suggested that tax exemptions and subsidies are equivalent. *E.g., Bob Jones University v. United States,* 461 U.S. 574, 591 (1983). We have not treated them as equivalent, however, in the Establishment Clause context, and with good reason. "In the case of direct subsidy, the state forcibly diverts the income of both believers and nonbelievers to churches. In the case of an exemption, the state merely refrains from diverting to its own uses income independently generated by the churches through voluntary contributions." Giannella, *Religious Liberty, Nonestablishment, and Doctrinal Development*, 81 HARV. L. REV. 513, 553 (1968). In *Walz* we pointed out that the *primary* effect of a tax exemption was not to sponsor religious activity but to "restric[t] the fiscal relationship between church and state" and to "complement and reinforce the desired separation insulating each from the other." [*Walz*] (BRENNAN, J., concurring).

Finally, and least persuasively of all, JUSTICE BRENNAN suggests that § 151.312 violates the "excessive government entanglement" aspect of *Lemon.*

It is plain that the exemption does not foster the sort of "comprehensive, discriminating, and continuing state surveillance" necessary to run afoul of that test. A State does not excessively involve itself in religious affairs merely by examining material to determine whether it is religious or secular in nature. In *Mueller* [v. *Allen*], for instance, we held that state officials' examination of textbooks to determine whether they were "books and materials used in the teaching of religious tenets, doctrines or worship" did not constitute excessive entanglement. I see no material distinction between that inquiry and the one Texas officials must make in this case. Moreover, here as in *Walz*, it is all but certain that elimination of the exemption will have the effect of *increasing* government's involvement with religion. The Court's invalidation of §151.312 ensures that Texas churches selling publications that promulgate their religion will now be subject to numerous statutory and regulatory impositions, including audits, requirements for the filing of security, reporting requirements, writs of attachment without bond, tax liens, and the seizure and sale of property to satisfy tax delinquencies.

NOTE ON THE TAX EXEMPTION FOR PARSONAGES

Justice White notes in his *Texas Monthly* dissent that the Internal Revenue Code has for many years provided a tax exemption for the value of parsonages provided by religious institutions to ministers of the gospel (defined to include rabbis and cantors). This exemption is the subject of a new statute and a recent lawsuit in the United States Court of Appeals for the Ninth Circuit.

The current version of the parsonage exemption provides that "in the case of a minister of the gospel, gross income does not include . . . the rental allowance paid to him as part of his compensation, to the extent used by him to rent or provide a home." 26 U.S.C. § 107(2). Unlike the typical property tax exemption for church property (and arguably just like the exemption invalidated in *Texas Monthly*), the parsonage exemption does not extend to any secular activity.

In *Warren v. C.I.R.*, 114 T.C. 343 (2000), a Baptist minister deducted approximately $80,000 per year in housing expenses for three tax successive tax years. During those same years he had other income ranging from $187,000 to $241,000. The Internal Revenue Service argued that the minister's parsonage exemption should be limited to the fair rental market value of the house, which in this case was significantly less than the actual expenses deducted by the minister. The Tax Court ruled against the I.R.S., holding that the parsonage exemption covered actual expenses, even if they far exceeded fair rental value of the property. The I.R.S. appealed to the United States Court of Appeals for the Ninth Circuit, which issued an extraordinary order asking the parties and a newly appointed amicus curiae to address the issue whether the parsonage exemption is constitutional in light of *Texas Monthly*. *See Warren v. C.I.R.*, 282 F.3d 1119 (9th Cir. 2002). Before the Ninth Circuit could adjudicate this issue, the parties settled the case and stipulated that the appeal be dismissed. *Warren v. C.I.R.*, 302 F.3d 1012 (9th Cir. 2002).

Meanwhile, on May 20, 2002, the President signed into law the "Clergy Housing Allowance Clarification Act of 2002," which adopts the I.R.S. interpretation of existing law and explicitly revises the existing parsonage exemption provision to make clear that future deductions taken under the provision should be limited to the fair rental value of the home. The new act applies to tax years beginning after December 31, 2001. Ironically, the new act also has a provision (Section 2(b)(3)) that seems intended to decide cases like *Warren* in favor of the taxpayer: "Except as provided in paragraph (2), notwithstanding any prior regulation, revenue ruling, or other guidance issued by the Internal Revenue Service, no person shall be subject to the limitations added to section 107 of such Code by this Act for any taxable year beginning before January 1, 2002." Whether Section 2(b)(3) actually settles the statutory interpretation dispute in cases like *Warren* depends on whether Section 2(b)(3) is ultimately deemed a legitimate retroactive change in the applicable substantive law, *see Robertson v. Seattle Audubon Soc.*, 503 U.S. 429 (1992), or an invalid attempt to impose a rule of decision on the courts, *see United States v. Klein*, 80 U.S. 128 (1872).

NOTE ON TAX EXPENDITURES AND RELIGION

Tax expenditure analysis has long been the subject of academic debate, and the Court's tax religious exemption decisions have also long been used as examples by proponents and opponents of the analysis. The leading opponent of tax expenditure analysis in this context is Boris Bittker. *See* Boris I. Bittker, *Churches, Taxes and the Constitution*, 78 YALE L.J. 1285 (1969). Bittker argues that not all tax expenditures are functionally equivalent to subsidies because the issue really turns on whether the property that is being "exempted" from taxes was ever considered part of the tax base at all. In other words, only some types of property are subject to tax; if the type of property subject to tax does not include categories of property to which churches logically belong, then the failure to collect taxes from the churches is merely a byproduct of defining the tax base, not a "tax subsidy." Proponents of tax expenditure analysis tend to criticize *Walz* on the ground that the tax exemption is financially equivalent to an outright subsidy. *See* Donna D. Adler, *The Internal Revenue Code, the Constitution, and the Courts: The Use of Tax Expenditure Analysis in Judicial Decision Making*, 28 WAKE FOREST L. REV. 855, 888 (1993) ("If a property tax of $100 were normally imposed on a property owner, for example, the church is in the same position whether the government actually transfers $100 to the church to pay the tax or merely relieves the church of paying the $100."). *See also* E.C. Lashbrooke, Jr., *An Economic and Constitutional Case for Repeal of the I.R.C. Section 170 Deduction for Charitable Contributions to Religious Organizations*, 27 DUQ. L. REV. 695 (1989). For an argument that the Court should take a case-by-case approach to these issues, *see* Edward A. Zelinsky, *Are Tax "Benefits" Constitutionally Equivalent to Direct Expenditures?*, 112 HARV. L. REV. 379 (1998). Under this approach, the Court would consider factors such as the permanence, eligibility, and quantity of every challenged tax. *See id.* at 400-01. Applying this analysis to *Walz*, Professor Zelinsky sees several elements that distinguish tax exemptions from traditional subsidies: the tax exemption at issue in *Walz* is permanent rather than reviewable annually; the exemption is automatically open to any qualifying institution, rather than targeted to specific institutions; and finally, the tax exemption is uncapped, rather than subject to a specific appropriation. *Id.* at 401-06. Based on this analysis, Zelinsky concludes that *Walz* was correctly decided.

B. DIRECT PUBLIC FINANCIAL SUPPORT FOR RELIGIOUS EDUCATION

EVERSON v. BOARD OF EDUCATION OF THE TOWNSHIP OF EWING
330 U.S. 1 (1947)

MR. JUSTICE BLACK delivered the opinion of the Court.

A New Jersey statute authorizes its local school districts to make rules and contracts for the transportation of children to and from schools. The appellee, a township board of education, acting pursuant to this statute, authorized reimbursement to parents of money expended by them for the bus transportation of their children on regular busses operated by the public transportation system. Part of this money was for the payment of transportation of some children in the community to Catholic parochial schools. These church schools give their students, in addition to secular education, regular religious instruction conforming to the religious tenets and modes of worship of the Catholic Faith. The superintendent of these schools is a Catholic priest.

The "establishment of religion" clause of the First Amendment means at least this: Neither a state nor the Federal Government can set up a church. Neither can pass laws which aid one religion, aid all religions, or prefer one religion over another. Neither can force nor influence a person to go to or to remain away from church against his will or force him to profess a belief or disbelief in any religion. No person can be punished for entertaining or professing religious beliefs or disbeliefs, for church attendance or non-attendance. No tax in any amount, large or small, can be levied to support any religious activities or institutions, whatever they may be called, or whatever form they may adopt to teach or practice religion. Neither a state nor the Federal Government can, openly or secretly, participate in the affairs of any religious organizations or groups and *vice versa.* In the words of Jefferson, the clause against establishment of religion by law was intended to erect "a wall of separation between church and State." *Reynolds v. United States.*

We must consider the New Jersey statute in accordance with the foregoing limitations imposed by the First Amendment. But we must not strike that state statute down if it is within the State's constitutional power even though it approaches the verge of that power. *See Interstate Ry. v. Massachusetts,* Holmes,

J., *supra* at 85, 88. New Jersey cannot consistently with the "establishment of religion" clause of the First Amendment contribute tax-raised funds to the support of an institution which teaches the tenets and faith of any church. On the other hand, other language of the amendment commands that New Jersey cannot hamper its citizens in the free exercise of their own religion. Consequently, it cannot exclude individual Catholics, Lutherans, Mohammedans, Baptists, Jews, Methodists, Non-believers, Presbyterians, or the members of any other faith, *because of their faith, or lack of it*, from receiving the benefits of public welfare legislation. While we do not mean to intimate that a state could not provide transportation only to children attending public schools, we must be careful, in protecting the citizens of New Jersey against state-established churches, to be sure that we do not inadvertently prohibit New Jersey from extending its general state law benefits to all its citizens without regard to their religious belief.

Measured by these standards, we cannot say that the First Amendment prohibits New Jersey from spending tax-raised funds to pay the bus fares of parochial school pupils as a part of a general program under which it pays the fares of pupils attending public and other schools. It is undoubtedly true that children are helped to get to church schools. There is even a possibility that some of the children might not be sent to the church schools if the parents were compelled to pay their children's bus fares out of their own pockets when transportation to a public school would have been paid for by the State. The same possibility exists where the state requires a local transit company to provide reduced fares to school children including those attending parochial schools, or where a municipally owned transportation system undertakes to carry all school children free of charge. Moreover, state-paid policemen, detailed to protect children going to and from church schools from the very real hazards of traffic, would serve much the same purpose and accomplish much the same result as state provisions intended to guarantee free transportation of a kind which the state deems to be best for the school children's welfare. And parents might refuse to risk their children to the serious danger of traffic accidents going to and from parochial schools, the approaches to which were not protected by policemen. Similarly, parents might be reluctant to permit their children to attend schools which the state had cut off from such general government services as ordinary police and fire protection, connections for sewage disposal, public highways and sidewalks. Of course, cutting off church schools from these services, so separate and so indisputably marked off from the religious function, would make it far more difficult for the schools to operate. But such is obviously not the purpose of the First Amendment. That Amendment requires the state to be a neutral in its relations with groups of religious believers and non-believers; it does not require the state to be their adversary. State power is no more to be used so as to handicap religions than it is to favor them.

This Court has said that parents may, in the discharge of their duty under state compulsory education laws, send their children to a religious rather than a public school if the school meets the secular educational requirements which the state has power to impose. *See Pierce v. Society of Sisters*, 268 U.S. 510. It appears that these parochial schools meet New Jersey's requirements. The State contributes no money to the schools. It does not support them. Its legislation, as applied, does no more than provide a general program to help parents get their children, regardless of their religion, safely and expeditiously to and from accredited schools.

The First Amendment has erected a wall between church and state. That wall must be kept high and impregnable. We could not approve the slightest breach. New Jersey has not breached it here.

MR. JUSTICE JACKSON, dissenting.

I.

If we are to decide this case on the facts before us, our question is simply this: Is it constitutional to tax this complainant to pay the cost of carrying pupils to Church schools of one specified denomination?

II.

Whether the taxpayer constitutionally can be made to contribute aid to parents of students because of their attendance at parochial schools depends upon the nature of those schools and their relation to the Church. The Constitution says nothing of education. It lays no obligation on the states to provide schools and does not undertake to regulate state systems of education if they see fit to maintain them. But they cannot, through school policy any more than through other means, invade rights secured to citizens by the Constitution of the United States. *West Virginia State Board of Education v. Barnette,* 319 U.S. 624. One of our basic rights is to be free of taxation to support a transgression of the constitutional command that the authorities "shall make no law respecting an establishment of religion, or prohibiting the free exercise thereof. . . ." U.S. Const., Amend. I.

The function of the Church school is a subject on which this record is meager. It shows only that the schools are under superintendence of a priest and that "religion is taught as part of the curriculum." But we know that such schools are parochial only in name — they, in fact, represent a world-wide and age-old policy of the Roman Catholic Church. Under the rubric "Catholic Schools," the Canon Law of the Church, by which all Catholics are bound, provides:

"1215. Catholic children are to be educated in schools where not only nothing contrary to Catholic faith and morals is taught, but rather in schools where religious and moral training occupy the first place. . . . (Canon 1372.)"

"1216. In every elementary school the children must, according to their age, be instructed in Christian doctrine.

"The young people who attend the higher schools are to receive a deeper religious knowledge, and the bishops shall appoint priests qualified for such work by their learning and piety. (Canon 1373.)"

"1217. Catholic children shall not attend non-Catholic, indifferent, schools that are mixed, that is to say, schools open to Catholics and non-Catholics alike. The bishop of the diocese only has the right, in harmony with the instructions of the Holy See, to decide under what circumstances, and with what safeguards to prevent loss of faith, it may be tolerated that Catholic children go to such schools. (Canon 1374.)"

"1224. The religious teaching of youth in any schools is subject to the authority and inspection of the Church.

"The local Ordinaries have the right and duty to watch that nothing is taught contrary to faith or good morals, in any of the schools of their territory.

"They, moreover, have the right to approve the books of Christian doctrine and the teachers of religion, and to demand, for the sake of safeguarding religion and morals, the removal of teachers and books. (Canon 1381.)" (Woywod, Rev. Stanislaus, The New Canon Law, under imprimatur of Most Rev. Francis J. Spellman, Archbishop of New York and others, 1940.)

It is no exaggeration to say that the whole historic conflict in temporal policy between the Catholic Church and non-Catholics comes to a focus in their respective school policies. The Roman Catholic Church, counseled by experience in many ages and many lands and with all sorts and conditions of men, takes what, from the viewpoint of its own progress and the success of its mission, is a wise estimate of the importance of education to religion. It does not leave the individual to pick up religion by chance. It relies on early and indelible indoctrination in the faith and order of the Church by the word and example of persons consecrated to the task.

Our public school, if not a product of Protestantism, at least is more consistent with it than with the Catholic culture and scheme of values. It is a relatively recent development dating from about 1840. It is organized on the premise that secular education can be isolated from all religious teaching so that the school can inculcate all needed temporal knowledge and also maintain a strict and lofty neutrality as to religion. The assumption is that after the individual has been instructed in worldly wisdom he will be better fitted to choose his religion. Whether such a disjunction is possible, and if possible whether it is wise, are questions I need not try to answer.

I should be surprised if any Catholic would deny that the parochial school is a vital, if not the most vital, part of the Roman Catholic Church. If put to the choice, that venerable institution, I should expect, would forego its whole service for mature persons before it would give up education of the young, and it would be a wise choice. Its growth and cohesion, discipline and loyalty, spring from its schools. Catholic education is the rock on which the whole structure rests, and to render tax aid to its Church school is indistinguishable to me from rendering the same aid to the Church itself.

III.

It is of no importance in this situation whether the beneficiary of this expenditure of tax-raised funds is primarily the parochial school and incidentally the pupil, or whether the aid is directly bestowed on the pupil with indirect benefits to the school. The state cannot maintain a Church and it can no more tax its citizens to furnish free carriage to those who attend a Church. The prohibition against establishment of religion cannot be circumvented by a subsidy, bonus or reimbursement of expense to individuals for receiving religious instruction and indoctrination.

The Court, however, compares this to other subsidies and loans to individuals and says, "Nor does it follow that a law has a private rather than a public purpose because it provides that tax-raised funds will be paid to reimburse individuals on account of money spent by them in a way which furthers a public program." Of course, the state may pay out tax-raised funds to relieve pauperism, but it may not under our Constitution do so to induce or reward piety. It may spend funds to secure old age against want, but it may not spend funds to secure religion against skepticism. It may compensate individuals for loss of employment, but it cannot compensate them for adherence to a creed.

It seems to me that the basic fallacy in the Court's reasoning, which accounts for its failure to apply the principles it avows, is in ignoring the essentially religious test by which beneficiaries of this expenditure are selected. A policeman protects a Catholic, of course — but not because he is a Catholic; it is because he is a man and a member of our society. The fireman protects the Church school — but not because it is a Church school; it is because it is property, part of the assets of our society. Neither the fireman nor the policeman has to ask before he renders aid "Is this man or building identified with the Catholic Church?" But before these school authorities draw a check to reimburse for a student's fare they must ask just that question, and if the school is a Catholic one they may render aid because it is such, while if it is of any other faith or is run for profit, the help must be withheld. To consider the converse of the Court's reasoning will best disclose its fallacy. That there is no parallel between police and fire protection and this plan of reimbursement is apparent from the incongruity of the limitation of this Act if applied to police and fire service. Could we sustain an Act that said the police shall protect pupils on the way to or from public schools and Catholic schools but not while going to and coming from other schools, and firemen shall extinguish a blaze in public or Catholic school buildings but shall not put out a blaze in Protestant Church schools or private schools operated for profit? That is the true analogy to the case we have before us and I should think it pretty plain that such a scheme would not be valid.

The Court's holding is that this taxpayer has no grievance because the state has decided to make the reimbursement a public purpose and therefore we are bound to regard it as such. I agree that this Court has left, and always should leave to each state, great latitude in deciding for itself, in the light of its own conditions, what shall be public purposes in its scheme of things. It may socialize utilities and economic enterprises and make taxpayers' business out of what conventionally had been private business. It may make public business of individual welfare, health, education, entertainment or security. But it cannot make public business of religious worship or instruction, or of attendance at religious institutions of any character. There is no answer to the proposition, more fully expounded by MR. JUSTICE RUTLEDGE, that the effect of the religious freedom Amendment to our Constitution was to take every form of propagation of religion out of the realm of things which could directly or indirectly be made public business and thereby be supported in whole or in part at taxpayers' expense. That is a difference which the Constitution sets up between religion and almost every other subject matter of legislation, a difference which goes to the very root of religious freedom and which the Court is overlooking today. This freedom was first in the Bill of Rights because it was first in the forefathers' minds; it was set forth in absolute terms, and its strength is its rigidity. It was intended not only to keep the states' hands out of religion, but to keep religion's hands off the state, and, above all, to keep bitter religious controversy out of public life by denying to every denomination any advantage from getting control of public policy or the public purse. Those great ends I cannot but think are immeasurably compromised by today's decision.

This policy of our Federal Constitution has never been wholly pleasing to most religious groups. They all are quick to invoke its protections; they all are irked when they feel its restraints. This Court has gone a long way, if not an unreasonable way, to hold that public business of such paramount importance as maintenance of public order, protection of the privacy of the home, and taxation may not be pursued by a state in a way that even indirectly will interfere with religious proselyting.

But we cannot have it both ways. Religious teaching cannot be a private affair when the state seeks to impose regulations which infringe on it indirectly, and a public affair when it comes to taxing citizens of one faith to aid another, or those of no faith to aid all. If these principles seem harsh in prohibiting aid to Catholic education, it must not be forgotten that it is the same Constitution that alone assures Catholics the right to maintain these schools at all when predominant local sentiment would forbid them. *Pierce v. Society of Sisters*, 268 U.S. 510. Nor should I think that those who have done so well without this aid would want to see this separation between Church and State broken down. If the state may aid these religious schools, it may therefore regulate them. Many groups have sought aid from tax funds only to find that it carried political controls with it.

But in any event, the great purposes of the Constitution do not depend on the approval or convenience of those they restrain. I cannot read the history of the struggle to separate political from ecclesiastical affairs, well summarized in the opinion of MR. JUSTICE RUTLEDGE in which I generally concur, without a conviction that the Court today is unconsciously giving the clock's hands a backward turn.

Mr. Justice Rutledge, with whom Mr. Justice Frankfurter, Mr. Justice Jackson and Mr. Justice Burton agree, dissenting.

IV.

[W]e are told that the New Jersey statute is valid in its present application because the appropriation is for a public, not a private purpose, namely, the promotion of education, and the majority accept this idea in the conclusion that all we have here is "public welfare legislation." If that is true and the Amendment's force can be thus destroyed, what has been said becomes all the more pertinent. For then there could be no possible objection to more extensive support of religious education by New Jersey.

If the fact alone be determinative that religious schools are engaged in education, thus promoting the general and individual welfare, together with the legislature's decision that the payment of public moneys for their aid makes their work a public function, then I can see no possible basis, except one of dubious legislative policy, for the state's refusal to make full appropriation for support of private, religious schools, just as is done for public instruction. There could not be, on that basis, valid constitutional objection.[2]

Of course paying the cost of transportation promotes the general cause of education and the welfare of the individual. So does paying all other items of educational expense. And obviously, as the majority say, it is much too late to urge that legislation designed to facilitate the opportunities of children to secure a secular education serves no public purpose. Our nation-wide system of public education rests on the contrary view, as do all grants in aid of education, public or private, which is not religious in character.

These things are beside the real question. They have no possible materiality except to obscure the all-pervading, inescapable issue. *Cf. Cochran v. Board of Education, supra.* Stripped of its religious phase, the case presents no substantial federal question. The public function argument, by casting the issue in terms of promoting the general cause of education and the welfare of the individual, ignores the religious factor and its essential connection with the transportation, thereby leaving out the only vital element in the case. So of course do the "public welfare" and "social legislation" ideas, for they come to the same thing.

---

[2] If it is part of the state's function to supply to religious schools or their patrons the smaller items of educational expense, because the legislature may say they perform a public function, it is hard to see why the larger ones also may not be paid. Indeed, it would seem even more proper and necessary for the state to do this. For if one class of expenditures is justified on the ground that it supports the general cause of education or benefits the individual, or can be made to do so by legislative declaration, so even more certainly would be the other. To sustain payment for transportation to school, for textbooks, for other essential materials, or perhaps for school lunches, and not for what makes all these things effective for their intended end, would be to make a public function of the smaller items and their cumulative effect, but to make wholly private in character the larger things without which the smaller could have no meaning or use.

We have here then one substantial issue, not two. To say that New Jersey's appropriation and her use of the power of taxation for raising the funds appropriated are not for public purposes but are for private ends, is to say that they are for the support of religion and religious teaching. Conversely, to say that they are for public purposes is to say that they are not for religious ones.

This is precisely for the reason that education which includes religious training and teaching, and its support, have been made matters of private right and function, not public, by the very terms of the First Amendment. That is the effect not only in its guaranty of religion's free exercise, but also in the prohibition of establishments. It was on this basis of the private character of the function of religious education that this Court held parents entitled to send their children to private, religious schools. *Pierce v. Society of Sisters, supra.* Now it declares in effect that the appropriation of public funds to defray part of the cost of attending those schools is for a public purpose. If so, I do not understand why the state cannot go farther or why this case approaches the verge of its power.

In truth this view contradicts the whole purpose and effect of the First Amendment as heretofore conceived. The "public function" — "public welfare" — "social legislation" argument seeks, in Madison's words, to "employ Religion [that is, here, religious education] as an engine of Civil policy." REMONSTRANCE, Par. 5. It is of one piece with the Assessment Bill's preamble, although with the vital difference that it wholly ignores what that preamble explicitly states.

Our constitutional policy is exactly the opposite. It does not deny the value or the necessity for religious training, teaching or observance. Rather it secures their free exercise. But to that end it does deny that the state can undertake or sustain them in any form or degree. For this reason the sphere of religious activity, as distinguished from the secular intellectual liberties, has been given the twofold protection and, as the state cannot forbid, neither can it perform or aid in performing the religious function. The dual prohibition makes that function altogether private. It cannot be made a public one by legislative act. This was the very heart of Madison's Remonstrance, as it is of the Amendment itself.

The reasons underlying the Amendment's policy have not vanished with time or diminished in force. Now as when it was adopted the price of religious freedom is double. It is that the church and religion shall live both within and upon that freedom. There cannot be freedom of religion, safeguarded by the state, and intervention by the church or its agencies in the state's domain or dependency on its largesse. MADISON'S REMONSTRANCE, Par. 6, 8. The great condition of religious liberty is that it be maintained free from sustenance, as also from other interferences, by the state. For when it comes to rest upon that secular foundation it vanishes with the resting. *Id.,* Par. 7, 8. Public money devoted to payment of religious costs, educational or other, brings the quest for more. It brings too the struggle of sect against sect for the larger share or for any. Here one by numbers alone will benefit most, there another. That is precisely the history of societies which have had an established religion and dissident groups. *Id.*, Par. 8, 11. It is the very thing Jefferson and Madison experienced and sought to guard against, whether in its blunt or in its more screened forms. *Ibid.* The end of such strife cannot be other than to destroy the cherished liberty. The dominating group will achieve the dominant benefit; or all will embroil the state in their dissensions. *Id.*, Par. 11.

Exactly such conflicts have centered of late around providing transportation to religious schools from public funds. The issue and the dissension work typically, in Madison's phrase, to "destroy that moderation and harmony which the forbearance of our laws to intermeddle with Religion, has produced amongst its several sects." *Id.*, Par. 11. This occurs, as he well knew, over measures at the very threshold of departure from the principle. *Id.*, Par. 3, 9, 11.

This is not therefore just a little case over bus fares. In paraphrase of Madison, distant as it may be in its present form from a complete establishment of religion, it differs from it only in degree; and is the first step in that direction. *Id.*, Par. 9. Today as in his time "the same authority which can force a citizen to contribute three pence only . . . for the support of any one [religious] establishment, may force him" to pay more; or "to conform to any other establishment in all cases whatsoever." And now, as then, "either . . . we must say, that the will of the Legislature is the only measure of their authority; and that in the plenitude of this authority, they may sweep away all our fundamental rights; or, that they are bound to leave this particular right untouched and sacred." REMONSTRANCE, Par. 15.

The realm of religious training and belief remains, as the Amendment made it, the kingdom of the individual man and his God. It should be kept inviolately private, not "entangled . . . in precedents" or confounded with what legislatures legitimately may take over into the public domain.

COMMITTEE FOR PUBLIC EDUCATION & RELIGIOUS LIBERTY v. NYQUIST
413 U.S. 756 (1973)

MR. JUSTICE POWELL delivered the opinion of the Court.

These cases raise a challenge under the Establishment Clause of the First Amendment to the constitutionality of a recently enacted New York law which provides financial assistance, in several ways, to nonpublic elementary and secondary schools in that State. The cases involve an intertwining of societal and constitutional issues of the greatest importance.

I

In May 1972, the Governor of New York signed into law several amendments to the State's Education and Tax Laws. The first five sections of these amendments established three distinct financial aid programs for nonpublic elementary and secondary schools.

The first section of the challenged enactment, entitled "Health and Safety Grants for Nonpublic School Children," provides for direct money grants from the State to "qualifying" nonpublic schools to be used for the "maintenance and repair of . . . school facilities and equipment to ensure the health, welfare and safety of enrolled pupils." A "qualifying" school is any nonpublic, nonprofit elementary or secondary school which "has been designated during the (immediately preceding) year as serving a high concentration of pupils from low-income families for purposes of Title IV of the Federal Higher Education Act of nineteen hundred sixty-five (20 U.S.C.A. § 425)." Such schools are entitled to receive a grant of $30 per pupil per year, or $40 per pupil per year if the facilities are more than 25 years old. Each school is required to submit to the Commissioner of Education an audited statement of its expenditures for maintenance and repair during the preceding year, and its grant may not exceed the total of such expenses. The Commissioner is also required to ascertain the average per-pupil cost for equivalent maintenance and repair services in the public schools, and in no event may the grant to nonpublic qualifying schools exceed 50% of that figure.

"Maintenance and repair" is defined by the statute to include "the provision of heat, light, water, ventilation and sanitary facilities; cleaning, janitorial and custodial services; snow removal; necessary upkeep and renovation of buildings, grounds and equipment; fire and accident protection; and such other items as the commissioner may deem necessary to ensure the health, welfare and safety of enrolled pupils." This section is prefaced by a series of legislative findings which shed light on the State's purpose in enacting the law. These findings conclude that the State "has a primary responsibility to ensure the health, welfare and safety of children attending . . . nonpublic schools"; that the "fiscal crisis in nonpublic education . . . has caused a diminution of proper maintenance and repair programs, threatening the health, welfare and safety of nonpublic school children" in low-income urban areas; and that "a healthy and safe school environment" contributes "to the stability of urban neighborhoods." For these reasons, the statute declares that "the state has the right to make grants for maintenance and repair expenditures which are clearly secular, neutral and non-ideological in nature."

The remainder of the challenged legislation — §§ 2 through 5 — is a single package captioned the "Elementary and Secondary Education Opportunity Program." It is composed, essentially, of two parts, a tuition grant program and a tax benefit program. Section 2 establishes a limited plan providing tuition reimbursements to parents of children attending elementary or secondary non- public schools. To quality under this section a parent must have an annual taxable income of less than $5,000. The amount of reimbursement is limited to $50 for each grade school child and $100 for each high school child. Each parent is required, however, to submit to the Commissioner of Education a verified statement containing a receipted tuition bill, and the amount of state reimbursement may not exceed 50% of that figure. No restrictions are imposed on the use of the funds by the reimbursed parents.

This section, like § 1, is prefaced by a series of legislative findings designed to explain the impetus for the State's action. Expressing a dedication to the "vitality of our pluralistic society," the findings state that a "healthy competitive and diverse alternative to public education is not only desirable but indeed vital to a state and nation that have continually reaffirmed the value of individual differences." The findings further emphasize that the right to select among alternative educational systems "is diminished or even denied to children of lower-income families, whose parents, of all groups, have the least options in determining where their children are to be educated." Turning to the public schools, the findings state that any "precipitous decline in the number of nonpublic school pupils would cause a massive increase in public school enrollment and costs," an increase that would "aggravate an already serious fiscal crises in public education" and would "seriously jeopardize quality education for all children." Based on these premises, the statute asserts the State's right to relieve the financial burden of parents who send their children to non-public schools through this tuition reimbursement program. Repeating the declaration contained in § 1, the findings conclude that "[s]uch assistance is clearly secular, neutral and nonideological."

The remainder of the "Elementary and Secondary Education Opportunity Program," contained in §§ 3, 4, and 5 of the challenged law, is designed to provide a form of tax relief to those who fail to qualify for tuition reimbursement. Under these sections parents may subtract from their adjusted gross income for state income tax purposes a designated amount for each dependent for whom they have paid at least $50 in nonpublic school tuition. If the taxpayer's adjusted gross income is less than $9,000 he may subtract $1,000 for each of as many as three dependents. As the taxpayer's income rises, the amount he may subtract diminishes. Thus, if a taxpayer has adjusted gross income of $15,000, he may subtract only $400 per dependent, and if his adjusted gross income is $25,000 or more, no deduction is allowed. The amount of the deduction is not dependent upon how much the taxpayer actually paid for nonpublic school tuition, and is given in addition to any deductions to which the taxpayer may be entitled for other religious or charitable contributions. As indicated in the memorandum from the Majority Leader and President pro tem of the Senate, submitted to each New York Legislator during consideration of the bill, the actual tax benefits under these provisions were carefully calculated in advance. Thus, comparable tax benefits pick up at approximately the point at which tuition reimbursement benefits leave off.

Although no record was developed in these cases, a number of pertinent generalizations may be made about the nonpublic schools which would benefit from these enactments. The District Court, relying on findings in a similar case recently decided by the same court, adopted a profile of these sectarian, nonpublic schools similar to the one suggested in the plaintiffs' complaint. Qualifying institutions, under all three segments of the enactment, could be ones that

> "(a) impose religious restrictions on admissions; (b) require attendance of pupils at religious activities; (c) require obedience by students to the doctrines and dogmas of a particular faith; (d) require pupils to attend instruction in the theology or doctrine of a particular faith; (e) are an integral part of the religious mission of the church sponsoring it; (f) have as a substantial purpose the inculcation of religious values; (g) impose religious restrictions on faculty appointments; and (h) impose religious restrictions on what or how the faculty may teach." 350 F. Supp. 655, 663.

Of course, the characteristics of individual schools may vary widely from that profile. Some 700,000 to 800,000 students constituting almost 20% of the State's entire elementary and secondary school population, attend over 2,000 nonpublic schools, approximately 85% of which are church affiliated. And while "all or practically all" of the 280 schools entitled to receive "maintenance and repair" grants "are related to the Roman Catholic Church and teach Catholic religious doctrine to some degree," institutions qualifying under the remainder of the statute include a substantial number of Jewish, Lutheran, Episcopal, Seventh Day Adventist, and other church-affiliated schools.[23]

II

Most of the cases coming to this Court raising Establishment Clause questions have involved the relationship between religion and education. Among these religion-education precedents, two general categories of cases may be identified: those dealing with religious activities within the public schools, and those involving public aid in varying forms to sectarian educational institutions. While the New York legislation places this case in the latter category, its resolution requires consideration, not only of the several aid-to-sectarian-education cases, but also of our other education precedents and of several important noneducation cases. For the now well-defined three-part test that has emerged from our decisions is a product of considerations derived from the full sweep of the Establishment Clause cases. Taken together, these decisions dictate that to pass muster under the Establishment Clause the law in question first must reflect a clearly secular legislative purpose, second, must have a primary effect that neither advances nor inhibits religion, and third, must avoid excessive government entanglement with religion.

[The Court held that "the State's interest in promoting pluralism and diversity among its public and nonpublic schools" was a valid secular purpose under *Lemon*.]

---

[23] In the fall of 1968, there were 2,038 nonpublic schools in New York State; 1,415 Roman Catholic; 164 Jewish; 59 Lutheran; 49 Episcopal; 37 Seventh Day Adventist; 18 other church affiliated; 296 without religious affiliation. N. Y. State Educ. Dept., Financial Support — Nonpublic Schools 3 (1969).

But the propriety of a legislature's purposes may not immunize from further scrutiny a law which either has a primary effect that advances religion, or which fosters excessive entanglements between Church and State. Accordingly, we must weigh each of the three aid provisions challenged here against these criteria of effect and entanglement.

A

The "maintenance and repair" provisions of § 1 authorize direct payments to nonpublic schools, virtually all of which are Roman Catholic schools in low-income areas. The grants, totaling $30 or $40 per pupil depending on the age of the institution, are given largely without restriction on usage. So long as expenditures do not exceed 50% of comparable expenses in the public school system, it is possible for a sectarian elementary or secondary school to finance its entire "maintenance and repair" budget from state tax-raised funds. No attempt is made to restrict payments to those expenditures related to the upkeep of facilities used exclusively for secular purposes, nor do we think it possible within the context of these religion-oriented institutions to impose such restrictions. Nothing in the statute, for instance, bars a qualifying school from paying out of state funds the salaries of employees who maintain the school chapel, or the cost of renovating classrooms in which religion is taught, or the cost of heating and lighting those same facilities. Absent appropriate restrictions on expenditures for these and similar purposes, it simply cannot be denied that this section has a primary effect that advances religion in that it subsidizes directly the religious activities of sectarian elementary and secondary schools.

The state officials nevertheless argue that these expenditures for "maintenance and repair" are similar to other financial expenditures approved by this Court. Primarily they rely on *Everson v. Board of Education*; *Board of Education v. Allen*; and *Tilton v. Richardson*. In each of those cases it is true that the Court approved a form of financial assistance which conferred undeniable benefits upon private, sectarian schools. But a close examination of those cases illuminates their distinguishing characteristics. In *Everson*, the Court, in a five-to-four decision, approved a program of reimbursements to parents of public as well as parochial schoolchildren for bus fares paid in connection with transportation to and from school, a program which the Court characterized as approaching the "verge" of impermissible state aid. In *Allen*, decided some 20 years later, the Court upheld a New York law authorizing the provision of *secular* textbooks for all children in grades seven through 12 attending public and nonpublic schools. Finally, in *Tilton*, the Court upheld federal grants of funds for the construction of facilities to be used for clearly *secular* purposes by public and nonpublic institutions of higher learning.

These cases simply recognize that sectarian schools perform secular, educational functions as well as religious functions, and that some forms of aid may be channeled to the secular without providing direct aid to the sectarian. But the channel is a narrow one, as the above cases illustrate. Of course, it is true in each case that the provision of such neutral, nonideological aid, assisting only the secular functions of sectarian schools, served indirectly and incidentally to promote the religious function by rendering it more likely that children would attend sectarian schools and by freeing the budgets of those schools for use in other nonsecular areas. But an indirect and incidental effect beneficial to religious institutions has never been thought a sufficient defect to warrant the invalidation of a state law. In *McGowan v. Maryland, supra*, Sunday Closing Laws were sustained even though one of their undeniable effects was to render it somewhat more likely that citizens would respect religious institutions and even attend religious services. Also, in *Walz v. Tax Comm'n, supra*, property tax exemptions for church property were held not violative of the Establishment Clause despite the fact that such exemptions relieved churches of a financial burden.

Tilton draws the line most clearly. While a bare majority was there persuaded, for the reasons stated in the plurality opinion and in Mr. Justice White's concurrence, that carefully limited construction grants to colleges and universities could be sustained, the Court was unanimous in its rejection of one clause of the federal statute in question. Under that clause, the Government was entitled to recover a portion of its grant to a sectarian institution in the event that the constructed facility was used to advance religion by, for instance, converting the building to a chapel or otherwise allowing it to be "used to promote religious interests." But because the statute provided that the condition would expire at the end of 20 years, the facilities would thereafter be available for use by the institution for any sectarian purpose. In striking down this provision, the plurality opinion emphasized that "[l]imiting the prohibition for religious use of the structure to 20 years obviously opens the facility to use for any purpose at the end of that period." And in that event, "the original federal grant will in part have the effect of advancing religion." If tax-raised funds may not be granted to institutions of higher learning where the possibility exists that those funds will be used to construct a facility utilized for sectarian activities 20 years hence, *a fortiori* they may not be distributed to elementary and secondary sectarian schools for the maintenance and repair of facilities without any limitations on their use. If the State may not erect buildings in which religious activities are to take place, it may not maintain such buildings or renovate them when they fall into disrepair.

It might be argued, however, that while the New York "maintenance and repair" grants lack specifically articulated secular restrictions, the statute does provide a sort of statistical guarantee of separation by limiting grants to 50% of the amount expended for comparable services in the public schools. The legislature's supposition might have been that at least 50% of the ordinary public school maintenance and repair budget would be devoted to purely secular facility upkeep in sectarian schools. The shortest answer to this argument is that the statute itself allows, as a ceiling, grants satisfying the entire "amount of expenditures for maintenance and repair of such school" providing only that it is neither more than $30 or $40 per pupil nor more than 50% of the comparable public school expenditures. Quite apart from the language of the statute, our cases make clear that a mere statistical judgment will not suffice as a guarantee that state funds will not be used to finance religious education. In *Earley v. DiCenso*, a companion case to *Lemon v. Kurtzman*, the Court struck down a Rhode Island law authorizing salary supplements to teachers of secular subjects. The grants were not to exceed 15% of any teacher's annual salary. Although the law was invalidated on entanglement grounds, the Court made clear that the State could not have avoided violating the Establishment Clause by merely assuming that its teachers would succeed in segregating "their religious beliefs from their secular educational responsibilities."

> "The Rhode Island Legislature has not, *and could not,* provide state aid on the basis of a mere assumption that secular teachers under religious discipline can avoid conflicts. The State *must be certain, given the Religion Clauses,* that subsidized teachers do not inculcate religion. . . ."

Nor could the State of Rhode Island have prevailed by simply relying on the assumption that, whatever a secular teacher's inabilities to refrain from mixing the religious with the secular, he would surely devote at least 15% of his efforts to purely secular education, thus exhausting the state grant. It takes little imagination to perceive the extent to which States might openly subsidize parochial schools under such a loose standard of scrutiny. *See also Tilton v. Richardson, supra.*

[Because the Court struck down the provisions in question under the secular effect analysis, it did not consider the third (administrative entanglement) prong of the *Lemon* test.]

B

New York's tuition reimbursement program also fails the "effect" test, for much the same reasons that govern its maintenance and repair grants. The state program is designed to allow direct, unrestricted grants of $50 to $100 per child (but no more than 50% of tuition actually paid) as reimbursement to parents in low-income brackets who send their children to nonpublic schools, the bulk of which is concededly sectarian in orientation. To qualify, a parent must have earned less than $5,000 in taxable income and must present a receipted tuition bill from a nonpublic school.

There can be no question that these grants could not, consistently with the Establishment Clause, be given directly to sectarian schools, since they would suffer from the same deficiency that renders invalid the grants for maintenance and repair. In the absence of an effective means of guaranteeing that the state aid derived from public funds will be used exclusively for secular, neutral, and nonideological purposes, it is clear from our cases that direct aid in whatever form is invalid. As Mr. Justice Black put it quite simply in *Everson*:

> "No tax in any amount, large or small, can be levied to support any religious activities or institutions, whatever they may be called, or

whatever form they may adopt to teach or practice religion." 330 U.S., at 16.

The controlling question here, then, is whether the fact that the grants are delivered to parents rather than schools is of such significance as to compel a contrary result. The State and intervenor-appellees rely on *Everson* and *Allen* for their claim that grants to parents, unlike grants to institutions, respect the "wall of separation" required by the Constitution. It is true that in those cases the Court upheld laws that provided benefits to children attending religious schools and to their parents: As noted above, in *Everson* parents were reimbursed for bus fares paid to send children to parochial schools, and in *Allen* textbooks were loaned directly to the children. But those decisions make clear that, far from providing a *per se* immunity from examination of the substance of the State's program, the fact that aid is disbursed to parents rather than to the schools is only one among many factors to be considered.

In *Everson*, the Court found the bus fare program analogous to the provision of services such as police and fire protection, sewage disposal, highways, and sidewalks for parochial schools. Such services, provided in common to all citizens, are "so separate and so indisputably marked off from the religious function," *id.*, at 18, that they may fairly be viewed as reflections of a neutral posture toward religious institutions. *Allen* is founded upon a similar principle. The Court there repeatedly emphasized that upon the record in that case there was no indication that textbooks would be provided for anything other than purely secular courses. "Of course books are different from buses. Most bus rides have no inherent religious significance, while religious books are common. However, the language of [the law under consideration] does not authorize the loan of religious books, and the State claims no right to distribute religious literature. . . . Absent evidence, we cannot assume that school authorities . . . are unable to distinguish between secular and religious books or that they will not honestly discharge their duties under the law."[38]

Although we think it clear, for the reasons above stated, that New York's tuition grant program fares no better under the "effect" test than its mainte-

---

[38] *Allen* and *Everson* differ from the present litigation in a second important respect. In both cases the class of beneficiaries included all schoolchildren, those in public as well as those in private schools. *See also Tilton v. Richardson, supra,* in which federal aid was made available to all institutions of higher learning, and *Walz v. Tax Comm'n, supra,* in which tax exemptions were accorded to all educational and charitable nonprofit institutions. We do not agree with the suggestion in the dissent of THE CHIEF JUSTICE that tuition grants are an analogous endeavor to provide comparable benefits to all parents of schoolchildren whether enrolled in public or nonpublic schools. 413 U.S., at 801-803. The grants to parents of private schoolchildren are given in addition to the right that they have to send their children to public schools 'totally at state expense.' And in any event, the argument proves too much, for it would also provide a basis for approving through tuition grants the *complete subsidization* of all religious schools on the ground that such action is necessary if the State is fully to equalize the position of parents who elect such schools — a result wholly at variance with the Establishment Clause.

nance and repair program, in view of the novelty of the question we will address briefly the subsidiary arguments made by the state officials and intervenors in its defense.

First, it has been suggested that it is of controlling significance that New York's program calls for *reimbursement* for tuition already paid rather than for direct contributions which are merely routed through the parents to the schools, in advance of or in lieu of payment by the parents. The parent is not a mere conduit, we are told, but is absolutely free to spend the money he receives in any manner he wishes. There is no element of coercion attached to the reimbursement, and no assurance that the money will eventually end up in the hands of religious schools. The absence of any element of coercion, however, is irrelevant to questions arising under the Establishment Clause. In *School District of Abington Township v. Schempp, supra*, it was contended that Bible recitations in public schools did not violate the Establishment Clause because participation in such exercises was not coerced. The Court rejected that argument, noting that while proof of coercion might provide a basis for a claim under the Free Exercise Clause, it was not a necessary element of any claim under the Establishment Clause. MR. JUSTICE BRENNAN'S concurring views reiterated the Court's conclusion:

> "Thus the short, and to me sufficient, answer is that the availability of excusal or exemption simply has no relevance to the establishment question, if it is once found that these practices are essentially religious exercises designed at least in part to achieve religious aims. . . ." *Id.*, at 288.

A similar inquiry governs here: if the grants are offered as an incentive to parents to send their children to sectarian schools by making unrestricted cash payments to them, the Establishment Clause is violated whether or not the actual dollars given eventually find their way into the sectarian institutions. Whether the grant is labeled a reimbursement, a reward, or a subsidy, its substantive impact is still the same. In sum, we agree with the conclusion of the District Court that "[w]hether he gets it during the current year, or as reimbursement for the past year, if of no constitutional importance."

Second, the Majority Leader and President pro tem of the State Senate argues that it is significant here that the tuition reimbursement grants pay only a portion of the tuition bill, and an even smaller portion of the religious school's total expenses. The New York statute limits reimbursement to 50% of any parent's actual outlay. Additionally, intervenor estimates that only 30% of the total cost of nonpublic education is covered by tuition payments, with the remaining coming from "voluntary contribution, endowments and the like." On the basis of these two statistics, appellees reason that the "maximum tuition reimbursement by the State is thus only 15% of educational costs in the nonpublic schools." And, "since the compulsory education laws of the State, by necessity require significantly more than 15% of school time to be devoted to teaching secular courses," the New York statute provides "a statistical guarantee of neutrality." It should readily be seen that this is simply another variant of the argument we have rejected as to maintenance and repair costs, and it can fare no better here. Obviously, if accepted, this argument would provide the foundation for massive, direct subsidization of sectarian elementary and secondary schools. Our cases, however, have long since foreclosed the notion that mere statistical assurances will suffice to sail between the Scylla and Charybodis of "effect" and "entanglement."

Finally, the State argues that its program of tuition grants should survive scrutiny because it is designed to promote the free exercise of religion. The State notes that only "low-income parents" are aided by this law, and without state assistance their right to have their children educated in a religious environment "is diminished or even denied." It is true, of course, that this Court has long recognized and maintained the right to choose nonpublic over public education. *Pierce v. Society of Sisters*, 268 U.S. 510 (1925). It is also true that a state law interfering with a parent's right to have his child educated in a sectarian school would run afoul of the Free Exercise Clause. But this Court repeatedly has recognized that tension inevitably exists between the Free Exercise and the Establishment Clauses, *e.g., Everson v. Board of Education*; *Walz v. Tax Comm'n,* and that it may often not be possible to promote the former without offending the latter. As a result of this tension, our cases require the State to maintain an attitude of "neutrality," neither "advancing" nor "inhibiting" religion. In its attempt to enhance the opportunities of the poor to choose between public and nonpublic education, the State has taken a step which can only be regarded as one "advancing" religion. However great our sympathy for the burdens experienced by those who must pay public school taxes at the same time that they support other schools because of the constraints of "conscience and discipline," and notwithstanding the "high social importance" of the State's purposes, neither may justify an eroding of the limitations of the Establishment Clause now firmly implanted.

C

Sections 3, 4, and 5 establish a system for providing income tax benefits to parents of children attending New York's nonpublic schools. In this Court, the parties have engaged in a considerable debate over what label best fits the New York law. Appellants insist that the law is, in effect, one establishing a system of tax "credits." The State and the intervenors reject that characterization and would label it, instead, a system of income tax "modifications." The Solicitor General, in an *amicus curiae* brief filed in this Court, has referred throughout to the New York law as one authorizing tax "deductions." The District Court majority found that the aid was "in effect a tax *credit*." Because of the peculiar nature of the benefit allowed, it is difficult to adopt any single traditional label lifted from the law of income taxation. It is, at least in its form, a tax deduction since it is an amount subtracted from adjusted gross income, prior to computation of the tax due. Its effect, as the District Court concluded, is more like that of a tax credit since the deduction is not related to the amount actually spent for tuition and is apparently designed to yield a predetermined amount of tax "forgiveness" in exchange for performing a specific act which the State desires to encourage — the usual attribute of a tax credit. We see no reason to select one label over another, as the constitutionality of this hybrid benefit does not turn in any event on the label we accord it. As MR. CHIEF JUSTICE BURGER's opinion for the Court in *Lemon v. Kurtzman* notes, constitutional analysis is not a "legalistic minuet in which precise rules and forms must govern." Instead we must "examine the form of the relationship for the light that it casts on the substance."

These sections allow parents of children attending nonpublic elementary and secondary schools to subtract from adjusted gross income a specified amount if they do not receive a tuition reimbursement under § 2, and if they have an adjusted gross income of less than $25,000. The amount of the deduction is unrelated to the amount of money actually expended by any parent on tuition, but is calculated on the basis of a formula contained in the statute. The formula is apparently the product of a legislative attempt to assure that each family would receive a carefully estimated net benefit, and that the tax benefit would be comparable to, and compatible with, the tuition grant for lower income families. Thus, a parent who earns less than $5,000 is entitled to a tuition reimbursement of $50 if he has one child attending an elementary, nonpublic school, while a parent who earns more (but less than $9,000) is entitled to have a precisely equal amount taken off his tax bill. Additionally, a taxpayer's benefit under these sections is unrelated to, and not reduced by, any deductions to which he may be entitled for charitable contributions to religious institutions.

In practical terms there would appear to be little difference, for purposes of determining whether such aid has the effect of advancing religion, between the tax benefit allowed here and the tuition grant allowed under § 2. The qualifying parent under either program receives the same form of encouragement and reward for sending his children to nonpublic schools. The only difference is that one parent receives an actual cash payment while the other is allowed to reduce by an arbitrary amount the sum he would otherwise be obliged to pay over to the State. We see no answer to Judge Hays' dissenting statement below that "[I]n both instances the money involved represents a charge made upon the state for the purpose of religious education."

Appellees defend the tax portion of New York's legislative package on two grounds. First, they contend that it is of controlling significance that the grants or credits are directed to the parents rather than to the schools. This is the same argument made in support of the tuition reimbursements and rests on the same reading of the same precedents of this Court, primarily *Everson* and *Allen*. Our treatment of this issue in Part II-B is applicable here and requires rejection of this claim. Second, appellees place their strongest reliance on *Walz v. Tax Comm'n, supra*, in which New York's property tax exemption for religious organizations was upheld. We think that *Walz* provides no support for appellees' position. Indeed, its rationale plainly compels the conclusion that New York's tax package violates the Establishment Clause.

Tax exemptions for church property enjoyed an apparently universal approval in this country both before and after the adoption of the First Amendment. The Court in *Walz* surveyed the history of tax exemptions and found that each of the 50 States has long provided for tax exemptions for places of worship, that Congress has exempted religious organizations from taxation for over three-quarters of a century, and that congressional enactments in 1802, 1813, and 1870 specifically exempted church property from taxation. In sum, the Court concluded that "[f]ew concepts are more deeply embedded in the fabric of our national life, beginning with pre-Revolutionary colonial times, than for the government to exercise at the very least this kind of benevolent neutrality toward churches and religious exercise generally." We know of no historical precedent for New York's recently promulgated tax relief program. Indeed, it seems clear that tax benefits for parents whose children attend parochial schools are a recent innovation, occasioned by the growing financial plight of such nonpublic institutions and designed, albeit unsuccessfully, to tailor state aid in a manner not incompatible with the recent decisions of this Court.

But historical acceptance without more would not alone have sufficed, as "no one acquires a vested or protected right in violation of the Constitution by long use." *Walz.* It was the reason underlying that long history of tolerance of tax exemptions for religion that proved controlling. A proper respect for both the Free Exercise and the Establishment Clauses compels the State to pursue a course of "neutrality" toward religion. Yet governments have not always pursued such a course, and oppression has taken many forms, one of which has been taxation of religion. Thus, if taxation was regarded as a form of "hostility" toward religion, "exemption constitute[d] a reasonable and balanced attempt to guard against those dangers." Special tax benefits, however, cannot be squared with the principle of neutrality established by the decisions of this Court. To the contrary, insofar as such benefits render assistance to parents who send their children to sectarian schools, their purpose and inevitable effect are to aid and advance those religious institutions.

Apart from its historical foundations, *Walz* is a product of the same dilemma and inherent tension found in most government-aid-to-religion controversies. To be sure, the exemption of church property from taxation conferred a benefit, albeit an indirect and incidental one. Yet that "aid" was a product not of any purpose to support or to subsidize, but of a fiscal relationship designed to minimize involvement and entanglement between Church and State. "The exemption," the Court emphasized, "tends to complement and reinforce the desired separation insulating each from the other." Furthermore, "[e]limination of the exemption would tend to expand the involvement of government by giving rise to tax valuation of church property, tax liens, tax foreclosures, and the direct confrontations and conflicts that follow in the train of those legal processes." The granting of the tax benefits under the New York statute, unlike the extension of an exemption, would tend to increase rather than limit the involvement between Church and State.

One further difference between tax exemption for church property and tax benefits for parents should be noted. The exemption challenged in *Walz* was not restricted to a class composed exclusively or even predominantly of religious institutions. Instead, the exemption covered all property devoted to religious, educational, or charitable purposes. As the parties here must concede, tax reductions authorized by this law flow primarily to the parents of children attending sectarian, nonpublic schools. Without intimating whether this factor alone might have controlling significance in another context in some future case, it should be apparent that in terms of the potential divisiveness of any legislative measure the narrowness of the benefited class would be an important factor.

In conclusion, we find the *Walz* analogy unpersuasive, and in light of the practical similarity between New York's tax and tuition reimbursement programs, we hold that neither form of aid is sufficiently restricted to assure that it will not have the impermissible effect of advancing the sectarian activities of religious schools.

ROEMER v. BOARD OF PUBLIC WORKS OF MARYLAND
426 U.S. 736 (1976)

MR. JUSTICE BLACKMUN announced the judgment of the Court and delivered an opinion in which THE CHIEF JUSTICE and MR. JUSTICE POWELL joined.

We are asked once again to police the constitutional boundary between church and state. Maryland, this time, is the alleged trespasser. It has enacted a statute which, as amended, provides for annual noncategorical grants to private colleges, among them religiously affiliated institutions, subject only to the restrictions that the funds not be used for "sectarian purposes."

I

The challenged grant program provides funding for "any private institution of higher learning within the State of Maryland," provided the institution is accredited by the State Department of Education, was established in Maryland prior to July 1, 1970, maintains one or more "associate of arts or baccalaureate degree" programs, and refrains from awarding "only seminarian or theological degrees." The aid is in the form of an annual fiscal year subsidy to qualifying colleges and universities. The formula by which each institution's entitlement is computed has been changed several times and is not independently at issue here. It now provides for a qualifying institution to receive, for each full-time student (excluding students enrolled in seminarian or theological academic programs), an amount equal to 15% Of the State's per-full-time-pupil appropriation for a student in the state college system. As first enacted, the grants were completely unrestricted. They remain noncategorical in nature, and a recipient institution may put them to whatever use it prefers, with but one exception. In 1972, following this Court's decisions in *Lemon v. Kurtzman* and *Tilton v.Richardson*, § 68 was added to the statute. It provides:

> "None of the moneys payable under this subtitle shall be utilized by the institutions for sectarian purposes."

The administration of the grant program is entrusted to the State's Board of Public Works "assisted by the Maryland Council for Higher Education."

The Council performs what the District Court described as a "two-step screening process" to insure compliance with the statutory restrictions on the grants. First, it determines whether an institution applying for aid is eligible at all, or is one "awarding primarily theological or seminary degrees." Several applicants have been disqualified at this stage of the process. Second, the Council requires that those institutions that are eligible for funds not put them to any sectarian use. An application must be accompanied by an affidavit of the institution's chief executive officer stating that the funds will not be used for sectarian purposes, and by a description of the specific nonsectarian uses that are planned. These may be changed only after written notice to the Council. By the end of the fiscal year the institution must file a "Utilization of Funds Report" describing and itemizing the use of the funds. The chief executive officer must certify the report and also file his own "Post- expenditure Affidavit," stating that the funds have not been put to sectarian uses. The recipient institution is further required to segregate state funds in a "special revenue account" and to identify aided nonsectarian expenditures separately in its budget. It must retain "sufficient documentation of the State funds expended to permit verification by the Council that funds were not spent for sectarian purposes." Any question of sectarian use that may arise is to be resolved by the Council, if possible, on the basis of information submitted to it by the institution and without actual examination of its books. Failing that, a "verification or audit" may be undertaken. The District Court found that the audit would be "quick and non-judgmental," taking one day or less.

In 1971, $1.7 million was disbursed to 17 private institutions in Maryland. The disbursements were under the statute as originally enacted, and were therefore not subject to § 68A's specific prohibition on sectarian use. Of the 17 institutions, five were church related, and these received $520,000 of the $1.7 million. A total of $1.8 million was to be awarded to 18 institutions in 1972, the second year of the grant program; of this amount, $603,000 was to go to church-related institutions. Before disbursement, however, this suit, challenging the grants as in violation of the Establishment Clause of the First Amendment, was filed. The $603,000 was placed in escrow and was so held until after the entry of the District Court's judgment on October 21, 1974. These and subsequent awards, therefore, are subject to [the statutory guidelines] and to the Council's procedures for insuring compliance therewith.

Plaintiffs in this suit, appellants here, are four individual Maryland citizens and taxpayers. Their complaint sought a declaration of the statute's invalidity, an order enjoining payments under it to church-affiliated institutions, and a declaration that the State was entitled to recover from such institutions any amounts already disbursed. In addition to the responsible state officials, plaintiff-appellants joined as defendants the five institutions they claimed were constitutionally ineligible for this form of aid: Western Maryland College, College of Notre Dame, Mount Saint Mary's College, Saint Joseph College, and Loyola College. Of these, the last four are affiliated with the Roman Catholic Church; Western Maryland was a Methodist affiliate. The District Court ruled with respect to all five. Western Maryland, however, has since been dismissed as a defendant-appellee. We are concerned, therefore, only with the four Roman Catholic affiliates.

II

A system of government that makes itself felt as pervasively as ours could hardly be expected never to cross paths with the church. In fact, our State and Federal Governments impose certain burdens upon, and impart certain benefits to, virtually all our activities, and religious activity is not an exception. The Court has enforced a scrupulous neutrality by the State, as among religions, and also as between religious and other activities, but a hermetic separation of the two is an impossibility it has never required. It long has been established, for example, that the State may send a cleric, indeed even a clerical order, to perform a wholly secular task. In *Bradfield v. Roberts*, 175 U.S. 291 (1899), the Court upheld the extension of public aid to a corporation which, although composed entirely of members of a Roman Catholic sisterhood acting "under the auspices of said church," was limited by its corporate charter to the secular purpose of operating a charitable hospital.

And religious institutions need not be quarantined from public benefits that are neutrally available to all. The Court has permitted the State to supply transportation for children to and from church-related as well as public schools. *Everson v. Board of Education*. It has done the same with respect to secular textbooks loaned by the State on equal terms to students attending both public and church-related elementary schools. *Board of Education v. Allen*, 392 U.S. 236 (1968). Since it had not been shown in *Allen* that the secular textbooks would be put to other than secular purposes, the Court concluded that, as in *Everson*, the State was merely "extending the benefits of state laws to all citizens." *Id.*, at 242. Just as *Bradfield* dispels any notion that a religious person can never be in the State's pay for a secular purpose, *Everson* and *Allen* put to rest any argument that the State may never act in such a way that has the incidental effect of facilitating religious activity. The Court has not been blind to the fact that in aiding a religious institution to perform a secular task, the State frees the institution's resources to be put to sectarian ends. If this were impermissible, however, a church could not be protected by the police and fire departments, or have its public sidewalk kept in repair. The Court never has held that religious activities must be discriminated against in this way.

Neutrality is what is required. The State must confine itself to secular objectives, and neither advance nor impede religious activity. Of course, that principle is more easily stated than applied. The Court has taken the view that a secular purpose and a facial neutrality may not be enough, if in fact the State is lending direct support to a religious activity. The State may not, for example, pay for what is actually a religious education, even though it purports to be paying for a secular one, and even though it makes its aid available to secular and religious institutions alike. The Court also has taken the view that the State's efforts to perform a secular task, and at the same time avoid aiding in the performance of a religious one, may not lead it into such an intimate relationship with religious authority that it appears either to be sponsoring or to be excessively interfering with that authority. In *Lemon I* as noted above, the Court distilled these concerns into a three-prong test, resting in part on prior case law, for the constitutionality of statutes affording state aid to church-related schools:

> "First, the statute must have a secular legislative purpose; second, its principal or primary effect must be one that neither advances nor inhibits religion . . .; finally, the statute must not foster 'an excessive government entanglement with religion.'" 403 U.S., at 612-613.

At issue in *Lemon I* were two state-aid plans, a Rhode Island program to grant a 15% supplement to the salaries of private, church-related school teachers teaching secular courses, and a Pennsylvania program to reimburse private church-related schools for the entire cost of secular courses also offered in public schools. Both failed the third part of the test, that of "excessive government entanglement." This part the Court held in turn required a consideration of three factors: (1) the character and purposes of the benefited institutions, (2) the nature of the aid provided, and (3) the resulting relationship between the State and the religious authority. As to the first of these, in reviewing the Rhode Island program, the Court found that the aided schools, elementary and secondary, were characterized by "substantial religious activity and purpose." They were located near parish churches. Religious instruction was considered "part of the total educational process." Religious symbols and religious activities abounded. Two-thirds of the teachers were nuns, and their operation of the schools was regarded as an "'integral part of the religious mission of the Catholic Church.'" The schooling came at an impressionable age. The form of aid also cut against the programs. Unlike the textbooks in *Allen* and the bus transportation in *Everson*, the services of the state-supported teachers could not be counted on to be purely secular. They were bound to mix religious teachings with secular ones, not by conscious design, perhaps, but because the mixture was inevitable when teachers (themselves usually Catholics) were "employed by a religious organization, subject to the direction and discipline of religious authorities, and work[ed] in a system dedicated to rearing children in a particular faith." The State's efforts to supervise and control the teaching of religion in supposedly secular classes would therefore inevitably entangle it excessively in religious affairs. The Pennsylvania program similarly foundered.

The Court also pointed to another kind of church-state entanglement threatened by the Rhode Island and Pennsylvania programs, namely, their "divisive political potential." They represented "successive and very likely permanent annual appropriations that benefit relatively few religious groups." Political factions, supporting and opposing the programs, were bound to divide along religious lines. This was "one of the principal evils against which the First Amendment was intended to protect." It was stressed that the political divisiveness of the programs was "aggravated . . . by the need for continuing annual appropriations."

In *Tilton v. Richardson*, a companion case to *Lemon I*, the Court reached the contrary result. The aid challenged in *Tilton* was in the form of federal grants for the construction of academic facilities at private colleges, some of them church related, with the restriction that the facilities not be used for any sectarian purpose.[17] Applying *Lemon I*'s three-part test, the Court found the purpose of the federal aid program there under consideration to be secular. Its primary effect was not the advancement of religion, for sectarian use of the facilities was prohibited. Enforcement of this prohibition was made possible by the fact that religion did not so permeate the defendant colleges that their religious and secular functions were inseparable. On the contrary, there was no evidence that religious activities took place in the funded facilities. Courses at the colleges were "taught according to the academic requirements intrinsic to the subject matter," and "an atmosphere of academic freedom rather than religious indoctrination" was maintained.

Turning to the problem of excessive entanglement, the Court first stressed the character of the aided institutions. It pointed to several general differences between college and precollege education: College students are less susceptible to religious indoctrination; college courses tend to entail an internal discipline that inherently limits the opportunities for sectarian influence; and a high degree of academic freedom tends to prevail at the college level. It found no evidence that the colleges in *Tilton* varied from this pattern. Though controlled and largely populated by Roman Catholics, the colleges were not restricted to adherents of that faith. No religious services were required to be attended. Theology courses were mandatory, but they were taught in an academic fashion, and with treatment of beliefs other than Roman Catholicism. There were no attempts to proselytize among students, and principles of academic freedom prevailed. With colleges of this character, there was little risk that religion would seep into the teaching of secular subjects, and the state surveillance necessary to separate the two, therefore, was diminished. The Court next looked to the type of aid provided, and found it to be neutral or nonideological in nature. Like the textbooks and bus transportation in *Allen* and *Everson*, but unlike the teachers' services in *Lemon I*, physical facilities were capable of being restricted

---

[17] The restriction, as imposed, was to remain in effect for 20 years following construction. Since the Court could not approve the facilities' sectarian use even after a 20-year period, it excised that time limitation from the statute. 403 U.S., at 682-684 (plurality opinion).

to secular purposes. Moreover, the construction grant was a one-shot affair, not involving annual audits and appropriations.

As for political divisiveness, no "continuing religious aggravation" over the program had been shown, and the Court reasoned that this might be because of the lack of continuity in the church-state relationship, the character and diversity of the colleges, and the fact that they served a dispersed student constituency rather than a local one. "[C]umulatively," all these considerations persuaded the Court that church-state entanglement was not excessive.

In *Hunt v. McNair*, 413 U.S. 734 (1973), the challenged aid was also for the construction of secular college facilities, the state plan being one to finance the construction by revenue bonds issued through the medium of a state authority. In effect, the college serviced and repaid the bonds, but at the lower cost resulting from the tax-free status of the interest payments. The Court upheld the program on reasoning analogous to that in *Tilton*. In applying the second of the *Lemon I*'s three-part test, that concerning "primary effect," the following refinement was added:

> "Aid normally may be thought to have a primary effect of advancing religion when it flows to an institution in which religion is so pervasive that a substantial portion of its functions are subsumed in the religious mission or when it funds a specifically religious activity in an otherwise substantially secular setting." 413 U.S., at 743.

Although the college which *Hunt* concerned was subject to substantial control by its sponsoring Baptist Church, it was found to be similar to the colleges in *Tilton* and not "pervasively sectarian." As in *Tilton*, state aid went to secular facilities only, and thus not to any "specifically religious activity."

Committee for Public Education v. Nyquist followed in *Lemon I*'s wake much as *Hunt* followed in *Tilton*'s. The aid in *Nyquist* was to elementary and secondary schools which, the District Court found, generally conformed to a "profile" of a sectarian or substantially religious school.[18] The state aid took three forms: direct subsidies for the maintenance and repair of buildings; reimbursement of parents for a percentage of tuition paid; and certain tax benefits for parents. All three forms of aid were found to have an impermissible primary effect. The maintenance and repair subsidies, being unrestricted, could be used for the upkeep of a chapel or classrooms used for religious instruction. The reimbursements and tax benefits to parents could likewise be used to support wholly religious activities.

---

[18] The elements of the "profile" were that the schools placed religious restrictions on admission and also faculty appointments; that they enforced obedience to religious dogma; that they required attendance at religious services and the study of particular religious doctrine; that they were an "integral part" of the religious mission of the sponsoring church; that they had religious indoctrination as a "substantial purpose"; and that they imposed religious restrictions on how and what the faculty could teach. 413 U.S., at 767-768.

[The Court then reviewed other cases similar to *Nyquist,* such as *Levitt v. Committee for Public Education*, 413 U.S. 472 (1973), and *Meek v. Pittenger*, 421 U.S. 349 (1975).]

So the slate we write on is anything but clean. Instead, there is little room for further refinement of the principles governing public aid to church-affiliated private schools. Our purpose is not to unsettle those principles, so recently reaffirmed, see *Meek v. Pittenger, supra,* or to expand upon them substantially, but merely to insure that they are faithfully applied in this case.

III

The first part of *Lemon I*'s three-part test is not in issue; appellants do not challenge the District Court's finding that the purpose of Maryland's aid program is the secular one of supporting private higher education generally, as an economic alternative to a wholly public system. The focus of the debate is on the second and third parts, those concerning the primary effect of advancing religion, and excessive church-state entanglement. We consider them in the same order.

A

While entanglement is essentially a procedural problem, the primary-effect question is the substantive one of what private educational activities, by whatever procedure, may be supported by state funds. *Hunt* requires (1) that no state aid at all go to institutions that are so "pervasively sectarian" that secular activities cannot be separated from sectarian ones, and (2) that if secular activities *can* be separated out, they alone may be funded.

(1) District Court's finding in this case was that the appellee colleges are not "pervasively sectarian." This conclusion it supported with a number of subsidiary findings concerning the role of religion on these campuses:

(a) Despite their formal affiliation with the Roman Catholic Church, the colleges are "characterized by a high degree of institutional autonomy." None of the four receives funds from, or makes reports to, the Catholic Church. The Church is represented on their governing boards, but, as with Mount Saint Mary's, "no instance of entry of Church considerations into college decisions was shown."

(b) The colleges employ Roman Catholic chaplains and hold Roman Catholic religious exercises on campus. Attendance at such is not required; the encouragement of spiritual development is only "one secondary objective" of each college; and "at none of these institutions does this encouragement go beyond providing the opportunities or occasions for religious experience." It was the District Court's general finding that "religious indoctrination is not a substantial purpose or activity of any of these defendants."

(c) Mandatory religion or theology courses are taught at each of the colleges, primarily by Roman Catholic clerics, but these only supplement a curriculum covering "the spectrum of a liberal arts program." Nontheology courses are taught in an "atmosphere of intellectual freedom" and without "religious pressures." Each college subscribes to, and abides by, the 1940 Statement of Principles on Academic Freedom of the American Association of University Professors.

(d) Some classes are begun with prayer. The percentage of classes in which this is done varies with the college, from a "minuscule" percentage at Loyola and Mount Saint Mary's, to a majority at Saint Joseph. There is no "actual college policy" of encouraging the practice. "It is treated as a facet of the instructor's academic freedom." Classroom prayers were therefore regarded by the District Court as "peripheral to the subject of religious permeation," as were the facts that some instructors wear clerical garb and some classrooms have religious symbols. The court concluded:

> "None of these facts impairs the clear and convincing evidence that courses at each defendant are taught 'according to the academic requirements intrinsic to the subject matter and the individual teacher's concept of professional standards.' [citing *Tilton v. Richardson*]."

In support of this finding the court relied on the fact that a Maryland education department group had monitored the teacher education program at Saint Joseph College, where classroom prayer is most prevalent, and had seen "no evidence of religion entering into any elements of that program."

(e) The District Court found that, apart from the theology departments, faculty hiring decisions are not made on a religious basis. At two of the colleges, Notre Dame and Mount Saint Mary's, no inquiry at all is made into an applicant's religion. Religious preference is to be noted on Loyola's application form, but the purpose is to allow full appreciation of the applicant's background. Loyola also attempts to employ each year two members of a particular religious order which once staffed a college recently merged into Loyola. Budgetary considerations lead the colleges generally to favor members of religious orders, who often receive less than full salary. Still, the District Court found that "academic quality" was the principal hiring criterion, and that any "hiring bias," or "effort by any defendant to stack its faculty with members of a particular religious group," would have been noticed by other faculty members, who had never been heard to complain.

(f) The great majority of students at each of the colleges are Roman Catholic, but the District Court concluded from a "thorough analysis of the student admission and recruiting criteria" that the student bodies "are chosen without regard to religion."

We cannot say that the foregoing findings as to the role of religion in particular aspects of the colleges are clearly erroneous. Appellants ask us to set those findings aside in certain respects. Not surprisingly, they have gleaned from this record of thousands of pages, compiled during several weeks of trial, occasional evidence of a more sectarian character than the District Court ascribes to the colleges. It is not our place, however, to reappraise the evidence, unless it plainly fails to support the findings of the trier of facts. That is certainly not the case here, and it would make no difference even if we were to second-guess the District Court in certain particulars. To answer the question whether an institution is so "pervasively sectarian" that it may receive no direct state aid of any kind, it is necessary to paint a general picture of the institution, composed of many elements. The general picture that the District Court has painted of the appellee institutions is similar in almost all respects to that of the church-affiliated colleges considered in *Tilton* and *Hunt*. We find no constitutionally significant distinction between them, at least for purposes of the "pervasive sectarianism" test.

(2) Having found that the appellee institutions are not "so permeated by religion that the secular side cannot be separated from the sectarian," the District Court proceeded to the next question posed by *Hunt*: whether aid in fact was extended only to "the secular side." This requirement the court regarded as satisfied by the statutory prohibition against sectarian use, and by the administrative enforcement of that prohibition through the Council for Higher Education. We agree. *Hunt* requires only that state funds not be used to support "specifically religious activity." It is clear that fund uses exist that meet this requirement. *See Tilton v. Richardson*; *Hunt v. McNair*. We have no occasion to elaborate further on what is and is not a "specifically religious activity," for no particular use of the state funds is set out in this statute. Funds are put to the use of the college's choice, provided it is not a sectarian use, of which the college must satisfy the Council. If the question is whether the statute sought to be enjoined authorizes state funds for "specifically religious activity," that question fairly answers itself. The statute in terms forbids the use of funds for "sectarian purposes," and this prohibition appears to be at least as broad as Hunt's prohibition of the public funding of "specifically religious activity." We must assume that the colleges, and the Council, will exercise their delegated control over use of the funds in compliance with the statutory, and therefore the constitutional, mandate. It is to be expected that they will give a wide berth to "specifically religious activity," and thus minimize constitutional questions.[22] Should

---

[22] The Council, at least, thus far has shown every sign of doing so. For example, appellants have pointed during this litigation to three assertedly sectarian uses in which state funds either have been or could be employed under this statute: the salaries of teachers teaching religion or theology courses, scholarships for students in religious studies, and maintenance of buildings used for religious activity. Brief for Appellants 50-55. (The alleged instances of actual use in these ways related to the 1971 funds.) However, the Council has now adopted regulations specifically prohibiting the use of state funds in these and other ways:

"A. Art. 77A, § 68A, Annotated Code of Maryland, prohibits recipient institutions from using State funds for 'sectarian purposes.' That provision generally proscribes the use of State funds to support religious instruction, religious worship, or other activities of a religious nature. Listed below are several potential uses of State funds which would violate the sectarian use prohibition. The list is not intended to be all-inclusive and, if an institution is in doubt whether any other possible use of the funds might violate the sectarian use prohibition, it should consult with and seek the advice of the Council in advance.

"(1) Student Aid: State Funds may not be used for student aid if the institution imposes

such questions arise, the courts will consider them. It has not been the Court's practice, in considering facial challenges to statutes of this kind, to strike them down in anticipation that particular applications may result in unconstitutional use of funds.

B

If the foregoing answer to the "primary effect" question seems easy, it serves to make the "excessive entanglement" problem more difficult. The statute itself clearly denies the use of public funds for "sectarian purposes." It seeks to avert such use, however, through a process of annual interchange proposal and approval, expenditure and review between the colleges and the Council. In answering the question whether this will be an "excessively entangling" relationship, we must consider the several relevant factors identified in prior decisions:

(1) First is the character of the aided institutions. This has been fully described above. As the District Court found, the colleges perform "essentially secular educational functions" that are distinct and separable from religious activity. This finding, which is a prerequisite under the "pervasive sectarianism" test to any state aid at all, is also important for purposes of the entanglement test because it means that secular activities, for the most part, can be taken at face value. There is no danger, or at least only a substantially reduced danger, that an ostensibly secular activity — the study of biology, the learning of a foreign language, an athletic event — will actually be infused with religious content or significance. The need for close surveillance of purportedly secular activities is correspondingly reduced. Thus the District Court found that in this case "there is no necessity for state officials to investigate the conduct of

---

religious restrictions or qualifications on eligibility for student aid, nor may they be paid to students then enrolled in a religious, seminarian or theological academic program.

"(2) Salaries: State funds may not be used to pay in whole or in part the salary of any person who is engaged in the teaching of religion or theology, who serves as chaplain or director of the campus ministry, or who administers or supervises any program of religious activities.

"(3) Maintenance and Repair: State funds may not be used to pay any portion of the cost of maintenance or repair of any building or facility used for the teaching of religion or theology or for religious worship or for any religious activity.

"(4) Utilities: If an institution has any building or facility that is used in whole or in part for the teaching of religion or theology or for religious worship or for any religious activity, State funds may not be used to pay utilities bills unless those buildings or facilities are separately metered. If buildings or facilities used for any religious purpose described in the preceding sentence are separately metered, the cost of providing heat, electricity, and water to those buildings or facilities cannot be paid with State funds.

"(5) Capital Construction and Improvements: If State funds are used to construct a new building or facility or to renovate an existing one, the building or facility may not be used for the teaching of religion or theology or for religious worship or for any religious activity at any time in the future." Regulation 01.03.06A.

particular classes of educational programs to determine whether a school is attempting to indoctrinate its students under the guise of secular education."

(2) As for the form of aid, we have already noted that no particular use of state funds is before us in this case. The *process* by which aid is disbursed, and a use for it chosen, is before us. We address this as a matter of the "resulting relationship" of secular and religious authority.

(3) As noted, the funding process is an annual one. The subsidies are paid out each year, and they can be put to annually varying uses. The colleges propose particular uses for the Council's approval, and, following expenditure, they report to the Council on the use to which the funds have been put.

We agree with the District Court that "excessive entanglement" does not necessarily result from the fact that the subsidy is an annual one. It is true that the Court favored the "one-time, single-purpose" construction grants in *Tilton* because they entailed "no continuing financial relationships or dependencies, no annual audits, and no government analysis of an institution's expenditures." The present aid program cannot claim these aspects. But if the question is whether this case is more like *Lemon I* or more like *Tilton* and surely that is the fundamental question before us the answer must be that it is more like *Tilton*.

(4) As for political divisiveness, the District Court recognized that the annual nature of the subsidy, along with its promise of an increasing demand for state funds as the colleges' dependency grew, aggravated the danger of "[p]olitical fragmentation . . . on religious lines." Nonetheless, the District Court found that the program "does not create a substantial danger of political entanglement." Several reasons were given. As was stated in *Tilton*, the danger of political divisiveness is "substantially less" when the aided institution is not an elementary or secondary school, but a college, "whose student constituency is not local but diverse and widely dispersed." Furthermore, political divisiveness is diminished by the fact that the aid is extended to private colleges generally, more than two-thirds of which have no religious affiliation; this is in sharp contrast to *Nyquist*, for example, where 95% of the aided schools were Roman Catholic parochial schools. Finally, the substantial autonomy of the colleges was thought to mitigate political divisiveness, in that controversies surrounding the aid program are not likely to involve the Catholic Church itself, or even the religious character of the schools, but only their "fiscal responsibility and educational requirements."

NOTES AND QUESTIONS ON THE CONCEPT OF "PERVASIVELY SECTARIAN"

The term "pervasively sectarian" refers to an institution in which the religious activities so pervade the institution's operation that religious and secular functions cannot be separated. Considering the heavily religious nature of the institutions deemed by the Court in *Roemer* not to be "pervasively sectarian," what more is needed to fall into that category? In *Columbia Union College v. Clarke*, 159 F.3d 151 (4th Cir. 1998), *cert. denied*, 527 U.S. 1013 (1999), the Fourth Circuit Court of Appeals reviewed a summary judgment motion denying a religiously affiliated college from receiving state scholarship money. In determining whether the college was "pervasively sectarian," the court noted the four general categories of scrutiny defined by the Supreme Court in *Roemer*: "(1) does the college mandate religious worship, (2) to what extent do religious influences dominate the academic curriculum, (3) how much do religious preferences shape the college's faculty hiring and student admission processes, and (4) to what degree does the college enjoy "institutional autonomy" apart from the church with which it is affiliated." *Id.* at 163. Despite extensive findings of fact by the district court on each of these factors, the court of appeals reversed the district court's grant of summary judgment against the school. The court expressed great reluctance to find the college pervasively sectarian.

> Neither the Supreme Court, nor any circuit court to our knowledge, has ever found a college to be pervasively sectarian. The decision is not a simple one. The criteria for assessing whether an institution is pervasively sectarian are complex, elusive, and heavily fact intensive. Given the "far-flung import" of this case . . . no court could or should decide whether Columbia Union is pervasively sectarian based solely on the evidence in this record, which is comprised almost exclusively of the college's written literature and policies. Controlling Supreme Court law, as well as common sense, mandate that a court review not only the college's written policies, but also its practices, to determine whether religious indoctrination pervades the institution.

Id. at 169. The dissent chided the majority for its unusually close attention to the details of every factor.

> As the majority concedes, the district court "took careful note of the appropriate areas of inquiry and conscientiously" considered evidence on each and every one of these factors. Among its more significant conclusions, the district court found that Columbia Union was closely affiliated with, if not to a great extent controlled by, the Seventh-day Adventist Church; that Columbia Union's religious mission is furthered in part by requirements that students attend weekly chapel sessions and worship options in the residence halls; and that descriptions of even the college's secular courses were pervaded with religious references. The district court concluded that, in combination, the undisputed evidence under the several factors supported the conclusion that Columbia Union is a pervasively sectarian institution. I believe that the considerable evidence relied upon by the district court revealed no genuine dispute of material fact and, therefore, was more than sufficient to establish that Columbia Union is a pervasively sectarian institution. By contrast, the majority erroneously flyspecks Columbia Union's characteristics. Rather than "paint[ing] a general picture of [Columbia

Union]," *Roemer* at 758, the majority picks and scratches at each individual factor. It is not surprising that it determines that no particular factor conclusively establishes Columbia Union's sectarian nature. After all, "[t]he relevant factors . . . are to be considered cumulatively." *Roemer* at 766. The majority's methodology, while not wholly irrelevant, is overly focused; it simply turns its microscope to too high a power.

Columbia Union, 159 F.3d at 174-75 (Wilkinson, J., dissenting).

For other examples of the application of this fact-intensive standard, *see Johnson v. Econ. Dev. Corp. of the County of Oakland*, 241 F.3d 501 (6th Cir. 2001) (college not pervasively sectarian); *Steele v. Indust. Dev. Bd. of Metro. Gov't of Nashville and Davidson County*, 117 F. Supp. 2d 693 (M.D. Tenn. 2000) (analyzing thirteen factors and concluding that college is pervasively sectarian).

C. INDIRECT PUBLIC FINANCIAL SUPPORT FOR RELIGIOUS EDUCATION

MUELLER v. ALLEN
463 U.S. 388 (1983)

JUSTICE REHNQUIST delivered the opinion of the Court.

Minnesota allows taxpayers, in computing their state income tax, to deduct certain expenses incurred in providing for the education of their children. Minn. Stat. § 290.09 subd. 22 (1982).[1] The United States Court of Appeals for the Eighth Circuit held that the Establishment Clause of the First and Fourteenth Amendments was not offended by this arrangement. We now affirm.

---

[1] Minn.Stat. § 290.09 subd. 22 (1982) permits a taxpayer to deduct from his or her computation of gross income the following:

> "Tuition and transportation expense. The amount he has paid to others, not to exceed $500 for each dependent in grades K to 6 and $700 for each dependent in grades 7 to 12, for tuition, textbooks and transportation of each dependent in attending an elementary or secondary school situated in Minnesota, North Dakota, South Dakota, Iowa, or Wisconsin, wherein a resident of this state may legally fulfill the state's compulsory attendance laws, which is not operated for profit, and which adheres to the provisions of the Civil Rights Act of 1964 and chapter 363. As used in this subdivision, 'textbooks' shall mean and include books and other instructional materials and equipment used in elementary and secondary schools in teaching only those subjects legally and commonly taught in public elementary and secondary schools in this state and shall not include instructional books and materials used in the teaching of religious tenets, doctrines or worship, the purpose of which is to inculcate such tenets, doctrines or worship, nor shall it include such books or materials for, or transportation to, extracurricular activities including sporting events, musical or dramatic events, speech activities, driver's education, or programs of a similar nature."

Minnesota, like every other state, provides its citizens with free elementary and secondary schooling. It seems to be agreed that about 820,000 students attended this school system in the most recent school year. During the same year, approximately 91,000 elementary and secondary students attended some 500 privately supported schools located in Minnesota, and about 95% of these students attended schools considering themselves to be sectarian.

Minnesota, by a law originally enacted in 1955 and revised in 1976 and again in 1978, permits state taxpayers to claim a deduction from gross income for certain expenses incurred in educating their children. The deduction is limited to actual expenses incurred for the "tuition, textbooks and transportation" of dependents attending elementary or secondary schools. A deduction may not exceed $500 per dependent in grades K through six and $700 per dependent in grades seven through twelve.[2]

Today's case is no exception to our oft-repeated statement that the Establishment Clause presents especially difficult questions of interpretation and application. It is easy enough to quote the few words comprising that clause —

---

[2] Both lower courts found that the statute permits deduction of a range of educational expenses. The District Court found that deductible expenses included:

"1. Tuition in the ordinary sense.

"2. Tuition to public school students who attend public schools outside their residence school districts.

"3. Certain summer school tuition.

"4. Tuition charged by a school for slow learner private tutoring services.

"5. Tuition for instruction provided by an elementary or secondary school to students who are physically unable to attend classes at such school.

"6. Tuition charged by a private tutor or by a school that is not an elementary or secondary school if the instruction is acceptable for credit in an elementary or secondary school.

"7. Montessori School tuition for grades K through 12.

"8. Tuition for driver education when it is part of the school curriculum."

514 F. Supp. 998, 1000.

The Court of Appeals concurred in this finding. In addition, the District Court found that the statutory deduction for "textbooks" included not only "secular textbooks" but also:

*"1. Cost of tennis shoes and sweat suits for physical education.

"2. Camera rental fees paid to the school for photography classes.

"3. Ice skates rental fee paid to the school.

"4. Rental fee paid to the school for calculators for mathematics classes.

"5. Costs of home economics materials needed to meet minimum requirements.

"6. Costs of special metal or wood needed to meet minimum requirements of shop classes.

"7. Costs of supplies needed to meet minimum requirements of art classes.

"8. Rental fees paid to the school for musical instruments.

"9. Cost of pencils and special notebooks required for class." *Ibid.*

The Court of Appeals accepted this finding.

"Congress shall make no law respecting an establishment of religion." It is not at all easy, however, to apply this Court's various decisions construing the Clause to governmental programs of financial assistance to sectarian schools and the parents of children attending those schools. Indeed, in many of these decisions "we have expressly or implicitly acknowledged that 'we can only dimly perceive the lines of demarcation in this extraordinarily sensitive area of constitutional law.'"

One fixed principle in this field is our consistent rejection of the argument that "any program which in some manner aids an institution with a religious affiliation" violates the Establishment Clause. For example, it is now well-established that a state may reimburse parents for expenses incurred in transporting their children to school, *Everson v. Board of Education*, and that it may loan secular textbooks to all schoolchildren within the state, *Board of Education v. Allen*, 392 U.S. 236 (1968).

Notwithstanding the repeated approval given programs such as those in *Allen* and *Everson*, our decisions also have struck down arrangements resembling, in many respects, these forms of assistance. *See, e.g., Lemon v. Kurtzman; Levitt v. Committee for Public Education*, 413 U.S. 472 (1972); *Meek v. Pittenger*, 421 U.S. 349 (1975); *Wolman v. Walter*, 433 U.S. 229, 237-238 (1977).[3] In this case we are asked to decide whether Minnesota's tax deduction bears greater resemblance to those types of assistance to parochial schools we have approved, or to those we have struck down. Petitioners place particular reliance on our decision in *Committee for Public Education v. Nyquist, supra,* where we held invalid a New York statute providing public funds for the maintenance and repair of the physical facilities of private schools and granting thinly disguised "tax benefits," actually amounting to tuition grants, to the parents of children attending private schools. As explained below, we conclude that § 290.09 subd. 22, bears less resemblance to the arrangement struck down in *Nyquist* than it does to assistance programs upheld in our prior decisions and those discussed with approval in *Nyquist*.

The general nature of our inquiry in this area has been guided, since the decision in *Lemon v. Kurtzman*, by the "three-part" test laid down in that case:

> "First, the statute must have a secular legislative purpose; second, its principal or primary effect must be one that neither advances nor inhibits religion . . .; finally, the statute must not foster 'an excessive government entanglement with religion.'" *Id.*, at 612-613.

---

[3] In *Lemon v. Kurtzman*, the Court concluded that the state's reimbursement of nonpublic schools for the cost of teacher's salaries, textbooks, and instructional materials, and its payment of a salary supplement to teachers in nonpublic schools, resulted in excessive entanglement of church and state. In *Levitt v. Committee for Public Education*, we struck down on Establishment Clause grounds a state program reimbursing nonpublic schools for the cost of teacher-prepared examinations. Finally, in *Meek v. Pittenger*, and *Wolman v. Walter*, we held unconstitutional a direct loan of instructional materials to nonpublic schools, while upholding the loan of textbooks to individual students.

While this principle is well settled, our cases have also emphasized that it provides "no more than [a] helpful signpost" in dealing with Establishment Clause challenges. With this caveat in mind, we turn to the specific challenges raised against § 290.09 subd. 22 under the *Lemon* framework.

Little time need be spent on the question of whether the Minnesota tax deduction has a secular purpose. Under our prior decisions, governmental assistance programs have consistently survived this inquiry even when they have run afoul of other aspects of the *Lemon* framework.

A State's decision to defray the cost of educational expenses incurred by parents — regardless of the type of schools their children attend — evidences a purpose that is both secular and understandable. An educated populace is essential to the political and economic health of any community, and a state's efforts to assist parents in meeting the rising cost of educational expenses plainly serves this secular purpose of ensuring that the state's citizenry is well-educated. Similarly, Minnesota, like other states, could conclude that there is a strong public interest in assuring the continued financial health of private schools, both sectarian and non-sectarian. By educating a substantial number of students such schools relieve public schools of a correspondingly great burden — to the benefit of all taxpayers. In addition, private schools may serve as a benchmark for public schools, in a manner analogous to the "TVA yardstick" for private power companies.

All these justifications are readily available to support § 290.09 subd. 22, and each is sufficient to satisfy the secular purpose inquiry of *Lemon*.

We turn therefore to the more difficult but related question whether the Minnesota statute has "the primary effect of advancing the sectarian aims of the nonpublic schools." *Lemon v. Kurtzman*. In concluding that it does not, we find several features of the Minnesota tax deduction particularly significant. First, an essential feature of Minnesota's arrangement is the fact that § 290.09 subd. 22 is only one among many deductions — such as those for medical expenses, and charitable contributions — available under the Minnesota tax laws.[5] Our decisions consistently have recognized that traditionally "[l]egislatures have especially broad latitude in creating classifications and distinctions in tax statutes," *Regan v. Taxation with Representation of Wash.*, 461 U.S. 540 (1983), in part because the "familiarity with local conditions" enjoyed by legislators especially enables them to "achieve an equitable distribution of the tax burden." *Madden v. Kentucky*, 309 U.S. 83, 87 (1940). Under our prior decisions, the Minnesota legislature's judgment that a deduction for educational expenses

---

[5] Deductions for charitable contributions, allowed by Minnesota law, Minn.Stat. § 290.21, include contributions to religious institutions, and exemptions from property tax for property used for charitable purposes under Minnesota law include property used for wholly religious purposes. In each case, it may be that religious institutions benefit very substantially from the allowance of such deductions. The Court's holding in *Walz v. Tax Commission*, 397 U.S. 664 (1970), indicates, however, that this does not require the conclusion that such provisions of a state's tax law violate the Establishment Clause.

fairly equalizes the tax burden of its citizens and encourages desirable expenditures for educational purposes is entitled to substantial deference.[6]

Other characteristics of § 290.09(22) argue equally strongly for the provision's constitutionality. Most importantly, the deduction is available for educational expenses incurred by all parents, including those whose children attend public schools and those whose children attend non-sectarian private schools or sectarian private schools. Just as in *Widmar v. Vincent* [*supra* Chapter 7], where we concluded that the state's provision of a forum neutrally "open to a broad class of nonreligious as well as religious speakers" does not "confer any imprimatur of State approval," so here: "the provision of benefits to so broad a spectrum of groups is an important index of secular effect."

In this respect, as well as others, this case is vitally different from the scheme struck down in *Nyquist*. There, public assistance amounting to tuition grants, was provided only to parents of children in *nonpublic* schools. This fact had considerable bearing on our decision striking down the New York statute at issue; we explicitly distinguished both *Allen* and *Everson* on the grounds that "In both cases the class of beneficiaries included *all* schoolchildren, those in public as well as those in private schools." Moreover, we intimated that "public assistance (e.g., scholarships) made available generally without regard to the sectarian- nonsectarian or public-nonpublic nature of the institution benefited," might not offend the Establishment Clause. We think the tax deduction adopted by Minnesota is more similar to this latter type of program than it is to the arrangement struck down in *Nyquist*. Unlike the assistance at issue in *Nyquist*, § 290.09 subd. 22, permits *all* parents — whether their children attend public school or private — to deduct their children's educational expenses. As *Widmar* and our other decisions indicate, a program, like § 290.09 subd. 22, that neutrally provides state assistance to a broad spectrum of citizens is not readily subject to challenge under the Establishment Clause.

---

[6] Our decision in *Nyquist* is not to the contrary on this point. We expressed considerable doubt there that the "tax benefits" provided by New York law properly could be regarded as parts of a genuine system of tax laws. Plainly, the outright grants to low-income parents did not take the form of ordinary tax benefits. As to the benefits provided to middle- income parents, the Court said:

> "The amount of the deduction is unrelated to the amount of money actually expended by any parent on tuition, but is calculated on the basis of a formula contained in the statute. The formula is apparently the product of a legislative attempt to assure that each family would receive a carefully estimated net benefit, and that the tax benefit would be comparable to, and compatible with, the tuition grant for lower income families."

Indeed, the question whether a program having the elements of a "genuine tax deduction" would be constitutionally acceptable was expressly reserved in *Nyquist, supra,* at 790, n. 49. While the economic consequences of the program in *Nyquist* and that in this case may be difficult to distinguish, we have recognized on other occasions that "the form of the [state's assistance to parochial schools must be examined] for the light that it casts on the substance." *Lemon v. Kurtzman*, 403 U.S., at 614. The fact that the Minnesota plan embodies a "genuine tax deduction" is thus of some relevance, especially given the traditional rule of deference accorded legislative classifications in tax statutes.

We also agree with the Court of Appeals that, by channeling whatever assistance it may provide to parochial schools through individual parents, Minnesota has reduced the Establishment Clause objections to which its action is subject. It is true, of course, that financial assistance provided to parents ultimately has an economic effect comparable to that of aid given directly to the schools attended by their children. It is also true, however, that under Minnesota's arrangement public funds become available only as a result of numerous, private choices of individual parents of school-age children. For these reasons, we recognized in *Nyquist* that the means by which state assistance flows to private schools is of some importance: we said that "the fact that aid is disbursed to parents rather than to . . . schools" is a material consideration in Establishment Clause analysis, albeit "only one among many to be considered." *Nyquist*. It is noteworthy that all but one of our recent cases invalidating state aid to parochial schools have involved the direct transmission of assistance from the state to the schools themselves. The exception, of course, was *Nyquist*, which, as discussed previously is distinguishable from this case on other grounds. Where, as here, aid to parochial schools is available only as a result of decisions of individual parents no "imprimatur of State approval" can be deemed to have been conferred on any particular religion, or on religion generally.

We find it useful, in the light of the foregoing characteristics of § 290.09 subd. 22, to compare the attenuated financial benefits flowing to parochial schools from the section to the evils against which the Establishment Clause was designed to protect. These dangers are well-described by our statement that "[w]hat is at stake as a matter of policy [in Establishment Clause cases] is preventing that kind and degree of government involvement in religious life that, as history teaches us, is apt to lead to strife and frequently strain a political system to the breaking point." It is important, however, to "keep these issues in perspective":

> "At this point in the 20th century we are quite far removed from the dangers that prompted the Framers to include the Establishment Clause in the Bill of Rights. *See Walz v. Tax Comm'n*, 397 U.S. 664, 668 (1970). The risk of significant religious or denominational control over our democratic processes — or even of deep political division along religious lines — is remote, and when viewed against the positive contributions of sectarian schools, and such risk seems entirely tolerable in light of the continuing oversight of this Court." *Wolman*, 433 U.S., at 263 (POWELL, J., concurring in part, concurring in the judgment in part, and dissenting in part).

The Establishment Clause of course extends beyond prohibition of a state church or payment of state funds to one or more churches. We do not think, however, that its prohibition extends to the type of tax deduction established by Minnesota. The historic purposes of the clause simply do not encompass the sort of attenuated financial benefit, ultimately controlled by the private choices of individual parents, that eventually flows to parochial schools from the neutrally available tax benefit at issue in this case.

Petitioners argue that, notwithstanding the facial neutrality of § 290.09 subd. 22, in application the statute primarily benefits religious institutions. Petitioners rely, as they did below, on a statistical analysis of the type of persons claiming the tax deduction. They contend that most parents of public school children incur no tuition expenses, *see* Minn. Stat. § 120.06, and that other expenses deductible under § 290.09 subd. 22, are negligible in value; moreover, they claim that 96% of the children in private schools in 1978-1979 attended religiously-affiliated institutions. Because of all this, they reason, the bulk of deductions taken under § 290.09(22) will be claimed by parents of children in sectarian schools. Respondents reply that petitioners have failed to consider the impact of deductions for items such as transportation, summer school tuition, tuition paid by parents whose children attended schools outside the school districts in which they resided, rental or purchase costs for a variety of equipment, and tuition for certain types of instruction not ordinarily provided in public schools.

We need not consider these contentions in detail. We would be loath to adopt a rule grounding the constitutionality of a facially neutral law on annual reports reciting the extent to which various classes of private citizens claimed benefits under the law. Such an approach would scarcely provide the certainty that this field stands in need of, nor can we perceive principled standards by which such statistical evidence might be evaluated. Moreover, the fact that private persons fail in a particular year to claim the tax relief to which they are entitled — under a facially neutral statute — should be of little importance in determining the constitutionality of the statute permitting such relief.

Finally, private educational institutions, and parents paying for their children to attend these schools, make special contributions to the areas in which they operate. "Parochial schools, quite apart from their sectarian purpose, have provided an educational alternative for millions of young Americans; they often afford wholesome competition with our public schools; and in some States they relieve substantially the tax burden incident to the operation of public schools." *Wolman*, at 262 (POWELL, J., concurring and dissenting). If parents of children in private schools choose to take especial advantage of the relief provided by § 290.09 subd. 22, it is no doubt due to the fact that they bear a particularly great financial burden in educating their children. More fundamentally, whatever unequal effect may be attributed to the statutory classification can fairly be regarded as a rough return for the benefits, discussed above, provided to the state and all taxpayers by parents sending their children to parochial schools. In the light of all this, we believe it wiser to decline to engage in the type of empirical inquiry into those persons benefited by state law which petitioners urge.[10]

---

[10] Our conclusion is unaffected by the fact that § 290.09, subd. 22, permits deductions for amounts spent for textbooks and transportation as well as tuition. In *Everson v. Board of Education*, 330 U.S. 1 (1947), we approved a statute reimbursing parents of all schoolchildren for the costs of transporting their children to school. Doing so by means of a deduction, rather than a direct grant,

Thus, we hold that the Minnesota tax deduction for educational expenses satisfies the primary effect inquiry of our Establishment Clause cases.

Turning to the third part of the *Lemon* inquiry, we have no difficulty in concluding that the Minnesota statute does not "excessively entangle" the state in religion. The only plausible source of the "comprehensive, discriminating, and continuing state surveillance" necessary to run afoul of this standard would lie in the fact that state officials must determine whether particular textbooks qualify for a deduction. In making this decision, state officials must disallow deductions taken from "instructional books and materials used in the teaching of religious tenets, doctrines or worship, the purpose of which is to inculcate such tenets, doctrines or worship." Minn. Stat. § 290.09 subd. 22. Making decisions such as this does not differ substantially from making the types of decisions approved in earlier opinions of this Court. In *Board of Education v. Allen,* 392 U.S. 236 (1968), for example, the Court upheld the loan of secular textbooks to parents or children attending nonpublic schools; though state officials were required to determine whether particular books were or were not secular, the system was held not to violate the Establishment Clause. The same result follows in this case.

JUSTICE MARSHALL, with whom JUSTICE BRENNAN, JUSTICE BLACKMUN and JUSTICE STEVENS join, dissenting.

I

B

1

The majority first attempts to distinguish *Nyquist* on the ground that Minnesota makes all parents eligible to deduct up to $500 or $700 for each dependent, whereas the New York law allowed a deduction only for parents whose children attended nonpublic schools. Although Minnesota taxpayers who send their children to local public schools may not deduct tuition expenses because they incur none, they may deduct other expenses, such as the cost of gym clothes, pencils, and notebooks, which are shared by all parents of school-age children. This, in the majority's view, distinguishes the Minnesota scheme from the law at issue in *Nyquist.*

That the Minnesota statute makes some small benefit available to all parents cannot alter the fact that the most substantial benefit provided by the statute is available only to those parents who send their children to schools that charge

---

only serves to make the state's action less objectionable. Likewise, in *Board of Education v. Allen,* 392 U.S. 236 (1968), we approved state loans of textbooks to all schoolchildren; although we disapproved, in *Meek v. Pittenger* and *Wolman v. Walter* direct loans of instructional materials to sectarian schools, we do not find those cases controlling. First, they involved assistance provided to the schools themselves, rather than tax benefits directed to individual parents. Moreover, we think that state assistance for the rental of calculators, ice skates, *ibid.,* tennis shoes, *ibid.,* and the like, scarcely poses the type of dangers against which the Establishment Clause was intended to guard.

tuition. It is simply undeniable that the single largest expense that may be deducted under the Minnesota statute is tuition. The statute is little more than a subsidy of tuition masquerading as a subsidy of general educational expenses. The other deductible expenses are *de minimis* in comparison to tuition expenses.

Contrary to the majority's suggestion, the bulk of the tax benefits afforded by the Minnesota scheme are enjoyed by parents of parochial school children not because parents of public school children fail to claim deductions to which they are entitled, but because the latter are simply *unable* to claim the largest tax deduction that Minnesota authorizes.[2] Fewer than 100 of more than 900,000 school-age children in Minnesota attend public schools that charge a general tuition. Of the total number of taxpayers who are eligible for the tuition deduction, approximately 96% send their children to religious schools.[3] Parents who send their children to free public schools are simply ineligible to obtain the full benefit of the deduction except in the unlikely event that they buy $700 worth of pencils, notebooks, and bus rides for their school-age children. Yet parents who pay at least $700 in tuition to nonpublic, sectarian schools can claim the full deduction even if they incur no other educational expenses.

That this deduction has a primary effect of promoting religion can easily be determined without any resort to the type of "statistical evidence" that the majority fears would lead to constitutional uncertainty. The only factual inquiry necessary is the same as that employed in *Nyquist* and *Sloan v. Lemon*, 413 U.S. 825 (1973): whether the deduction permitted for tuition expenses primarily benefits those who send their children to religious schools. In *Nyquist* we unequivocally rejected any suggestion that, in determining the effect of a tax statute, this Court should look exclusively to what the statute on its face purports to do and ignore the actual operation of the challenged provision. In determining the effect of the New York statute, we emphasized that "virtually all" of the schools receiving direct grants for maintenance and repair were Roman Catholic schools, that reimbursements were given to parents "who send their children to nonpublic schools, the bulk of which is concededly sectarian in orientation," that "it is precisely the function of New York's law to provide assistance to private schools, the great majority of which are sectarian," and that "tax reductions authorized by this law flow primarily to the parents of children attending sectarian, nonpublic schools." Similarly, in *Sloan v. Lemon*, 413 U.S., at 830, we considered important to our "consider[ation of] the new law's effect

---

[2] Even if the Minnesota statute allowed parents of public school students to deduct expenses that were likely to be equivalent to the tuition expenses of private school students, it would still be unconstitutional. Insofar as the Minnesota statute provides a deduction for parochial school tuition, it provides a benefit to parochial schools that furthers the religious mission of those schools. *Nyquist* makes clear that the State may not provide any financial assistance to parochial schools unless that assistance is limited to secular uses. 413 U.S., at 780-785.

[3] Indeed, in this respect the Minnesota statute has an even greater tendency to promote religious education than the New York statute struck down in *Nyquist*, since the percentage of private schools that are nonsectarian is far greater in New York than in Minnesota.

. . . [that] 'more than 90% of the children attending nonpublic schools in the Commonwealth of Pennsylvania are enrolled in schools that are controlled by religious institutions or that have the purpose of propagating and promoting religious faith.' "[4]

In this case, it is undisputed that well over 90% of the children attending tuition-charging schools in Minnesota are enrolled in sectarian schools. History and experience likewise instruct us that any generally available financial assistance for elementary and secondary school tuition expenses mainly will further religious education because the majority of the schools which charge tuition are sectarian. Because Minnesota, like every other State, is committed to providing free public education, tax assistance for tuition payments inevitably redounds to the benefit of nonpublic, sectarian schools and parents who send their children to those schools.

2

The majority also asserts that the Minnesota statute is distinguishable from the statute struck down in *Nyquist* in another respect: the tax benefit available under Minnesota law is a "genuine tax deduction," whereas the New York law provided a benefit which, while nominally a deduction, also had features of a "tax credit." Under the Minnesota law, the amount of the tax benefit varies directly with the amount of the expenditure. Under the New York law, the amount of deduction was not dependent upon the amount actually paid for tuition but was a predetermined amount which depended on the tax bracket of each taxpayer. The deduction was designed to yield roughly the same amount of tax "forgiveness" for each taxpayer.

This is a distinction without a difference. Our prior decisions have rejected the relevance of the majority's formalistic distinction between tax deductions and the tax benefit at issue in *Nyquist*. The deduction afforded by Minnesota law was "designed to yield a [tax benefit] in exchange for performing a specific act which the State desires to encourage." *Nyquist*. Like the tax benefit held impermissible in *Nyquist*, the tax deduction at issue here concededly was designed to "encourag[e] desirable expenditures for educational purposes." Of equal importance, as the majority also concedes, the "economic consequenc[e]" of these programs is the same, for in each case the "financial assistance provided to parents

---

[4] Similarly, in *Meek v. Pittenger*, 421 U.S., at 363, we held "that the direct loan of instructional material and equipment has the unconstitutional primary effect of advancing religion because of the predominantly religious character of the schools benefiting from the Act." *See id.*, at 366. We relied on a finding that "of the 1,320 nonpublic schools in Pennsylvania that ... qualify for aid under Act 195, more than 75% are church-related or religiously affiliated educational institutions." *Id.*, at 364. This could not possibly have been ascertained from the text of the facially neutral statute, but could only be determined on the basis of an "empirical inquiry." And in *Wolman v. Walter*, 433 U.S., at 234, the Court relied on a stipulation that "during the 1974-1975 school year there were 720 chartered nonpublic schools in Ohio. Of these, all but 29 were sectarian. More than 96% of the nonpublic enrollment attended sectarian schools, and more than 92% attended Catholic schools."

ultimately has an economic effect comparable to that of aid given directly to the schools." *See Walz v. Tax Comm'n* (opinion of Harlan, J.). It was precisely the substantive impact of the financial support, and not its particular form, that rendered the programs in *Nyquist* and *Sloan v. Lemon* unconstitutional.

C

The majority incorrectly asserts that Minnesota's tax deduction for tuition expenses "bears less resemblance to the arrangement struck down in *Nyquist* than it does to assistance programs upheld in our prior decisions and discussed with approval in *Nyquist.*" One might as well say that a tangerine bears less resemblance to an orange than to an apple. The two cases relied on by the majority, *Board of Education v. Allen* and *Everson v. Board of Education*, are inapposite today for precisely the same reasons that they were inapposite in *Nyquist.*

We distinguished these cases in *Nyquist*, and again in *Sloan v. Lemon*, 413 U.S., at 832. Financial assistance for tuition payments has a consequence that

> "is quite unlike the sort of 'indirect' and 'incidental' benefits that flowed to sectarian schools from programs aiding all parents by supplying bus transportation and secular textbooks for their children. *Such benefits were carefully restricted to the purely secular side of church-affiliated institutions* and provided no special aid for those who had chosen to support religious schools. Yet such aid approached the 'verge' of the constitutionally impermissible." *Sloan v. Lemon, supra,* at 832 (latter emphasis added).

As previously noted, the Minnesota tuition tax deduction is not available to *all* parents, but only to parents whose children attend schools that charge tuition, which are comprised almost entirely of sectarian schools. More importantly, the assistance that flows to parochial schools as a result of the tax benefit is not restricted, and cannot be restricted, to the secular functions of those schools.

II

In my view, Minnesota's tax deduction for the cost of textbooks and other instructional materials is also constitutionally infirm. The majority is simply mistaken in concluding that a tax deduction, unlike a tax credit or a direct grant to parents, promotes religious education in a manner that is only "attenuated." A tax deduction has a primary effect that advances religion if it is provided to offset expenditures which are not restricted to the secular activities of parochial schools.

The instructional materials which are subsidized by the Minnesota tax deduction plainly may be used to inculcate religious values and belief. In *Meek v. Pittenger*, 421 U.S., at 366, we held that even the use of "wholly neutral, secular instructional material and equipment" by church-related schools contributes to religious instruction because "'[t]he secular education those schools provide goes hand in hand with the religious mission that is the only reason for the schools' existence.'" In *Wolman v. Walter*, 433 U.S., at 249-250, we concluded that precisely the same impermissible effect results when the instructional materials are loaned to the pupil or his parent, rather than directly to the schools. We stated that "it would exalt form over substance if this distinction were found to justify a result different from that in *Meek*." *Id.*, at 250. It follows that a tax deduction to offset the cost of purchasing instructional materials for use in sectarian schools, like a loan of such materials to parents, "necessarily results in aid to the sectarian school enterprise as a whole" and is therefore a "substantial advancement of religious activity" that "constitutes an impermissible establishment of religion." *Meek v. Pittenger, supra,* at 366.

There is no reason to treat Minnesota's tax deduction for textbooks any differently. Secular textbooks, like other secular instructional materials, contribute to the religious mission of the parochial schools that use those books. Although this Court upheld the loan of secular textbooks to religious schools in *Board of Education v. Allen, supra,* the Court believed at that time that it lacked sufficient experience to determine "based solely on judicial notice" that "the processes of secular and religious training are so intertwined that secular textbooks furnished to students by the public [will always be] instrumental in the teaching of religion." This basis for distinguishing secular instructional materials and secular textbooks is simply untenable, and is inconsistent with many of our more recent decisions concerning state aid to parochial schools.

In any event, the Court's assumption in *Allen* that the textbooks at issue there might be used only for secular education was based on the fact that those very books had been chosen by the State for use in the public schools. In contrast, the Minnesota statute does not limit the tax deduction to those books which the State has approved for use in public schools. Rather, it permits a deduction for books that are chosen by the parochial schools themselves. Indeed, under the Minnesota statutory scheme, textbooks chosen by parochial schools but not used by public schools are likely to be precisely the ones purchased by parents for their children's use. Like the law upheld in *Board of Education v. Allen*, [Minnesota law authorizes] the State Board of Education to provide textbooks used in public schools to nonpublic school students. Parents have little reason to purchase textbooks that can be borrowed under this provision.

III

There can be little doubt that the State of Minnesota intended to provide, and has provided, "[s]ubstantial aid to the educational function of [church- related] schools," and that the tax deduction for tuition and other educational expenses "necessarily results in aid to the sectarian school enterprise as a whole." *Meek v. Pittenger, supra,* at 366. It is beside the point that the State may have legitimate secular reasons for providing such aid. In focusing upon the contributions made by church-related schools, the majority has lost sight of the issue before us in this case.

"The sole question is whether state aid to these schools can be squared with the dictates of the Religion Clauses. Under our system the choice has been made that government is to be entirely excluded from the area of religious instruction. . . . The Constitution decrees that religion must be a private matter for the individual, the family, and the institutions of private choice, and that while some involvement and entanglement are inevitable, lines must be drawn." *Lemon v. Kurtzman.*

In my view, the lines drawn in *Nyquist* were drawn on a reasoned basis with appropriate regard for the principles of neutrality embodied by the Establishment Clause. I do not believe that the same can be said of the lines drawn by the majority today. For the first time, the Court has upheld financial support for religious schools without any reason at all to assume that the support will be restricted to the secular functions of those schools and will not be used to support religious instruction. This result is flatly at odds with the fundamental principle that a State may provide no financial support whatsoever to promote religion. As the Court stated in *Everson*, and has often repeated,

"No tax in any amount, large or small, can be levied to support any religious activities or institutions, whatever they may be called, or whatever form they may adopt to teach or practice religion."

I dissent.

NOTES AND QUESTIONS ON *MUELLER* AND THE FILTERING OF GOVERNMENT MONEY TO RELIGIOUS INSTITUTIONS

Mueller inaugurates an analysis that has come to be one of the lodestars of the Court's modern government-financing Establishment Clause jurisprudence. The key to *Mueller* is that the Constitution does not prohibit government funds from being transferred to religious institutions as long as those funds are first filtered through the bank accounts of private individuals. Professor Laura S. Underkuffler has termed this theory "the theory of the individual as causative agent," and she argues that it does not logically justify large-scale government programs that have the effect of subsidizing religious education:

When we have, as in the voucher case, the payment of large amounts of public funds to institutions which perform vital public functions — when we have the payment of large amounts of public funds to institutions which are intended to accomplish, and which do accomplish, important state objectives and state goals — the fact that such money is channeled through a process of individual decisionmaking has little constitutional relevance. The theory of the individual as causative agent assumes that no state interest is involved in the activities that are undertaken by the ultimate beneficiaries of state funds. Indeed, when the state program involves the payment of a welfare check or the provision of a public forum for all comers, the state has no interest in the particular activities that its funding (ultimately) facilitates. Under an educational voucher plan, the situation is quite different. In that case, the choices that are made by individuals in distributing or using state funds are not made for purposes or for ends that are unrelated to state interests: they are made in execution of a program that is infused — both before and after the individual distributive decision — with vital state concerns. The individual decisions under voucher plans are not unrelated and unanticipated actions that break the connection between state payment and ultimate recipient; they are completely related, anticipated, and authorized actions, which accomplish the goal — the public funding of (public and private) education — that the government has previously identified. As a result, the Establishment Clause concerns that inhere in state-aid programs to religious institutions remain a vital part of these cases.

Laura S. Underkuffler, *Vouchers and Beyond: The Individual as Causative Agent in Establishment Clause Jurisprudence*, 75 IND. L.J. 167, 188 (2000). *See also* Steven K. Green, *Private School Vouchers and the Confusion Over "Direct" Aid*, 10 GEO. MASON U. CIV. RTS. L.J. 47 (1999-2000).

The Supreme Court seems to have rejected what Professor Underkuffler calls the "individual as causative agent theory" in the context of racially segregated education. Since *Brown v. Board of Education*, 347 U.S. 483 (1954), the government has not been permitted to operate racially segregated schools. In *Griffin v. County School Board of Prince Edward County*, 377 U.S. 218 (1964), the Supreme Court upheld a lower court order enjoining a local school board's attempt to shut down the public schools to avoid a court order mandating that the school desegregate. The Court also upheld an injunction prohibiting the school board from paying county tuition grants or giving tax exemptions to parents sending their children to segregated private schools. The Court held that it was impermissible for the government to perpetuate racial segregation in private schools "supported directly or indirectly by state or county funds." *Id.* at 232. Is the Court's refusal to distinguish between direct and indirect funding of segregated education inconsistent with the way the Court viewed the issue of direct and indirect funding of religious education in *Mueller*?

WITTERS v. WASHINGTON DEPARTMENT OF SERVICES FOR THE BLIND
474 U.S. 481 (1986)

JUSTICE MARSHALL delivered the opinion of the Court.

I

Petitioner Larry Witters applied in 1979 to the Washington Commission for the Blind for vocational rehabilitation services pursuant to Wash. Rev. Code § 74.16.181 (1981). That statute authorized the Commission, *inter alia,* to "[p]rovide for special education and/or training in the professions, business or trades" so as to "assist visually handicapped persons to overcome vocational handicaps and to obtain the maximum degree of self-support and self-care." *Ibid.* Petitioner, suffering from a progressive eye condition, was eligible for vocational rehabilitation assistance under the terms of the statute. He was at the time attending Inland Empire School of the Bible, a private Christian college in Spokane, Washington, and studying the Bible, ethics, speech, and church administration in order to equip himself for a career as a pastor, missionary, or youth director.

The Commission denied petitioner aid. It relied on an earlier determination embodied in a Commission policy statement that "[t]he Washington State constitution forbids the use of public funds to assist an individual in the pursuit of a career or degree in theology or related areas," and on its conclusion that petitioner's training was "religious instruction" subject to that ban. That ruling was affirmed by a state hearings examiner, who held that the Commission was precluded from funding petitioner's training "in light of the State Constitution's prohibition against the state directly or indirectly supporting a religion." The hearings examiner cited Wash. Const., Art. I, § 11, providing in part that "no public money or property shall be appropriated for or applied to any religious worship, exercise or instruction, or the support of any religious establishment," and Wash. Const., Art. IX, § 4, providing that "[a]ll schools maintained or supported wholly or in part by the public funds shall be forever free from sectarian control or influence." That ruling, in turn, was upheld on internal administrative appeal.

Petitioner then instituted an action in State Superior Court for review of the administrative decision; the court affirmed on the same state-law grounds cited by the agency. The State Supreme Court affirmed as well. The Supreme Court, however, declined to ground its ruling on the Washington Constitution. Instead, it explicitly reserved judgment on the state constitutional issue and chose to base its ruling on the Establishment Clause of the Federal Constitution. The court stated:

> "The Supreme Court has developed a 3-part test for determining the constitutionality of state aid under the establishment clause of the First Amendment. 'First, the statute must have a secular legislative purpose; second, its principal or primary effect must be one that neither advances nor inhibits religion . . . ; finally, the statute must not foster "an excessive government entanglement with religion."' *Lemon v. Kurtzman*, [403 U.S. 602, 612-613 (1971)]. To withstand attack under the establishment clause, the challenged state action must satisfy each of the three criteria."

The Washington court had no difficulty finding the "secular purpose" prong of that test satisfied. Applying the second prong, however, that of "principal or primary effect," the court held that "[t]he provision of financial assistance by the State to enable someone to become a pastor, missionary, or church youth director clearly has the primary effect of advancing religion." The court, therefore, held that provision of aid to petitioner would contravene the Federal Constitution. In light of that ruling, the court saw no need to reach the "entanglement" prong; it stated that the record was in any case inadequate for such an inquiry.

We granted certiorari, 471 U.S. 1002 (1985), and we now reverse.

II

We are guided, as was the court below, by the three-part test set out by this Court in *Lemon*. Our analysis relating to the first prong of that test is simple: all parties concede the unmistakably secular purpose of the Washington program. That program was designed to promote the well-being of the visually handicapped through the provision of vocational rehabilitation services, and no more than a minuscule amount of the aid awarded under the program is likely to flow to religious education. No party suggests that the State's "actual purpose" in creating the program was to endorse religion, or that the secular purpose articulated by the legislature is merely "sham."

The answer to the question posed by the second prong of the *Lemon* test is more difficult. We conclude, however, that extension of aid to petitioner is not barred on that ground either. It is well settled that the Establishment Clause is not violated every time money previously in the possession of a State is conveyed to a religious institution. For example, a State may issue a paycheck to one of its employees, who may then donate all or part of that paycheck to a religious institution, all without constitutional barrier; and the State may do so even knowing that the employee so intends to dispose of his salary. It is equally well-settled, on the other hand, that the State may not grant aid to a religious school, whether cash or inkind, where the effect of the aid is "that of a direct subsidy to the religious school" from the State. Aid may have that effect even though it takes the form of aid to students or parents. The question presented is whether, on the facts as they appear in the record before us, extension of aid to petitioner and the use of that aid by petitioner to support his religious education is a permissible transfer similar to the hypothetical salary donation described above, or is an impermissible "direct subsidy."

Certain aspects of Washington's program are central to our inquiry. As far as the record shows, vocational assistance provided under the Washington program is paid directly to the student, who transmits it to the educational institution of his or her choice. Any aid provided under Washington's program that ultimately flows to religious institutions does so only as a result of the genuinely independent and private choices of aid recipients.[4] Washington's program is "made available generally without regard to the sectarian-nonsectarian, or public-

---

[4] This is not the case described in *Grand Rapids School District v. Ball*, 473 U.S. 373, 396 (1985) (Where . . . no meaningful distinction can be made between aid to the student and aid to the school, 'the concept of a loan to individuals is a transparent fiction'"), quoting *Wolman v. Walter*, 433 U.S. 229, 264 (1977) (opinion of POWELL, J.); *see also Wolman, supra*, at 250.

nonpublic nature of the institution benefited," *Nyquist,* and is in no way skewed towards religion. It is not one of "the ingenious plans for channeling state aid to sectarian schools that periodically reach this Court." It creates no financial incentive for students to undertake sectarian education. It does not tend to provide greater or broader benefits for recipients who apply their aid to religious education, nor are the full benefits of the program limited, in large part or in whole, to students at sectarian institutions. On the contrary, aid recipients have full opportunity to expend vocational rehabilitation aid on wholly secular education, and as a practical matter have rather greater prospects to do so. Aid recipients' choices are made among a huge variety of possible careers, of which only a small handful are sectarian. In this case, the fact that aid goes to individuals means that the decision to support religious education is made by the individual, not by the State.

Further, and importantly, nothing in the record indicates that, if petitioner succeeds, any significant portion of the aid expended under the Washington program as a whole will end up flowing to religious education. The function of the Washington program is hardly "to provide desired financial support for nonpublic, sectarian institutions." The program, providing vocational assistance to the visually handicapped, does not seem well suited to serve as the vehicle for such a subsidy. No evidence has been presented indicating that any other person has ever sought to finance religious education or activity pursuant to the State's program. The combination of these factors, we think, makes the link between the State and the school petitioner wishes to attend a highly attenuated one.

On the facts we have set out, it does not seem appropriate to view any aid ultimately flowing to the Inland Empire School of the Bible as resulting from a *state* action sponsoring or subsidizing religion. Nor does the mere circumstance that petitioner has chosen to use neutrally available state aid to help pay for his religious education confer any message of state endorsement of religion. Thus, while *amici* supporting respondent are correct in pointing out that aid to a religious institution unrestricted in its potential uses, if properly attributable to the State, is "clearly prohibited under the Establishment Clause," because it may subsidize the religious functions of that institution, that observation is not apposite to this case. On the facts present here, we think the Washington program works no state support of religion prohibited by the Establishment Clause.[5]

III

We therefore reject the claim that, on the record presented, extension of aid under Washington's vocational rehabilitation program to finance petitioner's

---

[5] We decline to address the "entanglement" issue at this time. As a prudential matter, it would be inappropriate for us to address that question without the benefit of a decision on the issue below. Further, we have no reason to doubt the conclusion of the Washington Supreme Court that that analysis could be more fruitfully conducted on a more complete record.

training at a Christian college to become a pastor, missionary, or youth director would advance religion in a manner inconsistent with the Establishment Clause of the First Amendment. On remand, the state court is of course free to consider the applicability of the "far stricter" dictates of the Washington State Constitution, see *Witters v. Commission for the Blind*, 102 Wash. 2d, at 626,. It may also choose to reopen the factual record in order to consider the arguments made by respondent and discussed in nn. 3 and 5, *supra*. We decline petitioner's invitation to leapfrog consideration of those issues by holding that the Free Exercise Clause *requires* Washington to extend vocational rehabilitation aid to petitioner regardless of what the State Constitution commands or further factual development reveals, and we express no opinion on that matter.

JUSTICE POWELL, with whom THE CHIEF JUSTICE and JUSTICE REHNQUIST join, concurring.

[Justice Powell concurred, noting the omission of any reference to *Mueller v. Allen* in the Court's analysis, and arguing that *Mueller* strongly supports the *Witters* result.]

D. THE FRAMEWORK OF THE TRADITIONAL STANDARD: THE FEAR OF RELIGIOUS INCULCATION, ENDORSEMENT, AND SUBSIDY

SCHOOL DISTRICT OF THE CITY OF GRAND RAPIDS v. BALL
473 U.S. 373 (1985)

JUSTICE BRENNAN delivered the opinion of the Court.

The School District of Grand Rapids, Michigan, adopted two programs in which classes for nonpublic school students are financed by the public school system, taught by teachers hired by the public school system, and conducted in "leased" classrooms in the nonpublic schools. Most of the nonpublic schools involved in the programs are sectarian religious schools. This case raises the question whether these programs impermissibly involve the government in the support of sectarian religious activities and thus violate the Establishment Clause of the First Amendment.

I

A

At issue in this case are the Community Education and Shared Time programs offered in the nonpublic schools of Grand Rapids, Michigan. These programs, first instituted in the 1976-1977 school year, provide classes to nonpublic school students at public expense in classrooms located in and leased from the local nonpublic schools.

The Shared Time program offers classes during the regular schoolday that are intended to be supplementary to the "core curriculum" courses that the State of Michigan requires as a part of an accredited school program. Among the subjects offered are "remedial" and "enrichment" mathematics, "remedial" and "enrichment" reading, art, music, and physical education. A typical nonpublic school student attends these classes for one or two class periods per week; approximately "ten percent of any given nonpublic school student's time during the academic year would consist of Shared Time instruction." *Americans United for Separation of Church and State v. School Dist. of Grand Rapids*, 546 F. Supp. 1071, 1079 (WD Mich.1982). Although Shared Time itself is a program offered only in the nonpublic schools, there was testimony that the courses included in that program are offered, albeit perhaps in a somewhat different form, in the public schools as well. All of the classes that are the subject of this case are taught in elementary schools, with the exception of Math Topics, a remedial mathematics course taught in the secondary schools.

The Shared Time teachers are full-time employees of the public schools, who often move from classroom to classroom during the course of the schoolday. A "significant portion" of the teachers (approximately 10%) "previously taught in nonpublic schools, and many of those had been assigned to the same nonpublic school where they were previously employed." The School District of Grand Rapids hires Shared Time teachers in accordance with its ordinary hiring procedures. The public school system apparently provides all of the supplies, materials, and equipment used in connection with Shared Time instruction.

The Community Education program is offered throughout the Grand Rapids community in schools and on other sites, for children as well as adults. The classes at issue here are taught in the nonpublic elementary schools and commence at the conclusion of the regular schoolday. Among the courses offered are Arts and Crafts, Home Economics, Spanish, Gymnastics, Yearbook Production, Christmas Arts and Crafts, Drama, Newspaper, Humanities, Chess, Model Building, and Nature Appreciation. The District Court found that "[a]lthough certain Community Education courses offered at nonpublic school sites are not offered at the public schools on a Community Education basis, all Community Education programs are otherwise available at the public schools, usually as a part of their more extensive regular curriculum."

Community Education teachers are part-time public school employees. Community Education courses are completely voluntary and are offered only if 12 or more students enroll. Because a well-known teacher is necessary to attract the requisite number of students, the School District accords a preference in hiring to instructors already teaching within the school. Thus, "virtually every Community Education course conducted on facilities leased from nonpublic schools has an instructor otherwise employed full time by the same nonpublic school."

Both programs are administered similarly. The Director of the program, a public school employee, sends packets of course listings to the participating nonpublic schools before the school year begins. The nonpublic school administrators then decide which courses they want to offer. The Director works out an academic schedule for each school, taking into account, *inter alia,* the varying religious holidays celebrated by the schools of different denominations.

Nonpublic school administrators decide which classrooms will be used for the programs, and the Director then inspects the facilities and consults with Shared Time teachers to make sure the facilities are satisfactory. The public school system pays the nonpublic schools for the use of the necessary classroom space by entering into "leases" at the rate of $6 per classroom per week. The "leases," however, contain no mention of the particular room, space, or facility leased and teachers' rooms, libraries, lavatories, and similar facilities are made available at no additional charge. Each room used in the programs has to be free of any crucifix, religious symbol, or artifact, although such religious symbols can be present in the adjoining hallways, corridors, and other facilities used in connection with the program. During the time that a given classroom is being used in the programs, the teacher is required to post a sign stating that it is a "public school classroom."[2] However, there are no signs posted outside the school buildings indicating that public school courses are conducted inside or that the facilities are being used as a public school annex.

Although petitioners label the Shared Time and Community Education students as "part-time public school students," the students attending Shared Time and Community Education courses in facilities leased from a nonpublic school are the same students who attend that particular school otherwise. There is no evidence that any public school student has ever attended a Shared Time or Community Education class in a nonpublic school. The District Court found that "[t]hough Defendants claim the Shared Time program is available to all students, the record is abundantly clear that only nonpublic school students wearing the cloak of a 'public school student' can enroll in it." The District Court noted that "[w]hereas public school students are assembled at the public facility nearest to their residence, students in religious schools are assembled on the basis of religion without any consideration of residence or school district boundaries." Thus, "beneficiaries are wholly designated on the basis of religion," and these "public school" classes, in contrast to ordinary public school classes which are largely neighborhood based, are as segregated by religion as are the schools at which they are offered.[3]

---

[2] The signs read as follows: "GRAND RAPIDS PUBLIC SCHOOLS' ROOM. THIS ROOM HAS BEEN LEASED BY THE GRAND RAPIDS PUBLIC SCHOOL DISTRICT, FOR THE PURPOSE OF CONDUCTING PUBLIC SCHOOL EDUCATIONAL PROGRAMS. THE ACTIVITY IN THIS ROOM IS CONTROLLED SOLELY BY THE GRAND RAPIDS PUBLIC SCHOOL DISTRICT." App. 200.

[3] As would be expected, a large majority of the students attending religious schools belong to the denomination that controls the school. The District Court found, for instance, that approximately 85% of the students at the Catholic schools are Catholic. 546 F. Supp., at 1080.

Forty of the forty-one schools at which the programs operate are sectarian in character.[4] The schools of course vary from one another, but substantial evidence suggests that they share deep religious purposes. For instance, the Parent Handbook of one Catholic school states the goals of Catholic education as "[a] God oriented environment which *permeates* the total educational program," "[a] Christian atmosphere which guides and encourages participation in the church's commitment to social justice," and "[a] continuous development of knowledge of the Catholic faith, its traditions, teachings and theology." A policy statement of the Christian schools similarly proclaims that "it is not sufficient that the teachings of Christianity be a separate subject in the curriculum, but *the Word of God must be an all-pervading force in the educational program.*" These Christian schools require all parents seeking to enroll their children either to subscribe to a particular doctrinal statement or to agree to have their children taught according to the doctrinal statement. The District Court found that the schools are "pervasively sectarian," and concluded "without hesitation that the purposes of these schools is to advance their particular religions," and that "a substantial portion of their functions are subsumed in the religious mission."

II

B

Our inquiry must begin with a consideration of the nature of the institutions in which the programs operate. Of the 41 private schools where these "part-time public schools" have operated, 40 are identifiably religious schools. It is true that each school may not share all of the characteristics of religious schools. The District Court found, however, that "[b]ased upon the massive testimony and exhibits, the conclusion is inescapable that the religious institutions receiving instructional services from the public schools are sectarian in the sense that a substantial portion of their functions are subsumed in the religious mission." *See Hunt v. McNair*, 413 U.S. 734, 735 (1973); *Meek v. Pittenger* ("The very purpose of many of those schools is to provide an integrated secular and religious education"); *Walz v. Tax Comm'n* ("to assure future adherents to a particular faith" is "an affirmative if not dominant policy of church schools"). At the religious schools here — as at the sectarian schools that have been the subject of our past cases — "the secular education those schools provide goes hand in hand with the religious mission that is the only reason for the schools' existence. Within that institution, the two are inextricably intertwined." *Lemon v. Kurtzman.*

Given that 40 of the 41 schools in this case are thus "pervasively sectarian," the challenged public school programs operating in the religious schools may impermissibly advance religion in three different ways. First, the teachers participating in the programs may become involved in intentionally or inadvertently

---

[4] Twenty-eight of the schools are Roman Catholic, seven are Christian Reformed, three are Lutheran, one is Seventh Day Adventist, and one is Baptist.

inculcating particular religious tenets or beliefs. Second, the programs may provide a crucial symbolic link between government and religion, thereby enlisting — at least in the eyes of impressionable youngsters — the powers of government to the support of the religious denomination operating the school. Third, the programs may have the effect of directly promoting religion by impermissibly providing a subsidy to the primary religious mission of the institutions affected.

(1)

Although Establishment Clause jurisprudence is characterized by few absolutes, the Clause does absolutely prohibit government-financed or government-sponsored indoctrination into the beliefs of a particular religious faith. Such indoctrination, if permitted to occur, would have devastating effects on the right of each individual voluntarily to determine what to believe (and what not to believe) free of any coercive pressures from the State, while at the same time tainting the resulting religious beliefs with a corrosive secularism.

In *Meek v. Pittenger*, 421 U.S. 349 (1975), the Court invalidated a statute providing for the loan of state-paid professional staff — including teachers — to nonpublic schools to provide remedial and accelerated instruction, guidance counseling and testing, and other services on the premises of the nonpublic schools. Such a program, if not subjected to a "comprehensive, discriminating, and continuing state surveillance," *Lemon v. Kurtzman*, would entail an unacceptable risk that the state-sponsored instructional personnel would "advance the religious mission of the church-related schools in which they serve." *Meek*, 421 U.S., at 370. Even though the teachers were paid by the State, "[t]he potential for impermissible fostering of religion under these circumstances, although somewhat reduced, is nonetheless present." *Id.*, at 372. The program in *Meek*, if not sufficiently monitored, would simply have entailed too great a risk of state-sponsored indoctrination.

The programs before us today share the defect that we identified in *Meek*. With respect to the Community Education program, the District Court found that "virtually every Community Education course conducted on facilities leased from nonpublic schools has an instructor otherwise employed full time by the same nonpublic school." These instructors, many of whom no doubt teach in the religious schools precisely because they are adherents of the controlling denomination and want to serve their religious community zealously, are expected during the regular schoolday to inculcate their students with the tenets and beliefs of their particular religious faiths. Yet the premise of the program is that those instructors can put aside their religious convictions and engage in entirely secular Community Education instruction as soon as the schoolday is over. Moreover, they are expected to do so before the same religious school students and in the same religious school classrooms that they employed to advance religious purposes during the "official" schoolday. Nonetheless, as petitioners themselves asserted, Community Education classes are not specifically monitored for religious content.

We do not question that the dedicated and professional religious school-teachers employed by the Community Education program will attempt in good faith to perform their secular mission conscientiously. Nonetheless, there is a substantial risk that, overtly or subtly, the religious message they are expected to convey during the regular schoolday will infuse the supposedly secular classes they teach after school. The danger arises "not because the public employee [is] likely deliberately to subvert his task to the service of religion, but rather because the pressures of the environment might alter his behavior from its normal course." *Wolman v. Walter*, 433 U.S. 229, 247 (1977). "The conflict of functions inheres in the situation." *Lemon v. Kurtzman.*

The Shared Time program, though structured somewhat differently, nonetheless also poses a substantial risk of state-sponsored indoctrination. The most important difference between the programs is that most of the instructors in the Shared Time program are full-time teachers hired by the public schools. Moreover, although "virtually every" Community Education instructor is a full- time religious schoolteacher, only "[a] significant portion" of the Shared Time instructors previously worked in the religious schools.[7] Nonetheless, as with the Community Education program, no attempt is made to monitor the Shared Time courses for religious content.

Thus, despite these differences between the two programs, our holding in *Meek* controls the inquiry with respect to Shared Time, as well as Community Education. Shared Time instructors are teaching academic subjects in religious schools in courses virtually indistinguishable from the other courses offered during the regular religious schoolday. The teachers in this program, even more than their Community Education colleagues, are "performing important educational services in schools in which education is an integral part of the dominant sectarian mission and in which an atmosphere dedicated to the advancement of religious belief is constantly maintained." *Meek v. Pittenger.* Teachers in such an atmosphere may well subtly (or overtly) conform their instruction to the environment in which they teach, while students will perceive the instruction provided in the context of the dominantly religious message of the institution, thus reinforcing the indoctrinating effect. As we stated in *Meek*, "[w]hether the subject is 'remedial reading,' 'advanced reading,' or simply 'reading,' a teacher remains a teacher, and the danger that religious doctrine will become intertwined with secular instruction persists." Unlike types of aid that the Court has upheld, such as state-created standardized tests, *Committee for Public Education & Religious Liberty v. Regan*, or diagnostic services, *Wolman v. Walter*, there is a "substantial risk" that programs operating in this environment would "be used for religious educational purposes." *Committee for Public Education & Religious Liberty v. Regan.*

---

[7]Approximately 10% of the Shared Time instructors were previously employed by the religious schools, and many of these were reassigned back to the school at which they had previously taught.

The Court of Appeals of course recognized that respondents adduced no evidence of specific incidents of religious indoctrination in this case. But the absence of proof of specific incidents is not dispositive. When conducting a supposedly secular class in the pervasively sectarian environment of a religious school, a teacher may knowingly or unwillingly tailor the content of the course to fit the school's announced goals. If so, there is no reason to believe that this kind of ideological influence would be detected or reported by students, by their parents, or by the school system itself. The students are presumably attending religious schools precisely in order to receive religious instruction. After spending the balance of their schoolday in classes heavily influenced by a religious perspective, they would have little motivation or ability to discern improper ideological content that may creep into a Shared Time or Community Education course. Neither their parents nor the parochial schools would have cause to complain if the effect of the publicly supported instruction were to advance the schools' sectarian mission. And the public school system itself has no incentive to detect or report any specific incidents of improper state- sponsored indoctrination. Thus, the lack of evidence of specific incidents of indoctrination is of little significance.

(2)

Our cases have recognized that the Establishment Clause guards against more than direct, state-funded efforts to indoctrinate youngsters in specific religious beliefs. Government promotes religion as effectively when it fosters a close identification of its powers and responsibilities with those of any — or all — religious denominations as when it attempts to inculcate specific religious doctrines. If this identification conveys a message of government endorsement or disapproval of religion, a core purpose of the Establishment Clause is violated. As we stated in *Larkin v. Grendel's Den, Inc.*, 459 U.S. 116, 125-126 (1982): "[T]he mere appearance of a joint exercise of legislative authority by Church and State provides a significant symbolic benefit to religion in the minds of some by reason of the power conferred." *See also Widmar v. Vincent*, 454 U.S. 263, 274 (1981) (finding effect "incidental" and not "primary" because it "does not confer any imprimatur of state approval on religious sects or practices").

It follows that an important concern of the effects test is whether the symbolic union of church and state effected by the challenged governmental action is sufficiently likely to be perceived by adherents of the controlling denominations as an endorsement, and by the nonadherents as a disapproval, of their individual religious choices. The inquiry into this kind of effect must be conducted with particular care when many of the citizens perceiving the governmental message are children in their formative years. The symbolism of a union between church and state is most likely to influence children of tender years, whose experience is limited and whose beliefs consequently are the function of environment as much as of free and voluntary choice.

Our school-aid cases have recognized a sensitivity to the symbolic impact of the union of church and state. Grappling with problems in many ways parallel to those we face today, *McCollum v. Board of Education*, 333 U.S. 203 (1948), held that a public school may not permit part-time religious instruction on its premises as a part of the school program, even if participation in that instruction is entirely voluntary and even if the instruction itself is conducted only by nonpublic school personnel. Yet in *Zorach v. Clauson,* 343 U.S. 306 (1952), the Court held that a similar program conducted off the premises of the public school passed constitutional muster. The difference in symbolic impact helps to explain the difference between the cases. The symbolic connection of church and state in the *McCollum* program presented the students with a graphic symbol of the "concert or union or dependency" of church and state, *see Zorach*. This very symbolic union was conspicuously absent in the *Zorach* program.

In the programs challenged in this case, the religious school students spend their typical schoolday moving between religious school and "public school" classes. Both types of classes take place in the same religious school building and both are largely composed of students who are adherents of the same denomination. In this environment, the students would be unlikely to discern the crucial difference between the religious school classes and the "public school" classes, even if the latter were successfully kept free of religious indoctrination. As one commentator has written:

> "This pervasive [religious] atmosphere makes on the young student's mind a lasting imprint that the holy and transcendental should be central to all facets of life. It increases respect for the church as an institution to guide one's total life adjustments and undoubtedly helps stimulate interest in religious vocations. . . . In short, the parochial school's total operation serves to fulfill both secular and religious functions concurrently, and the two cannot be completely separated. Support of any part of its activity entails some support of the disqualifying religious function of molding the religious personality of the young student." Giannella, *Religious Liberty, Nonestablishment and Doctrinal Development: Part II. The Nonestablishment Principle*, 81 HARV. L. REV. 513, 574 (1968).

Consequently, even the student who notices the "public school" sign temporarily posted would have before him a powerful symbol of state endorsement and encouragement of the religious beliefs taught in the same class at some other time during the day.

As Judge Friendly, writing for the Second Circuit in the companion case to the case at bar, stated:

> "Under the City's plan public school teachers are, so far as appearance is concerned, a regular adjunct of the religious school. They pace the same halls, use classrooms in the same building, teach the same students, and confer with the teachers hired by the religious schools, many

of them members of religious orders. The religious school appears to the public as a joint enterprise staffed with some teachers paid by its religious sponsor and others by the public." *Felton v. Secretary, United States Dept. of Ed.,* 739 F. 2d 48, 67-68 (1984).

This effect — the symbolic union of government and religion in one sectarian enterprise — is an impermissible effect under the Establishment Clause.

(3)

In *Everson v. Board of Education*, the Court stated that "[n]o tax in any amount, large or small, can be levied to support any religious activities or institutions, whatever they may be called, or whatever form they may adopt to teach or practice religion." With but one exception, our subsequent cases have struck down attempts by States to make payments out of public tax dollars directly to primary or secondary religious educational institutions.

Aside from cash payments, the Court has distinguished between two categories of programs in which public funds are used to finance secular activities that religious schools would otherwise fund from their own resources. In the first category, the Court has noted that it is "well established . . . that not every law that confers an 'indirect,' 'remote,' or 'incidental' benefit upon religious institutions is, for that reason alone, constitutionally invalid." In such "indirect" aid cases, the government has used primarily secular means to accomplish a primarily secular end, and no "primary effect" of advancing religion has thus been found. On this rationale, the Court has upheld programs providing for loans of secular textbooks to nonpublic school students, *Board of Education v. Allen*, and programs providing bus transportation for nonpublic schoolchildren, *Everson v. Board of Education.*

In the second category of cases, the Court has relied on the Establishment Clause prohibition of forms of aid that provide "direct and substantial advancement of the sectarian enterprise." In such "direct aid" cases, the government, although acting for a secular purpose, has done so by directly supporting a religious institution. Under this rationale, the Court has struck down state schemes providing for tuition grants and tax benefits for parents whose children attend religious school, *see Sloan v. Lemon,* 413 U.S. 825 (1973); *Committee for Public Education & Religious Liberty v. Nyquist,* and programs providing for "loan" of instructional materials to be used in religious schools, *see Wolman v. Walter; Meek v. Pittenger.* In *Sloan* and *Nyquist,* the aid was formally given to parents and not directly to the religious schools, while in *Wolman* and *Meek,* the aid was in-kind assistance rather than the direct contribution of public funds. Nonetheless, these differences in form were insufficient to save programs whose effect was indistinguishable from that of a direct subsidy to the religious school.

Thus, the Court has never accepted the mere possibility of subsidization, as the above cases demonstrate, as sufficient to invalidate an aid program. On the other hand, this effect is not wholly unimportant for Establishment Clause purposes. If it were, the public schools could gradually take on themselves the entire responsibility for teaching secular subjects on religious school premises. The question in each case must be whether the effect of the proffered aid is "direct and substantial," or indirect and incidental. "The problem, like many problems in constitutional law, is one of degree."

We have noted in the past that the religious school has dual functions, providing its students with a secular education while it promotes a particular religious perspective. *See Mueller v. Allen*; *Board of Education v. Allen*. In *Meek* and *Wolman*, we held unconstitutional state programs providing for loans of instructional equipment and materials to religious schools, on the ground that the programs advanced the "primary, religion-oriented educational function of the sectarian school." *Cf. Wolman* (upholding provision of diagnostic services, which were "'general welfare services for children that may be provided by the State regardless of the incidental benefit that accrues to church-related schools'"). The programs challenged here, which provide teachers in addition to the instructional equipment and materials, have a similar — and forbidden — effect of advancing religion. This kind of direct aid to the educational function of the religious school is indistinguishable from the provision of a direct cash subsidy to the religious school that is most clearly prohibited under the Establishment Clause.

Petitioners claim that the aid here, like the textbooks in *Allen*, flows primarily to the students, not to the religious schools. Of course, all aid to religious schools ultimately "flows to" the students, and petitioners' argument if accepted would validate all forms of nonideological aid to religious schools, including those explicitly rejected in our prior cases. Yet in *Meek,* we held unconstitutional the loan of instructional materials to religious schools and in *Wolman*, we rejected the fiction that a similar program could be saved by masking it as aid to individual students. It follows *a fortiori* that the aid here, which includes not only instructional materials but also the provision of instructional services by teachers in the parochial school building, "inescapably [has] the primary effect of providing a direct and substantial advancement of the sectarian enterprise." Where, as here, no meaningful distinction can be made between aid to the student and aid to the school, "the concept of a loan to individuals is a transparent fiction." *Wolman v. Walter* (opinion of POWELL, J.).

Petitioners also argue that this "subsidy" effect is not significant in this case, because the Community Education and Shared Time programs supplemented the curriculum with courses not previously offered in the religious schools and not required by school rule or state regulation. Of course, this fails to distinguish the programs here from those found unconstitutional in *Meek*. As in *Meek*, we do not find that this feature of the program is controlling. First, there is no way of knowing whether the religious schools would have offered some or all of these courses if the public school system had not offered them first. The distinction between courses that "supplement" and those that "supplant" the regular curriculum is therefore not nearly as clear as petitioners allege. Second, although the precise courses offered in these programs may have been new to the participating religious schools, their general subject matter — reading, mathematics, etc. — was surely a part of the curriculum in the past, and the concerns of the Establishment Clause may thus be triggered despite the "supplemental" nature of the courses. Third, and most important, petitioners' argument would permit the public schools gradually to take over the entire secular curriculum of the religious school, for the latter could surely discontinue existing courses so that they might be replaced a year or two later by a Community Education or Shared Time course with the same content. The average religious school student, for instance, now spends 10% of the schoolday in Shared Time classes. But there is no principled basis on which this Court can impose a limit on the percentage of the religious schoolday that can be subsidized by the public school. To let the genie out of the bottle in this case would be to permit ever larger segments of the religious school curriculum to be turned over the public school system, thus violating the cardinal principle that the State may not in effect become the prime supporter of the religious school system.

JUSTICE O'CONNOR, concurring in the judgment in part and dissenting in part.

I dissent from the Court's holding that the Grand Rapids Shared Time program impermissibly advances religion. Nothing in the record indicates that Shared Time instructors have attempted to proselytize their students.

The Court relies on the District Court's finding that a "significant portion of the Shared Time instructors previously taught in nonpublic schools, and many of those had been assigned to the same nonpublic school where they were previously employed." In fact, only 13 Shared Time instructors have ever been employed by any parochial school, and only a fraction of those 13 now work in a parochial school where they were previously employed. The experience of these few teachers does not significantly increase the risk that the perceived or actual effect of the Shared Time program will be to inculcate religion at public expense. I would uphold the Shared Time program.

I agree with the Court, however, that the Community Education program violates the Establishment Clause. The record indicates that Community Education courses in the parochial schools are overwhelmingly taught by instructors who are current full-time employees of the parochial school. The teachers offer secular subjects to the same parochial school students who attend their regular parochial school classes. In addition, the supervisors of the Community Education program in the parochial schools are by and large the principals of the very schools where the classes are offered. When full-time parochial school teachers receive public funds to teach secular courses to their parochial school students under parochial school supervision, I agree that the program has the perceived and actual effect of advancing the religious aims of the church-related schools. This is particularly the case where, as here, religion pervades the curriculum and the teachers are accustomed to bring religion to play in everything they teach. I concur in the judgment of the Court that the Community Education program violates the Establishment Clause.

Chapter 9

GOVERNMENT FINANCIAL SUPPORT OF RELIGION: THE NEW STANDARD

In many ways, the cases in this chapter represent a constitutional revolution. As illustrated in various materials reproduced in previous chapters, the origins of the Establishment Clause were very closely bound up with popular resistance to government financing of religion. Government financing of religious activity As is in many ways the central issue in Establishment Clause jurisprudence. Douglas Laycock summed up the history in the excerpt reprinted in Chapter 1: "[T]here were widespread objections to tax support for churches. . . . This opposition forced the Framers' generation to think about the tax issue. Once they thought about it, they concluded that any form of tax support for churches violated religious liberty. By the time of the first amendment, church taxes were repealed or moribund outside New England, and they were not working well in the four New England states that still tried to collect them." *See* Laycock, *"Nonpreferential" Aid to Religion: A False Claim About Original Intent, supra* Chapter 1.

The cases reprinted here could augur a level of government financing of religious institutions never before seen in the modern era. Each of these decisions represents a sharp break with the past, and each of the decisions overrules existing caselaw or greatly expands concepts that had previously provided for only a narrow range of financing. *Agostini v. Felton* overrules *Grand Rapids v Ball,* and thus permits the direct provision of state-financed teachers to religious private schools. *Zelman v. Simmons-Harris* takes the parental-subsidy logic of *Mueller v. Allen* and expands it far beyond its original context. In *Mueller,* this logic was used to justify a fairly small-scale subsidy of expenses for secular school supplies and minor portions of private school tuition. In *Zelman,* the logic is used to justify a multi-million dollar program of subsidies to private schools, virtually all of which were religious. The only limit on the parental-subsidy model that remains after *Zelman* is the easily satisfied requirement that the subsidy program be cast in formally neutral terms, such that secular schools could also apply for a subsidy. Finally, *Mitchell v. Helms* overrules decades of precedents barring direct governmental subsidies to religious schools. In *Mitchell,* Justice O'Connor provided the fifth vote to uphold the direct subsidy program, but continued to insist that the Constitution prohibits religious schools receiving government money from diverting that money to explicitly religious purposes. With Justice O'Connor's departure from the Court, that remaining limit on direct government financing of religious education may no longer have the support of a majority of current Justices.

With the dilution of Establishment Clause protections in this area, litigants may increasingly turn to state constitutional protections of religious liberty. A section of this chapter addresses the so-called "Little Blaine Amendments," which will be a focal point of any state-court litigation in this area. Finally, as the Court has revamped the rules permitting the government to finance religious education, similar questions have been raised concerning the government's use of religious organizations to provide publicly financed social services. The final section of this chapter addresses issues relating to these programs, which have become known as "faith-based initiatives."

A. GOVERNMENT AID TO RELIGIOUS SCHOOLS

AGOSTINI v. FELTON
521 U.S. 203 (1997)

JUSTICE O'CONNOR delivered the opinion of the Court.

In *Aguilar v. Felton*, 473 U.S. 402 (1985) [the companion case to *Grand Rapids v. Ball*, *supra* Chapter 8], this Court held that the Establishment Clause of the First Amendment barred the city of New York from sending public school teachers into parochial schools to provide remedial education to disadvantaged children pursuant to a congressionally mandated program. On remand, the District Court for the Eastern District of New York entered a permanent injunction reflecting our ruling. Twelve years later, petitioners — the parties bound by that injunction — seek relief from its operation. Petitioners maintain that *Aguilar* cannot be squared with our intervening Establishment Clause jurisprudence and ask that we explicitly recognize what our more recent cases already dictate: *Aguilar* is no longer good law. We agree with petitioners that *Aguilar* is not consistent with our subsequent Establishment Clause decisions and further conclude that, on the facts presented here, petitioners are entitled under Federal Rule of Civil Procedure 60(b)(5) to relief from the operation of the District Court's prospective injunction.

I

In 1965, Congress enacted Title I of the Elementary and Secondary Education Act of 1965 to "provid[e] full educational opportunity to every child regardless of economic background." Toward that end, Title I channels federal funds, through the States, to "local educational agencies" (LEA's). The LEA's spend these funds to provide remedial education, guidance, and job counseling to eligible students. An eligible student is one (i) who resides within the attendance boundaries of a public school located in a low-income area, and (ii) who is failing, or is at risk of failing, the State's student performance standards. Title I funds must be made available to *all* eligible children, regardless of whether they attend public schools, and the services provided to children attending private schools must be "equitable in comparison to services and other benefits for public school children."

An LEA providing services to children enrolled in private schools is subject to a number of constraints that are not imposed when it provides aid to public schools. Title I services may be provided only to those private school students eligible for aid, and cannot be used to provide services on a "school-wide" basis. In addition, the LEA must retain complete control over Title I funds; retain title to all materials used to provide Title I services; and provide those services through public employees or other persons independent of the private school and any religious institution. The Title I services themselves must be "secular, neutral, and nonideological," and must "supplement, and in no case supplant, the level of services" already provided by the private school.

Petitioner Board of Education of the City of New York (Board), an LEA, first applied for Title I funds in 1966 and has grappled ever since with how to provide Title I services to the private school students within its jurisdiction. Approximately 10% of the total number of students eligible for Title I services are private school students. Recognizing that more than 90% of the private schools within the Board's jurisdiction are sectarian, the Board initially arranged to transport children to public schools for after-school Title I instruction. But this enterprise was largely unsuccessful. Attendance was poor, teachers and children were tired, and parents were concerned for the safety of their children. The Board then moved the after-school instruction onto private school campuses, as Congress had contemplated when it enacted Title I. After this program also yielded mixed results, the Board implemented the plan we evaluated in *Aguilar v. Felton*, 473 U.S. 402 (1985).

That plan called for the provision of Title I services on private school premises during school hours. Under the plan, only public employees could serve as Title I instructors and counselors. Assignments to private schools were made on a voluntary basis and without regard to the religious affiliation of the employee or the wishes of the private school. As the Court of Appeals in Aguilar observed, a large majority of Title I teachers worked in nonpublic schools with religious affiliations different from their own. The vast majority of Title I teachers also moved among the private schools, spending fewer than five days a week at the same school.

Before any public employee could provide Title I instruction at a private school, she would be given a detailed set of written and oral instructions emphasizing the secular purpose of Title I and setting out the rules to be followed to ensure that this purpose was not compromised. Specifically, employees would be told that (i) they were employees of the Board and accountable only to their public school supervisors; (ii) they had exclusive responsibility for selecting students for the Title I program and could teach only those children who met the eligibility criteria for Title I; (iii) their materials and equipment would be used only in the Title I program; (iv) they could not engage in team-teaching or other cooperative instructional activities with private school teachers; and (v) they could not introduce any religious matter into their teaching or become involved in any way with the religious activities of the private schools. All religious symbols were to be removed from classrooms used for Title I services. The rules acknowledged that it might be necessary for Title I teachers to consult with a student's regular classroom teacher to assess the student's particular needs and progress, but admonished instructors to limit those consultations to mutual professional concerns regarding the student's education. To ensure compliance with these rules, a publicly employed field supervisor was to attempt to make at least one unannounced visit to each teacher's classroom every month.

In 1978, six federal taxpayers — respondents here — sued the Board in the District Court for the Eastern District of New York. In a 5-to-4 decision, this Court affirmed on the ground that the Board's Title I program necessitated an "excessive entanglement of church and state in the administration of [Title I] benefits."

The Board, like other LEA's across the United States, modified its Title I program so it could continue serving those students who attended private religious schools. Rather than offer Title I instruction to parochial school students at their schools, the Board reverted to its prior practice of providing instruction at public school sites, at leased sites, and in mobile instructional units (essentially vans converted into classrooms) parked near the sectarian school. The Board also offered computer-aided instruction, which could be provided "on premises" because it did not require public employees to be physically present on the premises of a religious school.

It is not disputed that the additional costs of complying with *Aguilar*'s mandate are significant. Since the 1986-1987 school year, the Board has spent over $100 million providing computer-aided instruction, leasing sites and mobile instructional units, and transporting students to those sites. ($93.2 million spent between 1986-1987 and 1993-1994 school years); *id.*, at 336 (annual additional costs average around $15 million). Under the Secretary of Education's regulations, those costs "incurred as a result of implementing alternative delivery systems to comply with the requirements of *Aguilar v. Felton* " and not paid for with other state or federal funds are to be deducted from the federal grant before the Title I funds are distributed to any student. These "*Aguilar* costs" thus reduce the amount of Title I money an LEA has available for remedial education, and LEA's have had to cut back on the number of students who receive Title I benefits. From Title I funds available for New York City children between the 1986-1987 and the 1993-1994 school years, the Board had to deduct $7.9 million "off-the-top" for compliance with *Aguilar*. When *Aguilar* was handed down, it was estimated that some 20,000 economically disadvantaged children in the city of New York, and some 183,000 children nationwide, would experience a decline in Title I services. *See also* S.Rep. No. 100-222, p. 14 (1987) (estimating that Aguilar costs have "resulted in a decline of about 35 percent in the number of private school children who are served").

In October and December of 1995, petitioners — the Board and a new group of parents of parochial school students entitled to Title I services — filed motions in the District Court seeking relief under Federal Rule of Civil Procedure 60(b) from the permanent injunction entered by the District Court on remand from our decision in *Aguilar*. Petitioners argued that relief was proper under Rule 60(b)(5) and our decision in *Rufo v. Inmates of Suffolk County Jail*, 502 U.S. 367, 388 (1992), because the "decisional law [had] changed to make legal what the [injunction] was designed to prevent." Specifically, petitioners pointed to the statements of five Justices in *Board of Ed. of Kiryas Joel Village School Dist. v. Grumet*, 512 U.S. 687 (1994), calling for the overruling of *Aguilar*. The District Court denied the motion. The District Court recognized that petitioners, "at bottom," sought "a procedurally sound vehicle to get the [propriety of the injunction] back before the Supreme Court," and concluded that the "the Board ha[d] properly proceeded under Rule 60(b) to seek relief from the injunction." Despite its observations that "the landscape of Establishment Clause decisions has changed," and that "[t]here may be good reason to conclude that *Aguilar*'s demise is imminent," the District Court denied the Rule 60(b) motion on the merits because *Aguilar*'s demise had "not yet occurred." The Court of Appeals for the Second Circuit "affirmed substantially for the reasons stated in" the District Court's opinion. We now reverse.

II

The question we must answer is a simple one: Are petitioners entitled to relief from the District Court's permanent injunction under Rule 60(b)? Rule 60(b)(5), the subsection under which petitioners proceeded below, states:

> "On motion and upon such terms as are just, the court may relieve a party ... from a final judgment [or] order ... [when] it is no longer equitable that the judgment should have prospective application."

In *Rufo v. Inmates of Suffolk County Jail, supra*, at 384, we held that it is appropriate to grant a Rule 60(b)(5) motion when the party seeking relief from an injunction or consent decree can show "a significant change either in factual conditions or in law." A court may recognize subsequent changes in either statutory or decisional law. A court errs when it refuses to modify an injunction or consent decree in light of such changes.

Petitioners point to three changes in the factual and legal landscape that they believe justify their claim for relief under Rule 60(b)(5). They first contend that the exorbitant costs of complying with the District Court's injunction constitute a significant factual development warranting modification of the injunction. Petitioners also argue that there have been two significant legal developments since *Aguilar* was decided: a majority of Justices have expressed their views that *Aguilar* should be reconsidered or overruled; and *Aguilar* has in any event been undermined by subsequent Establishment Clause decisions, including *Witters v. Washington Dept. of Servs. for Blind* [*supra* Chapter 8], *Zobrest v. Catalina Foothills School Dist.*, 509 U.S. 1 (1993), and *Rosenberger v. Rector and Visitors of Univ. of Va.*, 515 U.S. 819 (1995).

Respondents counter that, because the costs of providing Title I services off-site were known at the time *Aguilar* was decided, and because the relevant case law has not changed, the District Court did not err in denying petitioners' motions. Obviously, if neither the law supporting our original decision in this litigation nor the facts have changed, there would be no need to decide the propriety of a Rule 60(b)(5) motion. Accordingly, we turn to the threshold issue whether the factual or legal landscape has changed since we decided *Aguilar*.

We agree with respondents that petitioners have failed to establish the significant change in factual conditions required by *Rufo*. Both petitioners and this Court were, at the time *Aguilar* was decided, aware that additional costs would be incurred if Title I services could not be provided in parochial school classrooms. That these predictions of additional costs turned out to be accurate does not constitute a change in factual conditions warranting relief under Rule 60(b)(5). Accord, *Rufo*, 502 U.S., at 385 ("Ordinarily . . . modification should not be granted where a party relies upon events that actually were anticipated at the time [the order was entered]").

We also agree with respondents that the statements made by five Justices in *Kiryas Joel* do not, in themselves, furnish a basis for concluding that our Establishment Clause jurisprudence has changed. In the course of our opinion, [f]ive Justices joined opinions calling for reconsideration of *Aguilar*. But the question of *Aguilar*'s propriety was not before us. The views of five Justices that the case should be reconsidered or overruled cannot be said to have effected a change in Establishment Clause law.

In light of these conclusions, petitioners' ability to satisfy the prerequisites of Rule 60(b)(5) hinges on whether our later Establishment Clause cases have so undermined *Aguilar* that it is no longer good law. We now turn to that inquiry.

III

A

In order to evaluate whether *Aguilar* has been eroded by our subsequent Establishment Clause cases, it is necessary to understand the rationale upon which *Aguilar*, as well as its companion case, *School Dist. of Grand Rapids v. Ball* rested.

In *Ball*, the Court evaluated two programs implemented by the School District of Grand Rapids, Michigan. The district's Shared Time program, the one most analogous to Title I, provided remedial and "enrichment" classes, at public expense, to students attending nonpublic schools. The classes were taught during regular school hours by publicly employed teachers, using materials purchased with public funds, on the premises of nonpublic schools. The Shared Time courses were in subjects designed to supplement the "core curriculum" of the nonpublic schools. Of the 41 nonpublic schools eligible for the program, 40 were "'pervasively sectarian'" in character — that is, "the purpos[e] of [those] schools [was] to advance their particular religions."

The Court conducted its analysis by applying the three-part test set forth in *Lemon v. Kurtzman*.

The Court acknowledged that the Shared Time program served a purely secular purpose, thereby satisfying the first part of the so-called *Lemon* test. Nevertheless, it ultimately concluded that the program had the impermissible effect of advancing religion.

The Court found that the program violated the Establishment Clause's prohibition against "government-financed or government-sponsored indoctrination into the beliefs of a particular religious faith" in at least three ways. First, drawing upon the analysis in *Meek v. Pittenger*, the Court observed that "the teachers participating in the programs may become involved in intentionally or inadvertently inculcating particular religious tenets or beliefs." *Meek* invalidated a Pennsylvania program in which full-time public employees provided supplemental "auxiliary services" — remedial and accelerated instruction, guidance counseling and testing, and speech and hearing services — to nonpublic school children at their schools. Although the auxiliary services themselves were secular, they were mostly dispensed on the premises of parochial schools, where "an atmosphere dedicated to the advancement of religious belief [was] constantly maintained." Instruction in that atmosphere was sufficient to create "[t]he potential for impermissible fostering of religion."

The Court concluded that Grand Rapids' program shared these defects. As in *Meek*, classes were conducted on the premises of religious schools. Accordingly, a majority found a "'substantial risk'" that teachers — even those who were not employed by the private schools — might "subtly (or overtly) conform their instruction to the [pervasively sectarian] environment in which they [taught]." The danger of "state-sponsored indoctrination" was only exacerbated by the school district's failure to monitor the courses for religious content. Notably, the Court disregarded the lack of evidence of any specific incidents of religious indoctrination as largely irrelevant, reasoning that potential witnesses to any indoctrination — the parochial school students, their parents, or parochial school officials — might be unable to detect or have little incentive to report the incidents.

The presence of public teachers on parochial school grounds had a second, related impermissible effect: It created a "graphic symbol of the 'concert or union or dependency' of church and state," especially when perceived by "children in their formative years." The Court feared that this perception of a symbolic union between church and state would "conve[y] a message of government endorsement . . . of religion" and thereby violate a "core purpose" of the Establishment Clause.

Third, the Court found that the Shared Time program impermissibly financed religious indoctrination by subsidizing "the primary religious mission of the institutions affected." The Court separated its prior decisions evaluating programs that aided the secular activities of religious institutions into two categories: those in which it concluded that the aid resulted in an effect that was "indirect, remote, or incidental" (and upheld the aid); and those in which it concluded that the aid resulted in "a direct and substantial advancement of the sectarian enterprise" (and invalidated the aid). In light of *Meek* and *Wolman,* Grand Rapids' program fell into the latter category. In those cases, the Court ruled that a state loan of instructional equipment and materials to parochial schools was an impermissible form of "direct aid" because it "advanced the primary, religion-oriented educational function of the sectarian school," by providing "in-kind" aid (*e.g.,* instructional materials) that could be used to teach religion and by freeing up money for religious indoctrination that the school would otherwise have devoted to secular education. Given the holdings in *Meek* and *Wolman,* the Shared Time program — which provided teachers as well as instructional equipment and materials — was surely invalid. The *Ball* Court likewise placed no weight on the fact that the program was provided to the student rather than to the school. Nor was the impermissible effect mitigated by the fact that the program only supplemented the courses offered by the parochial schools.

The New York City Title I program challenged in *Aguilar* closely resembled the Shared Time program struck down in *Ball,* but the Court found fault with an aspect of the Title I program not present in Ball: The Board had "adopted a system for monitoring the religious content of publicly funded Title I classes in the religious schools." Even though this monitoring system might prevent the Title I program from being used to inculcate religion, the Court concluded, as it had in *Lemon* and *Meek,* that the level of monitoring necessary to be "certain" that the program had an exclusively secular effect would "inevitably resul[t] in the excessive entanglement of church and state," thereby running afoul of *Lemon's* third prong. *Lemon* (invalidating Rhode Island program on entanglement grounds because "[a] comprehensive, discriminating, and continuing state surveillance will inevitably be required to ensure that th[e] restrictions [against indoctrination] are obeyed"); *Meek* (invalidating Pennsylvania program on entanglement grounds because excessive monitoring would be required for the State to be certain that public school officials do not inculcate religion). In the majority's view, New York City's Title I program suffered from the "same critical elements of entanglement" present in *Lemon* and *Meek*: the aid was provided "in a pervasively sectarian environment . . . in the form of teachers," requiring "ongoing inspection . . . to ensure the absence of a religious message." Such "pervasive monitoring by public authorities in the sectarian schools infringes precisely those Establishment Clause values at the root of the prohibition of excessive entanglement." The Court noted two further forms of entanglement inherent in New York City's Title I program: the "administrative cooperation" required to implement Title I services and the "dangers of political divisiveness" that might grow out of the day-to-day decisions public officials would have to make in order to provide Title I services.

Distilled to essentials, the Court's conclusion that the Shared Time program in *Ball* had the impermissible effect of advancing religion rested on three assumptions: (i) any public employee who works on the premises of a religious school is presumed to inculcate religion in her work; (ii) the presence of public employees on private school premises creates a symbolic union between church and state; and (iii) any and all public aid that directly aids the educational function of religious schools impermissibly finances religious indoctrination, even if the aid reaches such schools as a consequence of private decisionmaking. Additionally, in *Aguilar* there was a fourth assumption: that New York City's Title I program necessitated an excessive government entanglement with religion because public employees who teach on the premises of religious schools must be closely monitored to ensure that they do not inculcate religion.

B

Our more recent cases have undermined the assumptions upon which *Ball* and *Aguilar* relied. To be sure, the general principles we use to evaluate whether government aid violates the Establishment Clause have not changed since *Aguilar* was decided. For example, we continue to ask whether the government acted with the purpose of advancing or inhibiting religion, and the nature of that inquiry has remained largely unchanged. Likewise, we continue to explore whether the aid has the "effect" of advancing or inhibiting religion. What has changed since we decided *Ball* and *Aguilar* is our understanding of the criteria used to assess whether aid to religion has an impermissible effect.

1

As we have repeatedly recognized, government inculcation of religious beliefs has the impermissible effect of advancing religion. Our cases subsequent to *Aguilar* have, however, modified in two significant respects the approach we use to assess indoctrination. First, we have abandoned the presumption erected in *Meek* and *Ball* that the placement of public employees on parochial school grounds inevitably results in the impermissible effect of state-sponsored indoctrination or constitutes a symbolic union between government and religion. In *Zobrest v. Catalina Foothills School Dist.*, 509 U.S. 1 (1993), we examined whether the IDEA was constitutional as applied to a deaf student who sought to bring his state-employed sign-language interpreter with him to his Roman Catholic high school. We held that this was permissible, expressly disavowing the notion that "the Establishment Clause [laid] down [an] absolute bar to the placing of a public employee in a sectarian school." "Such a flat rule, smacking of antiquated notions of 'taint,' would indeed exalt form over substance." We refused to presume that a publicly employed interpreter would be pressured by the pervasively sectarian surroundings to inculcate religion by "add[ing] to [or] subtract[ing] from" the lectures translated. In the absence of evidence to the contrary, we assumed instead that the interpreter would dutifully discharge her responsibilities as a full-time public employee and comply with the ethical guidelines of her profession by accurately translating what was said. Because the only *government* aid in *Zobrest* was the interpreter, who was herself not inculcating any religious messages, no *government* indoctrination took place and we were able to conclude that "the provision of such assistance [was] not barred by the Establishment Clause." *Zobrest* therefore expressly rejected the notion — relied on in *Ball* and *Aguilar* — that, solely because of her presence on private school property, a public employee will be presumed to inculcate religion in the students. *Zobrest* also implicitly repudiated another assumption on which *Ball* and *Aguilar* turned: that the presence of a public employee on private school property creates an impermissible "symbolic link" between government and religion.

JUSTICE SOUTER contends that *Zobrest* did not undermine the "presumption of inculcation" erected in *Ball* and *Aguilar,* and that our conclusion to the contrary rests on a "mistaken reading" of *Zobrest*. In his view, *Zobrest* held that the Establishment Clause tolerates the presence of public employees in sectarian schools "only. . . in . . . limited circumstances" — *i.e.,* when the employee "simply translates for one student the material presented to the class for the benefit of all students." The sign-language interpreter in *Zobrest* is unlike the remedial instructors in *Ball* and *Aguilar* because signing, JUSTICE SOUTER explains, "[cannot] be understood as an opportunity to inject religious content in what [is] supposed to be secular instruction." He is thus able to conclude that *Zobrest* is distinguishable from — and therefore perfectly consistent with — *Ball* and *Aguilar*.

In *Zobrest*, however, we did not expressly or implicitly rely upon the basis JUSTICE SOUTER now advances for distinguishing *Ball* and *Aguilar*. If we had thought that signers had no "opportunity to inject religious content" into their translations, we would have had no reason to consult the record for evidence of inaccurate translations. The signer in *Zobrest* had the same opportunity to inculcate religion in the performance of her duties as do Title I employees, and there is no genuine basis upon which to confine *Zobrest*'s underlying rationale — that public employees will not be presumed to inculcate religion — to sign-language interpreters. Indeed, even the *Zobrest* dissenters acknowledged the shift *Zobrest* effected in our Establishment Clause law when they criticized the majority for "stray[ing] . . . from the course set by nearly five decades of Establishment Clause jurisprudence." (Blackmun, J., dissenting). Thus, it was *Zobrest* — and not this case — that created "fresh law." Our refusal to limit *Zobrest* to its facts despite its rationale does not, in our view, amount to a "misreading" of precedent.

Second, we have departed from the rule relied on in *Ball* that all government aid that directly aids the educational function of religious schools is invalid. In *Witters v. Washington Dept. of Servs. for Blind*, we held that the Establishment Clause did not bar a State from issuing a vocational tuition grant to a blind person who wished to use the grant to attend a Christian college and become a pastor, missionary, or youth director. Even though the grant recipient clearly would use the money to obtain religious education, we observed that the tuition grants were "'made available generally without regard to the sectarian-nonsectarian, or public-nonpublic nature of the institution benefited.'" The grants were disbursed directly to students, who then used the money to pay for tuition at the educational institution of their choice. In our view, this transaction was no different from a State's issuing a paycheck to one of its employees, knowing that the employee would donate part or all of the check to a religious institution. In both situations, any money that ultimately went to religious institutions did so "only as a result of the genuinely independent and private choices of" individuals. The same logic applied in *Zobrest*, where we allowed the State to provide an interpreter, even though she would be a mouthpiece for religious instruction, because the IDEA's neutral eligibility criteria ensured that the interpreter's presence in a sectarian school was a "result of the private decision of individual parents" and "[could] not be attributed to *state* decisionmaking." Because the private school would not have provided an interpreter on its own, we also concluded that the aid in *Zobrest* did not indirectly finance religious education by "reliev[ing] the sectarian schoo[l] of costs [it] otherwise would have borne in educating [its] students."

Zobrest and *Witters* make clear that, under current law, the Shared Time program in *Ball* and New York City's Title I program in *Aguilar* will not, as a matter of law, be deemed to have the effect of advancing religion through indoctrination. Indeed, each of the premises upon which we relied in *Ball* to reach a contrary conclusion is no longer valid. First, there is no reason to presume that, simply because she enters a parochial school classroom, a full-time public employee such as a Title I teacher will depart from her assigned duties and instructions and embark on religious indoctrination, any more than there was a reason in *Zobrest* to think an interpreter would inculcate religion by altering her translation of classroom lectures. Certainly, no evidence has ever shown that any New York City Title I instructor teaching on parochial school premises attempted to inculcate religion in students. Thus, both our precedent and our experience require us to reject respondents' remarkable argument that we must presume Title I instructors to be "uncontrollable and sometimes very unprofessional."

As discussed above, *Zobrest* also repudiates *Ball*'s assumption that the presence of Title I teachers in parochial school classrooms will, without more, create the impression of a "symbolic union" between church and state. JUSTICE SOUTER maintains that *Zobrest* is not dispositive on this point because *Aguilar*'s implicit conclusion that New York City's Title I program created a "symbolic union" rested on more than the presence of Title I employees on parochial school grounds. To him, Title I continues to foster a "symbolic union" between the Board and sectarian schools because it mandates "the involvement of public teachers in the instruction provided within sectarian schools," and "fus[es] public and private faculties." JUSTICE SOUTER does not disavow the notion, uniformly adopted by lower courts, that Title I services may be provided to sectarian school students in off-campus locations, even though that notion necessarily presupposes that the danger of "symbolic union" evaporates once the services are provided off-campus. Taking this view, the only difference between a constitutional program and an unconstitutional one is the location of the classroom, since the degree of cooperation between Title I instructors and parochial school faculty is the same no matter where the services are provided. We do not see any perceptible (let alone dispositive) difference in the degree of symbolic union between a student receiving remedial instruction in a classroom on his sectarian school's campus and one receiving instruction in a van parked just at the school's curbside. To draw this line based solely on the location of the public employee is neither "sensible" nor "sound," and the Court in *Zobrest* rejected it.

Nor under current law can we conclude that a program placing full-time public employees on parochial campuses to provide Title I instruction would impermissibly finance religious indoctrination. In all relevant respects, the provision of instructional services under Title I is indistinguishable from the provision of sign-language interpreters under the IDEA. Both programs make aid available only to eligible recipients. That aid is provided to students at whatever school they choose to attend. Although Title I instruction is provided to several students at once, whereas an interpreter provides translation to a single student, this distinction is not constitutionally significant. Moreover, as in *Zobrest*, Title I services are by law supplemental to the regular curricula. These services do not, therefore, "reliev[e] sectarian schools of costs they otherwise would have borne in educating their students."

JUSTICE SOUTER finds our conclusion that the IDEA and Title I programs are similar to be "puzzling," and points to three differences he perceives between the programs: (i) Title I services are distributed by LEA's "directly to the religious schools" instead of to individual students pursuant to a formal application process; (ii) Title I services "necessarily reliev[e] a religious school of 'an expense that it otherwise would have assumed'"; and (iii) Title I provides services to more students than did the programs in *Witters* and *Zobrest*. None of these distinctions is meaningful. While it is true that individual students may not directly apply for Title I services, it does not follow from this premise that those services are distributed "directly to the religious schools." In fact, they are not. No Title I funds ever reach the coffers of religious schools, and Title I services may not be provided to religious schools on a school-wide basis. Title I funds are instead distributed to a *public* agency (an LEA) that dispenses services directly to the eligible students within its boundaries, no matter where they choose to attend school. Moreover, we fail to see how providing Title I services directly to eligible students results in a greater financing of religious indoctrination simply because those students are not first required to submit a formal application.

We are also not persuaded that Title I services supplant the remedial instruction and guidance counseling already provided in New York City's sectarian schools. Although JUSTICE SOUTER maintains that the sectarian schools provide such services and that those schools reduce those services once their students begin to receive Title I instruction, his claims rest on speculation about the impossibility of drawing any line between supplemental and general education, and not on any evidence in the record that the Board is in fact violating Title I regulations by providing services that supplant those offered in the sectarian schools. We are unwilling to speculate that all sectarian schools provide remedial instruction and guidance counseling to their students, and are unwilling to presume that the Board would violate Title I regulations by continuing to provide Title I services to students who attend a sectarian school that has curtailed its remedial instruction program in response to Title I. Nor are we willing to conclude that the constitutionality of an aid program depends on the number of sectarian school students who happen to receive the otherwise neutral aid. *Zobrest* did not turn on the fact that James Zobrest had, at the time of litigation, been the only child using a publicly funded sign-language interpreter to attend a parochial school. Accord, *Mueller v. Allen* ("We would be loath to adopt a rule grounding the constitutionality of a facially neutral law on annual reports reciting the extent to which various classes of private citizens claimed benefits under the law").

What is most fatal to the argument that New York City's Title I program directly subsidizes religion is that it applies with equal force when those services are provided off-campus, and *Aguilar* implied that providing the services off-campus is entirely consistent with the Establishment Clause. JUSTICE SOUTER resists the impulse to upset this implication, contending that it can be justified on the ground that Title I services are "less likely to supplant some of what would otherwise go on inside [the sectarian schools] and to subsidize what remains" when those services are offered off campus. But JUSTICE SOUTER does not explain why a sectarian school would not have the same incentive to "make patently significant cut- backs" in its curriculum no matter where Title I services are offered, since the school would ostensibly be excused from having to provide the Title I-type services itself. Because the incentive is the same either way, we find no logical basis upon which to conclude that Title I services are an impermissible subsidy of religion when offered on-campus, but not when offered off-campus. Accordingly, contrary to our conclusion in *Aguilar*, placing full-time employees on parochial school campuses does not as a matter of law have the impermissible effect of advancing religion through indoctrination.

2

Although we examined in *Witters* and *Zobrest* the criteria by which an aid program identifies its beneficiaries, we did so solely to assess whether any use of that aid to indoctrinate religion could be attributed to the State. A number of our Establishment Clause cases have found that the criteria used for identifying beneficiaries are relevant in a second respect, apart from enabling a court to evaluate whether the program subsidizes religion. Specifically, the criteria might themselves have the effect of advancing religion by creating a financial incentive to undertake religious indoctrination. *Cf. Witters* (upholding neutrally available program because it did not "creat[e a] financial incentive for students to undertake sectarian education"); *Zobrest* (upholding neutrally available IDEA aid because it "creates no financial incentive for parents to choose a sectarian school"). This incentive is not present, however, where the aid is allocated on the basis of neutral, secular criteria that neither favor nor disfavor religion, and is made available to both religious and secular beneficiaries on a nondiscriminatory basis. Under such circumstances, the aid is less likely to have the effect of advancing religion. *See Widmar v. Vincent* ("The provision of benefits to so broad a spectrum of groups is an important index of secular effect").

In *Ball* and *Aguilar*, the Court gave this consideration no weight. Before and since those decisions, we have sustained programs that provided aid to *all* eligible children regardless of where they attended school. *See, e.g., Everson v. Board of Ed. of Ewing* (sustaining local ordinance authorizing all parents to deduct from their state tax returns the costs of transporting their children to school on public buses); *Board of Ed. of Central School Dist. No. 1 v. Allen* (sustaining New York law loaning secular textbooks to all children); *Mueller v. Allen* (sustaining Minnesota statute allowing all parents to deduct actual costs of tuition, textbooks, and transportation from state tax returns); *Witters* (sustaining Washington law granting all eligible blind persons vocational assistance); *Zobrest* (sustaining section of IDEA providing all "disabled" children with necessary aid).

Applying this reasoning to New York City's Title I program, it is clear that Title I services are allocated on the basis of criteria that neither favor nor disfavor religion. The services are available to all children who meet the Act's eligibility requirements, no matter what their religious beliefs or where they go to school. The Board's program does not, therefore, give aid recipients any incentive to modify their religious beliefs or practices in order to obtain those services.

3

We turn now to *Aguilar*'s conclusion that New York City's Title I program resulted in an excessive entanglement between church and state. Whether a government aid program results in such an entanglement has consistently been an aspect of our Establishment Clause analysis. We have considered entanglement both in the course of assessing whether an aid program has an impermissible effect of advancing religion, and as a factor separate and apart from "effect." Regardless of how we have characterized the issue, however, the factors we use to assess whether an entanglement is "excessive" are similar to the factors we use to examine "effect." That is, to assess entanglement, we have looked to "the character and purposes of the institutions that are benefited, the nature of the aid that the State provides, and the resulting relationship between the government and religious authority." Similarly, we have assessed a law's "effect" by examining the character of the institutions benefited (*e.g.,* whether the religious institutions were "predominantly religious"), and the nature of the aid that the State provided (*e.g.,* whether it was neutral and nonideological). Indeed, in *Lemon* itself, the entanglement that the Court found "independently" to necessitate the program's invalidation also was found to have the effect of inhibiting religion. Thus, it is simplest to recognize why entanglement is significant and treat it — as we did in *Walz* — as an aspect of the inquiry into a statute's effect.

Not all entanglements, of course, have the effect of advancing or inhibiting religion. Interaction between church and state is inevitable, and we have always tolerated some level of involvement between the two. Entanglement must be "excessive" before it runs afoul of the Establishment Clause.

The pre-*Aguilar* Title I program does not result in an "excessive" entanglement that advances or inhibits religion. As discussed previously, the Court's finding of "excessive" entanglement in *Aguilar* rested on three grounds: (i) the program would require "pervasive monitoring by public authorities" to ensure that Title I employees did not inculcate religion; (ii) the program required "administrative cooperation" between the Board and parochial schools; and (iii) the program might increase the dangers of "political divisiveness." Under our current understanding of the Establishment Clause, the last two considerations are insufficient by themselves to create an "excessive" entanglement. They are present no matter where Title I services are offered, and no court has held that Title I services cannot be offered off-campus. Further, the assumption underlying the first consideration has been undermined. In *Aguilar,* the Court presumed that full-time public employees on parochial school grounds would be tempted to inculcate religion, despite the ethical standards they were required to uphold. Because of this risk *pervasive* monitoring would be required. But after *Zobrest* we no longer presume that public employees will inculcate religion simply because they happen to be in a sectarian environment. Since we have abandoned the assumption that properly instructed public employees will fail to discharge their duties faithfully, we must also discard the assumption that *pervasive* monitoring of Title I teachers is required. There is no suggestion in the record before us that unannounced monthly visits of public supervisors are insufficient to prevent or to detect inculcation of religion by public employees. Moreover, we have not found excessive entanglement in cases in which States imposed far more onerous burdens on religious institutions than the monitoring system at issue here.

To summarize, New York City's Title I program does not run afoul of any of three primary criteria we currently use to evaluate whether government aid has the effect of advancing religion: it does not result in governmental indoctrination; define its recipients by reference to religion; or create an excessive entanglement. We therefore hold that a federally funded program providing supplemental, remedial instruction to disadvantaged children on a neutral basis is not invalid under the Establishment Clause when such instruction is given on the premises of sectarian schools by government employees pursuant to a program containing safeguards such as those present here. The same considerations that justify this holding require us to conclude that this carefully constrained program also cannot reasonably be viewed as an endorsement of religion. Accordingly, we must acknowledge that *Aguilar,* as well as the portion of *Ball* addressing Grand Rapids' Shared Time program, are no longer good law.

C

The doctrine of *stare decisis* does not preclude us from recognizing the change in our law and overruling *Aguilar* and those portions of *Ball* inconsistent with our more recent decisions. As we have often noted, "[s]*tare decisis* is not an inexorable command," but instead reflects a policy judgment that "in most matters it is more important that the applicable rule of law be settled than that it be settled right," That policy is at its weakest when we interpret the Constitution because our interpretation can be altered only by constitutional amendment or by overruling our prior decisions. Thus, we have held in several cases that *stare decisis* does not prevent us from overruling a previous decision where there has been a significant change in or subsequent development of our constitutional law. As discussed above, our Establishment Clause jurisprudence has changed significantly since we decided *Ball* and *Aguilar*, so our decision to overturn those cases rests on far more than "a present doctrinal disposition to come out differently from the Court of [1985]." We therefore overrule *Ball* and *Aguilar* to the extent those decisions are inconsistent with our current understanding of the Establishment Clause.

Nor does the "law of the case" doctrine place any additional constraints on our ability to overturn *Aguilar*. Under this doctrine, a court should not reopen issues decided in earlier stages of the same litigation. The doctrine does not apply if the court is "convinced that [its prior decision] is clearly erroneous and would work a manifest injustice." In light of our conclusion that *Aguilar* would be decided differently under our current Establishment Clause law, we think adherence to that decision would undoubtedly work a "manifest injustice," such that the law of the case doctrine does not apply.

IV

We therefore conclude that our Establishment Clause law has "significant[ly] change[d]" since we decided *Aguilar*. *See Rufo*, 502 U.S., at 384. We are only left to decide whether this change in law entitles petitioners to relief under Rule 60(b)(5). We conclude that it does. Our general practice is to apply the rule of law we announce in a case to the parties before us. We adhere to this practice even when we overrule a case.

We do not acknowledge, and we do not hold, that other courts should conclude our more recent cases have, by implication, overruled an earlier precedent. We reaffirm that "[i]f a precedent of this Court has direct application in a case, yet appears to rest on reasons rejected in some other line of decisions, the Court of Appeals should follow the case which directly controls, leaving to this Court the prerogative of overruling its own decisions." *Rodriguez de Quijas*, 490 U.S., at 484. Adherence to this teaching by the District Court and Court of Appeals in this case does not insulate a legal principle on which they relied from our review to determine its continued vitality. The trial court acted within its discretion in entertaining the motion with supporting allegations, but it was also correct to recognize that the motion had to be denied unless and until this Court reinterpreted the binding precedent.

Respondents and JUSTICE GINSBURG urge us to adopt a different analysis because we are reviewing the District Court's denial of petitioners' Rule 60(b)(5) motion for an abuse of discretion. It is true that the trial court has discretion, but the exercise of discretion cannot be permitted to stand if we find it rests upon a legal principle that can no longer be sustained. The standard of review we employ in this litigation does not therefore require us to depart from our general practice.

Respondents nevertheless contend that we should not grant Rule 60(b)(5) relief here, in spite of its propriety in other contexts. They contend that petitioners have used Rule 60(b)(5) in an unprecedented way — not as a means of *recognizing* changes in the law, but as a vehicle for *effecting* them. If we were to sanction this use of Rule 60(b)(5), respondents argue, we would encourage litigants to burden the federal courts with a deluge of Rule 60(b)(5) motions premised on nothing more than the claim that various judges or Justices have stated that the law has changed. See also post (GINSBURG, J., dissenting) (contending that granting Rule 60(b)(5) relief in this case will encourage "invitations to reconsider old cases based on 'speculat[ions] on chances from changes in [the Court's membership]'"). We think their fears are overstated. As we noted above, a judge's stated belief that a case should be overruled does not make it so.

Most importantly, our decision today is intimately tied to the context in which it arose. This litigation involves a party's request under Rule 60(b)(5) to vacate a continuing injunction entered some years ago in light of a bona fide, significant change in subsequent law. The clause of Rule 60(b)(5) that petitioners invoke applies by its terms only to "judgment[s] hav[ing] prospective application." Intervening developments in the law by themselves rarely constitute the extraordinary circumstances required for relief under Rule 60(b)(6), the only remaining avenue for relief on this basis from judgments lacking any prospective component. Our decision will have no effect outside the context of ordinary civil litigation where the propriety of continuing prospective relief is at issue. Given that Rule 60(b)(5) specifically contemplates the grant of relief in the circumstances presented here, it can hardly be said that we have somehow warped the Rule into a means of "allowing an 'anytime' rehearing."

Respondents further contend that "[p]etitioners' [p]roposed [u]se of Rule 60(b) [w]ill [e]rode the [i]nstitutional [i]ntegrity of the Court." Respondents do not explain how a proper application of Rule 60(b)(5) undermines our legitimacy. Instead, respondents focus on the harm occasioned if we were to overrule *Aguilar*. But as discussed above, we do no violence to the doctrine of *stare decisis* when we recognize bona fide changes in our decisional law. And in those circumstances, we do no violence to the legitimacy we derive from reliance on that doctrine.

As a final matter, we see no reason to wait for a "better vehicle" in which to evaluate the impact of subsequent cases on *Aguilar*'s continued vitality. To evaluate the Rule 60(b)(5) motion properly before us today in no way undermines "integrity in the interpretation of procedural rules" or signals any departure from "the responsive, non-agenda-setting character of this Court." Indeed, under these circumstances, it would be particularly inequitable for us to bide our time waiting for another case to arise while the city of New York labors under a continuing injunction forcing it to spend millions of dollars on mobile instructional units and leased sites when it could instead be spending that money to give economically disadvantaged children a better chance at success in life by means of a program that is perfectly consistent with the Establishment Clause.

JUSTICE SOUTER, with whom JUSTICE STEVENS and JUSTICE GINSBURG join, and with whom JUSTICE BREYER joins as to Part II, dissenting.

In this novel proceeding, petitioners seek relief from an injunction the District Court entered 12 years ago to implement our decision in *Aguilar v. Felton*, 473 U.S. 402 (1985). For the reasons given by JUSTICE GINSBURG, the Court's holding that petitioners are entitled to relief under Rule 60(b) is seriously mistaken. The Court's misapplication of the rule is tied to its equally erroneous reading of our more recent Establishment Clause cases, which the Court describes as having rejected the underpinnings of *Aguilar* and portions of *Aguilar*'s companion case, *School Dist. of Grand Rapids v. Ball*. The result is to repudiate the very reasonable line drawn in *Aguilar* and *Ball*, and to authorize direct state aid to religious institutions on an unparalleled scale, in violation of the Establishment Clause's central prohibition against religious subsidies by the government.

I respectfully dissent.

I

In both *Aguilar* and *Ball*, we held that supplemental instruction by public school teachers on the premises of religious schools during regular school hours violated the Establishment Clause. *Aguilar*, of course, concerned the very school system before us here and the same Title I program at issue now, under which local educational agencies receive public funds to provide remedial education, guidance and job counseling to eligible students including those attending religious schools. Immediately before *Aguilar*, New York City used Title I funds to provide guidance services and classes in remedial reading, remedial mathematics, and English as a second language to students at religious schools, as it did by sending employees of the public school system, including teachers, guidance counselors, psychologists, and social workers into the religious schools. *Ball* involved a program similar in many respects to Title I called Shared Time, under which the local school district provided religious school students with "supplementary" classes in their religious schools, taught by teachers who were full-time employees of the public schools, in subjects including remedial math and reading, art, music, and physical education.

We held that both schemes ran afoul of the Establishment Clause. The Shared Time program had the impermissible effect of promoting religion in three ways: first, state-paid teachers conducting classes in a sectarian environment might inadvertently (or intentionally) manifest sympathy with the sectarian aims to the point of using public funds for religious educational purposes; second, the government's provision of secular instruction in religious schools produced a symbolic union of church and state that tended to convey a message to students and to the public that the State supported religion; and, finally, the Shared Time program subsidized the religious functions of the religious schools by assuming responsibility for teaching secular subjects the schools would otherwise be required to provide. Our decision in *Aguilar* noted the similarity between the Title I and Shared Time programs, and held that the system New York City had adopted to monitor the religious content of Title I classes held in religious schools would necessarily result in excessive entanglement of church and state, and violate the Establishment Clause for that reason.

As I will indicate as I go along, I believe *Aguilar* was a correct and sensible decision, and my only reservation about its opinion is that the emphasis on the excessive entanglement produced by monitoring religious instructional content obscured those facts that independently called for the application of two central tenets of Establishment Clause jurisprudence. The State is forbidden to subsidize religion directly and is just as surely forbidden to act in any way that could reasonably be viewed as religious endorsement.

As is explained elsewhere, the flat ban on subsidization antedates the Bill of Rights and has been an unwavering rule in Establishment Clause cases, qualified only by the conclusion two Terms ago that state exactions from college students are not the sort of public revenues subject to the ban. *See Rosenberger v. Rector and Visitors of Univ. of Va.,* 515 U.S. 819 (1995) (SOUTER, J., dissenting). The rule expresses the hard lesson learned over and over again in the American past and in the experiences of the countries from which we have come, that religions supported by governments are compromised just as surely as the religious freedom of dissenters is burdened when the government supports religion. "When the government favors a particular religion or sect, the disadvantage to all others is obvious, but even the favored religion may fear being 'taint[ed] . . . with corrosive secularism.' The favored religion may be compromised as political figures reshape the religion's beliefs for their own purposes; it may be reformed as government largesse brings government regulation." *Lee v. Weisman* (Blackmun, J., concurring); *see also* MEMORIAL AND REMONSTRANCE AGAINST RELIGIOUS ASSESSMENTS 1785, *in* THE COMPLETE MADISON 299, 309 (S. Padover ed. 1953) ("Religion flourishes in greater purity, without than with the aid of Gov[ernment]"); M. HOWE, THE GARDEN AND THE WILDERNESS 6 (1965) (noting Roger Williams's view that "worldly corruptions . . . might consume the churches if sturdy fences against the wilderness were not maintained"). The ban against state endorsement of religion addresses the same historical lessons. Governmental approval of religion tends to reinforce the religious message (at least in the short run) and, by the same token, to carry a message of exclusion to those of less favored views. The human tendency, of course, is to forget the hard lessons, and to overlook the history of governmental partnership with religion when a cause is worthy, and bureaucrats have programs. That tendency to forget is the reason for having the Establishment Clause (along with the Constitution's other structural and libertarian guarantees), in the hope of stopping the corrosion before it starts.

What was significant in *Aguilar* and *Ball* about the placement of state-paid teachers into the physical and social settings of the religious schools was not only the consequent temptation of some of those teachers to reflect the schools' religious missions in the rhetoric of their instruction, with a resulting need for monitoring and the certainty of entanglement. What was so remarkable was that the schemes in issue assumed a teaching responsibility indistinguishable from the responsibility of the schools themselves. The obligation of primary and secondary schools to teach reading necessarily extends to teaching those who are having a hard time at it, and the same is true of math. Calling some classes remedial does not distinguish their subjects from the schools' basic subjects, however inadequately the schools may have been addressing them.

What was true of the Title I scheme as struck down in *Aguilar* will be just as true when New York reverts to the old practices with the Court's approval after today. There is simply no line that can be drawn between the instruction paid for at taxpayers' expense and the instruction in any subject that is not identified as formally religious. While it would be an obvious sham, say, to channel cash to religious schools to be credited only against the expense of "secular" instruction, the line between "supplemental" and general education is likewise impossible to draw. If a State may constitutionally enter the schools to teach in the manner in question, it must in constitutional principle be free to assume, or assume payment for, the entire cost of instruction provided in any ostensibly secular subject in any religious school. This Court explicitly recognized this in *Ball*, and although in *Aguilar* the Court concentrated on entanglement it noted the similarity to *Ball*, and Judge Friendly's opinion for the Second Circuit made it expressly clear that there was no stopping place in principle once the public teacher entered the religious schools to teach their secular subjects.

It may be objected that there is some subsidy in remedial education even when it takes place off the religious premises, some subsidy, that is, even in the way New York City has administered the Title I program after *Aguilar*. In these circumstances, too, what the State does, the religious school need not do; the schools save money and the program makes it easier for them to survive and concentrate their resources on their religious objectives. This argument may, of course, prove too much, but if it is not thought strong enough to bar even off-premises aid in teaching the basics to religious school pupils (an issue not before the Court in *Aguilar* or today), it does nothing to undermine the sense of drawing a line between remedial teaching on and off premises. The off-premises teaching is arguably less likely to open the door to relieving religious schools of their responsibilities for secular subjects simply because these schools are less likely (and presumably legally unable) to dispense with those subjects from their curriculums or to make patently significant cut-backs in basic teaching within the schools to offset the outside instruction; if the aid is delivered outside of the schools, it is less likely to supplant some of what would otherwise go on inside them and to subsidize what remains. On top of that, the difference in the degree of reasonably perceptible endorsement is substantial. Sharing the teaching responsibilities within a school having religious objectives is far more likely to telegraph approval of the school's mission than keeping the State's distance would do. This is clear at every level. As the Court observed in *Ball*, "[t]he symbolism of a union between church and state [effected by placing the public school teachers into the religious schools] is most likely to influence children of tender years, whose experience is limited and whose beliefs consequently are the function of environment as much as of free and voluntary choice." When, moreover, the aid goes overwhelmingly to one religious denomination, minimal contact between state and church is the less likely to feed the resentment of other religions that would like access to public money for their own worthy projects.

In sum, if a line is to be drawn short of barring all state aid to religious schools for teaching standard subjects, the *Aguilar-Ball* line was a sensible one capable of principled adherence. It is no less sound, and no less necessary, today.

II

The Court today ignores this doctrine and claims that recent cases rejected the elemental assumptions underlying *Aguilar* and much of *Ball*. But the Court errs. Its holding that *Aguilar* and the portion of *Ball* addressing the Shared Time program are "no longer good law," rests on mistaken reading.

A

Zobrest v. Catalina Foothills School Dist. held that the Establishment Clause does not prevent a school district from providing a sign-language interpreter to a deaf student enrolled in a sectarian school. The Court today relies solely on *Zobrest* to support its contention that we have "abandoned the presumption erected in *Meek* [v. *Pittenger*] and *Ball* that the placement of public employees on parochial school grounds inevitably results in the impermissible effect of state-sponsored indoctrination or constitutes a symbolic union between government and religion." *Zobrest*, however, is no such sanction for overruling *Aguilar* or any portion of *Ball*.

In *Zobrest* the Court did indeed recognize that the Establishment Clause lays down no absolute bar to placing public employees in a sectarian school, *Zobrest*, but the rejection of such a *per se* rule was hinged expressly on the nature of the employee's job, sign-language interpretation (or signing) and the circumscribed role of the signer. On this point (and without reference to the facts that the benefited student had received the same aid before enrolling in the religious school and the employee was to be assigned to the student not to the school) the Court explained itself this way: "[T]he task of a sign-language interpreter seems to us quite different from that of a teacher or guidance counselor. . . . Nothing in this record suggests that a sign-language interpreter would do more than accurately interpret whatever material is presented to the class as a whole. In fact, ethical guidelines require interpreters to 'transmit everything that is said in exactly the same way it was intended.'" The signer could thus be seen as more like a hearing aid than a teacher, and the signing could not be understood as an opportunity to inject religious content in what was supposed to be secular instruction. *Zobrest* accordingly holds only that in these limited circumstances where a public employee simply translates for one student the material presented to the class for the benefit of all students, the employee's presence in the sectarian school does not violate the Establishment Clause. *Cf. Lemon v. Kurtzman* ("[T]eachers have a substantially different ideological character from books [and] [i]n terms of potential for involving some aspect of faith or morals in secular subjects, a textbook's content is ascertainable, but a teacher's handling of a subject is not").

The Court, however, ignores the careful distinction drawn in *Zobrest* and insists that a full-time public employee such as a Title I teacher is just like the signer, asserting that "there is no reason to presume that, simply because she enters a parochial school classroom, . . . [this] teacher will depart from her assigned duties and instructions and embark on religious indoctrination. . . ." Whatever may be the merits of this position (and I find it short on merit), it does not enjoy the authority of *Zobrest*. The Court may disagree with *Ball*'s assertion that a publicly employed teacher working in a sectarian school is apt to reinforce the pervasive inculcation of religious beliefs, but its disagreement is fresh law.

The Court tries to press *Zobrest* into performing another service beyond its reach. The Court says that *Ball* and *Aguilar* assumed "that the presence of a public employee on private school property creates an impermissible 'symbolic link' between government and religion," and that *Zobrest* repudiated this assumption. First, *Ball* and *Aguilar* said nothing about the "mere presence" of public employees at religious schools. It was *Ball* that specifically addressed the point and held only that when teachers employed by public schools are placed in religious schools to provide instruction to students during the schoolday a symbolic union of church and state is created and will reasonably be seen by the students as endorsement; *Aguilar* adopted the same conclusion by reference. *Zobrest* did not, implicitly or otherwise, repudiate the view that the involvement of public teachers in the instruction provided within sectarian schools looks like a partnership or union and implies approval of the sectarian aim. On the subject of symbolic unions and the strength of their implications, the lesson of *Zobrest* is merely that less is less.

B

The Court next claims that *Ball* rested on the assumption that "any and all public aid that directly aids the educational function of religious schools impermissibly finances religious indoctrination, even if the aid reaches such schools as a consequence of private decisionmaking." After *Ball*, the opinion continues, the Court departed from the rule that "all government aid that directly aids the educational function of religious schools is invalid." But this mischaracterizes *Ball*'s discussion on the point, and misreads *Witters* and *Zobrest* as repudiating the more modest proposition on which *Ball* in fact rested.

Ball did not establish that "any and all" such aid to religious schools necessarily violates the Establishment Clause. It held that the Shared Time program subsidized the religious functions of the parochial schools by taking over a significant portion of their responsibility for teaching secular subjects. The Court noted that it had "never accepted the mere possibility of subsidization . . . as sufficient to invalidate an aid program," and instead enquired whether the effect of the proffered aid was "direct and substantial" (and, so, unconstitutional) or merely "indirect and incidental," (and, so, permissible) emphasizing that the question "is one of degree." *Witters* and *Zobrest* did nothing to repudiate the principle, emphasizing rather the limited nature of the aid at issue in each case as well as the fact that religious institutions did not receive it directly from the State. In *Witters*, the Court noted that the State would issue the disputed vocational aid directly to one student who would then transmit it to the school of his choice, and that there was no record evidence that "any significant portion of the aid expended under the Washington program as a whole will end up flowing to religious education." *Zobrest* also presented an instance of a single beneficiary, and emphasized that the student (who had previously received the interpretive services in a public school) determined where the aid would be used, that the aid at issue was limited, and that the religious school was "not relieved of an expense that it otherwise would have assumed in educating its students."

It is accordingly puzzling to find the Court insisting that the aid scheme administered under Title I and considered in *Aguilar* was comparable to the programs in *Witters* and *Zobrest*. Instead of aiding isolated individuals within a school system, New York City's Title I program before *Aguilar* served about 22,000 private school students, all but 52 of whom attended religious schools.[2] Instead of serving individual blind or deaf students, as such, Title I as administered in New York City before *Aguilar* (and as now to be revived) funded instruction in core subjects (remedial reading, reading skills, remedial mathematics, English as a second language) and provided guidance services. Instead of providing a service the school would not otherwise furnish, the Title I services necessarily relieved a religious school of "an expense that it otherwise would have assumed," and freed its funds for other, and sectarian uses.

Finally, instead of aid that comes to the religious school indirectly in the sense that its distribution results from private decisionmaking, a public educational agency distributes Title I aid in the form of programs and services directly to the religious schools. In *Zobrest* and *Witters*, it was fair to say that individual students were themselves applicants for individual benefits on a scale that could not amount to a systemic supplement. But under Title I, a local educational agency (which in New York City is the Board of Education) may receive federal funding by proposing programs approved to serve individ-

---

[2] The Court's refusal to recognize the extent of student participation as relevant to the constitutionality of an aid program ignores the contrary conclusion in *Witters* on this very point. *See* [*Witters*] (noting, among relevant factors, that "[n]o evidence ha[d] been presented indicating that any other person ha[d] ever sought to finance religious education or activity pursuant to the State's program").

ual students who meet the criteria of need, which it then uses to provide such programs at the religious schools; students eligible for such programs may not apply directly for Title I funds. The aid, accordingly, is not even formally aid to the individual students (and even formally individual aid must be seen as aid to a school system when so many individuals receive it that it becomes a significant feature of the system.

In sum, nothing since *Ball* and *Aguilar* and before this case has eroded the distinction between "direct and substantial" and "indirect and incidental." That principled line is being breached only here and now.

C

The Court notes that aid programs providing benefits solely to religious groups may be constitutionally suspect, while aid allocated under neutral, secular criteria is less likely to have the effect of advancing religion. The opinion then says that *Ball* and *Aguilar* "gave this consideration no weight," and accordingly conflict with a number of decisions. But what exactly the Court thinks *Ball* and *Aguilar* inadequately considered is not clear, given that evenhandedness is a necessary but not a sufficient condition for an aid program to satisfy constitutional scrutiny. Title I services are available to all eligible children regardless whether they go to religious or public schools, but, as I have explained elsewhere and am not alone in recognizing, that fact does not define the reach of the Establishment Clause. If a scheme of government aid results in support for religion in some substantial degree, or in endorsement of its value, the formal neutrality of the scheme does not render the Establishment Clause helpless or the holdings in *Aguilar* and *Ball* inapposite.

III

Finally, there is the issue of precedent. *Stare decisis* is no barrier in the Court's eyes because it reads *Aguilar* and *Ball* for exaggerated propositions that *Witters* and *Zobrest* are supposed to have limited to the point of abandoned doctrine. The Court's dispensation from *stare decisis* is, accordingly, no more convincing than its reading of those cases. Since *Aguilar* came down, no case has held that there need be no concern about a risk that publicly paid school teachers may further religious doctrine; no case has repudiated the distinction between direct and substantial aid and aid that is indirect and incidental; no case has held that fusing public and private faculties in one religious school does not create an impermissible union or carry an impermissible endorsement; and no case has held that direct subsidization of religious education is constitutional or that the assumption of a portion of a religious school's teaching responsibility is not direct subsidization.

The continuity of the law, indeed, is matched by the persistence of the facts. When *Aguilar* was decided everyone knew that providing Title I services off the premises of the religious schools would come at substantial cost in efficiency, convenience, and money. Title I had begun off the premises in New York, after all, and dissatisfaction with the arrangement was what led the City to put the public school teachers into the religious schools in the first place. When *Aguilar* required the end of that arrangement, conditions reverted to those of the past and they have remained unchanged: teaching conditions are often poor, it is difficult to move children around, and it costs a lot of money. That is, the facts became once again what they were once before, as everyone including the Members of this Court knew they would be. No predictions have gone so awry as to excuse the case from the claim of precedent, let alone excuse the Court from adhering to its own prior decision in this very litigation.

That is not to deny that the facts just recited are regrettable; the object of Title I is worthy without doubt, and the cost of compliance is high. In the short run there is much that is genuinely unfortunate about the administration of the scheme under *Aguilar*'s rule. But constitutional lines have to be drawn, and on one side of every one of them is an otherwise sympathetic case that provokes impatience with the Constitution and with the line. But constitutional lines are the price of constitutional government.

ZELMAN v. SIMMONS-HARRIS
536 U.S. 639 (2002)

CHIEF JUSTICE REHNQUIST delivered the opinion of the Court.

The State of Ohio has established a pilot program designed to provide educational choices to families with children who reside in the Cleveland City School District. The question presented is whether this program offends the Establishment Clause of the United States Constitution. We hold that it does not.

There are more than 75,000 children enrolled in the Cleveland City School District. The majority of these children are from low-income and minority families. Few of these families enjoy the means to send their children to any school other than an inner-city public school. For more than a generation, however, Cleveland's public schools have been among the worst performing public schools in the Nation. In 1995, a Federal District Court declared a crisis of magnitude and placed the entire Cleveland school district under state control. Shortly thereafter, the state auditor found that Cleveland's public schools were in the midst of a crisis that is perhaps unprecedented in the history of American education. Cleveland City School District Performance Audit 21 (Mar. 1996). The district had failed to meet any of the 18 state standards for minimal acceptable performance. Only 1 in 10 ninth graders could pass a basic proficiency examination, and students at all levels performed at a dismal rate compared with students in other Ohio public schools. More than two-thirds of high school students either dropped or failed out before graduation. Of those students who managed to reach their senior year, one of every four still failed to graduate. Of those students who did graduate, few could read, write, or compute at levels comparable to their counterparts in other cities.

It is against this backdrop that Ohio enacted, among other initiatives, its Pilot Project Scholarship Program. The program provides financial assistance to families in any Ohio school district that is or has been under federal court order requiring supervision and operational management of the district by the state superintendent. Cleveland is the only Ohio school district to fall within that category.

The program provides two basic kinds of assistance to parents of children in a covered district. First, the program provides tuition aid for students in kindergarten through third grade, expanding each year through eighth grade, to attend a participating public or private school of their parents choosing. Second, the program provides tutorial aid for students who choose to remain enrolled in public school.

The tuition aid portion of the program is designed to provide educational choices to parents who reside in a covered district. Any private school, whether religious or nonreligious, may participate in the program and accept program students so long as the school is located within the boundaries of a covered district and meets statewide educational standards. Participating private schools must agree not to discriminate on the basis of race, religion, or ethnic background, or to "advocate or foster unlawful behavior or teach hatred of any person or group on the basis of race, ethnicity, national origin, or religion." Any public school located in a school district adjacent to the covered district may also participate in the program. Adjacent public schools are eligible to receive a $2,250 tuition grant for each program student accepted in addition to the full amount of per-pupil state funding attributable to each additional student. All participating schools, whether public or private, are required to accept students in accordance with rules and procedures established by the state superintendent.

Tuition aid is distributed to parents according to financial need. Families with incomes below 200% of the poverty line are given priority and are eligible to receive 90% of private school tuition up to $2,250. For these lowest-income families, participating private schools may not charge a parental co-payment greater than $250. For all other families, the program pays 75% of tuition costs, up to $1,875, with no co-payment cap. These families receive tuition aid only if the number of available scholarships exceeds the number of low-income children who choose to participate. Where tuition aid is spent depends solely upon where parents who receive tuition aid choose to enroll their child. If parents choose a private school, checks are made payable to the parents who then endorse the checks over to the chosen school.

The tutorial aid portion of the program provides tutorial assistance through grants to any student in a covered district who chooses to remain in public school. Parents arrange for registered tutors to provide assistance to their children and then submit bills for those services to the State for payment. Students from low-income families receive 90% of the amount charged for such assistance up to $360. All other students receive 75% of that amount. The number of tutorial assistance grants offered to students in a covered district must equal the number of tuition aid scholarships provided to students enrolled at participating private or adjacent public schools.

The program has been in operation within the Cleveland City School District since the 1996-1997 school year. In the 1999-2000 school year, 56 private schools participated in the program, 46 (or 82%) of which had a religious affiliation. None of the public schools in districts adjacent to Cleveland have elected to participate. More than 3,700 students participated in the scholarship program, most of whom (96%) enrolled in religiously affiliated schools. Sixty percent of these students were from families at or below the poverty line. In the 1998-1999 school year, approximately 1,400 Cleveland public school students received tutorial aid. This number was expected to double during the 1999-2000 school year.

The program is part of a broader undertaking by the State to enhance the educational options of Cleveland's schoolchildren in response to the 1995 takeover. That undertaking includes programs governing community and magnet schools. Community schools are funded under state law but are run by their own school boards, not by local school districts. These schools enjoy academic independence to hire their own teachers and to determine their own curriculum. They can have no religious affiliation and are required to accept students by lottery. During the 1999-2000 school year, there were 10 start-up community schools in the Cleveland City School District with more than 1,900 students enrolled. For each child enrolled in a community school, the school receives state funding of $4,518, twice the funding a participating program school may receive.

Magnet schools are public schools operated by a local school board that emphasize a particular subject area, teaching method, or service to students. For each student enrolled in a magnet school, the school district receives $7,746, including state funding of $4,167, the same amount received per student enrolled at a traditional public school. As of 1999, parents in Cleveland were able to choose from among 23 magnet schools, which together enrolled more than 13,000 students in kindergarten through eighth grade. These schools provide specialized teaching methods, such as Montessori, or a particularized curriculum focus, such as foreign language, computers, or the arts.

In July 1999, respondents filed this action in United States District Court, seeking to enjoin the program on the ground that it violated the Establishment Clause of the United States Constitution. In December 2000, a divided panel of the Court of Appeals affirmed the judgment of the District Court, finding that the program had the primary effect of advancing religion in violation of the Establishment Clause.

The Establishment Clause of the First Amendment, applied to the States through the Fourteenth Amendment, prevents a State from enacting laws that have the purpose or effect of advancing or inhibiting religion. There is no dispute that the program challenged here was enacted for the valid secular purpose of providing educational assistance to poor children in a demonstrably failing public school system. Thus, the question presented is whether the Ohio program nonetheless has the forbidden effect of advancing or inhibiting religion.

To answer that question, our decisions have drawn a consistent distinction between government programs that provide aid directly to religious schools, *Mitchell v. Helms*; *Agostini, supra*; *Rosenberger v. Rector and Visitors of Univ. of Va.*, and programs of true private choice, in which government aid reaches religious schools only as a result of the genuine and independent choices of private individuals, *Mueller v. Allen*; *Witters v. Washington Dept. of Servs. for Blind*; *Zobrest v. Catalina Foothills School Dist.* While our jurisprudence with respect to the constitutionality of direct aid programs has changed significantly over the past two decades, our jurisprudence with respect to true private choice programs has remained consistent and unbroken. Three times we have confronted Establishment Clause challenges to neutral government programs that provide aid directly to a broad class of individuals, who, in turn, direct the aid to religious schools or institutions of their own choosing. Three times we have rejected such challenges.

[The Court then reviewed the holdings of *Mueller*, *Witters*, and *Zobrest*.]

Mueller, *Witters*, and *Zobrest* thus make clear that where a government aid program is neutral with respect to religion, and provides assistance directly to a broad class of citizens who, in turn, direct government aid to religious schools wholly as a result of their own genuine and independent private choice, the program is not readily subject to challenge under the Establishment Clause. A program that shares these features permits government aid to reach religious institutions only by way of the deliberate choices of numerous individual recipients. The incidental advancement of a religious mission, or the perceived endorsement of a religious message, is reasonably attributable to the individual recipient, not to the government, whose role ends with the disbursement of benefits.

We believe that the program challenged here is a program of true private choice, consistent with *Mueller*, *Witters*, and *Zobrest*, and thus constitutional. As was true in those cases, the Ohio program is neutral in all respects toward religion. It is part of a general and multifaceted undertaking by the State of Ohio to provide educational opportunities to the children of a failed school district. It confers educational assistance directly to a broad class of individuals defined without reference to religion, *i.e.*, any parent of a school-age child who resides in the Cleveland City School District. The program permits the participation of *all* schools within the district, religious or nonreligious. Adjacent public schools also may participate and have a financial incentive to do so. Program benefits are available to participating families on neutral terms, with no reference to religion. The only preference stated anywhere in the program is a preference for low-income families, who receive greater assistance and are given priority for admission at participating schools.

There are no "financial incentive[s] that ske[w] the program toward religious schools." *Witters*. Such incentives "[are] not present where the aid is allocated on the basis of neutral, secular criteria that neither favor nor disfavor religion, and is made available to both religious and secular beneficiaries on a nondiscriminatory basis." *Agostini*. The program here in fact creates financial *disincentives* for religious schools, with private schools receiving only half the government assistance given to community schools and one-third the assistance given to magnet schools. Adjacent public schools, should any choose to accept program students, are also eligible to receive two to three times the state funding of a private religious school. Families too have a financial disincentive to choose a private religious school over other schools. Parents that choose to participate in the scholarship program and then to enroll their children in a private school (religious or nonreligious) must copay a portion of the school's tuition. Families that choose a community school, magnet school, or traditional public school pay nothing. Although such features of the program are not necessary to its constitutionality, they clearly dispel the claim that the program "creates . . . financial incentive[s] for parents to choose a sectarian school." *Zobrest*.

Respondents suggest that even without a financial incentive for parents to choose a religious school, the program creates a public perception that the State is endorsing religious practices and beliefs. But we have repeatedly recognized that no reasonable observer would think a neutral program of private choice, where state aid reaches religious schools solely as a result of the numerous independent decisions of private individuals, carries with it the *imprimatur* of government endorsement. The argument is particularly misplaced here since the reasonable observer in the endorsement inquiry must be deemed aware of the history and context underlying a challenged program. Any objective observer familiar with the full history and context of the Ohio program would reasonably view it as one aspect of a broader undertaking to assist poor children in failed schools, not as an endorsement of religious schooling in general.

There also is no evidence that the program fails to provide genuine opportunities for Cleveland parents to select secular educational options for their school-age children. Cleveland schoolchildren enjoy a range of educational choices: They may remain in public school as before, remain in public school with publicly funded tutoring aid, obtain a scholarship and choose a religious school, obtain a scholarship and choose a nonreligious private school, enroll in a community school, or enroll in a magnet school. That 46 of the 56 private schools now participating in the program are religious schools does not condemn it as a violation of the Establishment Clause. The Establishment Clause question is whether Ohio is coercing parents into sending their children to religious schools, and that question must be answered by evaluating *all* options Ohio provides Cleveland schoolchildren, only one of which is to obtain a program scholarship and then choose a religious school.

JUSTICE SOUTER speculates that because more private religious schools currently participate in the program, the program itself must somehow discourage the participation of private nonreligious schools. But Cleveland's preponderance of religiously affiliated private schools certainly did not arise as a result of the program; it is a phenomenon common to many American cities. Indeed, by all accounts the program has captured a remarkable cross-section of private schools, religious and nonreligious. It is true that 82% of Cleveland's participating private schools are religious schools, but it is also true that 81% of private schools in Ohio are religious schools. To attribute constitutional significance to this figure, moreover, would lead to the absurd result that a neutral school-choice program might be permissible in some parts of Ohio, such as Columbus, where a lower percentage of private schools are religious schools, but not in inner-city Cleveland, where Ohio has deemed such programs most sorely needed, but where the preponderance of religious schools happens to be greater. *Cf.* Brief for State of Florida et al. as *Amici Curiae* 17 ([T]he percentages of sectarian to nonsectarian private schools within Florida's 67 school districts vary from zero to 100 percent). Likewise, an identical private choice program might be constitutional in some States, such as Maine or Utah, where less than 45% of private schools are religious schools, but not in other States, such as Nebraska or Kansas, where over 90% of private schools are religious schools.

Respondents and JUSTICE SOUTER claim that even if we do not focus on the number of participating schools that are religious schools, we should attach constitutional significance to the fact that 96% of scholarship recipients have enrolled in religious schools. They claim that this alone proves parents lack genuine choice, even if no parent has ever said so. We need not consider this argument in detail, since it was flatly rejected in *Mueller*, where we found it irrelevant that 96% of parents taking deductions for tuition expenses paid tuition at religious schools. Indeed, we have recently found it irrelevant even to the constitutionality of a direct aid program that a vast majority of program benefits went to religious schools. *See Agostini*; see also *Mitchell*. The constitutionality of a neutral educational aid program simply does not turn on whether and why, in a particular area, at a particular time, most private schools are run by religious organizations, or most recipients choose to use the aid at a religious school. As we said in *Mueller*, "[s]uch an approach would scarcely provide the certainty that this field stands in need of, nor can we perceive principled standards by which such statistical evidence might be evaluated."

This point is aptly illustrated here. The 96% figure upon which respondents and JUSTICE SOUTER rely discounts entirely (1) the more than 1,900 Cleveland children enrolled in alternative community schools, (2) the more than 13,000 children enrolled in alternative magnet schools, and (3) the more than 1,400 children enrolled in traditional public schools with tutorial assistance. Including some or all of these children in the denominator of children enrolled in non-traditional schools during the 1999-2000 school year drops the percentage enrolled in religious schools from 96% to under 20%. The 96% figure also represents but a snapshot of one particular school year. In the 1997-1998 school year, by contrast, only 78% of scholarship recipients attended religious schools. The difference was attributable to two private nonreligious schools that had accepted 15% of all scholarship students electing instead to register as community schools, in light of larger per-pupil funding for community schools and the uncertain future of the scholarship program generated by this litigation. Many of the students enrolled in these schools as scholarship students remained enrolled as community school students, thus demonstrating the arbitrariness of counting one type of school but not the other to assess primary effect. In spite of repeated questioning from the Court at oral argument, respondents offered no convincing justification for their approach, which relies entirely on such arbitrary classifications.

Respondents finally claim that we should look to *Committee for Public Ed. & Religious Liberty v. Nyquist,* to decide these cases. We disagree for two reasons. First, the program in *Nyquist* was quite different from the program challenged here. *Nyquist* involved a New York program that gave a package of benefits exclusively to private schools and the parents of private school enrollees. Although the program was enacted for ostensibly secular purposes, we found that its function was "*unmistakably* to provide desired financial support for nonpublic, sectarian institutions." Its genesis, we said, was that private religious schools faced increasingly grave fiscal problems. The program thus provided direct money grants to religious schools. It provided tax benefits unrelated to the amount of money actually expended by any parent on tuition, ensuring a windfall to parents of children in religious schools. It similarly provided tuition reimbursements designed explicitly to "offe[r] . . . an incentive to parents to send their children to sectarian schools." Indeed, the program flatly prohibited the participation of any public school, or parent of any public school enrollee. Ohio's program shares none of these features.

Second, were there any doubt that the program challenged in *Nyquist* is far removed from the program challenged here, we expressly reserved judgment with respect to a case involving some form of public assistance (*e.g.*, scholarships) made available generally without regard to the sectarian-nonsectarian, or public-nonpublic nature of the institution benefited. That, of course, is the very question now before us, and it has since been answered, first in *Mueller*, then in *Witters*, and again in *Zobrest*. To the extent the scope of *Nyquist* has remained an open question in light of these later decisions, we now hold that *Nyquist* does not govern neutral educational assistance programs that, like the program here, offer aid directly to a broad class of individual recipients defined without regard to religion.

In sum, the Ohio program is entirely neutral with respect to religion. It provides benefits directly to a wide spectrum of individuals, defined only by financial need and residence in a particular school district. It permits such individuals to exercise genuine choice among options public and private, secular and religious. The program is therefore a program of true private choice. In keeping with an unbroken line of decisions rejecting challenges to similar programs, we hold that the program does not offend the Establishment Clause.

JUSTICE O'CONNOR, concurring.

I

These cases are different from prior indirect aid cases in part because a significant portion of the funds appropriated for the voucher program reach religious schools without restrictions on the use of these funds. The share of public resources that reach religious schools is not, however, as significant as respondents suggest. Data from the 1999-2000 school year indicate that 82 percent of schools participating in the voucher program were religious and that 96 percent of participating students enrolled in religious schools, but these data are incomplete. These statistics do not take into account all of the reasonable educational choices that may be available to students in Cleveland public schools. When one considers the option to attend community schools, the percentage of students enrolled in religious schools falls to 62.1 percent. If magnet schools are included in the mix, this percentage falls to 16.5 percent.

Even these numbers do not paint a complete picture. The Cleveland program provides voucher applicants from low-income families with up to $2,250 in tuition assistance and provides the remaining applicants with up to $1,875 in tuition assistance. In contrast, the State provides community schools $4,518 per pupil and magnet schools, on average, $7,097 per pupil. Even if one assumes that all voucher students came from low-income families and that each voucher student used up the entire $2,250 voucher, at most $8.2 million of public funds flowed to religious schools under the voucher program in 1999-2000. Although just over one-half as many students attended community schools as religious private schools on the state fisc, the State spent over $1 million more on students in community schools than on students in religious private schools because per-pupil aid to community schools is more than double the per-pupil aid to private schools under the voucher program. Moreover, the amount spent on religious private schools is minor compared to the $114.8 million the State spent on students in the Cleveland magnet schools.

Although $8.2 million is no small sum, it pales in comparison to the amount of funds that federal, state, and local governments already provide religious institutions. Religious organizations may qualify for exemptions from the federal corporate income tax; the corporate income tax in many States; and property taxes in all 50 States; and clergy qualify for a federal tax break on income used for housing expenses. In addition, the Federal Government provides individuals, corporations, trusts, and estates a tax deduction for charitable contributions to qualified religious groups. Finally, the Federal Government and certain state governments provide tax credits for educational expenses, many of which are spent on education at religious schools.

Most of these tax policies are well established, yet confer a significant relative benefit on religious institutions. The state property tax exemptions for religious institutions alone amount to very large sums annually. For example, available data suggest that Colorado's exemption lowers that States tax revenues by more than $40 million annually; Maryland's exemption lowers revenues by more than $60 million; Wisconsin's exemption lowers revenues by approximately $122 million; and Louisiana's exemption, looking just at the city of New Orleans, lowers revenues by over $36 million. As for the Federal Government, the tax deduction for charitable contributions reduces federal tax revenues by nearly $25 billion annually, and it is reported that over 60 percent of household charitable contributions go to religious charities. Even the relatively minor exemptions lower federal tax receipts by substantial amounts. The parsonage exemption, for example, lowers revenues by around $500 million.

These tax exemptions, which have "much the same effect as [cash grants] . . . of the amount of tax [avoided]," are just part of the picture. Federal dollars also reach religiously affiliated organizations through public health programs such as Medicare and Medicaid, through educational programs such as the Pell Grant program, and the G.I. Bill of Rights, and through child care programs such as the Child Care and Development Block Grant Program (CCDBG). These programs are well-established parts of our social welfare system, and can be quite substantial.

A significant portion of the funds appropriated for these programs reach religiously affiliated institutions, typically without restrictions on its subsequent use. For example, it has been reported that religious hospitals, which account for 18 percent of all hospital beds nationwide, rely on Medicare funds for 36 percent of their revenue. Moreover, taking into account both Medicare and Medicaid, religious hospitals received nearly $45 billion from the federal fisc in 1998. Federal aid to religious schools is also substantial. Although data for all States is not available, data from Minnesota, for example, suggest that a substantial share of Pell Grant and other federal funds for college tuition reach religious schools. Roughly one-third or $27.1 million of the federal tuition dollars spent on students at schools in Minnesota were used at private 4-year colleges. The vast majority of these funds — $23.5 million — flowed to religiously affiliated institutions.

Against this background, the support that the Cleveland voucher program provides religious institutions is neither substantial nor atypical of existing government programs. While this observation is not intended to justify the Cleveland voucher program under the Establishment Clause, it places in broader perspective alarmist claims about implications of the Cleveland program and the Courts decision in these cases.

JUSTICE STEVENS, dissenting.

Is a law that authorizes the use of public funds to pay for the indoctrination of thousands of grammar school children in particular religious faiths a "law respecting an establishment of religion" within the meaning of the First Amendment? In answering that question, I think we should ignore three factual matters that are discussed at length by my colleagues.

First, the severe educational crisis that confronted the Cleveland City School District when Ohio enacted its voucher program is not a matter that should affect our appraisal of its constitutionality. In the 1999-2000 school year, that program provided relief to less than five percent of the students enrolled in the district's schools. The solution to the disastrous conditions that prevented over 90 percent of the student body from meeting basic proficiency standards obviously required massive improvements unrelated to the voucher program. Of course, the emergency may have given some families a powerful motivation to leave the public school system and accept religious indoctrination that they would otherwise have avoided, but that is not a valid reason for upholding the program.

Second, the wide range of choices that have been made available to students *within the public school system* has no bearing on the question whether the State may pay the tuition for students who wish to reject public education entirely and attend private schools that will provide them with a sectarian education. The fact that the vast majority of the voucher recipients who have entirely rejected public education receive religious indoctrination at state expense does, however, support the claim that the law is one "respecting an establishment of religion." The State may choose to divide up its public schools into a dozen different options and label them magnet schools, community schools, or whatever else it decides to call them, but the State is still required to provide a public education and it is the State's decision to fund private school education over and above its traditional obligation that is at issue in these cases.

Third, the voluntary character of the private choice to prefer a parochial education over an education in the public school system seems to me quite irrelevant to the question whether the government's choice to pay for religious indoctrination is constitutionally permissible. Today, however, the Court seems to have decided that the mere fact that a family that cannot afford a private education wants its children educated in a parochial school is a sufficient justification for this use of public funds.

For the reasons stated by JUSTICE SOUTER and JUSTICE BREYER, I am convinced that the Court's decision is profoundly misguided. Admittedly, in reaching that conclusion I have been influenced by my understanding of the impact of religious strife on the decisions of our forbears to migrate to this continent, and on the decisions of neighbors in the Balkans, Northern Ireland, and the Middle East to mistrust one another. Whenever we remove a brick from the wall that was designed to separate religion and government, we increase the risk of religious strife and weaken the foundation of our democracy.

JUSTICE SOUTER, with whom JUSTICE STEVENS, JUSTICE GINSBURG, and JUSTICE BREYER join, dissenting.

The Court's majority holds that the Establishment Clause is no bar to Ohio's payment of tuition at private religious elementary and middle schools under a scheme that systematically provides tax money to support the schools' religious missions. The occasion for the legislation thus upheld is the condition of public education in the city of Cleveland. The record indicates that the schools are failing to serve their objective, and the vouchers in issue here are said to be needed to provide adequate alternatives to them. If there were an excuse for giving short shrift to the Establishment Clause, it would probably apply here. But there is no excuse. Constitutional limitations are placed on government to preserve constitutional values in hard cases, like these.

The applicability of the Establishment Clause to public funding of benefits to religious schools was settled in *Everson*, which inaugurated the modern era of establishment doctrine. The Court stated the principle in words from which there was no dissent:

> "No tax in any amount, large or small, can be levied to support any religious activities or institutions, whatever they may be called, or whatever form they may adopt to teach or practice religion."

The Court has never in so many words repudiated this statement, let alone, in so many words, overruled *Everson*.

Today, however, the majority holds that the Establishment Clause is not offended by Ohio's Pilot Project Scholarship Program, under which students may be eligible to receive as much as $2,250 in the form of tuition vouchers transferable to religious schools. In the city of Cleveland the overwhelming proportion of large appropriations for voucher money must be spent on religious schools if it is to be spent at all, and will be spent in amounts that cover almost all of tuition. The money will thus pay for eligible students' instruction not only in secular subjects but in religion as well, in schools that can fairly be characterized as founded to teach religious doctrine and to imbue teaching in all subjects with a religious dimension. Public tax money will pay at a systemic level for teaching the covenant with Israel and Mosaic law in Jewish schools, the primacy of the Apostle Peter and the Papacy in Catholic schools, the truth of reformed Christianity in Protestant schools, and the revelation to the Prophet in Muslim schools, to speak only of major religious groupings in the Republic.

How can a Court consistently leave *Everson* on the books and approve the Ohio vouchers? The answer is that it cannot. It is only by ignoring *Everson* that the majority can claim to rest on traditional law in its invocation of neutral aid provisions and private choice to sanction the Ohio law. It is, moreover, only by ignoring the meaning of neutrality and private choice themselves that the majority can even pretend to rest today's decision on those criteria.

I

[Justice Souter reviewed many of the Court's financial assistance precedents and concluded:]

[I]t seems fair to say that it was not until today that substantiality of aid has clearly been rejected as irrelevant by a majority of this Court, just as it has not been until today that a majority, not a plurality, has held purely formal criteria to suffice for scrutinizing aid that ends up in the coffers of religious schools. Today's cases are notable for their stark illustration of the inadequacy of the majority's chosen formal analysis.

II

Although it has taken half a century since *Everson* to reach the majority's twin standards of neutrality and free choice, the facts show that, in the majority's hands, even these criteria cannot convincingly legitimize the Ohio scheme.

A

Consider first the criterion of neutrality. As recently as two Terms ago, a majority of the Court recognized that neutrality conceived of as evenhandedness toward aid recipients had never been treated as alone sufficient to satisfy the Establishment Clause, *Mitchell*. But at least in its limited significance, formal neutrality seemed to serve some purpose. Today, however, the majority employs the neutrality criterion in a way that renders it impossible to understand.

Neutrality in this sense refers, of course, to evenhandedness in setting eligibility as between potential religious and secular recipients of public money. Thus, for example, the aid scheme in *Witters* provided an eligible recipient with a scholarship to be used at any institution within a practically unlimited universe of schools; it did not tend to provide more or less aid depending on which one the scholarship recipient chose, and there was no indication that the maximum scholarship amount would be insufficient at secular schools. Neither did any condition of *Zobrest*'s interpreters subsidy favor religious education.

In order to apply the neutrality test, then, it makes sense to focus on a category of aid that may be directed to religious as well as secular schools, and ask whether the scheme favors a religious direction. Here, one would ask whether the voucher provisions, allowing for as much as $2,250 toward private school tuition (or a grant to a public school in an adjacent district), were written in a way that skewed the scheme toward benefiting religious schools.

This, however, is not what the majority asks. The majority looks not to the provisions for tuition vouchers, but to every provision for educational opportunity: "The program permits the participation of *all* schools within the district, [as well as public schools in adjacent districts], religious or nonreligious." The majority then finds confirmation that "participation of *all* schools" satisfies neutrality by noting that the better part of total state educational expenditure goes to public schools, thus showing there is no favor of religion.

The illogic is patent. If regular, public schools (which can get no voucher payments) "participate" in a voucher scheme with schools that can, and public expenditure is still predominantly on public schools, then the majority's reasoning would find neutrality in a scheme of vouchers available for private tuition in districts with no secular private schools at all. Neutrality as the majority employs the term is, literally, verbal and nothing more. This, indeed, is the only way the majority can gloss over the very nonneutral feature of the total scheme covering "*all* schools": public tutors may receive from the State no more than $324 per child to support extra tutoring (that is, the State's 90% of a total amount of $360), whereas the tuition voucher schools (which turn out to be mostly religious) can receive up to $2,250.

Why the majority does not simply accept the fact that the challenge here is to the more generous voucher scheme and judge its neutrality in relation to religious use of voucher money seems very odd. It seems odd, that is, until one recognizes that comparable schools for applying the criterion of neutrality are also the comparable schools for applying the other majority criterion, whether the immediate recipients of voucher aid have a genuinely free choice of religious and secular schools to receive the voucher money. And in applying this second criterion, the consideration of "*all* schools" is ostensibly helpful to the majority position.

B

The majority addresses the issue of choice the same way it addresses neutrality, by asking whether recipients or potential recipients of voucher aid have a choice of public schools among secular alternatives to religious schools. Again, however, the majority asks the wrong question and misapplies the criterion. The majority has confused choice in spending scholarships with choice from the entire menu of possible educational placements, most of them open to anyone willing to attend a public school. I say "confused" because the majority's new use of the choice criterion, which it frames negatively as "whether Ohio is coercing parents into sending their children to religious schools," ignores the reason for having a private choice enquiry in the first place. Cases since *Mueller* have found private choice relevant under a rule that aid to religious schools can be permissible so long as it first passes through the hands of students or parents. The majority's view that all educational choices are comparable for purposes of choice thus ignores the whole point of the choice test: it is a criterion for deciding whether indirect aid to a religious school is legitimate because it passes through private hands that can spend or use the aid in a secular school. The question is whether the private hand is genuinely free to send the money in either a secular direction or a religious one. The majority now has transformed this question about private choice in channeling aid into a question about selecting from examples of state spending (on education) including direct spending on magnet and community public schools that goes through no private hands and could never reach a religious school under any circumstance. When the choice test is transformed from where to spend the money to where to go to school, it is cut loose from its very purpose.

Defining choice as choice in spending the money or channeling the aid is, moreover, necessary if the choice criterion is to function as a limiting principle at all. If "choice" is present whenever there is any educational alternative to the religious school to which vouchers can be endorsed, then there will always be a choice and the voucher can always be constitutional, even in a system in which there is not a single private secular school as an alternative to the religious school. And because it is unlikely that any participating private religious school will enroll more pupils than the generally available public system, it will be easy to generate numbers suggesting that aid to religion is not the significant intent or effect of the voucher scheme.

That is, in fact, just the kind of rhetorical argument that the majority accepts in these cases. In addition to secular private schools (129 students), the majority considers public schools with tuition assistance (roughly 1,400 students), magnet schools (13,000 students), and community schools (1,900 students), and concludes that fewer than 20% of pupils receive state vouchers to attend religious schools. (In fact, the numbers would seem even more favorable to the majority's argument if enrollment in traditional public schools without tutoring were considered, an alternative the majority thinks relevant to the private choice enquiry.) JUSTICE O'CONNOR focuses on how much money is spent on each educational option and notes that at most $8.2 million is spent on vouchers for students attending religious schools, which is only 6% of the State's expenditure if one includes separate funding for Cleveland's community ($9.4 million) and magnet ($114.8 million) public schools. The variations show how results may shift when a judge can pick and choose the alternatives to use in the comparisons, and they also show what dependably comfortable results the choice criterion will yield if the identification of relevant choices is wide open. If the choice of relevant alternatives is an open one, proponents of voucher aid will always win, because they will always be able to find a "choice" somewhere that will show the bulk of public spending to be secular. The choice enquiry will be diluted to the point that it can screen out nothing, and the result will always be determined by selecting the alternatives to be treated as choices.

Confining the relevant choices to spending choices, on the other hand, is not vulnerable to comparable criticism. Although leaving the selection of alternatives for choice wide open, as the majority would, virtually guarantees the availability of a "choice" that will satisfy the criterion, limiting the choices to spending choices will not guarantee a negative result in every case. There may, after all, be cases in which a voucher recipient will have a real choice, with enough secular private school desks in relation to the number of religious ones, and a voucher amount high enough to meet secular private school tuition levels. But, even to the extent that choice-to-spend does tend to limit the number of religious funding options that pass muster, the choice criterion has to be understood this way in order, as I have said, for it to function as a limiting principle. Otherwise there is surely no point in requiring the choice to be a true or real or genuine one.

It is not, of course, that I think even a genuine choice criterion is up to the task of the Establishment Clause when substantial state funds go to religious teaching; the discussion in Part III, *infra,* shows that it is not. The point is simply that if the majority wishes to claim that choice is a criterion, it must define choice in a way that can function as a criterion with a practical capacity to screen something out.

If, contrary to the majority, we ask the right question about genuine choice to use the vouchers, the answer shows that something is influencing choices in a way that aims the money in a religious direction: of 56 private schools in the district participating in the voucher program (only 53 of which accepted voucher students in 1999-2000), 46 of them are religious; 96.6% of all voucher recipients go to religious schools, only 3.4% to nonreligious ones. Unfortunately for the majority position, there is no explanation for this that suggests the religious direction results simply from free choices by parents. One answer to these statistics, for example, which would be consistent with the genuine choice claimed to be operating, might be that 96.6% of families choosing to avail themselves of vouchers choose to educate their children in schools of their own religion. This would not, in my view, render the scheme constitutional, but it would speak to the majority's choice criterion. Evidence shows, however, that almost two out of three families using vouchers to send their children to religious schools did not embrace the religion of those schools. The families made it clear they had not chosen the schools because they wished their children to be proselytized in a religion not their own, or in any religion, but because of educational opportunity.

Even so, the fact that some 2,270 students chose to apply their vouchers to schools of other religions, might be consistent with true choice if the students "chose" their religious schools over a wide array of private nonreligious options, or if it could be shown generally that Ohio's program had no effect on educational choices and thus no impermissible effect of advancing religious education. But both possibilities are contrary to fact. First, even if all existing nonreligious private schools in Cleveland were willing to accept large numbers of voucher students, only a few more than the 129 currently enrolled in such schools would be able to attend, as the total enrollment at all nonreligious private schools in Cleveland for kindergarten through eighth grade is only 510 children, and there is no indication that these schools have many open seats. Second, the $2,500 cap that the program places on tuition for participating low-income pupils has the effect of curtailing the participation of nonreligious schools: nonreligious schools with higher tuition (about $4,000) stated that they could afford to accommodate just a few voucher students. By comparison, the average tuition at participating Catholic schools in Cleveland in 1999-2000 was $1,592, almost $1,000 below the cap.

Of course, the obvious fix would be to increase the value of vouchers so that existing nonreligious private and non-Catholic religious schools would be able to enroll more voucher students, and to provide incentives for educators to create new such schools given that few presently exist. Private choice, if as robust as that available to the seminarian in *Witters*, would then be true private choice under the majority's criterion. But it is simply unrealistic to presume that parents of elementary and middle schoolchildren in Cleveland will have a range of secular and religious choices even arguably comparable to the statewide program for vocational and higher education in *Witters*. And to get to that hypothetical point would require that such massive financial support be made available to religion as to disserve every objective of the Establishment Clause even more than the present scheme does.

There is, in any case, no way to interpret the 96.6% of current voucher money going to religious schools as reflecting a free and genuine choice by the families that apply for vouchers. The 96.6% reflects, instead, the fact that too few non-religious school desks are available and few but religious schools can afford to accept more than a handful of voucher students. And contrary to the majority's assertion, public schools in adjacent districts hardly have a financial incentive to participate in the Ohio voucher program, and none has. For the overwhelming number of children in the voucher scheme, the only alternative to the public schools is religious. And it is entirely irrelevant that the State did not deliberately design the network of private schools for the sake of channeling money into religious institutions. The criterion is one of genuinely free choice on the part of the private individuals who choose, and a Hobson's choice is not a choice, whatever the reason for being Hobsonian.

III

I do not dissent merely because the majority has misapplied its own law, for even if I assumed *arguendo* that the majority's formal criteria were satisfied on the facts, today's conclusion would be profoundly at odds with the Constitution. Proof of this is clear on two levels. The first is circumstantial, in the now discarded symptom of violation, the substantial dimension of the aid. The second is direct, in the defiance of every objective supposed to be served by the bar against establishment.

A

The scale of the aid to religious schools approved today is unprecedented, both in the number of dollars and in the proportion of systemic school expenditure supported. Each measure has received attention in previous cases. On one hand, the sheer quantity of aid, when delivered to a class of religious primary and secondary schools, was suspect on the theory that the greater the aid, the greater its proportion to a religious schools existing expenditures, and the greater the likelihood that public money was supporting religious as well as secular instruction.

On the other hand, the Court has found the gross amount unhelpful for Establishment Clause analysis when the aid afforded a benefit solely to one individual, however substantial as to him, but only an incidental benefit to the religious school at which the individual chose to spend the State's money.

The Cleveland voucher program has cost Ohio taxpayers $33 million since its implementation in 1996 ($28 million in voucher payments, $5 million in administrative costs), and its cost was expected to exceed $8 million in the 2001-2002 school year. These tax-raised funds are on top of the textbooks, reading and math tutors, laboratory equipment, and the like that Ohio provides to private schools, worth roughly $600 per child.

The gross amounts of public money contributed are symptomatic of the scope of what the taxpayers' money buys for a broad class of religious-school students. In paying for practically the full amount of tuition for thousands of qualifying students, the scholarships purchase everything that tuition purchases, be it instruction in math or indoctrination in faith. The consequences of substantial aid hypothesized in *Meek* are realized here: the majority makes no pretense that substantial amounts of tax money are not systematically underwriting religious practice and indoctrination.

B

It is virtually superfluous to point out that every objective underlying the prohibition of religious establishment is betrayed by this scheme, but something has to be said about the enormity of the violation. I anticipated these objectives earlier, in discussing *Everson*, which cataloged them, the first being respect for freedom of conscience. Jefferson described it as the idea that no one "shall be compelled to. . . support any religious worship, place, or ministry whatsoever," even a "teacher of his own religious persuasion," and Madison thought it violated by any authority "which can force a citizen to contribute three pence . . . of his property for the support of any. . . establishment." "Any tax to establish religion is antithetical to the command that the minds of men always be wholly free," *Mitchell*, 530 U.S., at 871. Madison's objection to three pence has simply been lost in the majority's formalism.

As for the second objective, to save religion from its own corruption, Madison wrote of the "'experience. . . that ecclesiastical establishments, instead of maintaining the purity and efficacy of Religion, have had a contrary operation.'" In Madison's time, the manifestations were "pride and indolence in the Clergy; ignorance and servility in the laity[,] in both, superstition, bigotry and persecution," in the 21st century, the risk is one of corrosive secularism to religious schools, and the specific threat is to the primacy of the schools' mission to educate the children of the faithful according to the unaltered precepts of their faith. Even "[t]he favored religion may be compromised as political figures reshape the religion's beliefs for their own purposes; it may be reformed as government largesse brings government regulation."

The risk is already being realized. In Ohio, for example, a condition of receiving government money under the program is that participating religious schools may not "discriminate on the basis of . . . religion," which means the school may not give admission preferences to children who are members of the patron faith; children of a parish are generally consigned to the same admission lotteries as non-believers. This indeed was the exact object of a 1999 amendment repealing the portion of a predecessor statute that had allowed an admission preference for "[c]hildren . . . whose parents are affiliated with any organization that provides financial support to the school, at the discretion of the school." Nor is the State's religious antidiscrimination restriction limited to student admission policies: by its terms, a participating religious school may well be forbidden to choose a member of its own clergy to serve as teacher or principal over a layperson of a different religion claiming equal qualification for the job. *Cf.* National Catholic Educational Association, Balance Sheet for Catholic Elementary Schools: 2001 Income and Expenses 25 (2001) (31% of [reporting Catholic elementary and middle] schools had at least one full-time teacher who was a religious sister). Indeed, a separate condition that "[t]he school . . . not . . . teach hatred of any person or group on the basis of . . . religion," could be understood (or subsequently broadened) to prohibit religions from teaching traditionally legitimate articles of faith as to the error, sinfulness, or ignorance of others, if they want government money for their schools.

For perspective on this foot-in-the-door of religious regulation, it is well to remember that the money has barely begun to flow. Prior examples of aid, whether grants through individuals or in-kind assistance, were never significant enough to alter the basic fiscal structure of religious schools; state aid was welcome, but not indispensable. But given the figures already involved here, there is no question that religious schools in Ohio are on the way to becoming bigger businesses with budgets enhanced to fit their new stream of tax-raised income. *See, e.g.*, People for the American Way Foundation, A Painful Price 5, 9, 11 (Feb. 14, 2002) (of 91 schools participating in the Milwaukee program, 75 received voucher payments in excess of tuition, 61 of those were religious and averaged $185,000 worth of overpayment per school, justified in part to "raise low salaries"). The administrators of those same schools are also no doubt following the politics of a move in the Ohio State Senate to raise the current maximum value of a school voucher from $2,250 to the base amount of current state spending on each public school student ($4,814 for the 2001 fiscal year). *See* Bloedel, Bill Analysis of S.B. No. 89, 124th Ohio Gen. Assembly, regular session 2001-2002 (Ohio Legislative Service Commission). Ohio, in fact, is merely replicating the experience in Wisconsin, where a similar increase in the value of educational vouchers in Milwaukee has induced the creation of some 23 new private schools, Public Policy Forum, Research Brief, vol. 90, no. 1, p.3 (Jan. 23, 2002), some of which, we may safely surmise, are religious. New schools have presumably pegged their financial prospects to the government from the start, and the odds are that increases in government aid will bring the threshold voucher amount closer to the tuition at even more expensive religious schools.

When government aid goes up, so does reliance on it; the only thing likely to go down is independence. If Justice Douglas in *Allen* was concerned with state agencies, influenced by powerful religious groups, choosing the textbooks that parochial schools would use, how much more is there reason to wonder when dependence will become great enough to give the State of Ohio an effective veto over basic decisions on the content of curriculums? A day will come when religious schools will learn what political leverage can do, just as Ohio's politicians are now getting a lesson in the leverage exercised by religion.

Increased voucher spending is not, however, the sole portent of growing regulation of religious practice in the school, for state mandates to moderate religious teaching may well be the most obvious response to the third concern behind the ban on establishment, its inextricable link with social conflict. As appropriations for religious subsidy rise, competition for the money will tap sectarian religion's capacity for discord. "Public money devoted to payment of religious costs, educational or other, brings the quest for more. It brings too the struggle of sect against sect for the larger share or for any. Here one by numbers alone will benefit most, there another."

JUSTICE BREYER has addressed this issue in his own dissenting opinion, which I join, and here it is enough to say that the intensity of the expectable friction can be gauged by realizing that the scramble for money will energize not only contending sectarians, but taxpayers who take their liberty of conscience seriously. Religious teaching at taxpayer expense simply cannot be cordoned from taxpayer politics, and every major religion currently espouses social positions that provoke intense opposition. Not all taxpaying Protestant citizens, for example, will be content to underwrite the teaching of the Roman Catholic Church condemning the death penalty. Nor will all of Americas Muslims acquiesce in paying for the endorsement of the religious Zionism taught in many religious Jewish schools, which combines "a nationalistic sentiment" in support of Israel with a "deeply religious" element. Nor will every secular taxpayer be content to support Muslim views on differential treatment of the sexes, or, for that matter, to fund the espousal of a wife's obligation of obedience to her husband, presumably taught in any schools adopting the articles of faith of the Southern Baptist Convention. Views like these, and innumerable others, have been safe in the sectarian pulpits and classrooms of this Nation not only because the Free Exercise Clause protects them directly, but because the ban on supporting religious establishment has protected free exercise, by keeping it relatively private. With the arrival of vouchers in religious schools, that privacy will go, and along with it will go confidence that religious disagreement will stay moderate.

* * *

If the divisiveness permitted by today's majority is to be avoided in the short term, it will be avoided only by action of the political branches at the state and national levels. Legislatures not driven to desperation by the problems of public education may be able to see the threat in vouchers negotiable in sectarian schools. Perhaps even cities with problems like Cleveland's will perceive the danger, now that they know a federal court will not save them from it.

JUSTICE BREYER, with whom JUSTICE STEVENS and JUSTICE SOUTER join, dissenting.

I

The First Amendment begins with a prohibition, that "Congress shall make no law respecting an establishment of religion," and a guarantee, that the government shall not prohibit "the free exercise thereof." These Clauses embody an understanding, reached in the 17th century after decades of religious war, that liberty and social stability demand a religious tolerance that respects the religious views of all citizens, permits those citizens to "worship God in their own way," and allows all families to "teach their children and to form their characters" as they wish. The Clauses reflect the Framers' vision of an American Nation free of the religious strife that had long plagued the nations of Europe. Whatever the Framers might have thought about particular 18th century school funding practices, they undeniably intended an interpretation of the Religion Clauses that would implement this basic First Amendment objective.

In part for this reason, the Court's 20th-century Establishment Clause cases — both those limiting the practice of religion in public schools and those limiting the public funding of private religious education — focused directly upon social conflict, potentially created when government becomes involved in religious education.

When it decided these 20th-century Establishment Clause cases, the Court did not deny that an earlier American society might have found a less clear-cut church/state separation compatible with social tranquility. Indeed, historians point out that during the early years of the Republic, American schools — including the first public schools — were Protestant in character. Their students recited Protestant prayers, read the King James version of the Bible, and learned Protestant religious ideals. Those practices may have wrongly discriminated against members of minority religions, but given the small number of such individuals, the teaching of Protestant religions in schools did not threaten serious social conflict.

The 20th-century Court was fully aware, however, that immigration and growth had changed American society dramatically since its early years. By 1850, 1.6 million Catholics lived in America, and by 1900 that number rose to 12 million. There were similar percentage increases in the Jewish population. Not surprisingly, with this increase in numbers, members of non-Protestant religions, particularly Catholics, began to resist the Protestant domination of the public schools. Scholars report that by the mid-19th century religious conflict over matters such as Bible reading grew intense, as Catholics resisted and Protestants fought back to preserve their domination. Dreading Catholic domination, native Protestants terrorized Catholics. In some States "Catholic students suffered beatings or expulsions for refusing to read from the Protestant Bible, and crowds . . . rioted over whether Catholic children could be released from the classroom during Bible reading."

II

The principle underlying these cases — avoiding religiously based social conflict — remains of great concern. As religiously diverse as America had become when the Court decided its major 20th-century Establishment Clause cases, we are exponentially more diverse today. America boasts more than 55 different religious groups and subgroups with a significant number of members. Major religions include, among others, Protestants, Catholics, Jews, Muslims, Buddhists, Hindus, and Sikhs. And several of these major religions contain different subsidiary sects with different religious beliefs. Newer Christian immigrant groups are "expressing their Christianity in languages, customs, and independent churches that are barely recognizable, and often controversial, for European-ancestry Catholics and Protestants."

Under these modern-day circumstances, how is the "equal opportunity" principle to work — without risking the "struggle of sect against sect" against which Justice Rutledge warned? School voucher programs finance the religious education of the young. And, if widely adopted, they may well provide billions of dollars that will do so. Why will different religions not become concerned about, and seek to influence, the criteria used to channel this money to religious schools? Why will they not want to examine the implementation of the programs that provide this money — to determine, for example, whether implementation has biased a program toward or against particular sects, or whether recipient religious schools are adequately fulfilling a program's criteria? If so, just how is the State to resolve the resulting controversies without provoking legitimate fears of the kinds of religious favoritism that, in so religiously diverse a Nation, threaten social dissension?

Consider the voucher program here at issue. That program insists that the religious school accept students of all religions. Does that criterion treat fairly groups whose religion forbids them to do so? The program also insists that no participating school "advocate or foster unlawful behavior or teach hatred of any person or group on the basis of race, ethnicity, national origin, or religion." And it requires the State to "revoke the registration of any school if, after a hearing, the superintendent determines that the school is in violation" of the program's rules. As one *amicus* argues, "it is difficult to imagine a more divisive activity than the appointment of state officials as referees to determine whether a particular religious doctrine teaches hatred or advocates lawlessness."

How are state officials to adjudicate claims that one religion or another is advocating, for example, civil disobedience in response to unjust laws, the use of illegal drugs in a religious ceremony, or resort to force to call attention to what it views as an immoral social practice? What kind of public hearing will there be in response to claims that one religion or another is continuing to teach a view of history that casts members of other religions in the worst possible light? How will the public react to government funding for schools that take controversial religious positions on topics that are of current popular interest — say, the conflict in the Middle East or the war on terrorism? Yet any major funding program for primary religious education will require criteria. And the selection of those criteria, as well as their application, inevitably pose problems that are divisive. Efforts to respond to these problems not only will seriously entangle church and state, but also will promote division among religious groups, as one group or another fears (often legitimately) that it will receive unfair treatment at the hands of the government.

In a society as religiously diverse as ours, the Court has recognized that we must rely on the Religion Clauses of the First Amendment to protect against religious strife, particularly when what is at issue is an area as central to religious belief as the shaping, through primary education, of the next generation's minds and spirits.

III

I concede that the Establishment Clause currently permits States to channel various forms of assistance to religious schools, for example, transportation costs for students, computers, and secular texts.

School voucher programs differ, however, in both *kind* and *degree* from aid programs upheld in the past. They differ in kind because they direct financing to a core function of the church: the teaching of religious truths to young children. For that reason the constitutional demand for "separation" is of particular constitutional concern.

Vouchers also differ in *degree*. The aid programs recently upheld by the Court involved limited amounts of aid to religion. But the majority's analysis here appears to permit a considerable shift of taxpayer dollars from public secular schools to private religious schools. That fact, combined with the use to which these dollars will be put, exacerbates the conflict problem. State aid that takes the form of peripheral secular items, with prohibitions against diversion of funds to religious teaching, holds significantly less potential for social division. In this respect as well, the secular aid upheld in *Mitchell* differs dramatically from the present case.

V

The Court, in effect, turns the clock back. It adopts, under the name of "neutrality," an interpretation of the Establishment Clause that this Court rejected more than half a century ago. In its view, the parental choice that offers each religious group a kind of equal opportunity to secure government funding overcomes the Establishment Clause concern for social concord. An earlier Court found that "equal opportunity" principle insufficient; it read the Clause as insisting upon greater separation of church and state, at least in respect to primary education. In a society composed of many different religious creeds, I fear that this present departure from the Court's earlier understanding risks creating a form of religiously based conflict potentially harmful to the Nation's social fabric. Because I believe the Establishment Clause was written in part to avoid this kind of conflict, and for reasons set forth by JUSTICE SOUTER and JUSTICE STEVENS, I respectfully dissent.

NOTES AND QUESTIONS ON *ZELMAN*

1. *Are there now two Establishment Clause standards — one for financing cases and one for symbolic endorsement cases?* Does the Court's *Zelman* decision introduce a serious disjunction between the Court's approach to religious financing issues and symbolic endorsement issues? In the school prayer context, the Court has definitively and repeatedly rejected the application of neutrality theory. The neutrality claim was a centerpiece of the school board's case in *Santa Fe Independent School District v. Doe* (*supra* Chapter 6). The school board's theory in that case was that since all students were given the opportunity to vote on the inclusion of prayer, the prayer policy was therefore "neutral" in the sense that it did not favor religion over secularism or vice versa. As the school board phrased the argument, the policy was "one of neutrality rather than endorsement." Six members of the Court rejected this argument, relying instead on the Court's assessment of an overall context that was basically foreordained to produce results favorable to religious speakers. This approach is fundamentally different than the approach taken by the Court in *Zelman*, where the overall context was dominated by the prevalence of religious private education, and therefore foreordained to produce a system in which almost all the voucher funds going to private schools would be funneled to religious schools.

A second possible inconsistency between the funding and school prayer/symbolic endorsement cases is the Court's very different approach to the issue of state action. In the funding case, the Court treats the decision to spend money on religious education as a purely private matter, which does not in any way involve the state with the religious institution. The *Zelman* dissenters argue that in any realistic assessment of the situation this is true only in the most formalistic sense — the state knows in advance where most of the funds are going, the state actors who propose the program therefore implicitly embrace this allocation of funds as a good idea, and the state checks cannot even be cashed unless they are cosigned by the religious institution — thus the funds are transferred directly from state coffers to the bank accounts of the religious institutions. In the school prayer/symbolic endorsement context, on the other hand, the Court has refused to engage in the same sort of formalistic neutrality. Again, in *Santa Fe* the school board argued that the speech involved there was not attributable to the state. As the school board put it, the "individual student [was] the 'circuit-breaker' in the process." And again, six members of the Court refused to accept this characterization, relying instead on an overall context that applied the "imprint of the state" to the individual student's prayer.

How can these different analyses be reconciled? Do we now have two different Establishment Clause standards?

2. *Zelman and the Revival of Direct Religious Establishments.* For the *Zelman* majority, the key factors in determining whether a state program passes constitutional muster is whether the program is "neutral," which in turn seems to mean that the (1) the selection of religious beneficiaries of government aid is made by private individuals rather than the government, and (2) all religions are permitted to partake of the government's largess.

Consider the following scenario: The Maryland state constitution of 1776 contained a provision stating that "the Legislature may, in their discretion, lay a general and equal tax, for the support of the Christian religion; leaving to each individual the power of appointing the payment of the money, collected from him, to the support of any particular place of worship or minister. . . ." Various statutes were proposed to implement this constitutional provision permitting a multiple governmental establishment of religion. One such proposed statute provided a tax to support all Christian denominations and exempted from the tax "anyone identifying himself as a 'Jew or Mohometan, or [declaring] that he does not believe in the Christian religion. . . .'" LEONARD LEVY, THE ESTABLISH- MENT CLAUSE: RELIGION AND THE FIRST AMENDMENT 48 (1986). According to Pro- fessor Levy's account, this proposal engendered tremendous opposition throughout Maryland. "A blizzard of newspaper articles and petitions con- demned the bill as a new establishment of religion and a violation of the Chris- tian spirit, asserted that establishments harmed religion, and darkly warned about an Episcopalian conspiracy to regain supremacy." *Id.* The bill was even- tually defeated by a two-to-one majority, and Maryland never did implement its constitutional authorization of religious establishment.

Suppose a state enacted a modern version of Maryland's constitutional pro- vision and proposed a similar implementing statute. Would such a state regime be constitutional under the *Zelman* neutrality theory? Under the Maryland plan, the selection of religious beneficiaries would be made by private individ- uals (since every citizen identifies the beneficiary of his or her religious tax) and all religions would be permitted to participate in the system (or refrain from doing so). Non-religious persons could opt out of the system by declaring them- selves unaffiliated to a religion. Thus, a modern version of the Maryland reli- gious establishment plan would seem to satisfy both requisites of *Zelman*-style neutrality. One key difference between the Maryland plan and the Cleveland voucher system upheld in *Zelman* is that the money in the Maryland plan would be transferred directly from the state to the religious organization, but at least one court has already held that *Zelman* does not prohibit the direct trans- fer of government funds to religious organizations as long as the program as a whole is "neutral." *See Freedom From Religion Found. v. McCallum*, which is discussed in the next note. Is there any other element in the *Zelman* majority opinion that can be used to avoid the conclusion that the Establishment Clause now permits eighteenth century-style multiple religious establishments?

3. *Subsequent Applications of Zelman. Zelman* is already being used outside the private school funding context to support other government programs pro- viding state money to religious organizations. In *Freedom From Religion Foun- dation, Inc. v. McCallum*, 324 F.3d 880 (7th Cir. 2003), for example, a unanimous panel of the Third Circuit Court of Appeals relied heavily on *Zelman* to uphold a Wisconsin state program providing public funds to Faith Works, a halfway house for paroled state prisoners. Faith Works is an explicitly religious organ- ization, which "encourages the offender to establish a personal relationship with God through the mediation of Jesus Christ." *Id.* at 881. State parole offi- cers recommend Faith Works to some parolees, but are required to identify the program's religious element and offer a secular halfway house as an alternative. The state waived its usual bidding requirements when it offered Faith Works a contract to participate in the halfway house program for parolees. According to the court, this was done because the religious group offered a nine-month residential program, whereas the secular groups offered only a three-month residential program. "The longer term makes Faith Works uniquely attractive to the correctional authorities because they believe that many offenders need the longer period of supervised residence in order to succeed in becoming reintegrated into civil society." *Id.* at 882.

The Court relied almost exclusively on *Zelman* to support its holding, even though — unlike the Cleveland school voucher program upheld in *Zelman* — the state in this case paid money directly to the religious organization. Despite the Supreme Court's heavy emphasis on this aspect of the Cleveland program, the Court in *McCallum* held that that the direct payment was not constitutionally significant.

> The practice challenged in the present case is similar. The state in effect gives eligible offenders "vouchers" that they can use to purchase a place in a halfway house, whether the halfway house is "parochial" or secular. We have put "vouchers" in scare quotes because the state has dispensed with the intermediate step by which the recipient of the publicly funded private service hands his voucher to the service provider. But so far as the policy of the establishment clause is concerned, there is no difference between giving the voucher recipient a piece of paper that directs the public agency to pay the service provider and the agency's asking the recipient to indicate his preference and paying the provider whose service he prefers.

Id. at 882.

Assuming that the Seventh Circuit panel in *McCallum* correctly interpreted *Zelman*, what restrictions remain on government financing of religious social programs? If government money does not have to be funneled to religious institutions through private individuals, and if the government can grant a religious program favorable treatment simply because the religious program is more comprehensive than secular alternatives, then does the ostensible requirement of governmental neutrality have any teeth? Does the Establishment Clause requirement of neutrality mean nothing more than that the state may not impose a legal mandate to attend a government-financed religious program? *McCallum* specifically holds that the government can recommend an overtly religious program over a secular program. Would the Establishment Clause likewise permit the government to "recommend" one religious sect's program over another if the government concludes that the preferred sect's program is more successful than others in curing an identified social ill (such as alcoholism or recidivism)? Does neutrality require the government to provide a truly viable secular alternative to a government-financed religious program, or is the formal availability of a secular alternative sufficient — even if the government itself admits that the secular alternative is not as "uniquely attractive" as the favored religious program?

MITCHELL v. HELMS
530 U.S. 793 (2000)

JUSTICE THOMAS announced the judgment of the Court and delivered an opinion, in which THE CHIEF JUSTICE, JUSTICE SCALIA, and JUSTICE KENNEDY join.

As part of a longstanding school-aid program known as Chapter 2, the Federal Government distributes funds to state and local governmental agencies, which in turn lend educational materials and equipment to public and private schools, with the enrollment of each participating school determining the amount of aid that it receives. The question is whether Chapter 2, as applied in Jefferson Parish, Louisiana, is a law respecting an establishment of religion, because many of the private schools receiving Chapter 2 aid in that parish are religiously affiliated. We hold that Chapter 2 is not such a law.

I

A

Chapter 2 of the Education Consolidation and Improvement Act of 1981 is a close cousin of the provision of the ESEA that we recently considered in *Agostini v. Felton*. Like the provision at issue in *Agostini*, Chapter 2 channels federal funds to local educational agencies (LEA's), which are usually public school districts, via state educational agencies (SEA's), to implement programs to assist children in elementary and secondary schools. Among other things, Chapter 2 provides aid

> "for the acquisition and use of instructional and educational materials, including library services and materials (including media materials), assessments, reference materials, computer software and hardware for instructional use, and other curricular materials."

LEA's and SEA's must offer assistance to both public and private schools (although any private school must be nonprofit). Participating private schools receive Chapter 2 aid based on the number of children enrolled in each school, and allocations of Chapter 2 funds for those schools must generally be "equal (consistent with the number of children to be served) to expenditures for programs . . . for children enrolled in the public schools of the [LEA]." LEA's must in all cases "assure equitable participation" of the children of private schools "in the purposes and benefits" of Chapter 2. Further, Chapter 2 funds may only "supplement and, to the extent practical, increase the level of funds that would . . . be made available from non-Federal sources."

Several restrictions apply to aid to private schools. Most significantly, the "services, materials, and equipment" provided to private schools must be "secular, neutral, and nonideological." In addition, private schools may not acquire control of Chapter 2 funds or title to Chapter 2 materials, equipment, or property. A private school receives the materials and equipment listed in by submitting to the LEA an application detailing which items the school seeks and how it will use them; the LEA, if it approves the application, purchases those items from the school's allocation of funds, and then lends them to that school.

In Jefferson Parish (the Louisiana governmental unit at issue in this case), as in Louisiana as a whole, private schools have primarily used their allocations for nonrecurring expenses, usually materials and equipment. In the 1986-1987 fiscal year, for example, 44% of the money budgeted for private schools in Jefferson Parish was spent by LEA's for acquiring library and media materials, and 48% for instructional equipment. Among the materials and equipment provided have been library books, computers, and computer software, and also slide and movie projectors, overhead projectors, television sets, tape recorders, VCR's, projection screens, laboratory equipment, maps, globes, filmstrips, slides, and cassette recordings.

It appears that, in an average year, about 30% of Chapter 2 funds spent in Jefferson Parish are allocated for private schools. For the 1985-1986 fiscal year, 41 private schools participated in Chapter 2. For the following year, 46 participated, and the participation level has remained relatively constant since then. Of these 46, 34 were Roman Catholic; 7 were otherwise religiously affiliated; and 5 were not religiously affiliated.

B

Respondents filed suit in December 1985, alleging, among other things, that Chapter 2, as applied in Jefferson Parish, violated the Establishment Clause of the First Amendment of the Federal Constitution. The case's tortuous history over the next 15 years indicates well the degree to which our Establishment Clause jurisprudence has shifted in recent times, while nevertheless retaining anomalies with which the lower courts have had to struggle.

[The original district judge assigned to the case held extensive hearings and granted summary judgment for the plaintiffs, holding the program unconstitutional under the secular effects prong of *Lemon v. Kurtzman*, along with cases like *Meek v. Pittenger* and *Wolman v. Walter*, in which the Supreme Court held unconstitutional programs that provided aid to religious schools in the form of materials other than books — indeed, many the same sorts of materials and equipment provided under Chapter 2. Two years later, the original judge died. During prejudgment motions, the new judge assigned to the case reversed the original ruling and held the programs constitutional. He relied on more recent cases such as *Zobrest v. Catalina Foothills School District* and *Rosenberger v. Rector and Visitors of University of Virginia*. The Fifth Circuit Court of Appeals reversed, holding that although inconsistent with later rulings, the holdings of *Meek* and *Wolman* were directly on point and had to be applied to Chapter 2.]

II.

The Establishment Clause of the First Amendment dictates that "Congress shall make no law respecting an establishment of religion." In the over 50 years since *Everson*, we have consistently struggled to apply these simple words in the context of governmental aid to religious schools. As we admitted in *Tilton v. Richardson*, 403 U.S. 672 (1971), "candor compels the acknowledgment that we can only dimly perceive the boundaries of permissible government activity in this sensitive area."

In *Agostini*, however, we brought some clarity to our case law, by overruling two anomalous precedents (one in whole, the other in part) and by consolidating some of our previously disparate considerations under a revised test. Whereas in *Lemon* we had considered whether a statute (1) has a secular purpose, (2) has a primary effect of advancing or inhibiting religion, or (3) creates an excessive entanglement between government and religion, in *Agostini* we modified *Lemon* for purposes of evaluating aid to schools and examined only the first and second factors. We acknowledged that our cases discussing excessive entanglement had applied many of the same considerations as had our cases discussing primary effect, and we therefore recast *Lemon*'s entanglement inquiry as simply one criterion relevant to determining a statute's effect. We also acknowledged that our cases had pared somewhat the factors that could justify a finding of excessive entanglement. We then set out revised criteria for determining the effect of a statute:

> "To summarize, New York City's Title I program does not run afoul of any of three primary criteria we currently use to evaluate whether government aid has the effect of advancing religion: It does not result in governmental indoctrination; define its recipients by reference to religion; or create an excessive entanglement."

In this case, our inquiry under *Agostini*'s purpose and effect test is a narrow one. Because respondents do not challenge the District Court's holding that Chapter 2 has a secular purpose, and because the Fifth Circuit also did not question that holding, we will consider only Chapter 2's effect. Further, in determining that effect, we will consider only the first two *Agostini* criteria, since neither respondents nor the Fifth Circuit has questioned the District Court's holding that Chapter 2 does not create an excessive entanglement. Considering Chapter 2 in light of our more recent case law, we conclude that it neither results in religious indoctrination by the government nor defines its recipients by reference to religion. We therefore hold that Chapter 2 is not a "law respecting an establishment of religion." In so holding, we acknowledge what both the Ninth and Fifth Circuits saw was inescapable — *Meek* and *Wolman* are anomalies in our case law. We therefore conclude that they are no longer good law.

A

As we indicated in *Agostini*, and have indicated elsewhere, the question whether governmental aid to religious schools results in governmental indoctrination is ultimately a question whether any religious indoctrination that occurs in those schools could reasonably be attributed to governmental action.

We have also indicated that the answer to the question of indoctrination will resolve the question whether a program of educational aid "subsidizes" religion, as our religion cases use that term.

In distinguishing between indoctrination that is attributable to the State and indoctrination that is not, we have consistently turned to the principle of neutrality, upholding aid that is offered to a broad range of groups or persons without regard to their religion. If the religious, irreligious, and areligious are all alike eligible for governmental aid, no one would conclude that any indoctrination that any particular recipient conducts has been done at the behest of the government. For attribution of indoctrination is a relative question. If the government is offering assistance to recipients who provide, so to speak, a broad range of indoctrination, the government itself is not thought responsible for any particular indoctrination. To put the point differently, if the government, seeking to further some legitimate secular purpose, offers aid on the same terms, without regard to religion, to all who adequately further that purpose, then it is fair to say that any aid going to a religious recipient only has the effect of furthering that secular purpose. The government, in crafting such an aid program, has had to conclude that a given level of aid is necessary to further that purpose among secular recipients and has provided no more than that same level to religious recipients.

As a way of assuring neutrality, we have repeatedly considered whether any governmental aid that goes to a religious institution does so "only as a result of the genuinely independent and private choices of individuals." We have viewed as significant whether the "private choices of individual parents," as opposed to the "unmediated" will of government, determine what schools ultimately benefit from the governmental aid, and how much. For if numerous private choices, rather than the single choice of a government, determine the distribution of aid pursuant to neutral eligibility criteria, then a government cannot, or at least cannot easily, grant special favors that might lead to a religious establishment. Private choice also helps guarantee neutrality by mitigating the preference for pre-existing recipients that is arguably inherent in any governmental aid program, *see, e.g.*, Gilder, *The Revitalization of Everything: The Law of the Microcosm*, HARV. BUS. REV. 49 (Mar./Apr.1988), and that could lead to a program inadvertently favoring one religion or favoring religious private schools in general over nonreligious ones.

The principles of neutrality and private choice, and their relationship to each other, were prominent not only in *Agostini*, but also in *Zobrest, Witters*, and *Mueller*.

Agostini's second primary criterion for determining the effect of governmental aid is closely related to the first. The second criterion requires a court to consider whether an aid program "define[s] its recipients by reference to religion." As we briefly explained in *Agostini*, this second criterion looks to the same set of facts as does our focus, under the first criterion, on neutrality, but the second criterion uses those facts to answer a somewhat different question — whether the criteria for allocating the aid "creat[e] a financial incentive to undertake religious indoctrination." In *Agostini* we set out the following rule for answering this question:

> "This incentive is not present, however, where the aid is allocated on the basis of neutral, secular criteria that neither favor nor disfavor religion, and is made available to both religious and secular beneficiaries on a nondiscriminatory basis. Under such circumstances, the aid is less likely to have the effect of advancing religion."

The cases on which *Agostini* relied for this rule, and *Agostini* itself, make clear the close relationship between this rule, incentives, and private choice. For to say that a program does not create an incentive to choose religious schools is to say that the private choice is truly "independent."

B

Respondents inexplicably make no effort to address Chapter 2 under the *Agostini* test. Instead, dismissing *Agostini* as factually distinguishable, they offer two rules that they contend should govern our determination of whether Chapter 2 has the effect of advancing religion. They argue first, and chiefly, that "direct, nonincidental" aid to the primary educational mission of religious schools is always impermissible. Second, they argue that provision to religious schools of aid that is divertible to religious use is similarly impermissible. Respondents' arguments are inconsistent with our more recent case law, in particular *Agostini* and *Zobrest*, and we therefore reject them.

1

Although some of our earlier cases, particularly *Ball*, did emphasize the distinction between direct and indirect aid, the purpose of this distinction was merely to prevent "subsidization" of religion. As even the dissent all but admits, our more recent cases address this purpose not through the direct/indirect distinction but rather through the principle of private choice, as incorporated in the first *Agostini* criterion (*i.e.,* whether any indoctrination could be attributed to the government). If aid to schools, even "direct aid," is neutrally available and, before reaching or benefiting any religious school, first passes through the hands (literally or figuratively) of numerous private citizens who are free to direct the aid elsewhere, the government has not provided any "support of religion." Although the presence of private choice is easier to see when aid literally passes through the hands of individuals — which is why we have mentioned directness in the same breath with private choice, there is no reason why the Establishment Clause requires such a form.

Indeed, *Agostini* expressly rejected the absolute line that respondents would have us draw. We there explained that "we have departed from the rule relied on in *Ball* that all government aid that directly assists the educational function of religious schools is invalid." *Agostini* relied primarily on *Witters* for this conclusion and made clear that private choice and neutrality would resolve the con-

cerns formerly addressed by the rule in *Ball*. It was undeniable in *Witters* that
the aid (tuition) would ultimately go to the Inland Empire School of the Bible
and would support religious education. We viewed this arrangement, however,
as no different from a government issuing a paycheck to one of its employees
knowing that the employee would direct the funds to a religious institution. Both
arrangements would be valid, for the same reason: "[A]ny money that ultimately went to religious institutions did so 'only as a result of the genuinely
independent and private choices of' individuals." In addition, the program in *Witters* was neutral.

As *Agostini* explained, the same reasoning was at work in *Zobrest*, where we
allowed the government-funded interpreter to provide assistance at a Catholic
school, "even though she would be a mouthpiece for religious instruction,"
because the interpreter was provided according to neutral eligibility criteria and
private choice. Therefore, the religious messages interpreted by the interpreter
could not be attributed to the government.

Of course, we have seen "special Establishment Clause dangers" when *money*
is given to religious schools or entities directly rather than, as in *Witters* and
Mueller, indirectly. But direct payments of money are not at issue in this case,
and we refuse to allow a "special" case to create a rule for all cases.

2

Respondents also contend that the Establishment Clause requires that aid to
religious schools not be impermissibly religious in nature or be divertible to religious use. We agree with the first part of this argument but not the second.
Respondents' "no divertibility" rule is inconsistent with our more recent case law
and is unworkable. So long as the governmental aid is not itself "unsuitable for
use in the public schools because of religious content," and eligibility for aid is
determined in a constitutionally permissible manner, any use of that aid to
indoctrinate cannot be attributed to the government and is thus not of constitutional concern. And, of course, the use to which the aid is put does not affect
the criteria governing the aid's allocation and thus does not create any impermissible incentive under *Agostini*'s second criterion.

Our recent precedents, particularly *Zobrest*, require us to reject respondents'
argument. For *Zobrest* gave no consideration to divertibility or even to actual
diversion. Had such things mattered to the Court in *Zobrest*, we would have
found the case to be quite easy — for *striking down* rather than, as we did,
upholding the program — which is just how the dissent saw the case. Quite
clearly, then, we did not, as respondents do, think that the *use* of governmental aid to further religious indoctrination was synonymous with religious indoctrination *by* the government or that such use of aid created any improper
incentives.

Similarly, had we, in *Witters*, been concerned with divertibility or diversion,
we would have unhesitatingly, perhaps summarily, struck down the tuition-
reimbursement program, because it was certain that Witters sought to partic-

ipate in it to acquire an education in a religious career from a sectarian institution. Diversion was guaranteed. *Mueller* took the same view as *Zobrest* and *Witters*, for we did not in *Mueller* require the State to show that the tax deductions were only for the costs of education in secular subjects. We declined to impose any such segregation requirement for either the tuition-expense deductions or the deductions for items strikingly similar to those at issue in Meek and Wolman, and here.

The issue is not divertibility of aid but rather whether the aid itself has an impermissible content. Where the aid would be suitable for use in a public school, it is also suitable for use in any private school. Similarly, the prohibition against the government providing impermissible content resolves the Establishment Clause concerns that exist if aid is actually diverted to religious uses. In *Agostini,* we explained *Zobrest* by making just this distinction between the content of aid and the use of that aid: "Because the only *government* aid in *Zobrest* was the interpreter, who was *herself not inculcating* any religious messages, no *government* indoctrination took place." *Agostini* also acknowledged that what the dissenters in *Zobrest* had charged was essentially true: *Zobrest* did effect a "shift . . . in our Establishment Clause law." The interpreter herself, assuming that she fulfilled her assigned duties, had "no inherent religious significance," and so it did not matter (given the neutrality and private choice involved in the program) that she "would be a mouthpiece for religious instruction." And just as a government interpreter does not herself inculcate a religious message — even when she is conveying one — so also a government computer or overhead projector does not itself inculcate a religious message, even when it is conveying one.

A concern for divertibility, as opposed to improper content, is misplaced not only because it fails to explain why the sort of aid that we have allowed is permissible, but also because it is boundless — enveloping all aid, no matter how trivial — and thus has only the most attenuated (if any) link to any realistic concern for preventing an "establishment of religion." Presumably, for example, government-provided lecterns, chalk, crayons, pens, paper, and paintbrushes would have to be excluded from religious schools under respondents' proposed rule. But we fail to see how indoctrination by means of (*i.e.,* diversion of) such aid could be attributed to the government. In fact, the risk of improper attribution is *less* when the aid lacks content, for there is no risk (as there is with books), of the government inadvertently providing improper content.

Finally, *any* aid, with or without content, is "divertible" in the sense that it allows schools to "divert" resources. Yet we have "'not accepted the recurrent argument that all aid is forbidden because aid to one aspect of an institution frees it to spend its other resources on religious ends.'" It is perhaps conceivable that courts could take upon themselves the task of distinguishing among the myriad kinds of possible aid based on the ease of diverting each kind. But it escapes us how a court might coherently draw any such line. It not only is far more workable, but also is actually related to real concerns about preventing advancement of religion by government, simply to require, as did *Zobrest, Agostini*, and *Allen*, that a program of aid to schools not provide improper content and that it determine eligibility and allocate the aid on a permissible basis.

C

The dissent serves up a smorgasbord of 11 factors that, depending on the facts of each case "in all its particularity," could be relevant to the constitutionality of a school-aid program. And those 11 are a bare minimum. We are reassured that there are likely more. Presumably they will be revealed in future cases, as needed, but at least one additional factor is evident from the dissent itself: The dissent resurrects the concern for political divisiveness that once occupied the Court but that post-*Aguilar* cases have rightly disregarded. While the dissent delights in the perverse chaos that all these factors produce, the Constitution becomes unnecessarily clouded, and legislators, litigants, and lower courts groan, as the history of this case amply demonstrates.

One of the dissent's factors deserves special mention: whether a school that receives aid (or whose students receive aid) is pervasively sectarian. The dissent is correct that there was a period when this factor mattered, particularly if the pervasively sectarian school was a primary or secondary school. But that period is one that the Court should regret, and it is thankfully long past.

There are numerous reasons to formally dispense with this factor. First, its relevance in our precedents is in sharp decline. Although our case law has consistently mentioned it even in recent years, we have not struck down an aid program in reliance on this factor since 1985, in *Aguilar* and *Ball*. *Agostini* of course overruled *Aguilar* in full and *Ball* in part, and today JUSTICE O'CONNOR distances herself from the part of *Ball* with which she previously agreed, by rejecting the distinction between public and private employees that was so prominent in *Agostini*.

Second, the religious nature of a recipient should not matter to the constitutional analysis, so long as the recipient adequately furthers the government's secular purpose. If a program offers permissible aid to the religious (including the pervasively sectarian), the areligious, and the irreligious, it is a mystery which view of religion the government has established, and thus a mystery what the constitutional violation would be. The pervasively sectarian recipient has not received any special favor, and it is most bizarre that the Court would, as the dissent seemingly does, reserve special hostility for those who take their religion seriously, who think that their religion should affect the whole of their lives, or who make the mistake of being effective in transmitting their views to children.

Third, the inquiry into the recipient's religious views required by a focus on whether a school is pervasively sectarian is not only unnecessary but also offensive. It is well established, in numerous other contexts, that courts should refrain from trolling through a person's or institution's religious beliefs. Yet that is just what this factor requires, as was evident before the District Court.

Although the dissent welcomes such probing, we find it profoundly troubling. In addition, and related, the application of the "pervasively sectarian" factor collides with our decisions that have prohibited governments from discriminating in the distribution of public benefits based upon religious status or sincerity.

Finally, hostility to aid to pervasively sectarian schools has a shameful pedigree that we do not hesitate to disavow. Although the dissent professes concern for "the implied exclusion of the less favored," the exclusion of pervasively sectarian schools from government-aid programs is just that, particularly given the history of such exclusion. Opposition to aid to "sectarian" schools acquired prominence in the 1870's with Congress' consideration (and near passage) of the Blaine Amendment, which would have amended the Constitution to bar any aid to sectarian institutions. Consideration of the amendment arose at a time of pervasive hostility to the Catholic Church and to Catholics in general, and it was an open secret that "sectarian" was code for "Catholic." *See generally* Green, *The Blaine Amendment Reconsidered*, 36 AM. J. LEGAL HIST. 38 (1992). Notwithstanding its history, of course, "sectarian" could, on its face, describe the school of any religious sect, but the Court eliminated this possibility of confusion when, in *Hunt v. McNair*, 413 U.S., at 743, it coined the term "pervasively sectarian" — a term which, at that time, could be applied almost exclusively to Catholic parochial schools and which even today's dissent exemplifies chiefly by reference to such schools.

In short, nothing in the Establishment Clause requires the exclusion of pervasively sectarian schools from otherwise permissible aid programs, and other doctrines of this Court bar it. This doctrine, born of bigotry, should be buried now.

III

[In applying the standard set forth above, the plurality then concluded that Chapter 2 is constitutional because aid] is allocated on the basis of neutral, secular criteria that neither favor nor disfavor religion, and is made available to both religious and secular beneficiaries on a nondiscriminatory basis [and the] program makes a broad array of schools eligible for aid without regard to their religious affiliations or lack thereof. [The plurality also concluded that] [b]ecause Chapter 2 aid is provided pursuant to private choices, it is not problematic that one could fairly describe Chapter 2 as providing 'direct' aid. . . . Like the Ninth Circuit, and unlike the dissent, we 'see little difference in loaning science kits to students who then bring the kits to school as opposed to loaning science kits to the school directly. [Finally, the plurality noted that] [t]he chief aid at issue is computers, computer software, and library books. The computers presumably have no pre-existing content, or at least none that would be impermissible for use in public schools. Respondents do not contend otherwise. Respondents also offer no evidence that religious schools have received software from the government that has an impermissible content.

Justice O'Connor, with whom Justice Breyer joins, concurring in the judgment.

I.

I write separately because, in my view, the plurality announces a rule of unprecedented breadth for the evaluation of Establishment Clause challenges to government school-aid programs. Reduced to its essentials, the plurality's rule states that government aid to religious schools does not have the effect of advancing religion so long as the aid is offered on a neutral basis and the aid is secular in content. The plurality also rejects the distinction between direct and indirect aid, and holds that the actual diversion of secular aid by a religious school to the advancement of its religious mission is permissible. Although the expansive scope of the plurality's rule is troubling, two specific aspects of the opinion compel me to write separately. First, the plurality's treatment of neutrality comes close to assigning that factor singular importance in the future adjudication of Establishment Clause challenges to government school-aid programs. Second, the plurality's approval of actual diversion of government aid to religious indoctrination is in tension with our precedents and, in any event, unnecessary to decide the instant case.

The clearest example of the plurality's near-absolute position with respect to neutrality is found in its following statement:

> "If the religious, irreligious, and areligious are all alike eligible for governmental aid, no one would conclude that any indoctrination that any particular recipient conducts has been done at the behest of the government. For attribution of indoctrination is a relative question. If the government is offering assistance to recipients who provide, so to speak, a broad range of indoctrination, the government itself is not thought responsible for any particular indoctrination. To put the point differently, if the government, seeking to further some legitimate secular purpose, offers aid on the same terms, without regard to religion, to all who adequately further that purpose, then it is fair to say that any aid going to a religious recipient only has the effect of furthering that secular purpose."

I agree with Justice Souter that the plurality, by taking such a stance, "appears to take evenhandedness neutrality and in practical terms promote it to a single and sufficient test for the establishment constitutionality of school aid." I do not quarrel with the plurality's recognition that neutrality is an important reason for upholding government-aid programs against Establishment Clause challenges. Our cases have described neutrality in precisely this manner, and we have emphasized a program's neutrality repeatedly in our decisions approving various forms of school aid. Nevertheless, we have never held that a government-aid program passes constitutional muster *solely* because of the neutral criteria it employs as a basis for distributing aid. For example, in *Agostini,* neutrality was only one of several factors we considered in determining that

New York City's Title I program did not have the impermissible effect of advancing religion. Indeed, given that the aid in *Agostini* had secular content and was distributed on the basis of wholly neutral criteria, our consideration of additional factors demonstrates that the plurality's rule does not accurately describe our recent Establishment Clause jurisprudence.

JUSTICE SOUTER provides a comprehensive review of our Establishment Clause cases on government aid to religious institutions that is useful for its explanation of the various ways in which we have used the term "neutrality" in our decisions. Even if we at one time used the term "neutrality" in a descriptive sense to refer to those aid programs characterized by the requisite equipoise between support of religion and antagonism to religion, JUSTICE SOUTER's discussion convincingly demonstrates that the evolution in the meaning of the term in our jurisprudence is cause to hesitate before equating the neutrality of recent decisions with the neutrality of old. As I have previously explained, neutrality is important, but it is by no means the only "axiom in the history and precedent of the Establishment Clause." Thus, I agree with JUSTICE SOUTER's conclusion that our "most recent use of 'neutrality' to refer to generality or evenhandedness of distribution . . . is relevant in judging whether a benefit scheme so characterized should be seen as aiding a sectarian school's religious mission, but this neutrality is not alone sufficient to qualify the aid as constitutional."

I also disagree with the plurality's conclusion that actual diversion of government aid to religious indoctrination is consistent with the Establishment Clause. Although "[o]ur cases have permitted some government funding of secular functions performed by sectarian organizations," our decisions "provide no precedent for the use of public funds to finance religious activities." At least two of the decisions at the heart of today's case demonstrate that we have long been concerned that secular government aid not be diverted to the advancement of religion. In both *Agostini,* our most recent school-aid case, and *Board of Ed. of Central School Dist. No. 1 v. Allen*, 392 U.S. 236 (1968), we rested our approval of the relevant programs in part on the fact that the aid had not been used to advance the religious missions of the recipient schools. Our decision in *Bowen v. Kendrick* also demonstrates that actual diversion is constitutionally impermissible. After concluding that the government-aid program in question was constitutional on its face, we remanded the case so that the District Court could determine, after further factual development, whether aid recipients had used the government aid to support their religious objectives. The remand would have been unnecessary if, as the plurality contends, actual diversion were irrelevant under the Establishment Clause.

The plurality bases its holding that actual diversion is permissible on *Witters* and *Zobrest*. Those decisions, however, rested on a significant factual premise missing from this case, as well as from the majority of cases thus far considered by the Court involving Establishment Clause challenges to school-aid programs. Specifically, we decided *Witters* and *Zobrest* on the understanding that the aid was provided directly to the individual student who, in turn, made the choice of where to put that aid to use. Accordingly, our approval of the aid in both cases relied to a significant extent on the fact that "[a]ny aid . . . that ultimately flows to religious institutions does so only as a result of the genuinely independent and private choices of aid recipients." This characteristic of both programs made them less like a direct subsidy, which would be impermissible under the Establishment Clause, and more akin to the government issuing a paycheck to an employee who, in turn, donates a portion of that check to a religious institution.

Like JUSTICE SOUTER, I do not believe that we should treat a per-capita-aid program the same as the true private-choice programs considered in *Witters* and *Zobrest*. First, when the government provides aid directly to the student beneficiary, that student can attend a religious school and yet retain control over whether the secular government aid will be applied toward the religious education. The fact that aid flows to the religious school and is used for the advancement of religion is therefore *wholly* dependent on the student's private decision. It is for this reason that in *Agostini* we relied on *Witters* and *Zobrest* to reject the rule "that all government aid that directly assists the educational function of religious schools is invalid."

Second, I believe the distinction between a per-capita school-aid program and a true private-choice program is significant for purposes of endorsement. In terms of public perception, a government program of direct aid to religious schools based on the number of students attending each school differs meaningfully from the government distributing aid directly to individual students who, in turn, decide to use the aid at the same religious schools. In the former example, if the religious school uses the aid to inculcate religion in its students, it is reasonable to say that the government has communicated a message of endorsement. Because the religious indoctrination is supported by government assistance, the reasonable observer would naturally perceive the aid program as *government* support for the advancement of religion. That the amount of aid received by the school is based on the school's enrollment does not separate the government from the endorsement of the religious message. The aid formula does not — and could not — indicate to a reasonable observer that the inculcation of religion is endorsed only by the individuals attending the religious school, who each affirmatively choose to direct the secular government aid to the school and its religious mission. No such choices have been made. In contrast, when government aid supports a school's religious mission only because of independent decisions made by numerous individuals to guide their secular aid to that school, "[n]o reasonable observer is likely to draw from the facts . . . an inference that the State itself is endorsing a religious practice or belief." Rather, endorsement of the religious message is reasonably attributed to the individuals who select the path of the aid.

Finally, the distinction between a per-capita-aid program and a true private-choice program is important when considering aid that consists of direct monetary subsidies. This Court has "recognized special Establishment Clause dangers where the government makes direct money payments to sectarian institutions." If, as the plurality contends, a per-capita-aid program is identical in relevant constitutional respects to a true private-choice program, then there is no reason that, under the plurality's reasoning, the government should be precluded from providing direct money payments to religious organizations (including churches) based on the number of persons belonging to each organization. And, because actual diversion is permissible under the plurality's holding, the participating religious organizations (including churches) could use that aid to support religious indoctrination. To be sure, the plurality does not actually hold that its theory extends to direct money payments. That omission, however, is of little comfort. In its logic — as well as its specific advisory language — the plurality opinion foreshadows the approval of direct monetary subsidies to religious organizations, even when they use the money to advance their religious objectives.

[Having rejected the plurality's approach, Justice O'Connor then applied the three criteria set forth in *Agostini*: "Looking to our recently decided cases, we articulated three primary criteria to guide the determination whether a government-aid program impermissibly advances religion: (1) whether the aid results in governmental indoctrination, (2) whether the aid program defines its recipients by reference to religion, and (3) whether the aid creates an excessive entanglement between government and religion." She concluded that the program satisfied all three criteria. "As in *Agostini*, the Chapter 2 aid is allocated on the basis of neutral, secular criteria; the aid must be supplementary and cannot supplant non-Federal funds; no Chapter 2 funds ever reach the coffers of religious schools; the aid must be secular; any evidence of actual diversion is *de minimis*; and the program includes adequate safeguards. Regardless of whether these factors are constitutional requirements, they are surely sufficient to find that the program at issue here does not have the impermissible effect of advancing religion. For the same reasons, 'this carefully constrained program also cannot reasonably be viewed as an endorsement of religion.' Accordingly, I concur in the judgment."]

JUSTICE SOUTER, with whom JUSTICE STEVENS and JUSTICE GINSBURG join, dissenting.

The establishment prohibition of government religious funding serves more than one end. It is meant to guarantee the right of individual conscience against compulsion, to protect the integrity of religion against the corrosion of secular support, and to preserve the unity of political society against the implied exclusion of the less favored and the antagonism of controversy over public support for religious causes.

These objectives are always in some jeopardy since the substantive principle of no aid to religion is not the only limitation on government action toward religion. Because the First Amendment also bars any prohibition of individual free exercise of religion, and because religious organizations cannot be isolated from the basic government functions that create the civil environment, it is as much necessary as it is difficult to draw lines between forbidden aid and lawful benefit. For more than 50 years, this Court has been attempting to draw these lines. Owing to the variety of factual circumstances in which the lines must be drawn, not all of the points creating the boundary have enjoyed self-evidence.

So far as the line drawn has addressed government aid to education, a few fundamental generalizations are nonetheless possible. There may be no aid supporting a sectarian school's religious exercise or the discharge of its religious mission, while aid of a secular character with no discernible benefit to such a sectarian objective is allowable. Because the religious and secular spheres largely overlap in the life of many such schools, the Court has tried to identify some facts likely to reveal the relative religious or secular intent or effect of the government benefits in particular circumstances. We have asked whether the government is acting neutrally in distributing its money, and about the form of the aid itself, its path from government to religious institution, its divertibility to religious nurture, its potential for reducing traditional expenditures of religious institutions, and its relative importance to the recipient, among other things.

In all the years of its effort, the Court has isolated no single test of constitutional sufficiency, and the question in every case addresses the substantive principle of no aid: what reasons are there to characterize this benefit as aid to the sectarian school in discharging its religious mission? Particular factual circumstances control, and the answer is a matter of judgment.

It is not just that a majority today mistakes the significance of facts that have led to conclusions of unconstitutionality in earlier cases, though I believe the Court commits error in failing to recognize the divertibility of funds to the service of religious objectives. What is more important is the view revealed in the plurality opinion, which espouses a new conception of neutrality as a practically sufficient test of constitutionality that would, if adopted by the Court, eliminate enquiry into a law's effects. The plurality position breaks fundamentally with Establishment Clause principle, and with the methodology painstakingly worked out in support of it.

[Justice Souter then provided a long description of the history of disputes over government financing of religious activities, culminating with a discussion of the various ways in which the Court has used the term "neutrality." Portions of this discussion are reproduced in Chapter 5, *infra*.]

II

B

The insufficiency of evenhandedness neutrality as a stand-alone criterion of constitutional intent or effect has been clear from the beginning of our interpretative efforts, for an obvious reason. Evenhandedness in distributing a benefit approaches the equivalence of constitutionality in this area only when the term refers to such universality of distribution that it makes no sense to think of the benefit as going to any discrete group. Conversely, when evenhandedness refers to distribution to limited groups within society, like groups of schools or schoolchildren, it does make sense to regard the benefit as aid to the recipients.

Hence, if we looked no further than evenhandedness, and failed to ask what activities the aid might support, or in fact did support, religious schools could be blessed with government funding as massive as expenditures made for the benefit of their public school counterparts, and religious missions would thrive on public money. This is why the consideration of less than universal neutrality has never been recognized as dispositive and has always been teamed with attention to other facts bearing on the substantive prohibition of support for a school's religious objective.

At least three main lines of enquiry addressed particularly to school aid have emerged to complement evenhandedness neutrality. First, we have noted that two types of aid recipients heighten Establishment Clause concern: pervasively religious schools and primary and secondary religious schools. Second, we have identified two important characteristics of the method of distributing aid: directness or indirectness of distribution and distribution by genuinely independent choice. Third, we have found relevance in at least five characteristics of the aid itself: its religious content; its cash form; its divertibility or actually diversion to religious support; its supplantation of traditional items of religious school expense; and its substantiality.

1

Two types of school aid recipients have raised special concern. First, we have recognized the fact that the overriding religious mission of certain schools, those sometimes called "pervasively sectarian," is not confined to a discrete element of the curriculum. Based on record evidence and long experience, we have concluded that religious teaching in such schools is at the core of the instructors' individual and personal obligations, cf. Canon 803, § 2, Text & Commentary 568 ("It is necessary that the formation and education given in a Catholic school be based upon the principles of Catholic doctrine; teachers are to be outstanding for their correct doctrine and integrity of life"), and that individual religious teachers will teach religiously. As religious teaching cannot be separated from secular education in such schools or by such teachers, we have concluded that direct government subsidies to such schools are prohibited because they will inevitably and impermissibly support religious indoctrination.

Second, we have expressed special concern about aid to primary and secondary religious schools. On the one hand, we have understood how the youth of the students in such schools makes them highly susceptible to religious indoctrination. On the other, we have recognized that the religious element in the education offered in most sectarian primary and secondary schools is far more intertwined with the secular than in university teaching, where the natural and academic skepticism of most older students may separate the two. Thus, government benefits accruing to these pervasively religious primary and secondary schools raise special dangers of diversion into support for the religious indoctrination of children and the involvement of government in religious training and practice.

2

We have also evaluated the portent of support to an organization's religious mission that may be inherent in the method by which aid is granted, finding pertinence in at least two characteristics of distribution. First, we have asked whether aid is direct or indirect, observing distinctions between government schemes with individual beneficiaries and those whose beneficiaries in the first instance might be religious schools. Direct aid obviously raises greater risks, although recent cases have discounted this risk factor, looking to other features of the distribution mechanism.

Second, we have distinguished between indirect aid that reaches religious schools only incidentally as a result of numerous individual choices and aid that is in reality directed to religious schools by the government or in practical terms selected by religious schools themselves. In these cases, we have declared the constitutionality of programs providing aid directly to parents or students as tax deductions or scholarship money, where such aid may pay for education at some sectarian institutions, but only as the result of "genuinely independent and private choices of aid recipients." We distinguished this path of aid from the route in *Ball* and *Wolman*, where the opinions indicated that "[w]here . . . no meaningful distinction can be made between aid to the student and aid to the school, the concept of a loan to individuals is a transparent fiction."

3

In addition to the character of the school to which the benefit accrues, and its path from government to school, a number of features of the aid itself have figured in the classifications we have made. First, we have barred aid with actual religious content, which would obviously run afoul of the ban on the government's participation in religion. In cases where we have permitted aid, we have regularly characterized it as "neutral" in the sense of being without religious content.

Second, we have long held government aid invalid when circumstances would allow its diversion to religious education. The risk of diversion is obviously high when aid in the form of government funds makes its way into the coffers of religious organizations, and so from the start we have understood the Constitution to bar outright money grants of aid to religion.

Divertibility is not, of course, a characteristic of cash alone, and when examining provisions for ostensibly secular supplies we have considered their susceptibility to the service of religious ends. In upholding a scheme to provide students with secular textbooks, we emphasized that "each book loaned must be approved by the public school authorities; only secular books may receive approval."

With the same point in mind, we held that buildings constructed with government grants to universities with religious affiliation must be barred from religious use indefinitely to prevent the diversion of government funds to religious objectives. We were accordingly constrained to strike down aid for repairing buildings of nonpublic schools because they could be used for religious education.

Third, our cases have recognized the distinction, adopted by statute in the Chapter 2 legislation, between aid that merely supplements and aid that supplants expenditures for offerings at religious schools, the latter being barred. Although we have never adopted the position that any benefit that flows to a religious school is impermissible because it frees up resources for the school to engage in religious indoctrination, from our first decision holding it permissible to provide textbooks for religious schools we have repeatedly explained the unconstitutionality of aid that supplants an item of the school's traditional expense.

Finally, we have recognized what is obvious (however imprecise), in holding "substantial" amounts of aid to be unconstitutional whether or not a plaintiff can show that it supplants a specific item of expense a religious school would have borne. [W]e invalidated the loan of instructional materials to religious schools because "faced with the substantial amounts of direct support authorized by [the program], it would simply ignore reality to attempt to separate secular educational functions from the predominantly religious role performed by many of Pennsylvania's church-related elementary and secondary schools and then characterize [the program] as channeling aid to the secular without providing direct aid to the sectarian."

C

This stretch of doctrinal history leaves one point clear beyond peradventure: together with James Madison we have consistently understood the Establishment Clause to impose a substantive prohibition against public aid to religion and, hence, to the religious mission of sectarian schools. Evenhandedness neutrality is one, nondispositive pointer toward an intent and (to a lesser degree) probable effect on the permissible side of the line between forbidden aid and general public welfare benefit. Other pointers are facts about the religious mission and education level of benefited schools and their pupils, the pathway by which a benefit travels from public treasury to educational effect, the form and content of the aid, its adaptability to religious ends, and its effects on school budgets. The object of all enquiries into such matters is the same whatever the particular circumstances: is the benefit intended to aid in providing the religious element of the education and is it likely to do so?

The substance of the law has thus not changed since *Everson*. Emphasis on one sort of fact or another has varied depending on the perceived utility of the enquiry, but all that has been added is repeated explanation of relevant considerations, confirming that our predecessors were right in their prophecies that no simple test would emerge to allow easy application of the establishment principle.

The plurality, however, would reject that lesson. The majority misapplies it.

III

A

The nub of the plurality's new position is this:

> "[I]f the government, seeking to further some legitimate secular purpose, offers aid on the same terms, without regard to religion, to all who adequately further that purpose, then it is fair to say that any aid going to a religious recipient only has the effect of furthering that secular purpose. The government, in crafting such an aid program, has had to conclude that a given level of aid is necessary to further that purpose among secular recipients and has provided no more than that same level to religious recipients."

As a break with consistent doctrine the plurality's new criterion is unequaled in the history of Establishment Clause interpretation. Simple on its face, it appears to take evenhandedness neutrality and in practical terms promote it to a single and sufficient test for the establishment constitutionality of school aid. Even on its own terms, its errors are manifold, and attention to at least three of its mistaken assumptions will show the degree to which the plurality's proposal would replace the principle of no aid with a formula for generous religious support.

First, the plurality treats an external observer's attribution of religious support to the government as the sole impermissible effect of a government aid scheme. While perceived state endorsement of religion is undoubtedly a relevant concern under the Establishment Clause, it is certainly not the only one. *Everson* made this clear from the start: secret aid to religion by the government is also barred. State aid not attributed to the government would still violate a taxpayer's liberty of conscience, threaten to corrupt religion, and generate disputes over aid. In any event, since the same-terms feature of the scheme would, on the plurality's view, rule out the attribution or perception of endorsement, adopting the plurality's rule of facial evenhandedness would convert neutrality into a dispositive criterion of establishment constitutionality and eliminate the effects enquiry directed by *Allen, Lemon*, and other cases. Under the plurality's rule of neutrality, if a program met the first part of the *Lemon* enquiry, by declining to define a program's recipients by religion, it would automatically satisfy the second, in supposedly having no impermissible effect of aiding religion.

Second, the plurality apparently assumes as a fact that equal amounts of aid to religious and nonreligious schools will have exclusively secular and equal effects, on both external perception and on incentives to attend different schools.

But there is no reason to believe that this will be the case; the effects of same-terms aid may not be confined to the secular sphere at all. This is the reason that we have long recognized that unrestricted aid to religious schools will support religious teaching in addition to secular education, a fact that would be true no matter what the supposedly secular purpose of the law might be.

Third, the plurality assumes that per capita distribution rules safeguard the same principles as independent, private choices. But that is clearly not so. We approved university scholarships in *Witters* because we found them close to giving a government employee a paycheck and allowing him to spend it as he chose, but a per capita aid program is a far cry from awarding scholarships to individuals, one of whom makes an independent private choice. Not the least of the significant differences between per capita aid and aid individually determined and directed is the right and genuine opportunity of the recipient to choose not to give the aid. To hold otherwise would be to license the government to donate funds to churches based on the number of their members, on the patent fiction of independent private choice.

The plurality's mistaken assumptions explain and underscore its sharp break with the Framers' understanding of establishment and this Court's consistent interpretative course. Under the plurality's regime, little would be left of the right of conscience against compelled support for religion; the more massive the aid the more potent would be the influence of the government on the teaching mission; the more generous the support, the more divisive would be the resentments of those resisting religious support, and those religions without school systems ready to claim their fair share.

B

[Justice Souter then discussed the divertibility and diversion of government aid to sectarian purposes in Chapter 2, concluding that the evidence required the program to be deemed unconstitutional.]

IV

The plurality would break with the law. The majority misapplies it. That misapplication is, however, the only consolation in the case, which reaches an erroneous result but does not stage a doctrinal coup. But there is no mistaking the abandonment of doctrine that would occur if the plurality were to become a majority. It is beyond question that the plurality's notion of evenhandedness neutrality as a practical guarantee of the validity of aid to sectarian schools would be the end of the principle of no aid to the schools' religious mission. And if that were not so obvious it would become so after reflecting on the plurality's thoughts about diversion and about giving attention to the pervasiveness of a school's sectarian teaching.

The plurality is candid in pointing out the extent of actual diversion of Chapter 2 aid to religious use in the case before us, and equally candid in saying it does not matter. To the plurality there is nothing wrong with aiding a school's religious mission; the only question is whether religious teaching obtains its tax support under a formally evenhanded criterion of distribution. The principle of no aid to religious teaching has no independent significance.

And if this were not enough to prove that no aid in religious school aid is dead under the plurality's First Amendment, the point is nailed down in the plurality's attack on the legitimacy of considering a school's pervasively sectarian character when judging whether aid to the school is likely to aid its religious mission. The relevance of this consideration is simply a matter of common sense: where religious indoctrination pervades school activities of children and adolescents, it takes great care to be able to aid the school without supporting the doctrinal effort. This is obvious. The plurality nonetheless condemns any enquiry into the pervasiveness of doctrinal content as a remnant of anti-Catholic bigotry (as if evangelical Protestant schools and Orthodox Jewish yeshivas were never pervasively sectarian), and it equates a refusal to aid religious schools with hostility to religion (as if aid to religious teaching were not opposed in this very case by at least one religious respondent and numerous religious *amici curiae* in a tradition claiming descent from Roger Williams). My concern with these arguments goes not so much to their details as it does to the fact that the plurality's choice to employ imputations of bigotry and irreligion as terms in the Court's debate makes one point clear: that in rejecting the principle of no aid to a school's religious mission the plurality is attacking the most fundamental assumption underlying the Establishment Clause, that government can in fact operate with neutrality in its relation to religion. I believe that it can, and so respectfully dissent.

NOTES AND QUESTIONS: A NEW STANDARD FOR PUBLIC FINANCING OF RELIGIOUS EDUCATION?

Agostini, *Zelman*, and *Mitchell* certainly change the landscape of public financing of religious education, but is it entirely clear how much of a change the cases have inaugurated? The clearest effect of the cases is to significantly loosen constraints on government aid to religious schools that supplants ordinary educational expenses the schools would otherwise have to shoulder themselves. Another clear effect is to reduce greatly the oversight of government employees working in religious environments. A final clear effect is to allow the government to provide religious schools a wide range of educational materials in addition to books. But aside from these specific changes in the rules regarding the administration of government aid programs, while Justice O'Connor remained on the Court it was perhaps equally significant that neither *Agostini* nor *Mitchell* overturned the portion of *Ball* that held the community education program unconstitutional. Nor did the majority in either case significantly change the basic rules regarding the application of the *Lemon* test. At the time they were issued, perhaps the most significant message of these cases was the conclusion of the majority in *Mitchell* (that is, the three dissenters plus O'Connor and Breyer) that the basic doctrine remained intact — i.e., the doctrine regarding the prohibition on aid to pervasively sectarian institutions, the need for more than a weak neutrality principle to guide Establishment Clause decisions (at least with regard to direct aid), and the range of factors relevant in considering whether a particular aid program violates Establishment Clause principles. Unfortunately for the Court's remaining separationists, the resistance to change rested on a slim one-vote majority, with Justice O'Connor as the lynchpin. Given their relatively scarce record on such issues, it is not yet entirely clear how the addition of Chief Justice Roberts and Justice Alito will change the rules in this area of Establishment Clause law. If these new Justices join Justices Kennedy, Scalia, and Thomas, then in the coming decade the doctrine involving government financing of religious institutions may change beyond all recognition.

In any event, the darker side of *Mitchell* is the emergence of what Justice Souter referred to as the "plurality's choice to employ imputations of bigotry and irreligion as terms in the Court's debate." The personalities and personal histories of the Justices have always been in the background of the great disputes on the Court, but the fact that the Justices' own specific religious affiliations and sentiments are being announced explicitly in the Court's opinions may bode ill for any future efforts to achieve even a rough consensus on the constitutional rules regarding church and state.

B. THE "LITTLE BLAINE" AMENDMENTS AND OTHER STATE LIMITS ON FINANCIAL AID TO RELIGION

The Court's focus on "neutrality" in *Zelman* raises the question whether state voucher programs *must* fund religious schools if they fund nonreligious private schools. Specifically, what are the implications of the Court's new "neutrality" theory for programs such as the Maine tuition reimbursement program, which permits only nonsectarian private schools to accept state money? The program was upheld against both Establishment and Free Exercise Clause challenges in *Strout v. Albanese*, 178 F.3d 57 (1st Cir.), *cert. denied,* 528 U.S. 931 (1999). In *Zelman* Justice Rehnquist emphasizes that the "Ohio program is neutral in all respects toward religion." Justice O'Connor's concurring opinion says that the secular effects prong of *Lemon* is applied by assessing "whether the program administers aid in a neutral fashion, without differentiation based on the religious status of beneficiaries or providers of services." Does Maine's program comply with a literal reading of this standard? If not, does *Zelman* effectively convert the Establishment Clause from a constitutional ban on state funding of religion into a constitutional mandate of state funding of religion? Recall in this regard the *Everson* Court's unanimous pronouncement that "No tax in any amount, large or small, can be levied to support any religious activities or institutions, whatever they may be called, or whatever they adopt to teach or practice religion." Is this principle now nothing more than a historical artifact?

These questions are especially important in light of numerous state constitutional provisions prohibiting government aid to religion. These state constitutional provisions are often referred to as "Little Blaine" amendments. The term refers to James G. Blaine, who was Speaker of the United States House of Representatives from 1869 to 1875. Blaine was also the unsuccessful Republican nominee for President in the 1884 election. While serving as Speaker, Blaine proposed what became known as the "Blaine Amendment" to the United States Constitution. There were actually several versions of what became known as the Blaine Amendment. The House version, which was introduced in 1875, stated:

> No State shall make any law respecting an establishment of religion, or prohibiting the free exercise thereof; and no money raised by taxation in any State for the support of public schools, or derived from any public fund therefor, nor any public lands devoted thereto, shall ever be under the control of any religious sect; nor shall any money so raised or lands so devoted be divided between religious sects or denominations.

The pertinent part of the Senate version stated:

> No state shall make any law respecting an establishment of religion or prohibiting the free exercise thereof. . . . No public property, and no public revenue of, nor any loan or credit . . . shall be appropriated to, or made to be used for, the support of any religious or antireligious sect, organization, or denomination or to promote its interests or tenets.

4 Cong. Rec. 205 (1875). (For other versions of the Amendment, *see* Steven K. Green, *The Blaine Amendment Reconsidered*, 36 AM. J. LEGAL HIST. 38, 47-66 (1992). Professor Green's article is probably the best general history of the Blaine Amendment and its political and legal context.) The proposed amendment to the United States Constitution obtained the requisite two-thirds majority in the House (by a vote of 180-7), but fell short in the Senate by a vote of 28-16 in favor of the amendment, with 27 members not voting. *See* Alfred W. Meyer, *The Blaine Amendment and the Bill of Rights*, 64 HARV. L. REV. 939, 942 (1951). Another effort to enact a constitutional amendment prohibiting government support for sectarian schools failed in 1889, but a version of the prohibition was included in the Enabling Act, which governed the process of introducing new states into the Union. The Act required the constitutions of newly admitted states to provide for "the establishment and maintenance of a system of public schools, which shall be open to all children . . . and free from sectarian control." *See* Enabling Act, ch. 180, § 4, 25 Stat. 676, 676-77 (1889). A total of 37 states now have some form of constitutional prohibition on aid to religious education, although the scope of these provisions and the circumstances in which they were adopted vary widely.

In recent years there has been an increasingly vigorous debate about the genesis of the federal Blaine Amendment and its state offshoots. Proponents of government aid to religious schools have emphasized that many of the nineteenth-century proposals to deny government money to sectarian schools were motivated by nativist and anti-Catholic sentiment. In his recent book, for example, Philip Hamburger argues that "Nativist Protestants . . . failed to obtain a federal constitutional amendment but, because of the strength of anti-Catholic feeling, managed to secure local versions of the Blaine Amendment in the vast majority of states." PHILIP HAMBURGER, SEPARATION OF CHURCH AND STATE 335 (2002). In reviewing the Arizona state constitution's version of the Blaine Amendment, the Arizona Supreme Court noted that "[t]he Blaine amendment was a clear manifestation of religious bigotry, part of a crusade manufactured by the contemporary Protestant establishment to counter what was perceived as a growing 'Catholic menace.'" *Kotterman v. Killian*, 972 P.2d 606, 624 (Ariz. 1999) (citing Joseph P. Viteritti, *Choosing Equality: Religious Freedom and Educational Opportunity Under Constitutional Federalism*, 15 YALE L. & POL'Y REV. 113, 146 (1996)). Meanwhile, Justice Thomas has contributed to the debate a blistering attack on both the nineteenth century Blaine Amendment and the twentieth century notion that the government should not finance pervasively sectarian schools:

> Opposition to aid to "sectarian" schools acquired prominence in the 1870's with Congress's consideration (and near passage) of the Blaine Amendment, which would have amended the Constitution to bar any aid to sectarian institutions. Consideration of the amendment arose at a time of pervasive hostility to the Catholic Church and to Catholics in general, and it was an open secret that "sectarian" was code for "Catholic." [Citing Green, *supra*.] Notwithstanding its history, of course, "sectarian" could, on its face, describe the school of any religious sect, but the Court eliminated this possibility of confusion when, in *Hunt v. McNair,* it coined the term "pervasively sectarian" — a term which, at that time, could be applied almost exclusively to Catholic parochial schools and which even today's dissent exemplifies chiefly by reference to such schools. . . .

> In short, nothing in the Establishment Clause requires the exclusion of pervasively sectarian schools from otherwise permissible aid programs, and other doctrines of this Court bar it. This doctrine, born of bigotry, should be buried now.

Mitchell v. Helms, 530 U.S. 793, 828-29 (2000) (plurality opinion).

There is some truth in all these allegations, but the story is much more complicated than the modern advocates of education and social service voucher programs acknowledge. There is no question that strong evidence exists of anti-Catholic bias among many supporters of the Blaine Amendment and its state equivalents. It is likewise unquestionable that Blaine himself used the Amendment as part of his campaign for the Republican nomination for President, and that the Amendment was a central part of the Republican Party's larger campaign against "Rum, Romanism, and Rebellion" at the end of the nineteenth century. *See* KIRK PORTER & DONALD JOHNSON, NATIONAL PARTY PLATFORMS 1840-

1964, 51-52 (1966). But it is historically inaccurate to characterize all, or even most, state no-aid provisions as the exclusive product of anti-Catholic animus. Public sentiment against government aid to religion, including religious education, has an extensive history in the United States that long predates large-scale Catholic immigration or the battle over the Blaine Amendment. Madison's famous admonition in the *Memorial and Remonstrance* (*see* Chapter 1 of the main text) that it would be impermissible for the government to collect even "three pence . . . for the support of any one establishment" is the most famous articulation of this sentiment.

Opposition to government funding of sectarian religious education was often merely a particular application of the broader resistance to public funding of religion generally. Contrary to Justice Thomas' assertion in *Mitchell*, "sectarian" was not necessarily code for "Catholic." Many of the early battles to defend publicly financed nonsectarian education against claims by religious schools took place in New York City, where the Free School Society operated nonsectarian schools and routinely opposed government financing of sectarian schools run by various Protestant sects. *See generally* WILLIAM OLAND BOURNE, HISTORY OF THE PUBLIC SCHOOL SOCIETY OF THE CITY OF NEW YORK (1870); JOHN WEBB PRATT, RELIGION, POLITICS, AND DIVERSITY: THE CHURCH-STATE THEME IN NEW YORK HISTORY (1967). One significant early dispute resulted in the New York City Common Council voting in 1825 to end the funding of religious charity schools. *See* BOURNE, *supra*, at 72-75; PRATT, *supra*, at 167. This occurred almost a decade before the first wave of Irish Catholic immigration and also years before the American Catholic Church made the decision to create a parochial school system. Many other states adopted their constitutional no-aid provisions prior to extensive Catholic immigration into those states or disputes over parochial education, and long before the Blaine Amendment was proposed at the federal level. Those states include Michigan (1835), Wisconsin (1848), Indiana (1851), Minnesota (1857), and Oregon (1857).

There is substantial evidence of public resistance to any state aid to religious education — not merely opposition to disfavored Catholics — even in states that adopted no-aid constitutional provisions after the Blaine Amendment. After discussing the more sordid history of the federal Blaine Amendment, for example, the Arizona Supreme Court acknowledged finding no evidence that similar bigotry motivated the drafters of the Arizona "Little Blaine" amendment. *Kotterman*, 972 P.2d at 624. One member of the Arizona court noted other evidence that the Arizona provision was motivated more by general separationist sentiment than anti-Catholic bigotry. "In contrast to the Blaine Amendment and constitutional amendments in states that discriminated against Catholics and promoted Protestantism through reading the King James Bible in schools, Arizona legislated against *all religious exercise*. . . ." *Kotterman*, 972 P.2d at 635 (Feldman, J., dissenting). Justice Feldman then quotes a 1918 report by the United States Bureau of Education:

Every school law since that of 1871 had contained provisions against the introduction of tracts or papers of a sectarian character into the public school, also against the teaching of any sectarian doctrine in them. For some reason this was not believed to be drastic enough, and a section was added to the law which provided for revoking teachers' certificates for using in their schools sectarian or denominational books, for teaching in them any sectarian doctrine, or for conducting any religious exercise therein. The lawmakers evidently aimed to relegate all religious teaching to the home and the church. The prohibiting of "religious exercises" in schools has met with strong condemnation from many Protestant church members, but with the variety of religious creeds represented in the Territory it is doubtful whether a better policy could have been found.

Stephen B. Weeks, United States Bureau Of Education, History Of Public School Education In Arizona 55 (Bulletin No. 17, 1918) (quoting Samuel Pressly McCrea, *Establishment of the Arizona School System, in* Biennial Report of the Superintendent of Public Instruction of the Territory of Arizona, for the Years Ending June 30, 1907 and June 30, 1908, at 121-22 (1908)). The Arizona experience is not uncommon. As one supporter of government aid to religious school admits, "It is one of the great ironies of American constitutional history that the Blaine Amendment, which erupted out of a spirit of religious bigotry and a politics that sought to promote Protestantism in public schools, eventually became an emblem of religious freedom in some states." Viteritti, *supra,* 15 YALE L. & POL'Y REV. 113, 147.

Few generalizations can be drawn from this history. To some extent, both sides in the current controversy are correct: On one hand, many people supported the federal and state Blaine Amendments because of hostility toward Catholics and the parochial school system; on the other hand, the no-aid principle predated this dispute by many decades and seems to have been the motivating factor behind many state provisions prohibiting the provision of government money to religious education.

These issues came to a head in litigation over the Washington state constitutional no-aid provision. The Ninth Circuit Court of Appeals held that this provision violated the Free Exercise Clause of the First Amendment, and the United States Supreme Court reversed. *Davey v. Locke,* 299 F.3d 748 (9th Cir. 2002), *rev'd,* 540 U.S. 712 (2004).

Article 1, Section 11 of the Washington state constitution provides:

Absolute freedom of conscience in all matters of religious sentiment, belief and worship, shall be guaranteed to every individual, and no one shall be molested or disturbed in person or property on account of religion; but the liberty of conscience hereby secured shall not be so construed as to excuse acts of licentiousness or justify practices inconsistent with the peace and safety of the state. No public money or property shall be appropriated for or applied to any religious worship, exercise or instruction, or the support of any religious establishment. . . .

In 1999 Washington created a new college scholarship program for students graduating in the top ten percent of their high school senior class. Students may use their scholarship money for any educational expense, including room and board, and students may attend any accredited public or private college or university within the state, including schools affiliated with religious organizations. Money awarded under this scholarship is limited, however, by a provision of the Washington Revised Code, which states that "[n]o aid shall be awarded to any student who is pursuing a degree in theology."

The plaintiff in the case was enrolled at Northwest College, an accredited institution affiliated with the Assembly of God. Students applying to Northwest are required to indicate "a personal commitment to Jesus Christ as Lord and Savior," and the college educates students from a "distinctly Christian" point of view. The plaintiff intended to become a minister, and therefore declared a double major in Pastoral Ministries and Business Management and Administration. At Northwest the Pastoral Ministries major is intended to prepare students to become Christian ministers. The state of Washington denied the plaintiff's application for a scholarship on the ground that his Pastoral Ministries major fell within the statutory prohibition on providing funds to students seeking theology degrees.

The Ninth Circuit held that Washington's refusal to award scholarships to theology majors violates the Free Exercise Clause of the First Amendment. The court relied heavily on *McDaniel v. Paty, infra* Chapter 11, and *Church of the Lukumi Babalu Aye, Inc. v. City of Hialeah, infra* Chapter 14. The court held that those cases impose a neutrality rule on the state allocation of funds, and therefore require states to allocate funds without regard to the religious nature of the recipient's activity. According to the court, the Washington policy "implicates the free exercise interests articulated in *Lukumi*" because it "is administered so as to disqualify only students who pursue a degree in theology from receiving its benefit." 299 F.3d at 753. The court also ruled that the Washington policy violates the First Amendment's free speech protections. The court reached this conclusion by treating the scholarship program as a public forum under *Rosenberger v. Rector and Visitors of the University of Virginia, supra* Chapter 7. Having characterized the scholarship program as a public forum, the court held that the restriction on the award of scholarship funds to theology students "necessarily communicates disfavor, and discriminates in distributing the subsidy in such a way as to suppress a religious point of view." 299 F.3d at 756. On this point, consider the following hypothetical: Suppose a state enacts a graduate education scholarship program that provided scholarships to all graduate students except those enrolled in law schools. Could law students sue to be included in the scholarship program? If not, then why does the Ninth Circuit grant theology students such a right in *Davey*? If so, then can states ever enact publicly funded benefits programs to target specific beneficiaries?

As this hypothetical indicates, one of the difficulties with the plaintiff's position in *Locke v. Davey* is defining a stopping point to his claim that constitutionally mandated neutrality requires the government to fund religious activity whenever it funds an analogous secular activity. This seems to have been what troubled the Court the most in *Locke.* During the oral argument, the following exchange occurred between the Justices (who are not identified in the official oral argument transcripts) and Jay Sekulow, the attorney for Mr. Davey:

> QUESTION: Suppose the — the state would say, we are going to fund professional education, lawyers, doctors, architects, engineers, but we're not going to fund people who are — who are in a divinity program. Would that qualify or would that fall also?

> MR. SEKULOW: Well, I think a program that were to just limit it to specific professions would not necessarily have to go towards theology. For instance, in a lot of states using that example, Justice Ginsburg, there is a shortage of nurses right now. And if the state were to adopt a program to fund education for nurses that included public and private schools, they don't have to bring theology —

> QUESTION: No, but it would include — my program includes all professions, save one, and — and that is ministry.

> MR. SEKULOW: Well, if it was as you described it, I would be here arguing the same point in this context. The idea that you would list all of the professions and then say we are going to fund everything but those students studying theology would be again that religious classification, and I would think unless the state could establish its compelling governmental interest —

Mr. Sekulow was also asked about the implications for *Zelman*-style voucher programs:

> QUESTION: Suppose a state has a school voucher program such as the Court indicated could be upheld in the Zelman case. Now, if the state decides not to give school vouchers for use in religious or parochial schools, do you take the position it must, that it has to do one or the other? It can have a voucher program, but if it does, it has to fund all private and religious schools with a voucher program?

> MR. SEKULOW: No, I think —

> QUESTION: Is that your position?

> MR. SEKULOW: No. The state —

> QUESTION: Well, why not? I mean, why wouldn't it follow from what you are saying today?

> MR. SEKULOW: For this reason. The state can set neutral and eligible criteria for admission as an eligible institution. Here it was accredita-

tion. Now, if the religious school, the school that was affiliated with the religious denomination met the general neutral eligibility requirement, and there was no countervailing Establishment Clause problems, yes, then it should —

QUESTION: I — I don't know what you mean. The state says all schools were going to have a program to give vouchers for use in all schools of a certain grade level, assuming the teachers are qualified to be teachers.

MR. SEKULOW: That —

QUESTION: Can they refrain from making that program available for use in religious schools?

MR. SEKULOW: I — I would think not. I think once it would go towards the private schools, as long as the eligibility —

QUESTION: So what you're urging here would have a major impact, then, would it not, on — on voucher programs?

MR. SEKULOW: Well, it would. I think a voucher program could be established that has a neutral criteria and if the private schools meet that criteria, including the private religious schools and there is no countervailing Establishment Clause problem, I wouldn't see any reason —

QUESTION: Well, but the only criteria that they have —

QUESTION: Sure — surely, the state can decide to fund only public schools.

MR. SEKULOW: Absolutely.

QUESTION: And it's only when it starts funding some private schools that you get into the religious question.

MR. SEKULOW: That's correct.

The implications of the arguments on behalf of Mr. Davey were too much for the Court's majority, which upheld the Washington program by a 7-2 vote.

LOCKE v. DAVEY
540 U.S. 712 (2004)

C HIEF J USTICE R EHNQUIST delivered the opinion of the Court.

The Religion Clauses of the First Amendment provide: "Congress shall make no law respecting an establishment of religion, or prohibiting the free exercise thereof." These two Clauses, the Establishment Clause and the Free Exercise Clause, are frequently in tension. Yet we have long said that "there is room for play in the joints" between them. In other words, there are some state actions permitted by the Establishment Clause but not required by the Free Exercise Clause.

This case involves that "play in the joints" described above. Under our Establishment Clause precedent, the link between government funds and religious training is broken by the independent and private choice of recipients. *See Zelman.* As such, there is no doubt that the State could, consistent with the Federal Constitution, permit Promise Scholars to pursue a degree in devotional theology, *see Witters*, and the State does not contend otherwise. The question before us, however, is whether Washington, pursuant to its own constitution, which has been authoritatively interpreted as prohibiting even indirectly funding religious instruction that will prepare students for the ministry, can deny them such funding without violating the Free Exercise Clause.

Davey urges us to answer that question in the negative. He contends that under the rule we enunciated in *Church of Lukumi Babalu Aye, Inc. v. Hialeah* [*see* Chapter 14], the program is presumptively unconstitutional because it is not facially neutral with respect to religion.[3] We reject his claim of presumptive unconstitutionality, however; to do otherwise would extend the *Lukumi* line of cases well beyond not only their facts but their reasoning. In *Lukumi*, the city of Hialeah made it a crime to engage in certain kinds of animal slaughter. We found that the law sought to suppress ritualistic animal sacrifices of the Santeria religion. In the present case, the State's disfavor of religion (if it can be called that) is of a far milder kind. It imposes neither criminal nor civil sanctions on any type of religious service or rite. It does not deny to ministers the right to participate in the political affairs of the community. And it does not require students to choose between their religious beliefs and receiving a government benefit. The State has merely chosen not to fund a distinct category of instruction.

JUSTICE SCALIA argues, however, that generally available benefits are part of the "baseline against which burdens on religion are measured." Because the Promise Scholarship Program funds training for all secular professions, JUSTICE SCALIA contends the State must also fund training for religious professions. But training for religious professions and training for secular professions are not fungible. Training someone to lead a congregation is an essentially religious endeavor. Indeed, majoring in devotional theology is akin to a religious calling as well as an academic pursuit. And the subject of religion is one in which both the United States and state constitutions embody distinct views — in favor of free exercise, but opposed to establishment — that find no counterpart with respect to other callings or professions. That a State would deal differently with religious education for the ministry than with education for other callings is a product of these views, not evidence of hostility toward religion.

---

[3] Davey, relying on *Rosenberger v. Rector and Visitors of Univ. of Va.*, contends that the Promise Scholarship Program is an unconstitutional viewpoint restriction on speech. But the Promise Scholarship Program is not a forum for speech. The purpose of the Promise Scholarship Program is to assist students from low- and middle-income families with the cost of postsecondary education, not to "'encourage a diversity of views from private speakers.'" Our cases dealing with speech forums are simply inapplicable.

Even though the differently worded Washington Constitution draws a more stringent line than that drawn by the United States Constitution, the interest it seeks to further is scarcely novel. In fact, we can think of few areas in which a State's antiestablishment interests come more into play. Since the founding of our country, there have been popular uprisings against procuring taxpayer funds to support church leaders, which was one of the hallmarks of an "established" religion. *See* R. Butts, The American Tradition in Religion and Education 15-17, 19-20, 26-37 (1950); F. Lambert, The Founding Fathers and the Place of Religion in America 188 (2003) ("In defending their religious liberty against overreaching clergy, Americans in all regions found that Radical Whig ideas best framed their argument that state-supported clergy undermined liberty of conscience and should be opposed"); *see also* J. Madison, Memorial and Remonstrance Against Religious Assessments (noting the dangers to civil liberties from supporting clergy with public funds).

Most States that sought to avoid an establishment of religion around the time of the founding placed in their constitutions formal prohibitions against using tax funds to support the ministry. *E.g.,* Ga. Const., Art. IV, § 5 (1789), *reprinted in* 2 Federal and State Constitutions, Colonial Charters and Other Organic Laws 789 (F. Thorpe ed. 1909) (reprinted 1993) ("All persons shall have the free exercise of religion, without being obliged to contribute to the support of any religious profession but their own"); Pa. Const., Art. II (1776) in 5 *id.,* at 3082 ("[N]o man ought or of right can be compelled to attend any religious worship, or erect or support any place of worship, or maintain any ministry, contrary to, or against, his own free will and consent"); N.J. Const., Art. XVIII (1776), in *id.,* at 2597 (similar); Del. Const., Art. I, §1 (1792), in 1 *id.,* at 568 (similar); Ky. Const., Art. XII, §3 (1792), in 3 *id.,* at 1274 (similar); Vt. Const., Ch. I, Art. 3 (1793), in 6 *id.,* at 3762 (similar); Tenn. Const., Art. XI, §3 (1796), in *id.,* at 3422 (similar); Ohio Const., Art. VIII, §3 (1802), in 5 *id.,* at 2910 (similar). The plain text of these constitutional provisions prohibited *any* tax dollars from supporting the clergy. We have found nothing to indicate, as Justice Scalia contends, that these provisions would not have applied so long as the State equally supported other professions or if the amount at stake was *de minimis.* That early state constitutions saw no problem in explicitly excluding *only* the ministry from receiving state dollars reinforces our conclusion that religious instruction is of a different ilk.[7]

---

[7] The *amici* contend that Washington's Constitution was born of religious bigotry because it contains a so-called "Blaine Amendment," which has been linked with anti-Catholicism. As the State notes and Davey does not dispute, however, the provision in question is not a Blaine Amendment. The enabling Act of 1889, which authorized the drafting of the Washington Constitution, required the state constitution to include a provision "for the establishment and maintenance of systems of public schools, which shall be . . . free from sectarian control." Act of Feb. 22, 1889, ch. 180, § 4, ¶ Fourth, 25 Stat. 676. This provision was included in Article IX, § 4, of the Washington Constitution ("All schools maintained and supported wholly or in part by the public funds shall be forever free from sectarian control or influence"), and is not at issue in this case. Neither Davey nor *amici* have established a credible connection between the Blaine Amendment and Article I, § 11, the relevant constitutional provision. Accordingly, the Blaine Amendment's history is simply not before us.

Far from evincing the hostility toward religion which was manifest in *Lukumi*, we believe that the entirety of the Promise Scholarship Program goes a long way toward including religion in its benefits. The program permits students to attend pervasively religious schools, so long as they are accredited. As Northwest advertises, its "concept of education is distinctly Christian in the evangelical sense." It prepares *all* of its students, "through instruction, through modeling, [and] through [its] classes, to use . . . the Bible as their guide, as the truth," no matter their chosen profession. And under the Promise Scholarship Program's current guidelines, students are still eligible to take devotional theology courses. Davey notes all students at Northwest are required to take at least four devotional courses, "Exploring the Bible," "Principles of Spiritual Development," "Evangelism in the Christian Life," and "Christian Doctrine," and some students may have additional religious requirements as part of their majors.

In short, we find neither in the history or text of Article I, § 11 of the Washington Constitution, nor in the operation of the Promise Scholarship Program, anything that suggests animus towards religion. Given the historic and substantial state interest at issue, we therefore cannot conclude that the denial of funding for vocational religious instruction alone is inherently constitutionally suspect.

Without a presumption of unconstitutionality, Davey's claim must fail. The State's interest in not funding the pursuit of devotional degrees is substantial and the exclusion of such funding places a relatively minor burden on Promise Scholars. If any room exists between the two Religion Clauses, it must be here. We need not venture further into this difficult area in order to uphold the Promise Scholarship Program as currently operated by the State of Washington.

The judgment of the Court of Appeals is therefore *Reversed*.

JUSTICE SCALIA, with whom JUSTICE THOMAS joins, dissenting.

I

We articulated the principle that governs this case more than 50 years ago in *Everson*:

> "New Jersey cannot hamper its citizens in the free exercise of their own religion. Consequently, it cannot exclude individual Catholics, Lutherans, Mohammedans, Baptists, Jews, Methodists, Non-believers, Presbyterians, or the members of any other faith, because of their faith, or lack of it, from receiving the benefits of public welfare legislation." *Id.*, at 16 (emphasis deleted).

When the State makes a public benefit generally available, that benefit becomes part of the baseline against which burdens on religion are measured; and when the State withholds that benefit from some individuals solely on the basis of religion, it violates the Free Exercise Clause no less than if it had imposed a special tax.

That is precisely what the State of Washington has done here. It has created a generally available public benefit, whose receipt is conditioned only on academic performance, income, and attendance at an accredited school. It has then carved out a solitary course of study for exclusion: theology. No field of study but religion is singled out for disfavor in this fashion. Davey is not asking for a special benefit to which others are not entitled. He seeks only *equal* treatment — the right to direct his scholarship to his chosen course of study, a right every other Promise Scholar enjoys.

In any case, the State already has all the play in the joints it needs. There are any number of ways it could respect both its unusually sensitive concern for the conscience of its taxpayers *and* the Federal Free Exercise Clause. It could make the scholarships redeemable only at public universities (where it sets the curriculum), or only for select courses of study. Either option would replace a program that facially discriminates against religion with one that just happens not to subsidize it. The State could also simply abandon the scholarship program altogether. If that seems a dear price to pay for freedom of conscience, it is only because the State has defined that freedom so broadly that it would be offended by a program with such an incidental, indirect religious effect.

What is the nature of the State's asserted interest here? It cannot be protecting the pocketbooks of its citizens; given the tiny fraction of Promise Scholars who would pursue theology degrees, the amount of any citizen's tax bill at stake is *de minimis*. It cannot be preventing mistaken appearance of endorsement; where a State merely declines to penalize students for selecting a religious major, "[n]o reasonable observer is likely to draw . . . an inference that the State itself is endorsing a religious practice or belief." Nor can Washington's exclusion be defended as a means of assuring that the State will neither favor nor disfavor Davey in his religious calling. Davey will throughout his life contribute to the public fisc through sales taxes on personal purchases, property taxes on his home, and so on; and nothing in the Court's opinion turns on whether Davey winds up a net winner or loser in the State's tax-and-spend scheme.

No, the interest to which the Court defers is not fear of a conceivable Establishment Clause violation, budget constraints, avoidance of endorsement, or substantive neutrality — none of these. It is a pure philosophical preference: the State's opinion that it would violate taxpayers' freedom of conscience *not* to discriminate against candidates for the ministry. This sort of protection of "freedom of conscience" has no logical limit and can justify the singling out of religion for exclusion from public programs in virtually any context. The Court never says whether it deems this interest compelling (the opinion is devoid of any mention of standard of review) but, self-evidently, it is not.

II

It may be that Washington's original purpose in excluding the clergy from public benefits was benign, and the same might be true of its purpose in maintaining the exclusion today. But those singled out for disfavor can be forgiven for suspecting more invidious forces at work. Let there be no doubt: This case is about discrimination against a religious minority. Most citizens of this country identify themselves as professing some religious belief, but the State's policy poses no obstacle to practitioners of only a tepid, civic version of faith. Those the statutory exclusion actually affects — those whose belief in their religion is so strong that they dedicate their study and their lives to its ministry — are a far narrower set. One need not delve too far into modern popular culture to perceive a trendy disdain for deep religious conviction. In an era when the Court is so quick to come to the aid of other disfavored groups, *see, e.g., Romer v. Evans,* 517 U.S. 620, 635 (1996), its indifference in this case, which involves a form of discrimination to which the Constitution actually speaks, is exceptional.

Today's holding is limited to training the clergy, but its logic is readily extendible, and there are plenty of directions to go. What next? Will we deny priests and nuns their prescription-drug benefits on the ground that taxpayers' freedom of conscience forbids medicating the clergy at public expense? This may seem fanciful, but recall that France has proposed banning religious attire from schools, invoking interests in secularism no less benign than those the Court embraces today. *See* Sciolino, *Chirac Backs Law To Keep Signs of Faith Out of School,* N.Y. TIMES, Dec. 18, 2003, p. A17, col. 1. When the public's freedom of conscience is invoked to justify denial of equal treatment, benevolent motives shade into indifference and ultimately into repression. Having accepted the justification in this case, the Court is less well equipped to fend it off in the future. I respectfully dissent.

NOTES

1. Locke v. Davey *and the Logic of Neutrality. Locke* holds that the theory of neutrality used by the Court in *Zelman* permits, but does not require, states to aid religion in a general aid program such as a scholarship or voucher scheme. Is the *Locke* majority's logic more compelling than that of the plaintiff and dissenters in that case? Is it fair to say that the Court has refashioned its neutrality theory into something more akin to a deconstitutionalization theory, under which most determinations about the proper financial relationship between church and state are made by political branches of government rather than the judiciary? Is this better or worse from the perspective of religious liberty? Recall Justice Souter's warning in *Zelman:* "As appropriations for religious subsidy rise, competition for the money will tap sectarian religion's capacity for discord. Public money devoted to payment of religious costs, educational or other, brings the quest for more. It brings too the struggle of sect against sect for the larger share or for any." Is the Court's reference to the "play in the joints" between the Establishment and Free Exercise Clauses simply another way of saying that the Court will no longer referee the sectarian competition for political largess?

2. *Does "Neutrality" Require States to Adopt Voucher Programs? Locke* seems to put to rest the implication some found in *Zelman* that states *must* enact voucher programs and include religious schools among the beneficiaries of those programs. For one version of this pre-*Locke* argument, *see* Mark Tushnet, *Vouchers After* Zelman, 2002 SUP. CT. REV. 1, 31-32:

> Public education is a system of subsidies available to every parent in the state. But, in states without voucher systems, education subsidies are not provided to parents who choose to send their children to private schools. As a result, there is a disparate impact on parents who send their children to religiously affiliated schools out of religious conviction. The only way a state could save money by subsidizing public but not private education is in the unlikely case that operating public schools is more efficient than operating private schools. Otherwise, subsidizing both simply transfers the expenditure from one line — "public education" — to another, the voucher program. Prior to *Zelman*, the justification for refusing to adopt a voucher program might have been to avoid violating the Constitution. Now that reason is unavailable. It may be that no other reason is available either.

If this reasoning were to have prevailed in *Locke*, what would have been left of Madison's "three pence" principle? Is imposing a tax to pay for the inculcation of religion in youngsters different from imposing a tax to support a church? Recall once again the view of religious establishment expressed by a unanimous Court in *Everson*: "No tax in any amount, large or small, can be levied to support any religious activities or institutions." In *Zelman*, the current majority on the Supreme Court seemed to renounce this principle by upholding the imposition of general taxes to support overtly religious education. In *Locke*, the Court seemed to step back from some of the implications of its earlier opinion. Is it fair to say that the modern Court has decided to rephrase the quote from *Everson* by replacing the word "can" with the word "must"?

C. PROVIDING PUBLIC SERVICES THROUGH RELIGIOUS INSTITUTIONS

BOWEN v. KENDRICK
487 U.S. 589 (1988)

CHIEF JUSTICE REHNQUIST delivered the opinion of the Court.

I

The Adolescent Family Life Act (AFLA or Act) was passed by Congress in 1981 in response to the "severe adverse health, social, and economic consequences" that often follow pregnancy and childbirth among unmarried adolescents. Like its predecessor, the Adolescent Health Services and Pregnancy Prevention and

Care Act of 1978, the AFLA is essentially a scheme for providing grants to public or nonprofit private organizations or agencies "for services and research in the area of premarital adolescent sexual relations and pregnancy." These grants are intended to serve several purposes, including the promotion of "self discipline and other prudent approaches to the problem of adolescent premarital sexual relations," the promotion of adoption as an alternative for adolescent parents, the establishment of new approaches to the delivery of care services for pregnant adolescents, and the support of research and demonstration projects "concerning the societal causes and consequences of adolescent premarital sexual relations, contraceptive use, pregnancy, and child rearing."

In pertinent part, grant recipients are to provide two types of services: "care services," for the provision of care to pregnant adolescents and adolescent parents, and "prevention services," for the prevention of adolescent sexual relations. While the AFLA leaves it up to the Secretary of Health and Human Services (the Secretary) to define exactly what types of services a grantee must provide, the statute contains a listing of "necessary services" that may be funded. These services include pregnancy testing and maternity counseling, adoption counseling and referral services, prenatal and postnatal health care, nutritional information, counseling, child care, mental health services, and perhaps most importantly for present purposes, "educational services relating to family life and problems associated with adolescent premarital sexual relations."

In drawing up the AFLA and determining what services to provide under the Act, Congress was well aware that "the problems of adolescent premarital sexual relations, pregnancy, and parenthood are multiple and complex." Indeed, Congress expressly recognized that legislative or governmental action alone would be insufficient:

> "[S]uch problems are best approached through a variety of integrated and essential services provided to adolescents and their families by other family members, religious and charitable organizations, voluntary associations, and other groups in the private sector as well as services provided by publicly sponsored initiatives."

Accordingly, the AFLA expressly states that federally provided services in this area should promote the involvement of parents, and should "emphasize the provision of support by other family members, religious and charitable organizations, voluntary associations, and other groups." The AFLA implements this goal by providing that demonstration projects funded by the government

> "shall use such methods as will strengthen the capacity of families to deal with the sexual behavior, pregnancy, or parenthood of adolescents and to make use of support systems such as other family members, friends, religious and charitable organizations, and voluntary associations."

In addition, AFLA requires grant applicants, among other things, to describe how they will, "as appropriate in the provision of services[,] involve families of adolescents[, and] involve religious and charitable organizations, voluntary associations, and other groups in the private sector as well as services provided by publicly sponsored initiatives." This broad-based involvement of groups outside of the government was intended by Congress to "establish better coordination, integration, and linkages" among existing programs in the community to aid in the development of "strong family values and close family ties," and to "help adolescents and their families deal with complex issues of adolescent premarital sexual relations and the consequences of such relations."

In line with its purposes, the AFLA also imposes limitations on the use of funds by grantees. First, the AFLA expressly states that no funds provided for demonstration projects under the statute may be used for family planning services (other than counseling and referral services) unless appropriate family planning services are not otherwise available in the community. Second, the AFLA restricts the awarding of grants to "programs or projects which do not provide abortions or abortion counseling or referral," except that the program may provide referral for abortion counseling if the adolescent and her parents request such referral. Finally, the AFLA states that "grants may be made only to projects or programs which do not advocate, promote, or encourage abortion."

Since 1981, when the AFLA was adopted, the Secretary has received 1,088 grant applications and awarded 141 grants. Funding has gone to a wide variety of recipients, including state and local health agencies, private hospitals, community health associations, privately operated health care centers, and community and charitable organizations. It is undisputed that a number of grantees or subgrantees were organizations with institutional ties to religious denominations.

II

The District Court in this lawsuit held the AFLA unconstitutional both on its face and as applied. Few of our cases in the Establishment Clause area have explicitly distinguished between facial challenges to a statute and attacks on the statute as applied. Several cases have clearly involved challenges to a statute "on its face." For example, in *Edwards v. Aguillard* we considered the validity of the Louisiana "Creationism Act," finding the Act "facially invalid." Indeed, in that case it was clear that only a facial challenge could have been considered, as the Act had not been implemented. Other cases, as well, have considered the validity of statutes without the benefit of a record as to how the statute had actually been applied. *See Wolman v. Walter; Committee for Public Education & Religious Liberty v. Nyquist.*

In other cases we have, in the course of determining the constitutionality of a statute, referred not only to the language of the statute but also to the manner in which it had been administered in practice. *Levitt v. Committee for Public Education & Religious Liberty,* 413 U.S. 472, 479 (1973); *Meek v. Pittenger. See also Grand Rapids School District v. Ball; Aguilar v. Felton.* In several cases we have expressly recognized that an otherwise valid statute authorizing grants might be challenged on the grounds that the award of a grant in a particular case would be impermissible. *Hunt v. McNair*, 413 U.S. 734 (1973), involved a challenge to a South Carolina statute that provided for the issuance of revenue bonds to assist "institutions of higher learning" in constructing new facilities. The plaintiffs in that case did not contest the validity of the statute as a whole, but contended only that a statutory grant to a religiously affiliated college would be invalid. In *Tilton v. Richardson*, 403 U.S. 672 (1971), the Court reviewed a federal statute authorizing construction grants to colleges exclusively for secular educational purposes. We rejected the contention that the statute was invalid "on its face" and "as applied" to the four church-related colleges that were named as defendants in the case. However, we did leave open the possibility that the statute might authorize grants which could be invalid, stating that "[i]ndividual projects can be properly evaluated if and when challenges arise with respect to particular recipients and some evidence is then presented to show that the institution does in fact possess" sectarian characteristics that might make a grant of aid to the institution constitutionally impermissible. *See also Roemer v. Maryland Bd. of Public Works* (upholding a similar statute authorizing grants to colleges against a "facial" attack and pretermitting the question whether "particular applications may result in unconstitutional use of funds").

There is, then, precedent in this area of constitutional law for distinguishing between the validity of the statute on its face and its validity in particular applications. Although the Court's opinions have not even adverted to (to say nothing of explicitly delineated) the consequences of this distinction between "on its face" and "as applied" in this context, we think they do justify the District Court's approach in separating the two issues as it did here.

This said, we turn to consider whether the District Court was correct in concluding that the AFLA was unconstitutional on its face. As in previous cases involving facial challenges on Establishment Clause grounds, *e.g., Edwards v. Aguillard*; *Mueller v. Allen*, we assess the constitutionality of an enactment by reference to the three factors first articulated in *Lemon v. Kurtzman*. Under the *Lemon* standard, which guides "[t]he general nature of our inquiry in this area," a court may invalidate a statute only if it is motivated wholly by an impermissible purpose, if its primary effect is the advancement of religion, or if it requires excessive entanglement between church and state. We consider each of these factors in turn.

As we see it, it is clear from the face of the statute that the AFLA was motivated primarily, if not entirely, by a legitimate secular purpose — the elimination or reduction of social and economic problems caused by teenage sexuality, pregnancy, and parenthood. Appellees cannot, and do not, dispute that, on the whole, religious concerns were not the sole motivation behind the Act, nor can it be said that the AFLA lacks a legitimate secular purpose. In the court below, however, appellees argued that the real purpose of the AFLA could only be understood in reference to the AFLA's predecessor, Title VI. Appellees contended that Congress had an impermissible purpose in adopting the AFLA because it specifically amended Title VI to increase the role of religious organizations in the programs sponsored by the Act. In particular, they pointed to the fact that the AFLA, unlike Title VI, requires grant applicants to describe how they will involve religious organizations in the programs funded by the AFLA.

The District Court rejected this argument, however, reasoning that even if it is assumed that the AFLA was motivated in part by improper concerns, the parts of the statute to which appellees object were also motivated by other, entirely legitimate secular concerns. We agree with this conclusion. As the District Court correctly pointed out, Congress amended Title VI in a number of ways, most importantly for present purposes by attempting to enlist the aid of not only "religious organizations," but also "family members . . . , charitable organizations, voluntary associations, and other groups in the private sector," in addressing the problems associated with adolescent sexuality. Congress' decision to amend the statute in this way reflects the entirely appropriate aim of increasing broad-based community involvement "in helping adolescent boys and girls understand the implications of premarital sexual relations, pregnancy, and parenthood." In adopting the AFLA, Congress expressly intended to expand the services already authorized by Title VI, to insure the increased participation of parents in education and support services, to increase the flexibility of the programs, and to spark the development of new, innovative services. These are all legitimate secular goals that are furthered by the AFLA's additions to Title VI, including the challenged provisions that refer to religious organizations. There simply is no evidence that Congress' "actual purpose" in passing the AFLA was one of "endorsing religion." Nor are we in a position to doubt that Congress' expressed purposes are "sincere and not a sham."

As usual in Establishment Clause cases, *see, e.g., Grand Rapids School District v. Ball; Mueller,* the more difficult question is whether the primary effect of the challenged statute is impermissible. Before we address this question, however, it is useful to review again just what the AFLA sets out to do. Simply stated, it authorizes grants to institutions that are capable of providing certain care and prevention services to adolescents. Because of the complexity of the problems that Congress sought to remedy, potential grantees are required to describe how they will involve other organizations, including religious organizations, in the programs funded by the federal grants. There is no requirement in the Act that grantees be affiliated with any religious denomination, although the Act clearly does not rule out grants to religious organizations. The services to be provided under the AFLA are not religious in character, nor has there been any suggestion that religious institutions or organizations with religious ties are uniquely well qualified to carry out those services. Certainly it is true that a substantial part of the services listed as "necessary services" under the Act involve some sort of education or counseling, but there is nothing inherently religious about these activities and appellees do not contend that, by themselves, the AFLA's "necessary services" somehow have the primary effect of advancing religion. Finally, it is clear that the AFLA takes a particular approach toward dealing with adolescent sexuality and pregnancy — for example, two of its stated purposes are to "promote self discipline and other prudent approaches to the problem of adolescent premarital sexual relations," and to "promote adoption as an alternative" — but again, that approach is not inherently religious, although it may coincide with the approach taken by certain religions.

Given this statutory framework, there are two ways in which the statute, considered "on its face," might be said to have the impermissible primary effect of advancing religion. First, it can be argued that the AFLA advances religion by expressly recognizing that "religious organizations have a role to play" in addressing the problems associated with teenage sexuality. Senate Report, at 16. In this view, even if no religious institution receives aid or funding pursuant to the AFLA, the statute is invalid under the Establishment Clause because, among other things, it expressly enlists the involvement of religiously affiliated organizations in the federally subsidized programs, it endorses religious solutions to the problems addressed by the Act, or it creates symbolic ties between church and state. Secondly, it can be argued that the AFLA is invalid on its face because it allows religiously affiliated organizations to participate as grantees or subgrantees in AFLA programs. From this standpoint, the Act is invalid because it authorizes direct federal funding of religious organizations which, given the AFLA's educational function and the fact that the AFLA's "viewpoint" may coincide with the grantee's "viewpoint" on sexual matters, will result unavoidably in the impermissible "inculcation" of religious beliefs in the context of a federally funded program.

We consider the former objection first. As noted previously, the AFLA expressly mentions the role of religious organizations in four places. It states (1) that the problems of teenage sexuality are "best approached through a variety of integrated and essential services provided to adolescents and their families by[, among others,] religious organization," (2) that federally subsidized services "should emphasize the provision of support by[, among others,] religious and charitable organizations," (3) that AFLA programs "shall use such methods as will strengthen the capacity of families . . . to make use of support systems such as . . . religious . . . organizations," and (4) that grant applicants shall describe how they will involve religious organizations, among other groups, in the provision of services under the Act.

Putting aside for the moment the possible role of religious organizations as grantees, these provisions of the statute reflect at most Congress' considered judgment that religious organizations can help solve the problems to which the AFLA is addressed. Nothing in our previous cases prevents Congress from making such a judgment or from recognizing the important part that religion or religious organizations may play in resolving certain secular problems. Particularly when, as Congress found, "prevention of adolescent sexual activity and adolescent pregnancy depends primarily upon developing strong family values and close family ties," it seems quite sensible for Congress to recognize that religious organizations can influence values and can have some influence on family life, including parents' relations with their adolescent children. To the extent that this congressional recognition has any effect of advancing religion, the effect is at most "incidental and remote." In addition, although the AFLA does require potential grantees to describe how they will involve religious organizations in the provision of services under the Act, it also requires grantees to describe the involvement of "charitable organizations, voluntary associations, and other groups in the private sector." In our view, this reflects the statute's successful maintenance of "a course of neutrality among religions, and between religion and non-religion," *Grand Rapids School District v. Ball.*

This brings us to the second ground for objecting to the AFLA: the fact that it allows religious institutions to participate as recipients of federal funds. The AFLA defines an "eligible grant recipient" as a "public or nonprofit private organization or agency" which demonstrates the capability of providing the requisite services. As this provision would indicate, a fairly wide spectrum of organizations is eligible to apply for and receive funding under the Act, and nothing on the face of the Act suggests it is anything but neutral with respect to the grantee's status as a sectarian or purely secular institution. *See* Senate Report, at 16 ("Religious affiliation is not a criterion for selection as a grantee . . ."). In this regard, then, the AFLA is similar to other statutes that this Court has upheld against Establishment Clause challenges in the past.

We note in addition that this Court has never held that religious institutions are disabled by the First Amendment from participating in publicly sponsored social welfare programs. To the contrary, in *Bradfield v. Roberts*, 175 U.S. 291 (1899), the Court upheld an agreement between the Commissioners of the District of Columbia and a religiously affiliated hospital whereby the Federal Government would pay for the construction of a new building on the grounds of the hospital. In effect, the Court refused to hold that the mere fact that the hospital was "conducted under the auspices of the Roman Catholic Church" was sufficient to alter the purely secular legal character of the corporation, particularly in the absence of any allegation that the hospital discriminated on the basis of religion or operated in any way inconsistent with its secular charter. In the Court's view, the giving of federal aid to the hospital was entirely consistent with the Establishment Clause, and the fact that the hospital was religiously affiliated was "wholly immaterial." The propriety of this holding, and the long history of cooperation and interdependency between governments and charitable or religious organizations is reflected in the legislative history of the AFLA. *See* S. Rep. No. 98-496, p. 10 (1984) ("Charitable organizations with religious affiliations historically have provided social services with the support of their communities and without controversy").

Of course, even when the challenged statute appears to be neutral on its face, we have always been careful to ensure that direct government aid to religiously affiliated institutions does not have the primary effect of advancing religion. One way in which direct government aid might have that effect is if the aid flows to institutions that are "pervasively sectarian." We stated in *Hunt* that "[a]id normally may be thought to have a primary effect of advancing religion when it flows to an institution in which religion is so pervasive that a substantial portion of its functions are subsumed in the religious mission. . . ."

The reason for this is that there is a risk that direct government funding, even if it is designated for specific secular purposes, may nonetheless advance the pervasively sectarian institution's "religious mission." *See Grand Rapids School District v. Ball* (discussing how aid to religious schools may impermissibly advance religion). Accordingly, a relevant factor in deciding whether a particular statute on its face can be said to have the improper effect of advancing religion is the determination of whether, and to what extent, the statute directs government aid to pervasively sectarian institutions. In *Grand Rapids School District*, for example, the Court began its "effects" inquiry with "a consideration of the nature of the institutions in which the [challenged] programs operate."

In this lawsuit, nothing on the face of the AFLA indicates that a significant proportion of the federal funds will be disbursed to "pervasively sectarian" institutions. Indeed, the contention that there is a substantial risk of such institutions receiving direct aid is undercut by the AFLA's facially neutral grant requirements, the wide spectrum of public and private organizations which are capable of meeting the AFLA's requirements, and the fact that, of the eligible religious institutions, many will not deserve the label of "pervasively sectarian."[12] This is not a case like *Grand Rapids*, where the challenged aid flowed almost entirely to parochial schools. In that case the State's "Shared Time" program was directed specifically at providing certain classes for nonpublic schools, and 40 of 41 of the schools that actually participated in the program were found to be "pervasively sectarian." Instead, this litigation more closely resembles *Tilton* and *Roemer*, where it was foreseeable that some proportion of the recipients of government aid would be religiously affiliated, but that only a small portion of these, if any, could be considered "pervasively sectarian." In those cases we upheld the challenged statutes on their face and as applied to the institutions named in the complaints, but left open the consequences which would ensue if they allowed federal aid to go to institutions that were in fact pervasively sectarian. As in *Tilton* and *Roemer*, we do not think the possibility that AFLA grants may go to religious institutions that can be considered "pervasively sectarian" is sufficient to conclude that no grants whatsoever can be given under the statute to religious organizations. We think that the District Court was wrong in concluding otherwise.

---

[12] The validity of this observation is borne out by the statistics for the AFLA program in fiscal year 1986. According to the record of funding for that year, some $10.7 million in funding was awarded under the AFLA to a total of 86 organizations. Of this, about $3.3 million went to 23 religiously affiliated grantees, with only $1.3 million of this figure going to the 13 projects that were cited by the District Court for constitutional violations. App. 748-756. Of these 13 projects, 4 appear to be state or local government organizations, and at least 1 is a hospital. *Id.*, at 755. Of the 13 religiously affiliated organizations listed, 2 are universities. *Id.*, at 756.

Nor do we agree with the District Court that the AFLA necessarily has the effect of advancing religion because the religiously affiliated AFLA grantees will be providing educational and counseling services to adolescents. Of course, we have said that the Establishment Clause does "prohibit government- financed or government-sponsored indoctrination into the beliefs of a particular religious faith," and we have accordingly struck down programs that entail an unacceptable risk that government funding would be used to "advance the religious mission" of the religious institution receiving aid. But nothing in our prior cases warrants the presumption adopted by the District Court that religiously affiliated AFLA grantees are not capable of carrying out their functions under the AFLA in a lawful, secular manner. Only in the context of aid to "pervasively sectarian" institutions have we invalidated an aid program on the grounds that there was a "substantial" risk that aid to these religious institutions would, knowingly or unknowingly, result in religious indoctrination. In contrast, when the aid is to flow to religiously affiliated institutions that were not pervasively sectarian, as in Roemer, we refused to presume that it would be used in a way that would have the primary effect of advancing religion. *Roemer* ("We must assume that the colleges . . . will exercise their delegated control over use of the funds in compliance with the statutory, and therefore the constitutional, mandate"). We think that the type of presumption that the District Court applied in this case is simply unwarranted. As we stated in *Roemer*: "It has not been the Court's practice, in considering facial challenges to statutes of this kind, to strike them down in anticipation that particular applications may result in unconstitutional use of funds."

We also disagree with the District Court's conclusion that the AFLA is invalid because it authorizes "teaching" by religious grant recipients on "matters [that] are fundamental elements of religious doctrine," such as the harm of premarital sex and the reasons for choosing adoption over abortion. On an issue as sensitive and important as teenage sexuality, it is not surprising that the Government's secular concerns would either coincide or conflict with those of religious institutions. But the possibility or even the likelihood that some of the religious institutions who receive AFLA funding will agree with the message that Congress intended to deliver to adolescents through the AFLA is insufficient to warrant a finding that the statute on its face has the primary effect of advancing religion. Nor does the alignment of the statute and the religious views of the grantees run afoul of our proscription against "fund[ing] a specifically religious activity in an otherwise substantially secular setting." The facially neutral projects authorized by the AFLA — including pregnancy testing, adoption counseling and referral services, prenatal and postnatal care, educational services, residential care, child care, consumer education, etc. — are not themselves "specifically religious activities," and they are not converted into such activities by the fact that they are carried out by organizations with religious affiliations.

As yet another reason for invalidating parts of the AFLA, the District Court found that the involvement of religious organizations in the Act has the imper-

684   GOVERNMENT FINANCIAL SUPPORT OF RELIGION   CH. 9

missible effect of creating a "crucial symbolic link" between government and religion. If we were to adopt the District Court's reasoning, it could be argued that any time a government aid program provides funding to religious organizations in an area in which the organization also has an interest, an impermissible "symbolic link" could be created, no matter whether the aid was to be used solely for secular purposes. This would jeopardize government aid to religiously affiliated hospitals, for example, on the ground that patients would perceive a "symbolic link" between the hospital — part of whose "religious mission" might be to save lives — and whatever government entity is subsidizing the purely secular medical services provided to the patient. We decline to adopt the District Court's reasoning and conclude that, in this litigation, whatever "symbolic link" might in fact be created by the AFLA's disbursement of funds to religious institutions is not sufficient to justify striking down the statute on its face.

A final argument that has been advanced for striking down the AFLA on "effects" grounds is the fact that the statute lacks an express provision preventing the use of federal funds for religious purposes. Clearly, if there were such a provision in this statute, it would be easier to conclude that the statute on its face could not be said to have the primary effect of advancing religion, but we have never stated that a statutory restriction is constitutionally required. The closest we came to such a holding was in *Tilton*, where we struck down a provision of the statute that would have eliminated Government sanctions for violating the statute's restrictions on religious uses of funds after 20 years. The reason we did so, however, was because the 20-year limit on sanctions created a risk that the religious institution would, after the 20 years were up, act as if there were no longer any constitutional or statutory limitations on its use of the federally funded building. This aspect of the decision in Tilton was thus intended to indicate that the constitutional limitations on use of federal funds, as embodied in the statutory restriction, could not simply "expire" at some point during the economic life of the benefit that the grantee received from the Government. In this litigation, although there is no express statutory limitation on religious use of funds, there is also no intimation in the statute that at some point, or for some grantees, religious uses are permitted. To the contrary, the 1984 Senate Report on the AFLA states that "the use of Adolescent Family Life Act funds to promote religion, or to teach the religious doctrines of a particular sect, is contrary to the intent of this legislation." We note in addition that the AFLA requires each grantee to undergo evaluations of the services it provides, and also requires grantees to "make such reports concerning its use of Federal funds as the Secretary may require." The application requirements of the Act, as well, require potential grantees to disclose in detail exactly what services they intend to provide and how they will be provided. These provisions, taken together, create a mechanism whereby the Secretary can police the grants that are given out under the Act to ensure that federal funds are not used for impermissible purposes. Unlike some other grant programs, in which aid might be given out in one-time grants without ongoing supervision by the Government, the programs established under the authority of the AFLA can be monitored to determine whether the funds are, in effect, being used by the grantees in such a way as to advance religion. Given this statutory scheme, we do not think that the absence of an express limitation on the use of federal funds for religious purposes means that the statute, on its face, has the primary effect of advancing religion.

This, of course, brings us to the third prong of the *Lemon* Establishment Clause "test" — the question whether the AFLA leads to "'an excessive government entanglement with religion.'" There is no doubt that the monitoring of AFLA grants is necessary if the Secretary is to ensure that public money is to be spent in the way that Congress intended and in a way that comports with the Establishment Clause. Accordingly, this litigation presents us with yet another "Catch-22" argument: the very supervision of the aid to assure that it does not further religion renders the statute invalid. For this and other reasons, the "entanglement" prong of the *Lemon* test has been much criticized over the years. Most of the cases in which the Court has divided over the "entanglement" part of the *Lemon* test have involved aid to parochial schools; in *Aguilar v. Felton,* for example, the Court's finding of excessive entanglement rested in large part on the undisputed fact that the elementary and secondary schools receiving aid were "pervasively sectarian" and had "'as a substantial purpose the inculcation of religious values.'" In *Aguilar*, the Court feared that an adequate level of supervision would require extensive and permanent on-site monitoring, and would threaten both the "freedom of religious belief of those who [were] not adherents of that denomination" and the "freedom of . . . the adherents of the denomination."

Here, by contrast, there is no reason to assume that the religious organizations which may receive grants are "pervasively sectarian" in the same sense as the Court has held parochial schools to be. There is accordingly no reason to fear that the less intensive monitoring involved here will cause the Government to intrude unduly in the day-to-day operation of the religiously affiliated AFLA grantees. Unquestionably, the Secretary will review the programs set up and run by the AFLA grantees, and undoubtedly this will involve a review of, for example, the educational materials that a grantee proposes to use. The Secretary may also wish to have Government employees visit the clinics or offices where AFLA programs are being carried out to see whether they are in fact being administered in accordance with statutory and constitutional requirements. But in our view, this type of grant monitoring does not amount to "excessive entanglement," at least in the context of a statute authorizing grants to religiously affiliated organizations that are not necessarily "pervasively sectarian."

In sum, in this somewhat lengthy discussion of the validity of the AFLA on its face, we have concluded that the statute has a valid secular purpose, does not have the primary effect of advancing religion, and does not create an excessive entanglement of church and state. We note, as is proper given the traditional presumption in favor of the constitutionality of statutes enacted by Congress, that our conclusion that the statute does not violate the Establishment Clause is consistent with the conclusion Congress reached in the course of its deliberations on the AFLA. As the Senate Committee Report states:

> "In the committee's view, provisions for the involvement of religious organizations [in the AFLA] do not violate the constitutional separation between church and state. Recognizing the limitations of Government in dealing with a problem that has complex moral and social dimensions, the committee believes that promoting the involvement of religious organizations in the solution to these problems is neither inappropriate or illegal." Senate Report, at 15-16.

For the foregoing reasons we conclude that the AFLA does not violate the Establishment Clause "on its face."

III

We turn now to consider whether the District Court correctly ruled that the AFLA was unconstitutional as applied.

On the merits of the "as applied" challenge, it seems to us that the District Court did not follow the proper approach in assessing appellees' claim that the Secretary is making grants under the Act that violate the Establishment Clause of the First Amendment. Although the District Court stated several times that AFLA aid had been given to religious organizations that were "pervasively sectarian," it did not identify which grantees it was referring to, nor did it discuss with any particularity the aspects of those organizations which in its view warranted classification as "pervasively sectarian." The District Court did identify certain instances in which it felt AFLA funds were used for constitutionally improper purposes, but in our view the court did not adequately design its remedy to address the specific problems it found in the Secretary's administration of the statute. Accordingly, although there is no dispute that the record contains evidence of specific incidents of impermissible behavior by AFLA grantees, we feel that this lawsuit should be remanded to the District Court for consideration of the evidence presented by appellees insofar as it sheds light on the manner in which the statute is presently being administered.

JUSTICE BLACKMUN, with whom JUSTICE BRENNNAN, JUSTICE MARSHALL, and JUSTICE STEVENS join, dissenting.

In 1981, Congress enacted the Adolescent Family Life Act (AFLA), thereby "involv[ing] families[,] . . . religious and charitable organizations, voluntary associations, and other groups," in a broad-scale effort to alleviate some of the problems associated with teenage pregnancy. It is unclear whether Congress ever envisioned that public funds would pay for a program during a session of which parents and teenagers would be instructed:

> "You want to know the church teachings on sexuality. . . . You are the church. You people sitting here are the body of Christ. The teachings of you and the things you value are, in fact, the values of the Catholic Church."

Or of curricula that taught:

> "The Church has always taught that the marriage act, or intercourse, seals the union of husband and wife, (and is a representation of their union on all levels.) Christ commits Himself to us when we come to ask for the sacrament of marriage. We ask Him to be active in our life. God is love. We ask Him to share His love in ours, and God procreates with us, He enters into our physical union with Him, and we begin new life."

Or the teaching of a method of family planning described on the grant application as "not only a method of birth regulation but also a philosophy of procreation," and promoted as helping "spouses who are striving . . . to transform their married life into testimony[,] . . . to cultivate their matrimonial spirituality[, and] to make themselves better instruments in God's plan," and as "facilitat[ing] the evangelization of homes."

Whatever Congress had in mind, however, it enacted a statute that facilitated and, indeed, encouraged the use of public funds for such instruction, by giving religious groups a central pedagogical and counseling role without imposing any restraints on the sectarian quality of the participation. As the record developed thus far in this litigation makes all too clear, federal tax dollars appropriated for AFLA purposes have been used, with Government approval, to support religious teaching. Today the majority upholds the facial validity of this statute and remands the action to the District Court for further proceedings concerning appellees' challenge to the manner in which the statute has been applied. Because I am firmly convinced that our cases require invalidating this statutory scheme, I dissent.

II

A central premise of the majority opinion seems to be that the primary means of ascertaining whether a statute that appears to be neutral on its face in fact has the effect of advancing religion is to determine whether aid flows to "pervasively sectarian" institutions. This misplaced focus leads the majority to ignore the substantial body of case law the Court has developed in analyzing programs providing direct aid to parochial schools, and to rely almost exclusively on the few cases in which the Court has upheld the supplying of aid to private colleges, including religiously affiliated institutions.

"Pervasively sectarian," a vaguely defined term of art, has its roots in this Court's recognition that government must not engage in detailed supervision of the inner workings of religious institutions, and the Court's sensible distaste for the "picture of state inspectors prowling the halls of parochial schools and auditing classroom instruction," Under the "effects" prong of the *Lemon* test, the Court has used one variant or another of the pervasively sectarian concept to explain why any but the most indirect forms of government aid to such institutions would necessarily have the effect of advancing religion. For example, in *Meek v. Pittenger*, the Court explained:

"[I]t would simply ignore reality to attempt to separate secular educational functions from the predominantly religious role performed by many of Pennsylvania's church-related elementary and secondary schools and to then characterize Act 195 as channeling aid to the secular without providing direct aid to the sectarian."

The majority first skews the Establishment Clause analysis by adopting a cramped view of what constitutes a pervasively sectarian institution. Perhaps because most of the Court's decisions in this area have come in the context of aid to parochial schools, which traditionally have been characterized as pervasively sectarian, the majority seems to equate the characterization with the institution. In support of that illusion, the majority relies heavily on three cases in which the Court has upheld direct government funding to liberal arts colleges with some religious affiliation, noting that such colleges were not "pervasively sectarian." But the happenstance that the few cases in which direct-aid statutes have been upheld have concerned religiously affiliated liberal arts colleges no more suggests that only parochial schools should be considered "pervasively sectarian," than it suggests that the only religiously affiliated institutions that may ever receive direct government funding are private liberal arts colleges. In fact, the cases on which the majority relies have stressed that the institutions' "*predominant* higher education mission is to provide their students with a *secular* education." In sharp contrast, the District Court here concluded that AFLA grantees and participants included "organizations with institutional ties to religious denominations *and corporate requirements that the organizations abide by and not contradict religious doctrines. In addition, other recipients of AFLA funds, while not explicitly affiliated with a religious denomination, are religiously inspired *and dedicated to teaching the dogma that inspired them.*" On a continuum of "sectarianum" running from parochial schools at one end to the colleges funded by the statutes upheld in *Tilton, Hunt,* and *Roemer* at the other, the AFLA grantees described by the District Court clearly are much closer to the former than to the latter.

More importantly, the majority also errs in suggesting that the inapplicability of the label is generally dispositive. While a plurality of the Court has framed the inquiry as "whether an institution is so 'pervasively sectarian' that it may receive no direct state aid of any kind," *Roemer,* the Court never has treated the absence of such a finding as a license to disregard the potential for impermissible fostering of religion. The characterization of an institution as "pervasively sectarian" allows us to eschew further inquiry into the use that will be made of direct government aid. In that sense, it is a sufficient, but not a necessary, basis for a finding that a challenged program creates an unacceptable Establishment Clause risk. The label thus serves in some cases as a proxy for a more detailed analysis of the institution, the nature of the aid, and the manner in which the aid may be used.

The voluminous record compiled by the parties and reviewed by the District Court illustrates the manner in which the AFLA has been interpreted and implemented by the agency responsible for the aid program, and eliminates whatever need there might be to speculate about what kind of institutions *might* receive funds and how they *might* be selected; the record explains the nature of the activities funded with Government money, as well as the content of the educational programs and materials developed and disseminated. There is no basis for ignoring the volumes of depositions, pleadings, and undisputed facts reviewed by the District Court simply because the recipients of the Government funds may not in every sense resemble parochial schools.

III

A

(1)

The District Court concluded that asking religious organizations to teach and counsel youngsters on matters of deep religious significance, yet expect them to refrain from making reference to religion is both foolhardy and unconstitutional. The majority's rejection of this view is illustrative of its doctrinal misstep in relying so heavily on the college-funding cases. The District Court reasoned:

> "To presume that AFLA counselors from religious organizations can put their beliefs aside when counseling an adolescent on matters that are part of religious doctrine is simply unrealistic. . . . Even if it were possible, government would tread impermissibly on religious liberty merely by suggesting that religious organizations instruct *on doctrinal matters* without any conscious or unconscious reference to that doctrine. Moreover, the statutory scheme is fraught with the possibility that religious beliefs might infuse instruction and never be detected by the impressionable and unlearned adolescent to whom the instruction is directed." (emphasis in original).

The majority rejects the District Court's assumptions as unwarranted outside the context of a pervasively sectarian institution. In doing so, the majority places inordinate weight on the nature of the institution receiving the funds, and ignores altogether the targets of the funded message and the nature of its content.

I find it nothing less than remarkable that the majority relies on statements expressing confidence that administrators of religiously affiliated liberal arts colleges would not breach statutory proscriptions and use government funds earmarked "for secular purposes only," to finance theological instruction or religious worship, in order to reject a challenge based on the risk of indoctrination inherent in "educational services relating to family life and problems associated with adolescent premarital sexual relations," or "outreach services to families of adolescents to discourage sexual relations among unemancipated minors." The two situations are simply not comparable.

The AFLA, unlike any statute this Court has upheld, pays for teachers and counselors, employed by and subject to the direction of religious authorities, to educate impressionable young minds on issues of religious moment. Time and again we have recognized the difficulties inherent in asking even the best-intentioned individuals in such positions to make "a total separation between secular teaching and religious doctrine." Where the targeted audience is composed of children, of course, the Court's insistence on adequate safeguards has always been greatest. In those cases in which funding of colleges with religious affiliations has been upheld, the Court has relied on the assumption that "college students are less impressionable and less susceptible to religious indoctrination. . . . The skepticism of the college student is not an inconsiderable barrier to any attempt or tendency to subvert the congressional objectives and limitations" (footnote omitted). *Tilton v. Richardson*, 403 U.S., at 686 (plurality opinion). *See also Widmar v. Vincent* [*supra* Chapter 7] ("University students are, of course, young adults. They are less impressionable than younger students and should be able to appreciate that the University's policy is one of neutrality toward religion").

(2)

By observing that the alignment of the statute and the religious views of the grantees do not render the AFLA a statute which funds "specifically religious activity," the majority makes light of the religious significance in the counseling provided by some grantees. Yet this is a dimension that Congress specifically sought to capture by enlisting the aid of religious organizations in battling the problems associated with teenage pregnancy. Whereas there may be secular values promoted by the AFLA, including the encouragement of adoption and premarital chastity and the discouragement of abortion, it can hardly be doubted that when promoted in theological terms by religious figures, those values take on a religious nature. Not surprisingly, the record is replete with observations to that effect.[9] It should be undeniable by now that religious dogma may not be employed by government even to accomplish laudable secular purposes such as "the promotion of moral values, the contradiction to the materialistic trends of

---

[9] The District Court's conclusion, which I find compelling, is that the AFLA requires teaching and counseling "on matters inseparable from religious dogma." 657 F. Supp., at 1565. This conclusion is borne out by statements of AFLA administrators and participants. For example, the Lyon County, Kan., Health Department's grant proposal acknowledges that "[s]uch sensitive and intimate material cannot be presented without touching on . . . religious beliefs." Record 155, Plaintiffs' Appendix, Vol. IV, p. 221. Patrick J. Sheeran, the Director of the Division of Program Development and Monitoring in the Office of Adolescent Pregnancy Programs explained:

> "Broadly speaking, I find it hard to find any kind of educational or value type of program that doesn't have some kind of basic religious or ethical foundation, and while a sex education class may be completely separate from a religious class, it might relate back to it in terms of principles that are embedded philosophically or theologically or religiously in another discipline." App. 122.

Mr. Sheeran's views were echoed by Dr. Paul Simmons, a Baptist clergyman and professor of Christian Ethics:

> "The very purpose of religion is to transmit certain values, and those values associated with sex, marriage, chastity and abortion involve religious values and theological or doc-

our times, the perpetuation of our institutions and the teaching of literature."
Abington School District v. Schempp (holding unconstitutional daily reading of
Bible verses and recitation of the Lord's Prayer in public schools); *Stone v. Graham* (holding unconstitutional posting of Ten Commandments despite nota-
tion explaining secular application thereof).

It is true, of course, that the Court has recognized that the Constitution does
not prohibit the government from supporting secular social-welfare services
solely because they are provided by a religiously affiliated organization. But
such recognition has been closely tied to the nature of the subsidized social
service: "the State may send a cleric, indeed even a clerical order, to perform a
wholly secular task" (emphasis added). *Roemer.* There is a very real and important difference between running a soup kitchen or a hospital, and counseling
pregnant teenagers on how to make the difficult decisions facing them. The
risk of advancing religion at public expense, and of creating an appearance
that the government is endorsing the medium and the message, is much greater
when the religious organization is directly engaged in pedagogy, with the
express intent of shaping belief and changing behavior, than where it is neutrally dispensing medication, food, or shelter.

There is also, of course, a fundamental difference between government's
employing religion *because* of its unique appeal to a higher authority and the
transcendental nature of its message, and government's enlisting the aid of
religiously committed individuals or organizations without regard to their sectarian motivation. In the latter circumstance, religion plays little or no role; it
merely explains why the individual or organization has chosen to get involved
in the publicly funded program. In the former, religion is at the core of the
subsidized activity, and it affects the manner in which the "service" is dispensed. For some religious organizations, the answer to a teenager's question
"Why shouldn't I have an abortion?" or "Why shouldn't I use barrier contra-
ceptives?" will undoubtedly be different from an answer based solely on secular
considerations.12 Public funds may not be used to endorse the religious message.

---

trinal issues. In encouraging premarital chastity, it would be extremely difficult for a religiously affiliated group not to impart its own religious values and doctrinal perspectives
when teaching a subject that has always been central to its religious teachings." *Id.,* at
597.

In any event, regardless of the efforts AFLA teachers and counselors may have undertaken in
attempting to separate their religious convictions from the advice they actually dispensed to participating teenagers, the District Court found that "the overwhelming number of comments shows
that program participants believed that these federally funded programs were also sponsored by the
religious denomination." 657 F. Supp., at 1566.

12 Employees of some grantees must follow the directives set forth in a booklet entitled "The Ethical and Religious Directives for Catholic Health Facilities," approved by the Committee on Doctrine
of the National Conference of Catholic Bishops. App. 526, 540-544. Solely because of religious dictates, some AFLA grantees teach and refer teenagers for only "natural family planning," which

NOTE ON CHARITABLE CHOICE AND "FAITH-BASED" SOCIAL SERVICES

During recent years there have been several proposals to increase the involvement of religious groups in the provision of social services. These proposals have generally been referred to by the term "charitable choice." This term was coined in the 1990s by John Ashcroft, then a United States Senator from Missouri. Ashcroft was a leading proponent of charitable choice in the Senate, and during his tenure there he attempted to attach charitable choice provisions to a wide range of federal legislation. Before leaving the Senate, Senator Ashcroft succeeded in adding charitable choice provisions to two pieces of federal legislation: The Welfare Reform Act of 1996 and the Health and Human Services Reauthorization Act of 1998. Each statute contains broad language directing the federal government (and the states that distribute the federal funds) to employ religious groups as well as secular groups to carry out the objectives of the federal program.

The language of the Welfare Reform Act provision is typical of charitable choice statutes. The purpose of the provision, according to the statute, is to "allow states to contract with religious organizations" to disburse welfare assistance "without impairing the religious character of such organizations." 42 U.S.C. § 604a(b). The provision generally prohibits both state and federal governments from refusing to use religious organizations to distribute aid, and guarantees the independence of religious organizations that want to participate in government aid programs. Certain types of government control over these organizations are specifically prohibited. The government is prohibited from regulating the internal governance of the organizations participating in public aid programs, and is also prohibited from interfering with the organizations' religious expression or their use of religious symbols or scripture. Although federal money cannot be used to pay for the religious aspects of church operations, the religious organizations distributing the funds can be overwhelmingly religious in nature.

Other bills currently pending before Congress go beyond the language of the Welfare Reform Act and would create even stronger connections between the religious objectives of church groups and government aid programs. One example of the stronger charitable choice language appeared in an early version of the American Community Renewal Act, which would provide government financial assistance to economically depressed communities. Under this provision (which was dropped from subsequent versions of the bill) church groups dis-

---

"has never been used successfully with teenagers," id., at 535, and may not refer couples to programs that offer artificial methods of birth control, because those programs conflict with the teachings of the Roman Catholic Church. Id., at 407, 628. One nurse mid-wife working at an AFLA program was even reprimanded for contravening the hospital's religious views on sex when she answered "yes" to a teenager who asked, as a medical matter, whether she could have sex during pregnancy. Id., at 552.

tributing federal aid could require individuals being treated for substance abuse to "actively participate in religious practice, worship and instruction and to follow the rules of behavior that are religious in content or origin." Similar language can be found in a bill introduced by Senator Spencer Abraham of Michigan in a bill addressing federally-financed drug treatment programs. Meanwhile, President Bush has created a special office in the White House to advance so-called "faith-based initiatives" similar to the proposals already pending in Congress.

None of the cases decided by the Supreme Court address these new, more intensively religious social service programs. At best there are suggestions in some of the existing cases, especially *Bowen v. Kendrick*. Note that the Court in *Bowen* emphasized that the AFLA was a broad statute that incorporated the services of a range of secular as well as religious community organizations. As the Court noted, "There is no requirement in the Act that grantees be affiliated with any religious denomination, although the Act clearly does not rule out grants to religious organizations. The services to be provided under the AFLA are not religious in character, nor has there been any suggestion that religious institutions or organizations with religious ties are uniquely well qualified to carry out those services." This is significantly different than charitable choice statutes, many of which specifically order the government to seek out religious organizations to participate in government aid programs.

Another factor that will enter into the courts' consideration of charitable choice legislation is the continuing debate in the Supreme Court over the significance of the "pervasively sectarian" factor. In recent years, the key vote on this issue has been Justice O'Connor, and until her departure from the Court, the prognosis for charitable choice proponents did not appear good. In her *Mitchell v. Helms* concurrence, O'Connor went out of her way to distance herself from the plurality's analysis — especially the plurality's abandonment of the rule against government money going to pervasively sectarian institutions. The reason O'Connor cited for refusing to join the plurality's analysis is that it "foreshadows the approval of direct monetary subsidies to religious organizations, even when they use the money to advance their religious objectives." This is precisely the problem posed by many applications of charitable choice legislation, although in light of *Bowen v. Kendrick*, any challenges to the legislation may have to be on an "as-applied" basis rather than in the context of a facial challenge to the statute as a whole. The most important question, however, is whether the Court's new Justices will carry forward Justice O'Connor's reluctance to approve large-scale government financing of religious activity in the context of social services operations.

Chapter 10

GOVERNMENT INVOLVEMENT IN RELIGIOUS DISPUTES

The cases in this chapter lie on the cusp between Establishment and Free Exercise Clause doctrine. These cases deal with legal disputes arising from internal disputes within religious organizations. The question in these cases is whether parties to these intra-church disputes may use the law to resolve issues of control over church authority and assets. Problems arise when authority and control are dictated by internal church rules that are theological in nature. In such cases, the courts have to decide how to address the issues of legal control without violating the church's constitutional rights to determine its internal structure free of government control or interference. The Supreme Court has taken two different approaches to this problem. The first approach, articulated in *Watson v. Jones* (which was based on federal common law, not on the First Amendment), was a rule of deference. Thus, under this approach, courts would defer to centralized ecclesiastical authorities in churches with hierarchical structures, and to local majority control in churches with congregational structures. In more recent years, the Court has moved to a principle that courts must apply "neutral principles" to resolve disputes over church property.

WATSON v. JONES
80 U.S. 679 (1871)

[This case arose from a dispute over the Walnut Street Presbyterian Church of Louisville, Kentucky. According to the Court, "With the outbreak of the war of the insurrection, and the action of it upon the subject of slavery, a very excited condition of things, originating with and influenced by that subject, manifested itself in the Walnut Street Church."

[This is how Justice Brandeis would later summarize the facts of *Watson v. Jones* in *Kedroff v. St. Nicholas Cathedral*, 344 U.S. 94, 111-13 (1952):

[*In May of 1865 the General Assembly, the highest judicatory of the church, made a declaration of loyalty to the Federal Government denouncing slavery, and directed that new members with contrary views should not be received. The Louisville Presbytery, the immediate superior of the Walnut Street Church, promptly issued a Declaration and Testimony, refusing obedience and calling for resistance to the alleged usurpation of authority. The Louisville Presbytery divided as did the Walnut Street Church and the proslavery group obtained admission into the Presbyterian Church of the Confederate States. In June 1867 the Presbyterian General Assembly for the United States declared the Presbytery and Synod recognized by the proslavery party were "in no sense a true and law-*

ful Synod and Presbytery in connection with and under the care and authority of the General Assembly of the Presbyterian Church in the United States of America." They were "permanently excluded from connection with or representation in the Assembly. By the same resolution the Synod and Presbytery adhered to by those whom [the proslavery party] opposed were declared to be the true and lawful Presbytery of Louisville, and Synod of Kentucky."

[*Litigation started in 1866 with a suit in the state court by certain of the antislavery group to have declared their right to act as duly elected additional elders "in the management of the church property for purposes of religious worship." As the Court of Appeals of Kentucky thought that certain acts of the Louisville Presbytery and the General Assembly of the United States, in pronouncing the additional elders duly elected, were void as beyond their functions, it refused the plea of the antislavery group and left the proslavery elders and trustees in control of the Walnut Street Church.*]

[*Thereupon a new suit,* Watson v. Jones, *was begun by alleged members of the church to secure the use of the Walnut Street Church for the antislavery group. This suit was to decide not the validity of an election of elders, but which one of two bodies should be recognized as entitled to the use of the Walnut Street Presbyterian Church.*]

[The material that follows is from the Court's opinion in *Watson.*]

MR. JUSTICE MILLER delivered the opinion of the Court.

The case before us is one of this class, growing out of a schism which has divided the congregation and its officers, and the presbytery and synod, and which appeals to the courts to determine the right to the use of the property so acquired. Here is no case of property devoted forever by the instrument which conveyed it, or by any specific declaration of its owner, to the support of any special religious dogmas, or any peculiar form of worship, but of property purchased for the use of a religious congregation, and so long as any existing religious congregation can be ascertained to be that congregation, or its regular and legitimate successor, it is entitled to the use of the property. In the case of an independent congregation we have pointed out how this identity, or succession, is to be ascertained, but in cases of this character we are bound to look at the fact that the local congregation is itself but a member of a much larger and more important religious organization, and is under its government and control, and is bound by its orders and judgments. There are in the Presbyterian system of ecclesiastical government, in regular succession, the presbytery over the session or local church, the synod over the presbytery, and the General Assembly over all. These are called, in the language of the church organs, "judicatories," and they entertain appeals from the decisions of those below, and prescribe corrective measures in other cases.

In this class of cases we think the rule of action which should govern the civil courts, founded in a broad and sound view of the relations of church and state under our system of laws, and supported by a preponderating weight of judicial authority is, that, whenever the questions of discipline, or of faith, or ecclesiastical rule, custom, or law have been decided by the highest of these church judicatories to which the matter has been carried, the legal tribunals must accept such decisions as final, and as binding on them, in their application to the case before them.

In this country the full and free right to entertain any religious belief, to practice any religious principle and to teach any religious doctrine which does not violate the laws of morality and property, and which does not infringe personal rights, is conceded to all. The law knows no heresy, and is committed to the support of no dogma, the establishment of no sect. The right to organize voluntary religious associations to assist in the expression and dissemination of any religious doctrine, and to create tribunals for the decision of controverted questions of faith within the association, and for the ecclesiastical government of all the individual members, congregations, and officers within the general association, is unquestioned. All who unite themselves to such a body do so with an implied consent to this government, and are bound to submit to it. But it would be a vain consent and would lead to the total subversion of such religious bodies, if any one aggrieved by one of their decisions could appeal to the secular courts and have them reversed. It is of the essence of these religious unions, and of their right to establish tribunals for the decision of questions arising among themselves, that those decisions should be binding in all cases of ecclesiastical cognizance, subject only to such appeals as the organism itself provides for.

Nor do we see that justice would be likely to be promoted by submitting those decisions to review in the ordinary judicial tribunals. Each of these large and influential bodies (to mention no others, let reference be had to the Protestant Episcopal, the Methodist Episcopal, and the Presbyterian churches), has a body of constitutional and ecclesiastical law of its own, to be found in their written organic laws, their books of discipline, in their collections of precedents, in their usage and customs, which as to each constitute a system of ecclesiastical law and religious faith that tasks the ablest minds to become familiar with. It is not to be supposed that the judges of the civil courts can be as competent in the ecclesiastical law and religious faith of all these bodies as the ablest men in each are in reference to their own. It would therefore be an appeal from the more learned tribunal in the law which should decide the case, to one which is less so.

[I]t is easy to see that if the civil courts are to inquire into all these matters, the whole subject of the doctrinal theology, the usages and customs, the written laws, and fundamental organization of every religious denomination may, and must, be examined into with minuteness and care, for they would become, in almost every case, the *criteria* by which the validity of the ecclesiastical decree would be determined in the civil court. This principle would deprive these bodies of the right of construing their own church laws, would open the way to all the evils which we have depicted as attendant upon the doctrine of Lord Eldon, and would, in effect, transfer to the civil courts where property rights were concerned the decision of all ecclesiastical questions.

And this is precisely what the Court of Appeals of Kentucky did in the case of *Watson v. Avery*. Under cover of inquiries into the jurisdiction of the synod and presbytery over the congregation, and of the General Assembly over all, it went into an elaborate examination of the principles of Presbyterian church government, and ended by overruling the decision of the highest judicatory of that church in the United States, both on the jurisdiction and the merits; and, substituting its own judgment for that of the ecclesiastical court, decides that ruling elders, declared to be such by that tribunal, are not such, and must not be recognized by the congregation, though four-fifths of its members believe in the judgment of the Assembly and desired to conform to its decree.

But we need pursue this subject no further. Whatever may have been the case before the Kentucky court, the appellants in the case presented to us have separated themselves wholly from the church organization to which they belonged when this controversy commenced. They now deny its authority, denounce its action, and refuse to abide by its judgments. They have first erected themselves into a new organization, and have since joined themselves to another totally different, if not hostile, to the one to which they belonged when the difficulty first began. Under any of the decisions which we have examined, the appellants, in their present position, have no right to the property, or to the use of it, which is the subject of this suit.

NOTE

Watson was decided long before the First Amendment was incorporated into the Fourteenth Amendment and thereby made applicable to the states. The case was based on common law, rather than constitutional law. In *Kedroff v. St. Nicholas Cathedral*, however, the Court suggested that the rule of deference to religious authorities also has some basis in constitutional principles:

> Ours is a government which by the "law of its being" allows no statute, state or national, that prohibits the free exercise of religion. There are occasions when civil courts must draw lines between the responsibilities of church and state for the disposition or use of property. Even in those cases when the property right follows as an incident from decisions of the church custom or law on ecclesiastical issues, the church rule controls. This under our Constitution necessarily follows in order that there may be free exercise of religion.

Kedroff, 344 U.S. at 120-21. The modern cases quoted below are all based on the assumption that the Free Exercise Clause provides the justification for judicial restraint in this area, and in some cases (such as Justice Rehnquist's dissent in *Milivojevich*) there are suggestions that if the courts defer too broadly to religious authorities, they may violate the Establishment Clause.

SERBIAN EASTERN ORTHODOX
DIOCESE v. MILIVOJEVICH
426 U.S. 696 (1976)

MR. JUSTICE BRENNAN delivered the opinion of the Court.

In 1963, the Holy Assembly of Bishops and the Holy Synod of the Serbian Orthodox Church (Mother Church) suspended and ultimately removed respondent Dionisije Milivojevich (Dionisije) as Bishop of the American-Canadian Diocese of that Church, and appointed petitioner Bishop Firmilian Ocokoljich (Firmilian) as Administrator of the Diocese, which the Mother Church then reorganized into three Dioceses. In 1964 the Holy Assembly and Holy Synod defrocked Dionisije as a Bishop and cleric of the Mother Church. In this civil action brought by Dionisije and the other respondents in Illinois Circuit Court, the Supreme Court of Illinois held that the proceedings of the Mother Church respecting Dionisije were procedurally and substantively defective under the internal regulations of the Mother Church and were therefore arbitrary and invalid. The State Supreme Court also invalidated the Diocesan reorganization into three Dioceses. We granted certiorari to determine whether the actions of the Illinois Supreme Court constituted improper judicial interference with decisions of the highest authorities of a hierarchical church in violation of the First and Fourteenth Amendments. We hold that the inquiries made by the Illinois Supreme Court into matters of ecclesiastical cognizance and polity and the court's actions pursuant thereto contravened the First and Fourteenth Amendments. We therefore reverse.

II.

The fallacy fatal to the judgment of the Illinois Supreme Court is that it rests upon an impermissible rejection of the decisions of the highest ecclesiastical tribunals of this hierarchical church upon the issues in dispute, and impermissibly substitutes its own inquiry into church polity and resolutions based thereon of those disputes. Consistently with the First and Fourteenth Amendments "civil courts do not inquire whether the relevant [hierarchical] church governing body has power under religious law [to decide such disputes]. . . . Such a determination . . . frequently necessitates the interpretation of ambiguous religious law and usage. To permit civil courts to probe deeply enough into the allocation of power within a [hierarchical] church so as to decide . . . religious law [governing church polity] . . . would violate the First Amendment in much the same manner as civil determination of religious doctrine." *Md. & Va. Churches v. Sharpsburg Church,* 396 U. S. 367, 369 (1970) (BRENNAN, J., concurring). For where resolution of the disputes cannot be made without extensive inquiry by civil courts into religious law and polity, the First and Fourteenth Amendments mandate that civil courts shall not disturb the decisions of the highest ecclesiastical tribunal within a church of hierarchical polity, but must accept such decisions as binding on them, in their application to the religious issues of doctrine or polity before them.

Resolution of the religious disputes at issue here affects the control of church property in addition to the structure and administration of the American-Canadian Diocese. This is because the Diocesan Bishop controls respondent Monastery of St. Sava and is the principal officer of respondent property-holding corporations. Resolution of the religious dispute over Dionisije's defrockment therefore determines control of the property. Thus, this case essentially involves not a church property dispute, but a religious dispute the resolution of which under our cases is for ecclesiastical and not civil tribunals. Even when rival church factions seek resolution of a church property dispute in the civil courts there is substantial danger that the State will become entangled in essentially religious controversies or intervene on behalf of groups espousing particular doctrinal beliefs. Because of this danger, "the First Amendment severely circumscribes the role that civil courts may play in resolving church property disputes." *Presbyterian Church v. Hull Church.* "First Amendment values are plainly jeopardized when church property litigation is made to turn on the resolution by civil courts of controversies over religious doctrine and practice. If civil courts undertake to resolve such controversies in order to adjudicate the property dispute, the hazards are ever present of inhibiting the free development of religious doctrine and of implicating secular interests in matters of purely ecclesiastical concern. . . . [T]he [First] Amendment therefore commands civil courts to decide church property disputes without resolving underlying controversies over religious doctrine." This principle applies with equal force to church disputes over church polity and church administration.

Although *Watson* [*v. Jones*] had left civil courts no role to play in reviewing ecclesiastical decisions during the course of resolving church property disputes, *Gonzalez* [*v. Archbishop*, 280 U.S. 1 (1929)] first adverted to the possibility of "marginal civil court review," in cases challenging decisions of ecclesiastical tribunals as products of "fraud, collusion, or arbitrariness." [A]lthough references to the suggested exception appear in opinions in cases decided since the *Watson* rule has been held to be mandated by the First Amendment, no decision of this Court has given concrete content to or applied the "exception." However, it was the predicate for the Illinois Supreme Court's decision in this case, and we therefore turn to the question whether reliance upon it in the circumstances of this case was consistent with the prohibition of the First and Fourteenth Amendments against rejection of the decisions of the Mother Church upon the religious disputes in issue.

The conclusion of the Illinois Supreme Court that the decisions of the Mother Church were "arbitrary" was grounded upon an inquiry that persuaded the Illinois Supreme Court that the Mother Church had not followed its own laws and procedures in arriving at those decisions. We have concluded that whether or not there is room for "marginal civil court review" under the narrow rubrics of "fraud" or "collusion" when church tribunals act in bad faith for secular purposes, no "arbitrariness" exception — in the sense of an inquiry whether the decisions of the highest ecclesiastical tribunal of a hierarchical church complied with church laws and regulations — is consistent with the constitutional mandate that civil courts are bound to accept the decisions of the highest judicatories of a religious organization of hierarchical polity on matters of discipline, faith, internal organization, or ecclesiastical rule, custom, or law. For civil courts to analyze whether the ecclesiastical actions of a church judicatory are in that sense "arbitrary" must inherently entail inquiry into the procedures that canon or ecclesiastical law supposedly requires the church judicatory to follow, or else into the substantive criteria by which they are supposedly to decide the ecclesiastical question. But this is exactly the inquiry that the First Amendment prohibits; recognition of such an exception would undermine the general rule that religious controversies are not the proper subject of civil court inquiry, and that a civil court must accept the ecclesiastical decisions of church tribunals as it finds them. *Watson* itself requires our conclusion in its rejection of the analogous argument that ecclesiastical decisions of the highest church judicatories need only be accepted if the subject matter of the dispute is within their "jurisdiction."

Indeed, it is the essence of religious faith that ecclesiastical decisions are reached and are to be accepted as matters of faith whether or not rational or measurable by objective criteria. Constitutional concepts of due process, involving secular notions of "fundamental fairness" or impermissible objectives, are therefore hardly relevant to such matters of ecclesiastical cognizance.

In short, under the guise of "minimal" review under the umbrella of "arbitrariness," the Illinois Supreme Court has unconstitutionally undertaken the resolution of quintessentially religious controversies whose resolution the First Amendment commits exclusively to the highest ecclesiastical tribunals of this hierarchical church. And although the Diocesan Bishop controls respondent Monastery of St. Sava and is the principal officer of respondent property-holding corporations, the civil courts must accept that consequence as the incidental effect of an ecclesiastical determination that is not subject to judicial abrogation, having been reached by the final church judicatory in which authority to make the decision resides.

III.

Similar considerations inform our resolution of the second question we must address — the constitutionality of the Supreme Court of Illinois' holding that the Mother Church's reorganization of the American-Canadian Diocese into three Dioceses was invalid because it was " 'in clear and palpable excess of its own jurisdiction.' " Essentially, the court premised this determination on its view that the early history of the Diocese "manifested a clear intention to retain independence and autonomy in its administrative affairs while at the same time becoming ecclesiastically and judicially an organic part of the Serbian Orthodox Church," and its interpretation of the constitution of the American-Canadian Diocese as confirming this intention. It also interpreted the constitution of the Serbian Orthodox Church, which was adopted after the Diocesan constitution, in a manner consistent with this conclusion.

This conclusion was not, however, explicitly based on the "fraud, collusion, or arbitrariness" exception. Rather, the Illinois Supreme Court relied on purported "neutral principles" for resolving property disputes which would "not in any way entangle this court in the determination of theological or doctrinal matters." Nevertheless the Supreme Court of Illinois substituted its interpretation of the Diocesan and Mother Church constitutions for that of the highest ecclesiastical tribunals in which church law vests authority to make that interpretation. This the First and Fourteenth Amendments forbid.

We will not delve into the various church constitutional provisions relevant to this conclusion, for that would repeat the error of the Illinois Supreme Court. It suffices to note that the reorganization of the Diocese involves a matter of internal church government, an issue at the core of ecclesiastical affairs.

As a practical matter the effect of the reorganization is a tripling of the Diocesan representational strength in the Holy Assembly and a decentralization of hierarchical authority to permit closer attention to the needs of individual congregations within each of the new Dioceses, a result which Dionisije and Diocesan representatives had already concluded was necessary. Whether corporate bylaws or other documents governing the individual property-holding corporations may affect any desired disposition of the Diocesan property is a question not before us.

MR. JUSTICE REHNQUIST, with whom MR. JUSTICE STEVENS joins, dissenting.

The Court's opinion, while long on the ecclesiastical history of the Serbian Orthodox Church, is somewhat short on the procedural history of this case. A casual reader of some of the passages in the Court's opinion could easily gain the impression that the State of Illinois had commenced a proceeding designed to brand Bishop Dionisije as a heretic, with appropriate pains and penalties. But the state trial judge in the Circuit Court of Lake County was not the Bishop of Beauvais, trying Joan of Arc for heresy; the jurisdiction of his court was invoked by petitioners themselves, who sought an injunction establishing their control over property of the American-Canadian Diocese of the church located in Lake County.

The jurisdiction of that court having been invoked for such a purpose by both petitioners and respondents, contesting claimants to Diocesan authority, it was entitled to ask if the real Bishop of the American-Canadian Diocese would please stand up. The protracted proceedings in the Illinois courts were devoted to the ascertainment of who that individual was, a question which the Illinois courts sought to answer by application of the canon law of the church, just as they would have attempted to decide a similar dispute among the members of any other voluntary association. The Illinois courts did not in the remotest sense inject their doctrinal preference into the dispute. They were forced to decide between two competing sets of claimants to church office in order that they might resolve a dispute over real property located within the State. Each of the claimants had requested them to decide the issue. Unless the First Amendment requires control of disputed church property to be awarded solely on the basis of ecclesiastical paper title, I can find no constitutional infirmity in the judgment of the Supreme Court of Illinois.

Unless civil courts are to be wholly divested of authority to resolve conflicting claims to real property owned by a hierarchical church, and such claims are to be resolved by brute force, civil courts must of necessity make some factual inquiry even under the rules the Court purports to apply in this case. We are told that "a civil court must accept the ecclesiastical decisions of church tribunals as it finds them." But even this rule requires that proof be made as to what these decisions are, and if proofs on that issue conflict the civil court will inevitably have to choose one over the other. In so choosing, if the choice is to be a rational one, reasons must be adduced as to why one proffered decision is to prevail over another. Such reasons will obviously be based on the canon law by which the disputants have agreed to bind themselves, but they must also represent a preference for one view of that law over another.

If civil courts, consistently with the First Amendment, may do that much, the question arises why they may not do what the Illinois courts did here regarding the defrockment of Bishop Dionisije, and conclude, on the basis of testimony from experts on the canon law at issue, that the decision of the religious tribunal involved was rendered in violation of its own stated rules of procedure.

There is nothing in this record to indicate that the Illinois courts have been instruments of any such impermissible intrusion by the State on one side or the other of a religious dispute. There is nothing in the Supreme Court of Illinois' opinion indicating that it placed its thumb on the scale in favor of the respondents. Instead that opinion appears to be precisely what it purports to be: an application of neutral principles of law consistent with the decisions of this Court. Indeed, petitioners make absolutely no claim to the contrary. They agree that the Illinois courts *should* have decided the issues which *they* presented; but they contend that in doing so those courts should have deferred entirely to the representations of the announced representatives of the Mother Church. Such blind deference, however, is counseled neither by logic nor by the First Amendment. To make available the coercive powers of civil courts to rubber-stamp ecclesiastical decisions of hierarchical religious associations, when such deference is not accorded similar acts of secular voluntary associations, would, in avoiding the free exercise problems petitioners envision, itself create far more serious problems under the Establishment Clause.

JONES v. WOLF
443 U.S. 595 (1979)

Mr. Justice Blackmun delivered the opinion of the Court.

This case involves a dispute over the ownership of church property following a schism in a local church affiliated with a hierarchical church organization. The question for decision is whether civil courts, consistent with the First and Fourteenth Amendments to the Constitution, may resolve the dispute on the basis of "neutral principles of law," or whether they must defer to the resolution of an authoritative tribunal of the hierarchical church.

I

The Vineville Presbyterian Church of Macon, Ga., was organized in 1904, and first incorporated in 1915. Its corporate charter lapsed in 1935, but was revived and renewed in 1939, and continues in effect at the present time.

The property at issue and on which the church is located was acquired in three transactions, and is evidenced by conveyances to the "Trustees of [or 'for'] Vineville Presbyterian Church and their successors in office," or simply to the "Vineville Presbyterian Church." The funds used to acquire the property were contributed entirely by local church members. Pursuant to resolutions adopted by the congregation, the church repeatedly has borrowed money on the property. This indebtedness is evidenced by security deeds variously issued in the name of the "Trustees of the Vineville Presbyterian Church," or, again, simply the "Vineville Presbyterian Church."

In the same year it was organized, the Vineville church was established as a member church of the Augusta-Macon Presbytery of the Presbyterian Church in the United States (PCUS). The PCUS has a generally hierarchical or connectional form of government, as contrasted with a congregational form. Under the polity of the PCUS, the government of the local church is committed to its Session in the first instance, but the actions of this assembly or "court" are subject to the review and control of the higher church courts, the Presbytery, Synod, and General Assembly, respectively. The powers and duties of each level of the hierarchy are set forth in the constitution of the PCUS, the Book of Church Order, which is part of the record in the present case.

On May 27, 1973, at a congregational meeting of the Vineville church attended by a quorum of its duly enrolled members, 164 of them, including the pastor, voted to separate from the PCUS. Ninety-four members opposed the resolution. The majority immediately informed the PCUS of the action, and then united with another denomination, the Presbyterian Church in America. Although the minority remained on the church rolls for three years, they ceased to participate in the affairs of the Vineville church and conducted their religious activities elsewhere.

In response to the schism within the Vineville congregation, the Augusta-Macon Presbytery appointed a commission to investigate the dispute and, if possible, to resolve it. The commission eventually issued a written ruling declaring that the minority faction constituted "the true congregation of Vineville Presbyterian Church," and withdrawing from the majority faction "all authority to exercise office derived from the [PCUS]." The majority took no part in the commission's inquiry, and did not appeal its ruling to a higher PCUS tribunal.

Representatives of the minority faction sought relief in federal court, but their complaint was dismissed for want of jurisdiction. They then brought this class action in state court, seeking declaratory and injunctive orders establishing their right to exclusive possession and use of the Vineville church property as a member congregation of the PCUS. The trial court, purporting to apply Georgia's "neutral principles of law" approach to church property disputes, granted judgment for the majority. The Supreme Court of Georgia, holding that the trial court had correctly stated and applied Georgia law, and rejecting the minority's challenge based on the First and Fourteenth Amendments, affirmed.

II

Georgia's approach to church property litigation has evolved in response to *Presbyterian Church v. Hull Church*. That case was a property dispute between the PCUS and two local Georgia churches that had withdrawn from the PCUS. The Georgia Supreme Court resolved the controversy by applying a theory of implied trust, whereby the property of a local church affiliated with a hierarchical church organization was deemed to be held in trust for the general church, provided the general church had not "substantially abandoned" the tenets of faith and practice as they existed at the time of affiliation. This Court reversed, holding that Georgia would have to find some other way of resolving church property disputes that did not draw the state courts into religious controversies. The Court did not specify what that method should be, although it noted in passing that "there are neutral principles of law, developed for use in all property disputes, which can be applied without 'establishing' churches to which property is awarded."

On remand, the Georgia Supreme Court concluded that, without the departure-from-doctrine element, the implied trust theory would have to be abandoned in its entirety. In its place, the court adopted what is now known as the "neutral principles of law" method for resolving church property disputes. The court examined the deeds to the properties, the state statutes dealing with implied trusts, and the Book of Church Order to determine whether there was any basis for a trust in favor of the general church. Finding nothing that would give rise to a trust in any of these documents, the court awarded the property on the basis of legal title, which was in the local church, or in the names of trustees for the local church.

The neutral-principles analysis was further refined by the Georgia Supreme Court in *Carnes v. Smith*, 236 Ga. 30, 222 S.E.2d 322, *cert. denied*, 429 U.S. 868 (1976). That case concerned a property dispute between The United Methodist Church and a local congregation that had withdrawn from that church. As in *Presbyterian Church II*, the court found no basis for a trust in favor of the general church in the deeds, the corporate charter, or the state statutes dealing with implied trusts. The court observed, however, that the constitution of The United Methodist Church, its Book of Discipline, contained an express trust provision in favor of the general church. On this basis, the church property was awarded to the denominational church.

In the present case, the Georgia courts sought to apply the neutral-principles analysis of *Presbyterian Church II* and *Carnes* to the facts presented by the Vineville church controversy. Here, as in those two earlier cases, the deeds conveyed the property to the local church. Here, as in the earlier cases, neither the state statutes dealing with implied trusts, nor the corporate charter of the Vineville church, indicated that the general church had any interest in the property. And here, as in *Presbyterian Church II*, but in contrast to *Carnes*, the provisions of the constitution of the general church, the Book of Church Order, concerning the ownership and control of property failed to reveal any language of trust in favor of the general church. The courts accordingly held that legal title to the property of the Vineville church was vested in the local congregation. Without further analysis or elaboration, they further decreed that the local congregation was represented by the majority faction, respondents herein.

III

The only question presented by this case is which faction of the formerly united Vineville congregation is entitled to possess and enjoy the property located at 2193 Vineville Avenue in Macon, Ga. There can be little doubt about the general authority of civil courts to resolve this question. The State has an obvious and legitimate interest in the peaceful resolution of property disputes, and in providing a civil forum where the ownership of church property can be determined conclusively.

It is also clear, however, that "the First Amendment severely circumscribes the role that civil courts may play in resolving church property disputes." Most importantly, the First Amendment prohibits civil courts from resolving church property disputes on the basis of religious doctrine and practice. As a corollary to this commandment, the Amendment requires that civil courts defer to the resolution of issues of religious doctrine or polity by the highest court of a hierarchical church organization. Subject to these limitations, however, the First Amendment does not dictate that a State must follow a particular method of resolving church property disputes. Indeed, "a State may adopt *any* one of various approaches for settling church property disputes so long as it involves no consideration of doctrinal matters, whether the ritual and liturgy of worship or the tenets of faith."

At least in general outline, we think the "neutral principles of law" approach is consistent with the foregoing constitutional principles. The primary advantages of the neutral-principles approach are that it is completely secular in operation, and yet flexible enough to accommodate all forms of religious organization and polity. The method relies exclusively on objective, well-established concepts of trust and property law familiar to lawyers and judges. It thereby promises to free civil courts completely from entanglement in questions of religious doctrine, polity, and practice. Furthermore, the neutral-principles analysis shares the peculiar genius of private-law systems in general — flexibility in ordering private rights and obligations to reflect the intentions of the parties. Through appropriate reversionary clauses and trust provisions, religious societies can specify what is to happen to church property in the event of a particular contingency, or what religious body will determine the ownership in the event of a schism or doctrinal controversy. In this manner, a religious organization can ensure that a dispute over the ownership of church property will be resolved in accord with the desires of the members.

This is not to say that the application of the neutral-principles approach is wholly free of difficulty. The neutral-principles method, at least as it has evolved in Georgia, requires a civil court to examine certain religious documents, such as a church constitution, for language of trust in favor of the general church. In undertaking such an examination, a civil court must take special care to scrutinize the document in purely secular terms, and not to rely on religious precepts in determining whether the document indicates that the parties have intended to create a trust. In addition, there may be cases where the deed, the corporate charter, or the constitution of the general church incorporates religious concepts in the provisions relating to the ownership of property. If in such a case the interpretation of the instruments of ownership would require the civil court to resolve a religious controversy, then the court must defer to the resolution of the doctrinal issue by the authoritative ecclesiastical body.

The dissent would require the States to abandon the neutral-principles method, and instead would insist as a matter of constitutional law that whenever a dispute arises over the ownership of church property, civil courts must defer to the "authoritative resolution of the dispute within the church itself." It would require, first, that civil courts review ecclesiastical doctrine and polity to determine where the church has "placed ultimate authority over the use of the church property." After answering this question, the courts would be required to "determine whether the dispute has been resolved within that structure of government and, if so, what decision has been made." They would then be required to enforce that decision. We cannot agree, however, that the First Amendment requires the States to adopt a rule of compulsory deference to religious authority in resolving church property disputes, even where no issue of doctrinal controversy is involved.

[In applying these principles to the facts of *Wolf*, the Court noted that] there are at least some indications that under Georgia law the process of identifying the faction that represents the Vineville church involves considerations of religious doctrine and polity. [I]f Georgia law provides that the identity of the Vineville church is to be determined according to the "laws and regulations" of the PCUS, then the First Amendment requires that the Georgia courts give deference to the presbyterial commission's determination of that church's identity. [The Court then remanded the case to Georgia courts for determination of what Georgia law required.]

MR. JUSTICE POWELL, with whom THE CHIEF JUSTICE, MR. JUSTICE STEWART, and MR. JUSTICE WHITE join, dissenting.

This case presents again a dispute among church members over the control of a local church's property. Although the Court appears to accept established principles that I have thought would resolve this case, it superimposes on these principles a new structure of rules that will make the decision of these cases by civil courts more difficult. The new analysis also is more likely to invite intrusion into church polity forbidden by the First Amendment.

I

Since 1872, disputes over control of church property usually have been resolved under principles established by *Watson v. Jones*. Under the new and complex, two-stage analysis approved today, a court instead first must apply newly defined "neutral principles of law" to determine whether property titled to the local church is held in trust for the general church organization with which the local church is affiliated. If it is, then the court will grant control of the property to the councils of the general church. If not, then control by the local congregation will be recognized. In the latter situation, if there is a schism in the local congregation, as in this case, the second stage of the new analysis becomes applicable. Again, the Court fragments the analysis into two substeps for the purpose of determining which of the factions should control the property.

As this new approach inevitably will increase the involvement of civil courts in church controversies, and as it departs from long-established precedents, I dissent.

A

The first stage in the "neutral principles of law" approach operates as a restrictive rule of evidence. A court is required to examine the deeds to the church property, the charter of the local church (if there is one), the book of order or discipline of the general church organization, and the state statutes governing the holding of church property. The object of the inquiry, where the title to the property is in the local church, is "to determine whether there [is] any basis for a trust in favor of the general church." The court's investigation is to be "completely secular," "rel[ying] exclusively on objective, well-established concepts of trust and property law familiar to lawyers and judges." Thus, where religious documents such as church constitutions or books of order must be examined "for language of trust in favor of the general church," "a civil court must take special care to scrutinize the document in purely secular terms, and not to rely on religious precepts in determining whether the document indicates that the parties have intended to create a trust." It follows that the civil courts using this analysis may consider the form of religious government adopted by the church members for the resolution of intrachurch disputes *only* if that polity has been stated, in express relation to church property, in the language of trust and property law.

One effect of the Court's evidentiary rule is to deny to the courts relevant evidence as to the religious polity — that is, the form of governance — adopted by the church members. The constitutional documents of churches tend to be drawn in terms of religious precepts. Attempting to read them "in purely secular terms" is more likely to promote confusion than understanding. Moreover, whenever religious polity has not been expressed in specific statements referring to the property of a church, there will be no evidence of that polity cognizable under the neutral-principles rule. Lacking such evidence, presumably a court will impose some rule of church government derived from state law. In the present case, for example, the general and unqualified authority of the Presbytery over the actions of the Vineville church had not been expressed in secular terms of control of its property. As a consequence, the Georgia courts could find no acceptable evidence of this authoritative relationship, and they imposed instead a congregational form of government determined from state law.

When civil courts step in to resolve intrachurch disputes over control of church property, they will either support or overturn the authoritative resolution of the dispute within the church itself. The new analysis, under the attractive banner of "neutral principles," actually invites the civil courts to do the latter. The proper rule of decision, that I thought had been settled until today, requires a court to give effect in all cases to the decisions of the church government agreed upon by the members before the dispute arose.

B

The Court acknowledges that the church law of the Presbyterian Church in the United States (PCUS), of which the Vineville church is a part, provides for the authoritative resolution of this question by the Presbytery. Indeed, the Court indicates that Georgia, consistently with the First Amendment, may adopt the *Watson v. Jones* rule of adherence to the resolution of the dispute according to church law — a rule that would necessitate reversal of the judgment for the respondents. But instead of requiring the state courts to take this approach, the Court approves as well an alternative rule of state law: the Georgia courts are said to be free to "adop[t] a presumptive rule of majority representation, defeasible upon a showing that the identity of the local church is to be determined by some other means." This showing may be made by proving that the church has "provid[ed], in the corporate charter or the constitution of the general church, that the identity of the local church is to be established in some other way."

On its face, this rebuttable presumption also requires reversal of the state court's judgment in favor of the schismatic faction. The polity of the PCUS commits to the Presbytery the resolution of the dispute within the local church. Having shown this structure of church government for the determination of the identity of the local congregation, the petitioners have rebutted any presumption that this question has been left to a majority vote of the local congregation.

The Court nevertheless declines to order reversal. Rather than decide the case here in accordance with established First Amendment principles, the Court leaves open the possibility that the state courts might adopt some restrictive evidentiary rule that would render the petitioners' evidence inadequate to overcome the presumption of majority control. But, aside from a passing reference to the use of the neutral-principles approach developed earlier in its opinion, the Court affords no guidance as to the constitutional limitations on such an evidentiary rule; the state courts, it says, are free to adopt any rule that is constitutional.

In essence, the Court's instructions on remand therefore allow the state courts the choice of following the long-settled rule of *Watson v. Jones* or of adopting some other rule — unspecified by the Court — that the state courts view as consistent with the First Amendment. Not only questions of state law but also important issues of federal constitutional law thus are left to the state courts for their decision, and, if they depart from *Watson v. Jones*, they will travel a course left totally uncharted by this Court.

IV

The principles developed in prior decisions thus afford clear guidance in the case before us. The Vineville church is Presbyterian, a part of the PCUS. The Presbyterian form of church government, adopted by the PCUS, is "a hierarchical structure of tribunals which consists of, in ascending order, (1) the Church Session, composed of the elders of the local church; (2) the Presbytery, composed of several churches in a geographical area; (3) the Synod, generally composed of all Presbyteries within a State; and (4) the General Assembly, the highest governing body." *Presbyterian Church v. Hull Church*. The Book of Church Order subjects the Session to "review and control" by the Presbytery in all matters, even authorizing the Presbytery to replace the leadership of the local congregation, to winnow its membership, and to take control of it. No provision of the Book of Church Order gives the Session the authority to withdraw the local church from the PCUS; similarly, no section exempts such a decision by the local church from review by the Presbytery.

Thus, while many matters, including the management of the church property, are committed in the first instance to the Session and congregation of the local church, their actions are subject to review by the Presbytery. Here, the Presbytery exercised its authority over the local church, removing the dissidents from church office, asserting direct control over the government of the church, and recognizing the petitioners as the legitimate congregation and Session of the Church. It is undisputed that under the established government of the Presbyterian Church — accepted by the members of the church before the schism — the use and control of the church property have been determined authoritatively to be in the petitioners. Accordingly, under the principles I have thought were settled, there is no occasion for the further examination of the law of Georgia that the Court directs. On remand, the Georgia courts should be directed to enter judgment for the petitioners.

NOTES

For a sampling of academic assessments of the church dispute cases, see Kent Greenawalt, *Hands Off! Civil Court Involvement in Conflicts over Religious Property*, 98 COLUM. L. REV. 1843 (1998); John H. Garvey, *Churches and the Free Exercise of Religion*, 4 NOTRE DAME J.L. ETHICS & PUB. POL'Y 567 (1990); Ira Mark Ellman, *Driven from the Tribunal: Judicial Resolution of Internal Church Disputes,* 69 CAL. L. REV. 1378 (1981).

Chapter 11

FREE EXERCISE: BASIC PRINCIPLES

In this chapter we return to the Free Exercise Clause principles that appeared in the theoretical discussions in Chapters 1 and 2. This chapter reviews the basic issues arising in Free Exercise Clause jurisprudence, and the next three chapters consider recent developments in this area. In reading the following materials, recall the questions raised earlier: Is there a relevant constitutional distinction between the theological and behavioral aspects of religion? Does accommodation of religion create Establishment Clause problems? What does the Free Exercise Clause add to the verbal and symbolic speech protections already offered by the Free Speech Clause? Also keep in mind throughout the Free Exercise materials the important distinction between accommodation of religion mandated by the Constitution, and accommodation of religion mandated by statutes such as the federal and state Religious Freedom Restoration Acts and the federal Religious Land Use and Institutionalized Persons Act. These statutes will be discussed in Chapter 14.

A. GOVERNMENT REGULATION OF UNUSUAL RELIGIOUS PRACTICES

REYNOLDS v. UNITED STATES
98 U.S. 145 (1879)

This is an indictment found in the District Court for the third judicial district of the Territory of Utah, charging George Reynolds with bigamy, in violation of sect. 5352 of the Revised Statutes, which, omitting its exceptions, is as follows:

> "Every person having a husband or wife living, who marries another, whether married or single, in a Territory, or other place over which the United States have exclusive jurisdiction, is guilty of bigamy, and shall be punished by a fine of not more than $500, and by imprisonment for a term of not more than five years."

MR. CHIEF JUSTICE WAITE delivered the opinion of the court.

On the trial, the plaintiff in error, the accused, proved that at the time of his alleged second marriage he was, and for many years before had been, a member of the Church of Jesus Christ of Latter-Day Saints, commonly called the Mormon Church, and a believer in its doctrines; that it was an accepted doctrine of that church "that it was the duty of male members of said church, circumstances permitting, to practice polygamy; . . . that this duty was enjoined by different books which the members of said church believed to be of divine origin, and among others the Holy Bible, and also that the members of the church believed that the practice of polygamy was directly enjoined upon the male members thereof by the Almighty God, in a revelation to Joseph Smith, the founder and prophet of said church; that the failing or refusing to practice polygamy by such male members of said church, when circumstances would admit, would be punished, and that the penalty for such failure and refusal would be damnation in the life to come." He also proved "that he had received permission from the recognized authorities in said church to enter into polygamous marriage; . . . that Daniel H. Wells, one having authority in said church to perform the marriage ceremony, married the said defendant on or about the time the crime is alleged to have been committed, to some woman by the name of Schofield, and that such marriage ceremony was performed under and pursuant to the doctrines of said church."

Upon this proof he asked the court to instruct the jury that if they found from the evidence that he "was married as charged — if he was married — in pursuance of and in conformity with what he believed at the time to be a religious duty, that the verdict must be "not guilty." This request was refused, and the court did charge "that there must have been a criminal intent, but that if the defendant, under the influence of a religious belief that it was right, — under an inspiration, if you please, that it was right, — deliberately married a second time, having a first wife living, the want of consciousness of evil intent — the want of understanding on his part that he was committing a crime — did not excuse him; but the law inexorably in such case implies the criminal intent."

Upon this charge and refusal to charge the question is raised, whether religious belief can be accepted as a justification of an overt act made criminal by the law of the land. The inquiry is not as to the power of Congress to prescribe criminal laws for the Territories, but as to the guilt of one who knowingly violates a law which has been properly enacted, if he entertains a religious belief that the law is wrong.

Congress cannot pass a law for the government of the Territories which shall prohibit the free exercise of religion. The first amendment to the Constitution expressly forbids such legislation. Religious freedom is guaranteed everywhere throughout the United States, so far as congressional interference is concerned. The question to be determined is, whether the law now under consideration comes within this prohibition.

The word "religion" is not defined in the Constitution. We must go elsewhere, therefore, to ascertain its meaning, and nowhere more appropriately, we think, than to the history of the times in the midst of which the provision was adopted. The precise point of the inquiry is, what is the religious freedom which has been guaranteed.

[The Court recounted the battle in Virginia over Patrick Henry's "bill establishing provision for teachers of the Christian religion."] At the next session the proposed bill was not only defeated, but another, "for establishing religious freedom," drafted by Mr. Jefferson, was passed. In the preamble of this act religious freedom is defined; and after a recital "that to suffer the civil magistrate to intrude his powers into the field of opinion, and to restrain the profession or propagation of principles on supposition of their ill tendency, is a dangerous fallacy which at once destroys all religious liberty," it is declared "that it is time enough for the rightful purposes of civil government for its officers to interfere when principles break out into overt acts against peace and good order." In these two sentences is found the true distinction between what properly belongs to the church and what to the State.

Polygamy has always been odious among the northern and western nations of Europe, and, until the establishment of the Mormon Church, was almost exclusively a feature of the life of Asiatic and of African people. At common law, the second marriage was always void, and from the earliest history of England polygamy has been treated as an offence against society. After the establishment of the ecclesiastical courts, and until the time of James I, it was punished through the instrumentality of those tribunals, not merely because ecclesiastical rights had been violated, but because upon the separation of the ecclesiastical courts from the civil the ecclesiastical were supposed to be the most appropriate for the trial of matrimonial causes and offences against the rights of marriage, just as they were for testamentary causes and the settlement of the estates of deceased persons.

By the statute of 1 James I, the offence, if committed in England or Wales, was made punishable in the civil courts, and the penalty was death. As this statute was limited in its operation to England and Wales, it was at a very early period re-enacted, generally with some modifications, in all the colonies. In connection with the case we are now considering, it is a significant fact that on the 8th of December, 1788, after the passage of the act establishing religious freedom, and after the convention of Virginia had recommended as an amendment to the Constitution of the United States the declaration in a bill of rights that "all men have an equal, natural, and unalienable right to the free exercise of religion, according to the dictates of conscience," the legislature of that State substantially enacted the statute of James I, death penalty included, because, as recited in the preamble, "it hath been doubted whether bigamy or polygamy be punishable by the laws of this Commonwealth." From that day to this we think it may safely be said there never has been a time in any State of the Union when polygamy has not been an offence against society, cognizable by the civil courts and punishable with more or less severity. In the face of all this evidence, it is impossible to believe that the constitutional guaranty of religious freedom was intended to prohibit legislation in respect to this most important feature of social life. Marriage, while from its very nature a sacred obligation, is nevertheless, in most civilized nations, a civil contract, and usually regulated by law. Upon it society may be said to be built, and out of its fruits spring social relations and social obligations and duties, with which government is necessarily required to deal. In fact, according as monogamous or polygamous marriages are allowed, do we find the principles on which the government of the people, to a greater or less extent, rests. Professor, Lieber says, polygamy leads to the patriarchal principle, and which, when applied to large communities, fetters the people in stationary despotism, while that principle cannot long exist in connection with monogamy. Chancellor Kent observes that this remark is equally striking and profound. An exceptional colony of polygamists under an exceptional leadership may sometimes exist for a time without appearing to disturb the social condition of the people who surround it; but there cannot be a doubt that, unless restricted by some form of constitution, it is within the legitimate scope of the power of every civil government to determine whether polygamy or monogamy shall be the law of social life under its dominion.

In our opinion, the statute immediately under consideration is within the legislative power of Congress. It is constitutional and valid as prescribing a rule of action for all those residing in the Territories, and in places over which the United States have exclusive control. This being so, the only question which remains is, whether those who make polygamy a part of their religion are excepted from the operation of the statute. If they are, then those who do not make polygamy a part of their religious belief may be found guilty and punished, while those who do, must be acquitted and go free. This would be introducing a new element into criminal law. Laws are made for the government of actions, and while they cannot interfere with mere religious belief and opinions, they may with practices. Suppose one believed that human sacrifices were a necessary part of religious worship, would it be seriously contended that the civil government under which he lived could not interfere to prevent a sacrifice? Or if a wife religiously believed it was her duty to burn herself upon the funeral pile of her dead husband, would it be beyond the power of the civil government to prevent her carrying her belief into practice?

So here, as a law of the organization of society under the exclusive dominion of the United States, it is provided that plural marriages shall not be allowed. Can a man excuse his practices to the contrary because of his religious belief? To permit this would be to make the professed doctrines of religious belief superior to the law of the land, and in effect to permit every citizen to become a law unto himself. Government could exist only in name under such circumstances.

A criminal intent is generally an element of crime, but every man is presumed to intend the necessary and legitimate consequences of what he knowingly does. Here the accused knew he had been once married, and that his first wife was living. He also knew that his second marriage was forbidden by law. When, therefore, he married the second time, he is presumed to have intended to break the law. And the breaking of the law is the crime. Every act necessary to constitute the crime was knowingly done, and the crime was therefore knowingly committed. Ignorance of a fact may sometimes be taken as evidence of a want of criminal intent, but not ignorance of the law. The only defense of the accused in this case is his belief that the law ought not to have been enacted. It matters not that his belief was a part of his professed religion: it was still belief, and belief only.

In *Regina v. Wagstaff* (10 Cox Crim. Cases, 531), the parents of a sick child, who omitted to call in medical attendance because of their religious belief that what they did for its cure would be effective, were held not to be guilty of manslaughter, while it was said the contrary would have been the result if the child had actually been starved to death by the parents, under the notion that it was their religious duty to abstain from giving it food. But when the offence consists of a positive act which is knowingly done, it would be dangerous to hold that the offender might escape punishment because he religiously believed the law which he had broken ought never to have been made. No case, we believe, can be found that has gone so far.

[Reynolds also objected that the trial court "directed the attention of the jury to the consequences of polygamy."]

The passage complained of is as follows: "I think it not improper, in the discharge of your duties in this case, that you should consider what are to be the consequences to the innocent victims of this delusion. As this contest goes on, they multiply, and there are pure-minded women and there are innocent children, — innocent in a sense even beyond the degree of the innocence of childhood itself. These are to be the sufferers; and as jurors fail to do their duty, and as these cases come up in the Territory of Utah, just so do these victims multiply and spread themselves over the land."

While every appeal by the court to the passions or the prejudices of a jury should be promptly rebuked, and while it is the imperative duty of a reviewing court to take care that wrong is not done in this way, we see no just cause for complaint in this case. Congress, in 1862 saw fit to make bigamy a crime in the Territories. This was done because of the evil consequences that were supposed to flow from plural marriages. All the court did was to call the attention of the jury to the peculiar character of the crime for which the accused was on trial, and to remind them of the duty they had to perform. There was no appeal to the passions, no instigation of prejudice. Upon the showing made by the accused himself, he was guilty of a violation of the law under which he had been indicted: and the effort of the court seems to have been not to withdraw the minds of the jury from the issue to be tried, but to bring them to it; not to make them partial, but to keep them impartial.

B. RELIGIOUS EXPRESSION AND THE FREE EXERCISE CLAUSE

CANTWELL v. CONNECTICUT
310 U.S. 296 (1940)

MR. JUSTICE ROBERTS, delivered the opinion of the Court.

Newton Cantwell and his two sons, Jesse and Russell, members of a group known as Jehovah's Witnesses, and claiming to be ordained ministers, were arrested in New Haven, Connecticut, and each was charged by information in five counts, with statutory and common law offenses. After trial in the Court of Common Pleas of New Haven County each of them was convicted.

On the day of their arrest the appellants were engaged in going singly from house to house on Cassius Street in New Haven. They were individually equipped with a bag containing books and pamphlets on religious subjects, a portable phonograph and a set of records, each of which, when played, introduced, and was a description of, one of the books. Each appellant asked the person who responded to his call for permission to play one of the records. If permission was granted he asked the person to buy the book described and, upon refusal, he solicited such contribution towards the publication of the pamphlets as the listener was willing to make. If a contribution was received a pamphlet was delivered upon condition that it would be read.

Cassius Street is in a thickly populated neighborhood, where about ninety per cent of the residents are Roman Catholics. A phonograph record, describing a book entitled "Enemies," included an attack on the Catholic religion. None of the persons interviewed were members of Jehovah's Witnesses.

The statute under which the appellants were charged provides:

"No person shall solicit money, services, subscriptions or any valuable thing for any alleged religious, charitable or philanthropic cause, from other than a member of the organization for whose benefit such person is soliciting or within the county in which such person or organization is located unless such cause shall have been approved by the secretary of the public welfare council. Upon application of any person in behalf of such cause, the secretary shall determine whether such cause is a religious one or is a bona fide object of charity or philanthropy and conforms to reasonable standards of efficiency and integrity, and, if he shall so find, shall approve the same and issue to the authority in charge a certificate to that effect. Such certificate may be revoked at any time. Any person violating any provision of this section shall be fined not more than one hundred dollars or imprisoned not more than thirty days or both."

The appellants claimed that their activities were not within the statute but consisted only of distribution of books, pamphlets, and periodicals. The State Supreme Court construed the finding of the trial court to be that "in addition to the sale of the books and the distribution of the pamphlets the defendants were also soliciting contributions or donations of money for an alleged religious cause, and thereby came within the purview of the statute." It overruled the contention that the Act, as applied to the appellants, offends the due process clause of the Fourteenth Amendment, because it abridges or denies religious freedom and liberty of speech and press. The court stated that it was the solicitation that brought the appellants within the sweep of the Act and not their other activities in the dissemination of literature. It declared the legislation constitutional as an effort by the State to protect the public against fraud and imposition in the solicitation of funds for what purported to be religious, charitable, or philanthropic causes.

The facts which were held to support the conviction of Jesse Cantwell on the fifth count were that he stopped two men in the street, asked, and received, permission to play a phonograph record, and played the record "Enemies," which attacked the religion and church of the two men, who were Catholics. Both were incensed by the contents of the record and were tempted to strike Cantwell unless he went away. On being told to be on his way he left their presence. There was no evidence that he was personally offensive or entered into any argument with those he interviewed.

The court held that the charge was not assault or breach of the peace or threats on Cantwell's part, but invoking or inciting others to breach of the peace, and that the facts supported the conviction of that offense.

First. We hold that the statute, as construed and applied to the appellants, deprives them of their liberty without due process of law in contravention of the Fourteenth Amendment. The fundamental concept of liberty embodied in that Amendment embraces the liberties guaranteed by the First Amendment. The First Amendment declares that Congress shall make no law respecting an establishment of religion or prohibiting the free exercise thereof. The Fourteenth Amendment has rendered the legislatures of the states as incompetent as Congress to enact such laws. The constitutional inhibition of legislation on the subject of religion has a double aspect. On the one hand, it forestalls compulsion by law of the acceptance of any creed or the practice of any form of worship. Freedom of conscience and freedom to adhere to such religious organization or form of worship as the individual may choose cannot be restricted by law. On the other hand, it safeguards the free exercise of the chosen form of religion. Thus the Amendment embraces two concepts, — freedom to believe and freedom to act. The first is absolute but, in the nature of things, the second cannot be. Conduct remains subject to regulation for the protection of society. The freedom to act must have appropriate definition to preserve the enforcement of that protection. In every case the power to regulate must be so exercised as not, in attaining a permissible end, unduly to infringe the protected freedom. No one would contest the proposition that a state may not, be statute, wholly deny the right to preach or to disseminate religious views. Plainly such a previous and absolute restraint would violate the terms of the guarantee. It is equally clear that a state may by general and non-discriminatory legislation regulate the times, the places, and the manner of soliciting upon its streets, and of holding meetings thereon; and may in other respects safeguard the peace, good order and comfort of the community, without unconstitutionally invading the liberties protected by the Fourteenth Amendment. The appellants are right in their insistence that the Act in question is not such a regulation. If a certificate is procured, solicitation is permitted without restraint but, in the absence of a certificate, solicitation is altogether prohibited.

The appellants urge that to require them to obtain a certificate as a condition of soliciting support for their views amounts to a prior restraint on the exercise of their religion within the meaning of the Constitution. The State insists that the Act, as construed by the Supreme Court of Connecticut, imposes no previous restraint upon the dissemination of religious views or teaching but merely safeguards against the perpetration of frauds under the cloak of religion. Conceding that this is so, the question remains whether the method adopted by Connecticut to that end transgresses the liberty safeguarded by the Constitution.

The general regulation, in the public interest, of solicitation, which does not involve any religious test and does not unreasonably obstruct or delay the collection of funds, is not open to any constitutional objection, even though the collection be for a religious purpose. Such regulation would not constitute a prohibited previous restraint on the free exercise of religion or interpose an inadmissible obstacle to its exercise.

It will be noted, However, that the Act requires an application to the secretary of the public welfare council of the State; that he is empowered to determine whether the cause is a religious one, and that the issue of a certificate depends upon his affirmative action. If he finds that the cause is not that of religion, to solicit for it becomes a crime. He is not to issue a certificate as a matter of course. His decision to issue or refuse it involves appraisal of facts, the exercise of judgment, and the formation of an opinion. He is authorized to withhold his approval if he determines that the cause is not a religious one. Such a censorship of religion as the means of determining its right to survive is a denial of liberty protected by the First Amendment and included in the liberty which is within the protection of the Fourteenth.

The State asserts that if the licensing officer acts arbitrarily, capriciously, or corruptly, his action is subject to judicial correction. Counsel refer to the rule prevailing in Connecticut that the decision of a commission or an administrative official will be reviewed upon a claim that "it works material damage to individual or corporate rights, or invades or threatens such rights, or is so unreasonable as to justify judicial intervention, or is not consonant with justice, or that a legal duty has not been performed." It is suggested that the statute is to be read as requiring the officer to issue a certificate unless the cause in question is clearly not a religious one; and that if he violates his duty his action will be corrected by a court.

To this suggestion there are several sufficient answers. The line between a discretionary and a ministerial act is not always easy to mark and the statute has not been construed by the State court to impose a mere ministerial duty on the secretary of the welfare council. Upon his decision as to the nature of the cause, the right to solicit depends. Moreover, the availability of a judicial remedy for abuses in the system of licensing still leaves that system one of previous restraint which, in the field of free speech and press, we have held inadmissible. A statute authorizing previous restraint upon the exercise of the guaranteed freedom by judicial decision after trial is as obnoxious to the Constitution as one providing for like restraint by administrative action.

Nothing we have said is intended even remotely to imply that, under the cloak of religion, persons may, with impunity, commit frauds upon the public. Certainly penal laws are available to punish such conduct. Even the exercise of religion may be at some slight inconvenience in order that the state may protect its citizens from injury. Without doubt a state may protect its citizens from fraudulent solicitation by requiring a stranger in the community, before permitting him publicly to solicit funds for any purpose, to establish his identity and his authority to act for the cause which he purports to represent. The State is likewise free to regulate the time and manner of solicitation generally, in the interest of public safety, peace, comfort or convenience. But to condition the solicitation of aid for the perpetuation of religious views or systems upon a license, the grant of which rests in the exercise of a determination by state authority as to what is a religious cause, is to lay a forbidden burden upon the exercise of liberty protected by the Constitution.

Second. We hold that, in the circumstances disclosed, the conviction of Jesse Cantwell on the fifth count must be set aside. Decision as to the lawfulness of the conviction demands the weighing of two conflicting interests. The fundamental law declares the interest of the United States that the free exercise of religion be not prohibited and that freedom to communicate information and opinion be not abridged. The State of Connecticut has an obvious interest in the preservation and protection of peace and good order within her borders. We must determine whether the alleged protection of the State's interest, means to which end would, in the absence of limitation by the Federal Constitution, lie wholly within the State's discretion, has been pressed, in this instance, to a point where it has come into fatal collision with the overriding interest protected by the federal compact.

Conviction on the fifth count was not pursuant to a statute evincing a legislative judgment that street discussion of religious affairs, because of its tendency to provoke disorder, should be regulated, or a judgment that the playing of a phonograph on the streets should in the interest of comfort or privacy be limited or prevented. Violation of an Act exhibiting such a legislative judgment and narrowly drawn to prevent the supposed evil, would pose a question differing from that we must here answer. Such a declaration of the State's policy would weigh heavily in any challenge of the law as infringing constitutional limitations. Here, however, the judgment is based on a common law concept of the most general and undefined nature.

[A] State may not unduly suppress free communication of views, religious or other, under the guise of conserving desirable conditions. Here we have a situation analogous to a conviction under a statute sweeping in a great variety of conduct under a general and indefinite characterization, and leaving to the executive and judicial branches too wide a discretion in its application.

Having these considerations in mind, we note that Jesse Cantwell, on April 26, 1938, was upon a public street, where he had a right to be, and where he had a right peacefully to impart his views to others. There is no showing that his deportment was noisy, truculent, overbearing or offensive. He requested of two pedestrians permission to play to them a phonograph record. The permission was granted. It is not claimed that he intended to insult or affront the hearers by playing the record. It is plain that he wished only to interest them in his propaganda. The sound of the phonograph is not shown to have disturbed residents of the street, to have drawn a crowd, or to have impeded traffic. Thus far he had invaded no right or interest of the public or of the men accosted.

The record played by Cantwell embodies a general attack on all organized religious systems as instruments of Satan and injurious to man; it then singles out the Roman Catholic Church for strictures couched in terms which naturally would offend not only persons of that persuasion, but all others who respect the honestly held religious faith of their fellows. The hearers were in fact highly offended. One of them said he felt like hitting Cantwell and the other that he was tempted to throw Cantwell off the street. The one who testified he felt like hitting Cantwell said, in answer to the question "Did you do anything else or have any other reaction?" "No, sir, because he said he would take the victrola and he went." The other witness testified that he told Cantwell he had better get off the street before something happened to him and that was the end of the matter as Cantwell picked up his books and walked up the street.

We find in the instant case no assault or threatening of bodily harm, no truculent bearing, no intentional discourtesy, no personal abuse. On the contrary, we find only an effort to persuade a willing listener to buy a book or to contribute money in the interest of what Cantwell, however misguided others may think him, conceived to be true religion.

In the realm of religious faith, and in that of political belief, sharp differences arise. In both fields the tenets of one man may seem the rankest error to his neighbor. To persuade others to his own point of view, the pleader, as we know, at times, resorts to exaggeration, to vilification of men who have been, or are, prominent in church or state, and even to false statement. But the people of this nation have ordained in the light of history, that, in spite of the probability of excesses and abuses, these liberties are, in the long view, essential to enlightened opinion and right conduct on the part of the citizens of a democracy.

The essential characteristic of these liberties is, that under their shield many types of life, character, opinion and belief can develop unmolested and unobstructed. Nowhere is this shield more necessary than in our own country for a people composed of many races and of many creeds. There are limits to the exercise of these liberties. The danger in these times from the coercive activities of those who in the delusion of racial or religious conceit would incite violence and breaches of the peace in order to deprive others of their equal right to the exercise of their liberties, is emphasized by events familiar to all. These and other transgressions of those limits the states appropriately may punish.

Although the contents of the record not unnaturally aroused animosity, we think that, in the absence of a statute narrowly drawn to define and punish specific conduct as constituting a clear and present danger to a substantial interest of the State, the petitioner's communication, considered in the light of the constitutional guarantees, raised no such clear and present menace to public peace and order as to render him liable to conviction of the common law offense in question.

McDANIEL v. PATY
435 U.S. 618 (1978)

MR. CHIEF JUSTICE BURGER announced the judgment of the Court and delivered an opinion in which MR. JUSTICE POWELL, MR. JUSTICE REHNQUIST, and MR. JUSTICE STEVENS joined.

The question presented by this appeal is whether a Tennessee statute barring "Minister[s] of the Gospel, or priest[s] of any denomination whatever" from serving as delegates to the State's limited constitutional convention deprived appellant McDaniel, an ordained minister, of the right to the free exercise of religion guaranteed by the First Amendment and made applicable to the States by the Fourteenth Amendment. The First Amendment forbids all laws "prohibiting the free exercise" of religion.

I

In its first Constitution, in 1796, Tennessee disqualified ministers from serving as legislators.[1] That disqualifying provision has continued unchanged since its adoption; it is now Art. 9, § 1, of the State Constitution. The state legislature applied this provision to candidates for delegate to the State's 1977 limited constitutional convention when it enacted ch. 848, § 4, of 1976 Tenn. Pub. Acts: "Any citizen of the state who can qualify for membership in the House of Representatives of the General Assembly may become a candidate for delegate to the convention. . . ."

---

[1] "Whereas Ministers of the Gospel are, by their profession, dedicated to God and the care of Souls, and ought not to be diverted from the great duties of their functions; therefore, no Minister of the Gospel, or priest of any denomination whatever, shall be eligible to a seat in either House of the Legislature." Tenn. Const., Art. VIII, § 1 (1796).

McDaniel, an ordained minister of a Baptist Church in Chattanooga, Tenn., filed as a candidate for delegate to the constitutional convention. An opposing candidate, appellee Selma Cash Paty, sued in the Chancery Court for a declaratory judgment that McDaniel was disqualified from serving as a delegate and for a judgment striking his name from the ballot.

II

A

The disqualification of ministers from legislative office was a practice carried from England by seven of the original States;[3] later six new States similarly excluded clergymen from some political offices. 1 A. STOKES, CHURCH AND STATE IN THE UNITED STATES 622 (1950) (hereafter STOKES). In England the practice of excluding clergy from the House of Commons was justified on a variety of grounds: to prevent dual officeholding, that is, membership by a minister in both Parliament and Convocation; to insure that the priest or deacon devoted himself to his "sacred calling" rather than to "such mundane activities as were appropriate to a member of the House of Commons"; and to prevent ministers, who after 1533 were subject to the Crown's powers over the benefices of the clergy, from using membership in Commons to diminish its independence by increasing the influence of the King and the nobility. *In re MacManaway*, [1951] A.C. 161, 164, 170-171.

The purpose of the several States in providing for disqualification was primarily to assure the success of a new political experiment, the separation of church and state. STOKES 622. Prior to 1776, most of the 13 Colonies had some form of an established, or government-sponsored, church. *Id.*, at 364-446. Even after ratification of the First Amendment, which prohibited the Federal Government from following such a course, some States continued pro-establishment provisions. *See id.*, at 408, 418-427, 444. Massachusetts, the last State to accept disestablishment, did so in 1833. *Id.*, at 426-427.

In light of this history and a widespread awareness during that period of undue and often dominant clerical influence in public and political affairs here, in England, and on the Continent, it is not surprising that strong views were held by some that one way to assure disestablishment was to keep clergymen out of public office. Indeed, some of the foremost political philosophers and statesmen of that period held such views regarding the clergy. Earlier, John Locke argued for confining the authority of the English clergy "within the bounds of the church, nor can it in any manner be extended to civil affairs; because the church itself is a thing absolutely separate and distinct from the commonwealth." 5 WORKS OF JOHN LOCKE 21 (C. Baldwin ed. 1824). Thomas Jefferson initially advocated such a position in his 1783 draft of a constitution for

---

[3] Maryland, Virginia, North Carolina, South Carolina, Georgia, New York, and Delaware. L. PFEFFER, CHURCH, STATE, AND FREEDOM 118 (Rev. ed. 1967). Three of these — New York, Delaware, and South Carolina — barred clergymen from holding any political office. *Ibid.*

Virginia. James Madison, however, disagreed and vigorously urged the position which in our view accurately reflects the spirit and purpose of the Religion Clauses of the First Amendment. Madison's response to Jefferson's position was:

> "Does not The exclusion of Ministers of the Gospel as such violate a fundamental principle of liberty by punishing a religious profession with the privation of a civil right? does it [not] violate another article of the plan itself which exempts religion from the cognizance of Civil power? does it not violate justice by at once taking away a right and prohibiting a compensation for it? does it not in fine violate impartiality by shutting the door [against] the Ministers of one Religion and leaving it open for those of every other." 5 WRITINGS OF JAMES MADISON 288 (G. Hunt ed. 1904).

Madison was not the only articulate opponent of clergy disqualification. When proposals were made earlier to prevent clergymen from holding public office, John Witherspoon, a Presbyterian minister, president of Princeton University, and the only clergyman to sign the Declaration of Independence, made a cogent protest and, with tongue in cheek, offered an amendment to a provision much like that challenged here:

> " 'No clergyman, of any denomination, shall be capable of being elected a member of the Senate or House of Representatives, because (here insert the grounds of offensive disqualification, which I have not been able to discover) Provided always, and it is the true intent and meaning of this part of the constitution, that if at any time he shall be completely deprived of the clerical character by those by whom he was invested with it, as by deposition for cursing and swearing, drunkenness or uncleanness, he shall then be fully restored to all the privileges of a free citizen; his offense [of being a clergyman] shall no more be remembered against him; but he may be chosen either to the Senate or House of Representatives, and shall be treated with all the respect due to his *brethren*, the other members of Assembly.' " STOKES 624-625.

As the value of the disestablishment experiment was perceived, 11 of the 13 States disqualifying the clergy from some types of public office gradually abandoned that limitation. New York, for example, took that step in 1846 after delegates to the State's constitutional convention argued that the exclusion of clergymen from the legislature was an "odious distinction." 2 C. LINCOLN, THE CONSTITUTIONAL HISTORY OF NEW YORK 111-112 (1906). Only Maryland and Tennessee continued their clergy-disqualification provisions into this century and, in 1974, a District Court held Maryland's provision violative of the First and Fourteenth Amendments' guarantees of the free exercise of religion. *Kirkley v. Maryland*, 381 F. Supp. 327. Today Tennessee remains the only State excluding ministers from certain public offices.

The essence of this aspect of our national history is that in all but a few States the selection or rejection of clergymen for public office soon came to be viewed as something safely left to the good sense and desires of the people.

B

This brief review of the history of clergy-disqualification provisions also amply demonstrates, however, that, at least during the early segment of our national life, those provisions enjoyed the support of responsible American statesmen and were accepted as having a rational basis. Against this background we do not lightly invalidate a statute enacted pursuant to a provision of a state constitution which has been sustained by its highest court. The challenged provision came to the Tennessee Supreme Court clothed with the presumption of validity to which that court was bound to give deference.

However, the right to the free exercise of religion unquestionably encompasses the right to preach, proselyte, and perform other similar religious functions, or, in other words, to be a minister of the type McDaniel was found to be. *Cantwell v. Connecticut.* Tennessee also acknowledges the right of its adult citizens generally to seek and hold office as legislators or delegates to the state constitutional convention. Yet under the clergy-disqualification provision, McDaniel cannot exercise both rights simultaneously because the State has conditioned the exercise of one on the surrender of the other. Or, in James Madison's words, the State is "punishing a religious profession with the privation of a civil right." 5 WRITINGS OF JAMES MADISON, *supra,* at 288. In so doing, Tennessee has encroached upon McDaniel's right to the free exercise of religion. "[T]o condition the availability of benefits [including access to the ballot] upon this appellant's willingness to violate a cardinal principle of [his] religious faith [by surrendering his religiously impelled ministry] effectively penalizes the free exercise of [his] constitutional liberties." *Sherbert v. Verner* [*infra* Chapter 12].

If the Tennessee disqualification provision were viewed as depriving the clergy of a civil right solely because of their religious beliefs, our inquiry would be at an end. The Free Exercise Clause categorically prohibits government from regulating, prohibiting, or rewarding religious beliefs as such. In *Torcaso v. Watkins*, the Court reviewed the Maryland constitutional requirement that all holders of "any office of profit or trust in this State" declare their belief in the existence of God. In striking down the Maryland requirement, the Court did not evaluate the interests assertedly justifying it but rather held that it violated freedom of religious belief.

In our view, however, *Torcaso* does not govern. By its terms, the Tennessee disqualification operates against McDaniel because of his *status* as a "minister" or "priest." The meaning of those words is, of course, a question of state law. And although the question has not been examined extensively in state-law sources, such authority as is available indicates that ministerial status is defined in terms of conduct and activity rather than in terms of belief. Because the Tennessee disqualification is directed primarily at status, acts, and conduct it is unlike the requirement in *Torcaso*, which focused on *belief*. Hence, the Free Exercise Clause's absolute prohibition of infringements on the "freedom to believe" is inapposite here.

This does not mean, of course, that the disqualification escapes judicial scrutiny or that McDaniel's activity does not enjoy significant First Amendment protection. The Court recently declared in *Wisconsin v. Yoder* [*infra* Chapter 13]:

> "The essence of all that has been said and written on the subject is that only those interests of the highest order and those not otherwise served can overbalance legitimate claims to the free exercise of religion."

Tennessee asserts that its interest in preventing the establishment of a state religion is consistent with the Establishment Clause and thus of the highest order. The constitutional history of the several States reveals that generally the interest in preventing establishment prompted the adoption of clergy disqualification provisions, *see* STOKES 622; Tennessee does not appear to be an exception to this pattern. There is no occasion to inquire whether promoting such an interest is a permissible legislative goal, however, for Tennessee has failed to demonstrate that its views of the dangers of clergy participation in the political process have not lost whatever validity they may once have enjoyed. The essence of the rationale underlying the Tennessee restriction on ministers is that if elected to public office they will necessarily exercise their powers and influence to promote the interests of one sect or thwart the interests of another, thus pitting one against the others, contrary to the anti-establishment principle with its command of neutrality. *See Walz v. Tax Comm'n* [*supra* Chapter 8]. However widely that view may have been held in the 18th century by many, including enlightened statesmen of that day, the American experience provides no persuasive support for the fear that clergymen in public office will be less careful of anti-establishment interests or less faithful to their oaths of civil office than their unordained counterparts.[9]

MR. JUSTICE BRENNAN, with whom MR. JUSTICE MARSHALL joins, concurring in the judgment.

Tennessee invokes the Establishment Clause to excuse the imposition of a civil disability upon those deemed to be deeply involved in religion. In my view, that Clause will not permit, much less excuse or condone, the deprivation of religious liberty here involved.

---

[9] The struggle for separation of church and state in Virginia, which influenced developments in other States — and in the Federal Government — was waged by others in addition to such secular leaders as Jefferson, Madison, and George Mason; many clergymen vigorously opposed any established church. *See* STOKES 366-379. This suggests the imprecision of any assumption that, even in the early days of the Republic, most ministers, as legislators, would support measures antithetical to the separation of church and state.

Fundamental to the conception of religious liberty protected by the Religion Clauses is the idea that religious beliefs are a matter of voluntary choice by individuals and their associations, and that each sect is entitled to "flourish according to the zeal of its adherents and the appeal of its dogma." *Zorach v. Clauson*, 343 U.S. 306, 313 (1952). Accordingly, religious ideas, no less than any other, may be the subject of debate which is "uninhibited, robust, and wide-open. . . ." *New York Times Co. v. Sullivan*, 376 U.S. 254, 270 (1964). Government may not interfere with efforts to proselyte or worship in public places. *Kunz v. New York,* 340 U.S. 290 (1951). It may not tax the dissemination of religious ideas. *Murdock v. Pennsylvania*, 319 U.S. 105 (1943). It may not seek to shield its citizens from those who would solicit them with their religious beliefs. *Martin v. City of Struthers*, 319 U.S. 141 (1943).

That public debate of religious ideas, like any other, may arouse emotion, may incite, may foment religious divisiveness and strife does not rob it of constitutional protection. *Cantwell v. Connecticut.* The mere fact that a purpose of the Establishment Clause is to reduce or eliminate religious divisiveness or strife, does not place religious discussion, association, or political participation in a status less preferred than rights of discussion, association, and political participation generally. "Adherents of particular faiths and individual churches frequently take strong positions on public issues including . . . vigorous advocacy of legal or constitutional positions. Of course, churches as much as secular bodies and private citizens have that right." *Walz v. Tax Comm'n* [*supra* Chapter 8].

The State's goal of preventing sectarian bickering and strife may not be accomplished by regulating religious speech and political association. The Establishment Clause does not license government to treat religion and those who teach or practice it, simply by virtue of their status as such, as subversive of American ideals and therefore subject to unique disabilities. Government may not inquire into the religious beliefs and motivations of officeholders — it may not remove them from office merely for making public statements regarding religion, or question whether their legislative actions stem from religious conviction.

In short, government may not as a goal promote "safe thinking" with respect to religion and fence out from political participation those, such as ministers, whom it regards as overinvolved in religion. Religionists no less than members of any other group enjoy the full measure of protection afforded speech, association, and political activity generally. The Establishment Clause, properly understood, is a shield against any attempt by government to inhibit religion as it has done here; *Abington School Dist. v. Schempp* [*supra* Chapter 6]. It may not be used as a sword to justify repression of religion or its adherents from any aspect of public life.[25]

---

[25] "In much the same spirit, American courts have not thought the separation of church and state to require that religion be totally oblivious to government or politics; church and religious groups in the United States have long exerted powerful political pressures on state and national legislatures, on subjects as diverse as slavery, war, gambling, drinking, prostitution, marriage, and education. To view such religious activity as suspect, or to regard its political results as automatically

Our decisions under the Establishment Clause prevent government from supporting or involving itself in religion or from becoming drawn into ecclesiastical disputes. These prohibitions naturally tend, as they were designed to, to avoid channeling political activity along religious lines and to reduce any tendency toward religious divisiveness in society. Beyond enforcing these prohibitions, however, government may not go. The antidote which the Constitution provides against zealots who would inject sectarianism into the political process is to subject their ideas to refutation in the marketplace of ideas and their platforms to rejection at the polls. With these safeguards, it is unlikely that they will succeed in inducing government to act along religiously divisive lines, and, with judicial enforcement of the Establishment Clause, any measure of success they achieve must be short-lived, at best.

WEST VIRGINIA STATE BOARD OF EDUCATION v. BARNETTE
319 U.S. 624 (1943)

MR. JUSTICE JACKSON delivered the opinion of the Court.

Following the decision by this Court on June 3, 1940, in *Minersville School District v. Gobitis*, 310 U.S. 586, the West Virginia legislature amended its statutes to require all schools therein to conduct courses of instruction in history, civics, and in the Constitutions of the United States and of the State "for the purpose of teaching, fostering and perpetuating the ideals, principles and spirit of Americanism, and increasing the knowledge of the organization and machinery of the government." Appellant Board of Education was directed, with advice of the State Superintendent of Schools, to "prescribe the courses of study covering these subjects" for public schools. The Act made it the duty of private, parochial and denominational schools to prescribe courses of study "similar to those required for the public schools."[1]

---

tainted, might be inconsistent with first amendment freedoms of religious and political expression — and might not even succeed in keeping religious controversy out of public life, given the 'political ruptures caused by the alienation of segments of the religious community.'" L. TRIBE, [AMERICAN CONSTITUTIONAL LAW (1978)], *supra* n. 20, § 14-12, pp. 866-867 (footnotes omitted).

[1] § 1734, West Virginia Code (1941 Supp.):

"In all public, private, parochial and denominational schools located within this state there shall be given regular courses of instruction in history of the United States, in civics, and in the constitutions of the United States and of the State of West Virginia, for the purpose of teaching, fostering and perpetuating the ideals, principles and spirit of Americanism, and increasing the knowledge of the organization and machinery of the government of the United States and of the state of West Virginia. The state board of education shall, with the advice of the state superintendent of schools, prescribe the courses of study covering these subjects for the public elementary and grammar schools, public high schools and state normal schools. It shall be the duty of the officials or boards having authority over the respective private, parochial and denominational schools to prescribe courses of study for the schools under their control and supervision similar to those required for the public schools."

The Board of Education on January 9, 1942, adopted a resolution containing recitals taken largely from the Court's *Gobitis* opinion and ordering that the salute to the flag become "a regular part of the program of activities in the public schools," that all teachers and pupils "shall be required to participate in the salute honoring the Nation represented by the Flag; provided, however, that refusal to salute the Flag be regarded as an Act of insubordination, and shall be dealt with accordingly."

Failure to conform is "insubordination" dealt with by expulsion. Readmission is denied by statute until compliance. Meanwhile the expelled child is "unlawfully absent" and may be proceeded against as a delinquent. His parents or guardians are liable to prosecution, and if convicted are subject to fine not exceeding $50 and jail term not exceeding thirty days.

Appellees, citizens of the United States and of West Virginia, brought suit in the United States District Court for themselves and others similarly situated asking its injunction to restrain enforcement of these laws and regulations against Jehovah's Witnesses. The Witnesses are an unincorporated body teaching that the obligation imposed by law of God is superior to that of laws enacted by temporal government. Their religious beliefs include a literal version of Exodus, Chapter 20, verses 4 and 5, which says: "Thou shalt not make unto thee any graven image, or any likeness of anything that is in heaven above, or that is in the earth beneath, or that is in the water under the earth; thou shalt not bow down thyself to them nor serve them." They consider that the flag is an "image" within this command. For this reason they refuse to salute it.

Children of this faith have been expelled from school and are threatened with exclusion for no other cause. Officials threaten to send them to reformatories maintained for criminally inclined juveniles. Parents of such children have been prosecuted and are threatened with prosecutions for causing delinquency.

There is no doubt that, in connection with the pledges, the flag salute is a form of utterance. Symbolism is a primitive but effective way of communicating ideas. The use of an emblem or flag to symbolize some system, idea, institution, or personality, is a short cut from mind to mind. Causes and nations, political parties, lodges and ecclesiastical groups seek to knit the loyalty of their followings to a flag or banner, a color or design. The State announces rank, function, and authority through crowns and maces, uniforms and black robes; the church speaks through the Cross, the Crucifix, the altar and shrine, and clerical raiment. Symbols of State often convey political ideas just as religious symbols come to convey theological ones. Associated with many of these symbols are appropriate gestures of acceptance or respect: a salute, a bowed or bared head, a bended knee. A person gets from a symbol the meaning he puts into it, and what is one man's comfort and inspiration is another's jest and scorn.

Over a decade ago Chief Justice Hughes led this Court in holding that the display of a red flag as a symbol of opposition by peaceful and legal means to organized government was protected by the free speech guaranties of the Constitution. *Stromberg v. California*, 283 U.S. 359. Here it is the State that employs a flag as a symbol of adherence to government as presently organized. It requires the individual to communicate by word and sign his acceptance of the political ideas it thus bespeaks. Objection to this form of communication when coerced is an old one, well known to the framers of the Bill of Rights.[13]

It is also to be noted that the compulsory flag salute and pledge requires affirmation of a belief and an attitude of mind. It is not clear whether the regulation contemplates that pupils forego any contrary convictions of their own and become unwilling converts to the prescribed ceremony or whether it will be acceptable if they simulate assent by words without belief and by a gesture barren of meaning. It is now a commonplace that censorship or suppression of expression of opinion is tolerated by our Constitution only when the expression presents a clear and present danger of action of a kind the State is empowered to prevent and punish. It would seem that involuntary affirmation could be commanded only on even more immediate and urgent grounds than silence. But here the power of compulsion is invoked without any allegation that remaining passive during a flag salute ritual creates a clear and present danger that would justify an effort even to muffle expression. To sustain the compulsory flag salute we are required to say that a Bill of Rights which guards the individual's right to speak his own mind, left it open to public authorities to compel him to utter what is not in his mind.

Whether the First Amendment to the Constitution will permit officials to order observance of ritual of this nature does not depend upon whether as a voluntary exercise we would think it to be good, bad or merely innocuous. Any credo of nationalism is likely to include what some disapprove or to omit what others think essential, and to give off different overtones as it takes on different accents or interpretations. If official power exists to coerce acceptance of any patriotic creed, what it shall contain cannot be decided by courts, but must be largely discretionary with the ordaining authority, whose power to prescribe would no doubt include power to amend. Hence validity of the asserted power to force an American citizen publicly to profess any statement of belief or to engage in any ceremony of assent to one presents questions of power that must be considered independently of any idea we may have as to the utility of the ceremony in question.

Nor does the issue as we see it turn on one's possession of particular religious views or the sincerity with which they are held. While religion supplies

---

[13] Early Christians were frequently persecuted for their refusal to participate in ceremonies before the statue of the emperor or other symbol of imperial authority. The story of William Tell's sentence to shoot an apple off his son's head for refusal to salute a bailiff's hat is an ancient one. 21 ENCYCLOPEDIA BRITANNICA (14th Ed.) 911, 912. The Quakers, William Penn included, suffered punishment rather than uncover their heads in deference to any civil authority. BRAITHWAITE, THE BEGINNINGS OF QUAKERISM (1912) 200, 229-230, 232, 233, 447, 451; Fox, QUAKERS COURAGEOUS (1941) 113.

appellees' motive for enduring the discomforts of making the issue in this case, many citizens who do not share these religious views hold such a compulsory rite to infringe constitutional liberty of the individual. It is not necessary to inquire whether non-conformist beliefs will exempt from the duty to salute unless we first find power to make the salute a legal duty.

The *Gobitis* decision, however, *assumed*, as did the argument in that case and in this, that power exists in the State to impose the flag salute discipline upon school children in general. The Court only examined and rejected a claim based on religious beliefs of immunity from an unquestioned general rule. The question which underlies the flag salute controversy is whether such a ceremony so touching matters of opinion and political attitude may be imposed upon the individual by official authority under powers committed to any political organization under our Constitution. We examine rather than assume existence of this power and, against this broader definition of issues in this case, re-examine specific grounds assigned for the *Gobitis* decision.

[T]his is the very heart of the *Gobitis* opinion[:] it reasons that "National unity is the basis of national security," that the authorities have "the right to select appropriate means for its attainment," and hence reaches the conclusion that such compulsory measures toward "national unity" are constitutional. Upon the verity of this assumption depends our answer in this case.

National unity as an end which officials may foster by persuasion and example is not in question. The problem is whether under our Constitution compulsion as here employed is a permissible means for its achievement.

Struggles to coerce uniformity of sentiment in support of some end thought essential to their time and country have been waged by many good as well as by evil men. Nationalism is a relatively recent phenomenon but at other times and places the ends have been racial or territorial security, support of a dynasty or regime, and particular plans for saving souls. As first and moderate methods to attain unity have failed, those bent on its accomplishment must resort to an ever-increasing severity. As governmental pressure toward unity becomes greater, so strife becomes more bitter as to whose unity it shall be. Probably no deeper division of our people could proceed from any provocation than from finding it necessary to choose what doctrine and whose program public educational officials shall compel youth to unite in embracing. Ultimate futility of such attempts to compel coherence is the lesson of every such effort from the Roman drive to stamp out Christianity as a disturber of its pagan unity, the Inquisition, as a means to religious and dynastic unity, the Siberian exiles as a means to Russian unity, down to the fast failing efforts of our present totalitarian enemies. Those who begin coercive elimination of dissent soon find themselves exterminating dissenters. Compulsory unification of opinion achieves only the unanimity of the graveyard.

It seems trite but necessary to say that the First Amendment to our Constitution was designed to avoid these ends by avoiding these beginnings. There is no mysticism in the American concept of the State or of the nature or origin of its authority. We set up government by consent of the governed, and the Bill of Rights denies those in power any legal opportunity to coerce that consent. Authority here is to be controlled by public opinion, not public opinion by authority.

The case is made difficult not because the principles of its decision are obscure but because the flag involved is our own. Nevertheless, we apply the limitations of the Constitution with no fear that freedom to be intellectually and spiritually diverse or even contrary will disintegrate the social organization. To believe that patriotism will not flourish if patriotic ceremonies are voluntary and spontaneous instead of a compulsory routine is to make an unflattering estimate of the appeal of our institutions to free minds. We can have intellectual individualism and the rich cultural diversities that we owe to exceptional minds only at the price of occasional eccentricity and abnormal attitudes. When they are so harmless to others or to the State as those we deal with here, the price is not too great. But freedom to differ is not limited to things that do not matter much. That would be a mere shadow of freedom. The test of its substance is the right to differ as to things that touch the heart of the existing order.

If there is any fixed star in our constitutional constellation, it is that no official, high or petty, can prescribe what shall be orthodox in politics, nationalism, religion, or other matters of opinion or force citizens to confess by word or act their faith therein. If there are any circumstances which permit an exception, they do not now occur to us.

We think the action of the local authorities in compelling the flag salute and pledge transcends constitutional limitations on their power and invades the sphere of intellect and spirit which it is the purpose of the First Amendment to our Constitution to reserve from all official control.

The decision of this Court in *Minersville School District v. Gobitis* and the holdings of those few *per curiam* decisions which preceded and foreshadowed it are overruled, and the judgment enjoining enforcement of the West Virginia Regulation is *Affirmed.*

MR. JUSTICE FRANKFURTER, dissenting.

One who belongs to the most vilified and persecuted minority in history is not likely to be insensible to the freedoms guaranteed by our Constitution. Were my purely personal attitude relevant I should whole-heartedly associate myself with the general libertarian views in the Court's opinion, representing as they do the thought and action of a lifetime. But as judges we are neither Jew nor Gentile, neither Catholic nor agnostic. We owe equal attachment to the Constitution and are equally bound by our judicial obligations whether we derive our citizenship from the earliest or the latest immigrants to these shores. As a member of this Court I am not justified in writing my private notions of policy into the Constitution, no matter how deeply I may cherish them or how mischievous I may deem their disregard. They duty of a judge who must decide which of two claims before the Court shall prevail, that of a State to enact and enforce laws within its general competence or that of an individual to refuse obedience because of the demands of his conscience, is not that of the ordinary person. It can never be emphasized too much that one's own opinion about the wisdom or evil of a law should be excluded altogether when one is doing one's duty on the bench. The only opinion of our own even looking in that direction that is material is our opinion whether legislators could in reason have enacted such a law. In the light of all the circumstances, including the history of this question in this Court, it would require more daring than I possess to deny that reasonable legislators could have taken the action which is before us for review. Most unwillingly, therefore, I must differ from my brethren with regard to legislation like this. I cannot bring my mind to believe that the "liberty" secured by the Due Process Clause gives this Court authority to deny to the State of West Virginia the attainment of that which we all recognize as a legitimate legislative end, namely, the promotion of good citizenship, by employment of the means here chosen.

When Mr. Justice Holmes, speaking for this Court, wrote that "it must be remembered that legislatures are ultimate guardians of the liberties and welfare of the people in quite as great a degree as the courts," *Missouri, K. & T. Ry. Co. v. May*, 194 U.S. 267, 270, he went to the very essence of our constitutional system and the democratic conception of our society. He did not mean that for only some phases of civil government this Court was not to supplant legislatures and sit in judgment upon the right or wrong of a challenged measure. He was stating the comprehensive judicial duty and rôle of this Court in our constitutional scheme whenever legislation is sought to be nullified on any ground, namely, that responsibility for legislation lies with legislatures, answerable as they are directly to the people, and this Court's only and very narrow function is to determine whether within the broad grant of authority vested in legislatures they have exercised a judgment for which reasonable justification can be offered.

The precise scope of the question before us defines the limits of the constitutional power that is in issue. The State of West Virginia requires all pupils to share in the salute to the flag as part of school training in citizenship. The present action is one to enjoin the enforcement of this requirement by those in school attendance. We have not before us any attempt by the State to punish disobedient children or visit penal consequences on their parents. All that is in question is the right of the State to compel participation in this exercise by those who choose to attend the public schools.

Under our constitutional system the legislature is charged solely with civil concerns of society. If the avowed or intrinsic legislative purpose is either to promote or to discourage some religious community or creed, it is clearly within the constitutional restrictions imposed on legislatures and cannot stand. But it by no means follows that legislative power is wanting whenever a general non-discriminatory civil regulation in fact touches conscientious scruples or religious beliefs of an individual or a group. Regard for such scruples or beliefs undoubtedly presents one of the most reasonable claims for the exertion of legislative accommodation. It is, of course, beyond our power to rewrite the State's requirement, by providing exemptions for those who do not wish to participate in the flag salute or by making some other accommodations to meet their scruples. That wisdom might suggest the making of such accommodations and that school administration would not find it too difficult to make them and yet maintain the ceremony for those not refusing to conform, is outside our province to suggest. Tact, respect, and generosity toward variant views will always commend themselves to those charged with the duties of legislation so as to achieve a maximum of good will and to require a minimum of unwilling submission to a general law. But the real question is, who is to make such accommodations, the courts or the legislature?

The constitutional protection of religious freedom terminated disabilities, it did not create new privileges. It gave religious equality, not civil immunity. Its essence is freedom from conformity to religious dogma, not freedom from conformity to law because of religious dogma. Religious loyalties may be exercised without hindrance from the state, not the state may not exercise that which except by leave of religious loyalties is within the domain of temporal power. Otherwise each individual could set up his own censor against obedience to laws conscientiously deemed for the public good by those whose business it is to make laws.

The essence of the religious freedom guaranteed by our Constitution is therefore this: no religion shall either receive the state's support or incur its hostility. Religion is outside the sphere of political government. This does not mean that all matters on which religious organizations or beliefs may pronounce are outside the sphere of government. Were this so, instead of the separation of church and state, there would be the subordination of the state on any matter deemed within the sovereignty of the religious conscience. Much that is the concern of temporal authority affects the spiritual interests of men. But it is not enough to strike down a non-discriminatory law that it may hurt or offend some dissident view. It would be too easy to cite numerous prohibitions and injunctions to which laws run counter if the variant interpretations of the Bible were made the tests of obedience to law. The validity of secular laws cannot be measured by their conformity to religious doctrines. It is only in a theocratic state that ecclesiastical doctrines measure legal right or wrong.

An act compelling profession of allegiance to a religion, no matter how subtly or tenuously promoted, is bad. But an act promoting good citizenship and national allegiance is within the domain of governmental authority and is therefore to be judged by the same considerations of power and of constitutionality as those involved in the many claims of immunity from civil obedience because of religious scruples.

That claims are pressed on behalf of sincere religious convictions does not of itself establish their constitutional validity. Nor does waving the banner of religious freedom relieve us from examining into the power we are asked to deny the states. Otherwise the doctrine of separation of church and state, so cardinal in the history of this nation and for the liberty of our people, would mean not the disestablishment of a state church but the establishment of all churches and of all religious groups.

The subjection of dissidents to the general requirement of saluting the flag, as a measure conducive to the training of children in good citizenship, is very far from being the first instance of exacting obedience to general laws that have offended deep religious scruples. Compulsory vaccination, food inspection regulations, the obligation to bear arms, testimonial duties, compulsory medical treatment — these are but illustrations of conduct that has often been compelled in the enforcement of legislation of general applicability even though the religious consciences of particular individuals rebelled at the exaction.

Law is concerned with external behavior and not with the inner life of man. It rests in large measure upon compulsion. Socrates lives in history partly because he gave his life for the conviction that duty of obedience to secular law does not presuppose consent to its enactment or belief in its virtue. The consent upon which free government rests is the consent that comes from sharing in the process of making and unmaking laws. The state is not shut out from a domain because the individual conscience may deny the state's claim. The individual conscience may profess what faith it chooses. It may affirm and promote that faith — in the language of the Constitution, it may "exercise" it freely — but it cannot thereby restrict community action through political organs in matters of community concern, so long as the action is not asserted in a discriminatory way either openly or by stealth. One may have the right to practice one's religion and at the same time owe the duty of formal obedience to laws that run counter to one's beliefs. Compelling belief implies denial of opportunity to combat it and to assert dissident views. Such compulsion is one thing. Quite another matter is submission to conformity of action while denying its wisdom or virtue and with ample opportunity for seeking its change or abrogation.

When dealing with religious scruples we are dealing with an almost numberless variety of doctrines and beliefs entertained with equal sincerity by the particular groups for which they satisfy man's needs in his relation to the mysteries of the universe. There are in the United States more than 250 distinctive established religious denominations. In the State of Pennsylvania there are 120 of these, and in West Virginia as many as 65. But if religious scruples afford immunity from civic obedience to laws, they may be invoked by the religious beliefs of any individual even though he holds no membership in any sect or organized denomination. Certainly this Court cannot be called upon to determine what claims of conscience should be recognized and what should be rejected as satisfying the "religion" which the Constitution protects. That would indeed resurrect the very discriminatory treatment of religion which the Constitution sought forever to forbid.

Of course patriotism cannot be enforced by the flag salute. But neither can the liberal spirit be enforced by judicial invalidation of illiberal legislation. Our constant preoccupation with the constitutionality of legislation rather than with its wisdom tends to preoccupation of the American mind with a false value. The tendency of focusing attention on constitutionality is to make constitutionality synonymous with wisdom, to regard a law as all right if it is constitutional. Such an attitude is a great enemy of liberalism. Particularly in legislation affecting freedom of thought and freedom of speech much which should offend a free-spirited society is constitutional. Reliance for the most precious interests of civilization, therefore, must be found outside of their vindication in courts of law. Only a persistent positive translation of the faith of a free society into the convictions and habits and actions of a community is the ultimate reliance against unabated temptations to fetter the human spirit.

Notes and Questions on the Free Speech Clause and Religious Expression

Despite the religious nature of the case, *Barnette* is actually a free speech decision, not a free exercise decision. *Cantwell* has obvious free speech overtones as well. Do these cases suggest that the Free Exercise Clause is often unnecessary to the protection of religious activites? Consider that the Court has expressly extended the protection of the Free Speech Clause to religious speech: "it is immaterial whether the beliefs sought to be advanced . . . pertain to political, economic, religious, or cultural matters." *NAACP v. Alabama ex rel. Patterson*, 357 U.S. 449, 460 (1958). *See also Thomas v. Collins*, 323 U.S. 516, 545 (1945) (Jackson, J., concurring) ("The very purpose of the First Amendment is to foreclose public authority from assuming a guardianship of the public mind through regulating the press, speech, and religion."). Outside the context of mandatory accommodations (*see Sherbert v. Verner, infra* Chapter 12), what does the Free Exercise Clause add to existing protections offered by a combination of First Amendment right of free association, *see Boy Scouts of Am. v. Dale*, 530 U.S. 640 (2000), vigorous advocacy, *see Brandenburg v. Ohio*, 395 U.S. 444 (1969), symbolic speech, *see Texas v. Johnson*, 491 U.S. 397 (1989), and expressive anonymity, *see McIntyre v. Ohio Elections Comm'n*, 514 U.S. 334, 345-346 (1995)? Under these cases, religious practitioners have the First Amendment expressive right to meet and proselytize (even anonymously), spread their religious message either orally or in writing, and make and worship images central to their faith. What more does the Free Exercise Clause add?

C. SYMBOLIC RELIGIOUS EXPRESSION AND THE MILITARY

GOLDMAN v. WEINBERGER
475 U.S. 503 (1986)

JUSTICE REHNQUIST delivered the opinion of the Court.

Petitioner S. Simcha Goldman contends that the Free Exercise Clause of the First Amendment to the United States Constitution permits him to wear a yarmulke while in uniform, notwithstanding an Air Force regulation mandating uniform dress for Air Force personnel. The District Court for the District of Columbia permanently enjoined the Air Force from enforcing its regulation against petitioner and from penalizing him for wearing his yarmulke. The Court of Appeals for the District of Columbia Circuit reversed on the ground that the Air Force's strong interest in discipline justified the strict enforcement of its uniform dress requirements. We granted certiorari because of the importance of the question and now affirm.

Petitioner Goldman is an Orthodox Jew and ordained rabbi. In 1973, he was accepted into the Armed Forces Health Professions Scholarship Program and placed on inactive reserve status in the Air Force while he studied clinical psychology at Loyola University of Chicago. During his three years in the scholarship program, he received a monthly stipend and an allowance for tuition, books, and fees. After completing his Ph.D. in psychology, petitioner entered active service in the United States Air Force as a commissioned officer, in accordance with a requirement that participants in the scholarship program serve one year of active duty for each year of subsidized education. Petitioner was stationed at March Air Force Base in Riverside, California, and served as a clinical psychologist at the mental health clinic on the base.

Until 1981, petitioner was not prevented from wearing his yarmulke on the base. He avoided controversy by remaining close to his duty station in the health clinic and by wearing his service cap over the yarmulke when out of doors. But in April 1981, after he testified as a defense witness at a court-martial wearing his yarmulke but not his service cap, opposing counsel lodged a complaint with Colonel Joseph Gregory, the Hospital Commander, arguing that petitioner's practice of wearing his yarmulke was a violation of Air Force Regulation (AFR) 35-10. This regulation states in pertinent part that "[h]eadgear will not be worn . . . [w]hile indoors except by armed security police in the performance of their duties."

Colonel Gregory informed petitioner that wearing a yarmulke while on duty does indeed violate AFR 35-10, and ordered him not to violate this regulation outside the hospital. Although virtually all of petitioner's time on the base was spent in the hospital, he refused. Later, after petitioner's attorney protested to the Air Force General Counsel, Colonel Gregory revised his order to prohibit petitioner from wearing the yarmulke even in the hospital. Petitioner's request to report for duty in civilian clothing pending legal resolution of the issue was denied. The next day he received a formal letter of reprimand, and was warned that failure to obey AFR 35-10 could subject him to a court-martial. Colonel Gregory also withdrew a recommendation that petitioner's application to extend the term of his active service be approved, and substituted a negative recommendation.

Our review of military regulations challenged on First Amendment grounds is far more deferential than constitutional review of similar laws or regulations designed for civilian society. The military need not encourage debate or tolerate protest to the extent that such tolerance is required of the civilian state by the First Amendment; to accomplish its mission the military must foster instinctive obedience, unity, commitment, and esprit de corps. The essence of military service "is the subordination of the desires and interests of the individual to the needs of the service." *Orloff v. Willoughby, supra*, 345 U.S., at 92.

These aspects of military life do not, of course, render entirely nugatory in the military context the guarantees of the First Amendment. But "within the military community there is simply not the same [individual] autonomy as there is in the larger civilian community." *Parker v. Levy, supra*, 417 U.S., at 751. In the context of the present case, when evaluating whether military needs justify a particular restriction on religiously motivated conduct, courts must give great deference to the professional judgment of military authorities concerning the relative importance of a particular military interest. Not only are courts "'ill-equipped to determine the impact upon discipline that any particular intrusion upon military authority might have,'" *Chappell v. Wallace*, 462 U.S., at 305, quoting Warren, *The Bill of Rights and the Military*, 37 N.Y.U. L. Rev. 181, 187 (1962), but the military authorities have been charged by the Executive and Legislative Branches with carrying out our Nation's military policy. "[J]udicial deference . . . is at its apogee when legislative action under the congressional authority to raise and support armies and make rules and regulations for their governance is challenged." *Rostker v. Goldberg*, 453 U.S. 57, 70 (1981).

The considered professional judgment of the Air Force is that the traditional outfitting of personnel in standardized uniforms encourages the subordination of personal preferences and identities in favor of the overall group mission. Uniforms encourage a sense of hierarchical unity by tending to eliminate outward individual distinctions except for those of rank. The Air Force considers them as vital during peacetime as during war because its personnel must be ready to provide an effective defense on a moment's notice; the necessary habits of discipline and unity must be developed in advance of trouble. We have acknowledged that "[t]he inescapable demands of military discipline and obedience to orders cannot be taught on battlefields; the habit of immediate compliance with military procedures and orders must be virtually reflex with no time for debate or reflection." *Chappell v. Wallace*, 462 U.S., at 300.

To this end, the Air Force promulgated AFR 35-10, a 190-page document, which states that "Air Force members will wear the Air Force uniform while performing their military duties, except when authorized to wear civilian clothes on duty." The rest of the document describes in minute detail all of the various items of apparel that must be worn as part of the Air Force uniform. It authorizes a few individualized options with respect to certain pieces of jewelry and hairstyle, but even these are subject to severe limitations. In general, authorized headgear may be worn only out of doors. Indoors, "[h]eadgear [may] not be worn . . . except by armed security police in the performance of their duties." A narrow exception to this rule exists for headgear worn during indoor religious ceremonies. In addition, military commanders may in their discretion permit visible religious headgear and other such apparel in designated living quarters and nonvisible items generally.

Petitioner Goldman contends that the Free Exercise Clause of the First Amendment requires the Air Force to make an exception to its uniform dress requirements for religious apparel unless the accouterments create a "clear danger" of undermining discipline and esprit de corps. He asserts that in general, visible but "unobtrusive" apparel will not create such a danger and must therefore be accommodated. He argues that the Air Force failed to prove that a specific exception for his practice of wearing an unobtrusive yarmulke would threaten discipline. He contends that the Air Force's assertion to the contrary is mere *ipse dixit,* with no support from actual experience or a scientific study in the record, and is contradicted by expert testimony that religious exceptions to AFR 35-10 are in fact desirable and will increase morale by making the Air Force a more humane place.

But whether or not expert witnesses may feel that religious exceptions to AFR 35-10 are desirable is quite beside the point. The desirability of dress regulations in the military is decided by the appropriate military officials, and they are under no constitutional mandate to abandon their considered professional judgment. Quite obviously, to the extent the regulations do not permit the wearing of religious apparel such as a yarmulke, a practice described by petitioner as silent devotion akin to prayer, military life may be more objectionable for petitioner and probably others. But the First Amendment does not require the military to accommodate such practices in the face of its view that they would detract from the uniformity sought by the dress regulations. The Air Force has drawn the line essentially between religious apparel that is visible and that which is not, and we hold that those portions of the regulations challenged here reasonably and evenhandedly regulate dress in the interest of the military's perceived need for uniformity. The First Amendment therefore does not prohibit them from being applied to petitioner even though their effect is to restrict the wearing of the headgear required by his religious beliefs.

JUSTICE STEVENS, with whom JUSTICE WHITE and JUSTICE POWELL join, concurring.

JUSTICE BRENNAN is unmoved by the Government's concern that "while a yarmulke might not seem obtrusive to a Jew, neither does a turban to a Sikh, a saffron robe to a Satchidananda Ashram-Integral Yogi, nor do dreadlocks to a Rastafarian." He correctly points out that "turbans, saffron robes, and dreadlocks are not before us in this case," and then suggests that other cases may be fairly decided by reference to a reasonable standard based on "functional utility, health and safety considerations, and the goal of a polished, professional appearance." As the Court has explained, this approach attaches no weight to the separate interest in uniformity itself. Because professionals in the military service attach great importance to that plausible interest, it is one that we must recognize as legitimate and rational even though personal experience or admiration for the performance of the "rag-tag band of soldiers" that won us our freedom in the Revolutionary War might persuade us that the Government has exaggerated the importance of that interest.

The interest in uniformity, however, has a dimension that is of still greater importance for me. It is the interest in uniform treatment for the members of all religious faiths. The very strength of Captain Goldman's claim creates the danger that a similar claim on behalf of a Sikh or a Rastafarian might readily be dismissed as "so extreme, so unusual, or so faddish an image that public confidence in his ability to perform his duties will be destroyed." If exceptions from dress code regulations are to be granted on the basis of a multifactored test such as that proposed by JUSTICE BRENNAN, inevitably the decisionmaker's evaluation of the character and the sincerity of the requester's faith — as well as the probable reaction of the majority to the favored treatment of a member of that faith — will play a critical part in the decision. For the difference between a turban or a dreadlock on the one hand, and a yarmulke on the other, is not merely a difference in "appearance" — it is also the difference between a Sikh or a Rastafarian, on the one hand, and an Orthodox Jew on the other. The Air Force has no business drawing distinctions between such persons when it is enforcing commands of universal application.

As the Court demonstrates, the rule that is challenged in this case is based on a neutral, completely objective standard — visibility. It was not motivated by hostility against, or any special respect for, any religious faith. An exception for yarmulkes would represent a fundamental departure from the true principle of uniformity that supports that rule. For that reason, I join the Court's opinion and its judgment.

JUSTICE BRENNAN, with whom JUSTICE MARSHALL joins, dissenting.

Simcha Goldman invokes this Court's protection of his First Amendment right to fulfill one of the traditional religious obligations of a male Orthodox Jew — to cover his head before an omnipresent God. The Court's response to Goldman's request is to abdicate its role as principal expositor of the Constitution and protector of individual liberties in favor of credulous deference to unsupported assertions of military necessity. I dissent.

I

In ruling that the paramount interests of the Air Force override Dr. Goldman's free exercise claim, the Court overlooks the sincere and serious nature of his constitutional claim. It suggests that the desirability of certain dress regulations, rather than a First Amendment right, is at issue. The Court declares that in selecting dress regulations, "military officials . . . are under no constitutional mandate to abandon their considered professional judgment." If Dr. Goldman wanted to wear a hat to keep his head warm or to cover a bald spot I would join the majority. Mere personal preferences in dress are not constitutionally protected. The First Amendment, however, restrains the Government's ability to prevent an Orthodox Jewish serviceman from, or punish him for, wearing a yarmulke.[1]

The Court also attempts, unsuccessfully, to minimize the burden that was placed on Dr. Goldman's rights. The fact that "the regulations do not permit the wearing of . . . a yarmulke," does not simply render military life for observant Orthodox Jews "objectionable." It sets up an almost absolute bar to the fulfillment of a religious duty. Dr. Goldman spent most of his time in uniform indoors, where the dress code forbade him even to cover his head with his service cap. Consequently, he was asked to violate the tenets of his faith virtually every minute of every workday.

II

A

Dr. Goldman has asserted a substantial First Amendment claim, which is entitled to meaningful review by this Court. The Court, however, evades its responsibility by eliminating, in all but name only, judicial review of military regulations that interfere with the fundamental constitutional rights of service personnel.

Our cases have acknowledged that in order to protect our treasured liberties, the military must be able to command service members to sacrifice a great many of the individual freedoms they enjoyed in the civilian community and to endure certain limitations on the freedoms they retain. Notwithstanding this acknowledgment, we have steadfastly maintained that "'our citizens in uniform may not be stripped of basic rights simply because they have doffed their civilian clothes.'" *Chappell v. Wallace,* 462 U.S. 296, 304 (1983) (quoting Warren, *The Bill of Rights and the Military,* 37 N.Y.U. L. Rev. 181, 188 (1962)). And, while we have hesitated, due to our lack of expertise concerning military affairs and our respect for the delegated authority of a coordinate branch, to strike down

---

[1] The yarmulke worn by Dr. Goldman was a dark-colored skullcap measuring approximately 5½ inches in diameter. Brief for Petitioner 3.

restrictions on individual liberties which could reasonably be justified as necessary to the military's vital function, we have never abdicated our obligation of judicial review.

Today the Court eschews its constitutionally mandated role. It adopts for review of military decisions affecting First Amendment rights a subrational-basis standard — absolute, uncritical "deference to the professional judgment of military authorities." If a branch of the military declares one of its rules sufficiently important to outweigh a service person's constitutional rights, it seems that the Court will accept that conclusion, no matter how absurd or unsupported it may be.

A deferential standard of review, however, need not, and should not, mean that the Court must credit arguments that defy common sense. When a military service burdens the free exercise rights of its members in the name of necessity, it must provide, as an initial matter and at a minimum, a *credible* explanation of how the contested practice is likely to interfere with the proffered military interest.[2] Unabashed *ipse dixit* cannot outweigh a constitutional right.

In the present case, the Air Force asserts that its interests in discipline and uniformity would be undermined by an exception to the dress code permitting observant male Orthodox Jews to wear yarmulkes. The Court simply restates these assertions without offering any explanation how the exception Dr. Goldman requests reasonably could interfere with the Air Force's interests. Had the Court given actual consideration to Goldman's claim, it would have been compelled to decide in his favor.

B

1

The Government maintains in its brief that discipline is jeopardized whenever exceptions to military regulations are granted. Service personnel must be trained to obey even the most arbitrary command reflexively. Non-Jewish personnel will perceive the wearing of a yarmulke by an Orthodox Jew as an unauthorized departure from the rules and will begin to question the principle of unswerving obedience. Thus shall our fighting forces slip down the treacherous slope toward unkempt appearance, anarchy, and, ultimately, defeat at the hands of our enemies.

The contention that the discipline of the Armed Forces will be subverted if Orthodox Jews are allowed to wear yarmulkes with their uniforms surpasses belief. It lacks support in the record of this case, and the Air Force offers no basis

---

2 I continue to believe that Government restraints on First Amendment rights, including limitations placed on military personnel, may be justified only upon showing a compelling state interest which is precisely furthered by a narrowly tailored regulation. *See, e.g., Brown v. Glines*, 444 U.S. 348, 367 (1980) (BRENNAN, J., dissenting). I think that any special needs of the military can be accommodated in the compelling-interest prong of the test. My point here is simply that even under a more deferential test Dr. Goldman should prevail.

for it as a general proposition. While the perilous slope permits the services arbitrarily to refuse exceptions requested to satisfy mere personal preferences, before the Air Force may burden free exercise rights it must advance, at the *very least*, a rational reason for doing so.

Furthermore, the Air Force cannot logically defend the content of its rule by insisting that discipline depends upon absolute adherence to whatever rule is established. If, as General Usher admitted at trial, App. 52, the dress code codified religious exemptions from the "no-headgear-indoors" regulation, then the wearing of a yarmulke would be sanctioned by the code and could not be considered an unauthorized deviation from the rules.

2

The Government also argues that the services have an important interest in uniform dress, because such dress establishes the preeminence of group identity, thus fostering esprit de corps and loyalty to the service that transcends individual bonds. In its brief, the Government characterizes the yarmulke as an assertion of individuality and as a badge of religious and ethnic identity, strongly suggesting that, as such, it could drive a wedge of divisiveness between members of the services.

First, the purported interests of the Air Force in complete uniformity of dress and in elimination of individuality or visible identification with any group other than itself are belied by the service's own regulations. The dress code expressly abjures the need for total uniformity:

> "(1) The American public and its elected representatives draw certain conclusions on military effectiveness based on what they see; that is, the image the Air Force presents. The image must instill public confidence and leave no doubt that the service member lives by a common standard and responds to military order and discipline.

> "(2) Appearance in uniform is an important part of this image. . . . Neither the Air Force nor the public expects absolute uniformity of appearance. Each member has the right, within limits, to express individuality through his or her appearance. However, the image of a disciplined service member who can be relied on to do his or her job excludes the extreme, the unusual, and the fad." AFR 35-10, ¶¶ 1-12a(1) and (2) (1978).

It cannot be seriously contended that a serviceman in a yarmulke presents so extreme, so unusual, or so faddish an image that public confidence in his ability to perform his duties will be destroyed. Under the Air Force's own standards, then, Dr. Goldman should have and could have been granted an exception to wear his yarmulke.

The dress code also allows men to wear up to three rings and one identification bracelet of "neat and conservative," but nonuniform, design. AFR 35-10, & 1-12b(1)(b) (1978). This jewelry is apparently permitted even if, as is often the case with rings, it associates the wearer with a denominational school or a religious or secular fraternal organization. If these emblems of religious, social, and ethnic identity are not deemed to be unacceptably divisive, the Air Force cannot rationally justify its bar against yarmulkes on that basis.

Moreover, the services allow, and rightly so, other manifestations of religious diversity. It is clear to all service personnel that some members attend Jewish services, some Christian, some Islamic, and some yet other religious services. Barracks mates see Mormons wearing temple garments, Orthodox Jews wearing tzitzit, and Catholics wearing crosses and scapulars. That they come from different faiths and ethnic backgrounds is not a secret that can or should be kept from them.

I find totally implausible the suggestion that the overarching group identity of the Air Force would be threatened if Orthodox Jews were allowed to wear yarmulkes with their uniforms. To the contrary, a yarmulke worn with a United States military uniform is an eloquent reminder that the shared and proud identity of United States serviceman embraces and unites religious and ethnic pluralism.

Finally, the Air Force argues that while Dr. Goldman describes his yarmulke as an "unobtrusive" addition to his uniform, obtrusiveness is a purely relative, standardless judgment. The Government notes that while a yarmulke might not seem obtrusive to a Jew, neither does a turban to a Sikh, a saffron robe to a Satchidananda Ashram-Integral Yogi, nor dreadlocks to a Rastafarian. If the Court were to require the Air Force to permit yarmulkes, the service must also allow all of these other forms of dress and grooming.

The Government dangles before the Court a classic parade of horribles, the specter of a brightly-colored, "rag-tag band of soldiers." Brief for Respondents 20. Although turbans, saffron robes, and dreadlocks are not before us in this case and must each be evaluated against the reasons a service branch offers for prohibiting personnel from wearing them while in uniform, a reviewing court could legitimately give deference to dress and grooming rules that have a *reasoned* basis in, for example, functional utility, health and safety considerations, and the goal of a polished, professional appearance.[4] AFR 35-10, ¶¶ 1-12a and 1-12a(1) (1978) (identifying neatness, cleanliness, safety, and military image as the four elements of the dress code's "high standard of dress and personal appearance"). It is the lack of any reasoned basis for prohibiting yarmulkes that is so striking here.

Furthermore, contrary to its intimations, the Air Force has available to it a familiar standard for determining whether a particular style of yarmulke is consistent with a polished, professional military appearance — the "neat and con-

---

[4] For example, the Air Force could no doubt justify regulations ordering troops to wear uniforms, prohibiting garments that could become entangled in machinery, and requiring hair to be worn short so that it may not be grabbed in combat and may be kept louse-free in field conditions.

servative" standard by which the service judges jewelry. AFR 35-10, ¶ 1-12b(1)(b) (1978). No rational reason exists why yarmulkes cannot be judged by the same criterion. Indeed, at argument Dr. Goldman declared himself willing to wear whatever style and color yarmulke the Air Force believes best comports with its uniform.

3

Department of Defense Directive 1300.17 (June 18, 1985) grants commanding officers the discretion to permit service personnel to wear religious items and apparel that are not visible with the uniform, such as crosses, temple garments, and scapulars. JUSTICE STEVENS favors this "visibility test" because he believes that it does not involve the Air Force in drawing distinctions among faiths. He rejects functional utility, health, and safety considerations, and similar grounds as criteria for religious exceptions to the dress code, because he fears that these standards will allow some servicepersons to satisfy their religious dress and grooming obligations, while preventing others from fulfilling theirs. But, the visible/not visible standard has that same effect. Furthermore, it restricts the free exercise rights of a larger number of servicepersons. The visibility test permits *only* individuals whose outer garments and grooming are indistinguishable from those of mainstream Christians to fulfill their religious duties. In my view, the Constitution requires the selection of criteria that permit the greatest possible number of persons to practice their faiths freely.

Implicit in JUSTICE STEVENS' concurrence, and in the Government's arguments, is what might be characterized as a fairness concern. It would be unfair to allow Orthodox Jews to wear yarmulkes, while prohibiting members of other minority faiths with visible dress and grooming requirements from wearing their saffron robes, dreadlocks, turbans, and so forth. While I appreciate and share this concern for the feelings and the free exercise rights of members of these other faiths, I am baffled by this formulation of the problem. What puzzles me is the implication that a neutral standard that could result in the disparate treatment of Orthodox Jews and, for example, Sikhs is *more* troublesome or unfair than the existing neutral standard that does result in the different treatment of Christians, on the one hand, and Orthodox Jews and Sikhs on the other. *Both* standards are constitutionally suspect; before either can be sustained, it must be shown to be a narrowly tailored means of promoting important military interests.

I am also perplexed by the related notion that for purposes of constitutional analysis religious faiths may be divided into two categories — those with visible dress and grooming requirements and those without. This dual category approach seems to incorporate an assumption that fairness, the First Amendment, and, perhaps, equal protection, require all faiths belonging to the same category to be treated alike, but permit a faith in one category to be treated differently from a faith belonging to the other category. The practical effect of this categorization is that, under the guise of neutrality and evenhandedness, majority religions are favored over distinctive minority faiths. This dual category analysis is fundamentally flawed and leads to a result that the First Amendment was intended to prevent. Under the Constitution there is only *one* relevant category — *all* faiths. Burdens placed on the free exercise rights of members of one faith must be justified independently of burdens placed on the rights of members of another religion. It is not enough to say that Jews cannot wear yarmulkes simply because Rastafarians might not be able to wear dreadlocks.

Unless the visible/not visible standard for evaluating requests for religious exceptions to the dress code promotes a significant military interest, it is constitutionally impermissible. JUSTICE STEVENS believes that this standard advances an interest in the "uniform treatment" of all religions. As I have shown, that uniformity is illusory, unless uniformity means uniformly accommodating majority religious practices and uniformly rejecting distinctive minority practices. But, more directly, Government agencies are not free to define their own interests in uniform treatment of different faiths. That function has been assigned to the First Amendment. The First Amendment requires that burdens on free exercise rights be justified by independent and important interests that promote the function of the agency. *See, e.g., United States v. Lee [infra* Chapter 13]; *Thomas v. Review Bd. of Indiana Employment Security Div. [infra* Chapter 12]; *Wisconsin v. Yoder [infra* Chapter 13]; *Sherbert v. Verner [infra* Chapter 12]. The only independent military interest furthered by the visibility standard is uniformity of dress. And, that interest, as I demonstrated in Part II-B(2), *supra,* does not support a prohibition against yarmulkes.

The Air Force has failed utterly to furnish a credible explanation why an exception to the dress code permitting Orthodox Jews to wear neat and conservative yarmulkes while in uniform is likely to interfere with its interest in discipline and uniformity. We cannot "distort the Constitution to approve all that the military may deem expedient." *Korematsu v. United States,* 323 U.S. 214, 244 (1944) (Jackson, J., dissenting). Under any meaningful level of judicial review, Simcha Goldman should prevail.

III

It is not the province of the federal courts to second-guess the professional judgments of the military services, but we are bound by the Constitution to assure ourselves that there exists a rational foundation for assertions of military necessity when they interfere with the free exercise of religion. "The concept of military necessity is seductively broad," *Glines,* 444 U.S., at 369 (BRENNAN, J., dissenting), and military decisionmakers themselves are as likely to succumb to its allure as are the courts and the general public. Definitions of necessity are influenced by decisionmakers' experiences and values. As a consequence, in pluralistic societies such as ours, institutions dominated by a majority are inevitably, if inadvertently, insensitive to the needs and values of minorities when these needs and values differ from those of the majority. The military, with its strong ethic of conformity and unquestioning obedience, may be particularly impervious to minority needs and values. A critical function of the Religion Clauses of the First Amendment is to protect the rights of members of minority religions against quiet erosion by majoritarian social institutions that dismiss minority beliefs and practices as unimportant, because unfamiliar. It is the constitutional role of this Court to ensure that this purpose of the First Amendment be realized.

The Court and the military services have presented patriotic Orthodox Jews with a painful dilemma — the choice between fulfilling a religious obligation and serving their country. Should the draft be reinstated, compulsion will replace choice. Although the pain the services inflict on Orthodox Jewish servicemen is clearly the result of insensitivity rather than design, it is unworthy of our military because it is unnecessary. The Court and the military have refused these servicemen their constitutional rights; we must hope that Congress will correct this wrong.

Chapter 12

FREE EXERCISE AS A SWORD: GOVERNMENT-MANDATED ACCOMMODATION IN EMPLOYMENT CONTEXTS

This chapter addresses constitutionally mandated accommodations of religion. In the cases below, courts have been asked to hold that the Free Exercise Clause requires government agencies to waive or modify requirements that conflict with the practices of religious individuals. In the early cases, such as *Sherbert v. Verner*, the accommodation imposed nothing more than a slight financial burden on the state fisc. In the later cases, however, the accommodation principle expanded to the point that the Supreme Court used the principle to justify a church's firing of a janitor who refused to join the church. *See Church of Latter Day Saints v. Amos, infra*. In light of these later cases, consider whether the accommodation of religion under the Free Exercise Clause raises Establishment Clause problems by permitting the state to provide certain benefits based on a person's (or group's) religious beliefs, while denying those same benefits to individuals or groups who have equally strong beliefs of a secular nature. Does this concern explain the Court's decision in *Thornton v. Caldor, infra*? Is *Thornton* consistent with *Sherbert*?

Keep in mind while reading this chapter and the next that the very different analysis in *Employment Division v. Smith*, Chapter 14, *infra*, casts into doubt much of what went before — although the *Smith* majority specifically left intact the holding of *Sherbert*.

A. ACCOMMODATION OF RELIGIOUS PRACTICES IN EMPLOYMENT

SHERBERT v. VERNER
374 U.S. 398 (1963)

MR. JUSTICE BRENNAN delivered the opinion of the Court.

Appellant, a member of the Seventh-day Adventist Church was discharged by her South Carolina employer because she would not work on Saturday, the Sabbath Day of her faith.[1] When she was unable to obtain other employment

---

[1] Appellant became a member of the Seventh-day Adventist Church in 1957, at a time when her employer, a textile-mill operator, permitted her to work a five-day week. It was not until 1959 that the work week was changed to six days, including Saturday, for all three shifts in the employer's

because from conscientious scruples she would not take Saturday work,[2] she filed a claim for unemployment compensation benefits under the South Carolina Unemployment Compensation Act. That law provides that, to be eligible for benefits, a claimant must be "able to work and . . . available for work"; and, further, that a claimant is ineligible for benefits "[I]f . . . he has failed, without good cause . . . to accept available suitable work when offered him by the employment office or the employer. . . ." The appellee Employment Security Commission, in administrative proceedings under the statute, found that appellant's restriction upon her availability for Saturday work brought her within the provision disqualifying for benefits insured workers who fail, without good cause, to accept "suitable work when offered . . . by the employment office or the employer. . . ." The Commission's finding was sustained by the Court of Common Pleas for Spartanburg County. That court's judgment was in turn affirmed by the South Carolina Supreme Court, which rejected appellant's contention that, as applied to her, the disqualifying provisions of the South Carolina statute abridged her right to the free exercise of her religion secured under the Free Exercise Clause of the First Amendment through the Fourteenth Amendment. The State Supreme Court held specifically that appellant's ineligibility infringed no constitutional liberties because such a construction of the statute "places no restriction upon the appellant's freedom of religion nor does it in any way prevent her in the exercise of her right and freedom to observe her religious beliefs in accordance with the dictates of her conscience."[4] We reverse.

---

mill. No question has been raised in this case concerning the sincerity of appellant's religious beliefs. Nor is there any doubt that the prohibition against Saturday labor is a basic tenet of the Seventh-day Adventist creed, based upon that religion's interpretation of the Holy Bible.

[2] After her discharge, appellant sought employment with three other mills in the Spartanburg area, but found no suitable five-day work available at any of the mills. In filing her claim with the Commission, she expressed a willingness to accept employment at other mills, or even in another industry, so long as Saturday work was not required. The record indicates that of the 150 or more Seventh-day Adventists in the Spartanburg area, only appellant and one other have been unable to find suitable non-Saturday employment.

[4] It has been suggested that appellant is not within the class entitled to benefits under the South Carolina statute because her unemployment did not result from discharge or layoff due to lack of work. It is true that unavailability for work for some personal reasons not having to do with matters of conscience or religion has been held to be a basis of disqualification for benefits. See, e.g., Judson Mills v. South Carolina Unemployment Compensation Comm'n, 204 S. C. 37, 28 S.E.2d 535; Stone Mfg. Co. v. South Carolina Employment Security Comm'n, 219 S.C. 239, 64 S.E.2d 644. But appellant claims that the Free Exercise Clause prevents the State from basing the denial of benefits upon the 'personal reason' she gives for not working on Saturday. Where the consequence of disqualification so directly affects First Amendment rights, surely we should not conclude that every "personal reason" is a basis for disqualification in the absence of explicit language to that effect in the statute or decisions of the South Carolina Supreme Court. Nothing we have found in the statute or in the cited decisions, cf. Lee v. Spartan Mills, 7 CCH Unemployment Ins. Rep. S.C. ¶ 8156 (C.P. 1944), and certainly nothing in the South Carolina Court's opinion in this case so construes the statute. Indeed, the contrary seems to have been that court's basic assumption, for if the eligibility provisions were thus limited, it would have been unnecessary for the court to have decided appellant's constitutional challenge to the application of the statute under the Free Exercise Clause.

I.

The door of the Free Exercise Clause stands tightly closed against any governmental regulation of religious *beliefs* as such, *Cantwell v. Connecticut*. Government may neither compel affirmation of a repugnant belief, *Torcaso v. Watkins*; nor penalize or discriminate against individuals or groups because they hold religious views abhorrent to the authorities, *Fowler v. Rhode Island*, 345 U.S. 67; nor employ the taxing power to inhibit the dissemination of particular religious views, *Murdock v. Pennsylvania,* 319 U.S. 105; *Follett v. McCormick*, 321 U.S. 573; *cf. Grosjean v. American Press Co.,* 297 U.S. 233. On the other hand, the Court has rejected challenges under the Free Exercise Clause to governmental regulation of certain overt acts prompted by religious beliefs or principles, for "even when the action is in accord with one's religious convictions, [it] is not totally free from legislative restrictions." *Braunfeld v. Brown,* 366 U.S. 599, 603. The conduct or actions so regulated have invariably posed some substantial threat to public safety, peace or order. *See, e.g., Reynolds v. United States; Jacobson v. Massachusetts,* 197 U.S. 11; *Prince v. Massachusetts,* 321 U.S. 158; *Cleveland v. United States,* 329 U.S. 14.

Plainly enough, appellant's conscientious objection to Saturday work constitutes no conduct prompted by religious principles of a kind within the reach of state legislation. If, therefore, the decision of the South Carolina Supreme Court is to withstand appellant's constitutional challenge, it must be either because her disqualification as a beneficiary represents no infringement by the State of her constitutional rights of free exercise, or because any incidental burden on the free exercise of appellant's religion may be justified by a "compelling state interest in the regulation of a subject within the State's constitutional power to regulate. . . ." *NAACP v. Button,* 371 U.S. 415, 438.

II.

We turn first to the question whether the disqualification for benefits imposes any burden on the free exercise of appellant's religion. We think it is clear that it does. In a sense the consequences of such a disqualification to religious principles and practices may be only an indirect result of welfare legislation within the State's general competence to enact; it is true that no criminal sanctions directly compel appellant to work a six-day week. But this is only the beginning, not the end, of our inquiry. For "[I]f the purpose or effect of a law is to impede the observance of one or all religions or is to discriminate invidiously between religions, that law is constitutionally invalid even though the burden may be characterized as being only indirect." *Braunfeld v. Brown, supra,* 366 U.S., at 607. Here not only is it apparent that appellant's declared ineligibility for benefits derives solely from the practice of her religion, but the pressure upon her to forego that practice is unmistakable. The ruling forces her to choose between following the precepts of her religion and forfeiting benefits, on the one hand, and abandoning one of the precepts of her religion in order to accept work, on the other hand. Governmental imposition of such a choice puts the same kind of burden upon the free exercise of religion as would a fine imposed against appellant for her Saturday worship.

Nor may the South Carolina court's construction of the statute be saved from constitutional infirmity on the ground that unemployment compensation benefits are not appellant's "right" but merely a "privilege." It is too late in the day to doubt that the liberties of religion and expression may be infringed by the denial of or placing of conditions upon a benefit or privilege. In *Speiser v. Randall,* 357 U.S. 513, we emphasized that conditions upon public benefits cannot be sustained if they so operate, whatever their purpose, as to inhibit or deter the exercise of First Amendment freedoms. We there struck down a condition which limited the availability of a tax exemption to those members of the exempted class who affirmed their loyalty to the state government granting the exemption. While the State was surely under no obligation to afford such an exemption, we held that the imposition of such a condition upon even a gratuitous benefit inevitably deterred or discouraged the exercise of First Amendment rights of expression and thereby threatened to "produce a result which the State could not command directly." 357 U.S., at 526. "To deny an exemption to claimants who engage in certain forms of speech is in effect to penalize them for such speech." *Id.,* 357 U.S., at 518. Likewise, to condition the availability of benefits upon this appellant's willingness to violate a cardinal principle of her religious faith effectively penalizes the free exercise of her constitutional liberties.

Significantly South Carolina expressly saves the Sunday worshiper from having to make the kind of choice which we here hold infringes the Sabbatarian's religious liberty. When in times of "national emergency" the textile plants are authorized by the State Commissioner of Labor to operate on Sunday, "no employee shall be required to work on Sunday . . . who is conscientiously opposed to Sunday work; and if any employee should refuse to work on Sunday on account of conscientious . . . objections he or she shall not jeopardize his or her seniority by such refusal or be discriminated against in any other manner." No question of the disqualification of a Sunday worshiper for benefits is likely to arise, since we cannot suppose that an employer will discharge him in violation of this statute. The unconstitutionality of the disqualification of the Sabbatarian is thus compounded by the religious discrimination which South Carolina's general statutory scheme necessarily effects.

III.

We must next consider whether some compelling state interest enforced in the eligibility provisions of the South Carolina statute justifies the substantial infringement of appellant's First Amendment right. It is basic that no showing merely of a rational relationship to some colorable state interest would suffice; in this highly sensitive constitutional area, "[o]nly the gravest abuses, endangering paramount interest, give occasion for permissible limitation," *Thomas v. Collins,* 323 U.S. 516, 530. No such abuse or danger has been advanced in the present case. The appellees suggest no more than a possibility that the filing of fraudulent claims by unscrupulous claimants feigning religious objections to

Saturday work might not only dilute the unemployment compensation fund but also hinder the scheduling by employers of necessary Saturday work. But that possibility is not apposite here because no such objection appears to have been made before the South Carolina Supreme Court, and we are unwilling to assess the importance of an asserted state interest without the views of the state court. Nor, if the contention had been made below, would the record appear to sustain it; there is no proof whatever to warrant such fears of malingering or deceit as those which the respondents now advance. Even if consideration of such evidence is not foreclosed by the prohibition against judicial inquiry into the truth or falsity of religious beliefs, *United States v. Ballard,* 322 U.S. 78 — a question as to which we intimate no view since it is not before us — it is highly doubtful whether such evidence would be sufficient to warrant a substantial infringement of religious liberties. For even if the possibility of spurious claims did threaten to dilute the fund and disrupt the scheduling of work, it would plainly be incumbent upon the appellees to demonstrate that no alternative forms of regulation would combat such abuses without infringing First Amendment rights.

In these respects, then, the state interest asserted in the present case is wholly dissimilar to the interests which were found to justify the less direct burden upon religious practices in *Braunfeld v. Brown, supra.* The Court recognized that the Sunday closing law which that decision sustained undoubtedly served "to make the practice of [the Orthodox Jewish merchants'] religious beliefs more expensive," 366 U.S., at 605. But the statute was nevertheless saved by a countervailing factor which finds no equivalent in the instant case — a strong state interest in providing one uniform day of rest for all workers. That secular objective could be achieved, the Court found, only by declaring Sunday to be that day of rest. Requiring exemptions for Sabbatarians, while theoretically possible, appeared to present an administrative problem of such magnitude, or to afford the exempted class so great a competitive advantage, that such a requirement would have rendered the entire statutory scheme unworkable. In the present case no such justifications underlie the determination of the state court that appellant's religion makes her ineligible to receive benefits.

IV.

In holding as we do, plainly we are not fostering the "establishment" of the Seventh-day Adventist religion in South Carolina, for the extension of unemployment benefits to Sabbatarians in common with Sunday worshipers reflects nothing more than the governmental obligation of neutrality in the face of religious differences, and does not represent that involvement of religious with secular institutions which it is the object of the Establishment Clause to forestall. See *School District of Abington Township v. Schempp* [*supra* Chapter 6]. Nor does the recognition of the appellant's right to unemployment benefits under the state statute serve to abridge any other person's religious liberties. Nor do we, by our decision today, declare the existence of a constitutional right to unemployment benefits on the part of all persons whose religious convictions are the cause of their unemployment. This is not a case in which an employee's religious convictions serve to make him a nonproductive member of society. Finally, nothing we say today constrains the States to adopt any particular form or scheme of unemployment compensation. Our holding today is only that South Carolina may not constitutionally apply the eligibility provisions so as to constrain a worker to abandon his religious convictions respecting the day of rest. This holding but reaffirms a principle that we announced a decade and a half ago, namely that no State may "exclude individual Catholics, Lutherans, Mohammedans, Baptists, Jews, Methodists, Non-believers, Presbyterians, or the members of any other faith, *because of their faith, or lack of it,* from receiving the benefits of public welfare legislation." *Everson v. Board of Education.*

In view of the result we have reached under the First and Fourteenth Amendments' guarantee of free exercise of religion, we have no occasion to consider appellant's claim that the denial of benefits also deprived her of the equal protection of the laws in violation of the Fourteenth Amendment.

Mr. Justice Stewart, concurring in the result.

Although fully agreeing with the result which the Court reaches in this case, I cannot join the Court's opinion. This case presents a double-barreled dilemma, which in all candor I think the Court's opinion has not succeeded in papering over. The dilemma ought to be resolved.

I.

Twenty-three years ago in *Cantwell v. Connecticut*, the Court said that both the Establishment Clause and the Free Exercise Clause of the First Amendment were made wholly applicable to the States by the Fourteenth Amendment. In the intervening years several cases involving claims of state abridgment of individual religious freedom have been decided here — most recently *Braunfeld v. Brown*, 366 U.S. 599, and *Torcaso v. Watkins*. During the same period "cases dealing with the specific problems arising under the 'Establishment' Clause which have reached this Court are few in number." The most recent are last Term's *Engel v. Vitale* and this Term's *Schempp* and *Murray* cases.

I am convinced that no liberty is more essential to the continued vitality of the free society which our Constitution guarantees than is the religious liberty protected by the Free Exercise Clause explicit in the First Amendment and imbedded in the Fourteenth. And I regret that on occasion, and specifically in *Braunfeld v. Brown, supra,* the Court has shown what has seemed to me a distressing insensitivity to the appropriate demands of this constitutional guarantee. By contrast I think that the Court's approach to the Establishment Clause has on occasion, and specifically in *Engel, Schempp* and *Murray*, been not only insensitive, but positively wooden, and that the Court has accorded to the Establishment Clause a meaning which neither the words, the history, nor the intention of the authors of that specific constitutional provision even remotely suggests.

But my views as to the correctness of the Court's decisions in these cases are beside the point here. The point is that the decisions are on the books. And the result is that there are many situations where legitimate claims under the Free Exercise Clause will run into head-on collision with the Court's insensitive and sterile construction of the Establishment Clause. The controversy now before us is clearly such a case.

Because the appellant refuses to accept available jobs which would require her to work on Saturdays, South Carolina has declined to pay unemployment compensation benefits to her. Her refusal to work on Saturdays is based on the tenets of her religious faith. The Court says that South Carolina cannot under these circumstances declare her to be not "available for work" within the meaning of its statute because to do so would violate her constitutional right to the free exercise of her religion.

Yet what this Court has said about the Establishment Clause must inevitably lead to a diametrically opposite result. If the appellant's refusal to work on Saturdays were based on indolence, or on a compulsive desire to watch the Saturday television programs, no one would say that South Carolina could not hold that she was not "available for work" within the meaning of its statute. That being so, the Establishment Clause as construed by this Court not only *permits* but affirmatively *requires* South Carolina equally to deny the appellant's claim for unemployment compensation when her refusal to work on Saturdays is based upon her religious creed. For, as said in *Everson v. Board of Education*, the Establishment Clause bespeaks "a government . . . stripped of all power . . . to support, or otherwise to assist any or all religions . . .," and no State "can pass laws which aid one religion. . . ." In Mr. Justice Rutledge's words, adopted by the Court today in *Schempp*, the Establishment Clause forbids "every form of public aid or support for religion." In the words of the Court in *Engel v. Vitale*, reaffirmed today in the *Schempp* case, the Establishment Clause forbids the "financial support of government" to be "placed behind a particular religious belief."

To require South Carolina to so administer its laws as to pay public money to the appellant under the circumstances of this case is thus clearly to require the State to violate the Establishment Clause as construed by this Court. This poses no problem for me, because I think the Court's mechanistic concept of the Establishment Clause is historically unsound and constitutionally wrong. I think the process of constitutional decision in the area of the relationships between government and religion demands considerably more than the invocation of broad-brushed rhetoric of the kind I have quoted. And I think that the guarantee of religious liberty embodied in the Free Exercise Clause affirmatively requires government to create an atmosphere of hospitality and accommodation to individual belief or disbelief. In short, I think our Constitution commands the positive protection by government of religious freedom — not only for a minority, however small — not only for the majority, however large — but for each of us.

South Carolina would deny unemployment benefits to a mother unavailable for work on Saturdays because she was unable to get a babysitter. Thus, we do not have before us a situation where a State provides unemployment compensation generally, and singles out for disqualification only those persons who are unavailable for work on religious grounds. This is not, in short, a scheme which operates so as to discriminate against religion as such. But the Court nevertheless holds that the State must prefer a religious over a secular ground for being unavailable for work — that state financial support of the appellant's religion is constitutionally required to carry out "the governmental obligation of neutrality in the face of religious differences. . . ."

Yet in cases decided under the Establishment Clause the Court has decreed otherwise. It has decreed that government must blind itself to the differing religious beliefs and traditions of the people. With all respect, I think it is the Court's duty to face up to the dilemma posed by the conflict between the Free Exercise Clause of the Constitution and the Establishment Clause as interpreted by the Court. It is a duty, I submit, which we owe to the people, the States, and the Nation, and a duty which we owe to ourselves. For so long as the resounding but fallacious fundamentalist rhetoric of some of our Establishment Clause opinions remains on our books, to be disregarded at will as in the present case, or to be undiscriminatingly invoked as in the *Schempp* case, so long will the possibility of consistent and perceptive decision in this most difficult and delicate area of constitutional law be impeded and impaired. And so long, I fear, will the guarantee of true religious freedom in our pluralistic society be uncertain and insecure.

Mr. Justice Harlan, whom Mr. Justice White joins, dissenting.

Today's decision is disturbing both in its rejection of existing precedent and in its implications for the future. The significance of the decision can best be understood after an examination of the state law applied in this case.

South Carolina's Unemployment Compensation Law was enacted in 1936 in response to the grave social and economic problems that arose during the depression of that period. As stated in the statute itself:

> "Economic insecurity due to unemployment is a serious menace to health, morals and welfare of the people of this State; *involuntary unemployment* is therefore a subject of general interest and concern . . .; the achievement of social security requires protection against this greatest hazard of our economic life; this can be provided by encouraging the employers *to provide more stable employment and by the systematic accumulation of funds during periods of employment to provide benefits for periods of unemployment,* thus maintaining purchasing power and limiting the serious social consequences of poor relief assistance." § 68-38. (Emphasis added.)

Thus the purpose of the legislature was to tide people over, and to avoid social and economic chaos, during periods when *work was unavailable*. But at the same time there was clearly no intent to provide relief for those who for purely personal reasons were or became *unavailable for work*. In accordance with this design, the legislature provided that "[a]n unemployed insured worker shall be eligible to receive benefits with respect to any week only if the Commission finds that . . . [h]e is able to work and is available for work. . . ." (Emphasis added.)

The South Carolina Supreme Court has uniformly applied this law in conformity with its clearly expressed purpose. It has consistently held that one is not "available for work" if his unemployment has resulted not from the inability of industry to provide a job but rather from personal circumstances, no matter how compelling. The reference to "involuntary unemployment" in the legislative statement of policy, whatever a sociologist, philosopher, or theologian might say, has been interpreted not to embrace such personal circumstances. *See, e.g., Judson Mills v. South Carolina Unemployment Compensation Comm'n,* 204 S.C. 37, 28 S.E.2d 535 (claimant was "unavailable for work" when she became unable to work the third shift, and limited her availability to the other two, because of the need to care for her four children).

In the present case all that the state court has done is to apply these accepted principles. Since virtually all of the mills in the Spartanburg area were operating on a six-day week, the appellant was "unavailable for work," and thus ineligible for benefits, when personal considerations prevented her from accepting employment on a full-time basis in the industry and locality in which she had worked. The fact that these personal considerations sprang from her religious convictions was wholly without relevance to the state court's application of the law. Thus in no proper sense can it be said that the State discriminated against the appellant on the basis of her religious beliefs or that she was denied benefits because she was a Seventh-day Adventist. She was denied benefits just as any other claimant would be denied benefits who was not "available for work" for personal reasons.

With this background, this Court's decision comes into clearer focus. What the Court is holding is that if the State chooses to condition unemployment compensation on the applicant's availability for work, it is constitutionally compelled to *carve out an exception* — and to provide benefits — for those whose unavailability is due to their religious convictions. Such a holding has particular significance in two respects.

First, despite the Court's protestations to the contrary, the decision necessarily overrules *Braunfeld v. Brown,* 366 U.S. 599, which held that it did not offend the "Free Exercise" Clause of the Constitution for a State to forbid a Sabbatarian to do business on Sunday. The secular purpose of the statute before us today is even clearer than that involved in *Braunfeld*. And just as in *Braunfeld* — where exceptions to the Sunday closing laws for Sabbatarians would have been inconsistent with the purpose to achieve a uniform day of rest and would have required case-by-case inquiry into religious beliefs — so here, an exception to the rules of eligibility based on religious convictions would necessitate judicial examination of those convictions and would be at odds with the limited purpose of the statute to smooth out the economy during periods of industrial instability. Finally, the indirect financial burden of the present law is far less than that involved in *Braunfeld*. Forcing a store owner to close his business on Sunday may well have the effect of depriving him of a satisfactory livelihood if his religious convictions require him to close on Saturday as well. Here we are dealing only with temporary benefits, amounting to a fraction of regular weekly wages and running for not more than 22 weeks. Clearly, any differences between this case and *Braunfeld* cut against the present appellant.

Second, the implications of the present decision are far more troublesome than its apparently narrow dimensions would indicate at first glance. The meaning of today's holding, as already noted, is that the State must furnish unemployment benefits to one who is unavailable for work if the unavailability stems from the exercise of religious convictions. The State, in other words, must *single out* for financial assistance those whose behavior is religiously motivated, even though it denies such assistance to others whose identical behavior (in this case, inability to work on Saturdays) is not religiously motivated.

It has been suggested that such singling out of religious conduct for special treatment may violate the constitutional limitations on state action. *See* Kurland, *Of Church and State and The Supreme Court*, 29 U. OF CHI. L. REV. 1; *cf. Cammarano v. United States*, 358 U.S. 498, 515 (concurring opinion). My own view, however, is that at least under the circumstances of this case it would be a permissible accommodation of religion for the State, if it chose to do so, to create an exception to its eligibility requirements for persons like the appellant. The constitutional obligation of "neutrality" is not so narrow a channel that the slightest deviation from an absolutely straight course leads to condemnation. There are too many instances in which no such course can be charted, too many areas in which the pervasive activities of the State justify some special provision for religion to prevent it from being submerged by an all-embracing secularism. The State violates its obligation of neutrality when, for example, it mandates a daily religious exercise in its public schools, with all the attendant pressures on the school children that such an exercise entails. *See Engel v. Vitale*; *School District of Abington Township v. Schempp*. But there is, I believe, enough flexibility in the Constitution to permit a legislative judgment accommodating an unemployment compensation law to the exercise of religious beliefs such as appellant's.

For very much the same reasons, however, I cannot subscribe to the conclusion that the State is constitutionally *compelled* to carve out an exception to its general rule of eligibility in the present case. Those situations in which the Constitution may require special treatment on account of religion are, in my view, few and far between, and this view is amply supported by the course of constitutional litigation in this area. *See, e.g., Braunfeld v. Brown*; *Cleveland v. United States*, 329 U.S. 14; *Prince v. Massachusetts*, 321 U.S. 158; *Jacobson v. Massa-*

chusetts, 197 U.S. 11; *Reynolds v. United States* [*supra* Chapter 11]. Such compulsion in the present case is particularly inappropriate in light of the indirect, remote, and insubstantial effect of the decision below on the exercise of appellant's religion and in light of the direct financial assistance to religion that today's decision requires.

THOMAS v. REVIEW BOARD
OF INDIANA EMPLOYMENT
450 U.S. 707 (1981)

CHIEF JUSTICE BURGER delivered the opinion of the Court.

We granted certiorari to consider whether the State's denial of unemployment compensation benefits to the petitioner, a Jehovah's Witness who terminated his job because his religious beliefs forbade participation in the production of armaments, constituted a violation of his First Amendment right to free exercise of religion.

I

Thomas terminated his employment in the Blaw-Knox Foundry & Machinery Co. when he was transferred from the roll foundry to a department that produced turrets for military tanks. He claimed his religious beliefs prevented him from participating in the production of war materials. The respondent Review Board denied him unemployment compensation benefits by applying disqualifying provisions of the Indiana Employment Security Act.

Thomas, a Jehovah's Witness, was hired initially to work in the roll foundry at Blaw-Knox. The function of that department was to fabricate sheet steel for a variety of industrial uses. On his application form, he listed his membership in the Jehovah's Witnesses, and noted that his hobbies were Bible study and Bible reading. However, he placed no conditions on his employment; and he did not describe his religious tenets in any detail on the form.

Approximately a year later, the roll foundry closed, and Blaw-Knox transferred Thomas to a department that fabricated turrets for military tanks. On his first day at this new job, Thomas realized that the work he was doing was weapons related. He checked the bulletin board where in-plant openings were listed, and discovered that all of the remaining departments at Blaw-Knox were engaged directly in the production of weapons. Since no transfer to another department would resolve his problem, he asked for a layoff. When that request was denied, he quit, asserting that he could not work on weapons without violating the principles of his religion. The record does not show that he was offered any nonweapons work by his employer, or that any such work was available.

Upon leaving Blaw-Knox, Thomas applied for unemployment compensation benefits under the Indiana Employment Security Act. At an administrative hearing where he was not represented by counsel, he testified that he believed that contributing to the production of arms violated his religion. He said that when he realized that his work on the tank turret line involved producing weapons for war, he consulted another Blaw-Knox employee — a friend and fellow Jehovah's Witness. The friend advised him that working on weapons parts at Blaw-Knox was not "unscriptural." Thomas was not able to "rest with" this view, however. He concluded that his friend's view was based upon a less strict reading of Witnesses' principles than his own.

When asked at the hearing to explain what kind of work his religious convictions would permit, Thomas said that he would have no difficulty doing the type of work that he had done at the roll foundry. He testified that he could, in good conscience, engage indirectly in the production of materials that might be used ultimately to fabricate arms — for example, as an employee of a raw material supplier or of a roll foundry.

The hearing referee found that Thomas' religious beliefs specifically precluded him from producing or directly aiding in the manufacture of items used in warfare. He also found that Thomas had terminated his employment because of these religious convictions. The referee reported:

> "Claimant continually searched for a transfer to another department which would not be so armament related; however, this did not materialize, and prior to the date of his leaving, claimant requested a layoff, which was denied; and on November 6, 1975, *claimant did quit due to his religious convictions.*"

The referee concluded nonetheless that Thomas' termination was not based upon a "good cause [arising] in connection with [his] work," as required by the Indiana unemployment compensation statute. Accordingly, he was held not entitled to benefits. The Review Board adopted the referee's findings and conclusions, and affirmed the denial of benefits.

The Indiana Court of Appeals reversed the decision of the Review Board. The Supreme Court of Indiana, dividing 3-2, vacated the decision of the Court of Appeals, and denied Thomas benefits. With reference to the Indiana unemployment compensation statute, the court said:

> "It is not intended to facilitate changing employment or to provide relief for those who quit work voluntarily for personal reasons. Voluntary unemployment is not compensable under the purpose of the Act, which is to provide benefits for persons unemployed through no fault of their own.
>
> "Good cause which justifies voluntary termination must be job- related and objective in character." *Id.,* at — , 391 N.E.2d, at 1129 (footnotes omitted).

The court held that Thomas had quit voluntarily for personal reasons, and therefore did not qualify for benefits.

In discussing the petitioner's free exercise claim, the court stated: "A personal philosophical choice rather than a religious choice, does not rise to the level of a first amendment claim." The court found the basis and the precise nature of Thomas' belief unclear — but it concluded that the belief was more "personal philosophical choice" than religious belief. Nonetheless, it held that, even assuming that Thomas quit for religious reasons, he would not be entitled to benefits: under Indiana law, a termination motivated by religion is not for "good cause" objectively related to the work.

The Indiana court concluded that denying Thomas benefits would create only an indirect burden on his free exercise right and that the burden was justified by the legitimate state interest in preserving the integrity of the insurance fund and maintaining a stable work force by encouraging workers not to leave their jobs for personal reasons.

Finally, the court held that awarding unemployment compensation benefits to a person who terminates employment voluntarily for religious reasons, while denying such benefits to persons who terminate for other personal but nonreligious reasons, would violate the Establishment Clause of the First Amendment.

II

Only beliefs rooted in religion are protected by the Free Exercise Clause, which, by its terms, gives special protection to the exercise of religion. *Sherbert v. Verner, supra*; *Wisconsin v. Yoder*. The determination of what is a "religious" belief or practice is more often than not a difficult and delicate task, as the division in the Indiana Supreme Court attests. However, the resolution of that question is not to turn upon a judicial perception of the particular belief or practice in question; religious beliefs need not be acceptable, logical, consistent, or comprehensible to others in order to merit First Amendment protection.

In support of his claim for benefits, Thomas testified:

"Q. And then when it comes to actually producing the tank itself, hammering it out; that you will not do. . . .

"A. That's right, that's right when . . . I'm daily faced with the knowledge that these are tanks. . . .

. . . .

"A. I really could not, you know, conscientiously continue to work with armaments. It would be against all of the . . . religious principles that . . . I have come to learn. . . ." 271 Ind., at ___, 391 N. E. 2d, at 1132.

Based upon this and other testimony, the referee held that Thomas "quit due to his religious convictions." The Review Board adopted that finding, and the finding is not challenged in this Court.

The Indiana Supreme Court apparently took a different view of the record. It concluded that "although the claimant's reasons for quitting were described as religious, it was unclear what his belief was, and what the religious basis of his belief was." In that court's view, Thomas had made a merely "personal philosophical choice rather than a religious choice."

In reaching its conclusion, the Indiana court seems to have placed considerable reliance on the facts that Thomas was "struggling" with his beliefs and that he was not able to "articulate" his belief precisely. It noted, for example, that Thomas admitted before the referee that he would not object to

> "working for United States Steel or Inland Steel . . . produc[ing] the raw product necessary for the production of any kind of tank . . . [because I] would not be a direct party to whoever they shipped it to [and] would not be . . . chargeable in . . . conscience. . . ."

The court found this position inconsistent with Thomas' stated opposition to participation in the production of armaments. But Thomas' statements reveal no more than that he found work in the roll foundry sufficiently insulated from producing weapons of war. We see, therefore, that Thomas drew a line, and it is not for us to say that the line he drew was an unreasonable one. Courts should not undertake to dissect religious beliefs because the believer admits that he is "struggling" with his position or because his beliefs are not articulated with the clarity and precision that a more sophisticated person might employ.

The Indiana court also appears to have given significant weight to the fact that another Jehovah's Witness had no scruples about working on tank turrets; for that other Witness, at least, such work was "scripturally" acceptable. Intrafaith differences of that kind are not uncommon among followers of a particular creed, and the judicial process is singularly ill equipped to resolve such differences in relation to the Religion Clauses. One can, of course, imagine an asserted claim so bizarre, so clearly nonreligious in motivation, as not to be entitled to protection under the Free Exercise Clause; but that is not the case here, and the guarantee of free exercise is not limited to beliefs which are shared by all of the members of a religious sect. Particularly in this sensitive area, it is not within the judicial function and judicial competence to inquire whether the petitioner or his fellow worker more correctly perceived the commands of their common faith. Courts are not arbiters of scriptural interpretation.

The narrow function of a reviewing court in this context is to determine whether there was an appropriate finding that petitioner terminated his work because of an honest conviction that such work was forbidden by his religion. Not surprisingly, the record before the referee and the Review Board was not made with an eye to the microscopic examination often exercised in appellate judicial review. However, judicial review is confined to the facts as found and conclusions drawn. On this record, it is clear that Thomas terminated his employment for religious reasons.

III

A

More that 30 years ago, the Court held that a person may not be compelled to choose between the exercise of a First Amendment right and participation in an otherwise available public program. A state may not

> "exclude individual Catholics, Lutherans, Mohammedans, Baptists, Jews, Methodists, Non-believers, Presbyterians, or the members of any other faith, because of their faith, or lack of it, from receiving the benefits of public welfare legislation." *Everson v. Board of Education.*

Later, in *Sherbert*, the Court examined South Carolina's attempt to deny unemployment compensation benefits to a Sabbatarian who declined to work on Saturday. In sustaining her right to receive benefits, the Court held:

> "The ruling [disqualifying Mrs. Sherbert from benefits because of her refusal to work on Saturday in violation of her faith] forces her to choose between following the precepts of her religion and forfeiting benefits, on the one hand, and abandoning one of the precepts of her religion in order to accept work, on the other hand. Governmental imposition of such a choice puts the same kind of burden upon the free exercise of religion as would a fine imposed against [her] for her Saturday worship." 374 U.S., at 404.

The respondent Review Board argues, and the Indiana Supreme Court held, that the burden upon religion here is only the indirect consequence of public welfare legislation that the State clearly has authority to enact. "Neutral objective standards must be met to qualify for compensation." Indiana requires applicants for unemployment compensation to show that they left work for "good cause in connection with the work."

A similar argument was made and rejected in *Sherbert*, however. It is true that, as in *Sherbert*, the Indiana law does not compel a violation of conscience. But, "this is only the beginning, not the end, of our inquiry." In a variety of ways we have said that "[a] regulation neutral on its face may, in its application, nonetheless offend the constitutional requirement for governmental neutrality if it unduly burdens the free exercise of religion." *Wisconsin v. Yoder*. Cf. *Walz v. Tax Comm'n.*

Here, as in *Sherbert*, the employee was put to a choice between fidelity to religious belief or cessation of work; the coercive impact on Thomas is indistinguishable from *Sherbert*, where the Court held:

> "[N]ot only is it apparent that appellant's declared ineligibility for benefits derives solely from the practice of her religion, but the pressure upon her to forego, that practice is unmistakable."

Where the state conditions receipt of an important benefit upon conduct proscribed by a religious faith, or where it denies such a benefit because of conduct mandated by religious belief, thereby putting substantial pressure on an adherent to modify his behavior and to violate his beliefs, a burden upon religion exists. While the compulsion may be indirect, the infringement upon free exercise is nonetheless substantial.

The respondents also contend that Sherbert is inapposite because, in that case, the employee was dismissed by the employer's action. But we see that Mrs. Sherbert was dismissed because she refused to work on Saturdays after the plant went to a 6-day workweek. Had Thomas simply presented himself at the Blaw-Knox plant turret line but refused to perform any assigned work, it must be assumed that he, like Sherbert, would have been terminated by the employer's action, if no other work was available. In both cases, the termination flowed from the fact that the employment, once acceptable, became religiously objectionable because of changed conditions.

B

The mere fact that the petitioner's religious practice is burdened by a governmental program does not mean that an exemption accommodating his practice must be granted. The state may justify an inroad on religious liberty by showing that it is the least restrictive means of achieving some compelling state interest. However, it is still true that "[t]he essence of all that has been said and written on the subject is that only those interests of the highest order . . . can overbalance legitimate claims to the free exercise of religion." *Wisconsin v. Yoder.*

The purposes urged to sustain the disqualifying provision of the Indiana unemployment compensation scheme are twofold: (1) to avoid the widespread unemployment and the consequent burden on the fund resulting if people were permitted to leave jobs for "personal" reasons; and (2) to avoid a detailed probing by employers into job applicants' religious beliefs. These are by no means unimportant considerations. When the focus of the inquiry is properly narrowed, however, we must conclude that the interests advanced by the State do not justify the burden placed on free exercise of religion.

There is no evidence in the record to indicate that the number of people who find themselves in the predicament of choosing between benefits and religious beliefs is large enough to create "widespread unemployment," or even to seriously affect unemployment — and no such claim was advanced by the Review Board. Similarly, although detailed inquiry by employers into applicants' religious beliefs is undesirable, there is no evidence in the record to indicate that such inquiries will occur in Indiana, or that they have occurred in any of the states that extend benefits to people in the petitioner's position. Nor is there any reason to believe that the number of people terminating employment for religious reasons will be so great as to motivate employers to make such inquiries.

Neither of the interests advanced is sufficiently compelling to justify the burden upon Thomas' religious liberty. Accordingly, Thomas is entitled to receive benefits unless, as the respondents contend and the Indiana court held, such payment would violate the Establishment Clause.

IV

The respondents contend that to compel benefit payments to Thomas involves the State in fostering a religious faith. There is, in a sense, a "benefit" to Thomas deriving from his religious beliefs, but this manifests no more than the tension between the two Religion Clauses which the Court resolved in *Sherbert*:

> "In holding as we do, plainly we are not fostering the 'establishment' of the Seventh-day Adventist religion in South Carolina, for the extension of unemployment benefits to Sabbatarians in common with Sunday worshipers reflects nothing more than the governmental obligation of neutrality in the face of religious differences, and does not represent that involvement of religious with secular institutions which it is the object of the Establishment Clause to forestall." *Sherbert v. Verner.*

Unless we are prepared to overrule *Sherbert, supra,* Thomas cannot be denied the benefits due him on the basis of the findings of the referee, the Review Board, and the Indiana Court of Appeals that he terminated his employment because of his religious convictions.

JUSTICE REHNQUIST, dissenting.

The Court today holds that the State of Indiana is constitutionally required to provide direct financial assistance to a person solely on the basis of his religious beliefs. Because I believe that the decision today adds mud to the already muddied waters of First Amendment jurisprudence, I dissent.

I

The Court correctly acknowledges that there is a "tension" between the Free Exercise and Establishment Clauses of the First Amendment of the United States Constitution. Although the relationship of the two Clauses has been the subject of much commentary, the "tension" is a fairly recent vintage, unknown at the time of the framing and adoption of the First Amendment. The causes of the tension, it seems to me, are threefold. First, the growth of social welfare legislation during the latter part of the 20th century has greatly magnified the potential for conflict between the two Clauses, since such legislation touches the individual at so many points in his life. Second, the decision by this Court that the First Amendment was "incorporated" into the Fourteenth Amendment and thereby made applicable against the States similarly multiplied the number of instances in which the "tension" might arise. The third, and perhaps most important, cause of the tension is our overly expansive interpretation of *both* Clauses. By broadly construing both Clauses, the Court has constantly narrowed the channel between the Scylla and Charybdis through which any state or federal action must pass in order to survive constitutional scrutiny.

None of these developments could have been foreseen by those who framed and adopted the First Amendment. The First Amendment was adopted well before the growth of much social welfare legislation and at a time when the Federal Government was in a real sense considered a government of limited delegated powers. Indeed, the principal argument against adopting the Constitution *without* a "Bill of Rights" was not that such an enactment would be *undesirable* but that it was *unnecessary* because of the limited nature of the Federal Government. So long as the Government enacts little social welfare legislation, as was the case in 1791, there are few occasions in which the two Clauses may conflict. Moreover, as originally enacted, the First Amendment applied only to the Federal Government, not the government of the States. The Framers could hardly anticipate the "selective incorporation" doctrine adopted by the Court, a decision which greatly expanded the number of statutes which would be subject to challenge under the First Amendment. Because those who drafted and adopted the First Amendment could not have foreseen either the growth of social welfare legislation or the incorporation of the First Amendment into the Fourteenth Amendment, we simply do not know how they would view the scope of the two Clauses.

II

The decision today illustrates how far astray the Court has gone in interpreting the Free Exercise and Establishment Clauses of the First Amendment. Although the Court holds that a State is constitutionally required to provide direct financial assistance to persons solely on the basis of their religious beliefs and recognizes the "tension" between the two Clauses, it does little to help resolve that tension or to offer meaningful guidance to other courts which must decide cases like this on a day-by-day basis. Instead, it simply asserts that there is no Establishment Clause violation here and leaves the tension between the two Religion Clauses to be resolved on a case-by-case basis. As suggested above, however, I believe that the "tension" is largely of this Court's own making, and would diminish almost to the vanishing point if the Clauses were properly interpreted.

Just as it did in *Sherbert v. Verner,* the Court today reads the Free Exercise Clause more broadly than is warranted. As to the proper interpretation of the Free Exercise Clause, I would accept the decision of *Braunfeld v. Brown,* 366 U.S. 599 (1961), and the dissent in *Sherbert.* In *Braunfeld,* we held that Sunday closing laws do not violate the First Amendment rights of Sabbatarians. Chief Justice Warren explained that the statute did not make unlawful any religious practices of appellants; it simply made the practice of their religious beliefs more expensive. We concluded that "[t]o strike down, without the most critical scrutiny, legislation which imposes only an indirect burden on the exercise of religion, *i.e.* legislation which does not make unlawful the religious practice itself, would radically restrict the operating latitude of the legislature." 366 U.S., at 606. Likewise in this case, it cannot be said that the State discriminated against Thomas on the basis of his religious beliefs or that he was denied benefits *because* he was a Jehovah's Witness. Where, as here, a State has enacted a general statute, the purpose and effect of which is to advance the State's secular goals, the Free Exercise Clause does not in my view require the State to conform that statute to the dictates of religious conscience of any group. As Justice Harlan recognized in his dissent in *Sherbert v. Verner:* "Those situations in which the Constitution may require special treatment on account of religion are . . . few and far between." Like him I believe that although a State could choose to grant exemptions to religious persons from state unemployment regulations, a State is not constitutionally compelled to do so.[2]

The Court's treatment of the Establishment Clause issue is equally unsatisfying. Although today's decision requires a State to provide direct financial assistance to persons solely on the basis of their religious beliefs, the Court nonetheless blandly assures us, just as it did in *Sherbert,* that its decision "plainly" does not foster the "establishment" of religion. I would agree that the Establishment Clause, properly interpreted, would not be violated if Indiana voluntarily chose to grant unemployment benefits to those persons who left their jobs for religious reasons. But I also believe that the decision below is inconsistent with many of our prior Establishment Clause cases. Those cases, if faithfully applied, would require us to hold that such voluntary action by a State *did* violate the Establishment Clause.

JUSTICE STEWART noted this point in his concurring opinion in *Sherbert.* He observed that decisions like *Sherbert,* and the one rendered today, squarely conflict with the more extreme language of many of our prior Establishment Clause cases. In *Everson v. Board of Education,* the Court stated that the Establishment Clause bespeaks a "government . . . stripped of all power . . . to support, or otherwise to assist any or all religions . . . ," and no State "can pass laws which aid one religion . . . [or] all religions." In *Torcaso v. Watkins* the Court asserted that the government cannot "constitutionally pass laws or impose requirements which aid all religions as against non-believers." And in *Abington*

---

2 To the extent *Sherbert* was correctly decided, it might be argued that cases such as *McCollum v. Board of Education,* 333 U.S. 203 (1948); *Engel v. Vitale,* 370 U.S. 421 (1962); *Abington School District v. Schempp,* 374 U.S. 203 (1963); *Lemon v. Kurtzman,* 403 U.S. 602 (1971); and *Committee for Public Education v. Nyquist,* 413 U.S. 756 (1973), were wrongly decided. The "aid" rendered to religion in these latter cases may not be significantly different, in kind or degree, than the "aid" afforded Mrs. Sherbert or Thomas. For example, if the State in *Sherbert* could not deny compensation to one refusing work for religious reasons, it might be argued that a State may not deny reimbursement to students who choose for religious reasons to attend parochial schools. The argument would be that although a State need not allocate any funds to education, once it has done so, it may not require any person to sacrifice his religious beliefs in order to obtain an equal education. *See Lemon, supra,* at 665 (opinion of WHITE, J.); *Nyquist, supra,* at 798-805 (opinion of BURGER, C.J.). There can be little doubt that to the extent secular education provides answers to important moral questions without reference to religion or teaches that there are no answers, a person in one sense sacrifices his religious belief by attending secular schools. And even if such "aid" were not constitutionally compelled by the Free Exercise Clause, Justice Harlan may well have been right in *Sherbert* when he found sufficient flexibility in the Establishment Clause to permit the States to voluntarily choose to grant such benefits to individuals.

School District v. Schempp the Court adopted Justice Rutledge's words in *Everson* that the Establishment Clause forbids "'every form of public aid or support for religion.'" *See also Engel v. Vitale.*

In recent years the Court has moved away from the mechanistic "no-aid-to-religion" approach to the Establishment Clause and has stated a three-part test to determine the constitutionality of governmental aid to religion. *See Lemon v. Kurtzman.* First, the statute must serve a secular legislative purpose. Second, it must have a "primary effect" that neither advances nor inhibits religion. And third, the State and its administration must avoid excessive entanglement with religion.

It is not surprising that the Court today makes no attempt to apply those principles to the facts of this case. If Indiana were to legislate what the Court today requires — an unemployment compensation law which permitted benefits to be granted to those persons who quit their jobs for religious reasons — the statute would "plainly" violate the Establishment Clause as interpreted in such cases as *Lemon* and *Nyquist*. First, although the unemployment statute as a whole would be enacted to serve a secular legislative purpose, the proviso would clearly serve only a religious purpose. It would grant financial benefits for the sole purpose of accommodating religious beliefs. Second, there can be little doubt that the primary effect of the proviso would be to "advance" religion by facilitating the exercise of religious belief. Third, any statute including such a proviso would surely "entangle" the State in religion far more than the mere grant of tax exemptions, as in *Walz*, or the award of tuition grants and tax credits, as in *Nyquist*. By granting financial benefits to persons solely on the basis of their religious beliefs, the State must necessarily inquire whether the claimant's belief is "religious" and whether it is sincerely held. Otherwise any dissatisfied employee may leave his job without cause and claim that he did so because his own particular beliefs required it.

It is unclear from the Court's opinion whether it has temporarily retreated from its expansive view of the Establishment Clause, or wholly abandoned it. I would welcome the latter. Just as I think that Justice Harlan in *Sherbert* correctly stated the proper approach to free exercise questions, I believe that JUSTICE STEWART, dissenting in *Abington School District v. Schempp*, accurately stated the reach of the Establishment Clause. He explained that the Establishment Clause is limited to "government support of proselytizing activities of religious sects by throwing the weight of secular authorit[ies] behind the dissemination of religious tenets." Conversely, governmental assistance which does not have the effect of "inducing" religious belief, but instead merely "accommodates" or implements an independent religious choice does not impermissibly involve the government in religious choices and therefore does not violate the Establishment Clause of the First Amendment. I would think that in this case, as in *Sherbert*, had the State voluntarily chosen to pay unemployment compensation benefits to persons who left their jobs for religious reasons, such aid would be constitutionally permissible because it redounds directly to the benefit of the individual.

In sum, my difficulty with today's decision is that it reads the Free Exercise Clause too broadly and it fails to squarely acknowledge that such a reading conflicts with many of our Establishment Clause cases. As such, the decision simply exacerbates the "tension" between the two Clauses. If the Court were to construe the Free Exercise Clause as it did in *Braunfeld* and the Establishment Clause as JUSTICE STEWART did in *Schempp*, the circumstances in which there would be a conflict between the two Clauses would be few and far between. Although I heartily agree with the Court's tacit abandonment of much of our rhetoric about the Establishment Clause, I regret that the Court cannot see its way clear to restore what was surely intended to have been a greater degree of flexibility to the Federal and State Governments in legislating consistently with the Free Exercise Clause. Accordingly, I would affirm the judgment of the Indiana Supreme Court.

ESTATE OF THORNTON v. CALDOR, INC.
472 U.S. 703 (1985)

CHIEF JUSTICE BURGER delivered the opinion of the Court.

I

In early 1975, petitioner's decedent Donald E. Thornton began working for respondent Caldor, Inc., a chain of New England retail stores; he managed the men's and boys' clothing department in respondent's Waterbury, Connecticut, store. At that time, respondent's Connecticut stores were closed on Sundays pursuant to state law.

In 1977, following the state legislature's revision of the Sunday-closing laws, respondent opened its Connecticut stores for Sunday business. In order to handle the expanded store hours, respondent required its managerial employees to work every third or fourth Sunday. Thornton, a Presbyterian who observed Sunday as his Sabbath, initially complied with respondent's demand and worked a total of 31 Sundays in 1977 and 1978. In October 1978, Thornton was transferred to a management position in respondent's Torrington store; he continued to work on Sundays during the first part of 1979. In November 1979, however, Thornton informed respondent that he would no longer work on Sundays because he observed that day as his Sabbath; he invoked the protection of Conn. Gen. Stat. § 53-303e(b) (1985), which provides:

> "No person who states that a particular day of the week is observed as his Sabbath may be required by his employer to work on such day. An employee's refusal to work on his Sabbath shall not constitute grounds for his dismissal."

Thornton rejected respondent's offer either to transfer him to a management job in a Massachusetts store that was closed on Sundays, or to transfer him to a nonsupervisory position in the Torrington store at a lower salary. In March 1980, respondent transferred Thornton to a clerical position in the Torrington store; Thornton resigned two days later and filed a grievance with the State Board of Mediation and Arbitration alleging that he was discharged from his manager's position in violation of Conn. Gen. Stat. § 53-303e(b) (1985).

Respondent defended its action on the ground that Thornton had not been "discharged" within the meaning of the statute; respondent also urged the Board to find that the statute violated Article 7 of the Connecticut Constitution as well as the Establishment Clause of the First Amendment.

After holding an evidentiary hearing the Board evaluated the sincerity of Thornton's claim and concluded it was based on a sincere religious conviction; it issued a formal decision sustaining Thornton's grievance. The Board framed the statutory issue as follows: "If a discharge for refusal to work Sunday hours occurred and Sunday was the Grievant's Sabbath . . .," § 53-303e(b) would be violated; the Board held that respondent had violated the statute by "discharg[ing] Mr. Thornton as a management employee for refusing to work . . . [on] Thornton's . . . Sabbath." The Board ordered respondent to reinstate Thornton with backpay and compensation for lost fringe benefits. The Superior Court, in affirming that ruling, concluded that the statute did not offend the Establishment Clause.

The Supreme Court of Connecticut reversed, holding the statute did not have a "clear secular purpose."

II

Under the Religion Clauses, government must guard against activity that impinges on religious freedom, and must take pains not to compel people to act in the name of any religion. In setting the appropriate boundaries in Establishment Clause cases, the Court has frequently relied on our holding in *Lemon*, *supra*, for guidance, and we do so here. To pass constitutional muster under *Lemon* a statute must not only have a secular purpose and not foster excessive entanglement of government with religion, its primary effect must not advance or inhibit religion.

The Connecticut statute challenged here guarantees every employee, who "states that a particular day of the week is observed as his Sabbath," the right not to work on his chosen day. The State has thus decreed that those who observe a Sabbath any day of the week as a matter of religious conviction must be relieved of the duty to work on that day, no matter what burden or inconvenience this imposes on the employer or fellow workers. The statute arms Sabbath observers with an absolute and unqualified right not to work on whatever day they designate as their Sabbath.

In essence, the Connecticut statute imposes on employers and employees an absolute duty to conform their business practices to the particular religious practices of the employee by enforcing observance of the Sabbath the employee unilaterally designates. The State thus commands that Sabbath religious concerns automatically control over all secular interests at the workplace; the statute takes no account of the convenience or interests of the employer or those of other employees who do not observe a Sabbath. The employer and others must adjust their affairs to the command of the State whenever the statute is invoked by an employee.

There is no exception under the statute for special circumstances, such as the Friday Sabbath observer employed in an occupation with a Monday through Friday schedule — a school teacher, for example; the statute provides for no special consideration if a high percentage of an employer's work force asserts rights to the same Sabbath. Moreover, there is no exception when honoring the dictates of Sabbath observers would cause the employer substantial economic burdens or when the employer's compliance would require the imposition of significant burdens on other employees required to work in place of the Sabbath observers.[9] Finally, the statute allows for no consideration as to whether the employer has made reasonable accommodation proposals.

This unyielding weighting in favor of Sabbath observers over all other interests contravenes a fundamental principle of the Religion Clauses, so well articulated by Judge Learned Hand:

> "The First Amendment . . . gives no one the right to insist that in pursuit of their own interests others must conform their conduct to his own religious necessities." *Otten v. Baltimore & Ohio R. Co.*, 205 F.2d 58, 61 (CA2 1953).

As such, the statute goes beyond having an incidental or remote effect of advancing religion. *See, e.g., Roemer v. Maryland Bd. of Public Works, infra* Chapter 8; *Board of Education v. Allen*, 392 U.S. 236 (1968). The statute has a primary effect that impermissibly advances a particular religious practice.

JUSTICE O'CONNOR, with whom JUSTICE MARSHALL joins, concurring.

The Court applies the test enunciated in *Lemon v. Kurtzman* and concludes that Conn. Gen. Stat. § 53-303e(b) (1985) has a primary effect that impermissibly advances religion. I agree, and I join the Court's opinion and judgment. In

---

[9] Section 53-303e(b) gives Sabbath observers the valuable right to designate a particular weekly day off — typically a weekend day, widely prized as a day off. Other employees who have strong and legitimate, but non-religious, reasons for wanting a weekend day off have no rights under the statute. For example, those employees who have earned the privilege through seniority to have weekend days off may be forced to surrender this privilege to the Sabbath observer; years of service and payment of "dues" at the workplace simply cannot compete with the Sabbath observer's absolute right under the statute. Similarly, those employees who would like a weekend day off, because that is the only day their spouses are also not working, must take a back seat to the Sabbath observer.

my view, the Connecticut Sabbath law has an impermissible effect because it conveys a message of endorsement of the Sabbath observance.

All employees, regardless of their religious orientation, would value the benefit which the statute bestows on Sabbath observers — the right to select the day of the week in which to refrain from labor. Yet Connecticut requires private employers to confer this valued and desirable benefit only on those employees who adhere to a particular religious belief. The statute singles out Sabbath observers for special and, as the Court concludes, absolute protection without according similar accommodation to ethical and religious beliefs and practices of other private employees. There can be little doubt that an objective observer or the public at large would perceive this statutory scheme precisely as the Court does today. The message conveyed is one of endorsement of a particular religious belief, to the detriment of those who do not share it. As such, the Connecticut statute has the effect of advancing religion, and cannot withstand Establishment Clause scrutiny.

I do not read the Court's opinion as suggesting that the religious accommodation provisions of Title VII of the Civil Rights Act of 1964 are similarly invalid. These provisions preclude employment discrimination based on a person's religion and require private employers to reasonably accommodate the religious practices of employees unless to do so would cause undue hardship to the employer's business. 42 U.S.C. §§ 2000e(j) and 2000e-2(a)(1). Like the Connecticut Sabbath law, Title VII attempts to lift a burden on religious practice that is imposed by *private* employers, and hence it is not the sort of accommodation statute specifically contemplated by the Free Exercise Clause. The provisions of Title VII must therefore manifest a valid secular purpose and effect to be valid under the Establishment Clause. In my view, a statute outlawing employment discrimination based on race, color, religion, sex, or national origin has the valid secular purpose of assuring employment opportunity to all groups in our pluralistic society. Since Title VII calls for reasonable rather than absolute accommodation and extends that requirement to all religious beliefs and practices rather than protecting only the Sabbath observance, I believe an objective observer would perceive it as an anti-discrimination law rather than an endorsement of religion or a particular religious practice.

B. CONFLICTS BETWEEN THE ACCOMMODATION OF RELIGIOUS GROUPS AND RELIGIOUS INDIVIDUALS

CHURCH OF LATTER DAY SAINTS v. AMOS
483 U.S. 327 (1987)

JUSTICE WHITE delivered the opinion of the Court.

Section 702 of the Civil Rights Act of 1964, 78 Stat. 255, as amended, 42 U.S.C. § 2000e-1, exempts religious organizations from Title VII's prohibition against discrimination in employment on the basis of religion.[1] The question presented is whether applying the § 702 exemption to the secular nonprofit activities of religious organizations violates the Establishment Clause of the First Amendment. The District Court held that it does. We reverse.

I

The Deseret Gymnasium (Gymnasium) in Salt Lake City, Utah, is a nonprofit facility, open to the public, run by the Corporation of the Presiding Bishop of The Church of Jesus Christ of Latter-day Saints (CPB), and the Corporation of the President of The Church of Jesus Christ of Latter-day Saints (COP). The CPB and the COP are religious entities associated with The Church of Jesus Christ of Latter-day Saints (Church), an unincorporated religious association sometimes called the Mormon or LDS Church.[3]

Appellee Mayson worked at the Gymnasium for some 16 years as an assistant building engineer and then as building engineer. He was discharged in 1981 because he failed to qualify for a temple recommend, that is, a certificate that he is a member of the Church and eligible to attend its temples.[4]

II

"This Court has long recognized that the government may (and sometimes must) accommodate religious practices and that it may do so without violating

---

[1] Section 702 provides in relevant part:

"This subchapter [i.e., Title VII of the Civil Rights Act of 1964, 42 U.S.C. § 2000e *et seq.*] shall not apply . . . to a religious corporation, association, educational institution, or society with respect to the employment of individuals of a particular religion to perform work connected with the carrying on by such corporation, association, educational institution, or society of its activities."

[3] The CPB and the COP are "corporations sole" organized under Utah law to perform various activities on behalf of the Church. Both corporations are tax-exempt, nonprofit religious entities under § 501(c)(3) of the Internal Revenue Code. Appellees do not contest that the CPB and the COP are religious organizations for purposes of § 702.

[4] Temple recommends are issued only to individuals who observe the Church's standards in such matters as regular church attendance, tithing, and abstinence from coffee, tea, alcohol, and tobacco.

the Establishment Clause." *Hobbie v. Unemployment Appeals Comm'n of Fla.*, 480 U.S. 136, 144-145 (1987) (footnote omitted). It is well established, too, that "[t]he limits of permissible state accommodation to religion are by no means co-extensive with the noninterference mandated by the Free Exercise Clause." *Walz v. Tax Comm'n.* There is ample room under the Establishment Clause for "benevolent neutrality which will permit religious exercise to exist without sponsorship and without interference." At some point, accommodation may devolve into "an unlawful fostering of religion," but these are not such cases, in our view.

The private appellants contend that we should not apply the three-part *Lemon* approach, which is assertedly unsuited to judging the constitutionality of exemption statutes such as § 702. The argument is that an exemption statute will always have the effect of advancing religion and hence be invalid under the second (effects) part of the *Lemon* test, a result claimed to be inconsistent with cases such as *Walz v. Tax Comm'n, supra*, which upheld property tax exemptions for religious organizations. The first two of the three Lemon factors, however, were directly taken from pre-*Walz* decisions, and *Walz* did not purport to depart from prior Establishment Clause cases, except by adding a consideration that became the third element of the *Lemon* test. In any event, we need not reexamine *Lemon* as applied in this context, for the exemption involved here is in no way questionable under the *Lemon* analysis.

Lemon requires first that the law at issue serve a "secular legislative purpose." This does not mean that the law's purpose must be unrelated to religion — that would amount to a requirement "that the government show a callous indifference to religious groups," *Zorach v. Clauson*, 343 U.S. 306, 314 (1952), and the Establishment Clause has never been so interpreted. Rather, *Lemon's* "purpose" requirement aims at preventing the relevant governmental decisionmaker — in this case, Congress — from abandoning neutrality and acting with the intent of promoting a particular point of view in religious matters.

Under the *Lemon* analysis, it is a permissible legislative purpose to alleviate significant governmental interference with the ability of religious organizations to define and carry out their religious missions. Appellees argue that there is no such purpose here because § 702 provided adequate protection for religious employers prior to the 1972 amendment, when it exempted only the religious activities of such employers from the statutory ban on religious discrimination. We may assume for the sake of argument that the pre-1972 exemption was adequate in the sense that the Free Exercise Clause required no more. Nonetheless, it is a significant burden on a religious organization to require it, on pain of substantial liability, to predict which of its activities a secular court will consider religious. The line is hardly a bright one, and an organization might understandably be concerned that a judge would not understand its religious tenets and sense of mission. Fear of potential liability might affect the way an organization carried out what it understood to be its religious mission.

After a detailed examination of the legislative history of the 1972 amendment, the District Court concluded that Congress' purpose was to minimize governmental "interfer[ence] with the decision-making process in religions." We agree with the District Court that this purpose does not violate the Establishment Clause.

The second requirement under *Lemon* is that the law in question have "a principal or primary effect . . . that neither advances nor inhibits religion." Undoubtedly, religious organizations are better able now to advance their purposes than they were prior to the 1972 amendment to § 702. But religious groups have been better able to advance their purposes on account of many laws that have passed constitutional muster: for example, the property tax exemption at issue in *Walz v. Tax Comm'n, supra*, or the loans of schoolbooks to school-children, including parochial school students, upheld in *Board of Education v. Allen*, 392 U.S. 236 (1968). A law is not unconstitutional simply because it *allows* churches to advance religion, which is their very purpose. For a law to have forbidden "effects" under *Lemon*, it must be fair to say that the *government itself* has advanced religion through its own activities and influence. As the Court observed in *Walz*, "for the men who wrote the Religion Clauses of the First Amendment the 'establishment' of a religion connoted sponsorship, financial support, and active involvement of the sovereign in religious activity."

The District Court appeared to fear that sustaining the exemption would permit churches with financial resources impermissibly to extend their influence and propagate their faith by entering the commercial, profit-making world. The cases before us, however, involve a nonprofit activity instituted over 75 years ago in the hope that "all who assemble here, and who come for the benefit of their health, and for physical blessings, [may] feel that they are in a house dedicated to the Lord." These cases therefore do not implicate the apparent concerns of the District Court. Moreover, we find no persuasive evidence in the record before us that the Church's ability to propagate its religious doctrine through the Gymnasium is any greater now than it was prior to the passage of the Civil Rights Act in 1964. In such circumstances, we do not see how any advancement of religion achieved by the Gymnasium can be fairly attributed to the Government, as opposed to the Church.[15]

---

[15] Undoubtedly, Mayson's freedom of choice in religious matters was impinged upon, but it was the Church (through the COP and the CPB), and not the Government, who put him to the choice of changing his religious practices or losing his job. This is a very different case than *Estate of Thornton v. Caldor, Inc.,* 472 U.S. 703 (1985). In *Caldor,* the Court struck down a Connecticut statute prohibiting an employer from requiring an employee to work on a day designated by the employee as his Sabbath. In effect, Connecticut had given the force of law to the employee's designation of a Sabbath day and required accommodation by the employer regardless of the burden which that constituted for the employer or other employees. *See Hobbie v. Unemployment Appeals Comm'n of Fla.*, 480 U.S. 136, 145, n. 11 (1987). In the present cases, appellee Mayson was not legally obligated to take the steps necessary to qualify for a temple recommend, and his discharge was not required by statute. We find no merit in appellees' contention that § 702 "impermissibly delegates governmental power to religious employees and conveys a message of governmental endorsement of religious discrimination."

We find unpersuasive the District Court's reliance on the fact that § 702 singles out religious entities for a benefit. Although the Court has given weight to this consideration in its past decisions, it has never indicated that statutes that give special consideration to religious groups are *per se* invalid. That would run contrary to the teaching of our cases that there is ample room for accommodation of religion under the Establishment Clause. Where, as here, government acts with the proper purpose of lifting a regulation that burdens the exercise of religion, we see no reason to require that the exemption comes packaged with benefits to secular entities.

We are also unpersuaded by the District Court's reliance on the argument that § 702 is unsupported by long historical tradition. There was simply no need to consider the scope of the § 702 exemption until the 1964 Civil Rights Act was passed, and the fact that Congress concluded after eight years that the original exemption was unnecessarily narrow is a decision entitled to deference, not suspicion.

Appellees argue that § 702 offends equal protection principles by giving less protection to the employees of religious employers than to the employees of secular employers. Appellees rely on *Larson v. Valente*, 456 U.S. 228, 246 (1982), for the proposition that a law drawing distinctions on religious grounds must be strictly scrutinized. But *Larson* indicates that laws discriminating *among* religions are subject to strict scrutiny, and that laws "affording a uniform benefit to *all* religions" should be analyzed under *Lemon*. In cases such as these, where a statute is neutral on its face and motivated by a permissible purpose of limiting governmental interference with the exercise of religion, we see no justification for applying strict scrutiny to a statute that passes the *Lemon* test. The proper inquiry is whether Congress has chosen a rational classification to further a legitimate end. We have already indicated that Congress acted with a legitimate purpose in expanding the § 702 exemption to cover all activities of religious employers. To dispose of appellees' equal protection argument, it suffices to hold — as we now do — that as applied to the nonprofit activities of religious employers, § 702 is rationally related to the legitimate purpose of alleviating significant governmental interference with the ability of religious organizations to define and carry out their religious missions.

It cannot be seriously contended that § 702 impermissibly entangles church and state; the statute effectuates a more complete separation of the two and avoids the kind of intrusive inquiry into religious belief that the District Court engaged in in this case. The statute easily passes muster under the third part of the *Lemon* test.

JUSTICE BRENNAN, with whom JUSTICE MARSHALL joins, concurring in the judgment.

I write separately to emphasize that my concurrence in the judgment rests on the fact that these cases involve a challenge to the application of § 702's categorical exemption to the activities of a *nonprofit* organization. I believe that the particular character of nonprofit activity makes inappropriate a case-by-case determination whether its nature is religious or secular.

These cases present a confrontation between the rights of religious organizations and those of individuals. Any exemption from Title VII's proscription on religious discrimination necessarily has the effect of burdening the religious liberty of prospective and current employees. An exemption says that a person may be put to the choice of either conforming to certain religious tenets or losing a job opportunity, a promotion, or, as in these cases, employment itself.[1] The potential for coercion created by such a provision is in serious tension with our commitment to individual freedom of conscience in matters of religious belief.

At the same time, religious organizations have an interest in autonomy in ordering their internal affairs, so that they may be free to:

> "select their own leaders, define their own doctrines, resolve their own disputes, and run their own institutions. Religion includes important communal elements for most believers. They exercise their religion through religious organizations, and these organizations must be protected by the [Free Exercise] [C]lause." Laycock, *Towards a General Theory of the Religion Clauses: The Case of Church Labor Relations and the Right to Church Autonomy*, 81 COLUM. L. REV. 1373, 1389 (1981).

See also Serbian Eastern Orthodox Diocese v. Milivojevich, 426 U.S. 696 (1976) (church has interest in effecting binding resolution of internal governance disputes); *Kedroff v. Saint Nicholas Cathedral*, 344 U.S. 94 (1952) (state statute

---

[1] The fact that a religious organization is permitted, rather than required, to impose this burden is irrelevant; what is significant is that the burden is the effect of the exemption. *See Lemon v. Kurtzman*, 403 U.S. 602, 612 (1971). An exemption by its nature merely permits certain behavior, but that has never stopped this Court from examining the *effect* of exemptions that would free religion from regulations placed on others. *See, e.g., United States v. Lee*, 455 U.S. 252, 261 (1982) ("Granting an exemption from social security taxes to an employer operates to impose the employer's religious faith on the employees"); *Walz v. Tax Comm'n*, 397 U.S. 664, 674 (1970) (legislative purpose in granting tax exemption not determinative; "[w]e must also be sure that the end result — the effect — is not an excessive government entanglement with religion"); *see also Wisconsin v. Yoder*, 406 U.S. 205, 220-221 (1972) ("The Court must not ignore the danger that an exception from a general obligation of citizenship on religious grounds may run afoul of the Establishment Clause"). This approach reflects concern not only about the impact of exemptions on others, but also awareness that:

> "Government promotes religion as effectively when it fosters a close identification of its powers and responsibilities with those of any — or all — religious denominations as when it attempts to inculcate specific religious doctrines. If this identification conveys a message of government endorsement . . . of religion, a core purpose of the Establishment Clause is violated." *Grand Rapids School Dist. v. Ball,* 473 U.S. 373, 389 (1985).

In these cases, as JUSTICE O'CONNOR cogently observes in her concurrence, "[t]he Church had the power to put [appellee] Mayson to a choice of qualifying for a temple recommend or losing his job because the Government had lifted from religious organizations the general regulatory burden imposed by § 702."

purporting to transfer administrative control from one church authority to another violates Free Exercise Clause). For many individuals, religious activity derives meaning in large measure from participation in a larger religious community. Such a community represents an ongoing tradition of shared beliefs, an organic entity not reducible to a mere aggregation of individuals. Determining that certain activities are in furtherance of an organization's religious mission, and that only those committed to that mission should conduct them, is thus a means by which a religious community defines itself. Solicitude for a church's ability to do so reflects the idea that furtherance of the autonomy of religious organizations often furthers individual religious freedom as well.

The authority to engage in this process of self-definition inevitably involves what we normally regard as infringement on free exercise rights, since a religious organization is able to condition employment in certain activities on subscription to particular religious tenets. We are willing to countenance the imposition of such a condition because we deem it vital that, if certain activities constitute part of a religious community's practice, then a religious organization should be able to require that only members of its community perform those activities.

This rationale suggests that, ideally, religious organizations should be able to discriminate on the basis of religion *only* with respect to religious activities, so that a determination should be made in each case whether an activity is religious or secular. This is because the infringement on religious liberty that results from conditioning performance of *secular* activity upon religious belief cannot be defended as necessary for the community's self-definition. Furthermore, the authorization of discrimination in such circumstances is not an accommodation that simply enables a church to gain members by the normal means of prescribing the terms of membership for those who seek to participate in furthering the mission of the community. Rather, it puts at the disposal of religion the added advantages of economic leverage in the secular realm. As a result, the authorization of religious discrimination with respect to nonreligious activities goes beyond reasonable accommodation, and has the effect of furthering religion in violation of the Establishment Clause. *See Lemon v. Kurtzman.*

What makes the application of a religious-secular distinction difficult is that the character of an activity is not self-evident. As a result, determining whether an activity is religious or secular requires a searching case-by-case analysis. This results in considerable ongoing government entanglement in religious affairs. Furthermore, this prospect of government intrusion raises concern that a religious organization may be chilled in its free exercise activity. While a church may regard the conduct of certain functions as integral to its mission, a court may disagree. A religious organization therefore would have an incentive to characterize as religious only those activities about which there likely would be no dispute, even if it genuinely believed that religious commitment was important in performing other tasks as well. As a result, the community's process of self-definition would be shaped in part by the prospects of litigation. A case-by-case analysis for all activities therefore would both produce excessive government entanglement with religion and create the danger of chilling religious activity.

The risk of chilling religious organizations is most likely to arise with respect to *nonprofit* activities. The fact that an operation is not organized as a profit-making commercial enterprise makes colorable a claim that it is not purely secular in orientation. In contrast to a for-profit corporation, a non-profit organization must utilize its earnings to finance the continued provision of the goods or services it furnishes, and may not distribute any surplus to the owners. *See generally* Hansmann, *The Role of Nonprofit Enterprise*, 89 YALE L.J. 835 (1980). This makes plausible a church's contention that an entity is not operated simply in order to generate revenues for the church, but that the activities themselves are infused with a religious purpose. Furthermore, unlike for-profit corporations, nonprofits historically have been organized specifically to provide certain community services, not simply to engage in commerce. Churches often regard the provision of such services as a means of fulfilling religious duty and of providing an example of the way of life a church seeks to foster.

Nonprofit activities therefore are most likely to present cases in which characterization of the activity as religious or secular will be a close question. If there is a danger that a religious organization will be deterred from classifying as religious those activities it actually regards as religious, it is likely to be in this domain. This substantial potential for chilling religious activity makes inappropriate a case-by-case determination of the character of a nonprofit organization, and justifies a categorical exemption for nonprofit activities. Such an exemption demarcates a sphere of deference with respect to those activities most likely to be religious. It permits infringement on employee free exercise rights in those instances in which discrimination is most likely to reflect a religious community's self-definition. While not every nonprofit activity may be operated for religious purposes, the likelihood that many are makes a categorical rule a suitable means to avoid chilling the exercise of religion.[6]

Sensitivity to individual religious freedom dictates that religious discrimination be permitted only with respect to employment in religious activities. Concern for the autonomy of religious organizations demands that we avoid the entanglement and the chill on religious expression that a case-by-case determination would produce. We cannot escape the fact that these aims are in tension. Because of the nature of nonprofit activities, I believe that a categorical exemption for such enterprises appropriately balances these competing concerns. As a result, I concur in the Court's judgment that the nonprofit Deseret

---

[6] It is also conceivable that some for-profit activities could have a religious character, so that religious discrimination with respect to these activities would be justified in some cases. The cases before us, however, involve a nonprofit organization; I believe that a *categorical* exemption authorizing discrimination is particularly appropriate for such entities, because claims that they possess a religious dimension will be especially colorable.

Gymnasium may avail itself of an automatic exemption from Title VII's proscription on religious discrimination.

JUSTICE O'CONNOR concurring in the judgment.

Although I agree with the judgment of the Court, I write separately to note that this action once again illustrates certain difficulties inherent in the Court's use of the test articulated in *Lemon v. Kurtzman*. As a result of this problematic analysis, while the holding of the opinion for the Court extends only to non-profit organizations, its reasoning fails to acknowledge that the amended § 702, 42 U.S.C. § 2000e-1 raises different questions as it is applied to profit and non-profit organizations.

In *Wallace v. Jaffree*, I noted a tension in the Court's use of the *Lemon* test to evaluate an Establishment Clause challenge to government efforts to accommodate the free exercise of religion:

> "On the one hand, a rigid application of the *Lemon* test would invalidate legislation exempting religious observers from generally applicable government obligations. By definition, such legislation has a religious purpose and effect in promoting the free exercise of religion. On the other hand, judicial deference to all legislation that purports to facilitate the free exercise of religion would completely vitiate the Establishment Clause. Any statute pertaining to religion can be viewed as an 'accommodation' of free exercise rights." *Wallace v. Jaffree*, 472 U.S., at 82.

In my view, the opinion for the Court leans toward the second of the two unacceptable options described above. While acknowledging that "[u]ndoubtedly, religious organizations are better able now to advance their purposes than they were prior to the 1972 amendment to § 702," the Court seems to suggest that the "effects" prong of the *Lemon* test is not at all implicated as long as the government action can be characterized as "allowing" religious organizations to advance religion, in contrast to government action directly advancing religion. This distinction seems to me to obscure far more than to enlighten. Almost any government benefit to religion could be recharacterized as simply "allowing" a religion to better advance itself, unless perhaps it involved actual proselytization by government agents. In nearly every case of a government benefit to religion, the religious mission would not be advanced if the religion did not take advantage of the benefit; even a direct financial subsidy to a religious organization would not advance religion if for some reason the organization failed to make any use of the funds. It is for this same reason that there is little significance to the Court's observation that it was the Church rather than the Government that penalized Mayson's refusal to adhere to Church doctrine. The Church had the power to put Mayson to a choice of qualifying for a temple recommend or losing his job because *the Government* had lifted from religious organizations the general regulatory burden imposed by § 702.

The necessary first step in evaluating an Establishment Clause challenge to a government action lifting from religious organizations a generally applicable regulatory burden is to recognize that such government action does have the effect of advancing religion. The necessary second step is to separate those benefits to religion that constitutionally accommodate the free exercise of religion from those that provide unjustifiable awards of assistance to religious organizations. As I have suggested in earlier opinions, the inquiry framed by the *Lemon* test should be "whether government's purpose is to endorse religion and whether the statute actually conveys a message of endorsement." *Wallace.* To ascertain whether the statute conveys a message of endorsement, the relevant issue is how it would be perceived by an objective observer, acquainted with the text, legislative history, and implementation of the statute. Of course, in order to perceive the government action as a permissible accommodation of religion, there must in fact be an identifiable burden *on the exercise of religion* that can be said to be lifted by the government action. The determination whether the objective observer will perceive an endorsement of religion "is not a question of simple historical fact. Although evidentiary submissions may help answer it, the question is, like the question whether racial or sex-based classifications communicate an invidious message, in large part a legal question to be answered on the basis of judicial interpretation of social facts." *Lynch v. Donnelly.*

The above framework, I believe, helps clarify why the amended § 702 raises different questions as it is applied to nonprofit and for-profit organizations. As JUSTICE BRENNAN observes in his concurrence: "The fact that an operation is not organized as a profit-making commercial enterprise makes colorable a claim that it is not purely secular in orientation." These cases involve a Government decision to lift from a nonprofit activity of a religious organization the burden of demonstrating that the particular nonprofit activity is religious as well as the burden of refraining from discriminating on the basis of religion. Because there is a probability that a nonprofit activity of a religious organization will itself be involved in the organization's religious mission, in my view the objective observer should perceive the Government action as an accommodation of the exercise of religion rather than as a Government endorsement of religion.

It is not clear, however, that activities conducted by religious organizations solely as profit-making enterprises will be as likely to be directly involved in the religious mission of the organization. While I express no opinion on the issue, I emphasize that under the holding of the Court, and under my view of the appropriate Establishment Clause analysis, the question of the constitutionality of the § 702 exemption as applied to for-profit activities of religious organizations remains open.

FRAZEE v. ILLINOIS DEPARTMENT OF EMPLOYMENT SECURITY
489 U.S. 829 (1989)

JUSTICE WHITE delivered the opinion of the Court.

The Illinois Unemployment Insurance Act provides that "[a]n individual shall be ineligible for benefits if he has failed, without good cause, either to apply for available, suitable work when so directed . . . or to accept suitable work when offered him. . . ." In April 1984, William Frazee refused a temporary retail position offered him by Kelly Services because the job would have required him to work on Sunday. Frazee told Kelly that, as a Christian, he could not work on "the Lord's day." Frazee then applied to the Illinois Department of Employment Security for unemployment benefits claiming that there was good cause for his refusal to work on Sunday. His application was denied. Frazee appealed the denial of benefits to the Department of Employment Security's Board of Review, which also denied his claim. The Board of Review stated: "When a refusal of work is based on religious convictions, the refusal must be based upon some tenets or dogma accepted by the individual of some church, sect, or denomination, and such a refusal based solely on an individual's personal belief is personal and noncompelling and does not render the work unsuitable." The Board of Review concluded that Frazee had refused an offer of suitable work without good cause. The Circuit Court of the Tenth Judicial Circuit of Illinois, Peoria County, affirmed, finding that the agency's decision was "not contrary to law nor against the manifest weight of the evidence," thereby rejecting Frazee's claim based on the Free Exercise Clause of the First Amendment.

Frazee's free exercise claim was again rejected by the Appellate Court of Illinois, Third District. The court characterized Frazee's refusal to work as resting on his "personal professed religious belief," and made it clear that it did "not question the sincerity of the plaintiff." It then engaged in a historical discussion of religious prohibitions against work on the Sabbath and, in particular, on Sunday. Nonetheless, the court distinguished *Sherbert v. Verner*; *Thomas v. Review Bd. of Indiana Employment Security Div.*; and *Hobbie v. Unemployment Appeals Comm'n of Florida,* 480 U.S. 136 (1987), from the facts of Frazee's case. Unlike the claimants in *Sherbert, Thomas,* and *Hobbie,* Frazee was not a member of an established religious sect or church, nor did he claim that his refusal to work resulted from a "tenet, belief or teaching of an established religious body." To the Illinois court, Frazee's position that he was "a Christian" and as such felt it wrong to work on Sunday was not enough. For a Free Exercise Clause claim to succeed, said the Illinois Appellate Court, "the injunction against Sunday labor must be found in a tenet or dogma of an established religious sect. [Frazee] does not profess to be a member of any such sect." The Illinois Supreme Court denied Frazee leave to appeal.

We have had more than one occasion before today to consider denials of unemployment compensation benefits to those who have refused work on the basis of their religious beliefs. In *Sherbert v. Verner,* the Court held that a State could not "constitutionally apply the eligibility provisions [of its unemployment-compensation program] so as to constrain a worker to abandon his religious convictions respecting the day of rest." *Thomas v. Review Bd. of Indiana Employment Security Div., supra,* also held that the State's refusal to award unemployment compensation benefits to one who terminated his job because his religious beliefs forbade participation in the production of armaments violated the First Amendment right to free exercise. Just two years ago, in *Hobbie v. Unemployment Appeals Comm'n of Florida, supra,* Florida's denial of unemployment compensation benefits to an employee discharged for her refusal to work on her Sabbath because of religious convictions adopted subsequent to employment was also declared to be a violation of the Free Exercise Clause. In each of these cases, the appellant was "forced to choose between fidelity to religious belief and . . . employment," and we found "the forfeiture of unemployment benefits for choosing the former over the latter brings unlawful coercion to bear on the employee's choice" In each of these cases, we concluded that the denial of unemployment compensation benefits violated the Free Exercise Clause of the First Amendment of the Constitution, as applied to the States through the Fourteenth Amendment.

It is true, as the Illinois court noted, that each of the claimants in those cases was a member of a particular religious sect, but none of those decisions turned on that consideration or on any tenet of the sect involved that forbade the work the claimant refused to perform. Our judgments in those cases rested on the fact that each of the claimants had a sincere belief that religion required him or her to refrain from the work in question. Never did we suggest that unless a claimant belongs to a sect that forbids what his job requires, his belief, however sincere, must be deemed a purely personal preference rather than a religious belief. Indeed, in *Thomas,* there was disagreement among sect members as to whether their religion made it sinful to work in an armaments factory; but we considered this to be an irrelevant issue and hence rejected the State's submission that unless the religion involved formally forbade work on armaments, Thomas' belief did not qualify as a religious belief. Because Thomas unquestionably had a sincere belief that his religion prevented him from doing such work, he was entitled to invoke the protection of the Free Exercise Clause.

There is no doubt that "[o]nly beliefs rooted in religion are protected by the Free Exercise Clause." Purely secular views do not suffice. Nor do we underestimate the difficulty of distinguishing between religious and secular convictions and in determining whether a professed belief is sincerely held. States are clearly entitled to assure themselves that there is an ample predicate for invoking the Free Exercise Clause. We do not face problems about sincerity or about the religious nature of Frazee's convictions, however. The courts below did not question his sincerity, and the State concedes it. Furthermore, the Board of Review characterized Frazee's views as "religious convictions," and the Illinois

Appellate Court referred to his refusal to work on Sunday as based on a "personal professed religious belief."[1]

Frazee asserted that he was a Christian, but did not claim to be a member of a particular Christian sect. It is also true that there are assorted Christian denominations that do not profess to be compelled by their religion to refuse Sunday work, but this does not diminish Frazee's protection flowing from the Free Exercise Clause. *Thomas* settled that much. Undoubtedly, membership in an organized religious denomination, especially one with a specific tenet forbidding members to work on Sunday, would simplify the problem of identifying sincerely held religious beliefs, but we reject the notion that to claim the protection of the Free Exercise Clause, one must be responding to the commands of a particular religious organization. Here, Frazee's refusal was based on a sincerely held religious belief. Under our cases, he was entitled to invoke First Amendment protection.[2]

The State does not appear to defend this aspect of the decision below. In its brief and at oral argument, the State conceded that the Free Exercise Clause does not demand adherence to a tenet or dogma of an established religious sect. Instead, the State proposes its own test for identifying a "religious" belief, asserts that Frazee has not met such a test, and asks that we affirm on this basis. We decline to address this submission; for as the case comes to us, Frazee's conviction was recognized as religious but found to be inadequate because it was not claimed to represent a tenet of a religious organization of which he was a member. That ground for decision was clearly erroneous.

The State offers no justification for the burden that the denial of benefits places on Frazee's right to exercise his religion. The Illinois Appellate Court ascribed great significance to America's weekend way of life. The Illinois court asked: "What would Sunday be today if professional football, baseball, basketball, and tennis were barred. Today Sunday is not only a day for religion, but for recreation and labor. Today the supermarkets are open, service stations dispense fuel, utilities continue to serve the people and factories continue to belch smoke and tangible products," concluding that "[i]f all Americans were to abstain from working on Sunday, chaos would result." We are unpersuaded, however, that there will be a mass movement away from Sunday employ if William Frazee succeeds in his claim.

---

[1] From the very first report of the Illinois Division of Unemployment Insurance claims adjudicator, Frazee's refusal of Sunday work has been described as "due to his religious convictions." In his application for reconsideration of the referee's determination, Frazee stated: "I refused the job which required me to work on Sunday based on Biblical principles, scripture Exodus 20: 8, 9, 10: 'Remember the Sabbath day by keeping it holy. Six days you shall labour and do all your work but the seventh day is a Sabbath to the Lord your God. On it you shall not do any work.'"

[2] We noted in *Thomas v. Review Bd. of Indiana Employment Security Div.*, 450 U.S. 707, 715 (1981), that an asserted belief might be "so bizarre, so clearly nonreligious in motivation, as not to be entitled to protection under the Free Exercise Clause." But that avails the State nothing in this case. As the discussion of the Illinois Appellate Court itself indicates, claims by Christians that their religion forbids Sunday work cannot be deemed bizarre or incredible.

As was the case in *Thomas* where there was "no evidence in the record to indicate that the number of people who find themselves in the predicament of choosing between benefits and religious beliefs is large enough to create 'widespread unemployment,' or even to seriously affect unemployment," there is nothing before us in this case to suggest that Sunday shopping, or Sunday sporting, for that matter, will grind to a halt as a result of our decision today. And, as we have said in the past, there may exist state interests sufficiently compelling to override a legitimate claim to the free exercise of religion. No such interest has been presented here.

Chapter 13

THE ACCOMMODATION PRINCIPLE WRIT LARGE: FREE EXERCISE AS A DEFENSE TO GENERAL LEGAL OBLIGATIONS

Sherbert v. Verner, Chapter 12, *supra*, marks the beginning of the Court's effort to enforce a constitutionally mandated principle requiring government agencies to accommodate the practices of religious adherents by mediating or waiving otherwise applicable legal requirements. Prior to *Sherbert*, the Court took a very narrow view of claims that the Free Exercise Clause required the government to avoid conflicts between general legal obligations and religious practices. Some of these earlier cases had a very harsh effect. For example, after the Court rejected an Establishment Clause challenge to Sunday closing laws, *see McGowan v. Maryland*, 366 U.S. 420 (1961), it also rejected the Free Exercise claim of Orthodox Jewish store owners that the Sunday closing laws should not apply to them. The store owners argued that the Sunday closing laws severely impaired their ability to earn a livelihood, since — unlike Christian store owners — members of the Jewish faith were unable to open their stores on Saturday without violating religious rules against working on the Sabbath. *See Braunfeld v. Brown*, 366 U.S. 599 (1961). The Court's response to this claim was blunt:

> To strike down, without the most critical scrutiny, legislation which imposes only an indirect burden on the exercise of religion, i.e., legislation which does not make unlawful the religious practice itself, would radically restrict the operating latitude of the legislature. . . . Consequently, it cannot be expected, much less required, that legislators enact no law regulating conduct that may in some way result in an economic disadvantage to some religious sects and not to others because of the special practices of the various religions. We do not believe that such an effect is an absolute test for determining whether the legislation violates the freedom of religion protected by the First Amendment.

In *Sherbert*, the Supreme Court retreated substantially from this broad deference to legislative prerogatives. But even after *Sherbert*, the Court repeatedly expressed reluctance to intrude in the day-to-day operation of government and the implementation of religiously-neutral government policies. This Chapter provides a cross-section of cases in which the Court considered Free Exercise accommodation claims against generally applicable legal obligations. The results in these cases are less uniform than the results in the employment cases. Consider whether the two sets of cases are consistent. Consider also whether the results of the cases are adequately explained in *Employment Division v. Smith*, Chapter 14, *infra*.

WISCONSIN v. YODER
406 U.S. 205 (1972)

MR. CHIEF JUSTICE BURGER delivered the opinion of the Court.

On petition of the State of Wisconsin, we granted the writ of certiorari in this case to review a decision of the Wisconsin Supreme Court holding that respondents' convictions for violating the State's compulsory school-attendance law were invalid under the Free Exercise Clause of the First Amendment to the United States Constitution made applicable to the States by the Fourteenth Amendment. For the reasons hereafter stated we affirm the judgment of the Supreme Court of Wisconsin.

Respondents Jonas Yoder and Wallace Miller are members of the Old Order Amish religion, and respondent Adin Yutzy is a member of the Conservative Amish Mennonite Church. They and their families are residents of Green County, Wisconsin. Wisconsin's compulsory school-attendance law required them to cause their children to attend public or private school until reaching age 16 but the respondents declined to send their children, ages 14 and 15, to public school after they complete the eighth grade. The children were not enrolled in any private school, or within any recognized exception to the compulsory-attendance law, and they are conceded to be subject to the Wisconsin statute.

On complaint of the school district administrator for the public schools, respondents were charged, tried, and convicted of violating the compulsory-attendance law in Green County Court and were fined the sum of $5 each. Respondents defended on the ground that the application of the compulsory-attendance law violated their rights under the First and Fourteenth Amendments. The trial testimony showed that respondents believed, in accordance with the tenets of Old Order Amish communities generally, that their children's attendance at high school, public or private, was contrary to the Amish religion and way of life. They believed that by sending their children to high school, they would not only expose themselves to the danger of the censure of the church community, but, as found by the county court, also endanger their own salvation and that of their children. The State stipulated that respondents' religious beliefs were sincere.

In support of their position, respondents presented as expert witnesses scholars on religion and education whose testimony is uncontradicted. They expressed their opinions on the relationship of the Amish belief concerning school attendance to the more general tenets of their religion, and described the impact that compulsory high school attendance could have on the continued survival of Amish communities as they exist in the United States today. The history of the Amish sect was given in some detail, beginning with the Swiss Anabaptists of the 16th century who rejected institutionalized churches and sought to return to the early, simple, Christian life de-emphasizing material success, rejecting the competitive spirit, and seeking to insulate themselves from the modern world. As a result of their common heritage, Old Order Amish communities today are characterized by a fundamental belief that salvation requires life in a church community separate and apart from the world and worldly influence. This concept of life aloof from the world and its values is central to their faith.

A related feature of Old Order Amish communities is their devotion to a life in harmony with nature and the soil, as exemplified by the simple life of the early Christian era that continued in America during much of our early national life. Amish beliefs require members of the community to make their living by farming or closely related activities. Broadly speaking, the Old Order Amish religion pervades and determines the entire mode of life of its adherents. Their conduct is regulated in great detail by the *Ordnung*, or rules, of the church community. Adult baptism, which occurs in late adolescence, is the time at which Amish young people voluntarily undertake heavy obligations, not unlike the Bar Mitzvah of the Jews, to abide by the rules of the church community.

Amish objection to formal education beyond the eighth grade is firmly grounded in these central religious concepts. They object to the high school, and higher education generally, because the values they teach are in marked variance with Amish values and the Amish way of life; they view secondary school education as an impermissible exposure of their children to a "wordly" influence in conflict with their beliefs. The high school tends to emphasize intellectual and scientific accomplishments, self-distinction, competitiveness, worldly success, and social life with other students. Amish society emphasizes informal learning-through-doing; a life of "goodness," rather than a life of intellect; wisdom, rather than technical knowledge, community welfare, rather than competition; and separation from, rather than integration with, contemporary worldly society.

Formal high school education beyond the eighth grade is contrary to Amish beliefs, not only because it places Amish children in an environment hostile to Amish beliefs with increasing emphasis on competition in class work and sports and with pressure to conform to the styles, manners, and ways of the peer group, but also because it takes them away from their community, physically and emotionally, during the crucial and formative adolescent period of life. During this period, the children must acquire Amish attitudes favoring manual work and self-reliance and the specific skills needed to perform the adult role of an Amish farmer or housewife. They must learn to enjoy physical labor. Once a child has learned basic reading, writing, and elementary mathematics, these traits, skills, and attitudes admittedly fall within the category of those best learned through example and "doing" rather than in a classroom. And, at this time in life, the Amish child must also grow in his faith and his relationship to the Amish community if he is to be prepared to accept the heavy obligations imposed by adult baptism. In short, high school attendance with teachers who are not of the Amish faith — and may even be hostile to it — interposes a serious barrier to the integration of the Amish child into the Amish religious community. Dr. John Hostetler, one of the experts on Amish society, testified that the modern high school is not equipped, in curriculum or social environment, to impart the values promoted by Amish society.

The Amish do not object to elementary education through the first eight grades as a general proposition because they agree that their children must have basic skills in the "three R's" in order to read the Bible, to be good farmers and citizens, and to be able to deal with non-Amish people when necessary in the course of daily affairs. They view such a basic education as acceptable because it does not significantly expose their children to worldly values or interfere with their development in the Amish community during the crucial adolescent period. While Amish accept compulsory elementary education generally, wherever possible they have established their own elementary schools in many respects like the small local schools of the past. In the Amish belief higher learning tends to develop values they reject as influences that alienate man from God.

On the basis of such considerations, Dr. Hostetler testified that compulsory high school attendance could not only result in great psychological harm to Amish children, because of the conflicts it would produce, but would also, in his opinion, ultimately result in the destruction of the Old Order Amish church community as it exists in the United States today. The testimony of Dr. Donald A. Erickson, an expert witness on education, also showed that the Amish succeed in preparing their high school age children to be productive members of the Amish community. He described their system of learning through doing the skills directly relevant to their adult roles in the Amish community as "ideal" and perhaps superior to ordinary high school education. The evidence also showed that the Amish have an excellent record as law-abiding and generally self-sufficient members of society.

Although the trial court in its careful findings determined that the Wisconsin compulsory school-attendance law "does interfere with the freedom of the Defendants to act in accordance with their sincere religious belief" it also concluded that the requirement of high school attendance until age 16 was a "reasonable and constitutional" exercise of governmental power, and therefore denied the motion to dismiss the charges. The Wisconsin Circuit Court affirmed the convictions. The Wisconsin Supreme Court, however, sustained respondents' claim under the Free Exercise Clause of the First Amendment and reversed the convictions. A majority of the court was of the opinion that the State had failed to make an adequate showing that its interest in "establishing and maintaining an educational system overrides the defendants' right to the free exercise of their religion."

I

There is no doubt as to the power of a State, having a high responsibility for education of its citizens, to impose reasonable regulations for the control and duration of basic education. *See, e.g., Pierce v. Society of Sisters*, 268 U.S. 510, 534 (1925). Providing public schools ranks at the very apex of the function of a State. Yet even this paramount responsibility was, in *Pierce*, made to yield to the right of parents to provide an equivalent education in a privately operated system. There the Court held that Oregon's statute compelling attendance in a public school from age eight to age 16 unreasonably interfered with the interest of parents in directing the rearing of their off-spring, including their education in church-operated schools. As that case suggests, the values of parental direction of the religious upbringing and education of their children in their early and formative years have a high place in our society. *See also Ginsberg v. New York,* 390 U.S. 629, 639 (1968); *Meyer v. Nebraska,* 262 U.S. 390 (1923); *cf. Rowan v. United States Post Office Dept.,* 397 U.S. 728 (1970). Thus, a State's interest in universal education, however highly we rank it, is not totally free from a balancing process when it impinges on fundamental rights and interests, such as those specifically protected by the Free Exercise Clause of the First Amendment, and the traditional interest of parents with respect to the religious upbringing of their children so long as they, in the words of *Pierce,* "prepare [them] for additional obligations."

It follows that in order for Wisconsin to compel school attendance beyond the eighth grade against a claim that such attendance interferes with the practice of a legitimate religious belief, it must appear either that the State does not deny the free exercise of religious belief by its requirement, or that there is a state interest of sufficient magnitude to override the interest claiming protection under the Free Exercise Clause.

The essence of all that has been said and written on the subject is that only those interests of the highest order and those not otherwise served can overbalance legitimate claims to the free exercise of religion. We can accept it as settled, therefore, that, however strong the State's interest in universal compulsory education, it is by no means absolute to the exclusion or subordination of all other interests.

II

We come then to the quality of the claims of the respondents concerning the alleged encroachment of Wisconsin's compulsory school-attendance statute on their rights and the rights of their children to the free exercise of the religious beliefs they and their forbears have adhered to for almost three centuries. In evaluating those claims we must be careful to determine whether the Amish religious faith and their mode of life are, as they claim, inseparable and interdependent. A way of life, however virtuous and admirable, may not be interposed as a barrier to reasonable state regulation of education if it is based on purely secular considerations; to have the protection of the Religion Clauses, the claims must be rooted in religious belief. Although a determination of what is a "religious" belief or practice entitled to constitutional protection may present a most delicate question, the very concept of ordered liberty precludes allowing every person to make his own standards on matters of conduct in which society as a whole has important interests. Thus, if the Amish asserted their claims because of their subjective evaluation and rejection of the contemporary secular values accepted by the majority, much as Thoreau rejected the social values of his time and isolated himself at Walden Pond, their claims would not rest on a religious basis. Thoreau's choice was philosophical and personal rather than religious, and such belief does not rise to the demands of the Religion Clauses.

Giving no weight to such secular considerations, however, we see that the record in this case abundantly supports the claim that the traditional way of life of the Amish is not merely a matter of personal preference, but one of deep religious conviction, shared by an organized group, and intimately related to daily living. That the Old Order Amish daily life and religious practice stem from their faith is shown by the fact that it is in response to their literal interpretation of the Biblical injunction from the Epistle of Paul to the Romans, "be not conformed to this world. . . ." This command is fundamental to the Amish faith. Moreover, for the Old Order Amish, religion is not simply a matter of theocratic belief. As the expert witnesses explained, the Old Order Amish religion pervades and determines virtually their entire way of life, regulating it with the detail of the Talmudic diet through the strictly enforced rules of the church community.

The record shows that the respondents' religious beliefs and attitude toward life, family, and home have remained constant — perhaps some would say static — in a period of unparalleled progress in human knowledge generally and great changes in education. The respondents freely concede, and indeed assert as an article of faith, that their religious beliefs and what we would today call "life style" have not altered in fundamentals for centuries. Their way of life in a church-oriented community, separated from the outside world and "worldly" influences, their attachment to nature and the soil, is a way inherently simple and uncomplicated, albeit difficult to preserve against the pressure to conform. Their rejection of telephones, automobiles, radios, and television, their mode of dress, of speech, their habits of manual work do indeed set them apart from much of contemporary society; these customs are both symbolic and practical.

As the society around the Amish has become more populous, urban, industrialized, and complex, particularly in this century, government regulation of human affairs has correspondingly become more detailed and pervasive. The Amish mode of life has thus come into conflict increasingly with requirements of contemporary society exerting a hydraulic insistence on conformity to majoritarian standards. So long as compulsory education laws were confined to eight grades of elementary basic education imparted in a nearby rural schoolhouse, with a large proportion of students of the Amish faith, the Old Order Amish had little basis to fear that school attendance would expose their children to the worldly influence they reject. But modern compulsory secondary education in rural areas is now largely carried on in a consolidated school, often remote from the student's home and alien to his daily home life. As the record so strongly shows, the values and programs of the modern secondary school are in sharp conflict with the fundamental mode of life mandated by the Amish religion; modern laws requiring compulsory secondary education have accordingly engendered great concern and conflict. The conclusion is inescapable that secondary schooling, by exposing Amish children to worldly influences in terms of attitudes, goals, and values contrary to beliefs, and by substantially interfering with the religious development of the Amish child and his integration into the way of life of the Amish faith community at the crucial adolescent stage of development, contravenes the basic religious tenets and practice of the Amish faith, both as to the parent and the child.

The impact of the compulsory-attendance law on respondents' practice of the Amish religion is not only severe, but inescapable, for the Wisconsin law affirmatively compels them, under threat of criminal sanction, to perform acts undeniably at odds with fundamental tenets of their religious beliefs. *See Braunfeld v. Brown.* Nor is the impact of the compulsory-attendance law confined to grave interference with important Amish religious tenets from a subjective point of view. It carries with it precisely the kind of objective danger to the free exercise of religion that the First Amendment was designed to prevent. As the record shows, compulsory school attendance to age 16 for Amish children carries with it a very real threat of undermining the Amish community and religious practice as they exist today; they must either abandon belief and be assimilated into society at large, or be forced to migrate to some other and more tolerant region.

In sum, the unchallenged testimony of acknowledged experts in education and religious history, almost 300 years of consistent practice, and strong evidence of a sustained faith pervading and regulating respondents' entire mode of life support the claim that enforcement of the State's requirement of compulsory formal education after the eighth grade would gravely endanger if not destroy the free exercise of respondents' religious beliefs.

III

Neither the findings of the trial court nor the Amish claims as to the nature of their faith are challenged in this Court by the State of Wisconsin. Its position is that the State's interest in universal compulsory formal secondary education to age 16 is so great that it is paramount to the undisputed claims of respondents that their mode of preparing their youth for Amish life, after the traditional elementary education, is an essential part of their religious belief and practice. Nor does the State undertake to meet the claim that the Amish mode of life and education is inseparable from and a part of the basic tenets of their religion — indeed, as much a part of their religious belief and practices as baptism, the confessional, or a Sabbath may be for others.

Wisconsin concedes that under the Religion Clauses religious beliefs are absolutely free from the State's control, but it argues that "actions," even though religiously grounded, are outside the protection of the First Amendment. But our decisions have rejected the idea that religiously grounded conduct is always outside the protection of the Free Exercise Clause. It is true that activities of individuals, even when religiously based, are often subject to regulation by the States in the exercise of their undoubted power to promote the health, safety, and general welfare, or the Federal Government in the exercise of its delegated powers. But to agree that religiously grounded conduct must often be subject to the broad police power of the State is not to deny that there are areas of conduct protected by the Free Exercise Clause of the First Amendment and thus beyond the power of the State to control, even under regulations of general applicability. *E.g., Sherbert v. Verner; Murdock v. Pennsylvania,* 319 U.S. 105 (1943); *Cantwell v. Connecticut.* This case, therefore, does not become easier because respondents were convicted for their "actions" in refusing to send their children to the public high school; in this context belief and action cannot be neatly confined in logic-tight compartments.

Nor can this case be disposed of on the grounds that Wisconsin's requirement for school attendance to age 16 applies uniformly to all citizens of the State and does not, on its face, discriminate against religions or a particular religion, or that it is motivated by legitimate secular concerns. A regulation neutral on its face may, in its application, nonetheless offend the constitutional requirement for governmental neutrality if it unduly burdens the free exercise of religion. *Sherbert v. Verner; cf. Walz v. Tax Commission.* The Court must not ignore the danger that an exception from a general obligation of citizenship on religious grounds may run afoul of the Establishment Clause, but that danger cannot be allowed to prevent any exception no matter how vital it may be to the protection of values promoted by the right of free exercise. By preserving doctrinal flexibility and recognizing the need for a sensible and realistic application of the Religion Clauses

> "we have been able to chart a course that preserved the autonomy and freedom of religious bodies while avoiding any semblance of established religion. This is a 'tight rope' and one we have successfully traversed." *Walz v. Tax Commission.*

We turn, then, to the State's broader contention that its interest in its system of compulsory education is so compelling that even the established religious practices of the Amish must give way. Where fundamental claims of religious freedom are at stake, however, we cannot accept such a sweeping claim; despite its admitted validity in the generality of cases, we must searchingly examine the interests that the State seeks to promote by its requirement for compulsory education to age 16, and the impediment to those objectives that would flow from recognizing the claimed Amish exemption. *See, e.g., Sherbert v. Verner; Martin v. City of Struthers,* 319 U.S. 141 (1943); *Schneider v. State,* 308 U.S. 147 (1939).

The State advances two primary arguments in support of its system of compulsory education. It notes, as Thomas Jefferson pointed out early in our history, that some degree of education is necessary to prepare citizens to participate effectively and intelligently in our open political system if we are to preserve freedom and independence. Further, education prepares individuals to be self-reliant and self-sufficient participants in society. We accept these propositions.

However, the evidence adduced by the Amish in this case is persuasively to the effect that an additional one or two years of formal high school for Amish children in place of their long-established program of informal vocational education would do little to serve those interests. Respondents' experts testified at trial, without challenge, that the value of all education must be assessed in terms of its capacity to prepare the child for life. It is one thing to say that compulsory education for a year or two beyond the eighth grade may be necessary when its goal is the preparation of the child for life in modern society as the majority live, but it is quite another if the goal of education be viewed as the preparation of the child for life in the separated agrarian community that is the keystone of the Amish faith.

The State attacks respondents' position as one fostering "ignorance" from which the child must be protected by the State. No one can question the State's duty to protect children from ignorance but this argument does not square with the facts disclosed in the record. Whatever their idiosyncrasies as seen by the majority, this record strongly shows that the Amish community has been a highly successful social unit within our society, even if apart from the conventional "mainstream." Its members are productive and very law-abiding members of society; they reject public welfare in any of its usual modern forms. The Congress itself recognized their self-sufficiency by authorizing exemption of such groups as the Amish from the obligation to pay social security taxes.

It is neither fair nor correct to suggests that the Amish are opposed to education beyond the eighth grade level. What this record shows is that they are opposed to conventional formal education of the type provided by a certified high school because it comes at the child's crucial adolescent period of religious development. Dr. Donald Erickson, for example, testified that their system of learning-by-doing was an "ideal system" of education in terms of preparing Amish children for life as adults in the Amish community, and that "I would be inclined to say they do a better job in this than most of the rest of us do." As he put it, "These people aren't purporting to be learned people, and it seems to mc the self-sufficiency of the community is the best evidence I can point to — whatever is being done seems to function well."

We must not forget that in the Middle Ages important values of the civilization of the Western World were preserved by members of religious orders who isolated themselves from all worldly influences against great obstacles. There can be no assumption that today's majority is "right" and the Amish and others like them are "wrong." A way of life that is odd or even erratic but interferes with no rights or interests of others is not to be condemned because it is different.

The State, however, supports its interest in providing an additional one or two years of compulsory high school education to Amish children because of the possibility that some such children will choose to leave the Amish community, and that if this occurs they will be ill-equipped for life. The State argues that if Amish children leave their church they should not be in the position of making their way in the world without the education available in the one or two additional years the State requires. However, on this record, that argument is highly speculative. There is no specific evidence of the loss of Amish adherents by attrition, nor is there any showing that upon leaving the Amish community Amish children, with their practical agricultural training and habits of industry and self-reliance, would become burdens on society because of educational shortcomings. Indeed, this argument of the State appears to rest primarily on the State's mistaken assumption, already noted, that the Amish do not provide any education for their children beyond the eighth grade, but allow them to grow in "ignorance." To the contrary, not only do the Amish accept the necessity for formal schooling through the eighth grade level, but continue to provide what has been characterized by the undisputed testimony of expert educators as an "ideal" vocational education for their children in the adolescent years.

There is nothing in this record to suggest that the Amish qualities of reliability, self-reliance, and dedication to work would fail to find ready markets in today's society. Absent some contrary evidence supporting the State's position, we are unwilling to assume that persons possessing such valuable vocational skills and habits are doomed to become burdens on society should they determine to leave the Amish faith, nor is there any basis in the record to warrant a finding that an additional one or two years of formal school education beyond the eighth grade would serve to eliminate any such problem that might exist.

Insofar as the State's claim rests on the view that a brief additional period of formal education is imperative to enable the Amish to participate effectively and intelligently in our democratic process, it must fall. The Amish alternative to formal secondary school education has enabled them to function effectively in their day-to-day life under self-imposed limitations on relations with the world, and to survive and prosper in contemporary society as a separate, sharply identifiable and highly self-sufficient community for more than 200 years in this country. In itself this is strong evidence that they are capable of fulfilling the social and political responsibilities of citizenship without compelled attendance beyond the eighth grade at the price of jeopardizing their free exercise of religious belief. When Thomas Jefferson emphasized the need for education as a bulwark of a free people against tyranny, there is nothing to indicate he had in mind compulsory education through any fixed age beyond a basic education. Indeed, the Amish communities singularly parallel and reflect many of the virtues of Jefferson's ideal of the "sturdy yeoman" who would form the basis of what he considered as the ideal of a democratic society. Even their idiosyncratic separateness exemplifies the diversity we profess to admire and encourage.

The requirement for compulsory education beyond the eighth grade is a relatively recent development in our history. Less than 60 years ago, the educational requirements of almost all of the States were satisfied by completion of the elementary grades, at least where the child was regularly and lawfully employed. The independence and successful social functioning of the Amish community for a period approaching almost three centuries and more than 200 years in this country are strong evidence that there is at best a speculative gain, in terms of meeting the duties of citizenship, from an additional one or two years of compulsory formal education. Against this background it would require a more particularized showing from the State on this point to justify the severe interference with religious freedom such additional compulsory attendance would entail.

We should also note that compulsory education and child labor laws find their historical origin in common humanitarian instincts, and that the age limits of both laws have been coordinated to achieve their related objectives. In the context of this case, such considerations, if anything, support rather than detract from respondents' position. The origins of the requirement for school attendance to age 16, an age falling after the completion of elementary school but before completion of high school, are not entirely clear. But to some extent such laws reflected the movement to prohibit most child labor under age 16 that culminated in the provisions of the Federal Fair Labor Standards Act of 1938. It is true, then, that the 16-year child labor age limit may to some degree derive from a contemporary impression that children should be in school until that age. But at the same time, it cannot be denied that, conversely, the 16-year education limit reflects, in substantial measure, the concern that children under that age not be employed under conditions hazardous to their health, or in work that should be performed by adults.

In these terms, Wisconsin's interest in compelling the school attendance of Amish children to age 16 emerges as somewhat less substantial than requiring such attendance for children generally. For, while agricultural employment is not totally outside the legitimate concerns of the child labor laws, employment of children under parental guidance and on the family farm from age 14 to age 16 is an ancient tradition that lies at the periphery of the objectives of such laws. There is no intimation that the Amish employment of their children on family farms is in any way deleterious to their health or that Amish parents exploit children at tender years. Any such inference would be contrary to the record before us. Moreover, employment of Amish children on the family farm does not present the undesirable economic aspects of eliminating jobs that might otherwise be held by adults.

IV

Contrary to the suggestion of the dissenting opinion of MR. JUSTICE DOUGLAS, our holding today in no degree depends on the assertion of the religious interest of the child as contrasted with that of the parents. It is the parents who are subject to prosecution here for failing to cause their children to attend school, and it is their right of free exercise, not that of their children, that must determine Wisconsin's power to impose criminal penalties on the parent. The dissent argues that a child who expresses a desire to attend public high school in conflict with the wishes of his parents should not be prevented from doing so. There is no reason for the Court to consider that point since it is not an issue in the case. The children are not parties to this litigation. The State has at no point tried this case on the theory that respondents were preventing their children from attending school against their expressed desires, and indeed the record is to the contrary. The State's position from the outset has been that it is empowered to apply its compulsory-attendance law to Amish parents in the same manner as to other parents — that is, without regard to the wishes of the child. That is the claim we reject today.

Our holding in no way determines the proper resolution of possible competing interests of parents, children, and the State in an appropriate state court proceeding in which the power of the State is asserted on the theory that Amish parents are preventing their minor children from attending high school despite their expressed desires to the contrary. Recognition of the claim of the State in such a proceeding would, of course, call into question traditional concepts of parental control over the religious upbringing and education of their minor children recognized in this Court's past decisions. It is clear that such an intrusion by a State into family decisions in the area of religious training would give rise to grave questions of religious freedom comparable to those raised here and those presented in *Pierce v. Society of Sisters*, 268 U.S. 510 (1925). On this record we neither reach nor decide those issues.

The State's argument proceeds without reliance on any actual conflict between the wishes of parents and children. It appears to rest on the potential that exemption of Amish parents from the requirements of the compulsory-education law might allow some parents to act contrary to the best interests of their children by foreclosing their opportunity to make an intelligent choice between the Amish way of life and that of the outside world. The same argument could, of course, be made with respect to all church schools short of college. There is nothing in the record or in the ordinary course of human experience to suggest that non-Amish parents generally consult with children of ages 14-16 if they are placed in a church school of the parents' faith.

Indeed it seems clear that if the State is empowered, as *parens patriae*, to "save" a child from himself or his Amish parents by requiring an additional two years of compulsory formal high school education, the State will in large measure influence, if not determine, the religious future of the child. Even more markedly than in *Prince*, therefore, this case involves the fundamental interest of parents, as contrasted with that of the State, to guide the religious future and education of their children. The history and culture of Western civilization reflect a strong tradition of parental concern for the nurture and upbringing of their children. This primary role of the parents in the upbringing of their children is now established beyond debate as an enduring American tradition. If not the first, perhaps the most significant statements of the Court in this area are found in *Pierce v. Society of Sisters*, in which the Court observed:

> "Under the doctrine of *Meyer v. Nebraska*, 262 U.S. 390, we think it entirely plain that the Act of 1922 unreasonably interferes with the liberty of parents and guardians to direct the upbringing and education of children under their control. As often heretofore pointed out, rights guaranteed by the Constitution may not be abridged by legislation

which has no reasonable relation to some purpose within the competency of the State. The fundamental theory of liberty upon which all governments in this Union repose excludes any general power of the State to standardize its children by forcing them to accept instruction from public teachers only. The child is not the mere creature of the State; those who nurture him and direct his destiny have the right, coupled with the high duty, to recognize and prepare him for additional obligations." 268 U.S., at 534-535.

The duty to prepare the child for "additional obligations," referred to by the Court, must be read to include the inculcation of moral standards, religious beliefs, and elements of good citizenship. *Pierce,* of course, recognized that where nothing more than the general interest of the parent in the nurture and education of his children is involved, it is beyond dispute that the State acts "reasonably" and constitutionally in requiring education to age 16 in some public or private school meeting the standards prescribed by the State.

However read, the Court's holding in *Pierce* stands as a charter of the rights of parents to direct the religious upbringing of their children. And, when the interests of parenthood are combined with a free exercise claim of the nature revealed by this record, more than merely a "reasonable relation to some purpose within the competency of the State" is required to sustain the validity of the State's requirement under the First Amendment. To be sure, the power of the parent, even when linked to a free exercise claim, may be subject to limitation under *Prince* if it appears that parental decisions will jeopardize the health or safety of the child, or have a potential for significant social burdens. But in this case, the Amish have introduced persuasive evidence undermining the arguments the State has advanced to support its claims in terms of the welfare of the child and society as a whole. The record strongly indicates that accommodating the religious objections of the Amish by forgoing one, or at most two, additional years of compulsory education will not impair the physical or mental health of the child, or result in an inability to be self-supporting or to discharge the duties and responsibilities of citizenship, or in any other way materially detract from the welfare of society.

In the fact of our consistent emphasis on the central values underlying the Religion Clauses in our constitutional scheme of government, we cannot accept a *parens patriae* claim of such all-encompassing scope and with such sweeping potential for broad and unforeseeable application as that urged by the State.

V

For the reasons stated we hold, with the Supreme Court of Wisconsin, that the First and Fourteenth Amendments prevent the State from compelling respondents to cause their children to attend formal high school to age 16. Our disposition of this case, however, in no way alters our recognition of the obvious fact that courts are not school boards or legislatures, and are ill-equipped to determine the "necessity" of discrete aspects of a State's program of compulsory education. This should suggest that courts must move with great circumspection in performing the sensitive and delicate task of weighing a State's legitimate social concern when faced with religious claims for exemption from generally applicable education requirements. It cannot be overemphasized that we are not dealing with a way of life and mode of education by a group claiming to have recently discovered some "progressive" or more enlightened process for rearing children for modern life.

Aided by a history of three centuries as an identifiable religious sect and a long history as a successful and self-sufficient segment of American society, the Amish in this case have convincingly demonstrated the sincerity of their religious beliefs, the interrelationship of belief with their mode of life, the vital role that belief and daily conduct play in the continued survival of Old Order Amish communities and their religious organization, and the hazards presented by the State's enforcement of a statute generally valid as to others. Beyond this, they have carried the even more difficult burden of demonstrating the adequacy of their alternative mode of continuing informal vocational education in terms of precisely those overall interests that the State advances in support of its program of compulsory high school education. In light of this convincing showing, one that probably few other religious groups or sects could make, and weighing the minimal difference between what the State would require and what the Amish already accept, it was incumbent on the State to show with more particularity how its admittedly strong interest in compulsory education would be adversely affected by granting an exemption to the Amish. *Sherbert v. Verner.*

Nothing we hold is intended to undermine the general applicability of the State's compulsory school-attendance statutes or to limit the power of the State to promulgate reasonable standards that, while not impairing the free exercise of religion, provide for continuing agricultural vocational education under parental and church guidance by the Old Order Amish or others similarly situated. The States have had a long history of amicable and effective relationships with church-sponsored schools, and there is no basis for assuming that, in this related context, reasonable standards cannot be established concerning the content of the continuing vocational education of Amish children under parental guidance, provided always that state regulations are not inconsistent with what we have said in this opinion.

MR. JUSTICE DOUGLAS, dissenting in part.

I

I agree with the Court that the religious scruples of the Amish are opposed to the education of their children beyond the grade schools, yet I disagree with the Court's conclusion that the matter is within the dispensation of parents alone. The Court's analysis assumes that the only interests at stake in the case are those of the Amish parents on the one hand, and those of the State on the other. The difficulty with this approach is that, despite the Court's claim, the parents are seeking to vindicate not only their own free exercise claims, but also those of their high-school-age children.

It is argued that the right of the Amish children to religious freedom is not presented by the facts of the case, as the issue before the Court involves only the Amish parents' religious freedom to defy a state criminal statute imposing upon them an affirmative duty to cause their children to attend high school.

First, respondents' motion to dismiss in the trial court expressly asserts, not only the religious liberty of the adults, but also that of the children, as a defense to the prosecutions. It is, of course, beyond question that the parents have standing as defendants in a criminal prosecution to assert the religious interests of their children as a defense.[1] Although the lower courts and a majority of this Court assume an identity of interest between parent and child, it is clear that they have treated the religious interest of the child as a factor in the analysis.

Second, it is essential to reach the question to decide the case, not only because the question was squarely raised in the motion to dismiss, but also because no analysis of religious-liberty claims can take place in a vacuum. If the parents in this case are allowed a religious exemption, the inevitable effect is to impose the parents' notions of religious duty upon their children. Where the child is mature enough to express potentially conflicting desires, it would be an invasion of the child's rights to permit such an imposition without canvassing his views. As in *Prince v. Massachusetts,* 321 U.S. 158, it is an imposition resulting from this very litigation. As the child has no other effective forum, it is in this litigation that his rights should be considered. And, if an Amish child desires to attend high school, and is mature enough to have that desire respected, the State may well be able to override the parents' religiously motivated objections.

Religion is an individual experience. It is not necessary, nor even appropriate, for every Amish child to express his views on the subject in a prosecution of a single adult. Crucial, however, are the views of the child whose parent is the subject of the suit. Frieda Yoder has in fact testified that her own religious views are opposed to high-school education. I therefore join the judgment of the Court as to respondent Jonas Yoder. But Frieda Yoder's views may not be those of Vernon Yutzy or Barbara Miller. I must dissent, therefore, as to respondents Adin Yutzy and Wallace Miller as their motion to dismiss also raised the question of their children's religious liberty.

---

[1] Thus, in *Prince v. Massachusetts,* 321 U.S. 158, a Jehovah's Witness was convicted for having violated a state child labor law by allowing her nine-year-old niece and ward to circulate religious literature on the public streets. There, as here, the narrow question was the religious liberty of the adult. There, as here, the Court analyzed the problem from the point of view of the State's conflicting interest in the welfare of the child. But, as MR. JUSTICE BRENNAN, speaking for the Court, has so recently pointed out, "The Court [in *Prince*] implicitly held that the custodian had standing to assert alleged freedom of religion . . . rights of the child that were threatened in the very litigation before the Court and that the child had no effective way of asserting herself." *Eisenstadt v. Baird,* 405 U.S. 438, 446 n. 6. Here, as in Prince, the children have no effective alternate means to vindicate their rights. The question, therefore, is squarely before us.

II

This issue has never been squarely presented before today. Our opinions are full of talk about the power of the parents over the child's education. *See Pierce v. Society of Sisters,* 268 U.S. 510; *Meyer v. Nebraska,* 262 U.S. 390. And we have in the past analyzed similar conflicts between parent and State with little regard for the views of the child. *See Prince v. Massachusetts, supra.* Recent cases, however, have clearly held that the children themselves have constitutionally protectible interests.

These children are "persons" within the meaning of the Bill of Rights. We have so held over and over again. In *Haley v. Ohio,* 332 U.S. 596, we extended the protection of the Fourteenth Amendment in a state trial of a 15-year-old boy. In *In re Gault,* 387 U.S. 1, 13, we held that "neither the Fourteenth Amendment nor the Bill of Rights is for adults alone." In *In re Winship,* 397 U.S. 358, we held that a 12-year-old boy, when charged with an act which would be a crime if committed by an adult, was entitled to procedural safeguards contained in the Sixth Amendment.

In *Tinker v. Des Moines Independent Community School District,* 393 U.S. 503, we dealt with 13-year-old, 15-year-old, and 16-year-old students who wore armbands to public schools and were disciplined for doing so. We gave them reflief, saying that their First Amendment rights had been abridged.

> "Students in school as well as out of school are "persons" under our Constitution. They are possessed of fundamental rights which the State must respect, just as they themselves must respect their obligations to the State."

In *Board of Education v. Barnette* we held that school-children, whose religious beliefs collided with a school rule requiring them to salute the flag, could not be required to do so. While the sanction included expulsion of the students and prosecution of the parents, the vice of the regime was its interference with the child's free exercise of religion. We said: "Here . . . we are dealing with a compulsion of students to declare a belief." In emphasizing the important and delicate task of boards of education we said:

> "That they are educating the young for citizenship is reason for scrupulous protection of Constitutional freedoms of the individual, if we are not to strangle the free mind at its source and teach youth to discount important principles of our government as mere platitudes."

On this important and vital matter of education, I think the children should be entitled to be heard. While the parents, absent dissent, normally speak for the entire family, the education of the child is a matter on which the child will often have decided views. He may want to be a pianist or an astronaut or an oceanographer. To do so he will have to break from the Amish tradition.[2]

---

[2] A significant number of Amish children do leave the Old Order. Professor Hostetler notes that "[t]he loss of members is very limited in some Amish districts and considerable in others."

It is the future of the student, not the future of the parents, that is imperiled by today's decision. If a parent keeps his child out of school beyond the grade school, then the child will be forever barred from entry into the new and amazing world of diversity that we have today. The child may decide that that is the preferred course, or he may rebel. It is the student's judgment, not his parents', that is essential if we are to give full meaning to what we have said about the Bill of Rights and of the right of students to be masters of their own destiny.[3] If he is harnessed to the Amish way of life by those in authority over him and if his education is truncated, his entire life may be stunted and deformed. The child, therefore, should be given an opportunity to be heard before the State gives the exemption which we honor today.

The views of the two children in question were not canvassed by the Wisconsin courts. The matter should be explicitly reserved so that new hearings can be held on remand of the case.

III

I think the emphasis of the Court on the "law and order" record of this Amish group of people is quite irrelevant. A religion is a religion irrespective of what the misdemeanor or felony records of its members might be. I am not at all sure how the Catholics, Episcopalians, the Baptists, Jehovah's Witnesses, the Unitarians, and my own Presbyterians would make out if subjected to such a test. It is, of course, true that if a group or society was organized to perpetuate crime and if that is its motive, we would have rather startling problems akin to those that were raised when some years back a particular sect was challenged here as operating on a fraudulent basis. *United States v. Ballard*, 322 U.S. 78. But no such factors are present here, and the Amish, whether with a high or low

---

J. HOSTETLER, AMISH SOCIETY 226 (1968). In one Pennsylvania church, he observed a defection rate of 30%. *Ibid.* Rates up to 50% have been reported by others. Casad, *Compulsory High School Attendance and the Old Order Amish: A Commentary on* State v. Garber, 16 KAN. L. REV. 423, 434 n. 51 (1968).

[3] The court below brushed aside the students' interests with the offhand comment that "[w]hen a child reaches the age of judgment, he can choose for himself his religion." 49 Wis. 2d 430, 440, 182 N.W.2d 539, 543. But there is nothing in this record to indicate that the moral and intellectual judgment demanded of the student by the question in this case is beyond his capacity. Children far younger than the 14- and 15-year-olds involved here are regularly permitted to testify in custody and other proceedings. Indeed, the failure to call the affected child in a custody hearing is often reversible error. *See, e.g., Callicott v. Callicott*, 364 S.W.2d 455 (Civ. App. Tex.) (reversible error for trial judge to refuse to hear testimony of eight-year-old in custody battle). Moreover, there is substantial agreement among child psychologists and sociologists that the moral and intellectual maturity of the 14-year-old approaches that of the adult. *See, e.g.,* J. PIAGET, THE MORAL JUDGMENT OF THE CHILD (1948); D. ELKIND, CHILDREN AND ADOLESCENTS 75-80 (1970); Kohlberg, *Moral Education in the Schools: A Development View, in* R. MUUSS, ADOLESCENT BEHAVIOR AND SOCIETY 193, 199-200 (1971); W. KAY, MORAL DEVELOPMENT 172-183 (1968); A. GESELL & F. ILG, YOUTH: THE YEARS FROM TEN TO SIXTEEN 175-182 (1956). The maturity of Amish youth, who identify with and assume adult roles from early childhood, *see* M. GOODMAN, THE CULTURE OF CHILDHOOD 92-94 (1970), is certainly not less than that of children in the general population.

criminal record,[5] certainly qualify by all historic standards as a religion within the meaning of the First Amendment.

The Court rightly rejects the notion that actions, even though religiously grounded, are always outside the protection of the Free Exercise Clause of the First Amendment. In so ruling, the Court departs from the teaching of *Reynolds v. United States*, where it was said concerning the reach of the Free Exercise Clause of the First Amendment, "Congress was deprived of all legislative power over mere opinion, but was left free to reach actions which were in violation of social duties or subversive of good order." In that case it was conceded that polygamy was a part of the religion of the Mormons. Yet the Court said, "It matters not that his belief [in polygamy] was a part of his professed religion: it was still belief and belief only."

Action, which the Court deemed to be antisocial, could be punished even though it was grounded on deeply held and sincere religious convictions. What we do today, at least in this respect, opens the way to give organized religion a broader base than it has ever enjoyed; and it even promises that in time *Reynolds* will be overruled.

In another way, however, the Court retreats when in reference to Henry Thoreau it says his "choice was philosophical and personal rather than religious, and such belief does not rise to the demands of the Religion Clauses." That is contrary to what we held in *United States v. Seeger*, where we were concerned with the meaning of the words "religious training and belief" in the Selective Service Act, which were the basis of many conscientious objector claims. We said:

> "Within that phrase would come all sincere religious beliefs which are based upon a power or being, or upon a faith, to which all else is subordinate or upon which all else is ultimately dependent. The test might be stated in these words: A sincere and meaningful belief which occupies in the life of its possessor a place parallel to that filled by the God of those admittedly qualifying for the exemption comes within the statutory definition. This construction avoids imputing to Congress an intent to classify different religious beliefs, exempting some and excluding others, and is in accord with the well-established congressional policy of

---

[5] The observation of Justice Heffernan, dissenting below, that the principal opinion in his court portrayed the Amish as leading a life of "idyllic agrarianism," is equally applicable to the majority opinion in this Court. So, too, is his observation that such a portrayal rests on a "mythological basis." Professor Hostetler has noted that "[d]rinking among the youth is common in all the large Amish settlements." AMISH SOCIETY 283. Moreover, "[I]t would appear that among the Amish the rate of suicide is just as high, if not higher, than for the nation." *Id.*, at 300. He also notes an unfortunate Amish "preoccupation with filthy stories," *id.*, at 282, as well as significant "rowdyism and stress." *Id.*, at 281. These are not traits peculiar to the Amish, of course. The point is that the Amish are not people set apart and different.

equal treatment for those whose opposition to service is grounded in their religious tenets."

Welsh v. United States was in the same vein, the Court saying:

"In this case, Welsh's conscientious objection to war was undeniably based in part on his perception of world politics. In a letter to his local board, he wrote:

"I can only act according to what I am and what I see. And I see that the military complex wastes both human and material resources, that it fosters disregard for (what I consider a paramount concern) human needs and ends; I see that the means we employ to 'defend' our 'way of life' profoundly change that way of life. I see that in our failure to recognize the political, social, and economic realities of the world, we, *as a nation*, fail our responsibility *as a nation*."

The essence of Welsh's philosophy, on the basis of which we held he was entitled to an exemption, was in these words:

"I believe that human life is valuable in and of itself; in its living; therefore I will not injure or kill another human being. This belief (and the corresponding 'duty' to abstain from violence toward another person) is not 'superior to those arising from any human relation.' On the contrary: *it is essential to every human relation.* I cannot, therefore, conscientiously comply with the Government's insistence that I assume duties which I feel are immoral and totally repugnant."

I adhere to these exalted views of "religion" and see no acceptable alternative to them now that we have become a Nation of many religions and sects, representing all of the diversities of the human race.

UNITED STATES v. LEE
455 U.S. 252 (1982)

CHIEF JUSTICE BURGER delivered the opinion of the Court

I

Appellee, a member of the Old Order Amish, is a farmer and carpenter. From 1970 to 1977, appellee employed several other Amish to work on his farm and in his carpentry shop. He failed to file the quarterly social security tax returns required of employers, withhold social security tax from his employees, or pay the employer's share of social security taxes.

In 1978, the Internal Revenue Service assessed appellee in excess of $27,000 for unpaid employment taxes; he paid $91 — the amount owed for the first quarter of 1973 — and then sued in the United States District Court for the Western District of Pennsylvania for a refund, claiming that imposition of the social security taxes violated his First Amendment free exercise rights and those of his Amish employees.

The District Court held the statutes requiring appellee to pay social security and unemployment insurance taxes unconstitutional as applied. The court noted that the Amish believe it sinful not to provide for their own elderly and needy and therefore are religiously opposed to the national social security system. The court also accepted appellee's contention that the Amish religion not only prohibits the acceptance of social security benefits, but also bars all contributions by Amish to the social security system. The District Court observed that in light of their beliefs, Congress has accommodated self-employed Amish and self-employed members of other religious groups with similar beliefs by providing exemptions from social security taxes. 26 U.S.C. § 1402(g). The court's holding was based on both the exemption statute for the self-employed and the First Amendment; appellee and others "who fall within the carefully circumscribed definition provided in 1402(g) are relieved from paying the employer's share of [social security taxes] as it is an unconstitutional infringement upon the free exercise of their religion."

II

The exemption provided by § 1402(g) is available only to self-employed individuals and does not apply to employers or employees. Consequently, appellee and his employees are not within the express provisions of § 1402(g). Thus any exemption from payment of the employer's share of social security taxes must come from a constitutionally required exemption.

A

The preliminary inquiry in determining the existence of a constitutionally required exemption is whether the payment of social security taxes and the receipt of benefits interferes with the free exercise rights of the Amish. The Amish believe that there is a religiously based obligation to provide for their fellow members the kind of assistance contemplated by the social security system. Although the Government does not challenge the sincerity of this belief, the Government does contend that payment of social security taxes will not threaten the integrity of the Amish religious belief or observance. It is not within "the judicial function and judicial competence," however, to determine whether appellee or the Government has the proper interpretation of the Amish faith; "[c]ourts are not arbiters of scriptural interpretation." *Thomas v. Review Bd. of Indiana Employment Security Div.*, 450 U.S. 707, 716 (1981). We therefore accept appellee's contention that both payment and receipt of social security benefits is forbidden by the Amish faith. Because the payment of the taxes or receipt of benefits violates Amish religious beliefs, compulsory participation in the social security system interferes with their free exercise rights.

The conclusion that there is a conflict between the Amish faith and the obligations imposed by the social security system is only the beginning, however, and not the end of the inquiry. Not all burdens on religion are unconstitutional.

The state may justify a limitation on religious liberty by showing that it is essential to accomplish an overriding governmental interest.

B

Because the social security system is nationwide, the governmental interest is apparent. The social security system in the United States serves the public interest by providing a comprehensive insurance system with a variety of benefits available to all participants, with costs shared by employers and employees. The social security system is by far the largest domestic governmental program in the United States today, distributing approximately $11 billion monthly to 36 million Americans. The design of the system requires support by mandatory contributions from covered employers and employees. This mandatory participation is indispensable to the fiscal vitality of the social security system. "[W]idespread individual voluntary coverage under social security . . . would undermine the soundness of the social security program." S. Rep. No. 404, 89th Cong., 1st Sess., pt. 1, p. 116 (1965). Moreover, a comprehensive national social security system providing for voluntary participation would be almost a contradiction in terms and difficult, if not impossible, to administer. Thus, the Government's interest in assuring mandatory and continuous participation in and contribution to the social security system is very high.

C

The remaining inquiry is whether accommodating the Amish belief will unduly interfere with fulfillment of the governmental interest. In *Braunfeld v. Brown*, 366 U.S. 599, 605 (1961), this Court noted that "to make accommodation between the religious action and an exercise of state authority is a particularly delicate task . . . because resolution in favor of the State results in the choice to the individual of either abandoning his religious principle or facing . . . prosecution." The difficulty in attempting to accommodate religious beliefs in the area of taxation is that "we are a cosmopolitan nation made up of people of almost every conceivable religious preference." *Braunfeld, supra,* at 606. The Court has long recognized that balance must be struck between the values of the comprehensive social security system, which rests on a complex of actuarial factors, and the consequences of allowing religiously based exemptions. To maintain an organized society that guarantees religious freedom to a great variety of faiths requires that some religious practices yield to the common good. Religious beliefs can be accommodated, but there is a point at which accommodation would "radically restrict the operating latitude of the legislature." *Braunfeld, supra,* at 606.

Unlike the situation presented in *Wisconsin v. Yoder, supra,* it would be difficult to accommodate the comprehensive social security system with myriad exceptions flowing from a wide variety of religious beliefs. The obligation to pay the social security tax initially is not fundamentally different from the obligation to pay income taxes; the difference — in theory at least — is that the social security tax revenues are segregated for use only in furtherance of the statutory program. There is no principled way, however, for purposes of this case, to distinguish between general taxes and those imposed under the Social Security Act. If, for example, a religious adherent believes war is a sin, and if a certain percentage of the federal budget can be identified as devoted to war-related activities, such individuals would have a similarly valid claim to be exempt from paying that percentage of the income tax. The tax system could not function if denominations were allowed to challenge the tax system because tax payments were spent in a manner that violates their religious belief. Because the broad public interest in maintaining a sound tax system is of such a high order, religious belief in conflict with the payment of taxes affords no basis for resisting the tax.

III

Congress has accommodated, to the extent compatible with a comprehensive national program, the practices of those who believe it a violation of their faith to participate in the social security system. In § 1402(g) Congress granted an exemption, on religious grounds, to self-employed Amish and others. Confining the § 1402(g) exemption to the self-employed provided for a narrow category which was readily identifiable. Self-employed persons in a religious community having its own "welfare" system are distinguishable from the generality of wage earners employed by others.

Congress and the courts have been sensitive to the needs flowing from the Free Exercise Clause, but every person cannot be shielded from all the burdens incident to exercising every aspect of the right to practice religious beliefs. When followers of a particular sect enter into commercial activity as a matter of choice, the limits they accept on their own conduct as a matter of conscience and faith are not to be superimposed on the statutory schemes which are binding on others in that activity. Granting an exemption from social security taxes to an employer operates to impose the employer's religious faith on the employees. Congress drew a line in § 1402(g), exempting the self-employed Amish but not all persons working for an Amish employer. The tax imposed on employers to support the social security system must be uniformly applicable to all, except as Congress provides explicitly otherwise.

BOB JONES UNIVERSITY v. UNITED STATES
461 U.S. 574 (1983)

CHIEF JUSTICE BURGER delivered the opinion of the Court.

I

A

Until 1970, the Internal Revenue Service granted tax-exempt status to private schools, without regard to their racial admissions policies, under § 501(c)(3) of the Internal Revenue Code, and granted charitable deductions for contributions to such schools under § 170 of the Code.

On January 12, 1970, a three-judge District Court for the District of Columbia issued a preliminary injunction prohibiting the IRS from according tax-exempt status to private schools in Mississippi that discriminated as to admissions on the basis of race. Thereafter, in July 1970, the IRS concluded that it could "no longer legally justify allowing tax-exempt status [under § 501(c)(3)] to private schools which practice racial discrimination." At the same time, the IRS announced that it could not "treat gifts to such schools as charitable deductions for income tax purposes [under § 170]." By letter dated November 30, 1970, the IRS formally notified private schools, including those involved in this case, of this change in policy, "applicable to all private schools in the United States at all levels of education."

The revised policy on discrimination was formalized in Revenue Ruling 71-447:

> "Both the courts and the Internal Revenue Service have long recognized that the statutory requirement of being 'organized and operated exclusively for religious, charitable, . . . or educational purposes' was intended to express the basic common law concept [of 'charity']. . . . All charitable trusts, educational or otherwise, are subject to the requirement that the purpose of the trust may not be illegal or contrary to public policy."

Based on the "national policy to discourage racial discrimination in education," the IRS ruled that "a [private] school not having a racially nondiscriminatory policy as to students is not 'charitable' within the common law concepts reflected in sections 170 and 501(c)(3) of the Code."

B

No. 81-3, Bob Jones University v. United States

Bob Jones University is a nonprofit corporation located in Greenville, South Carolina. Its purpose is "to conduct an institution of learning . . . , giving special emphasis to the Christian religion and the ethics revealed in the Holy Scriptures." The corporation operates a school with an enrollment of approximately 5,000 students, from kindergarten through college and graduate school. Bob Jones University is not affiliated with any religious denomination, but is dedicated to the teaching and propagation of its fundamentalist Christian religious beliefs. It is both a religious and educational institution. Its teachers are required to be devout Christians, and all courses at the University are taught according to the Bible. Entering students are screened as to their religious beliefs, and their public and private conduct is strictly regulated by standards promulgated by University authorities.

The sponsors of the University genuinely believe that the Bible forbids interracial dating and marriage. To effectuate these views, Negroes were completely excluded until 1971. From 1971 to May 1975, the University accepted no applications from unmarried Negroes, but did accept applications from Negroes married within their race.

Following the decision of the United States Court of Appeals for the Fourth Circuit in *McCrary v. Runyon*, 515 F. 2d 1082 (1975), *aff'd* 427 U.S. 160 (1976), prohibiting racial exclusion from private schools, the University revised its policy. Since May 29, 1975, the University has permitted unmarried Negroes to enroll; but a disciplinary rule prohibits interracial dating and marriage. That rule reads:

"There is to be no interracial dating

"1. Students who are partners in an interracial marriage will be expelled.

"2. Students who are members of or affiliated with any group or organization which holds as one of its goals or advocates interracial marriage will be expelled.

"3. Students who date outside their own race will be expelled.

"4. Students who espouse, promote, or encourage others to violate the University's dating rules and regulations will be expelled."

The University continues to deny admission to applicants engaged in an interracial marriage or known to advocate interracial marriage or dating.

Until 1970, the IRS extended tax-exempt status to Bob Jones University under § 501(c)(3). By the letter of November 30, 1970, that followed the injunction issued in *Green v. Kennedy*, 309 F. Supp. 1127 (DC 1970), the IRS formally notified the University of the change in IRS policy, and announced its intention to challenge the tax-exempt status of private schools practicing racial discrimination in their admissions policies.

Thereafter, on April 16, 1975, the IRS notified the University of the proposed revocation of its tax-exempt status. On January 19, 1976, the IRS officially revoked the University's tax-exempt status, effective as of December 1, 1970, the day after the University was formally notified of the change in IRS policy. The University subsequently filed returns under the Federal Unemployment Tax Act for the period from December 1, 1970, to December 31, 1975, and paid a tax totaling $21.00 on one employee for the calendar year of 1975. After its request for a refund was denied, the University instituted the present action, seeking to recover the $21.00 it had paid to the IRS. The Government counterclaimed for unpaid federal unemployment taxes for the taxable years 1971 through 1975, in the amount of $489,675.59, plus interest.

III

Petitioners contend that, even if the Commissioner's policy is valid as to nonreligious private schools, that policy cannot constitutionally be applied to schools that engage in racial discrimination on the basis of sincerely held religious beliefs.[28] As to such schools, it is argued that the IRS construction of

---

[28] The District Court found, on the basis of a full evidentiary record, that the challenged practices of petitioner Bob Jones University were based on a genuine belief that the Bible forbids

§ 170 and § 501(c)(3) violates their free exercise rights under the Religion Clauses of the First Amendment. This contention presents claims not heretofore considered by this Court in precisely this context.

This Court has long held the Free Exercise Clause of the First Amendment an absolute prohibition against governmental regulation of religious beliefs. As interpreted by this Court, moreover, the Free Exercise Clause provides substantial protection for lawful conduct grounded in religious belief. However, "[n]ot all burdens on religion are unconstitutional. . . . The state may justify a limitation on religious liberty by showing that it is essential to accomplish an overriding governmental interest." *United States v. Lee.*

On occasion this Court has found certain governmental interests so compelling as to allow even regulations prohibiting religiously based conduct. In *Prince v. Massachusetts*, 321 U.S. 158 (1944), for example, the Court held that neutrally cast child labor laws prohibiting sale of printed materials on public streets could be applied to prohibit children from dispensing religious literature. The Court found no constitutional infirmity in "excluding [Jehovah's Witness children] from doing there what no other children may do." *Id.,* at 170. *See also Reynolds v. United States; United States v. Lee; Gillette v. United States.* Denial of tax benefits will inevitably have a substantial impact on the operation of private religious schools, but will not prevent those schools from observing their religious tenets.

The governmental interest at stake here is compelling. As discussed in Part II-B, *supra,* the Government has a fundamental, overriding interest in eradicating racial discrimination in education[29] — discrimination that prevailed, with official approval, for the first 165 years of this Nation's constitutional history. That governmental interest substantially outweighs whatever burden denial of tax benefits places on petitioners' exercise of their religious beliefs. The interests asserted by petitioners cannot be accommodated with that compelling governmental interest, see *United States v. Lee;* and no "less restrictive means," see *Thomas v. Review Board of Indiana Employment Security Div., supra,* 450 U.S., at 718, are available to achieve the governmental interest.[30]

---

interracial dating and marriage. 468 F. Supp., at 894. We assume, as did the District Court, that the same is true with respect to petitioner Goldsboro Christian Schools. *See* 436 F. Supp., at 1317.

[29] We deal here only with religious *schools* — not with churches or other purely religious institutions; here, the governmental interest is in denying public support to racial discrimination in education. As noted earlier, racially discriminatory schools "exer[t] a pervasive influence on the entire educational process," outweighing any public benefit that they might otherwise provide, *Norwood v. Harrison,* 413 U.S. 455, 469 (1973). *See generally* Simon, [*The Tax-Exempt Status of Racially Discriminatory Religious Schools,* 36 TAX L. REV. 477, 485-489 (1981), at] 495-496.

[30] Bob Jones University also contends that denial of tax exemption violates the Establishment Clause by preferring religions whose tenets do not require racial discrimination over those which believe racial intermixing is forbidden. It is well settled that neither a State nor the Federal Government may pass laws which "prefer one religion over another," *Everson v. Board of Education,* but "[i]t is equally true" that a regulation does not violate the Establishment Clause merely because it "happens to coincide or harmonize with the tenets of some or all religions." *McGowan v. Maryland,* 366 U.S. 420, 442 (1961). *See Harris v. McRae,* 448 U.S. 297, 319-320 (1980). The IRS policy at issue

JIMMY SWAGGART MINISTRIES v. BOARD OF EQUALIZATION OF CALIFORNIA

493 U.S. 378 (1990)

JUSTICE O'CONNOR delivered the opinion of the Court.

This case presents the question whether the Religion Clauses of the First Amendment prohibit a State from imposing a generally applicable sales and use tax on the distribution of religious materials by a religious organization.

I

California's Sales and Use Tax Law requires retailers to pay a sales tax "[f]or the privilege of selling tangible personal property at retail." A "sale" includes any transfer of title or possession of tangible personal property for consideration.

The use tax, as a complement to the sales tax, reaches out-of-state purchases by residents of the State. It is "imposed on the storage, use, or other consumption in this state of tangible personal property purchased from any retailer," at the same rate as the sales tax (6 percent). Although the use tax is imposed on the purchaser, it is generally collected by the retailer at the time the sale is made. Neither the State Constitution nor the State Sales and Use Tax Law exempts religious organizations from the sales and use tax, apart from a limited exemption for the serving of meals by religious organizations.

During the tax period in question (1974 to 1981), appellant Jimmy Swaggart Ministries was a religious organization incorporated as a Louisiana nonprofit corporation and recognized as such by the Internal Revenue Service pursuant to § 501(c)(3) of the Internal Revenue Code of 1954, and by the California State Controller pursuant to the Inheritance Tax and Gift Tax Laws of the State of California. Appellant's constitution and bylaws provide that it "is called for the purpose of establishing and maintaining an evangelistic outreach for the worship of Almighty God." This outreach is to be performed "by all available means, both at home and in foreign lands," and

> "shall specifically include evangelistic crusades; missionary endeavors; radio broadcasting (as owner, broadcaster, and placement agency); television broadcasting (both as owner and broadcaster); and audio production and reproduction of music; audio production and reproduction of preaching; audio production and reproduction of teaching; writing,

---

here is founded on a "neutral, secular basis," *Gillette v. United States*, 401 U.S. 437, 452 (1971), and does not violate the Establishment Clause. *See generally* U.S. Comm'n on Civil Rights, Discriminatory Religious Schools and Tax Exempt Status 10-17 (1982). In addition, as the Court of Appeals noted, "the uniform application of the rule to all religiously operated schools *avoids* the necessity for a potentially entangling inquiry into whether a racially restrictive practice is the result of sincere religious belief." [*United States v. Bob Jones Univ.*], 639 F.2d 147, 155 (4th Cir. 1980) (emphasis in original). *Cf. NLRB v. Catholic Bishop of Chicago*, 440 U.S. 490 (1979). *But see generally* Note, 90 YALE L.J. 350 (1980).

printing and publishing; and, any and all other individual or mass media methods that presently exist or may be devised in the future to proclaim the good news of Jesus Christ."

From 1974 to 1981, appellant conducted numerous "evangelistic crusades" in auditoriums and arenas across the country in cooperation with local churches. During this period, appellant held 23 crusades in California — each lasting 1 to 3 days, with one crusade lasting 6 days — for a total of 52 days. At the crusades, appellant conducted religious services that included preaching and singing. Some of these services were recorded for later sale or broadcast. Appellant also sold religious books, tapes, records, and other religious and nonreligious merchandise at the crusades.

Appellant also published a monthly magazine, "The Evangelist," which was sold nationwide by subscription. The magazine contained articles of a religious nature as well as advertisements for appellant's religious books, tapes, and records. The magazine included an order form listing the various items for sale in the particular issue and their unit price, with spaces for purchasers to fill in the quantity desired and the total price. Appellant also offered its items for sale through radio, television, and cable television broadcasts, including broadcasts through local California stations.

In 1980, appellee Board of Equalization of the State of California (Board) informed appellant that religious materials were not exempt from the sales tax and requested appellant to register as a seller to facilitate reporting and payment of the tax. Appellant responded that it was exempt from such taxes under the First Amendment. In 1981, the Board audited appellant and advised appellant that it should register as a seller and report and pay sales tax on all sales made at its California crusades. The Board also opined that appellant had a sufficient nexus with the State of California to require appellant to collect and report use tax on its mail-order sales to California purchasers.

Based on the Board's review of appellant's records, the parties stipulated "that [appellant] sold for use in California tangible personal property for the period April 1, 1974, through December 31, 1981, measured by payment to [appellant] of $1,702,942.00 for mail order sales from Baton Rouge, Louisiana and $240,560.00 for crusade merchandise sales in California." These figures represented the sales and use in California of merchandise with specific religious content — Bibles, Bible study manuals, printed sermons and collections of sermons, audiocassette tapes of sermons, religious books and pamphlets, and religious music in the form of songbooks, tapes, and records. Based on the sales figures for appellant's religious materials, the Board notified appellant that it owed sales and use taxes of $118,294.54, plus interest of $36,021.11, and a penalty of $11,829.45, for a total amount due of $166,145.10. Appellant did not contest the Board's assessment of tax liability for the sale and use of certain nonreligious merchandise, including such items as "T-shirts with JSM logo, mugs, bowls, plates, replicas of crown of thorns, ark of the covenant, Roman coin, candlesticks, Bible stand, pen and pencil sets, prints of religious scenes, bud vase, and communion cups."

Appellant filed a petition for redetermination with the Board, reiterating its view that the tax on religious materials violated the First Amendment. Following a hearing and an appeal to the Board, the Board deleted the penalty but otherwise redetermined the matter without adjustment in the amount of $118,294.54 in taxes owing, plus $65,043.55 in interest. Pursuant to state procedural law, appellant paid the amount and filed a petition for redetermination and refund with the Board. The Board denied appellant's petition, and appellant brought suit in state court, seeking a refund of the tax paid.

The trial court entered judgment for the Board, ruling that appellant was not entitled to a refund of any tax. The California Court of Appeal affirmed, and the California Supreme Court denied discretionary review. We noted probable jurisdiction and now affirm.

II

Appellant relies almost exclusively on our decisions in *Murdock v. Pennsylvania*, 319 U.S. 105 (1943), and *Follett v. McCormick*, 321 U.S. 573, 576 (1944), for the proposition that a State may not impose a sales or use tax on the evangelical distribution of religious material by a religious organization. Appellant contends that the State's imposition of use and sales tax liability on it burdens its evangelical distribution of religious materials in a manner identical to the manner in which the evangelists in *Murdock* and *Follett* were burdened.

We reject appellant's expansive reading of *Murdock* and *Follett* as contrary to the decisions themselves. In *Murdock*, we considered the constitutionality of a city ordinance requiring all persons canvassing or soliciting within the city to procure a license by paying a flat fee. Reversing the convictions of Jehovah's Witnesses convicted under the ordinance of soliciting and distributing religious literature without a license, we explained:

> "The hand distribution of religious tracts is an age-old form of missionary evangelism . . . [and] has been a potent force in various religious movements down through the years. This form of evangelism is utilized today on a large scale by various religious sects whose colporteurs carry the Gospel to thousands upon thousands of homes and seek through personal visitations to win adherents to their faith. It is more than preaching; it is more than distribution of religious literature. It is a combination of both. Its purpose is as evangelical as the revival meeting. This form of religious activity occupies the same high estate under the First Amendment as do worship in the churches and preaching in the pulpits." 319 U.S., at 108-109 (footnotes omitted).

Accordingly, we held that "spreading one's religious beliefs or preaching the Gospel through distribution of religious literature and through personal visitations is an age-old type of evangelism with as high a claim to constitutional protection as the more orthodox types."

We extended *Murdock* the following Term by invalidating, as applied to "one who earns his livelihood as an evangelist or preacher in his home town," an ordinance (similar to that involved in *Murdock*) that required all booksellers to pay a flat fee to procure a license to sell books. *Follett v. McCormick*, 321 U.S., at 576. Reaffirming our observation in *Murdock* that "'the power to tax the exercise of a privilege is the power to control or suppress its enjoyment,'" we reasoned that "[t]he protection of the First Amendment is not restricted to orthodox religious practices any more than it is to the expression of orthodox economic views. He who makes a profession of evangelism is not in a less preferred position than the casual worker."

Our decisions in these cases, however, resulted from the particular nature of the challenged taxes — flat license taxes that operated as a prior restraint on the exercise of religious liberty. In *Murdock*, for instance, we emphasized that the tax at issue was "a license tax — a flat tax imposed on the exercise of a privilege granted by the Bill of Rights," and cautioned that "[w]e do not mean to say that religious groups and the press are free from all financial burdens of government. . . . We have here something quite different, for example, from a tax on the income of one who engages in religious activities or a tax on property used or employed in connection with those activities." In *Follett*, we reiterated that a preacher is not "free from all financial burdens of government, including taxes on income or property" and, "like other citizens, may be subject to *general* taxation."

Significantly, we noted in both cases that a primary vice of the ordinances at issue was that they operated as prior restraints of constitutionally protected conduct:

> "In all of these cases [in which license taxes have been invalidated] the issuance of the permit or license is dependent on the payment of a license tax. And the license tax is fixed in amount and unrelated to the scope of the activities of petitioners or to their realized revenues. It is not a nominal fee imposed as a regulatory measure to defray the expenses of policing the activities in question. It is in no way apportioned. It is a flat license tax levied and collected as a condition to the pursuit of activities whose enjoyment is guaranteed by the First Amendment. Accordingly, *it restrains in advance those constitutional liberties of press and religion and inevitably tends to suppress their exercise.* That is almost uniformly recognized as the inherent vice and evil of this flat license tax." *Murdock, supra*, 319 U.S., at 113-114.

See also Follett, supra, 321 U.S., at 577 ("The exaction of a tax as a condition to the exercise of the great liberties guaranteed by the First Amendment is as obnoxious as the imposition of a censorship or a previous restraint") (citations omitted). Thus, although *Murdock* and *Follett* establish that appellant's form of religious exercise has "as high a claim to constitutional protection as the more orthodox types," *Murdock, supra*, 319 U.S., at 110, those cases are of no further help to appellant. Our concern in *Murdock* and *Follett* — that a flat license tax would act as a *precondition* to the free exercise of religious beliefs — is simply not present where a tax applies to all sales and uses of tangible personal property in the State.

We also note that just last Term a plurality of the Court rejected the precise argument appellant now makes. In *Texas Monthly, Inc. v. Bullock*, JUSTICE BRENNAN, writing for three Justices, held that a state sales tax exemption for religious publications violated the Establishment Clause. In so concluding, the plurality further held that the Free Exercise Clause did not prevent the State from withdrawing its exemption, noting that "[t]o the extent that our opinions in *Murdock* and *Follett* might be read . . . to suggest that the States and the Federal Government may never tax the sale of religious or other publications, we reject those dicta." JUSTICE WHITE, concurring in the judgment, concluded that the exemption violated the Free Press Clause because the content of a publication determined its tax-exempt status. JUSTICE BLACKMUN, joined by JUSTICE O'CONNOR, concurred in the plurality's holding that the tax exemption at issue in that case contravened the Establishment Clause, but reserved the question whether "the Free Exercise Clause requires a tax exemption for the sale of religious literature by a religious organization; in other words, defining the ultimate scope of *Follett* and *Murdock* may be left for another day." In this case, of course, California has not chosen to create a tax exemption for religious materials, and we therefore have no need to revisit the Establishment Clause question presented in *Texas Monthly*.

We do, however, decide the free exercise question left open by JUSTICE BLACKMUN's concurrence in *Texas Monthly* by limiting *Murdock* and *Follett* to apply only where a flat license tax operates as a prior restraint on the free exercise of religious beliefs. As such, *Murdock* and *Follett* plainly do not support appellant's free exercise claim. California's generally applicable sales and use tax is not a flat tax, represents only a small fraction of any retail sale, and applies neutrally to all retail sales of tangible personal property made in California. California imposes its sales and use tax even if the seller or the purchaser is charitable, religious, nonprofit, or state or local governmental in nature. Thus, the sales and use tax is not a tax on the right to disseminate religious information, ideas, or beliefs *per se*; rather, it is a tax on the privilege of making retail sales of tangible personal property and on the storage, use, or other consumption of tangible personal property in California. For example, California treats the sale of a Bible by a religious organization just as it would treat the sale of a Bible by a bookstore; as long as both are in-state retail sales of tangible personal property, they are both subject to the tax regardless of the motivation for the sale or the purchase. There is no danger that appellant's religious activity is being singled out for special and burdensome treatment.

Moreover, our concern in *Murdock* and *Follett* that flat license taxes operate as a precondition to the exercise of evangelistic activity is not present in this case, because the registration requirement, and the tax itself do not act as prior restraints — no fee is charged for registering, the tax is due regardless of preregistration, and the tax is not imposed as a precondition of disseminating the message. Thus, unlike the license tax in *Murdock*, which was "in no way apportioned" to the "realized revenues" of the itinerant preachers forced to pay the tax, the tax at issue in this case is akin to a generally applicable income or property tax, which *Murdock* and *Follett* specifically state may constitutionally be imposed on religious activity.

There is no evidence in this case that collection and payment of the tax violates appellant's sincere religious beliefs. California's nondiscriminatory Sales and Use Tax Law requires only that appellant collect the tax from its California purchasers and remit the tax money to the State. The only burden on appellant is the claimed reduction in income resulting from the presumably lower demand for appellant's wares (caused by the marginally higher price) and from the costs associated with administering the tax. [T]o the extent that imposition of a generally applicable tax merely decreases the amount of money appellant has to spend on its religious activities, any such burden is not constitutionally significant.

At bottom, though we do not doubt the economic cost to appellant of complying with a generally applicable sales and use tax, such a tax is no different from other generally applicable laws and regulations — such as health and safety regulations — to which appellant must adhere.

We therefore conclude that the collection and payment of the generally applicable tax in this case imposes no constitutionally significant burden on appellant's religious practices or beliefs. The Free Exercise Clause accordingly does not *require* the State to grant appellant an exemption from its generally applicable sales and use tax. Although it is of course possible to imagine that a more onerous tax rate, even if generally applicable, might effectively choke off an adherent's religious practices, we face no such situation in this case. Accordingly, we intimate no views as to whether such a generally applicable tax might violate the Free Exercise Clause.

BOWEN v. ROY
476 U.S. 693 (1986)

Chief Justice Burger announced the judgment of the Court and delivered the opinion of the Court with respect to Parts I and II, and an opinion with respect to Part III, in which Justice Powell and Justice Rehnquist join.

The question presented is whether the Free Exercise Clause of the First amendment compels the Government to accommodate a religiously based objection to the statutory requirements that a Social Security number be provided by an applicant seeking to receive certain welfare benefits and that the States use these numbers in administering the benefit programs.

I

Appellees Stephen J. Roy and Karen Miller applied for and received benefits under the Aid to Families with Dependent Children program and the Food Stamp program. They refused to comply, however, with the requirement that participants in these programs furnish their state welfare agencies with the Social Security numbers of the members of their household as a condition of receiving benefits. Appellees contended that obtaining a Social Security number for their 2-year-old daughter, Little Bird of the Snow, would violate their Native American religious beliefs. The Pennsylvania Department of Public Welfare thereafter terminated AFDC and medical benefits payable to appellees on the child's behalf and instituted proceedings to reduce the level of food stamps that appellees' household was receiving. Appellees then filed this action against the Secretary of the Pennsylvania Department of Public Welfare, the Secretary of Health and Human Services, and the Secretary of Agriculture, arguing that the Free Exercise Clause entitled them to an exemption from the Social Security number requirement. In their complaint, appellees stated that "[t]he sole basis" for the denial of welfare benefits was "Mr. Roy's refusal to obtain a Social Security Number for Little Bird of the Snow," and thus requested injunctive relief, damages, and benefits. In the statement of "undisputed facts," the parties agreed that Little Bird of the Snow did not have a Social Security number.

At trial, Roy testified that he had recently developed a religious objection to obtaining a Social Security number for Little Bird of the Snow.[2] Roy is a Native American descended from the Abenaki Tribe, and he asserts a religious belief that control over one's life is essential to spiritual purity and indispensable to "becoming a holy person." Based on recent conversations with an Abenaki chief, Roy believes that technology is "robbing the spirit of man." In order to prepare his daughter for greater spiritual power, therefore, Roy testified to his belief that he must keep her person and spirit unique and that the uniqueness of the Social Security number as an identifier, coupled with the other uses of the number over which she has no control, will serve to "rob the spirit" of his daughter and prevent her from attaining greater spiritual power.

For purposes of determining the breadth of Roy's religious concerns, the trial judge raised the possibility of using the phonetics of his daughter's name to derive a Social Security number. Although Roy saw "a lot of good" in this suggestion, he stated it would violate his religious beliefs because the special number still would apply uniquely and identify her. Roy also testified that his religious objection would not be satisfied even if the Social Security Administration appended the daughter's full tribal name to her Social Security number.

---

[2] Roy and Miller both have Social Security numbers. They also obtained a Social Security number for their 5-year-old daughter Renee at some time prior to the present dispute.

In Roy's own testimony, he emphasized the evil that would flow simply from *obtaining* a number.[3] On the last day of trial, however, a federal officer inquired whether Little Bird of the Snow already had a Social Security number; he learned that a number had been assigned — under first name "Little," middle name "Bird of the Snow," and last name "Roy."

The Government at this point suggested that the case had become moot because, under Roy's beliefs, Little Bird of the Snow's spirit had already been "robbed." Roy, however, was recalled to the stand and testified that her spirit would be robbed only by "use" of the number. Since no known use of the number had yet been made, Roy expressed his belief that her spirit had not been damaged. The District Court concluded that the case was not moot because of Roy's beliefs regarding "use" of the number. *See Roy v. Cohen*, 590 F. Supp. 600, 605 (MD Pa. 1984) (finding of fact 33) ("Roy believes that the establishment of a social security number for Little Bird of the Snow, without more, has not 'robbed her spirit,' but widespread use of the social security number by the federal or state governments in their computer systems would have that effect").

After hearing all of the testimony, the District Court denied appellees' request for damages and benefits, but granted injunctive relief. Based on the testimony of the Government's experts and the obvious fact that many people share certain names, the District Court found that "[u]tilization in the computer system of the name of a benefit recipient alone frequently is not sufficient to ensure the proper payment of benefits." The court nevertheless concluded that the public "interest in maintaining an efficient and fraud resistant system can be met without requiring use of a social security number for Little Bird of the Snow," elaborating:

> "It appears to the Court that the harm that the Government might suffer if [appellees] prevailed in this case would be, at worst, that one or perhaps a few individuals could fraudulently obtain welfare benefits. Such a result would obtain only if (1) Little Bird of the Snow attempted fraudulently to obtain welfare benefits or someone else attempted fraudulently to obtain such benefits using Little Bird of the Snow's name *and* (2) identification procedures available to the Defendants that do not require utilization of a social security number failed to expose the fraud. This possibility appears to the Court to be remote."

---

[3] "[Q.] Mr. Roy, could you explain why obtaining a Social Security Number for Little Bird of the Snow would be contrary to your religious beliefs as a native Abenaki?

"A. Yes. Because we felt that this number would be used to rob her of her ability to have greater power in that this number is a unique number. It serves unique purposes. It's applied to her and only her; and being applied to her, that's what offends us, and we try to keep her person unique, and we try to keep her spirit unique, and we're scared that if we were to use this number, she would lose control of that and she would have no ability to protect herself from any evil that that number might be used against her."

Citing our decision in *United States v. Lee*, the court entered an injunction containing two basic components. *First*, the Secretary of Health and Human Services was "permanently restrained from making any use of the social security number which was issued in the name of Little Bird of the Snow Roy and from disseminating the number to any agency, individual, business entity, or any other third party." *Second*, the federal and state defendants were enjoined until Little Bird of the Snow's 16th birthday from denying Roy cash assistance, medical assistance, and food stamps "because of the [appellees'] refusal to provide a social security number for her."

We noted probable jurisdiction, and we vacate and remand.

II

Appellees raise a constitutional challenge to two features of the statutory scheme here. They object to Congress' requirement that a state AFDC plan "*must* . . . provide (A) that, *as a condition of eligibility* under the plan, *each* applicant for or recipient of aid shall furnish to the State agency his social security account number." They also object to Congress' requirement that "such State agency *shall utilize* such account numbers . . . in the administration of such plan." We analyze each of these contentions, turning to the latter contention first.

Our cases have long recognized a distinction between the freedom of individual belief, which is absolute, and the freedom of individual conduct, which is not absolute. This case implicates only the latter concern. Roy objects to the statutory requirement that state agencies "shall utilize" Social Security numbers not because it places any restriction on what he may believe or what he may do, but because he believes the use of the number may harm his daughter's spirit.

Never to our knowledge has the Court interpreted the First Amendment to require the Government *itself* to behave in ways that the individual believes will further his or her spiritual development or that of his or her family. The Free Exercise Clause simply cannot be understood to require the Government to conduct its own internal affairs in ways that comport with the religious beliefs of particular citizens. Just as the Government may not insist that appellees engage in any set form of religious observance, so appellees may not demand that the Government join in their chosen religious practices by refraining from using a number to identify their daughter. "[T]he Free Exercise Clause is written in terms of what the government cannot do to the individual, not in terms of what the individual can extract from the government." *Sherbert v. Verner*.

As a result, Roy may no more prevail on his religious objection to the Government's use of a Social Security number for his daughter than he could on a sincere religious objection to the size or color of the Government's filing cabinets. The Free Exercise Clause affords an individual protection from certain forms of governmental compulsion; it does not afford an individual a right to dictate the conduct of the Government's internal procedures.

The Federal Government's use of a Social Security number for Little Bird of the Snow does not itself in any degree impair Roy's "freedom to believe, express, and exercise" his religion. Consequently, appellees' objection to the statutory requirement that each state agency "shall utilize" a Social Security number in the administration of its plan is without merit. It follows that their request for an injunction against use of the Social Security number in processing benefit applications should have been rejected. We therefore hold that the portion of the District Court's injunction that permanently restrained the Secretary from making any use of the Social Security number that had been issued in the name of Little Bird of the Snow Roy must be vacated.

III

Roy also challenges Congress' requirement that a state AFDC plan *"must . . . provide (A) that, as a condition of eligibility* under the plan, *each* applicant for or recipient of aid *shall furnish* to the State agency his social security account number."* The First Amendment's guarantee that "Congress shall make no law . . . prohibiting the free exercise" of religion holds an important place in our scheme of ordered liberty, but the Court has steadfastly maintained that claims of religious conviction do not automatically entitle a person to fix unilaterally the conditions and terms of dealings with the Government. Not all burdens on religion are unconstitutional. *See Reynolds v. United States.* This was treated recently in *United States v. Lee:*

> "To maintain an organized society that guarantees religious freedom to a great variety of faiths requires that some religious practices yield to the common good. Religious beliefs can be accommodated, but there is a point at which accommodation would 'radically restrict the operating latitude of the legislature.'"

The statutory requirement that applicants provide a Social Security number is wholly neutral in religious terms and uniformly applicable. There is no claim that there is any attempt by Congress to discriminate invidiously or any covert suppression of particular religious beliefs. The administrative requirement does not create any danger of censorship or place a direct condition or burden on the dissemination of religious views. It does not intrude on the organization of a religious institution or school. It may indeed confront some applicants for benefits with choices, but in no sense does it affirmatively compel appellees, by threat of sanctions, to refrain from religiously motivated conduct or to engage in conduct that they find objectionable for religious reasons. Rather, it is appellees who seek benefits from the Government and who assert that, because of certain religious beliefs, they should be excused from compliance with a condition that is binding on all other persons who seek the same benefits from the Government.

This is far removed from the historical instances of religious persecution and intolerance that gave concern to those who drafted the Free Exercise Clause of the First Amendment. *See generally* M. MALBIN, RELIGION AND POLITICS: THE

INTENTIONS OF THE AUTHORS OF THE FIRST AMENDMENT (1978). We are not unmindful of the importance of many government benefits today or of the value of sincerely held religious beliefs. However, while we do not believe that no government compulsion is involved, we cannot ignore the reality that denial of such benefits by a uniformly applicable statute neutral on its face is of a wholly different, less intrusive nature than affirmative compulsion or prohibition, by threat of penal sanctions, for conduct that has religious implications.

This distinction is clearly revealed in the Court's opinions. Decisions rejecting religiously based challenges have often recited the fact that a mere denial of a governmental benefit by a uniformly applicable statute does not constitute infringement of religious liberty. In *Hamilton v. Regents of University of California*, 293 U.S. 245 (1934), for example, the Court rejected a religious challenge by students to military courses required as part of their curriculum, explaining:

> "The fact that they are able to pay their way in this university but not in any other institution in California is without significance upon any constitutional or other question here involved. California has not drafted or called them to attend the university. They are seeking education offered by the State and at the same time insisting that they be excluded from the prescribed course solely upon grounds of their religious beliefs and conscientious objections to war. . . ."

In cases upholding First Amendment challenges, on the other hand, the Court has often relied on the showing that compulsion of certain activity with religious significance was involved. In *West Virginia Bd. of Ed. v. Barnette*, for example, the Court distinguished the earlier Hamilton holding and upheld a challenge to a flag salute requirement:

> "Here . . . we are dealing with a compulsion of students to declare a belief. . . . This issue is not prejudiced by the Court's previous holding that where a State, without compelling attendance, extends college facilities to pupils who voluntarily enroll, it may prescribe military training as part of the course without offense to the Constitution. It was held that those who take advantage of its opportunities may not on ground of conscience refuse compliance with such conditions. In the present case attendance is not optional."

The distinction between governmental compulsion and conditions relating to governmental benefits contained in these two cases was emphasized by JUSTICE BRENNAN in his concurring opinion in *Abington School District v. Schempp*:

> "The different results of [*Hamilton* and *Barnette*] are attributable only in part to a difference in the strength of the particular state interests which the respective statutes were designed to serve. Far more significant is the fact that *Hamilton* dealt with the voluntary attendance at college of young adults, while *Barnette* involved the compelled attendance of young children at elementary and secondary schools. This distinction warrants a difference in constitutional results."

We have repeatedly emphasized this distinction: In rejecting a Free Exercise challenge in *Bob Jones University v. United States*, for example, we observed that the "[d]enial of tax benefits will inevitably have a substantial impact on the operation of private religious schools, but will not prevent those schools from observing their religious tenets."

We conclude then that government regulation that indirectly and incidentally calls for a choice between securing a governmental benefit and adherence to religious beliefs is wholly different from governmental action or legislation that criminalizes religiously inspired activity or inescapably compels conduct that some find objectionable for religious reasons. Although the denial of government benefits over religious objection can raise serious Free Exercise problems, these two very different forms of government action are not governed by the same constitutional standard. A governmental burden on religious liberty is not insulated from review simply because it is indirect, but the nature of the burden is relevant to the standard the government must meet to justify the burden.

The general governmental interests involved here buttress this conclusion. Governments today grant a broad range of benefits; inescapably at the same time the administration of complex programs requires certain conditions and restrictions. Although in some situations a mechanism for individual consideration will be created, a policy decision by a government that it wishes to treat all applicants alike and that it does not wish to become involved in case-by-case inquiries into the genuineness of each religious objection to such condition or restrictions is entitled to substantial deference. Moreover, legitimate interests are implicated in the need to avoid any appearance of favoring religious over nonreligious applicants.

The test applied in cases like *Wisconsin v. Yoder*, is not appropriate in this setting. In the enforcement of a facially neutral and uniformly applicable requirement for the administration of welfare programs reaching many millions of people, the Government is entitled to wide latitude. The Government should not be put to the strict test applied by the District Court; that standard required the Government to justify enforcement of the use of Social Security number requirement as the least restrictive means of accomplishing a compelling state interest.[17] Absent proof of an intent to discriminate against particular religious beliefs or against religion in general, the Government meets its burden when it demonstrates that a challenged requirement for governmental benefits, neutral

---

[17] It is readily apparent that virtually *every* action that the Government takes, no matter how innocuous it might appear, is potentially susceptible to a Free Exercise objection. For example, someone might raise a religious objection, based on Norse mythology, to filing a tax return on a Wednesday (Woden's day). Accordingly, if the dissent's interpretation of the Free Exercise Clause is to be taken seriously, then the Government will be unable to enforce any generally applicable rule unless it can satisfy a federal court that it has a "compelling government interest." While libertarians and anarchists will no doubt applaud this result, it is hard to imagine that this is what the Framers intended.

and uniform in its application, is a reasonable means of promoting a legitimate public interest.

Here there is nothing whatever suggesting antagonism by Congress towards religion generally or towards any particular religious beliefs. The requirement that applicants provide a Social Security number is facially neutral and applies to all applicants for the benefits involved. Congress has made no provision for individual exemptions to the requirement in the two statutes in question. Indeed, to the contrary, Congress has specified that a state AFDC plan "*must . . .* provide (A) that, *as a condition of eligibility* under the plan, *each* applicant for or recipient of aid *shall* furnish to the State agency his social security account number," and that "[s]tate agencies *shall* (1) *require, as a condition of eligibility* for participation in the food stamp program, that *each* household member furnish to the State agency their social security account number." Nor are these requirements relics from the past; Congress made the requirement mandatory for the Food Stamp program in 1981. Congress also recently extended to several other aid programs the mandatory requirement that the States use Social Security numbers in verifying eligibility for benefits.

The Social Security number requirement clearly promotes a legitimate and important public interest. No one can doubt that preventing fraud in these benefits programs is an important goal.

We also think it plain that the Social Security number requirement is a reasonable means of promoting that goal. The programs at issue are of truly staggering magnitude. Each year roughly 3.8 million families receive $7.8 billion through federally funded AFDC programs and 20 million persons receive $11 billion in food stamps. The Social Security program itself is the largest domestic governmental program in the United States today, distributing approximately $51 billion monthly to 36 million recipients. Because of the tremendous administrative problems associated with managing programs of this size, the District Court found that

> "Social security numbers are used in making the determination that benefits in the programs are properly paid and that there is no duplication of benefits or failure of payment. . . . Utilization in the computer system of the name of a benefit recipient alone frequently is not sufficient to ensure the proper payment of benefits."

Social Security numbers are unique numerical identifiers and are used pervasively in these programs. The numbers are used, for example, to keep track of persons no longer entitled to receive food stamps because of past fraud or abuses of the program. Moreover, the existence of this unique numerical identifier creates opportunities for ferreting out fraudulent applications through computer "matching" techniques. One investigation, "Project Match," compared federal employee files against AFDC and Medicaid files to determine instances of Government employees receiving welfare benefits improperly. Data from 26 States were examined, and 9,000 individuals were identified as receiving duplicate welfare payments. While undoubtedly some fraud escapes detection in spite of such investigations, the President's Private Sector Survey on Cost Control, known more popularly as the "Grace Commission," recently reported that matching "is the Federal Government's most cost-effective tool for verification or investigation in the prevention and detection of fraud, waste and abuse."

The importance of the Social Security number to these matching techniques is illustrated by the facts of this case. The District Court found that "efficient operation of these [matching] programs requires the use of computer systems that utilize unique numerical identifiers such as the social security number." It further found that exempting even appellees alone from this requirement could result in "one or perhaps a few individuals . . . fraudulently obtain[ing] welfare benefits," a prospect the court termed "remote." The District Court's assessment of this probability seems quite dubious. But in any event, we know of no case obligating the Government to tolerate a slight risk of "one or perhaps a few individuals" fraudulently obtaining benefits in order to satisfy a religious objection to a requirement designed to combat that very risk. Appellees may not use the Free Exercise Clause to demand Government benefits, but only on their own terms, particularly where that insistence works a demonstrable disadvantage to the Government in the administration of the programs.

As the Court has recognized before, given the diversity of beliefs in our pluralistic society and the necessity of providing governments with sufficient operating latitude, some incidental neutral restraints on the free exercise of religion are inescapable. As a matter of legislative policy, a legislature might decide to make religious accommodations to a general and neutral system of awarding benefits, "[b]ut our concern is not with the wisdom of legislation but with its constitutional limitation." *Braunfeld v. Brown*, 366 U.S. 599, 608 (1961) (plurality opinion). We conclude that the Congress' refusal to grant appellees a special exemption does not violate the Free Exercise Clause.

JUSTICE BLACKMUN, concurring in part.

I join only Parts I and II of the opinion written by THE CHIEF JUSTICE.

Since the proceedings on remand might well render unnecessary any discussion of whether appellees constitutionally may be required to provide a social security number for Little Bird of the Snow in order to obtain government assistance on her behalf, that question could be said not to be properly before us. I nonetheless address it, partly because the rest of the Court has seen fit to do so, and partly because I think it is not the kind of difficult constitutional question that we should refrain from deciding except when absolutely necessary. Indeed, for the reasons expressed by JUSTICE O'CONNOR, I think the question requires nothing more than a straightforward application of *Sherbert, Thomas,* and *Wisconsin v. Yoder*. If it proves necessary to reach the issue on remand, I agree with JUSTICE O'CONNOR that, on the facts as determined by the District Court, the Government may not deny assistance to Little Bird of the Snow solely because her parents' religious convictions prevent them from supplying the Government with a social security number for their daughter.

JUSTICE STEVENS, concurring in part and concurring in the result.

As the Court holds in Part II of its opinion, which I join, the first claim must fail because the Free Exercise Clause does not give an individual the right to dictate the Government's method of recordkeeping. The second claim, I submit, is either moot or not ripe for decision.

JUSTICE O'CONNOR, with whom JUSTICE BRENNAN and JUSTICE MARSHALL join, concurring in part and dissenting in part.

I join Parts I and II of THE CHIEF JUSTICE's opinion and I would vacate only a portion of the injunction issued by the District Court.

II

Once it has been shown that a governmental regulation burdens the free exercise of religion, "only those interests of the highest order and those not otherwise served can over-balance legitimate claims to the free exercise of religion." *Wisconsin v. Yoder*. This Court has consistently asked the Government to demonstrate that unbending application of its regulation to the religious objector "is essential to accomplish an overriding governmental interest," *United States v. Lee*, or represents "the least restrictive means of achieving some compelling state interest," *Thomas v. Review Bd., supra*, 450 U.S., at 718. *See also Braunfeld v. Brown*, 366 U.S. 599, 607 (1961); *Sherbert v. Verner*. Only an especially important governmental interest pursued by narrowly tailored means can justify exacting a sacrifice of First Amendment freedoms as the price for an equal share of the rights, benefits, and privileges enjoyed by other citizens.

Granting an exemption to Little Bird of the Snow, and to the handful of others who can be expected to make a similar religious objection to providing the Social Security number in conjunction with the receipt of welfare benefits, will not demonstrably diminish the Government's ability to combat welfare fraud. The District Court found that the governmental appellants had hardly shown that a significant number of other individuals were likely to make a claim similar to that at issue here:

> "There have been four reported cases involving challenges to the social security number requirement for welfare benefits based upon the contention that the number violates sincerely held religious beliefs of the welfare recipient."

The danger that a religious exemption would invite or encourage fraudulent applications seeking to avoid cross-matching performed with the use of Social Security numbers is remote on the facts as found by the District Court: few would-be lawbreakers would risk arousing suspicion by requesting an exemption granted only to a very few. And the sincerity of appellees' religious beliefs is here undisputed. There is therefore no reason to believe that our previous standard for determining whether the Government must accommodate a free exercise claim does not apply.

Here, although prevention of welfare fraud is concededly a compelling interest, the Government asserts only administrative efficiency as its reason for refusing to exempt appellees from furnishing the Social Security number. The District Court found that assertion sorely wanting, and our conclusion that part of the resulting injunction was overbroad only makes the Government's assertion less plausible. Surely the fact that the Court was willing in *Bob Jones University* to give overriding weight to the Government's interest in eradicating the scourge of racial discrimination does not mean that the Court must also give overriding weight to the unanchored anxieties of the welfare bureaucracy.

JUSTICE WHITE, dissenting.

Being of the view that *Thomas v. Review Bd. of Indiana Employment Security Div.*, 450 U.S. 707 (1981), and *Sherbert v. Verner*, control this case, I cannot join the Court's opinion and judgment.

LYNG v. NORTHWEST INDIAN CEMETERY PROTECTIVE ASSOCIATION
485 U.S. 439 (1988)

JUSTICE O'CONNOR delivered the opinion of the Court.

This case requires us to consider whether the First Amendment's Free Exercise Clause prohibits the Government from permitting timber harvesting in, or constructing a road through, a portion of a National Forest that has traditionally been used for religious purposes by members of three American Indian tribes in northwestern California. We conclude that it does not.

I

As part of a project to create a paved 75-mile road linking two California towns, Gasquet and Orleans, the United States Forest Service has upgraded 49 miles of previously unpaved roads on federal land. In order to complete this project (the G-O road), the Forest Service must build a 6-mile paved segment through the Chimney Rock section of the Six Rivers National Forest. That section of the forest is situated between two other portions of the road that are already complete.

In 1977, the Forest Service issued a draft environmental impact statement that discussed proposals for upgrading an existing unpaved road that runs through the Chimney Rock area. In response to comments on the draft statement, the Forest Service commissioned a study of American Indian cultural and religious sites in the area. The Hoopa Valley Indian Reservation adjoins the Six Rivers National Forest, and the Chimney Rock area has historically been used for religious purposes by Yurok, Karok, and Tolowa Indians. The commissioned study, which was completed in 1979, found that the entire area "is significant as an integral and indispensable part of Indian religious conceptualization and practice." Specific sites are used for certain rituals, and "successful use of the [area] is dependent upon and facilitated by certain qualities of the physical environment, the most important of which are privacy, silence, and an undisturbed natural setting." The study concluded that constructing a road along any of the available routes "would cause serious and irreparable damage to the sacred areas which are an integral and necessary part of the belief systems and lifeway of Northwest California Indian peoples." Accordingly, the report recommended that the G-O road not be completed.

In 1982, the Forest Service decided not to adopt this recommendation, and it prepared a final environmental impact statement for construction of the road. The Regional Forester selected a route that avoided archeological sites and was removed as far as possible from the sites used by contemporary Indians for specific spiritual activities. Alternative routes that would have avoided the Chimney Rock area altogether were rejected because they would have required the acquisition of private land, had serious soil stability problems, and would in any event have traversed areas having ritualistic value to American Indians. At about the same time, the Forest Service adopted a management plan allowing for the harvesting of significant amounts of timber in this area of the forest. The management plan provided for one-half mile protective zones around all the religious sites identified in the report that had been commissioned in connection with the G-O road.

III

A

The Free Exercise Clause of the First Amendment provides that "Congress shall make no law . . . prohibiting the free exercise [of religion]." It is undisputed that the Indian respondents' beliefs are sincere and that the Government's proposed actions will have severe adverse effects on the practice of their religion. Those respondents contend that the burden on their religious practices is heavy enough to violate the Free Exercise Clause unless the Government can demonstrate a compelling need to complete the G-O road or to engage in timber harvesting in the Chimney Rock area. We disagree.

In *Bowen v. Roy*, we considered a challenge to a federal statute that required the States to use Social Security numbers in administering certain welfare programs. Two applicants for benefits under these programs contended that their religious beliefs prevented them from acceding to the use of a Social Security number for their 2-year-old daughter because the use of a numerical identifier would "'rob the spirit' of [their] daughter and prevent her from attaining greater spiritual power." Similarly, in this case, it is said that disruption of the natural environment caused by the G-O road will diminish the sacredness of the area in question and create distractions that will interfere with "training and ongoing religious experience of individuals using [sites within] the area for personal medicine and growth . . . and as integrated parts of a system of religious belief and practice which correlates ascending degrees of personal power with a geographic hierarchy of power." The Court rejected this kind of challenge in *Roy*:

> "The Free Exercise Clause simply cannot be understood to require the Government to conduct its own internal affairs in ways that comport with the religious beliefs of particular citizens. Just as the Government may not insist that [the Roys] engage in any set form of religious observance, so [they] may not demand that the Government join in their chosen religious practices by refraining from using a number to identify their daughter. . . .
>
> ". . . The Free Exercise Clause affords an individual protection from certain forms of governmental compulsion; it does not afford an individual a right to dictate the conduct of the Government's internal procedures."

The building of a road or the harvesting of timber on publicly owned land cannot meaningfully be distinguished from the use of a Social Security number in *Roy*. In both cases, the challenged Government action would interfere significantly with private persons' ability to pursue spiritual fulfillment according to their own religious beliefs. In neither case, however, would the affected individuals be coerced by the Government's action into violating their religious beliefs; nor would either governmental action penalize religious activity by denying any person an equal share of the rights, benefits, and privileges enjoyed by other citizens.

We are asked to distinguish this case from *Roy* on the ground that the infringement on religious liberty here is "significantly greater," or on the ground that the Government practice in *Roy* was "purely mechanical" whereas this case involves "a case-by-case substantive determination as to how a particular unit of land will be managed." Similarly, we are told that this case can be distinguished from *Roy* because "the government action is not at some physically removed location where it places no restriction on what a practitioner may do." The State suggests that the Social Security number in Roy "could be characterized as interfering with Roy's religious tenets from a subjective point of view, where the government's conduct of 'its own internal affairs' was known to him only secondhand and did not interfere with his ability to practice his religion." In this case, however, it is said that the proposed road will "physically destro[y] the environmental conditions and the privacy without which the [religious] practices cannot be conducted."

These efforts to distinguish *Roy* are unavailing. This Court cannot determine the truth of the underlying beliefs that led to the religious objections here or in *Roy*, *see Hobbie v. Unemployment Appeals Comm'n of Fla.*, 480 U.S. 136, 144, n. 9 (1987), and accordingly cannot weigh the adverse effects on the appellees in *Roy* and compare them with the adverse effects on the Indian respondents. Without the ability to make such comparisons, we cannot say that the one form of incidental interference with an individual's spiritual activities should be subjected to a different constitutional analysis than the other.

Respondents insist, nonetheless, that the courts below properly relied on a factual inquiry into the degree to which the Indians' spiritual practices would become ineffectual if the G-O road were built. They rely on several cases in which this Court has sustained free exercise challenges to government programs that interfered with individuals' ability to practice their religion. *See Wisconsin v. Yoder; Sherbert v. Verner; Thomas v. Review Board, Indiana Employment Security Div.* (denial of unemployment benefits to applicant whose religion forbade him to fabricate weapons); *Hobbie* (denial of unemployment benefits to religious convert who resigned position that required her to work on the Sabbath).

Even apart from the inconsistency between *Roy* and respondents' reading of these cases, their interpretation will not withstand analysis. It is true that this Court has repeatedly held that indirect coercion or penalties on the free exercise of religion, not just outright prohibitions, are subject to scrutiny under the First Amendment. Thus, for example, ineligibility for unemployment benefits, based solely on a refusal to violate the Sabbath, has been analogized to a fine imposed on Sabbath worship. *Sherbert.* This does not and cannot imply that incidental effects of government programs, which may make it more difficult to practice certain religions but which have no tendency to coerce individuals into acting contrary to their religious beliefs, require government to bring forward a compelling justification for its otherwise lawful actions. The crucial word in the constitutional text is "prohibit": "For the Free Exercise Clause is written in terms of what the government cannot do to the individual, not in terms of what the individual can exact from the government." *Sherbert* (Douglas, J., concurring).

Whatever may be the exact line between unconstitutional prohibitions on the free exercise of religion and the legitimate conduct by government of its own affairs, the location of the line cannot depend on measuring the effects of a governmental action on a religious objector's spiritual development. The Government does not dispute, and we have no reason to doubt, that the logging and road-building projects at issue in this case could have devastating effects on traditional Indian religious practices. Those practices are intimately and inextricably bound up with the unique features of the Chimney Rock area, which is known to the Indians as the "high country." Individual practitioners use this area for personal spiritual development; some of their activities are believed to be critically important in advancing the welfare of the Tribe, and indeed, of mankind itself. The Indians use this area, as they have used it for a very long time, to conduct a wide variety of specific rituals that aim to accomplish their religious goals. According to their beliefs, the rituals would not be efficacious if conducted at other sites than the ones traditionally used, and too much disturbance of the area's natural state would clearly render any meaningful continuation of traditional practices impossible. To be sure, the Indians themselves were far from unanimous in opposing the G-O road, and it seems less than certain that construction of the road will be so disruptive that it will doom their religion. Nevertheless, we can assume that the threat to the efficacy of at least some religious practices is extremely grave.

Even if we assume that we should accept the Ninth Circuit's prediction, according to which the G-O road will "virtually destroy the . . . Indians' ability to practice their religion," the Constitution simply does not provide a principle that could justify upholding respondents' legal claims. However much we might wish that it were otherwise, government simply could not operate if it were required to satisfy every citizen's religious needs and desires. A broad range of government activities — from social welfare programs to foreign aid to conservation projects — will always be considered essential to the spiritual well-being of some citizens, often on the basis of sincerely held religious beliefs. Others will find the very same activities deeply offensive, and perhaps incompatible with their own search for spiritual fulfillment and with the tenets of their religion. The First Amendment must apply to all citizens alike, and it can give to none of them a veto over public programs that do not prohibit the free exercise of religion. The Constitution does not, and courts cannot, offer to reconcile the various competing demands on government, many of them rooted in sincere religious belief, that inevitably arise in so diverse a society as ours. That task, to the extent that it is feasible, is for the legislatures and other institutions. *Cf.* THE FEDERALIST No. 10 (suggesting that the effects of religious factionalism are best restrained through competition among a multiplicity of religious sects).

One need not look far beyond the present case to see why the analysis in *Roy*, but not respondents' proposed extension of *Sherbert* and its progeny, offers a sound reading of the Constitution. Respondents attempt to stress the limits of the religious servitude that they are now seeking to impose on the Chimney Rock area of the Six Rivers National Forest. While defending an injunction against logging operations and the construction of a road, they apparently do not *at present* object to the area's being used by recreational visitors, other Indians, or forest rangers. Nothing in the principle for which they contend, however, would distinguish this case from another lawsuit in which they (or similarly situated religious objectors) might seek to exclude all human activity but their own from sacred areas of the public lands. The Indian respondents insist that "[p]rivacy during the power quests is required for the practitioners to maintain the purity needed for a successful journey." Similarly: "The practices conducted in the high country entail intense meditation and require the practitioner to achieve a profound awareness of the natural environment. Prayer seats are oriented so there is an unobstructed view, and the practitioner must be surrounded by *undisturbed* naturalness." No disrespect for these practices is implied when one notes that such beliefs could easily require de facto beneficial ownership of some rather spacious tracts of public property. Even without anticipating future cases, the diminution of the Government's property rights, and the concomitant subsidy of the Indian religion, would in this case be far from trivial: the District Court's order permanently forbade commercial timber harvesting, or the construction of a two-lane road, anywhere within an area covering a full 27 sections (i.e. more than 17,000 acres) of public land.

The Constitution does not permit government to discriminate against religions that treat particular physical sites as sacred, and a law prohibiting the Indian respondents from visiting the Chimney Rock area would raise a different set of constitutional questions. Whatever rights the Indians may have to the use of the area, however, those rights do not divest the Government of its right to use what is, after all, its land. *Cf. Bowen v. Roy* (O'CONNOR, J., concurring in part and dissenting in part) (distinguishing between the Government's use of information in its possession and the Government's requiring an individual to provide such information).

C

The dissent proposes an approach to the First Amendment that is fundamentally inconsistent with the principles on which our decision rests. Notwithstanding the sympathy that we all must feel for the plight of the Indian respondents, it is plain that the approach taken by the dissent cannot withstand analysis. On the contrary, the path towards which it points us is incompatible with the text of the Constitution, with the precedents of this Court, and with a responsible sense of our own institutional role.

The dissent begins by asserting that the "constitutional guarantee we interpret today . . . is directed against *any* form of government action that frustrates or inhibits religious practice." The Constitution, however, says no such thing. Rather, it states: "Congress shall make no law . . . *prohibiting* the free exercise [of religion]." U.S. Const., Amdt. 1 (emphasis added).

As we explained above, *Bowen v. Roy* rejected a First Amendment challenge to Government activities that the religious objectors sincerely believed would "'"rob the spirit" of [their] daughter and prevent her from attaining greater spiritual power. The dissent now offers to distinguish that case by saying that the Government was acting there "in a purely internal manner," whereas land-use decisions "are likely to have substantial external effects." Whatever the source or meaning of the dissent's distinction, it has no basis in *Roy*. Robbing the spirit of a child, and preventing her from attaining greater spiritual power, is both a "substantial external effect" and one that is remarkably similar to the injury claimed by respondents in the case before us today. The dissent's reading of *Roy* would effectively overrule that decision, without providing any compelling justification for doing so.

The dissent also misreads *Wisconsin v. Yoder*. The statute at issue in that case prohibited the Amish parents, on pain of criminal prosecution, from providing their children with the kind of education required by the Amish religion. The statute directly compelled the Amish to send their children to public high schools "contrary to the Amish religion and way of life." The Court acknowledged that the statute might be constitutional, *despite* its coercive nature, if the State could show with sufficient "particularity how its admittedly strong interest in compulsory education would be adversely affected by granting an exemption to the Amish." The dissent's out-of-context quotations notwithstanding, there is nothing whatsoever in the *Yoder* opinion to support the proposition that the "impact" on the Amish religion would have been constitutionally problematic if the statute at issue had not been coercive in nature.

Perceiving a "stress point in the longstanding conflict between two disparate cultures," the dissent attacks us for declining to "balanc[e] these competing and potentially irreconcilable interests, choosing instead to turn this difficult task over to the Federal Legislature." Seeing the Court as the arbiter, the dissent proposes a legal test under which it would decide which public lands are "central" or "indispensable" to which religions, and by implication which are "dispensable" or "peripheral," and would then decide which government programs are "compelling" enough to justify "infringement of those practices." We would accordingly be required to weigh the value of every religious belief and practice that is said to be threatened by any government program. Unless a "showing of 'centrality, is nothing but an assertion of centrality, the dissent thus offers us the prospect of this Courts holding that some sincerely held religious beliefs and practices are not "central" to certain religions, despite protestations to the contrary from the religious objectors who brought the lawsuit. In other words, the dissent's approach would require us to rule that some religious adherents misunderstand their own religious beliefs. We think such an approach cannot be squared with the Constitution or with our precedents, and that it would cast the Judiciary in a role that we were never intended to play.

JUSTICE BRENNAN, with whom JUSTICE MARSHALL and JUSTICE BLACKMUN join, dissenting.

I

For at least 200 years and probably much longer, the Yurok, Karok, and Tolowa Indians have held sacred an approximately 25-square-mile area of land situated in what is today the Blue Creek Unit of Six Rivers National Forest in northwestern California. As the Government readily concedes, regular visits to this area, known to respondent Indians as the "high country," have played and continue to play a "critical" role in the religious practices and rituals of these Tribes. Those beliefs, only briefly described in the Court's opinion, are crucial to a proper understanding of respondents' claims.

As the Forest Service's commissioned study, the Theodoratus Report, explains, for Native Americans religion is not a discrete sphere of activity separate from all others, and any attempt to isolate the religious aspects of Indian life "is in reality an exercise which forces Indian concepts into non- Indian categories." Thus, for most Native Americans, "[t]he area of worship cannot be delineated from social, political, cultur[al], and other areas o[f] Indian lifestyle." A pervasive feature of this lifestyle is the individual's relationship with the natural world; this relationship, which can accurately though somewhat incompletely be characterized as one of stewardship, forms the core of what might be called, for want of a better nomenclature, the Indian religious experience. While traditional Western religions view creation as the work of a deity "who institutes natural laws which then govern the operation of physical nature," tribal religions regard creation as an on-going process in which they are morally and religiously obligated to participate. Native Americans fulfill this duty through ceremonies and rituals designed to preserve and stabilize the earth and to protect humankind from disease and other catastrophes. Failure to conduct these ceremonies in the manner and place specified, adherents believe, will result in great harm to the earth and to the people whose welfare depends upon it.

In marked contrast to traditional Western religions, the belief systems of Native Americans do not rely on doctrines, creeds, or dogmas. Established or universal truths — the mainstay of Western religions — play no part in Indian faith. Ceremonies are communal efforts undertaken for specific purposes in accordance with instructions handed down from generation to generation. Commentaries on or interpretations of the rituals themselves are deemed absolute violations of the ceremonies, whose value lies not in their ability to explain the natural world or to enlighten individual believers but in their efficacy as protectors and enhancers of tribal existence. *Ibid.* Where dogma lies at the heart of Western religions, Native American faith is inextricably bound to the use of land. The site-specific nature of Indian religious practice derives from the Native American perception that land is itself a sacred, living being. Rituals are performed in prescribed locations not merely as a matter of traditional orthodoxy, but because land, like all other living things, is unique, and specific sites possess different spiritual properties and significance. Within this belief system, therefore, land is not fungible; indeed, at the time of the Spanish colonization of the American Southwest, "all . . . Indians held in some form a belief in a sacred and indissoluble bond between themselves and the land in which their settlements were located."

For respondent Indians, the most sacred of lands is the high country where, they believe, prehuman spirits moved with the coming of humans to the Earth. Because these spirits are seen as the source of religious power, or "medicine," many of the tribes' rituals and practices require frequent journeys to the area. Thus, for example, religious leaders preparing for the complex of ceremonies that underlie the Tribes' World Renewal efforts must travel to specific sites in the high country in order to attain the medicine necessary for successful renewal. Similarly, individual tribe members may seek curative powers for the healing of the sick, or personal medicine for particular purposes such as good luck in singing, hunting, or love. A period of preparation generally precedes such visits, and individuals must select trails in the sacred area according to the medicine they seek and their abilities, gradually moving to increasingly more powerful sites, which are typically located at higher altitudes. Among the most powerful of sites are Chimney Rock, Doctor Rock, and Peak 8, all of which are elevated rock outcroppings.

According to the Theodoratus Report, the qualities "of silence, the aesthetic perspective, and the physical attributes, are an extension of the sacredness of [each] particular site." The act of medicine making is akin to meditation: the individual must integrate physical, mental, and vocal actions in order to communicate with the prehuman spirits. As a result, "successful use of the high country is dependent upon and facilitated by certain qualities of the physical environment, the most important of which are privacy, silence, and an undisturbed natural setting." Although few Tribe members actually make medicine at the most powerful sites, the entire Tribe's welfare hinges on the success of the individual practitioners.

Beginning in 1972, the Forest Service began preparing a multiple-use management plan for the Blue Creek Unit. The plan's principal features included the harvesting of 733 million board feet of Douglas fir over an 80-year period and the completion of a 6-mile segment of paved road running between two northern California towns, Gasquet and Orleans (the G-O road). The road's primary purpose was to provide a route for hauling the timber harvested under the management plan; in addition, it would enhance public access to the Six Rivers and other national forests, and allow for more efficient maintenance and fire control by the Forest Service itself. In the mid-1970's, the Forest Service circulated draft environmental impact statements evaluating the effects of several proposed routes for the final segment of the G-O road, including at least two that circumnavigated the high country altogether. Ultimately, however, the Service settled on a route running along the Chimney Rock Corridor, which traverses the Indians' sacred lands.

II

C

In the final analysis, the Court's refusal to recognize the constitutional dimension of respondents' injuries stems from its concern that acceptance of respondents' claim could potentially strip the Government of its ability to manage and use vast tracts of federal property. In addition, the nature of respondents' site-specific religious practices raises the specter of future suits in which Native Americans seek to exclude all human activity from such areas. These concededly legitimate concerns lie at the very heart of this case, which represents yet another stress point in the longstanding conflict between two disparate cultures — the dominant Western culture, which views land in terms of ownership and use, and that of Native Americans, in which concepts of private property are not only alien, but contrary to a belief system that holds land sacred. Rather than address this conflict in any meaningful fashion, however, the Court disclaims all responsibility for balancing these competing and potentially irreconcilable interests, choosing instead to turn this difficult task over to the Federal Legislature. Such an abdication is more than merely indefensible as an institutional matter: by defining respondents' injury as "nonconstitutional," the Court has effectively bestowed on one party to this conflict the unilateral authority to resolve all future disputes in its favor, subject only to the Court's toothless exhortation to be "sensitive" to affected religions. In my view, however, Native Americans deserve — and the Constitution demands — more than this.

Prior to today's decision, several Courts of Appeals had attempted to fashion a test that accommodates the competing "demands" placed on federal property by the two cultures. Recognizing that the Government normally enjoys plenary authority over federal lands, the Courts of Appeals required Native Americans to demonstrate that any land-use decisions they challenged involved lands that were "central" or "indispensable" to their religious practices. Although this requirement limits the potential number of free exercise claims that might be brought to federal land management decisions, and thus forestalls the possibility that the Government will find itself ensnared in a host of Lilliputian lawsuits, it has been criticized as inherently ethnocentric, for it incorrectly assumes that Native American belief systems ascribe religious significance to land in a traditionally Western hierarchical manner. It is frequently the case in constitutional litigation, however, that courts are called upon to balance interests that are not readily translated into rough equivalents. At their most absolute, the competing claims that both the Government and Native Americans assert in federal land are fundamentally incompatible, and unless they are tempered by compromise, mutual accommodation will remain impossible.

I believe it appropriate, therefore, to require some showing of "centrality" before the Government can be required either to come forward with a compelling justification for its proposed use of federal land or to forego that use altogether. "Centrality," however, should not be equated with the survival or extinction of the religion itself. In *Yoder*, for example, we treated the objection to the compulsory school attendance of adolescents as "central" to the Amish faith even though such attendance did not prevent or otherwise render the practice of that religion impossible, and instead simply threatened to "undermine" that faith. Because of their perceptions of and relationship with the natural world, Native Americans consider all land sacred. Nevertheless, the Theodoratus Report reveals that respondents here deemed certain lands more powerful and more directly related to their religious practices than others. Thus, in my view, while Native Americans need not demonstrate, as respondents did here, that the Government's land-use decision will assuredly eradicate their faith, I do not think it is enough to allege simply that the land in question is held sacred. Rather, adherents challenging a proposed use of federal land should be required to show that the decision poses a substantial and realistic threat of frustrating their religious practices. Once such a showing is made, the burden should shift to the Government to come forward with a compelling state interest sufficient to justify the infringement of those practices.

The Court today suggests that such an approach would place courts in the untenable position of deciding which practices and beliefs are "central" to a given faith and which are not, and invites the prospect of judges advising some religious adherents that they "misunderstand their own religious beliefs." In fact, however, courts need not undertake any such inquiries: like all other religious adherents, Native Americans would be the arbiters of which practices are central to their faith, subject only to the normal requirement that their claims be genuine and sincere. The question for the courts, then, is not whether the Native American claimants understand their own religion, but rather whether they have discharged their burden of demonstrating, as the Amish did with respect to the compulsory school law in *Yoder*, that the land-use decision poses a substantial and realistic threat of undermining or frustrating their religious practices. Ironically, the Court's apparent solicitude for the integrity of religious belief and its desire to forestall the possibility that courts might second-guess the claims of religious adherents leads to far greater inequities than those the Court postulates: today's ruling sacrifices a religion at least as old as the Nation itself, along with the spiritual well-being of its approximately 5,000 adherents, so that the Forest Service can build a 6-mile segment of road that two lower courts found had only the most marginal and speculative utility, both to the Government itself and to the private lumber interests that might conceivably use it.

Similarly, the Court's concern that the claims of Native Americans will place "religious servitudes" upon vast tracts of federal property cannot justify its refusal to recognize the constitutional injury respondents will suffer here. It is true, as the Court notes, that respondents' religious use of the high country requires privacy and solitude. The fact remains, however, that respondents have never asked the Forest Service to exclude others from the area. Should respondents or any other group seek to force the Government to protect their religious practices from the interference of private parties, such a demand would implicate not only the concerns of the Free Exercise Clause, but also those of the Establishment Clause as well. That case, however, is most assuredly not before us today, and in any event cannot justify the Court's refusal to acknowledge that the injuries respondents will suffer as a result of the Government's proposed activities are sufficient to state a constitutional cause of action.

NOTES ON CONSTITUTIONAL DEFENSES TO TORT LIABILITY AGAINST CHURCHES

1. *Tort Liability for Sexual Abuse by Church Personnel.* In recent years, several churches, and particularly the Catholic Church, have been subject to a growing number of legal claims by alleged victims of sexual abuse by church personnel, including priests and ministers. These claims have led to frequent litigation over the issue of whether the Constitution immunizes churches from liability for tort claims. In general, courts have refused to immunize churches from liability where the facts giving rise to the tort pertain to conduct that does not involve the courts in the assessment of religious doctrine. Most sexual abuse cases fall into this category.

Legal claims against churches for sexual abuse committed by church employees have been brought under a range of different tort theories, including breach of fiduciary duty, negligent hiring or supervision, respondeat superior, and agency liability. In some states, the doctrine of charitable immunity has been employed to bar tort liability against churches for tortious acts of sexual abuse committed by church employees. Although the common law doctrine of charitable immunity has fallen from favor, a few states have enacted statutory versions of the immunity. *See, e.g.,* the New Jersey statutory version of charitable immunity, N.J. STAT. ANN. § 2A:53A-7a (2004), which grants entities immunity from suit by beneficiaries of that entity if the entity is a "nonprofit corporation, society or association organized exclusively for religious, charitable or educational purposes."

Most of the states that do not recognize charitable immunity have also been reluctant to grant churches broad constitutional immunity from tort liability arising out of sexual abuse by church personnel. The general thrust of the opinions denying immunity to churches in these cases is that tort liability for sexual abuse does not require the courts to review church doctrine and therefore does not interfere with the churches' constitutionally protected religious practices. A representative sample of this approach appears in a recent ruling by the Florida Supreme Court rejecting both Establishment and Free Exercise Clause defenses to a claim brought against the Archdiocese of Miami for a priest's sexual abuse of a minor:

> In this case, the Church Defendants do not claim that the underlying acts of its priest in committing sexual assault and battery was governed by sincerely held religious beliefs or practices. Nor do they claim that the reason they failed to exercise control over [the priest] was because of sincerely held religious beliefs or practices. Therefore, it appears that the Free Exercise Clause is not implicated in this case because the conduct sought to be regulated; that is, the Church Defendants' alleged negligence in hiring and supervision is not rooted in religious belief. Moreover, even assuming an "incidental effect of burdening a particular religious practice," the parishioners' cause of action for negligent hiring and supervision is not barred because it is based on neutral application of principles of tort law. *See Lukumi Babalu Aye,* 508 U.S. at 531. Through neutral application of principles of tort law, we thus give no greater or lesser deference to tortious conduct committed on third parties by religious organizations than we do to tortious conduct committed on third parties by non-religious entities.

Malicki v. Doe, 814 So. 2d 347, 360-61 (Fla. 2002).

The most sensitive constitutional issues relate to claims of breach of fiduciary duty, since proof of a fiduciary relationship requires the factfinder to analyze the duties and responsibilities of the religious official under the official's governing religious doctrine, and also requires the factfinder to assess the specific relationship between religious officials and their parishioners. Nevertheless, most courts permit these claims to go forward. In rejecting a free exercise defense to a breach of fiduciary duty claim based on child sexual abuse by a priest, the United States Court of Appeals for the Second Circuit noted:

> [U]nder the Constitution, "[t]he law knows no heresy, and is committed to the support of no dogma, the establishment of no sect." *Watson v. Jones*, 80 U.S. (13 Wall.) 679, 728 (1871). That is now an American truism, but it is unrelated to this appeal. Where a person's beliefs are alleged to give rise to a special legal relationship between him and his church, we may be required to consider with other relevant evidence the nature of that person's beliefs in order properly to determine whether the asserted relationship in fact exists. In doing so, we judge nothing to be heresy, support no dogma, and acknowledge no beliefs or practices of any sect to be the law. . . . [W]e find no merit to the Diocese's claim that the judgment violated the First Amendment by determining the Diocese's obligations to its parishioners as a matter of church doctrine. Martinelli's claim was brought under Connecticut law, not church law; church law is not ours to assess or to enforce. Martinelli's claim neither relied upon nor sought to enforce the duties of the Diocese according to religious beliefs, nor did it require or involve a resolution of whether the Diocese's conduct was consistent with them. The jury's consideration of church doctrine here was both permissible under First Amendment principles and required by Connecticut law.

Martinelli v. Bridgeport Roman Catholic Diocesan Corp., 196 F.3d 409, 431 (2d Cir. 1999). *See also Olson v. First Church of the Nazarene*, 661 N.W.2d 254, 266 (Minn. Ct. App. 2003) ("the district court has subject-matter jurisdiction over claims that a religious employer is vicariously liable, liable for negligent retention, or liable for negligent supervision for a cleric's sexual penetration of a person while the cleric was providing ongoing, private spiritual advice, aid, or comfort to that person").

On the other hand, in a significant minority of jurisdictions courts have upheld constitutional defenses to sexual abuse-related tort claims against churches. In one case, for example, a federal district court rejected a negligent hiring and supervision claim against a church in a sexual abuse suit on the ground that both the Establishment and Free Exercise Clauses bar a court from intruding into sensitive employment matters as they relate to priests and other religious personnel.

> The choice of individuals to serve as ministers is one of the most fundamental rights belonging to a religious institution. It is one [of] the most important exercises of a church's freedom from government control. For this Court to insert itself into the process by which priests are chosen would substantially burden these Defendants' free exercise of a crucial power to control the future of the church and therefore constitute interference with the practice of their religion.

It would also cause excessive entanglement in church operations by fostering inappropriate government involvement. The application of even general tort law principles to church procedures on the choice of priests would require an inquiry into present practices with an intent to pass on their reasonableness. Such court examination and oversight of internal church policies would constitute an encroachment on the church's religious functions.

Ayon v. Gourley, 47 F. Supp. 2d 1246, 1250 (D. Colo. 1998), *aff'd*, 185 F.3d 873 (10th Cir. 1999). Other examples of decisions rejecting on constitutional grounds liability against churches in sexual abuse cases include *Dausch v. Rykse*, 52 F.3d 1425, 1429 (7th Cir. 1994); *L.L.N. v. Clauder*, 563 N.W.2d 434, 445 (Wis. 1997); *Bryan R. v. Watchtower Bible & Tract Soc'y of N.Y., Inc.*, 738 A.2d (Me. 1999).

2. *Clergy Malpractice and Other Torts.* The weight of a church's constitutional defense to tort liability depends heavily on how closely the allegedly tortious behavior can be related to the central teachings of the faith. Consider the issue of shunning. In *Paul v. Watchtower Bible and Tract Society of New York, Inc.*, 819 F.2d 875 (9th Cir.), *cert. denied*, 484 U.S. 926 (1987), a panel of the United States Court of Appeals for the Ninth Circuit ruled that the Jehovah's Witness Church has "a constitutionally protected privilege to engage in the practice of shunning." *Id.* at 876.

Courts also tend to rely on constitutional defenses to reject tort claims that are based on the negative psychological effects of the counseling activities of church personnel. During the 1980s, plaintiffs attempted to convince courts to create an independent tort of clergy malpractice to address such harms. To date, every court that has been asked to recognize an independent tort of clergy malpractice has refused to do so, and claims for clergy malpractice that are cast in the form of negligence and breach of fiduciary duty torts generally suffer the same fate. For a recent example of a church's successful Establishment Clause defense against a clergy malpractice claim based on negligence, *see Franco v. The Church of Jesus Christ of Latter-Day Saints*, 21 P.3d 198 (Utah 2001). In this case, the Utah Supreme Court rejected a negligence claim brought against a church and its officials based on injuries the plaintiff allegedly suffered as a result of flawed advice she received during ecclesiastical counseling. The Court based its decision on the third, entanglement prong of the three-part *Lemon v. Kurtzman* analysis. *See* Chapter 5, Section A. The court ruled that:

> [I]t is well settled that civil tort claims against clerics that require the courts to review and interpret church law, policies, or practices in the determination of the claims are barred by the First Amendment under the entanglement doctrine. . . . For, as the Supreme Court stated in *Kedroff v. St. Nicholas Cathedral*, 344 U.S. 94 (1952), churches must have "power to decide for themselves, free from state interference, matters of church government as well as those of faith and doctrine." *Id.* at 116. . . . [C]ourts throughout the United States have uniformly rejected claims for clergy malpractice under the First Amendment. . . . These

courts have generally held that a determination of such claims would necessarily entangle the courts in the examination of religious doctrine, practice, or church polity — an inquiry that we have already explained is prohibited by the Establishment Clause.

Franco, 21 P.3d at 203-04.

Like the Utah court in *Franco*, most courts attempt to reconcile their uniform rejection of an independent clergy malpractice tort with their increasing tendency to ascribe liability in sexual abuse and other ordinary tort cases by referring to the reluctance to recognize any claim that requires judicial review of religious doctrine. Thus, tort liability is permitted where non-religious "neutral principles" can be employed. This is how the New Jersey Supreme Court describes the relevant standard:

> A court may not inquire into the validity of a religious belief or practice that prompts the challenged conduct. *United States v. Ballard*, 322 U.S. 78 (1944). A court, however, may apply neutral principles of law to decide an issue that does not implicate religious doctrine. *See Elmora Hebrew Ctr. Inc. v. Fishman*, 125 N.J. 404, 413, 593 A.2d 725 (1991) (stating "religious parties or institutions are not . . . less entitled to civil adjudication of secular legal questions"). Neutral principles "are wholly secular legal rules whose application to religious parties or disputes does not entail theological or doctrinal evaluations." *Id.* at 414-15, 593 A.2d 725. Only "when the underlying dispute turns on doctrine or polity" should a court refuse to enforce secular rights. *Welter v. Seton Hall Univ.*, 128 N.J. 279, 293, 608 A.2d 206 (1992).

F.G. v. MacDonell, 696 A.2d 697 (N.J. 1997).

Despite this common explanation, the distinction between theologically dictated church behavior and ordinary conduct subject to "wholly secular legal rules" is not always easy to discern. This dilemma is suggested by one of the most noted clergy malpractice decisions. *See Nally v. Grace Cmty. Church*, 763 P.2d 948 (Cal. 1988). In this case, the California Supreme Court rejected a tort action against church counselors who had been counseling a depressed young parishioner. The young parishioner eventually committed suicide, and his parents sued the church and the counselors. The court rejected the parents' claim and held that pastoral counselors have no duty to refer potentially suicidal persons to professional therapists.

The facts of *Nally* are complicated by the fact that the suicidal parishioner in that case had actually received (and in some cases rejected) psychological care. The court's denial of liability can also be explained in part by the court's practical concern about the difficulties of articulating a standard of care in such actions. But given somewhat more extreme circumstances, does the result in *Nally* always make sense? If religious practitioners convince a desperately ill member of their faith who is under their care to forego mainstream medical treatment that a reasonable person would understand is highly effective in treating the ailment in question, should the religious practitioners be immune from the same legal responsibilities that apply to everyone else in society? If so, why? Do the courts treat the sexual abuse cases differently from cases like *Nally* because no disputed church doctrine is at issue in the sexual abuse cases, or rather because the sexual abuse cases involve the misuse of religious authority (i.e., the authority exercised by a priest or minister) to harm a third party? If the sexual abuse cases are explained as misuse of authority/harm cases, are cases like *Nally* really that different?

Chapter 14

THE FREE EXERCISE CLAUSE AFTER *EMPLOYMENT DIVISION v. SMITH*

In many respects, *Employment Division v. Smith* is a revolution in Free Exercise jurisprudence. It casts into doubt the validity of the more than thirty-year-old principle that the Free Exercise Clause requires the government to accommodate religious practitioners by exempting them from certain general legal obligations. *Smith* casts doubt upon both the theory and the holdings of many of the cases discussed in the previous three Chapters. Many religious groups were outraged by the Court's decision in *Smith*, and Congress responded by enacting the Religious Freedom Restoration Act. In *Boerne v. Flores, infra*, the Court struck down RFRA on the grounds that Congress had exceeded its authority under Section 5 of the Fourteenth Amendment. Proponents of RFRA then redrafted the statute in response to the Court's decision, and a much more narrowly focused version of that redrafted statute has now been enacted into law in the form of the Religious Land Use and Institutionalized Persons Act (RLUIPA). This Chapter includes a large portion of the *Smith* decision, an excerpt from *Boerne*, post-*Boerne* academic assessments of RFRA, and excerpts and explanations of RLUIPA. The Chapter also includes an excerpt from *Church of the Lukumi Babalu Aye v. Hialeah*, which sketches the parameters of the post-*Smith* Free Exercise Clause.

A. *SMITH* AND THE NARROWING OF THE ACCOMMODATION PRINCIPLE

EMPLOYMENT DIVISION, DEPARTMENT OF HUMAN RESOURCES OF OREGON v. SMITH
494 U.S. 872 (1990)

JUSTICE SCALIA delivered the opinion of the Court.

I

Oregon law prohibits the knowing or intentional possession of a "controlled substance" unless the substance has been prescribed by a medical practitioner. The law defines "controlled substance" as a drug classified in Schedules I through V of the Federal Controlled Substances Act, as modified by the State Board of Pharmacy. Persons who violate this provision by possessing a controlled substance listed on Schedule I are "guilty of a Class B felony." As compiled by the State Board of Pharmacy under its statutory authority, Schedule

I contains the drug peyote, a hallucinogen derived from the plant *Lophophora williamsii Lemaire.*

Respondents Alfred Smith and Galen Black (hereinafter respondents) were fired from their jobs with a private drug rehabilitation organization because they ingested peyote for sacramental purposes at a ceremony of the Native American Church, of which both are members. When respondents applied to petitioner Employment Division (hereinafter petitioner) for unemployment compensation, they were determined to be ineligible for benefits because they had been discharged for work-related "misconduct." The Oregon Court of Appeals reversed that determination, holding that the denial of benefits violated respondents' free exercise rights under the First Amendment.

The Oregon Supreme Court held that respondents' religiously inspired use of peyote fell within the prohibition of the Oregon statute, which "makes no exception for the sacramental use" of the drug. It then considered whether that prohibition was valid under the Free Exercise Clause, and concluded that it was not. The court therefore reaffirmed its previous ruling that the State could not deny unemployment benefits to respondents for having engaged in that practice.

II

Respondents' claim for relief rests on our decisions in *Sherbert v. Verner* [*supra* Chapter 12], *Thomas v. Review Bd. of Indiana Employment Security Div.* [*supra* Chapter 12], and *Hobbie v. Unemployment Appeals Comm'n of Florida,* 480 U.S. 136 (1987), in which we held that a State could not condition the availability of unemployment insurance on an individual's willingness to forgo conduct required by his religion. As we observed in *Smith I,* however, the conduct at issue in those cases was not prohibited by law. We held that distinction to be critical, for "if Oregon does prohibit the religious use of peyote, and if that prohibition is consistent with the Federal Constitution, there is no federal right to engage in that conduct in Oregon," and "the State is free to withhold unemployment compensation from respondents for engaging in work-related misconduct, despite its religious motivation." Now that the Oregon Supreme Court has confirmed that Oregon does prohibit the religious use of peyote, we proceed to consider whether that prohibition is permissible under the Free Exercise Clause.

A

The Free Exercise Clause of the First Amendment . . . means, first and foremost, the right to believe and profess whatever religious doctrine one desires. Thus, the First Amendment obviously excludes all "governmental regulation of religious *beliefs* as such." *Sherbert v. Verner* [*supra* Chapter 12]. The government may not compel affirmation of religious belief, punish the expression of religious doctrines it believes to be false, impose special disabilities on the basis of religious views or religious status, or lend its power to one or the other side in controversies over religious authority or dogma.

But the "exercise of religion" often involves not only belief and profession but the performance of (or abstention from) physical acts: assembling with others for a worship service, participating in sacramental use of bread and wine, proselytizing, abstaining from certain foods or certain modes of transportation. It would be true, we think (though no case of ours has involved the point), that a State would be "prohibiting the free exercise [of religion]" if it sought to ban such acts or abstentions only when they are engaged in for religious reasons, or only because of the religious belief that they display. It would doubtless be unconstitutional, for example, to ban the casting of "statues that are to be used for worship purposes," or to prohibit bowing down before a golden calf.

Respondents in the present case, however, seek to carry the meaning of "prohibiting the free exercise [of religion]" one large step further. They contend that their religious motivation for using peyote places them beyond the reach of a criminal law that is not specifically directed at their religious practice, and that is concededly constitutional as applied to those who use the drug for other reasons. They assert, in other words, that "prohibiting the free exercise [of religion]" includes requiring any individual to observe a generally applicable law that requires (or forbids) the performance of an act that his religious belief forbids (or requires). As a textual matter, we do not think the words must be given that meaning. It is no more necessary to regard the collection of a general tax, for example, as "prohibiting the free exercise [of religion]" by those citizens who believe support of organized government to be sinful, than it is to regard the same tax as "abridging the freedom . . . of the press" of those publishing companies that must pay the tax as a condition of staying in business. It is a permissible reading of the text, in the one case as in the other, to say that if prohibiting the exercise of religion (or burdening the activity of printing) is not the object of the tax but merely the incidental effect of a generally applicable and otherwise valid provision, the First Amendment has not been offended.

Our decisions reveal that the latter reading is the correct one. We have never held that an individual's religious beliefs excuse him from compliance with an otherwise valid law prohibiting conduct that the State is free to regulate. On the contrary, the record of more than a century of our free exercise jurisprudence contradicts that proposition. As described succinctly by Justice Frankfurter in *Minersville School Dist. Bd. of Ed. v. Gobitis,* 310 U.S. 586, 594-595 (1940): "Conscientious scruples have not, in the course of the long struggle for religious toleration, relieved the individual from obedience to a general law not aimed at the promotion or restriction of religious beliefs. The mere possession of religious convictions which contradict the relevant concerns of a political society does not relieve the citizen from the discharge of political responsibilities (footnote omitted)." We first had occasion to assert that principle in *Reynolds v. United States,* where we rejected the claim that criminal laws against polygamy could not be constitutionally applied to those whose religion commanded the practice. "Laws," we said, "are made for the government of actions, and while they cannot interfere with mere religious belief and opinions, they may with practices. . . . Can a man excuse his practices to the contrary because of his religious belief? To permit this would be to make the professed doctrines of religious belief superior to the law of the land, and in effect to permit every citizen to become a law unto himself."

Subsequent decisions have consistently held that the right of free exercise does not relieve an individual of the obligation to comply with a "valid and neutral law of general applicability on the ground that the law proscribes (or prescribes) conduct that his religion prescribes (or proscribes)."

Our most recent decision involving a neutral, generally applicable regulatory law that compelled activity forbidden by an individual's religion was *United States v. Lee*. There, an Amish employer, on behalf of himself and his employees, sought exemption from collection and payment of Social Security taxes on the ground that the Amish faith prohibited participation in governmental support programs. We rejected the claim that an exemption was constitutionally required. There would be no way, we observed, to distinguish the Amish believer's objection to Social Security taxes from the religious objections that others might have to the collection or use of other taxes. "If, for example, a religious adherent believes war is a sin, and if a certain percentage of the federal budget can be identified as devoted to war-related activities, such individuals would have a similarly valid claim to be exempt from paying that percentage of the income tax. The tax system could not function if denominations were allowed to challenge the tax system because tax payments were spent in a manner that violates their religious belief." *Cf. Hernandez v. Commissioner*, 490 U.S. 680 (1989) (rejecting free exercise challenge to payment of income taxes alleged to make religious activities more difficult).

The only decisions in which we have held that the First Amendment bars application of a neutral, generally applicable law to religiously motivated action have involved not the Free Exercise Clause alone, but the Free Exercise Clause in conjunction with other constitutional protections, such as freedom of speech and of the press, *see Cantwell v. Connecticut* (invalidating a licensing system for religious and charitable solicitations under which the administrator had discretion to deny a license to any cause he deemed nonreligious); *Murdock v. Pennsylvania*, 319 U.S. 105 (1943) (invalidating a flat tax on solicitation as applied to the dissemination of religious ideas); *Follett v. McCormick*, 321 U.S. 573 (1944) (same), or the right of parents, acknowledged in *Pierce v. Society of Sisters*, 268 U.S. 510 (1925), to direct the education of their children, *see Wisconsin v. Yoder* (invalidating compulsory school-attendance laws as applied to Amish parents who refused on religious grounds to send their children to school). Some of our cases prohibiting compelled expression, decided exclusively upon free speech grounds, have also involved freedom of religion, *cf. Wooley v. Maynard*, 430 U.S. 705 (1977) (invalidating compelled display of a license plate slogan that offended individual religious beliefs); *West Virginia Bd. of Education v. Barnette* (invalidating compulsory flag salute statute challenged by religious objectors). And it is easy to envision a case in which a challenge on freedom of association grounds would likewise be reinforced by Free Exercise

Clause concerns. *Cf. Roberts v. United States Jaycees*, 468 U.S. 609, 622 (1984) ("An individual's freedom to speak, to worship, and to petition the government for the redress of grievances could not be vigorously protected from interference by the State [if] a correlative freedom to engage in group effort toward those ends were not also guaranteed").

The present case does not present such a hybrid situation, but a free exercise claim unconnected with any communicative activity or parental right. Respondents urge us to hold, quite simply, that when otherwise prohibitable conduct is accompanied by religious convictions, not only the convictions but the conduct itself must be free from governmental regulation. We have never held that, and decline to do so now. There being no contention that Oregon's drug law represents an attempt to regulate religious beliefs, the communication of religious beliefs, or the raising of one's children in those beliefs, the rule to which we have adhered ever since *Reynolds* plainly controls. "Our cases do not at their farthest reach support the proposition that a stance of conscientious opposition relieves an objector from any colliding duty fixed by a democratic government." *Gillette v. United States*, 401 U.S., at 461.

B

Respondents argue that even though exemption from generally applicable criminal laws need not automatically be extended to religiously motivated actors, at least the claim for a religious exemption must be evaluated under the balancing test set forth in *Sherbert v. Verner*. Under the *Sherbert* test, governmental actions that substantially burden a religious practice must be justified by a compelling governmental interest. Applying that test we have, on three occasions, invalidated state unemployment compensation rules that conditioned the availability of benefits upon an applicant's willingness to work under conditions forbidden by his religion. *See Sherbert v. Verner* [*supra* Chapter 12]; *Thomas v. Review Bd. of Indiana Employment Security Div.* [*supra* Chapter 12]; *Hobbie v. Unemployment Appeals Comm'n of Florida*, 480 U.S. 136 (1987). We have never invalidated any governmental action on the basis of the *Sherbert* test except the denial of unemployment compensation. Although we have sometimes purported to apply the *Sherbert* test in contexts other than that, we have always found the test satisfied, *see United States v. Lee*; *Gillette v. United States*, 401 U.S. 437 (1971). In recent years we have abstained from applying the *Sherbert* test (outside the unemployment compensation field) at all. In *Bowen v. Roy*, we declined to apply *Sherbert* analysis to a federal statutory scheme that required benefit applicants and recipients to provide their Social Security numbers. The plaintiffs in that case asserted that it would violate their religious beliefs to obtain and provide a Social Security number for their daughter. We held the statute's application to the plaintiffs valid regardless of whether it was necessary to effectuate a compelling interest. In *Lyng v. Northwest Indian Cemetery Protective Assn.*, we declined to apply *Sherbert* analysis to the Government's logging and road construction activities on lands used for religious purposes by several Native American Tribes, even though it was undisputed that the activities "could have devastating effects on traditional Indian religious practices." In *Goldman v. Weinberger,* we rejected application of the *Sherbert* test to military dress regulations that forbade the wearing of yarmulkes. In *O'Lone v. Estate of Shabazz*, 482 U.S. 342 (1987), we sustained, without mentioning the *Sherbert* test, a prison's refusal to excuse inmates from work requirements to attend worship services.

Even if we were inclined to breathe into *Sherbert* some life beyond the unemployment compensation field, we would not apply it to require exemptions from a generally applicable criminal law. The *Sherbert* test, it must be recalled, was developed in a context that lent itself to individualized governmental assessment of the reasons for the relevant conduct. As a plurality of the Court noted in *Roy,* a distinctive feature of unemployment compensation programs is that their eligibility criteria invite consideration of the particular circumstances behind an applicant's unemployment: "The statutory conditions [in *Sherbert* and *Thomas*] provided that a person was not eligible for unemployment compensation benefits if, 'without good cause,' he had quit work or refused available work. The 'good cause' standard created a mechanism for individualized exemptions." *Bowen v. Roy* (opinion of Burger, C.J., joined by Powell and REHNQUIST, JJ.). *See also Sherbert* (reading state unemployment compensation law as allowing benefits for unemployment caused by at least some "personal reasons"). As the plurality pointed out in *Roy,* our decisions in the unemployment cases stand for the proposition that where the State has in place a system of individual exemptions, it may not refuse to extend that system to cases of "religious hardship" without compelling reason.

Whether or not the decisions are that limited, they at least have nothing to do with an across-the-board criminal prohibition on a particular form of conduct. Although, as noted earlier, we have sometimes used the *Sherbert* test to analyze free exercise challenges to such laws, see *United States v. Lee; Gillette v. United States, supra*, 401 U.S., at 462, we have never applied the test to invalidate one. We conclude today that the sounder approach, and the approach in accord with the vast majority of our precedents, is to hold the test inapplicable to such challenges. The government's ability to enforce generally applicable prohibitions of socially harmful conduct, like its ability to carry out other aspects of public policy, "cannot depend on measuring the effects of a governmental action on a religious objector's spiritual development." *Lyng.* To make an individual's obligation to obey such a law contingent upon the law's coincidence with his religious beliefs, except where the State's interest is "compelling" — permitting him, by virtue of his beliefs, "to become a law unto himself," *Reynolds v. United States* — contradicts both constitutional tradition and common sense.[1]

The "compelling government interest" requirement seems benign, because it is familiar from other fields. But using it as the standard that must be met before the government may accord different treatment on the basis of race, or

---

[1] JUSTICE O'CONNOR seeks to distinguish *Lyng v. Northwest Indian Cemetery Protective Assn.*, 485 U.S. 439 (1988), and *Bowen v. Roy*, 476 U.S. 693 (1986), on the ground that those cases involved the

before the government may regulate the content of speech, is not remotely comparable to using it for the purpose asserted here. What it produces in those other fields — equality of treatment and an unrestricted flow of contending speech — are constitutional norms; what it would produce here — a private right to ignore generally applicable laws — is a constitutional anomaly.

Nor is it possible to limit the impact of respondents' proposal by requiring a "compelling state interest" only when the conduct prohibited is "central" to the individual's religion. It is no more appropriate for judges to determine the "centrality" of religious beliefs before applying a "compelling interest" test in the free exercise field, than it would be for them to determine the "importance" of ideas before applying the "compelling interest" test in the free speech field. What principle of law or logic can be brought to bear to contradict a believer's assertion that a particular act is "central" to his personal faith? Judging the centrality of different religious practices is akin to the unacceptable "business of evaluating the relative merits of differing religious claims." As we reaffirmed only last Term, "[i]t is not within the judicial ken to question the centrality of particular beliefs or practices to a faith, or the validity of particular litigants' interpretations of those creeds." *Hernandez v. Commissioner*, 490 U.S., at 699. Repeatedly and in many different contexts, we have warned that courts must not presume to determine the place of a particular belief in a religion or the plausibility of a religious claim.[4]

If the "compelling interest" test is to be applied at all, then, it must be applied across the board, to all actions thought to be religiously commanded. Moreover, if "compelling interest" really means what it says (and watering it down here would subvert its rigor in the other fields where it is applied), many laws

---

government's conduct of "its own internal affairs," which is different because, as Justice Douglas said in *Sherbert*, "'the Free Exercise Clause is written in terms of what the government cannot do to the individual, not in terms of what the individual can exact from the government.'" But since Justice Douglas voted with the majority in *Sherbert*, that quote obviously envisioned that what "the government cannot do to the individual" includes not just the prohibition of an individual's freedom of action through criminal laws but also the running of its programs (in *Sherbert*, state unemployment compensation) in such fashion as to harm the individual's religious interests. Moreover, it is hard to see any reason in principle or practicality why the government should have to tailor its health and safety laws to conform to the diversity of religious belief, but should not have to tailor its management of public lands, *Lyng,* or its administration of welfare programs, *Roy.*

[4] While arguing that we should apply the compelling interest test in this case, JUSTICE O'CONNOR nonetheless agrees that "our determination of the constitutionality of Oregon's general criminal prohibition cannot, and should not, turn on the centrality of the particular religious practice at issue." This means, presumably, that compelling interest scrutiny must be applied to generally applicable laws that regulate or prohibit any religiously motivated activity, no matter how unimportant to the claimant's religion. Earlier in her opinion, however, JUSTICE O'CONNOR appears to contradict this, saying that the proper approach is "to determine whether the burden on the specific plaintiffs before us is constitutionally significant and whether the particular criminal interest asserted by the State before us is compelling." "Constitutionally significant burden" would seem to be "centrality" under another name. In any case, dispensing with a "centrality" inquiry is utterly unworkable. It would require, for example, the same degree of "compelling state interest" to impede the practice of throwing rice at church weddings as to impede the practice of getting married in church. There is no way out of the difficulty that, if general laws are to be subjected to a "religious

will not meet the test. Any society adopting such a system would be courting anarchy, but that danger increases in direct proportion to the society's diversity of religious beliefs, and its determination to coerce or suppress none of them. Precisely because "we are a cosmopolitan nation made up of people of almost every conceivable religious preference," and precisely because we value and protect that religious divergence, we cannot afford the luxury of deeming *presumptively invalid*, as applied to the religious objector, every regulation of conduct that does not protect an interest of the highest order. The rule respondents favor would open the prospect of constitutionally required religious exemptions from civic obligations of almost every conceivable kind — ranging from compulsory military service, *see, e.g., Gillette v. United States*, 401 U.S. 437 (1971), to the payment of taxes, see, e.g., *United States v. Lee, supra;* to health and safety regulation such as manslaughter and child neglect laws, *see, e.g., Funkhouser v. State,* 763 P.2d 695 (Okla.Crim.App.1988), compulsory vaccination laws, *see, e.g., Cude v. State,* 237 Ark. 927, 377 S.W.2d 816 (1964), drug laws, *see, e.g., Olsen v. Drug Enforcement Administration,* 279 U.S.App.D.C. 1 (1989), and traffic laws, *see Cox v. New Hampshire,* 312 U.S. 569 (1941); to social welfare legislation such as minimum wage laws, *see Tony and Susan Alamo Foundation v. Secretary of Labor,* 471 U.S. 290 (1985), child labor laws, *see Prince v. Massachusetts,* 321 U.S. 158 (1944), animal cruelty laws, *see, e.g., Church of the Lukumi Babalu Aye Inc. v. City of Hialeah,* 723 F.Supp. 1467 (SD Fla.1989), *cf. State v. Massey,* 229 N.C. 734, 51 S.E.2d 179, *appeal dism'd,* 336 U.S. 942 (1949), environmental protection laws, *see United States v. Little,* 638 F.Supp. 337 (Mont.1986), and laws providing for equality of opportunity for the races, *see, e.g., Bob Jones University v. United States,* 461 U.S. 574, 603-604 (1983). The First Amendment's protection of religious liberty does not require this.[5]

Values that are protected against government interference through enshrinement in the Bill of Rights are not thereby banished from the political process. Just as a society that believes in the negative protection accorded to the press by the First Amendment is likely to enact laws that affirmatively foster the dis-

---

practice" exception, *both* the importance of the law at issue *and* the centrality of the practice at issue must reasonably be considered.

Nor is this difficulty avoided by JUSTICE BLACKMUN'S assertion that "although . . . courts should refrain from delving into questions whether, as a matter of religious doctrine, a particular practice is 'central' to the religion, . . . I do not think this means that the courts must turn a blind eye to the severe impact of a State's restrictions on the adherents of a minority religion." *Post,* at 1621 (dissenting opinion). As JUSTICE BLACKMUN'S opinion proceeds to make clear, inquiry into "severe impact" is no different from inquiry into centrality. He has merely substituted for the question "How important is X to the religious adherent?" the question "How great will be the harm to the religious adherent if X is taken away?" There is no material difference.

[5] JUSTICE O'CONNOR contends that the "parade of horribles" in the text only "demonstrates . . . that courts have been quite capable of . . . strik[ing] sensible balances between religious liberty and competing state interests." *Post,* at 1612-1613 (opinion concurring in judgment). But the cases we cite have struck "sensible balances" only because they have all applied the general laws, despite the claims for religious exemption. In any event, JUSTICE O'CONNOR mistakes the purpose of our parade: it is not to suggest that courts would necessarily permit harmful exemptions from these laws (though they might), but to suggest that courts would constantly be in the business of determining

semination of the printed word, so also a society that believes in the negative
protection accorded to religious belief can be expected to be solicitous of that
value in its legislation as well. It is therefore not surprising that a number of
States [such as Arizona, Colorado, and New Mexico] have made an exception to
their drug laws for sacramental peyote use. But to say that a nondiscriminatory
religious-practice exemption is permitted, or even that it is desirable, is not to
say that it is constitutionally required, and that the appropriate occasions for
its creation can be discerned by the courts. It may fairly be said that leaving
accommodation to the political process will place at a relative disadvantage
those religious practices that are not widely engaged in; but that unavoidable
consequence of democratic government must be preferred to a system in which
each conscience is a law unto itself or in which judges weigh the social importance of all laws against the centrality of all religious beliefs.

* * *

Because respondents' ingestion of peyote was prohibited under Oregon law,
and because that prohibition is constitutional, Oregon may, consistent with the
Free Exercise Clause, deny respondents unemployment compensation when
their dismissal results from use of the drug. The decision of the Oregon
Supreme Court is accordingly reversed.

JUSTICE O'CONNOR, with whom JUSTICE BRENNAN, JUSTICE MARSHALL, and
JUSTICE BLACKMUN join as to Parts I and II, concurring in the judgment.
[Although JUSTICE BRENNAN, JUSTICE MARSHALL, and JUSTICE BLACKMUN join
Parts I and II of this opinion, they do not concur in the judgment.]

Although I agree with the result the Court reaches in this case, I cannot join
its opinion. In my view, today's holding dramatically departs from well-settled
First Amendment jurisprudence, appears unnecessary to resolve the question
presented, and is incompatible with our Nation's fundamental commitment to
individual religious liberty.

II

The Court today extracts from our long history of free exercise precedents the
single categorical rule that "if prohibiting the exercise of religion . . . is . . .
merely the incidental effect of a generally applicable and otherwise valid provision, the First Amendment has not been offended." Indeed, the Court holds
that where the law is a generally applicable criminal prohibition, our usual
free exercise jurisprudence does not even apply. To reach this sweeping result,
however, the Court must not only give a strained reading of the First Amend-

---

whether the "severe impact" of various laws on religious practice (to use JUSTICE BLACKMUN's terminology *post*, at 1621) or the "constitutiona[l] significan[ce]" of the "burden on the specific plaintiffs" (to use JUSTICE O'CONNOR's terminology *post*, at 1611) suffices to permit us to confer an
exemption. It is a parade of horribles because it is horrible to contemplate that federal judges will
regularly balance against the importance of general laws the significance of religious practice.

ment but must also disregard our consistent application of free exercise doctrine to cases involving generally applicable regulations that burden religious conduct.

A

The Free Exercise Clause of the First Amendment commands that "Congress shall make no law . . . prohibiting the free exercise [of religion]." In *Cantwell v. Connecticut,* we held that this prohibition applies to the States by incorporation into the Fourteenth Amendment and that it categorically forbids government regulation of religious beliefs. As the Court recognizes, however, the "free *exercise*" of religion often, if not invariably, requires the performance of (or abstention from) certain acts. *Cf.* 3 A NEW ENGLISH DICTIONARY ON HISTORICAL PRINCIPLES 401-402 (J. Murray ed. 1897) (defining "exercise" to include "[t]he practice and performance of rites and ceremonies, worship, etc.; the right or permission to celebrate the observances (of a religion)" and religious observances such as acts of public and private worship, preaching, and prophesying). "[B]elief and action cannot be neatly confined in logic-tight compartments." *Wisconsin v. Yoder*. Because the First Amendment does not distinguish between religious belief and religious conduct, conduct motivated by sincere religious belief, like the belief itself, must be at least presumptively protected by the Free Exercise Clause.

The Court today, however, interprets the Clause to permit the government to prohibit, without justification, conduct mandated by an individual's religious beliefs, so long as that prohibition is generally applicable. But a law that prohibits certain conduct — conduct that happens to be an act of worship for someone — manifestly does prohibit that person's free exercise of his religion. A person who is barred from engaging in religiously motivated conduct is barred from freely exercising his religion. Moreover, that person is barred from freely exercising his religion regardless of whether the law prohibits the conduct only when engaged in for religious reasons, only by members of that religion, or by all persons. It is difficult to deny that a law that prohibits religiously motivated conduct, even if the law is generally applicable, does not at least implicate First Amendment concerns.

The Court responds that generally applicable laws are "one large step" removed from laws aimed at specific religious practices. The First Amendment, however, does not distinguish between laws that are generally applicable and laws that target particular religious practices. Indeed, few States would be so naive as to enact a law directly prohibiting or burdening a religious practice as such. Our free exercise cases have all concerned generally applicable laws that had the effect of significantly burdening a religious practice. If the First Amendment is to have any vitality, it ought not be construed to cover only the extreme and hypothetical situation in which a State directly targets a religious practice. As we have noted in a slightly different context, " '[s]uch a test has no basis in precedent and relegates a serious First Amendment value to the barest level of minimum scrutiny that the Equal Protection Clause already provides.' " *Hobbie v. Unemployment Appeals Comm'n of Florida*, 480 U.S. 136, 141-142 (1987) (quoting *Bowen v. Roy*, 476 U.S. 693, 727 (1986) (O'CONNOR, J., concurring in part and dissenting in part)).

To say that a person's right to free exercise has been burdened, of course, does not mean that he has an absolute right to engage in the conduct. Under our established First Amendment jurisprudence, we have recognized that the freedom to act, unlike the freedom to believe, cannot be absolute. *See, e.g., Cantwell; Reynolds v. United States.* Instead, we have respected both the First Amendment's express textual mandate and the governmental interest in regulation of conduct by requiring the government to justify any substantial burden on religiously motivated conduct by a compelling state interest and by means narrowly tailored to achieve that interest. The compelling interest test effectuates the First Amendment's command that religious liberty is an independent liberty, that it occupies a preferred position, and that the Court will not permit encroachments upon this liberty, whether direct or indirect, unless required by clear and compelling governmental interests "of the highest order," *Yoder.* "Only an especially important governmental interest pursued by narrowly tailored means can justify exacting a sacrifice of First Amendment freedoms as the price for an equal share of the rights, benefits, and privileges enjoyed by other citizens." *Roy* (opinion concurring in part and dissenting in part).

The Court attempts to support its narrow reading of the Clause by claiming that "[w]e have never held that an individual's religious beliefs excuse him from compliance with an otherwise valid law prohibiting conduct that the State is free to regulate." But as the Court later notes, as it must, in cases such as *Cantwell* and *Yoder* we have in fact interpreted the Free Exercise Clause to forbid application of a generally applicable prohibition to religiously motivated conduct. Indeed, in *Yoder* we expressly rejected the interpretation the Court now adopts:

> "[O]ur decisions have rejected the idea that religiously grounded conduct is always outside the protection of the Free Exercise Clause. It is true that activities of individuals, even when religiously based, are often subject to regulation by the States in the exercise of their undoubted power to promote the health, safety, and general welfare, or the Federal Government in the exercise of its delegated powers. But to agree that religiously grounded conduct must often be subject to the broad police power of the State is not to deny that there are areas of conduct protected by the Free Exercise Clause of the First Amendment and thus beyond the power of the State to control, *even under regulations of general applicability*. . . .

> ". . . A regulation neutral on its face may, in its application, nonetheless offend the constitutional requirement for government neutrality if it unduly burdens the free exercise of religion."

The Court endeavors to escape from our decisions in *Cantwell* and *Yoder* by labeling them "hybrid" decisions, but there is no denying that both cases expressly relied on the Free Exercise Clause, and that we have consistently regarded those cases as part of the mainstream of our free exercise jurisprudence. Moreover, in each of the other cases cited by the Court to support its categorical rule, we rejected the particular constitutional claims before us only after carefully weighing the competing interests. *See Prince v. Massachusetts*, 321 U.S. 158, 168-170 (1944) (state interest in regulating children's activities justifies denial of religious exemption from child labor laws); *Braunfeld v. Brown*, 366 U.S. 599, 608-609 (1961) (plurality opinion) (state interest in uniform day of rest justifies denial of religious exemption from Sunday closing law); *Gillette, supra*, 401 U.S., at 462 (state interest in military affairs justifies denial of religious exemption from conscription laws); *Lee* (state interest in comprehensive Social Security system justifies denial of religious exemption from mandatory participation requirement). That we rejected the free exercise claims in those cases hardly calls into question the applicability of First Amendment doctrine in the first place. Indeed, it is surely unusual to judge the vitality of a constitutional doctrine by looking to the win-loss record of the plaintiffs who happen to come before us.

B

Respondents, of course, do not contend that their conduct is automatically immune from all governmental regulation simply because it is motivated by their sincere religious beliefs. The Court's rejection of that argument might therefore be regarded as merely harmless dictum. Rather, respondents invoke our traditional compelling interest test to argue that the Free Exercise Clause requires the State to grant them a limited exemption from its general criminal prohibition against the possession of peyote. The Court today, however, denies them even the opportunity to make that argument, concluding that "the sounder approach, and the approach in accord with the vast majority of our precedents, is to hold the [compelling interest] test inapplicable to" challenges to general criminal prohibitions.

In my view, however, the essence of a free exercise claim is relief from a burden imposed by government on religious practices or beliefs, whether the burden is imposed directly through laws that prohibit or compel specific religious practices, or indirectly through laws that, in effect, make abandonment of one's own religion or conformity to the religious beliefs of others the price of an equal place in the civil community. As we explained in *Thomas*:

> "Where the state conditions receipt of an important benefit upon conduct proscribed by a religious faith, or where it denies such a benefit because of conduct mandated by religious belief, thereby putting substantial pressure on an adherent to modify his behavior and to violate his beliefs, a burden upon religion exists."

A State that makes criminal an individual's religiously motivated conduct burdens that individual's free exercise of religion in the severest manner possible, for it "results in the choice to the individual of either abandoning his religious principle or facing criminal prosecution." *Braunfeld, supra,* 366 U.S., at 605. I would have thought it beyond argument that such laws implicate free exercise concerns.

Indeed, we have never distinguished between cases in which a State conditions receipt of a benefit on conduct prohibited by religious beliefs and cases in which a State affirmatively prohibits such conduct. The *Sherbert* compelling interest test applies in both kinds of cases. As I noted in *Bowen v. Roy* :

> "The fact that the underlying dispute involves an award of benefits rather than an exaction of penalties does not grant the Government license to apply a different version of the Constitution. . . .

> ". . . The fact that appellees seek exemption from a precondition that the Government attaches to an award of benefits does not, therefore, generate a meaningful distinction between this case and one where appellees seek an exemption from the Government's imposition of penalties upon them." 476 U.S., at 731-732 (opinion concurring in part and dissenting in part).

I would reaffirm that principle today: A neutral criminal law prohibiting conduct that a State may legitimately regulate is, if anything, more burdensome than a neutral civil statute placing legitimate conditions on the award of a state benefit.

Legislatures, of course, have always been "left free to reach actions which were in violation of social duties or subversive of good order." *Reynolds*. Yet because of the close relationship between conduct and religious belief, "[i]n every case the power to regulate must be so exercised as not, in attaining a permissible end, unduly to infringe the protected freedom." *Cantwell*. Once it has been shown that a government regulation or criminal prohibition burdens the free exercise of religion, we have consistently asked the government to demonstrate that unbending application of its regulation to the religious objector "is essential to accomplish an overriding governmental interest," *Lee,* or represents "the least restrictive means of achieving some compelling state interest," *Thomas*. To me, the sounder approach — the approach more consistent with our role as judges to decide each case on its individual merits — is to apply this test in each case to determine whether the burden on the specific plaintiffs before us is constitutionally significant and whether the particular criminal interest asserted by the State before us is compelling. Even if, as an empirical matter, a government's criminal laws might usually serve a compelling interest in health, safety, or public order, the First Amendment at least requires a case-by-case determination of the question, sensitive to the facts of each particular claim. *Cf. McDaniel,* 435 U.S., at 628, n. 8 (plurality opinion) (noting application of *Sherbert* to general criminal prohibitions and the "delicate balancing required by our decisions in" *Sherbert* and *Yoder*). Given the range of conduct that a State might legitimately make criminal, we cannot assume, merely because a law carries criminal sanctions and is generally applicable, that the First

Amendment *never* requires the State to grant a limited exemption for religiously motivated conduct.

Moreover, we have not "rejected" or "declined to apply" the compelling interest test in our recent cases. Recent cases have instead affirmed that test as a fundamental part of our First Amendment doctrine. The cases cited by the Court signal no retreat from our consistent adherence to the compelling interest test. In both *Bowen v. Roy* and *Lyng v. Northwest Indian Cemetery Protective Assn.*, for example, we expressly distinguished *Sherbert* on the ground that the First Amendment does not "require the Government *itself* to behave in ways that the individual believes will further his or her spiritual development. . . . The Free Exercise Clause simply cannot be understood to require the Government to conduct its own internal affairs in ways that comport with the religious beliefs of particular citizens." *Roy*. This distinction makes sense because "the Free Exercise Clause is written in terms of what the government cannot do to the individual, not in terms of what the individual can exact from the government." *Sherbert* (Douglas, J., concurring). Because the case *sub judice*, like the other cases in which we have applied *Sherbert*, plainly falls into the former category, I would apply those established precedents to the facts of this case.

Similarly, the other cases cited by the Court for the proposition that we have rejected application of the *Sherbert* test outside the unemployment compensation field are distinguishable because they arose in the narrow, specialized contexts in which we have not traditionally required the government to justify a burden on religious conduct by articulating a compelling interest. *See Goldman v. Weinberger* ("Our review of military regulations challenged on First Amendment grounds is far more deferential than constitutional review of similar laws or regulations designed for civilian society"); *O'Lone v. Estate of Shabazz*, 482 U.S. 342, 349 (1987) ("[P]rison regulations alleged to infringe constitutional rights are judged under a 'reasonableness' test less restrictive than that ordinarily applied to alleged infringements of fundamental constitutional rights") (citation omitted). That we did not apply the compelling interest test in these cases says nothing about whether the test should continue to apply in paradigm free exercise cases such as the one presented here.

The Court today gives no convincing reason to depart from settled First Amendment jurisprudence. There is nothing talismanic about neutral laws of general applicability or general criminal prohibitions, for laws neutral toward religion can coerce a person to violate his religious conscience or intrude upon his religious duties just as effectively as laws aimed at religion. Although the Court suggests that the compelling interest test, as applied to generally applicable laws, would result in a "constitutional anomaly," the First Amendment unequivocally makes freedom of religion, like freedom from race discrimination and freedom of speech, a "constitutional nor[m]," not an "anomaly." Nor would application of our established free exercise doctrine to this case necessarily be incompatible with our equal protection cases. We have in any event recognized that the Free Exercise Clause protects values distinct from those protected by the Equal Protection Clause. *See Hobbie*, 480 U.S., at 141-142. As the language of the Clause itself makes clear, an individual's free exercise of religion is a preferred constitutional activity. *See, e.g.,* McConnell, *Accommodation of Religion*, 1985 S. Ct. Rev. 1, 9 ("[T]he text of the First Amendment itself 'singles out' religion for special protections"); P. Kauper, Religion and the Constitution 17 (1964). A law that makes criminal such an activity therefore triggers constitutional concern — and heightened judicial scrutiny — even if it does not target the particular religious conduct at issue. Our free speech cases similarly recognize that neutral regulations that affect free speech values are subject to a balancing, rather than categorical, approach. The Court's parade of horribles not only fails as a reason for discarding the compelling interest test, it instead demonstrates just the opposite: that courts have been quite capable of applying our free exercise jurisprudence to strike sensible balances between religious liberty and competing state interests.

Finally, the Court today suggests that the disfavoring of minority religions is an "unavoidable consequence" under our system of government and that accommodation of such religions must be left to the political process. In my view, however, the First Amendment was enacted precisely to protect the rights of those whose religious practices are not shared by the majority and may be viewed with hostility. The history of our free exercise doctrine amply demonstrates the harsh impact majoritarian rule has had on unpopular or emerging religious groups such as the Jehovah's Witnesses and the Amish. Indeed, the words of Justice Jackson in *West Virginia State Bd. of Ed. v. Barnette* (overruling *Minersville School Dist. v. Gobitis*, 310 U.S. 586 (1940)) are apt:

> "The very purpose of a Bill of Rights was to withdraw certain subjects from the vicissitudes of political controversy, to place them beyond the reach of majorities and officials and to establish them as legal principles to be applied by the courts. One's right to life, liberty, and property, to free speech, a free press, freedom of worship and assembly, and other fundamental rights may not be submitted to vote; they depend on the outcome of no elections."

See also United States v. Ballard, 322 U.S. 78, 87 (1944) ("The Fathers of the Constitution were not unaware of the varied and extreme views of religious sects, of the violence of disagreement among them, and of the lack of any one religious creed on which all men would agree. They fashioned a charter of government which envisaged the widest possible toleration of conflicting views"). The compelling interest test reflects the First Amendment's mandate of preserving religious liberty to the fullest extent possible in a pluralistic society. For the Court to deem this command a "luxury," is to denigrate "[t]he very purpose of a Bill of Rights."

III

The Court's holding today not only misreads settled First Amendment precedent; it appears to be unnecessary to this case. I would reach the same result applying our established free exercise jurisprudence.

B

Thus, the critical question in this case is whether exempting respondents from the State's general criminal prohibition "will unduly interfere with fulfillment of the governmental interest." *Lee.* Although the question is close, I would conclude that uniform application of Oregon's criminal prohibition is "essential to accomplish" its overriding interest in preventing the physical harm caused by the use of a Schedule I controlled substance. Oregon's criminal prohibition represents that State's judgment that the possession and use of controlled substances, even by only one person, is inherently harmful and dangerous. Because the health effects caused by the use of controlled substances exist regardless of the motivation of the user, the use of such substances, even for religious purposes, violates the very purpose of the laws that prohibit them. *Cf. State v. Massey,* 229 N.C. 734, 51 S.E.2d 179 (denying religious exemption to municipal ordinance prohibiting handling of poisonous reptiles), *appeal dism'd sub nom. Bunn v. North Carolina,* 336 U.S. 942 (1949). Moreover, in view of the societal interest in preventing trafficking in controlled substances, uniform application of the criminal prohibition at issue is essential to the effectiveness of Oregon's stated interest in preventing any possession of peyote. *Cf. Jacobson v. Massachusetts,* 197 U.S. 11 (1905) (denying exemption from smallpox vaccination requirement).

For these reasons, I believe that granting a selective exemption in this case would seriously impair Oregon's compelling interest in prohibiting possession of peyote by its citizens. Under such circumstances, the Free Exercise Clause does not require the State to accommodate respondents' religiously motivated conduct. Unlike in *Yoder,* where we noted that "[t]he record strongly indicates that accommodating the religious objections of the Amish by forgoing one, or at most two, additional years of compulsory education will not impair the physical or mental health of the child, or result in an inability to be self-supporting or to discharge the duties and responsibilities of citizenship, or in any other way materially detract from the welfare of society," a religious exemption in this case would be incompatible with the State's interest in controlling use and possession of illegal drugs.

Respondents contend that any incompatibility is belied by the fact that the Federal Government and several States provide exemptions for the religious use of peyote, *see* 21 CFR § 1307.31 (1989); 307 Ore., at 73, n. 2, 763 P. 2d, at 148, n. 2 (citing 11 state statutes that expressly exempt sacramental peyote use from criminal proscription). But other governments may surely choose to grant an exemption without Oregon, with its specific asserted interest in uniform application of its drug laws, being *required* to do so by the First Amendment.

Respondents also note that the sacramental use of peyote is central to the tenets of the Native American Church, but I agree with the Court that because " '[i]t is not within the judicial ken to question the centrality of particular beliefs or practices to a faith,' " our determination of the constitutionality of Oregon's general criminal prohibition cannot, and should not, turn on the centrality of the particular religious practice at issue. This does not mean, of course, that courts may not make factual findings as to whether a claimant holds a sincerely held religious belief that conflicts with, and thus is burdened by, the challenged law. The distinction between questions of centrality and questions of sincerity and burden is admittedly fine, but it is one that is an established part of our free exercise doctrine, and one that courts are capable of making.

I would therefore adhere to our established free exercise jurisprudence and hold that the State in this case has a compelling interest in regulating peyote use by its citizens and that accommodating respondents' religiously motivated conduct "will unduly interfere with fulfillment of the governmental interest." *Lee.* Accordingly, I concur in the judgment of the Court.

JUSTICE BLACKMUN, with whom JUSTICE BRENNAN and JUSTICE MARSHALL join, dissenting.

This Court over the years painstakingly has developed a consistent and exacting standard to test the constitutionality of a state statute that burdens the free exercise of religion. Such a statute may stand only if the law in general, and the State's refusal to allow a religious exemption in particular, are justified by a compelling interest that cannot be served by less restrictive means.

Until today, I thought this was a settled and inviolate principle of this Court's First Amendment jurisprudence. The majority, however, perfunctorily dismisses it as a "constitutional anomaly." As carefully detailed in JUSTICE O'CONNOR's concurring opinion, the majority is able to arrive at this view only by mischaracterizing this Court's precedents.

This distorted view of our precedents leads the majority to conclude that strict scrutiny of a state law burdening the free exercise of religion is a "luxury" that a well-ordered society cannot afford, and that the repression of minority religions is an "unavoidable consequence of democratic government." I do not believe the Founders thought their dearly bought freedom from religious persecution a "luxury," but an essential element of liberty — and they could not have thought religious intolerance "unavoidable," for they drafted the Religion Clauses precisely in order to avoid that intolerance.

For these reasons, I agree with JUSTICE O'CONNOR's analysis of the applicable free exercise doctrine, and I join parts I and II of her opinion. I do disagree, however, with her specific answer to that question.

I

The State proclaims an interest in protecting the health and safety of its citizens from the dangers of unlawful drugs. It offers, however, no evidence that the religious use of peyote has ever harmed anyone. The factual findings of other courts cast doubt on the State's assumption that religious use of peyote is harmful. *See State v. Whittingham,* 19 Ariz. App. 27, 30 (1973) ("[T]he State failed to prove that the quantities of peyote used in the sacraments of the Native American Church are sufficiently harmful to the health and welfare of the participants so as to permit a legitimate intrusion under the State's police power"); *People v. Woody,* 61 Cal. 2d 716, 722-723, 40 Cal.Rptr. 69, 74 (1964) ("[A]s the Attorney General . . . admits, . . . the opinion of scientists and other experts is 'that peyote . . . works no permanent deleterious injury to the Indian' ").

The carefully circumscribed ritual context in which respondents used peyote is far removed from the irresponsible and unrestricted recreational use of unlawful drugs.[6] The Native American Church's internal restrictions on, and supervision of, its members' use of peyote substantially obviate the State's health and safety concerns. *See Olsen, id.,* at 10, 878 F.2d, at 1467 (" 'The Administrator [of the Drug Enforcement Administration (DEA)] finds that . . . the Native American Church's use of peyote is isolated to specific ceremonial occasions,' " and so " 'an accommodation can be made for a religious organization which uses peyote in circumscribed ceremonies' " (quoting DEA Final Order)); *id.,* at 7, 878 F.2d, at 1464 ("[F]or members of the Native American Church, use of peyote outside the ritual is sacrilegious"); *Woody,* 61 Cal. 2d, at 721, 394 P.2 d, at 817 ("[T]o use peyote for nonreligious purposes is sacrilegious"); R. JULIEN, A PRIMER OF DRUG ACTION 148 (3d ed. 1981) ("[P]eyote is seldom abused by members of the Native American Church"); Slotkin, *The Peyote Way, in* TEACHINGS FROM THE AMERICAN EARTH 96, 104 (D. Tedlock & B. Tedlock eds. 1975) ("[T]he Native American Church . . . refuses to permit the presence of curiosity seekers at its rites, and vigorously opposes the sale or use of Peyote for non-sacramental purposes"); Bergman, *Navajo Peyote Use: Its Apparent Safety,* 128 AM.J. PSYCHIATRY 695 (1971) (Bergman).[7]

Moreover, just as in *Yoder,* the values and interests of those seeking a religious exemption in this case are congruent, to a great degree, with those the

---

[6] In this respect, respondents' use of peyote seems closely analogous to the sacramental use of wine by the Roman Catholic Church. During Prohibition, the Federal Government exempted such use of wine from its general ban on possession and use of alcohol. *See* National Prohibition Act, Title II, § 3, 41 Stat. 308. However compelling the Government's then general interest in prohibiting the use of alcohol may have been, it could not plausibly have asserted an interest sufficiently compelling to outweigh Catholics' right to take communion.

[7] The use of peyote is, to some degree, self-limiting. The peyote plant is extremely bitter, and eating it is an unpleasant experience, which would tend to discourage casual or recreational use. *See State v. Whittingham,* 19 Ariz. App. 27, 30, 504 P.2d 950, 953 (1973) (" '[P]eyote can cause vomiting by reason of its bitter taste' "); E. ANDERSON, PEYOTE: THE DIVINE CACTUS 161 (1980) ("[T]he eating of peyote usually is a difficult ordeal in that nausea and other unpleasant physical manifestations occur regularly. Repeated use is likely, therefore, only if one is a serious researcher or is devoutly involved in taking peyote as part of a religious ceremony"); Slotkin, *The Peyote Way, in* TEACHINGS FROM THE AMERICAN EARTH 96, 98 (D. Tedlock & B. Tedlock eds. 1975) ("[M]any find it bitter, inducing indigestion or nausea").

State seeks to promote through its drug laws. *See Yoder* (since the Amish accept formal schooling up to 8th grade, and then provide "ideal" vocational education, State's interest in enforcing its law against the Amish is "less substantial than . . . for children generally"). Not only does the church's doctrine forbid nonreligious use of peyote; it also generally advocates self-reliance, familial responsibility, and abstinence from alcohol. *See* Brief for Association on American Indian Affairs et al. as *Amici Curiae* 33-34 (the church's "ethical code" has four parts: brotherly love, care of family, self-reliance, and avoidance of alcohol (quoting from the church membership card)); *Olsen*, 279 U.S.App. D. C., at 7 (the Native American Church, "for all purposes other than the special, stylized ceremony, reinforced the state's prohibition"); *Woody*, 61 Cal. 2d, at 721-722, n. 3 ("[M]ost anthropological authorities hold Peyotism to be a positive, rather than negative, force in the lives of its adherents . . . the church forbids the use of alcohol . . ."). There is considerable evidence that the spiritual and social support provided by the church has been effective in combating the tragic effects of alcoholism on the Native American population. Two noted experts on peyotism, Dr. Omer C. Stewart and Dr. Robert Bergman, testified by affidavit to this effect on behalf of respondent Smith before the Employment Appeal Board. *See also* E. ANDERSON, PEYOTE: THE DIVINE CACTUS 165-166 (1980) (research by Dr. Bergman suggests "that the religious use of peyote seemed to be directed in an ego-strengthening direction with an emphasis on interpersonal relationships where each individual is assured of his own significance as well as the support of the group"; many people have "'come through difficult crises with the help of this religion. . . . It provides real help in seeing themselves not as people whose place and way in the world is gone, but as people whose way can be strong enough to change and meet new challenges'" (quoting Bergman 698)); Pascarosa & Futterman, *Ethnopsychedelic Therapy for Alcoholics: Observations in the Peyote Ritual of the Native American Church*, 8 J. OF PSYCHEDELIC DRUGS, No. 3, p. 215 (1976) (religious peyote use has been helpful in overcoming alcoholism); Albaugh & Anderson, *Peyote in the Treatment of Alcoholism among American Indians*, 131 AM. J. PSYCHIATRY 1247, 1249 (1974) ("[T]he philosophy, teachings, and format of the [Native American Church] can be of great benefit to the Indian alcoholic"); *see generally* O. STEWART, PEYOTE RELIGION 75 et seq. (1987) (noting frequent observations, across many tribes and periods in history, of correlation between peyotist religion and abstinence from alcohol). Far from promoting the lawless and irresponsible use of drugs, Native American Church members' spiritual code exemplifies values that Oregon's drug laws are presumably intended to foster.

NOTES ON THE FALLOUT FROM *SMITH*

1. *Academic criticism of Smith.* The Supreme Court's *Smith* decision has generated vigorous opposition in both Congress and academia. Congress responded to *Smith* by passing the Religious Freedom Restoration Act, which is addressed in *Boerne, infra*. Academics responded in the law reviews. For a representative sample of critical treatments of *Smith*, see Frederick Mark Gedicks,

The Normalized Free Exercise Clause: Three Abnormalities, 75 IND. L.J. 77 (2000); Douglas Laycock, *The Remnants of Free Exercise*, 1990 SUP. CT. REV. 1; Michael W. McConnell, *Free Exercise Revisionism and the Smith Decision*, 57 U. CHI. L. REV. 1109 (1990); Steven D. Smith, *The Rise and Fall of Religious Freedom in Constitutional Discourse*, 140 U. PA. L. REV. 149 (1991); David E. Steinberg, *Rejecting the Case Against the Free Exercise Exemption: A Critical Assessment*, 75 B.U. L. REV. 241, 268-76 (1995).

2. *Academic support for Smith.* Some commentators have defended the *Smith* decision (although not always its reasoning). *See* William P. Marshall, *In Defense of Smith and Free Exercise Revisionism*, 58 U. CHI. L. REV. 308 (1991); William P. Marshall, *The Case Against the Constitutionally Compelled Free Exercise Exemption*, 40 CASE W. RES. L. REV. 357 (1990); Suzanna Sherry, *Lee v. Weisman: Paradox Redux*, 1992 SUP. CT. REV. 123. *See also* Steven G. Gey, *Why is Religion Special?: Reconsidering the Accommodation of Religion under the Religion Clauses of the First Amendment*, 52 U. PITT. L. REV. 75 (1990) (pre-*Smith* argument against accommodation principle). For a comprehensive (and critical) treatment of religious accommodation generally, see MARCI A. HAMILTON, GOD VS. THE GAVEL: RELIGION AND THE RULE OF LAW (2005).

B. THE INITIAL STATUTORY RESPONSE TO *SMITH*

CITY OF BOERNE v. FLORES
521 U.S. 507 (1997)

JUSTICE KENNEDY delivered the opinion of the Court.

A decision by local zoning authorities to deny a church a building permit was challenged under the Religious Freedom Restoration Act of 1993 (RFRA), 42 U.S.C. § 2000bb *et seq.* The case calls into question the authority of Congress to enact RFRA. We conclude the statute exceeds Congress' power.

I

Situated on a hill in the city of Boerne, Texas, some 28 miles northwest of San Antonio, is St. Peter Catholic Church. Built in 1923, the church's structure replicates the mission style of the region's earlier history. The church seats about 230 worshippers, a number too small for its growing parish. Some 40 to 60 parishioners cannot be accommodated at some Sunday masses. In order to meet the needs of the congregation the Archbishop of San Antonio gave permission to the parish to plan alterations to enlarge the building.

A few months later, the Boerne City Council passed an ordinance authorizing the city's Historic Landmark Commission to prepare a preservation plan with proposed historic landmarks and districts. Under the ordinance, the Commission must preapprove construction affecting historic landmarks or buildings in a historic district.

Soon afterwards, the Archbishop applied for a building permit so construction to enlarge the church could proceed. City authorities, relying on the ordinance and the designation of a historic district (which, they argued, included the church), denied the application. The Archbishop brought this suit challenging the permit denial in the United States District Court for the Western District of Texas.

The complaint contained various claims, but to this point the litigation has centered on RFRA and the question of its constitutionality. The Archbishop relied upon RFRA as one basis for relief from the refusal to issue the permit. The District Court concluded that by enacting RFRA Congress exceeded the scope of its enforcement power under § 5 of the Fourteenth Amendment. The court certified its order for interlocutory appeal and the Fifth Circuit reversed, finding RFRA to be constitutional. We . . . now reverse.

II

Congress enacted RFRA in direct response to the Court's decision in *Employment Div., Dept. of Human Resources of Oregon v. Smith*. There we considered a Free Exercise Clause claim brought by members of the Native American Church who were denied unemployment benefits when they lost their jobs because they had used peyote. Their practice was to ingest peyote for sacramental purposes, and they challenged an Oregon statute of general applicability which made use of the drug criminal. In evaluating the claim, we declined to apply the balancing test set forth in *Sherbert v. Verner*, under which we would have asked whether Oregon's prohibition substantially burdened a religious practice and, if it did, whether the burden was justified by a compelling government interest. We stated:

> "[G]overnment's ability to enforce generally applicable prohibitions of socially harmful conduct . . . cannot depend on measuring the effects of a governmental action on a religious objector's spiritual development. To make an individual's obligation to obey such a law contingent upon the law's coincidence with his religious beliefs, except where the State's interest is 'compelling' . . . contradicts both constitutional tradition and common sense."

The application of the *Sherbert* test, the *Smith* decision explained, would have produced an anomaly in the law, a constitutional right to ignore neutral laws of general applicability. The anomaly would have been accentuated, the Court reasoned, by the difficulty of determining whether a particular practice was central to an individual's religion. We explained, moreover, that it "is not within the judicial ken to question the centrality of particular beliefs or practices to a faith, or the validity of particular litigants' interpretations of those creeds."

The only instances where a neutral, generally applicable law had failed to pass constitutional muster, the *Smith* Court noted, were cases in which other constitutional protections were at stake. In *Wisconsin v. Yoder*, for example, we invalidated Wisconsin's mandatory school-attendance law as applied to Amish parents who refused on religious grounds to send their children to school. That case implicated not only the right to the free exercise of religion but also the right of parents to control their children's education.

The *Smith* decision acknowledged the Court had employed the *Sherbert* test in considering free exercise challenges to state unemployment compensation rules on three occasions where the balance had tipped in favor of the individual. *See Sherbert; Thomas v. Review Bd. of Indiana Employment Security Div.; Hobbie v. Unemployment Appeals Comm'n of Fla.,* 480 U.S. 136 (1987). Those cases, the Court explained, stand for "the proposition that where the State has in place a system of individual exemptions, it may not refuse to extend that system to cases of religious hardship without compelling reason." By contrast, where a general prohibition, such as Oregon's, is at issue, "the sounder approach, and the approach in accord with the vast majority of our precedents, is to hold the test inapplicable to [free exercise] challenges." *Smith* held that neutral, generally applicable laws may be applied to religious practices even when not supported by a compelling governmental interest.

Four Members of the Court disagreed. They argued the law placed a substantial burden on the Native American Church members so that it could be upheld only if the law served a compelling state interest and was narrowly tailored to achieve that end. JUSTICE O'CONNOR concluded Oregon had satisfied the test, while Justice Blackmun, joined by Justice Brennan and Justice Marshall, could see no compelling interest justifying the law's application to the members.

These points of constitutional interpretation were debated by Members of Congress in hearings and floor debates. Many criticized the Court's reasoning, and this disagreement resulted in the passage of RFRA. Congress announced:

"(1) [T]he framers of the Constitution, recognizing free exercise of religion as an unalienable right, secured its protection in the First Amendment to the Constitution;

"(2) laws 'neutral' toward religion may burden religious exercise as surely as laws intended to interfere with religious exercise;

"(3) governments should not substantially burden religious exercise without compelling justification;

"(4) in *Employment Division v. Smith,* 494 U.S. 872 (1990), the Supreme Court virtually eliminated the requirement that the government justify burdens on religious exercise imposed by laws neutral toward religion; and

"(5) the compelling interest test as set forth in prior Federal court rulings is a workable test for striking sensible balances between religious liberty and competing prior governmental interests." 42 U.S.C. § 2000bb(a).

The Act's stated purposes are:

> "(1) to restore the compelling interest test as set forth in *Sherbert v. Verner*, 374 U.S. 398 (1963) and *Wisconsin v. Yoder*, 406 U.S. 205 (1972) and to guarantee its application in all cases where free exercise of religion is substantially burdened; and

> "(2) to provide a claim or defense to persons whose religious exercise is substantially burdened by government." § 2000bb(b).

RFRA prohibits "[g]overnment" from "substantially burden[ing]" a person's exercise of religion even if the burden results from a rule of general applicability unless the government can demonstrate the burden "(1) is in furtherance of a compelling governmental interest; and (2) is the least restrictive means of furthering that compelling governmental interest." § 2000bb-1. The Act's mandate applies to any "branch, department, agency, instrumentality, and official (or other person acting under color of law) of the United States," as well as to any "State, or . . . subdivision of a State." § 2000bb-2(1). The Act's universal coverage is confirmed in § 2000bb-3(a), under which RFRA "applies to all Federal and State law, and the implementation of that law, whether statutory or otherwise, and whether adopted before or after [RFRA's enactment]." In accordance with RFRA's usage of the term, we shall use "state law" to include local and municipal ordinances.

III

A

Under our Constitution, the Federal Government is one of enumerated powers. The judicial authority to determine the constitutionality of laws, in cases and controversies, is based on the premise that the "powers of the legislature are defined and limited; and that those limits may not be mistaken, or forgotten, the constitution is written." *Marbury v. Madison.*

Congress relied on its Fourteenth Amendment enforcement power in enacting the most far reaching and substantial of RFRA's provisions, those which impose its requirements on the States. The Fourteenth Amendment provides, in relevant part:

> "Section 1. . . . No State shall make or enforce any law which shall abridge the privileges or immunities of citizens of the United States; nor shall any State deprive any person of life, liberty, or property, without due process of law; nor deny to any person within its jurisdiction the equal protection of the laws.

> . . . .

> "Section 5. The Congress shall have power to enforce, by appropriate legislation, the provisions of this article."

The parties disagree over whether RFRA is a proper exercise of Congress' § 5 power "to enforce" by "appropriate legislation" the constitutional guarantee that no State shall deprive any person of "life, liberty, or property, without due process of law" nor deny any person "equal protection of the laws."

In defense of the Act respondent contends, with support from the United States as amicus, that RFRA is permissible enforcement legislation. Congress, it is said, is only protecting by legislation one of the liberties guaranteed by the Fourteenth Amendment's Due Process Clause, the free exercise of religion, beyond what is necessary under *Smith*. It is said the congressional decision to dispense with proof of deliberate or overt discrimination and instead concentrate on a law's effects accords with the settled understanding that § 5 includes the power to enact legislation designed to prevent as well as remedy constitutional violations. It is further contended that Congress' § 5 power is not limited to remedial or preventive legislation.

Congress' power under § 5, however, extends only to "enforc[ing]" the provisions of the Fourteenth Amendment. The Court has described this power as "remedial." The design of the Amendment and the text of § 5 are inconsistent with the suggestion that Congress has the power to decree the substance of the Fourteenth Amendment's restrictions on the States. Legislation which alters the meaning of the Free Exercise Clause cannot be said to be enforcing the Clause. Congress does not enforce a constitutional right by changing what the right is. It has been given the power "to enforce," not the power to determine what constitutes a constitutional violation. Were it not so, what Congress would be enforcing would no longer be, in any meaningful sense, the "provisions of [the Fourteenth Amendment]."

While the line between measures that remedy or prevent unconstitutional actions and measures that make a substantive change in the governing law is not easy to discern, and Congress must have wide latitude in determining where it lies, the distinction exists and must be observed. There must be a congruence and proportionality between the injury to be prevented or remedied and the means adopted to that end. Lacking such a connection, legislation may become substantive in operation and effect. History and our case law support drawing the distinction, one apparent from the text of the Amendment.

B

Regardless of the state of the legislative record, RFRA cannot be considered remedial, preventive legislation, if those terms are to have any meaning. RFRA is so out of proportion to a supposed remedial or preventive object that it cannot be understood as responsive to, or designed to prevent, unconstitutional behavior. It appears, instead, to attempt a substantive change in constitutional protections. Preventive measures prohibiting certain types of laws may be appropriate when there is reason to believe that many of the laws affected by the congressional enactment have a significant likelihood of being unconstitutional. *See City of Rome,* 446 U.S., at 177 (since "jurisdictions with a demonstrable history of intentional racial discrimination . . . create the risk of purposeful discrimination" Congress could "prohibit changes that have a discriminatory impact" in those jurisdictions). Remedial legislation under § 5 "should be adapted to the mischief and wrong which the [Fourteenth] [A]mendment was intended to provide against." *Civil Rights Cases*, 109 U.S., at 13.

RFRA is not so confined. Sweeping coverage ensures its intrusion at every level of government, displacing laws and prohibiting official actions of almost every description and regardless of subject matter. RFRA's restrictions apply to every agency and official of the Federal, State, and local Governments. RFRA applies to all federal and state law, statutory or otherwise, whether adopted before or after its enactment. RFRA has no termination date or termination mechanism. Any law is subject to challenge at any time by any individual who alleges a substantial burden on his or her free exercise of religion.

The stringent test RFRA demands of state laws reflects a lack of proportionality or congruence between the means adopted and the legitimate end to be achieved. If an objector can show a substantial burden on his free exercise, the State must demonstrate a compelling governmental interest and show that the law is the least restrictive means of furthering its interest. Claims that a law substantially burdens someone's exercise of religion will often be difficult to contest. Requiring a State to demonstrate a compelling interest and show that it has adopted the least restrictive means of achieving that interest is the most demanding test known to constitutional law. If " 'compelling interest' really means what it says . . . many laws will not meet the test. . . . [The test] would open the prospect of constitutionally required religious exemptions from civic obligations of almost every conceivable kind." [*Smith.*] Laws valid under *Smith* would fall under RFRA without regard to whether they had the object of stifling or punishing free exercise. We make these observations not to reargue the position of the majority in *Smith* but to illustrate the substantive alteration of its holding attempted by RFRA. Even assuming RFRA would be interpreted in effect to mandate some lesser test, say one equivalent to intermediate scrutiny, the statute nevertheless would require searching judicial scrutiny of state law with the attendant likelihood of invalidation. This is a considerable congressional intrusion into the States' traditional prerogatives and general authority to regulate for the health and welfare of their citizens.

JUSTICE STEVENS, concurring.

In my opinion, the Religious Freedom Restoration Act of 1993 (RFRA) is a "law respecting an establishment of religion" that violates the First Amendment to the Constitution.

If the historic landmark on the hill in Boerne happened to be a museum or an art gallery owned by an atheist, it would not be eligible for an exemption from the city ordinances that forbid an enlargement of the structure. Because the landmark is owned by the Catholic Church, it is claimed that RFRA gives its owner a federal statutory entitlement to an exemption from a generally applicable, neutral civil law. Whether the Church would actually prevail under the statute or not, the statute has provided the Church with a legal weapon that no atheist or agnostic can obtain. This governmental preference for religion, as opposed to irreligion, is forbidden by the First Amendment. *Wallace v. Jaffree.*

JUSTICE SCALIA, with whom JUSTICE STEVENS joins, concurring in part.

I write to respond briefly to the claim of JUSTICE O'CONNOR's dissent (hereinafter "the dissent") that historical materials support a result contrary to the one reached in *Employment Div., Dept. of Human Resources of Oregon v. Smith.* We held in *Smith* that the Constitution's Free Exercise Clause "does not relieve an individual of the obligation to comply with a 'valid and neutral law of general applicability on the ground that the law proscribes (or prescribes) conduct that his religion prescribes (or proscribes).'" The material that the dissent claims is at odds with *Smith* either has little to say about the issue or is in fact more consistent with *Smith* than with the dissent's interpretation of the Free Exercise Clause. The dissent's extravagant claim that the historical record shows *Smith* to have been wrong should be compared with the assessment of the most prominent scholarly critic of *Smith*, who, after an extensive review of the historical record, was willing to venture no more than that "constitutionally compelled exemptions [from generally applicable laws regulating conduct] were *within the contemplation* of the framers and ratifiers *as a possible interpretation* of the free exercise clause." McConnell, *The Origins and Historical Understanding of Free Exercise of Religion*, 103 HARV. L. REV. 1409, 1415 (1990) (emphasis added); *see also* Hamburger, *A Constitutional Right of Religious Exemption: An Historical Perspective*, 60 GEO. WASH. LAW REV. 915 (1992) (arguing that historical evidence supports *Smith*'s interpretation of free exercise).

The historical evidence marshalled by the dissent cannot fairly be said to demonstrate the correctness of *Smith*; but it is more supportive of that conclusion than destructive of it. And, to return to a point I made earlier, that evidence is not compatible with any theory I am familiar with that has been proposed as an alternative to *Smith*. The dissent's approach has, of course, great popular attraction. Who can possibly be against the abstract proposition that government should not, even in its general, nondiscriminatory laws, place unreasonable burdens upon religious practice? Unfortunately, however, that abstract proposition must ultimately be reduced to concrete cases. The issue presented by *Smith* is, quite simply, whether the people, through their elected representatives, or rather this Court, shall control the outcome of those concrete cases. For example, shall it be the determination of this Court, or rather of the people, whether (as the dissent apparently believes) church construction will be exempt from zoning laws? The historical evidence put forward by the dissent does nothing to undermine the conclusion we reached in *Smith*: It shall be the people.

JUSTICE O'CONNOR, with whom JUSTICE BREYER joins except as to [a portion] of Part I, dissenting.

I dissent from the Court's disposition of this case. I agree with the Court that the issue before us is whether the Religious Freedom Restoration Act (RFRA) is a proper exercise of Congress' power to enforce § 5 of the Fourteenth Amendment. But as a yardstick for measuring the constitutionality of RFRA, the Court uses its holding in *Employment Div., Dept. of Human Resources of Oregon v. Smith*, the decision that prompted Congress to enact RFRA as a means of more rigorously enforcing the Free Exercise Clause. I remain of the view that *Smith* was wrongly decided, and I would use this case to reexamine the Court's holding there. Therefore, I would direct the parties to brief the question whether *Smith* represents the correct understanding of the Free Exercise Clause and set the case for reargument. If the Court were to correct the misinterpretation of the Free Exercise Clause set forth in *Smith*, it would simultaneously put our First Amendment jurisprudence back on course and allay the legitimate concerns of a majority in Congress who believed that *Smith* improperly restricted religious liberty. We would then be in a position to review RFRA in light of a proper interpretation of the Free Exercise Clause.

JUSTICE SOUTER, dissenting.

I have serious doubts about the precedential value of the *Smith* rule and its entitlement to adherence. These doubts are intensified today by the historical arguments going to the original understanding of the Free Exercise Clause presented in JUSTICE O'CONNOR's dissent, which raises very substantial issues about the soundness of the *Smith* rule. But without briefing and argument on the merits of that rule (which this Court has never had in any case, including *Smith* itself, *see Lukumi*, at 571-572), I am not now prepared to join JUSTICE O'CONNOR in rejecting it or the majority in assuming it to be correct. In order to provide full adversarial consideration, this case should be set down for reargument permitting plenary reexamination of the issue.

NOTES ON *BOERNE*

1. *Boerne as an example of "antidisestablishmentarianism."* Consider Jeb Rubenfeld's explanation of the result in *Boerne*:

> Already RFRA's chief supporters have urged Congress to reenact RFRA's protections for religion by compiling a more "careful record" or by invoking different bases of congressional power. In this debate over the reach of section 5 and other grants of federal legislative power — the same debate that engrossed commentators on RFRA before the statute reached the Court — a more important point will be missed.
>
> RFRA violated the Establishment Clause, and a new RFRA modified along the lines suggested above would also violate the Establishment Clause. It is not, however, as some have argued, that RFRA was so pro-

tective of religion that it amounted to an establishment in its own right. But if RFRA did not establish religion, how could it have violated the Establishment Clause? By seeking to dictate church-state relations.

Although many have forgotten it, the First Amendment, under which Congress can "make no law *respecting* an establishment of religion," does not only prohibit Congress from establishing religion; it prohibits Congress from dictating to the states how to legislate religion. The First Amendment excludes Congress from an entire legislative subject matter. Congress may not dictate a position on religion to individuals, and it may not dictate a position on religion to the states.

RFRA did so. RFRA was the first-ever direct effort by Congress to prescribe a regulatory framework governing church-state relations for the country. It marked a massive, unprecedented shift in the triangular relation among the federal government, the state governments, and religion. It was a law quintessentially respecting establishment: RFRA was a congressional effort to dictate the terms of religious neutrality to which state law must conform.

But RFRA not only sought to regulate a subject matter from which Congress is expressly excluded. RFRA was also *dis*establishing. It required states to abolish the favoritism of majority religious practices that their laws of general applicability inevitably effect. In this way, RFRA violated the First Amendment's specific *antidisestablishmentarian* requirement. RFRA would therefore have been unconstitutional even if it had fallen within Congress's section 5 powers, and it will still be unconstitutional if reenacted along the lines its supporters now propose.

Disabling Congress from dictating church-state relations is not a matter of protecting state sovereignty, in the sense of carving out a domain in which states are to have supreme legislative authority. If Congress could dictate church-state relations, even in the name of religious diversity and religious neutrality, Congress would have the power to intercede directly and profoundly into the nation's religious life. Paradoxical though it may seem, antidisestablishmentarianism is essential to the fundamental constitutional separation of religion and government.

Jeb Rubenfeld, *Antidisestablishmentarianism: Why RFRA Really Was Unconstitutional*, 95 MICH. L. REV. 2347, 2349-50 (1997).

2. *State RFRAs.* Keep in mind that although *Boerne* holds RFRA unconstitutional, at least as applied to states, many states themselves have adopted RFRAs. Eugene Volokh argues that these state RFRAs (and the federal RFRA if it applies to the federal government) should be viewed as imposing a "common-law exemption model." Under this model, "courts decide in the first instance whether an exemption is to be granted. But because RFRAs may be revised by the legislature, the courts' decisions aren't final. Ultimately, the tough calls will be governed by the political process, just as they have been in the common-law system under which American law has generally evolved." Eugene Volokh, *A Common-Law Model For Religious Exemptions*, 46 UCLA L. REV. 1465, 1469 (1999).

3. *Historical Preservation Laws and the Establishment Clause.* For a good analysis of the church/state problems posed by historical preservation laws, see Ira C. Lupu & Robert W. Tuttle, *Historical Preservation Grants to Houses of Worship: A Case Study in the Survival of Separationism*, 43 B.C. L. REV. 1139 (2002). Two different dilemmas present themselves in this context. On the one hand, many states have programs subsidizing the maintenance of historically significant structures, which in the religious context raises concerns about government funding of sectarian activity. On the other hand, land use laws often strictly regulate historically significant structures, in ways that limit the uses of those structures. This is the problem raised (albeit on statutory grounds) in *Boerne.* Professors Lupu and Tuttle analyze the ways in which the Establishment Clause theoretical approaches of separationism and neutrality apply to these two problems and arrive at an elegant solution: They argue that the most logical way to address the problems of historical preservation laws and churches is to distinguish between the inside and the outside of religious structures. They argue that the interiors of religious structures are far more likely to be closely connected to the spiritual enterprise of the church and are far more likely to contain liturgically important features. Thus it usually will be inappropriate for the government to regulate the inside of these structures, but also inappropriate for the government to subsidize the inside of the structures. Conversely, the outside of religious structures "are visible to passersby and constitute part of the historically significant design features of the property or neighborhood," *id.* at 1173, which renders the outside of a church appropriately subject to more government regulation, but also worthy of government financial support for the aesthetic benefit of the community at large.

4. *The Continued Applicability of RFRA to the Federal Government.* One question left unanswered by *Boerne* is whether RFRA is constitutional as applied to the internal operations of the federal government. *Boerne* dealt only with Congress' power to regulate the states under authority granted by Section 5 of the Fourteenth Amendment. The unanswered question was whether Congress also had power under Article I to apply RFRA restrictions to federal action. Although some lower courts split on this issue, *compare United States v. Sandia*, 6 F. Supp. 2d 1278 (D.N.M. 1997) (RFRA unconstitutional as applied to the federal government), *with Young v. Crystal Evangelical Free Church*, 141 F.3d 854, 856 (8th Cir. 1998), *cert. denied*, 525 U.S. 811 (1998) (RFRA constitutional as applied to the federal government), the Supreme Court has recently applied RFRA to prevent the federal government from enforcing the Controlled Substances Act by punishing the religious use of a hallucinogenic tea.

GONZALES v. O CENTRO ESPIRITA BENEFICENTE UNIAO DO VEGETAL
126 S. Ct. 1211, 163 L. Ed. 2d 1017 (2006)

CHIEF JUSTICE ROBERTS delivered the opinion of the Court.

A religious sect with origins in the Amazon Rainforest receives communion by drinking a sacramental tea, brewed from plants unique to the region, that contains a hallucinogen regulated under the Controlled Substances Act by the Federal Government. The Government concedes that this practice is a sincere exercise of religion, but nonetheless sought to prohibit the small American branch of the sect from engaging in the practice, on the ground that the Controlled Substances Act bars all use of the hallucinogen. The sect sued to block enforcement against it of the ban on the sacramental tea, and moved for a preliminary injunction.

It relied on the Religious Freedom Restoration Act of 1993, which prohibits the Federal Government from substantially burdening a person's exercise of religion, unless the Government "demonstrates that application of the burden to the person" represents the least restrictive means of advancing a compelling interest. 42 U.S.C. § 2000bb-1(b). The District Court granted the preliminary injunction, and the Court of Appeals affirmed. We granted the Government's petition for certiorari. Before this Court, the Government's central submission is that it has a compelling interest in the *uniform* application of the Controlled Substances Act, such that no exception to the ban on use of the hallucinogen can be made to accommodate the sect's sincere religious practice. We conclude that the Government has not carried the burden expressly placed on it by Congress in the Religious Freedom Restoration Act, and affirm the grant of the preliminary injunction.

I

[The Court recounted *Smith* and the passage of RFRA.]

At a hearing on the preliminary injunction, the Government conceded that the challenged application of the Controlled Substances Act would substantially burden a sincere exercise of religion by the UDV. The Government argued, however, that this burden did not violate RFRA, because applying the Controlled Substances Act in this case was the least restrictive means of advancing three compelling governmental interests: protecting the health and safety of UDV members, preventing the diversion of *hoasca* from the church to recreational users, and complying with the 1971 United Nations Convention on Psychotropic Substances, a treaty signed by the United States and implemented by the Act.

The District Court heard evidence from both parties on the health risks of *hoasca* and the potential for diversion from the church. The Government presented evidence to the effect that use of *hoasca*, or DMT more generally, can cause psychotic reactions, cardiac irregularities, and adverse drug interactions. The UDV countered by citing studies documenting the safety of its sacramental use of *hoasca* and presenting evidence that minimized the likelihood of the health risks raised by the Government. With respect to diversion, the Government pointed to a general rise in the illicit use of hallucinogens, and cited interest in the illegal use of DMT and *hoasca* in particular; the UDV emphasized the thinness of any market for *hoasca*, the relatively small amounts of the substance imported by the church, and the absence of any diversion problem in the past.

The District Court concluded that the evidence on health risks was "in equipoise," and similarly that the evidence on diversion was "virtually balanced." In the face of such an even showing, the court reasoned that the Government had failed to demonstrate a compelling interest justifying what it acknowledged was a substantial burden on the UDV's sincere religious exercise.

[After rejecting the government's argument that "such evidentiary equipoise is an insufficient basis for issuing a preliminary injunction," the Court turned to the government's arguments on the merits of enforcing the Controlled Substances Act.]

III

The Government's second line of argument rests on the Controlled Substances Act itself. The Government contends that the Act's description of Schedule I substances as having "a high potential for abuse," "no currently accepted medical use in treatment in the United States," and "a lack of accepted safety for use . . . under medical supervision," by itself precludes any consideration of individualized exceptions such as that sought by the UDV. The Government goes on to argue that the regulatory regime established by the Act — a "closed" system that prohibits all use of controlled substances except as authorized by the Act itself, "cannot function with its necessary rigor and comprehensiveness if subjected to judicial exemptions." According to the Government, there would be no way to cabin religious exceptions once recognized, and "the public will misread" such exceptions as signaling that the substance at issue is not harmful after all. Under the Government's view, there is no need to assess the particulars of the UDV's use or weigh the impact of an exemption for that specific use, because the Controlled Substances Act serves a compelling purpose and simply admits of no exceptions.

A

RFRA, and the strict scrutiny test it adopted, contemplate an inquiry more focused than the Government's categorical approach. RFRA requires the Government to demonstrate that the compelling interest test is satisfied through application of the challenged law "to the person" — the particular claimant whose sincere exercise of religion is being substantially burdened. 42 U.S.C. § 2000bb-1(b). RFRA expressly adopted the compelling interest test "as set forth in *Sherbert v. Verner*, and *Wisconsin v. Yoder*." In each of those cases, this

Court looked beyond broadly formulated interests justifying the general applicability of government mandates and scrutinized the asserted harm of granting specific exemptions to particular religious claimants. In *Yoder,* for example, we permitted an exemption for Amish children from a compulsory school attendance law. We recognized that the State had a "paramount" interest in education, but held that "despite its admitted validity in the generality of cases, we must searchingly examine the interests that the State seeks to promote . . . and the impediment to those objectives that would flow from recognizing *the claimed Amish exemption*." The Court explained that the State needed "to show with more particularity how its admittedly strong interest . . . would be adversely affected by granting an exemption *to the Amish*."

In *Sherbert,* the Court upheld a particular claim to a religious exemption from a state law denying unemployment benefits to those who would not work on Saturdays, but explained that it was not announcing a constitutional right to unemployment benefits for "*all* persons whose religious convictions are the cause of their unemployment." The Court distinguished the case "in which an employee's religious convictions serve to make him a nonproductive member of society." [*S*]*ee also Smith* (O'CONNOR, J., concurring in judgment) (strict scrutiny "at least requires a case-by-case determination of the question, sensitive to the facts of each particular claim"). Outside the Free Exercise area as well, the Court has noted that "[c]ontext matters" in applying the compelling interest test, *Grutter v. Bollinger,* 539 U.S. 306, 327 (2003), and has emphasized that "strict scrutiny *does* take 'relevant differences' into account — indeed, that is its fundamental purpose," *Adarand Constructors, Inc. v. Pena,* 515 U.S. 200, 228 (1995).

B

Under the more focused inquiry required by RFRA and the compelling interest test, the Government's mere invocation of the general characteristics of Schedule I substances, as set forth in the Controlled Substances Act, cannot carry the day. It is true, of course, that Schedule I substances such as DMT are exceptionally dangerous. Nevertheless, there is no indication that Congress, in classifying DMT, considered the harms posed by the particular use at issue here — the circumscribed, sacramental use of *hoasca* by the UDV. Congress' determination that DMT should be listed under Schedule I simply does not provide a categorical answer that relieves the Government of the obligation to shoulder its burden under RFRA.

This conclusion is reinforced by the Controlled Substances Act itself. The Act contains a provision authorizing the Attorney General to "waive the requirement for registration of certain manufacturers, distributors, or dispensers if he finds it consistent with the public health and safety." 21 U.S.C. § 822(d). The fact that the Act itself contemplates that exempting certain people from its requirements would be "consistent with the public health and safety" indicates that congressional findings with respect to Schedule I substances should not carry the determinative weight, for RFRA purposes, that the Government would ascribe to them.

And in fact an exception has been made to the Schedule I ban for religious use. For the past 35 years, there has been a regulatory exemption for use of peyote — a Schedule I substance — by the Native American Church. *See* 21 CFR § 1307.31 (2005). In 1994, Congress extended that exemption to all members of every recognized Indian Tribe. *See* 42 U.S.C. § 1996a(b)(1). Everything the Government says about the DMT in *hoasca* — that, as a Schedule I substance, Congress has determined that it "has a high potential for abuse," "has no currently accepted medical use," and has "a lack of accepted safety for use . . . under medical supervision," 21 U.S.C. § 812(b)(1) — applies in equal measure to the mescaline in peyote, yet both the Executive and Congress itself have decreed an exception from the Controlled Substances Act for Native American religious use of peyote. If such use is permitted in the face of the congressional findings in § 812(b)(1) for hundreds of thousands of Native Americans practicing their faith, it is difficult to see how those same findings alone can preclude any consideration of a similar exception for the 130 or so American members of the UDV who want to practice theirs. *See Church of Lukumi Babalu Aye, Inc. v. Hialeah* ("It is established in our strict scrutiny jurisprudence that 'a law cannot be regarded as protecting an interest 'of the highest order' . . . when it leaves appreciable damage to that supposedly vital interest unprohibited.'").

The Government responds that there is a "unique relationship" between the United States and the Tribes, but never explains what about that "unique" relationship justifies overriding the same congressional findings on which the Government relies in resisting any exception for the UDV's religious use of *hoasca*. In other words, if any Schedule I substance is in fact *always* highly dangerous in any amount no matter how used, what about the unique relationship with the Tribes justifies allowing their use of peyote? Nothing about the unique political status of the Tribes makes their members immune from the health risks the Government asserts accompany any use of a Schedule I substance, nor insulates the Schedule I substance the Tribes use in religious exercise from the alleged risk of diversion.

The Government argues that the existence of a *congressional* exemption for peyote does not indicate that the Controlled Substances Act is amenable to *judicially crafted* exceptions. RFRA, however, plainly contemplates that *courts* would recognize exceptions — that is how the law works. *See* 42 U.S.C. § 2000bb-1(c) ("A person whose religious exercise has been burdened in violation of this section may assert that violation as a claim or defense in a judicial proceeding and obtain appropriate relief against a government"). Congress' role in the peyote exemption — and the Executive's, *see* 21 CFR § 1307.31 (2005) — confirms that the findings in the Controlled Substances Act do not preclude exceptions altogether; RFRA makes clear that it is the obligation of the courts to consider whether exceptions are required under the test set forth by Congress.

C

The well-established peyote exception also fatally undermines the Government's broader contention that the Controlled Substances Act establishes a closed regulatory system that admits of no exceptions under RFRA. The Government argues that the effectiveness of the Controlled Substances Act will be "necessarily . . . undercut" if the Act is not uniformly applied, without regard to burdens on religious exercise. The peyote exception, however, has been in place since the outset of the Controlled Substances Act, and there is no evidence that it has "undercut" the Government's ability to enforce the ban on peyote use by non-Indians.

The Government points to some pre-*Smith* cases relying on a need for uniformity in rejecting claims for religious exemptions under the Free Exercise Clause. . . . Here the Government's argument for uniformity is different; it rests not so much on the particular statutory program at issue as on slippery-slope concerns that could be invoked in response to any RFRA claim for an exception to a generally applicable law. The Government's argument echoes the classic rejoinder of bureaucrats throughout history: If I make an exception for you, I'll have to make one for everybody, so no exceptions. But RFRA operates by mandating consideration, under the compelling interest test, of exceptions to "rule[s] of general applicability." 42 U.S.C. § 2000bb-1(a).

We reaffirmed just last Term the feasibility of case-by-case consideration of religious exemptions to generally applicable rules. In *Cutter v. Wilkinson* [*infra* this Chapter], we held that the Religious Land Use and Institutionalized Persons Act of 2000, which allows federal and state prisoners to seek religious accommodations pursuant to the same standard as set forth in RFRA, does not violate the Establishment Clause. We had "no cause to believe" that the compelling interest test "would not be applied in an appropriately balanced way" to specific claims for exemptions as they arose. Nothing in our opinion suggested that courts were not up to the task.

* * *

The Government repeatedly invokes Congress' findings and purposes underlying the Controlled Substances Act, but Congress had a reason for enacting RFRA, too. Congress recognized that "laws 'neutral' toward religion may burden religious exercise as surely as laws intended to interfere with religious exercise," and legislated "the compelling interest test" as the means for the courts to "strike sensible balances between religious liberty and competing prior governmental interests."

We have no cause to pretend that the task assigned by Congress to the courts under RFRA is an easy one. Indeed, the very sort of difficulties highlighted by the Government here were cited by this Court in deciding that the approach later mandated by Congress under RFRA was not required as a matter of constitutional law under the Free Exercise Clause. *See Smith.* But Congress has determined that courts should strike sensible balances, pursuant to a compelling interest test that requires the Government to address the particular practice at issue. Applying that test, we conclude that the courts below did not err in determining that the Government failed to demonstrate, at the preliminary injunction stage, a compelling interest in barring the UDV's sacramental use of *hoasca*.

NOTE

For academic arguments that RFRA should be held unconstitutional as applied to the federal government, see Christopher L. Eisgruber & Lawrence G. Sager, *Why the Religious Freedom Restoration Act is Unconstitutional*, 69 N.Y.U. L. REV. 437, 470 (1994) ("By demanding that the Court use constitutional concepts according to statutory instruction, Congress interferes with the judiciary's authority and obligation to develop an autonomous jurisprudence."); Marci A. Hamilton, City of Boerne v. Flores: *A Landmark for Structural Analysis*, 39 WM. & MARY L. REV. 699, 718-21 (1998); Marci A. Hamilton, *The Religious Freedom Restoration Act is Unconstitutional, Period*, 1 U. PA. J. CONST. L. 1, 14-19 (1998). For a defense of RFRA as applied to the federal government, see Ira C. Lupu, *Why the Congress Was Wrong and the Court Was Right — Reflections on City of Boerne v. Flores*, 39 WM. & MARY L. REV. 793, 810 (1998) ("If Congress is empowered to create prisons, as surely it is, then Congress may accommodate religion in those prisons beyond what the Free Exercise Clause requires — up to the limit of what the Establishment Clause forbids. Congress may regulate the federal government more broadly than it regulates state government — in this context, more broadly than the substantive rights protected by the First Amendment. RFRA as applied to the federal government, therefore, does not threaten the Court's *Marbury* function in the manner suggested by RFRA as applied to the states through the Fourteenth Amendment's enforcement power.").

For one of the more interesting contributions to the scholarly literature on what remains of RFRA, see Gregory P. Magarian, *How to Apply the Religious Freedom Restoration Act to Federal Law Without Violating the Constitution*, 99 MICH. L. REV. 1903 (2001). Magarian offers a nuanced view of the constitutional issues surrounding the application of RFRA to the federal government. On the one hand, Magarian disagrees with scholars such as Eisgruber and Sager, who argue that RFRA is unconstitutional on its face as applied to the federal government. On the other hand, "[a]lthough I reject arguments that RFRA is facially invalid under the Establishment Clause, I believe a freewheeling regime of purely religious exemptions would offend both Establishment Clause doctrine and separationist principle. . . . These protections would improperly privilege religion, because they would inequitably relieve believers of constraints from which many nonbelievers might also prefer to be free." *Id.* at 1977. Magarian offers two possible approaches to the interpretation of RFRA that would avoid this Establishment Clause problem.

The "libertarian" approach would have the courts expansively interpret the statutory term "religion." Drawing on the conscientious objector cases excerpted *supra* Chapter 3, the "meaning of 'religion' in the text of RFRA should be understood to encompass all deeply held conscientious beliefs, whether or not the believers profess faith in a supreme being." *Id.* at 1978. The alternative "restrictive" approach would prohibit the courts from enforcing accommodations that extended favorable treatment to religious groups or individuals. The scope of RFRA would be substantially narrowed under this alternative approach, but it would still have an effect in two categories of cases. First, under this approach courts could prohibit the federal government from engaging in "neutral state action that, over a range of cases, disproportionately burdens some religions — typically minority religions — while expressly or implicitly accommodating others." *Id.* at 1993. Second, under this approach courts could grant what Magarian calls "idiosyncratic accommodations," "where granting a religious believer's request for accommodation would neither deny adherents of any other religions, or of no religion, any benefit that they want and have a factual basis for claiming, nor impose substantial costs on nonbeneficiaries." *Id.* at 1995-96. The first approach would significantly broaden the scope of RFRA; the second approach would significantly narrow the scope of the statute. Either of Magarian's approaches would arguably satisfy the as-applied Establishment Clause problem with RFRA, but would either approach satisfy the statute's supporters? Is it likely the courts would apply a *Seeger*-style accommodation standard to the general range of federal government obligations?

C. LIMITATIONS ON *SMITH*: THE "NEUTRAL AND GENERALLY APPLICABLE" REQUIREMENT

CHURCH OF THE LUKUMI BABALU AYE v. CITY OF HIALEAH
508 U.S. 520 (1993)

JUSTICE KENNEDY delivered the opinion of the Court, except as to Part II-A-2.

I

A

This case involves practices of the Santeria religion, which originated in the 19th century. When hundreds of thousands of members of the Yoruba people were brought as slaves from western Africa to Cuba, their traditional African religion absorbed significant elements of Roman Catholicism. The resulting syncretion, or fusion, is Santeria, "the way of the saints." The Cuban Yoruba express their devotion to spirits, called *orishas*, through the iconography of Catholic saints, Catholic symbols are often present at Santeria rites, and Santeria devotees attend the Catholic sacraments.

The Santeria faith teaches that every individual has a destiny from God, a destiny fulfilled with the aid and energy of the *orishas*. The basis of the Santeria religion is the nurture of a personal relation with the *orishas*, and one of the principal forms of devotion is an animal sacrifice. The sacrifice of animals as part of religious rituals has ancient roots. Animal sacrifice is mentioned throughout the Old Testament, and it played an important role in the practice of Judaism before destruction of the second Temple in Jerusalem. In modern Islam, there is an annual sacrifice commemorating Abraham's sacrifice of a ram in the stead of his son.

According to Santeria teaching, the *orishas* are powerful but not immortal. They depend for survival on the sacrifice. Sacrifices are performed at birth, marriage, and death rites, for the cure of the sick, for the initiation of new members and priests, and during an annual celebration. Animals sacrificed in Santeria rituals include chickens, pigeons, doves, ducks, guinea pigs, goats, sheep, and turtles. The animals are killed by the cutting of the carotid arteries in the neck. The sacrificed animal is cooked and eaten, except after healing and death rituals.

Santeria adherents faced widespread persecution in Cuba, so the religion and its rituals were practiced in secret. The open practice of Santeria and its rites remains infrequent. The religion was brought to this Nation most often by exiles from the Cuban revolution. The District Court estimated that there are at least 50,000 practitioners in South Florida today.

B

Petitioner Church of the Lukumi Babalu Aye, Inc. (Church), is a not-for-profit corporation organized under Florida law in 1973. The Church and its congregants practice the Santeria religion. The president of the Church is petitioner Ernesto Pichardo, who is also the Church's priest and holds the religious title of *Italero*, the second highest in the Santeria faith. In April 1987, the Church leased land in the City of Hialeah, Florida, and announced plans to establish a house of worship as well as a school, cultural center, and museum. Pichardo indicated that the Church's goal was to bring the practice of the Santeria faith, including its ritual of animal sacrifice, into the open. The Church began the process of obtaining utility service and receiving the necessary licensing, inspection, and zoning approvals. Although the Church's efforts at obtaining the necessary licenses and permits were far from smooth, it appears that it received all needed approvals by early August 1987.

The prospect of a Santeria church in their midst was distressing to many members of the Hialeah community, and the announcement of the plans to open a Santeria church in Hialeah prompted the city council to hold an emergency public session on June 9, 1987. The resolutions and ordinances passed at that and later meetings are set forth in the Appendix following this opinion.

A summary suffices here, beginning with the enactments passed at the June 9 meeting. First, the city council adopted Resolution 87-66, which noted the "concern" expressed by residents of the city "that certain religions may propose to engage in practices which are inconsistent with public morals, peace or safety," and declared that "[t]he City reiterates its commitment to a prohibition against any and all acts of any and all religious groups which are inconsistent with public morals, peace or safety." Next, the council approved an emergency ordinance, Ordinance 87-40, which incorporated in full, except as to penalty, Florida's animal cruelty laws. Among other things, the incorporated state law subjected to criminal punishment "[w]hoever . . . unnecessarily or cruelly . . . kills any animal."

The city council desired to undertake further legislative action, but Florida law prohibited a municipality from enacting legislation relating to animal cruelty that conflicted with state law. To obtain clarification, Hialeah's city attorney requested an opinion from the attorney general of Florida as to whether [Florida law] prohibited "a religious group from sacrificing an animal in a religious ritual or practice" and whether the city could enact ordinances "making religious animal sacrifice unlawful." The attorney general responded in mid-July. He concluded that the "ritual sacrifice of animals for purposes other than food consumption" was not a "necessary" killing and so was prohibited by [Florida law]. The attorney general appeared to define "unnecessary" as "done without any useful motive, in a spirit of wanton cruelty or for the mere pleasure of destruction without being in any sense beneficial or useful to the person killing the animal." He advised that religious animal sacrifice was against state law, so that a city ordinance prohibiting it would not be in conflict.

The city council responded at first with a hortatory enactment, Resolution 87-90, that noted its residents' "great concern regarding the possibility of public ritualistic animal sacrifices" and the state-law prohibition. The resolution declared the city policy "to oppose the ritual sacrifices of animals" within Hialeah and announced that any person or organization practicing animal sacrifice "will be prosecuted."

In September 1987, the city council adopted three substantive ordinances addressing the issue of religious animal sacrifice. Ordinance 87-52 defined "sacrifice" as "to unnecessarily kill, torment, torture, or mutilate an animal in a public or private ritual or ceremony not for the primary purpose of food consumption," and prohibited owning or possessing an animal "intending to use such animal for food purposes." It restricted application of this prohibition, however, to any individual or group that "kills, slaughters or sacrifices animals for any type of ritual, regardless of whether or not the flesh or blood of the animal is to be consumed." The ordinance contained an exemption for slaughtering by "licensed establishment[s]" of animals "specifically raised for food purposes." Declaring, moreover, that the city council "has determined that the sacrificing of animals within the city limits is contrary to the public health, safety, welfare and morals of the community," the city council adopted Ordinance 87-71. That ordinance defined sacrifice as had Ordinance 87-52, and then provided that "[i]t shall be unlawful for any person, persons, corporations or associations to sacrifice any animal within the corporate limits of the City of Hialeah, Florida." The final Ordinance, 87-72, defined "slaughter" as "the killing of animals for food" and prohibited slaughter outside of areas zoned for slaughterhouse use. The ordinance provided an exemption, however, for the slaughter or processing for sale of "small numbers of hogs and/or cattle per week in accordance with an exemption provided by state law." All ordinances and resolutions passed the city council by unanimous vote. Violations of each of the four ordinances were punishable by fines not exceeding $500 or imprisonment not exceeding 60 days, or both.

II

In addressing the constitutional protection for free exercise of religion, our cases establish the general proposition that a law that is neutral and of general applicability need not be justified by a compelling governmental interest even if the law has the incidental effect of burdening a particular religious practice. *Employment Div., Dept. of Human Resources of Ore. v. Smith.* Neutrality and general applicability are interrelated, and, as becomes apparent in this case, failure to satisfy one requirement is a likely indication that the other has not been satisfied. A law failing to satisfy these requirements must be justified by a compelling governmental interest and must be narrowly tailored to advance that interest. These ordinances fail to satisfy the Smith requirements. We begin by discussing neutrality.

A

At a minimum, the protections of the Free Exercise Clause pertain if the law at issue discriminates against some or all religious beliefs or regulates or prohibits conduct because it is undertaken for religious reasons. Indeed, it was "historical instances of religious persecution and intolerance that gave concern to those who drafted the Free Exercise Clause." These principles, though not often at issue in our Free Exercise Clause cases, have played a role in some. In *McDaniel v. Paty*, for example, we invalidated a State law that disqualified members of the clergy from holding certain public offices, because it "impose[d] special disabilities on the basis of . . . religious status." On the same principle, in *Fowler v. Rhode Island* we found that a municipal ordinance was applied in an unconstitutional manner when interpreted to prohibit preaching in a public park by a Jehovah's Witness but to permit preaching during the course of a Catholic mass or Protestant church service. *Cf. Larson v. Valente*, 456 U.S. 228 (1982) (state statute that treated some religious denominations more favorably than others violated the Establishment Clause).

1

The record in this case compels the conclusion that suppression of the central element of the Santeria worship service was the object of the ordinances. First, though use of the words "sacrifice" and "ritual" does not compel a finding of improper targeting of the Santeria religion, the choice of these words is support for our conclusion. There are further respects in which the text of the city council's enactments discloses the improper attempt to target Santeria. Resolution 87-66, adopted June 9, 1987, recited that "residents and citizens of the City of

Hialeah have expressed their concern that certain religions may propose to engage in practices which are inconsistent with public morals, peace or safety," and "reiterate[d]" the city's commitment to prohibit "any and all [such] acts of any and all religious groups." No one suggests, and on this record it cannot be maintained, that city officials had in mind a religion other than Santeria.

It becomes evident that these ordinances target Santeria sacrifice when the ordinances' operation is considered. Apart from the text, the effect of a law in its real operation is strong evidence of its object. To be sure, adverse impact will not always lead to a finding of impermissible targeting. For example, a social harm may have been a legitimate concern of government for reasons quite apart from discrimination. *McGowan v. Maryland*, 366 U.S., at 442. *See, e.g., Reynolds v. United States; Davis v. Beason*, 133 U.S. 333 (1890). *See also* Ely, *Legislative and Administrative Motivation in Constitutional Law*, 79 YALE L.J. 1205, 1319 (1970). The subject at hand does implicate, of course, multiple concerns unrelated to religious animosity, for example, the suffering or mistreatment visited upon the sacrificed animals and health hazards from improper disposal. But the ordinances when considered together disclose an object remote from these legitimate concerns. The design of these laws accomplishes instead a "religious gerrymander," an impermissible attempt to target petitioners and their religious practices.

It is a necessary conclusion that almost the only conduct subject to Ordinances 87-40, 87-52, and 87-71 is the religious exercise of Santeria church members. The texts show that they were drafted in tandem to achieve this result. We begin with Ordinance 87-71. It prohibits the sacrifice of animals, but defines sacrifice as "to unnecessarily kill . . . an animal in a public or private ritual or ceremony not for the primary purpose of food consumption." The definition excludes almost all killings of animals except for religious sacrifice, and the primary purpose requirement narrows the proscribed category even further, in particular by exempting kosher slaughter. We need not discuss whether this differential treatment of two religions is itself an independent constitutional violation. *Cf. Larson v. Valente*, 456 U.S., at 244-246. It suffices to recite this feature of the law as support for our conclusion that Santeria alone was the exclusive legislative concern. The net result of the gerrymander is that few if any killings of animals are prohibited other than Santeria sacrifice, which is proscribed because it occurs during a ritual or ceremony and its primary purpose is to make an offering to the orishas, not food consumption. Indeed, careful drafting ensured that, although Santeria sacrifice is prohibited, killings that are no more necessary or humane in almost all other circumstances are unpunished.

Operating in similar fashion is Ordinance 87-52, which prohibits the "possess [ion], sacrifice, or slaughter" of an animal with the "inten[t] to use such animal for food purposes." This prohibition, extending to the keeping of an animal as well as the killing itself, applies if the animal is killed in "any type of ritual" and there is an intent to use the animal for food, whether or not it is in fact consumed for food. The ordinance exempts, however, "any licensed [food] establishment" with regard to "any animals which are specifically raised for food purposes," if the activity is permitted by zoning and other laws. This exception, too, seems intended to cover kosher slaughter. Again, the burden of the ordinance, in practical terms, falls on Santeria adherents but almost no others: If the killing is — unlike most Santeria sacrifices — unaccompanied by the intent to use the animal for food, then it is not prohibited by Ordinance 87-52; if the killing is specifically for food but does not occur during the course of "any type of ritual," it again falls outside the prohibition; and if the killing is for food and occurs during the course of a ritual, it is still exempted if it occurs in a properly zoned and licensed establishment and involves animals "specifically raised for food purposes." A pattern of exemptions parallels the pattern of narrow prohibitions. Each contributes to the gerrymander.

Ordinance 87-40 incorporates the Florida animal cruelty statute. Its prohibition is broad on its face, punishing "[w]hoever . . . unnecessarily . . . kills any animal." The city claims that this ordinance is the epitome of a neutral prohibition. The problem, however, is the interpretation given to the ordinance by respondent and the Florida attorney general. Killings for religious reasons are deemed unnecessary, whereas most other killings fall outside the prohibition. The city, on what seems to be a *per se* basis, deems hunting, slaughter of animals for food, eradication of insects and pests, and euthanasia as necessary. There is no indication in the record that respondent has concluded that hunting or fishing for sport is unnecessary. Indeed, one of the few reported Florida cases decided under [the Florida statute] concludes that the use of live rabbits to train greyhounds is not unnecessary. *See Kiper v. State*, 310 So. 2d 42 (Fla. App.), *cert. denied*, 328 So. 2d 845 (Fla. 1975). Further, because it requires an evaluation of the particular justification for the killing, this ordinance represents a system of "individualized governmental assessment of the reasons for the relevant conduct," *Employment Div., Dept. of Human Resources of Ore. v. Smith.* As we noted in *Smith*, in circumstances in which individualized exemptions from a general requirement are available, the government "may not refuse to extend that system to cases of 'religious hardship' without compelling reason." Respondent's application of the ordinance's test of necessity devalues religious reasons for killing by judging them to be of lesser import than nonreligious reasons. Thus, religious practice is being singled out for discriminatory treatment.

We also find significant evidence of the ordinances' improper targeting of Santeria sacrifice in the fact that they proscribe more religious conduct than is necessary to achieve their stated ends. It is not unreasonable to infer, at least when there are no persuasive indications to the contrary, that a law which visits "gratuitous restrictions" on religious conduct, *McGowan v. Maryland*, 366 U.S., at 520 (opinion of Frankfurter, J.), seeks not to effectuate the stated governmental interests, but to suppress the conduct because of its religious motivation.

The legitimate governmental interests in protecting the public health and preventing cruelty to animals could be addressed by restrictions stopping far short of a flat prohibition of all Santeria sacrificial practice. If improper disposal, not the sacrifice itself, is the harm to be prevented, the city could have imposed a general regulation on the disposal of organic garbage. It did not do so. Indeed, counsel for the city conceded at oral argument that, under the ordinances, Santeria sacrifices would be illegal even if they occurred in licensed, inspected, and zoned slaughterhouses. Thus, these broad ordinances prohibit Santeria sacrifice even when it does not threaten the city's interest in the public health. The District Court accepted the argument that narrower regulation would be unenforceable because of the secrecy in the Santeria rituals and the lack of any central religious authority to require compliance with secular disposal regulations. It is difficult to understand, however, how a prohibition of the sacrifices themselves, which occur in private, is enforceable if a ban on improper disposal, which occurs in public, is not. The neutrality of a law is suspect if First Amendment freedoms are curtailed to prevent isolated collateral harms not themselves prohibited by direct regulation.

Under similar analysis, narrower regulation would achieve the city's interest in preventing cruelty to animals. With regard to the city's interest in ensuring the adequate care of animals, regulation of conditions and treatment, regardless of why an animal is kept, is the logical response to the city's concern, not a prohibition on possession for the purpose of sacrifice. The same is true for the city's interest in prohibiting cruel methods of killing. Under federal and Florida law and Ordinance 87-40, which incorporates Florida law in this regard, killing an animal by the "simultaneous and instantaneous severance of the carotid arteries with a sharp instrument" — the method used in kosher slaughter — is approved as humane. The District Court found that, though Santeria sacrifice also results in severance of the carotid arteries, the method used during sacrifice is less reliable and therefore not humane. If the city has a real concern that other methods are less humane, however, the subject of the regulation should be the method of slaughter itself, not a religious classification that is said to bear some general relation to it.

Ordinance 87-72 — unlike the three other ordinances — does appear to apply to substantial nonreligious conduct and not to be overbroad. For our purposes here, however, the four substantive ordinances may be treated as a group for neutrality purposes. Ordinance 87-72 was passed the same day as Ordinance 87-71 and was enacted, as were the three others, in direct response to the opening of the Church. It would be implausible to suggest that the three other ordinances, but not Ordinance 87-72, had as their object the suppression of religion. We need not decide whether the Ordinance 87-72 could survive constitutional scrutiny if it existed separately; it must be invalidated because it functions, with the rest of the enactments in question, to suppress Santeria religious worship.

2

That the ordinances were enacted " 'because of,' not merely 'in spite of,' " their suppression of Santeria religious practice is revealed by the events preceding their enactment. Although respondent claimed at oral argument that it had experienced significant problems resulting from the sacrifice of animals within the city before the announced opening of the Church, Tr. of Oral Arg. 27, 46, the city council made no attempt to address the supposed problem before its meeting in June 1987, just weeks after the Church announced plans to open. The minutes and taped excerpts of the June 9 session, both of which are in the record, evidence significant hostility exhibited by residents, members of the city council, and other city officials toward the Santeria religion and its practice of animal sacrifice. The public crowd that attended the June 9 meetings interrupted statements by council members critical of Santeria with cheers and the brief comments of Pichardo with taunts. When Councilman Martinez, a supporter of the ordinances, stated that in prerevolution Cuba "people were put in jail for practicing this religion," the audience applauded. Taped excerpts of Hialeah City Council Meeting, June 9, 1987.

Other statements by members of the city council were in a similar vein. For example, Councilman Martinez, after noting his belief that Santeria was outlawed in Cuba, questioned: "[I]f we could not practice this [religion] in our homeland [Cuba], why bring it to this country?" Councilman Cardoso said that Santeria devotees at the Church "are in violation of everything this country stands for." Councilman Mejides indicated that he was "totally against the sacrificing of animals" and distinguished kosher slaughter because it had a "real purpose." The "Bible says we are allowed to sacrifice an animal for consumption," he continued, "but for any other purposes, I don't believe that the Bible allows that." The president of the city council, Councilman Echevarria, asked: "What can we do to prevent the Church from opening?"

Various Hialeah city officials made comparable comments. The chaplain of the Hialeah Police Department told the city council that Santeria was a sin, "foolishness," "an abomination to the Lord," and the worship of "demons." He advised the city council: "We need to be helping people and sharing with them the truth that is found in Jesus Christ." He concluded: "I would exhort you . . . not to permit this Church to exist." The city attorney commented that Resolution 87-66 indicated: "This community will not tolerate religious practices which are abhorrent to its citizens. . . ." Similar comments were made by the deputy city attorney. This history discloses the object of the ordinances to target animal sacrifice by Santeria worshippers because of its religious motivation.

3

In sum, the neutrality inquiry leads to one conclusion: The ordinances had as their object the suppression of religion. The pattern we have recited discloses animosity to Santeria adherents and their religious practices; the ordinances by their own terms target this religious exercise; the texts of the ordinances were gerrymandered with care to proscribe religious killings of animals but to exclude almost all secular killings; and the ordinances suppress much more religious conduct than is necessary in order to achieve the legitimate ends asserted in their defense. These ordinances are not neutral, and the court below committed clear error in failing to reach this conclusion.

B

We turn next to a second requirement of the Free Exercise Clause, the rule that laws burdening religious practice must be of general applicability. *Employment Div., Dept. of Human Resources of Ore. v. Smith*. All laws are selective to some extent, but categories of selection are of paramount concern when a law has the incidental effect of burdening religious practice. The Free Exercise Clause "protect[s] religious observers against unequal treatment," and inequality results when a legislature decides that the governmental interests it seeks to advance are worthy of being pursued only against conduct with a religious motivation.

Respondent claims that Ordinances 87-40, 87-52, and 87-71 advance two interests: protecting the public health and preventing cruelty to animals. The ordinances are underinclusive for those ends. They fail to prohibit nonreligious conduct that endangers these interests in a similar or greater degree than Santeria sacrifice does. The underinclusion is substantial, not inconsequential. Despite the city's proffered interest in preventing cruelty to animals, the ordinances are drafted with care to forbid few killings but those occasioned by religious sacrifice. Many types of animal deaths or kills for nonreligious reasons are either not prohibited or approved by express provision. For example, fishing — which occurs in Hialeah, *see* A. KHEDOURI & F. KHEDOURI, SOUTH FLORIDA INSIDE OUT 57 (1991) — is legal. Extermination of mice and rats within a home is also permitted. Florida law incorporated by Ordinance 87-40 sanctions euthanasia of "stray, neglected, abandoned, or unwanted animals"; destruction of animals judicially removed from their owners "for humanitarian reasons" or when the animal "is of no commercial value"; the infliction of pain or suffering "in the interest of medical science"; the placing of poison in one's yard or enclosure; and the use of a live animal "to pursue or take wildlife or to participate in any hunting," and "to hunt wild hogs."

The ordinances are also underinclusive with regard to the city's interest in public health, which is threatened by the disposal of animal carcasses in open public places and the consumption of uninspected meat. Neither interest is pursued by respondent with regard to conduct that is not motivated by religious conviction. The health risks posed by the improper disposal of animal carcasses are the same whether Santeria sacrifice or some nonreligious killing preceded it. The city does not, however, prohibit hunters from bringing their kill to their houses, nor does it regulate disposal after their activity. Despite substantial testimony at trial that the same public health hazards result from improper disposal of garbage by restaurants, restaurants are outside the scope of the ordinances. Improper disposal is a general problem that causes substantial health risks, but which respondent addresses only when it results from religious exercise.

We conclude, in sum, that each of Hialeah's ordinances pursues the city's governmental interests only against conduct motivated by religious belief. The ordinances "ha[ve] every appearance of a prohibition that society is prepared to impose upon [Santeria worshippers] but not upon itself." *Florida Star v. B.J.F.,* 491 U.S. 524, 542 (1989) (SCALIA, J., concurring in part and concurring in judgment). This precise evil is what the requirement of general applicability is designed to prevent.

III

A law burdening religious practice that is not neutral or not of general application must undergo the most rigorous of scrutiny. To satisfy the commands of the First Amendment, a law restrictive of religious practice must advance "'interests of the highest order'" and must be narrowly tailored in pursuit of those interests. *McDaniel v. Paty*, quoting *Wisconsin v. Yoder*. The compelling interest standard that we apply once a law fails to meet the *Smith* requirements is not "water[ed] . . . down" but "really means what it says." *Employment Div., Dept. of Human Resources of Ore. v. Smith*. A law that targets religious conduct for distinctive treatment or advances legitimate governmental interests only against conduct with a religious motivation will survive strict scrutiny only in rare cases. It follows from what we have already said that these ordinances cannot withstand this scrutiny.

First, even were the governmental interests compelling, the ordinances are not drawn in narrow terms to accomplish those interests. As we have discussed, all four ordinances are overbroad or underinclusive in substantial respects. The proffered objectives are not pursued with respect to analogous non-religious conduct, and those interests could be achieved by narrower ordinances that burdened religion to a far lesser degree. The absence of narrow tailoring suffices to establish the invalidity of the ordinances.

Respondent has not demonstrated, moreover, that, in the context of these ordinances, its governmental interests are compelling. Where government restricts only conduct protected by the First Amendment and fails to enact feasible measures to restrict other conduct producing substantial harm or alleged harm of the same sort, the interest given in justification of the restriction is not compelling. It is established in our strict scrutiny jurisprudence that "a law cannot be regarded as protecting an interest 'of the highest order' . . . when it leaves appreciable damage to that supposedly vital interest unprohibited." *Florida Star v. B.J.F., supra*, 491 U.S., at 541-542 (SCALIA, J., concurring in part and concurring in judgment) (citation omitted). As we show above, *see supra*, at 21-24, the ordinances are underinclusive to a substantial extent with respect to each of the interests that respondent has asserted, and it is only conduct motivated by religious conviction that bears the weight of the governmental restrictions. There can be no serious claim that those interests justify the ordinances.

D. NEW STATUTORY RESPONSE TO *SMITH*

Douglas Laycock
Testimony to the Senate Judiciary Committee
Wednesday, October 1, 1997

Thank you for the opportunity to testify this morning on possible Congressional responses to *City of Boerne v. Flores*.

I was appellate counsel for Archbishop Flores in that case. I have taught and written about the law of religious liberty for twenty years, and in recognition of my scholarly work, I have been elected a Fellow of the American Academy of Arts and Sciences. I hold the Alice McKean Young Regents Chair in Law at The University of Texas at Austin, but of course The University of course takes no position on any issue before the Committee. This statement is submitted in my personal capacity as a scholar.

I. The Shrinking of Congressional Power

City of Boerne v. Flores, 117 S. Ct. 2157 (1997), holds that the Religious Freedom Restoration Act is unconstitutional as applied to state and local governments. The decision is based on newly announced limits to Congressional power to enforce the Fourteenth Amendment. The decision does not affect RFRA's application to federal law, which is based on Article I powers and in no way depends on the Fourteenth Amendment. The Administration shares my view that federal applications of RFRA are unaffected.

When the Supreme Court announces a limit on the powers of Congress or of the states, it is central to our system of government that the Court's decision is entitled to obedience. The Court itself is entitled to respect, and I do not doubt that the Justices believe they have delivered the best possible interpretation of the Constitution. But respect does not mean immunity from criticism, and the *Boerne* opinion has serious problems. I briefly note those problems here, because they complicate the task of assessing what Congressional power remains.

I confidently testified in earlier hearings that Congress had power to enact RFRA. Either I badly misunderstood the law, or the Court has changed the law. I take some comfort from the fact that six appellate courts considered the constitutionality of RFRA prior to the Supreme Court's decision in *Boerne*, and all six upheld the Act. Five of these decisions upheld RFRA as applied to state or local law. Four of these decisions came from federal courts of appeals, and each of these was written by a well-respected conservative judge appointed by Ronald Reagan — Patrick Higginbotham, Richard Posner, John Noonan, and James Buckley. I think that *Boerne* has dramatically changed the law, but if not, I am not the only one who was confused. *Boerne* significantly limits Congress's independent power to protect the civil liberties of the American people. With respect to the states, that power is expressly granted by the Enforcement

Clauses of the Thirteenth, Fourteenth, and Fifteenth Amendments. That power is no constitutional anomaly; it is as central to our system of government as the Supreme Court's power to invalidate statutes. Governmental power in our system is separated and divided so that each branch has the power and the duty to protect liberty. The Supreme Court has announced a different vision, and Congress must obey, but it need not be persuaded.

The choice between these competing visions of separation of powers will continue to be litigated, because the *Boerne* opinion announces a vague standard of uncertain scope, and because plausible readings of that standard call in question the validity of many other Acts of Congress. The Court reaffirms that Congressional power to enforce the Fourteenth Amendment includes power to enforce rights incorporated into that Amendment from elsewhere in the Constitution, 117 S. Ct. at 2163-64, and it reaffirms that Congress may "prohibit" conduct which is not itself unconstitutional." *Id.* at 2163. But Congress may prohibit such conduct only as a means to "deter" or remed[y] "constitutional violations" as defined by the Court, *id.*, and "there must be a congruence and proportionality between the injury to be prevented or remedied and the means adapted to that end." *Id.* at 2164. "The line is not easy to discern, and Congress must have wide latitude in determining where it lies." *Id.* But here, the Court determined that "RFRA is so out of proportion to a supposed remedial or preventive object that it cannot be understood as responsive to, or designed to prevent, unconstitutional behavior." *Id.* at 2170.

This standard seems to require an empirical judgment: Congressional enforcement legislation is valid if the number of violations of the Constitution as interpreted by the Court is sufficiently large in proportion to the number of violations of the statute. The Court plainly believed that this proportion is small in the case of RFRA, and that it was larger in the case of other enforcement legislation previously upheld. But the Court had no data on any of these proportions, and it made its guesses about the number of free exercise violations without addressing a significant disagreement about what would count as a violation. The facts relevant to this proportion did not get much attention in the briefing, because no one had reason to anticipate that such facts would be dispositive. In any event, facts about the relative magnitude of societal problems should be legislative facts, not judicial ones.

The standard of "congruence and proportionality" is inherently vague, and the litigation process is probably incapable of producing good data on the relevant proportions. Under this standard, it is little more than guesswork to decide which enforcement legislation is valid and which invalid. With respect to future legislation, Congress would be well advised to compile a detailed factual record of constitutional violations as the Court defines them. With respect to past enforcement legislation, we may expect constitutional challenges to the Voting Rights Amendments of 1982, to the Civil Rights Acts of 1964 as it applies to state and local employment, to the Pregnancy Discrimination Act as it applies to state and local government, to the Civil Rights Act of 1991, to the Violence

Against Women Act, and generally to all other enforcement legislation that has not already been upheld by the Supreme Court. I have no better data than the Court, but reading in the reported cases suggests that for many of these statutes, the proportion of constitutional violations to statutory violations is far smaller than for RFRA. The Court avoided this difficulty by simply not discussing these statutes; it focused instead on the Voting Rights Act of 1965, which is unique among modem civil rights legislation in the magnitude of the constitutional problem to which it responded.

Of course *Boerne* is not the only recent decision restricting Congressional power, and it is not the only recent decision overruling or distinguishing away past precedent. Constitutional law is changing, and what Congress has power to do based on past precedent it may not have power to do after the Court's next decision. My earlier testimony that RFRA would be valid demonstrates that I have little power to predict how far the Court will cut back. What I can do is outline Congressional responses that are clearly constitutional under existing precedent.

I would also note that the Coalition that came together to support RFRA, both in and out of Congress, would not agree on the appropriate scope of Congressional power in other areas of regulation. Some parts of the Coalition would undoubtedly prefer to see Congress less active in

some areas of regulation. But I think that all parts of this Coalition agree that Congress should not lose its power, and Congress should not abandon the effort, to protect basic human liberties that are explicitly guaranteed in the text of the Constitution. That is the wrong place to cut back on Congressional power.

II. The Shrinking of Religious Liberty

Religious liberty is far less secure today, under the rule of *Employment Division v. Smith*, 494 U.S. 872 (1990), than it appeared to be last spring under RFRA. But it is not obvious just how much protection has been removed. The meaning of *Smith* is disputed, and under *Boerne*, that dispute is relevant to the scope of Congressional power.

In 1990, in the immediate wake of *Smith*, I noted deep ambiguities in the *Smith* opinion:

> "*Smith* announces a general rule that the Free Exercise Clause provides no substantive protection for religious conduct. It also notes enough exceptions and limitations to swallow most of its new rule. Everything seems to depend on judicial willingness to enforce the exceptions and police the neutrality requirement." Douglas Laycock, *The Remnants of Free Exercise*, 1990 SUP. CT. REV. 1, 54.

Hearings on RFRA were held in 1991 and 1992. At that time, the few lower court decisions under *Smith* were giving it the worst possible interpretation. Neither the exceptions nor the neutrality requirement appeared to have any content. Even laws that expressly applied only to churches or only to religious practices were being held neutral and generally applicable. And RFRA's advocates naturally emphasized this worst case scenario, which maximized the need for legislative remedies.

This legislative record was held against RFRA in *Boerne*. The Court inferred that Congress did not really believe that there are many violations of *Smith* in America today. In the Court's view, the hearing record showed that even Congress believed that the proportion of constitutional violations to RFRA violations would be small. And it followed, in the Court's view, that Congress was not interested in facilitating the proof of *Smith* violations, but in reaching other conduct that even Congress did not believe violated the Constitution as interpreted in *Smith*.

But in the meantime, the Court decided *Church of the Lukumi Babalu Aye v. City of Hialeah*, 508 U.S. 520 (1993), and gave real content to the requirements of neutrality and general applicability. *Lukumi* compared the local ordinances regulating religious practices to a broad range of other state and local laws dealing with analogous secular conduct and with secular conduct that caused analogous harms. It wrote into holding Smith's dictum that if a state permits exceptions for secular conduct, it must have compelling reason for refusing exceptions for analogous religious conduct. 508 U.S. at 537.

Some lower court interpretations of *Smith* began to change in light of *Lukumi*. One district court held that a rule requiring all university freshmen to live in the dorm was not neutral and generally applicable, because nearly a third of freshmen were covered by various exceptions.

The Free Exercise Clause — not RFRA — therefore required an exception for a freshman who wanted to live in a religious group house. *Rader v. Johnston*, 924 F. Supp. 1540 (D. Neb. 1996). Another district court held that a landmarking law was not neutral and generally applicable, because it contained three exceptions for various secular situations. The Free Exercise Clause — not RFRA — therefore required an exception for a church stuck with a useless landmark. *Keeler v. City of Cumberland*, 940 F. Supp. 879 (D. Md. 1996).

If these decisions are good law, and I think they are, then there are many violations of *Smith* in the land. Federal, state, and local laws are full of exceptions for influential secular interests. Moreover, the details of federal, state, and local laws are frequently filled in through individualized processes that provide ample opportunity to exempt favored interests and refuse exemptions to less favored interests, often including religious practice. Where a law has secular exceptions or an individualized exemption process, any burden on religion requires compelling justification under reasonable interpretations of *Smith*.

The problem, of course, is that these violations are difficult to litigate. There is room for endless argument whether the secular exception is really analogous to the claimed religious exception, and whether the lawmaking and exemption process is really individualized. In the very best case, all free exercise litigation will be far more complicated and expensive, and many good claims will be lost. In the more likely case, courts will defer to regulators and only the most egregious discrimination against religion will ever be adjudicated.

There is also continued dispute about the meaning of *Smith* even in principle. The discrimination against religious practice in *Lukumi* was so extreme that it can be distinguished from the more widespread discrimination of the sort found in *Rader* and *Keeler*. In its discussion of *Smith* in *Boerne*, the Court reaffirmed the hybrid rights exception to *Smith*, and it reaffirmed the rule that exemptions for secular hardship require exemptions for religious hardship. 117 S. Ct. at 2161. But when it considered whether RFRA was a proportionate response to violations of *Smith*, it used the phrase "religious bigotry" as a shorthand for what *Smith* required. *Id.* at 2171. This shorthand made it easier to argue that RFRA was a disproportionate response to a small number of actual violations, but as a summary of *Smith*, it is either inaccurate or a term of art. The word "bigotry" never appears in either the *Smith* or *Lukumi* opinions; the *Smith-Lukumi* test is an objective test of differential treatment, not a subjective test of governmental motive. "Religious bigotry" must be a label for unjustified differential treatment of religion; we should not assume that the new phrase was meant to change the *Smith-Lukumi* standard without explanation and once again dramatically shrink constitutional protection for religious liberty without briefing or argument. Lower court judges will almost never find a *Smith* violation if they conclude that doing so requires them to find state or local officials guilty of religious bigotry in a subjective sense.

I explain this ambiguity in detail that may be excessive, because it is critical both to the scope of remaining free exercise protection and to the scope of Congressional power. Loose congressional rhetoric to the effect that *Smith* eliminates nearly all protection for free exercise can actually shrink Congressional power, as *Boerne* illustrates. Congressional fact-finding preliminary to enforcement legislation must focus on regulatory fields in which violations of *Smith* may be widespread but are difficult to prove. The more such regulatory fields there are, the greater the reach of Congress's power to enforce the Fourteenth Amendment right to free exercise. Whether there are many such regulatory fields or few depends on whether we take seriously the exceptions to *Smith* and the requirement of neutrality and general applicability. Senators must resist the temptation to bash the Court by exaggerating the harm it has caused; the unexaggerated harm is quite enough to justify Congressional response.

III. What Congress Can Do Now

Congress can no longer enact a general solution to the problem of free exercise law. But it can enact a series of overlapping partial solutions that would collectively provide substantial protection for religious practice.

1. The Commerce Power. Congress could enact RFRA's level of protection for religious practices in or affecting commerce. The statute would provide that any religious practice in or affecting commerce is exempt from burdens imposed by state and local legislation, except where the regulating jurisdiction demonstrates that the application of the burden to the individual serves a compelling government interest by the least restrictive means. The models here are the Privacy Protection Act of 1980, 42 U.S.C. 2000aa (1994), protecting papers and documents in preparation for a publication in or affecting commerce, and the public accommodations title of the Civil Rights Act of 1964, 42 U.S.C. 2000a (1994), forbidding racial and religious discrimination in places of public accommodation affecting commerce, and irrefutably presuming that commerce is affected by any hotel and by any restaurant that serves interstate travelers.

The public accommodations law is particularly instructive as to Congressional power. Congress's first public accommodations law was the Civil Rights Act of 1875, enacted to enforce the Thirteenth and Fourteenth Amendments. The Supreme Court struck that law down as beyond the enforcement power. *Civil Rights Cases*, 109 U.S. 3 (1883). Congress's second public accommodations law was the Civil Rights Act of 1964, enacted with substantially the same scope in practical effect but pursuant to the commerce power. This Act was upheld in *Katzenbach v. McClung*, 379 U.S. 294 (1964), and *Heart of Atlanta Motel v. United States*, 379 U.S. 241 (1964).

Congress did not enact the public accommodations law to maximize the sale of barbecue sauce. Rather, it enacted the public accommodations law because it was morally right, and it used the Commerce Clause because that was an available means to the end. Similarly here, protecting the religious practices of the American people is morally right, and to the extent that those practices affect commerce, the Commerce Clause is an available means to the end.

After *United States v. Lopez*, 514 U.S. 549 (1995), I doubt that the commerce power can reach religious practices that do not affect a commercial transaction. But many religious practices do affect commercial transactions. When burdensome regulation prevents a church from building a house of worship, as in *Boerne*, tens of thousands or even millions of dollars of commerce are prevented from happening. When a Roman Catholic hospital loses its accreditation in obstetrics because it refuses to teach abortion techniques in violation of its religious commitments, all the services and all the instruction its obstetrics program would have provided are prevented or diverted to other sites. If the hospital succumbs to state coercion and agrees to teach abortion techniques, the resulting abortions are themselves a service provided in commerce, and that commerce is diverted to the Catholic hospital from other sites.

It should not matter whether commercial transactions are prevented entirely, diverted from one provider to another, coerced, or changed in some other way: in all these cases, commerce is affected. The Court has long held that production of goods and services affects commerce, that individual transactions are within the commerce power if all such transactions cumulatively affect commerce, and that Congress can regulate commerce for moral or other non-economic motives. Unless we see dramatic changes in Commerce Clause doctrine, Congress can protect many religious practices under the Commerce Clause.

It would simplify litigation of the affecting-commerce issue if Congress enacted definitions or presumptions. For example, Congress could create presumptions that the practices of religious institutions affect commerce, and that religious practices that use goods or services regularly bought and sold in commerce affect commerce. It would be prudent to specify that Congress is exercising the commerce power to the full constitutional limit.

2. *The Spending Power*. Congress could enact RFRA's level of protection for religious practices burdened by the rules of any program receiving federal financial assistance. No person could be excluded from participation in, or denied the benefits of, or otherwise subjected to discrimination, or have their religious practice burdened, under any program or activity receiving federal financial assistance, because of a religious practice, unless application of the burden to the person served a compelling interest by the least restrictive means. The leading models here are Title VI of the Civil Rights Act of 1964, 42 U.S.C. 2000d (1994), forbidding racial discrimination in federally assisted programs, similar civil rights statutes modeled on Title VI and protecting other classes, and the Equal Access Act, 20 U.S.C. 4071 et seq. (1994), protecting student speech in federally assisted secondary schools. It would better serve the bill's purposes to confine the reach of this spending power provision to recipients of federal money who act under color of law; this bill should not become embroiled in debates over regulation of religious entities that deliver federally financed social services.

Congressional power to attach conditions to federal spending has been recognized since *Steward Machine Co. v. Davis*, 301 U.S. 548 (1937). But conditions on federal grants must be "Related to the federal interest in particular national projects or programs." *South Dakota v. Dole*, 483 U.S. 203, 207 (1987). Federal aid to one program does not empower Congress to demand compliance with RFRA in other programs. But within a single program, this requirement is easily satisfied. The federal interest is that the intended beneficiaries of federal programs not be excluded because of their religious practice. Congress should include language modeled on 42 U.S.C. 2000d-4a (1994), which defines the scope of aided programs for purposes of the obligation to refrain from burdening religious practices.

Conditions on federal grants must also be clearly stated. They are in the nature of a contract, and state and local entities are entitled to know what obligations they are assuming before they accept the federal money. *Suter v. Artist M.*, 503 U.S. 347, 356 (1992); *Pennhurst State School & Hospital v. Halderman*, 451 U.S. 1, 17 (1981). This requirement can easily be satisfied by careful drafting.

A Spending Clause statute could protect many religious individuals who are subject to bureaucratic authority in federally assisted programs. Many of these cases will involve individual devotions or observance that do not lead to any commercial transaction and do not plausibly affect commerce. Thus, a Spending

Clause statute and a Commerce Clause statute are complementary. Together they would address a large portion of the problem.

3. The Enforcement Power. City of Boerne v. Flores does not deprive Congress of all power to protect religious exercise under its power to enforce the Fourteenth Amendment. Congress can enact legislation to assist the enforcement of the Free Exercise Clause as the Court interprets it, providing stronger remedies and facilitating proof of violations in cases where proof is difficult. If the connection between judicial interpretation and Congressional legislation is not obvious, Congress should make a clear record that its legislation is directed to deterring or remedying violations that, if all the facts could be readily proved, the Court would recognize as constitutional violations under *Employment Division v. Smith*. Plainly the Court means to require a more detailed factual record than Congress compiled for RFRA, and although constitutionality should not depend on what Congress thinks, Congressional rhetoric should put more emphasis on addressing free exercise violations as the Court understands them.

I doubt that the Court would uphold a re-enactment of RFRA under the Enforcement Clause no matter how good a record Congress compiled. But the Court should uphold burden of proof provisions, which simply reallocate the risk of factual error in cases where it is impossible to be certain whether government did or did not violate the Constitution as the Court interprets it. And the Court may well uphold more particularized statutes directed to particular problems, if the Congress and the religious and civil liberties community do their homework and make their record.

The clearest example is land use regulation, which has enormous disparate impact on churches, which is administered through highly discretionary and individualized processes that leave ample room for deliberate but hidden discrimination, and where there is substantial evidence of widespread hostility to non-mainstream churches and some hostility to all churches. Here are some facts that have already been documented:

a. In the City of New York, churches are landmarked at a rate forty-two times higher than secular properties. *N.J. L'Heureux, Jr., Ministry v. Mortar. A Landmark Conflict, in* DEAN M. KELLEY, ED., GOVERNMENT INTERVENTION IN RELIGIOUS AFFAIRS 2 at 164, 168 (1986).

b. In the City of Chicago and some of its suburbs, zoning regulation is administered in such a way that it is nearly impossible to start a new church without consent of surrounding owners, and this consent is so often withheld that finding a site for a new church is often impossible, especially in the case of churches not affiliated with a well-known denomination. Many of the resulting lawsuits are not about efforts to build new structures, but simply efforts to rent and occupy a storefront. I believe the same problem exists elsewhere, but it is well documented in and around Chicago. If the Committee will call the attorneys for these churches as witnesses, it can learn the details. Some of this discrimination can be proved; some of it cannot be. But so many churches would not be investing so much effort in litigation if there were no serious difficulties in locating sites.

c. Denominations that account for only 9% of the population account for about half the reported church zoning cases. That is, the zoning process disproportionately excludes small and unfamiliar faiths. This discrimination is often unprovable in any individual case, but when large numbers of cases are examined, the pattern is clear. These data are gathered in the Brief of the Church of Jesus Christ of Latter-Day Saints as Amicus Curiae in *City of Boerne v. Flores*.

d. Journalists have reported that new suburbs on the fringe of urban growth often exclude churches, even from mainstream denominations. R. Gustav Neibuhr, *Here is the Church; As for the People, They're Picketing It*, WALL ST. J. at A1 (Nov. 20, 1991).

e. The process of administering zoning laws and the process of designating landmarks are highly individualized. Standards tend to be vague and manipulable; zoning for a parcel is easily changed if those in power desire to change it. Many key decisions are made at the level of individual parcels in applications for special permits or variances or in votes on zoning changes or in landmark designations. In Boerne for example, St. Peter's Church was added to the historic district by a separate ordinance that applied only to St. Peter's and to no other property. These land-use laws are often not neutral and they are almost never generally applicable in any meaningful sense. Thus, the resulting burdens on churches should be subject to strict scrutiny under *Employment Division v. Smith*. There are *Smith* violations here that are difficult to prove, and that is an appropriate case for enforcement legislation even under *Boerne*. Indeed, to subject the location of churches to the zoning and landmarking procedures in many jurisdictions is to subject the First Amendment right to gather for worship to a standardless licensing scheme, in violation of settled principles developed under the Free Speech Clause. *See, e.g.*, *City of Lakewood v. Plain Dealer Publishing Co.*, 486 U.S. 750 (1988); *Griffin v. City of Lovell*, 303 U.S. 444 (1938).

It is vague standards and discretionary decisions [that] give religious prejudice a chance to operate not just in the zoning cases, but also in may other cases. Vague standards and discretionary decisions are quite common in governmental organizations. In nearly all the cases in which schools penalize the religious practices of students, or government agencies penalize the religious practices of government employees or beneficiaries of the agency's program, the relevant administrator has a large element of discretion in making the rule, interpreting the rule, and choosing when to enforce the rule. The particular disputes in these cases cover a wide range of issues, which makes them hard to generalize about, but they have in common that the administrator's attitude towards the religious practice inevitably influences his exercise of discretion.

It commonly happens that the administrator's attitude towards the religious practice is negative. At least some Americans are hostile to religion generally;

more are hostile to particular religions; many believe that religion should be kept wholly private and are hostile to its public manifestation. Many believers have experienced this hostility, and sympathetic observers have seen it in operation; the hearing process can easily gather anecdotal evidence. Systematic quantitative evidence is scarcer, partly because the studies have not been done, and partly because few people consciously admit to bigotry even when they are guilty. Despite these difficulties, the Gallup Poll has gathered some remarkably revealing information.

In 1993, 45% of Americans admitted to "mostly unfavorable" or "very unfavorable" opinions of "religious fundamentalists," and 86% admitted to mostly or very unfavorable opinions of "members of religious cults or sects." George Gallup, Jr., Gallup Poll: Public Opinion 1993 at 75-76, 78 (1994).

In 1989, 30% of Americans said they would not like to have "religious fundamentalists" as neighbors, and 62% said they would not like to have "members of minority religious sects or cults" as neighbors. By contrast, only 12% admitted that they would not like to have "blacks" as neighbors. George Gallup Jr., The Gallup Poll: Public Opinion 1989 at 63, 67 (1990).

It is a reasonable inference that at least a comparable percentage of government administrators hold these hostile views toward religious fundamentalists and members of minority sects. In fact, the proportion of hostile government administrators is probably higher, because it is the experience of many believers that these hostile attitudes are more common among persons in elite positions. If 45% or more of government administrators hold unfavorable opinions of religious fundamentalists and members of minority sects, and if these administrators have broad discretion to deal with persons under their supervision, then half or more of administrative decisions about the religious practices of these religious minorities are infected by these hostile attitudes.

If all the facts were known and provable, administrative action so motivated would generally violate the Free Exercise Clause as interpreted by the Supreme Court. A recent example where the facts could be proved is *Rader v. Johnston*, 924 F. Supp. 1540 (D. Neb. 1996), in which the district judge found that the testimony of high ranking university officials (the Chancellor and the Vice Chancellor for Student Affairs) "manifested a degree of antipathy toward members of [Christian Student Fellowship]. " *Id.* at 1554. The issue was a rule requiring all freshmen to live in the residence halls; the administration had allowed secular exceptions but it refused to allow freshmen to live in a religious group house under supervision of a pastor. Plaintiff objected to the rampant sex and drugs in the residence halls; the Chancellor testified that religious students who objected to the residence halls should not attend the University.

But proving this hostility in any individual case is difficult, principally because administrators cover their tracks with rationalizations for their decision, but also because judges are reluctant to draw the inference even when the evidence is available. Judges are reluctant to impute bad motive to government officials. And although it is indelicate to say so, there is no reason to think that judges as a group are more sympathetic than the population to fundamentalists and members of minority sects. It is a reasonable inference from the Gallup data that 45% or more of judges also hold unfavorable views of these religious minorities. Most of these judges strive to be fair to all litigants who come before them, but they too have discretion, and facts are always disputed and uncertain. Their assessment of the facts and of the administrator's motivations is inevitably affected by their views of the religious practice at issue. If the judge were sure of the facts and convinced of the administrator's improper motivation, of course he would find a constitutional violation. But it is hard to be sure, and so he gives the administrator the benefit of the doubt.

I would add to the record one recent incident in my own experience. I attended a luncheon for representatives of philanthropic organizations in Texas. These people were highly educated, economically successful, well-meaning, genteel, genuinely devoted to helping a broad range of causes. Their desire to do good and to help people was similar to that of many well-motivated government administrators. The luncheon speaker introduced her talk by telling two Baptist jokes, jokes that drew their humor from a caricatured version of Baptist theological teaching in one case and of Baptist moral teaching in the other. The audience laughed appreciatively both times. I was surely not the only person in the room who thought the jokes objectionable, but no one objected, and more than enough people laughed heartily to make the jokes successful.

It is inconceivable to me that the speaker would have told ethnic jokes to that audience, or that the audience would have laughed appreciatively if she had. Ethnic jokes would have drawn an embarrassed silence, a few nervous titters, exchanges of shocked or disapproving looks. But it is acceptable in many educated circles to make fun of traditional religious believers.

Attitudes such as those reflected in that lunch and in the Gallup Poll data infect the discretionary decisions of thousands of government administrators throughout the land. So if all the facts were known in every case, widespread violations of the Constitution as the Court interprets it can be found in the discretionary decisions of government bureaucracies, including schools and social welfare agencies. Land use regulation is just the most visible and best documented example. Religious liberty groups get many such complaints, and if some of those groups have maintained good files, they could document examples.

Another set of decision-makers entrusted with effectively unreviewable discretion is juries. Civil juries review religions and religious practices in a wide range of cases, including suits by disaffected members objecting to religious teaching or practice, suits for personal injury and other torts, and suits by individuals whose religious practice somehow becomes an issue in the case. Of course some of the claims against churches are legitimate and meritorious; others are thinly disguised attacks on religious beliefs and practices. But lawyers who have tried these cases say that whatever the formal rule of law and whatever the nature of the claim, a key issue is what the jury thinks of the religion and the religious practice. I and others can identify lawyers who have tried many of these cases; one of them should be invited to testify at a future hearing.

4. The Power to Make Federal Law. Congress has undoubted power to determine the scope and reach of federal statutes and regulations. Congress can therefore provide that federal law shall not be interpreted to substantially burden a religious practice unless necessary to serve a compelling state interest. *EEOC v. Catholic University,* 83 F.3d 455, 469-70 (D.C. Cir. 1996). Nothing in *Boerne* casts any doubt on this proposition. Rather, the opinion reaffirms that "When Congress acts within its sphere of power and responsibilities, it has not just the right but the duty to make its own informed judgment on the meaning and force of the Constitution." 117 S. Ct. 2171. There is therefore no reason to doubt that RFRA is valid with respect to federal law, although the challenge will be made and courts will have to decide the issue again.

It would be prudent for Congress to reaffirm its view that RFRA is still in effect with respect to federal law, either by joint resolution or in a savings clause in any new legislation, or by an explicit amendment to RFRA as an existing federal statute. Otherwise, we will have to spend time litigating whether the passage of legislation to replace the invalidated part of RFRA was an implied repeal of the valid part.

There may also be need for more specific federal legislation directed at particular problems. For example, trustees in bankruptcy persist in filing fraudulent transfer claims against churches to recover ordinary-course pre-bankruptcy contributions, and many lower courts are rejecting RFRA defenses, even though the only appellate holding allows the RFRA defense. *In re Young,* 82 F.3d 1407 (8th Cir. 1996), *vacated on other grounds,* 117 S. Ct. 2502 (1997). The general language of RFRA has not been enough to avoid repeated litigation, even though the burden of refunding old contributions long since spent should be obvious to anyone.

Indeed, these are cases that could be resolved under the Free Exercise Clause as interpreted in Smith. The generally applicable rule in bankruptcy is that the debtor has control of his funds and may dissipate them prior to bankruptcy, with the result that creditors generally go unpaid. Creditors cannot recover funds gambled away at casinos, because the debtor gets entertainment value and a chance to win money, *In re Chamakos,* 69 F.3d 769 (6th Cir. 1995), but many lower courts hold that the debtor gets nothing in exchange for his weekly contribution to his church.

Congress can solve this problem and largely end this litigation with a specific amendment to the Bankruptcy Code protecting ordinary-course charitable contributions made in good faith. Congress could at the same time address the related problem of whether debtors who choose to make voluntary partial payments to their creditors under chapter 13 can continue to contribute to their church. I am sure there are other specific issues in federal law, but these bankruptcy issues are ripe for resolution because they have already caused much litigation.

5. *Remedies.* Any legislation to protect religious liberty should provide explicit remedies. RFRA's provisions for individual rights of action for damages, injunctions, and attorneys' fees are a reasonable model. The Court generally assumes that you did not mean for your laws to be enforced unless you tell it otherwise. It is particularly important to provide for private enforcement in Spending Clause legislation; it is extremely unlikely that any federal grant will be revoked because of one or a few incidents of suppressing religious practice.

THE RELIGIOUS LIBERTY PROTECTION ACT
105th CONGRESS, 2d Session HR 4019

IN THE HOUSE OF REPRESENTATIVES

June 9, 1998

Mr. CANADY of Florida (for himself and Mr. NADLER) introduced the following bill; which was referred to the Committee on the Judiciary

A BILL

To protect religious liberty.

Be it enacted by the Senate and House of Representatives of the United States of America in Congress assembled,

SECTION 1. SHORT TITLE.

This Act may be cited as the "Religious Liberty Protection Act of 1998".

SECTION 2. PROTECTION OF RELIGIOUS EXERCISE.

(a) GENERAL RULE — Except as provided in subsection (b), a government shall not substantially burden a person's religious exercise —

(1) in a program or activity, operated by a government, that receives Federal financial assistance; or

(2) in or affecting commerce with foreign nations, among the several States, or with the Indian tribes; even if the burden results from a rule of general applicability.

(b) EXCEPTION — A government may substantially burden a person's religious exercise if the government demonstrates that application of the burden to the person —

(1) is in furtherance of a compelling governmental interest; and

(2) is the least restrictive means of furthering that compelling governmental interest.

(c) FUNDING NOT AFFECTED — Nothing in this section shall be construed to authorize the United States to deny or withhold Federal financial assistance as a remedy for a violation of this Act.

(d) STATE POLICY NOT COMMANDEERED — A government may eliminate the substantial burden on religious exercise by changing the policy that results in the burden, by retaining the policy and exempting the religious exercise from that policy, or by any other means that eliminates the burden.

(e) DEFINITIONS — As used in this section —

(1) the term "government" means a branch, department, agency, instrumentality, subdivision, or official of a State (or other person acting under color of State law);

(2) the term "program or activity" means a program or activity as defined in paragraph (1) or (2) of section 606 of the Civil Rights Act of 1964 (42 U.S.C. 2000d-4a); and

(3) the term "demonstrates" means meets the burdens of going forward with the evidence and of persuasion.

SECTION 3. ENFORCEMENT OF THE FREE EXERCISE CLAUSE.

(a) PROCEDURE — If a claimant produces prima facie evidence to support a claim of a violation of the Free Exercise Clause, the government shall bear the burden of persuasion on all issues relating to the claim, except any issue as to the existence of the burden on religious exercise.

(b) LAND USE REGULATION —

(1) LIMITATION ON LAND USE REGULATION — No government shall impose a land use regulation that —

(A) substantially burdens religious exercise, unless the burden is the least restrictive means to prevent substantial and tangible harm to neighboring properties or to the public health or safety;

(B) denies religious assemblies a reasonable location in the jurisdiction; or

(C) excludes religious assemblies from areas in which nonreligious assemblies are permitted.

(2) FULL FAITH AND CREDIT — Adjudication of a claim of a violation of this subsection in a non-Federal forum shall be entitled to full faith and credit in a Federal court only if the claimant had a full and fair adjudication of that claim in the non-Federal forum.

(3) NONPREEMPTION — Nothing in this subsection shall preempt State law that is equally or more protective of religious exercise.

(4) NONAPPLICATION OF OTHER PORTIONS OF THIS ACT — Section 2 does not apply to land use regulation.

SECTION 4. JUDICIAL RELIEF.

(a) CAUSE OF ACTION — A person may assert a violation of this Act as a claim or defense in a judicial proceeding and obtain appropriate relief against a government. Standing to assert a claim or defense under this section shall be governed by the general rules of standing under article III of the Constitution.

(b) ATTORNEYS' FEES — Section 722(b) of the Revised Statutes (42 U.S.C. 1988(b)) is amended —

(1) by inserting "the Religious Liberty Protection Act of 1998," after " Religious Freedom Restoration Act of 1993,"; and

(2) by striking the comma that follows a comma.

(c) PRISONERS — Any litigation under this Act in which the claimant is a prisoner shall be subject to the Prison Litigation Reform Act of 1995 (including provisions of law amended by that Act).

(d) LIABILITY OF GOVERNMENTS —

(1) LIABILITY OF STATES — A State shall not be immune under the 11th amendment to the Constitution from a civil action, for a violation of the Free Exercise Clause under section 3, including a civil action for money damages.

(3) LIABILITY OF THE UNITED STATES — The United States shall not be immune from a civil action, for a violation of the Free Exercise Clause under section 3, including a civil action for money damages.

SECTION 5. RULES OF CONSTRUCTION.

(a) RELIGIOUS BELIEF UNAFFECTED — Nothing in this Act shall be construed to authorize any government to burden any religious belief.

(b) RELIGIOUS EXERCISE NOT REGULATED — Nothing in this Act shall create any basis for regulation of religious exercise or for claims against a religious organization, including any religiously affiliated school or university, not acting under color of law.

(c) CLAIMS TO FUNDING UNAFFECTED — Nothing in this Act shall create or preclude a right of any religious organization to receive funding or other assistance from a government, or of any person to receive government funding for a religious activity, but this Act may require government to incur expenses in its own operations to avoid imposing a burden or a substantial burden on religious exercise.

(d) OTHER AUTHORITY TO IMPOSE CONDITIONS ON FUNDING UNAFFECTED — Nothing in this Act shall —

(1) authorize a government to regulate or affect, directly or indirectly, the activities or policies of a person other than a government as a condition of receiving funding or other assistance; or

(2) restrict any authority that may exist under other law to so regulate or affect, except as provided in this Act.

(e) EFFECT ON OTHER LAW — Proof that a religious exercise affects commerce for the purposes of this Act does not give rise to any inference or presumption that the religious exercise is subject to any other law regulating commerce.

(f) SEVERABILITY — If any provision of this Act or of an amendment made by this Act, or any application of such provision to any person or circumstance, is held to be unconstitutional, the remainder of this Act, the amendments made by this Act, and the application of the provision to any other person or circumstance shall not be affected.

SECTION 6. ESTABLISHMENT CLAUSE UNAFFECTED.

Nothing in this Act shall be construed to affect, interpret, or in any way address that portion of the first amendment to the Constitution prohibiting laws respecting an establishment of religion (referred to in this section as the "Establishment Clause"). Granting government funding, benefits, or exemptions, to the extent permissible under the Establishment Clause, shall not constitute a violation of this Act. As used in this section, the term "granting", used with respect to government funding, benefits, or exemptions, does not include the denial of government funding, benefits, or exemptions.

SECTION 7. AMENDMENTS TO RELIGIOUS FREEDOM RESTORATION ACT.

(a) DEFINITIONS — Section 5 of the Religious Freedom Restoration Act of 1993 (42 U.S.C. 2000bb-2) is amended —

(1) in paragraph (1), by striking "a State, or subdivision of a State" and inserting "a covered entity or a subdivision of such an entity";

(2) in paragraph (2), by striking "term" and all that follows through "includes" and inserting term "'covered entity' means"; and

(3) in paragraph (4), by striking all after "means," and inserting "an act or refusal to act that is substantially motivated by a religious belief, whether or not the act or refusal is compulsory or central to a larger system of religious belief.".

(b) CONFORMING AMENDMENT — Section 6(a) of the Religious Freedom Restoration Act of 1993 (42 U.S.C. 2000bb-3(a)) is amended by striking "and State".

SECTION 8. DEFINITIONS.

As used in this Act —

    (1) the term "religious exercise" means an act or refusal to act that is substantially motivated by a religious belief, whether or not the act or refusal is compulsory or central to a larger system of religious belief;

    (2) the term "Free Exercise Clause" means that portion of the first amendment to the Constitution that proscribes laws prohibiting the free exercise of religion and includes the application of that proscription under the 14th amendment to the Constitution; and

    (3) except as otherwise provided in this Act, the term "government" means a branch, department, agency, instrumentality, subdivision, or official of a State, or other person acting under color of State law, or a branch, department, agency, instrumentality, subdivision, or official of the United States, or other person acting under color of Federal law.

Marci A. Hamilton
***Testimony to the Senate Committee
on the Judiciary***
Tuesday, June 23, 1998

S. 1248, The Religious Liberty Protection Act of 1998

Thank you, Mr. Chairman and members of the Committee, for inviting me to speak today on this important constitutional law topic. I am a Professor of Law at Benjamin N. Cardozo School of Law, Yeshiva University, where I specialize in constitutional law. I was also the lead counsel for the City of Boerne, Texas in the case that ultimately invalidated the Religious Freedom Restoration Act (RFRA). *See Boerne v. Flores*, 117 S. Ct. 2157 (1997). I have devoted the last five years of my life to writing about, lecturing on, and litigating the Religious Freedom Restoration Act and similar religious liberty legislation in the states. For the record, I am a religious believer.

As you know, the *Boerne v. Flores* decision unequivocally rejected RFRA. Not a single member of the Supreme Court defended the law in either the majority, the concurrences, or the dissents. The Court's decision was not a result of any hostility on the part of the Court toward this body. That is evident in its calm, evenhanded tone. Nor was it the result of mistaken understandings of its own precedents. The decision was inevitable. Contrary to Professor Laycock's and the Congressional Research Service's confident assurances in the RFRA legislative record, RFRA was plainly ultra vires.

Today I am here to tell you that I believe that RLPA violates the Constitution. That this bill, which is a slap in the face of the Framers and the Constitution, is receiving a hearing indicates that what I say today may   not make much difference. If Congress wants to be perceived as the savior of religious liberty and wants to defer to the most powerful coalition of religions in this country's history, there is absolutely nothing that I can do about it. Thus, I will not offer detailed critique of each of this bill's glaring constitutional errors. Instead, I will offer a summary of those errors.

Then I will share with you the interests that will be hurt by granting religion this unprecedented quantum of power against the government. I represent none of these interests, but I have heard their stories in my travels around the country these five years.

RLPA's Most Severe Constitutional Defects

[1] RLPA Violates the Separation of Powers. Like RFRA, RLPA is an undisguised attempt to reverse the Supreme Court's interpretation of the Free Exercise Clause in *Employment Division v. Smith*, 494 U.S. 872 (1990), and to take over the Court's core function of interpreting the Constitution. *See* Secs. 2(a) and 3(a). For a clear discussion explaining why this is beyond Congress's power, *see Boerne v. Flores*, 117 S. Ct. at 2172.

[2] RLPA Violates the Constitution's Ratification Procedures. Like RFRA, RLPA attempts to amend the Constitution by a majority vote, bypassing Article V's required ratification procedures in direct violation of *Marbury v. Madison*, 5 U.S. (1 Cranch) 137 (1803). For a plain discussion in which the Court reasserts its allegiance to *Marbury*, *see Boerne v. Flores*, 117 S. Ct. at 2168.

Professor Douglas Laycock tilts at windmills when he attempts to argue that the test instituted by RLPA (and RFRA), the compelling interest/least restrictive means test, was the test regularly employed in all free exercise cases before 1990. He neglects to mention *Turner v. Safley*, 482 U.S. 78 (1987), which makes explicit that strict scrutiny does not apply in the prison context or any of other cases in which the Court demonstrated great deference to government interests. *See, e.g., Goldman v. Weinberger*, 475 U.S. 503 (1986); *Bowen v. Roy*, 476 U.S. 693 (1986). Whatever Professor Laycock's interpretation of the Supreme Court's free exercise jurisprudence may be, the Supreme Court itself made absolutely clear in *Boerne v. Flores* that the least restrictive means test is "a requirement that was not used in the pre-Smith jurisprudence RFRA purported to codify."117 S. Ct. at 2171.

[3] RLPA Is an Assault on States' Rights. Despite its rote recitation of language from cases addressing federalism issues, *see, e.g.,* Sec. 2(d) ("state policy not commandeered"), this bill federalizes local land use law and (if good law) would eviscerate one of the final strongholds of local government. It violates the letter and the spirit of the modern Court's emerging structural constitutional jurisprudence. *See Printz v. United States,* 117 S. Ct. 2365 (1997); *United States v. Lopez*, 514 U.S. 549 (1995); *New York v. U.S.*, 505 U.S. 144 (1992). If good law,

RLPA's micromanagement of local land use law would set the pace for an expansive invasion of state and local government authority. If RLPA becomes law, it will haunt any representative who attempts to climb onto the limited federal government platform.

[4] RLPA Fails to Satisfy the Enumerated Power Requirement. RLPA is ultra vires. There is not a single statute that provides a model for RLPA's claim to be grounded in either the Spending Clause or the Commerce Clause. Congress has not identified any specific arena of spending or commerce. Rather, it has identified all religious conduct as its target and attempted to cover as much religious conduct as possible by casting a net over all federal spending and commerce. *See* Hearings, H.R. 4019, The Religious Liberty Protection Act, Subcommittee on the Constitution, House Committee on the Judiciary (June 16, 1998). Like RFRA, its obvious purpose is to displace the Supreme Court's interpretation of the Free Exercise Clause in as many fora as possible. It is a transparent end-run around the Supreme Court's criticism of RFRA in *Boerne v. Flores*.

The specious argument that Congress may grant religion this windfall under the Commerce Clause because religion generates commerce attempts to transform the First Amendment, a limitation on congressional power, into an enumerated power.

[5] RLPA Violates the Establishment Clause. RLPA privileges religion over all other interests in the society. While the Supreme Court indicated in *Smith* that tailored exemptions from certain laws for particular religious practices might pass muster, it has never given any indication that legislatures have the power to privilege religion across-the-board in this way. RFRA's and RLPA's defenders rely on Corporation of the *Presiding Bishop v. Amos*, 483 U.S. 327 (1987), for the proposition that government may enact exemptions en masse. This is a careless reading of the case, which stands for the proposition that religion may be exempted from a particular law (affecting employment) if such an exemption is necessary to avoid excessive entanglement between church and state. RLPA, like RFRA, creates, rather than solves, entanglement problems. RLPA, which was drafted by religion for the purpose of benefiting religion and has the effect of privileging religion in a vast number of scenarios, violates the Establishment Clause. For the Court's most recent explanation of the Establishment Clause, see *Agostini v. Felton*, 117 S. Ct. 1997 (1997).

The following is a list of interests that will be affected adversely if RLPA is adopted, because it elevates religion above all other societal interests. As Oregon recently discovered when a prosecutor attempted to prosecute a religious community for the deaths of three children, particular exemptions from general laws can have real consequences. This is a zero-sum game: by granting religion expansive new power against generally applicable, neutral laws, Congress inevitably subtracts from the liberty accorded other societal interests.

Before blindly passing this law with its mandate to exempt religion from general laws in an infinite number of scenarios, Congress should know that it risks responsibility for harming the following constituencies:

[1] Children in religions that advocate and practice abuse

[2] Women in religions that advocate male domination

[3] Children in religions that refuse medical treatment, including immunizations

[4] Pediatricians, who have lobbied vigorously for mandatory immunizations

[5] The handicapped, women, minorities, and homosexuals, whose interests are currently protected by anti-discrimination laws and may well be trumped by religions exercising the compelling interest/least restrictive means test

[6] Departments of correction and prison officials attempting to ensure order in prisons populated by increasingly violent criminals

[7] Artistic and historical preservation interests, including whole communities that depend on historical districts for revenue and jobs

[8] Neighborhoods attempting to enforce neutral rules regulating congestion, building size, lot size, and on- and off-street parking

[9] School boards desperately attempting to ensure order and safety in the public schools

[10] State, local, and municipal officials who will be forced to bear the cost of accommodating every religious request (whether from a mainstream religion or a cult) or bear the cost of litigating refusals to do so. Last, but not least, citizens who will bear the extreme increase in litigation costs created by these new rights coupled to an attorney's fees provision (a virtual invitation to sue).

In sum, RLPA is no better than RFRA. In fact, it is worse. Congress has a duty to investigate its wide-ranging effects with care before taking this plainly unconstitutional path.

For those who take comfort from the fact that RLPA is supported by a wide cross-section of religions, I leave you with the words of Framer Rufus King, one of the youngest members of the Constitutional Convention but a Harvard graduate who was highly respected on structural issues:

"[I]f the clergy combine, they will have their influence on government."

THE RELIGIOUS LAND AND INSTITUTIONALIZED PERSONS ACT
42 U.S.C. § 2000cc

After the RLPA failed to move beyond a favorable vote of the House of Representatives, Congress enacted and President Clinton signed a more tightly focused version of the statute. The statute is known as the "Religious Land Use and Institutionalized Persons Act," 42 U.S.C. § 2000cc. Consider whether this narrow statute cures the problems identified by Professor Hamilton. Note especially the constitutional powers used by Congress — the Commerce Clause and the Spending Clause — not Section Five of the Fourteenth Amendment.

The first part of the act protects property used by religious groups:

(a) Substantial burdens.

(1) General rule. No government shall impose or implement a land use regulation in a manner that imposes a substantial burden on the religious exercise of a person, including a religious assembly or institution, unless the government demonstrates that imposition of the burden on that person, assembly, or institution —

(A) is in furtherance of a compelling governmental interest; and

(B) is the least restrictive means of furthering that compelling governmental interest.

(2) Scope of application. This subsection applies in any case in which —

(A) the substantial burden is imposed in a program or activity that receives Federal financial assistance, even if the burden results from a rule of general applicability;

(B) the substantial burden affects, or removal of that substantial burden would affect, commerce with foreign nations, among the several States, or with Indian tribes, even if the burden results from a rule of general applicability; or

(C) the substantial burden is imposed in the implementation of a land use regulation or system of land use regulations, under which a government makes, or has in place formal or informal procedures or practices that permit the government to make, individualized assessments of the proposed uses for the property involved.

(b) Discrimination and exclusion.

(1) Equal terms. No government shall impose or implement a land use regulation in a manner that treats a religious assembly or institution on less than equal terms with a nonreligious assembly or institution.

(2) Nondiscrimination. No government shall impose or implement a land use regulation that discriminates against any assembly or institution on the basis of religion or religious denomination.

(3) Exclusions and limits. No government shall impose or implement a land use regulation that —

(A) totally excludes religious assemblies from a jurisdiction; or

(B) unreasonably limits religious assemblies, institutions, or structures within a jurisdiction.

The second part of the statute deals with the religious practices of institutionalized persons.

(a) General rule. No government shall impose a substantial burden on the religious exercise of a person residing in or confined to an institution, as defined in section 2 of the Civil Rights of Institutionalized Persons Act (42 U.S.C. 1997), even if the burden results from a rule of general applicability, unless the government demonstrates that imposition of the burden on that person —

(1) is in furtherance of a compelling governmental interest; and

(2) is the least restrictive means of furthering that compelling governmental interest.

(b) Scope of application. This section applies in any case in which —

(1) the substantial burden is imposed in a program or activity that receives Federal financial assistance; or

(2) the substantial burden affects, or removal of that substantial burden would affect, commerce with foreign nations, among the several States, or with Indian tribes.

NOTES ON **RLUIPA**

1. *The RLUIPA Land Use Provisions — Statutory Claims.* Religious individuals and organizations seeking to enforce RLUIPA have fared very well under the land use provisions of the statute. Although the issues are interlinked, and tend to be discussed together, there are four separate matters requiring analysis under the land use provisions of RLUIPA: Does the private activity burdened by the government constitute "religious exercise"? Does the regulation constitute a "substantial burden"? Is the burden justified by a compelling interest? And is the burden the least restrictive means of protecting that interest? In addition to these issues, recall that the statute contains three specific limitations on government action affecting religious land use. These specific limits (1) require governments to treat religion on equal terms with other activities, (2) prohibit governments from discriminating against religious institutions, and (3) prohibit governments from totally excluding or unreasonably limiting religious institutions or structures within a jurisdiction. Most of these terms are interpreted in fairly straightforward ways, although there is no grand theory unifying the analysis. Here are several examples of cases involving each issue:

A. *What is a religious exercise?*

RLUIPA itself defines religious exercise very broadly. According to Section 8 of the statute, "religious exercise" includes "any exercise of religion, whether or not compelled by, or central to, a system of religious belief." The statute also states that "[t]he use, building, or conversion of real property for the purpose of religious exercise shall be considered to be religious exercise of the person or entity that uses or intends to use the property for that purpose." Most of the cases discussing this issue involve the operation of a facility for religious purposes or the conversion of a preexisting facility for use in religious activity, including religious education. *See, e.g., Midrash Sephardi, Inc. v. Town of Surfside*, 366 F.3d 1214 (11th Cir. 2004), *cert. denied*, 543 U.S. 1146 (2005); *San Jose Christian Coll. v. City of Morgan Hill*, 360 F.3d 1024 (9th Cir. 2004) (converting a hospital into a religious college). If a building is being used for any sort of religious purpose, the "religious exercise" requirement is satisfied. *But see Grace United Methodist Church v. City of Cheyenne*, 235 F. Supp. 2d 1186, 1196-97 (D. Wyo. 2002) (holding that it is a question of fact for the jury whether a day care center operated by a church was intended to be religious in nature and therefore a "religious exercise").

C. *What is a substantial burden?*

There is a large amount of litigation over the meaning of a "substantial burden," and many courts have imported into RLUIPA the interpretations courts previously applied to the same term in RFRA. *See Marria v. Broaddus*, 200 F. Supp. 2d 280, 298 (S.D.N.Y. 2002); *Charles v. Verhagen*, 220 F.Supp.2d 937 (W.D.Wis. 2002), *aff'd*, 348 F.3d 601 (7th Cir. 2003). Under RFRA, the interpretations of the term "substantial burden" included: (1) a narrow standard adopted by the Fourth, Ninth, and Eleventh Circuits, *see Mack v. O'Leary*, 80 F.3d 1175, 1178 (9th Cir. 1996) ("substantial burden" is "one that either compels the religious adherent to engage in conduct that his religion forbids (such as eating pork, for a Muslim or Jew) or forbids him to engage in conduct that his religion requires (such as prayer)"); (2) an intermediate standard adopted by the Sixth Circuit, *see Abdur-Rahman v. Mich. Dept. of Corr.*, 65 F.3d 489, 491-92 (6th Cir. 1995) ("substantial burden" is a burden on a practice that is "essential" or "fundamental" to the religion); and (3) a broad standard, adopted by the Eighth and Tenth Circuits, *see Brown-El v. Harris*, 26 F.3d 68, 70 (8th Cir.1994) ([A] "substantial burden" is an action that forces religious adherents to "refrain from religiously motivated conduct").

These variations on the theme of "substantial burden" are replicated in the RLUIPA decisions. The Eleventh Circuit recently ruled on the meaning of the term "substantial burden" in RLUIPA. According to the Eleventh Circuit:

> [A] "substantial burden" must place more than an inconvenience on religious exercise; a "substantial burden" is akin to significant pressure which directly coerces the religious adherent to conform his or her behavior accordingly. Thus, a substantial burden can result from pres-

sure that tends to force adherents to forego religious precepts or from pressure that mandates religious conduct.

Midrash Sephardi, Inc. v. Town of Surfside, 366 F.3d 1214, 1227 (11th Cir. 2004), *cert. denied*, 125 543 U.S. 1146 (2005). In applying this standard, the court held that a town ordinance excluding churches and synagogues from the business district did not constitute a substantial burden, even though the ordinance effectively forced members of a Synagogue to walk farther than would otherwise be necessary. "While we certainly sympathize with those congregants who endure Floridian heat and humidity to walk to services, the burden of walking a few extra blocks, made greater by Mother Nature's occasional incorrigibility, is not 'substantial' within the meaning of RLUIPA." *Midrash*, 366 F.3d at 1228.

Different circuits have phrased the standard for assessing a "substantial burden" under RLUIPA in somewhat different ways from the Eleventh Circuit (and somewhat different ways from their description of the same term as used in RFRA). The Ninth Circuit, for example, has described a "substantial burden" as "a significantly great restriction or onus" on religious exercise. *San Jose Christian Coll. v. City of Morgan Hill*, 360 F.3d 1024, 1034-35 (9th Cir. 2004). The Seventh Circuit has phrased the standard in somewhat different terms. To the Seventh Circuit, a "substantial burden" is one that "necessarily bears direct, primary, and fundamental responsibility for rendering religious exercise — including the use of real property for the purpose thereof within the regulated jurisdiction generally — effectively impracticable." *Civil Liberties for Urban Believers (CLUB) v. Chicago*, 342 F.3d 752, 761 (7th Cir. 2003), *cert. denied*, 541 U.S. 1096 (2004). The Eleventh Circuit has specifically rejected the Seventh Circuit's description of the standard in *CLUB* on the ground that it would "render § b(3)'s total exclusion prohibition meaningless." *Midrash*, 366 F.3d at 1227.

These standards are all somewhat different, but it is difficult to describe those differences systematically, or even to identify precisely where similar facts might lead to different results under the different standards. All the courts seem to accept that zoning laws may impose some burden on religious enterprises, but there is no consistent calculus to measure how to reconcile the different goals and objectives advanced by local governments and the countervailing interests of religious groups. As one illustration of the difficulty posed in these cases, the district court in *Westchester Day School v. Village of Mamaroneck*, 280 F. Supp. 2d 230 (S.D.N.Y. 2003), held that the denial of a zoning permit to increase the size of a religious school substantially burdened the religious practitioners precisely because it prohibited them from growing. Of course, this will always be the case whenever a religious institution is denied a permit to expand its facilities; thus, if limits on growth are deemed "substantial burdens," then the plaintiffs will always satisfy that part of the RLUIPA analysis, and the true measure of an RLUIPA case will rest on the government's ability to muster a compelling interest that will satisfy the court. The court of appeals vacated the district court's judgment on other grounds, but it also expressed the opinion in dicta that the district court had interpreted the substantial burden component of RLUIPA too broadly. Part of the court of appeals' rationale was based on a concern with government favoritism of religion under such a broad reading of the statute. "[I]f RLUIPA means what the district court believes it does, a serious question arises whether it goes beyond the proper function of protecting the free exercise of religion into the constitutionally impermissible zone of entwining government with religion in a manner that prefers religion over irreligion and confers special benefits on it." *Westchester Day Sch. v. Vill. of Mamaroneck*, 386 F.3d 183, 190 (2d Cir. 2004).

D. *What Constitutes a Compelling Interest and a Least Restrictive Means?*

Once again, the courts have not described either of these terms precisely. Generally, health and safety concerns are deemed "compelling," *see Murphy v. Zoning Comm'n of the Town of New Milford*, 148 F. Supp. 2d 173 (D. Conn. 2001), while traffic and parking concerns are occasionally viewed as not compelling. *See Westchester Day Sch. v. Vill. of Mamaroneck*, 280 F. Supp. 2d 230 (S.D.N.Y. 2003), *judgment vacated and remanded for trial*, 386 F.3d 183 (2d Cir. 2004). The cases more often turn on the least restrictive means analysis. For example, in *Elsinore Christian Ctr. v. City of Lake Elsinore*, 270 F. Supp. 2d 1163 (C.D. Cal. 2003), the court ruled that curing "urban blight" was a compelling interest, but rejected the city's claim that denying a church a permit that would allow the city to evict a food market from the downtown area was the least restrictive means of carrying out the city's interest in redevelopment. Again, little can be said to provide much substance to the meaning of these terms. The cases are heavily fact-specific, and depend largely on whether the plaintiffs can describe to the courts other methods of achieving the government's stated goal. (The court in *Elsinore Christian Ctr.* later vacated its order on constitutional grounds, holding that RLUIPA exceeded Congress's powers under both Section 5 and the Commerce Clause. *See Elsinore Christian Ctr. v. City of Lake Elsinore*, 291 F. Supp. 2d 1083 (C.D. Cal. 2003).)

E. *"Equal Terms" and Discrimination*

One of the few definitive statements that can be made about the application of the RLUIPA land-use provisions is that the courts tend to focus on the equal treatment of religious and non-religious property. *See San Jose Christian Coll. v. City of Morgan Hill*, 360 F.3d 1024 (9th Cir. 2004); *Civil Liberties for Urban Believers (CLUB) v. City of Chicago*, 342 F.3d 752 (7th Cir. 2003), *cert. denied*, 541 U.S. 1096 (2004). In particular, courts have been especially reluctant to permit cities to favor commercial over religious uses of land. *See, e.g., Cottonwood Christian Ctr. v. Cypress Redevelopment Agency*, 218 F. Supp. 2d 1203 (C.D. Cal. 2002).

Because courts tend to focus on the disparate treatment of religious and non-religious activities, many of these cases get decided under the discrimination and "equal terms" provisions of RLUIPA. The Eleventh Circuit recently addressed the discrimination and "equal terms" analysis in *Midrash*. Although the Eleventh Circuit in *Midrash* held that the exclusion of churches and synagogues from the business district did not constitute a substantial burden under RLUIPA, it also found that the "equal terms" part of the statute was violated by another part of the town's ordinance, which permitted private clubs and other secular assemblies in the same downtown area from which the ordinance excluded religious assemblies. The question was whether a private club was an "assembly or institution" subject to the "equal terms" portion of the statute. The court held that private clubs, churches, and synagogues all fell under the umbrella of "assembly or institution" as those terms are used in RLUIPA, and therefore had to be treated on "equal terms." In elaborating on this holding, the Eleventh Circuit held that this portion of the statute codifies the jurisprudence of *Smith* and *Church of the Lukumi Babalu Aye,* which emphasizes that a law targeting a particular religion was not neutral and therefore was not a law of general applicability subject to the lenient *Smith* analysis. Thus, the compelling interest analysis applies whenever a law does not treat similarly situated religious and secular enterprises on "equal terms."

For a detailed discussion of the relationship between the "substantial obstacle" and equal terms/discrimination portions of the statute, *see Sts. Constantine and Helen Greek Orthodox Church v. City of New Berlin*, 396 F.3d 895 (7th Cir. 2005). According to this opinion, the "substantial obstacle" portion of the statute "backstops the explicit prohibition of religious discrimination in the later section of the Act." *Id.* at 900. Thus, "substantial obstacle" means something different than (indeed, something more protective than) a simple ban on discrimination. On the other hand, although this phrasing of the relationship between the "substantial obstacle" and equal terms/discrimination portions of the statute makes it seem that the "substantial obstacle" portion of the statute is more protective of religious activity, note the contrary implications of *Midrash*. In *Midrash*, the court rejected the "substantial obstacle" claim and granted the equal terms/discrimination claim.

F. *Applying RLUIPA: An Example*

A recent federal district court decision in Connecticut provides an example of the potential scope of RLUIPA claims in the land use context. In *Murphy v. Zoning Commission of the Town of New Milford*, 148 F. Supp. 2d 173 (D. Conn. 2001), Mr. Murphy held weekly group prayer meetings in his home for up to sixty people at a time. Murphy's home was located in a residential neighborhood, at the end of a cul-de-sac. During the prayer meetings, attendees would park their cars "'anywhere they could' . . . '[o]ut in the circle down the street, in the backyard, in the driveways, in their yard, [or] in the front lawn.'" *Id.* at 176. After multiple complaints from neighbors, the local zoning board sent Murphy a cease and desist letter. Murphy's house was zoned for use as a single-family dwelling, and the applicable zoning regulations did not permit large group meetings. The board did not prohibit prayer meetings at Murphy's house altogether, but rather ordered Murphy to limit future meetings to no more than twenty-five people.

Murphy sued the town, claiming that the town's attempt to enforce its zoning law restrictions against him violated his rights under RLUIPA and the Free Exercise Clause. The district court granted a preliminary injunction barring the town from enforcing its zoning regulation against Murphy's weekly meetings. The court first found that the town's action substantially burdened the religious practices in question. The court relied primarily on testimony that some individuals had become afraid to attend the prayer meetings for fear they would be arrested because of the complaints of Murphy's neighbors. "Foregoing or modifying the practice of one's religion because of governmental interference or fear of punishment by the government is precisely the type of 'substantial burden' Congress intended to trigger the RLUIPA's protections; indeed, it is the concern which impelled adoption of the First Amendment." *Id.* at 189.

Having determined that the town substantially burdened plaintiff's religious practice, the court then turned to the question whether the burden was justified by a compelling interest that the town pursued in a manner least restrictive to the religious practice. Although the court found that the protection of residential areas through zoning regulations did constitute a compelling interest, it ruled against the town on the least restrictive means aspect of the analysis. The court noted that although the town was mainly concerned with the number of cars on the residential street, the town's order was framed in terms of the number of people attending the meeting. The court then concluded by urging the town officials to enter into a dialogue with local residents to fashion a voluntary compromise between the parties and quoted scripture to guide them in this process: "'In everything do to others as you would have them do to you; for this is the law and the prophets.' Matthew 7:12; *see also* Luke 6:31." *Id.* at 191 n.15.

2. *The RLUIPA Institutionalized Persons Provisions — Statutory Claims.* Unlike the land use cases, claims brought under the institutionalized persons section of have been mostly unsuccessful. *See, e.g., Adkins v. Kaspar*, 393 F.3d 559 (5th Cir. 2004), *cert. denied,* 73 U.S.L.W. 3709 (U.S. June 6, 2005) (No. 04-1347) (holding that a prison regulation prohibiting a religious group from observing a weekly Sabbath and assorted other holy days did not substantially burden the prisoner's religious practice under RLUIPA). Many prisoner claims have been dismissed on procedural grounds or involve the denial of summary judgment motions by prisoners. There are, however, a growing number of exceptions to this trend. One typical exception is *Mayweathers v. Terhune*, 328 F. Supp. 2d 1086 (E.D. Cal. 2004), in which the court found RLUIPA violated by prison rules requiring Muslim prisoners to shave their beards and punishing Muslim prisoners for missing work assignments to attend hour-long Sabbath meetings. Other decisions reach the merits of the RLUIPA claim, only to deny the prisoner legal relief. *See, e.g., Dunlap v. Losey*, No. 01-2586, 2002 U.S. App. LEXIS 9636 (6th Cir. May 15, 2002) (unpublished opinion) (denying a prisoner his request for access to hardcover Bibles). Still other courts have held that RLUIPA claims raise genuine issues of material fact justifying denial of summary judgment for the government, without reaching the ultimate merits of the RLUIPA claims. *See Murphy v. Missouri Dept. of Corr.* 372 F.3d 979 (8th Cir.), *cert. denied*, 543 U.S 991 (2004) (prison's refusal to grant group worship rights to whites-only religious group raised genuine issues of material fact regarding substantial burden); *Coronel v. Paul*, 316 F. Supp. 2d 868 (D. Ariz. 2004) (refusal to permit pagan inmate to attend religious functions of other groups raised genuine issues of material fact regarding substantial burden). It is not yet possible to generalize from these disparate cases about the broad meaning or application of RLUIPA in the prison context; the cases are very fact-specific, and cases are often decided inconsistently with other cases that seem to have similar facts. Many lower courts defer broadly to the security concerns and judgments of prison authorities, and the Supreme Court recently endorsed this tendency when it rejected a constitutional challenge to the prison provisions of RLUIPA in *Cutter v. Wilkinson*.

E. THE ESTABLISHMENT CLAUSE CHALLENGE TO RLUIPA

CUTTER v. WILKINSON
125 S. Ct. 2113 (2005)

JUSTICE GINSBURG delivered the opinion of the Court.

Plaintiffs below, petitioners here, are current and former inmates of institutions operated by the Ohio Department of Rehabilitation and Correction and assert that they are adherents of "nonmainstream" religions: the Satanist, Wicca, and Asatru religions, and the Church of Jesus Christ Christian. They complain that Ohio prison officials, in violation of RLUIPA, have failed to accommodate their religious exercise.

The appeals court held, as the prison officials urged, that the portion of RLUIPA applicable to institutionalized persons violates the Establishment Clause. We reverse the Court of Appeals' judgment.

"This Court has long recognized that the government may . . . accommodate religious practices . . . without violating the Establishment Clause." Just last Term, in *Locke v. Davey,* the Court reaffirmed that "there is room for play in the joints between" the Free Exercise and Establishment Clauses, allowing the government to accommodate religion beyond free exercise requirements, without offense to the Establishment Clause. *Id.*, at 718 (quoting *Walz* [*supra* Chapter 8]). "At some point, accommodation may devolve into 'an unlawful fostering of religion.'" *Corporation of Presiding Bishop of Church of Jesus Christ of Latter-day Saints v. Amos* [*supra* Chapter 12]. But § 3 of RLUIPA, we hold, does not, on its face, exceed the limits of permissible government accommodation of religious practices.

I.

A.

RLUIPA is the latest of long-running congressional efforts to accord religious exercise heightened protection from government-imposed burdens, consistent with this Court's precedents. Ten years before RLUIPA's enactment, the Court held, in *Employment Div., Dept. of Human Resources of Ore. v. Smith,* that the First Amendment's Free Exercise Clause does not inhibit enforcement of otherwise valid laws of general application that incidentally burden religious conduct. The Court recognized, however, that the political branches could shield religious exercise through legislative accommodation, for example, by making an exception to proscriptive drug laws for sacramental peyote use.

Responding to *Smith,* Congress enacted the Religious Freedom Restoration Act of 1993. In *City of Boerne,* this Court invalidated RFRA as applied to States and their subdivisions, holding that the Act exceeded Congress' remedial powers under the Fourteenth Amendment.[2] Congress again responded, this time by enacting RLUIPA. Less sweeping than RFRA, and invoking federal authority under the Spending and Commerce Clauses, RLUIPA targets two areas: Section 2 of the Act concerns land-use regulation,[3] §3 relates to religious exercise by institutionalized persons.

Before enacting §3, Congress documented, in hearings spanning three years, that "frivolous or arbitrary" barriers impeded institutionalized persons' religious exercise. To secure redress for inmates who encountered undue barriers to their religious observances, Congress carried over from RFRA the "compelling governmental interest"/"least restrictive means" standard. Lawmakers anticipated, however, that courts entertaining complaints under § 3 would accord "due deference to the experience and expertise of prison and jail administrators."

II.

A.

The Religion Clauses of the First Amendment provide: "Congress shall make no law respecting an establishment of religion, or prohibiting the free exercise thereof." The first of the two Clauses, commonly called the Establishment Clause, commands a separation of church and state. The second, the Free Exercise Clause, requires government respect for, and noninterference with, the

---

[2] RFRA, Courts of Appeals have held, remains operative as to the Federal Government and federal territories and possessions. *See O'Bryan v. Bureau of Prisons,* 349 F.3d 399, 400-401 (7th Cir. 2003); *Guam v. Guerrero,* 290 F.3d 1210, 1220-1222 (9th Cir. 2002); *Kikumura v. Hurley,* 242 F.3d 950, 958-960 (10th Cir. 2001); *In re Young,* 141 F.3d 854, 858-863 (8th Cir. 1998). This Court, however, has not had occasion to rule on the matter.

[3] Section 2 of RLUIPA is not at issue here. We therefore express no view on the validity of the part of the Act.

religious beliefs and practices of our Nation's people. While the two Clauses express complementary values, they often exert conflicting pressures.[6]

Our decisions recognize that "there is room for play in the joints" between the Clauses, some space for legislative action neither compelled by the Free Exercise Clause nor prohibited by the Establishment Clause. *See, e.g., Smith* ("[A] society that believes in the negative protection accorded to religious belief can be expected to be solicitous of that value in its legislation . . . ."); *Amos* (Federal Government may exempt secular nonprofit activities of religious organizations from Title VII's prohibition on religious discrimination in employment); *Sherbert v. Verner*, (Harlan, J., dissenting) ("The constitutional obligation of 'neutrality' is not so narrow a channel that the slightest deviation from an absolutely straight course leads to condemnation.") In accord with the majority of Courts of Appeals that have ruled on the question, we hold that § 3 of RLUIPA fits within the corridor between the Religion Clauses: On its face, the Act qualifies as a permissible legislative accommodation of religion that is not barred by the Establishment Clause.

Foremost, we find RLUIPA's institutionalized-persons provision compatible with the Establishment Clause because it alleviates exceptional government-created burdens on private religious exercise. Furthermore, the Act on its face does not founder on shoals our prior decisions have identified: Properly applying RLUIPA, courts must take adequate account of the burdens a requested accommodation may impose on nonbeneficiaries, and they must be satisfied that the Act's prescriptions are and will be administered neutrally among different faiths.[8]

Section 3 covers state-run institutions — mental hospitals, prisons, and the like — in which the government exerts a degree of control unparalleled in civilian society and severely disabling to private religious exercise. RLUIPA thus protects institutionalized persons who are unable freely to attend to their religious needs and are therefore dependent on the government's permission and accommodation for exercise of their religion.[10]

---

[6] [RELOCATED FOOTNOTE.] *Lemon* stated a three-part test: "First, the statute must have a secular legislative purpose; second, its principal or primary effect must be one that neither advances nor inhibits religion; finally, the statute must not foster an excessive government entanglement with religion." We resolve this case on other grounds.

[8] Directed at obstructions institutional arrangements place on religious observances, RLUIPA does not require a State to pay for an inmate's devotional accessories. *See, e.g., Charles v. Verhagen*, 348 F.3d 601, 605 (7th Cir. 2003) (overturning prohibition on possession of Islamic prayer oil but leaving inmate-plaintiff with responsibility for purchasing the oil).

[10] Respondents argue, in line with the Sixth Circuit, that RLUIPA goes beyond permissible reduction of impediments to free exercise. The Act, they project, advances religion by encouraging prisoners to "get religion," and thereby gain accommodations afforded under RLUIPA. Brief for Respondents 15-17; *see* 349 F.3d, at 266 ("One effect of RLUIPA is to induce prisoners to adopt or feign religious belief in order to receive the statute's benefits."). While some accommodations of reli-

We note in this regard the Federal Government's accommodation of religious practice by members of the military. In *Goldman v. Weinberger,* we held that the Free Exercise Clause did not require the Air Force to exempt an Orthodox Jewish officer from uniform dress regulations so that he could wear a yarmulke indoors. Congress responded to *Goldman* by prescribing that "a member of the armed forces may wear an item of religious apparel while wearing the uniform," unless "the wearing of the item would interfere with the performance [of] military duties [or] the item of apparel is not neat and conservative."

We do not read RLUIPA to elevate accommodation of religious observances over an institution's need to maintain order and safety. Our decisions indicate that an accommodation must be measured so that it does not override other significant interests. In *Caldor,* the Court struck down a Connecticut law that "arm[ed] Sabbath observers with an absolute and unqualified right not to work on whatever day they designate[d] as their Sabbath." We held the law invalid under the Establishment Clause because it "unyielding[ly] weigh[ted]" the interests of Sabbatarians "over all other interests."

We have no cause to believe that RLUIPA would not be applied in an appropriately balanced way, with particular sensitivity to security concerns. While the Act adopts a "compelling governmental interest" standard, "[c]ontext matters" in the application of that standard.[11] Lawmakers supporting RLUIPA were mindful of the urgency of discipline, order, safety, and security in penal institutions. They anticipated that courts would apply the Act's standard with "due deference to the experience and expertise of prison and jail administrators in establishing necessary regulations and procedures to maintain good order, security and discipline, consistent with consideration of costs and limited resources."

---

gious observance, notably the opportunity to assemble in worship services, might attract joiners seeking a break in their closely guarded day, we doubt that all accommodations would be perceived as "benefits." For example, congressional hearings on RLUIPA revealed that one state corrections system served as its kosher diet "a fruit, a vegetable, a granola bar, and a liquid nutritional supplement — each and every meal."

The argument, in any event, founders on the fact that Ohio already facilitates religious services for mainstream faiths. The State provides chaplains, allows inmates to possess religious items, and permits assembly for worship.

[11] The Sixth Circuit posited that an irreligious prisoner and member of the Aryan Nation who challenges prison officials' confiscation of his white supremacist literature as a violation of his free association and expression rights would have his claims evaluated under the deferential rational-relationship standard described in *Turner v. Safley,* 482 U.S. 78 (1987). A member of the Church of Jesus Christ Christian challenging a similar withholding, the Sixth Circuit assumed, would have a stronger prospect of success because a court would review his claim under RLUIPA's compelling-interest standard. 349 F.3d, at 266 (citing *Madison v. Riter,* 240 F. Supp. 2d 566, 576 (W.D. Va. 2003)). Courts, however, may be expected to recognize the government's countervailing compelling interest in not facilitating inflammatory racist activity that could imperil prison security and order. *Cf. Reimann v. Murphy,* 897 F. Supp. 398, 402-403 (E.D. Wis. 1995) (concluding, under RFRA, that excluding racist literature advocating violence was the least restrictive means of furthering the compelling state interest in preventing prison violence); *George v. Sullivan,* 896 F. Supp. 895, 898 (W.D. Wis. 1995) (same).

Finally, RLUIPA does not differentiate among bona fide faiths. It confers no privileged status on any particular religious sect, and singles out no bona fide faith for disadvantageous treatment.

B.

The Sixth Circuit misread our precedents to require invalidation of RLUIPA as "impermissibly advancing religion by giving greater protection to religious rights than to other constitutionally protected rights." Our decision in *Amos* counsels otherwise. There, we upheld against an Establishment Clause challenge a provision exempting "religious organizations from Title VII's prohibition against discrimination in employment on the basis of religion." The District Court in *Amos*, reasoning in part that the exemption improperly "single[d] out religious entities for a benefit," had "declared the statute unconstitutional as applied to secular activity." Religious accommodations, we held, need not "come packaged with benefits to secular entities."

Were the Court of Appeals' view the correct reading of our decisions, all manner of religious accommodations would fall. Congressional permission for members of the military to wear religious apparel while in uniform would fail, *see* 10 U.S.C. § 774, as would accommodations Ohio itself makes. Ohio could not, as it now does, accommodate "traditionally recognized" religions: The State provides inmates with chaplains "but not with publicists or political consultants," and allows "prisoners to assemble for worship, but not for political rallies."

In upholding RLUIPA's institutionalized-persons provision, we emphasize that respondents "have raised a facial challenge to [the Act's] constitutionality, and have not contended that under the facts of any of [petitioners'] specific cases . . . [that] applying RLUIPA would produce unconstitutional results." The District Court, noting the underdeveloped state of the record, concluded: A finding "that it is *factually impossible* to provide the kind of accommodations that RLUIPA will require without significantly compromising prison security or the levels of service provided to other inmates" cannot be made at this juncture. *Id.*, at 848 (emphasis added).[13] We agree.

Should inmate requests for religious accommodations become excessive, impose unjustified burdens on other institutionalized persons, or jeopardize the effective functioning of an institution, the facility would be free to resist the imposition. In that event, adjudication in as-applied challenges would be in order.

[Justice Thomas's concurring opinion is discussed in Chapter 1.]

---

[13] Respondents argue that prison gangs use religious activity to cloak their illicit and often violent conduct. The instant case was considered below on a motion to dismiss. Thus, the parties' conflicting assertions on this matter are not before us. It bears repetition, however, that prison security is a compelling state interest, and that deference is due to institutional officials' expertise in this area. Further, prison officials may appropriately question whether a prisoner's religiosity, asserted as the basis for a requested accommodation, is authentic. Although RLUIPA bars inquiry into whether a particular belief or practice is "central" to a prisoner's religion, *see* 42 U.S.C. § 2000cc-5(7)(A), the Act does not preclude inquiry into the sincerity of a prisoner's professed religiosity.

Notes on *Cutter*

1. *Cutter and the Permissible Scope of Mandatory Statutory Accommodation.* In holding that Section 3 of RLUIPA is compatible with the Establishment Clause, the Court emphasizes that the statute "alleviates exceptional government-created burdens on private religious exercise." Would the Court reach the same conclusion regarding a statute that accommodated religious practitioners by alleviating private burdens on religious exercise? *See Thornton v. Caldor, supra* Chapter 12, in which the Court struck down a Connecticut statute requiring all employers to accommodate every employee's observance of the Sabbath. According to the Court in *Caldor*, "[t]his unyielding weighting in favor of Sabbath observers over all other interests contravenes a fundamental principle of the Religion Clauses, so well articulated by Judge Learned Hand: 'The First Amendment . . . gives no one the right to insist that in pursuit of their own interests others must conform their conduct to his own religious necessities.'" Does *Cutter* cast doubt on this part of *Caldor*? (Note that in *Cutter* the Court does not discuss the broader principle of *Caldor*, but rather distinguishes *Caldor* on the ground that unlike RLUIPA, the statute in *Caldor* inflexibly favored the interests of Sabbatarians "over all other interests.")

2. *Cutter and* Turner v. Safley. Notice that although the Court upholds the application of the statutory strict scrutiny standard in *Cutter*, it also goes out of its way to recognize the necessity of deferring to the prison authorities in matters of prison order and security. Recall that in *O'Lone v. Shabazz, supra* Chapter 3, the Court upheld prison policies that prevented Muslim prisoners from attending religious services on the ground that these policies were necessary for order and security within the prison. *Shabazz* was an application of a constitutional standard applicable to prison regulations in general, which was set forth in *Turner v. Safley, supra* Chapter 3. Under the *Turner* standard, prison regulations are permitted if they are "reasonably related to legitimate penological interests," even if those regulations implicate the prisoners' constitutional rights. Although this is a much lower formal standard than the strict scrutiny analysis set forth on the face of RLUIPA, is there any notable distinction between the deference provided to prison officials under *Turner* and the "particular sensitivity to security concerns" and the "due deference to the experience and expertise of prison and jail administrators in establishing necessary regulations and procedures to maintain good order, security and discipline," which the Court in *Cutter* says is part of the RLUIPA standard?

3. *The Applicability of the Cutter Logic Beyond the Prison Context.* Is *Cutter* a broad general statement favoring government accommodation of religion, or is the holding in that case tied closely to the prison context? A consistent theme running throughout the Court's decision in *Cutter* relates to the singular nature of state control over the religious practices of prisoners. As the Court notes, "Section 3 covers state-run institutions — mental hospitals, prisons, and the like — in which the government exerts a degree of control unparalleled in civilian society and severely disabling to private religious exercise." Is this emphasis sufficient to distinguish the prison provisions of RLUIPA from the land-use provisions? The Court asserts in *Cutter* that prisoners are "unable freely to attend to their religious needs and are therefore dependent on the government's permission and accommodation for exercise of their religion." Does the fact that churches have significant political and financial resources to facilitate the exercise of their faith in the civilian context distinguish land-use controls from prison regulations?

Is the possibility of religious favoritism stronger in the land-use than the institutionalized-persons context? Reconsider the district court's decision in *Murphy v. Zoning Commission*, which is cited earlier in this Chapter in the discussion of land-use statutory considerations. It is unlikely the court in *Murphy v. Zoning Commission* would have ruled against the city on First Amendment free speech grounds if Murphy had held similar-sized weekly political meetings inside his house. But if that is true, then this ruling raises the possibility that RLUIPA favors religious association and expression over association and expression of other types, in violation of the Establishment Clause. In other contexts, discrimination in favor of religion has been viewed as a violation of the Establishment Clause. *See Texas Monthly v. Bullock, supra* Chapter 8 (striking down a Texas statute exempting religious publications from a general sales tax provision).

The constitutionality of the RLUIPA land-use provisions was not at issue in *Murphy*, but other courts have rejected Establishment Clause claims against those provisions. In *Midrash Sephardi, Inc. v. Town of Surfside*, 366 F.3d 1214 (11th Cir. 2004), the Eleventh Circuit Court of Appeals rejected both *Boerne* and Establishment Clause challenges to RLUIPA. The case involved a synagogue's challenge to a local zoning ordinance that prohibited churches and synagogues from operating in the downtown business district. In rejecting the city's constitutional claims, the Eleventh Circuit agreed with the United States government's contention that RLUIPA was a legitimate exercise of Congress's power to protect "the non-discrimination principles embodied in the Free Exercise and the Establishment Clauses of the First Amendment, as well as the Equal Protection Clause of the Fourteenth Amendment." *Id.* at 1238. With regard to the Establishment Clause claim, the court likewise rejected the city's argument that the statute gave an impermissible special preference to religious interests. "[C]ontrary to Surfside's assertions, RLUIPA does not allow religious assemblies to avoid the application of zoning regulations. RLUIPA does not impose affirmative duties on states that would require them to facilitate or subsidize the exercise of religion. RLUIPA instead calls for exactly the opposite — forbidding states from imposing impermissible burdens on religious worship." *Id.* at 1241.

A federal district court in Pennsylvania reached a similar result. *See Freedom Baptist Church of Delaware Cty v. Township of Middletown*, 204 F. Supp. 2d 857 (E.D. Pa. 2002). This decision involved a township's constitutional defenses to a church's RLUIPA challenge to certain zoning rules imposed on churches built within the township. In a somewhat diffuse opinion, the district court refused to address a township's Establishment Clause argument against the statute because the court concluded that the statute is a legitimate codification of free exercise protections. The court did address the township's claims under the Commerce Clause and Section 5 of the Fourteenth Amendment, holding that Congress had ample grounds under both provisions to justify statutory protection of religious organizations from land use rules of state and local governments. The Court based its conclusions under the Commerce Clause on broad deference to Congress's factual findings. With regard to the Fourteenth Amendment, the court avoided the negative implications of *Boerne* by noting that "[a]fter *Smith* was decided, the Supreme Court confirmed that the presence of 'individualized assessments' remains of constitutional significance in Free Exercise cases even outside the unemployment compensation arena [citing *Church of the Lukumi Babalu Aye*]." *Id.* at 868. The court upheld RLUIPA by reading the portion of RLUIPA that was based on the Fourteenth Amendment to prohibit only this sort of "individualized assessment."

4. *Other Potential Constitutional Problems with RLUIPA.* Note that the Establishment Clause is only one of several potential constitutional problems with RLUIPA. The Court declined to rule on the Petitioners' argument that in passing RLUIPA, Congress exceeded its authority under the Spending or Commerce Clauses because these issues had not been addressed by the court of appeals. The Court also declined to rule on the state's argument that RLUIPA interfered with state sovereignty interests under the Tenth Amendment. Although the majority does not intimate how it would ultimately view these issues, Justice Thomas suggests in his *Cutter* concurrence that RLUIPA "may well exceed Congress' authority under either the Spending Clause or the Commerce Clause."

Table of Cases

References are to pages. Locations of principal cases appear in italics.

INDEX

[References are to page numbers.]

A

ACCESS BY RELIGIOUS GROUPS TO PUBLIC FACILITIES (See EQUAL OR OPEN ACCESS)

ACCOMMODATION OF RELIGION
Anti-accommodationists, response to 69-77
Arguments against . . . 60-69
Arguments supporting . . . 53-57
Definition of religion . . . 98
Employment Division v. Smith (See FREE EXERCISE CLAUSE)
Legal obligations, free exercise clause as defense to (See FREE EXERCISE CLAUSE)
McConnell, *Accommodation of Religion: An Update and Response to Critics* . . . 69-77
Narrow definition and application of accommodation principle . . . 64-69
Philosophical approaches to role of religion in modern constitutional democracy . . 86-91
Secular republic, in favor of (See SECULAR REPUBLIC)
Sherbert v. Verner . . . 749-759; 787

AD HOC APPROACH
Board of Education of Kiryas Joel v. Grumet . . . 290-293
Establishment Clause standards . . 289-294

ADOLESCENT FAMILY LIFE ACT (AFLA)
Grants to nonprofit private organizations or agencies . . . 675-691

AID TO RELIGION (See GOVERNMENT FINANCIAL SUPPORT OF RELIGION)

AMISH BELIEVERS
Compulsory school attendance laws, violations of . . . 788-805
Social Security taxes, refusal to file returns and withhold taxes . . . 805-808

B

BIOLOGY VS. CREATIONISM (See CREATIONISM AS RELIGION)

C

CHAPLAINS
Congressional chaplains (See CONGRESSIONAL CHAPLAINS)
State legislatures, chaplain paid by 388-393
Student council chaplain at football games, prayer initiated by . . . 365-374

CHARITABLE CHOICE
Generally . . . 692-693

CHRISTMAS DISPLAYS
Nativity scenes (See NATIVITY SCENES)
Tree on public grounds . . . 398-426

CHURCH PROPERTY DISPUTES (See DISPUTES BETWEEN RELIGIOUS FACTIONS, GOVERNMENT INVOLVEMENT IN)

CLERGY MALPRACTICE
Constitutional defenses to tort liability . . . 840-842

COERCION ANALYSIS
Broad coercion . . . 247-249
Establishment Clause standard . . . 253-258
Gey, S. G., *Religious Coercion and the Establishment Clause* . . . 225-229; 258-275
Holiday religious displays . . . 262-265
McConnell, M. W., *Coercion: The Lost Element of Establishment* . . . 253-258
Narrow coercion . . . 249-275
Prayer in public schools . . . 265-275; 319-336

COLLEGES AND UNIVERSITIES (See UNIVERSITIES AND COLLEGES)

COMMENCEMENT EXERCISES (See SCHOOL PRAYER CASES, subhead: Graduation prayers)

CONGRESSIONAL CHAPLAINS
Government endorsement of religion 397-398
Madison's *Detached Memorandum* . . . 44-46

CONSCIENTIOUS OBJECTOR CASES
Generally . . . 129-130
United States v. Seeger . . . 102-118
Welsh v. United States . . . 118-123

CREATIONISM AS RELIGION
Arkansas's anti-evolution statute 155-162
Carter, *Evolutionism, Creationism, and Treating Religion as a Hobby* . . . 182-183
Edwards v. Aguillard . . . 162-181
Epperson v. Arkansas . . . 155-162
"Intelligent design" . . . 183-192
Kansas state board of education's attempts to remove references to evolution . . 184-186
Louisiana statute requiring balanced treatment for creation science and evolution . . . 162-181

CRÈCHES (See NATIVITY SCENES)

[References are to page numbers.]

[References are to page numbers.]

[References are to page numbers.]

[References are to page numbers.]

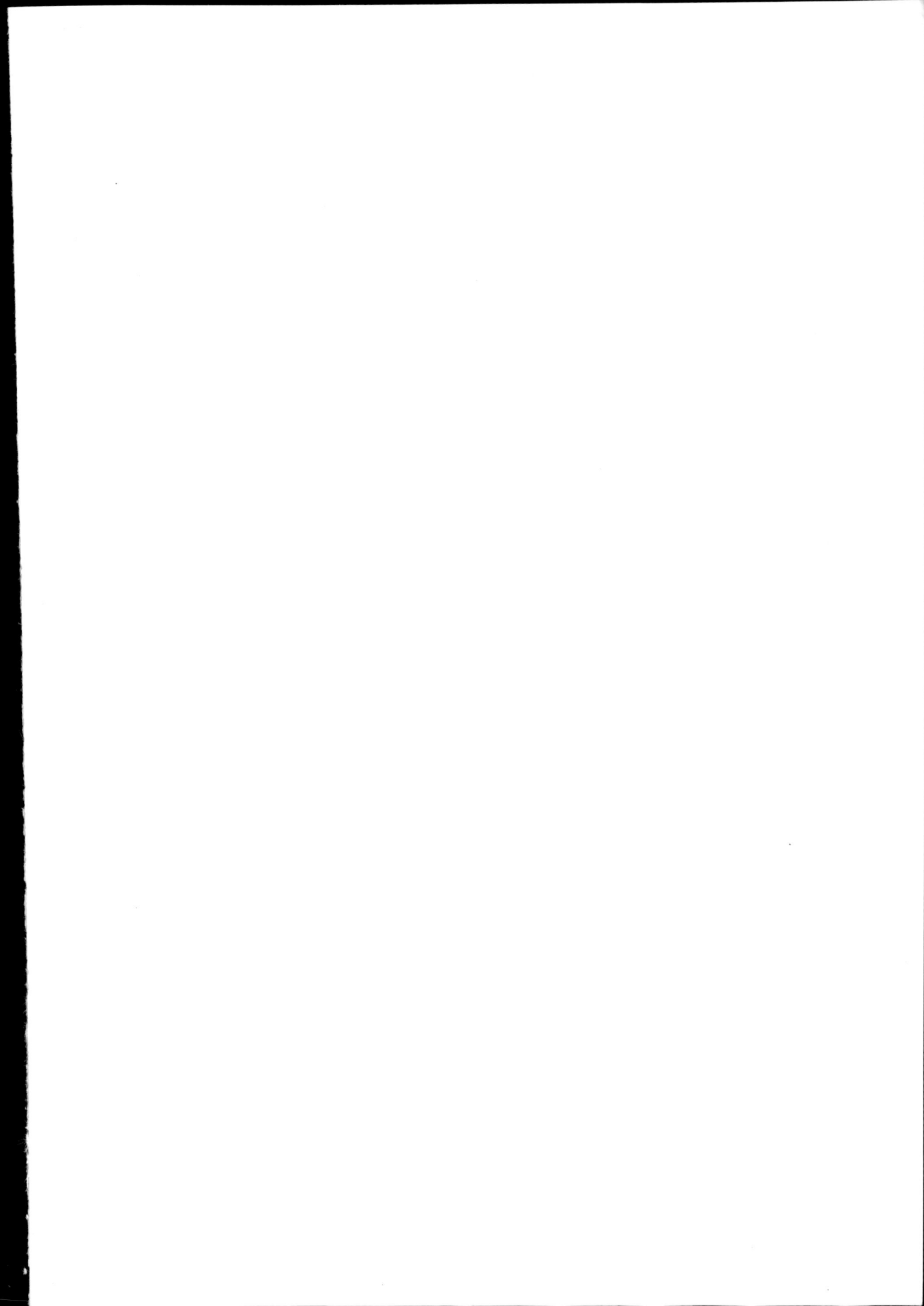